Poetry Criticism

Guide to Gale Literary Criticism Series

For criticism on	Consult these Gale series
Authors now living or who died after December 31, 1959	*CONTEMPORARY LITERARY CRITICISM (CLC)*
Authors who died between 1900 and 1959	*TWENTIETH-CENTURY LITERARY CRITICISM (TCLC)*
Authors who died between 1800 and 1899	*NINETEENTH-CENTURY LITERATURE CRITICISM (NCLC)*
Authors who died between 1400 and 1799	*LITERATURE CRITICISM FROM 1400 TO 1800 (LC)* *SHAKESPEAREAN CRITICISM (SC)*
Authors who died before 1400	*CLASSICAL AND MEDIEVAL LITERATURE CRITICISM (CMLC)*
Black writers of the past two hundred years	*BLACK LITERATURE CRITICISM (BLC)*
Authors of books for children and young adults	*CHILDREN'S LITERATURE REVIEW (CLR)*
Dramatists	*DRAMA CRITICISM (DC)*
Hispanic writers of the late nineteenth and twentieth centuries	*HISPANIC LITERATURE CRITICISM (HLC)*
Native North American writers and orators of the eighteenth, nineteenth, and twentieth centuries	*NATIVE NORTH AMERICAN LITERATURE (NNAL)*
Poets	*POETRY CRITICISM (PC)*
Short story writers	*SHORT STORY CRITICISM (SSC)*
Major authors from the Renaissance to the present	*WORLD LITERATURE CRITICISM, 1500 TO THE PRESENT (WLC)*

Poetry Criticism

Excerpts from Criticism of the Works of the Most Significant and Widely Studied Poets of World Literature

VOLUME 17

Carol T. Gaffke
Margaret Haerens
Editors

GALE

DETROIT · NEW YORK · TORONTO · LONDON

STAFF

Carol T. Gaffke, Margaret Haerens *Editors*

Kathy Darrow, Drew Kalasky, Michael L. Lablanc,
Damon Z. Percy, Susan Salas, Andrew Spongberg, Larry Trudeau,
Associate Editors

Susan Trosky, *Permissions Manager*
Kimberly F. Smilay, *Permissions Specialist*

Sarah Chesney, Diane Cooper, Edna Hedblad, Michele Lonoconus,
Maureen Puhl, Shalice Shah,
Permissions Associates

Steve Cusack, Kelly Quin,
Permissions Assistants

Victoria B. Cariappa, *Research Manager*

Julie C. Daniel, Tamara C. Nott, Michele P. Pica,
Norma Sawaya, Cheryl L. Warnock, *Research Associates*

Mary Beth Trimper, *Production Director*
Deborah Milliken, *Production Assistant*

Sherrell Hobbs, *Macintosh Artist*
Randy Bassett, *Image Database Supervisor*
Robert Duncan, *Scanner Operator*
Pamela Hayes, *Photography Coordinator*

Library of Congress Catalog Card Number 91-118494
ISBN 0-7876-0957-9
ISSN 1052-4851

Printed in the United States of America
Published simultaneously in the United Kingdom
by Gale Research International Limited
(An affiliated company of Gale Research Inc.)
10 9 8 7 6 5 4 3

Contents

Preface

A Comprehensive Information Source on World Poetry

*P*oetry Criticism *(PC)* provides substantial critical excerpts and biographical information on poets throughout the world who are most frequently studied in high school and undergraduate college courses. Each *PC* entry is supplemented by biographical and bibliographical material to help guide the user to a fuller understanding of the genre and its creators. Although major poets and literary movements are covered in such Gale Literary Criticism Series as *Contemporary Literary Criticism (CLC)*, *Twentieth-Century Literary Criticism (TCLC)*, *Nineteenth-Century Literature Criticism (NCLC)*, *Literature Criticism from 1400 to 1800 (LC)*, and *Classical and Medieval Literature Criticism (CMLC)*, *PC* offers more focused attention on poetry than is possible in the broader, survey-oriented entries on writers in these Gale series. Students, teachers, librarians, and researchers will find that the generous excerpts and supplementary material provided by *PC* supply them with the vital information needed to write a term paper on poetic technique, to examine a poet's most prominent themes, or to lead a poetry discussion group.

Coverage

In order to reflect the influence of tradition as well as innovation, poets of various nationalities, eras, and movements are represented in every volume of *PC*. Each author entry presents a historical survey of the critical response to that author's work; the length of an entry reflects the amount of critical attention that the author has received from critics writing in English and from foreign critics in translation. Since many poets have inspired a prodigious amount of critical explication, *PC* is necessarily selective, and the editors have chosen the most significant published criticism to aid readers and students in their research. In order to provide these important critical pieces, the editors will sometimes reprint essays that have appeared in previous volumes of Gale's Literary Criticism Series. Such duplication, however, never exceeds fifteen percent of a *PC* volume.

Organization

Each *PC* author entry consists of the following components:

- **Author Heading:** the name under which the author wrote appears at the beginning of the entry, followed by birth and death dates. If the author wrote consistently under a pseudonym, the pseudonym will be listed in the author heading and his or her legal name given in parentheses in the lines immediately preceding the Introduction. Uncertainty as to birth or death dates is indicated by question marks.

- **Introduction:** a biographical and critical essay introduces readers to the author and the critical discussions surrounding his or her work.

- **Author Portrait:** a photograph or illustration of the author is included when available.

- **Principal Works:** the author's most important works are identified in a list ordered chronologically by first publication dates. The first section comprises poetry collections and book-length poems. The second section gives information on other major works by the author. For foreign authors, original foreign-language publication information is provided, as well as the best and most complete English-language editions of their works.

- **Criticism:** critical excerpts chronologically arranged in each author entry provide perspective on changes in critical evaluation over the years. All individual titles of poems and poetry collections by the author featured in the entry are printed in boldface type to enable a reader to ascertain without difficulty the works under discussion. For purposes of easy identification, the critic's name and the publication date of the essay are given at the beginning of each piece of criticism. Unsigned criticism is preceded by the title of the journal in which it originally appeared. Publication information (such as publisher names and book prices) and parenthetical numerical references (such as footnotes or page and line references to specific editions of a work) have been deleted at the editor's discretion to enable smoother reading of the text.

- **Explanatory Notes:** introductory comments preface each critical excerpt, providing several types of useful information, including: the reputation of a critic, the importance of a work of criticism, and the specific type of criticism (biographical, psychoanalytic, historical, etc.).

- **Author Commentary:** insightful comments from the authors themselves and excerpts from author interviews are included when available.

- **Bibliographical Citations:** information preceding each piece of criticism guides the interested reader to the original essay or book.

- **Further Reading:** bibliographic references accompanied by descriptive notes at the end of each entry suggest additional materials for study of the author. Boxed material following the Further Reading provides references to other biographical and critical series published by Gale.

Other Features

Cumulative Author Index: comprises all authors who have appeared in Gale's Literary Criticism Series, along with cross-references to such Gale biographical series as *Contemporary Authors* and *Dictionary of Literary Biography*. This cumulated index enables the user to locate an author within the various series.

Cumulative Nationality Index: includes all authors featured in *PC,* arranged alphabetically under their respective nationalities.

Cumulative Title Index: lists in alphabetical order all individual poems, book-length poems, and collection titles contained in the *PC* series. Titles of poetry collections and separately published poems are printed in italics, while titles of individual poems are printed in roman type with quotation marks. Each title is followed by the author's name and the volume and page number corresponding to the location of commentary on specific works. English-language translations of original foreign-language titles are cross-referenced to the foreign titles so that all references to discussion of a work are combined in one listing.

Citing *Poetry Criticism*

When writing papers, students who quote directly from any volume in the Literary Criticism Series may use the following general formats to footnote reprinted criticism. The first example pertains to material drawn from periodicals, the second to material reprinted from books:

[1]David Daiches, "W. H. Auden: The Search for a Public," *Poetry* LIV (June 1939), 148-56; excerpted and reprinted in *Poetry Criticism*, Vol. 1, ed. Robyn V. Young (Detroit: Gale Research, 1990), pp. 7-9.

[2]Pamela J. Annas, *A Disturbance in Mirrors: The Poetry of Sylvia Plath* (Greenwood Press, 1988); excerpted and reprinted in *Poetry Criticism*, Vol. 1, ed. Robyn V. Young (Detroit: Gale Research, 1990), pp. 410-14.

Comments Are Welcome

Readers who wish to suggest authors to appear in future volumes, or who have other suggestions, are cordially invited to contact the editors.

Acknowledgments

The editors wish to thank the copyright holders of the excerpted criticism included in this volume and the permissions managers of many book and magazine publishing companies for assisting us in securing reproduction rights. We are also grateful to the staffs of the Detroit Public Library, the Library of Congress, the University of Detroit Mercy Library, Wayne State University Purdy/Kresge Library Complex, and the University of Michigan Libraries for making their resources available to us. Following is a list of the copyright holders who have granted us permission to reproduce material in this volume of *PC*. Every effort has been made to trace copyright, but if omissions have been made, please let us know.

COPYRIGHTED EXCERPTS IN *PC*, VOLUME 17, WERE REPRODUCED FROM THE FOLLOWING PERIODICALS:

The American Book Review, v. 10, September-October, 1988.© 1988 by *The American Book Review.* Reproduced by permission.—*American Poetry,* v. 5, Fall, 1987.© 1987 by Lee Bartlett and Peter White. All rights reserved.Reproduced by permission.—*The American Poetry Review,* v. 22, November-December, 1993 for "Kin and Kin: The Poetry of Lucille Clifton" by Alicia Ostriker. Copyright © 1993 by World Poetry, Inc.Reproduced by permission of the author.—*The American Society Legion of Honor Magazine,* v. 32, 1961 for "Victor Hugo's Poetics" by Michael Riffaterre. © copyright by *The American Society of the French Legion of Honor Magazine* 1961. Reproduced by permission of the author.—*Callaloo,* v. 6, 1983 for a review of "Two-Headed Woman" by Marilyn Nelson Waniek. Copyright © 1983 by Charles H. Rowell. All rights reserved.Reproduced by permission of the author.—*Canadian Journal of Italian Studies,* v. 5, Fall, 1981-Winter, 1982. Copyright 1982, Stelio Cro. Reproduced by permission. *Chicago Sunday Tribune Magazine of Books,* May 12, 1963 for "Rugged Poetry Imbued with Spirit of the Hawk" by Stephen Spender. Reproduced by courtesy of Faber and Faber Ltd. and the Literary Estate of Stephen Spender.—*CLA Journal,* v. XXX, March, 1987.Copyright, 1987 by The College Language Association. Used by permission of The College Language Association.—*Contemporary Literature,* v. 16, Autumn, 1975. © 1975 by the Board of Regents of the University of Wisconsin System. Reproduced by permission of The University of Wisconsin Press.—*Critical Quarterly,* v. 17, Summer, 1975. © Manchester University Press 1975.Reproduced by permission of Basil Blackwell Limited.—*ELH,* v. 39, June, 1972. Copyright © 1972 by The Johns Hopkins University Press. All rights reserved. Reproduced by permission.—*Encounter,* v. XXXV, December, 1970 for a review of "The Way of a World" by Ronald Hayman. © 1970 by the author. Reproduced by permission of the author.—*English Literary Renaissance,* v. 4, Winter, 1974.Copyright © 1974 by *English Literary Renaissance.* Reproduced by permission.—*Essays in Criticism,* v. IX, April, 1959 for "See, and Relieve" by Donald Davie. Reproduced by permission of the Editors of *Essays in Criticism* and Carcanet Press Limited (Manchester). / v. XVIII, January, 1968 for "The Poetry of Ben Jonson" by G. A. E. Parfitt. Reproduced by permission of the *Editors of Essays in Criticism* and the author.—*Forum Italicum,* v. IX, December, 1975. Copyright © 1975 by *Forum Italicum.* Reproduced by permission.—*French Forum,* v. 6, May, 1981.Copyright 1981 by French Forum, Inc. Reproduced by permission.—*The Georgia Review,* v. XXXII, Summer, 1978. Copyright, 1978, by the University of Georgia. Reproduced by permission.—*Hungry Mind Review,* Winter, 1994-95.Reproduced by permission.—*The Iowa Review,* v. 1, Spring, 1970 for "Calvin Bedient on Charles Tomlinson" by Calvin Bedient. Copyright © 1970 by The University of Iowa. Reproduced by permission of the author.—*Italian Quarterly,* vs. XXI-XXII, Fall, 1980-Winter, 1981; v. XXXI, Winter-Spring, 1990. Copyright © 1981, 1990 by *Italian Quarterly.* Both reproduced by permission.—*The Kenyon Review,* n.s. v. XIV, Summer, 1992 for a review of "Quilting:Poems, 1987-1990" by Leslie Ullman. Copyright 1992 by Kenyon College. All rights reserved. Reproduced by permission of the author.—*The Lion and the Unicorn,* n. 10, 1986. Copyright © 1986 by The Johns Hopkins University Press. Reproduced by permission.—*London Review of Books,* v. 17, July 6, 1995 for "Stirring Your Tea Is Only a Normal Activity If You Stop Doing It Relatively Quickly" by John Redmond. Appears here by permission of the *London Review of Books* and the author.—*Mid-American Review,* v. XIV, 1994 for "Healing Our Wounds: The Direction of Difference in the Poetry of Lucille Clifton and Judith Johnson" by Jean Anaporte-Easton.Copyright © 1994 by the author.Reproduced by the author.—*The Midwest Quarterly,* v. XXX, Spring, 1989. Copyright, 1989, by *The Midwest Quarterly,* Pittsburg State University. Reproduced

COPYRIGHTED EXCERPTS IN *PC*, VOLUME 17, WERE REPRODUCED FROM THE FOLLOWING BOOKS:

PHOTOGRAPHS AND ILLUSTRATIONS APPEARING IN *PC*, VOLUME 17, WERE RECEIVED FROM THE FOLLOWING SOURCES:

Cassian, Nina photograph. (c) Nancy Crampton. Reproduced by permission.

Hugo, Victor-Marie, photograph. The Granger Collection, New York. Reproduced by permission.

Jeffers, Robinson, photograph. AP/Wide World Photos. Reproduced by permission.

Ortiz, Simon, photograph by Nancy Crampton. Reproduced by permission.

Pasolini, Pier Paolo, photograph by Lutfi Ozkok. Reproduced by permission.

Tomlinson, Charles, photograph. Matrix International, Inc. Reproduced by permission.

Nina Cassian
1924-

Romanian poet, playwright, short story writer, illustrator, composer, journalist, critic, and translator.

INTRODUCTION

Regarded as one of Romania's most prominent literary figures, Cassian has created a large and varied body of work, the main concern of which is passion: passion as desire and passion as suffering. Cassian's poems are marked especially by their physicality; they are intensely personal, rhythmically complex, and dynamic works that move easily from love to hate, from tenderness to severity. Cassian's dramatic poetry vividly portrays life experience. As Cassian notes, *"Poetry is not to transcend life or to transform it, but it is life. . . . Art is as alive as an animal."*

Biographical Information

Cassian was born to working class parents in Galati, a town at the mouth of the Danube. By the time Cassian was eleven, she and her parents had moved twice, first to Brasov, a city in Transylvania, and then to Bucharest, Romania. These shifts in locale supplied Cassian with access to a wide variety of peoples, landscapes, and celebrations in which she reveled as a child. Cassian started playing piano, composing music, and writing poems at a very young age, and in high school she excelled in these arts—along with painting and foreign languages—to the detriment of her other studies. The rise of fascism in Romania, which forced her to leave her studies at the Pompilian Institute and attend a Jewish girls' school, led Cassian to embrace a staunch Communism. In 1943, Cassian married Vladimir Colin, a Jewish Communist poet, whom she divorced five years later to marry Alexandru Stefanescu, a Christian ten years her senior. She remained married to Stefanescu until his death in 1985. Cassian's creative output suffered in the early 1950s as a result of trying to change her writing style in response to a ruling of the Communist Party which deemed her poetry "decadent." A slight—and temporary—erosion of severe Stalinist Communism in the late 1950s allowed Cassian a period of great creativity and productivity. As a visiting professor of creative writing at New York University in 1985, Cassian was awarded both a Yaddo Fellowship and a Fulbright Fellowship. Later that year, Cassian was informed that a long-time friend, Gheorghe Ursu, had been arrested for keeping a political diary, a diary that contained unpermitted, satirical pieces written by Cassian. Ursu died as a result of injuries sustained during his interrogation. Cassian subsequently received political asylum in the United States. She currently lives and works in New York.

Major Works

Cassian's first collection of poems, *La scara 1/1* (1948; *On the Scale of 1/1*), was denounced by the Communist Party, which claimed the work did not follow properly the Party's principles. In subsequent collections, including *Sufletul nostru* (1949; *Our Soul*), *An viu, nouu sute si saptesprezece* (1949; *Vital Year, 1917*), and *Tinerete* (1953; *Youth*), Cassian attempted to adhere to the Party doctrine she admired. In these works Cassain tried to use simpler vocabulary and avoid metaphorical language as the Communist government preferred. Cassian now rejects these works for aesthetic reasons. With the loosening of restrictions in the late 1950's, Cassian wrote a number of books in which the pleasures of the body are prevalent; these volumes include *Singele* (1966; *Blood*), *Destinele paralele* (1967; *Parallel Destinies*), *Marea conjugare* (1971; *The Big Conjugation*), and the award-winning *Numaratoarea inversa* (1983; *Countdown*). In 1982, Cassian was awarded the Bucharest Writers Association Award for *De indurare* (1981; *Mercy*). *Call Yourself Alive?* (1988) collects love poems from various periods of Cassian's literary career. In Cassain's later works, including the award-winning *Life Sentence* (1990) and

Cheerleader for a Funeral (1992), the poet considers the theme of ageing along with her usual themes of passion, love, loss, and suffering.

Critical Reception

Cassian's work is admired by critics for the same reasons that it was disapproved of by Romania's Communist government; it is both highly personal and highly courageous. While she has been written out of the literary history of her native Romania, Cassian is greatly admired by literary critics who frequently comment upon the strength and the intensity of emotion in her work. Although critics are wary of the difficulties of translating Cassian's rhythms and word-play into English, all agree that the available translations are high-quality, capable of transferring much of the charged energy which defines Cassian's work.

PRINCIPAL WORKS

Poetry

La scara 1/1 [*On the Scale of 1/1*] 1948
An viu, noua sute si saptesprezece [*Vital Year, 1917*] 1949
Cintece pentru republica [*Songs for the Republic*] 1949
Sufletul nostru [*Our Soul*] 1949
Horea nu mai este singur [*Horea Not Alone Anymore*] 1952
Tinerete [*Youth*] 1953
Versuri alese [*Selected Poems*] 1955
Dialogul vintului cu marea: motive bulgare [*The Dialogue of the Wind and Sea: Bulgarian Motives*] 1957
Virstele anului [*The Measures of the Year*] 1957
Sarbatorile zilnice [*Everyday Holidays*] 1961
Spectacol in aer liber [*Outdoor Performance—A Monograph of Love*] 1961
Cele mai frumoase poezii [*The Most Beautiful Poems*] 1963
Sa ne facem daruri [*Gift Giving*] 1963
Disciplina harfei [*The Discipline of the Harp*] 1965
Singele [*Blood*] 1966
Destinele paralele [*Parallel Destinies*] 1967
Ambitus [*Ambit*] 1969
Cronofagie, 1944-1969 [*Chronophagy, 1944-1969*] 1970
Marea conjugare [*The Big Conjugation*] 1971
Recviem [*Requiem*] 1971
Loto-poeme [*Lottery Poems*] 1972
O suta de Poeme [*100 Poems*] 1974
Spectacol in aer liber—o alta monografie a dragostei [*Outdoor Performance—Another Monograph of Love*] 1974
Suave 1977
Viraje [*Orbits*] 1978
De indurare [*Mercy*] 1981
Lady of Miracles 1982
Jocuri de vacanta [*Parlour Games*] (poetry and prose) 1983
Numaratoarea inversa [*Countdown*] 1983
Call Yourself Alive?: Love Poems of Nina Cassian 1988
Life Sentence: Selected Poems 1990
Cheerleader for a Funeral 1992

Other Major Works

Ce-a vazut Oana: versui si cintece [*What Oana Saw: Poems and Songs*] (juvenilia) 1952
Florile patriei [*Flowers of the Homeland*] (juvenilia) 1954
Nica fara frica [*Fearless Niki*] (juvenilia) 1956
Bot Gros, catel fricos [*Big Muzzle, the Fearful Puppy*] (juvenilia) 1957
Printul Miorlau [*Prince Miaow*] (juvenilia) 1957
Chipuri hazlii pentru copii [*Funny Faces for Kids*] (juvenilia) 1958
Aventurile lui Trompisor [*The Adventures of Trunky the Elephant*] (juvenilia) 1959
Incura-lume [*The Mischief Maker*] (juvenilia) 1961
Curcubeu [*Rainbow*] (juvenilia) 1962
Elefantelul curios [*The Curious Little Elephant*, adaptor; from a story by Kipling] (juvenilia) 1964
Pisica de una singura [*The Cat Alone*, adaptor; from a story by Kipling] (juvenilia) 1967
Povestea a doi pui do tigru numiti Ninigra si Aligru (juvenilia) 1969; published in journal *The Lion and the Unicorn* as "Tigrino and Tigrene," 1987
Atit de grozava si adio: confidente ficitve [*You're Wonderful—Adieu: Fictitious Confidences*] (prose) 1971; revised edition, *Confidente fictive* [*Fictitious Confidences*], 1976
Pisica la televizor [*T.V. Cat*] (juvenilia) 1971
Ninigra si Aligru [*Tigrino and Tigrene*] (juvenilia) 1972
Intre noi copiii [*Between Us Kids*] (juvenilia) 1974
Naca fara frica [*Fearless Niki*] (juvenilia) 1984

CRITICISM

Nina Cassian with Geraldine DeLuca and Roni Natov (interview date 1986)

SOURCE: "Writing Children's Literature in Romania: An Interview with Nina Cassian," in *The Lion and the Unicorn*, Vol. 10, 1986, pp. 108-11.

[*In the following interview, Cassian discusses her work in children's literature and her work's reception in Romania.*]

[DeLuca]: *Would you like to talk about the children's books you have written and about why you wrote them?*

[Cassian]: I don't have children. If I write for them, I write for the child inside adults too. I am sure the way children react to my books—very warmly indeed—is due, especially, to the fact that I tried, and perhaps succeeded, in keeping intact the feelings of my own childhood and adolescence, the candor, the capacity for continually discovering the world. It is a cruelty anyway to divide our lives, which are so short, into periods. We have approximately seventy to eighty years to live and we insist on cutting them into childhood, adolescence, young adulthood, maturity, senility, and so forth. It's not only cruel, it's not real. I see life as a unique gesture from beginning to end. I think we can live our lives like those chess players playing several games of chess simultaneously, but we are expected to be excellent chess players! I don't give up what I have already lived, and if I am a real artist I live also in times I haven't reached yet. So being still a child, I address myself to myself and, of course, to those who are more entitled to call themselves children than I am.

The first children's book I wrote was not really written by choice but from necessity. It was in 1950, during the dogmatic period in Romania. Socialist realism was, unfortunately, characterized by the restraining of structures and styles and vocabulary. During that period I lost my appetite for writing poetry. I did write some poems in the politically approved manner because I tried to be a "faithful child of the party." I had become a member of the Communist Party in 1940 when I was 15 years old. There was fascism and war in my country and I wanted to sacrifice myself for the happiness of humanity! So when I was asked to write in a rigid and simplified manner, I tried to do my best, but after awhile, I switched to literature for children because it was the only field where metaphors were still allowed, where imagination was tolerated and assonance was permitted. (It sounds crazy: what has assonance to do with the communist catechism?!)

[Natov]: *Do you always write in verse?*

If I were very proud—and I'm not—I could quote Ovid who said: *"Quidquid tentabam dicere versus erat,"* which means, "Everything I tried to say became verse." No, I wrote two books of short stories but I mainly write and translate poetry. I also think that children are attracted by poetry with its rhyme and rhythm, especially in the early years: it's like playing and it's easy to memorize. That doesn't mean that children (mostly boys perhaps) do not also enjoy adventure stories (which I write . . . in verse). The only prose I loved in my childhood was the fairy tales with their poetical halo.

[Natov]: *Are you still writing poems for children?*

My most recent story in verse was published last year. It is called, **"Copper Red and the Seven Dachsies."** "Dachsies" is a shorter name for dachshund and, except for the title, the book has nothing to do with "Snow White and the Seven Dwarfs." Since I have been in New York, I have translated one of my stories into English with a Romanian friend. It is a story about two little tigers, a bestseller in Romania.

[DeLuca]: *Is most of your poetry for children narrative poetry?*

No, not really. One of my books, for instance, a cycle called **"Prince Meow,"** is a sort of "inventory of bad children." The general tendency or prejudice or superstition in children's literature is to deal with good, nice, kind, pleasing children, even if we know, and they know too, that they can be, now and then, lazy, cruel, or liars.

[Natov]: *What are your bad children like?*

Well, there's the whining kid (Prince Meow), the child who plays the soldier with a trumpet and a drum while—and because—papa is reading a book, the one who dreams of being a great sailor but complains that the water he washes himself with is too cold, the child who forgets everything and has no sense of order, the "Sour Cream Princess," a coquette, who just looks in the mirror and is unwilling to do any work, the boy who won't take anything seriously, the lazy one who lies in bed waiting for the ripe fruit to drop into his mouth, the cruel one who terrorizes animals, the one so very slow that he falls asleep in the middle of a sentence, etc., etc.

I wrote this book to deal with reality, for educational purposes, and for fun. Children loved it because they recognized those "nasty children" from their experience, because they know themselves, and because they appreciated my tender irony toward them.

[DeLuca]: *Do you have a sense of the quality of Romanian children's literature in general?*

Almost all the great writers—our greatest poet (Eminescu), our greatest playwright (I. L. Caragiale), our greatest fiction writer (Sadoveanu)—also wrote for children. If I cannot mention many resounding successes today, I don't think we have many competitors in the field of poetry for adults and classical music.

[DeLuca]: *Do a lot of people read poetry in Romania?*

Not anymore. The pretext is "lack of paper." My story about the two little tigers has been reprinted three times, with about 30,000 copies each time. It could have been reprinted ten times more. Are the publishers such poor businessmen? It's hard to believe. I rather expect it's the generally decreasing interest in and care for culture and especially artistic achievements.

[DeLuca]: *Is there literature for children in the schools?*

It's not taught in schools, if that's what you mean. I deplore the low quality of almost all the recent literary selections included in the textbooks. A didactic, conventional, so-called "patriotic" poetry predominates, in elementary schools as well as in high schools. When my "dachsies" appeared, it was like a carnival in Rio, even though the book has a repulsive aspect, the paper is incredibly bad, the illustrations inadequate. It not only vanished from the bookstores in a couple of days, but parents and children called me for weeks telling me how happy they were about it.

[DeLuca]: *Do you think Romanians particularly appreciate books because they are feeling oppressed?*

The connection is not so simple and mechanical. Let's say it's rather a kind of compensation. In a consumer-oriented society, people are just invaded—and sometimes confused—by the offer. In my country, things are so limited, the necessary objects so dramatically reduced, that people focus on what can easily be bought—books are pretty affordable—and also on what cannot be bought or sold, on what is priceless, like love and friendship and spiritual values. That's nice and sane, but I hate to think that it happens only because they have no choice. I still hope that life can be well balanced.

Fleur Adcock (essay date 1988)

SOURCE: An introduction to *Call Yourself Alive?: Love Poems of Nina Cassian,* Forest Books, 1988, pp. vii-ix.

[*In the following introduction to* Call Yourself Alive?, *Adcock praises the physicality of Cassian's poems. Adcock also notes that while the translations are very good, they cannot quite convey Cassian's "expertise in the more subtle and flexible rhythms of spoken language" that the original poems display*.]

Nina Cassian is a notable phenomenon in Romanian literature: a poet remarkable for the vigour, the sensuality and indeed the savagery of her work, but also an intellectual, a critic, a journalist, and a writer of fiction and of books for children. Side by side with this prolific literary career she has also had a parallel career as a composer, with a sideline in book illustration. But it is as a poet that she is best known, with an established international reputation. She has been publishing poetry for forty years: the earliest poem in this book [*Call Yourself Alive?*] dates from 1947, the latest from 1987. This selection concentrates on her love poetry, with love being interpreted in its widest sense: not only sexual passion, but love of life, of freedom, and, in the splendidly sensuous final poem, of her own language.

Cassian never lets us forget that we have bodies, and that all our living has to be done through them and in them. Mysterious and powerful events happen to people's bodies in her poems.

—*Fleur Adcock*

Perhaps the most immediately striking feature of these poems is their startling physicality: Cassian never lets us forget that we have bodies, and that all our living has to be done through them and in them. Mysterious and powerful events happen to people's bodies in her poems. In "**Temptation**", which opens this collection, the temptress promises her lover:

you'll feel your pores opening
like fish mouths, and you'll actually be able to hear
your blood surging through all those lanes.

In the tenderly and almost ritualistically erotic "**The First and Last Night of Love**" the woman sees 'strange pale herbs dried beneath her hands' where she has touched the man's hair. In "**The Rainmaker**" the speaker tells her lover:

Your arms pour down my body,
your eyes rinse my throat,
. . .
Water-tassels hang from the ends of my fingers.

And in "**Romance**"—in which, as so often in Cassian's poems, love has turned to something more like hate—the speaker says:

Forgive me for making you weep,
I should have murdered you,
I should have dragged out your soul
and battered you with it.

There is a good deal of blood in these poems—rather more than is fashionable nowadays, perhaps, but Nina Cassian is not concerned with anything so superficial as fashion.

All the poems I have quoted so far date from the 1960s. In some of her more recent work, Cassian's concern with the physical takes on a new aspect, when she turns to the process of her own ageing. In "**Nude**" she writes:

I stroll the beach
with this useless frame
like a piece of scrap . . .

In "**Mud**" she sees herself as a crocodile ready to snap, but:

Nothing happens.
I'm just an old woman.

There is despair here, but in a wonderful poem written at about the same time (1983) she has a more positive vision of her ageing self:

In a solar grand old age
cheerful flies pester me
because I smell of honey and sea.

Her awareness of the body's progression through the stages of life also extends backwards, to the years of childhood, in the joyfully celebratory "**Part of a Bird**".

English-speaking readers will find a great deal to enjoy in these translations, but they will partially be deprived of one pleasure: the finely-judged metrical patterns and often rhyming forms of the originals. A great deal of the rhythm and form of Nina Cassian's poetry comes across in Andrea Deletant's and Brenda Walker's sensitive and faithful translations, and the full force of their emotional impact is present, but it is impossible to convey in English the full technical skill of the originals. Cassian has an excellent ear for rhythm—a quality which may possibly be related to her talents as a composer, but has a lot to do with a different expertise in the more subtle and flexible rhythms of spoken language.

The arrangement of the book is thematic rather than chronological, but the dates of the individual poems (bearing in mind that they are only a selection from a lifetime's work) reveal an illuminating pattern: a handful from the 1940s and '50s, a rich gathering from the 1960s, one single example from 1971, and then, after what appears to have been a lull, an abundant harvest from the years since 1980. It is particularly exciting to see so many new poems. They are interspersed throughout the book, but there is also a large cluster of them in the final section, reflecting Nina Cassian's experiences since she left Romania for the United States in 1985. Some express the pain of exile; one or two grieve for the deaths of loved ones:

> The immigration office is not the ideal place
> to keen your dead

some are celebrations of the language she has left behind, as in **"Licentiousness"**, where she tells of:

> the clitoris in my throat
> vibrating, sensitive, pulsating,
> exploding in the orgasm of Romanian.

But there is also a sense of her looking ahead, tentatively but with a stoical courage, to whatever her new life may bring. At the end of **"The Immigration Department"** she writes:

> With the glasses of my loved one
> on my famous nose,
> I'm waiting, waiting,
> for centuries, always waiting
> to be called
> by the clerk.

And in **"Tapestry"** we see her stance as that of a figure in a heraldic picture, threatened but still heroic:

> With one foot in the grave
> and the other on the tiger skin
> —that's how I see myself, defeated and triumphant
> in this hunting scene.

It is appropriate that the skin in the image is that of a tiger—an animal which could serve as a symbol for this fierce, lithe, beautifully constructed and uncompromising poetry.

Lesley Chamberlain (essay date 1989)

SOURCE: "Letters After Love," in *Times Literary Supplement*, February 24, 1989, p. 200.

[*In the following excerpt, Chamberlain favorably reviews* Call Yourself Alive? *and finds the collection a refined and emotive look at human experience.*]

The refinement and strength of feeling which distinguish contemporary Romanian poetry have an eminent representative in Nina Cassian, who in this collection of poems from four decades translates her daily joys and disappointments into a glacial, hard-edged, barely real landscape. In **"Winter Event"** (1947) the snow throws into relief the fire and dazzle of a kiss glimpsed and heard like a passing fox. **"The cold"** of twenty years later describes a shameful contraction of humanity. The failure to forge bonds, our barely concealed lust for each other's blood ("Cold's lifestyle produces a strange impression of order") are mitigated by convention, "the pale, sweet sister of the law, / making it easier for us, if not to live, / at least, to survive".

A poem from 1965, **"I wanted to stay in September"**, locates Cassian at her most happily sensual, knowing the nearness of cold but living in an easier season, "with one hand in the trees—the other / in the greying sand, to slip / along with summer into autumn". Yet she is "fated to be uprooted from landscapes / with an unprepared soul", and with that wrench we are in the emotional country that most of these poems occupy, after-love. **"Letters"** (1967) conveys the purged alertness Cassian repeatedly feels after an ending—to love, hope, youth or summer. As Fleur Adcock points out in her brief introduction and biographical sketch, these poems are about love of freedom, life and language, not only sexual love. They reverberate with the resourcefulness and inventiveness which makes us go on living greedily despite pain, and these are the qualities which make Cassian's voice an impressively energetic one.

> Water's getting dearer
> I'd better learn
> To swim in dust
> And drink mud.

Moreover she has a very determined impatience: "I can't lose time like this any longer, / forced to feel pain—ashamed to respond."

> These poems are about love of freedom, life and language, not only sexual love. They reverberate with the resourcefulness and inventiveness which makes us go on living greedily despite pain, and these are the qualities which make Cassian's voice an impressively energetic one.
>
> —*Lesley Chamberlain*

Cassian emigrated to the United States in 1985, and her mixed experience of loss and positive uncertainty is reflected in her latest work. "The clerk won't be convinced

/ of my metaphors", she writes in **"The Immigration Department"**, and as she waits in the queue she almost wishes to be refused entry as a poet, writing in parenthesis, "hope unbalances me". One is bound to wonder how much the memory of Romania's astringent political circumstances, supplying real material deprivation to echo every emotional loss, and obliging poets to take what refuge they can from censorship, will remain with Cassian; such conditions pushed her, early on, towards a surreally suggestive language. A recent poem, **"Fog"** (1987), is reminiscent of an emergency which could occur anywhere, though it fits the present shutdown state of her native country well:

> Fog obliterating colours,
> greying characters;
> If I dig the fog with my hands
> I'll come across other hands digging towards me.

Exile too must have been a familiar experience before Cassian left. She writes of the lonely intricacies of free expression, as in a foreign land the phrases continue to swell, "exploding in the orgasm of Romanian".

Marguerite Dorian (essay date 1990)

SOURCE: A review of *Call Yourself Alive?: Love Poems of Nina Cassian,* in *World Literature Today,* Winter, 1990, pp. 92-3.

[*In the following review, Dorian praises the way in which Cassian's poetry captures the "wonderfully shocking metamorphoses and mutations of words and feelings, of people and objects."*]

Nina Cassian is a prolific poet with a large number of verse collections (***On the Scale 1/1, Songs for the Republic, The Ages of the Year, The Daily Holidays, Outdoor Show, Parallel Destinies, The Discipline of the Harp, Chronophagia, Ambitus, Lotto-Poems, Counting Backward,*** et cetera) and with a definite place in the generation of Romanian poets who began publishing at the end of the last war. Her poetry takes shape at the intersection of lucidity ("the platinum scalpel with which / I attempt the surgery of truth") with the games of imagination, the enticing, wonderfully shocking metamorphoses and mutations of words and feelings, of people and objects.

Taking the latitude and longitude of Cassian's work is no simple matter, however; for just as the charmed reader believes he is holding the map of the poet's passions and problems, she makes an about-face, scorns his admiration with an ironic grin, eludes him, reappears as fury, feline lover, murderess, buffoon, or ship's figurehead bringing in a new cargo of inventions, offering new projects and proposals. She may undertake "an anthology of hand motions" or, to punish her lover, decide to unscrew his head: "From now on—that's where you start—at the knot in your tie." Ready for tumultuous celebrations and longed-for communions, she may arrive bearing fantastic gifts but would also smuggle in the threat of "adamant truths." Her

ironic list of temptations, drawn for a reluctant lover, offers life at an altitude and an intensity of giant dimensions, her hunger for living and experiment unsatiable: "Call yourself alive? I promise you / you'll be deafened by dust falling on the furniture / you'll feel your eyebrows turning to two gashes / and every memory you have—will begin / at Genesis."

Cassian's world appears in savage flux and reflux, inventing, dismantling, and reinventing itself with mischievous and sober variations, but its energy radiates from a constant center: the miracle of love. Absorbed by love and loving, devoured by it and devouring too, ferocious and cajoling, hunter and hunted, she knows all its nuances: hate-love, antilove, rejection and ecstasy, love under the surgery of the platinum scalpel ("We lived like two monsters / on the back of our young years"), sensual love ("lazy blood, like a resin / ran through us both"), or touchingly ridiculous love ("coming home through the drizzle / love with light shoes / with a blue-green scarf / and which still won't believe / in cold--and walks for hours, / coughing and sneezing"). She is Eve consumed by the memory of being one with her man's body and by the longing to be "enfolded back into his ribs," only to move on, impatient with love's imperfection and discordances: "I can't lose time like this any longer / and I'll take myself higher than you and beyond." We are offered the rediscovery of a lost Atlantis of love, which has disappeared from the poetry of contemporary European women. There are a few instances, as in the poem **"The First and Last Night of Love,"** when lovemaking with its cosmic beat, its thrilling and sad vibrations, seems to have been reinvented by Cassian. The night "is a symbol inhaled very slowly"; the lovers enter the threatening world of a Cocteau-like fairy tale, and their love gestures are reviving the discovery of love at the beginning of the world. Cassian's mourning poems, ferocious and tender, are also intense love poems. She mourns aloud, with the gestures of the heroines of classical Greek tragedies, drawing the entire world into the vortex of her pain.

How much of Cassian's tumultuous and original voice is made available to the English-speaking reader by *Call Yourself Alive?* Definitely some of it. The collection offers sixty poems translated by the same Deletant-Walker team which so far has given us six books of Romanian verse, and once more the work is done sensitively and respectfully. The problems of finding English correspondences for the rhymes and rhythms of Romanian poetry, where the "discipline of the harp" is rigorous and rhyming is a tradition informed with culture, remain to be discussed elsewhere. A good many of Cassian's poems are games delighting in words and language and show her Meistersinger's virtuosity. They had to be eliminated from consideration. In exchange we are offered a number of her latest poems; they open a new cycle in the work and life of the poet, who in 1985 left Romania and now lives in New York. The time of Cassian's exquisite games is receding, lacerated by memories of love and death, under the growing shadow of aging, in alien cities ("it is Christmas in mid-America"), like a Christmas decoration: "I rotate but without air / without delicate tinkling, hung from the ceiling." Still, her poetry remains indomitable. Wounded by time, by the loss of country and language, impatient with such absurdities as consolation and reasonableness, she challenges God the way she would challenge one of her reluctant lovers: "If you really exist—show up / as a bear, a goat, a pilot / come with eyes, mouth, voice /—demand something from me, / force me to sacrifice myself, / take me in your arms, protect me from above, feed me with the seventh part of a fish, / hiss at me, reanimate my fingers, / refill me with aromas, with astonishment /—resurrect me."

William Jay Smith (essay date 1990)

SOURCE: An Introduction, in *Life Sentence: Selected Poems,* W.W. Norton and Company, 1990, pp. xv-xxiv.

[*In this introduction to* Life Sentence, *Smith praises Cassian's intensity, gives an overview of pervading themes in her work, and offers biographical information on the poet.*]

Nina Cassian comes to us, even in translation, as a poet of tremendous range and vitality. We are at once aware of her antecedents: a modernist, nurtured on those French poets who, through T. S. Eliot and Ezra Pound, helped to change the shape of twentieth-century poetry in England and America, she is at the same time very much the product of Romania. Her poetry has something of the clear line and the strikingly simple texture of her countryman, Brancusi, and, like him, her sophistication is grounded in folklore. There is great variety to her work and a comic spirit that recalls the theater of the absurd of her other countryman, Ionesco. Her themes are eternal, love and loss, life and death, and they are communicated with an immediacy as rare as it is compelling. Hers is a passionate commitment in the greatest tradition of lyric poetry. For this poet, life is indeed a tragic sentence. But the sentence that she composes in answer to life is made up of clean Latin vowels, with rational syllables "trying to clear the occult mind." Only in poetry does she reach "the word, the inhabited homestead." And in poetry she takes her reader with her.

Nina Cassian composes poetry by "tea-light," in a golden zone of "pure burning amber." And in that golden light she explores the physicality of love. As with Sappho, the sight of the lover is overpowering.

>Your eyes make the air pulse,
>they electrify the house,
>the drawers open, rugs flood
>down the stairs like a river.
>Your star-like teeth
>rip open my heart like lightning.

And when the lover has departed:

>the air whistled as if clutching a line
>of a thousand arrows never reaching their target.

and the cruelty of the departed lover circles the poet's head "like a bright rotting halo." Rejected in love, the poet feels her arms like anchors trail at her side and she chokes on an "Isadora-scarf" of smoke from her cigarette:

>Void. Loneliness . . .
>search is pointless—
>all that is true
>are my doubts:
>How real are you?
>How real were you?

Everything in Cassian's poetry has its precise sensory description:

>A rug of dead butterflies at my feet,
>dead and limp
>(they don't experience rigor mortis).

The widow smells "incitingly / of absence:"

>A dog sniffs at her solitude
>and takes off yelping.

The memory of childhood is intense and physical:

>Even now my breast bone's aching
>when I remember how I was running
>because the smell of petunias invaded everything.

Her poems are filled with creatures—birds, domestic, exotic, and fantastic—with squirrels, rabbits, monkeys. Here is a living, moving world (the poet is in orbit), where even the smallest sensation is penetrating and where she is "deafened by dust falling on the furniture," and where she experiences love in

>long knives in the night,
>beaks by the window . . .

and sees terror

>in the long, rough, white thread
>through aunt's needle—
>the fly's legs rubbing against each other.

The wheel of the ship on which she finds herself stranded

>rests like a spider
>fixed on my wooden sky . . .

Even the poet's devotion to language is precise and physical; she speaks of the

>clitoris in my throat
>vibrating, sensitive, pulsating,
>exploding in the orgasm of Romanian.

For all the immediacy of Nina Cassian's poetry (and this immediacy and sensory appeal have made her a brilliant writer for children), her tone is never confessional but rather intense and direct and without self-pity. In her celebrated "**Self-Portrait**" she compares her strange triangular face to the figurehead on the prow of a pirate ship. She is vulnerable but proud; her totem bird is the swan, but a swan with a big bill, half-bird, half-woman, graceful and mysterious. Nina Cassian's friend Petre Solomon has given us this description of the poet when she first began to publish:

> Although she had not yet published her verses in a volume, Nina's poems in various magazines of the time signaled a characteristically lyrical voice—it was strong and acute, in harmony with her whole iconoclastical generation. To her outstanding intelligence, an inimitable gift for cutting and explosive statement could be added. Equally talented in poetry, music, and painting (she had taken classes from Löwendal and Maxy), Nina even had an extraordinary gift for acting in public or during our literary sessions in the circle of her numerous intimate friends. Nina's presence in a group of otherwise heterogeneous individuals acted always as a unifying factor, as a social "glue" of immediate effect. It was enough that she appear among such a group for everyone to become lively, as they discovered elective affinities. Improvising or playing Debussy, Bartók, or Constantin Silvestri on the piano, Nina would find herself the center of attention, which she could also capture through other means, especially brilliant conversation. Having a complex because of her Dantesque profile, Nina always tried to prove the superiority of her intellect in an aggressive manner, devised to disarm those who might have been paying heed to her "ugliness" (which was in fact mostly imaginary).

When I first met her in Bucharest in 1970, I found Nina Cassian very much the center of her circle, as Petre Solomon describes her, a charming and witty companion, but not in the least aggressively intellectual. Nor did I find anything ugly in her Dantesque profile: on the contrary, it seemed only to enhance her charm and elegance and to make her totally unlike anyone else.

Nina Cassian (Renée Annie Ştefănescu) was born November 27, 1924, at Galati, a city on the Danube. She would discover the charm of this city later during several short vacations because her family moved when she was two years old to Brasov, an ancient city at the base of Mount Timpa in Transylvania. It was here that Coresi in 1560 published a Romanian translation of the *Gospels,* the first major book in Romanian. "Brasov provided me," Nina Cassian has written, "with an ideal setting, the halo of an Austro-Hungarian 'burg': heavy wooden gates concealing mysterious interior courtyards; the majestic Black Church; narrow lanes paved with stones from the river climbing toward the mountain—and green mists on the wooded peaks; sumptuous winters; cold, sparkling well springs; glades with translucent flowers; strong downpours; vivid, scented air. I was a happy child." The town had a mixed population of Romanians, Germans, Hungarians, and Jews. "I moved among all these different peoples, learning their languages and making friends," she continues. "It is not too farfetched to think that it was this eclectic background that molded my internationalist feeling, never allowing me to lose a sense of the specific character of the respective peoples—quite the contrary—and protecting me from any

prejudices and chauvinist narrow-mindedness. As a child, this amounted to observing every religious holiday as it came along so that the whole year was for me a perpetual celebration. I was particularly fond of the celebration of the Saint Nicholas of Austrian tradition. I enjoyed setting my little shoes on the windowsill and in the morning finding them brimming over with candies and, especially, with scarlet cellophane bags from which little red velvet devils holding tiny golden pitchforks were grinning at me. Of course, I waited with equal impatience for the ceremony of trimming the Christmas tree and for Easter, with its snowdrops, chocolate rabbits, and little eggs of blue, pink, purple sugar. My parents were not religious so even the Jewish traditions that were preserved in our home had for me a quality of entertaiment and culinary ecstasy rather than of spiritual fulfillment."

When she was five years old, she had her first piano lessons and composed her first waltz; she also learned to read and wrote her first poem. Her parents had little formal education but her father became a reputable translator from French and German and the author of a fine version of Poe's "The Raven." She went through the primary grades in the Jewish school affiliated with the Synagogue of Brasov; her summers were spent in Constanta, where she discovered a beach "still savage and abundant with giant dunes, and the multicolored atmosphere of a cosmopolitan city, the bead curtains at the entrances of the barber shops, the cafés, the wave-washed piers, the harbor, the statue of Ovid who found himself exiled to these inhospitable shores when Constanta was still called Tomi and in whose cold winters wine would freeze in goblets."

When she was eleven, her family moved to Bucharest, where her father was unemployed for along period of time and where the family moved from boarding house to boarding house, each one shabbier than the last. She began her high-school studies at the Pompilian Institute, where French was taught intensively. It was a school for young ladies of good families but which occasionally accepted a few of more modest backgrounds. She was an unexceptional student, having no appetite for disciplined study with the exception of foreign languages, music and drawing, subjects that would always salvage her grade average. When Romania embraced Fascism, she was expelled from the Pompilian Institute and required to register at a high school for Jewish girls. While still a student, she became an ardent Communist, embracing a doctrine that she felt promised to solve all problems. "I am not the only person in history," she has said, "who came to see an ideal turned into its very opposite."

In January 1943, at the age of eighteen, she married Vladimir (Jany) Colin, a handsome young Jewish Communist poet and an admirer of modern, especially French, poetry. But in 1948, when she was 23 she met Al. I. (Ali) Ştefănescu, a Christian ten years older than she, a thin, wrinkled little man ("the old Child" he had been called when young), who had been orphaned at the age of nine. He had worked his way through the university to become a teacher of French and an editor of the review, *Contemporanul,* and later a critic and novelist. She divorced Colin and married Ştefănescu. It was perhaps the total differ-ence in their backgrounds that intensified the magnetism that drew them together and kept them together for three and a half decades until his death.

After the turmoil of World War II and just before meeting Ştefănescu, Nina Cassian published her first book, ***On the Scale of One to One,*** a volume inspired by the *poètes fantaisistes,* Max Jacob, Toulet, and Apollinaire. Cassian had already translated a number of French poets as well as the *Gallow Songs* of Christian Morgenstern. In her teens, when she began to write seriously, Cassian had been influ-enced by Mihai Eminescu (1850-89), the great Romantic, and later by Tudor Arghezi (1880-1967), whose rich metaphorical language held her attention. But, as with many other Romanian poets, it was the work of Ion Barbu (1885-1961), that truly revolutionized her style. Barbu, a math-ematician, whose real name was Dan Barbilian, was as hermetic as Mallarmé and as original. Barbu's work, as well as that of the French poets she emulated, led her in this early volume to a concentrated form of surrealism. There are surrealist touches throughout the work of Nina Cassian, but she has made it clear that she never wholly espoused surrealist doctrine. Her surrealism is close to that found in Romanian folklore. Like Ionesco, Nina Cassian owes something to Urmuz (1883-1923), whose rich bur-lesque spirit inspired the surrealists. The Castle Never-more in her poem is straight out of Edgar Allan Poe, but it is also rooted in Transylvania, the home of Vlad the Impaler, the fifteenth-century Prince of Wallachia. Vampires flicker through her poetry, which is replete at times with blood and terror, but is often edged with gallows humor, and, more often than not, with a touch of the absurd.

Vampires flicker through Cassian's poetry, which is replete at times with blood and terror, but is often edged with gallows humor, and, more often than not, with a touch of the absurd.

—William Jay Smith

Because of her first book, Nina Cassian was attacked by the authorities as an enemy of the people. She tried to change her style and follow the party line. She cut back on her vocabulary and attempted to use only words that the masses could understand with no metaphorical language whatever. And yet similes would appear all the same. In one poem she described Lenin sitting at his desk while the light filtering through the window turned his inkwell into a great blue light bulb. The poem caused a scandal: she was accused of wishing to write about the ink and the lightbulb and of using Lenin merely as a pretext. With sincerity and conviction, she wrote four more books, which she now rejects aesthetically. Her conscience was clear, but her talent was in eclipse. What fantasy she had left went into her books for children, in which she could in-dulge her word play. Finally between 1955 and 1957 she found that she could not write at all. She turned for a while to composing; musical notes, she said, could not be found in the dictionary and she could not be accused of making allusions in her musical compositions.

In 1957 there was a thaw; Stalin had died. "Words I had banished and despised came back to me little by little," Nina has said. "Then it was an avalanche—books, books, books, one after another. And again, poetry. We had five wonderful years from 1965 to 1970. We enjoyed an amazing freedom, and we all used this freedom to write as we wished." The seventies, however, were more restricted and more chaotic. Nina Cassian turned again to musical com-position, but continued to publish poetry, children's books, and film criticism.

When Nina Cassian came to this country in 1985, it never occurred to her that she might not return to Romania. Invited to teach a course in Creative Writing at New York University, she arrived in September and began the semester with every indication that her stay here would be a pleasant one. Her husband of many years, Al. J. Ştefănescu, had died several months before, and she welcomed the change of scene and the challenge of meeting and working with American writers and students. She was informed almost at once that she would receive the Fulbright fellowship which had been awarded to her earlier but which the Romanian authorities had never told her about. After such a happy beginning, she found within two months that it would be impossible under any circumstances to return to Romania.

During the summer of 1985, her friend of many years, Gheorghe Ursu, an engineer and amateur of the arts, had been questioned by the police and had ultimately been set free. Ursu was an old friend; Nina Cassian had shared summer vacations with him in a fishing village, of which she has spoken in her reminiscences of Paul Celan. They had often joked and shared, as old friends do, their feelings about literature, life, and the political scene. In New York Nina Cassian heard that Ursu had again been arrested. In his office the police had discovered a diary that he had kept for forty years. It was an important, expressive, thor-ough document, in which he had put down every aspect of his life, and in which he had committed the indiscretion of mentioning his close friends by name. Nina Cassian learned that she was not only named but that pointed satirical and often scathing verses in which she had lampooned the authorities had been carefully copied out and their author clearly identified. As a result, Ursu, she learned, had been questioned in detail about her. He had subsequently been tortured, and after another month, he died. It was clear that now she could not return to Bucharest. "A poet never leaves his country, his territory, his language, of his or her own free will," Nina Cassian has told me, "but I had no choice." She requested political asylum in this country, and her request was granted.

The nightmare that she had delineated so splendidly in her poems—the ship of her country dead-still in the water with no helmsman to guide it, the syllables of the lie outlined on the leader's lips—were no longer merely imaginative projections; they were absolute reality. Argue with chaos though she might, in poetry she had won but in life she had lost. Her life sentence, like death itself, was confirmed when at Christmas 1987, she learned that the authorities had put a seal on the house that she had left behind in Bucharest; they had emptied it of all its contents, all her manuscripts, letters, drawings, paintings, notebooks, musical compositions, her entire library and her most precious personal mementos from her school days and her travels, the entire accumulation of a rich and full literary life. What has happened to all these things no one knows. She has been written out of her country's literature, its anthologies, its histories, its textbooks. Her books, even her totally apolitical children's books, have all been withdrawn from circulation. At present she is a nonperson; she does not exist. As in one of her poems, the tables have been wiped clean. The only other similar instance in recent literary history that I know of is that of Aldous Huxley, who watched his house in the hills above Los Angeles burn to the ground with all the writings he had retained since his boyhood together with the journals that his wife had kept during her entire life. Like Nina, Huxley was beginning life again, *tabula rasa.* But Nina was beginning life again in another country, with another language very different from her own. It would not be an easy adjustment.

When I was in Bucharest again last February, I saw a number of the friends of Nina Cassian who had surrounded her on my previous visit in 1970. Her absence left a terrible gap. Without her, something of the cultural fabric of her country, of which she had been so vital a part, seemed to have come unglued.

Because Nina Cassian is herself a brilliant translator, she has understood the difficulty of assembling this selection of her poems in English. Some poems have had to be omitted because the resonance and the allusions of the original could not be carried over. Nina Cassian often employs intricate verse forms, rich in rhymes. Richard Wilbur and Dana Gioia have succeeded brilliantly in retaining exactly the rhyme schemes of the poems they have translated; and many others have also given close approximations of the original form. But because rhyme is much more difficult in English than in Romanian, some translators have had to abandon it completely in order to convey the force and meaning of the original poem. The author has permitted, and even encouraged, her translators to take considerable liberty as long as they did not violate the spirit of her work. It is surely a tribute to the validity of Nina Cassian's poetry that that spirit has come through so well in so many of the versions of these poet-translators, each with his or her own distinctive style.

Constance Hunting   (essay date 1991)

SOURCE: "Methods of Transport," in *Parnassus,* Vol. 16, No. 2, pp. 377-88.

[In this excerpt, Hunting investigates and applauds the energy and techniques in Life Sentence.*]*

Tietjens, Monroe, Bullis, Bollingen, Loines, Shelley, Crane, Lilly—what a long train of prizes and awards for the engine of poetry to pull! During a distinguished career, Mona Van Duyn has won them all. As well, she is a member of the National Institute of Arts and Letters and a chancellor of the Academy of American Poets. Then there are the fellowships and the honorary degrees. . . . A very long train indeed, traveling a steady track through a reliable landscape. For thirty years we have been privileged to watch its progress.

Now, rushing from another horizon, around a curve of history, suddenly appears on a quite different track a locomotive so powerful, so sweeping in speed and force, as to remind one of an iron Pegasus, pulling along with seeming effortlessness a train of assorted brightly painted and loosely coupled cars. Whereas its American counterpart travels through level heartlands, this exotic manifestation seems to have in the eye of its headlight the reflection of a landscape of violent juxtapositions, forests, rivers, mountains, steppes impinging on and jostling one another. Such is the impression made by the poetry of Nina Cassian, for over forty years a leading literary figure of Romania with an increasing reputation in Europe and in parts of the English-speaking world.

Their age is very nearly the only thing these two poets have in common; the other is, of course, their sex. Van Duyn was born in Waterloo, Iowa, in 1921, Cassian in Galati, a city on the Danube, in 1924. Van Duyn has published seven volumes of poetry, of which *Near Changes* is the most recent; save for criticism and reviews, all of her published work is poetry. For twenty years she served as editor, with her husband, Jarvis Thurston, of *Perspective: A Quarterly of Literature,* the magazine they founded in 1947. Cassian has published more than fifty books, including works of fiction and books and puppet plays for children; ***Life Sentence: Selected Poems*** is the first major collection of her poetry to appear in America, although a few translations have been published through the valiant small press. The translations in the present volume have been made by American poets, some of whom worked directly with her, and by the poet herself. Cassian is also a composer of music, and has been a journalist, film critic, and translator of, among others, Shakespeare, Brecht, Mayakovsky, and Molière.

To attempt to balance without falsely reconciling two such disparate poets and their offerings of works and days would seem a daunting, even a misguided task. Better, perhaps, to begin with distinctions of a general nature than with particulars of sought similarity. For example, there are words—and there is language. There are poems—and there is poetry. Between these two poets, there is much to choose.

Whereas Van Duyn's poems move mainly on a horizontal plane, their internal emotional fuel augmented by injections of energy from outside intellectual and historical sources, Nina Cassian's poems in ***Life Sentence*** go up like rockets to flower and burst in showers of sparks against a universal night sky. Sent up from blood-soaked earth like signals of transcendence into poetry's pure atmosphere, they are fueled by the pulse of a single human heart compelled by love of it to celebrate a tragic world.

First, then, momentum. Second, variety. Cassian's subjects occur at any and every instant of her terrifically aware existence, as these randomly chosen opening lines attest: "The lighthouse there at Cape Crepuscular / sends out signals: the weather is getting rough" (from **"The Troubled Bay"**); "The orbit I describe in my environment, / cautiously, so as not to strike birds with my forehead" (from **"Orbits"**); "I wake up and say: I'm through" (from **"Morning Exercises"**); "The word was uttered: let us break its neck" (from **"Game Mistress"**)—open *Life Sentence* anywhere and electrifying images coruscate on the page. Not that the poems are all whoosh and glitter. Many are so quiet that the breaking of a heart may be heard:

> Ready for goodbye, although the moon is rising.
> Ready for goodbye, although the tea is boiling.
> Ready for goodbye, although the wind is pouring
> its triumphant notes into the air.
> Ready for goodbye, although my sister's mother
> carries in her womb a lovely daughter.
> Ready for goodbye.
> 　　("**Ready for Goodbye**," trans. William Jay Smith)

But always they breathe out the sense of an ascending spirit.

Although her poetry has certain affinities with that of Rilke, for example, or of Milosz, and shares their heritage of European Romanticism, it is more transparent in texture than Rilke's, which can become opalescent at the edges, and generally less spacious in contour than Milosz's. And although her antecedents include the French Symbolists who, as William Jay Smith points out in his graceful and erudite Introduction to this selection, influenced Eliot and Pound, she is preeminently herself—not her "own person," as current jargon has it, but her self, Cassian, for poetry as a bird is for the sky.

Van Duyn has a strong sense of the poem as incentive: By molding her experiences into art and offering the poem as a "valentine" to her audience ("the world"), she may cause its members to look at their own experiences in a new way and, perhaps, to act on their findings. "This effort," she has remarked, "assumes a caring about other human beings, a caring which is a form of love." ["Mona Van Duyn," *CA* Interview, by Jean W. Ross, *Contemporary Authors,* New Revision Series, volume 7 (1982), pp. 505-7]. Hence her predilection for multiple examples and rhetorical figurations: They are, in effect, teaching devices. Cassian would agree that the business of poetry is "to put order in the chaos of appearances," but her ideas on the nature of poetry differ from Van Duyn's in that she sees the poem not as illustrative or conversionary means but as a form of life itself: "Poetry is not to transcend life or to transform it, but it *is* life. It doesn't change its structure of being alive, of being organic. Art is as alive as an animal" [Nina Cassian, Interview by Ricia Gordon, transcript, 1987]. To Cassian, poetry has a listening ear.

If art is "as alive as an animal," Cassian is not out to capture it but to release it from its cage of propriety. Freed, it assumes protean shapes. Metaphor becomes metamorphosis:

> My hands creep forward on the hot sand
> to unknown destinations;
> perhaps to the shoreline,
> perhaps to the arms from which they were severed
> and which lie on the beach
> like two decapitated eels.
> 　　("**Sands,**" trans. Naomi Lazard)

Surrealistic, yes; but note the viewpoint, which never deviates from beach level and thus provides stability, so that the poem may "creep forward" with the bodiless "hands" towards the culminating transformation of the shocking final image. Yet the image as image is not final, but goes on replicating itself in the reader's consciousness. Agreed, we say, that hands would wish to rejoin their arms; agreed, that arms without hands might resemble eels. If hands join arms, do hands become the equivalent of heads? For these are "decapitated" eels. If arms have heads, then arms, the bodies of eels, are comparable to human trunks. Are hands, then, the equivalent of intelligence? More than that, for hands also "feel." Hands "think," besides, through touch. So the reader continues, after the poem has left the page, simultaneously thinking and feeling toward it, feeling the exhilaration of thought. As the internal configurations of the poem alter, its observer and companion is changed as well, becoming not only witness to but in his own way participant in the pageant of mutability.

A less violent, ultimately more playful metamorphosis occurs in **"The Couple,"** in which Cassian seems to be setting out to describe a pair of swans:

> Necks crossed, then parallel,
> they float in slow motion
> white and hazel
> mingling their blond contrasts,
> their floating heads
> watching the world from lunar heights,
> their fragile legs like antennae,
> the bones of their foreheads
> breathing sadness and exile . . .

Of course there are clues: "lunar heights," "fragile legs." But so persuasive are such phrases as "they float in slow motion," "floating heads," and that first color adjective "white" that the reader persists in his initial avian impression; furthermore, if he's read Yeats, "sadness and exile" carry irresistible echoes of "The Wild Swans at Coole." And Cassian allows his persistence to continue:

> . . . as they circle in their dismal arena,
> straining upward to escape
> as if pulled by invisible leashes
> in love with their heads
> but hating their captive bodies.
> They separate, they follow
> like the languid hours

of the final days
of an extinct species—

We have taken in the details Cassian has given, we have experienced the motion of the lines, and we see nothing, or almost nothing, but swans, floating on a round pond ("their dismal arena" may be weedy) in the dream of a picture. Then Cassian, in Christopher Hewitt's translation, gives us her final word: ". . . giraffes!" In turning birds into animals, Cassian astonishes not the poem, but *us*. The exclamation point is for *us*: how blind, how gullible, we are! how limited our notions have been! If not swans, then giraffes, Cassian seems to say; or, swans *and* giraffes. Nothing could be simpler, once we have been shown. After all, do we not mingle Linnaean sub-kingdoms?

What might be called the principle of metamorphosis is found throughout *Life Sentence*. In the long poem **"Cold,"** for example, the title quality is made masculine: "He's immutable, self-centered, he doesn't communicate," while "convention," common courtesy, is assigned the feminine gender: "she is the one who asks for our handshake, / for uttering 'good day' and 'good night.'" In **"Kisses,"** the "hundreds, thousands" of these become, with a swiftness that defies ordinary logic, "my fruits, squirrels, carnations, / rivers—my knives!" Yet never does the reader feel the associations to be random; rather, his sense is that each has a history within the situation being so rapidly delineated. In **"Postmeridian,"** the inaction of waiting without anticipation "expands chairs, / flattens the telephone," changes the attributes of physical objects. It is not amorphousness of images that Cassian explores and emphasizes, but coherence of all things animate and inanimate. As she asks in **"Cold,"** "[W]ho could name the place where something begins to change?"

"Part of a Bird," a long, sustained, ecstatic flight of a poem, is perhaps the best exemplar of Cassian's technique of transformation through continual shifts of immediate sensory perception; the poem's off and flying from its title on to its last, questioning line. So pulsing is Cassian's memory of childhood that "Even now my breast bone's aching / when I remember how I was running / because the smell of petunias invaded everything." The poem is in seven unnumbered sections, four long and three successively shorter, the last consisting of a single question. The four long sections contain two or three sentences each, sentences which in their swift spiraling out, their enjambments, and their fairly sparse but natural use of "and" as joiner and leader at once, are only lightly stopped before taking off again—the effect of the punctuation mark being more a dip in flight than a landing. As the sections become briefer, the mind of the poem appears to slow, its words to become more hesitant: "And after that . . . / What was I saying?"; "And after that . . . / —Where was I?" Ellipses are introduced to suggest uncertainty; the vehicle loses altitude, yaws slightly, seems unsure of that destination toward which it has until now been speeding with such assurance. But with the last repetition of "And after that,"

phrased not as an expression of hesitation but as a question which invites more experience, the poem swoops upward with a fresh vigor: "And after that?" The translators, Brenda Walker and Andrea Deletant, seem to have followed Cassian's original with rapt scrupulousness. The result is that **"Part of a Bird"** is, even in translation, virtuosic in all respects, not least in its syntactical brilliance.

In fact, Cassian seems to have inspired in all of her translators here the passionate respect that poets give to a superlative practitioner of their shared art. Thus they are able to approach her work with their own best strengths. Poets will often turn to translating as a spur to or refreshment of their own work; the translators of *Life Sentence,* however, uniformly show unusual devotion to revealing and illuminating the unique forces which propel Cassian's living forms. Although some of the poems initially chosen to be presented in this selection had to be omitted because, as Smith has it in his Introduction, "the resonance and the allusions of the original[s] could not be carried over" into English, the recognition of these difficulties speaks excellently for the sensitivity of editor and translators alike. Smith goes on to report that Cassian, herself a translator of note, "has permitted, and even encouraged, her translators to take considerable liberty as long as they did not violate the spirit of her work." Thus such interpreters as Richard Wilbur and Dana Gioia have been able to keep their translations in strict accordance with Cassian's rhyme schemes, others have been able to approximate them, and still others have elected to emphasize meaning rather than arrangement. The list of translators is also a list of distinguished American poets, among them Stanley Kunitz, Ruth Whitman, and Carolyn Kizer; by investing their own talents in *Life Sentence,* they have produced a treasure. As Cassian has said elsewhere concerning what may be lost in translations of her poems, "I'm not limited to my own music. . . . I'm open to all the tunes in the world" [Interview by Ricia Gordon, transcript, 1987].

Can we draw these two disparate poets closer together by speaking of exile? It is easy, perhaps too easy, to say that all poets, all artists, are in some way exiles, outsiders by temperament, choice, or happenstance. Cassian is, of course, a literal exile, her house in Bucharest emptied and sealed, her name written out of her country's literature. She lives now in New York City; in Romania, Nina Cassian does not exist.

On the surface, Mona Van Duyn's life would seem to admit of none of the exigencies of exile. Longtime residence in St. Louis, Missouri; longtime academic surroundings; consistent, cumulative progress of poetic career. One has the sense, with this American poet, of hardwon and possibly rueful wisdom. Exile of a non-literal sort may occur within safety. There is something appealing in Van Duyn's assessment of her professional achievement: "I've just tried to write the way I thought was best and the way I *could* write" ["Mona Van Duyn," *CA* Interview, by Jean W. Ross, *Contemporary Authors,* New Revision Series, vol. 7 (1982), pp. 505-07].

At this chronologically similar stage of their work, both poets have a keen perception of their relationship to time. Van Duyn feels that "the ideas have become so scarce, so few and far between these last few years." Cassian observes, "You need some detachment and time to look and consider what really happened. If you are under pressure you are a slave of what's happening; you are not the master" [Interview by Ricia Gordon, transcript, 1987]. Even an instant requires time; even revelation requires mastery. For a poet there are many methods of transport. In her poem **"The Troubled Bay,"** Nina Cassian writes:

> I knew, as I swam at length far out from shore,
> thinking of poets and so much in their debt,
> having absorbed a hundred poems or more,
> I'd have to write, or drown in one, myself.

It is, indeed, a life sentence.

Lawrence Sail (essay date 1991)

SOURCE: A review of *Life Sentence: Selected Poems,* in *Stand Magazine,* Vol. 16, No. 2, Autumn, 1991, pp. 13-14.

[*In this review, Cassian's* Life Sentence: Selected Poems *is praised as "a remarkable book, full of joyous energy, utterly honest, and without self-pity."*]

Nina Cassian's life has been disrupted . . . , but as the poems in *Life Sentence* show clearly, nothing has succeeded in vanquishing her zestful brio. Whether recalling childhood, as in the fine poem **"Part of a Bird"**, a free monologue which finally dissolves into humorous non-remembering as if distracted by its own attempt to summon the past, whether describing her own face ('Disjointed shape I'm destined to carry around'), or writing of the implications of love, as in **"Kisses"** ('heavy, slow, hurtful / where blood, voice and memory all take part'), a sense of relish is never far away. Her real subject is indeed love—its delights, but even more its blank aftermath and its hurts. Images of fragmentation and dismemberment are strikingly recurrent, as are those of birds and of flight, the attempt to escape upwards. In one poem which combines both, **"Fable"**, an angel has its wings cut off and is told by God, 'aesthetics doesn't matter here, / only your ability to master imbalance.' Echoes of Baudelaire's albatross—but Cassian's poem ends with a characteristic lack of pretension, as the fallen angel is mistaken for a stork by those who see it land on a roof. In another poem Cassian sees herself as disabled by 'at least three major afflications' which she defines as 'Pride, Loneliness and Art'. The truth is that this is a remarkable book, full of joyous energy, utterly honest and without self-pity. Let the translators also have their due: no less than twenty of them have been at work here, yet the poems read seamlessly. This alone suggests that the Poetry Book Society's Translation Award, given to the book, is well merited. It is also, of course, a real compliment to the poet.

Marguerite Dorian (essay date 1994)

SOURCE: A review of *Cheerleader for a Funeral,* in *World Literature Today,* Vol. 68, No. 4, Winter, 1994, p. 110.

[*In this review, Dorian praises the seductive variety of* Cheerleader for a Funeral, *in which the author treats the themes of love, loss, and growing older both humorously and seriously.*]

Is there life after death—and poetry writing after emigration? With her fourth collection of poems in English translation—following *Lady of Miracles* (1985), *Call Yourself Alive?* (1988), and *Life Sentence* (1990)—Nina Cassian, the Romanian poet and author of over fifty books of verse and prose who in 1985 asked for political asylum in this country, gives an affirmative answer as she consolidates her postemigration literary career. *Cheerleader for the Funeral* collects a number of Cassian's earlier poems (some, like **"Dialectic"** or **"Dance,"** were written as early as 1963), together with a few recent pieces, among which three poems have been written directly in English, a triumph every exiled poet dreams of at some time or other.

Because the poems are not dated, one cannot find out more about the osmosis between poetry writing and living in a new language and a new tradition of poetry, or at what cost the writing of poetry in exile has been accomplished. New and old poetry blend well together here, however, partly because the selection for translation has been skillfully done, but mostly because, from the start of her career, in 1947, in her best pieces, Cassian already had the premonition of the funeral—the funeral of love, of stability, of illusion. Her fear of being stagnant, frozen, that her lyric sources would dry out—a fear which at times takes the form of a great appetite for life, for experience   would drive her back and forth between polarized attitudes and would contribute to the restless, anxious lucidity of her poetry. Her anthological volume *Chronophagia* (Bucharest, 1970) was a passionate and fierce confrontation with Time and its undoings: lovers leave, or, better yet, they bore you and must be abandoned ("Goodbye—no sequel to the fairy tale / tin man with rigid joints covered with dust"); castles burn down, the first night of love is also the last, seasons and landscapes holding the lovers in their fold wilt and disintegrate.

The memorable great celebrations Cassian's poetry has given us, her moments of recovery and regeneration, have been episodic and almost always eroded by the sharp tooth of lucidity. "I do not know how much Time ate from me to feed its abstraction," she tells us in the preface to *Chronophagia,* "nor how much I feasted on it, digested it to turn it into substance, nor if our confrontation is a fight, a polemic or maybe an embrace, hurting like an assassination." In her latest poems her old struggle with Time has remained just as courageous, even as the attack strategy was insidiously modified: the earlier predatory embrace, the frontal assault, is now an intense jeering and mocking of pain, hers and others'; she is the noisy disturber of solemnities and rituals, the "cheerleader for the funeral."

The grace with which some of her new poems accept aging—"I am no longer twenty! . . . / . . . rising from the foam of approximations . . . / I face the unseen side of the world / until fireworks of meaning / illuminate my feast!"— is suspect (Cassian always mocked wisdom, despised caution, and denounced serenity), and the attitude is soon contradicted elsewhere: by a disturbing *Totentanz* scene where "you'll hear my cells cracking / before the appearance of my perfected skeleton," when "the most elaborate dignity / is invaded by the sordid swarm / (bred in a fly's intestine)"; by a terrifying negative of Snow White's classic chromolithograph, "the artificial paradise / of tiny old men," where "Pitch-Black / is dead / in her grown-up bed."

Still, Cassian's celebrated humor with its whole family of nuances—sarcasm, often directed at herself ("the ridiculous beret / on my oblong skull / —like a minuscule hat / on a circus dog"), contempt, and, with them, her freedom and her wonderful impertinence—is intact. With one single verse, like a laser beam, she can still blow to powder the ridiculous lover zealouslyperforming a Chaplinesque suite for his beloved: "he unscrewed mountains . . . jumped in the street with one sock tied to another . . . but then his ego began to sneeze." With her old appetite for play, which gave her poetry a certain weightlessness at such moments and made it immensely entertaining, she might pause for a prank or two. She holds imaginary dialogues with **"Madame Decrepitude,"** aspiring to be "a fringe on your lampshade"; the cuckoo clock "has brownish testicles / heavy with time's semen"; the sound of unknown English words makes its very own hilarious sense to her ("is 'glibly' a squirrel? . . . is 'perfunctory' the dining room / of an abbey?"). Then she can descend abruptly to her gravest

tones; she might take up again her old motif, the sea, on which she has played many erotic variations and which has been a cohesive force holding the couple together throughout difficulties, "caught together in this slice of sea / like a rock, like an eternal / kernel." Once kin to its vast force, she would now seek in it a potential final refuge from the polarities of passion, longing "to communicate through the sea / ear to ear / fish to fish / . . . to forget the breathing / the to-ing and fro-ing / of our restless souls."

With her kit of casting spells, the liquid jewels of her imagery, and some colored streamers saved from her old, beloved surrealistic games—"my fingers don't flow anymore / under the broken bridges of my rings"—Cassian remains an unabashed seducer but also a reflexive woman and a poet organically welded to poetry. Brenda Walker's continuous contact with Romanian poetry, which she translates and publishes regularly, makes the translations lively and inventive.

FURTHER READING

CRITICISM

Cassian, Nina. "Notes on Romanian Poetry." *Parnassus* 18, No. 2 and Vol. 19, No. 1: 58-80.
    Overview of major figures and trends in twentieth century poetry, focusing on the effects of rise of repressive government regimes in the mid-twentieth century.

Lucille Clifton
1936-

American poet, autobiographer, and author of children's books.

INTRODUCTION

A prolific author whose works frequently concern the well-being of black families and youths, Clifton is highly praised for her strong affirmation of African-American culture. She is one of the most accessible poets to emerge from the generation of writers influenced in the late 1960s and early 1970s by the Black Arts Movement's belief that artistic expression would assist Black Americans both in personal and social achievements. Her reputation has increased steadily since her first book of poems appeared. Her poems explore the African American experience, particularly the role and influence of matriarchy, providing strong, diverse social role models. Characteristically, and at her best, Clifton creates technically accomplished poems that use neither punctuation nor capitalization. Her strong and purposeful voice is expressed through common language, thus making her poetry available to a wide audience.

Biographical Information

Born Lucille Sayles in the Buffalo suburb of Depew, New York, in 1936, Clifton was the child of working-class parents whose storytelling kept alive a family history that connected Clifton to her Dahomey, West Africa, ancestors. While attending Howard University in Washington, DC, in 1953, she met and was influenced by dramatist and poet Amiri Baraka (formerly LeRoi Jones) and poet Sterling Brown. In 1955 she transferred to Fredonia State Teachers College, during which time she met her future husband, Fred, then a philosophy professor at the nearby University of Buffalo. While at Fredonia, she fostered her interest in drama and experimented with poetic forms, exploring lyrical and aural rhythms that would later characterize her work. In 1969, after nearly fifteen years of marriage and motherhood, she offered her first submission of poems to Robert Hayden, a respected African-American poet, resulting in her receipt of the YW-YMCA Poetry Center Discovery Award—an achievement that was followed by the publication of her first poetry collection, *Good Times: Poems,* which was hailed as one of the best books of 1969 by the *New York Times.* In 1976, Clifton produced *Generations: A Memoir.* This autobiography and family history brought wider attention both to her and to her work. It was later included with a selection of her earlier poems in *Good Woman: Poems and a Memoir.* In addition to her poetry, Clifton has written more than a dozen children's books, all of which give depth and dignity to the lives of African-American children living in the

inner city and help these children to understand their world. A Pulitzer Prize nominee and recipient of National Endowment for the Arts grants, Clifton, a long-time resident of Baltimore, is Poet Laureate of Maryland.

Major Works

Clifton's first book, *Good Times,* garnered considerable attention from critics, especially African-American commentators, who lauded her strength and celebration in the face of social adversity. One of Clifton's most popular and best-received collections is *Good Woman: Poems and a Memoir, 1969-1980.* It contains selections from her first four books of poems as well as her 1976 autobiographical study *Generations: A Memoir,* which traces her family line back to its African roots and shows how family, especially wise and strong matriarchies, have shaped the African-American experience. *Next: New Poems* has been praised for its range of subject matter, from terminal illness and suffering (both local and global), to poems of growth and change within both self and family. With *Next,* Clifton leaves behind her early manner of mythologizing herself and begins to become more human, more accessible to her reader. Showing Clifton as a poet at the peak of her art, *Quilting: Poems 1987-1990* is a work that was constructed in sections derived from traditional quilting patterns (Catalpa Flower, Eight-pointed Star, and Tree of Life) and which praises matriarchy, feminine strengths, and the individual.

Critical Reception

Although some reviewers found her earlier books of poems overly critical of white society, her reputation has grown progressively and touched increasingly wider audiences. Her poems have continued to explore and expand upon themes of family, strong female models, religious influences and interpretation, and her consistent optimism and belief in human will when faced with adversities such as family illness, death, and the dynamics and tensions of social change. Clifton has been often compared to other African American women poets of her generation, such as June Jordon, Ai, Nikki Giovanni, Audre Lourde, or Maya Angelou. The most striking comparison has been to Gwendolyn Brooks, who was Poet Laureate of her own state, Illinois. Both poets speak of family, matriarchy, children, and the value of both the artist and the individual in stylistically simple poems that use ordinary language spiced with speech patterns from folk songs, spirituals, and African-American idioms.

PRINCIPAL WORKS

Poetry

Good Times: Poems 1969
Good News about the Earth 1972
An Ordinary Woman 1974
Two-Headed Woman 1980
Good Woman: Poems and a Memoir, 1969-1980 1987
Next: New Poems 1988
Quilting: Poems 1987-1990 1991
The Book of Light 1993
The Terrible Stories 1996

Juvenile Fiction

The Black BCs 1970
Some of the Days of Everett Anderson 1970
Everett Anderson's Christmas Coming 1971
All Us Come Cross the Water 1973
The Boy Who Didn't Believe in Spring 1973
Don't You Remember? 1973
Good, Says Jerome 1973
Everett Anderson's Year 1974
The Times They Used to Be 1974
My Brother Fine with Me 1975
Everett Anderson's Friend 1976
Three Wishes 1976

Amifika 1977
Everett Anderson's 1 2 3 1977
Everett Anderson's Nine Month Long 1978
The Lucky Stone 1979
My Friend Jacob 1980
Sonora Beautiful 1981
Everett Anderson's Goodbye 1983

Other

Generations: A Memoir 1976

CRITICISM

Ralph J. Mills, Jr. (essay date 1973)

SOURCE: A review of *Good News about the Earth,* in *Poetry,* Vol. 122, No. 2, May, 1973, pp. 107-08.

[*In the following review of* Good News about the Earth, *Mills discusses Clifton's work as a poetry of reality and of affirmation.*]

Those who found Lucille Clifton's **Good Times** an amazing volume marking the discovery of one of the best new black poets will surely not be disappointed by **Good News about the Earth,** which she has divided into three sections: *"About the Earth," "Heroes,"* and *"Some Jesus,"* the latter consisting of poems on Old and New Testament themes, beginning with Adam and Eve and concluding in a **"Spring Song"** which follows some Easter pieces:

> the green of Jesus
> is breaking the ground
> and the sweet
> smell of delicious Jesus
> is opening the house and
> the dance of Jesus music
> has hold of the air and
> the world is turning
> in the body of Jesus and
> the future is possible.

Here is Mrs. Clifton's deft, economical, poised lyricism moving with the directness of finely turned speech yet eschewing any sort of artificiality. Donald Hall has recently said that black poetry is "a poetry of reality", "of character, attending to qualities like courage, defiance and tenderness", and his words could find no better illustration than the work of Lucille Clifton. She focuses on the events of the day, the killings at Kent State, on black figures of prominence and tragedy, such as Malcolm X, Angela Davis, Bobby Seale, Eldridge Cleaver; and a desire for and evocation of her African heritage, in all its natural luxuriance, fills several poems. But Mrs. Clifton's poetic range goes beyond matters of black pride and tradition to embrace the entire world, human and non-human, in the deep affirmation she makes in the teeth of negative evidence. She is a master of her style, with its spare, elliptical, idiomatic, rhythmical speech, and of prophetic warning in the same language:

After Kent State

only to keep
his little fear
he kills his cities
and his trees
even his children oh
people
white ways are
the way of death
come into the
Black
and live

If, as Donald Hall suggests, black poets probably will write some of the most significant poetry in America in the last third of the century, Lucille Clifton will hold an enviable place among them.

Chad Walsh on Clifton's "double vision":

In the long run, the most invigorating thing happening to American poetry may be the birth or discovery of a black cultural consciousness. Already it has produced impressive results, ranging from the explosive poems of a Don L. Lee to the lyrical bittersweet verse of an Alice Walker. Lucille Clifton's *Good Times* introduces another important talent. Affirming blackness more than it denounces whiteness, the book somehow reveals joy in the midst of misery. The vignette of an eviction in "**The 1st**" dramatizes the double vision of the author:

What I remember about that day
is boxes stacked across the walk
and couch springs curling through the air
and drawers and tables balanced on the curb
and us, hollering,
leaping up and around
happy to have a playground;

nothing about the emptied rooms
nothing about the emptied family

Chad Walsh, in The Washington Post Book
World, *March 8, 1970.*

Kossia Orloff (essay date 1982)

SOURCE: A review of *Two-Headed Woman,* in *National Forum,* Vol. 62, No. 3, Summer, 1982, p. 49

[*In the follow review of Two-Headed woman, Orloff believes that Clifton's theme of spiritual unity is the unifying force of her work.*]

in this garden
growing
following strict orders
following the Light
see the sensational
two-headed woman
one face turned outward
one face
swiveling slowly in

The image and statement of this untitled poem, as well as its circular structure and its position in the collection define the cyclical nature of *Two-Headed Woman*. The poem, which is the first in Part 2, points back to Part 1, where Clifton celebrates her physical self, and forward to the more introspective sections. By the end of the collection, as a result of the introspection, Clifton has taken on direction. Now she speaks of herself as "a circular stair . . . turning."

The motive force for the "Swiveling slowly in" (and indeed for the collection as a whole) is Clifton's need to define herself. Her primary method is to define her relationship with a community of women.

She thinks of herself and her mother:

twenty-one years of my life you have been
the lost color in my eye. my secret blindness,
all my seeings turned grey with your going.
mother, i have worn your name like a shield.
it has torn but protected me all these years

. . . . .

. . . i am not grown away from you
whatever i say. (february 13, 1980)

She bonds herself with her mother and daughter and by so doing turns loss into gain.

i was born with twelve fingers
like my mother and my daughter.

. . . . .

somebody was afraid we would learn to cast
spells
and our wonders were cut off
but they didn't understand
the powerful memory of ghosts. now
we take what we want
with invisible fingers
and we connect
my dead mother my live daughter and me
through our terrible shadowy hands.

(untitled)

Equally significant in Clifton's search for her self is her creation of historic sisterhood to nourish her.

> say skinny manysided tall on the ball
> brown downtown woman
> last time i saw you was on the corner of
> pyramid and sphinx
>
> . . . . .
>
> sister, sister,
> i been waiting for you.
>
> ("to merle," Part 1)

Balancing the merle poem is the luminous **"to joan,"** where Clifton asks, if in "the whisper of french grass . . . sounding now like a windsong . . . did you never hear . . . among beloved others . . . sister sister . . . my voices my voices?" (Part 3)

Her central identification, though, is with Mary, which she explores in a cycle of poems. This cycle, at the structural center of the collection, is the most telling, since it is equally the psychological center of the work. Clifton emphasizes the connection in two ways: she gives Mary roles similar to her own and has Mary speak in black-accented English. She thereby brings Mary not only into her own time but particularly into her own space. "joseph, i afraid of stars . . . i hands keep moving toward i breasts" **("holy night")**.

Concomitant with Clifton's establishing her own authenticity is her authenticating a mutually nurturant sisterhood, both by bringing her heritage into the present and becoming herself a vital presence in the past. This impetus toward confluence and identity appears in the very first poem, **"lucy and her girls"**—

> lucy is the ocean
> extended by
> her girls
> are the river
> fed by
> lucy
> is the sun
> reflected through
> her girls
> are the moon
> lighted by
> lucy
> is the history of
> her girls
> are the place where
> lucy
> was going.—

and is redefined in the last.

This psychological transcendence of time, finally is a transcendence of the psychological into the spiritual, explicit in her overtly religious poems, implicit in the others. Clifton's expression of her spiritual unity with women (**"lucy**

and her girls"**), both framing and punctuating the collection, is the underlying unifying force in her work.

Marilyn Nelson Waniek (essay date 1983)

SOURCE: A review of *Two-Headed Woman,* in *Callaloo,* Vol. 6, No. 1, 1983, pp. 160-62.

[*Below, poet and critic Waniek reviews the visionary and transcendent nature of Clifton's poems in* Two-Headed Woman.]

Lucille Clifton is a visionary poet. Her vision, however, is one of sanity, connectedness, light. She can write poems which are bright little gems of perceptive observation. As the mother of a large family (a fact important to much of her work) she may have been forced to work on small canvases. The result in her best poems, of which there are many, is similar to that of a laser beam. In *Two-Headed Woman,* her third collection of poetry, Clifton asserts her belief in personalism by affirming herself and her family and by exposing her exterior and interior lives to the the piercing light of her poems.

Clifton first pays "homage to mine" by affirming her decision to be mother, to reach thus backward into her family and racial history and forward into the unknown. In **"Lucy and Her Girls"** she celebrates this connectedness:

> lucy is the ocean
> extended by
> her girls
> are the river
> fed by
> lucy
> is the sun
> reflected through
> her girls
> are the moon
> lighted by
> lucy
> is the history of
> her girls
> are the place where
> lucy
> was going

The poem is a serious game whose intent is the exploration of the interrelatedness of generations. In the strongest poems of this collection, among them the humorous **"homage to my hips"** and **"what the mirror said,"** the delightful **"to merle"** and the moving **"poems on my fortieth birthday . . ."** and **"forgiving my father,"** Clifton's voice is similarly delicate and clear.

> i went into my mother as
> some souls go into a church,
> for the rest only. but there
> even there, from the belly of a
> poor woman who could not save herself

i was pushed without my permission
into a tangle of birthdays.
listen, eavesdroppers, there is no such thing
as a bed without affliction;
the bodies all may open wide but
you enter at your own risk.

> **("to the unborn and waiting children")**

As indicated by the two poems quoted here in full, Clifton is doing something small but monumental; hers is a poetry of transcendence, a glimpse into another world of light and promise. One feels in the latter sections of the book that Clifton is groping for a language equal to her vision. She comes closest in some of the poems in the impressive "island mary" sequence. Here is Clifton's Annunciation:

winged women who saying
"full of grace" and like.
was light beyond sun and words
of a name and a blessing.
winged women to only i.
i joined them, whispering
yes.

> **("mary's dream")**

Clifton wants to convey to the reader a sense of the "angels" she has seen, her proof of the continuity of life, of the immortality of the individual soul. She has, she tells us, *seen* this:

someone calling itself Light
has opened my inside.
i am flooded with brilliance
mother,

someone of it is answering to
your name.

> **("mother, i am mad")**

Hers is a poetry of transcendence, a glimpse into another world of light and promise.

—*Marilyn Nelson Waniek*

Lucille Clifton's poetry is direct, filled with conviction, and touched to its heart by human sympathy. The poems which do not ring true are rare, though they nonetheless weaken this otherwise excellent collection. Here, for example, is one whose central metaphor is a songwriter's cliche:

the once and future dead
who learn they will be white men
weep for their history. we call it
rain.

> **("the once and future dead")**

The brevity of some of the poems makes them thin, but the substance of the best of them is so compressed that they are weighty and thought-provoking. Lucille Clifton is a fine writer and a beautiful soul.

Lucille Clifton   (essay date 1984)

SOURCE: "A Simple Language," *in Black Women Writers (1950-1980): A Critical Evaluation,* edited by Mari Evans, Anchor Press/Double, 1984, pp. 137-38

[*Here, Clifton describes her views of her role in society and the ideology and methods behind her poetry*]

I write the way I write because I am the kind of person that I am. My styles and content stem from my experience. I grew up a well-loved child in a loving family and so I have always known that being very poor, which we were, had nothing to do with lovingness or familyness or character or any of that. This doesn't mean that I or we were content with whatever we had and never hoped tried worked at having more. It means that we were quite clear that what we had didn't have anything to do with what we were. We were/are quite sure that we were/are among the best of people and not having any money had nothing to do with that. Other people's opinions didn't influence us about that. We were quite sure. When I write, especially for children, I try to get that across, that being poor or whatever your circumstance, you are capable of being the best of people and that best, as a human, does not come from the outside in, it comes from the inside out.

I use a simple language. I have never believed that for anything to be valid or true or intellectual or "deep" it had to first be complex. I deliberately use the language that I use. Sometimes people have asked me when I was going to try something hard or difficult, as if my work sprang from my ignorance. I like to think that I write from my knowledge not my lack, from my strength not my weakness. I am not interested if anyone knows whether or not I am familiar with big words, I am interested in trying to render big ideas in a simple way. I am interested in being understood not admired. I wish to celebrate and not be celebrated (though a little celebration is a lot of fun).

I am a woman and I write from that experience. I am a Black woman and I write from that experience. I do not feel inhibited or bound by what I am. That does not mean that I have never had bad scenes relating to being Black and/or a woman, it means that other people's craziness has not managed to make me crazy. At least not in their way because I try very hard not to close my eye to my own craziness nor to my family's, my sex's, nor my race's. I don't believe that I should only talk about the beauty and strength and good-ness of my people but I do believe that if we talk about our room for improvement we should do it privately. I don't believe in public family fights. But I do think sometimes a good fight is cleansing. We are not perfect people. There are no perfect people.

I have been a wife for over twenty years. We have parented six children. Both these things have brought me great joy. I try to transmit the possible joy in my work. This does not mean that there have been no dark days; it means that they have not mattered. In the long run. I try to write about looking at the long run.

I have been writing things down all my life. I was first published in 1969 due to the efforts of Robert Hayden and Carolyn Kizer among others. I did not try to be published; it wasn't something that I thought that much about. I had had a short short story published in an issue of *Negro Digest* magazine earlier in the sixties. That had been my try.

I use a simple language. I have never believed that for anything to be valid or true or intellectual or "deep" it had to first be complex.

—Lucille Clifton

When my first book was published I was thirty-three years old and had six children under ten years old. I was too busy to take it terribly seriously. I was very happy and proud of course, but had plenty of other things to think about. It was published by Random House and that seemed to bother some of my friends. At first my feelings were a little hurt that anyone would even be concerned about it but I got over that. I decided that if something doesn't matter, it really doesn't matter. Sometimes I think that the most anger comes from ones who were late in discovering that when the world said nigger it meant them too. I grew up knowing that the world meant me too but that was the world's insanity and not mine. I have been treated in publishing very much like other poets are treated, that is, not really very well. I continue to write since my life as a human only includes my life as a poet, it doesn't depend on it.

I live in Baltimore and so I do not have sustained relationships with many of my peers. I am friends with a lot of the people who do what I do but my public and private lives tend to be separate. At home I am wife and mama mostly. My family has always come first with me. This is my choice due to my personal inclination. As the children have grown up I have been able to travel more and I enjoy it. I very much enjoy the public life and I also very much enjoy the private.

My family tends to be a spiritual and even perhaps mystical one. That certainly influences my life and my work. I write in the kitchen or wherever I happen to be though I do have a study. I write on a typewriter rather than in longhand. My children think of me as a moody person; I am shy and much less sunny than I am pictured. I draw my own conclusions and do not believe everything I am told. I am not easily fooled. I do the best I can. I try.

Haki Madhubuti (essay date 1984)

SOURCE: "Lucille Clifton: Warm Water, Greased Legs, and Dangerous Poetry," *Black Women Writers (1950-1980): A Critical Evaluation,* edited by Mari Evans, Anchor Press/Doubleday, 1984, pp. 150-60

[*In the following essay, poet, critic, and educator Madhubuti discusses the language and cultural sensitivity of Clifton's poetry*]

In everything she creates, this Lucille Clifton, a writer of no ordinary substance, a singer of faultless ease and able storytelling, there is a message. No slogans or billboards, but words that are used refreshingly to build us, make us better, stronger, and whole. Words that defy the odds and in the end make us wiser.

Lucille Clifton is a woman of majestic presence, a full-time wife, over-time mother, part-time street activist and writer of small treasures (most of her books are small but weighty). That she is not known speaks to, I feel, her preoccupation with truly becoming a full Black woman and writer. Celebrity,—that is, people pointing you out in drugstores and shopping malls—does not seem to interest her. When she was almost assured of becoming the poet laureate of Maryland, she wrote Gwendolyn Brooks (poet laureate of Illionis) asking if she should consider such a position. I suggest that she really wanted to know: (1) Are there any advantages in the position for her people? and (2) Would she significantly have to change her life by accepting the honor? Brooks' response was, "It is what you make of it." Clifton accepted.

The city of Baltimore, where she and her family reside, does not figure heavily in her work. The "place" of her poetry and prose is essentially urban landscapes that are examples of most Black communities in this country. Clifton's urge is to live, is to conquer oppressive and nonnatural spaces. Her poetry is often a conscious, quiet introduction to the real world of Black sensitivities. Her focus and her faces are both the men and the women connected and connecting; the children, the family, the slave-like circumstances, the beauty, and the raw and most important the hideouts of Black people to Black people.

Her poetry is emotion-packed and musically fluent to the point of questioning whether a label on it would limit one's understanding. Her first book of poetry, **Good Times,** cannot be looked upon as simply a "first" effort. The work is unusually compacted and memory-evoking.

There is no apology for the Black condition. There is an awareness and a seriousness that speak to "houses straight as / dead men." Clifton's poems are not vacant lots; the mamas and daddies are not forgotten human baggages to be made loose of and discarded. Much of today's writing, especially much of that being published by Black women writers, seems to invalidate Black men or make small of them, often relegating them to the position of white sexual renegades in Black faces.

No such cop-out for Clifton. There is no misrepresentation of the men or women. And one wouldfind it extremely difficult to misread Clifton. She is not a "complicated" writer in the traditional Western sense. She is a writer of complexity, and she makes her readers work and think. Her poetry has a quiet force without being pushy or alien. Whether she is cutting through family relationships, surviving American racial attitudes, or just simply renewing love ties, she puts something heavy on your mind. The great majority of her published poetry is significant. At the base of her work is concern for the Black family, especially the destruction of its youth. Her eye is for the uniqueness of our people, always concentrating on the small strengths that have allowed us to survive the horrors of Western life.

Her treatment of Black men is unusually significant and sensitive. I feel that part of the reason she treats men fairly and with balance in her work is her relationship with her father, brothers, husband, and sons. Generally, positive relationships produce positive results.

> my daddy's fingers move among the couplers
> chipping steel and skin
> and if the steel would break
> my daddy's fingers might be men again.

Lucille Clifton is often calling for the men to be Black men. Asking and demanding that they seek and be more than expected. Despite her unlimited concern for her people, she does not box herself into the corner of preaching at them or of describing them with metaphors of belittlement. Clifton has a fine, sharp voice pitched to high C and tuned carefully to the frequency of the Black world. She is a homeland technician who has not allowed her "education" to interfere with her solos.

The women of *Good Times* are strong and Dahomey-made, are imposing and tragic, yet givers of love. Unlike most of us, Clifton seemed to have taken her experiences and observations and squeezed the knowledge from them, translating them into small and memorable lessons:

> . . . surrounded by the smell
> of too old potato peels
> you wet brown bag of a woman
> who used to be the best looking gal in Georgia
> used to be called the Georgia Rose
> I stand up
> through your destruction
> I stand up

Standing up is what *Good Times* is about. However, Clifton can beat you up with a poem; she can write history into four stanzas and bring forth reaction from the most hardened nonreader. Listen to the story of Robert:

> Was born obedient
> without questions
> did a dance called
> Picking grapes
> Sticking his butt out

> for pennies
> Married a master
> who whipped his head
> until he died
> until he died
> the color of his life
> was nigger.

There is no time frame in such a poem. Such poems do not date easily. Robert is 1619 and 1981, is alive and dying on urban streets, in rural churches and corporate offices. "Niggers" have not disappeared; some of them (us) are now being called by last names and are receiving different types of mind whippings, mind whippings that achieve the same and sometimes greater results.

Her originality is accomplished with everyday language and executed with musical percussion, pushed to the limits of poetic possibilities.

—*Haki Madhubuti*

Clifton is a Black cultural poet. We see in her work a clear transmission of values. It is these values that form the base of a developing consciousness of struggle. She realizes that we do have choices that can still be exercised. Hers is most definitely to fight. From page to page, from generation to generation, the poems cry out direction, hope, and future. One of the best examples of this connecting force is from her book *An Ordinary Woman*; the poem is **"Turning."**

> Turning into my own
> turning on in
> to my own self
> at last
> turning out of the
> white cage, turning out of the
> lady cage
> turning at last
> on a stem like a black fruit
> in my own season
> at last.

It is the final voyage into oneself that is the most difficult. Then there comes the collective fight, the dismantling of the real monsters outside. But first we must become whole again. The true undiluted culture of a people is the base of wholeness. One way toward such wholeness is what Stephen Henderson calls "saturation," the giving and defining of Blackness through proclaiming such experiences as legitimate and necessary, whereas the Black poetic experience used often enough becomes natural and expected. Clifton "saturates" us in a way that forces us to look at ourselves in a different and more profound way. For every weakness, she points to a strength; where there are negatives she pulls and searches for the positives. She has not let the low ebbs of life diminish her talents or toughness. She is always looking for the good, the best, but not naïvely so. Her work is realistic and burning with the energy of renewal.

Clifton is an economist with words; her style is to use as few words as possible. Yet she is effective because, despite consciously limiting her vocabulary, she has defined her audience. She is not out to impress, or to showcase the scope of her lexicon. She is communicating ideas and concepts. She understands that precise communication is not an easy undertaking; language, at its root, seeks to express emotion, thought, action. Most poetry writing (other than the blues) is foreign to the Black community. It is nearly impossible to translate to the page the changing linguistic nuances or the subtleties of body language Blacks use in everyday conversation; the Black writer's task is an extremely complicated and delicate one. But understand me, Clifton does not write down to us, nor is she condescending or patronizing with her language. Most of her poems are short and tight, as is her language. Her poems are well-planned creations, and as small as some of them are, they are not cloudy nor rainy with words for words' sake. The task is not to fill the page with letters but to challenge the mind:

> What I remember about that day
> is boxes stacked across the walk
> and couch springs curling through the air
> and drawers and tables balanced on the curb
> and us, hollering,
> leaping up and around
> happy to have a playground
> nothing about the emptied rooms
> nothing about the emptied family

Her originality is accomplished with everyday language and executed with musical percussion, pushed to the limits of poetic possibilities. Lucille Clifton is a lover of life, a person who feels her people. Her poems are messages void of didacticism and needless repetition. Nor does she shout or scream the language at you; her voice is birdlike but loud and high enough to pierce the ears of dogs. She is the quiet warrior, and, like the weapons of all good warriors, her weapons can hurt, kill, and protect.

Andrea Benton Rushing (essay date 1985)

SOURCE: "Lucille Clifton: A Changing Voice for Changing Times," in *Coming to Light: American Women Poets in the Twentieth Century,* edited by Diane Wood Middlebrook and Marilyn Yalom, The University of Michigan Press, 1985, pp. 214-22

[*Here, Rushing examines Clifton's relationship to the Black Arts Movement and comments on Clifton's poetic representation of women.*]

Like all the other contemporary African-American women poets, Clifton was deeply affected by the Black Arts

movement of the sixties and seventies. Although subsequent experiences like the women's movement and her own heightened religious consciousness have also left their imprint on her, we must consider that soul-changing crusade the crucible which most searingly shaped her art.

A concomitant of the separatist Black Power campaign, the Black Arts movement enlisted such cultural workers as musicians, visual artists, and writers to address the masses of African-Americans about the liberation struggles which confronted them. Propelled by slogans like "I'm Black and I'm proud" and "Black is beautiful," artists pronounced European and Euro-American critical norms inadequate yardsticks for African-American creations and viewed African-American arts as cultural tools with which to destroy three centuries of racial oppression and degradation.

While many bourgeois Euro-American and African-American readers and critics deplored the rage, obscenity, and violence of "New Breed" poetry, respected African-American critics like Bernard Bell, Hoyt Fuller, Addison Gayle, and George Kent recognized its merits. More importantly, young African-Americans in pool rooms and bars (as well as on street corners and college campuses) read it attentively and imitated it widely. . . . According to [Stephen Henderson in his essay "Understanding the New Black Poetry"] both oral and written African-American poetry clusters around the motif of political, sexual, and spiritual liberation. In analyzing structure, Henderson terms it the poetry's reflection of spoken language and performed music. "Whenever Black poetry is most distinctively and effectively Black, it derives its form from . . . Black speech and Black music." Saturation is Henderson's rubric for "the communication of Blackness in a given situation and the sense of fidelity to the observed and intuited truth of the Black Experience."

Clifton's early verse clearly indicates the influence of the Black Arts movement. In accord with its dictates about how poetry should raise the cultural and political consciousness of "the Black community," Clifton dedicates ***Good News About the Earth*** to those killed in student uprisings at Orangeburg, South Carolina, and Jackson, Mississippi. It contains an apology to the militant Black Panther Party.

> i became a woman
> during the old prayers
> among the ones who wore
> bleaching cream to bed
> and all my lessons stayed
> i was obedient
> but brothers i thank you
> for these mannish days
> i remember agin the wise one
> old and telling of suicides
> refusing to be slaves
> i had forgotten and
> brothers i thank you
> i praise you
> i grieve my whiteful ways

The volume also features verse to Angela Davis, Eldridge Cleaver, and Bobby Seale. In addition to treating these political subjects, Clifton mirrors the tenets of the Black Arts movement by directing herself to a general African-American audience using the grammar, vocabulary, and rhythm of idiomatic African-American speech. Interestingly, none of Clifton's verse on these vivid figures parallels so many of the tributes to them in relying on typographical quirks, like capitalized words and slashes, or haranguing either African-American or Euro-American readers.

In light of Clifton's later poetry, it is crucial to indicate the ways in which her early work diverges from the creations of her contemporaries. Many of the women poets who came to prominence during the sixties and seventies shocked readers. Despite their slight stature and (in a few cases) bourgeois upbringing, they mirrored the strident stance, profane language, and violent imagery of urban, male poetry. Part of my interest in Clifton's lyrical verse arises from my admiration for the acumen with which she found her own voice during a turbulent period when so many poets sounded the same chords of outrage and militancy. Rather than merely imitating the sarcasm and fury of male poets, Clifton anticipated the concern with women's issues which is—like opposition to the war in Vietnam, support of homosexuals' rights, and the crusade for environmental protection—in deep, though often unacknowledged, debt to the strategies and moral vision of the Civil Rights and Black Power campaigns. Furthermore, while other poets have tended to focus on historical figures such as Harriet Tubman, Sojourner Truth, Frederick Douglass, and Malcolm X, Clifton anticipated Alex Haley's *Roots* in personalizing history and using her own natal family as a symbol of the anguish and triumph of the African-American experience. Moreover, in an era when many African-American nationalists were harshly critical of their accommodating "Uncle Tom" and "Aunt Jemima" elders, the "opiate" of African-American Christianity, and the Anglo-Saxon proper names which are a living legacy of chattel slavery and cultural assimilation, Clifton wrote in a different key. While others complained of their elders' failures, she celebrated her ancestors, while others converted to Islam, she wrote about the life-giving power of African-American religion; and, though others assumed African and Arabic names, Clifton justified her own.

> light
> on my mother's tongue
> breaks through her soft
> extravagant hip
> into life.
> Lucille
> she calls the light,
> which was the name
> of the grandmother
> who waited by the crossroads
> in Virginia
> and shot the whiteman off his horse,
> . . . . .
> mine already is
> an Afrikan name.

Beginning with an allusion to the origins of the name "Lucille" in the Latin for "bright light," Clifton goes on to affirm a throbbing connection between Africa, the slave experience, and her own twentieth-century life.

Despite the considerable achievements of *Good Times, Good News About the Earth,* and *Generations,* it is with the publication of *An Ordinary Woman* and *Two-Headed Woman* that Clifton strides to center stage among contemporary African-American poets. These two fine collections parse the female sector of African-American life and give vivid testimony to the terse brilliance which alerted readers of her early work to Clifton's enormous potential. Not only do they explore a broad swath of rarely examined experience; they do so in an appealing personal voice with an attractive infusion of self-revelation and wit. By now, all the major contemporary African-American women poets have written verse about women's lives: the mother-daughter dyad, heterosexual relations, oppressive standards of female beauty, and loneliness are common themes. The verse is often autobiographical, its saturation in African and African-American culture is explicit, and its tone varies from aggrieved to nostalgic to exultant. Several things set Clifton's work apart from the strophes of others. First, she has written more poems about women's lives than any other African-American poet except Gwendolyn Brooks. Second, she has consistently done so in the African-American demotic with sinewy diction, a confiding voice, and stark imagery.

With the Kali poems in *An Ordinary Woman,* Clifton makes a bold innovation in poetic presentation of African-American women. Rather than limning heroic embodiments of female power and triumph, or depicting lifelike women victimized by parents, racism, poverty, and sexism, Clifton invokes an aboriginal ebony-faced Indian goddess associated with blood, violence, and murder. Since the paternal slave ancestor Clifton celebrates in her memoir, *Generations,* came from Dahomey, with its well-known tradition of heroic women, Clifton could have crafted poems around an African-based tradition. In turning to Kali, however, she frees herself from the feminist tendency to see women as hapless victims and explores the psychic tensions of an introspective modern woman negotiating the dramatic changes in contemporary attitudes about culture, race, and gender at the same time that she juggles the roles of daughter, sister, artist, wife, and mother. Written in standard English, these lyrics differ from Clifton's earlier work in syntax and diction; they are also tighter and more forceful. Like her earlier work, however, they also employ short lines, few rhymes, brief stanzas, and recurring images of women's blood and bones. The three Kali poems are striking enough to be quoted at length.

Kali

> queen of fatality, she
> determines the destiny
> of things. nemesis.
> the permanent guest
> within ourselves.
> woman of warfare,

of the chase, bitch
of blood sacrifice and death.
dread mother. the mystery
ever present in us and
outside us. the
terrible Hindu Woman God
Kali.
who is Black.

The Coming of Kali

it is the Black God, Kali,
a woman God and terrible
with her skulls and breasts.
i am one side of your skin,
she sings, softness is the other,
you know you know me well, she sings,
you know you know me well.

Calming Kali

be quiet awful woman,
lonely as hell,
and i will comfort you
when i can
and give you my bones
and my blood to feed on.
gently gently now
awful woman,
i know i am your sister.

In these poems, Clifton juxtaposes archetypal imagery about female generative and destructive power and insists on the tense mystery implicit in that union of opposites. Furthermore, she combines awe about Kali's violence and power with a fierce, almost protective, tenderness toward the fearful figure she refers to as "sister."

The thematic connections between *Two-Headed Woman* and Clifton's previous verse are immediately apparent. The opening **"homage to mine"** section demonstrates her continuing attention to family and friends and religious themes. In other ways, however, Clifton's latest volume of verse marks some sort of threshold experience for her. Unlike most other African-American women poets of the sixties and seventies, Clifton's marriage has been stable, and she has had six children. None of her verse articulates either the strains between men and women or the loneliness which often characterizes the work of other female poets, and her sons and daughters have been sources of pleasure and affirmation for her. A pivotal poem in *Two-Headed Woman* indicates new timbres in her life.

the light that came to lucille clifton came in a shift of knowing when even her fondest sureties faded away. it was the summer she understood that she had not understood and was not mistress even of her own off eye. then the man escaped throwing away his tie and she could see the peril of an unexamined life.

Here the poet's children grow up, her husband "escapes," and (despite all the introspective verse she has written)

she terms her life "unexamined." One indication of the difference between the texture of *An Ordinary Woman* and *Two-Headed Woman* is that while the former invokes Kali to personify the furious tensions between women's creative and destructive powers, the latter concentrates on the smaller (though equally intense) landscape of one woman's searching psyche.

see the sensational
two-headed woman
one face turned outward
one face
swiveling slowly in.

Another indication of the difference appears in the religious verse in the volume. On the one hand, Clifton uses a lower-class Caribbean accent rather than the African-American idiom in which she usually writes. On the other, she concentrates on the near ineffability of the interface between divine call and human response. Many of her religious poems are about Mary. Rather than depicting her as the wise poised figure of Renaissance painting, Clifton portrays her as an uneducated young girl inexplicably chosen for miraculous experience. . . .

holy night

joseph, i afraid of stars,
their brilliant seeing.
so many eyes, such light.
joseph, i cannot still these limbs,
i hands keep moving toward i breasts,
so many stars. so bright.

Clifton's focus on Mary not only reflects her heightened concern with extraordinary religious experience but also resonates with the emphasis on motherhood which has characterized poetry about her family.

One comes away from Clifton's powerful recent verse knowing that while it shares its lyric qualities, lucidity, and compression with her earlier work, it also marks significant steps beyond her past achievements. Using many of the same tools which molded the stanzas of *Good Times* and *Good News About the Earth* and maintaining her interest in female experience, Clifton has broadened her range and deepened her perspective.

Marilyn Hacker (essay date 1988)

SOURCE: A review of *Next,* in *The Woman's Review of Books,* Vol. 5, Nos. 10-11, July, 1988, p. 24.

[*Poet and critic Marilyn Hacker calls Clifton's style in* Next *one of astonishing economy and her theme one of asserting the connecting spirit.*]

Lucille Clifton's sixth book, *Next,* has been much better served by Boa Editions. Her spare, sometimes gnomic poems stand in the middle of their sufficient space, and can sink in. Clifton is a poet of astonishing economy: five or ten pared lines can tell volumes.

> i am the sieve she strains from
> little by little
> every day
>
> i am the rind
> she is discarding.
>
> i am the riddle
> she is trying to answer.
>
> something is moving
> in the water.
> she is the hook.
> i am the line.
>
>   (**"4 daughters"**)

Lorine Neidecker and Hilda Morley limn in such strokes; Clifton contains, though, in her craft, the force, anger and hope of the Afro-American experience.

She also renders character with precision. Readers of her earlier books will recognize some of the ancestors and companions whose images Clifton had previously etched: her mother Thelma, her husband Fred, the twelve-fingered Dahomey foremothers. Their lives and deaths counterpoint farther-flung presences: Crazy Horse and Black Buffalo Woman, Winnie Mandela, the women of Lebanon and Johannesburg.

The book's first section takes a global perspective, from Johannesburg to Jonestown to Nagasaki to the Middle Passage; its concentration is on women of color suffering violence they did not incite, a celebration of their wisdom and connection:

> this is the tale
> i keep on telling
> trying to get it right:
> the feast of women,
> the feeding
> and being fed.
>
>   (**"this is the tale"**)

The book's second section is a brave and devastating roll-call of elegies: deaths, the messages of the departed, the resurrecting power of words and names:

> White Buffalo Woman who brought the pipe
> Black Buffalo Woman and Black Shawl
> sing the names of the women sing
> the power of name in the women sing
> the name i have saved for my daughter sing
> her name to the ties and baskets and
> the red tailed hawk will take her name and
> sing her power to Wakan Tanka sing
> the name of my daughter sing she is
> They Are Afraid Of Her.
>
>   (**"crazy horse names his daughter"**)

"The death of crazy horse" and **"the message of crazy horse,"** whose "medicine is strong in the Black basket of these fingers," are followed by the early death and testament of Thelma Sayles, the poet's mother, and the death, from leukemia, of a 21-year-old woman:

> i can hear her repeating my dates:
> 1962 to 1982 or 3. mother
> forgive me, mother believe
> i am trying to make old bones.
>
>   (**"she won't ever forgive me"**)

And then, in a honed sequence of five poems, Clifton tells of the death, also of cancer, of Fred Clifton, her husband, at the age of 49:

> i seemed to be drawn
> to the center of myself
> leaving the edges of me
> in the hands of my wife
>
> . . .
>
> . . . rising and turning
> through my skin
> there was all around not the
> shapes of things
> but oh, at last, the things
> themselves.
>
>   (**"the death of fred clifton"**)

The cumulative effect Clifton achieves through these testimonies, these elegies, is not despair, though grief fueled their making, but a mustering of strength and belief in the unkillable connecting spirit. Clifton mythologizes herself: that is, she illuminates her surroundings and history from within in a way that casts light on much beyond. She does this with penetrating brevity in a verse that mirrors speech as a Japanese ink drawing mirrors a mountain.

Doris Earnshaw (essay date 1988)

SOURCE: A review of *Good Woman: Poems and a Memoir 1969-1980* and *Next: New Poems,* in *World Literature Today,* Vol. 62, No. 3, Summer, 1988, p. 459.

[*Earnshaw praises Clifton's constancy in speaking victoriously for downtrodden people.*]

Like Nelly Sachs, whose *O the Chimneys* won a Nobel Prize for the German poet, Lucille Clifton arose from dreadful national experience to speak for all downtrodden people. Unlike Sachs, however, Clifton can speak victoriously about the survival through slavery of her family, although "even the good parts was awful." In *Generations,* a collection of autobiographical pieces published by Random House in 1976 and reprinted now in *good woman,* Clifton traces her lineage to her great-great-grandmother Mammy Ca'line, "born free in Afrika in 1822 died free in America in 1910." This absorbing biography makes her aware that slavery was a temporary experience; the power of Dahomey women goes on to her children's children's generation.

Clifton gives us details of her links with slave history. She carried with her to Howard University some doilies crocheted by a Miss Washington, born in slavery, whose mother had held her up to wave as Mr. Lincoln came by in a parade. Clifton's great-grandmother Lucy had shot and killed a white man, the father of her son. Lucy was the first black woman legally hanged in the state of Virginia—the honor of a trial accorded on the strength of Mammy Ca'line's reputation. Told this story by her daddy, Lucille Clifton asked for proof. Her daddy said, "In history, even the lies are true."

The volume *good woman* also brings together all of Clifton's previously published books of poetry: *Good Times, Good News about the Earth, An Ordinary Woman,* and *Two-Headed Woman*. Her short poems range in tone from irony and satire to direct appeals for political change. She bids us remember the natural world in **"Generation"**: "and the generations of rice / of coal / of grasshoppers // by their indivisibility / denounce us." Several series of poems on Bible heroes, on Jesus, and on the "disabled" approach the tone of the passionate prayers, as in **"for the blind."**

> you will enter morning
> without error.
> you will stand in a room
> where you have never lingered.
> . . . your fingers will shine
> with recognition
> your eyes will open
> with delight.

In the collection *Next: New Poems* Clifton writes of her dreams, her daughters and sons, her illness, her husband, her experience "in white america" reading poetry to college audiences. She writes, "it is late / in white america. / i stand / in the light of the / 7-11 / looking out toward / the church / and for a moment only / i feel the reverberation / of myself / in white america / a black cat / in the belfry / hanging / and / ringing."

William J. Harris (essay date 1988)

SOURCE: "True Names," in *American Book Review,* Vol. 10, No. 4, September-October, 1988, p. 7.

[*In the following review of* Good Woman: Poems and a Memoir 1969-1980, *critic William Harris discusses the lyrical and textured style of Clifton's work.*]

Lucille Clifton is a poet who has grown a great deal over the course of her career. In the late 1960s she began as a good poet of the New Black Renaissance, but she was in no way an equal to such accomplished artists of the period as Amiri Baraka, Nikki Giovanni, or Don L. Lee (Haki R. Madhubuti). Many of her early poems were too simple and easy; however, she stubbornly kept producing books of poems and they have dramatically improved; in fact, her poems have metamorphosed from flat and plain to lyric and textured. Furthermore, with her prose memoir,

Generations: A Memoir, she made a quantum leap into a new mature and powerful style; and happily, the books of poems that followed maintain, for the most part, the same level of excellence. In *Generations: A Memoir* and *Next,* her best book of poems to date, we see an artist come into her own, and to watch that transformation is an instructive and joyous occasion for any one devoted to the art of poetry.

Her first book is typical of the black militant 1960s, a period that produced many poets but few with staying power. The typical poem of the time was ethnic in character and political in agenda. The aesthetic of the 1960s forced the black artist to reawaken to a sense of his or her own cultural possibilities, to explore his or her own tradition instead of somebody else's. Unfortunately, integral to the black aesthetic of the time was the desire to denigrate the white tradition. In her first book Clifton wrote the obligatory antiwhitie poem, today as dated as any other cliché or fashionable period piece.

> pity this poor animal
> who has never gone beyond
> the ape herds gathered around the fires of europe
>
> all he knows how to do
> is huddle with others
> in straight haired grunt clusters
> to keep warm

Unlike Baraka, she could not hate with style or lyricism.

In Clifton's second book, *good news about the earth,* she becomes more self-consciously a woman poet, a black woman poet. One main mission of her poetry is to celebrate and explore the experiences of ordinary black women, including herself and her mother. And ironically, one prime experience of being an ordinary woman is

> i had expected more than this.
> i had not expected to be
> an ordinary woman

Clifton is sincerely committed to communicating to the "brother on the street"—therefore, the language is straightforward, but unlike Langston Hughes she too often fails to embody profundity in simplicity, and unlike Giovanni she lacks both sassiness and jazzy flavor. Sometimes, however, she does successfully absorb the poetics of the street and achieves complexity in simplicity—especially in such series poems as her character studies of street kids, in the buffalo soldiers poems, and in **"listen children,"** in which she uses the native rhythms and form of a child's game to eloquently make her point:

> listen children
> keep this in the place
> you have for keeping
> always
> keep it all ways
>
> we have never hated black

listen

we have been ashamed
hopeless tired mad
but always
all ways
we loved us

we have always loved each other
children all ways

pass it on

With the publication of *Generations: A Memoir* Clifton becomes a poet in prose. She expands her black aesthetic to include language as rich as Shakespeare and the Bible, a language that is as truly representative of black folk as any other. In fact, much of the richness of the tale comes from the poet recreating her father's speech; she has called him a great storyteller. Perhaps, in trying to record and remember his speech she learned the trick of great storytelling. Anyway, within the black literary tradition we find this grand style in Baldwin, Martin Luther King, Morrison, and Baraka, to name a few. Clifton's new work is filled with such lines as "Smoke was hanging over Buffalo like judgment." But to get a real sense of the power of this memoir you must read large sections, which do not lend themselves to short quotation. All the lushness of language and imagery that the reader wanted in the poetry is present in the prose. This little book ranks with such prose classics as Gwendolyn Brooks's *Maud Martha*—however, it is a much sweeter work since it is about love among generations of black people instead of the complexities of black marriage—and Baraka's modernist masterpiece, *The System of Dante's Hell*. Clifton declares that the main theme of the book is "The generations of white folks are just people but the generations of colored folks are families."

Two-Headed Woman was the next book published after the memoir. It is ambitious, with a few first-rate poems such as **"sonora desert poem."** Yet, assuming that the books were published in the order that they were composed, she does not gain full mastery of the poetic medium until her next volume, appropriately called *Next*. Perhaps the mastery of prose in poetry led to the mastery of poetry in poetry. This book includes such lovely and moving poems as **"the death of fred clifton,"** the cancer poems about her mother, Thelma, and **"this is the tale,"** and there are striking and lyric lines on almost every page except for the last section. The volume abounds with such lines as:

this belief
in the magic of whiteness,
that it is the smooth
pebble in your hand,

Clifton writes an endstopped free verse which needs little punctuation. Over her career she has written basically the same free verse line, but she has become more and more skilled at it, and in recent years the line now bears a denser vocabulary and imagery. As I briefly mentioned before, she writes poems in groups, series poems. In these she takes a poetic idea and develops it over a number of poems. For example, she writes a series of poems about the Bible and another about body parts. The series poems allow her to develop a complicated subject in a simple way—that is, individual poems add up to a complex experience. The prime example of this is the buffalo poems.

In a poem called **"the making of poems,"** she declares:

the reason why i do it
though i fail and fail
in the giving of true names
is i am adam and his mother
and these failures are my job.

This credo, this idea of continuing in the face of failure to name the world, is a heroic and a dignified act and one that has paid off, since Clifton has achieved much in her persistence. This reviewer anxiously awaits Lucille Clifton's next book. She has survived the 1960s and has grown into a mature and impressive poet.

Liz Rosenberg   (essay date 1989)

SOURCE: "Simply American and Mostly Free," in *The New York Times Book Review*, February 19, 1989, p. 24.

[*Below, Rosenberg sees Clifton as a storyteller whose work is rooted in her own personal history*]

The writer Clarence Major once noted that black American poetry is almost always, in some sense, a reaction to slavery—and therefore often concerns itself with the right to Being. Lucille Clifton is a poet who grapples mightily with such questions. Her poetry is direct and clear: full of humor and forthrightness, tenderness and anger. She has no sentimental hankering after the past: "'Oh slavery, slavery,' my Daddy would say. 'It ain't something in a book, Lue. Even the good parts was awful.'"

Her work is grounded in her own personal history, revealed most beautifully in the long memoir at the end of *Good Woman: Poems and a Memoir*. A sure sense of self reverberates throughout her poetry. . . .

Ms. Clifton resists, undermines myths of hierarchy, placement, entitlement (many of her poems are untitled), privilege—hers is a poetry of democracy, full of jumpy and lovely music:

say skinny manysided tall on the ball
brown downtown woman
last time i saw you was on the corner of
pyramid and sphinx.

She is a storyteller, as is clear throughout *Good Woman*.

. . . I was in the kitchen washing dishes and all of a sudden I heard my Mama start screaming and fall down

on the floor and I ran into the room and she was
rolling on the floor and Daddy hadn't touched her, she
had just started screaming and rolling on the floor.
'What have you done to her,' I hollered. Then 'What
should I do, what should I do?' And Daddy said 'I
don't know, I don't know, I don't know, she's crazy,'
and went out. When he left, Mama lay still, and then
sat up and leaned on me and whispered, 'Lue, I'm just
tired, I'm just tired.'

All of Ms. Clifton's best work falls into this space between comedy and tragedy—even melodrama. Her concerns are both earthbound and mystical, and what may
appear stylistically simple is, upon close examination, an
effort to free the true voice clear and plain. BOA Editions has simultaneously issued a book of her most recent poetry, *Next*. The poems here are about death and
loss, in which: "the one in the next bed is dying. / mother
we are all next. or next." The loss is not only personal,
but spreads outward:

> it is late
> in white america.
> i stand
> in the light of the
> 7-11
> looking out toward
> the church
> and for a moment only
> i feel the reverberation
> of myself
> in white america
> a black cat
> in the belfry
> hanging
> and
> ringing.

Ms. Clifton's poetry is big enough to accommodate sorrow
and madness and yet her vision emerges as overwhelmingly
joyous and calm:

> Things don't fall apart. Things hold. Lines connect in
> thin ways that last and last and lives become generations
> made out of pictures and words just kept. 'We come
> out of it better than they did, Lue,' my Daddy said,
> and I watch my six children and know we did. They
> walk with confidence through the world, free sons and
> daughters of free folk, for my Mama told me that
> slavery was a temporary thing, mostly we was free and
> she was right.

Bruce Bennett (essay date 1992)

SOURCE: "Preservation Poets," in *The New York Times
Book Review,* March 1, 1992, pp. 22-3.

[*Below, poet and critic Bennett discusses Clifton's thematic exploration of cultural and personal history in*
Quilting: Poems 1987-90.]

Readers familiar with Ms. Clifton will find in *Quilting,*
her seventh book of poetry, the kind of work they expect
from her: poems of witness on racial themes; celebrations of women; personal poems of self, family and her
vocation as poet; visionary poems taking off from the
Bible. She is a passionate, mercurial writer, by turns
angry, prophetic, compassionate, shrewd, sensuous, vulnerable and funny.

The title and construction of *Quilting* suggest its strategy;
four of the book's five sections—"Log Cabin," "Catalpa
Flower," "Eight-Pointed Star" and "Tree of Life"—are
named for traditional quilt designs and represent a stitching
together of various, and varicolored, pieces of an individual
life (the fifth section, "Prayer," consists of a single poem).
Yet the movement and effect of the whole book communicate the sense of a journey, of exploring, opening up,
testing, as the poet recognizes and accepts that she is on
the verge of something new.

"Log Cabin" begins by defining the past as "a monstrous
unnamed baby" the poet has taken to breast. She names
the baby History and observes her becoming "more human . . . learning language . . . remembering faces, names
and dates." She warns, "when she is strong enough to
travel / on her own, beware, she will." Naming as recla-
mation and recovery becomes a primary theme: there are
poems "for hector peterson, aged 13 / first child killed in
soweto riot, 1976," for the women not even listed in the
inventory of slaves, for "aunt nanny," a Maryland slave
whose "own sweet human name" was never recorded.
Several poems are dedicated to or allude to black men
and women whose names are well known: Amiri Baraka,
Nelson and Winnie Mandela, Fannie Lou Hamer, W. E.
B. Du Bois.

The poem **"White Lady"**—the term is identified as "a
street name for cocaine"—blisteringly attacks the drug
culture:

> white lady
> you have chained our sons
> in the basement
> of the big house
> white lady
> you have walked our daughters
> out into the streets
> white lady
> what do we have to pay
> to repossess our children
> white lady
> what do we have to owe
> to own our own at last

While claiming for herself the right to confer and restore
names, Ms. Clifton resists categorization by others, however well-meaning: "the merely human / is denied me
still / and i am now no longer beast / but saint"; "Log
Cabin" concludes with the defiant poem **"Defending My
Tongue"** "what i be talking about / can be said in this
language / only this tongue / be the one that understands
/ what i be talking about."

"Catalpa Flower" shifts the focus to women, their qualities and nature, their physical, psychological and spiritual beings. **"Nude Photograph"** hymns

> the woman's
> soft and vulnerable body,
> every where on her turning
> round into another
> where shadows on her
> promising mysterious places
> promising the answers to
> questions impossible to ask.

"Sleeping Beauty" dramatizes a sensual awakening and its consequences. After the near-ecstatic **"Poem in Praise of Menstruation"** come poems about men's contradictory nurturing and destructive qualities, others about the current political state of America and, as one title has it, about **"The Beginning of the End of the World."**

The third section, "Eight-Pointed Star," is the most personally revealing, and surprising. **"Wild Blessings"** testifies to the poet's ambivalence toward her own "gift of understanding"; in **"Water Sign Woman,"** she characterizes the peculiar situation of "the feel things woman . . . the woman who feels everything." Both at home and not at home among her fellow poets, she describes in **"Grandma, We Are Poets"** the poet's activity, in terms relating to autism.

Having acknowledged, in **"To My Friend, Jerina,"** that she has been an incest victim, in the next poem, **"Lot's Wife 1988,"** she declares herself responsible for preserving her family's name and its past. Then she adores her grandchildren, bids farewell to her uterus, writes the rollicking poems **"To My Last Period"** and **"Wishes for Sons"** ("bring them to gynecologists / not unlike themselves") and love poems to her late husband, interspersing these with poems of longing, sexual desire and awareness of new possibilities for life.

In **"The Mother's Story,"** she—"one black girl from buffalo"—is the beneficiary of a fairy godmother who "filled [her] ear with light," thereby linking her with Lucifer, the light-bearing fallen angel, the embodiment of creative and sexual energy who is the hero of the marvelous fourth sequence. "Tree of Life." Yet it is the woman Eve who leads Adam and Lucifer (**"clay and morning star"**) "past the winged gate / into the unborn world" where "chaos fell away / before her like a cloud / and everywhere seemed light." *Quilting* leaves the reader certain that Lucille Clifton is headed somewhere, and will, like her Lucifer, illuminate the way as she goes along.

Leslie Ullman (essay date 1992)

SOURCE: A review of *Quilting: Poems 1987-1990*, in *The Kenyon Review*, Vol. XIV, No. 3, Summer, 1992, pp. 178-80.

[*Critic and poet Ullman discusses how Clifton's poems in* Quilting: Poems 1987-1990 *echo the speech patterns of African-American idioms, folk songs, and spirituals.*]

Lucille Clifton's seventh collection [*Quilting: Poems 1987-1990*] offers a poet who lives multiple lives and is of multiple, often contradictory minds, as an African-American and a woman living the "inexplicable life" of a poet. The book's title and its sections named after quilt patterns ("CatalpaFlower," "Eight-pointed Star," "Tree of Life") supply a visual metaphor for the vibrant wholeness of vision the book achieves through its many patterns of speech and points of focus, but "quilting" is not a necessary device for making it all work. Clifton's vision, as we have come to know it in her earlier work as well, is large, diffuse, and sensual, always empathic, and often fierce in the deft, sultry manner of a lioness stalking and striking.

These poems do not depart significantly in style or music from Clifton's earlier work. They are mostly brief, driving to the quick of what she has to say, and many echo the sometimes-defiant, sometimes-celebratory rhythms and speech patterns of African-American idioms, folk songs, and spirituals. The presence behind the poems, however, speaks from new depths presaged by poems such as **"to my last period,"** where the poet who paid bold "homage" to her hips in an earlier collection now acknowledges the passing of her body to a more autumnal time, a somber maturity:

> well girl, goodbye,
> after thirty-eight years.
> thirty-eight years and you
> never arrived
> splendid in your red dress
> without trouble for me
> somewhere, somehow.
>
> now it is done,
> and i feel just like
> the grandmothers who,
> after the hussy has gone,
> sit holding her photograph
> and sighing, *wasn't she*
> *beautiful? wasn't she beautiful?*

In this collection, Clifton begins to emerge as a crone-figure: not in the sense of having lost sensual connection to the body, but rather as taking on the role of an elder, a custodian of records, a visionary who understands both the doomed and redemptive sides of mankind. Her visionary presence especially informs the brilliant series of poems spoken by Adam, Eve, and Lucifer in the book's final section, "Tree of Life," which resurrects the first terror, the first wonder, and the first relentless urge towards life which still nourish and torment us, though we often forget it.

Eve yields not so much to temptation as to the pure truth Lucifer tells her in a dream: "it is your own lush self / you hunger for / he whispers lucifer / honey-tongue" (**"eve's version"**). Adam reels under the dawning sense of separation within himself, the burden of his missing rib, as he acknowledges "some need in me / struggling to roar through my / mouth into a name / this creation is so fierce / i would rather have been born" (**"adam thinking"**). Lucifer flashes through these poems as "the bearer of lightning / and of lust," sensuous and fallen (**"lucifer understanding at last"**). He leaves the angels, his former compatriots, bereft of something vital: "in / perpetual evening . . . all of us / going about our / father's business / less radiant / less sure" (**"whispered to lucifer"**).

Clifton addresses her role as spokeswoman for the past in an untitled poem at the start of this collection when she says: "I am often accused of tending to the past / as if I . . . sculpted it / with my own hands." She goes on to assert, however, that the past simply waited for her to come, "a monstrous unnamed baby" which she "took to breast," named "History," and allowed to grow on its own:

> she is more human now,
> learning language everyday,
> remembering faces, names and dates.
> when she is strong enough to travel
> on her own, beware, she will.

In addition to her resurrection of mankind's first gestures, Clifton isolates small pieces of the recent past and gives them dimension in the many poems she dedicates to others: the first child killed in the 1976 Soweto riot (". . . and there was light around the young / boy hector peterson dead in soweto and still among us / yes," from **"poem beginning in no and ending in yes"**); Nelson and Winnie Mandela ("walk out old chief, old husband, / enter again your own wife," from **"february 11, 1990"**); a friend dead from cancer (**"4/25/89 late"**), her grandmother (**"grandma, we are poets"**), and others.

Clifton reopens the past especially effectively in several poems set on old plantations, where she wanders through a slave cabin or an old cemetery, resurrecting from scanty evidence the outer lives and sometimes the inner lives of slave women who lived and died anonymously. In the beam of her attention, these women briefly and indelibly reclaim their place in history: "nobody mentioned slaves / yet the curious tools / shine with your fingerprints," she says in **"at the cemetery, walnut grove plantation, south carolina, 1989."** And she concludes with an incantation that works as invocation, honoring the space on each tombstone where a name should be:

> tell me your dishonored names.
> here lies
> here lies
> here lies
> here lies
> hear

Naming arises throughout this volume as Clifton's urgent and healing task, both on behalf of the nameless who have lived bravely, and also as part her own ongoing struggle to have her language be heard on its own terms. Inspecting an old bench in the poem, **"slave cabin, sotterly plantation, maryland, 1989,"** Clifton reflects on the woman who sat there day after day, rounding and polishing its wood with the press of her bottom, "feet dead against the dirty floor / humming for herself humming / her own sweet human name." Clifton's own task, despite her acclaim as a poet, involves her in a similar isolation, the malaise of not being heard on her own terms: ". . . even the best believe / they have that right, / believe that / what they say i mean / is what i mean / as if words only matter in the world they know" (**"note to my self"**).

In the quietly defiant poem titled **"grandma we are poets,"** Clifton spins a definition of herself as a poet from definitions for the word *autism* taken from *Webster's New Universal Dictionary* and the *Random House Encyclopedia.* Against the notion of "state of mind / characterized by daydreaming" she writes, "say rather / i imagined myself / in the place before / language imprisoned itself / in words." Against the notion of "failure to use language normally," she writes, "say rather that labels / and names rearranged themselves / into description / so that what i saw / i wanted to say". . . .

These are not arrogant poems, but each one is effortlessly honest, implying hers and others' quiet victories against great odds. Clifton speaks from the freedom of an individual who acknowledges her full female self, including the losses suffered by heart and body. Like the menstrual blood she describes in **"poem in praise of menstruation,"** her poems are both dark and nourishing, painful and life-giving, a "wild river" that "flows also / through animals / beautiful and faithful and ancient / and female and brave."

David Kirby (essay date 1993)

SOURCE: A review of *The Book of Light,* in *The New York Times Book Review,* April 18, 1993, pp. 15-16.

[*Here, poet and critic David Kirby applauds the humanity of Clifton's poetry in* The Book of Light.]

Ms. Clifton finds beauty in actual people and places. In **"thel"** (uncapitalized, like the other poems in this collection), she speaks of someone who "was my first landscape," a "sweet attic of a woman. / 'repository of old songs." The speakers in Ms. Clifton's poems are usually heading home. In **"the yeti poet returns to his village to tell his story,"** the speaker retreats from "the shrunken world / of hairless men" and makes his way back "to this wilderness / where we know where we are / what we are." Thus the yeti poet defines himself only in the embraces of his hirsute peers.

And in **"the women you are accustomed to,"** Ms. Clifton pointedly rejects some chilly beauties in favor of a little funky human warmth:

> wearing that same black dress . . .
> their bronzed hair set in perfect place;
> these women gathered in my dream
> to talk their usual talk,

their conversation spiked with the names
of avenues in France.

and when i asked them what the hell,
they shook their marble heads
and walked erect out of my sleep,
back into a town which knows
all there is to know
about the cold outside, while i relaxed
and thought of you.
your burning blood, your dancing tongue.

When larger-than-life figures appear in *The Book of Light,*
Ms. Clifton cuts them down to size. In one poem, Atlas is
just a working stiff who has learned to carry the world
"the way a poor man learns / to carry everything," and in
another, Superman turns out to be "only clark kent /
after all." Even Lucifer is, not the Prince of Darkness, but just
"a sleek old / traveler." Yet this leveling act is less a
diminution of the gods than it is a reminder that our lives
are not controlled from on high, after all. There is a God
in these poems, but that God is silent. Everything else—
everything we can affect ourselves, in other words—is
noisy, human and hot.

Alicia Ostriker (essay date 1993)

SOURCE. "Kin and Kin: The Poetry of Lucille Clifton,"
in *American Poetry Review,* Vol. 22, No. 6, November/
December 1993, pp. 41-8.

[*Here poet and critic Ostriker calls Clifton a minimalist artist whose small poems encompass grand
themes.*]

Lucille Clifton's writing is deceptively simple. The poems
are short, unrhymed, the lines typically between four and
two beats. The sentences are usually declarative and direct,
the punctuation light, the diction a smooth mix of standard
English with varying styles and degrees of black vernacular. Almost nothing (including "i" and beginnings of
sentences) is capitalized. Some poems have titles, others
do not, a fact which may disconcert the reader, and is
probably intended to. Marilyn Hacker has written that
Clifton's poems remind her, in grace and deftness, of
Japanese ink drawings. They remind me of a drum held in
a woman's lap. The woman sits on a plain wooden chair,
or on the earth. A community surrounds her. She slaps the
drum with her bare hands. "Oh children," she says in the
title poem of Clifton's first book, "think about the good
times."

The work of a minimalist artist like Clifton makes empty
space resonate. A spacious silence is not mere absence of
noise, but locates us as it were on a cosmic stage. We are
meant to understand the unsaid, to take our humble places
with a sense of balance and belonging instead of the anxiety
and alienation promoted by more conspicuously sublime
and ambitious artistries. Omissions, as Marianne Moore
remarks in quite another context, are not accidents; and as

William Carlos Williams observes, in this mode, perfection is basic. Whatever the content of a particular piece,
we should experience the craftsmanship of the minimalist
as a set of unerring gestures governed by a constraining
and shaping discipline, so habitual it seems effortless.

While the white space in such art stands for the largeness
of space and time in which we human creatures find ourselves, the figured space stands for thick experience—
experience which has been philosophically contemplated
for an extended period. The artist, having patiently learned
something quite exact about the dynamics of reality, offers
it in concentrated form.

A byproduct of this concentration may be humor, the sacred
levity associated with adepts in numerous traditions of
religious art. Think of the Zen image of the laughing monk;
John Cage's playfulness; the jokes of the thirteenth-century
Sufi poet Rumi, or those in the Chasidic stories told by
Martin Buber; the trickster pranks of Coyote in Native
American folktales, or Monkey King leaping to the end of
the universe and peeing on the Buddha's little finger in a
Chinese tale; remember the boyishly erotic mischievousness of the young Krishna in Hindu mythology. Then think
of how Clifton fuses high comedy and high seriousness
when she describes the poetic vocation, a topic most poets
approach with a solemnity proportional to their/our insecurity. Clifton's **"admonitions,"** the last poem in *good
times,* ends:

> children
> when they ask you
> why is your mama so funny
> say
> she is a poet
> she don't have no sense

Another early poem about her vocation is "prayer," which
asks an unnamed listener to "lighten up," wonders why his
hand is so heavy on "just poor / me," and receives a
response which makes this poem cunningly parallel John
Milton's famous complaint of blindness:

> answer
>
> this is the stuff
> i made the heroes out of
> all the saints
> and prophets and things
> had to come by
> this

Has Clifton read Milton's sonnet, which questions how
God can exact the "day-labor" of poetry from a blind
man, and ends in the famous "They also serve who only
stand and wait"? Whether she has or not, what impresses
me (and makes me laugh) is the identical structure of these
two poems in which the poet interrogates God's fairness
and gets fairly answered—and the marvelous freshness of
Clifton's version. It thrills me as an American that this
sacred conversation, this *de profundis,* can occur in my
American language that, as Marianne Moore says, cats

and dogs can read. I enjoy the down-home familiarity between Clifton and her God; I applaud a woman lining herself up with the heroes and prophets; and I feel, as well, for her struggle—which is not Milton's blindness, or Gerard Manley Hopkins's conviction of sin, but an American black woman's struggle which I can guess at. In a much later piece, "the making of poems," humility and comic afflatus again meet:

> the reason why i do it
> though i fail and fail
> in the giving of true names
> is i am adam and his mother
> and these failures are my job.

What does it mean when a woman calls herself "adam and his mother"? The mother could be Eve, or a nameless pre-monotheistic goddess, or just any mother doing her homely work—and that conflation of myth and modernity is part of the joke. Making the poet double-gendered is another part. "True names" registers the archaic notion that language is not arbitrary, that poetry names essences of things—while the poet's failure, it seems to me, conflates individual inadequacy with the imperfect meshing of signifiers and signified in a non-mythic world. How *could* "adam and his mother" find language for the way we live in the twentieth century? Still, they have to try. As with the simple double gesture of "this" to stand for the hardship God inflicts on saints and prophets, the idea of the poet's work as an impossible yet sacred task is effectively rendered in the plainest of language—right down to calling it not a task but a job. "The making of poems" demystifies poetic labor and dignifies maternal and manly labor. What these poems tell us is that high and low things can meet, along with the union of the holy and the comic, if one knows enough about both.

ii

Let me talk a little more about meetings and mergings in Clifton, how they bely the poetry's apparent simplicity, and how they feed its spirituality. Born in upper New York State in 1936, Lucille Clifton was the daughter of Sam Clifton, a steel worker, and Thelma Louise, who died at age forty-four. She was the great-granddaughter of Caroline Sale, a Virginia midwife who remembered Africa, the slave ship, and walking from New Orleans to Virginia at the age of eight. She attended Howard University and Fredonia State Teacher's College, met and was influenced by Leroi Jones, Ishmael Reed, Gwendolyn Brooks. Reed showed some of her poems to Langston Hughes, who published them in an anthology. Robert Hayden sent some to Carolyn Kizer, who sent them to the 1969 YM-WHA Discovery contest, which Clifton won. Her first book of poems was selected by *The New York Times* as one of the ten best books of that same year.

Clifton began writing during the explosive Black Arts movement of the late 1960's and early 1970's, and her early subjects include the memory of slavery, the facts of poverty, urban riots. She mourns assassinated black leaders and praises live ones, tells family stories, records her womanly conversion from bleaching cream and "whiteful ways" to the love of blackness. Black anger and black pride stand at the core of her work. Her family memoir, *Generations,* begins with an epigraph from the Book of Job: "Lo, mine eye hath seen all this, mine ear hath heard and understood it. What ye know, the same do I know also; I am not inferior unto you." The second epigraph, which forms a powerful refrain both in the memoir and in Clifton's poems, quotes "Mammy Ca'line": "Get what you want, you from Dahomey women."

The black inheritance joins others. Walt Whitman's transcendental expansiveness and Emily Dickinson's verbal compression feel uniquely wedded in Clifton. Epigraphs from Whitman mark the sections of *Generations,* and the elliptical Emily might well consider the intensely playful Lucille one of her daughters. Audrey McCluskey notices her Dickinsonian "simultaneous acknowledgment of pain and possibility"; I notice the ghost of the Dickinson who felt the size of her small life swelling like horizons in her breast, and "sneered—softly—'small!'" Technically, the contemporary poet she most resembles in cadence, quality of ellipsis, and syntactic ambiguity, is Robert Creeley, though unlike Creeley's her verse feels not ascetic or spare but fully embodied, thickly material, communal.

An early instance of her communality would be Clifton's much anthologized **"miss rosie"**:

> when i watch you
> wrapped up like garbage
> sitting, surrounded by the smell
> of too old potato peels
> or
> when i watch you
> in your old man's shoes
> with the little toe cut out
> sitting, waiting for your mind
> like next week's grocery
> i say
> when i watch you
> you wet brown bag of a woman
> who used to be the best looking gal in georgia
> used to be called the Georgia Rose
> i stand up
> through your destruction
> i stand up

Structurally, this poem resembles a Shakespeare sonnet. The thrice-repeated "when i watch you" works in fact like Sonnet 64's triple "When I have seen . . ." to produce, section by section, a crescendo of urgency. The verb "watch," like "have seen," implies a sustained attentiveness. Unlike Shakespeare's verb, it also implies intimacy: it tells us that the speaker and the object of her gaze are neighbors. The poem's music is a matter of subtle assonances, alliterations, repetitions: notice the p's, s's and o's in "wrapped up . . . sitting, surrounded, smell . . . old potato peels," then the o's going into the next stanza, with the w's of "watch . . . with . . . waiting . . . weeks" and the off-rhyme of "cut out," and the third stanza's chiasmus of w's and b's in "wet brown bag of a woman." Notice how the cadences vary but at intervals coalesce into the adjacent stresses of "wrapped up . . . too old . . . old man's shoes . . . toe cut out . . . next week's grocery . . . wet brown bag," how the quasi-stanzaic units lengthen and grow increasingly emphatic, while the masculine endings are increasingly softened by feminine ones. The object of the gaze, the wasted woman, woman-as-garbage, is like the "ruin" of Shakespeare's sonnet, that makes him "ruminate." Beauty decays. Only what time destroys for Shakespeare is for Clifton destroyed by time and poverty joined.

Clifton's closing triplet, like a Shakespearean couplet, throws the poem into another gear. We move abruptly from sitting to standing. You to me. Destruction to survival. Clifton's whiplash has a tightness like Shakespeare's paradoxical sonnet endings: "To love that well which thou must leave ere long." "This thought is as a death, which cannot choose / But weep to have that which it fears to lose." But can we define Clifton's tone? Grief, shame and compassion govern this poem, we might say, and resolution governs its close. Yet the poem is cruel as well, and I do not think it is simply a matter of facing, confronting, the cruelty of age and poverty. The speaker keeps her distance in the poem. She watches, doesn't touch. Neither is it a protest poem. What of the pivotal preposition "through"? Difficult to pin down, it can mean "despite." Though you fail, I endure. Or it can imply duration or submission. I endure your destruction as if it were a storm pelting me. The gesture signals homage, a salute, almost a military standing at attention. I stand up for you, for your rights, in your honor. Yet "through" can also mean "because of." Your destruction precipitates or causes my survival, my will to survive. I do this for (or instead of) you. I do it because you don't, I triumph because you fail, and even in some sense thanks to your failure.

The reader of **"miss rosie"** need not be aware of the poem's technical subtlety or its emotional and moral ambiguity; in fact, the subtlety and ambiguity speak precisely to what we habitually repress from consciousness. At the obvious level of content, the poem makes us look at what we might prefer not to see: the condition of poverty and hopelessness. At another level it lets us see ourselves—and the awful complexity of our connection to others.

Forster's "Only connect" could be Clifton's motto. Other poets' juvenilia may elaborate the postures of a solitary or romantically alienated self, but Clifton is already maternal, daughterly, a voice at once personal and collective, rooted and relational. The "good times" of her first title poem describe an evening when the family is drunk and dancing in the kitchen because the rent is paid, the lights are back on, and an uncle has hit the numbers. The poem urges "oh children / think about the good times" in a voice that could be either rejoicing or begging, and which invites us to the party yet asks us to recognize ("think") how that party is circled by pain. An early ecological poem, **"generations,"** begins by invoking the responsibilities of "people who are going to be / in a few years / bottoms of trees," and ends by warning that "the generations of rice / of coal / of grasshoppers // by their invisibility / de-

nounce us." In her kitchen cutting greens, Clifton observes, "i hold their bodies in obscene embrace . . . and the kitchen twists dark on its spine / and i taste in my natural appetite / the bond of live things everywhere."

Her family poems brim with linkages. Poems to and about her mother proliferate, and spin through yearning, rue, rivalry, and passionate identification. Her father is adored, pitied, rebuked. Her daughters are "my girls / my almost me" and then "my dearest girls / my girls / my more than me." Or, in a rondeau of relation, "lucy is the ocean / extended by / her girls / are the river / fed by / lucy / is the sun / reflected through / her girls. . . ." She addresses her heroines Harriet Tubman, Sojourner Truth and her own grandmother, with the refrain "if i be you." In sum, she assumes connection where the dualisms of our culture assume separation—between self and other, humans and nature, male and female, public and private life, pleasure and pain—and what emanates from her mixings, like the wave of energy released when atoms fuse, is something like joy. This is true even when, or especially when, the experience that feeds the poems is of "blood and breaking."

The other side of Clifton's impulse to connect is the almost gnostic impulse to look inward. In the early work the most obvious form this impulse takes is her stress on memory, and the connection to ancestry and to an Africa that "all of my bones remember." Less conspicuously, she contemplates mental process itself, wondering what kinds of knowledge—material and spiritual, external and internal—may be available to us, what the difference is between appearance and reality. Her first poem about her mother's early death expresses puzzlement as much as pain:

> seemed like what she touched was hers
> seemed like what touched her couldn't hold,
> she got us almost through the high grass
> then seemed like she turned around and ran
> right back in
> right back on in

Her first poem about her father, describing his work, asks

> what do my daddy's fingers
> know about grace?
> what do the couplers know
> about being locked together?

A poem about an abortion asks

> what did i know about waters rushing back
> what did i know about drowning
> or being drowned

The implication is that truth is always somewhere deeper than words or even actions. In sex a husband "fills / his wife with children and / with things she never knew." Knowledge is also "the life thing in us . . . call it craziness . . . call it whatever you have to / call it anything." The female body is her primary teacher: "i entered the earth in / a woman jar . . . and it has made me / wise." The name her mother gave her, Lucille, means "light," and the poet views her own birth as a symbol of light breaking. Clifton celebrates the six fingers she had on each hand at birth, her nappy hair and her free hips, her body like a city, her tasty and electric sexuality. And again and again she uses the key figure of "turning" to express her need for inner life:

> turning out of the
> white cage, turning out of the
> lady cage
> turning at last
> on a stem like a black fruit
>
> if in the middle of my life
> i am turning the final turn
> into the shining dark
>
> see the sensational
> two-headed woman
> one face turned outward
> one face
> swiveling slowly in

For what the poet discovers within is a woman's epistemology, the radiant life of the spirit.

The source of Clifton's spiritual strength is black. It is also what she calls, punning on her own name, "the light." It comes, as she has her John the Baptist say in the "some jesus" poems, "in blackness like a star."

"Some jesus," the first of Clifton's revisionist religious sequences, begins like this:

> adam and eve
>
> the names
> of the things
> bloom in my mouth
>
> my body opens
> into brothers

You have to read that twice, I think, before you realize how simply and stunningly androgynous a poem it is—how lucidly it represents what Robert Hass, speaking of Rilke, calls "the pull inward, the erotic pull of the other we sense buried in the self," but represents it as achieved, not merely desired. The poet distinguishes male and female selves, voices, roles, but doesn't separate them from each other or from herself: she is both, they are both she. Casually proceeding then to inhabit the male personae of Cain, Moses, Solomon, Job, Daniel and Jonah, Clifton's voice in the New Testament section of this sequence section slides into the voice of a John who could be in Galilee or Philadelphia praising a savior—

> he be calling the people brother
> even in the prison
> even in the jail

then into the voice of a Mary whose annunciation is erotic, a kiss "as soft as cotton / over my breasts / all shiny

bright," a disciple who doesn't mind "laughing like god's fool / behind this jesus," a Lazarus whose raising is also a promise of revolution,

> whoever say
> dust must be dust
> don't see the trees
> smell rain
> remember africa

a Jesus on "good friday" who says "i rise up above myself / like a fish flying // men will be gods / if they want it," and a final "spring song" celebrating the green rebirth of "delicious Jesus." Gloria Ashaka has observed that Clifton feminizes, Africanizes, eroticizes and makes mystical the Biblical stories she uses. My own guess is that she is probably recovering and restoring forms of myth and worship which white tradition has all but erased, and that her intimacy or fusion with biblical personae fulfills on the stage of the inner life what her "if i be you" does with the kin of her outer life.

As her career proceeds, Clifton's spirituality grows bolder and more syncretic. In **"to a dark moses"** of Clifton's third book, *an ordinary woman*

> you are the one
> i am lit for.
> come with your rod
> that twists
> and is a serpent.
> i am the bush.
> i am burning.
> i am not consumed.

If we take this poem literally, and why should we not, God is a black woman who is also Lucille Clifton. In the sequence of Kali poems it is indeed "a woman god and terrible / with her skulls and breasts," who pushes past the poet's fear and resistance, enters her bones, and forces her to say "i know i am your sister." Admitting the goddess of death as a portion of herself—of ourselves—is Clifton's most radical move in *an ordinary woman.* The poet's next book, *two-headed woman,* includes a sequence of eight poems voicing the life of Mary in a dialect that thickens toward Caribbean, implies a braiding of Christianity and Rastafarianism, and emphatically fuses eroticism and spirituality, exaltation and fear, with her increasingly characteristic light imagery:

> joseph, i cannot still these limbs,
> i hands keep moving toward i breasts,
> so many stars. so bright.
> joseph, is wind burning from east
> joseph, i shine, oh joseph, oh
> illuminated night.

Clifton also lets us feel the human pain of this "chosen" woman whose womb blossoms then dies. Mary's mother Anna wants to "fight this thing." Mary in her last poem has become a weary "old creature" wondering "could i have walk away when voices / singing in my sleep," prophetically worrying about another girl whom a star might choose.

At about this time Clifton's spirituality unmoors itself from scripture. **"Breaklight"** testifies to a visionary synesthesia of inner light and language: "light keeps on breaking" with the spirit voices of "other nations," trees, water, which the poet mysteriously understands—and then the light reveals itself as the hesitant fears of the poet's dead mother. Uncannily parallel to Dylan Thomas's "Light bre.' ; where no sun shines," the poem opens itself to a kind of holy breaking and entering. That process, writ large and terrifying, becomes the theme of "the light that came to lucille clifton," the final sequence in *two-headed woman*. These excruciating poems delineate the poet's experiences of incandescent light infused with soft voices which at first make her fear madness. Only gradually does she identify the voices of light as wingless angels, as parents, as the dead: "in populated air / our ancestors continue . . . i have heard / their shimmering voices / singing."

Numerous writers have testified to the force of religion in Afro-American writing. "Mystical longings, a desire to transcend empirical boundaries and material limitations are . . . the entrancing essence of Afro-America," writes Houston Baker. Derek Walcott notes, "I have never separated the writing of poetry from prayer." Toni Morrison, Alice Walker, Toni Cade Bambara, Paule Marshall and Audre Lorde are a few of the black writers who make visionary sutures of material and spiritual existence. Yet I think no other writer approaches Clifton's capacity to carry us from fragmentation to wholeness. Thus in the poem elliptically entitled **"I at creation,"** in her 1987 volume *Next,* when she begins with "i and my body," we might think of the traditional duality of body and soul, but Clifton draws them coupled instead of adversarial. Here is the whole poem:

> and i and my body rise
> with the dusky beasts
> with eve and her brother
> to gasp in
> the unsubstantial air
> and evenly begin the long
> slide out of paradise.
> all life is life.
> all clay is kin and kin.

The moment of "creation" here is both past and continuous; it is inseparable from and contiguous with a departure from (not "loss" of) paradise; it perhaps includes the creation of the poem; it is the trauma and triumph of birth, and all creatures share it. At the same time there are the muted ironies, the understanding that a black woman is to be identified with "dusky beasts," but then again with "eve and her brother," and the tacit argument for kinship made by the assonance of "beasts," "eve," "evenly." The assonance of "i" and "rise" at the poem's opening (rise like bread? like new-made creatures? like the newborn from the womb? like the dead at the resurrection? like any person in the morning after sleep?) returns with the "slide" from "paradise" and is reinforced in the next line, which then yields to the alliteration of the final line, as if an argument were being closed. Isn't it closed? Isn't it obvious? The poem's physicality is one with its logic. As readers we

perceive ourselves rising amid a multitude of others, gasping like newborns, sliding involuntarily, and arriving at what feels like certain knowledge. The experience of creation, coterminous with the shedding of safety, is the one touch of nature which unifies the world—and the poet makes it seem the most natural thing in the world. . . .

Part of what separates white from black America, I suspect, is that if whites actually tried to imagine being black, we'd go mad with pain and rage. To be privileged is to be fragile. Clifton, on the other hand, defines herself without raising her voice:

> i got a long memory
> and i come from a line
> of black and going on women
> who got used to making it through murdered sons

She defines, in a tone of patient explanation, what young black males feel:

> they act like they don't love their country
> no
> what it is
> is they found out
> their country don't love them.

Clifton's stance toward white culture varies from the wry mockery of the first poem in *good times,* with its double sneer at repression and euphemism,

> in the inner city
> or
> like we call it
> home
> we think a lot about uptown
> and the silent nights
> and the houses straight as dead men
> and the pastel lights

to the scornful pity of **"after kent state,"** written after National Guardsmen shot four students demonstrating against the invasion of Cambodia during the Vietnam War,

> only to keep
> his little fear
> he kills his cities
> and his trees
> even his children oh
> people
> white ways are
> the ways of death

to a bit of acerbic mythmaking:

> the once and future dead
> who learn they will be white men
> weep for their history. we call it
> rain

The book title *good news about the earth* comes from a poem which predicts the destruction of white men by mountains and waters, enabling their bodies to join those of Native Americansbroken on the Trail of Tears, slaves melted into the ocean floor of Middle Passage. The celebratory and affirmative Clifton possesses this calm judge at her core, just as the Christian Clifton contains a black and ruthless Hindu goddess.

In *next* (1987), a series of poems on South Africa, and another on the death of Crazy Horse, join poems about Gettysburg, Buchenwald, Nagasaki, Jonestown, and the Shatila massacre in Lebanon, indicting "the extraordinary evil in ordinary men." These in turn join a set of anguished poems describing a young girl's struggle with leukemia, some luminously elegiac poems about the death of Clifton's husband Fred, some communings with her dead mother, a rueful sequence about doing poetry readings "in white america," the "shapeshifter poems" on incest, the "california lessons" on race and karma. Though a book filled with grief and grievances, it makes room for the pleasure of grandchildren; it also makes room for a meditation on the poet's own capacity for cruelty—a poem about killing cockroaches. In one mischievous poem, **"my dream about being white,"** the poet imagines herself with "no lips, no behind, hey" wearing white history—

> but there's no future
> in those clothes
> so i take them off and
> wake up
> dancing.

Quilting: poems 1987-1990, Clifton's boldest book, continues her meditations on history, loss, tragedy. Her affirmation of the body continues in two glorious poems on menstruation, **"poem in praise of menstruation,"** and **"to my last period,"** followed by the hilarious **"wishes for sons,"** which fantasizes for them cramps, the last tampon, one week early, one week late, hot flashes and clots, and gynecologists resembling themselves.

Among the things of the spirit, her largest and loveliest work now is the ten-poem "Tree of Life" sequence, a lyric re-imagining of the role of Lucifer in Eden. "How art thou fallen from heaven, oh Lucifer, son of the morning," cries Isaiah. Clifton's version of the myth makes Lucifer (Lat. "light-bringer") at once light, lightning, and snake, servant of God, illuminator of mankind.

As in the "some jesus" poems, the poet speaks through plural voices which seem to inhabit her. Hers is the voice of the mystified angels describing Lucifer's creation and fall in the first three poems, then woman's sensuous voice in **"eve's version"** and man's sensually and intellectually desperate one in **"adam thinking."** Most fascinatingly, her voice is also Lucifer's.

Clifton's possession of and by the spirit of Lucifer, whose name echoes hers, and who is "six-fingered" like her, is an identification with masculine creativity. When the rather neoplatonic seraphim ponder "was it the woman / en-

ticed you to leave us," Lucifer confirms and globalizes his sexuality:

> bearer of lightning
> and of lust
>
> thrust between the
> legs of the earth
> into this garden
>
> phallus and father
> doing holy work
>
> oh sweet delight
> oh eden

The trajectory of "Tree of Life" is from heaven to earth, creation to final day, ignorance to knowledge. Part of its charm is its teasing allusiveness, its indeterminacies and uncertainties. When the "shine" of Lucifer's birth seems too much for "one small heaven," should we be reminded of the breaking of vessels which in kabbala is the moment of creation? When Lucifer leaves heaven in shadow,

> and even the
> solitary brother
> has risen from his seat
> of stones he is holding
> they say a wooden stick
> and pointing toward
> a garden,

is the brother (never mentioned again) Death, or Christ, or the original black man? Is the stick the tree of life, the cross, or both? The unidentified speaker of **"the garden of delight"**—sixth poem in the sequence—invokes possible Edens of earth, air, fire and water "for some," using an alchemical scheme, concluding with the quintessential Eden of the poet:

> and for some
> certain only of the syllables
> it is the element they
> search their lives for
>
> eden
>
> for them
> it is a test

Ambiguities converge here. First, that poets may find Eden only in certain syllables (not all of them), or that syllables are the only things they are certain of. Then, that they spend their lives searching, or that they search *within* their lives. Is Eden, then, internal or external? Do words lead to it, or is it embodied in them? Is the test finding Eden, or living in it?

In the penultimate poem, uncertainty moves toward certitude. Eve has whispered her knowledge of names to Adam, and the unidentified voice describes the threesome of "the story thus far." As in Clifton's earlier **"creation,"** the time might be the year zero, or the day before yesterday: "so they went out / clay and morning star / following the bright back / of the woman." (I recall, in this vista, Whitman's Adam with his Eve "by my side or back of me . . . or in front, and I following her.") As they pass the gate "into the unborn world," the imagery grows brighter, chaos falls away, "and everywhere seemed light / seemed glorious / seemed very eden." Again the fall is not a fall but a birth; the light of Eros and knowledge still surrounds the protagonists, or *seems* to. The "seemed," though inconspicuous, is crucial. Not until the final poem do uncertainties crown themselves assured. In the sequence's last poem, **"lucifer speaks in his own voice,"** the light-bringer-snake knows he has done God's will and is

> certain of a
> graceful bed
> and a soft caress
> along my long belly
> at endtime,

but only in the final lines does his voice finally merge with the poet's, as if to summarize her career so far:

> illuminate i could
> and so
> illuminate i did.

That is the simplest possible description of Clifton's work.

Jean Anaporte-Easton   (essay date 1994)

SOURCE: "Healing Our Wounds: The Direction of Difference in the Poetry of Lucille Clifton and Judith Johnson," in *Mid-American Review*, Vol. XIV, No. 2, 1994, pp. 78-82.

[*In the essay below, Anaporte-Easton cites Clifton's thematic healing of the disparity between the mind, spirit, and the body.*]

The distinctive quality of Clifton's voice comes from her ability to ground her art in an imagery of the body and physical reality. Through the Mary poems, Clifton re-inscribes Christianity with the sacred wisdom of women's physical and emotional experience just as she expands the imagery of Judaism and Christianity to suggest African-American as well as white culture. Prior to the Mary poems in a series called *some jesus*, Clifton transposes details of Christian mythology associated with white culture into the physical terms of Black culture: Collard greens, beets, and turnips replace palm leaves on the path of the triumphal entry; Moses is "an old man / leaving slavery"; John the Baptist announces "somebody coming in blackness / like a star / and the world be a great bush / on his head / and his eyes be fire / in the city . . ." (*An Ordinary Woman*). The Mary poems transpose the birth story one step further so that it centers on

Anna, Mary's mother; Mary; and the wingless angels who bring voices and visions. Women, the birth-givers, become the source of the spirit manifest on earth.

The first thing the Mary poems accomplish then is a reclaiming of the body as a base for spirituality. For to tell the birth story from a woman's point of view is to talk about bodies:

> father
> i am not equal to the faith required.
> i doubt.
> i have a woman's certainties;
> bodies pulled from me,
> pushed into me.
> bone flesh is what i know
>
>   (**"confession"**)

For women, birth is unavoidably about the body—theirs, opening wider than we imagine possible (a miracle equal to wingless angels) to let a new being slide out. Moreover, when Mary and her mother dream, they experience it physically as "burning" the ear, "breaking" the eye:

> this one lie down on grass.
> this one old men will follow
> calling mother mother.
> she womb will blossom then die.
> this one she hide from evening.
> at a certain time when she hear something
> it will burn her ear.
> at a certain place when she see something
> it will break her eye.
>
>   (**"the astrologer predicts at mary's birth"**)

The response extends beyond recognition to activity. Physical activity and images in Clifton's poetry give presence to ideas and states of being. The poem just quoted begins with the image of lying down in grass, an action associated with connection, receptivity, lovemaking, birthing. The following poem, **"anna speaks of the childhood of mary her daughter,"** draws us in with the image of familiar domestic activity—rising early and scrubbing—and suggests as well the furious activity that keeps anxiety at bay:

> we rise up early and
> we work. work is the medicine
> for dreams.
>   that dream
> i am having again;
> she washed in light,
> whole world bowed to its knees,
> she on a hill looking up,
> face all long tears.
>   and shall i give her up
> to dream then? i fight this thing.
> all day we scrubbing scrubbing.

The scrubbing is women's work—washing clean. The physicality of the activity carries over to the dream event of Mary "washed in light." The world's homage is im-aged as the world kneeling. This ritual gesture echoes the necessary gesture of kneeling to scrub. In this way, Clifton joins the spiritual and the physical worlds. Mary's grief at the crucifixion is "long tears," both because of the physical act of looking up at the hill, and because of the intensity and depth of her grief. The idioms of ears "burning" or of "cutting" or "breaking" the eye give us physical reference points for being at home in this an-cient story of miracle while the Biblical context lifts the sayings out of ordinary experience so they regain their power as metaphor. We read them literally again as in the beginning.

The distinctive quality of Clifton's voice comes from her ability to ground her art in an imagery of the body and physical reality.

—Jean Anaport-Easton

Inevitably Clifton links spiritual and physical desire. On facing pages in *good woman* there is an image of Mary "whispering / yes" to the angels and an image of a shep-herd "who hears in his herding / his mother whisper my son my son." A series of concrete images prepare for the shepherd:

> like a pot turned on the straw
> nuzzled by cows and an old man
> dressed like a father, like a loaf
> a poor baker sets in the haystack to cool
> like a shepherd who hears in his herding
> his mother whisper my son my son.

The comparisons ground the manger story in earthy, sex-ual associations. In this version of the birth story, a wom-an's desire for a child and her faith in strange dreams elicit the spirit made flesh. But the desire for the child is also sexual desire. In **"holy night,"** even the rhythm and imagery suggest sexual ecstasy:

> joseph, i cannot still these limbs,
> i hands keep moving toward i breasts,
> so many stars. so bright.
> joseph, is wind burning from east
> joseph, i shine, oh joseph, oh
> illuminated night.

For Joseph, too, the sexual and spiritual trembling are one:

> so even when my fingers tremble
> on mary
> my mouth cries only
> Jesus Jesus Jesus

Here is a birth story that fuses the severed realms—mind and body, black and white, heaven and earth. This healing curves back to make scrubbing not just a way of dealing with apprehension but a spiritual act, accept-ing—or being—and doing at once. As the story of two women brooding and bringing to fruition a holy vision the Mary poems model a process for living at once as individuals and in community, on the planes of the earthly and spiritual worlds, scrubbing and dreaming and saying "yes."

Clifton doesn't argue with the traditional, patriarchal story of the immaculate conception. She uses what she believes and re-visions the rest. Because her poems are stories or slices of stories we already know, sanctioned by time and religion, we enter into her telling ready to accept what she says. Yet when Clifton tells a story, she refocuses or chang-es details, inching it toward her vision: the Son of God is first the son of a mortal woman, and a real shepherd as well: "like a shepherd who hears in his herding / his mother whisper my son my son"; Joseph's reverence for his son is manifest in his love-making; the Christmas Star in Clif-ton's story is part of Mary's sexual ecstasy. Finally, Clif-ton's use of body imagery is a form of argument pulling us kinesthetically into her world.

FURTHER READING

CRITICISM

Review of *Good News about the Earth*. *Booklist* 69, No.1, (1 September 1972): 21.
   Analysis of Clifton's use of structure in her books.

Carruth, Hayden. Review of *Good Times*. *The Hudson Review* 23, No. 1 (Spring 1970): 182.
   Praises Clifton for her craftsmanship as a writer.

Johnson, Joyce. "The Theme of Celebration in Lucille Clifton's Poetry." *Pacific Coast Philology* XVIII, Nos. 1 & 2 (November 1983): 70-6.
   Discusses Clifton's rejection of negative stereotypes in her portrayals of Black neighborhoods.

Kazemek, Francis E., and Rigg, Pat. "Four Poets: Modern Poetry in the Adult Literacy Classroom." *Journal of Reading* 30, No. 3 (December 1986): 218-25.
   Explores the readability of several twentieth-century American idiom poets, including Clifton.

Kuzma, Greg. Review of *Next*. *The Georgia Review* XLIII, No. 3 (Fall 1988): 628-30.
   Examines the style and themes of Clifton's poems.

Lang, E. K. "Making Each Word Count." *The Christian Science Monitor* 80, No. 49 (5 February 1988): B3.
   Collection of statements from an interview with Clifton on art, priorities, celebrity and accomplishments.

Lazar, Hank. "Blackness Blessed: The Writings of Lucille Clifton." *The Southern Review* 25, No. 3 (July 1989): 760-70. Explores the political content and aesthetic accomplishments of Clifton's poetry and children's literature.

Scarupa, Harriet Jackson. "Lucille Clifton: Making the World 'Poem-Up'." *Ms.* 5, No. 4 (October 1976): 118, 120, 123. Recounts a visit to Clifton's Baltimore home, noting elements of Clifton's family history and her philosophy of writing.

Additional coverage of Clifton's life and career is contained in the following sources published by Gale Research: *Black Literature Criticism,* **Vol. 1;** *Black Writers,* **Vol. 2;** *Children's Literature Review,* **Vol. 5;** *Contemporary Authors,* **Vols. 49-52;** *Contemporary Authors New Revision Series,* **Vols. 2, 24, 42;** *Contemporary Literary Criticism,* **Vols. 19, 66;** *Dictionary of Literary Biography,* **Vols. 5, 41;** *Major Authors and Illustrators for Children and Young Adults;* *Major 20th-Century Writers;* **and** *Something about the Author,* **Vols. 20, 69.**

Victor Hugo
1802-1885

(Full name Victor Marie Hugo) French poet, dramatist, novelist, essayist, and critic.

INTRODUCTION

Hugo is considered one of the leaders of the Romantic movement in French literature as well as one of its most prolific and versatile authors. Although chiefly known outside France for the novels *Notre Dame de Paris* (1831; *The Hunchback of Notre Dame*) and *Les misérables* (1862; *Les Misérables*), he is renowned in his own country primarily for his contributions as a Romantic poet. Hugo's verse has been favorably compared to the works of William Shakespeare, Dante, and Homer; and he has influenced such diverse poets as Charles Baudelaire, Alfred Lord Tennyson, and Walt Whitman. Hugo's technical virtuosity, stylistic experimentation, startling range of emotion, and variety and universality of his themes not only established him as a leader of the French Romantic school but anticipated modern poetry.

Biographical Information

Born into a military family, Hugo traveled extensively during his childhood until age twelve when his parents separated. He settled with his mother in Paris, where he attended school and attained literary recognition at a young age. In 1819, Hugo founded with his brothers a prominent literary journal, *Le conservateur littéraire,* and published his first volume of poetry, *Odes et poésies diverses* (1822). This volume, which celebrated the monarchy, earned him a pension from French king Louis XVIII and enabled him to marry his childhood sweetheart Adèle Foucher. Hugo's home was the center of intellectual activity, and he counted among his devoted friends literary critic Charles Sainte-Beuve and writer Théophile Gautier. In 1841, Hugo was elected to the Académie française, and four years later he was made a peer. Hugo was also elected to the National Assembly in 1848, when Louis's regime collapsed and Louis Napoléon Bonaparte established the Second Republic. Distressed by Napolèan's dictorial ambitions, which were made evident when Napoléan seized power in a coup d'etat in 1851, Hugo fled to Belgium. He then moved to the English Channel island of Jersey and, later, to the island of Guernsey; he lived in exile on the islands for eighteen years. There he conducted séances, wrote speeches and appeals concerning world politics, and published some of his greatest poetical works. Hugo returned to Paris a day after the Third Republic was proclaimed in 1870 as a national hero. He continued to write prolifically even as he became increasingly detached from the outside world. When he died in 1885, Hugo was given a state

funeral and was eventually buried in the Panthéon, though his body was transported in a poor man's hearse in accordance with his last wishes.

Major Works

Hugo's early verse consists primarily of odes, ballads, and lyrics. His odes, which are collected in such volumes as *Odes* (1823) and *Nouvelles odes* (1824), were written in the neoclassical style and contain traditional poetic devices. In his ballads, Hugo used more experimental forms of versification and began to address such romantic themes as faith, love, and nature. He explained in the preface to *Odes et ballades* (1826) that the ballad form was a "capricieux" or whimsical genre that lent itself to the telling of superstitions, legends, popular traditions, and dreams. Hugo continued his experiments with versification in *Les orientales* (1829; *Eastern Lyrics*), which is set in North Africa and the Near East and focuses on such subjects as the Greek war of independence, passionate love, and exotic cultures. Considered a protest against the materialism of western society, this volume was extremely popular and widely read in France.

Hugo's lyric poetry of the 1830s primarily addressed such themes as nature, love, and death in a style that was both personal and uninhibted. Collections of this period include *Les feuilles d'automne* (1831), *Les chants du crépuscule* (1835; *Songs of Twilight*), *Les voix intérieures* (1837), and *Les rayons et les ombres* (1840). Edward K. Kaplan has noted that these four collections "are unified by the poet's discovery of faith through uncertainty and doubt. Not a Christian faith, but a modern faith which understood anxiety as an approopriate response to rapid social, political, and intellectual change."

During the 1840s, Hugo concentrated on his social and political activities and published little poetry. In the 1850s, however, when he lived in exile on the islands of Jersey and Guernsey, Hugo wrote *Les contemplations* (1856) and the three-volume collection *La légende des siécles* (1859-1883; *The Legend of the Centuries*). Both of these works have been hailed as poetic masterpieces and are considered among Hugo's best works. *Les contemplations,* which explores the metaphysical aspects of death and life as well as the mysteries of human consciousness, is divided into two parts. "Autarefois" celebrates innocence, youth, love, and creation, while "Aujourd'hui" reveals Hugo's grief over the drowning death of his daughter Léopoldine in 1843 and addresses such issues as the incomprehensibility of the universe, religion, and good and evil. *La légende des siècles* presents a panorama of human history from the Old Testament to the nineteenth century. Hugo wrote that he intended the work to trace "the development of the human race over the centuries, mankind rising out of the shadows on its way to the ideal, the paradisiacal transfiguration of earthy hell, the low, the perfect coming to full bloom of freedom."

Hugo's later poetry comprises a diverse body of work. *Les chansons des rues et des bois* (1865) consists of light and fanciful pieces; *L'Année terrible* (1872) centers on French history, particularly the establishment of the Third Republic in 1870; and *L'art d'être grand-père* (1877) contains poems that reflect Hugo's delight in his grandchildren Georges and Jeanne. *La fin de Satan,* which Hugo worked on from 1854 to 1860, was published posthumously in 1886. Considered a theological epic poem, this volume depicts Satan accepting God's offer to return to heaven.

Critical Reception

At the time of Hugo's death, many of the works that were praised upon their publication were still highly regarded; *La légende des siècles,* for example, was pronounced "the greatest work of the century" by Algernon Charles Swinburne in 1886 and is still favorably compared to John Milton's *Paradise Lost* by late twentieth-century critics such as John Porter Houston. Although scholars have faulted the romantic excesses and pretentiousness sometimes evident in Hugo's writing, they are often more forgiving of his sentimentalism when it is conveyed with the grace, power, and technical virtuosity

that characterizes much of his poetry. What has most hampered the pace of Hugo scholarship in English-speaking countries has been the lack, inadequacy, and inaccessibility of critical editions and translations of Hugo's poetry; in recent decades, however, Hugo's works have inspired international scholarly activity.

PRINCIPAL WORKS

Poetry

Odes et poésies diverses 1822
Odes 1823
Nouvelles odes 1824
Odes et ballades 1826
Les orientales [*Eastern Lyrics*] 1829
Les feuilles d'automne 1831
Les chants du crépuscule [*Songs of Twilight*] 1835
Les voix intérieures 1837
Les rayons et les ombres 1840
Les châtiments 1853
Les contemplations 1856
La légende des siècles. 3 vols. [*The Legend of the Centuries*] 1859-1883
Les chansons des rues et des bois 1865
L'Année terrible 1872
L'art d'être grand-père 1877
Le pape 1878
La pitié supreme 1879
L'Âne 1880
Religions et religion 1880
Les quatre vents de l'esprit 1881
La fin de Satan 1886
Toute la lyre 2 vols. 1888-1898
Dieu 1891
Les années funestes 1898
Derniere gerbe 1902
Océan 1942
Tas de pierres 1942

Other Major Works

Han d'Islande [*Hans of Iceland*] (novel) 1823
Cromwell [*Cromwell*] (drama) 1827
Le dernier jour d'un condamné [*The Last Day of a Condemned*] (novel) 1829
Hernani [*Hernani*] (drama) 1830
Marion de Lorme [*The King's Edict*] (drama) 1831
Notre Dame de Paris [*The Hunchback of Notre Dame*] (novel) 1831
Le roi s'amuse [*The King's Fool*] (drama) 1832
Lucrèce Borgia [*Lucretia Borgia*] (drama) 1833
Marie Tudor (drama) 1833
Angélo, tyran de padoue (drama) 1835
Ruy Blas [*Ruy Blas*] (drama) 1838
Les burgraves (drama) 1843
Les misérables [*Les Misérables*] (novel) 1862
William Shakespeare [*William Shakespeare*] (criticism) 1864

Les travailleurs de la mer [*The Toilers of the Sea*] (novel)
  1866
L'homme qui rit [*The Man Who Laughs*] (novel) 1869
Quatrevingt-treize [*Ninety-three*] (novel) 1874
Torquemade (drama) 1882
Le théâtre en liberté (drama) 1886
Choses vues [*Things Seen*] (essays) 1887
Amy Robsart. Les jumeaux (drama) 1889

CRITICISM

Joseph Mazzini (essay date 1838)

SOURCE: "On the Poems of Victor Hugo," in *Life and
Writings of Joseph Mazzini,* Volume II, Smith, Elder, and
Company, 1890, pp. 257-303.

[*In the following excerpt, taken from an essay originally
published in* British and Foreign Review *in 1838, Mazzini
discusses the faults and limitations of Hugo's poetry, stating that "his words are cold, fleshless, desolate; at times
even imbued with a bitterness quite incomprehensible in
a poet who has so often been called religious."*]

I have not leisure here to analyze completely any of Victor
Hugo's poems. But let the reader open any one of his
collections, **Les Feuilles d'Automne** excepted, and peruse
the first piece that offers. An attentive examination, guided
by the notions here thrown out, will show the idea fet-
tered, bound down by the form which it ought to govern,—
the mind in some sort absorbed by matter, which matter it
ought to seize upon, pervade at every pore, and shine
through brilliantly, like flame through alabaster,—it will
show how Victor Hugo appears to me always to descend
from the deity to the symbol, instead of rising, as I conceive poetry always should, from the symbol to the deity.

If this be the prevalent habit of Victor Hugo, if it be the
characteristic of his poetry, dominant over all his conceptions, it is evident what must be the result in the poet's
mind as relates to man, to his business on earth, and to
God. Never generalize; never embrace life in its universality, or man in his functions relative to humanity; contemplate the former only in its several isolated manifestations, and in the latter seek only his individuality:—and
thus place man in presence of God. What feeling can you
deduce, if not a feeling of weakness, of absolute impotence? What destiny can be imagined as the lot of the
human creature upon earth, if not a destiny of resignation
and inaction? immensity crushes the individual. The finite
contending with the infinite can engender nothing but doubt
and scepticism for the strong, for those that wrestle,—
nothing for the feeble but blind submission, the passive
resignation of the East.

Now all this to be found in the poetry of Victor Hugo.
Humanity plays no part in his verses. Of the three points
of the triangle he retains only two, *i.e.,* God and man. The
intervening step, which alone could bring the one nearer

to the other, being thus suppressed, nothing is left to man
but the consciousness of his inability ever to attain to the
infinite object of his desires. He sinks into lethargy, faint-
heartedness and insuperable ignorance; the noise of events
oppresses him; life appears to him as an inexplicable
enigma, as a development of aimless activity.

> Helas! helas! tout travaille
> Sous tes yeux ô Jéhovah!
> De quelque côté qu'on aille,
> Partout un flot qui tressaille,
> Partout un homme qui va!
>   Ou vas-tu?—Vers la nuit noire.
>
> Ou vas-tu?—Vers le grand jour.
>
> Toi?—Je cherche s'il faut croire.
>
> Et toi?—Je vais à la gloire.
> Et toi?—Je vais à l'amour.
>
>   Vous allez tous à la tombe!
>
> Vous allez à l'inconnu!
>
> Aigle, vautour, ou colombe,
> Vous allez où tout retombe
> Et d'ou rien n'est revenu!
>
>   *Voix Intérieures,* xvii.

> Alas! alas! 'Tis labour all,
> Jehovah, underneath thine eye;
> And wheresoe'er our footsteps fall,
> Are quivering billows that appal
> Men hurrying onward eagerly.
>   Where goest thou?—Tow'rds darksome night
> Where goest thou?—Tow'rds lightsome day.
> And thou?—I seek what creed is right.
> And thou?—I follow glory bright.
> And thou?—I go where love bears sway.
>   Ye are all hast'ning to the tomb,
> All going to th' unknown, the fear'd.
> Dove, eagle, all by certain doom
> Seek the devouring gulf of gloom,
> Whence nothing ever reappear'd.
>
>   *Voix Intérieures,* xvii.

Ask not of Victor Hugo and his lays an increase of energy
wherewith to strive against the evil existing in the world.
Ask not of him advice respecting the path you must follow
to arrive at truth. Ask not of him even consolation amidst
your sufferings. He has nothing of the kind to give. His
words are cold, fleshless, desolate; at times even imbued
with a bitterness quite incomprehensible in a poet who has
so often been called religious.

> Cet ordre auquel tu t' opposes
> T'enveloppe et t'eugloutit.
>
> Mortel, plains-toi, si tu l'oses;
> Au Dieu qui fit ces deux choses
> Le ciel grand, l'homme petit!

Chacun, qu'il doute ou qu'il nie,
Lutte en frayant sou chemin;
Et l'eternelle harmonie
Pèse comme une ironie
Sur tout ce tumulte humain!

Into that Order, which in vain
Ye strive against, ye're swallow'd all;
Fond mortals, if ye dare, complain
To God, who fashion'd for his reign
The heavens so great, and man so small!

Each one toils onward strugglingly,
Whether he doubt, deny, or trust;
And th' everlasting harmony
Weighs like a bitter mockery
On human tumult, human dust.

Is this religion? Can this be the true God, the God whom we all seek—this terrible, mysterious, inaccessible God who seems to sport with his human work, who so fearfully resembles the pagan *Fate?* Can we adore God whilst despising his creature? Can we love him whilst knowing of him only his power? How, then, does he manifest himself in this world of ours (which also is his thought), if all be error, doubt, and darkness? Has life been given to us as—

"A tale . . .
    Told by an idiot, . . .
    Signifying nothing?"

[*Macbeth*]

Or as a mission of useful works, of progressive perfectibility, to be discharged, as the means of approximation to God himself? Would God have placed us here below had we not been designed to achieve something in this world; in a word, to act? And do not human actions hence acquire a high value, as the only means we possess of elevating ourselves towards God? Wherefore, then, incessantly endeavour to blight them by your scorn? Why despise what God himself does not despise, since it is by our actions that he judges whether we deviate from or strive to follow his law? Can you not magnify the Creator without outraging his creature? Can you not speak of God without trembling? For you tremble whenever you name him, and we imbibe from your lays a terror of infinity which enervates us, mutilates our faculties and arrests us in the midst of our finest bursts of self-devotion, of our holiest hopes. You recoil with a cry of terror from the invisible, because in its depths you have caught a glimpse of eternity (*Feuilles d'Automne,* xxix.); you fear the grave (*Ib.* vi.-xiii. xiv., etc.); you fear oblivion. Have you then no immortality within yourself? Is not this existence, for you as it is for us, a mere episode in the soul's life? What matters it to you though the man who has emitted a great idea should, in his turn, be obliterated? Does he not live on in that very idea which nothing can obliterate? Does he not live in the spark of good, in the fraction of perfectibility, which he has, by this idea, introduced into the hearts of his brethren? Has he not fulfilled his mission by contributing his share towards the fecundation of that flower of humanity which is to blossom in God? Tell us something of his future

prospects. Tell us the futurity of the martyr; tell us what every drop of blood, every tear shed for the good of mankind, weighs in the balance of humanity's destinies. We are already so little disposed to self-devotion; our only great faculties, those of enthusiasm, of self-sacrifice, of love, of poetry, are already so feeble, so chilled by the wind of egotism blowing from without; and you come to freeze them yet more, impelling them to dash themselves, on the one side against a tomb, on the other against a heaven of brass, closed alike against faith and intellect! Poet, is this your ministry? Is it thus you think to accomplish a work of rehabilitation?

This is what souls endowed with a genuine sense of religion, whatever be their number at the present day, are entitled to ask of Victor Hugo. This is also, as I believe, the secret of the indifference which, as well in France as elsewhere, has succeeded to the enthusiasm once excited by every lay of the poet. It is not, as one of his critics appears to insinuate, because Victor Hugo has deserted Aristotle and Boileau, and revolted from the *great age,* that the public has in its turn deserted him: it is because he has not kept his promises; because he said, "I will remake art; I will renew its alliance with spirituality and religion;" and, instead of fulfilling his programme, has merely battered down the older art: then, when he was expected to rebuild, has fallen back either into extinguished creeds or into scepticism; because he has subjected art to the worship of sensation, has sacrificed to materialism, and made himself, in some sort, a heathen poet. And herein he is behind his age; for the age, amidst all its egotism and its theories of self-interest, is nevertheless actuated by spiritual instincts, is tormented with a sense of its want of belief, and of social belief, which, despite all efforts at counteraction, must augment from day to day, and will imperatively claim a solution which the poetry of Victor Hugo is incapable of supplying.

And, after all, is not this new theory of art for art's sake, in which M. Victor Hugo's loftier views have ended, which he has frequently advanced as an axiom, and almost always practised in his compositions, a compromise with the times of materialism, of literary paganism? Does not this theory involve the negation of a permanent social object, the negation of a universal life and unity; and, in the application of pure individualism to art, the death of all faith, of all acknowledged law of progression? The first, the only, the real fall of M. Victor Hugo was the development of this, now irrevocable, tendency to stagnate in individuality; to base all poetry upon the human *Ego,* whilst the epoch requires more. Hence his terrors and his doubts. Hence his disposition to look down upon all that is human, to supersede as far as possible in his works the man by the thing, the artist by the monument, the intelligent being by the first abstract idea,—antiquity, annihilation, or any other that offers. Hence, also, when he is compelled, whether by circumstances or by the real splendour of an action, to celebrate man, he can find only a brilliant, but unsubstantial and selfish, crown to allot him: to wit, *glory;* glory to Napoleon, glory to the July martyrs. Hence, when he speaks of suicide (*Chants du Crépuscule,* xiii.), he cannot find a single consolatory expression for the suffering spirit that is almost ready to desert its post; not one word of duty; not one tone to reprobate the egotism of dying to escape from sorrow, whilst the age offers so many ways of both living and dying for others. "A hazardous problem," says he; obscure questions, mediating upon which the poet is "driven to roam the livelong night through the streets of Paris." Doubt therefore—always doubt. And man must indeed always appear enveloped in doubt so long as he is not contemplated from the point of view of humanity. From the species only can the law governing the individual be learned. Only by taking the idea of man's mission here upon earth as our starting-point, are religion, philosophy, or poetry at the present day possible.

An objective poet, a poet of sensations and analysis, Victor Hugo paints nature such as he sees her, presenting her beauties one by one, minutely, accurately, as if reflected in a mirror. But—with some few exceptions, as, *e.g.,* v. and xxxviii. *Feuilles d' Automne*—ask not of him to seek in her anything beyond forms. Never does it occur to him to look deeper for the sense of those forms, for the harmony that must needs exist between man and nature; never to contemplate the latter as *the drapery of eternal thought,* to borrow Herder's expression. Thus his pictures are seldom more than fine copies. Imitation of nature is as much his school as that of those *classicist* poets against whom he so vehemently battles. In his verses the whole material universe appears only a horizon, *formed to our wish,* as Fenelon said, *for the delight of our eyes.*

As the poet of individuality, wanting an unitary, universal conception, unable to become either an educator or a prophet of the future, Victor Hugo reflects without embellishing, and repeats without explaining; he follows the course of events, but never directs or foresees them. In his *Autumnal Leaves,* he has said that love, the tomb, life, glory, the wave, the sunbeam, and breath alike and successively make his *crystal soul* sparkle and vibrate. Again, in the prelude to the **"Lays of Twilight,"** he avers,—

> Le poète, en ses chants où l'amertume abonde,
> Reflétait, écho triste et calm cependant,
> Tout ce que l'ame rêve et tout ce que le monde
> Chante, bégaie ou dit dans l'ombre en l'attendant!

> The bard, in lays with bitter feelings fraught,
> Echoed his tones, while grief, yet calmness, mark
> All the soul dreams, all that the world e'er thought,
> Sang, stammer'd, said, whilst waiting in the dark.

This is indeed M. Victor Hugo's poetry, painted with a single stroke; his muse *is waiting* in the *dark.*

It is not in a period of transition, like ours, characterised by an immense disproportion betwixt the soul's wants and reality; it is not in times when all things—war and peace, sorrow and joy, earth and heaven, speak of the future,—when every living being asks himself, "Whither are we going? What is to become of us?" that poetry, living upon disdain and insulation, or waiting tremblingly in the dark, can aspire to the honours of lasting celebrity, of lasting

influence over men. In these days we set the poet a larger task. We exact of him that he should either guide us, or that he should modestly withdraw into obscurity. These last forty or fifty years have left around us a great void of creeds, of virtues, and of poetry. A very fatal divorce has taken place between genius and the public. The heart of the former is no longer full of faith, of love for the latter; nor has the latter respect for, or sympathy with, the former. Calculations, analysis, and the spirit of prose overflow; they threaten to stifle the holy devotion, the holy enthusiasm that form the pinions upon which the human soul rises towards God. There is nothing in all this to astonish the man who can extricate himself from actual existence to take more comprehensive views, especially if he think less of his sufferings than of his duties. This state of society, which is not new in the history of the world, which must recur as often as a great work of destruction shall have been accomplished, and a great work of renovation shall be upon the eve of accomplishment, is an additional prhis state subsists, the poet's is a solemn mission; the more so, because, through the slow operation of centuries, his voice is, at the present day, heard, not by his countrymen alone, but by all nations.

Now, if art would re-establish its influence, its fallen worship, it must burst forth from this state of anarchy or of indifference to the great things acting, or about to be acted, in the world; it must no longer withdraw to one side, but stand in the centre, swaying the heart of the social impulse. Art must no longer simply reflect reality without addition or modification, must no longer merely count the wounds affronting its eye; art must now whilst sounding those wounds with fearless hand, do that which shall determine men to heal them. Art must not say, "All is evil," and sink into despair; for well has Jean Paul declared, "Despair is the true atheism." Art must say, "There is evil here," and still must hope. Art must not, either in misanthropy or in the prudery or virtue, shun the fallen and corrupt creature; but accost it mercifully and devotedly, endeavoring to raise and purify it by a breath of innocence, of religion, and of poetry, and by revelations concerning its origin, its terrestrial lot, and its futurity. Whilst pointing out to man the arena assigned to his labour, art must teach him, not his weakness, but his strength; must inspire him, not with faint-heartedness, but with energy and a vigorous will. Are we in the desert? Are our steps in danger of being bewildered amidst the night of scepticism? Then be art our pillar of fire, guiding us to our promised land! We shall be found true believers, submissive and grateful.

But in order to be all this, must art undergo a complete revolution? Must the point of view, thestarting-post and the goal, be all simultaneously changed? Have we reached the point when, one epoch of art being exhausted, it must undergo a metamorphosis, or perish? Can all that has been done in literature during the third of a century which has just elapsed, all that we judged to be revolution, have been a mere work of reform, a return to independence, to literary freedom, opening the way, but leaving everything still to be done? Can this chance to be the secret of the despondence into which all the poets of the era in question finally sink, when they discover that, though powerful to destroy, they are impotent to construct; and of the scepticism of a generation that has not found in them the promised realisation of hope?

For the present I do no more than throw out these questions. They appear to me important in reference to the future prospects of art, and I would fain recommend them to the attention of our poets.

North American Review (review date 1855)

SOURCE: "Genius and Writings of Victor Hugo," in *North American Review,* Vol. 81, October, 1855, pp. 324-46.

[*In this excerpt, the critic offers a laudatory review of Hugo's verse up to and including* Les châtiments.]

[If] the genius of Victor Hugo is great as a novelist, it is still greater as a poet. And he seems to be almost equally distinguished in the lyric and the dramatic schools of poetry. His first publication was the **Odes et Ballades,** a volume strewn with beautiful verses, inspired with a religious and royalist enthusiasm. His next volume of lyric poetry was **Les Orientales,**—differing widely in form and substance from any of his other works. This collection, the idea of which was a sudden fantasy which flashed across his mind one evening in connection with some reminiscence of Spain, depicts Moorish and Oriental life in its many romantic phases. Here his lyrical power appears in its greatest lustre. The French language had never before arrived at such a degree of flexibility and beauty of poetic diction. Never were poems so distinguished for harmony, delicacy, smoothness of rhythm, richness of coloring, and profusion of imagery. In another publication, **Les Feuilles d'Automne,** Victor Hugo cultivates a different field of fancy. In these poems, the strains are pure and simple, the sentiments calm, tender, and domestic. They are chiefly of a religious tendency, diversified with glowing, spontaneous effusions of youthful hopes and affections. One of them, entitled "**La Prière pour tous,**" is one of the most touching devotional poems we have ever read, and leaves Pope's "Universal Prayer" at a cold and impassable distance. In his **Chants du Crépuscule,—Twilight Songs,**—our poet sings of the emotions that assail us in the twilight of life, when the hope of earthly happiness is gone, and the soul is absorbed in contemplation of the eternal change. Some of the finest specimens of psychological poetry which the present century has produced are to be found in this volume. It would be erroneous to suppose that these various collections of poems are loose and desultory pieces thrown at random into a volume. On the contrary, each has a special object, and represents a particular idea.

Les Voix Intérieures, which followed the **Twilight Songs,** are a series of poems devoted to the family affections. But unfortunately the lustre of the poet's genius seems here to desert him, and he has many feeble and poor lines. Amid numerous faulty and irregular compositions, marked by wild eccentricity, only a few gleam as bright and lustrous gems. On the appearance of this volume, the warmest admirers of Victor Hugo stood mute with sorrow and chagrin. His vein seemed exhausted, and France began to deplore the premature decline of her most brilliant poetic star. This proved, however, too hasty an impression, as the poet afterward demonstrated by the publication of **Les Rayons et les Ombres,** in which he seems to have surpassed all his former efforts. As a whole, it is undoubtedly to be considered his most faultless production, since every poem it contains beams with intelligence and genius. "There is infinite sweetness, pathos, and harmony in these poems. Pensive, serene, and peaceful glides along—among homely haunts, by the household hearth, amid the fields, the hamlets, and the woods—the verse that elsewhere rolls its mighty stream around kings and conquerors, triumphs and trophies, shattered thrones and contending factions. There is no lack of variety in his poetry. Few are the children of song in whom will be found a greater diversity of matter, a more free and facile multiformity of style." *Ennui* is a state of feeling never produced in his readers, and the charge of mechanical structure and wearisome monotony of rhythm, so often brought against French poetry, applies to none of his poems.

The latest lyric production of Victor Hugo is a volume of political poems, entitled **Châtiments,** printed at Jersey in 1853, and published at Geneva. This little volume is a collection of lyrics in various metres, all bearing upon the recent political events in France. In it he takes up the burden of his next preceding work, *Napoléon le Petit,* and summons the Emperor to the bar of justice, in the most thrilling and powerful verse which has ever flowed from his pen. Although the book may be termed a monody, in which the author sings the requiem of French liberty, it yet partakes of that infinite variety of treatment which characterizes all his works. Now we hear a melodious wail over the dead body of some exiled republican; now, a fierce upbraiding of imperial treachery; now, a lofty and musical apostrophe to the martyrs of the 4th of December; now, a sharp, short satire, aimed at some courtly debauchee, every rhyme in which bites to the quick; and now, an impassioned call to the republicans to keep alive their faith and courage.

Charles Baudelaire (essay date 1861)

SOURCE: "Victor Hugo," in *Baudelaire as a Literary Critic: Selected Essays,* translated by Lois Boe Hyslop and Francis E. Hyslop, Jr., Pennsylvania State University Press, 1964, pp. 233-47.

[*A French poet and critic, Baudelaire is best known for his poetry collection* Les fleurs de mal, *which is considered among the most influential works of French verse. In the following excerpt, which was originally published in* La revue fantaisiste *in 1861, he offers praise for Hugo, citing the poet's universality and greatness of theme.*]

For many years now Victor Hugo has no longer been in our midst. I remember the time when his figure was one of those most frequently encountered among the crowds, and many times I wondered, seeing him appear so often amid holiday excitement or in the silence of some lonely spot, how he could reconcile the needs of his incessant work with the sublime but dangerous taste for strolling and for reverie. This apparent contradiction is evidently the result of a well ordered life and of a strong spiritual constitution which permits him to work while walking, or rather to be able to walk while he is working. At all times, in all places, under the light of the sun, in the surging crowds, in the sanctuaries of art, beside dusty bookstalls exposed to the wind, Victor Hugo, serene and thoughtful, seemed to say to external nature: "Fix yourself in my eyes so that I may remember you."

At the time of which I am speaking, a time when he exercised a real dictatorship in literary matters, I occasionally encountered him in the company of Edouard Ourliac, through whom I also met Pétrus Borel and Gérard de Nerval. He seemed to me very affable, very powerful, always in control of his feelings, and relying on a restricted wisdom made up of a few irrefutable axioms. For a long time he had shown, not only in his books but also in the adornment of his personal life, a great taste for the monuments of the past, for picturesque furniture, china, engravings, and for all the mysterious and brilliant décor of earlier times. The critic whose eye overlooks this detail would not be a real critic; for not only does this taste for the beautiful and even for the strange as expressed through the plastic, confirm the literary character of Victor Hugo; not only did it confirm his revolutionary, or rather regenerative doctrine, but also it appeared as the indispensable complement of a universal poetic character. It is all very well that Pascal, fired by asceticism, should have persisted in living thereafter within four bare walls furnished with cane chairs, and that a priest of Saint-Roch (I no longer remember which one) should have had all his furniture sold at auction, to the horror of all prelates fond of comfort; that is all beautiful and great. But if I see a man of letters who is not oppressed by poverty neglect things that delight the eye and entertain the imagination, I am tempted to believe that he is a very incomplete man of letters, to say the least.

Victor Hugo was, from the onset, the man who was best endowed and most obviously chosen to express in poetry what I shall call *the mystery of life*.

—*Charles Baudelaire*

Today when we glance over the recent poetry of Victor Hugo, we see that he has remained what he was, a thoughtful wanderer, a solitary man, yet in love with life, a contemplative and inquiring mind. But it is no longer in the wooded and flowering outskirts of the great city, on the rough embankments of the Seine, in paths swarming with children that he sets his feet and eyes to wander. Like Demosthenes, he talks with the wind and the waves; formerly he roamed alone in places seething with human life; today he walks in solitudes peopled with his thoughts. And so he is perhaps even greater and more remarkable. The colors of his dreams have taken on a solemn hue and his voice has grown deeper in rivaling that of the Ocean. But there as here, he still seems to us like a statue of Meditation in movement.

In the days, already so distant, of which I was speaking, happy days when men of letters formed a society sorely missed by its survivors, who will never again find its equal, Victor Hugo was the one to whom everyone turned, seeking the watchword. Never was royalty more legitimate, more natural, more acclaimed by gratitude, more confirmed by the impotence of rebellion. When one recalls what French poetry was before he appeared, and what a rejuvenation it has undergone since he came; when one imagines how insignificant it would have been without him, how many mysterious and profound sentiments that have been given expression would have remained unvoiced, how many intellects he has discovered, how many men made famous by him would have remained obscure, itis impossible not to consider him as one of those rare, providential minds who bring about the salvation of all men in the literary order, as others do in the moral order and still others in the political order. The movement created by Victor Hugo still continues under our eyes. That he has received powerful support no one will deny; but if today mature men, young people, and society women have a feeling for good poetry, for poetry that is profoundly rhythmic and intensely colored, if the public taste has again risen to pleasures it had forgotten, it is Victor Hugo to whom the credit belongs. It is, moreover, through his powerful instigation that erudite and enthusiastic architects are repairing our cathedrals and preserving our ancient monuments of stone. No one will hesitate to admit this except those for whom justice is not a pleasure.

I can speak only very briefly in this article about his poetic faculties. Doubtless, in some matters I shall merely be summarizing many excellent things that have already been said; perhaps I shall have the good fortune to give them greater emphasis.

Victor Hugo was, from the outset, the man who was best endowed and most obviously chosen to express in poetry what I shall call *the mystery of life*. Nature which lies before us, no matter where we turn, and which envelops us like a mystery, shows herself under several simultaneous aspects, each of which, to the extent that it is more intelligible, more perceptible to us, is reflected more intensely in our hearts: form, attitude and movement, light and color, sound and harmony. The music of Victor Hugo's verses is adapted to the profound harmonies of nature; as a sculptor, he carves into his stanzas the unforgettable form of things; as a painter, he illuminates them with the right color. And the three impressions penetrate the reader's mind simultaneously, as if they came directly from nature. From this triple impression comes *the morality of things*. No artist is more universal than he, more suited to put himself in contact with the forces of universal life, more inclined to bathe ceaselessly in nature. Not only does he express precisely and translate literally what is clearly and distinctly visible, but he expresses with an *indispensable obscurity* what is obscure and vaguely revealed. His works abound in extraordinary features of the kind which we could call *tours de force,* if we did not know that they are essentially natural to him. The poetry of Victor Hugo can translate for the human soul not only the most direct pleasures that it draws from visible nature but also the most fleeting, the most complicated, the most moral (I am purposely using the word moral) sensations which are transmitted to it by visible substance, by inanimate or what is called inanimate nature; it can translate not only the form of substance exterior to man, vegetable or mineral, but also its aspect, its expression, its sadness, its tenderness, its exultant joy, its repulsive hate, its charm or its horror; in short, in other words, all that is human in every imaginable thing and also all that is divine, sacred, or diabolic.

Those who are not poets do not understand these things. Fourier appeared one day, a littletoo pompously, to reveal to us the mysteries of *analogy.* I do not deny the importance of some of his small discoveries, although I believe that his mind was too attached to material accuracy not to make mistakes and to attain straight off the moral certitude of intuition. With the same care he could have revealed to us all the excellent poets whose works educate the reading public as much as the contemplation of nature. Moreover, Swedenborg, who possessed a much greater soul, had already taught us that *heaven is a very great man*; that everything, form, movement, number, color, perfume, in the *spiritual* as well as in the *natural* world, is significant, monstration of universal truth to man's facial conformation, had translated for us the spiritual meaning of contour, of form, of dimension. If we broaden the demonstration (not only have we the right, but it would be infinitely difficult to do otherwise), we arrive at this truth that everything is hieroglyphic, and we know that symbols are only relatively obscure, that is to say according to the mind's purity, good will, or native insight. Now, what is a poet (I am using the word in its broadest sense) if not a translator, a decipherer? Among the best poets, there are no metaphors, comparisons, or epithets which are not adapted with mathematical exactitude to the particular circumstance, because these comparisons, metaphors, and epithets are drawn from the inexhaustible storehouse of *universal analogy* and cannot be found elsewhere. Now let me ask if, after a careful search, one will find, not in our history only but in the history of all peoples, many poets who, like Victor Hugo, contain so magnificent a repertory of human and divine analogies. I have read in the Bible about a prophet who was asked by God to devour a book. I do not know in what world Victor Hugo has previously consumed the dictionary of the language which he was called upon to speak, but I see that the French lexicon, as he uses it, has become a world, a colorful, melodious, and moving universe. Through what sequence of historical circumstances, philosophical destinies, sidereal conjunctions this man was born among us, I haven't the least idea, and I do not think it is my duty to examine it here. Perhaps it is simply because Germany had Goethe, and England Shakespeare and Byron, that Victor Hugo was rightfully owed to France. I see from the history of

peoples that each in its turn is called to conquer the world; perhaps the same thing is true of poetic domination as is true of rule by the sword.

From his ability to absorb the life around him, unique in its amplitude, as well as from his powerful faculty of meditation, Victor Hugo has become a very extraordinary poetic character, questioning, mysterious, and, like nature itself, vast and detailed, serene and agitated. Voltaire did not see mystery in anything, or at least in very few things. But Victor Hugo does not cut the Gordian knot of things with Voltaire's military dispatch; his keenly perceptive senses reveal abysses to him; he sees mystery everywhere. And indeed, where doesn't it exist? From it derives the sense of fright that penetrates several of his most beautiful poems; from it come those turbulent verses that rise and fall, those masses of stormy images carried along with the speed of a fleeing chaos; from it come those frequent repetitions of words, all destined to express the captivating shadows or the enigmatic countenance of mystery.

Thus Victor Hugo possesses not only greatness but universality. How varied is his repertory and, although always *one* and compact, how many-sided it is! I don't know if, among art lovers, there are many like me, but I can't help being extremely annoyed when I hear people speak of a landscapist (however perfect he may be), of a painter of animals or a painter of flowers with the same enthusiasm that might be used in praising a universal painter (that is to say a real painter) such as Rubens, Veronese, Velásquez or Delacroix. It seems to me, in fact, that he who does not know how to paint everything can not be called a painter. The renowned men whom I have just named expressperfectly everything that each of the specialists expresses and, in addition, they possess an imagination and a creative faculty which speaks vigorously to the minds of all men. The moment you wish to give me the idea of a perfect artist, my mind does not stop at perfection in one genre, but it immediately conceives the necessity of perfection in all genres. The same thing is true of literature in general and of poetry in particular. He who is not capable of painting everything, palaces and hovels, feelings of tenderness and of cruelty, circumscribed family affection and universal charity, the charm of plant life and the miracles of architecture, all that which is most pleasant and all that which is most horrible, the inner meaning and the external beauty of every religion, the moral and physical aspect of every nation, everything in short from the visible to the invisible, from heaven to hell—such a person, I say, is not really a poet in the broadest sense of the word and according to the heart of God. You say of one: he is a poet of the *home* or of the family; of another: he is a poet of love; and of another: he is a poet of glory. But by what right do you thus limit the range of each artist's talent? Do you mean to say that he who has extolled glory is *for that very reason* unsuited to celebrate love? You thereby invalidate the universal meaning of the word *poetry.* If you do not merely want to suggest that circumstances which have nothing to do with the poet have thus far confined him to one speciality, I shall always believe that you are speaking of a poor poet, of an incomplete poet, however clever he may be in *his* genre.

Ah! in the case of Victor Hugo we do not have to point out these distinctions, for his genius is without limits. Here we are dazzled, enchanted, and enveloped as if by life itself. The transparent air, the domed sky, the outline of a tree, the gaze of an animal, the silhouette of a house are painted in his books with the brush of an accomplished landscapist. In everything he puts the palpitation of life. If he paints the sea, no *seascape* will equal his. The ships which furrow its surface or which cut through its foam will have, more than those of any other painter, the appearance of fierce combatants, the character of will and of animality which mysteriously emerges from a geometric and mechanical apparatus of wood, iron, ropes and canvas; a monstrous animal created by man to which the wind and the waves add the beauty of movement.

As for love, war, family pleasures, the sorrows of the poor, national splendors, all that which is peculiar to man and which constitutes the domain of the genre painter and of the history painter, what have we seen that is richer and more concrete than the lyrical poetry of Victor Hugo? If space allowed, this would doubtless be the occasion to analyze the moral atmosphere which hovers and moves through his poems and which derives very obviously from the author's own temperament. It seems to me that it is unmistakably characterized by a love which makes no distinction between what is very strong and what is very weak, and that the attraction exercised over the poet by these two extremes stems from a single source, which is the very strength, the primordial vigor with which he is endowed. Strength delights and intoxicates him; he approaches it as if it were a brother: fraternal affection. Thus he is irresistibly attracted to every symbol of the infinite, the sea, the sky; to all the ancient representatives of strength, Homeric, or Biblical giants, paladins, knights; to enormous and fearful beasts. He makes child's play of fondling what would frighten weaker hands; he moves about in immensity without vertigo. On the other hand, but through a different tendency, whose source is, however, the same, the poet always shows warm compassion for all that is weak, lonely, sorrowful, for all that is fatherless: a paternal attraction. The man of strength, who senses a brother in all that is strong, sees his children in all that has need of protection or consolation. It is from strength itself and from the certainty that it gives to one who possesses it that the spirit of justice and of charity is derived. Thus in the poems of Victor Hugo there constantly occur those notes of love for fallen women, for the poor who are crushed in the cogwheels of society, for the animals that are martyrs of our gluttony and despotism. Few people have noticed the magic charm which kindness adds to strength and which is so frequently seen in the works of our poet. A smile and a tear on the face of a colossus is an almost divine form of originality. Even in his short poems devoted to sensual love, in those verses so voluptuous and so melodious in their melancholy, may be heard, like the continuous accompaniment of an orchestra, the deep voice of charity. Beneath the lover one senses a father and a protector. It is not a matter here of that sermonizing morality which, with its pedantic air and its didactic tone, can spoil the most beautiful piece of poetry but of an implicit morality which slips unnoticed into poetic matter like imponderable fluids into the machinery of the world. Morality does not enter into this art as its avowed purpose; it is intermingled with it and lost sight of, as in life itself. The poet is unintentionally a moralist through the abundance and plenitude of nature.

The excessive, the immense are the natural domain of Victor Hugo; he moves in it as if in his native atmosphere. The genius which he has always displayed in painting *all the monstrosity* surrounding man is truly prodigious. But it is especially in recent years that he has experienced the metaphysical influence emanating from all these things; the curiosity of an Oedipus obsessed by innumerable Sphinxes. Who does not remember **"La Pente de la Rêverie,"** done so long ago? A large part of his recent work seems to be the natural yet vast development of the faculty which gave birth to this fascinating poem. One might say that from that time on the poet's reverie has been interrupted more and more frequently by questioning and that in his eyes all aspects of nature are constantly bristling with problems. How has the father who is one been able to engender duality, and how has he been finally metamorphosed into endless numbers? Mystery! Must or can the infinite totality of numbers be again concentrated into the original unity? Mystery! The suggestive contemplation of the heavens occupies an immense and dominant place in the most recent works of the poet. Whatever the subject treated, the heavens dominate and rise above it like a changeless dome where mystery and light hover together, where mystery scintillates, where mystery invites curious reverie, where mystery dispels discouraged thought. Ah, even today, in spite of Newton and in spite of Laplace, astronomical certainty is not so great that reverie cannot find a place for itself among the vast lacunae still unexplored by modern science. Very rightly the poet lets his thought wander in an intoxicating labyrinth of speculations. There is not a problem that has been discussed or attacked, no matter when or by what philosophy, that has not inevitably come to demand its place in the works of the poet. Are the world of the stars and the world of souls finite or infinite? Is there a continuous bringing forth of beings in the vast cosmos as there is in the finite world? Would that which we are tempted to take for an infinite multiplication of beings be only a circulatory movement bringing these same beings back to life at times and under conditions marked by a supreme and all-embracing law?

Would matter and movement be only the respiration and inspiration of a God who brings forth worlds and then calls them back in turn to his bosom? Will all that which is multiple become one and will our universe and all those which we see suspended around us come to be replaced one day by new universes springing forth from the thought of Him whose sole happiness and sole function are to create unceasingly? And will not conjecture on the moral significance, on the intended purpose of all these worlds, our unknown neighbors, also naturally take its place in the immense domains of poetry?

Heavenly bodies, stars, suns, constellations, with your germinations, blossomings, flowerings, eruptions that are successive, simultaneous, slow or sudden, progressive or complete, are you simply forms of the life of God, or habitations prepared by his goodness or his justice for souls whom he wishes to educate and to gradually bring near himself? Worlds eternally studied, unknown perhaps forever, speak, have you your paradises, hells, purgatories, prisons, villas, palaces, etc.? . . . Would there be anything so *extravagant,* so monstrous, so exceeding the rightful limits of poetic conjecture in believing that there may spring forth from the limbo of the future new systems and clusters of planets which will assume unexpected forms, adopt unforeseen combinations, undergo unrecorded laws, imitate all the providential vagaries of a geometry too vast and too complicated for understanding? I insist on the word *conjecture* which serves to define fairly satisfactorily the extrascientific character of all poetry. In the hands of a poet other than Victor Hugo, such themes and such subjects could too easily have taken on a didactic form, which is the greatest enemy of true poetry. To recount in verse *known* laws governing the movement of the moral or sidereal world is to describe what has been discovered and what falls completely under the scientist's telescope or compass; it is to confine oneself to tasks pertaining to science, to encroach on its functions, and to encumber its traditional language with the superfluous and, in this case, dangerous embellishment of rhyme; but to give oneself up to all the reveries suggested by the infinite spectacle of life on earth and in the heavens is the legitimate right of anyone, consequently of the poet who is empowered to translate into a magnificent language, other than prose and music, the eternal conjectures of inquiring humanity. In describing what is, the poet is degraded and descends to the level of the professor; in recounting the possible he remains faithful to his function; he is a collective soul who questions, who weeps, who hopes and who sometimes finds the answer.

The music of Victor Hugo's verses is adapted to the profound harmonies of nature; as a sculptor, he carves into his stanzas the unforgettable form of things; as a painter, he illuminates them with the right color.

—*Charles Baudelaire*

A new proof of the same infallible taste is revealed in the latest work which Victor Hugo has offered for our pleasure. I am referring to *La Légende des Siècles*. Except at a nation's dawn, when poetry is both the expression of its soul and the repertory of its knowledge, history put into verse is a deviation from the laws which govern the two genres, history and poetry; it is an outrage against the two Muses. In periods of great culture there comes about in the spiritual world a division of work which strengthens and perfects each part; and he who then tries to create an epic poem as it was understood by younger nations, runs the risk of diminishing the magic effect of poetry, if only

through the intolerable length of the work, and of robbing history of a part of the wisdom and sobriety which older nations demand of it. Usually it results in nothing more than tedious nonsense. In spite of all the well meaning efforts of a French philosopher [Edgar Quinet] who believed that, without long-standing talent and without prolonged study, one could suddenly put poetry at the service of a poetic thesis, Napoleon, even today, is too much a part of history to be made into a legend. It is no more permissible than it is possible for man, even a man of genius, to artificially move back the centuries in that way. Such an idea could occur only to a philosopher, a professor, in other words to a man withdrawn from life. When in his first poems Victor Hugo tries to show us Napoleon as a legendary character, he is still a Parisian speaking, a contemporary who is deeply moved and lost in dreams; he evokes the legend that is *possible* in the future; he does not reduce it by his own authority to a past state.

Now, to come back to *La Légende des Siècles,* Victor Hugo has created the only epic poetry that could have been created by a man of his time for the readers of his time. First, the poems composing the work are usually short, and even the brevity of some is no less extraordinary than their power. This is already an important consideration, which is evidence of a complete understanding of all the possibilities of modern poetry. Next, wishing to create a modern epic poem, in other words a poem that has its source or rather its pretext in history, he carefully refrained from borrowing anything from history except that which it can rightfully and profitably lend to poetry. I am referring to legends, myths, fables which are, as it were, condensations of national life, deep reservoirs where sleep the blood and tears of peoples. Finally, he has not celebrated any particular nation or the passion of any particular century in his verse; he has risen at once to one of those philosophical heights from which the poet can survey the whole evolution of humanity with a glance that is impartially curious, angry, or compassionate. The majesty with which he has made the centuries pass before us like ghosts emerging from a wall, the complete command with which he has set them in motion, each with its correct costume, its true appearance, its authentic behavior is something which we have all seen. The sublime and subtle art, the terrible familiarity with which this magician has made the Centuries speak and gesticulate, would not be impossible for me to explain; but what I am especially anxious to point out is that this art could only move comfortably in a legendary milieu and that (putting aside the talents of the magician) it is the choice of the terrain that has facilitated the unfolding of the spectacle.

From his distant exile, toward which our eyes and ears are turned, the beloved and venerated poet has announced new poems. In recent years he has proved to us that the domain of poetry, however limited it may be, is nonetheless, by the law of genius, almost limitless. In what order of things, by what new means will he renew his proof? Will he wish hereafter to borrow unknown delights, for example, from buffoonery, (I am choosing at random), from immortal gaiety, from joy, from the supernatural, from the magical and from the marvelous, endowed by him with that immense, superlative character with which he can endow all things? It is not in the province of criticism to say; but what criticism can affirm without fear of being mistaken, because it has already seen successive proofs, is that he is one of those rare mortals, even more rare in the literary world than in any other, who draw new strength from the years and who, through an endlessly repeated miracle, continue growing younger and more vigorous until death.

Edward Dowden   (review date 1873)

SOURCE: "The Poetry of Victor Hugo," in *Studies in Literature: 1789-1877*, Kegan Paul, Trench and Company, 1889, pp. 428-67.

[*In this excerpt from a review originally published in 1873, Dowden traces Hugo's development as a poet.*]

The career of Victor Hugo naturally divides itself into three periods—first, that in which the poet was still unaware of his true self, or seeking that true self failed to find it; secondly, that presided over by the Hugoish conception of beauty; thirdly, that dominated by the Hugoish conception of the sublime. *Les Orientales* marks the limit of the first period; the transition from the second to the third, which begins to indicate itself in *Les Rayons et les Ombres,* is accomplished in *Les Contemplations*. The third period is not closed; at the present moment we have the promise from Victor Hugo of important works in verse and prose. Possibly, any hypothesis as to the orbit he describes is still premature.

In a divided household the boy Victor naturally inclined towards the side of his mother, and from her he inherited the monarchical tradition. From Chateaubriand he learned to recognize the literary advantages offered by neo-Catholicism, and under his influence the Voltairean royalism of Victor Hugo's earlier years was transformed into the Christian royalism which was to do service for the writer of odes under the Restoration. The boy ambitious of literary distinction, and furnished with literary instincts and aptitudes, but as yet unprovided with subjects for song from his own experience, must look about in the world to find subjects. He needs something to declaim against, and something to celebrate. The Revolution satisfies one of these requirements, and the monarchy the other. The vantage-ground of a creed is now gained; the dominant conception of his poetry declares itself to him; he is to be the singer of the restored Christian monarchy. If history would only supply themes, he is now prepared to take them up and execute brilliant variations upon them. And history is disposed to assist him. What more fortunate subject can there be for a neo-Catholic royalist ode than the birth of a Christian duke, unless it be the baptism of a Christian duke, or the consecration of a Christian king? Happy age when dukes are born and baptized, and when a philosophic poet of the age of twenty resolves to "solemnize some of

the principal memorials of our epoch which may serve as lessons to future societies." Happy age when atheist and regicide hide their heads, when the flood of Revolution has subsided, and the bow appears in the clouds! Highly favoured nation upon whom the presence of a Bourbon confers prosperity and peace, with all the Christian graces, and all the theological virtues:—

O, que la Royauté, peuples, est douce et belle!

In these odes the king is the terrestrial God; and God is the *grand monarque* who rules in the skies. If not the very same, he is a descendant not far removed from the aged and amiable God, something between a Pope and an Emperor, of the mediæval period, seated upon a throne, with a bird above his head, and his Son by his side, a courtly archangel on his right hand, and on the left a prophet, listening to harps, while Madame the Mother of God stands by, hand on breast. He is the God who was careful to punish the men of the Convention, and pulled down Napoleon from his high place; the God who chose Charles X. as the man after his own heart. If to disbelieve in this author of nature and moral governor of the universe be atheism, Victor Hugo is at present an atheist.

But the political and religious significance of these early poems was in truth a secondary affair. To reform the rhythm of French verse, to enrich its rhymes, to give mobility to the cesura, to carry the sense beyond the couplet, to substitute definite and picturesque words in place of the *fadeurs* of classical mythology and vague poetical periphrasis—these were matters awakening keener interest than the restoration of a dynasty or the vindicating of a creed. To denounce the Revolution was well; but how much higher and more divine to bring togther in brilliant consonance two unexpected words! Gustave Planche, reviewing at a later period this literary movement, and pronouncing in his magisterial way that the movement was primarily one of style, not of thought, recalls as a trivial circumstance, which however serves to characterize the time, that the ultimate word, the supreme term of literary art, was—"*la ciselure.*" The glow of Royalist fervour was somewhat of a painted fire; the new literary sensations were accompanied by thrills of pleasure which were genuine and intense.

Before 1828, Victor Hugo's royalist fervour had certainly lost some of its efficiency for the purposes of literature. The drama of *Cromwell* had been published in the previous year; and the poet was in open revolt against the great monarchical period of French art—the age of Racine. Either the births and baptisms of dukes occurred less frequently than heretofore, or Victor Hugo was less eager to celebrate them. But if his early faith was falling piece by piece, no new faith as yet came to replace the old, unless it were the artist's faith of "art for art." Accordingly, Victor Hugo in the forefront of his next lyrical volume—*Les Orientales*—proclaims in a high tone the independence of the poet from the trammels of belief. Let no one question him about the subjects of his singing,—if the manner be faultless, that is all which can be required of him. He will not now "endeavour to be useful," he will not attempt "to solemnize some of the principal memorials of our epoch which may serve as lessons to future societies." Farewell to the safe anchorage of neo-Catholicism! "Let the poet go where he pleases, and do what he pleases: such is the law. Let him believe in one God, or in many; in Pluto or in Satan, ... or in nothing; . . . . let him go north or south, west or east; let him be ancient or modern . . . He is free." What appropriateness was there in these *Orientales* in the midst of the grave preoccupations of the public mind! To what does the Orient rhyme? What consonance has it with anything? The author replies that "he does not know; the fancy took him; and took him in a ridiculous fashion enough, when, last summer, he was going to see a sunset." There was another sunset which Victor Hugo witnessed before long—the setting in a stormy sky of the ancient monarchy of France. Then, too, he thought of the East, and began that greater series of *Orientales,* those songs of the sunrise of the Republic, which still vibrate in the air. These last came not through caprice, but of necessity, and the only freedom which the poet has since claimed has been the freedom of service to his ideas and of fidelity to his creed.

The poems, *"Les Orientales,"* correspond with the announcements of the preface. They are miracles of colour and of sound. They shine and sparkle, and gleam like fiery opals, sapphires, and rubies. They startle the French muse, accustomed to the classic lyre or pastoral pipe, with the sound of sackbut, psaltery, dulcimer, and all kinds of music. Our eyes and ears are filled with vivid sensation. Does it greatly matter that they remain remote from our imaginative reason, our understanding heart, our conscience? The desires we possess for splendour and harmony are gratified: why should we demand anything further? Victor Hugo, still unprovided with sufficient subjects from his personal experience, and finding the monarchical pageant grow somewhat tarnished, had turned to Greece and Spain. With Spain the recollections of his boyhood connected him. Greece was a fashion of theperiod. The struggle with the Turkish power had surrounded the names of places and persons with associations which were effective with the popular imagination. Lord Byron had put his misanthropic hero into eastern costumes. The properties—jerreed, tophaïke, ataghan, caftan, the jewel of Giamschid, the throne of Eblis—took the taste of the period. The plash of the sack which contains a guilty wife in the still waters of the Bosphorus—the bearded heads attached to the Seraglio walls, and left as food for crows—these were thrilling sensations offered by eastern poetry. "Conscience," "imaginative reason," "understanding heart," what metaphysical jargon is this? Pedantry! we need colour and harmony; we demand a nervous excitation. And in truth, Victor Hugo had advanced a step, for he had lost a faith, and gained a style.

The more ambitious efforts of the years immediately following the publication of *Les Orientales* were in the direction of the theatre, and to the same period belongs the novel *Notre-Dame de Paris,* in which the mediævalism of the writer is no longer political, or religious, if it ever were such, but is purely æsthetical, supplying him with the rich and picturesque background before which his figures move. It was a fortunate circumstance for his lyrical poetry that it ceased to be the chief instrument of his ambition. Any deliberate attempt to surpass *Les Orientales* would have overleaped itself, and fallen on the other side. No pyrotechnic art could send up fiery parachutes or showers of golden rain higher than the last. But if instead of the fantastic blossoms of the pyrotechnist he were to bring together true flowers of the meadows, and leaves of the forest trees, the nosegay might have a grace and sweetness of its own. *Les Feuilles d'Automne* was published in the month of November 1831, and Victor Hugo notes as curious the contrast between the tranquillity of his verses and the feverish agitation of the minds of men. "The author feels in abandoning this useless book to the popular wave, which bears away so many better things, a little of the melancholy pleasure one experiences in flinging a flower into a torrent and watching what becomes of it."

There is an autumn in early manhood out of which a longer summer, or a spring of more rapturous joy, may be born. One period of life has been accomplished; better things may come, but there must be an abandonment of the old; a certain radiance fades away; it is a season of recollection; our eye has kept watch over the mortality of man; we know the "Soothing thoughts that spring out of human suffering." It was at this period that Wordsworth wrote his "Ode on the Intimations of Immortality." It was at this period that Victor Hugo wrote *Les Feuilles d'Automne*. No other volume of his poetry is marked by the same grave and tender self-possession; there is sadness in it, but not the ecstasy of grief; there is joy, but a wise and tempered joy. The calm of *Les Rayons et les Ombres* may be more profound; it is at all events a different calm—that of one who has the parting with youth well over, who has gone forward with confidence, and discovered the laws of the new order of existence and found them to be good. In *Les Rayons et les Ombres* the horizon is wider and the sky more blue; nature knows the great secret, and smiles. There is something pathetic in the calm of the earlier volume; something pathetic even in the shouts and laughter of the children which ring through it, though they ring clear and sweet as the bells upon the mules of Castile and Aragon.

Victor Hugo, who heretofore had for the most part been looking eagerly abroad for ambitious motives for song, now in *Les Feuilles d'Automne* very quietly folded the wing, dropped down, and found himself. Memories of his childhood, his mother's love and solicitude for her frail infant, the house at Blois where his father came to rest after the wars, the love-letters of thirteen years ago, his daughter at her evening prayer, the beauty of many sunsets, the voice of the sea heard from highheadlands, the festival of the starry heaven above, and, below, the human watcher, a "vain shadow, obscure and taciturn," yet seeming for a moment "the mysterious king of this nocturnal pomp,"— these and such as these are the themes over which the poet lingers with a grave sadness and joy. The feeling for external nature throughout is fervent, but large and pure. The poet stands in the presence of nature, and receives her precious influences; he is not yet enveloped by her myriad forces and made one with them; neither does he yet stand at odds with her, the human will contending in titanic struggle with the ἀνάγκη of natural law. God in these poems is a beneficent Father.

But now, again, Victor Hugo looked abroad. In *Les Orientales* he had treated subjects remote from his personal history. *Les Feuilles d'Automne* was a record of private joys and sorrows. In *Les Chants du Crépuscule* the personal and impersonal have met in living union; the individual appears, but his individuality is important less for its own sake than because it reflects the common spiritual characteristics of the period. The faith of France in her restored monarchy, her monarchy by divine right, had waned, and finally become extinct; and with the faith of France, that also of her chief poet. Many things had been preparing his spirit to accept the democratic movement of modern society. The literary war in which he had been engaged was a war of independence; it cultivated the temper of revolt, disdain of authority, self-confidence and a forward gaze into the future. None but a literary Danton could have dared in French alexandrines to name by its proper name *le cochon*. The noblesse of the poetical vocabulary had been rudely dealt with by Victor Hugo; and a rough swarm of words, which in a lexicon would have been branded with the obelus, now forced their way into the luxurious tenements of aristocratic noun-substantive and adjective. Victor Hugo had said to verse, "Be free;" to the words of the dictionary, "Be republican, fraternise, for you are equal." And in the enfranchisement of speech, was not thought enfranchised also? The poet had eloquently vindicated the rights of the grotesque in art. My Lady Beauty was no more needful to the world than her humorous clown; Quasimodo's face looked forth from the cathedral door, and vindicated all despised and insulted things. It was inevitable that the literary revolution should coalesce with the political revolution. Moreover, the monarchy had discredited itself,—it had been the agent of disorder; and the People had made itself beautiful by the virtue of the days of July.

Yet when the first acclamations which greeted a constitutional king had died away, there came a season of hesitation and surmise, a season of distrust. The dawn had seemed to open before men's eyes; and now again it was twilight—twilight of religious doubt, twilight of political disquietude. *Les Chants du Crépuscule* corresponds to this moment of welter and relapse in the wave of thought. Incertitude within, a vaporous dimness without—such is the stuff out of which this poetry has shaped itself; and the poet himself, hearing "Yes," and "No," cried by conflicting voices, is neither one of those who deny nor one of those who affirm. He is one of those who hope. The mysterious light upon the edge of the horizon, like the distant fire of a forge at night, is it the promise of the dawn, or the last brightness of receding day? Is the voice of Ocean a voice of joy or of fear? What is this murmur which rises from the heart of man?—a song, or perhaps a cry?

Notwithstanding the doubtful accent of *Les Chants du Crépuscule,* this volume leaves little uncertainty as to the direction in which the poet is tending. He is one of those who hope; and with Victor Hugo to hope is already half to believe. His former royalist Catholic convictions were not savagely demolished. They remained as a sacred and poetic ruin, appealing, as ruins do, to the sense in us of pathos and pity; but they exercised no authority over the will or the masculine part of the imagination. In *Les Chants du Crépuscule* we can discern this imagination venturing itself into the presence of the popular life and movement, and arrested and aroused by the new and marvellous objects which became visible. An exiled king is deserving of a respectful and sympathising gaze; but see, the billowy inundation of the people, the irresistible advance! and listen, the rumours, the terror, the joy, the mystery of the wind and of these waves that roll before it; the stormy murmur of the people around each great idea! Here is space, and strength, and splendour for the imagination to delight in, more satisfying to it than the livery of courtiers and the ceremonial of state days. And upon the other hand—(for what could Victor Hugo's imagination effect without a contrast?)—observe the gloomy faces of the enemies of liberty and of the people; not kings (for kings were not all tyrants in 1835), but the pernicious counsellors of kings, fulfilled with perjury and boldness, "unhappy, who believed in their dark error that one morning they could take the freedom of the world like a bird in a snare." The material of much future prophecy, triumphant and indignant, lies already in existence here.

But Victor Hugo was not going to allow his poetry to become the instrument of party politics. He must not allow the harmony of his nature to be violated. He must maintain his soul above the tumult; unmoved himself, he must be austere and indulgent to others. He must belong to all parties by their generous, and to no party by its vicious sides. His grave respect for the people must be united with scorn for mobs and mob leaders. He must live with external nature as well as with man. He may safely point out errors in little human codes if he contemplate by day and by night the text of the divine and eternal codes. And holding himself thus above all that is merely local and transitory, his poetry must be the portrait—profoundly faithful—of himself, such a portrait of his own personality being perhaps the largest and most universal work which a thinker can give to the world.

Such was the spirit in which *Les Voix Intérieures* and *Les Rayons et les Ombres* were written. It was a time of high resolves, and of successful conduct of his moral nature. And what gives joy and what restores faith like successful conduct of the moral nature? We cannot trace each step of the progress from *Les Chants du Crépuscule* to *Les Rayons et les Ombres,* but we can see that the progress was accomplished. The twilight had dissipated itself, and it was the dawn indeed which came, and not the darkness. Human love seemed to grow a more substantial and a diviner thing. Beside the light of their own beauty there was an "auxiliar light," illuminating the faces of the flowers. Some counter-charm of space and hollow sky had been found:

> Let no one ask me how it came to pass;
> It seems that I am happy, that to me

A livelier emerald twinkles in the grass,
A purer sapphire melts into the sea.

Nature which had been a tender mother, now becomes a strong and beautiful bride, with embracing arms, who has need of her eager lover the poet. God, who had been a beneficent father, is now something more than can be expressed by any human relation: He is joy, and law, and light. God and nature and man have approached and play through one another. What a moment ago wasdivine grace, is now light, and as it touches the heart it again changes into love, and once more is transformed from love to faith and hope. There is an endless interchange of services between all forces and objects spiritual and material. Nothing in the world is single. Small is great, and great is small. Below the odour of a rose-bud lies an abyss—the whole mysterious bosom of the earth,—and above it in the beauty of a woman's bending face, and the soul behind that face, rises an unfathomable heaven. The calm of *Les Rayons et les Ombres,* if it is profound, is also passionate. This is that "high mountain apart," the mountain of transfiguration. They who ascend there say, "It is good for us to be here," not knowing what they say: presently they come down from the mountain, with human help for those who are afflicted and diseased,—help which to some seems supernatural, and which assuredly those who have remained below are not always able to afford.

In the autumn of 1843, Léopoldine, daughter of Victor Hugo, and Charles Vacquerie, who had been her husband during some few spring and summer months, were drowned. After the Coup d'État of December 2, the poet became an exile from France. In 1853 was published in Brussels the volume entitled *Les Châtiments*. In 1856 (twelve years had elapsed since his daughter's death) appeared the two volumes of *Les Contemplations*.

Joy had been Victor Hugo's preparation for his great sorrow. Had a blow so sudden and dreadful fallen before his soul had been tempered and purified by joy, the soul might have been crushed into formless apathy, or shattered into fragments. But because joy and love and faith had maintained his nature in a state of high efficiency, because every part of it was now vital and sensitive, he was fitted to endure the blow. Extreme anguish can be accepted as a bitter gift if it comes from the hands of Life; martyrdom is unendurable only by one who is already half deceased, and little sensitive to pain. *Les Contemplations* is the lyrical record of twenty-five years. More than any other of Victor Hugo's collections of poetry it holds, as in a rocky chalice, the gathered waters of his life. "The author has allowed the book to form itself, so to speak, within him. Life, filtering drop by drop through events and sufferings, has deposited it in his heart." These deep waters have slowly amassed themselves in the soul's secret places. *Les Contemplations* completes the series of personal memorials which had preceded it by one more comprehensive than all the rest. Here nothing is absent—reminiscences of school-boy years, youth, the loves and fancies, the gaiety and the illusions of youth, the literary warfare of early manhood, and the pains and delights of poetical creation, friendship, sorrow, the innocent mirth of children, the tumult of life, the intense silence of the grave, the streams, the fields, the flowers, the tumbling of desolate seas, the songs of birds, solitude, the devout aspiration, doubt and the horror of doubt, the eager assault of the problems Whence? and Whither? and Wherefore? and the baffled vision and arrested foot there upon "the brink of the infinite." Into this book the sunlight and clear azure have gone; the storm and the mists. But when these, its tributaries, demand each the book as of right belonging to itself, when the forest claims it, and the blossoming meadowland, and the star, and the great winds, and the heaven, and the tempestuous sea, and the nests of birds—the poet refuses all these; he gives it to the tomb. An exiled man, he cannot now lay a flower upon his children's grave; he can only send to them his soul.

The first three books contain poems of many moods of joy. The fourth book includes the poems which recall all his daughter's sweetness and pretty ways in childhood—poems of a lovely purity and sadness. The father waits in his study for the morning visit of his child; she enters with her "Bonjour, mon petit père," takes his pen, opens his books, sits upon his bed, disturbs his papers, andis gone like a flying bird. Then his work begins more joyously, and on some page scribbled with her childish arabesques, or crumpled by her little hands, come the sweetest verses of his song. How the winter evenings passed with grammar and history lessons, and the four children at his knee, while their mother sat near and friends were chatting by the hearth! And those summer walks of the father, thirty years of age, and the daughter, ten, coming home by moonlight, when the moths were brushing the window panes. And the sight of the two fair children's heads stooping over the Bible, the elder explaining, and the younger listening, while their hands wandered from page to page over Moses, and Solomon, and Cyrus, and Moloch, and Leviathan, and Jesus. And she is dead; and to set over against all these, there is the walk begun at dawn, by forest, by mountain; the man silent, with eyes which see no outward thing, solitary, unknown, with bent back and crossed hands, and the day seeming to him like the night; and then when the evening gold is in the sky unseen, and the distant sails are descending towards Harfleur, the arrival, and a bunch of green holly and blossoming heath to lay upon the tomb.

Once more as the poems close Victor Hugo attains to peace. But it is not the peace of *Les Rayons et les Ombres,* the calm of the high table-lands of joy, the calm of a halt in clear air and under the wide and luminous sky. It is rather the peace of swiftest motion, the sleep of an orb spinning onward through space. For now the stress of life has become very urgent. Joy and sorrow are each intenser than before, and are scarcely tolerable. That atom, the human will, while still retaining consciousness and individuality, is enveloped by forces material and spiritual, and whirled onward with them in unfaltering career towards their goal. Odours, songs, the blossoms of flowers, the chariots of the suns, the generations of men, the religions and philosophies of races, the tears of a father over his dead child, winters and summers, the snows, and clouds, and rain, and among all these the individual soul, hasten forward with incredible speed and with an equal repose to that of the whirlpool's edge toward some divine issue. If the gloom is great, so is the splendour. We, poor mortals, gazing Godward are blind; yet we who are blind are dazzled as we gaze. The poems of later date in these volumes bear tokens of strain: the stress of life has become too intense, and the art of the poet, it may be, suffers in consequence. Shakspere was able, after enduring the visions of Lear upon the heath, and Othello by the bedside, to retire to a little English country town, and enjoy the quiet dignity of a country gentleman. Not all great artists are so framed. With Beethoven in his later period the passion of sound became overmastering, and almost an agony of delight. With Turner in his later period, the splendour of sunlight almost annihilated his faculty of vision. Blake's songs of Innocence and of Experience became mysterious prophecies of good and evil, of servitude and freedom, of heaven and hell. With Victor Hugo the joy and the sorrow of the world have been too exceedingly strong, and his art has had to endure a strain.

Les Châtiments, published some years earlier than *Les Contemplations,* belongs by its subject to a later period of Victor Hugo's life. His private sorrow was for a time submerged by the flood of indignation let loose against the public malefactor. In the last poem of an earlier collection Victor Hugo had spoken of three great voices which were audible within him, and which summoned him to the poet's task. One was the voice of threatening, of protest and malediction against baseness and crime, the voice of the muse who visited Jeremiah and Amos: the second was all gentleness and pity and pleading on behalf of the ignorance and errors of men: the third was the voice of the Absolute, the Most-High, of Pan, of Vishnu, who is affected neither by love nor hatred, to whom death is no less acceptable than life, who includes what seems to us crime as contentedly as what we call virtue. Now, for a season, Victor Hugo listened eagerly to what the first of these three voices had to say. It was the hour for art to rise and show that it is no dainty adornment of life, but an armed guardian of the land. "The rhetoricians coldly say, 'The poet is an angel; he soars, ignoring Fould, Magnan, Morny, Maupas; he gazes with ecstacy up the serene night.' No! so long as you are accomplices of these hideous crimes, which step by step I track, so long as you spread your veils over these brigands, blue heavens, and suns and stars, I will not look upon you." *Les Châtiments* is the roaring of an enraged lion. One could wish that the poet kept his indignation somewhat more under control. He is not Apollo shooting the faultless and shining shafts against Python, but a *Jupiter tonans,* a little robustious, and whirling superabundant thunderbolts with equal violence in every direction. It is now the chief criminal, the Man of December, now it is the jackals who form his body-guard, now the prostitute priest, now the bribed soldier, now the *bon bourgeois,* devotee of the god *Boutique* and on each and all descend the thunderbolts, with a rattling hail of stinging epithets, and with fire that runs and leaps. This eruption, which is meant to overwhelm the gewgaw Empire, goes on fulgurantly, resoundingly and not without scoriæ and smoke. Victor Hugo's faith in the people and in the future remains unshaken. "Progress," "Liberty," "Humanity,"

remain more than ever magic watchwords. The volume which opens with **"Nox"**—the blackness of that night of violence and treason—closes with **"Lux",** the dreadful shining of the coming day of Freedom. "Doubt not; let us believe, let us wait. God knows how to break the teeth of Nero as the panther's teeth. Let us have faith, be calm, and go onward." Let us not slay this man; let us keep him alive—"Oh, a superb chastisement? Oh! if one day he might pass along the highway naked, bowed down, trembling, as the grass trembles to the wind, under the execration of the whole human race." . . . "People, stand aside! this man is marked with the sign. Let Cain pass; he belongs to God."

And now Victor Hugo's gaze travelled from his own period backward over the universal history of man. Was this triumph of evil for a season, with tyranny and corruption and luxury in the high places, and fidelity, and truth, and virtue, and loyalty to great ideas cast out, fading on remote and poisonous shores, or languishing in dungeons,—was this a new thing in the world's history? The exile in the solitude of his rocky island, and encircled by the moaning seas, loses the tender and graceful aspect of things. As he looks backward through all time, what does he perceive? Always the weak oppressed by the strong, the child cast out of his heritage by violent men, the innocent entrapped by the crafty, the light-hearted girl led blindfold to her doom, old age insulted and thrust away by youth, the fratricide, the parricide, the venal priest on one side of the throne, and the harlot queening it on the other, the tables full of vomit and filthiness, the righteous sold for silver, the wicked bending their bow to cast down the poor and needy. While he gazes, the two passions which had filled *Les Châtiments* from the beginning to the end, the passions of Hatred and of Hope, condense and materialize themselves, and take upon them two forms—the one, that of the tyrant, the proud wrong-doer; the other, that of the Justiciary, the irresistible avenger of wrong. *La Légende des Siècles* is the imaginative record of the crimes and the overthrow of tyrants. If no collection of Victor Hugo's poetry formed itself so quietly and truly, gathering drop by drop, as *Les Contemplations,* there is none which is so much the product of resolution and determined energy as this, *La Légende des Siècles,* which next followed. These poems are not lyrical outflowings of sorrow and of joy. The poet, with the design of shaping a great whole out of many parts, chooses from a wide field the subject of each brief epic; having chosen his subject, he attacks it with the utmost vigour and audacity, determined to bring it into complete subjection to his imagination. Breaking into a new and untried province of art now when his sixtieth year was not distant, Victor Hugo never displayed more ambition or greater strength. The alexandrine in his hands becomes capable of any and every achievement; its even stepping is heard only when the poet chooses; now it is a winged thing and flies; now it advances with the threatening tread of Mozart's *commandatore.*

Occasional episodes, joyous or graciously tender, there are in *La Légende des Siècles.* The rapture of creation when the life of the first man-child was assured, the sleep of Boaz, Jesus in the house of Martha and Mary, the calm death of the eastern prophet, the gallantry of the little page Aymerillot who took Narbonne, the Infanta with the rose in her tiny hand, the fisherman who welcomes the two orphan children, and will toil for them as for his own—these relieve the gloom. But the prominent figures (and sometimes they assume Titanic size) are those of the great criminals and the great avengers—Cain, pursued by the eye of God, Canute, the seven evil uncles of the little King of Galicia, Joss the great and Zeno the little, but equal in the instincts of the tiger, Ratbert and his court of titled robbers and wanton women, Philip the Second, the Spanish inquisitors and baptizers of mountains—where shall we look for moral support against the cruelty and the treachery and the effrontery of these? Only in the persons of the avengers,—Roland whirling Durandal in the narrow gorge, Eviradnus standing over the body of the sleeping countess, or shooting the corpses of the two defeated wretches down their hideous *oubliette*—only in these and in the future when all dark shadows of crime and of sorrow shall have passed for ever away.

It is to be noted of **La Légende des Siècles** that the aspect of nature as an antagonist of the will of man, or as Victor Hugo would grandiosely express it, as "one form of the triple ἀνάγκη," that aspect presented with such force and infinite detail in *Les Travailleurs de la Mer,* and in the earlier chapters of *L'Homme qui Rit,* appears distinctly in some of these brief epic records of human struggle and human victory or defeat.

La Légende des Siècles and the volume which next followed become each more striking by the contrast they present. Victor Hugo has somewhere told us how one day he went to see the lion of Waterloo; the solitary and motionless figure stood dark against the sky, and the poet stepped up the little hillock and stood within its shadow. Suddenly he heard a song; it was the voice of a robin who had built her nest in the great mouth of the lion. **Les Chansons des Rues et des Bois** viewed in relation to *La Légende des Siècles* resembles this nest in the lion's mouth. The volume was indeed a piquant surprise to those who had watched the poet's career through its later period, and who took the trouble to surmise about his forthcoming works. After the tragic legends came these slight caprices. The songs (while their tone and colour are very different from those of Victor Hugo's youth) are a return to youth by the subjects of many of them, and by the circumstance that once again, as in the **Odes** and **Les Orientales,** style becomes a matter of more importance than the idea. These later feats of style are the more marvellous through their very slightness and curious delicacy. Pegasus, who has been soaring, descends and performs to a miracle the most exquisite circus accomplishments. Language, metre, and meaning seem recklessly to approach the brink of irretrievable confusion; yet the artist never practised greater strictness, or attained greater precision, because here more than elsewhere these were indispensable. All styles meet in mirthful reunion. Virgil walks side by side with Villon; Lalage and Jeanneton pour the wine; King David is seen behind the trees staring at Diana, and Actæon from the housetop at Bathsheba; the spider spins his web to catch the flying rhymes from Minerva's indignant nose to the bald head of St. Paul.

Yet all the while an ideal of beauty floats over this *Kermesse;* the goddesses do not lose their heavenly splendour; the sky bends overhead; the verse, while it sips its coffee, retains the fragrance of the dew. As to idea—the idea of such songs as these is that they shall have no idea. Enough of the mystery of life and death, the ascending scale of beings, the searching in darkness, the judicial pursuit of evil! Enough of visions on the mountain heights, of mysterious sadness by the sea! Let us live, and adjourn all these; adjourn this measureless task, adjourn Satan, and Medusa, and say to the Sphinx "Go by, I am gossiping with the rose." Friend, this interlude displeases you. What is to be done? The woods are golden. Up goes the notice-board, "Out for a holiday." I want to laugh a little in the fields. What! must I question the corn-cockle about eternity? Must I show a brow of night to the lily and the butterfly? Must I terrify the elm and the lime, the reeds and rushes, by hanging huge problems over the nests of little birds? Should I not be a hundred leagues from good sense if I were to go explaining to the wagtails the Latin of the *Dies Iræ?* Such is the mirthful spirit of the book; not mirth in the "happy, prompt, instinctive way of youth;" but the wilfulness prepense of one who seeks relief from thought and passion. The apparent recrudescence of sensuality in some of these songs is not an affair of the senses at all, but of the fancy: or if the eye is inquisitive and eager, it is because the vague bewildering consciousness of youthful pleasure is absent.

Such songs as these could be no more than an interlude in the literary life of Victor Hugo. But the transition becomes tragic when we pass from **Les Chansons des Rues et des Bois** to **L'Année terrible**. The holiday in the woods is indeed over, and all laughter and sportive ways. The fields are trampled by the steady battalions of the invaders. The streets have a grave and anxious air. Paris, the heroic city, the city of liberty, the capital of the world, where Danton thundered, and Molière shone, and Voltaire jested, Paris is enduring her agony. But the empire has fallen. The imperial bandit "passes along the highway naked, bowed down, trembling, as the grass trembles to the wind, under the execration of the whole human race." And Victor Hugo stands in republican France.

L'Année terrible is a record for the imagination, complete in every important particular, of the history of Paris, from August 1870 to July 1871; and with the life of Paris, the personal life of the poet is intertwined inseparably, and for ever. Great joy, the joy of an exile restored to his people, the joy of a patriot who has witnessed the overthrow of a corrupt and enervating despotism, and who is proud of the heroic attitude of the besieged city—such joy is mingled with the great sorrow of his country's defeat and dismemberment. He is sustained by his confidence in the future, and in the ultimate victory of the democratic ideas which form his faith; though once or twice this confidence seems for a moment shaken by the rude assault of facts. The extravagance of his love and devotion to France, the extravagance of his scorn and hatred of the invader, must be pardoned, if they need pardon—and passed by. When will a poet arise who shall unite the most accurate perception of facts as they really are—exaggerating nothing, diminishing nothing—with the most ardent passion; who shall be judicial and yet the greatest of lovers? He indeed will make such passion as that of Victor Hugo look pale. Yet the wisdom and charity and moderation of many poems of *L'Année terrible* must not be overlooked: nor the freedom of the poet from party spirit. He is a Frenchman throughout; not a man of the Commune, nor a man of Versailles. The most precious poems of the book are those which keep close to facts rather than concern themselves with ideas. The sunset seen from the ramparts, the floating bodies of the Prussians borne onward by the Seine, caressed and kissed and still swayed on by the eddying water, the bomb which fell near the old man's feet while he sat where had been the convent of the Feuillantines, and where he had walked under the trees in Aprils long ago, holding his mother's hand, the petroleuse dragged like a chained beast through the scorching streets of Paris, the gallant boy who came to confront death beside his friends,—memories of these it is which haunt us when we have closed the book. Of these—and of the little limbs, and transparent fingers and baby smile and murmur like the murmur of bees, and the face changed from rosy health to a pathetic paleness, of the one-year-old grandchild, too soon to become an orphan.

In the works of 1877 no new direction has been taken; but splendours and horrors, heroisms and shames still fill up the legendary record of the centuries; and amidst these glories and dishonours of adult manhood, shines the divine innocence of the child.

Henry James (review date 1877)

SOURCE: "Hugo's Légende des Siècles," in *Literary Reviews and Essays,* edited by Albert Mordell, Twayne Publishers, 1957, pp. 136-38.

[*In following review of* La légende des siècles, *which was originally published in* The Nation *in May 3, 1877, James discusses Hugo's strengths and weaknesses as a poet.*]

From the very flattering notices which the English journals have accorded to the new volumes of Victor Hugo's *Légende des Siècles,* it is apparent that the writer has lately become almost the fashion in England—a fact to be attributed in a measure to the influence of the "æsthetic" school, or, to speak more correctly, probably, of Mr. Swinburne, who, as we know, swears by Victor Hugo, and whose judgments seem to appeal less forcibly to the English sense of humor than they do to a corresponding quality on this side of the Atlantic. Be this as it may, however, Victor Hugo's new volumes are as characteristic as might have been expected—as violent and extravagant in their faults, and in their fine passages as full of imaginative beauty. Apropos of the sense of humor, the absence of this quality is certainly Victor Hugo's great defect—the only limitation (it must be confessed it is a very serious one) to his imaginative power. It should teach him occasionally to kindle Mr. Ruskin's "lamp of sacrifice." This "nouvelle série" of the *Légende des Siècles* is not a con-

tinuation of the first group of poems which appeared under this name: it is rather a return to the same ground, the various categories under which the first poems appeared being supplied with new recruits. These categories are too numerous to be mentioned here; they stretch from the creation of the world to the current year of grace. It is an immense plan, and shows on the author's part not only an extraordinary wealth of imagination, but a remarkable degree of research. It is true that Victor Hugo's researches are often rather pedantically exhibited; no poet was ever so fond of queer proper names, dragged together from dusty corners of history and legend, and strung together rhythmically—often with a great deal of ingenuity. He is too fond of emulating Homer's catalogue of the ships. But he has what the French call an extraordinary *scent* for picturesque subjects. These two volumes contain many examples of it; the story, for instance, of a certain king of Arragon who gives his son a blow on the cheek, whereupon the proud and sensitive young man, outraged, retires into the desert. The father, aggrieved at his desertion and greatly sorrowing, descends into the sepulchral crypt where his own father is buried, and there, apostrophizing the bronze statue on his tomb, complains of the young man's ingratitude and weeps. After this has gone on some time he feels, in the darkness, the statuestroke his cheek tenderly with its great hand. "L'Aigle du Casque," one of the best things in the two volumes, is the tale of a certain Northumbrian baron of the dark ages, Lord Tiphaine—Victor Hugo's English names are always very queer. He has a duel with a young Scotch noble—a delicate stripling many years his junior, and on the latter taking fright and fleeing from him, he pursues him a whole summer's day, over hill and dale, and at last overtakes him and murders him. The story of the chase and its various episodes is a specimen of Victor Hugo at his best. When the brutal Northumbrian has hacked his victim to death the brazen eagle perched upon his helmet suddenly becomes animate, utters in a rancorous scream its detestation of the dead, bends over and with its beak and talons tears his face to pieces, and then spreading its wings sails majestically away. Victor Hugo excels in leading a long narrative piece of verse up to a startling climax of this kind, related in the half-dozen closing lines. These volumes contain the usual proportion of fulsome adulation of Paris and of the bloodiest chapters in its history—that narrow Gallomania which makes us so often wonder at times, not whether the author is, after all, a great poet, but whether he is not very positively and decidedly a small poet. But, outside of this, this new series of what is probably his capital work contains plenty of proofs of his greatness—passages and touches of extraordinary beauty. No poet has written like Victor Hugo about children, and the second of these volumes contains a masterpiece of this kind. "Petit Paul" is simply the history of a very small child whose mother dies and whose father takes a second wife—a coarse, hard woman, who neglects the little boy. Before his father's second marriage he has been much with his grandfather, who delights in him— "Oh! quel céleste amour entre ces deux bonshommes." The grandfather dies and is buried, to Paul's knowledge, in the village churchyard. The stepmother comes; the child's life is miserably changed, and at last, one winter's night, he starts out, and not having been missed, is found the next morning dead in the snow at the closed gate of the cemetery. We must quote the lines in which the author describes him while he is meditating this attempt to rejoin his grandfather, the other *bonhomme;* on hearing his step-mother caress his step-brother, lately born:

> Paul se souvenait avec la quantité
> De mémoire qu'auraient les agneaux et les roses
> Qu'il s'était entendu dire les mêmes choses.
> Il prenait dans un coin, à terre, ses repas;
> Il etait devenu muet, ne parlait pas.
> Ne pleurait plus. L'enfance est parfois sombre et
>   forte,
> Souvent il regardait lugubrement la porte.

Algernon Charles Swinburne (review date 1883)

SOURCE: "Victor Hugo: La Légende des Siècles," in *Fortnightly Review,* Vol. XXXIV, 1883, pp. 497-520.

[*Swinburne was an English poet, dramatist, and critic. Though renowned in his lifetime for his lyric poetry, he is remembered today primarily for his rejection of Victorian mores. In the following excerpt, taken from a discussion of* La légende des siècles, *Swinburne lavishes praise on the work, favorably comparing it to the works of William Shakespeare and Dante.*]

The greatest work of the century [*La Légende des Siècles*] is now at length complete. It is upwards of twenty-four years since the first part of it was sent home to France from Guernsey. Eighteen years later we received a second instalment of the yet unexhausted treasure. And here, at the age of eighty-one, the sovereign poet of the world has placed the coping-stone on the stateliest of spiritual buildings that ever in modern times has been reared for the wonder and the worship of mankind.

Those only to whom nothing seems difficult because nothing to them seems greater than themselves could find it other than an arduous undertaking to utter some word of not unworthy welcome and thanksgiving when their life is suddenly enriched and brightened by such an addition to its most precious things as the dawn of a whole new world of song—and a world that may hold its own in heaven beside the suns created or evoked by the fiat of Shakespeare or of Dante. To review the *Divine Comedy,* to dispose of *Hamlet* in the course of a leading article, to dispatch in a few sentences the question of *Paradise Lost* and its claim to immortality, might seem easy to judges who should feel themselves on a level with the givers of these gifts; for others it could be none the less difficult to discharge this office because the gift was but newly given. One minor phase of the difficulty which presents itself is this: the temporary judge, self-elected to pass sentence on any supreme achievement of human power, must choose on which horn of an inevitable dilemma he may prefer to run the risk of impalement. If, recognising in this new master-work an equal share of the highest qualities possible to man with that possessed and manifested by any previous

writer of now unquestioned supremacy, he takes upon himself to admit, simply and honestly, that he does recognise this, and cannot choose but recognise it, he must know that his judgment will be received with no more tolerance or respect, with no less irritation and derision, than would have been, in Dante's time, the judgment of a critic who should have ventured to rank Dante above Virgil, in Shakespeare's time of a critic who should have dared to set Shakespeare beside Homer. If, on the other hand, he should abstain with all due discretion from any utterance or any intimation of a truth so ridiculous and untimely, he runs the sure and certain risk of leaving behind him a name to be ranked, by all who remember it at all, with those which no man mentions without a smile of compassion or of scorn, according to the quality of error discernible in the critic's misjudgment: innocent and incurable as the confidence of a Johnson or a Jeffrey, venomous and malignant as the rancour of Sainte-Beuve or Gifford. Of these two dangers I choose the former; and venture to admit, in each case with equal diffidence, that I do upon the whole prefer Dante to any Cino or Cecco, Shakespeare to all the Greenes and Peeles and Lillys, Victor Hugo to all or any, of their respective times. The reader who has no tolerance for paradox or presumption has therefore fair warning to read no further.

Auguste Vacquerie, of all poets and all men living the most worthy to praise the greatest poet of his century, has put on record long ago, with all the vivid ardour of his admirable style, an experience of which I now am but too forcibly reminded. He was once invited by Victor Hugo to choose among the manuscripts of the master's unpublished work, from the drawers containing respectively some lyric or dramatic or narrative masterpiece, of which among the three kinds he would prefer to have a sample first. Unable to select, he touched a drawer at random, which contained the opening chapters of a yet unfinished story—*Les Misérables.* If it is no less hard to choose where to begin in a notice of the *Légende des Siècles*—to decide what star in all this thronged and living heaven should first attract the direction of our critical telescope—it is on the other hand no less certain that on no side can the telescope be misdirected. From the miraculous music of a legendary dawn, when the first woman felt first within her the movement of her first-born child, to the crowning vision of ultimate justice made visible and material in the likeness of the trumpet of doom, no radiance or shadow of days or nights intervening, no change of light or cadence of music in all the tragic pageant of the centuries, finds less perfect expression and response, less absolute refraction or reflection than all that come and go before or after it. History and legend, fact and vision, are fused and harmonised by the mastering charm of moral unity in imaginative truth. There is no more possibility of discord or default in this transcendent work of human power than in the working of those powers of nature which transcend humanity. In the first verses of the overture we hear such depth and height of music, see such breadth and splendour of beauty, that we know at once these cannot but continue to the end; and from the end, when we arrive at the goal of the last line, we look back and perceive that it has been so. Were this overture but a thought less perfect, a shade less triumphant, we might doubt if what was to follow it could be as perfect and triumphant as itself. We might begin—and indeed, as it is, there are naturally those who have begun—to debate with ourselves or to dispute with the poet as to the details of his scheme, the selection of his types, the propriety of his method, the accuracy of his title. There are those who would seem to infer from the choice of this title that the book is, in the most vulgar sense, of a purely legendary cast; who object, for example, that a record of unselfish and devoted charity shown by the poor to the poor is, happily, no "legend." Writers in whom such self-exposure of naked and unashamed ignorance with respect to the rudiments of language is hardly to be feared have apparently been induced or inclined to expect some elaborate and orderly review of history, some versified chronicle of celebrated events and significant epochs, such as might perhaps be of subsidiary or supplementary service in the training of candidates for a competitive examination; and on finding something very different from this have tossed head and shrugged shoulder in somewhat mistimed impatience, as at some deception or misnomer on the great author's part which they, as men of culture and understanding, had a reasonable right to resent. The book, they affirm, is a mere agglomeration of unconnected episodes, irrelevant and incoherent, disproportionate and fortuitous, chosen at random by accident or caprice; it is not one great palace of poetry, but a series or congeries rather of magnificently accumulated fragments. It may be urged in answer to this impeachment that the unity of the book is not logical but spiritual; its diversity is not accidental or chaotic, it is the result and expression of a spontaneous and perfect harmony, as clear and as profound as that of the other greatest works achieved by man. To demonstrate this by rule and line of syllogism is no present ambition of mine. A humbler, a safer, and perhaps a more profitable task would be to attempt some flying summary, some glancing revision of the three great parts which compose this mightiest poem of our age; or rather, if this also should seem too presumptuous an aspiration, to indicate here and there the points to which memory and imagination are most fain to revert most frequently and brood upon them longest, with a deeper delight, a more rapturous reverence, than waits upon the rest. Not that I would venture to assert or to insinuate that there is in any poem of the cycle any note whatever of inferiority or disparity; but having neither space nor time nor power to speak, however inadequately, of each among the hundred and thirty-eight poems which compose the now perfect book, I am compelled to choose, not quite at random, an example here and there of its highest and most typical qualities. In the first book, for instance, of the first series, the divine poem on Ruth and Boaz may properly be taken as representative of that almost indefinable quality which hitherto has seemed more especially the gift of Dante: a fusion, so to speak, of sublimity with sweetness, the exaltation of loveliness into splendour and simplicity into mystery, such as glorifies the close of his *Purgatory* and the opening of his *Paradise*. Again, the majestic verses which bring Mahomet before us at his end strike a deeper impression into thememory than is left by the previous poem on the raising of Lazarus; and when we pass into the cycle of heroic or chivalrous legend we find those poems the loftiest and the loveliest which have in

them most of that prophetic and passionate morality which makes the greatest poet, in this as in some other ages, as much a seer as a singer, an evangelist no less than an artist. Hugo, for all his dramatic and narrative mastery of effect, will always probably remind men rather of such poets as Dante or Isaiah than of such poets as Sophocles or Shakespeare. We cannot of course imagine the Florentine or the Hebrew endowed with his infinite variety of sympathies, of interests, and of powers; but as little can we imagine in the Athenian such height and depth of passion, in the Englishman such unquenchable and sleepless fire of moral and prophetic faith. And hardly in any one of these, though Shakespeare may perhaps be excepted, can we recognise the same buoyant and childlike exultation in such things as are the delight of a high-hearted child—in free glory of adventure and ideal daring, in the triumph and rapture of reinless imagination, which gives now and then some excess of godlike empire and superhuman kingship to their hands whom his hands have created, to the lips whose life is breathed into them from his own. By the Homeric stature of the soul he measures the capacity of the sword. And indeed it is hardly in our century that men who do not wish to provoke laughter should venture to mock at a poet who puts a horde to flight before a hero, or strikes down strongholds by the lightning of a single will. No right and no power to disbelieve in the arm of Hercules or the voice of Orpheus can rationally remain with those who have seen Garibaldi take a kingdom into the hollow of his hand, and not one man but a whole nation arise from the dead at the sound of the word of Mazzini.

Two out of the five heroic poems which compose the fourth book of the first series will always remain types of what the genius of Hugo could achieve in two opposite lines. All the music of morning, all the sunshine of romance, all the sweetness and charm of chivalry, will come back upon all readers at the gracious and radiant name of **"Aymerillot";** all the blackness of darkness, rank with fumes of blood and loud with cries of torment, which covers in so many quarters the history, not romantic but actual, of the ages called ages of faith, will close in upon the memory which reverts to the direful **"Day of Kings"**. The sound of the final note struck in the latter poem remains in the mind as the echo of a crowning peal of thunder in the ear of one entranced and spell-stricken by the magnetism of storm. The Pyrenees belong to Hugo as the western coasts of Italy, Neapolitan or Tuscan, belong to Shelley; they can never again be done into words and translated into music as for once they have been by these. It can hardly be said that he who knows the Pyrenees has read Victor Hugo; but certainly it may be said that he who knows Victor Hugo has seen the Pyrenees. From the author's prefatory avowal that his book contains few bright or smiling pictures, a reader would never have inferred that so many of its pages are fragrant with all the breath and radiant with all the bloom of April or May among the pine-woods and their mountain lawns, ablaze with ardent blossom and astir with triumphant song. Tragedy may be hard at hand, with all the human train of sorrows and passions and sins; but the glory of beauty, the loveliness of love, the exultation of noble duty and lofty labour in a stress of arduous joy, these are the influences that pervade the world and permeate the air of the poems which deal with the Christian cycle of heroic legend, whose crowning image is the ideal figure of the Cid. To this highest and purest type of mediæval romance or history the fancy of the great poet whose childhood was cradled in Spain turns and returns throughout the course of his threefold masterpiece with an almost national pride and passion of sublime delight. Once in the first part and once in the third his chosen hero is set before us in heroic verse, doing menial service for his father in his father's house, and again, in a king's palace, doing for humanity thesovereign service of tyrannicide. But in the second part it seems as though the poet could hardly, with his fullest effusion of lyric strength and sweetness, do enough to satisfy his loving imagination of the perfect knight, most faithful and most gentle and most terrible, whom he likens even to the very Pic du Midi in its majesty of solitude. Each fresh blast of verse has in it the ring of a golden clarion which proclaims in one breath the honour of the loyal soldier and the dishonour of the disloyal king. There can hardly be in any language a more precious and wonderful study of technical art in verse of the highest kind of simplicity than this *Romancero du Cid,* with its jet of luminous and burning song sustained without lapse or break through sixteen "fyttes" of plain brief ballad metre. It is hard to say whether the one only master of all forms and kinds of poetry that ever left to all time the proof of his supremacy in all has shown most clearly by his use of its highest or his use of its simplest forms the innate and absolute equality of the French language as an instrument for poetry with the Greek of Æschylus and of Sappho, the English of Milton and of Shelley.

But among all Hugo's romantic and tragic poems of mediæval history or legend the two greatest are in my mind **"Eviradnus"** and **"Ratbert"**. I cannot think it would be rash to assert that the loveliest love-song in the world, the purest and keenest rapture of lyric fancy, the sweetest and clearest note of dancing or dreaming music, is that which rings for ever in the ear which has once caught the matchless echo of such lines as these that must once more be quoted, as though all the world of readers had not long since known them by heart:—

> Viens, sois tendre, je suis ivre.
> O les verts taillis mouillés!
> Ton souffle te fera suivre
> Des papillons réveillés.
>
>   . . . . .
>
> Allons-nous-en par l'Autriche!
> Nous aurons l'aube à nos fronts;
> Je serai grand, et toi riche,
> Puisque nous nous aimerons.
>
>   . . . . .
>
> Tu seras dame, et moi comte;
> Viens, mon cœur s'épanouit,
> Viens, nous conterons ce conte
> Aux étoiles de la nuit.

The poet would be as sure of a heavenly immortality in the hearts of men as any lyrist of Greece itself, who should only have written the fourteen stanzas of the song from which I have ventured to choose these three. All the sounds and shadows of a moonlit wilderness, all the dews and murmurs and breaths of midsummer midnight, have become for once articulate in such music as was never known even to Shakespeare's forest of Arden. In the heart of a poem so full of tragedy and terror that Hugo alone could have brightened it with his final touch of sunrise, this birdlike rapture breaks out as by some divine effect of unforbidden and blameless magic.

And yet, it may be said or thought, the master of masters has shown himself even greater in **"Ratbert"** than in **"Eviradnus"**. This most tragic of poems, lit up by no such lyric interlude, stands unsurpassed even by its author for tenderness, passion, divine magnificence of righteous wrath, august and pitiless command of terror and pity. From the kingly and priestly conclave of debaters more dark than Milton's to the superb admonition of loyal liberty in speech that can only be silenced by murder, and again from the heavenly and heroic picture of childhood worshipped by old age to the monstrous banquet of massacre, when the son of the prostitute has struck his perjured stroke of state, the poem passes through a change of successive pageants each fuller of splendour and wonder, of loveliness or of horror, than the last. But the agony of the hero over the little corpse of the child murdered with her plaything in her hand—the anguish that utters itself as in peal upon peal of thunder, broken by sobs of storm—the full crash of the final imprecation, succeeded again by such unspeakably sweet and piteous appeal to the little dead lips and eyes that would have answered yesterday—and at last the one crowning stroke of crime which calls down answerable stroke of judgment from the very height of heaven, for the comfort and refreshment and revival of all hearts — these are things of which no praise can speak aright. Shakespeare only, were he living, would be worthy to write on Hugo's Fabrice as Hugo has written on Shakespeare's Lear. History will forget the name of Bonaparte before humanity forgets the name of Ratbert.

But if this be the highest poem of all for passion and pathos and fire of terrible emotion, the highest in sheer sublimity of imagination is to my mind **"Zim-Zizimi."** Again and again, in reading it for the first time, one thinks that surely now the utmost height is reached, the utmost faculty revealed, that can be possible for a spirit clothed only with human powers, armed only with human speech. And always one finds the next step forward to be yet once more a step upward, even to the very end and limit of them all. Neither in Homer nor in Milton, nor in the English version of Job or Ezekiel or Isaiah, is the sound of the roll and surge of measured music more wonderful than here. Even after the vision of the tomb of Belus the miraculous impression of splendour and terror, distinct in married mystery, and diverse in unity of warning, deepens and swells onward like a sea till we reach the incomparable psalm in praise of the beauty and the magic of womanhood made perfect and made awful in Cleopatra, which closes in horror at the touch of a hand more powerful than

Orcagna's. The walls of the Campo Santo are fainter preachers and feebler pursuivants of the triumph of death than the pages of the poem which yet again renews its note of menace after menace and prophecy upon prophecy till the end. There is probably not one single couplet in all this sweet and bitter roll of song which could have been written by any poet less than the best or lower than the greatest of all time.

At every successive stage of his task, the man who undertakes to glance over this great cycle of poems must needs incessantly call to mind the most worn and hackneyed of all quotations from its author's works—"J'en passe, et des meilleurs." There is here no room, as surely there should nowhere now be any need, to speak at any length of the poems in which Roland plays the part of protagonist; first as the beardless champion of a five days' fight, and again as the deliverer whose hand could clear the world of a hundred human wolves in one continuous sword-sweep. There ishardly time allowed us for one poor word or two of tribute to such a crowning flower of song as **"La Rose de l'Infante,"** with its parable of the broken Armada made manifest in a wrecked fleet of drifting petals; to the superb and sonorous chant of the buccaneers, in which all the noise of lawless battle and stormy laughter passes off into the carol of mere triumphant love and trust; or even to the whole inner cycle of mystic and primæval legend which seeks utterance for the human sense of oppression or neglect by jealous or by joyous gods; for the wild profound revolt of riotous and trampled nature, the agony and passion and triumph of invincible humanity, the protest and witness of enduring earth against the passing shades of heaven, the struggle and the plea of eternal manhood against all transient forces of ephemeral and tyrannous godhead. Within the orbit of this epicycle one poem only of the first part, a star of strife and struggle, can properly be said to revolve; but the light of that planet has fire enough to animate with its reflex the whole concourse of stormy stars which illuminate the world-wide wrestle of the giants with the gods. The torch of revolt borne by the transfigured satyr, eyed like a god and footed like a beast, kindles the lamp of hopeful and laborious rebellion which dazzles us in the eye of the Titan who has seen beyond the world. In the song that struck silence through the triumph of amazed Olympus there is a sound and air as of the sea or the Book of Job. There may be something of Persian or Indian mysticism, there is more of universal and imaginative reason, in the great allegoric myth which sets forth here how the half-brute child of one poor planet has in him the seed, the atom, the principle of life everlasting, and dilates in force of it to the very type and likeness of the eternal universal substance which is spirit or matter of life; and before the face of his transfiguration the omnipresent and omnipotent gods who take each their turn to shine and thunder are all but shadows that pass away. Since the Lord answered Job out of the whirlwind no ear has heard the burst of such a song; but this time it is the world that answers out of its darkness the lords and gods of creed and oracle, who have mastered and have not made it. And in the cry of its protest and the prophecy of its advance there is a storm of swelling music which is as the sound of the strength of rollers after the noise of the rage of breakers.

Richard Aldington (essay date 1926)

SOURCE: "Victor Hugo and *La Légende des Siècles,*" in *Literary Studies and Reviews,* Dial Press, 1926, pp. 253-63.

[*In the following mixed review, Aldington faults Hugo's naïveté, mawkishness, and tendency to copy other poets but praises his humanism.*]

La Légende des siècles was designed by its author as an Epic of Progress. It was published in 1859, so that only sixty years elapsed between its first appearance and its inclusion in the series of "Grands Écrivains de la France," which is a kind of final homage to the illustrious. Yet, if one may judge from the date at the end of M. Paul Berret's excellent introduction, this edition would have appeared in 1914 had the publication not been delayed by a grand expression of Progress. A curious coincidence that this magniloquent praise of Progress should have been delayed six years by a European war; that this homage should be paid it at the very moment when its main idea is heavily discredited.

Hugo's faith in mechanically propelled vehicles as an evidence of Progress (the capital "P" seems as appropriate as in thc allied Podsnappery), as a proof of civilization, even as being civilization itself, is childish and commonplace, though he was not the only one to mistake the husk for the kernel, the science of mechanics for the art of life. His Satyr prophesies railways in these words—

> Qui sait si quelque jour on ne te verra pas,
> Fier, suprême, atteler les forces de l'abîme,
> Et, dérobant l'éclair à l'Inconnu sublime,
> Lier ce char d'un autre à des chevaux à toi?

He describes the *Great Eastern* steamship as—

> . . . un monstre à qui l'eau sans bornes fut promise,
> Et qui longtemps, Babel des mers, eut Londres entier
> Levant les yeux dans l'ombre au pied de son chantier,
> Effroyable, à sept mâts mêlant cinq cheminées
> Qui hennissaient au choc des vagues effrénées.

And his description of an aeronaut as a "fier cocher Du char aérien que l'éther voit marcher" is even more amusing. Fier cocher! And he seems to have thought a dirigible could fly to Sirius and back—

> Ciel! ainsi, comme on voit aux voûtes des celliers
> Les noirceurs qu'en rôdant tracent les chandeliers,
>   On pourrait, sous les bleus pilastres,
> Deviner qu'un enfant de la terre a passé,
> A ce que le flambeau de l'homme aurait laissé
>   De fumeé au plafond des astres!

Yet, even though the naïveté of Hugo's faith in machines is ridiculous, though his Progress is now a demolished illusion, is his epic necessarily valueless? We do not believe in Homer's gods or Dante's theology, yet we do not deny that the *Iliad* and the *Commedia* are great poems. Lucretius made a great poem out of philosophic doubt, Dante out of religious belief; but it is not necessary to agree with either to appreciate his poem. In fact, when we find any person who does not admire both the *De rerum Natura* and the *Commedia Divina* we know that such a one is defective in taste and sensibility. We do not go to poetry for science. All Hugo's unfortunate cumber of balloons and railways and *Great Eastern* steamers is only worse than Milton's cannons and bridge over chaos because they are made a more important part of his work by the Frenchman. In reading *La Légende des Siècles* we must not be worried by accessories to which the author gave a disproportionate attention; we must not even trouble about the truth or falsity of his main theme. We must look for other qualities and other excellences.

What was fine in Hugo was his love of human beings, his persuasion that on the whole men are more good than bad, his hatred of oppression, meanness, cruelty, and greed, his humanity and sympathy, his gifts as an imaginative writer. You may show that his Progress was principally the popular self-deception of the last century, that he was melodramatic, a wind-bag, that he humbugged himself, that he plagiarised shamefully, that his erudition was a sham and his local details a mere collection of bric-à-brac; and when all that is said and proved it has not destroyed Victor Hugo, it has not contaminated the essence of his poetry. You cannot dispose of passages like the following by simply calling them rhetorical—

Oh! les lugubres nuits! Combats dans la bruine!
La nuée attaquant, farouche, la ruine!
Un ruissellement vaste, affreux, torrentiel,
Descend des profondeurs furieuses du ciel;
Le burg brave la nue; on entend les gorgones
Aboyer aux huit coins de ses tours octogones;
Tous les monstres sculptés sur l'édifice épars,
Grondent, et les lions de pierre des remparts
Mordent la brume, l'air et l'onde, et les tarrasques
Battent de l'aile au souffle horrible des bourrasques;
L'âpre averse en fuyant vomit sur les griffons;
Et sous la pluie entrant par les trous des plafonds,
Les guivres, les dragons, les méduses, les drées,
Grincent des dents au fond des chambres effondrées....

Nor is it a complete criticism to say that "**Les Pauvres Gens**" and similar poems are sentimental. There is something real in lines like these—

La mère, se sentant mourir, leur avait mis
Sa mante sur les pieds et sur le corps sa robe,
Afin que, dans cette ombre où la mort nous dérobe,
Ils ne sentissent plus la tiédeur qui décroit,
Et pour qu'ils eussent chaud pendant qu'elle aurait froid.

Add to these the portrait of Philip II of Spain in "**La Rose et l'Infante**," the parricide's spirit under the rain of blood, the scene in the great hall in "**Eviradnus**," the lugubrious warnings of the ten sphinxes, the dramatic lines in "**Le Petit Roi de Galicie**," when

Le chevalier leva lentement sa visière:
Je m'appelle Roland, pair de France, dit-il . . .

and they still are only part of the fine things scattered through the pages of *La Légende des Siècles*.

After reading these passages most people who are not affected with excessive modernity will agree that Hugo was a poet. But if we are to keep a just sense of proportion we cannot compare him with the greater poets already mentioned. Still less can we speak of him as French enthusiasts, who think he is like Shakespeare but rather better. *La Légende des Siècles* is not an epic at all; it is a collection of dramatic and narrative poems. If they are to be compared with anything it is with *Men and Women* and *Poems and Ballads*. And Hugo is not always up to that standard. Too often he strikes an English reader as an inferior Browning writing in the style of an inferior Swinburne. He is less subtle than the author of *In a Balcony*; and he never wrote anything so sustained, so eloquent, and so harmonious as *Atalanta in Calydon*. Modesty and self-depreciation were not characteristics of Hugo; the kind of poem Browning was content to call a dramatic lyric Hugo called an epic. He had a mania for the grand and sublime, which too often with him meant the grandiose and the rhetorical. He tried to match himself with Shakespeare, but his best is not equal to Shakespeare's second best. He caught from Chateaubriand tricks of eloquence and phrase-making which do not always lead to complete sincerity. After Hugo, it is small wonder we had M. Jules Romains asking for poetry to be "nu et sobre." Hugo adopted the attitude of a prophet, of an inspired guider of weak humanity, a most difficult part to sustain before an enlightened public. Modern curiosity is too unscrupulous, criticism too searching, means of information too common for any man to be able to pose so grandly with success. We know too much about Hugo to be able to take him at his own estimate.

What was fine in Hugo was his love of human beings, his persuasion that on the whole men are more good than bad, his hatred of oppression, meanness, cruelty, and greed, his humanity and sympathy.

—*Richard Aldington*

It makes no difference to one's estimate of Hugo's genius to learn that he collected much of his information from Moréri's dictionary, that he used that information carelessly, that his poems are full of blunders, anachronisms, sonorous names which mean nothing. One does not even object to his numerous plagiarisms from less-known contemporaries. But he cannot be exonerated when he is cheap or silly or a dupe, for such defects seriously mar his work. There is no doubt that Hugo was deceived by table-rappings. The spirits of Molière, Shakespeare, Dante, Æschylus, a toad, the lion of Androcles, the Angel of Light, all dictated poems (written in French) in the style of Victor

Hugo, containing the ideas in which he was then interested. He seems never to have regarded these manifestations with anything but credulous awe; never to have suspected that they might be a subconscious thought transference through that "marvellous medium," Charles Hugo. The influences of these séances may be traced in "**Le Satyre**" and particularly in "**Plein Ciel**" and "**Plein Mer**." The pontifical and raving manner so displeasing in Hugo came from the fact that he regarded himself as inspired by God. M. Louis Barthou possesses a photograph of Hugo in an ecstatic pose with half-shut eyes, inscribed in the poet's handwriting: "V. Hugo écoutant Dieu."

If Hugo was a dupe in such matters, he was cheap in his snarlings at Napoleon III. It is the privilege of poets and prophets to denounce kings and governments, but not from motives of disappointed ambition. M. Berret tries to excuse Hugo by saying he was "always a liberal"; but why did he wait until he had been several times passed over for Cabinet rank before he found it out? Like Chateaubriand before him, he was corroded by disappointed political ambitions. "That is the speech of a man who has tried vainly for thirty years to enter the Cabinet," said Montalembert after hearing the famous denunciation of Napoléon le Petit. Unhappily, Montalembert was right. Who now can avoid a feeling of irritation at these furious denunciations of wounded vanity masquerading as an altruistic passion for the public welfare?

> Oh! pourquoi la souffrance et pourquoi la laideur?
> Hélas! le bas-empire est couvert d'Augustules,
> Les Césars de forfaits, les crapauds de pustules. . . .

Excellent invective, but how much more convincing if the author had not first vainly tried for a portfolio from Augustule.

Even Hugo's humanitarianism was a little silly. M. Berret tells an anecdote of a dinner scene. The Master says: "I saved a lizard to-day." Someone else says: "I saved a spider"; someone else: "I saved a crab." Then everyone tells in turn how he did it, and the Master concludes: "That lizard, that crab, etc., will open for us the gates of paradise." Yet the scrupulous prophet, who saved lizards, must have held human life rather cheap, judging from the rivers of blood shed in his words. There are few so blood-thirsty as your really tender humanitarian. This credulity, this cheapness, this sentimentality, have left their mark in Hugo's poems. What could be more deplorable than the famous ass?

> Cet âne abject, souillé, meutri sous le bâton
> Est plus saint que Socrate et plus grand que Platon.

Or the bathos of this couplet—

> Un seul instant d'amour rouvre l'Eden fermé:
> Un porceau secouru pèse un monde opprimé.

Both of which are mawkish lies.

Victor Hugo was a poetic demagogue. It was therefore no more possible for him to be sincere than it is for other demagogues. We must look in his works for the many magnificent passages when the poet spoke and the demagogue was silent.

Geoffrey Brereton (essay date 1956)

SOURCE: "Victor Hugo," in *An Introduction to the French Poets: Villon to the Present Day*, Methuen and Company, 1956, pp. 119-36.

[*In the following excerpt, Brereton surveys Hugo's poetry, comparing his works to those of such other French poets as Charles Baudelaire and Alphonse de Lamartine.*]

Rather than a work, the writings of Hugo are a territory— so vast and so strongly characterized that few readers can pass through it and remain neutral. They are forced into adopting an attitude either of excessive admiration or of hostility.

Besides his four great and several lesser novels, a considerable body of shorter and more occasional prose-writings, and eleven dramas of which seven are in verse, Hugo published in his life-time a dozen main collections of poetry. . . .

As a boy of sixteen Victor Hugo won the Golden Amaranth offered by the *Académie des jeux floraux de Toulouse*. It was an academic prize for a stiff and academic poem, '**Les Vierges de Verdun**', and those characteristics persisted in most of the verse contained in his first published volume of 1822, *Les Odes et poésies diverses*. Two subsequent volumes completed a work which Hugo finally republished under the collective title of *Odes et ballades*. The *Odes* were declamatory historical pieces, but the *Ballades* were based on legend and folklore and were recounted with a certain warmth and fantasy, as in the English ballad. By concentrating on these qualities, Hugo went on to produce *Les Orientales*. Their appearance in December 1828 marked a second stage in the progress of French Romanticism hardly less significant than 1820 had been with *Les Méditations*.

Les Orientales are romantic in both the literary and the popular senses. Their setting is ostensibly that most colourful of all regions—the East. But Hugo's Orient extended little further east than Istanbul and for the most part it was North African Arabic and Spanish. His stay in Madrid as a boy, his reading of the *Romancero*—that great storehouse of medieval Spanish ballads—the poems of Byron, and the splendour of summer sunsets over Paris—these were the chief sources of his 'local colour'. From such materials he built up an exotic-seeming world which warmed the imagination without overtaxing it. Lamartine's evocations of nature had been based on landscapes which, however mistily, he had observed. Hugo was bound by no such limitations. Rather than the Lake of Annecy, he could describe the Alhambra by moonlight, or the Nile whipped by a desert wind:

On entendait mugir le simoun meurtrier,
Et sur les cailloux blancs les écailles crier
    Sous le ventre des crocodiles.
Les obélisques gris s'élançaient d'un seul jet.
Comme une peau de tigre, au couchant s'allongeait
    Le Nil jaune, tacheté d'îles.

By means of this synthetic Orientalism, Hugo treated the kind of subjects that Delacroix treated in painting—the sack of eastern towns, foaming steeds and mustachioed janissaries, languishing harem-queens, minarets and palm-trees. None of it was entirely new, for even Racine, in *Bajazet,* had written on an 'eastern' subject. The novel of the first half of the seventeenth century (de Gomberville and Madeleine de Scudéry) had used similarly exotic settings, while in the eighteenth century Orientalism had permeated both novel and drama. But not poetry. And, besides this, Hugo's handling of such themes was more full-blooded and was carried out with a conscious intention of revolt. His avoidance of Greek and Latin subjects was deliberate. It enabled him to contrast his own work with that of the drier writers of the two previous centuries and so exaggerate the distinction between the coldness of the Classics and the warmth of the Romantics. Having applied his new principles to the theory of the drama in the preface to his unacted play *Cromwell* in 1827, he went on to state his conception of poetry in the shorter preface to the **Orientales**:

> The author is not unaware that many critics will think him rash and absurd to desire for France a literature comparable to a medieval town. It is one of the maddest ideas that one could have. It means openly desiring disorder, abundance, eccentricity, bad taste. How much better is a fine, regular nudity, high walls entirely *plain*, as they say, with a few sober ornaments *in good taste*— scrolls and ovals, a bronze garland for the cornices, a marble ceiling with cherubs' heads for the vaulting! The Palace of Versailles, the Place Louis XV [Place de la Concorde], the Rue de Rivoli—there you have it. That gives you a nice literature ruled on the line.
>
> Other nations say Homer, Dante, Shakespeare. We say Boileau.

If Hugo had added Corneille, Molière, Racine, La Bruyère, Lesage, his argument would have been considerably weakened, but he and his contemporaries were irked more by the hand of a debased classicism which had grown academic than by the original masters. Though overstated, their protest was genuine.

By this time Hugo was a sufficiently accomplished poet to lead his own revolt. The verse of **Les Orientales** shows great virtuosity in the handling of rhythm and metre. Technically, he is both varied and sure. He can write plain rollicking poems of the ballad type:

> Don Rodrigue est à la chasse.
> Sans épée et sans cuirasse
> Un jour d'été, vers midi,
> Sous la feuillée et sur l'herbe
> Il s'assied l'homme superbe,
> Don Rodrigue le hardi.

He can also accomplish a metrical *tour de force* like **'Les Djinns'**, which swells through seven changes of metre to its climax, then diminishes through the same changes in reverse until it dies away in the two-syllable lines with which it began:

> On doute
> La nuit . . .
> J'écoute:
> Tout fuit,
> Tout passe;
> L'espace
> Efface
> Le bruit.

It was artificial, but it was a change—as Hugo intended— from Boileau, and even from Chénier and Lamartine. At some periods poetry should be sublime, at others exploratory and sensitive, but this was a time when a poet's most urgent duty was to be read. If we look on the early Hugo as a great resuscitator, shocking French poetry back to life by methods which his contemporaries were too fastidious or too slow to apply, we shall be doing him justice.

His metrical revolution was completed by an attack on the 'regular' alexandrine. He began to break it up, to displace the caesura from the exact middle of the line and to carry on his sentences over the rhyme from one line to the next (*enjambement*). Other poets around and before him had done the same, but an 'irregularity' which in Racine, La Fontaine or even Chénier is something of an event, in Hugo is a characteristic. His most conspicuous challenge to the belated classicists was made in his drama *Hernani,* of which the opening lines:

> Serait-ce déjà lui? C'est bien à l'escalier
> Dérobé . . .

caused, according to Théophile Gautier, almost a riot in the audience.

After this, Hugo was ready to exploit the positions he had conquered. In his four great books of lyric verse—on which the least contestable part of his reputation is based—he writes with the same metrical freedom and originality, but with less desire to startle. He has grown accustomed to his own virtuosity, and in its place two different monsters are beginning to take shape: one is the personality of Hugo, and the other his windy, thundering rhetoric. But in the eighteen-thirties their outline was not yet perfectly clear, and to discuss them now would be to anticipate.

The four books reflect a certain growth in maturity from the first to the last, but in essentials they form a single body of poetry, beginning with **Les Feuilles d'automne** in 1831, through **Les Chants du crépuscule** (1835) and **Les Voix intérieures** (1837), to **Les Rayons et les ombres** of 1840. These poems are nearly all personal, in a perfectly open way. Whether Hugo speaks in the first person, or renames himself 'the poet' or Olympio—or, more familiarly, Ol—there is no real concealment that he is expressing the spontaneous reactions of Hugo. Spontaneity in love, in his response to nature, in his views on political questions, in his impressions of past ages (**'Le Passe'**, **'La Statue'**), expressed with that amazing fluency which caused Barrès to dub him 'Le maître des mots français.' Unsubtle and uninhibited, he gives himself away with the lavishness of a born showman. There is something for everyone, even the most fastidious if they happen to come his way, for who can really resist the lure of so opulent a sensuality? His emotional gusto is not forced. He believes in it completely, and why not, since these are the feelings which carry most conviction with the common man? His sensual approach is a universal approach, whether he is writing to Juliette such a lyric as:

Puisque j'ai mis ma lèvre à ta coupe encor pleine,
Puisque j'ai dans tes mains posé mon front pâli,
Puisque j'ai respiré parfois la douce haleine
De ton âme, parfum dans l'ombre enseveli . . .

with its mounting accumulation of *puisque's* which is a hallmark of his rhetoric; or whether, more delicately, he is describing a luminous midsummer night as in the short **'Nuits de juin',** or regretting past happiness, as in **'Tristesse d'Olympio',** or apostrophizing the ghosts of drowned sailors, as in **'Oceano Nox'**:

On s'entretient de vous parfois dans les veillées.
Maint joyeux cercle, assis sur des ancres rouillées,
Mêle encor quelque temps vos noms d'ombre
    couverts
Aux rires, aux refrains, aux récits d'aventures,
Aux baisers qu'on dérobe à vos belles futures,
Tandis que vous dormez dans les goëmons verts.

On demande:—Où sont-ils? sont-ils rois dans
    quelque île?
Nous ont-ils délaissés pour un bord plus fertile?—
Puis votre souvenir même est enseveli.
Le corps se perd dans l'eau, le nom dans la
    mémoire.
Le temps, qui sur toute ombre en jette une plus
    noire,
Sur le sombre océan jette le sombre oubli.

What has been most admired in these poems, and what remains, are the great commonplaces of feeling, expressed with more richness and a stronger *souffle* than in Lamartine. Hugo insists too much, it is agreed, but without him some of the most moving and lovely sentiments of ordinary humanity would have been left without adequate expression. This was no doubt his greatest achievement, and one which is easy to overlook unless it is replaced in its historical context. We have grown so used to supposing that normal 'poetic' diction is like this (ordinary speech emotionally heightened by rhyme and rhythm and by an occasional admixture of oratory) that we forget that for a hundred and fifty years before Hugo (in French poetry at least) it was not so. Poetry used a language composed of special ingredients which were out of reach of the average education. The opposition aroused in the twentieth century by various poetic techniques sometimes indiscriminately

classed as 'modern' is due largely to a return to pre-Romantic practice. The film-star who was everyone's darling suddenly turns highbrow, or develops complicated sensibilities which cannot be expressed in the language to which we have grown accustomed. In the eighteen-thirties this was a new language of which Hugo can justly be considered to have been the father. But to-day . . . to-day it belongs to the world. To tear something from the world before it has finished chewing it is to invite those bellows of indignation still heard even now, though more faintly as time passes. In other terms, Hugo was too successful for the well-being of the Muse. He democratized her, as he claimed, leaving it painfully difficult for her to alter her status in the future.

If after this Victor Hugo had died, or had ceased writing for good, he would have taken his place with the three other great Romantics on about equal terms—a less tortured poet than Vigny, less limpid than Lamartine, heavier yet less passionate than Musset—but a necessary member of the quartet to complete its combined range. We have to consider whether, by beginning to publish and write again after a ten-years' break, he increased his poetic stature.

There can be little doubt about *Les Contemplations*. At first sight these poems—nearly all composed between 1840 and 1852 (they were published in 1856)—continue the personal, lyric manner of the earlier volumes. They are divided into two parts by a page left blank except for the words: 'Quatre Septembre 1843,' and the tragedy of Léopoldine's death becomes the leitmotiv of the poems grouped after it. Hugo's new attitude of despair is summed up in the poem **'Veni, vidi, vixi'**:

Puisque l'espoir serein dans mon âme est vaincu,
Puisqu'en cette saison des parfums et des roses,
O ma fille! j'aspire à l'ombre où tu reposes,
Puisque mon coeur est mort, j'ai bien assez vécu.

Yet it is doubtful if the blow of his daughter's death alone accounts for the underlying difference between these poems and, say, *Les Rayons et les ombres*. Something besides a tragic accident had occurred since 1840, and that was the natural cessation of the young Romantic's inner source of poetry. He had exhausted the novelty of sensual experience and was prepared to 'contemplate' it rather than to express it directly. The poems of the first part of *Les Contemplations* are invectives such as **'Réponse à un acte d'accusation'** or **'A propos d'Horace,'** quiet records of daily life or of communings with nature, searchings after the destiny of man, eclogues where the inspiration is still erotic, songs where it is more generally sentimental. An act or an impression is now the material for a poem; it no longer is a poem of itself, spontaneously.

The second part of *Les Contemplations* confirms the evidence of the first. Here are verses of subdued pathos, laments, nightmare speculations on death and eternity.

Hugo's chief poems on the death of Léopoldine (**'A Villequier,' 'Demain dès l'aube,' 'Paroles sur la dune'**) stand as great 'commonplace' pieces beside his own **'Tristesse** d'Olympio', Lamartine's 'Le Vallon', or Tennyson's 'In Memoriam':

> J'entends le vent dans l'air, la mer sur le récif,
>   L'homme liant la gerbe mûre;
> J'écoute, et je confronte en mon esprit pensif
>   Ce qui parle à ce qui murmure;
>
> Et je reste parfois couché sans me lever
>   Sur l'herbe rare de la dune,
> Jusqu'à l'heure où l'on voit apparaître et rêver
>   Les yeux sinistres de la lune.
>
> . . . Comme le souvenir est voisin du remord!
>   Comme à pleurer tout nous ramène!
> Et que je te sens froide en te touchant, ô mort,
>   Noir verrou de la porte humaine!
>
> Et je pense, écoutant gémir le vent amer,
>   Et l'onde aux plis infranchissables;
> L'été rit, et l'on voit sur le bord de la mer
>   Fleurir le chardon bleu des sables.

Such poems form an essential part of a nation's stock of distinguished verse on universal themes. The word 'classic', in one of its most important senses, must certainly be applied to them. But they are elegiac rather than lyric. They are bets on immortality at such short odds that, thoughsuccessful, they do not thrill very much. It is when an outside chance like **'Bateau ivre'** comes off that the heart is astonished and uplifted. But for the obvious futility of the living advising the dead and the critic the poet, one would say that Hugo ought to have devoted the whole of his second literary existence to this quieter and safer vein. We should then have had two very good poets instead of one vast but uneven writer. At the cost of a narrowing of range we should have been rid of a great mass of repetitive verbiage and should have been able to see some rare blooms of impersonal art. We should have had sharper satire in *Les Châtiments* to give point to its great Meissonier pictures of battles and defeats, and we might have had an unquestionable masterpiece in *La Légende des siècles*.

Hugo attempted more things than he achieved successfully, yet in his totality he was unlike any other poet and in his own specialty he could be magnificent.

—Geoffrey Brereton

This was Hugo's epic of humanity, as *Les Visions* was to have been Lamartine's and *L'Histoire de France* was Michelet's. A fruit of his first years in the Channel Islands, the first volume was published in 1859. By that date the whole work had been conceived, through the second and third volumes followed only in 1877 and 1883. Its very loose theme is the progress of the human spirit from the

earliest days of the Creation, as described in the Bible, through the ancient civilizations of Assyria and Egypt to the European Middle Ages, finally reaching forward into a cloudy future with the poems *Dieu* and *La Fin de Satan,* which were published posthumously. The grand design was a noble one typical of the aspirations of the mid-nineteenth century, though it took no account of the evolutionist conception of history which was already well established by the time the second volume of *La Légende* appeared. Apart from this, Hugo's knowledge of history and prehistory was too incomplete for his work to be more than a series of dips into a huge bran-tub of legend, mythology and literature out of which almost anything might come.

The resulting poems are best appreciated as separate *tableaux*—far more fluent than Vigny's evocations of the past, yet, in their totality, far less memorable. The most impressive have been skimmed by anthologists and the traditional choices are sound—**'La Conscience,' 'Booz endormi,' 'Le Satyre,' 'La Rose de l'Infante'** foremost among them. Of the many others, few are entirely first-rate, some are ridiculous, but most repay reading for the occasional strange or startling passages which they contain. As random examples from the second volume there is the story of Zim-Zizimi, a kind of Sardanapalus who conquers the world only to be snuffed out by a supernatural force:

> Il a dompté Bagdad, Trébizonde et Mossul
> Que conquit le premier Duilius, ce consul
> Qui marchait précédé de flûtes tibicines;
> Il a soumis Gophna, les forêts abyssines,
> L'Arabie, où l'aurore a d'immenses rougeurs,
>   . . . Et le Sahara fauve, où l'oiseau vert asfir
> Vient becqueter la mouche aux pieds des
>   dromadaires.

A few pages further on is the legend of Sultan Mourad, a blood-thirsty tyrant who in his lifetime has slain thousands of human beings. In his last hours he relieves the sufferings of a pig, and when he appears before the Judgment Seat this single good deed saves him:

> Soudain, du plus profond des nuits, sur la nuée,
> Une bête difforme, affreuse, exténuée,
> Un être abject et sombre, un pourceau, s'éleva,
> Ouvrant un œil sanglant qui cherchait Jéhovah.
>   . . . Le pourceau misérable et Dieu se regardèrent.

During and after the composition of *La Légende des siècles,* the torrent of other poems continued. They were collected in *Les Chansons des rues et des bois* (1865), which were chiefly light pieces, *L'Art d'être grand père* (1877), familiar poems reflecting his delight in his grandchildren Georges and Jeanne, several volumes of philosophic and religious poems (some perhaps deserve to be called mystical) running from *La Pitié suprême* (1879) to *Les Quatre Vents de l'esprit* (1881) and prolonged in the posthumous *Fin de Satan* and *Dieu,* and in certain pieces of *Toute la lyre* (1888-93). There are also the patriotic verse of *L'Année terrible* (1872) and the Republican, anti-clerical tirades of *Les Années funestes* (1898). Many of these pieces deserve to be read more than they are. While some are senile vapourings, others are illuminations of the human mind, and the poet—unselective by temperament—often mingles the two in the same poem.

There are three levels of approach to Hugo. If one cannot penetrate to the third, it is perhaps best to stay on the first. One then remains free to appreciate, without hindrance or annoyance, some three or four dozen poems including all those which we have mentioned by their title.

But by penetrating beyond this, the reader becomes inescapably conscious of the poison which flows through all Hugo's work—the personality of Victor Hugo. It is this Hugo who writes with affectionate pride of himself in the first poem of *Les Feuilles d'automne,* who at the age of twenty-eight weeps over his love-letters written ten years before—not because they recall the woman he wrote them to, but because they recall his own younger self—who addresses to Juliette that cruelly patronizing poem, **'Oh, n'insultez jamais une femme qui tombe!'** and the greater cruelty of

> Quand tu me parles de gloire,
> Je souris amèrement.
> Cette voix que tu veux croire,
> Moi, je sais qu'elle ment.

Hugo, who had tasted the delights of fame, could now preach disdain of such vanities to the woman whose stage ambitions he had stifled. This was the Hugo who kept human beings as pets, so long as they would perform for him, and posed as a martyr in the exile to which he condemned not only himself, but his entire family—with the result that his younger daughter was finally driven into madness. (There is plenty of grief in his verse for the dead Léopoldine, 'cet autre moi-même,' but not a word of sympathy for the unfortunate Adèle, who dared to defy him.) Finally there is themegalomaniac's self-identification with God, easily discoverable in his later poems and well illustrated by his remark to a tongue-tied workman who approached him in his old age: *'N'ayez pas peur. Je ne suis qu'un homme.'*

This ridiculously inflated egoism cannot be ignored, because Hugo makes it the basis of his theory and practice. Once realized by the reader, it can be seen to be everywhere, and then every line he writes is suspect. 'Hélas!' he writes in the preface to *Les Contemplations,* 'quand je vous parle de moi, je vous parle de vous.' But this is precisely what he never succccds in doing. Never was a writer more lacking in his perception of the feelings of others, yet few writers have based so much of their work on their personal relationships. Those he loved go in alive and come out as wax models, labelled *the fiancée, the mistress, the dead daughter, the grandchild,* with hardly a name or a human face among them. The only living presence in that booming echo-room is Hugo's.

But is it? What was Victor Hugo? If there is no satisfactory answer, does not that explain everything? Cocteau summed up the matter when he remarked: *Hugo était un fou qui se croyait Hugo.* Suppose that the whole of Hugo's life, and his work which was so closely bound to it, was a series of impersonations of some ideal figure: the Lover, the Poet, the Seer, the Exile, the Democrat, the Grand Old Man, the God-inspired. That would explain our exasperation with his egotism, which is not of itself an unusual or repulsive quality in literature and is not displeasing in a Villon, a Rousseau, or a Verlaine. But if the ego is placed at the centre of the work, and there is nothing at the centre of the ego, disappointment is inevitable.

We now reach the third level, which transcends the usual limits of literary appreciation. Certain critics have suggested that at the centre of the Hugolian ego was God, or a god. This would make of Hugo one of the great mystics and of his cloud-capped, thundering rhetoric a sublime attempt to express the inexpressible.

While only a celestial judge would be really competent to decide whether this is true or false, we can at least see how it may affect our opinion of Hugo as a poet. What appear most important in this light are not the plainly sensual earlier poems, not the picture-poems, but some of the later *Contemplations* and the pantheistic (or deistic?) broodings expressed intermittently from then until his death in such poems as **'Religio,' 'Ce que dit la bouche d'ombre,' 'La Vision des montagnes,'** or *Dieu,* of which the final lines are:

> Veux-tu planer plus haut que la sombre nature?
> Veux-tu dans la lumière inconcevable et pure
> Ouvrir tes yeux, par l'ombre affreuse appesentis?
> Le veux-tu? Réponds.
> —Oui, criai-je.
>   Et je sentis
> Que la création tremblait comme une toile.
> Alors levant un bras et d'un pan de son voile
> Couvrant tous les objets terrestres disparus,
> Il [the angel] me toucha le front du doigt.
>   Et je mourus.

One would read with closer attention Hugo's description of the Day of Judgment, comparing it perhaps to d'Aubigné's description:

> On comprenait que tant que ce clairon suprême
> Se tairait, le sépulcre, obscur, raidi, béant,
> Garderait l'attitude horrible du néant,
>   . . . Mais qu'à l'heure où soudain, dans l'espace
>   sans rives,
> Cette trompette vaste et sombre sonnerait,
> On verrait, comme un tas d'oiseaux d'une forêt,
> Toutes les âmes, cygne, aigle, éperviers, colombes,
> Frémissantes, sortir du tremblement des tombes,
> Et tous les spectres faire un bruit de grandes eaux,
> Et se dresser, et prendre à la hâte leurs os,
> Tandis qu'au fond, au fond du gouffre, au fond du
>   rêve,
> Blanchissant l'absolu, comme un jour qui se lève,
> Le front mystérieux du Juge apparaîtrait!

And, reading on in the same long poem, one would wonder whether, and in what sense, Hugo had *seen* the immense trumpet of the final angel, with its symbolic dimensions—or whether it was just another instrument forged by his excessive mastery of words:

> Pensif, je regardais l'incorruptible airain . . .
> Sa dimension vague, ineffable, spectrale,
> Sortant de l'éternel, entrait dans l'absolu.
> Pour pouvoir mesurer ce tube, il eût fallu
> Prendre la toise au fond du rêve, et la coudée
> Dans la profondeur trouble et sombre de l'idée;
> Un de ses bouts touchait le bien, l'autre le mal;
> Et sa longueur allait de l'homme à l'animal,
> Quoiqu'on ne vît point là d'animal et point
>   d'homme;
> Couché sur terre, il eût joint Eden à Sodome.
>
> Son embouchure, gouffre où plongeait mon regard,
> Cercle de l'Inconnu ténébreux et hagard,
> Pleine de cette horreur que le mystère exhale,
> M'apparaissait ainsi qu'une offre colossale
> D'entrer dans l'ombre où Dieu même est évanoui.
> Cette gueule, avec l'air d'un redoutable ennui
> Morne, s'élargissait sur l'homme et la nature;
> Et cette épouvantable et muette ouverture
> Semblait le bâillement noir de l'éternité.

Reported or invented? The answer matters a great deal. In its absence one can certainly surrender oneself to a shudder—of some magnitude, but which never goes as near the nerve as the *frisson nouveau* which Hugo himself acutely detected in Baudelaire and such as is contained in Baudelaire's *Le Gouffre* or *L'Irrémédiable*.

In a less cosmic vein, Hugo also has his surprises for those who would confine him to the sensual platitude. There is this Blake-like verse to the **'Horse'**, from *Les Chansons des rues et des bois*:

> Monstre, à présent reprends ton vol.
> Approche que je te déboucle.
> Je te lâche, ôte ton licol,
> Rallume en tes yeux l'escarboucle.

And this from the first stanza of **'Crépuscule'**, in *Les Contemplations*:

> L'étang mystérieux, suaire aux blanches moires,
> Frissonne: au fond du bois la clairière apparaît;
> Les arbres sont profonds et les branches sont noires;
> Avez-vous vu Vénus à travers la forêt?

And this, which foreshadows Baudelaire:

> Et la vase—fond morne, affreux, sombre et dormant,
> Où des reptiles noirs fourmillent vaguement.
>   (**Les Rayons et les ombres**)

In justice to Hugo such poems should be even better known, and a considerable volume could be made from them. Taken in isolation and subjected to examination by an expert alienist, they might enable us to decide whether Hugo, who is known to have been on the verge of madness in 1855, became or remained technically mad—and not merely in Cocteau's half-joking sense—like his brother Eugène and his daughter Adèle. The usual view is that he recovered most of his sanity after a period of intense spiritual concentration and solitude, with which went adventures into spiritualism (the table-turning séances held in Guernsey) and some initiation into the Oriental religions. In that case, his remarkable self-identification with the forces of nature grew out of a perhaps superficial study of Buddhism, and once again he is the *écho sonore* and not the creative spirit.

Certainly the voice of the earlier Hugo persists, now amplified, in his later poems, and the mere hint of those swelling tones causes the too experienced reader to wince away. Perhaps it will be less apparent to some future generation which, knowing nothing of his biography, having lost three-quarters of his work, and reading what they have in the wrong chronological order, will be inclined to set him without reserve on the level of Virgil and Dante. Hugo badly needs a new 'legend', based quite unscientifically on his work and as little as possible on the known facts of his biography.

Hugo never asked or doubted where he stood, but his compatriots have constantly asked the question, not without a certain embarrassment. Gide's: *'Le plus grand poète français, hélas,'* best sums up their perplexities. Putting aside for the moment the seer, the satyr and the democrat, each of whom deserve their separate admirations, we have a poet who, in spite of his compelling eloquence, suffers from the very serious fault that his verse is static. Except in a small number of his best poems, there is no development from stanza to stanza, or from image to image, but only a constant variation of words and images all expressing the same concept. In Hugo's mind, ideas did not beget ideas: words begat words. He saw his outline too clearly before he began to write and his poems, instead of being a chain or a spiral of discoveries shared by the reader, are one long circling round in search of a better formula. And his megalomania compels him to efface nothing, because his first formulation, as much as his last, was part of Hugo. Ironically enough, he almost obeys Boileau's precept of

> Avant donc que d'écrire, apprenez à penser.

But their kinship is concealed by the immense verbal richness with which Hugo floods and covers the single concept with which he starts and ends. Instead of the organic movement which good poetry ought to have, there is only a series of resounding hammer-blows on the same spot. The stationariness of the concepts contrasted with the mechanically rapid flow of the rhythms and the rhetoric points to a disunity between Hugo's thought and his medium, and is the chief reason why he cannot be considered a supremely great artist.

But is he still, for all his faults, the greatest French poet? He has in him the elements of half a dozen poets, none of whom he surpasses on their own relatively narrow ground.

We have pointed to certain foreshadowings or reminiscences of Baudelaire but such passages would be eclipsed or ignored in the work of Baudelaire as a whole. We have quoted examples of Hugo's shorter strophes. . . . Many of Hugo's verses, particularly in *La Légende des siècles,* have a strong Parnassian tinge, but placed beside the exact and powerful work of Leconte de Lisle their weakness becomes apparent.

As a writer of light poetry Hugo is often charming. Many of his songs have grace and wit, as in:

> Moi, seize ans, et l'air morose,
> Elle, vingt; ses yeux brillaient.
> Les rossignols chantaient Rose,
> Et les merles me sifflaient.

Or, more sentimental:

> Et j'entendais, parmi le thym et le muguet,
> Les vagues violons de la mère Saguet.

But next to Musset, the master of this genre, how heavy and fumbling is Hugo. How pompously he writes to his mistress:

> Tu peux, comme il te plaît, me faire jeune ou vieux.
> Comme le soleil fait serein ou pluvieux
> L'azur dont il est l'âme et que sa clarté dore,
> Tu peux m'emplir de brume ou m'inonder d'aurore,

while Musset carelessly, almost mockingly, observes:

> Oui, femmes, quoi qu'on puisse dire,
> Vous avez le fatal pouvoir
> De nous jeter par un sourire
> Dans l'ivresse ou le désespoir.

Hugo consistently ignores the golden rule of love-poetry, whether light or serious, which is to write of the beloved and not of the lover, and in one more instance we must confront him with a poet who was a master of that art. Hugo writes '**A une femme**':

> Enfant! si j'étais roi, je donnerais l'empire,
> Et mon char, et mon sceptre, et mon peuple à
> genoux,
> Et ma couronne d'or, et mes bains de porphyre,
> Et mes flottes, à qui la mer ne peut suffire,
> Pour un regard de vous!
>
> Si j'étais Dieu, la terre et l'air avec les ondes,
> Les anges, les démons courbés devant ma loi,
> Et le profond chaos aux entrailles fécondes,
> L'éternité, l'espace, et les cieux, et les mondes,
> Pour un baiser de toi!

> *(Les Feuilles d'automne)*

Ronsard, promising little less, writes in an entirely different spirit and his final sestet saves everything:

> Si j'étais Jupiter, maîtresse, vous seriez
> Mon épouse Junon; si j'étais roi des ondes,

> Vous seriez ma Téthys, reine des eaux profondes,
> Et pour votre palais le monde vous auriez.
>
> Si le monde était mien, avec moi vous tiendriez
> L'empire de la Terre aux mamelles fécondes,
> Et dessus un beau coche, en longues tresses
> blondes,
> Par le peuple en honneur Déesse vous iriez.
>
> Mais je ne suis pas Dieu, et si ne le puis être;
> Le ciel pour vous servir seulement m'a fait naître,
> De vous seule je prends mon sort aventureux.
> Vous êtes tout mon bien, mon mal, et ma fortune:
> S'il vous plaît de m'aimer, je deviendrai Neptune,
> Tout Jupiter, tout roi, tout riche et tout heureux.

Yet to conclude that Hugo was jack-of-all-trades and master of none would be an absurd under-estimate. He attempted more things than he achieved successfully, yet in his totality he was unlike any other poet and in his own speciality—the voice of Jupiter-Prometheus—he could be magnificent. Perhaps as the nineteenth century recedes still further from us and takes on more of the attributes of a teeming, boisterous second Renaissance, Hugo will be prized as its most perfect representative.

Paul Valéry   (essay date 1958)

SOURCE: "Victor Hugo, Creator through Form," in *The Art of Poetry,* translated by Denise Folliot, Vintage Books, 1958, pp. 251-59.

[*In this essay, Valéry discusses the enduring quality of Hugo's poetic genius.*]

Victor Hugo is said to be dead, to have been dead for fifty years. . . . But an impartial observer would not be so sure. Only the other day he was being attacked just as though he were alive. An attempt was being made to destroy him. That is a strong proof of existence. However, I grant that he is dead: though not, I am convinced, to the point some say he is and wish he were.

When, half a century after his disappearance, a writer still provokes heated discussion, one may be free from anxiety about his future. There are centuries of vigor ahead of him. His future will settle down into a fairly regular cycle of phases of *indifference* and phases of *favor,* moments of devotion and periods of neglect. For the duration of fame this is a stable condition. It has become *periodic.*

And so one author takes his place as a sun or planet in the literary firmament, whereas another, who was his rival and who originally shone no less brightly than he, passes by and escapes us—like a meteor, a luminous incident that will never recur.

Victor Hugo, a meteor in 1830, did not stop growing and shedding light until his death. At that time one might have wondered what would become of the prodigious phenomenon of his renown and influence. Time seemed, at first to work against them. Other poets appeared; they created new poetic fashions and new desires in the public. On the other hand, critics, men of various degrees of intelligence, dared to examine the enormous work without indulgence. What would become of that immense, almost monstrous glory?

We now know. Hugo, the meteor, the dazzling phenomenon who filled a whole century with his extraordinary radiance, but who, as has happened with so many others, might have gradually become dimmer and burnt out and entered forever the night of oblivion—Hugo today appears to us one of the greatest stars in the literary sky, a Saturn or a Jupiter in the system of the world of the mind.

When a man's work has reached this exalted rank, it acquires this very remarkable characteristic, that all the attacks of which it may henceforth be the object, the denunciation of the errors that sully it (and they are made the most of), the blemishes one finds in it, are infinitely more helpful than harmful. It is not hurt by them so much as revived and as it were rejuvenated. Its enemies are only apparent enemies; in reality, they aid it powerfully to attract still more attention and to overcome once more the truly great enemy of the written word: *oblivion.* Once a certain threshold is crossed, therefore, all the effort expended against a man's work only strengthens its established existence, directs public opinion to it, and forces the public once more to recognize in it *a certain enduring principle* against which objections, mockery, analysis itself, can do nothing.

Further, one could well assert that at this stage the faults of the work, when they are as outstanding as the work itself, act as foils to its beauties and, moreover, provide criticism with opportunities for easy triumphs, for which in the end the work may be grateful.

But what is this enduring principle, this curious quality which preserves writings from being entirely effaced, endows them with a value very similar to that of gold, since, sustained by it, they oppose the effects of time by some kind of marvelous incorruptibility?

Here is the reply, whose excellent formula I take from Mistral. "Form alone exists," said the great poet of Provence. "Only form preserves the works of the mind."

To demonstrate the truth of this simple and profound saying, it is enough to notice that primitive literature, which is not *written,* which is kept and transmitted only by the actions of a living being, by a system of exchanges between the speaking voice, the hearing, and the memory, is necessarily a rhythmical, sometimes rhyming, literature, provided with every means that words afford for creating a memory of itself, for getting itself retained and imprinted on the mind. Everything that seems precious enough to preserve is put in the form of a poem, in epochs that do not yet know how to invent material signs. In the form of a poem: that is, one finds *rhythm, rhymes, meter, symmetry of figures, antitheses,* and all those means which are the essential characteristics of *form.* The *form* of a work, then, is the sum of its perceptible characteristics, whose physical action

compels recognition and tends to resist all those varying causes of dissolution which threaten the expressions of thought, whether it be inattention, forgetfulness, or even the objections that may arise against it in the mind. As stress and weather perpetually tax the architect's building, so time works against the writer's productions. But time is only an abstraction. It is the sequence of men, events, tastes, fashions, and tend to render it uninteresting or naïve or obscure or tedious or absurd. But experience shows that all these causes of neglect cannot destroy a really assured form. Form alone can indefinitely guard a work against the fluctuations in taste and culture, against the novelty and charm of works produced after it.

Finally, so long as the last judgment of works by the quality of their form has not been made, there exists a confusion of values. Does one ever know who will endure? A writer may, in his day, enjoy the greatest favor, excite the liveliest interest, and exert immense influence: his final destiny is not in the least sealed by this happy success. It always happens that this fame, even if justified, loses all those reasons for existing which depend only on the *spirit* of an age. The *new* becomes *old; strangeness* is imitated and surpassed; *passion* changes its expression; *ideas* become widespread; *manners* worsen. The work that was only *new, passionate, significant of the ideas* of a period can and must perish. But, on the contrary, if its author has been able to give it an effective form, he will have built upon the constant nature of man, on the structure and function of the human organism, on life itself. He will thus have forearmed his work against the diversity of impressions, the inconstancy of ideas, the essential mobility of the mind. Nay, more, an author who imparts to his compositions this deep-seated power thereby shows an unusual vitality and physical energy. A vitality and energy that involve sensuousness, an abundance of dominant bodily rhythms, the unlimited resources of the individual being, confidence in his strength and intoxication with the abuse of strength— are not these the very characteristic powers of Victor Hugo's genius?

Hugo can risk all the darts of criticism, face all the reproaches, present his adversaries with many arguments against himself, be prodigal of errors; one may well point out in his work many weaknesses and blemishes, even great ones. Thanks to the magnificence of what remains, these are only spots on the sun.

What is more, this work and this fame have often, and without perishing, undergone the severest test that can affect a man's work and fame. Even before the poet's death, other poets, lesser perhaps, but poets of the rarest quality, were already publishing works of a delicacy or violence or profundity or a new magic that one did not find in his. One might think that this novelty, these marvels of perfection or surangeness or charm, would attenuate, would weaken the great man's dominion over poetry. This result was all the more probable in that they all derived more or less openly from him. Everyone knows that to aim at not following or imitating someone is still in some way to imitate him. The mirror reverses images.

Hugo, however, endures and has power still. My invariable experience confirms this: each time I happen—*I who was so charmed, forty-five years ago, by the magic of the enchanters of that epoch*—each time I happen to open a volume by Hugo, I always find, in turning over a few pages, enough to fill me with admiration.

But I must explain in a few words how this great poetic force began, established, and developed itself.

In the first half of the nineteenth century, the matter of form, whose importance I have tried to show, was widely neglected. Purity, richness, and propriety of language, and the musical quality of verse were little sought after. Facility won the day. But facility, when it is not divine, is disastrous. The romantics generally were concerned with acting almost exclusively on the first impulse of the soul, whose emotions they tried to communicate without considering the reader's resistance, without bothering about the formal conditions I have mentioned. They put their trust in vehemence, intensity, singularity, the naked force of their feeling: they did not wait to organize its expression. Their verses are astonishingly unequal, their vocabulary vague, their images often imprecise or traditional. The immense resources of language and poetics were unknown to them; or else they thought them hindrances, bars to the possession of genius. These are naïve conceptions—of a detestable slackness. We recognize today to what extent very great poets, men like Lamartine, Musset, Vigny himself, suffer and will suffer more and more from having neglected all these things. This is easily verified by considering the events that followed. One then observes that although these poets have given riseto innumerable imitators, they have found no one to *continue* their *work;* that is, no one could develop the ideas and technical qualities that they did not possess. They gave us something to imitate but nothing to learn.

But Hugo arose among them. He noted their verbal insufficiency and the decadent state of the art of verse that all the triumphs of his rivals did not hide from so profound a connoisseur. For that is what Hugo is. Nothing is more significant than his choice of his true masters: Virgil and, above all, Horace, among the Latin authors. In France he cultivated most fruitfully the most substantial and the richest writers we have, of whom many are little known and read, some literally unknown. I refer to the poets and prose writers of the end of the sixteenth century and the beginning of the seventeenth, whose influence on Hugo is undoubted and from one of whom, the obscurest of all, he even borrowed one or two pages. If one goes back from Racine to Ronsard, one notices that the vocabulary is richer, the forms are firmer and more varied. Corneille, du Bartas, d'Aubigné were for Hugo models that in his mind he must have opposed to Racine. Hugo, like all true poets, is a critic of the first rank. His criticism is exerted through fact, and the fact is that he very soon opposed to the weaknesses of his rivals the resources of an art that he was to develop by incessant exercise until the end of his career.

Yes, in him the artist is dominant. For more than sixty years he spent from five until noon each day at his poet's workbench. He spent himself in assaults on the ease and difficulties of a calling that came more and more to be his own creation. Picture this inventor at work. I mean just that: inventor; for with him the invention of form is as stimulating and urgent as the invention of images and themes. From the time of the **Odes** and the **Orientales,** he seems to take pleasure in imagining unusual and sometimes baroque types of poems. But he thus trained himself in all the possibilities of his art. Madame Simone will recite the **'Djinns'** to you wonderfully. This poem is one of the many exercises he performed in order to become master of the universe of verbal effects. Sometimes he reaches an extreme and, indeed, somewhat perilous point. He came to be able to solve, or to think he could solve, all problems not only of art but of thought through the action and artifices of his rhetoric. Just as he knows how to describe, or rather to create, the prodigious presence of all visible things, and makes a sky, a tempest, a Cirque de Gavarnie, a Titan, so he boldly deals with the Universe, God, life, and death with extraordinary and sometimes stupefying freedom. Here criticism gets its chance. It can easily point out monsters of absurdity and puerility in these sequences of magnificent alexandrines. But perhaps in its zeal it does not see that a very profound lesson is hidden in this sometimes startling manner of attacking, or rather of assaulting, every possible question and of resolving them between two rhymes, usually rich. Indeed, whatever may be the problems that puzzle the mind, whatever the solutions it decides to give them, they are in the end (if it is able to give them expression) only combinations of words, arrangements of terms whose elements lie in the alphabetical chaos of a dictionary. Mallarmé said to me one evening, rather jestingly, that if there were a world mystery it could be contained in an article of the *Figaro.* Hugo, perhaps, flattered himself unconsciously that he had written or could one day write that particular page. . . .

Although he did not write it, he wrote others. This man ran through the whole universe of vocabulary; he tried every genre, from the ode to the satire, from the drama to the novel, criticism, and oratory. Nothing, indeed, is finer than to see him unfold his incomparable faculty of organizing verses and words. In our language the capacity for saying everything in correct verse has never been possessed and exercised to the same extent. To the point of abuse, perhaps. Hugo is, in a way, too strong not to abuse his power. He transmutes everything he wishes into poetry. In the use of poetic form he finds the means of imparting a strange life to everything. For him there are no inanimate objects. There is no abstraction he cannot make speak, sing, lament, or threaten, and yet with him there is no verse that is not a verse. Not one error of form. This is because with him form is the supreme mistress. The action that makes form is entirely predominant in him. This sovereign form is in some way stronger than himself; he is as it were possessed by poetic language. What we call Thought becomes in him, by a strange and very instructive reversal of function . . . thought becomes in him the means and not the aim of expression. Often with him the development of a poem is visibly deduced from a wonderful accident of language that has occurred in his mind. The case of Hugo merits long and deep reflections that I cannot even touch upon here.

But how can one, in speaking of this extraordinary man, conclude without invoking his own voice, surely the finest verses he wrote and perhaps the finest ever written. Here they are: they end the piece he wrote, at the age of seventy, on the death of Théophile Gautier:

Passons, car c'est la loi; nul ne peut s'y soustraire;
Tout penche, et ce grand siécle avec tous ses rayons
Entre en cette ombre immense où, pâles, nous
    fuyons.
Oh! quel farouche bruit font dans le crépuscule
Les chênes qu'on abat pour le bûcher d'Hercule!
Les chevaux de la Mort se mettent á hennir
Et sont joyeux, car l'âge éclatant va finir;
Ce siècle altier qui sut dompter le vent contraire
Expire . . . O Gautier! toi, leur égal et leur frère,
Tu pars aprés Dumas, Lamartine et Musset.
L'onde antique est tarie où l'on rajeunissait;
Comme il n'est plus de Styx, il n'est plus de
    Jouvence.
Le dur faucheur avec sa large lame avance,
Pensif et pas à pas, vers le reste du blé;
C'est mon tour; et la nuit emplit mon œil troublé
Qui, devinant hélas! l'avenir des colombes
Pleure sur des berceaux et sourit á des tombes.

Michael Riffaterre   (essay date 1961)

SOURCE: "Victor Hugo's Poetics," in *The American Society Legion of Honor Magazine,* Vol. 32, No. 3, 1961, pp. 181-96.

[*In the essay below, Riffaterre offers his interpretation of Hugo's philosophy of poetics.*]

As any poetics must be, Hugo's is inseparable from a certain theory of inspiration, since the nature of his inspiration affects a writer's techniques.

The poet finds inspiration in what surrounds him. His concern is with the "mysteries which rise to blind him . . . every morning with the sun, every evening with the stars." But Hugo goes far beyond contemplation and meditation upon the spectacle of nature: "the horizon darkens and contemplation becomes vision;" in fact, as early as the time of his first travels to see the world, when he composed *Le Rhin,* his exercises in imagination, and sometimes in hallucination, in the face of nature foreshadow the methods of a Rimbaud.

The poet's task is not only to see the world as a Baudelairean forest of symbols, like the seer who deciphers God's intentions in the book of the universe. He must not merely let himself be penetrated by reality, *he* must penetrate it, and prolong it, so to speak, in the direction sketched out by God: "the vast yearning for what could be, such is a poet's perpetual obsession. What could be in nature, what could be in destiny." In short, the poet must continue the work of divine creation where ascertainable truth gives place to potential truth: "what is it to look at the ocean,

compared with looking at the possible!" It is this rivalry with God—"the poet putting himself in the place of destiny"—this going beyond, which engenders beauty: "in art, however lofty the truth, beauty is still higher."

Prisoner as he is within the boundaries of reality, the poet can find his escape toward the possible only through supernaturalism, "the part of nature that is beyond our senses." To reach it the poet must use observation, imagination and intuition. Here is a sensualist theory of knowledge: nature is the object of imagination, imagination being the interiorization of the world perceived by the senses; mankind is the object of observation, but mankind is still nature, observed in man; "supernaturalism" is the object of intuition. Intuition, or conjecture, makes the poet kin to the scientist, with the difference that the latter's work remains to be perfected, whereas a poem is a final and perfect form. Conjecture is, we might say, an extrapolation from the given of the senses, or, again, a conception of possible infinity inferred from a finite given: "nature mirrored by the soul is more abysmal than when seen directly . . . This reflection . . . is an augmentation of reality." Infinity is the only reality, be it called God or moral ideal or absolute, or simply consciousness of what is beyond man, a consciousness which in itself makes him great and is the source of all poetry.

Any esthetics which limits Beauty by certain definitions or by the application of certain rules negates infinity and sterilizes imagination. This is the case with French classicism. Even irregularity can be a part of true poetry; in one of his drafts, under the title *The Infinite in Art,* Hugo sketches a theory of the baroque: "What makes the charm of irregularity? apparently irregularity is unfinishedness, and in unfinishedness there is infinity." Even ugliness or evil can be part of poetry: "What we call evil we should perhaps call good if we could see the beginning and the end of it. Evil, whether in nature or in destiny, is a thing mysteriously begun by God which stretches beyond us into the invisible . . . Some apparent ugliness . . . is really part of a supreme beauty."

The poet, therefore, eager to contemplate the absolute, must cast away any preconceived esthetics. He must be sure not to let literary tradition interpose itself between him and nature. Not only must he not restrict his inspiration to the beaten path, he has to be more than original. For an original poet may still follow guides and models; in order to create a beauty that can be called his own, it is then sufficient if he has personal traits of style: thus Vergil imitating Homer. Such beauty, however, quickly fades from imitation to imitation, and Hugo often compares "original" poets to moons more and more pallidly reflecting other moons of an invisible sun (here we recognize a personal version of a criticism frequently levelled at classicism by the Romantics). The true mark of poetic genius is thus not originality but "primitiveness." The word has no chronological connotation: "one can be primitive in any epoch: whoever draws direct inspiration from man is primitive." Molière is in *Amphitryon* only original, in the *Misanthrope* he is primitive. The poet copies from life, and his art does not lie in stylistic devices but in *idées-mères,* that is, in archetypes: "What is the use of copying books, copying poets, copying things already done, when you are rich with the enormous richness of the possible, when all the imaginable is yours, when you have before you, at your disposal, the whole dark chaos of types." Let us note the word: the poet does not grope about at random but knows how to select characters representative of fundamental traits of the human mind. Such characters Hugo calls prototypes or "Adams," each of them representing a whole psychological family. Nowhere more clearly than in this theory of types do we see what he means when he says that the poet continues the work of God: "the types are cases foreseen by God; genius actualizes them."

The type lives more intensely than real people do; it is not an abstraction but the union of converging psychological forces all the more powerful because concentrated within the narrow channel of a single passion; the type is a life, but a life in the form of a monomania. Don Juan, for example, epitomizes, in a figure always and everywhere valid, not only the seducer in his various forms but one kind of appetite, just as Macbeth symbolizes another sort of appetite, that of men who are nothing but a blind, insatiable hunger: the conquerors, the ambitious.

These types are powerful poetically because they embody anxieties and desires which man has felt and repressed since his remote beginnings. All these types have the same "point of departure, since they all have the same human heart." By comparing the actualizations of the same types in various cultures, by comparing Priam and Lear, for instance, Hugo easily traces their enduring quality to deep psychological roots: the types are the "points of intersection of creative forces," they all have something of the "same subterranean before-life shadowiness." Never perhaps until C. G. Jung do we find the concept of archetypes of the collective unconscious so clearly formulated.

This underlines how important it is for the poet to be docile to the suggestions of his unconscious, to what Hugo calls the "unknown collaboration." Communication with the mind's depths is indeed a true mark of genius: "what pedants call caprice, what fools call folly, what the ignorant call hallucination . . . this strange openness to the breath of the unknown is necessary to the deeper life of art." It demands of the poet good faith, a kind of naive acceptance of his mind's phantasms: Shakespeare believes in them, Molière does not; therefore the spectre of Elsinore imposes itself upon the reader, whereas the animated statue of the *Commandeur in Don Juan* looks only like what it is, a theatrical machine. Communication with the depths is achieved through meditation, for a time in Hugo's case through turning tables, but above all through night or day dreams (among his papers he left a number of "verses written while sleeping"). More than any other Romantic, more than Charles Nodier, the man who convinced him that the visions of sleep are not errors but knowledge, Hugo believes that "the phenomena of sleep put the invisible part of man in communication with the invisible part of nature." He underscores the fact that dreams permit the poet to perceive what conscious thought represses: "what we unjustly thrust out of our thoughts takes refuge in dreams." In fact, Hugo does not recoil from conclusions such as we might find in modern psychoanalytical writings: John wrote the *Apocalypse* because he was the "old virgin," and "love, unsatisfied anduncontented, changes at the end of life into a sinister disgorging of chimeras."

The respect the poet must feel for the "unknown collaboration" and the attention he turns to whatever in nature escapes our senses, sets up what we might call a "binary" poetics. That is, everything is conceived and expressed in terms of contrasts, in pairs. To begin with, the intellectual process of the creative genius is twofold: he uses logic, on the one hand, to apprehend whatever in this world is accessible to reason or at any rate to sensory perception, and on the other hand "caprice," which is to say fantasy, imagination. And reality is characterized by a fundamental duality, by the coexistence of contraries: the tritest of these are the facile oppositions which seem to delight God, a naive author, though they would incur the scorn of critics— night and day, mountain and valley. This universal duality is the physical confirmation of a Manicheism always present in Hugo's mind. Duality is above all the point in common between art and nature: "the ubiquitous antinomy . . . the ego and the non-ego, the objective and the subjective . . . such is the dark burning conflict, the ceaseless ebb and flow . . . the stupendous apparent antagonism from which a Rembrandt draws his chiaroscuro." This is to say that the artist has at his disposal the same devices as God: the "perpetual confrontation between contraries is the essence of life, in poetry as in Creation." Antithesis is at the same time an organizing principle of the cosmos and the basic figure of rhetoric—a special case of inseparability of form and content, on which more later. Antithesis is not a facile device of rhetorical amplification, as the adversaries of Romanticism have contended, but the graphic symbol of the great metaphysical dichotomy. The poet concentrates on this dichotomy, since it is his task to oppose "the invisible truth to superficial reality," since he has two ears for listening to life and to death, since poetry expresses man and man is "a double being, the boundary of two worlds. On this side of him is physical matter; beyond him, mystery . . . The luminous world is the one we do not see. Our eyes of flesh see only the night." Hugo, in a passage on St. Paul—where, incidentally, God's grace is defined in the same terms as is poetic inspiration elsewhere—attributes to the apostle the dual spiritual life he himself experienced: "half his thought is on earth, and half in the Unknown, and you would say at times that verse responds to verse through the dark wall of the sepulchre." Of course this "binary" poetic approach is not limited to the expression of opposition between visible and invisible; it gives structure to the whole of Hugo's inspiration; he constantly alternates between power and grace, between visionary anguish and the fantasy best exemplified by the *Chansons des Rues et des Bois*; his favorite symbols, such as the image of the two slopes of a mountain which he uses so often, emphasize the faculty which sets the poet apart: that of seeing at the same time the surface of things and their depths.

Neither the role of the unseen collaboration nor any structural identity between nature and art implies that the poet does no more than transcribe an inspiration which is beyond his control. On the contrary, only will power can create a masterpiece: "the will to beauty combined with the will to truth . . . This twofold intuition of the ideal civilizes man by making God manifest, and amends the relative by confronting it with the absolute." True, the content of a poem must be such that "one can never contemplate it without discovering new horizons filled with the mysterious radiance of infinity." Yet form demands an "austere precision," for if the ideal must have some indefiniteness, Beauty "needs contours." The poet of genius turns off his *furor poeticus* whenever he feels like it. The poet is enslaved only by his own idea; it is no sooner conceived than it focuses the entire force of his will: "however disturbing or formidable it may be, the poet follows up his idea to the bitter end, without pity for his fellow man." The poet must keep control of the unconscious forces that drive him: Shake-speare's chief merit, for instance, is that he is "a dreamer stronger than his dream;"Hugo often insists that madness is the abyss awaiting many thinkers who seek to draw knowledge from the oneiric world. Of the three physiological centers which condition literary creativity—brain, heart and belly—the last is the treacherous one: it degrades; this is why sensual poetry offers a spectrum ranging all the way from the *Song of Songs* to off-color doggerel: "Volupté remplace Volonté." Thus will-created art is perforce moral art, poetry being conscience. Hence poetic creation is a kind of heroism, or at least an act of missionary spirit, a pre-Sartrian engagement: "Destiny, especially other people's, must not be taken lightly . . . Any meditation of a sane, straight mind leads to a dim awakening of responsibility. To live is to be engaged."

In the concrete realization of the work of art, this self-mastery is exercised in two directions; first, it maintains immediate contact between the deep sources of poetry and their stylistic expression—an expression which must exert maximal effect on the reader. Second, it aims at creating a reality more real than that surrounding us, by making form more perfectly adequate to thought—the poet has within him "a reflector, observation, and a condenser, emotion."

An effective image, a good symbol, for instance, must have outward justification, appropriateness, naturalness and similitude; it is natural that Don Quixote, being a knight, should ride a horse, and despite Sancho's promotion to squirehood, his jackass mount reminds us that he is just a peasant after all. But in the same way that the phenomena of God's Creation conceal His intention, the poet's symbols serve as a mere facade for the deeper world of his poetic intention. Cervantes invented Sancho as the incarnation of common sense: he "sets him astride Ignorance, and . . . to Heroism he gives Fatigue as a mount. Thus he draws . . . the two profiles of Man and parodies them, sparing the sublime as little as he spares the grotesque . . . Enthusiasm takes the field, and Irony falls into step." The shape of everything, animate and inanimate, has a meaning which the poet's intuition makes clear; his own symbols are as rigorously shaped: in **Dieu,** for instance, where each dogma is symbolized by a different winged creature, infamous

birds represent the lowest grade in the spiritual ascension, and the griffin, a triple animal, symbolizes Christianity, etc.

Thus form is inseparable from idea. This is true also of prosody, because there must be harmony between feelings expressed and the metre chosen: so that "drama more closely resembles nature" and reflects changes in emotional stress, the poet passes from one rhythm to another: "hence the use of the anapest for the chorus, of the iamb for dialogue and the trochee for passion;" a spondaic line of Lucretius, for example, because of its long syllables, looks almost monstrous and full of shadow. But these correspondences are still superficial; the true value of rhythm lies in the fact that it is the form the divine order of the universe takes in poetry. This order Hugo, following the esoteric writers of his time, calls Number: "number reveals itself to art through rhythm, which is the heartbeat of infinity." It is difficult not to balk at such formulas. It is one thing to say that poetry depends on number just as science does; it is something else to state blandly that number governs metre and "the iridescence of imagination," differential calculus and poetic archetypes. The temptation is great to suspect that Hugo is here indulging in mere verbalism. Nothing of the sort: we must not take him too literally. The use of the word *nombre* is not excessive; it is purely incantatory. There are words that make him dizzy, that are like chinks in the wall of reality. Hugo counts on such words to awaken his readers' metaphysical anxiety, to revive in our reasonable world the idea of the Unknown: this method will be taken up again by the Surrealists. But the word *nombre,* for all its poetic haze, has a precise meaning, which is *order.* Hugo has a definition for it: "order is the full development of every man's faculties in accordance with the diameter Nature and Providence have given him."

It follows for Hugo that there is an ideal form for the expression of any idea, a form that is consequently inseparable from the idea: "it is a mistake to believe that an idea can be rendered in several different ways . . . An idea can be expressed only one way." This ideal was to be Flaubert's as well, and it seems to contradict the endless synonymic amplifications so typical of Hugo's own style. Actually he is not groping about for the right phrase, he is exercising a faculty which he sees as the "very essence of poetry," the faculty of "casting light upon all kindred ideas encircling a central idea."

On the other hand, "the idea without the word would be an abstraction; the word without the idea would be noise." Their fusion is no superimposition but an identification, and to separate the two elements would be to vivisect them. In the three stages of poetic genesis, as Hugo sees it—the act of imagination, which conceives, the act of creation, which organizes, and the act of production, which weaves the initial concept into the cloth of the poem—there is nowhere a simple adding of form to content, but rather an exteriorization of content, which makes it visible and palpable. This stamps the idea with the seal of the poet, with what Hugo calls his idiosyncracy, that is to say his style.

It is in the word, the smallest component of style, that this idiosyncrasy is most manifest: "genius . . . thinks the word simultaneously with the idea. Hence these deeper meanings inherent in the word." Hugo recognized the importance of verbal obsessions, both as signs enabling the reader to identify a style, and as indices of the writer's deeper preoccupations; these signs are the more striking because they reflect streams of thought which underlie the more superficial meaning: they are a "sudden blossoming out of the unknown." More generally, the power of words arises from the discrepancy between the immensity of man's inner world and the paucity of the lexicon: to each single word corresponds a wealth of meanings: "sometimes in order to find a substitute for a word you will need a whole sentence." The great writer reveals more of a word's inner meaning than language ordinarily does. The only shoals to be avoided are inappropriate and improper words, and also those which have been worn out by too great success (this includes some of Hugo's own early neologisms).

Because of the part played by words in style, the latter is rigidly conditioned by language. This does not detract from the author's originality, since much of it lies in the effects he is able to draw from semantic contrasts and extensions of meaning: the appropriateness of a word in context is often its impropriety in language; this makes a deeper impression on the reader, since it violates his habits. Thus form is not only the aptest expression of content, it is also built in such a unique and characteristic fashion that permanence is guaranteed which will resist any distorting substitution and will insure the same effects on successive generations of readers. This is also the purpose of the formal restrictions of verse: we should not look upon these restrictions as added obstacles or artificial constraints; like syntax or vocabulary, they are natural and necessary linguistic forms: rhyme after all is as natural in poetic style as the echo is in nature. The structure of the language does orient the development of poetry: Hugo paints a vivid picture of the literary paralysis which follows upon the phonetic decay of a language. According to climate, a language has a predominance of vowels or consonants, and therefore different criteria of poetic beauty: Northern, consonantic languagesemphasize harmony; Southern, vocalic languages emphasize melody.

A writer chooses his words with a view to effects in a context, not within the confines of a vocabulary previously weeded, as the classicists would have it: what would you think of a botanical handbook which excluded certain plants! The appropriateness of any word is entirely dependent upon the context: when Beaumarchais calls his Suzanne Suzon or Suzette, the three possibilities offered by the language, because of their opposition in the text of the *Mariage de Figaro,* have a comparative value found nowhere else, expressing as they do three different psychological aspects of the character.

The fundamental criterion of Hugo's poetics is thus the prevailing importance of the work as an organic whole over any intrinsic value its components might have in other contexts. The poem is a closed world, which dictates its own standards and yardsticks; it is an "entity like nature." Little matter if it shocks tastes for which it was not created. What counts is its harmony in relation to itself. The savage story of Iphigenia, for instance, is beauty and verisimilitude in the wild world of Aeschylus' kings of prey; the same story becomes revolting when garbed in the polite conventions of Racine. Thanks to this concept of the poetic work as an autonomous body, what would be normally considered a defect becomes in this singular whole a stress, an accent: the only real defect is a lacuna in the ensemble. It all comes back to "giving each component the amount of space it demands." True, these quantities, if translated from a work of genius into any other context might seem extreme or excessive. But it is precisely this excessiveness, this *quid divinum,* as Hugo calls it, that sublimizes reality. Vergil may be accused of servile flattering when he sets Augustus among the constellations. This is moral weakness in the eyes of men. But the reader, bewitched by style, steps into the world of poetry, leaving behind all moral considerations belonging to the ordinary world: "il entre en vision, le prodigieux ciel s'ouvre au-dessus de lui."

Robert T. Denommé (essay date 1969)

SOURCE: "Victor Hugo and the Prophetic Vision," in *Nineteenth-Century French Romantic Poets,* Southern Illinois University Press, 1969, pp. 91-129.

[*In the following essay, Denommé examines Hugo's poetic oeuvre, stating that it is representative of the development of French Romanticism. The critic concludes: "Hugo's poetry invites us to strip away the restrictions dictated to us by practical reason and experience in order to view the world more directly with our emotions."*]

The widespread association still made today between the name of Victor Hugo and the term Romanticism attests to the prominence that he enjoyed within the movement both in France and on the Continent during the nineteenth century. The wide range of his poetry from the early academic declamations of **"Les Vierges de Verdun"** ("The Virgins of Verdun") to the cabalistic symbolism of the posthumously-published collections, *La Fin de Satan* (*The End of Satan*) and *Dieu* (*God*) recounts the history and the development of French Romanticism in the most tellingly comprehensive terms we have. The seventeen volumes of poems that were published during Hugo'slong lifetime (1802-85) and shortly after his death unfold both his evolution and that of French poetry from the neo-Classicism and the social Romanticism of the first part of the century to the school of Art for Art's sake and the Symbolism or Modernism of the last five decades. The entire gamut of Hugo's verse is rescued from the limitations of his thought and messages; the power of his imagination and the suggestiveness of his imagery are discernible traits that characterize a significant number of his poems in such widely divergent collections as *Odes et Ballades* (1826), *Les Orientales* (1829), *Les Voix intérieures* (*Inner Voices*) (1837), *Les Châtiments* (1853) and *Les Contemplations* (1856). The last two volumes of poetry and the unfinished epic, *La Légende des siècles* (1859 and 1885) constitute Hugo's greatest legacy to the French Romantic movement and to the restoration of lyricism in France during the nineteenth century. Despite whatever embarrassing pretentiousness may have dictated the poet's intention in these collections, their undeniably convincing and moving lyrical strain overshadow such shortcomings and make their reading an enjoyable and worthwhile experience.

It has already been stated that the originality of French Romanticism rests much less on the idealism of its messages than on the manner in which such idealism is conceived and expressed. The whole history of western thought and civilization reveals the efforts of mankind to derive a meaningful sense of unity and balance from the confusion of a world that asserts itself in terms that are mostly fragmentary and heterogeneous. The evolution of social, political, and religious institutions from ancient times to the French Revolution records the various solutions attained by man in his attempts to explain the enigma of man in the universe. Such views were necessarily geared, in varying degrees, to the existing structure of the time, and whatever reforms were advocated were understandably defined and limited by such frames of reference. The French Revolution was a categorical rejection of the Old Order for its inability to provide and maintain an equilibrium that could meet the requirements of a society that had grown significantly more complex. In its dramatic rejection of the literary principles that guided and dictated French expression since the seventeenth century, Romanticism emerged as the literary corollary of the social and political revolution of 1789. Dismissing the purely rationalistic tenets of the Enlightenment as inadequate to shape modern thought, the French Romanticists sought the extension of expression through their recognition of the roles of instinct, intuition, and inspiration in the cognitive process. The appendage of such faculties to reason, they maintained, would permit man to attain knowledge that was more comprehensive. This view, somewhat cautiously and conditionally endorsed in the verse of Lamartine and Vigny, was destined to receive its fullest statement in the poetry of Victor Hugo. The study of the poet's slow progression to such an attitude constitutes a study of Hugo's verse from his beginnings in 1820 to the early 1840's which marked the turning point in his life and work.

The completed version of *Odes et Ballades* (1828) includes poems published earlier under various titles in 1822, 1824, and 1826. The collection of 1828 affords us the opportunity of examining the technical and intellectual development that took place in the poet's early career. The odes and ballads that constitute the final version of 1828 underscore Hugo's sustained political and religious conservatism even though they serve as a subtle delineation of his evolution from neo-Classicism to a moderately-stated acceptance of some of the innovations of Romanticism. Such obvious odes as the **"Mort du duc de Berry"** ("Death of the Duke of Berry") and **"Naissance du duc de Bordeaux"** ("Birth of the Duke of Bordeaux") bespeak the kind of official and circumstantial flavor that hardly qualifies them to be considered lyrical expressions. The nostalgic Bonapartist ode to heroic action in **"Mon Enfance"** (1823) ("My Childhood") is already a moderately effective personal statement of the *mal du siècle* experienced by the poet when he calls to mind the glory and excitement associated with the Imperial regime. The ode, **"A. M. Alphonse de L[amartine]"** composed in October of 1825 strikes a revealing chord in the development of Hugo's poetics. Advising Lamartine that he must ignore the criticism and lack of understanding of the "epicureans" that prefer to read voluptuous verse, he goes on to define the nature of true lyric poetry:

> Telle est la majesté de tes concerts suprêmes,
> Que tu sembles savoir comment les anges mêmes
> Sur des harpes du ciel laissent errer leurs doigts!
> On dirait que Dieu même, inspirant ton audace,
> Parfois dans le désert t'apparaît face à face,
>   Et qu'il te parle avec la voix!

> ["Such is the majesty of your supreme concerts, that you seem to know even how the angels manipulate their fingers on the harps of heaven! One would think that even God, the inspiration of your boldness, appears to you from time to time in the desert, and that he speaks to you with the voice that is manifest in your verse!"]

Whatever else, *Les Orientales* liberated French versification of its restrictive use of vocabulary and of the stiffness of its metrical system. Aside from a group of poems inspired by the Greek War for Independence, most of the verse in the collection is impregnated more with a sense of the picturesque than with any profoundly personal emotion. As the newly recognized leader of the Romanticists, Hugo asserts himself as the spokesman for the repressed victims of the Greek Revolution in such poems as **"Têtes du serail"** ("Heads in the Harema") and **"Mazeppa"** and **"L'Enfant grect"** ("The Greek Child"), no doubt influenced by Eugène Delacroix's *The Massacres of Scio*, painted in 1824. The orientalism of Hugo is, in fact, his imaginative description of the Spain that he had visited during his youth while his father, the General Hugo, was stationed near Madrid. Complicated by his later readings and his interest in the Near East, the Orient depicted in *Les Orientales* is one imbued with fantasy. Whatever falseness may be discernible in his interpretation of the East is to a large degree compensated by the vividness and suggestiveness of his imagery. The mosques, gardens, and steps that he describes are conveyed in such picturesque language that we are ready to ignore their essentially Spanish flavor.

The Preface to *Les Orientales,* in the tracks of the explosive *Préface de Cromwell* of 1827, proclaims the freedom and gratuity of art in terms that predicted the later pronouncements of Théophile Gautier, the chief exponent of art for art's sake during the 1830's: "Let the poet go where he wishes, doing what he likes; that is the only rule. The poet is free." Such statements mark his evolution from literary conservatism to the expansiveness and freedom of Romanticism. With characteristic verve for masking fact and testimony in order to make his point with more *éclat* than precision, Hugo bemoans the lack of greatness in

French literature in the following terms: "Other nations say: Homer, Dante, Shakespeare. We say: Boileau."

Les Orientales reveal Hugo's unmistakable mastery of French versification. Indeed, the most sustained single impression that is conveyed to the reader is the poet's masterful handling of the formal elements that constitute the collection. The poem, **"Les Djinns,"** for instance, contains seven different types of metre that ascend and then descend from the climax that is achieved in precisely the eighth strophe. The "Djinns" for Hugo represent the evil spirits of the night as they approach with terrifying intensity and gradually disappear in the distant calm. The poem is little more than a technical *tour de force*. As with so many poems that make up *Les Orientales,* the idea in the poem seems to weave itself gradually into the imagery. In other words, the inspiration or the basic idea emerges as an obvious extension of the principal images. The cadences and the increasing and decreasing sonorities produced in **"Les Djinns"** remind us, to an extent, of the effect that is achieved in Ravel's *Bolero*. Like the *Bolero,* also, **"Les Djinns"** is more attractive and pleasing for its novelty than for the theme that it actually unfolds. Yet, the poem does betray Hugo's unfailing sense of instinct; the dramatic form of **"Les Djinns"** does blend neatly with the sense of fright and terror that he meant to portray. The imagery of the poem, the haunting crescendoes and decrescendoes contribute to the kind of purely external musical effects of this minor verbal symphony.

The poetry of Victor Hugo way be viewed as a rejection of the rationalistic principle as too narrowly exclusive as an adequate guide for the acquisition of the depths of truth and wisdom.

—Robert T. Denommé

The mournful strain detectable in some of the verse of *Les Voix intérieures* (1837) is a projection of the kind of poignancy which Hugo's poetry will achieve with sustained force during his years of exile on the islands of Jersey and Guernsey. The death of the last Bourbon king, Charles X, the admitted infidelity of his wife with Sainte-Beuve, the passing of his brother, Eugéne, all served to unnerve the poet and to increase his already noticeable sense of insecurity to the point where he felt compelled to voice his almost paranoiac complaint in a poem addressed to his *alter ego,* **"A Olympio."** For the most part, the lyricism of *Les Voix intérieures* is somber. Yet such rêverie discernible in **"La Vache,"** for instance, announces the kind of attitude toward nature which the poet comes to adopt in **"Tristesse d'Olympio"** of the collection, *Les Rayons et les Ombres*. The last volume of poems to appear before his exile, *Les Rayons et les Ombers* (1840) reveals Hugo's slow evolution toward an increasing acceptance of the creeds and aesthetic codes of the French Romanticists. Somewhat more imbued with the social humanitarianism

of his noted counterparts, the overall effect of the collection is more purely lyrical than it is utilitarian. Among the best-known love poems of Hugo, and of all French poetry for that matter, is **"Tristesse d'Olympio"** ("Olympio's Lament"), composed in 1837 and inserted into the volume of 1840. Written with his mistress, Juliette Drouet, in mind, **"Tristesse d'Olympio"** is an evocation of the places where Hugo had spent many happy moments in the valley southwest of the city of Paris. His return to the property of the Bertin family provokes a meditation upon the passage of time that is underscored with sadness and regret. Yet the poem is far from conveying a pessimistic message; in the face of the seeming indifference of nature, Hugo expresses faith in the power and durability of the humanmemory to conserve the fleeting moments of happiness experienced by man. At the time of its composition in 1837, Hugo had not suffered the loss of his mistress; the anguish of **"Tristesse d'Olympio"** is prompted by the realization that his love for her has become transformed with the passing of time. The external natural setting of the Bièvre valley, recently rejuvenated by the spring, serves as an annoying reminder to the poet that his experience is doomed to disappear into cruel anonymity in the great receptacle of nature.

"Tristesse d'Olympio" illustrates one of the most popular themes of French Romanticism: the attempt to achieve both an ideal and permanent expression of human love. The resultant anguish and agony suffered by the poet when he recognizes that his efforts meet with failure constitute one of the major motifs of Romantic love poetry. Like Lamartine before him, Hugo expressly isolates his passion in nature, far from the crass considerations of a bustling and pragmatic world. Too, by so situating his love experience in a natural setting, he is more easily capable of conjuring up an association of purity and innocence, thus succeeding in appealing to a greater majority of his readers for sympathy. If Lamartine resolved the problem of the disconcerting transitoriness of human experience through the transfiguration of his love for Madame Charles, Hugo attempts to solve the problem by calling our attention to the more positive value to be found in remembrance and recollection. **"Tristesse d'Olympio"** is comprised of some thirty strophes, which may be divided into five parts, each of which may be considered as logical developments leading up to the resolution of the problem which Hugo presents. The first two strophes, serving as an introduction, reveal to us the slightly melancholic poet revisiting the scene of his love experience. These strophes constitute somewhat the reversal of the pathetic fallacy: nature does not reflect the sadness of the poet. The introductory strophes act, then, as a kind of prelude to the theme developed by the poem as a whole. The negatives of the first three lines are counteracted by the positive statements contained in the next nine lines which act as effective antitheses. The vague and general language of the introductory strophes conveys an almost religious atmosphere which is, to a degree, cancelled out by the documented inventory of realistic details which roughly comprise the make-up of strophes three through seven and constitute the second part of **"Tristesse d'Olympio."** The elaborate listing of things, specifically familiar to Juliette Drouet and to Hugo, is prompted by the desire to conjure up the past that is no more. But the poet's present frame of reference as he views the nature setting prevents him from resurrecting the past successfully. This idea is brought forth in the sixth strophe; only his thoughts attempt to fly on wounded wings—they, like the dead leaves on the ground which the poet moves with his feet will never become green or alive again.

> Les feuilles qui gisaient dans le bois solitaire,
> S'efforçant sous ses pas de s'élever de terre,
>   Couraient dans le jardin;
> Ainsi, parfois, quand l'âme est triste, nos pensées
> S'envolent un moment sur leurs ailes blessées,
>   Puis retombent soudain.

["The leaves which were strewn on the ground of the solitary woods, trying under his feet to rise from the ground, flurried about in the garden; thus, sometimes, when the heart is sad, our thoughts take flight for a moment on their wounded wings, then fall down again, suddenly."]

Part Three (strophes eight and nine) utters the poet's plea: is he a pariah, an outcast? The answer is provided him in strophes ten through fifteen which constitute the fourth part of the poem. Nature has changed; the poet recalls the past situation and attempts to relate it to the present; the idea of change is reiterated and effectively conveyed by the repetition and the variations on the single word, change. Part Five, beginning with strophe fifteen introduces the theme of death within the natural setting which undergoes continual change. The reminder "For no one here on earth ever ends or achieves the changes" imparts the final message of "Tristesse d'Olympio:" death ends everything; we all awaken at the same place in the dream. What nature has given to the two lovers, nature has taken from them.

"Tristesse d'Olympio" achieves through the clever counterpointing of negations and affirmations a novel interpretation of the passing of time. Nature is but an externalization of the human psychological process. In his aging maturity, man recalls in sadness the extinguishing dream of the romantic love he experienced when he contemplates the scene of his experiences. But he realizes that nature, however sympathetic it may have appeared to him at the moment of earlier happiness, will not bear witness for him. Hugo concludes with the thought that man has no need of nature to safeguard and preserve his experience. The essence of the experience, abstracted through time, lies in the heart of man. Remembrance is sweetened and ripened by his reminiscence; in a sense, he has vanquished both time and nature since the memory of his romantic love finds its lasting crystallization within himself.

Despite its obvious length, the love poem preserves its unity of thought and theme development. The poet's predilection for antitheses to impart his thoughts is given prominent display in the poem. Technically, **"Tristesse d'Olympio"** reveals Hugo's special talent for varying the rhythm of his verses to correspond or harmonize with the various shadings in the theme that is expressed. Hugo breaks the traditional caesura of the alexandrine with frequent irregularity in order to vary his rhythms and fit them to the moods of the individual strophes of the poem.

"Fonction du poète" and **"Sagesse"** ("Wisdom"), strategically placed at the beginning and at the end of *Les Rayons et les Ombres,* underscore the social and metaphysical dimensions already perceptible in Hugo's poetical creed by 1840. The two poems may be considered as part of the elaborate theoretical amplification that dictated the nature of Hugo's later and best-known verse. Like the "Moïse" of Vigny, **"Fonction du poète"** and **"Sagesse"** asserted the poet's superiority, but unlike Vigny, Hugo tended to view the resultant isolation experienced by the poet less dramatically and more constructively. The poet's momentary withdrawal from the tainted limitation of society afforded him the opportunity to communicate with the forces of nature in order to decipher the secret mysteries of the universe. Such a sense of isolation was permeated with the poet's burning desire to solve the enigma of human destiny and summarily dismissed the haughty and disdainful aloofness advocated by Chateaubriand's *René*. Hugo's poet has more in common with Senancour's protagonist, *Obermann,* who explained his withdrawal from society in the following terms: "I do not wish to enjoy life, I want to hope, I would like to know." With Lamartine's "Réponse à Némésis" ("Answer to Nemesis") (1831), **"Fonction du poète"** hurled a blanket condemnation of the purely egotistical stance advocated by René who does not seek to understand men:

> Dieu le veut, dans les temps contraires,
> Chacun travaille et chacun sert,
> Malheur à qui dit à ses frères:
> Je retourne dans le désert!
> Malheur à qui prend ses sandales
> Quand les haines et les scandales
> Tourmentent le peuple agité!
> Honte au penseur qui se mutile
> Et s'en va, chanteur inutile,
> Par la porte de la cité!

["God wishes that in troubled times everyone must work, everyone must serve. Woe on him who tells his brothers: I am returning into the desert! Woe on him who takes up his sandals when hatred and scandal torture a beleaguered people! Shame on the thinker who mutilates himself by going away outside the gates of the city, a useless singer of songs!"]

Unlike Vigny, but more like Lamartine, Hugo invests a religious or metaphysical ingredient into the poet's function. Nature, as a direct manifestation of God, remains the poet's greatest source of inspiration. The poet's enthusiasm for nature enables him to read and decipher the divine answer to the mysteries of the universe; thus, he becomes the Orphic interpreter of the earth for his fellow man. Hugo speaks of the poet's communion with nature in the first part of **"Fonction du poète"** as the divine bow of the great lyre. This relationship is, of course, intuitively felt and experienced by the poet. Of technical interest is Hugo's increasing reliance upon the technique of antitheses to delineate the theme and message of his poem. The use of such categorical language is to a large extent related to the reassurance with which his poetical creed endows him. There can be no mistaking the function of the poet: he must become the leader of the people, the prophet, and fashioner of the new society that must be created; in Hugo's own words, the poet is the man of utopias who, like the prophet, shares in the comprehensive vision that must guide humanity. Unlike his fellow man, his eyes pierce the veils of an inner, superior vision that he shares with God. The poem, **"Sagesse,"** bearing the subtitle, "A Mademoiselle Louise B.," links the poet's function with that of the prophet: the poet's destiny is to become a thinker, to be a magus and a king, to be the alchemist who from nature and the world extracts God and reveals him to the people.

Despite his increasing awareness of the social and political problems that beset France during the 1830's and 1840's, Hugo resisted committing himself in outright fashion to any specific position until August 1848 when he openly campaigned in his newspaper, *L'Evénement,* in behalf of Louis Napoleon's candidacy to the presidency of the Second Republic. The failure of his play, *Les Burgraves* (March 1843) left him disgusted with the French theatre and he published little or nothing during the years immediately following. The tragic loss of his daughter, Léopoldine, who drowned as a result of a boating accident at Villequier on her honeymoon trip with her husband, Charles Vacquerie, on 4 September of the same year drained Hugo of his literary ambitions and energies for many months. Named a peer of France in 1845, he became more absorbed with the political destiny of France, assuming moderately liberal views. Elected mayor of the Eighth *Arondissement* in Paris during 1848, Hugo became the champion of the poor and the oppressed, pronounced himself against capital punishment, and advocated freedom in education. At work on his monumental social novel, *Les Misérables,* Hugo soon detected in the president of the Republic for whom he had campaigneda dangerous usurper of power. Seven months prior to the *coup d'état* of December 1851, Hugo's newspaper, *L'Evénement,* was ordered confiscated by the reigning prince, Louis Napoleon. Such an unexpected reprisal confirmed Hugo as a staunch apostle of liberal republicanism and inspired his vituperative attack upon the emperor, *Après Auguste, Augustule (After Caesar Augustus, little Augustus)* later in that year. His declared opposition to the emperor, crystallized in his membership on the *Comité d'insurrection,* ended in his official expulsion from France in January of 1852. Fleeing at first to Brussels, Hugo finally found refuge on the island of Jersey (1852-55), then on the nearby Channel island of Guernsey (1855-70), where he, his family, and Juliette Drouet lived separated from their native France. Far from distracting him to the point of inactivity, the eighteen years of exile endured by Hugo confirmed and reinforced his sense of purpose and mission as a writer. At the urging of his friend, Pierre Leroux, he solemnly and formally resolved to dedicate all of his literary efforts to the service of humanity. The exile years inspired Hugo with the kind of fervor and intensity, heretofore absent in his earlier poetical collections, that won for such volumes as **Châtiments, Les Contempla-**

tions and **La Légende des siècles** a place of true distinction in French and western European lyricism during the nineteenth century.

The reign of Louis Napoleon III as second Emperor of France during the years 1851-70 struck a death blow to the French social Romanticists whose works advocated progress and humanitarianism. The strictly imposed censorship during the 1850's left such writers little choice: they could either accept exile and continue their moral and social preachments on foreign territory, or they could withdraw into relative quiet and isolation and practice the kind of literature that posed no threat to the newly-established status quo of the Second Empire. With the exception of such writers as Hugo, Pierre Leroux, and Emile de Girardin, the greatest majority of Romanticists elected to remain in France, diverting their literary talents in the Parnassianism developed by Théophile Gautier and the staunchest advocates of art for art's sake. From his house overlooking the sea in Guernsey, Hugo held to the Saint-Simonian conception of the social function of poetry, complicating his aesthetic creed with his personal notion of the prophetic power of the poet who was both the new priest and magus. His attraction to the magnetism, illuminism, and spiritualism, rampant in certain literary circles in the 1840's and 1850's, was destined to endow his lyricism with greater urgency and intensity than had been manifested before his exile in 1851.

Composed at Jersey during 1852 and 1853, **Les Châtiments,** Hugo's collection of violently effective attacks upon Louis Napoleon and the Second Empire, must be regarded as an impressive masterpiece of satirical lyricism. **Les Châtiments** translate the poet's howling scorn for the Emperor whose blatant usurpation of power in 1851 divested France of her freedom and condemned Hugo to the excruciating pain of exile from his native land. Hugo's anger, as it finds expression in the various pieces that constitute **Les Châtiments,** betrays his personal revulsion against the nephew of Napoleon I as well as the anguish and frustration that he experiences over the scandalous curtailment or deprivation of civil liberty in the France of the Second Empire. The epic and lyrical elements so prominently evident in **Les Châtiments** combine with the obvious political satire to make of the work the greatest and fullest expression of Hugo's talent as a poet up to this point. There can be no serious questioning of the author's sincerity of intention and the truthfulness of his expression in the many violent and often vituperative satirical poems in the collection. Even a cursory reading of the satires conveys the impression of intensity of feeling and emotion that doubtlessly dictated most of the poems. We are far from the amusing mockery of Voltaire in this collection; there can be nomistaking the fury that inspires the poet's attacks against everyone and everything that is symbolically associated with the regime of Napoleon III. The object of Hugo's derision is far from limited to the person of the Emperor; generals, clergymen, politicians, and writers who by their actions or silence acquiesced in the dictatorship bear the brunt of Hugo's often brutal attacks.

Part Four of the section entitled, "Ainsi les plus abjects" ("Thus, the Most Contemptible Ones"), characterizes the kind of lyricism underlying the often very angry and vituperative satire of *Les Châtiments*. Hugo's conviction that France's progress has been cruelly and arbitrarily thwarted by the usurpation of Louis Napoleon's power with the proclamation of the Second Empire in 1852 is conveyed with sustained explicitness throughout the section, so much so, in fact, that the poet's anger appears situated or influenced by an almost hallucinatory setting of hysteria and disorder. Hugo refers to a situation that has today fallen into the realm of history; his poem recalls events that appear more colored by the power of his imagination than by the facts revealed in existing records. There can be no denying the effectiveness of his satirical comments since they are so inextricably intertwined with his own strong emotions and reactions. The author's invective embraces in somewhat devastating language all those who by omission or commission allowed the Second Empire to be proclaimed. Hugo refers to the plebiscite of 2 December 1852 and decries the fear, greed, and stupidity that motivated or intimidated the will of the people to approve and proclaim the Empire of Napoleon III. "Ainsi les plus abjects" rails at the perpetrators of the downfall of France without the slightest restraint or exception. The section may be considered as a huge antithesis between the forces of evil, delineated with such categorical denunciations, and the forces of good, conspicuously absent but implied in the tremulous words of the satirist himself:

Ils ont voté!
       Troupeau que la peur mène paître
Entre le sacristain et le garde champêtre.
Vous qui, pleins de terreur, voyez, pour vous
    manger,
Pour manger vos maisons, vos bois, votre verger,
Vos meules de luzerne et vos pommes à cidre,
S'ouvrir tous les matins les machoires d'une hydre;
Braves gens, qui croyez en vos foins et mettez
De la religion dans vos propriétés;
Ames que l'argent touche et que l'or fait dévotes;
Maires narquois, traînant vos paysans aux votes;
Marguilliers aux regards vitreux; curés camus
Hurlant à vos lutrins: *Daemonem laudamus*;
Sots, [. . .]
Invalides, lions transformés en toutous;
Niais, pour qui cet homme est sauveur; vous tous
Est-ce que vous croyez que la France, c'est vous,
Que vous êtes le peuple, et que jamais vous eûtes
Le droit de nous donner un maître, ô tas de brutes?

["They have voted! Oh! Flock which is brought to pasture in fear under the direction of the church sexton and the village policeman, you, who are filled with terror, just look at the great jawsof the hydra open wide every morning to devour you, your homes, your woods, your orchards, your lucerne millstones, and your cider apples; good people, who believe in your farmlands and who so conveniently append religion to your sense of property; souls that are affected by the sight of money and whose devotion is increased by gold; bantering mayors, dragging your peasants to the voting place; Councilmen with glassy stares; snubnosed priests howling in your pulpits: *We praise the Devil:* fools, [. . .] invalids, lions transformed into bowwows; simpletons, for whom this man is a redeemer, all of you, do you think, really, that you represent France, that you are the people, and that you ever possessed the right to give us a master, you bunch of animals?"]

The three hundred and eighty six lines that constitute "L'Expiation" ("The Atonement") illustrate Hugo's remarkable talent for blending satire with epic elements. Although completed in 1852, "L'Expiation" is to a large extent a reworking of Hugo's earlier speech denouncing Louis Napoleon in July of the preceding year, "What! After Caesar Augustus, little Augustus! / What! Just because / We Have Had the Great Napoleon, / Must We Now Have Napoleon the Little One!" On the surface, the poem, in true epic fashion, recalls the exploits and the destiny of Napoleon. Although Hugo speaks in admiring terms about the first Napoleon, he ascribes his need for atonement to the fact that his coup d'état during the Revolution deprived France of its civil and political liberty. The contrasts with Napoleon III are in ample evidence; compared to the magnitude of his uncle's accomplishments, Louis Napoleon and his empire of 1852-70 appear as a lamentably ironic parody of the great Napoleonic era that opened the nineteenth century. Hugo deftly evokes the great army in the cruel snows of Russia, and the defeat suffered at Waterloo as well as Napoleon's death at Saint-Helena. In Hugo's poem, the great Emperor is made to question God if the various defeats he has experienced are a form of chastisement for whatever sins he may have committed against mankind. A voice from the shadows assures him that his downfall does not constitute the atonement that he must endure to repair the evil that he may have committed. Napoleon awakens from the dead, finally, to receive the chastisement reserved for him: the realization that his name and his fame is ignominiously exploited by his nephew. The last section of "L'Expiation" affords Hugo the opportunity to catalogue his scorn and contempt for the Second Empire. The juxtaposition of the two Napoleons is both clever and effective, since the life and the deeds of each serves as an antithesis to the other. Too, the poet of "L'Expiation" is enabled to voice his condemnation of authoritarianism with considerable dramatic effect by describing the downfall of the former and predicting the forthcoming demise of the latter. At the same time, Hugo's venemous hatred for Louis Napoleon accounts for much of the emotional lyricism. Again, the poet's personal reaction leads him to construct his epic-satire with striking metaphors and antitheses, as in the following lines:

Ton nom leur sert de lit, Napoléon premier.
On voit sur Austerlitz un peu de leur fumier.
Ta gloire est un gros vin dont leur honte se grise.

["Napoleon I, they use your name for a bed. We can see in Austerlitz a bit of their manure. Your glory is a great wine by which their shame becomes fuddled."]

Hugo is at his best in *Les Châtiments* when he depicts the present by evoking events of history with epic touches. His talent, made obvious in such successful pieces as

"L'Expiation," predicts the effectiveness of his unfinished epic, *La Légende des siècles*. His propensity for amplification and exaggeration enables him to conceive of his heroes in nearly superhuman terms physically as well as morally; his Napoleon in "L'Expiation," for example, is a highly idealized conception of the historical figure, much more in tune with the poet's vivid imagination than rooted in fact or acceptable documentation. Conversely, his enemies, such as they are evoked in *Les Châtiments,* are portrayed as cruel monsters and emerge more as hallucinatory figures than as credible persons. The presentation that results is a strangely impressive blend of lyrical and epic satire that helps us to understand the nature of Hugo's conception of Romanticism. The fury and rage expressed against Louis Napoleon and his regime is sporadically relieved by confessional poems of considerably less violence which underscore more directly Hugo's sense of loss and suffering in his long exile from his native France. "Chanson," composed in Jersey in 1853, is the poet's mournful reverie of a France that he knew in earlier days. Such lyrical expression of his nostalgia for his country fits neatly in the overall pattern of *Les Châtiments*: it recalls the ills of the Second Empire with more subtlety and indirection and lends variety to the collection of poems decrying the reign of Louis Napoleon:

...Je meurs de ne plus voir les champs
Où je regardais l'aube naître,
De ne plus entendre les chants
Que j'entendais de ma fenêtre.
Mon âme est où je ne puis être.
Sous quatre planches de sapin,
Enterrez-moi dans la prairie.
On ne peut pas vivre sans pain;
On ne peut pas non plus vivre sans la patrie.—

[" . . . I die from not being able to see the fields where I used to watch the dawn rise, from not being able to hear the songs that I used to hear from my window. My heart is where I cannot be. Bury me under four planks of pine in the prairie. One cannot live without bread; one cannot live either without his country."]

Les Châtiments illustrates Hugo's strengths and weaknesses as an artist. The great variety of expression in the poems attests eloquently to his technical genius, but the almost excessive venom detectable in many instances unveils the weaknesses evident in his own character. Although his images and his metaphors strike the reader with stunning force, they also serve as a constant reminder that the views and arguments presented are so exclusively and narrowly dependent upon the poet's single-minded reactions. Were it not for the dazzling display of poetic versatility so prominent in *Les Châtiments,* the collection, taken in its entirety, would likely have disintegrated into a monotonous litany of complaints and accusations. The kind of Romantic lyricism so evident in the volume stems, in part, from Hugo's exalted sense of indignation which, at certain intervals, suggests an effacement of time and space. At such moments, *Les Châtiments* translates unquestionably profoundly-felt emotions which by stirring recollections of the past excite the creation of intense lyricism at the moment of composition.

When *Les Contemplations* were originally published in two volumes in 1856, the first volume bore the title, *Autrefois* (*In Times Past*), and the second, *Aujourd'hui* (*Today*). Hugo explained in his preface that the poems presented in the first volume were the result of his poetic efforts prior to the tragic death of his daughter, Léopoldine, in 1843, and that the poems included in the second volume recorded directly or indirectly his reactions to the event during the following twelve years. The poet's claim is more interesting than it is wholly reliable; at least, it reveals the dominant source of inspiration for his most universally acclaimed collection, *Les Contemplations*. The same preface discusses the basic thematic structure of the six books that comprise the collection: "It begins with a smile, continues with a sob, and ends with a resounding clamor of the bugle arising from the abyss." The first three books, "Aurore" ("Dawn"); "L'Ame en fleur" ("The Budding Heart") and "Les Luttes et les rêves" ("Struggles and Dreams") are often successful evocations of happy experiences and balanced meditations on human suffering; many of the poems assume the various forms of narratives, descriptive tableaux, elegies, and songs, as well as moral and didactic pieces that recall Hugo's earlier *Les Voix intérieures*. The last three books, especially "Pauca Meae" ("A Few Verses for Mine," Hugo's dead daughter, Léopoldine) and "Au Bord de l'infini" ("At the Edge of the Infinite"), Books Four and Six respectively, reveal a lyricism and a philosophical dimension unmatched in the poet's entire literary production. Hugo's expression of grief over the death of his daughter and his protest against his forced exile become welded to metaphysical considerations which make of *Les Contemplations* the most compelling collection of French Romantic poems.

In September of 1853, Madame de Girardin, the former Delphine Gay, introduced the grieving Hugo and his family to the turning tables or the ouija boards that issued messages from beyond the grave through the efforts of mediums. Prior to 1853, again through the intermediation of Madame de Girardin, Hugo had already attracted the attention of the illuminist-artist, the former priest, Alphonse-Louis Constant, better known by his pseudonym, Eliphas Lévi, who attempted to prove that cabalistic doctrine was at the root of all occult thought. Gustave Simon describes the 11 September 1853 séance in the living room of Marine-Terrace when Hugo and his family believed they made contact with the deceased Léopoldine. Several other attempts at contact were made in which Hugo transcribed the messages he thought had been communicated to him. Nor was contact established only with Hugo's daughter; the poet of *Les Contemplations* believed he communicated with the spirits of Moses, Shakespeare, and Luther as well as a variety of somewhat lesser known historical figures. Gwendolyn Bays points out that the séances were not resumed after Hugo was forced to leave Jersey for Guernsey in 1855, presumably on the order of the poet's doctor who feared that his patient's mental health would become severely endangered by his persistence in such activities. Whatever else, these experiences with the voices and spirits from the great beyond provided Hugo with the assurances necessary for him to evolve the tenets of his newly-found religion in which he assumed the role of priest and magus.

Declarations of his new religiosity appear in such collections as Books Four and Six of *Les Contemplations, Dieu,* and *La Fin de Satan.*

There can be little doubt that Hugo's brushes with the occult forces of spiritualism and the ouija boards are responsible for the amplification and the intensification of his conception of the poet's function after 1853. Not only is the emotional quality in the poems concerning his deceased daughter charged with greater poignancy and authenticity, but there is also ample evidence of Hugo's growing need to expand the scope of his poetic vision in the first three books of *Les Contemplations* as well. His exper-iences with occult forces rescued Hugo from the despair and discouragement brought on by his exile, and they provided him with the sense of direction that enabled him to assert himself with sustained assurance. The knowledge that had been revealed to him during the spiritualist séances convinced him that he had found at last the key to the mystery of the universe. This secret he wished to convey to his fellow man by assuming the role of a prophet, elected specifically by God, to collaborate in the work of making known the way to man's redemption. The twenty-sixth poem, found in Book Two, entitled **"Crépuscule"** ("Twlight"), allegedly completed in August of 1854, is one of the more obvious attempts on the part of Hugo to reach out for the kind of supra-terrestrial knowledge provided him in such séances.

"Crépuscule" is ostensibly a meditation on the nature of human love. Hugo's contemplation of love takes place on an absolute level since he strives to balance it with the idea of death and the complete destiny of man. The first lines plunge the reader immediately into the unreal setting of the supernatural world:

> L'étang mystérieux, suaire aux blanches moires,
> Frissonne; au fond du bois la clairière apparaît;
> Les arbres sont profonds et les branches sont noires;
> Avez-vous vu Vénus à travers la forêt?

> ["The mysterious pond, a shroud for the watery substances, shivers; in the depths of the woods a clearing appears; the trees are thick and the branches are black; have you seen Venus anywhere in the forest?"]

The title, "Twilight," announces mystery, and the alexandrine lines aptly convey the sense of gravity that permeates the poem. The setting is rather one of a séance: "shroud" carries with it a suggestion of the dead, and the luminous quality perceptible in the undulating white moires conveys the idea of life within the shadows and points to the possible presence of spirits. This strophe portrays something considerably more than the poet's melancholia; the question posed in the fourth line, "Have you seen Venus?," translates the nature of Hugo's vision: he wishes to know and so he asks the question that will penetrate the secrets of the unknown. To an extent, we may characterize **"Crépuscule"** as a visionary or hallucinatory poem; we may detect the fusion of material and spiritual elements as

the poet's attempt to bridge the gap between the known visible world and the mysterious invisible world of the dead. Nor is matter simply relegated to the natural order in Hugo's poem: the highly imaginative use of images succeeds in suggesting such an ethereal setting that the imagery becomes a part of the vision itself—the invisible, spiritual world made visible. The thickness of the trees and the black branches, Hugo's setting for the lovers who are walking, issue a call beyond the visible reality to the unreal or supernatural world suggested by the "shroud" and the "watery white substances."

The secret of God is revealed to the two lovers by the blade of grass encountered in the third stanza. Nature as represented by the blade of grass is transformed by Hugo into a supernatural agent which becomes the main protagonist in this visionary poem. The poet, here the lovers, enters into communion with it in order to receive some kind of answer to the cosmic enigma of human life and death. The revelation contained in the first line of the fourth strophe constitutes the theme of **"Crépuscule:"** "God wants us to have loved." Life and death are joined only by love which provides the single, continuous line to eternity. The dead pray for the living; death transforms love into prayer. The last three strophes close the curtain to the vision: the glowworm alluded to in the fifthstrophe represents the bridge between the natural and supernatural orders by evoking the countryside and by suggesting the idea of the buried ones. The torch light symbolizes love transformed into prayer after death; the grass and the tomb quiver and become silent. The revelation is completed and the hand of the supernatural draws the curtain as everything returns once again to the natural order.

> Les mortes d'aujourd'hui furent jadis les belles.
> Le ver luisant dans l'ombre erre avec son flambeau.
> Le vent fait tressaillir, au milieu des javelles,
> Le brin d'herbe, et Dieu fait tressaillir le tombeau.

> ["The dead women of today were the beautiful women of yesteryear. The glowworm in the shadows roams with his torch light. In the midst of the bundles of wheat, the wind causes the blade of grass to quiver and God causes the tomb to throb."]

"Crépuscule" dramatically underscores the intimately personal nature of the religiosity that resulted from Hugo's experiences with the turning tables of Jersey and the spiritualist séances of the early 1850's. Hugo's religious belief is largely dictated by his need to be consoled and reassured in his personal life. The religious beliefs that he evolved became an integral part of his poetic creed which he unhesitatingly expounded in his poems from then on. However unorthodox or extreme his views of "visions" may appear to us as they find expression in his poetic production, they are nearly always related in some fashion and to some degree to the recognizable, conventional world of reality. The fact that his religious inspiration is so directly connected with his own experience prevents Hugo from embarking with any sustained degree upon a completely hallucinated realm of the imagination. His mystical illusion always refers itself eventually, however briefly, to realistic elements which heighten the reader's fascination. There exists in such poems an immediacy or urgency of expression that makes them resemble the poetry of such modernists as Baudelaire and Rimbaud. The presence of such a visionary poem as **"Crépuscule"** in the second book of *Les Contemplations* points out Hugo's literary progression from the kind of carefully rearranged recollections found in his **"Tristesse d'Olympio,"** for instance. The sense of frenzy, excitement, and immediacy which emerges from **"Crépuscule"** foreshadows the manner of the later French Symbolists.

It would be a gross exaggeration to assume that all of the poems in *Les Contemplations* reveal such metaphysica verse signed before and after 1843 assumes the tone of simple elegy. The third poem of the section entitled "Aurore," called simply, **"Mes deux Filles"** ("My Two Daughters"), is a case in point. More than direct descriptions of his daughters, Léopoldine and Adèle, the poem is somewhat impressionistic in that the images constitute a dreamy, moody setting for the two girls. The familiar but clever contrast between the white carnations, the dusk, and the butterfly suggests with effective indirectness the idea of the charm and the delicacy possessed by the two girls. The mood of Hugo at the writing of the poem is injected with unobtrusiveness; as a result, the portrait of Léopoldine and Adèle is conveyed in unusually quiet yet eloquent terms. By contrast, such direct didacticism as the lengthy **"Réponse à un acte d'accusation"** was meant as a reply to the charges contained in Alexandre Duval's pamphlet that he held a perverted influence on French letters. There can be little mistaking the programmic tone of the piece; Hugo defines the intention of his poetry with such bluntness that the poem verges on the bombastic. Ironically, the revolutionary aims of Romanticism are defined and described in the extreme language that characterizes his own Romanticwriting.

> Lanterne dans la rue, étoile au firmament.
> Elle entre aux profondeurs du langage insondable,
> Elle souffle dans l'art, porte-voix formidable;
> Et, c'est Dieu qui le veut . . .

> ["A lantern in the street, a star in the firmament. She [the literary revolution] enters into the depths of the fathomless language, she breathes into art, the tremendous megaphone, and, it is God that wishes it so . . ."]

Book Four, entitled, "Pauca Meae," contains without a doubt the most touchingly effective lyricism in Hugo's entire poetic output. The poems in this section recall the memory of his daughter, Léopoldine, who succumbed under tragic circumstances while Hugo was on a trip in the Pyrenees in September of 1843. By and large, the poems contain none of the despairing and inconsolable grief which the poet is reputed to have borne in the year immediately following the accident. The poems which constitute "Pauca Meae" are rather eloquent yet emotional meditations that evoke the memory of his daughter; they more frequently than not assume the form of simple and direct elegies. Despite the tone of relative restraint that may be discerned,

the poems translate Hugo's grief in heartrending terms whose sincerity of expression cannot be questioned. The rhythmic harmony of the majority of these verses combines with often striking imagery from which the intensity of the poet's total emotional experience may be deciphered. The father's despair over the loss of his beloved child is counterbalanced with quiet effectiveness by his heroic attempts at resignation. The sense of revolt that he experiences is ultimately assuaged by the appeasement he finally attains in such humble and quivering resignation. The poems unfold most eloquently Hugo's talent and genius as a lyricist principally because they are almost completely devoid of the pretentiousness of the verbal or pseudo-intellectual polemics that mar so much of his other verse. The poems in this section constitute one of Hugo's most distinguished poetic legacies for posterity.

Of the seventeen poems that celebrate the memory of Léopoldine, **"A Villequier,"** composed for the first anniversary of her death, 4 September 1844, and expanded somewhat in 1846, is Hugo's most perfectly achieved expression of paternal grief. The prayerful tone of restraint and resignation invites the kind of pathos seldom elicited with such force in the poetry of Victor Hugo. The skillful alternation of the familiar stanza forms of the elegy provides the variety of rhythm necessary to sustain the emotional warmth and development of the contemplation. The juxtaposition of such different stanza forms has the effect of a counterpoint between the alternating moods of doubt, revolt, resignation, and appeasement. The poet's heavy reliance upon antitheses stems more from the nature of his inspiration and conviction than upon any willful intent to produce dazzling and startling effects. There can be no doubting Hugo's genuineness or sincerity in the poem; despite its ultimate restraint, **"A Villequier"** conveys the sense of catastrophic loss produced by the death of his eldest daughter. Yet the poem is not entirely freed of the poet's own idea of his importance as an educator of the masses, even though, admittedly, the apostrophe is convincingly enough joined to the main theme of the elegy to prevent it from attaining any overbearing dimension.

> Je vous supplie, ô Dieu! de regarder mon âme,
>   Et de considérer
> Qu'humble comme un enfant et doux comme une femme,
>   Je viens vous adorer!

> Considérez encor que j'avais, dès l'aurore,
> Travaillé, combattu, pensé, marché, lutté
> Expliquant la nature à l'homme qui l'ignore,
> Eclairant toute chose avec votre clarté;
> Que j'avais, affrontant la haine et la colère,
>   Fait ma tâche ici-bas,
> Que je ne pouvais pas m'attendre à ce salaire . . .

> ["O God! I beg you to look into my soul, and to consider that, with the humility of a child and the gentleness of a woman, I come to worship you! Consider again that, from the dawn, I have worked, fought, thought, marched, struggled, explaining nature to man from whom it escapes, illuminating everything

with your light; that, confronting hatred and anger, I had accomplished my duty here on earth, and that I could not expect this reward . . ."]

Like the poems, **"Trois Ans après"** ("Three Years After") and **"Mors"** ("Death"), **"A Villequier"** translates what Pierre Moreau has termed the "positive force" of the human memory and imagination which has produced in "Pauca Meae" the reflection of Hugo's richly complicated soul state.

Like the majority of the Romantic poets, Hugo considered the forces of nature as the expression of the will of God which revealed crucial secrets of the meaning of the universe to man. The poem, **"Mugitusque Boum"** ("The Boom of the Oxen"), the title and theme of which is partly inspired by Vergil's *Georgics,* is the lyrical expression of Hugo's belief that the principle of love is contained within the bosom of the animate and inanimate elements of nature. In **"Mugitusque Boum,"** it is the voice of the oxen that teaches man: "To love unceasingly, to love always, and to love again." The inspiration of the piece may be easily traced to Hugo rather than to Vergil who is indirectly extolled. The statement of Hugo's personal vision of the universe is readily discernible: man tends to be dominated by nature into which he gradually becomes absorbed whereby he is enabled to achieve his own self-definition.

Hugo's experiences with the occult forces and spiritualism at Jersey during 1853 further complicated and deepened his conception of the poet as prophet or magus, an idea that he had suggested in *Les Voix intérieures* of 1837 and which had been shared, in varying degrees, with most of the French Romantic poets. The seven hundred and ten lines that comprise **"Les Mages,"** completed in April of 1855, describe the function and responsibility of the poet as interpreter of the voices of God, Nature, and Humanity. Again, the assurances of the superiority of the vision which Hugo believes he possesses, thanks to his spiritualist conversations with the great men of history, leave their imprint upon the seventy-one strophes by conveying the immediacy of an impression or experience rather than the balanced or ordered refashioning of a past emotion or feeling. The theme of **"Les Mages"**—that the superior man, the thinker, the scholar must through the articulate expression of their genius guide humanity toward its betterment and solve the most pressing enigmas of the universe—announces the tenor of Hugo's unfinished, yet nevertheless, monumental epic, *La Légende des siècles.* The almost interminable listing of the eighty names approved by the poet as priests intermediary between God and mankind is a fairly comprehensive review of the world's greatest artists, scientists, and scholars up to the time. The thirtieth strophe speaks of the poet's inherited gift from God to decipher the mysteries of nature for his fellow man; despite its programmic appeal, Hugo's talent as a lyricist is still very much in evidence:

Comme ils regardent, ces messies!
Oh! comme ils songent, effarés!
Dans les ténèbres épaissies
Quels spectateurs démesurés!
Oh! que de têtes stupéfaites!

Poètes, apôtres, prophètes,
Méditant, parlant, écrivant,
Sous des suaires, sous des voiles,
Les plis des robes pleins d'étoiles,
Les barbes au gouffre du vent!

["How they gaze, these messiahs! Oh! how they think, bewildered! in the thickening darknesses, what inordinate spectators they are! Oh! what astounding heads they have! Poets, apostles, prophets, meditating, speaking, writing, under shrouds, under veils, the folds of their gowns are filled with stars, their beards are filled with the abyss of the wind!"]

The collaboration between the magus-prophet and God which Hugo implies in **"Les Mages"** as well as elsewhere in *Les Contemplations* is momentarily challenged by the poet himself when he decreed the following formula to his fellow poets so that in times of stress they might affirm their wills to the acquisition of truth whatever the cost: "He must steal the eternal fire from the austere heavens, conquer his own mystery and steal from God." When the poem, **"Ibo"** ("I Shall Go"), was first published in *Les Contemplations,* the poet was decried for his haughtiness and audacity. Hugo's intention was misunderstood, for **"Ibo"** was meant as an affirmation of the poet's resolve to persist in his lonely quest for knowledge and truth. If the poem is seen as an expression of the defiance, such as we find in the poems of Baudelaire and Rimbaud, for example, it is important to observe that Hugo chooses to emphasize in his poem the constructive aspect of the poet's willful alienation from convention and tradition. The *poètes maudits* of the Parnassian and Symbolist schools emphasized, by contrast, the sense of decadence and disintegration experienced by the poet as a result of his revolt.

"Ibo" leads logically to **"Ce que dit la Bouche d'ombre"** ("What the Voice from the Abyss Decrees"). The seven hundred and eighty-six lines that comprise this long poem provide us with a summation of Hugo's somewhat cosmogonic solution to the fundamental problems besetting man. Most likely completed in 1854 and presented as the poet's philosophic conclusion to the six books of *Les Contemplations,* **"Ce que dit la Bouche d'ombre"** makes it plain that Hugo's alleged communication with the spirits of the departed at Jersey confirmed the views that he expounded in his poetry. Despite the pseudo-metaphysical intentions of **"Ce que dit la Bouche d'ombre,"** the powerful manipulation or transposition of ideas with striking imagery rescues this impressive piece from any kind of overbearing pretentiousness and bequeaths to it a memorable lyrical quality. Hugo's cosmogonic system is an entirely personal one, dictated by his own need to assuage the grief and despair engendered by the death of his daughter, and his banishment from France by Louis Napoleon and the regime of the Second Empire. The poem is in fact a treatise on the problem of death and the destiny of man after death. Hugo evolves his own conception of eternity and links it to the origin and nature of evil in the universe. Rejecting the view that punishment, like reward, is something eternal, he explains evil as something heavily engrossed in matter that aspires through human and temporary forms of chastisement to the perfection of the spirit; he establishes the uninterrupted chain of beings wherein the deceased evil doers may expiate their wrongs. Hugo's conception of the transmigration of souls in the universe causes him to see nature through the magnified vision of hallucination.

> Oh! que la terre est froide et que les rocs sont durs!
> Quelle muette horreur dans les halliers obscurs!
> Les pleurs noirs de la nuit sur la colombe blanche
> Tombent; le vent met nue et torture la branche;
> Quel monologue affreux dans l'arbre aux rameaux
>   verts!
> Quel frisson dans l'herbe! Oh! quels yeux fixes
>   ouverts
> Dans les cailloux profonds, oubliettes des âmes!
> C'est une âme que l'eau scie en ses froides lames;
> C'est une âme que fait ruisseler le pressoir.
> Ténèbres! l'univers est hagard.

> ["Oh! how cold is the earth and how hard are the rocks! What silent horror resides in the hidden thickets! The black cries of the night fall upon the white dove; the wind strips and tortures the tree branch. What a horrible monologue takes place in the tree with the green branches! What a shudder runs through the grass! Oh! what fixed open eyes are in the underlying pebbles, dungeons of souls! The water saws a soul in its cold lamina; it is a soul that causes the wine press to trickle. Darknesses! the universe is haggard."]

The punishment of the wicked, however, is terminal as Hugo cries out: "there is no eternal hell!" Hell on earth is destined to be eventually transformed into the Edens of heaven, and the work of the genius, the prophet and the poet is to lead mankind slowly to that evolution.

The beliefs expressed in *Les Contemplations* by and large incited the poet to assume a role of leadership in world affairs. As self-appointed arbiter, he intervened with astonishing effrontery in domestic and international issues to the point where he became eventually known throughout the Western World. With all the assurance of a patriarch, from his residence overlooking the ocean at Guernsey, Hugo addressed pleas to the Swiss in behalf of the abolition of capital punishment, encouraged the Mexicans to do battle against Napoleon III, and reminded England of its duty toward the Irish. Like the philosophy presented in *Les Contemplations,* Hugo's advice elicited the mixed reactions of its receivers. The reception of the poet's advice as well as of his latest collection of poems perhaps contains the most telling clue of the nature of his work. Whatever may be said of the vagueness of his metaphysical revelations or visions, *Les Contemplations* translates admirably the poet's complete lack of concern for the accepted criteria by which reality is judged or measured. In Books Four and Six especially of his collection, the rational substratum is meager to the point of being completely overcome by the poet's delirium and emotion. We are a long way from the reasonable epigrams of Voltaire and other exponents of the rationalist interpretation of the Enlightenment in Hugo's *Les Contemplations*. The visionary aspects, frequently conveyed with convincing sincerity, make it plain that the poet's sensitivity was considerably sharpened by the long exile and isolation endured in the

Channel Islands. Much of the lyricism of *Les Contemplations* is endowed with a force that is as sweeping as it is suggestive. If the collection still commands our attention and elicits our interest, it is rather for the manner in which the principal poems are expressed than for any explicit theme or message which they may impart. For their undeniably personal strain and emotional scope, *Les Contemplations* serves as an excellent example of what we mean when we speak of Romantic poetry. For the sense of immediacy and urgency which so many of the poems convey, *Les Contemplations* serves as a valid illustration of the kind of verse that represents a transition from Romanticism to Modern poetry.

The poetic form perhaps best attuned to the Romantic mind or temper was the epic, and such French Romanticists as Lamartine and Vigny experimented with it without succeeding in achieving any special distinction. For the more visionary Hugo, however, with a comprehensive view of humanity to relate to his readers, the epic form proved to be a challenge which he met with daring and achieved for himself, in so doing, a measure of greatness as an epic poet. Published in three series, 1859, 1873, and 1877, *La Légende des siècles* constitutes in actual fact a series of episodes or "lesser epics" which purport to commemorate the major events and institutions that have shaped humanity from the days of the Old Testament to the nineteenth century. Finally joined together in a collective edition in 1885, *La Légende des siècles* was originally meant to contain the crowning poems, *La Fin de Satan* and *Dieu* which remained uncompleted and whose fragments were published posthumously. Hugo's conception of the epic differs considerably from that of his predecessors in that like his counterpart, Lamartine, in the fragments of *Les Visions,* Hugo believed that the whole history of humanity could be achieved through the composition of individual poems linked together by a fundamental theme or thesis. *La Légende des siècles* traces the ascension of man from the darkness of ignorance to the light of progress and humanitarianism, and may be considered as a logical corollary to the apocalyptic poem in *Les Contemplations,* **"Ce que dit la Bouche d'ombre."** Hugo's comprehensive intention in the vast epic is perhaps best stated by himself in the 1859 perface to the First Series: "To express humanity in a kind of cyclic work; to portray it successively and simultaneously from all aspects, the historical, the legendary, the philosophical, the religious, and the scientific, all of which eventually fuse into a single and immense movement of ascension toward enlightenment."

H. J. Hunt points out that if **"Ce que dit la Bouche d'ombre"** revealed the secret of man as an individual, Hugo still sought to explain the unity of the human race as he saw it in history and created his epic to meet this end. The many episodic poems that constitute *La Légende des siècles* are in fact bound together by three doctrinal sections that set forth the poet's interpretation of the progress of man in time. "La Vision d'où est sorti ce Livre" ("The Vision out of Which Was Born this Book"), "Le Satyre," and "Pleine Mer—Plein Ciel" ("Full Ocean—Full Sky") explain the core of Hugo's epic on humanity.

The vastness of such an enterprise afforded Hugo ample opportunity to inject into the series the degree of magnitude of his own vision of humanity. *La Légende des siècles* is underscored with the poet's own political and social views; numerous poems are little more than vitriolic attacks upon kings, princes, and emperors as the repressive forces that prevented mankind for so long from ascending to an enlightened state. Conversely, the almost purely lyrical treatment of the plight of the poor in such notable sections as "Les pauvres Gens" ("The Poor People") in the 1859 series, is striking by its eloquence. Metaphysical allusions to the mysterious, the infinite, and the supernatural abound; Hugo preaches a kind of deistic devotion to God. *La Légende des siècles* may be likened to a group of uneven tableaux or frescos, some impressive and others merely banal or childish, that often capture the sense of the picturesque. The poet's temperament is easily visible in the great canvases which he paints; his predilection for conceiving reality and super-reality in antithetical strokes is readily discernible throughout the three series of poems. Nearly everything is contrasted in terms of good and evil, darkness and light, ignorance and truth. Yet such simplicity of conception is more frequently than not overridden by his outstanding genius to invent metaphors and analogies that lend to the epic tales a sense of virtually overwhelming lyricism. Hugo's imaginative powers were well adapted to the epic genre; his tendency to magnify and amplify endows such biblical and legendary figures as Boaz and Roland, with a sense of grandiose majesty. Yet he manages to transform those elements of magic and the miraculous usually associated with the epic into highly suggestive symbols that represent the various stages in man's attempt to understand the mysteries of the universe that will enable him to ascend to light and perfection.

Among the most celebrated poems in *La Légende des siècles* that best demonstrate Hugo's talent for evoking biblical events with great vividness yet with considerable directness of expression are **"Booz endormi"** ("Boaz Asleep") and **"La Conscience,"** both of them from the first series of poems published in 1859. **"Booz endormi"** is a beautifully achieved evocation from the *Book of Ruth* of the union of Boaz and Ruth from which was destined to emerge the lineage of David and Christ. Hugo's treatment of the biblical passage is a christianization of the Old Testament. The elliptic nature of **"Booz endormi"** announces rather the message of the Incarnation of the God-Man through the intercession of the race founded by Boaz and Ruth. **"La Conscience"** is a much more orthodox portrayal of the guilt suffered by Cain: Hugo stresses, rather, the vigilant eye of God pursuing Cain as the awakening of conscience in man.

Central to an adequate understanding of the scope and purpose of *La Légende des siècles* is the long poem, **"Le Satyre"** which Hugo placed alone under the multiple sub-heading, *Sixteenth Century: Renaissance and Paganism.* So strategically placed at the center of the three series, **"Le Satyre"** may be said to be the synthesis of the poet's philosophical and metaphysical doctrine. The satyr in Hugo's epic is presented as a mythological character—half-animal, half-man; he symbolizes the metamorphosis of man's ascension from matter to spirit. The Satyr, in the end, is changed into a giant, whose immense proportions are meant to suggest those of the universe itself. The Satyr's song before the gods on Mount Olympus relates the struggle of man against their tyranny for freedom and enlightenment. The spirit of man finally comes to dominate the repressive and dogmatic spirit of a useless deity. **"Le Satyre"** is divided into four sections, the first of which is appropriately entitled, "Le Bleu" ("The Blue") since it amusingly evokes the gods gathered on Mount Olympus before whom is brought the Satyr who had been caught observing Psyche bathing. The haughty gods condescend to forgive him for his boldness if he will sing for them. The Satyr's song constitutes the three remaining parts of the poem. Accompanying himself on the flute which he has borrowed from Mercury, the Satyr begins his song with "Le Noir" ("The Black") which narrates the creation of earth, and reiterates Hugo's favorite thesis: that from the inert and unconscious matter emerges life and the consciousness of man. The second song of the Satyr, "Le Sombre," celebrates the effort of man struggling to overcome the heaviness of matter to attain enlightenment, while the third song, constituting the last part of the poem, entitled, "L'Etoilé" ("The Starred") predicts or prophesizes the ultimate success of man in his struggle to rid himself of the shackles of ignorance from the meaningless deity by the achievement of liberty. **"Le Satyre"** represents man's deliverance from the superstitions and the fears that have repressed his expression of freedom and have limited his quest for true enlightenment. Hugo has cleverly made his faun represent the spirit of the Renaissance with its insatiable curiosity for knowledge. In the end, the Satyr assumes the proportion of a Gargantuan giant, towering the silly gods, representing dogmatic religion, who are gathered on Mount Olympus. **"Le Satyre"** expresses the triumph of the spirit of enlightened man over the despotism of the narrow, binding dogmatism that stunted the growth of humanity until the Renaissance. It reveals Hugo's curious blend of the non-transformist interpretation of evolution with his personal metaphysics, partly inspired in turn by Saint-Simonian idealism; the faun sings of the genesis of man in "Le Sombre" in the following terms:

> Oui, peut-être on verra l'homme devenir loi,
> Terrasser l'élément sous lui, saisir et tordre
> Cette anarchie au point d'en faire jaillir l'ordre,
> Le saint ordre de paix, d'amour et d'unité,
> Dompter tout ce qui l'a jadis persécuté,
> Se construire à lui-même une étrange monture
> Avec toute la vie et toute la nature . . .

> ["Yes, perhaps we will see man become the law, overwhelm the elements under him, seize and twist his anarchy to the point of springing order from it, the holy order of peace, love and unity, subdue everything which formerly persecuted him, and build by himself a strange stock with all of life and all of nature . . ."]

In Hugo's estimation, the evil that is present in creation stems from its material texture; **"Le Satyre"** makes evil synonymous with matter, and the problem remains for man to rid himself of this imperfection before he may truly ascend to an enlightened state. As Hunt maintains, the enfranchisement of man is achieved through the discovery of the laws which govern matter which enable him to harness it for his own purposes and thus allows him to follow his own destiny. The gods assembled on Mount Olympus symbolize the principle of limitation, fear, and ignorance from which the half-animal, half-man, the satyr, must free himself and mankind to permit the new reign of enlightenment. The final words of the satyr's song translate the exultation of mankind in its deliverance from the peril and darkness of ignorance.

> Place au fourmillement éternel des cieux noirs,
> Des cieux bleus, des midis, des aurores, des soirs!
> Place à l'atome saint qui brûle ou qui ruisselle!
> Place au rayonnement de l'âme universelle!
> Un roi c'est de la guerre, un dieu c'est de la nuit.
> Liberté, vie et foi sur le dogme détruit!
> Partout une lumière et partout un génie!
> Amour! tout s'entendra, tout étant harmonie!
> L'azur du ciel sera l'apaisement des loups.
> Place à Tout! Je suis Pan; Jupiter! à genoux.

["Make way for the eternal coming and going of the black heavens, of the blue skies, the noonday suns, the dawns and the evenings! Make way for the holy atom that burns or trickles! Make way for the radiation of the universal soul! A king means war, a god means the darkness of the night. Freedom, life and faith become superimposed on the destroyed dogma! Everywhere glows a light and everywhere glows a genius! Love. There will be understanding everywhere, since all is harmony! The azure-blue sky will be the appeasement of the wolves. Make way for Everything! I am Pan; Jupiter! get down on your knees."]

Except for the poems, *La Fin de Satan* and *Dieu,* published in their incomplete format after Hugo's death in 1885, Hugo's verse as typified in such collections as *L'Art d'être grand-père* (*The Art of Being a Grandfather*), published in 1877, and *Toute la Lyre* (*The Whole Song*), published posthumously in 1888, became considerably tempered and overshadowed by the earlier appearances of *Les Châtiments, Les Contemplations* and *La Légende des siècles.* Both *La Fin de Satan* and *Dieu* take up the message of the unfinished epic, and had they been completed by Hugo, they would likely have been inserted into the three series of poems to round out the epic cycle. *La Fin de Satan,* in a manner somewhat reminiscent of Milton and Blake, transforms Lucifer into an angel of deliverance and liberty. *Dieu* is the attainment of man's enlightenment through his containment of matter which causes the imperfection and evil of the world.

Despite his repeated claims of total and comprehensive vision of the universe, Hugo as a poet stirs the interest and enthusiasm of his readers more for the forceful and vivid manner of his expression than for the doctrines which may emanate from his poems. For the most part, his poetry represents the essence of French Romanticism. His conception or perception of knowledge transcends the rationalistic realm without however totally disregarding it in order to reach out into the intuitive and instinctive world of the subconscious as well as the conscious. Hugo's poetry invites us to strip away the restrictions dictated to us by practical reason and experience in order to view the world more directly with our emotions and our subconscious aspiration toward perfect knowledge and happiness. As such, his poetry moves in the direction of the modernism unleashed by the "acceleration of history" beginning with the French Revolution. The poetry of Victor Hugo may be viewed as a rejection of the rationalistic principle as too narrowly exclusive as an adequate guide for the acquisition of the depths of truth and wisdom. Whatever may be said of the nature of the "truths" or "visions" unveiled in Hugo's poetry, it must be admitted that his poetry does satisfy a partial need to visualize the world with more unity and homogeneity. A reading of Hugo's better verse affords us the opportunity to enrich, from time to time, with our imagination an otherwise bland and exasperating perception of the world by reason and practical experience alone.

Laurence M. Porter (essay date 1978)

SOURCE: "The Sublimity of Hugo's Odes," in *The Renaissance of the Lyric in French Romanticism: Elegy, "Poëme" and Ode,* French Forum Publishers, 1978, pp. 75-106.

[*In this excerpt, Porter examines the ways in which Hugo transformed the ode genre during the early and middle phases of his career.*]

Those contemporaries who were sympathetic to French Romanticism considered that it had revitalized three poetic genres: ode, elegy, and "Poëme." Later in the century, a neo-elegiac strain continues in the love poems of Baudelaire and Verlaine; a neo-epic tendency persists in Leconte de Lisle; and many romantic verse epics of redemption were composed; but the ode came eventually to predominate in nineteenth-century French literature. Such, at least, is the opinion of the poet Banville, who surveyed post-revolutionary poetry in 1871: "l'Ode, je le répète, une dernière fois, a absorbé tous les genres poétiques [. . .] elle est devenue toute la poésie moderne." A dramatization of the poet's creative powers became relatively more prominent in poetry, in comparison to the depiction of private emotions and to the relation of a collective adventure in a timebound setting. [Vigny] moved steadily in this direction. "L'Esprit pur" and even "La Maison du Berger" could be defined as odes. But Hugo was a much more prolific and consistent writer of poems that are unequivocally odes. His treatment of the sublime is the key to his innovations in and renewal of the genre.

Traditional Neoclassical French literary theory distinguished three types of ode according to their tone and subject. The Anacreontic Ode praised wine, women, and song. The Horatian Ode treated a wide variety of subjects with a relatively informal diction. The Pindaric heroic Ode, characterized by a "noble and elevated" tone, dealt with poetic and religious inspiration, moral exhortation, and the destinies of dynasties and nations.

Hugo's early odes, composed between 1816 and 1828, are generally of the Pindaric type. At first glance they seem static, outmoded, and uninteresting, "a curiously petrified form of neoclassical diction in which the middle and low styles have been forgotten and only the noble tone survives, forcing all subjects into its mold." From this viewpoint, the *Orientales* of 1829 emerge as the first great liberation of Hugo's artistic imagination in verse. A closer look at the early odes, however, reveals that "les promesses du vrai Hugo, du visionnaire et du mystique des *Contemplations,* sont, ici, plus perceptibles qu'en aucun autre recueil antérieur à l'exil—*Les Rayons et les Ombres* étant mis hors de pair." Granted that the early Hugo remains mainly within the limited compass of the heroic ode, he nevertheless transforms it decisively during his first few years as a poet.

The essence of the heroic ode was traditionally considered to reside in the "sublime." The concept of the sublime (applied to epics and to tragedies as well as to the ode) was most fully developed by "Longinus" in the third century A.D. Down through the eighteenth century, few later commentators went far beyond him. Longinus explains that the sublime aims at transcending the human condition, either by evoking a superhuman scale and an ideal of divinity which embodies the incontaminate, or by repressing the undesirable weaknesses of humanity—lamentation, pain and fear. Examples given by Longinus and his followers fall into two main categories: the spatial, and the temporal sublime. The spatial sublime evokes the might and vastness of the gods. Olympus trembles when Jupiter nods; the coursers of Neptune leap to the horizon with a single bound. The spatial sublime can be summed up by the metaphor that the world is the house of the gods.

The temporal sublime appears in the heroic human resolve which defies death. This defiance affirms moral qualities which transcend the limits of our mortality. The poet further transcends mortality by commemorating these qualities in the monument of art. So Achilles chooses a short, glorious life over a long and obscure one; Ajax implores the gods to dispel the clouds which hide and protect the Trojans so that he can return to battle, even if the gods then intend to slay him; old Horace, asked what he expected his son to do alone against three warriors, other than running away, replies: "Qu'il mourût." Early in his poetic practice, Hugo renovated both spatial and temporal sublime, discovering devices which characterize the greatest odes ("**Les Mages**"; "**Le Satyre**"; "**Plein Ciel**") of his maturity.

Once the vitality of classical pagan mythology declined, the hero of the ode, epic, or tragedy no longer could affirm his timeless human virtues by defying hostile gods (of course there are striking exceptions to this statement, such as Sartre's *Les Mouches*). So there arose the "moral ode" of the eighteenth century. It sought the temporal sublime on an abstract plane. The poet demonstrated his imaginative power by personifying in detail those virtues which are our immortal part. Hugo follows this tradition in his very early "**Ode à l'Amitié**" (1816: *Cahier de Vers français*). He begins with an apostrophe to this "adorable divinité," and after two *exempla* repeats the apostrophe.

The power of friendship makes men lay down their life for their friends.

The moral ode transcends the fear of death and other base emotions, not by depicting a struggle against a personified human or divine enemy, but by creating episodic, personified anti-heroes who serve to embody human weakness. The moral ode characteristically portrays this anti-self, and ritually expels him from the world of the poem, just before the culmination of heroic resolve with which the ode ends. This resolve is usually expressed through an appeal to some spiritual power to maintain the poet in the happiness of virtue: So Hugo's long second apostrophe to *L'Amitié* concludes:

> Loin de toi ces vils scélérats
> Qui n'ont jamais senti tes charmes,
> Et ne jouissent ici-bas
> Que par la terreur et les larmes!
> Ce n'est point auprès de Plutus,
> Dans les palais et le tumulte,
> Que tu rassembles sous ton culte
> Ceux qui chérissent les vertus.
> Plaise aux dieux que de ce bonheur,
>
> . . . . .
>
> Je puisse enivrer mon cœur.
>
> . . . . .

The "**Dernier jour du monde**," also composed in 1816, carries to its logical extreme the tendency of the moral ode to polarize good and evil with clear-cut moral judgments. God appears on His throne to mete out reward and punishment. Even some stanzas are divided in half to separate the wicked from the virtuous. Later, a heavily sarcastic passage of "**La Bande noire**" will grant the anti-self the unusual privilege of elaborating an anti-ode of its own (*Odes* Book II, number 3). Nobody believes the things a moral ode condemns—sin, cruelty, greed, and cowardice—are desirable, but the ode exhorts us to virtue and demands an active response to the good by dramatizing the repellent nature of its contrary.

Both moral and heroic odes seek to assure the immortality of the poet as well as of the hero. First the creative act associates the poet with lasting material achievements or with timeless moral excellence. Then he proclaims the word more real than the deed. As Vigny put it in "L'Esprit pur," speaking of his noble ancestors, "C'est en vain que d'eux tous le sang m'a fait descendre: / Si j'écris leur histoire, ils descendront de moi." Ever since Pindar, the ode writer had stressed the poet's power to confer or withhold immortality.

Hugo quickly abandoned the moral ode in its traditional form. From late 1818 to early 1821, most of his odes are politically inspired by events such as the Vendée massacres, the assassination of the Duc de Berry, the birth of the Duc de Bordeaux, and the re-erection of Henri IV's statue. But even these odes, mainly referring to the recent past, sometimes transcend it to achieve a refinement of the temporal sublime. First he associates heroic deeds with an implied *Exegi monumentum* topos, suggesting once again that the poem is more important than the history whose memory it preserves; and then he promotes the poem itself from the status of a monument to that of the monument of a monument—a superlative of immortality. By making his poem commemorate not a man, but a monument to a man, Hugo transcends the *Exegi monumentum* topos which leaves the poem itself subject metaphorically to the risks of deterioration and oblivion. Consider **"A la Colonne de la Place Vendôme"** (*Odes* III, 7), or the last stanza of **"Le Rétablissement de la Statue de Henri IV"** (*Odes* I, 6):

Un jour (mais repoussons tout présage funeste!)
Si des ans ou du sort les coups encor vainqueurs
Brisaient de notre amour le monument modeste,
    Henri, tu vivrais dans nos cœurs;
Cependant que du Nil les montagnes altières,
Cachant cent royales poussières,
    Du monde inutile fardeau,
Du temps et de la mort attestent le passage,
Et ne sont déjà plus, à l'œil ému du sage,
    Que la ruine d'un tombeau.

After having described the return of his statue, with magical powers of moral inspiration, Hugo dismisses the statues of the bad rulers or anti-selves which it is the ode's business to purge. These endure, forgotten, in the larval form of meaningless dilapidated pyramids, "la ruine d'untombeau." Thus Hugo suggests the superlative of a superlative: death squared. But the undefined eternity of loyalty in "our hearts" survives both the boundary of life marked by the tombstone, and the span of known human history which marks the boundary of the life of monuments. The title of the poem, and the *projet* (memorializing a memorial) which that title represents, promote the poem beyond a mere restatement of the *Ubi sunt* topos to the rank of an assurance of the eternity of the poetic vision.

Often the early Hugo confers immortality upon his verse much more explicitly. The ode poet's traditional role of making heroes' fame live forever appears only optatively in the **"Ode à l'Amitié"** when Hugo speaks of Castor and Pollux, Orestes and Pylade:

Puissent vos noms, amis constans,
Couverts d'une éternelle gloire,
Passer au temple de mémoire,
Jusqu'aux derniers de nos enfans.

Of course the poem itself is a room of this temple. **"Le Temps et les Cités"** affirms the poet's immortality more directly by contrasting material monuments, and the mountains themselves—all of which must eventually fall—with genius. "Ilion fut, Homère existe."

[. . .] d'une cité périssable
Si le sort compte les instans,
Il est un pouvoir plus durable
Qui seul peut défier le Tems;
C'est le Génie

Then in **"Le Désir de la Gloire—Ode"** (1818), Hugo confers immortality upon himself rather than on Homer, though he remains in the conditional. And soon an open-ended equation of the spatial sublime leads him to a superlative of the temporal sublime of poetic immortality. He describes the seven planets revolving around the sun:

Et peut-être cet astre immense
Ressent lui-même la puissance
D'un astre plus immense encor.

    . . . . .

Astres, dont le feu nous éclaire,
Parlez, avez-vous un Homère
Dont le nom vive plus que vous?

As the vastness of the solar system is in proportion to the entire universe, so is Homer's fame in proportion to the glory Hugo desires. After this grandiose vision, however, the effect of the poem trails off through ninety more lines.

Religious inspiration comes to dominate political inspiration in the *Odes* early in 1821. Hugo had allied himself with the ultraroyalists, becoming their main poetic spokesman. But their overreaction to the murder of the Duc de Berry made allegiance to their cause seem less attractive. At the same time, Lamennais's religious writings began to influence Hugo (in July 1820 he uses a Lamennais text as an epigraph to an ode to Chateaubriand), and he became acquainted with Lamennais personally in the spring of 1821. His mother's death in June of that year reinforced his meditative tendencies. The preface to the *Nouvelles Odes,* dated February 1824, reflects his new orientation: "Il ne sera jamais l'écho d'aucune parole, si ce n'est de celle de Dieu." But when Hugo attempts literally to put this intention into practice, by having God speak in his odes, he mars them with anticlimax similar to that of **"Le Désir de la Gloire,"** by continuing the poem after the divine words have been uttered (compare the effective sobriety of having God speak only seven words at the conclusion of *La Fin de Satan*). He obviates this difficulty, in his more successful odes, by not depicting God directly. Instead, he imbues history with a spiritual significance, under the influence of Joseph de Maistre, Saint-Simon, Ballanche, Lamennais, and the articles by Baron Eckstein which he admiringly published in *Le Drapeau Blanc,* and which introduced him to the ideas of Schlegel, Fichte, and Schelling. Hugo spiritualizes history by combining two familiar topoi: *Exegi monumentum,* and hopes for the future of mankind. Antithesis effectuates this combination in the third stanza of **"La Bande noire"** (*Odes* II, 3): "vieux monuments d'un peuple enfant." The vast span of civilization coextensive with the life of the monuments—themselves nearly immortal in comparison with individual human lives—merely corresponds to the childhood of humanity, evolving through eons towards an as yet undefined maturity.

It is in the domain of the spatial sublime that Hugo's innovations proved most effective. The implied metaphor that "the world is the gods' house" was renewed in Christian visions of a Last Judgment and Apocalypse, and in eighteenth-century Deistic visions of the plurality of worlds, but the poetic vision of these systems remained static, confined within the limits of a known cosmology. Eventually Hugo transcends these limits by no longer naming the vaster theater to which his metaphors of expansion point. And rather than simply shifting suddenly from the human to the divine spatial perspective (a shift accomplished in the traditional ode with the exclamation "Que vois-je!" and the like), he will depict the human as dynamically expanding until it attains and then exceeds the proportions of the divine: "Et, si vous aboyez, tonnerres, / Je rugirai" (**"Ibo," *Les Contemplations***). Thus the imagination comes to mediate between visionary consciousness and the phenomenal world. It preserves Nature from apocalyptic destruction and sustains a dialectical relationship between mind and nature, while keeping both intact.

The static form of the sublime spatial metaphor, with its abrupt shift of perspective, appears in Hugo's **"Dernier jour du monde"** written in 1816. The vision is related from the viewpoint of a resurrected man. "Où suis-je? Quelle main me rend à la lumière?" the ode begins. God appears; earth trembles; chaos engulfs the universe; and the spatial sublime leads to frozen time: "le Temps dort et s'arrête / Sur le trône du ciel." Christian cosmology here imposes an ultimate limit on poetic vision.

The poetry of Hugo's maturity at times simply suggests the implications of such expansive figures—God is the Selfhood of the infinite—more eloquently, frequently, and clearly. He speaks, for example, of "l'immensité qui n'est qu'un œil sublime" (**"Pleurs dans la nuit," *Les Contemplations***). Elsewhere, combining the spatial with the temporal sublime, he declares:

Le vent de l'infini sur ce monde souffla.
Il a sombré. . . .

. . . . .

Qu'est-ce que le simoun a fait du grain de sable?
Cela fut. C'est passé. Cela n'est plus ici.
(**"Pleine Mer," *Légende***)

But he transcends this cosmic framework even in the early odes (*a*) by creating an open-ended version of the motif of proportions and (*b*) by leading the imagination from the spatial sublime to a dynamic, evolving continuum of heroic resolve for the future.

So **"A la Colonne de la Place Vendôme"** (*Odes*) describes the huge column as only a small part of a fallen empire unimaginably vaster. The Vergilian epigraph "parva magnis" emphasizes the motif of proportions, which will recur, for example, in the magnificent expatiation **"Magnitudo parvi"** of the *Contemplations*. In the latter poem, the world of the human imagination symbolized by the shepherd's fire is vaster than the stars. In **"A la Colonne,"** a scale yet vaster than the Napoleonic empire is implied when Hugo compares the column itself to a warrior. As much as the column is greater than a single human, so much greater

than the empire of Napoleon would be an undefined empire of the imagination, conquered by an army of such columns which the poet had brought back to life.

Again, and similarly, the connotations of warlike valor and the active verbs associated with the key metaphor of **"Aux ruines de Montfort-L'Amaury"** (*Odes*)—the town as sword—removes the limits from the movement of visionary expansion. This expansion represents only an initial expression of soldierly resolve, the prelude to great exploits in a theater unimaginably vaster than the physical world itself:

Je médite longtemps, en mon cœur replié;
Et la ville, à mes pieds, d'arbres enveloppée,
Etend ses bras en croix et s'allonge en épée,
Comme le fer d'un preux dans la plaine oublié.

This time, nostalgia aborted the prophetic adventure, which was to achieve its plenitude only in the poetry of Hugo's exile. Otherwise, he might well have continued:

I will not cease from Mental Fight,
Nor shall my Sword sleep in my hand
Till we have built Jerusalem
In England's green and pleasant land.
(Blake, *Milton*, preface)

What warrior would take Hugo's sword-town in hand, and what would be his battle? It has been described: "The ancient struggle between man and spirit-influence—that is, of man for self-dependence—is continuing in a more intimate way. What do the spirits want? Always the same: man's fall, his ontic degradation. How does humanism deal with that? By sending against them the thunderbolt of hermeneutic degradation." Hugo will finally dramatize this humanistic strategy in what is perhaps his greatest poem, **"Le Satyre."** Summoned before the Olympian gods, the humble faun sings. And as he sings, he grows and swells until the gods shrink into insignificance:

L'avenir [. . .]
C'est l'élargissement dans l'infini sans fond,
C'est l'esprit pénétrant de toutes parts la chose!
On mutile l'effet en limitant la cause;
Monde, tout le mal vient de la forme des dieux.
On fait du ténébreux avec le radieux;
Pourquoi mettre au-dessus de l'Etre, des fantômes?
(*Légende*)

Blake said this often, but he couldn't have put it better.

The royal road past the divine to a humanistic perspective is the archetype of Inversion ("to see the World in a Grain of Sand") implied by the motif of proportion, as stated and illustrated, for example, in **"A la Colonne de la Place Vendôme."** What seemed bad, proves good. (What seemed enormous, proves small. What seemed insignificant, proves important, etc. For countless examples, see Christ's sayings in the Gospels, passim.) It was Hugo's explicit statement of the archetype of Inversion in the early odes which inspired him, apparently, to discover a new verbal dimension beyond spatial vastness, and thus to overcome the power of the gods. **"A M. de Chateaubriand"** (*Odes*) praises that minister for resigning from the government in 1824. Material renunciation leads to a moral triumph. "Chacun de tes revers pour ta gloire est compté [. . .] Tomber plus haut encore que tu n'étais monté!" Here the archetype of Inversion functions to transfer the perception of vastness from the objective to the subjective plane. Then the "beyonding" effect of the sublime will not depend on the existence of a God or gods, the theater of whose action is larger than ours, but rather on the creative fiat of the poetic imagination. God is in us, not "up there."

Thus the mechanism of transcendence is shifted from the continual evocation of mythological beings, personified abstractions, and angels or spirits (which persist to create the beyonding effect as late as the poetry of Baudelaire and of the early Mallarmé) to the poet's manipulation of syntax. So, at the beginning of this same ode to Chateaubriand, Hugo writes:

> Il est des astres, rois des cieux étincelants,
> Mondes volcans jetés parmi les autres mondes,
>> Qui volent dans les nuits profondes,
>
> . . . . .
>
> Le génie a partout des symboles sublimes.

As far as I know, "mondes volcans" is Hugo's earliest use of the "metaphor maxima," the juxtaposition of noun with noun in violation of ordinary French syntax, which has attracted much attention in the *Contemplations* and later collections. (In English, on the contrary, the juxtaposition of noun and noun—e.g. houseboat, boathouse—is so common that some computer programs for machine translation do not distinguish between English nouns and adjectives, calling both parts of speech "nadjes.") Clearly the metaphor maxima arises from placing a noun in apposition to another ("des astres, rois"), for in this situation French drops the article before the second noun, removing a barrier to its assimilation with the first. This condensation may seem trivial, but it is not. First, by violating normal syntax it implies a poetic vision which normal syntax cannot adequately communicate. It shows rather than tells the topos of inexpressibility. Second, without the metaphor maxima Hugo would have to express the sublime equation in a sentence with verb and subject ("The world is a volcano"). By condensing this equation to the single unit of two noun/adjectives, he frees the surrounding syntax. This syntax then no longer constitutes a mechanism ending with and limited by the metaphor maxima. It becomes capable of maneuvering that metaphor in the context of a vaster vision ("The world-volcano flies").

In this way the poet acquires limitless possibilities for displacing or transforming metaphorical immensity through his use of verbs. He ("le génie," above) rather than a god becomes the master of time and space, through his use of language ("des symboles"). The final step in this process will be to subject the entire known universe to the dynamic

dominion of syntax: **"L'hydre Univers tordant son corps écaillé d'astres" "Ce que dit la Bouche d'Ombre,"** (*Les Contemplations*). The metaphor maxima becomes an "être verbal" (e.g. the familiar "knife without a handle, whose blade is missing"), a concept which exists across our ordinary categories for experience—abstract and concrete, moral and physical, being and non-being—and thus dramatizes the transcending power of the creative imagination at work in a universe of words.

Hugo's theoretical statements in his prefaces to the *Odes* clearly show that he associates the Ode form with the Ancien Régime. Progressively as he evolves from monarchical views towards liberalism, he experiences the ode as inadequate for his poetic vision. His earliest definition of the ode proclaims quite conventionally that it "avec majesté célèbre les exploits / Des dieux, des conquérants, des héros et des rois" (**"Régles de l'Ode"**). His 1822 preface reaffirms the reactionary viewpoint that "l'histoire des hommes ne présente de poésie que jugée due haut des idées monarchiques et des croyances religieuses." And again in 1823 he advocates replacing pagan mythology with Christian dogma in an attempt to support and console French monarchical society "qui sort, encore toute chancelante, des saturnales de l'athéisme et de l'anarchie."

The reactionary reign of Charles X made Hugo change his mind. From late in 1821, moreover, he had been prepared for a change of heart by a progressive reconciliation with his father, who had been a general under Napoleon. The 1826 preface no longer casts a nostalgic backward glance at the Ancien Régime. Hugo, now chafing under the restraint of the ode's historical associations with a political system from which he is coming to wish himself free, simply defines the genre so broadly that his definition becomes meaningless. The ode reflects "toute inspiration purement religieuse, toute étude purement antique, toute traduction d'un événement contemporain ou d'une impression personnelle." Already in 1825, moreover, the weakening of Hugo's religious faith and his desire for a larger public led him to bid farewell—for a time—to visionary poetry. The October 1825 ode **"A M. Alponse de L[amartine]"** which introduces the third book of odes exclaims "Ah! nous ne sommes plùs au temps où le poète / Parlait au ciel en prêtre, a la terre en prophète!" and yields the palm to Hugo's friendly rival. No later poem in the *Odes et Ballades* proclaims the poet's prophetic mission, describes the abysses which open to his visionary gaze, nor invokes God or History.

The 1828 preface traces the evolution of his choice of subjects for the ode from historical (Books I-III) to "sujets de fantaisie" (Book IV), to "impressions personnelles" (Book V). With the *ballades* of Book VI and the *Orientales* of 1829 he abandons the formal designation of "ode" altogether: since "tout a droit dc cité en poésie" (1829), any generic label seems overly restrictive. Until the *Feuilles d'automne,* published in 1831, Hugo marks time with prosodic virtuosity, exoticism, and the light fantastic. The *Ballades* and *Orientales* show Hugo turning his attention away from France and from the decaying political influence of the aristocracy and monarchists with whom he had allied himself. The very act of juxtaposing the playful *Ballades* with the serious *Odes* in 1828 reflects a certain depreciation of the latter in Hugo's mind.

Nevertheless, to call to mind the features of the ode is to perceive more clearly the imaginative origins of the great poetry of the exile period. There Hugo multiplies original versions of the sublime suggested by his discoveries in the early odes. But beyond that, several other possibilities inherent in the ode, suggested but not exploited in the 1820's, receive a detailed imaginative development in the 1850's: the excoriation of the scapegoat figure (*Les Châtiments*); the redemption of the scapegoat (*Les Contemplations; La Fin de Satan*); the extension of the static temporal sublime into the dynamic future of humanity (*La Légende des siècles*); and the dramatization of an inexhaustibly unfolding poetic vision (*Dieu*).

After 1828, Hugo's transformation of the Ode passes through two main phases: generally speaking, the middle period collections—*Les Feuilles d'Automne, Les Chants du Crépuscule, Les Voix intérieures,* and *Les Rayons et les Ombres*—reverse the traditional arrangement of (*a*) inspiration from a superior order, and (*b*) report of the resulting vision. Hugo's growing democratic sensibilities now preclude his presenting himself as an intellectual or spiritual aristocrat at the outset of the poems. Instead, an imaginative encounter with the physical world leads him and the reader together towards the visionary insight suggested at the conclusion of the poems. Not having received an initial revelation, the poet can no longer play the role of Christ and Judge, self-confidently separating the sheep from the goats. Generalized metaphors of light and darkness replace the overtly judgmental polarities of hero and scapegoat, good and evil. To counterbalance this diminution of poetic prestige, Hugo reverses the relationship between poet and nature. Rather than nature being a source of inspiration for the poet, she receives a revelation from him. And it remains apparent that the implied author—as distinguished from the lyric self—has undergone a visionary experience by the beginning of the poems; allusions to it are insinuated into the initial sections of the poem, by descriptive details which imply an overarching harmony into which the polar oppositions of good and evil have been subsumed. Thus **"La Vache"** of *Les Voix intérieures* is compared both to a doe and to a leopard; her hide combines the colors white and russet red (ice and fire); and her barnyard contains both a sedentary old man and noisy children, before the visionary climax which equates her to universal nature. Hugo's rural landscape with figures revives, both in theme and subject, the seventeenth and eighteenth-century descriptive poetry which celebrated the cosmic order of *concordia discors*.

In 1823, **"Le Poète"** (*Odes*) already anticipates standing the ode on its head: inspiration and the message from a higher order occur at the very end of the poem. The first section evokes the poet's solitary condition; the second complains that he must live amidst the frivolous crowd; the third tells that crowd to leave him in

peace, because he is divinely inspired; and the fourth shows him appearing among mankind once more, bearing a transcendent revelation: "son front porte tout un Dieu!" **"Extase"** in 1828 (*Orientales*) is the first poem in which the poet's contemplation of nature, rather than the dictation of a Muse, leads to spiritual revelation. The stars and the waves beneath them proclaim the presence of God: "Mes yeux plongeaient plus loin que le monde réel."

In **"Pan"** of *Les Feuilles d'Automne,* the poet becomes the interpreter as well as the recipient of messages from a panpsychic nature, of "le mot mystérieux que chaque voix bégaie." He invites other poets to mingle their souls with creation. In an inversion of the poet-as-Aeolian-harp topos, nature metaphorically becomes a keyboard passively responding to the poet's strong fingers. As Pierre Albouy comments, here.

> Hugo renoue avec la haute ambition du poète 'vates' qui s'exprimait dans les *Odes*; à nouveau, le poète est défini comme un être 'sacré,' dont la mission consiste à traduire en langage humain ce 'verbe' divin qu'est la nature. Le poème annonce ainsi, lointainement, les Mages, et, aussi, par le symbole du dieu Pan, le mythe du Satyre, dans *la Légende des Siècles*.

The poet's mental processes are compared in detail to natural processes, and nature imitates him as much as he imitates her, in **"Dictée en présence du glacier du Rhône"** and **"La Pente de la Rêverie"** of *Les Feuilles d'Automne*. In the latter poem,

> La Seine, ainsi que moi, laissait son flot vermeil
> Suivre nonchalamment sa pente, et le soleil
> Faisait évaporer à la fois sur les grèves
> L'eau du fleuve en brouillards et ma pensée en
>   rêves!

Fused with nature, the poet no longer can hold himself aloof, a detached intellect, to judge and condemn the anti-selves of the traditional ode. In **"Ce qu'on entend sur la montagne,"** for example (July 1829; *Les Feuilles d'Automne,*), he distinguishes both a hymn of praise and a wail of lamentation emanating from the landscape. But now he feels sympathy for the dark world of suffering.

In short, Hugo's middle-period poetry adopts a three-fold rather than a two-fold vision. He undertakes a mission of mediation and reconciliation, rather than simply discriminating between black and white, evil and good. His habit of tripartite thinking is evident in *La Préface de Cromwell* (1827) and in the preface to *Les Voix intérieures,* but it becomes associated with a hierarchy of soul, mind, and body only in the **"Prélude"** of the *Chants du Crépuscule*. The poet as mind mediates between the soul and body. He echoes "tout ce que le monde [the body] / Chante [the soul] dans l'ombre en attendant!" The word "Crépuscule," which can mean either pre-dawn or dusk, also transcends a simple binary opposition of light and darkness, as Hugo insists in his preface:

Tout aujourd'hui, dans les idées comme dans les choses, dans la société comme dans l'individu, est à l'état de crépuscule. De quelle nature est ce crépuscule? de quoi sera-t-il suivi? . . . La société attend que ce qui est à l'horizon s'allume tout à fait ou s'éteigne complètement.

The preface likewise transcends the opposition of Good and Evil: "Dans ce livre . . . il y a tous les contraires, le doute et le dogme, le jour et la nuit . . . Le poète n'est pourtant, lui, ni de ceux qui nient, ni de ceux qui affirment. Il est de ceux qui espèrent." And in the liminal **"Prélude,"** the nearest approach to an anti-self is the uncertain poets and priests who seek a revelation and a new role. Hugo's poet-persona of the middle period odes seeks to penetrate a mystery rather than to distribute praise and blame.

Edward K. Kaplan (essay date 1981)

SOURCE: "Victor Hugo and the Poetics of Doubt: The Transition of 1835-1837," in *French Forum,* Vol. 6, No. 2, May, 1981, pp. 140-53.

[*In the essay below, Kaplan examines how various "political, moral, and religious upheavals" in Hugo's life are reflected in his early lyric collections.*]

Victor Hugo's post-exile religious ideas are well known, as is the anguish at their foundation. Critics tend to prefer **Les Contemplations,** which is organized around Léopoldine's death in 1843, and the ambitious metaphysical epics which follow. Yet his earlier four lyrical collections—**Les Feuilles d'automne** (1831), **Les Chants du crépuscule** (1835), **Les Voix intérieures** (1837), and **Les Rayons et les ombres** (1840)—trace an equally radical realignment of the poet's literary persona: Hugo was becoming detached from his royalism and Catholic faith, reflecting the crises of meaning which pervaded the July Monarchy. His brother's madness and death (in 1837), the suicides of several friends, guilt and anger at his and his wife's infidelities also echo political, moral, and religious upheavals. A new poetics—and Olympio, Hugo's permanent persona—emerge from that transition.

Hugo's four pre-exile collections are unified by the poet's discovery of faith through uncertainty and doubt. Not a Christian faith, but a modern faith which understands anxiety as an appropriate response to rapid social, political, and intellectual change. Using a gross biographical fact we can hypothesize an intentional progression from **Les Chants du crépuscule** (1835) to **Les Voix intérieures** (1837): Hugo composed his two great poems on doubt in the fall of 1835—**"Que nous avons le doute en nous"** (dated 13 October) and **"Pensar, Dudar"** (dated 8 September). He distributed them in different books. **"Que nous avons le doute en nous,"** a negative view of doubt, appears at the end of **Les Chants du crépuscule,** whereas his positive acceptance of doubt, **"Pensar, Dudar,"** almost concludes **Les Voix intérieures.** The biographical facts simply confirm a rhetorical reading: a traditional apologetic strategy forms the four collections into one spiritual itinerary.

Hugo develops the *topos* of the descent into hell as preparation for redemption to affirm doubt as the only path to modern faith. To do this he must transform his readers' consciousness. The Romantic poet confronts his century's proud rationalism as did Pascal, whose *Pensée* 72 (in the Brunschwicg numbering) transports the skeptic into the sublime world of the two infinites in order to produce a humble receptivity to the divine:

Qui se considérera de la sorte s'effraiera de soi-même, et, se considérant soutenu dans la masse que la nature lui a donné, entre ces deux abîmes de l'infini et du néant, il tremblera dans la vue de ces merveilles; et je crois que sa curiosité se changeant en admiration, il sera plus disposé à les contempler en silence qu'à les rechercher avec présomption.

Hugo evokes terror and uncertainty which imitate the trembling of Pascal's philosopher, "égaré dans ce canton détourné de la nature." Hugo challenges philosophical doubt with esthetic intuitions of nature's sublime inscrutability. Feelings of terror provoke his and the reader's conversion, literally, by scaring the daylights out of them. From the darkness will emerge a complex sense of the sacred.

The poet exemplifies a modern faith when he extracts meaning (and beauty) from confusion. Hugo stresses such words as *doute, vague, ombre, nuit,* and especially *crépuscule* ambiguously to characterize both intellectual uncertainty and the terror of otherness or non-being. Esthetic doubt draws from the pictorial *chiaroscuro* to evoke emotions of fear, whereas ontological doubt, which provokes similar emotions, conveys the person's uncertainty about reality itself. Hugo's apologetic strategy hinges upon the confusion of esthetic and ontological doubt, the translation of a vague feeling into a metaphysical insight. The poet's great accomplishment was to blend these two dimensions of doubt in a new poetry of commitment.

Paul Bénichou, in his seminal study, *Le Sacre de l'écrivain,* demonstrates the crucial importance of doubt in Romantic reflection on poetry and faith. Lamartine exemplifies the inseparability of doubt and belief as he ambiguously deplores the skepticism of Lord Byron in "L'Homme" (*Méditations poétiques,* 1820). But Hugo illustrates a more explicitly positive approach. This emerging liberal view was prepared by the philosopher Théodore Jouffroy in his famous pronouncement "Comment les dogmes finissent," first published in *Le Globe* in 1825. Jouffroy describes his era's "anxiety of emptiness and meaninglessness" as a conflict between skepticism and nostalgia for an expired faith. During the Restoration, serious debate was followed by polemics which degenerated into mockery; nevertheless, as Jouffroy maintains, the need to believe persisted: "Le doute est un état qui ne peut nous plaire que comme l'absence d'une fausse croyance dont nous nous sentons délivrés." Restoration liberals understood the true function of doubt: "A eux se dévoile l'énigme qui avait échappé aux autres; à eux le doute ne paraît plus la révolution, mais sa préparation." Far from increasing lethargy and escapism, doubt stimulated indignation against the emptiness of the present; those who courageously acknowledged the crisis could face the future. Victor Hugo's poet-prophet anticipates the modern "existential" courage that accepts doubt as a step towards knowledge and confronts meaninglessness with an enthusiastic commitment to life.

Hugo's enthusiastic faith did not spring full grown from his tremendous ego. It developed fitfully through the disappointment and sadness which permeate the first lyrical collection, *Les Feuilles d'automne*. The famous **"Pente de la rêverie"** (no. 29) anticipates his post-exile method of discovering vast historical frescoes and suggests that the subconscious can engender vision. ButHugo begins to exploit the struggle of doubt and faith in *Les Chants du crépuscule*. Doubt is the fundamental paradox of the age: on the one hand, it signifies anguish about the absence of transcendent meaning, despair about the death of religion; on the other hand, doubt liberates the mind from narrow preconceptions. Doubt can unveil the universe. Through radical doubt, Hugo will discover the depths of his genius. Olympio will illuminate the darkness.

The thematic symmetry of *Les Chants du crépuscule* anticipates the unity of the whole series. Its first and penultimate poems—**"Prélude"** and **"Que nous avons le doute en nous"** (no. 38)—elaborate the theme of the ambiguous dawn: the question as to whether the twilight is a death or a new beginning. Imagery of *clair/obscur* links several dimensions of doubt: the political, intellectual, religious, psychological, and ontological. "Tout aujourd'hui, dans les idées comme dans les choses, dans la société comme dans l'individu, est à l'état de crépuscule. De quelle nature est ce crépuscule? de quoi sera-t-il suivi?" Here doubt signifies anxiety about the future.

But poetry is better served by psychological reactions to ideas; Hugo's imagery joins the inner and outer dimensions to make social analysis reciprocal with feelings: "c'est cet étrange état crépusculaire de l'âme et de la société dans le siècle où nous vivons; c'est cette brume au dehors, cette incertitude au dedans; c'est ce je ne sais quoi d'à demi éclairé qui nous environne." Hugo mixes his antithèses: "ces cris d'espoir mêlés d'hésitation, ces chants d'amour coupés de plaintes, cette sérénité pénétrée de tristesse," etc. His imagery of mixture encompasses the complexities of "cette époque livrée à l'attente et à la transition."

Hugo's **"Prélude"** establishes that imagery and defines its meaning. Pictorial and affective mixtures evoke what Tillich calls the anxiety of emptiness and meaninglessness, an appropriate reaction to a state of rapid and chaotic social change. Hugo's refrain "Tout s'y mêle" focuses upon that anxiety as a desire for meaning:

> Seigneur! est-ce vraiment l'aube qu'on voit éclore?
> Oh! l'anxiété croît de moment en moment.
>
> · · · · ·
>
> Dans l'âme et sur la terre effrayant crépuscule!

The technical term *anxiété* connects to the imagery of ambiguous dawn to the inner life. According to the *Larous-*

se du XIXᵉ siècle, "anxiété" refers to a "tourment d'esprit, causé principalement par l'incertitude." Doubt is the result, not the cause (as Hugo's Catholic opponents believed), of that cultural transition.

Doubt includes three separable conflicts: (1) the incapacity to embrace cherished inherited ideas ("Croyances, passions, désespoir, espérances"), (2) anguish about the future ("c'est peut-être le soir qu'on prend pour une aurore!") and (3) intellectual skepticism, the true enemy of modern faith because it resists hope:

> Et l'homme qui gémit à côté de la chose;
> Car dans ce siècle, en proie aux sourires moqueurs,
> Toute conviction en peu d'instants dépose
> Le doute, lie affreuse, au fond de tous les cœurs!

Hugo sharply opposes *conviction* to *doute*. *Conviction* combines intellectual certainty and the active adhesion of the will to an ideal; the opposite is cynicism which can lead to despair. Both appear as an ironic *sourire moqueur*. Hugo attacks irony which separates an individual from the shared dilemma; irony implies, in his view, a willful hardness of heart that destroys moral solidarity.

Two consecutive poems, both dedicated to Louise Bertin, formulate the potentials of doubt. The first, **"A Mademoiselle Louise B."** (no. 37), opposes the young woman's wisdom and serenity to the poet's horror of time and human frailty. In the second poem, **"Que nous avons le doute en nous,"** Hugo explores the negative associations of doubt. The poet's conquest of the anxiety of doubt should inspire his nation.

Disbelief is the fundamental problem, whether it be willful incredulity or an incapacity to believe. **"Que nous avons le doute en nous"** assimilates ideological uncertainty and psychological anguish. The first six stanzas present the poet's interior twilight as a desire for faith:

> Si vous me demandez, vous muse, à moi poète,
> D'où vient qu'un rêve obscur semble agiter mes
>   jours,
> Que mon front est couvert d'ombres, et que
>   toujours,
> Comme un rameau dans l'air, ma vie est inquiète;
>
> Pourquoi je cherche un sens au murmure des vents;
>
> · · · · ·
>
> Je vous dirai qu'en moi je porte un ennemi,
> Le doute, qui m'emmène errer dans le bois sombre,
> Spectre myope et sourd, qui, fait de jour et
>   d'ombre,
> Montre et cache à la fois toute chose à demi!

The word *doute* is emphasized by the enjambment. Doubt is an enemy, but it also implies a positive restlessness, as suggested by the italicized words: "un rêve obscur semble *agiter* mes jours . . . ma vie est *inquiète* . . . je *cherche un sens* au murmure des vents." This "enemy" generates curiosity and effort; it is concern about the future.

The text then recapitulates three objects of yearning: a divine plan for humanity, an historical pattern that rises above political upheavals, authentic intimacy between men and women. The first two seem out of reach, and Hugo maintains a grim vision of the antagonism between flesh and spirit; mankind's internal contradiction is inescapable:

> Un instinct qui bégaye, en mes sens prisonnier,
> Près du besoin de croire un désir de nier,
> Et l'esprit qui ricane auprès du cœur qui pleure!

Doubt is the legacy of the age: "Le doute! mot funèbre." The passions of sensuality and the desire for money nurture moral indifference, yet that very egotism leads to despair (see **"A un riche,"** no. 19). The political discontinuity augments the personal conflict: "C'est notre mal à nous, enfants des passions . . . A nous dont le berceau . . . Vogua sur le flot noir des révolutions." Two lines summarize the emptiness felt by the *enfant du siècle*: "Nous portons dans nos cœurs le cadavre pourri / De la religion qui vivait dans nos pères."

Hugo's solution is individualistic. He withdraws from the social arena and makes of his intimate life the growing edge: "Heureux qui peut aimer, et qui dans la nuit noire, / Tout en cherchant la foi, peut rencontrer l'amour!" Philosophical hope must repose on interpersonal love when God remains aloof. "Aimer, c'est la moitié de croire" is the didactic conclusion of *Les Chants du crépuscule*.

Although Hugo took his moral seriously, the final poem, **"Date Lilia,"** endows it with a curious ambiguity. The malicious Sainte-Beuve remarked that this tribute was Hugo's guilt offering to the "faithful" spouse for his liaison with Juliette. *Les Chants du crépuscule* ends with an ideal image of bourgeois love: "Une femme au front pur, au pas grave, aux doux yeux, / Que suivent quatre enfants dont le dernier chancelle." Yet Hugo admits that he too *chancelle* and that his wife understands his guilt: "Celle qui, lorsqu'au mal, pensif, je m'abandonne, / Seule peut me punir et seule me pardonne." The poet seems to blame his sexual infidelity and insensitivity to his family's companionship on his penchant to dream. And he strives, perhaps in vain, to reconcile the opposition in the final line: "La fleur est de la terre et le parfum des cieux!" *Les Chants du crépuscule* leaves behind a subtle, but significant, question about love and marriage as solutions to France's weak faith.

Hugo consolidates his mission and dramatizes the ontological sources of his poetic vision in *Les Voix intérieures*. The poet is a civilizer who echoes three voices—*le foyer, le champ, la rue*—in the Preface and in the optimistic first poem, **"Ce siècle est grand et fort."** The disequilibrium of the poem's structure, however, reflects the disequilibrium of his faith. The first ten stanzas celebrate the century's intellectual and technological progress, while in the final stanza, it evokes a spiritual deficit:

> Dans tout ce grand éclat d'un siècle éblouissant,
> Une chose, ô Jésus, en secret m'épouvante,
> C'est l'écho de ta voix qui va s'affaiblissant.

Of course Hugo seeks to replace the official savior and the priest with the poet-*vates*. He counterpoises modern anxiety to the expired faith in order to promote his solution.

The poet intends to resolve his and his nation's intellectual twilight through an interpretation of nature, for nature represents that which is independent of the human mind. Nature becomes a source of faith because it is God's book and the poet its most perceptive reader. Poem no. 19, **"A un riche,"** defines the pre-Baudelairian correspondences which make such spiritual knowledge possible: "Tout objet dont le bois se compose répond / A quelque objet pareil dans la forêt de l'âme." The reciprocity is exact. The garden as metonymy for the wood, the wood for the forest, and the forest for nature ingeneral will symbolize the human condition. Obscure nature, then, reflects human obscurity. Hugo's great task is to discover in and through nature a meaning beyond anxiety.

Two emblematic poems, early in *Les Voix intérieures,* explore the twilight of the spirit. Jean Gaudon has analyzed parallels between **"A Virgile"** (no. 7) and **"A Albert Dürer"** (no. 10) and has traced Hugo's inspiration from Virgil through Dürer and Piranese. Further analysis reveals the ontological dimension. Doubt, in these two twilight poems, conveys the poet's uncertainty about reality itself. As he questions his very rationality, as doubt becomes absolute, poetic vision emerges. These poems effect a crucial transition from an intellectual dilemma to an esthetic solution.

"A Virgile" dramatizes the genesis of poetry. It follows the day from morning to sunset and moonlit solitude. The poet leaves Paris, "cette ville au cri sinistre et vain," which represents the emptiness of a "superior" civilization: "Lutèce . . . / Qui jette aujourd'hui . . . / Plus de clarté qu'Athène et plus de bruit que Rome." The poet internalizes the dawn as he sets out with his mistress, "Avec l'amour au cœur et l'aube dans les yeux." He can then confront the darkness.

The two final stanzas illustrate how twilight opens the poet's visionary eyes. Virgil inspires Hugo to experience reality as a mixture of known and unknown. The terror of that ontological doubt stimulates special intuitions. First, female sensitivity actualizes nature's silences: "Elle aime comme nous, maître, ces douces voix [de la nature]"; the surroundings which Juliette, Virgil, and the modern poet love are then unveiled by the evening, "quand le couchant morne a perdu sa rougeur." In the atmosphere of uncertainty, nature becomes animated and its hidden consciousness manifest:

> Les marais irrités des pas du voyageur,
> Et l'humble chaume, et l'antre obstrué d'herbe
>   verte,
> Et qui semble une bouche avec terreur ouverte,

The poet projects his anxiety on nature, for one would expect people to be terrified, not the landscape. Yet Hugo retains the comparison "qui semble une bouche" to rationalize his vision of the night's ambiguity. This is what the esthetic experience reveals.

Nature differentiates itself further from the poet in the final stanza. But with the help of his partners, Juliette and Virgil, he discerns nature's *secrète attitude,* that is, its innate psychological disposition:

> Nous irons tous les trois, c'est-à-dire tous deux,
> Dans ce vallon sauvage, et de la solitude,
> Rêveurs, nous surprendrons la secrète attitude.

Rêveur describes the contemplative or visionary mode of intuition developed more fully after the exile. Nature's consciousness is so hidden ("secrète") that the conventional hyperbole of black darkness fails to convey its *mixture* of realities "dans la *brune* clairière" (my italics). According to his special vision, the spectacle steals the initiative from the spectator: "Dans la brune clairière où l'arbre au tronc noueux / Prend le soir un profil humain et monstrueux. . . ."

This is one of the earliest appearances of Hugo's characteristic anthropomorphism when nature notonly becomes human, it menaces. The paradoxical "humain *et* monstrueux" expresses the poet's troubled identification with nature's unconscious. Ontological doubt then awakens. The text's progression delineates a method: in four lines solitude leads to dream, nature's secret feelings are perceived in the uncertain darkness, human and extraordinary shapes evoke a terror which suggests the sacred.

When reality itself is thrown into question, poetry is born. Frightful otherness whets the poet's appetite, which, in turn, engenders images. Hugo illustrates the positive thrust of anxiety in a Virgilian idiom as he becomes prepared to *see*, in exterior nature, what he had remembered from literature.

> Et, l'oreille tendue à leurs vagues chansons,
> Dans l'ombre, au clair de lune, à travers les
>   buissons,
> Avides, nous pourrons voir à la dérobée
> Les satyrs dansants qu'imite Alphésibée.

The profusion of *clair/obscur* images makes the poet *avide.* The visual ambiguity incites the imagination to transform reality. Hugo's faith in the possible reenactment of Virgil's *Bucolics* represents his limitless poetic power.

The parallel poem **"A Albert Durer"** (no. 10) continues where **"A Virgile"** left off. It is a visionary manifesto. Hugo identifies with Albert Dürer, "vieux peintre pensif," who already *sees* the images hidden in the mystery:

> On devine, devant tes tableaux qu'on vénère,
> Que dans les noirs taillis ton œil visionnaire
> Voyait distinctement, par l'ombre recouverts,
> Le faune aux doigts palmés, le sylvain aux yeux
>   verts,
> Pan. . . .

The paradoxical formulation "Voyait *distinctement,* par *l'ombre* recouverts" imitates the artist's "œil visionnaire" which enlarges reality. As nature's veil becomes translucent, the poet formulates an ontology of mixture: "Une forêt pour toi, c'est un monde hideux. / Le songe et le réel s'y mêlent tous les deux".

Hugo's *fantastique* insinuates supernatural beings into a realistic framework, but the next lines deepen the ambiguity. The poet questions nature's very status:

> Là se penchent rêveurs les vieux pins, les grands
>   ormes
> Dont les rameaux tordus font cent coudes difformes,
> Et dans ce groupe sombre agité par le vent
> Rien n'est tout à fait mort ni tout à fait vivant.

Hugo fully experiences nature's autonomy. The realistic explanation "ce groupe sombre agité par le vent" lends credibility to the intuition; but the trees, not only the poet, are *rêveurs.* Imaginationpenetrates, it does not deform, reality.

This is the crucial moment of Hugo's apologetic strategy. Just as esthetic ambiguity in **"A Virgile"** stimulates poetic vision, so, in **"A Albert Durer,"** esthetic *and ontological* ambiguity reveals a metaphysics. The poet effects a synthesis of esthetic and metaphysical intuitions of mystery and otherness: "Rien n'est tout à fait mort, ni tout à fait vivant." The texts realize that synthesis through images which provoke feelings of *horror,* what Rudolf Otto, in *The Idea of the Holy,* calls the *mysterium tremendum,* religious dread. (Hugo had named it in **Les Contemplations**.) According to Otto, experiences of the scared include "the peculiar quality of the 'uncanny' and ['awesome'] which survives with the quality of exaltedness and sublimity . . . ." The sacred is both attractively fascinating and repulsively alien.

How does the *mysterium tremendum* relate to doubt? Doubt is the incapacity to believe. If a person wants to believe and cannot, anxiety and terror may arise. Doubt, then, from the perspective of the seeker of faith, can become an intuition of divine otherness, of God's inaccessibility to the intellect. Religious dread, as well, includes a frightful intuition of God's transcendence and overwhelming power. That is why Hugo's images of the uncanny can prepare readers to imagine a divine presence hidden in nature.

Hugo identifies with Dürer's sacred. The final stanza describes how the artist is inspired by horror and dread:

> Aux bois, ainsi que toi, je n'ai jamais erré,
> Maître, sans qu'en mon cœur l'horreur ait pénétré,
> Sans voir tressaillir l'herbe, et, par le vent bercées,
> Pendre à tous les rameaux de confuses pensées.

Hugo anticipates Baudelaire's formulation "La nature est un Temple" which emits "de confuses paroles" as he begins in fear and trembling and ends in curiosity. The text passes from animism to a more precise suggestion that the trees' "confuses pensées" are the occult pages of nature's book (the variant "d'ineffables pensées" stresses the transcendent character of the message). The detail "par le vent agités"—which parallels "ce groupe sombre agité par le vent"—again rationalizes this vision of the sacred.

The apologetic goal is fulfilled: use nature to clarify the human dilemma. Emotions of the uncanny mediate the transition. Hugo leaps from doubt into faith:

> Dieu seul, ce grand témoin des faits mystérieux,
> Dieu seul le sait, souvent, en de sauvages lieux,
> J'ai senti, moi qu'échauffe une secrète flamme,
> Comme moi palpiter et vivre avec une âme,
> Et rire, et se parler dans l'ombre à demi-voix,
> Les chênes monstrueux qui remplissent les bois.

Hugo confidently asserts that nature and mankind speak the same language, since their soulis, at bottom, identical. Anxiety had conveyed this truth by forcing the poet to participate in multi-dimensional nature. The forest tells those who doubt to trust the unknown.

Two consecutive poems near the end of *Les Voix intérieures* resolve the problematic of doubt: **"Après une lecture de Dante"** and **"Pensar, Dudar"** (nos. 27 and 28). The first combines the insights of the bucolic Virgil with those of the frightful Dürer as it elaborates the forest as allegory of the human condition; Dante both interprets the world and inspires readers. It is significant that these three poems (which evoke Virgil, Dürer, and Dante) explicitly continue literary or artistic works which already interpret human mysteries; Hugo allegorically repeats already allegorical texts.

"Après une lecture de Dante" begins with a translation of the symbolism shared by the two poets:

> Quand le poète peint l'enfer, il peint sa vie:
> Sa vie, ombre qui fuit de spectres poursuivie;
> Forêt mystérieuse où ses pas effrayés
> S'égarent à tâtons hors des chemins frayés;

This accumulation of frightful, vague, and dark images evokes intellectual doubt which wanders without tradition ("hors des chemins frayés") in quest of an elusive faith. The first long stanza allegorizes the sins of lust, vengeance, fear, poverty, luxury, avarice, and hatred. Fantastic hallucinations concretize chaotic feelings of a life without predictable meaning:

> Noir voyage obstrué de rencontres difformes;
> Spirale aux bords douteux, aux profondeurs
>   énormes,
> Dont les cercles hideux vont toujours plus avant
> Dans une ombre où se meut l'enfer vague et vivant!
> Cette rampe se perd dans la brume indécise;

Hugo multiplies feelings of intellectual and emotional insecurity ("aux bords douteux," "cercles hideux," "la brume indécise") and combines them with a sense of objective danger ("l'enfer vague et vivant"). Not only is mankind lost, but it stands helpless before a hostile, unknowable will.

Nevertheless, the poet-guide who undergoes life's horrors rises above paralyzing anxiety. The despair of a lost soul does not condemn the enlightened prophet:

> [Dante, poète inspiré,]
> Vous nous montrez toujours debout à votre droite
> Le génie au front calme, aux yeux pleins de rayons,
> Le Virgile serein qui dit: Continuons!

Hugo, Dante, and Virgil share their interior light with troubled readers. **"Après une lecture de Dante"** condenses the entire series as it recapitulates a fourfold movement: (1) anxiety and horror at human folly and perversity, (2) objective acknowledgement of suffering, (3) gathering of personal faith through detachment, (4) writing which represents a hopeful commitment to the future.

"Pensar, Dudar" reiterates the itinerary. No escape is possible; the realistic goal is to understand and accept doubt. The first stanza analyzes the psycho-physiological experience:

> C'est l'âpre anxiété qui nous tient aux entrailles,
> C'est la fatale angoisse et le trouble profond
> Qui fait que notre cœur en abîmes se fond,
> Quand un matin le sort, qui nous a dans sa serre,
> Nous mettant face à face avec notre misère,
> Nous jette brusquement, lui notre maître à tous,
> Cette question sombre:—Ame, que croyez-vous?

Hugo's subtle phenomenology of anxiety reflects his esthetics of horror: both provoke somatic reactions, "aux entrailles"; both are intuitions of intrinsic precariousness ("la fatale angoissse"). Like Pascal, Hugo evokes God's distance as we face "l'infirmité de toute notre race."

Mankind is frail, subjected to chance, and our inescapable anxiety appropriately reflects the limits of reason. For Hugo, the incapacity to believe points to the real inscrutability of the world. But there is a positive side. Doubt is the philosophical counterpart of esthetic admiration:

> C'est l'hésitation redoutable et profonde
> Qui prend, devant ce sphinx qu'on appelle le
>   monde,
> Notre esprit effrayé plus encor qu'ébloui,
> Qui n'ose dire non et ne peut dire oui!

The world as forest of symbols becomes a sphinx, a sublime enigma whose solution eludes common mortals. The mind remains cowed rather than being inspired by admiration: "Notre esprit [est] effrayé plus encore qu'ébloui."

The proud are not the only victims, for even the wise person, free from tyrannical passions, remains unsatisfied: "Lui, ce cœur sans désirs, sans fautes et sans peines? / Il pense, il rêve, il doute . . . O ténèbres humaines!" Hugo challenges readers—as did Pascal in *Pensée* 72 on the two infinities—to transform terror into humble awe, the precondition of faith.

Hugo draws a vivid picture of the century as a "frêle esquif démâté" and mortals as "matelots furieux." Images of darkness, madness, and terror evoke the disorder of the age. The poet provides "une boussole," "un port"; he must become "un phare." He will rewrite the "livre déchiré" and unify the nation. He will resolve the contradition of "l'effroi" and "l'espoir." Hugo reinvents for himself "Ce mot d'espoir écrit sur la dernière page" and, challenging the incoherent present, commits himself to the future.

Hugo relentlessly repudiates nineteenth-century skepticism. Ten more stanzas explore the relationship between thought and doubt. The two final stanzas of **"Pensar, Dudar"** refine the polarity of belief and doubt by combining humility and awe. Hugo rejects once and for all proud, destructive skepticism: "Rire, et conclure tout par la négation, / Comme c'est plus aisé, c'est ce que font les hommes." Modern faith must acknowledge that the path to God must, at some crucial point, bypassreason. The conclusion seems to feature resignation, but closer scrutiny reveals its complexity:

> Il suffit que chaque âme en recueille une goutte [de
>   la vérité],
> Même à l'erreur mêlée! Hélas! Tout homme en soi
> Porte un obscur repli qui refuse la foi.

Thinking remains ambivalent, for it both conceives the ideal and questions it. But there is an alternative to despair—dread, a mixture of respect and terror before the mystery: "Dieu! la mort! mots sans fond qui cachent un abîme! / L'épouvante [variant: L'anxiété] saisit le cœur le plus sublime / Dès qu'il s'est hasardé sur de si grandes caux." Anxiety is the necessary threshold to the holy.

Hugo's religious anxiety combines resignation, terror, and hope. The mind will cure its relative impotence if the heart perceives its divine foundation:

> Il n'est pas de croyant si pur et si fidèle
> Qui ne tremble et n'hésite à de certains moments.
> Quelle âme est sans faiblesse et sans accablements?
> Enfants! résignons-nous et suivons notre route.
> Tout corps traîne son ombre, et tout esprit son
>   doute.

This acceptance does not exclude effort nor does it cease to challenge. The poem's penultimate line, in fact, stresses the activist imperative: "résignons-nous *et suivons notre route,*" which echoes Virgil's "Continuons!" in **"Après une lecture de Dante."** The voyage requires courage, however, for doubt and pain are as inseparable as body and mind. Even the purest of believers carries his burden of dread.

Hugo consolidates his mission when he resolves the problem of doubt. **"Pensar, Dudar"** is followed by only four other poems in *Les Voix intérieures*. The spiritual itinerary is complete. Readers conclude that doubt and thought are inseparable, but that the struggle can release a rich flow of creative energy. Hugo's terror passes from esthetic titillation to participation in the sacred. The poet's conscious understanding of mystery somewhat paradoxically endows him with the confidence to reconcile himself with his brother's madness and death (in poem 29) and to formulate his

permanent persona, Olympio. Finally, he announces his militancy, boldly, and somewhat violently, in the last poem, **"O muse, contiens-toi! muse aux hymnes d'airain."** The fourth volume, *Les Rayons et les ombres* (1840), repeats those commitments in the famous manifestoes, **"Fonction du poète"** (no. 1), **"Tristesse d'Olympio"** (no. 34), and the final poem, **"Sagesse"** (no. 44). The Romantic prophet has emerged from the ambiguous dawn.

John E. Coombes (essay date 1993)

SOURCE: "State, Self and History in Victor Hugo's *L'Année Terrible,*" in *Studies in Romanticism,* Vol. 32, No. 3, Fall, 1993, pp. 367-78.

[*In the essay below, Coombes discusses Hugo's treatment of history and politics in* L'Année terrible.]

Hugo's last major poem sequence, and perhaps the last major poetic statement of European romanticism [*L'Année terrible*], was written in 1870-72, throughout the historical events with which it is concerned: the Franco-Prussian war, the Commune and their aftermath. Its articulation upon those events is thus very different from that of Wordsworth's *The Prelude,* with its attempt at a monolithic tranquillity of retrospection upon the Revolution, or indeed—to cite a less evidently conservative/conservatory instance—Heine's *Deutschland, Ein Wintermärchen,* generated out of the depressing yet constant condition of political exile.

Rather, the conditions of writing of *L'Année Terrible*—from the last months of Republican exile in Jersey through residence in the Paris of siege and civil war, to brief renewed exile in, and expulsion from, Belgium after the Commune—resemble the vicissitudes of that other great epic of mixed political hope and despair, *Paradise Lost.* And indeed, in its invective power, its coruscations and intercalations of mythology, its problematic convictions of righteousness, *L'Année Terrible* deserves the epithet "Miltonic," with its further connotations of classical virtue and the imperatives of resistance to political degeneracy, as specified in Hugo's **"Prologue":**

> La république anglaise expire, se dissout,
> Tombe, et laisse Milton derrière elle debout;
> La foule a disparu, mais le penseur demeure

> [The English republic fades, dissolves,
> Falls, leaves Milton standing there;
> The crowd has disappeared, the thinker remains]

Particularly, the negotiations in Hugo's work, of poetic/textual truth and political/historical fact, are oblique. The text contains relatively little explicit reference to the "major" historical events with which it is closely involved; historical references, obscure to the modern reader, are often made in passing with the result that recourse to the footnotes of a scholarly edition has the effect of engendering, for the reader, a certain sense of fragmentariness, of structured chaos both within the writing and in its further communication. In general, the relation of text and context in *L'Année Terrible* comes to seem very like that perceived in those configurations of ground and figure with which we are all familiar, those complementary silhouettes where each constitutes the other by its momentary absence and where the branches of a tree may, in the blinking of an eye, be transformed into a donkey's head, and vice versa. Such a paradoxical relationship—arguably the condition of all textuality, particularly evident here—is signally achieved in the three poems of invective against the hapless and subsequently (deservedly) obscure general Trochu (Janvier V **"Sommation"**; Janvier XII; Juin XVII). In the first, a "Sommation" of extreme agitated tension, directed at the unnamed but identifiable military butt, deployment of proto-expressionist chiaroscuro effects enacts the contrast between action and inaction, popular will and military timidity:

> L'heure est sombre; il s'agit de sauver l'empyrée
> Qu'une nuée immonde et triste vient ternir,
> De dégager le bleu lointain de l'avenir,
> Et de faire une guerre implacable à l'abîme.

> [The hour is dark; now to save the firmament
> Threatened by a ghastly deadening cloud,
> To free the future's distant blue,
> and fight to the end against the abyss.]

The tendency of the poem is to cast its ostensible historical subject, Trochu, into a gulf of nothingness (it is notable to what extent familiar Hugolian imagery—"gouffre," "abîme," "ombre"—gains a new preponderance throughout the text); the corresponding imaging of inchoate viscosity has more in common with Rimbaud (and later Sartre and Malraux) than with the relatively stable identities of earlier romantic utterance:

> Quand tous les êtres bas, visqueux, abjects, jaloux,
> L'affreux lynx, le chacal boiteux, l'hyène obscène,
> L'aspic lâche, ont pu, grâce à la brume malsaine,
> Sortir rôder, glisser, ramper, boire du sang . . .

> [When all those creatures, vile, viscous, abject,
>   jealous
> Hideous lynx, lame jackal, obscene hyena,
> Creeping asp, have, through the foetid mist
> Come to slide, slither, crawl, suck blood . . .]

Similarly, in the second poem against Trochu-Tartuffe—"ce pauvre homme" (Janvier XII)—the motor forces of history, "Audace, Humanité, Volonté, Liberté," are juxtaposed/deadlocked against the personality of their conjunctural bearer, "dont le suprême instinct serait d'être immobile" ["whose primordial instinct would seem to be remaining still"]; the resultant articulation is of madness, nothingness:

> . . . notre démence,
> Devant le noir nadir et le zénith vermeil,
> Ajoute un chien d'aveugle aux chevaux du soleil.

> [. . . our madness
> Before the black nadir and the crimson zenith,
> Sends a blind man's dog towards the horses of the
>   sun.]

Intriguingly, Trochu's last poetic (dis)appearance (in Juin XVM) involves his reduction to a suggestive epistemological trace, to the status—in a brilliantly apposite pun—of the past participle of the invented verb *tropchoir* (to fall too far); a reflexive evocation of the collapse, not only of the ruling state order and its dominant notions of subjectivity, but of its very possibilities for signification itself.

The eclipse of the established, individualist, notion of the subject and of his/her language is central to the work as a whole; *L'Année Terrible* may be seen, indeed, as a notation of the disintegration of the romantic ideology of subjectivity and its quasi-mythological certainties under the pressure of events, notably the transition from foreign to civil war and the accompanying destabilization of perceptions of self and world as political discourses.

Thus the Prologue, **"Les 7 500 000 oui (Publié en Mai 1870)"**—ostensibly an attack on Napoléon III's last, successful, plebiscite—articulates at a high level of concentration the contradictions of liberal romantic Republicanism; it may be seen, in major ways, to assert the continuation from exile of the Second Republic which had been Hugo's project ever since the *Coup d'état.* In it we find much classic Republican élitism, manifest in the familiarly Olympian self-imaging of the poet:

> La foule passe, crie, appelle, pleure, fuit;
> Versons sur ses douleurs la pitié fraternelle.

> [The crowd goes by, shouts, calls out, weeps, flees;
> Let us assuage its pain with fraternal pity.]

Romantic poetic subjectivity is, then, initially manifest in a distanced sympathy for the coherent entity represented by the "peuple," as against the inchoate anarchy of the (lumpenproletarian) "foule." The uncertainty of the distinction was to be made explicit by Marx in his text on the Commune, *The Civil War In France,* where capacity for both "the highest and the lowest deeds" is ascribed to the lumpenproletariat; it is, moreover, reminiscent of perennial tensions in the romantic social thinking of 1848, of Michelet, Renan, George Sand. To the suggested plenitude of "le peuple"—"Ce vieux dormeur d'airain"—however, is counterposed "la foule," as later in Yeats, seen as fluctuating and contradictory, as ". . . la sombre faiblesse et . . . la force sombre." More socially specific, yet suffused with a certain conservatism, is the critique of modern individualist rootlessness as the product of capitalist property-relations:

> Ah! le premier venu, bourgeois ou paysan
> L'un égoiste et l'autre aveugle, parlons-en!

> [Oh! anyone at all, bourgeois or peasant
> Whether selfish or blind, let us speak of them!]

Yet running counter to this ideological set we perceive in the text a latent critique of it; a critique which, in its self-betraying language, may be seen, for instance, to demonstrate through its deployment of an obscure imagery which approaches oxymoron, the insubstantiality of Olympian "truth" as a commodity to be distributed rather than a process collectively elaborated:

> La vérité, voilà le grand encens austère
> Qu'on doit à cette masse où palpite un mystère.
>
> [See now the truth, great austere incense
> Owed to the masses throbbing with mystery.]

The distanced formulations of post-enlightenment optimism can still be made with notable banality:

> On interrompt Jean Huss; soit; Luther continue
> La lumière est toujours par quelque bras tenue . . .
> Des justes sortiront de la foule asservie
> Iront droit au sépulcre et quitteront la vie.
>
> [Maybe Jan Huss is stopped; but Luther carries on
> The light is always passed on from hand to hand . . .
> Just men will come out from the oppressed masses
> To go to the tomb, give up their life]

Yet their notional effect is subsequently undercut by a dynamic and graphic realization of the workings of ideology itself:

> L'ombre?
> . . . On dirait que la vie éternelle recule
> La neige fait, niveau hideux du crépuscule,
> On ne sait quel sinistre abaissement des monts;
> Nous nous sentons mourir si nous nous endormons;
>   on ne distingue plus son chemin. Tout est
>   piège.
> [
> The dark?
> . . . It is as if life eternal slips away
> The snow, dread surface of the dusk,
> Bears ominously down upon the hills;
> We feel that sleeping we are already dead
>   . . . We can no longer find our way. All's a trap.]

The perceived drive towards nothingness "—[la] mort à la vertu donne un baiser farouche" ["death gives a wild kiss to virtue"]—outruns the text's manifest assertion of reformist palliatives, just as fluid contortions of language and imagery outrun banal assertion:

> Qui donc s'est figuré
> . . . Que j'entrasse au cachot s'il entre au cabanon!
> [Who had ever thought
> . . . that I should go to the dungeon as he to the madhouse!]

Thus does the verse attain the contradictory position which its ostensible discourse ascribes to "le premier venu," the average individual representative of the nineteenth-century status quo: "Il est sa propre insulte et sa propre ironie"

["He is his own insult, his own irony"]. Such fluctuations and contradictions extend across the corpus of **L'Année Terrible** as a whole, their critical and problematic nature becoming increasingly evident. Thus in the sequence "Août" we have, repeatedly, the arresting sense of the writing of a new conjuncture, the impact of *total* war as the consequence of Napoleon III's modern manipulation of mass politics as disorientation and dream:

> Jamais les siècles le passé,
> L'histoire n'avaient vu ce spectacle insensé,
> Ce vertige, ce rêve, un homme qui lui-même,
> . . . Prend la peine d'ouvrir sa fosse . . .
>
> [Never had centuries past,
> Had history seen this senseless spectacle
> This dizzying dream, a man himself,
> . . . Working to open up his tomb . . .]

The perennial structured confusions of the late Napoleonic project are of course innovatory; their dimensions are more systematically explored both in Hugo's *Histoire d'un Crime* and in Marx's *Eighteenth Brumaire of Louis Bonaparte;* their significance for developments of right-wing totalitarianism in the twentieth century is now apparent. Yet at this point the discourse presented in opposition is still one of liberal balance; Hugo's elegiac suggestion of a decline from the status of the Napoleon for whom "le côté de clarté cachait le côté d'ombre" ["the side of light hid the side of darkness"] seems a notable escape from contemporary engagement into past myth.

In the same way we perceive in Octobre III—a poem notably shackled, so to speak, by residual bourgeois ideology—a retreat, a considerable reduction of dynamic range; first the Miltonic imaging of the chaos of battle, in which the rapid intermingling of concepts and levels ensures that chaos becomes not merely the topic but the condition of the poem:

> Le gouffre est comme un mur énorme de fumée
> Où fourmille on ne sait quelle farouche armée;
> . . . Et les bruits infernaux et les bruits souterrains
> Se mêlent, et, hurlant au fond de la géhenne,
> Les tonnerres ont l'air de bêtes à la chaîne.
> . . . Et ce chaos s'acharne à tuer cette sphère.
> Lui frappe avec la flamme, elle avec la lumière.
>
> [The gulf is like a massive wall of smoke
> In which some wild army rages;
> . . . And sounds infernal, subterranean
> Are mingled, and, shrieking in hellish depths,
> Thunder has the sound of beasts enchained,
> . . . Such chaos seeks to kill the very sphere.
> Which, struck by its flame, strikes back with light.]

But then follows the imposition of uncertain stability, implicit—if momentary—confirmation of a pathetically serene liberal ideology:

> Tout à coup un rayon sort par une trouée
> Une crinière en feu, par les vents secouée,
> Apparaît . . . le voilà!

[A sudden shaft of light shines through a crack
A fiery mane, swept by the winds,
Comes forth . . . see!]

In the opposite direction, however, we observe in the series "Novembre" and "Décembre" the eventual eclipse of a series of articulations of conventional bourgeois moralism. In **"Du haut de la muraille de Paris"** (Novembre I), notably, is to be found a reversionary poetic tendency more characteristic of Vigny than Hugo. Here, evocation of the twilight is anything but conventionally harmonious,

La nuit se fermait ainsi qu'une prison
. . . Le couchant n'était plus qu'une lame sanglante

[Night closed in like a prison
. . . The setting sun just a dripping blade]

yet the last stanza obliterates the immediacy of the effects which precede it by a dogmatic specification of explicit significance: "Cela faisait penser à quelque grand duel . . ." ["It called to mind some great duel . . ."].

The procedure—of dogmatic pedagogics rather than of poetic logic—has its correlatives in the inadequate, explicit politics of much of the series, with their simple manicheism ("Paris diffamé à Berlin"), banal moralism ("A tous ces princes") and—perhaps the nadir of the tendency—the vindictive banality of "En voyant flotter sur la Seine des cadavres prussiens":

'Allons chez la prostituée
. . . Paris, cette ville publique,
. . . Nous ouvrira ses bras . . .'
Et la Seine son lit.

['Let us go whoring
. . . Paris, strumpet city,
. . . Will open her arms to us . . .'
And the Seine her bed.]

But against such an image of Paris must be set the emergent notation of the city as collective subjectivity. Already apparent in **"Lettre à une femme"** (Janvier II) in which poetic Olympian individuality is occluded—"On est un peuple, on est un monde, on est une âme" ["Being a people, being a world, being a soul"]—the tendency is later more fully manifest, not just as a mode of being, but in a sense of shared practice:

Ce tumulte enseignant la science aux savants
Ce grand lever d'aurore au milieu des vivants.
(Janvier 1871, IV)

[This tumult teaching science to the scholar
This great dawning in the middle of the living.]

Such a perception of the transformation of "normal" human and social relations may be seen to provide the narrative context for the negative primordial charge of three centrally important poems, **"Sommation," "Une bombe aux Feuillantines,"** and **"Le Pigeon"** (Janvier 1871, V, VI, VII). Here we have a coruscation of expressionist effects *avant la lettre*—of light and dark, of emptiness, focus and flux, of presence and absence, infinite space and minute detail (**"Le pigeon"**)—which collectively constitutes a clear notation of political and cultural crisis to which received notions of writing are clearly no longer adequate.

The nature of the crisis—and of the work's figuration of it—is already apparent in the positive centrality of **"Loi de formation du progrès"** (Février V). The significance of the poem may be seen, in a sense, as the transition it effects from the world of 1848 to the world of the Commune, from the abstract post-enlightenment suggestion, reminiscent of Pope and Voltaire, of

quelque but final, dont notre humble prunelle
N'aperçoit même pas la lueur éternelle,
[Some final end, whose everlasting light
Cannot be glimpsed by our humble gaze]

to the implicit and forceful denunciation of such abstractions as projections of order, authority and social privilege:

Qui se promènera dans les éternités
Comme dans les jardins de Versailles Lenôtre?

[Who shall stroll through eternity
As did Lenôtre in the gardens of Versailles?]

From the distanced assertion of Olympian judgment

On voit la loi de paix, de vie et bonté
Pardessus l'infini dans les prodiges luire

[The law of peace, of life, of goodness
Is seen to shine beyond infinity in its marvels]

to the evocation of the self as discontinuous, problematic:

La loi!
Qui la connaît? Quelqu'un parmi nous, hors de soi,
Comme en soi . . .
A-t-il percé ce gouffre?

[The law!
Who knows it? Who amongst us, beside himself,
As in himself . . .
Has penetrated this chasm?]

From affirmation of the isolate self to that of positive human relations through and with others, the poem significantly moves from its earlier bland assertion that slavery is at least an advance on cannibalism to a final denunciation of imperialism very different in tone:

Le plus grand siècle peut avoir son heure immonde;
Parfois sur tous les points du globe un fléau
gronde.

[The greatest age of all may have its darkest hour;
And all across the globe rumbles the scourge's
sound.]

From these central movements on, reversion to liberal individualist discourse in *L'Année Terrible* is increasingly disrupted, offset, outweighed by radical shifts in understanding in which "literature" and "politics" are often merged. Thus, characteristically, the bloody repression of the Commune is denounced as "Alceste . . . aujourd'hui fusillé par Philinte" ["Alceste today . . . shot down by Philinte"], a Rousseauesque reading of Molière which breaks drastically with bourgeois notions of good sense and rationality. Thus does the poem **"Les fusillés"** (Juin XII) proclaim its indivisible radicalism; further, it incorporates a shift to a point in political understanding (of the "otherness" of opposing classes and their forms of reason) unrivalled in contemporary writing (or indeed in the early sequences of the work itself).

A stupendous realization of empathy with the Communard insurgents is throughout apparent:

Il semble
qu ils ont hâte de fuir un monde âpre, incomplet.

[It seems
They long to leave a world so harsh, so
    incomplete.]

(Politicization of romantic notions of totality)

. . . ils ne tiennent pas à la vie; elle est faite
De façon qu'il leur est égal de s'en aller.

[They do not care for life; it is such
That they do not mind leaving it behind.]

(Discretion and laconic respect);

Ils sont étrangers à tout ce qui se passe.

[They are apart from everything that happens.]

(Recognition of alienation both as a social variable and as an ontological category);

Etre avec nous, cela les étouffait.
Ils partent.

[Being with us stifled them
They leave.]

(Recognition of the writer's social distance; an elegy rather than an affirmation).

Moments such as these are indeed extraordinary. They culminate in the transformation of the Hugolian trope of "l'abîme" into the realization that this abyss is indeed the hell of oppressive social relations. And the transforming recognition is complemented by that of the narrating subject as, necessarily, the bearer of privilege. The import of such a transformation—how far, so to speak, the poem has come—may be demonstrated by a comparison of two poems, **"Choix entre deux pations"** (September I) and **"A qui la faute?"** (Juin VIII), which use virtually identical effects of narrative retardation to achieve their effect.

In the first, a contrived and rather effete climax is achieved by the brief exclamation—"O ma mère!"—which constitutes the entirety of the poem's second part ("A la France"), the first part consisting of a lengthy enumeration of the qualities of German culture ("A L'Allemagne"). The touching simplicity of conventional patriotism is quite evidently the sought-after effect, and no doubt achieved within its limits which are, after all, merely those of ritual confirmation. In the later poem, the narrator's interrogation of a Communard who has just set fire to a library carries an altogether different impact. Here, the contrast between the interrogator's prolonged, sonorous, idealist abstractions

"As-tu donc oublié que ton libérateur,
C'est le livre?"
["Can you have forgotten that the book
Is your liberator?"]

and the worker's one line reply—"Je ne sais pas lire" ["I cannot read"]—points to the material superficiality of pretentions to exclusive cultural power in a situation where two divergent class-discourses, two languages, can have little contact. Clearly, between the two poems the discourse of nation has been supplanted by the discourse of class; a manner of discursive disruption emerges which, in its laconic questioning of the axiomatic validity of established notions of language and culture themselves, looks forward notably to the poetry of Brecht.

In **"Flux et reflux"** (Juillet II), the awareness of discontinuity and structural diversity which we have already noted is warranted, amplified, by a consciousness of the significance of *will* as a necessary shaping principle, if human experience is not to be enclosed in a mechanistic fatalism:

Ces flux et ces reflux,
Ces recommencements, ces combats, sont voulus.

[These ebbs and flows
These new beginnings, struggles, all are willed.]

Stress on the will as a determinant natural factor, paradoxical though it may seem, places Hugo's poem here in a line of rational materialist thinking that leads from Marx to Gramsci and Althusser. In the same text, notably, the awareness of possible universal degeneracy—

Le pauvre a le haillon, le riche a le lambeau,
Rien d'entier pour personne; et sur tous l'ombre
    infâme.

[To the poor his rags, to the rich his tatters,
Nothing whole for anyone; and over all the dread
    shadow.]

—has evident affinities with Marx's warning of the possible "common ruin of all classes," the very antithesis of the mechanistic optimism so perennially ascribed to revolutionary thinking.

The alternative to such a distortion is suggested, finally, in Hugo's articulation of a revolutionary, collective optimism far removed from the text's initially distanced representation of the "peuple," in **"Le Procès à la Révolution"** where material conflict rather than abstract harmony is frankly asserted as the motor of history:

> Le monde ténébreux râle; que d'agonies!
> Il fait jour, c'est affreux! . . .
> Le rayon sans pitié prend l'ombre et la dévore . . .

> [The world of shadows slowly rattles out its last!
> And now the dreadful birth of day! . . .
> Its heartless light seizes and devours the gloom . . .]

Darkness at noon? At any event, the collusive stance of individualist romanticism has been supplanted by a discourse revolutionary in both procedure and effect.

FURTHER READING

Biography

Houston, John Porter. *Victor Hugo*. Revised. Boston: Twayne, 1988, 167 p.
    Concise study of Hugo's life and works, with an emphasis on his poetry. Includes selected bibliography.

Josephson, Matthew. *Victor Hugo: A Realistic Biography of the Great Romantic*. Garden City, N.Y.: Doubleday, Doran & Co., 1942, 514 p.
    Detailed biography in which Josephson considers Hugo "one of the greatest exemplars of the sedentary, meditative type of man, turning from his study to service in public life."

Marzials, Frank T. *Life of Victor Hugo*. London: Walter Scott, 1888, 254 p.
    General biography which includes an early bibliography of works by and about Hugo.

Maurois, André. *Olympio: The Life of Victor Hugo*. translated by Gerard Hopkins. New York: Harper & Brothers, 1956, 498 p.
    Definitive biography. Maurois calls Hugo the greatest of all French poets and states that "we need to know the story of his life if we are to understand his tormented genius to the full."

Criticism

Babuts, Nicolae. "Hugo's *La fin de satan:* The Identity Shift." *Symposium* 36, No. 2 (Summer 1981): 91-101.
    Analysis of *La fin de Satan* in which Babuts states: "I propose to show that Hugo's capacity to form bonds of identity with the fallen archangel has its beginnings in the act of meditation, and that it is a part of a prevailing creative behavior in which the poet assumes the identity of the protagonist."

Bach, Raymond. "*Les Contemplations* or Paternity Regained." *Romanic Review* 82, No. 3 (May 1991): 297-316.
    Provides a reading of *Les contemplations* as spiritual autobiography, basing his argument on the fact that Hugo's eldest child died when he was writing this work.

Bailey, John C. "Victor Hugo." In *The Claims of French Poetry: Nine Studies in the Greater French Poets*, pp. 177-244. London: Archibald Constable and Co., 1907.
    Positive evaluation of Hugo's poetry, in which Bailey compares Hugo's works to the writings of William Shakespeare, John Milton, Alfred Tennyson, and others.

Burt, E. S. "Hallucinatory History: Hugo's *Révolution*." *Modern Language Notes* 105, No. 5 (December 1990): 965-91.
    Examines Hugo's treatment of history in *Révolution*, stating "the question to be pursued in what follows . . . is the question of what poems have to say about the pressures in language toward reference and signification, as also what they have to say about their historicity."

Grant, Richard B. "Progress, Pessimism, and Revelation in Victor Hugo's *Dieu*." *Nineteenth Century French Studies* 17, No. 1 (Fall/Winter 1988-1989): 44-57.
    Addresses the difficulties associated with interpreting Hugo's unfinished poetic work *Dieu*, which the poet left with three possible endings.

———. "Sequence and Theme in Victor Hugo's *Les Orientales*." *PMLA* 94, No. 5 (October 1979): 894-908.
    Offers a fresh perspective on Hugo's *Les orientales*, based on the discovery of a new pattern among the poems.

Greenberg, Wendy Nicholas. *The Power of Rhetoric: Hugo's Metaphor and Poetics*. New York: Peter Lang, 1985, 143 p.
    Analyzes formal aspects of Hugo's lyrical poetry, including structure, extended metaphor, and symbolization.

Houston, John Porter. "Hugo's Later Poetry." In *The Demonic Imagination: Style and Theme in French Romantic Poetry*, pp. 140-71. Baton Rouge: Louisiana State University Press, 1969.
    Examines the theological concepts underlying *Dieu, La fin de satan*, and *La légende des siècles*.

Kessler, Joan C. "'Cette Babel du monde': Visionary Architecture in the Poetry of Victor Hugo." *Nineteenth Century French Studies* 19, No. 3 (Spring 1991): 417-31.
    Analyzes the architectural imagery in such poems as "Le feu du ciel," "La pente," and "La vision."

Longfellow, Henry Wadsworth. "Victor-Marie Hugo." In *The Poets and Poetry of Europe*, p. 494. London: C. S. Francis and Company, 1855.
    Briefly praises Hugo's poetry.

Martin, Eva. "Victor Hugo: Poet, Patriot, Philosopher (1802-1885)." *The Hibbert Journal* XLIV (October 1945): 69-75.
    Laudatory overview of Hugo's life and career.

Nash, Suzanne. *Les Contemplations of Victor Hugo: An Allegory of the Creative Process*. Princeton: Princeton University Press, 1976, 229 p.

Attempts to distinguish Hugo's contributions to modernist poetics, which historically have been overlooked by English critics.

———. "Victor Hugo's *Odes et ballades* and the Romantic Lyric." *Michigan Romance Studies* IX (1989): 73-95.
Reevaluates *Odes et ballades* and examines the influence of the works on future experiments in the poetic genre.

Peyre, Henri. *Victor Hugo: Philosophy and Poetry.* Translated by Roda P. Roberts. University: University of Alabama Press, 1980, 132 p.
Discusses Hugo's ideas on such subjects as prayer, evil, and immortality.

Poulet, Georges. "Hugo." In *The Interior Distance.* Translated by Elliott Coleman, pp. 153-87. Baltimore: The Johns Hopkins Press, 1952.
Examines spatial imagery in Hugo's poetry and prose.

Prais, Henry. "The Lilith Myth in Victor Hugo's *La Fin de Satan* and Its Source." In *Myth and Legend in French Literature: Essays in Honour of A. J. Steele,* edited by Keith Aspley, David Bellos, and Peter Sharratt, pp. 155-72. London: Modern Humanities Research Association, 1982.
Examines Hugo's interpretation of the biblical myth of Lilith in *La fin de Satan.*

Riffaterre, Michael. "The Poem as Representation: A Reading of Hugo." In *Text Production,* translated by Terese Lyons, pp. 181-201. New York: Columbia University Press, 1983.
Detailed reading of Hugo's poem, "Ecrit sur la vitre d'une fenêtre flamande" from *Les rayons et les ombers.* Riffaterre states: "I am concerned with seeing how the utterance . . . submits to the imperatives of semantic and formal associations among words."

Swinburne, Algernon Charles. "The Work of Victor Hugo." In *The Complete Works of Algernon Charles Swinburne: Prose Works,* Vol. III, edited by Sir Edmund Gosse and Thomas James Wise, pp. 13-111. London: William Heinemann Ltd., 1926.
Discusses and praises Hugo's poetry.

Taylor, Bayard. "Victor Hugo." In *Critical Essays and Literary Notes,* pp. 37-54. New York: G. P. Putnam's Sons, 1880.
Mixed review of *La légende des siècles.*

Ward, Patricia A. "La Légende des Siècles." In *The Medievalism of Victor Hugo,* pp. 84-99. University Park: Pennsylvania State University Press, 1975.
Discusses Hugo's portrayal of the Middle Ages in *La légende des siècles.*

Wellek, Rene. "Stendhal and Hugo." In *A History of Modern Criticism Vol. II: The Romantic Age,* pp. 241-58. New Haven: Yale University Press, 1955.
Analysis of Hugo's theories of poetry within the context of French Romanticism.

Additional coverage of Author's life and career is contained in the following sources published by Gale Research: *Nineteenth Century Literature Criticism,* Vols. 3, 10, 21; *DISCovering Authors;* *DISCovering Authors: Dramatists Module;* *DISCovering Authors: Most-Studied Authors Module;* *DISCovering Authors: Novelists Module;* *DISCovering Authors: Poets Module;* *World Literature Criticism, 1500 to Present;* *Dictionary of Literary Biography,* Vol. 119; and *Something About the Author,* Vol. 47.

Robinson Jeffers
1887-1962

(Full name John Robinson Jeffers) American poet, playwright, and essayist.

INTRODUCTION

Jeffers is a controversial figure in twentieth-century American poetry whose prophetic admonitions against modern civilization have attracted both critical censure and admiration. He is perhaps best known for long dramatic narrative poems in which he combined brutal imagery with a somber tone and dense syntax to explore unsettling topics. Guided by his philosophy of "inhumanism," which he defined as "a shifting of emphasis and significance from man to not-man; the rejection of human solipsism and recognition of the transhuman magnificence," Jeffers contrasted the strength and enduring beauty of nature with a tragic vision of human suffering and inconsequence. Incorporating structures and themes from Greek drama, the Bible, and Eastern mysticism, and influenced by such thinkers as Lucretius, Arthur Schopenhauer, and Friedrich Nietzsche, Jeffers drew upon science, history, nature, and contemporary events for subject material. Jeffers was also inspired by the landscape and legends of southern California's Monterey coast, where he lived throughout his adult life.

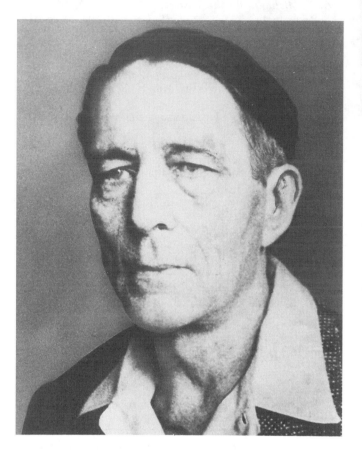

Biographical Information

Jeffers was born in Pittsburgh, Pennsylvania. He was tutored by his father, a Presbyterian preacher and theologian, in various languages, the classics, and the Bible before being sent to boarding schools in Switzerland and Germany. Following his graduation from Occidental College in 1905, Jeffers earned a master's degree in literature from the University of Southern California; he later spent several years studying medicine at USC and forestry at the University of Washington. A modest inheritance enabled Jeffers and his wife to settle on an isolated plot of coastal land in Carmel, California, where he built a stone house and tower overlooking the Pacific Ocean and devoted himself to his art. After suffering from numerous illnesses later in his life, Jeffers died in 1962.

Major Works

Jeffers's first two books, *Flagons and Apples* (1912) and *Californians* (1916), are generally considered derivative and undistinguished. *Roan Stallion, Tamar and Other Poems* (1925), which was originally published at Jeffers's own expense as *Tamar and Other Poems* (1924), exhibits a significant advance from his earlier work. Rejecting traditional modes, Jeffers utilizes simple, declarative, and often colloquial language as well as long narrative forms, while exploring sexual themes that display the influence of Sigmund Freud, Carl Jung, and Havelock Ellis. "Tamar," for example, illustrates the folly of incest through a tragic tale of sexual passion between a sister and her brother. Based on a story from the second book of Samuel, "Tamar" combines California locales with biblical diction and themes. "Roan Stallion" centers on a woman whose abusive husband is killed by her horse when she flees to the animal for protection. After slaying the horse in retaliation for the death of her husband, the woman realizes that she has destroyed the embodiment of her freedom. Her subsequent anguish symbolizes the suffering that humanity inflicts upon itself when it squanders opportunities for change and improvement. "The Tower beyond Tragedy" is drawn from Aeschylus's *Oresteia,* in which Orestes kills his mother to avenge her murder of his father, Agamemnon. In his version, Jeffers focuses on the character of Cassandra whom Agamemnon obtains as spoil from his victory at Troy and who prophesies many of the grim events that follow. Jeffers's Cassandra foretells not only the fall of old empires, as in the Greek myth, but that of future civilizations. Some of the shorter lyrics in this collection describe southern California's terrain and display Jeffers's knowledge of biology, astronomy, and physics.

The Women at Point Sur (1927) is a complex dramatic narrative poem that is considered one of Jeffers's most controversial works. Described by Dwight McDonald as "a witches' dance of incest, suicide, madness, adultery and Lesbianism," this piece relates the story of Barclay, a Christian minister whose disillusionment with the war that claimed his only son turns him from theology. Abandoning his wife and church, Barclay withdraws to the Carmel coast, where he seeks to establish a new religion based on the external world. He is distracted from his intention, however, by overbearing narcissism and lust for his daughter. Barclay eventually goes insane, and following an orgy of destruction, he wanders off to die in the hills. Modern in its use of science for poetic material and its candid, realistic concern with sex, *The Women at Point Sur* satirizes human self-importance and explores harmful aspects of civilization.

Cawdor and Other Poems (1928) is regarded by some critics as Jeffers's finest single volume. The title poem of this collection is based on the plot of Euripides's *Hippolytus,* in which Hippolytus is cursed by Aphrodite with the physical love of Phaedra, his stepmother. When Phaedra hangs herself in grief over her stepson's resistance to her advances, Hippolytus is driven from Athens by his father, whose prayers are fulfilled when his son is dragged to death by his own horses. This book also contains several short verses in unrhymed forms that focus upon the benefits of death over life. The title piece of *Dear Judas and Other Poems* (1929) dramatizes the crucifixion of Jesus Christ by adapting elements of Japanese Noh theater. Narrated by the ghosts of Jesus, the Virgin Mary, and Judas, "Dear Judas" exhibits Jeffers's most sustained concern with human emotion. This volume also includes "The Loving Shepherdess," a dramatic narrative about a long-suffering young woman who roams the southern California coast. During her travels, she encounters a friendly vaquero to whom she relates the events which have led to her tragic predicament. *Descent to the Dead: Poems Written in Ireland and Great Britain* (1931) contains sixteen short poems written in stately verse that feature local color and lore. In the title piece of *Thurso's Landing and Other Poems* (1932), Jeffers recounts the tale of an unhappily married couple whose passion is unable to save them from misery and confusion. *Give Your Heart to the Hawks and Other Poems* (1933) presents a psychological portrait of a strong-willed man who is driven insane by remorse for the murder of his brother. This volume also includes several short pieces that are predominantly concerned with themes of death and resurrection, poems from *Descent to the Dead,* and "At the Fall of an Age," which concerns the death of Helen on the island of Rhodes twenty years after the fall of Troy.

In *Solstice and Other Poems* (1935), Jeffers presents a modern version of the Greek legend of Medea based on an account by Euripides. This volume also contains the long narrative "At the Birth of an Age." Derived from the final sections of the Teutonic epic the *Nibelungenlied,* this poem portrays a petty argument between three sibling leaders of a small Germanic tribe and their sister. Jeffers overshadows the individual personalities of his characters by emphasizing the enormous consequences of their small-minded conduct. The title piece of *Such Counsels You Gave to Me and Other Poems* (1937) features a modern version of a traditional Scottish ballad in which the protagonist's medical acumen provides Jeffers with a vehicle for demonstrating his knowledge of science. Also included in this volume are short poems concerning Jeffers's refusal to align himself with any particular economic, social, or political movement, a position for which he was frequently criticized. *Be Angry at the Sun* (1941) contains several controversial portraits of Adolf Hitler, whom Jeffers considered historically necessary and simultaneously fascinating and disgusting. In *The Double Axe and Other Poems* (1948), Jeffers utilizes elements of Eastern ideology to convey the alienation and hatred experienced by many veterans of war. The title poem of this collection is a tale of a young soldier who returns from the dead to confront and kill his father, who had sent him into battle during World War II. This volume also features the philosophical poem "The Inhumanist," in which Jeffers expounds his fundamental convictions. In the final collection published during his lifetime, *Hungerfield and Other Poems* (1954), which was inspired by his wife's death in 1950, Jeffers portrays death as a welcome respite from life's distress.

Critical Reception

Critical reaction to Jeffers's work has fluctuated greatly. During the 1920s and early 1930s, Jeffers was hailed as among the greatest living American writers; *Time* magazine, which is often considered a barometer of popular achievement, placed him on its cover in 1932. During the Depression and World War II, however, Jeffers suffered a reversal of literary reputation that critics variously attribute to his unpopular social and political views, the diminishing quality of his verse, and the rise of New Criticism. Since his death, Jeffers's work has undergone extensive reevaluation, and several of his shorter poems, including "Shine, Perishing Republic," "Boats in a Fog," and "To the Stone-Cutters," remain essential to anthologies of American verse. Mercedes Cunningham Monjian concluded in 1958: "Whatever the future holds for this poet, our own age is still awed by the magnificent talent and effort of a burdened mind struggling to free humanity from the shackles of an impoverished self-love, and the myths to which he believes it gave birth."

PRINCIPAL WORKS

Poetry

Flagons and Apples 1912
Californians 1916
Tamar and Other Poems 1924
Roan Stallion, Tamar and Other Poems 1925
The Women at Point Sur 1927
Cawdor and Other Poems 1928
Poems 1928

Other Major Works

CRITICISM

Harriet Monroe (review date 1926)

SOURCE: A review of *Roan Stallion, Tamar and Other Poems,* in *Poetry,* Vol. 28, June, 1926, pp. 160-64.

[*In the following review of* Roan Stallion, Tamar and Other Poems, *Monroe disparages the long poems in the volume but praises such short poems as "Woodrow Wilson" and "Night."*]

"Tamar" and all the final three-fifths of this book [***Roan Stallion, Tamar and Other Poems***] were exhaustively reviewed by James Daly in *Poetry* [in August, 1925] so that the present writer need only record her hearty agreement with that review, her recognition of the "deep poetic compulsion" in Mr. Jeffers' usually distinguished art. All the more is it to be regretted that the title-poem of this larger book, if not 'prentice-work dug up and retouched, as I suspect, is of a quality quite unworthy of the author of **"Tamar."** But it is doubtful whether even the most accomplished artistry would excuse the deliberate choice of so revolting a subject. Apparently Mr. Jeffers wanted

to see how far he could go with himself and his newly acquired public; and we may be permitted to express a hope that the poet has now registered his final limit in a direction so repellant to modern taste.

Mr. Jeffers was brought up on classic literature, his father being a professor of Greek; therefore the class of subjects under discussion may come to his mind more naturally than to another's. But whereas to the Greek poet all the pagan energies of life were open ground for his spirit, ground almost sanctified by his myth-haunted religion, to a poet of our time and country it is impossible to explore certain jungles in the old simple and natural way. He has to force himself in; he is conscious of breathing noxious vapors in a dark melodrama of evil. The Greek audience accepted quite simply the horror as well as the beauty of its inherited myths; but the world has lived a number of centuries since then, and all the dark power of Mr. Jeffers cannot quite persuade us to swallow his modern tales of abnormal passion with the simple inherited faith of a more primitive time. The danger is that such a preoccupation may make his majestic art an anachronism, without vitality enough to endure.

In **"The Tower Beyond Tragedy"** the subject is appropriately Greek—the Clytemnestra story—and the poet's version, while too expansive, has passages of splendid eloquence, done in huge pounding rhythms like the Pacific at Carmel. Here are nine lines of Cassandra's despair:

> For me there is no mountain firm enough,
> The storms of light beating on the headlands,
> The storms of music undermine the mountains, they stumble and fall
> inward.
> Such music the stars
> Make in their courses, the vast vibration
> Plucks the iron heart of the earth like a harp-string.
> Iron and stone core, O stubborn axle of the earth, you also
> Dissolving in a little time like salt in water. . . .

This Cassandra ranges over the centuries; her prophecies reach out to the day "when America has eaten Europe and takes tribute of Asia, when the ends of the world grow aware of each other."

One turns with relief to the shorter poems which follow these. Here we have a stern and stately beauty, the expression of a harsh loneliness of soul which has studied the world afar off as it communed with sea and mountains. Perhaps this brief one, **"Joy,"** will suggest the sweep of this poet's imagination and the temper of his spirit; also his way of striking off vivid images in lines of mournful music:

> Though joy is better than sorrow, joy is not great;
> Peace is great, strength is great.
> Not for joy the stars burn, not for joy the vulture
> Spreads her gray sails on the air
> Over the mountain; not for joy the worn mountain
> Stands, while years like water

Trench his long sides. "I am neither mountain nor
  bird
Nor star; and I seek joy."
The weakness of your breed: yet at length quietness
Will cover those wistful eyes.

Not that Mr. Jeffers has been unobservant of passing events, or unpitiful of human agony. In **"Woodrow Wilson,"** a dialogue between "It" and the hero's death-enfranchised soul, we have a really noble tribute, a high recognition of tragedy. Here are the first two of the eight stanzas:

It said "Come home, here is an end, a goal,
Not the one raced for, is it not better indeed?
  Victory you know requires
Force to sustain victory, the burden is never
  lightened, but final defeat
Buys peace: you have praised peace, peace without
  victory."

He said "It seems I am traveling no new way,
But leaving my great work unfinished how can I
  rest? I enjoyed a vision,
Endured betrayal, you must not ask me to endure
  final defeat,
Visionless men, blind hearts, blind mouths, live
  still."

I should like to quote lengthily from **"Night,"** with its proud recognition of newly discovered immensities of space—

A few centuries
Gone by, was none dared not to people
The darkness beyond the stars with harps and
  habitations.
But now, dear is the truth. Life is grown sweeter
  and lonelier,
And death is no evil.

"The Torch-bearer's Race" shows man "at the world's end," where, all coasts and jungles explored, he is daring the air, "feet shaking earth off." But the poet reminds him:

In the glory of that your hawk's dream
Remember that the life of mankind is like the life
  of a man, a flutter from
  darkness to darkness
Across the bright hair of a fire.

Brooding on his rock over "the deep dark-shining Pacific," this poet has watched the course of stars and nations, and the music of his verse has acquired large rhythms. What he thinks of his own nation in its hour of splendor he tells in the poem **"Shine, Perishing Republic,"** which may be quoted as of immediate interest, and representative of his art in one of its less detached moods:

While this America settles in the mould of its
  vulgarity, heavily thickening
  to empire,
And protest, only a bubble in the molten mass, pops

and sighs out, and
  the mass hardens,
I sadly smiling remember that the flower fades to
  make fruit, the fruit rots
  to make earth.
Out of the mother; and through the spring
  exultances, ripeness and
  decadence; and home to the mother.

You making haste haste on decay: not blameworthy;
  life is good, be it
  stubbornly long or suddenly
A mortal splendor: meteors are not needed less than
  mountains: shine,
  perishing republic.

But for my children, I would have them keep their
  distance from the
  thickening center; corruption
Never has been compulsory, when the cities lie at
  the monster's feet
  there are left the mountains.

And boys, be in nothing so moderate as in love of
  man, a clever servant,
  insufferable master.
There is the trap that catches noblest spirits, that
  caught—they
  say—God, when he walked on earth.

A poet of extraordinary power is Mr. Jeffers, with perhaps a purple pride in the use of it.

Morton Dauwen Zabel (review date 1929)

SOURCE: A review of *Cawdor and Other Poems*, in *Poetry*, Vol. 33, No. 6, 1929, pp. 336-40.

[*In the mixed review of* Cawdor and Other Poems *below, Zabel praises Jeffers's technical skill as a poet but questions his detached treatment of such themes as fear and violence.*]

The theme of Robinson Jeffers' new poem ["**Cawdor**"] is the tragedy of a woman who meets the passion and selfish pride of men on their own terms, but finds herself the victim of an unimagined lust whose end comes only with the hideous defeat of those who caused her own humiliation. Even this curt summary is sufficient to indicate that **"Cawdor"** shares with **"Tamar," "Roan Stallion,"** and *The Women at Point Sur* those properties of tragic violence and broad dramatic conflict which we have come to regard as this poet's particular marks. The sensitiveness to all the forces of ancient terror, the infinite pathos of human blindness and vanity, and the strange unerring ways of biological and psychological life—these came out in that first obscure volume which gave us, five years ago, a new and remarkable writer. Since then it has become customary to think of Mr. Jeffers as the only one of our contemporary artists who has plunged bravely into the darkest waters of experience and found there the incalculable tides and currents which the Greeks tried to fathom. The comparison with Euripides has been inevitable, not only because of the subject-matter of these narratives, but also because of their style. And critics have even found occasion to point out the essential dissimilarity of Mr. Jeffers' work to that of the Greeks: its lack of real penetration, its barren spirit, its dearth of the pity which an instinct for scientific curiosity has denied him. Meanwhile Mr. Jeffers continues to write, probably quite uninfluenced by the mandates of his readers and eager to complete a body of work which he outlined long ago and determined to see to its end.

It is not necessary to deny Jeffers' work the truth and beauty which it unquestionably has. Any individual reader may fail to discover here a genuine reality, but that after all remains the failure of the individual reader.

—Morton Dauwen Zabel

It is not necessary to deny his work the truth and beauty which it unquestionably has. Any individual reader may fail to discover here a genuine reality, but that after all remains the failure of the individual reader. When work shows, as this does, ringing eloquence combined with a passionate search for honor, we are quite safe in crediting the author with some of the final attributes of genius. His shortcomings are to be credited largely to an age which has disestablished many of the relationships and laws whereby it was possible for former generations to think of life in terms of noble pity and grief. The very factors which make it possible for Mr. Jeffers to stand apart from our huge cities, our political warfare and our industrial vanity allow him to indulge in a kind of oracular aloofness. The disclosures of science have armed him with a seer-like omnipotence from which he looks down on the swarming efforts of man. He is not one of the struggling millions, like Sandburg or our other city poets. He is no road-side humanitarian, like Frost. Therefore he scorns to extend the hand of compassion to his creatures; he allows them to murder, to blind themselves, to wound and mutilate their bodies, and to break their fearful hearts.

When, in the course of his mounting drama, he stops to comment, it is with an almost disinterested candor:

The nerves of man after they die dream dimly
And dwindle into their peace; they are not very
    passionate,
And what they had was mostly spent while they
    lived.
They are sieves for leaking desire, they have many
    pleasures
And conversations; their dreams too are like that.

Or, translating science into a more fantastic imagery, he speaks with the calm demeanor of a laboratory worker:

In their deaths they dreamed a moment, the unspent
    chemistry
Of life resolving its powers; some in the cold star-
    gleam,
Some in the cooling darkness in the crushed skull.
But shine and shade were indifferent to them, their
    dreams
Determined by temperatures, access of air,
Wetness or drying, as the work of the autolytic
Enzymes of the last hunger hasted or failed.

The mistake behind this lies in the fact that, instead of writing poetry wholly in the spirit of modern reason and logic, he has endeavored to combine these factors with antique dramaturgy. His obsession for heroic violence and the grand passion of the Greeks furnishes him with wild and massive themes, and the comments of science seem very weak and puny in the midst of them. He wrote one masterpiece **"The Tower Beyond Tragedy."** The lesson in singleness of motive there presented has not served him very faithfully.

But **"Cawdor"** has passages of magnificence not often found in poetry today. Some of the early pictures of the Pacific coast and the redwood forests, the sweeping fires and gaunt ranges, are unforgettable. Where the ocean beats on the rocks three people hunt for sea-food:

They went to the waste of the ebb under the cliff,
Stone wilderness furred with dishevelled weed, but
    under each round
    black-shouldered stone universes
Of color and life, scarlet and green sea-urchins,
    violet and rose anemones,
    wave-purple urchins,
Red starfish, tenacle-rayed pomegranate-color sun-
    disks, shelled worms
    tuft-headed with astonishing
Flower-spray, pools of live crystal, quick eels
    plunged in the crevices. . . .

And, since this is a narrative poem, it must be said that few others of our time can compare with it for technical skill. The interest is consistent, the movement certain, and the shaping coherent. The characters of Fera Martial and Cawdor suffer because they are charged with too much purpose and too futile a passion; but the girl Michal and the inviolate brother Hood are alive with sympathy, and the minor figures have much variety and picturesque charm. Certain details are worked out with a sure touch. At one point Fera goes dizzy:

She felt
Her knees failing, and a sharp languor
Melt through her body; she saw the candle-flame
    (she had set the candle
    on the little table) circling
In a short orbit, and Cawdor's face waver, strange
    heavy face with the
    drooping brows and confused eyes. . . .

And many incidents are amazingly sharp in definition.

There are shorter poems in this book, notably a fine elegy on George Sterling, which aid in showing Mr. Jeffers' complete mastery of his instrument. His line may often be regular blank-verse, but it can swell into a full diapason of great power.

Yvor Winters (review date 1930)

SOURCE: A review of *Dear Judas,* in *Poetry,* Vol. 35, No. V, February, 1930, pp. 279-86.

[*Winters was a prominent American poet and critic who maintained that all good literature must serve a conscious moral purpose. In the negative review of* Dear Judas *below, he examines the themes and narrative structures in the volume, concluding that Jeffers's "aims are badly thoughtful and are essentially trivial."*]

It is difficult to write of Mr. Jeffers' latest book [*Dear Judas*] without discussing his former volumes; after his first collection he deals chiefly with one theme in all of his poems; and all of his works illustrate a single problem, a spiritual malady of considerable significance. Mr. Jeffers is theologically a kind of monist; he envisages, as did Wordsworth, Nature as Deity; but his Nature is the Nature of the physics textbook and not of the rambling botanist—Mr. Jeffers seems to have taken the terminology of modern physics more literally than it is meant by its creators. Nature, or God, is thus a kind of self-sufficient mechanism, of which man is an offshoot, but from which man is cut off by his humanity (just what gave rise to this humanity, which is absolutely severed from all connection with God, is left for others to decide): there is consequently no mode of communication between the consciousness of man and the mode of existence of God; God is praised adequately only by the screaming demons that make up the atom. Man, if he accepts this dilemma as necessary, is able to choose between two modes of action: he may renounce God and rely on his humanity, or he may renounce his humanity and rely on God.

Mr. Jeffers preaches the second choice: union with God, oblivion, the complete extinction of one's humanity, is the only good he is able to discover; and life, as such, is "incest," an insidious and destructive evil. So much, says Mr. Jeffers by implication, for Greek and Christian ethics. Now the mysticism of, say, San Juan de la Cruz offers at least the semblance of a spiritual, a human, discipline as a preliminary to union with Divinity; but for Mr. Jeffers a simple and mechanical device lies always ready; namely, suicide, a device to which he has not resorted.

In refusing to take this logical step, however, Mr. Jeffers illustrates one of a very interesting series of romantic compromises. The romantic of the ecstatic-pantheist type denies life, yet goes on living; nearly all romantics decry the intellect and philosophy, yet they offer justifications (necessarily foggy and fragmentary) of their attitude; they deride literary "technique" (the mastery of, and development of the sensitivity to, relationships between words, so that these relationships may extend almost illimitably the vocabulary) yet they write (of necessity, carelessly, with small efficiency). Not all romantics are guilty of all of these confusions, nor, doubtless, is Mr. Jeffers; but all of these confusions are essentially romantic—they are very natural developments of moral monism. And Mr. Jeffers, having decried human life as such, and having denied the worth of the rules of the game, endeavors to write narrative and dramatic poems—poems, in other words, dealing with people who are playing the game. Jesus, the hero of **"Dear Judas,"** speaking apparently for Mr. Jeffers, says that the secret reason for the doctrine of forgiveness is that all men are driven by the mechanism-God to act as they do, that they are entirely helpless; yet he adds in the next breath that this secret must be guarded, for if it were given out, men would run amuck, would get out of hand—*they would begin acting differently.*

The Women at Point Sur is a perfect laboratory of Mr. Jeffers' philosophy. Barclay, an insane divine, preaches Mr. Jeffers' religion, and his disciples, acting upon it, become emotional mechanisms, lewd and twitching conglomerations of plexi, their humanity annulled. Human experience, in these circumstances, having necessarily and according to the doctrine no meaning, there can be and is no necessary sequence of events: every act is equivalent to every other; every act is at the peak of hysteria; most of the incidents could be shuffled around into varying sequences without violating anything save, perhaps, Mr. Jeffers' private sense of their relative intensity. Since the poem is his, of course, such a private sense is legitimate enough; the point is that this is not a narrative, nor a dramatic, but a lyrical criterion. A successful lyrical poem of one hundred and seventy-five pages is unlikely, for the essence of lyrical expression is concentration, but it is at least theoretically possible. The difficulty is that the lyric achieves its effect by the generalization of emotion (that is, by the separation of the emotion from the personal history that gives rise to it in actual concrete experience) and by the concentration of expression. Narrative can survive in a measure without concentration, or intensity of detail, provided the narrative logic is detailed and compelling, as in the case of Balzac, though it is only wise to add that this occurs most often in prose. Now Mr. Jeffers, as I have pointed out, has abandoned narrative logic with the theory of ethics, and he has never achieved, in addition, a close and masterly style. His writing is loose, turgid, and careless; like most anti-intellectualists, he relies on his feelings alone and has no standard of criticism for them outside of themselves. There are occasional good flashes in his poems, and to these I shall return later, but they are very few, are very limited in their range of feeling and in their subject matter, and they are very far between. Mr. Jeffers has no remaining method of sustaining his lyric, then, other than the employment of an accidental (i.e., non-narrative) chain of anecdotes (i.e., details that are lyrically impure); his philosophical doctrine and his artistic dilemma alike decree that these shall be anecdotes of hysteria. By this method Mr. Jeffers continually *lays claim* to a high pitch of emotion which has no narrative support (that is, support of the inevitable accumulation of experience), nor lyrical support (that is, support of the intense perception of pure, or transferable, emotion), which has, in short, no support at all, and which is therefore simply unmastered and self-inflicted hysteria.

"**Cawdor**" alone of Mr. Jeffers' poems contains a plot that in its rough outlines might be sound, and [*Cawdor and other Poems*] likewise contains his best poetry; the poem as a whole, and in spite of the confused treatment of the woman, is moving, and the lines describing the seals at dawn are fine, as are the two or three last lines of the apotheosis of the eagle. Most of the preceding material in the latter passage, however, like most of the material in the sections that give Mr. Jeffers' notions of the post-mortem experience of man, are turgid, repetitious, arbitrary, and unconvincing. The plot itself is blurred for lack of stylistic finish (that is, for lack of ability on the part of the poet to see every detail of sense and movement incisively down to the last preposition, the last comma, as every detail *is* seen in Racine or Shakespeare); and it remains again a fair question whether a moral monist *can* arrive at any clear conclusions about the values of a course of action, since he denies the existence of any conceivable standard of values within the strict limits of human life as such. In "**The Tower Beyond Tragedy**" Mr. Jeffers takes a ready-made plot, the Clytemnestra-Orestes situation, which is particularly strong dramatically, because Orestes is forced to choose between two sins, the murder of his mother and the refusal to avenge his father. But at the very last moment, in Mr. Jeffers' version, Orestes is converted to Mr. Jeffers' religion and goes off explaining (to Electra, who has just tried to seduce him) that though men may think he is fleeing before the furies he is really just drifting up to the mountains to meditate on the stars; and the preceding action is, of course, rendered morally and emotionally meaningless.

In the latest volume, the title poem, "**Dear Judas,**" is a kind of dilution of *The Women at Point Sur,* with Jesus as Barclay, and with a less detailed background. Mr. Jeffers' mouthpiece and hero, Jesus, is little short of revolting as he whips reflexively from didactic passion to malice, self-justification, and vengeance. The poem shares the structural principles, or lack of them, of *The Women at Point Sur;* and it has no quotable lines, save, possibly, the last three, which are, however, heavy with dross. "**The Loving Shepherdess,**" the other long poem of the present volume, deals with a girl who knows herself doomed to die at a certain time in childbirth, and who wanders over the countryside caring for a small and diminishing flock of sheep in an anguish of devotion. The events here again are anecdotal and reversible, and the emotion is lyrical or nothing. The theme had two possibilities: the poet could have immersed the girl in a dream of approaching death, or he could have immersed her in the sentimental pathos of the immediate situation. There are moments when he seems to be trying for the former effect, but his perceptions are not fine enough and the mass of anecdotal detail is too heavy; the poem succeeds in being no more than a very Wordsworthian embodiment of a kind of maudlin humanitarianism—which is a curious but not an unexpected

outcome of Mr. Jeffers' sentimental misanthropy. The heroine is turned cruelly from door to door, and the sheep fall one by one before the reader's eyes, the doors and the sheep constituting the bulk of the anecdotal material; till finally the girl dies in a ditch in an impossible effort to give birth to her child.

There are occasional good flashes in Jeffers' poems, but they are very few, are very limited in their range of feeling and in their subject matter, and they are very far between.

—*Yvor Winters*

The short poems in the book deal with themes that Mr. Jeffers has handled better before. He has written here and there impressive lines descriptive of the sea and its rocks, and of dying birds of prey. "**Hurt Hawks II,**" in the *Cawdor* volume, is the most perfect short poem and is quite fine; there are excellent lines scattered through other pieces. These poems are, however, limited both in paraphrasable content and in experiential implication: they glorify brute nature and annihilation and are numb to the intricacies of human feeling; they share in the latter respect the limitations of all mystical poetry. Mr. Jeffers' insistence on another of his favorite lyrical themes, his own aloofness, is becoming, by dint of repetition, almost embarrassing; one has the constant feeling that he is trying to bully the reader into accepting him at his own evaluation.

Self-repetition has been the inevitable effect of anti-intellectualist doctrine on all of its supporters. If life is valued, explored, subdivided, and defined, poetic themes are infinite in number; if life is denied, the only theme is the rather sterile and monotonous one of the denial. Similarly, those poets who flee from form, which is infinitely variable, since every form is a definite and an individual thing, can achieve only the uniformity of chaos; and those individuals who endeavor to escape morality, which is personal form and controlled direction, can, in the very nature of things, achieve nothing save the uniformity of mechanism. One might classify Mr. Jeffers as a "great failure" if one meant by the phrase that he had wasted unusual talents; but not if one meant that he had failed in a major effort, for his aims are badly thoughtful and are essentially trivial.

Robert Penn Warren (review date 1937)

SOURCE: A review of *Solstice and Other Poems,* in *Poetry,* Vol. XLIX, No. V, February, 1937, pp. 279-82.

[*In the following mixed review of* Solstice and Other Poems, *Warren states that "this collection brings nothing new."*]

It is not probable that *Solstice and Other Poems* will do much to alter the reputation of Robinson Jeffers, for this collection brings nothing new. It is hard to say what kind of newness we expect when we pick up another volume by an established poet whose work we have read in the past. To expect something new need not brand one as light-minded and frivolous, even though the appetite for novelty, once out of hand and without center, is a dangerous thing for poets and readers of poetry, and accounts perhaps for the fickleness of the public, the hysteria of reviewers, and the random experimentation of the poets themselves. Need-less to say, when we pick up that recent book of the es-tablished poet, we expect something not new; we expect some characteristic turn of mind, a development of facul-ties with which we are already acquainted, a flavor of the old idiom—on the whole, a continuity of some kind, for we do not like to feel that the poet in his new self has betrayed the poet in his old self more glibly and irrespon-sibly than we would do so. If the new self has betrayed the old self too readily, we are inclined to suspect that the poet never did mean what he said, that he is merely a clever eclectic, and that we were deluded in our former estimate; if the poet's experience of his poetry was mean-ingless, perhaps ours was meaningless too, and we our-selves should reconsider. But we also demand in the new book something new, a new formulation of the old qualities, perhaps, but that at least, and a somewhat lively sense of potential variety in experience. We do not like to feel that, though we can predict the beginnings, we can predict the ends. If not new concepts, we want at least new percepts to keep us awake and to feed the understanding by their just relations to, and embodiments of, the old concepts.

The present book contains a great deal of self-imitation. The title poem, **"Solstice"** is like nothing so much as an ether dream Jeffers might have about some of his own poetry. The stereotypes of situation and language are here without the interest that was now and then achieved in **"Tamar," "The Roan Stallion,"** or *The Women at Point Sur.* In relation to the better of the earlier narratives the present one is repetition without direction. Waiving any question of the basic theme and impulse in the work of Jeffers, one might say that the only probable escape from this vice of self-imitation would be by a process of em-phasizing and exploring the aspect of special character instead of the aspect of the general symbol on which Jeffers' poetry is so largely based. For these symbols have them-selves been stereotyped. Our interest in the symbolic force of these narratives might be refreshed if we could be made to apprehend more intimately the persons as persons. All of this merely goes to say that Jeffers is often deficient in the dramatic sense; and this deficiency is more than of trifling importance in a writer who sets out to be a dramatic and narrative poet. The figures, gigantic, terrifying, and parabolical, are often on the verge of sinking back, again to be undifferentiated, into the general and often vague matrix of emotion from which they are shaped.

"At the Birth of an Age," a much more interesting poem than **"Solstice,"** suffers less from this situation. The strictly dramatic part of the poem gives the story of Gudrun's self-conflict in relation to her brothers, Gunnar, Hoegni,

and Carling, who are finally killed, not because she clearly wills her revenge for the death of Sigurd, but because she stands in vacillation after they have been lured to the camp of Attila's Horde. After Gudrun herself is dead, and the action proper is complete, the spirit of Gudrun, various choruses of spirits and voices, and the Hanged God, moralize the meaning of the preceding events and of life in general. The poet has assisted in pointing the rather inadequate communication coming from the spirit world by providing an introductory note on the meaning of the poem:

> The theme of self-contradiction and self-frustration, in Gudrun's naturem intends to express a characteristic quality of this culture-age, which I think should be called the Christian age, for it is conditioned by Christianity, and—except for a few centuries' lag—concurrent with it. Its civilization is the greatest, but also the most bewildered and self-contradictory, the least integrated, in some phases the most ignoble, that has ever existed. All these qualities together with the characteristic restlessness of the age, its energy, its extremes of hope and fear, its passion for discovery, I think are bred from the tension between its two poles, of Western blood and superimposed Oriental religion.. . . This tension is really the soul of the age, which will begin to die when it ceases.

The first half of the poem has some of the most effective dramatic writing in Jeffers' work, and some of the most sharply visualized scenes. The action, as action, is given a real psychological focus in Gudrun. But the idea in the introductory note is not satisfactorily assimilated into the action—is not really dramatized—and the rhetorical fury of the last half, with occasional bursts of moving phrase, scarcely welds the materials of the poem into a whole.

On the whole, the short poems in the present volume compare less favorably with earlier pieces of the same nature than does **"At the Birth of an Age"** with previous long pieces. Jeffers has done several extremely effective short pieces, but the short poem usually shows him at his most turgid and feeble. When the support of a narrative interest is withdrawn, as in the short poems, Jeffers is ordinarily unable to achieve the concentration of interest in detail that gives the short poem its power. His short poems tend to be fragmentary comments, gnomic utter-ances without adequate context.

Delmore Schwartz (review date 1939)

SOURCE: "The Enigma of Robinson Jeffers," in *Poetry,* Vol. 55, Part 1, October, 1939, pp. 30-8.

[In this excerpt from a review of The Selected Poetry of Robinson Jeffers, *Schwartz discusses Jeffers's treatment of such themes as science, war, and nature.]*

Although only half of his poetry is here [in *The Selected Poetry of Robinson Jeffers*] and the important poem called *The Women at Point Sur* is omitted, evidently because "it is the least liked and the least understood" of his poems, nevertheless this selection presents a sufficient span of writing in its six hundred pages to give any reader a just conception of what Jeffers has done. Above all, this selection invites a brief consideration and judgment of Jeffers' work as a whole, especially with regard to its sources.

At least one source is the scientific picture of the universe which was popular and "advanced" thought until a few short years ago. The versions of the implications of 19th-century science afforded by writers like Haeckel and Huxley seemed to create a picture of the world in which there was no room for most human values. The world was a wound-up machine or a whirling mass of chemical elements which stretched out without end and without purpose. No Deity assured justice or love or immortality, but the infinite emptiness reported by astronomy and the survival of the fittest of Darwinism seemed to comprise a definite and indubitable answer to human effort and belief. This is the world-view which has been the basis, in part, of the work of many other and quite different authors. It is to be found in the novels of Theodore Dreiser, in the plays of Bernard Shaw, in the criticism of H. L. Mencken (who suggests Nietzsche as an early and much more serious example), in the early philosophical writing of Bertrand Russell, in the poetry of Archibald MacLeish, and Joseph Wood Krutch's *The Modern Temper,* where it is explicitly announced that such things as love and tragedy and all other specifically human values are not possible to modern man. Russell suggests I. A. Richards, whose "sincerity ritual" to test the genuineness of a poem operates in part by envisaging the meaninglessness of the universe in the above sense, and Krutch suggests some of the best poems of Mark Van Doren, where the emptiness of the sky is the literal theme.

When Jeffers says in his foreword and in a number of his poems that he wishes to avoid lies, what he means by lies are all beliefs which would somehow deny or ameliorate this world-view. When he speaks repeatedly of stars, atoms, energy, rocks, science, and the power of Nature, it is the Nature of 19th-century science which he has in mind and which obsesses him. For Wordsworth, but a hundred years before, Nature was an image of the highest values; for Jeffers it has become merely a huge background which proffers only one delight, annihilation, and which makes human beings seem to him puny and disgusting beasts whose history is the tiniest cosmic incident.

But Jeffers' disgust with human beings seems to have another and less intellectual source. The poems he has written about Woodrow Wilson and Clemenceau and the brutality of modern warfare suggest that the source of his obsession with human violence was the World War. Here again parallels plead to be mentioned, as if an age were an organic entity, for one remembers that other writers who came to young manhood during the war, William Faulkner, Eugene O'Neill, Ernest Hemingway, have been similarly obsessed with violence, cruelty, rape, murder, and destruction. The California coast which serves as a background for Jeffers, and to which he came, he says, by pure accident, provides a third dominant element. "The strange,

introverted, and storm-twisted beauty of Point Lobos," as Jeffers' stage-set for his narrative poems, is merely another example of how birds, or perhaps one should say, hawks, of a feather flock together.

The world-picture of 19th-century science, the World War, and Jeffers' portion of the Pacific Coast are not, however, merely sources of his work, but actually, with little disguise, the substance of his poems. Of these three elements, the cosmology in question has definitely been discarded with the radical progress of science and scientific thought, and with the recognition that some of the supposed implications of 19th-century science were only the emotions of those who had lost their childhood faith or been dismayed by the bigness of the universe, as if bigness were an especially significant aspect. The World War too turns out not to have been either merely a display of human brutality or the crusade of an idealist, as Jeffers seems to take it to be when he writes of Wilson; but something quite different. And as for Point Lobos, one may very well question whether it can be accepted as a more accurate exhibit of Nature than Wordsworth's Lake Country, the state of Connecticut, or the city of New York. Such a question is to be raised only when the poet takes his landscape as being of universal significance.

The point involved is one of truth, the truth not of ultimate beliefs, but given facts. The poetry of Jeffers represents for the most part a response to the particular facts just mentioned. But if the facts are poorly envisaged, how adequate can the response be? Stated in terms of ideas, Jeffers' response is an ideology. Stated in terms of the emotions, his response is hysterical. Human beings are often brutal, Nature is sometimes violent, and life is indeed a mystery, but to respond as Jeffers does by rejecting humanity and saluting the peace of death is to come to a conclusion which is not only barren, a result which pleases Jeffers, but also false, and thus in the end without interest and without value.

This falsity has various consequences which define it precisely. There is no need to raise the usual and banal objections, to argue like a schoolboy over whether or not Jeffers is self-contradictory in denying human freedom and presenting characters who choose their actions, or to urge the contradiction of writing poetry which will only be read by the species which is being rejected, or to howl with facile radicalism that this tragic attitude is made possible by an income. It would be simple for the admirer of Jeffers to answer each of these accusations. But what cannot be adequately defended are the consequences in the poetry itself, both in the lyrics where we are presumably to get a representation of emotion and in the narrative poems where we ought to be getting a representation of human action.

The narrative poems constitute the major part of Jeffers' work and it is upon them that the weight of untruth is most unfortunate. In **"The Tower Beyond Tragedy,"** for example, the alternatives presented to the hero are: either incest or a complete rupture with humanity. One needs no knowledge of the Agamemnon story to know that this is not a genuine tragic dilemma, either for Orestes or for any other human being. And again in **"Roan Stallion,"** the two alternatives presented to the heroine, either sexual intercourse with a drunken and brutish husband or with a horse, are not mutually exhaustive of all possible choices, and the dénouement is not made more plausible when the stallion kills the man, in obedience to nothing but the doctrinal requirements of the poet. What happens in both stories and throughout the narrative writing is not only not true of human life even at its most monstrous—such untruth might conceivably be justified as an extreme use of symbols—but the untruth is essentially a matter of the contexts provided by the poet, the situations which he has furnished for his characters. Orestes' choice is unjustified by the character he has been given and the life which confronts him, and the heroine of **"Roan Stallion"** is untrue in the same literal sense, both characters being compelled to their acts by nothing but the emotion of the poet, an emotion utterly removed from their lives and differently motivated.

The same lack is present in the lyrics, and as in the narratives it was a narrative lack, so in the lyrics what is absent betrays itself in lyrical terms. The following poem, **"Science,"** is worth quoting as an example to justify this judgment and also as a typical statement of doctrine:

> Man, introverted man, having crossed
> In passage and but a little with the nature of things
>   this latter century
> Has begot giants; but being taken up
> Like a maniac with self-love and inward conflicts
>   cannot manage his hybrids.
> Being used to deal with edgeless dreams,
> Now he's bred knives on nature turns them also
>   inward: they have thirsty
>   points though.
> His mind forbodes his own destruction;
> Actaeon who saw the goddess naked among leaves
>   and his hounds tore him.
> A little knowledge, a pebble from the shingle,
> A drop from the oceans: who would have dreamed
>   this infinitely little too much?

What is to be noted here is the number of shifts the poet finds necessary in order to state the observation which concerns him. The machines of science which man cannot manage are named as giants, hybrids, knives. The knowledge of science which makes possible these machines is successively compared to a vision of Diana, a pebble, and a drop of water. The classical allusion to Actaeon's vision of the goddess is also in abrupt disjunction with the previous metaphor, man as a dreamer who has bred knives and as an introvert who has begotten giants. There is no rule or law which makes it impossible for a poet to go from one metaphor to another even in a very short poem, but such a transit can only be justified if it accomplishes some expressive purpose. Here the shifts, however, weaken each metaphor, preventing the reader from getting a clear picture of a thing, process or condition, by means of which to grasp the notion and the emotion in question. Actaeon's vision of Diana is plainly not at all symmetrical with man

as a begetter of dangerous giants. And the reason for this disorder is the desire of the poet to state an emotion about modern industrialism or armament in terms of the belief—too general to be meaningful—that knowledge is a dangerous thing for man. If the emotion were justified by a fact, then the fact would provide the emotion with adequate lyrical terms. But, to repeat, since the fact was imperfectly envisaged and the poet saw modern industrialism merely as an instance of incestuous brutality (man is introverted, self-loving, and thus incestuous for Jeffers), the emotion could not command the metaphors which would make it consistent and vivid upon the page.

The argument may seem theoretical and had better be made more evident and more lucid by comparison. Lear upon the heath with Kent and the fool represents a vision of the cruelty of the human heart which is in every sense more appalling than any equivalent desolation to be found in Jeffers. And yet the difference in literary terms is immense. The poet has managed to adhere to the formal burden of the play and of blank verse, he has provided a suitable individuation for the main characters, and he has not found it necessary to resort to continuous physical violence in order to present the emotion he feels about the human heart. A further point to be made, probably by the open-eyed optimist, is that Kent, the faithful friend, does accompany Lear upon the heath, and Cordelia does balance the cruelty of Goneril and Regan at the plausible ratio of two-to-one. One could scarcely consider *King Lear* a play in which it is affirmed that God's in His heaven and all's well with the world. Nor could one conceivably affirm that the poet was engaged in telling comforting lies about the human species. But the play is nevertheless a representation of life which can stand as a measure of what one means by the whole truth when one is confronted by such writers as Jeffers. Two other relevant touchstones may be mentioned in passing, *Moby Dick,* in which there is a similar regard for Nature, and the writing of Pascal in which the astronomical diminution of man is considered in its implication as to man's importance in the universe.

The mention of Shakespeare, however, may suggest a fundamental difficulty with the critical method which is being used. If the poet is examined by his ability to present the truth, and if many of his formal defects are attributed to emotions which spring from a distorted view of particular facts, then what is one to say when a ghost or witch appears in Shakespeare, or when in some respect the poet's substance is a response to beliefs about the world which the reader does not find acceptable? The problem of belief in poetry makes its inevitable re-appearance, like an unwanted cat. Without wishing to raise the whole subject, the answer here seems fairly plain. The predicament of Hamlet does not depend in the least upon the actuality of ghosts (a question about which there is no need to be dogmatic), and in general, most great poetry does not depend upon the truth of its philosophical beliefs, although it requires them as a structure and a framework. But in Jeffers the beliefs about the world and the consequent emotions are the substance of the poetry, and the observations of land and sea and the narrative characters are merely the means, which reverses the relationship. In the *Inferno,* the

Christian system helps to make possible a vision of human beings; in Jeffers, the human beings are there to make possible a vision of Jeffers' ideas of the world. Hence the literary critic is pressed to judge the ideas and the emotion which they occasion. It might also seem that Jeffers is being taken too literally, that his avowed rejection of humanity is "really" a subliminal disguise; and his hatred of cities might be understood as a social reaction. But in Jeffers, as opposed to other poets, it is impossible to make such a translation without ceasing to be a literary critic and becoming biographer, psychoanalyst, or sociologist. The substance of the poetry is his emotion about humanity and the wide world. The poet's business is to *see,* by means of words, and we can only judge him by what he presents as seen.

One is permitted to adopt any belief, attitude, or emotion that especially pleases one. But when one begins to act upon belief or emotion, and in particular when one begins to write poetry, a million more considerations, in addition to the few already mentioned, intrude of necessity. When one attempts to write narrative poems about human beings, the obligation of a sufficient knowledge of human beings intervenes, the necessity of a definite measure of rhythm descends upon one, and literature as an organic tradition enters upon the scene. Jeffers undoubtedly has a keen sense for the landscape and seascape he writes about and he is by no means without a knowledge of human beings. But on the basis of detesting humanity, the natural tendency is to turn away from a strict view of human beings as they actually are and to regard a concern with literature, *technically,* as being at best unnecessary, at worst a hindrance. The result is that the characters Jeffers writes about tend to become repetitive abstractions, and the long line of Jeffers' verse is corrupted repeatedly by the most gauche inconsistencies of rhythm. The causal sequence seems indubitable. The poet has decided that the emotion he feels is strong enough to justify any manipulation of characters; and the breaches of consistency in his rhythm appear to him to be merely a "literary" or formal matter:

> I say
> Humanity is the mould to break away from, the
> 　crust to break through,
> 　　the coal to break into fire,
> The atom to be split . . .

and the poet is breaking away from literature as well as humanity in his poems, which we are asked to accept as literature, and in which we are presumably presented with humanity.

Stephen Spender (review date 1963)

SOURCE: A review of *The Beginning and the End and Other Poems,* in *Chicago Tribune Magazine of Books,* May 12, 1963, p. 3.

[*In the review below, Spender extols the "ruggedness" and "grandeur" of Jeffers's poetry but disagrees with the poet's "abdication" of human consciousness.*]

Robinson Jeffers lived in vast scenery opposite the vast Pacific on the coast of Monterey where he built with his own hands a tower in which he lived. His poetry is rugged as the hills of that landscape, with lines ragged as that ocean, and the spirit of the poet is most often likened in his poetry to a hawk. On the whole it provokes awe and enthusiasm, but it is not poetry to live with, because it lacks intimacy.

It is like a net with too wide a mesh which only catches the most cosmic experiences and the most ultimate feelings. Most of us, altho we may have such feelings, live most of our lives experiencing and feeling thru a smaller mesh, which is the scale of our own bodies, families, occupations. We do not live on rocky cliffs, under vast skies, and over great oceans. We do not act like hawks.

Death, however, is both an extreme and a universal situation, and these last poems of Jeffers, [in *The Beginning and the End and Other Poems*], in which he is largely concerned with his own approaching death, in which he discovers a metaphor for the approaching end of the world, imminent as a result of nuclear fission, are extremely moving. They may well be his best poetry.

They are written by a poet who remains completely in command of his own technical and intellectual resources. Jeffers shows an ability to express ideas which are derived from reading modern scientific works, which is very rare in modern poetry.

Lines such as these about the "volcanic earth" are both exact and exhilarating:

> 　　She was like a mare in her heat eyeing the
> 　　stallion,
> Screaming for life in the womb; her atmosphere
> Was the breath of her passion: not the blithe air
> Men breathe and live, but marsh-gas, ammonia,
> 　sulphured hydrogen,
> Such poison as our remembering bodies return to
> When they die and decay and the end of life
> Meets its beginning.

The view of life expressed here is tragic, heroic, but ultimately rather detached. Jeffers tends to see the earth in relation to the cosmos, history in relation to infinity. Destruction and defeat, indeed civilization itself, therefore, are not very important. What matters is affirmation, courage, a gesture of cosmic defiance:

> 　　　　　Man's life's
> Too common to be lamented; and if they died after
> 　a while in their beds
> It would be nearly as painful—death's never
> 　pleasant.
> May the terror be brief—but for a people to be
> 　defeated is worse.

I happen to disagree with this, because I think that consciousness is what gives significance to the universe, and for this reason it is not valuable to measure or weigh immensity against the littleness and brevity of man.

Without consciousness time and space would be meaning-less, and meaning is what we exist for. Until it is proved that there is a super-consciousness inhabiting some other planet, the heroics of a poet such as Jeffers merely recommend the abdication of consciousness. But even if one rejects hisphilosophy, these poems confront one with final issues to choose among. They have imaginative grandeur.

James Dickey (review date 1964)

SOURCE: A review of *The Beginning and the End and Other Poems,* in *Poetry,* Vol. 103, No. 5, February, 1964, pp. 316-24.

[*Dickey was an American poet and critic. In the excerpt below, he suggests that despite Jeffers's conspicuous flaws, he is a poet of greatness and power.*]

Now that Robinson Jeffers is dead, his last poems have been issued, culled from hand-written manuscripts by his sons and his secretary, Though some of the pieces [in ***The Beginning and the End and Other Poems***] were obviously left unfinished—there are several different ones which have the same passages in them—it is worth noting that they are actually no more or less "finished" than the poems Jeffers published in book after book while he lived. This is typical of Jeffers' approach to poetry, I think; he had, as someone remarked of Charles Ives, "the indifference of greatness." Yet now, in some fashion, we must come to terms with Jeffers, for he somehow cannot be dismissed as lesser men—and no doubt better poets—can. As obviously flawed as he is, Jeffers is cast in a large mold; he fills a position in this country that would simply have been an empty gap without him: that of the poet as prophet, as large-scale philosopher, as doctrine-giver. This is a very real, very old and honorable function for poets, and carries with it a *tone* that has, but for Jeffers, not been much heard among us, in our prevailing atmosphere of ironic shrugs and never-too-much. Admittedly a great deal of bad poetry in all ages has been written from such a stance, but that does not invalidate the idea, or take from Jeffers the credit that is duly his. Surely he provides us with plenty to carp about: his oracular moralizing, his cruel and thoroughly repellent sexuality, his dreadful lapses of taste when he seems simply to throw back his head and howl, his slovenly diction, the eternal sameness of his themes, the amorphous sprawl of his poems on the page. The sheer power and drama of some of Jeffers' writing, however, still carries the day despite everything, and this is not so much because of the presence of the Truth that Jeffers believes he has got hold of but because of what might be called the embodiment of that Truth: Jeffers' gorgeous panorama of *big* imagery, his galaxies, suns, seas, cliffs, continents, mountains, rivers, flocks of birds gigantic schools of fish, and so on. His Truth is hard to swallow—try looking at your children and drawing comfort from Jeffers' "inhumanism"—but one cannot shake off Jeffers' vision as one can the carefully prepared surprises of many of the neatly packaged stanzas we call "good poems"; it is too deeply disturbing and too powerfully stated. One

thinks, uneasily, that the prophetic tone may be more than just a tone, remembering that Jeffers was telling us long before Hiroshima that the ultimate and of science, of knowledge and tool-using, is not comfort and convenience (how he despises such ideals!) but unrelieved tragedy. It is extraordinarily strange how the more awful and ludicrous aspects of the romic age have come to resemble Jeffers' poems. In a film like *Mondo Cane,* for example, one sees the dying sea-turtles, disoriented by the Bikini blasts until they cannot even find the Pacific Ocean, crawling inland to die in the desert, in the blazing sand they think is water, and the hundreds-of-miles-long trail of dead butterflies, the seabirds trying to hatch atom-sterilized eggs, and one thinks compulsively of Jeffers. Few visions have been more desperate than his, and few lives organized around such austere principles. It seems to me that we must honor these things, each in his own way.

Robert Boyers (essay date 1969)

SOURCE: "A Sovereign Voice: The Poetry of Robinson Jeffers," in *Sewanee Review,* Vol. LXXVII, No. 1, Winter, 1969, pp. 487-507.

[*In the following essay, Boyers provides a reexamination of Jeffers's poetry, focusing in particular on "the ferocity of the critical reaction against Jeffers" since the late 1940s.*]

A generation of critics and observers has agreed to bestow upon Robinson Jeffers the gravest sentence the critical imagination can conceive, the conclusion of ultimate irrelevance for both his life and his work. And though Jeffers, dead now since 1962, never gave a damn about either criticism or the critical imagination, nor for that matter about responses to his own poetry, those of us who continue to find in Jeffers a good deal to study and admire ought to speak out a little in his behalf from time to time. The propitiatory ritual need not always be wholly gratuitous, after all, and one has reason to fear that the inevitable decline in Jeffers's reputation may not contain within it the seed of some future revival.

Already the figure of Jeffers as a kind of gloomy apparition haunting the parapets of the stone tower he built and lived in has come to assume nearly mythical dimensions, and his isolation from the movements, whether artistic or political, of his time has been too easily attributed to savage intemperance or to idiotic philosophic ideologies relating to the doctrine of inhumanism. Indeed, more than any other poet of the modernist or post-modernist periods, Jeffers has served as a whipping boy to a variety of well-placed poets and critics who have found it stimulating to deal with him exclusively on their terms, though never on his. Thus, for Mr. Yvor Winters, Jeffers's poetry presented a simple spectacle of "unmastered and self-inflicted hysteria" working upon concerns that were "essentially trivial." For Randall Jarrell, an infinitely more gifted and judicious writer than Winters, Jeffers's poetry demonstrated that "the excesses of modernist poetry are the necessary concomitants of the excesses of late-capitalist society," and what is more set up "as a nostalgically awaited goal the war of all against all." For Kenneth Rexroth, whose championing of the most defiantly mediocre talents on the West Coast is notorious and might at least have extended to a major talent like Jeffers's, his poetry is "shoddy and pretentious," with "high-flown statements indulged in for their melodrama alone."

There is no single source for such misstatements and half-truths, and it would seem clear that any correctives would lie in the direction of Jeffers's verse itself, illuminated in part by the interesting documents that have been recently brought to light. And in turning to Jeffers and his work it is also useful to acknowledge that distinctions must be made and retained, in discussing what is fine and what is not, for Jeffers wrote a great deal in the course of a professional career that spanned fifty years, and he was not always a meticulous nor especially prudent craftsman. Clearly he did not linger over brief passages to the degree Ezra Pound might have urged him to, and he felt none of theurgency to revise and refine his work that is characteristic of modern poets as diverse as Eliot and Marianne Moore. Not that Jeffers is crude, or simple-minded, for he is not. Jeffers knew his gift and trusted his ability to give it adequate expression. As to whether that expression was sometimes more than adequate, he would leave it to others more anxious about such questions than he to decide.

In fact, the ferocity of the critical reaction against Jeffers that really began to set in after the end of World War II is in certain respects explicable in terms of the adulatory sympathies his earlier verse inspired in a number of people who might have been expected to know better. One of Jeffers's most consistent admirers, Mark Van Doren, in the foreword to Jeffers's *Selected Letters,* concludes with the line: "Homer and Shakespeare. In what more fitting company could we leave him?" Such conjunctions are not likely to sit well with more balanced observers of our poetry, and there is no doubt that Jeffers was frequently embarrassed by attempts to claim more for his achievement than it could realistically support. No doubt there is in Jeffers's best work a peculiarly sovereign quality, peculiar in our time at least, an ability to make large statements on large questions with little of the customary qualification and caution we have come to accept as almost obligatory in our serious literature. Only Jeffers's concerns are so much less varied, the range of his poetic devices so limited by contrast with Eliot's and Yeats's and Auden's, the generosity of his commitments so restricted by his fear of excessive involvement with other human beings as reflected in his poetry and in personal documents. Even in the case of Jeffers's characters in the long narratives, which would seem to confer some degree of similitude with Homeric figures, his creations do not really warrant such a comparison, for the memorable characters are largely maniacal, gripped by obsessions that never really evoked what Jeffers thought they would. Unable clearly to distinguish his own views from those of his characters in ambitious works like *The Women at Point Sur,* perhaps because he never fully considered the long-range implications of his sentiments and avowals, Jeffers

could do no more than "look grim" when confronted by articulate critics of his narratives, "and assure them that my hero was crazy but I am not." The Homeric perspective can by no means be equated with such a muddle.

In a way it is unfortunate that Jeffers wrote any long narratives at all, for none succeed, and for reasons that need hardly be elaborated in detail. Structurally, they are sound enough, but the texture of these poems is swollen by effusions of philosophizing and by attempts to impose representative signification on characters and actions which are so extraordinary as to be either ludicrous or simply shocking. Not that any serious reader is going to rush shrieking from the room at the mention of a little incest at a time when every perversion has been relieved by repetition and familiarity of its capacity to extract from readers even a bit of a chill. What is shocking in Jeffers's narratives, from **"Tamar"** through the later poems, is the author's contention of symptomatic and representative status for the perverse obsessions of his characters. Obviously the single-mindedness of Jeffers's pursuit of his themes in the long poems ought to dispel any notion that he indulged his fantasies in the interests of melodrama alone, as Rexroth claimed. Jeffers simply thought he had hit upon a fruitful means for engaging the most profound problem he could imagine: the relationship of the individual to his time, and the uses and limitations of human freedom.

Only **"Roan Stallion"** among Jeffers's narratives would seem to provide the consistently varied texture that is requisite in a long poem, but even here one finds it difficult to accept Jeffers at his own estimate, and in the terms of his advocates. While the entire poem is powerful, and not at all absurdas some have claimed, the whole fails to sustain particular elements in the imagery. The magnificent evocation of the roan stallion as a symbol of male potency is quite as fine in its way as D. H. Lawrence's comparable use of horses in his novel *The Rainbow,* published ten years before Jeffers's poem. But the eroticism in these passages of **"Roan Stallion"** is not clearly related to the basic thrust of the poem, which cannot be taken to be an indictment of male potency in general. If, as Jeffers wrote in a letter, "the woman fell in love with the stallion because there was no one else she could fall in love with," why is her attraction to the horse evoked in literally sexual terms? Unabashed sexuality the woman had had a good deal of, and there was no reason for her to be drawn to the horse for more of the same. Familiarity with Jeffers's universe, with the universe created by his many poems, suggests that the stallion was to call to mind qualities quite distinct from pure sexuality, though related, and yet these qualities are never sufficiently identified. The figure refuses to yield its latent connotations, and is distinguished by an opacity that characterizes the image rather than the symbol. In this respect Jeffers's failure has a good deal in common with much of the narrative poetry produced in the Romantic period. In each there is a strong lyrical element which calls into question the poet's center of interest, and the consequent interest of readers. While the structure of the work naturally tends to focus attention on the unfolding of events in the phenomenal world, the poet's interest seems always elsewhere, in the emotions that give rise to action and in abstract conceptions of fate and will. Poets find themselves more immediately and intimately involved in their characters than they ought to be in narrative poems, unable to decide where their creations begin and they leave off. W. H. Auden has lately described Byron's failure in poems like *Childe Harold* in such terms, and post-Romantic critics like Bradley have been similarly concerned with these matters.

In short, then, for a number of reasons, Jeffers devoted a great deal of his time and energy to the cultivation of a sub-genre, narrative poetry, to which his gifts were not especially adaptable. What is also distressing, though, is that the attention Jeffers has received has been so disproportionately weighted in the direction of these failed narratives, and that his stock has fallen so badly as a result. It is as though there had been a tacit agreement among all influential parties that Jeffers's shorter poems should be looked upon as nothing more than adjunct to the narratives, perhaps even as something less, as filler for the volumes his publishers issued with remarkable regularity for so many years. As it is, Jeffers's short poems, many of them rather lengthy by standards of the conventional lyric, will fill an enormous volume when they are collected, and an impressive volume it will be, for at his best Jeffers could blend passion and restraint, image and statement, contempt and admiration, as few poets of any time have been able to, and often with a music so ripe and easy that it is able to impress itself upon our senses without our ever remarking its grace and majesty, its sureness of touch. How better to know what we mean when we speak of such qualities than to locate them in those poems whose perfection of form and control of tone set them apart from the rest of the poet's work? I would select the following as representative of Jeffers at his best, in an order I might recommend to a skeptical and rather hard-nosed student whom I especially wanted Jeffers to reach: **"Ossian's Grave," "The Broadstone," "The Low Sky," "Antrim," "A Little Scraping," "November Surf," "Hurt Hawks," "Fire on the Hills," "Ante Mortem," "Post Mortem," "Credo," "Rearmament," "Haunted Country," "Return," "The Treasure," "Practical People," "The Maid's Thought," "To the Stone-Cutters," "The Cruel Falcon."**

No doubt I have neglected someone's favorites in drawing up such a list, but consensus is not what matters here. I am sure that responsible arguments might be made for poems like **"The Purse Seine"** and **"Shine, Perishing Republic,"** which have been frequently anthologized, or for a sobering longer poem like **"Hellenistics,"** so earnestly extolled by Brother Antoninus; but each of these has a ponderousness that is somehow too reminiscent of the longer poems, an indulgence of the explicit statement that runs against the grain of the hard, oblique quality we are given to demand of the poetry we admire. Of course there are many fine things in many of the poems I have rejected, if we may use so strong a word: one thinks of the weaving of exclamations in and out of **"The Purse Seine,"** the parallelisms binding the otherwise loosely flowing, open-ended line structures, the colorful images sheathed in the poet's wonder, quietly unfolding a vision of entrapment that is to stand in analogy to our own:

> I cannot tell you
> How beautiful the scene is, and a little terrible,
> then, when the
>   crowded fish
> Know they are caught, and wildly beat from one
>   wall to the other
>   of their closing destiny the phosphorescent
> Water to a pool of flame, each beautiful slender
>   body sheeted with
>   flame, like a live rocket
> A comet's tail wake of clear yellow flame; while
>   outside the narrowing
> Floats and cordage of the net great sea-lions come
>   up to watch,
> Sighing in the dark; the vast walls of night
> Stand erect to the stars.

How starkly these fine lines contrast with Jeffers's attempts to draw his analogy, with the crude simplifications of a political and social reality that leads to confusion and a blunting of those energies the poem had quietly released: "I cannot tell you how beautiful the city appeared, and a little terrible. / I thought, we have geared the machines and locked all together into interdependence; we have built the great cities; now / There is no escape. We have gathered vast populations incapable of free survival, insulated / From the strong earth." What can one say to all this as poetry, except that it is disastrous to use inflated rhetorical expressions of the sort represented in this sampling without some sense of irony, of the disparity between the more poetic language one familiarly relies upon and the gross sociologisms Jeffers would permit to roughen the texture of the verse.

There is, we have been given to understand, a certain ignominy readily to be associated with the use of the term "poetic language," and it ought perhaps to be justified in connection with a poet like Jeffers who has been accused of shoddy versification and pretentious inflation of imagery and rhetoric. Clearly, it would seem, what is shoddy can never be poetic, since what is poetic is always to some degree conscious, restrained, elegant, and delivers up its meanings in terms that are pleasurable wholly apart from what is being delivered or represented. The experienced reader of poetry will usually have little difficulty in distinguishing what is shoddy from what is not. In the matter of pretension there may be a good deal of difficulty that will be less securely resolved. Pretension, after all, has to do with qualities that may be largely extrinsic to the poetry itself, with an attitude or pose that may be justly or unjustly presumed to have dictated not only the broad contours of a poem, but its particular words and images. Often, one may safely predict, the presumption of general attitudes by readers will have little to do with what actually inheres in a given body of work, but will be used to explain or to justify an antipathy which may have more to do with the limitations of a reader than with the failings of a poet. Surely Yvor Winters's abstract identification of mysticism with muddle is fundamentally responsible for his inability to achieve even an elementary understanding of Jeffers, whose poetry evinces a materialism that is distinctly removed from the kind of mysticism to which Winters so objected.

Given his constitutional incapacity to apprehend as genuine any perspective on human life other than his own, Winters found in Jeffers's work a muddle, and it was inevitable that he should then seek to wither his adversary by the positing of mysticism as the source of his defection from authenticity.

But as to the question of what does and does not constitute poetic language, one may concede that critics of Jeffers have on occasion found fruitful grounds for argument. There is a good deal of pretension in the narratives, where prophetic rant frequently mounts to a kind of hysteria that has very little to do with the appeal poetry is to make to our senses. John Crowe Ransom has written that "the poetic consideration of the ethical situation is our contemplation and not our exercise of will, and therefore qualitatively a very different experience: knowledge without desire." I am not certain that I like the Aristotelian antithesis between knowledge and desire, but Mr. Ransom's formularization will do for our purposes. What is pretentious in the work of art, Mr. Ransom's statement suggests, is its attempt to be more than it can be, to *do* where its function is primarily to *be*. Which is not to say that a work of art, in particular the poem, cannot represent a position, take sides, for obviously it can, but if it does it must do so almost in spite of itself. What is important about it is the metamorphic flexibility which facilitates the passage of our imagination into and out of a number of conditions of being, for without such passage, and without real variety, there will be no tension, and no intensity of concern on our part. One thinks of Keats's famous letter in which he describes the poetical character: "it is not itself—it has no self—it is everything and nothing." That is to say, the poet is conceived in terms of a neutrality that permits him to assume qualities of the objects he contemplates.

What does such speculation lead us to conclude about those elements in Jeffers's work which have been vigorously assailed? Again, distinctions must be kept in mind. In what sense can Jeffers's work be said to suffer from pretension? It is pretentious when it ceases to control those elements of will that stand behind any creative act, elements which for the most part cannot be permitted to govern the nature or intensity of the poet's expression. Only the precise materials the poet uses can legitimately determine the intensity of expression and the poet's posture, for in its own terms the poem posits a world of its own, a word-world, if you will, which stands not so much in imitation of the phenomenal world we inhabit, as it stands merely in analogy to it. Given such a relationship, degrees of intensity and tonal qualities of a poem cannot be said to issue legitimately from contemplation of a reality which is not that poem's authentic reality. We take for examination a brief poem from Jeffers's final volume, entitled **"Unnatural Powers"**:

> For fifty thousand years man has been dreaming of powers
> Unnatural to him: to fly like the eagles—this groundling!
>   —to breathe under the seas, to voyage to the moon,

> To launch like the sky-god intolerable thunder-bolts:
>   now he has got them.
> How little he looks, how desperately scared and excited,
>   like a poisonous insect, and no God pities him.

The poem has the merit of focusing in brief compass what may be said of Jeffers's failures in a great many short poems. The poet here stands not within his poem, as Keats would have had him, not dissolved in the terms of his saying; nor does he stand beside his materials, gently or fiercely ordering, arranging them as Wallace Stevens would characteristically reveal himself handling the creatures of his own imagination; nor does Jeffers even stand here above his materials, for to stand above would be to retain some manner of relation. Jeffers here stands without the substance of his poem, not above or aloof, but apart. The words are connected by a will that is in no way implicated in the words themselves, so that the ordering, the structuring, of sentiments cannot be judged except by reference to that will, which we can have no way of knowing. The poem calls neither for understanding, nor for contemplation, but for simple assent, for a process of suspension in which the reader ceases to be himself, and gives himself wholly, not to the poem, but to the poet. To abandon one's self-possession temporarily, as to suspend disbelief, is to participate in a ritual which calls upon our instincts of generosity in the interests of a pleasure and enlightenment that are ideally to repay our gesture. The work of art requests, as it were implicitly, that we be generous in the interests of our senses. At his worst, and even to some extent when he is not writing badly at all, Jeffers insists that we agree to heed what he says though there be nothing in it for us, not even the extension or stimulation of our imagination. Utterly without art, and without sympathy either for us or for the materials he manipulates, Jeffers coldly mocks our foibles, our dreams, our delusions. The ideological content of Jeffers's fine poetry here hardens into a mannered response to experience, so that no valid experience is lived through in the poem. What we have is a system of response, but nothing valid or poetically real to respond *to*. Confronted by such poems as **"Unnatural Powers,"** we can have no alternative but to speak of arrogance and pretension.

How much less we are disposed to object to Jeffers's poetry when he reminds us of his mortality. We remain wary of prophecy in general, and of false prophets in particular, but we consent nonetheless to attend to Jeffers's prophetic rigors on occasion, perhaps even to be a little moved by the spectacle of a man obviously concerned for a purity of spirit, an integrity so hard for any man to come by. We are moved, for example, by **"Shine, Perishing Republic,"** a poem too familiar to quote. It is not one of Jeffers's best things, but there is a fine tolerance for humankind in this poem that is attractive and that we respond to repeatedly. The theme of the poem is, after all, not so very new or terrible, having to do with the corruption of institutionalized life in the modern world, the tendency of mass culture to absorb protest and distinction and to heighten vulgarity in its citizens. Yeats had no less to say of such matters than Jeffers, and one need only think of those unbelievably awful poems of Lawrence's on the beastly bourgeoisie to realize how conventional among recent poets these concerns of Jeffers's have been. In fact, what is most responsible for the effectiveness Jeffers's poem has is the relatively understated quality it shares with some of the leaner lyrics that are not as well known. It is as though Jeffers were here dealing with realities too long pondered and accepted to fight over, and the assimilation of these contemporary realities to the perspective of eternal recurrence, ripeness and decay, allows Jeffers to speak of them with a calmness we admire. The poet's accents are firm, rather than petulantly defiant, as he counsels his children on the course he would have them follow: "Corruption / Never has been compulsory, when the cities lie at the monster's feet there are left the mountains." There is something almost plaintive in those words "there are left the mountains," the procession of weak accents falling towards the final unaccented syllable, suggesting the encouragement of an option that is to be embraced only after others have been definitively abandoned, as they had been perhaps too casually by Jeffers himself.

What **"Shine, Perishing Republic"** lacks is a richness of sound and of metaphor. The language of the poem is not very interesting at all, dealing rather broadly in abstractions which yet do not confound, but which evoke, really, only other abstractions. If America is settling, as the poet claims, ". . . in the mould of its vulgarity, heavily thickening to empire, / And protest, only a bubble in the molten mass, pops and sighs out, and the mass hardens . . . ," we can be expected to feel nothing more than modest dismay, for our sympathies have not been engaged by anything more than an issue, nicely stated, but hardly made manifest. And nowhere does the poem improve upon this initial evocation, the poet settling for modest effects, again largely concerned with assent rather than with intensifying our experience of a reality we are presumed to recognize as pertinent to our own.

I have no doubt whatever that Jeffers was more than aware of his inclination towards prophetic abstraction, towards the hollow exclamation patently ringing with WISDOM, as he was aware of a solemnity in his own demeanor that could degenerate into sententiousness in the poetry. But a brief sonnet like Jeffers's **"Return"** is so perfect in its way that to read it, again and again, is to forget Jeffers's faults, and to wonder how a hard-boiled materialist often abused for the purple pride of his verse could manage to sound so much like Whitman, and yet like the Jeffers who was always so different from Whitman.

> A little too abstract, a little too wise,
> It is time for us to kiss the earth again,
> It is time to let the leaves rain from the skies,
> Let the rich life run to the roots again.
> I will go down to the lovely Sur Rivers
> And dip my arms in them up to the shoulders.
> I will find my accounting where the alder leaf
>   quivers
> In the ocean wind over the river boulders.
> I will touch things and things and no more
>   thoughts,
> That breed like mouthless May-flies darkening the
>   sky,

> The insect clouds that blind our passionate hawks
> So that they cannot strike, hardly can fly.
> Things are the hawk's food and noble is the
>   mountain, Oh noble
> Pico Blanco, steep sea-wave of marble.

Here at last is a poetry of sensation, of touch, in which form is meaning and substance, in which a restless and mobile imagery is the very whole and perfect embodiment of emotion. Here the poet feels not about his materials, but into and through them—things are his message, and as the poet thinks things he makes a poem. He has seen that to the degree that he thinks primarily thoughts he will cease to be a poet, and become a philosopher, a spokesman, a critic, anything but a poet. Does it matter that there is a minimum of paraphrasable content in such a poem, as Winters argued against Jeffers's output generally? I think not, for then, what would we do with a Herrick, or with a lyricist like Hardy, were we forced to consider the content of a poem as the quantity of ideas to be gathered therefrom? And indeed, what more is Jeffers saying but "no more thoughts"—not absolutely and forever, but now, when we embody a poem, allow an image to course through and work upon our sensibilities, when we would be reverently humble, and grateful to life for what it is, which is more than we usually deserve. How marvelous Jeffers's image of thoughts as a swarm of "mouthless May-flies," and we need hardly remind ourselves how often our poets have railed against the intellect that darkens the possibilities of human feeling, that distracts and weakens both passion and pleasure. Are such commonplaces banal? Not as Jeffers has them in **"Return"** and in his better poems, for Jeffers here proceeds through an intuition that is more than an assertion of will. He is not a poet of the world, but of a world *he* knew well, a world partial at best, but firmly gripped and eagerly loved, and his ability to make it known and real for others is a measure of his success as a poet.

Who among us that has read Jeffers with devotion, though critically, will not confess to an admiration for a man who could so charge a created universe with a network of images so consistently developed, so densely woven into the very fabric of the verse? Who more earnestly than Jeffers has confronted the frailty of our lives, and engaged more desperately the attempt to reorient our customary perspectives, to take us beyond pain into praise and wonder? Jeffers knew all too well how men could suffer, and did, and he knew why they suffered, and his awareness rarely failed to leave him either angry or amused, or both, for he felt that most human suffering was the result of unwarranted expectations, foolish illusions. His entire career was dedicated to the chastisement of a pity he felt, and knew others felt, for he did not believe that pity was an essentially human quality, though for the most part peculiar to our kind. He felt that pity, and the suffering it often implied, was a product not of human emotion, but of human civilization, and with this he had no sympathy at all. Against this civilization, the pride of western man with its "little empty bundles of enjoyment," Jeffers set the figure of the hawk, the eagle, the falcon, the vulture, predators all, and cast them winging alternately amidst towering rocks and seething waters, landscapes of permanence and of violent energy. The ambience of Jeffers's poems is characteristically stark, though rarely barren, and one has in them a sense of granitic harshness, as of objects tempered in a flame so blazing as to burn away all that is ephemeral and soft, and pitying, everything in a word that is simply and merely human. But Jeffers's poetry is neither anti-human, nor inhuman. It plainly works itself out within a system of values which includes much that is human, in terms of what we are capable of responding to at our most intense. As one would expect in a created universe of considerable density, though not of great complexity, there is a recurrence of specific symbols within the pervasive imagery of the poems, and a consequent cross-fertilization of meanings, so that we are presented a vision of experience that is everywhere interfused, a frame of reference that cuts across entire groups of poems. Everywhere meanings seem to beckon away beyond themselves, so that in Jeffers's finished works there is rarely an impression of a static quality, despite the weight of particular images.

Here is an irregular sonnet entitled **"The Cruel Falcon,"** which ought to help us with some of the things we have been saying:

> Contemplation would make a good life, keep it
>   strict, only
> The eyes of a desert skull drinking the sun,
> Too intense for flesh, lonely
> Exultations of white bone;
> Pure action would make a good life, let it be
>   sharp—
> Set between the throat and the knife.
> A man who knows death by heart
> Is the man for that life.
> In pleasant peace and security
> How suddenly the soul in a man begins to die.
> He shall look up above the stalled oxen
> Envying the cruel falcon,
> And dig under the straw for a stone
> To bruise himself on.

With this extraordinary performance we move more securely into that created universe which we know with every accent as Jeffers's. The setting is harsh, the features of the landscape characteristic in the marmoreal coldness of their surfaces, the poetic energies intensely abiding in the carefully chiselled phrases. What we have here is not the movement and vitality of life, but of an art that enhances life by appropriating its features in the interests of a vision at once more passionate and more lovely than any vision of life itself. Here is not that looseness of texture which even discerning readers like Brother Antoninus have sought to legitimize in their defenses of Jeffers, for Jeffers knew that as a poet and as a man he could achieve liberation only through scrupulous concern for style, for form. There are no paradoxes in this mature vision, so finely wrought, no telling nuances to qualify the poet's commitment; but everything is precisely placed, distributed its proper weight, and there are elements of style so subtly woven into the poem's basic

structure that they largely escape observation. Notice the delicacy with which Jeffers effects tense shifts in this poem, moving from the conditional into the hortatory, to the present indicative, to the future tense where he rests his case. It is a little triumph of the prophetic voice, urging without sinister overtones, stealthily proclaiming its insights without violence, for it has earned the privilege of prophecy by the substantiveness and accuracy of its representations in the course of the poem.

The language of **"The Cruel Falcon"** is, as we have intimated, perfectly accurate, and if this language is without that exotic strangeness we so admire in a Stevens, its dismissal of abstraction and of the commonplace routines of experience is impressive enough. And what precisely does Jeffers mean when he admonishes us to "keep it strict," to speculate on the contours of a "pure action," to abandon the "pleasant peace and security" that is the extinction of the soul? I do not know why critical observers have found it so difficult to explain these admonitions, why they have resorted to the interpretation of inhumanism to explain the work of a man all too frail, too human, and in his way enamored of a beauty our best men have long sought to capture and identify. Jeffers's concern in his poems is with the liberation of spirit from what is gross. Human flesh is gross, the conventions by which men cultivate the pleasures of flesh utterly ingenious and thoroughly destructive of alternative values. Jeffers's concern is with a resurrection of spirit out of the ashes of human display, a religious concern, and frequently expressed in terms that have their source in religious archetypes. The chastisement of flesh has, after all, been a staple feature of religious practice for any number of millennia, though Jeffers's extension of this tradition has its unique attributes. For Jeffers the God who creates and observes His universe cares not what we do, so long as we do it well, so long as life is clean and vibrant with energy and possibilities of renewal, so long as it is whole, sufficient unto itself like the rocks Jeffers loved to contemplate, like the white bone of the desert skull in his poem, freed of gross desire, liberated to "lonely exultations."

If Jeffers is truly a religious poet, he can be said to worship largely at the altar of art, for his resolution of the problems of spirit is really an aesthetic resolution, just as his politics, if he did indeed have a politics, is fundamentally determined by an aesthetic response to the world. Jeffers did not disparge human life but the ways in which human beings could destroy their world, and each other. There is nothing barbaric or fascistic about these lines from **"November Surf,"** generated by the poet's disgusted observation of the summer refuse that litters the clean surfaces of his beloved shoreline, with its smoldering waves and granite promontories:

> The earth, in her childlike prophetic sleep,
> Keeps dreaming of the bath of a storm that prepares
>   up the long coast
> Of the future to scour more than her sea-lines:

The cities gone down, the people fewer and the
hawks more numerous,
The rivers mouth to source pure; when the two-
footed
Mammal, being someways one of the nobler
animals, regains
The dignity of room, the value of rareness.

It is distressing that at this late date one should feel it
necessary to defend such writing, when its intentions are
so clear, and so fundamentally decent. Perhaps the crucial
words in the passage are "childlike," "dignity," "rareness."
Yeats would have understood Jeffers's meanings without
any difficulty whatever, and though the Irish poet could
speak in certain poems of "all hatred driven hence," and
of the blight that is arrogance, he knew the value of passions bordering on violence, and of sudden purgation. And
just as Yeats could speak of ceremonies of innocence, so
Jeffers sanctifies the "childlike prophetic sleep" of the
elemental, innocent in its contentment with the wholeness,
the unity of all things. For Jeffers the cities of man, representing industrial civilization, are a violation, an index
to the disharmony and spurious competitiveness that have
always distinguished our species. In the perspective of
Jeffers's poems, human life is a defilement of all that is
dignified and whole, and we are to listen to him not because he says we should, but because the poetic manifestations of his vision are sufficient to his message. How
easy it is to ridicule Jeffers, to parody his preference of a
hawk to a man, but given the terms of his vision there is
nothing in this to mock. For poetry is not a program, not
a series of proposals which are literally to be carried over
into the domain of normal human activity. Brother An
toninus has written eloquently on these matters: "We must
not shut ourselves off from the archetypal sources in [an
artist's] vision by virtue of [our] revulsion from their social
consequences when attempted politically in our time." The
poet "makes his vision permanent by virtue of its inherent
aesthetic, which protects it from misapplication in the
phenomenal world, because once it is translated into another
idiom it vanishes."

**The felicities of Jeffers's poetry ought no
longer to be denied, but received with
gratitude. If he was not among our
supreme poets, they have been few who
were his equals.**

—*Robert Boyers*

Jeffers's exaltation of the hawk, then, is not an exaltation
of a naked violence that will see the destruction of man by
man, but an exaltation of nature, of need, of instinct. For
Jeffers the instinct of the hawk is tolerable, even majestic,
because it does not seek to aggrandize itself at the expense of creation—it strikes according to its need and

within a framework that does not threaten the fundamental
harmony of other things. Its rarity he saw as a quality
intrinsic to its nature, associated also with its reasonable
relationship to its surroundings. At the point where the
environment could not support increasing numbers of the
species, the species by a law intrinsic to its nature would
cease to multiply: a matter not of will but of nature. How
different is man, clamoring for a little space, killing for
programs and ideologies. And anthropological investigations into the similarity of human and animal aggressions,
explanations of territoriality as a fundamental impulse of
all life, would have left Jeffers no less secure in his mounting
of the distinction, for Jeffers's thesis was developed not
as fact but as intuition. In the development of an ideal of
what is beautiful and can authentically be meaningful to
men, Jeffers's vision resists the disparagements of scientific
critiques.

Jeffers does not succumb, it must be said, to pure aestheticism. His indictments of mass man, which is to say
of man in our time, are not without a measure of conventionally *human* sentiment, and a number of the poems
evoke a tension in which the resort to aestheticism is
viewed as an element of necessity rather than of will or
choice. The conflict in Jeffers is powerfully dramatized
in the poem **"Rearmament,"** a poem in whose broadly
undulating rhythms and the sweep of its long line the
very quality and substance of Jeffers's message is embodied and reflected:

These grand and fatal movements toward death: the
grandeur of the mass
Makes pity a fool, the tearing pity
For the atoms of the mass, the persons, the victims,
makes it seem monstrous
To admire the tragic beauty they build.
It is beautiful as a river flowing or a slowly
gathering
Glacier on a high mountain rock-face,
Bound to plow down a forest, or as frost in
November,
The gold and flaming death-dance for leaves,
Or a girl in the night of her spent maidenhood,
bleeding and kissing.
I would burn my right hand in a slow fire
To change the future . . . I should do foolishly. The
beauty of modern
Man is not in the persons but in the
Disastrous rhythm, the heavy and mobile masses,
the dance of the
Dream-led masses down the dark mountain.

The rhetorical aspects of this poem are not so subdued as
they might be, but a poem dealing with the disastrous
currents of an entire civilization heading toward ruin need
not apologize for a vocabulary that includes such terms as
"fatal," "tearing pity," "monstrous," and "disastrous." It is
a poem that teaches us a good deal about the function of
art, or at least of an art that would transcend our sufferings
and the evils we promote. It is an example of an art that
through identification with the impersonal roots of all
human behavior, of all activity in this universe, permits us

to contemplate the reality of our foolishness and mortality without much pain, but with praise forming at the lips. Here, perhaps more clearly than in any other poem, Jeffers makes clear what we ought to have known even in his lesser work. To attribute, as Jeffers does, foolishness to the instinct to "burn my right hand in a slow fire / To change the future" is not to consign oneself to the perdition of the heartless, but to seek to forge out of futility a perspective in which futility can be relieved of its manifest failures, purified, rhythmically interpolated into a pattern in which it has meaning as part of that process that is life on this planet. The detachment that makes most great art possible is not heartless, nor is the distancing that is the process of the historical perspective, and that consigns to men the relative insignificance they deserve in the scheme of things, without its virtue. Throughout his career Jeffers tried to resolve the ambiguities of his vision in a direction that would take him further and further from concern with his fellows. How successful he was we can see in **"Rearmament,"** with its persisting ambiguities and unresolved tensions. What is unmistakable, though, is the poet's steadfast refusal to counsel violence among men, and his ability to achieve a perspective wherein the violence men would and did commit could be made tolerable, in a way even absorbed into the universe as an element of necessity. It is nothing less than a tragic vision, and if Jeffers in his poetry could not sufficiently examine and evoke the larger potentialities of man within his limitations, as could a Yeats, he did at least project a vision worthy of our attention, and capable of giving pleasure. The felicities of Jeffers's poetry ought no longer to be denied, but received with gratitude. If he was not among our supreme poets, they have been few who were his equals.

William H. Nolte (essay date 1978)

SOURCE: "Robinson Jeffers Redivivus," in *Georgia Review*, Vol. 32, No. 2, Summer, 1978, pp. 429-34.

[*In the essay below, Nolte surveys critical reception to Jeffers's work, concluding that after many years of suffering critical disdain, his reputation is once again on the rise.*]

When Robinson Jeffers died in 1962 his reputation was probably at its lowest ebb in nearly forty years—since, to be precise, the publication (at his own expense) of *Tamar and Other Poems* (1924), a volume that at first seemed to have been stillborn. Through one of those happy accidents that now and again occur in the literary world the book was brought to the attention of various influential critics—notably, Mark Van Doren, James Rorty, and Babette Deutsch—who praised it so enthusiastically that a new and expanded edition, *Roan Stallion, Tamar and Other Poems,* followed a year later under the imprint of Boni and Liveright, then one of the most prestigious of American publishers. Few volumes of poetry in our history have been greeted with such ecstatic praise from important critics or have met with such demand by the reading public. H. L. Mencken expressed the consensus in the concluding remark of his brief review in the *American Mercury*: "Now

that success has come to him at last, it seems to be solid and promises to be enduring." As book followed book (Jeffers was extremely prolific), that praise remained constant. I doubt that Dwight MacDonald surprised very many readers when, in a long two-part article in 1930, he called Jeffers the greatest poet America had yet produced, adding that he was not only "the most brilliant master of verse among contemporary poets, but his is also incomparably the broadest and most powerful personality." From such a pinnacle of renown there was no way to go but down.

Considering his rejection of all mass beliefs and faiths, his extraordinary individualism, and his abhorrence of all intrusions on his privacy, one might marvel that Jeffers gained so large an audience in the 1920's and 1930's, when he was featured on the cover of *Time* magazine (in 1932 with the publication of *Thurso's Landing and Other Poems*). At the time only T. S. Eliot, who now is in at least partial eclipse, offered competition for the laurel as our most important serious poet. In an article in *Saturday Review of Literature* (9 March 1935), Niven Busch marveled at the sale of Jeffers' books: "Although he has never written anything designed for a restful afternoon in a hammock, he has not, in the last nine years, written anything which sold less than six editions, and [*Roan Stallion, Tamar and Other Poems*] zoomed through fourteen, and this month received the accolade of inclusion in the Modern Library." His manuscripts and the early editions of his books were then bringing higher prices than those of any other living poet.

After a sharp decline in popularity just before, during, and after World War II, Jeffers' stock has in recent years been on the rise again both at home and abroad. His out-of-print volumes, for example, are once more in great demand. One bookfinder (with House of Books, Ltd.) wrote me in 1966: "Jeffers books which a few years ago were found all over at fairly reasonable prices have suddenly disappeared and when available the prices have skyrocketed." New editions are appearing and then selling out almost at once. In the last ten years translations of his poetry have been very well received on the Continent, and especially in Iron Curtain countries, where he is probably the favorite American poet. (Incidentally, Ezra Pound's daughter translated some of his poetry into Italian.)

When Gilbert Highet wrote over twenty years ago that the critical neglect of Jeffers constituted the greatest shame in American letters, he expressed a view that I have heard numerous times since. Indeed, the constantly reiterated query about why Jeffers is not more read today makes me wonder if he isn't the most widely read "unread" poet in world literature. Poetry anthologies are once again giving him prominent place; critical studies are appearing almost yearly; and, as I said before, his out-of-print volumes are being reissued by different publishers. The times, I am convinced, are now catching up with what was most timeless in his verse. Even his political views, the central cause of his temporary decline, now seem much less radical than before. If the events that occasioned the verse are dated, the poetic personality or voice has upon it a dateless stamp.

While it is true that most major writers go through a "cooling period" following their days among us and are then resurrected within ten or twenty years, Jeffers' reputation went into eclipse while he was still living and writing. True enough, *Hungerfield and Other Poems* (1954) and the posthumous *The Beginning and the End and Other Poems* (1963) were well received, but they did little to send readers back to the earlier volumes or make them forget the causes for his being out of favor. That the causes for that decline were primarily political was, of course, apparent to readers at the time. Jeffers would doubtless have enjoyed the irony implicit in the fact that at least part of the new interest in his work centers in the ideological and political views for which he was roundly condemned thirty years ago. As Jeffers put it in **"The Bowl of Blood,"** written just before our entry into the European war: "The present is always a crisis; people want a partisan cry, not judgment." Needless to say, Jeffers gave the latter, for which he was summarily sent to Coventry. In brief, his reputation was a (temporary) casualty of the European holocaust. Had he remained silent, his renown would not have suffered. As it was, he spoke out loudly and clearly—both before and after the War. While lamenting, in a prefatory note to *Be Angry at the Sun and Other Poems* (1941), "the obsession with contemporary history that pins many of these pieces to the calendar, like butterflies to cardboard," Jeffers refused to remain silent before the gathering storm in Europe, which he knew would eventually involve America: "Poetry is not private monologue," he wrote in his note, "but I think it is not public speech either; and in general it is the worse for being timely. . . . Yet it is right that a man's views be expressed, though the poetry suffer for it. Poetry should represent the whole mind; if part of the mind is occupied unhappily, so much the worse. And no use postponing the poetry to a time when these storms may have passed, for I think we have but seen a beginning of them; the calm to look for is the calm at the whirlwind's heart." The "calm" that Jeffers found and reported was not at all to the liking of most of his fellows who were caught in the whirlwind.

If his poetry written just before the War made many people uneasy, that which he wrote during and just after the conflict caused critics, in self-defense actually, to attack him with an unprecedented fury. Not even Whitman received so much abuse during his long lifetime. To read today those old reviews that greeted *The Double Axe and Other Poems* (1948) is both a sobering and an enlightening experience. People wanted to believe that the war effort constituted a moral mission, a kind of twentieth-century Crusade against the forces of Darkness, and that, moreover, an allied victory would usher in a lasting period of peace on earth, if not necessarily good will among all men. For Jeffers to drop his stink bomb into the midst of those who were celebrating a "moral" victory and forgetting the dead was simply unforgivable. Even his publisher, Random House, attached to the book a pious disclaimer of his political views, and has since refused, in the face of a clear public demand, to keep his books in print. Only *The Selected Poetry of Robinson Jeffers,* published in 1938 and now it its fifteenth print-

ing, and the Vintage paperback edition of *Selected Poems* (1965) are available from that publisher. Just recently, in James Shebl's *In This Wild Water* (1976), have we been given a full account of the editorial disagreements between poet and publisher—an account that leaves no doubt that the publisher behaved in a churlish fashion in suppressing various of the poems and insisting on changes in numerous others; but then one could hardly expect an entrepreneur like Bennett Cerf to comprehend a poet like Jeffers. Still, I cannot help feeling some sympathy for the publisher, who knew, after all, that *The Double Axe* was probably the most incendiary volume of verse ever printed on these shores; it was and is certainly the most scathing indictment of war and war-mongers ever composed by an American. That the first part ("The Love and the Hate") of the title poem drips with venom and hatred is certainly obvious to anyone who can read; that the second part ("The Inhumanist") is Jeffers' most serene, and even at times humorous, work was less obvious thirty years ago. It may be that the visceral clout of the first part prevented readers from understanding the poem in its entirety.

No doubt about it though: Jeffers was a good hater. Indeed, one of his most admirable qualities, to me at least, was his titanic hatred of buncombe, hypocrisy, and what Francis Bacon called the Idols of the Marketplace. One must go back to Swift, who also served time as a *persona non grata,* to find his equal as master of vitriol. Jeffers knew, of course, that his long views that is, his insistence on placing things in the context of history, coupled with his refusal to ascribe eternal significance to temporal affairs—would cause readers to misunderstand his work and/or condemn him for saying what only a few could bear to hear. He has in fact been misunderstood by many critics from the beginning of his career, or at least since the 1920's when his mature verse first appeared. I doubt that even Eliot has been the subject of so much errant interpretation, since once Eliot's *manner* has been plumbed his verse can be generally understood. Jeffers' difficulty rests not so much with any stylistic barrier he imposes between himself and the reader as it does with the philosophical content of the verse. In a word, Jeffers is disturbing, and we consciously or unconsciously seek to avoid that which is unsettling either by denying its validity or misrepresenting its meaning. He was, moreover, a bit inhuman: he refused to tell lies. And for that refusal he knew he would pay dearly, at least during his lifetime. He says as much in various of the "apologies" he wrote, perhaps most clearly in **"Self-Criticism in February,"** published in 1937:

> The bay is not blue but sombre yellow
> With wrack from the battered valley, it is speckled
>   with violent foam-heads
> And tiger-striped with long lovely storm-shadows.
> *You love this better than the other mask; better*
>   *eyes than yours*
> *Would feel the equal beauty in the blue.*
> *It is certain you have loved the beauty of storm*
>   *disproportionately.*

But the present time is not pastoral, but founded
On violence, pointed for more massive violence:
  perhaps it is not
Perversity but need that perceives the storm-beauty.
*Well, bite on this: your poems are too full of ghosts
  and demons,*
And people like phantoms—how often life's are—
*And passion so strained that the clay mouths go
  praying for destruction—*
Alas, it is not unusual in life;
To every soul at some time. *But why insist on it?
  And now*
For the worst fault: you have never mistaken
Demon nor passion nor idealism for the real God.
Then what is most disliked in those verses
Remains most true. *Unfortunately. If only you could
  sing*
That God is love, or perhaps that social
Justice will soon prevail. I can tell lies in prose.

Jeffers believed, however, that future readers—the only readers, he insisted, that should concern the poet—would be better able to discern the meaning of his poetry than were his contemporaries, who were too caught up in the passions of the present and, above all, too imprisoned by anthropocentrism to analyze coldly either the world they inhabited or the values they professed. I think it beyond a peradventure that Jeffers was our most far-sighted poet; and nearly the whole of his work concerns the values that men hold, usually to their detriment and despair.

Now, thirty years after the flap over *The Double Axe,* a new edition has been made available by W. W. Norton, issued under the old Liveright imprimatur, along with two other long out-of-print volumes, *The Women at Point Sur* and *Dear Judas and Other Poems,* originally published by Liveright in 1927 and 1929 respectively. Identical in format and beautifully printed from the original plates on thick paper, the editions contain uniformly excellent editorial and critical contributions by William Everson, Robert J. Brophy, Bill Hotchkiss, and Tim Hunt. The reappearance after so many years of these three extraordinary volumes offers additional evidence that Jeffers is undergoing a renaissance greater than that of any other modern poet. His cooling period over, Jeffers now occupies a solid niche in the pantheon of great poets.

Terry Beers   (essay date 1987)

SOURCE: "Robinson Jeffers and the Canon," in *American Poetry,* Vol. 5, No. 1, Fall, 1987, pp. 4-16.

[*In the following essay, Beers examines the negative reaction to Jeffers's poetry among the New Critics and suggests that feminist and deconstructionist critical approaches may be more receptive to his work.*]

The poetry of Robinson Jeffers has drawn from critics some of the most vicious—and arguably some of the most entertaining—condemnations afforded to any modern body of literature. At midcentury, R. P. Blackmur attempted to anticipate future critics by predicting which poets of the twentieth century then known to him would enjoy lasting reputations. He finds fault with a wide variety of writers, among them Auden, Empson, and Housman, only to conclude that "all of them are better than the flannel-mouthed inflation in the metric of Robinson Jeffers with his rugged rock-garden violence." Not many years later, Kenneth Rexroth added his voice to the vociferous anti-Jeffers crowd while reviewing Radcliffe Squires' source study of Jeffers, and again the condemnation is nothing it not extreme:

> In my opinion Jeffers's verse is shoddy and pretentious and the philosophizing is nothing but posturing. His reworking of Greek tragic plots makes me shudder at their vulgarity, the coarsening of language, and the tawdriness of the paltry insight into the great ancient meanings.

But as all Jeffers scholars would agree, these are mild expressions of dislike, comparatively weak heirs to a tradition established two decades earlier by Yvor Winters, whose disdain for Jeffers' verse was as constant and abiding as the coastal headlands in which Jeffers set his narrative poetry. As Rexroth himself has noticed, Winters' attacks were the most devastating in modern criticism, helping to push Jeffers' reputation—then at its height—into a steady decline.

Winters poisonous antipathy first emerged in reviews of *Dear Judas and Other Poems* (1929) and *Thurso's Landing and Other Poems* (1932). Of the former, Winters claimed the work had "no quotable lines, save possibly the last three, which are, however, heavy with dross." Of the latter, he claimed that the writing could hardly be equalled for "clumsiness and emptiness," a claim that led him to a characteristically unequivocal judgment: "The book is composed almost wholly of trash." Winters' invective was not limited to reviews, of course, and his disdain for Jeffers' verse found expression again in an essay "The Experimental School in American Poetry":

> *The Women at Point Sur* [1927] is a perfect laboratory of Mr. Jeffers' philosophy and a perfect example of his narrative method. Barclay, an insane divine, preaches Mr. Jeffers' religion, and his disciples, acting upon it, become emotional mechanisms, lewd and twitching conglomerations of plexuses, their humanity annulled.

As Squires has wryly observed, "It is impossible to improve on Winters' diction when he is inspired by indignation."

Of course these condemnations were no more extreme than the praise of some of the most influential reviewers of the time, including Mark Van Doren, who said of *Tamar* (1924), "Few [volumes] are as rich with the beauty and strength which belong to genius alone." Many of Jeffers' early critics were moved by his compelling imagery and the depth of his philosophic conviction, intangible qualities which gave Jeffers his "power." Harriet Monroe, though by no means an enthusiastic admirer, claimed that Jeffers was nevertheless a "poet of extraordinary power." Granville Hicks, reviewing **Thurso's Landing,** named the same quality: "There is, one cannot deny, a kind of validity in this and all of Jeffers's poems; such power was not born of self-deceit." Babette Deutsch found it in **Solstice and Other Poems** (1935): "The poem which opens Jeffers' latest volume restates his familiar themes, with no loss of power, and with the additional interest of a greater technical variety." And Van Doren, while offering only qualified praise of **Point Sur,** carefully reports: "I have read it with thrills of pleasure at its power and beauty." Whatever the qualities of Jeffers' verse, one must evidently agree with Rolfe Humphries' claim that Jeffers "either knocks you or leaves you cold," a claim that on the surface explains much about Jeffers' critics: Winters was left practically freezing, while other critics, both before and since, have fallen like tenpins.

Extreme critical disagreements like these invite our attention not only for what they reveal about particular works, but also for what they reveal about the critical environment in which they are expressed, the values and procedures by which critics make and defend their judgments, and as a result, the question of whether or not particular writers are widely read within the academy. These are central concerns for Jeffers scholars, especially if they are to have comprehensive answers to two fundamental questions. First, why isn't Jeffers' poetry more respected and more often taught within the academy, especially since some influential critics recognize its extraordinary power? Second, will the academy eventually bestow the respect that it has so far stubbornly withheld?

These two questions presuppose the assumption that Jeffers' work draws scant critical attention, and at first glance such an assumption seems dangerous. In 1978 William Nolte mused, "The constantly reiterated query why Jeffers is not more often read today makes me wonder if he it not the most widely read 'unread' poet in world literature." Earlier, Bill Hotchkiss had pointed to a flurry of activity in the seventeen years following the publication of Rexroth's "decline of the poet" article—the book-length studies of Jeffers' work, the reissue of some Jeffers volumes, and the publication of Jeffers' selected correspondence—to support his assertion that "someone is reading Robinson Jeffers." And in 1976 Robert Brophy expressed the cautious hopes of Jeffers critics by noting a significant increase in Jeffers dissertations and articles since the mid-sixties and remarking upon the passing of a generation of biased or hostile critics.

The regeneration of Jeffers scholarship in the sixties and seventies, moreover, seems to have established a receptive environment for continuing scholarship in the present decade. A glance through those numbers of the *Robinson Jeffers Newsletter* published in the last six years reveals that scholars continue to serve Jeffers' poetry by publishing hitherto unpublished correspondence, checklists, and notes

of bibliographical and biographical interest; that Stanford University Press has contracted for the **Complete Works**; and that work has begun on at least one scholarly biography. Articles and dissertations about Jeffers' work continue to appear; Cambridge University Press recently published Robert Zaller's Freudian study of Jeffers' poetry, *Cliffs of Solitude: A Reading of Robinson Jeffers*; and, of course, there are the celebrations and scholarly work planned to coincide with the centenary of Jeffers' birth in 1987. Robinson Jeffers is being read, but how much and by whom?

According to notes in *RJN,* the first five years of this decade have produced only four dissertations on or dealing with Robinson Jeffers, and in three of these studies, Jeffers is only one of two or more poets being compared under a general rubric such as "long narrative poems" or "the problem of rationalism." Because of their scope, these dissertations may indeed serve Jeffers scholarship by flagging the attention of scholars who otherwise take no notice of a Jeffers dissertation. Even so, the relatively small number of recent Jeffers dissertations leaves unfulfilled the optimism felt by earlier critics.

The first of the two questions I posed above—why isn't the poetry of Robinson Jeffers more respected by the academy?—can now be seen in more complicated ways, for as I have shown, the reputation of Robinson Jeffers languishes despite ongoing scholarship sympathetic to Jeffers' poetry and despite the passing of the hostile critics to which Brophy has alluded. Hotchkiss offers a partial answer, conjecturing that critics like Rexroth have done little more than follow the lead of their fire-breathing predecessors and echo their judgements. But this explanation—positing a sort of critical inertia whereby opinions set in motion are not easily deflected—seems inadequate when we realize that not only has a generation of hostile critics passed, but those critics largely represented a mode of critical perception that in recent years has been challenged, some believe overthrown.

I am referring, of course, to the New Criticism, that movement of critics dominating English studies in the middle decades of this century. There is no question that these critics are responsible for the neglect of Jeffers' poetry by the academy: Alex Vardamis' bibliography shows that many influential New Critics—for example, R. P. Blackmur, Robert Penn Warren, and Yvor Winters—condemned Jeffers' poetry, while others demonstrated their indifference through silence. The only influential New Critic to offer a sympathetic opinion is Allen Tate, who refers to Jeffers in familiar terms as "a poet of great power."

Although the approaches of these critics differed, they collectively strived for an almost scientific objectivity in order to isolate poems—verbal artifacts serving as the practical objects of literary study—from a host of correlative matters, including the specific intentions of their authors and the affective responses of their readers. Thus despite their internecine differences, the New Critics actively sought a common goal. Cleanth Brooks, with characteristic common sense, puts it best in *The Well-Wrought Urn*:

I insist that to treat the poems discussed primarily as poems is a proper emphasis and very much worth doing. For we have gone to school to the anthropologists and the cultural historians assiduously, and we have learned their lesson almost too well. We have learned it so well that the danger now, it seems to me, is not that we will forget the differences between poems of different historical periods, but that we may forget those qualities which they have in common.

In recent years, New Criticism has suffered from the attacks of critics like E. D. Hirsch, who argues that the isolation of a privileged text from the intention of its author leaves no compelling criterion by which to judge the validity of an interpretation; of critics like Stanley Fish, who is suspicious of the idea that poems are objective literary artifacts; and of scores of deconstructionists, reader-response theorists, and linguistic and language-philosophy critics who reject the notion that literary texts "contain" specific literary qualities or demarcate specific boundaries for linguistic meaning. As a result, most agree that contemporary skepticism has discredited New Criticsm as a theory of interpretive practice. But according to William Cain, despite the news of its demise, New Criticism still exerts a vital influence within the academy:

> It is the New Criticism that defines and gives support to the central job of work that we perform: "practical criticism," the "close reading" of literary texts. . . . If a new theory cannot generate close readings, if it fails the test of practical criticism, if it seems unable to make us understand the classic texts in new ways and appears unlikely to function well in the classroom, then it is usually judged to be irrelevant.

Accepting Cain's thesis goes a long way toward a clearer, more comprehensive explanation of why Jeffers' reputation languishes. Not only have some critics tended to accept the extreme judgments of influential predecessors, but the stubborn tendency of critical practice to do close readings, whatever the dominant theoretical mode, has often tended to put critical approaches on a competitive footing, each approach vying for validity by attempting to create new, insightful readings of already canonical texts. A classic example is Roland Barthes' reading of Balzac's novella, *Sarrasine,* where despite the fact that Barthes denigrates the conventional quality of "readerly" classical texts, he shows that an innovative, structuralist reading can transform that text into a "writerly" one, dependent upon changing social codes and their idiosyncratic application by a reader. Thus as long as contemporary critical movements still center on close reading, they have no urgent need to reform the canon. But as we shall see, the pressures for reform are building.

If I have complicated the original question, it is only to offer a comprehensive answer: despite the decline of New Criticism, the academy in general largely ignores Jeffers' poetry because there has been little impetus, thanks to the continued practice of "close reading," to attend to non-canonical works, to question the canon as it has been shaped by the New Critics. At best, Jeffers' poetry remains on the periphery as an example of "Experimentation in Poetry," as William Stafford (perhaps echoing Yvor Winters) classified it in his anthology *Twentieth Century American Writing*; at worst, it is completely ignored, as in the first edition of *The Norton Anthology of American Literature*.

But despite institutional lethargy, some critics do challenge the shape of our literary canon. Many of these challenges stem from sometimes unpopular political and social imperatives—imperatives felt, for example, by critics of Feminist and Minority literatures especially, who point to the inherent prejudices of a literary canon dominated by white, male authors. But other challenges originate when these and other critics extend the founding assumptions of their preferred critical principles to question the very idea of a literary canon, especially one based upon qualities supposedly inherent in the works that it would include. Rather than the mere passing of hostile critics, or the undoubted fact that Jeffers' poetry continues to attract the interest of some intrepid and talented literary scholars, I believe the challenge to the idea of an authoritative literary "canon" offers the best hope if the academy in general is to extend to Jeffers' work a greater measure of respect.

The philosopher Richard Bernstein sees recent interest in modern hermeneutics as potentially transforming how we view the sciences and the humanities: "what has happened is that thinkers in diverse fields, working on a variety of different problems, have come to share many of the insights, emphases, and concerns of contemporary, philosophic hermeneutics"; included is new skepticism toward what Bernstein calls an underlying Cartesian anxiety, a "seductive Either/Or. *Either* there is some support for our being, a fixed foundation for our knowledge, *or* we cannot escape the forces of darkness that envelop us with madness, with intellectual and moral chaos." Bernstein believes Gadamer has shown a way to destroy the dichotomy, for it objectivism is a myth—because "objective" facts are constituted by the presuppositions which precede them—the resulting relativism is not therefore arbitrary: "Gadamer reminds us that we belong to a tradition, history, and language before they belong to us."

One way or another, many critical modes reject the Cartesian dichotomy and recognize (in some cases celebrate) a principled relativism. For example, deconstructionists set out, says Jonathan Culler, to show how discourse undermines the philosophy it asserts by identifying the rhetorical operations that produce the grounds for argument, the key concept or premise. Meaning—and the elements of a text that serve it—depends upon convention and contextual factors which themselves are inexhaustible, though not necessarily arbitrary and thereby unprincipled. Like the New Critics, deconstructionists perform a sort of "close reading," but to a different purpose: instead of identifying in particular works supposedly objective features "common" to good poems, deconstructionists celebrate the processes by which language avoids such certainty, by which it remains always equivocal. Some reader-response theorists, too, question the objectivity of literary qualities either by emphasizing readers' contributions to the constitution of the literary work or by emphasizing that the constitution of the work is constrained by conventions and interpretive procedures extrinsic to the text. Taken together, these modes of critical analysis make of literature an always open category by destroying the objectivist notion that special literary qualities inhere within canonical works.

Partly as a result of these theoretical and philosophical shifts (even more compelling, it seems to me, because they derive from concerns not particularly limited to literary study) we can more easily see canons for what they really are: "what other people, once powerful, have made and what should now be opened up, demystified, or eliminated altogether." Once theory overturns the assumption of objective literary values inherent in poetic works, the New Critics' de facto exclusion of Jeffers from the canon need no longer be questioned from within their exclusionary model of criticism; instead, the question of Jeffers' literary value may be reconsidered in light of new theories with their criteria for rigorous analysis and their theoretical openness to a better understanding of the dynamics of canon formation.

Reconsidering Jeffer's reputation in terms of contemporary critical modes, however, assumes that his poetry will hold interest for the critics who practice them. The potential certainly exists, and I will here point to two possibilities.

I agree with Elaine Showalter that feminist criticism focusing on, among other things, the ways in which a given text may awaken readers to the significance of its sexual codes may in fact tend to "naturalize women's victimization making it the inevitable and obsessive topic of discussion." This objection, however, need not imply (nor is it meant to) that there is no value in such readings, and many of Jeffers' poems lend themselves naturally to an analysis of gender roles and the power structures encoded by them through strong female characters and Jeffers' own philosophy of Inhumanism, which looks skeptically upon humanity's solipsism.

For instance, Jeffers' narrative poem **"Solstice,"** a modern re-working of the Medea myth, explores the philosophy of Inhumanism through the central character, Madrone Bothwell, who laments her own humanity excessively. Madrone (the Medea figure of the poem) wishes to protect her children from their estranged father, Bothwell (the Jason figure), who serves as an emblem of the self-absorbed human world through his hopes for his children. He wishes for them "radio, motion-pictures, books, / The school, the church. And when they're old enough to go to college."

Feminist critics will especially notice that Madrone's excessive hatred of humanity only makes sense when set within a restricted world of human concerns, which Jeffers, following a sort of symbolic-realism, represents in terms of patriarchal forces: Bothwell and his retinue of male allies, who collectively signify a patriarchal society's support for Bothwell's claim upon the children. The tragedy of Madrone, who escapes her dilemma by slaying her children and taking her own life, stems not only from her excessive hatred of humanity, but also from the reluctance

of a patriarchal human world, threatened by her rejection, to let her or her children escape its self-interest. Jeffers' Inhumanism, which insists upon humanity's place within the natural cosmos and the attendant reification of human values necessary to accept that place, defines the moderate stance that neither side accepts. Thus an analysis of this text with special attention to the roles of gender would demonstrate not only how the text rejects the narrowness of human concerns for the transcendent values of the natural world, but also how it comments implicitly on patriarchal structures which authorize human values. Other Jeffers texts, for example **"Roan Stallion,"** seem to me susceptible to the same mode of analysis, revealing Jeffers to be a much more complex critic of the human condition than some detractors discern, especially those who, like Rexroth, see in his poetry only a "paltry insight into the great ancient meanings."

Deconstructionist critics, too, might discover an interest in Jeffers' work, finding a rich source of rhetorical paradox through exploring the question of how Jeffers' poetry, intended to focus attention on the transcendent natural world, actually questions the possibility of such a focus since it depends upon a system of language conventions and interpretive practices that derive from human value systems. Such an analysis might begin by noticing how the word that Jeffers chose to signify his philosophy, Inhumanism, introduces a surprising indeterminacy. Jeffers intended the word to represent values that were "not human," in the sense that they were of a greater order; but some readers may read the word as "not human," in the sense of lacking kindness or sympathy, as expressing a love for cruelty. Such readings often seem authorized by Jeffers' appreciation of natural events and his refusal to project human sentimentality into natural scenes. For instance, in the short poem **"Fire on the Hills"** Jeffers writes, "Beauty is not always lovely; the fire was beautiful, the terror / Of the deer was beautiful," lines which may strike some readers as a gruesome celebration of destruction and terror. In any case, Jeffers' terms for his poetic philosophy can now be seen to function more subtly. First, it signifies a complex of transcendent, "inhuman" values of a greater order than the more parochial human values which we uncritically and often unknowingly accept. Second, it demonstrates to readers, forced to disentangle the term "Inhumanism" from its historical and apparently legitimate usages, how deeply they are enmeshed in their own human value system.

Deconstructive analyses might also focus on specific works—both the longer narratives and the shorter lyrics—to show, for example, how narrative intrusions in these poems perform similar functions by simultaneously asserting the primacy of the natural order and demonstrating the difficulty of apprehending it, since these narrative intrusions often argue for a shift to an inhuman perspective even while calling attention to the humanity of the narrative voice. A specific example comes easily to mind, a passage from Jeffers' narrative poem, **"Roan Stallion"**:

> Humanity is
> the start of the race; I say
> Humanity is the mould to break away from, the

crust to break
 through, the coal to break into fire,
The atom to be split.
   Tragedy that breaks man's face and a white
 fire flies out of it; vision that fools him
Out of his limits, desire that fools him out of his
 limits, unnatural
 crime, inhuman science,
Slit eyes in the mask; wild loves that leap over the
 walls of nature,
 the wild fence-vaulter science,
Useless intelligence of far stars, dim knowledge of
 the spinning
 demons that make an atom,
These break, these pierce, these deify, praising their
 God shrilly
 with fierce voices: not in a man's shape
He approves the praise, he that walks lightning-
 naked on the
 Pacific, that laces the suns with planets,
The heart of the atom with electrons: what is
 humanity in this
 cosmos? For him, the last
Least taint of a trace in the dregs of the solution;
 for itself, the
 mould to break away from, the coal
To break into fire, the atom to be split.

The passage serves several functions, including, according to Brophy, serving as a chronic pronouncement urging that "man willingly submit himself to an expansion of his human nature." Consequently, the passage slows the narrative pace by asking readers to suspend their attention to narrative events and instead attend to an inhuman vision of deity, "not in a man's shape." Yet the very power of the language to affirm a deep conviction in the perspective for which it pleads—partly represented by the image of a God who "walks lightning-naked on the Pacific"—plays a subtle trick on readers, for that power draws attention to itself, to the humanity of the narrative voice, and thus to the eventual realization that the author and the reader are both trapped in a human linguistic system that makes the shift of perspective that Inhumanism demands a difficult act of will, if not an impossible one. The text itself, then, demonstrates the human predicament as forcefully as the story which it tells: just as the protagonist California is moved by "some obscure human fidelity" to destroy the roan stallion which represents her vision of God, readers are moved by the same obscure human fidelity to listen to the compelling voice of the narrator. Attending to the humanity within pronouncements seemingly functioning to implicate determinate, transcendent principles helps readers to question the felicity of language intended to direct attention away from the human world and reveals in Jeffers' poetry a quality that enriches reading.

Whatever the mode of analysis—deconstruction, feminist, reader-response, or even sympathetic "close reading" in the style of New Criticism—I believe Jeffers' reputation may benefit: not only because contemporary critical methods may lead to compelling readings of Jeffers texts, perhaps finding in their reading a greater complexity and a more subtle aesthetic than many in the academy previously have recognized, but also because the plurality of critical methods and their collective rejection of the objectivist myth guarantee that we can no longer naively accept canons formed in the tradition of Matthew Arnold's dictum, "the best that has been thought or said," for we no longer can be confident that the meaning of "best" is somehow an absolute.

Jeffers once wrote, "Poetry is less bound by circumstances than any of the arts; it does not need tangible materials; good poetry comes almost directly from a man's mind and senses and bloodstream, and no one can predict the man." I will concede that no one can predict the man, but as for the other point, Jeffers was dead wrong: poetry, like any mode of discourse, is certainly bound by circumstances. The reputations of few other poets demonstrate this so clearly as does that of Robinson Jeffers, a writer who found extraordinary power in poetic forms that defied the critical formalism of his age. We can hope, however, that with the decline of that formalism, Jeffers' poetry may be appreciated within the academy more fully and taught with the intelligence, verve, and dedication that it deserves.

Robert Brophy (essay date 1987)

SOURCE: "Robinson Jeffers," in *A Literary History of the American West,* Texas Christian University Press, 1987, pp. 398-415.

[*In the essay below, Brophy places Jeffers's work in the context of the American West, concluding "the westering experience was for [Jeffers] the exemplar of all journeys. Western motifs gave him vehicles for a larger philosophizing."*]

Jeffers's themes are . . . consistent from the beginning of his mature period (*Tamar,* 1924) till the end of his life (*The Beginning and the End,* 1963). He was a pantheist who believed that God is the evolving universe, a self-torturing god who discovers himself in the violent change which is at the center of life's dynamic. One need not go far in Jeffers to find that all his images are cyclic: cycle is the truth of the stars, the life of the planet, the fate of man, insect, and flower. Cycle moves through birth, growth, fullness, decay, and death. In ritual terms cycle translates into sacrifice (fragmentation of each entity at the cycle's end) and sacrament (reintegration and rebirth). For him, being involves change which is brought about only by violence and pain because each form resists its own dissolution. These realities, though customarily repugnant to man, are essential to beauty and divinity. For Jeffers there is only matter and energy; there is no spirit, or soul, or immortality (these being merely men's attempts to escape the cycle). God endures forever; man is a temporary phenomenon, something of an anomaly in the universe because of his megalomanic self-regard. But man is also unique, able to reflect on God. In fact man is, for the cosmic moment he endures, one of God's sense organs (**"The Beginning and the End"**).

Consciousness is a universal quality of the cosmos, but man's participation in it will pass (**"Credo"**); beauty survives man's faculty to perceive it. Death is at the end of each cycle, ending the individual existence; the material from each man's body is reassimilated into soil and air (**"Hungerfield"**). Man's energy sometimes endures for a moment after death, like a St. Elmo's fire, in psychic phenomena. The world in its various rhythms is determined. The universe expands and collapses, oceans condense and evaporate, mountains and civilizations rise and fall; nations emerge and grow old. The mass of men is fated in its course, but the individual can choose to remove himself from the breaking wave, can stand apart and contemplate instead of being blindly caught. God himself (the pronoun of course is an anomaly) is in no way like man; he is savage, indifferent, and wild (**"Hurt Hawks"**), encompassing both good and evil. If seen wholly, all things are sacred and in harmony. Evil itself is only part of the mosaic of beauty, indicating the close of the cycle (**"The Answer"**).

To Jeffers the task of living a "good life" lies principally in detachment from insane desires for power, wealth, and permanence, in a measured indifference to pain, joy, or success, and in a turning outward to God who is "all things." Wisdom, a word little used in his poetry except in irony (**"Wise Men in Their Bad Hours"**) means cosmic perspective (**"Signpost"**) and unfocusing from mankind (Jeffers's "inhumanism"). Peace, as cessation from strife, is an illusion in life. True peace is found in death; in life it can be anticipated in a stoic balance which discounts man's innate anxieties for immortality, invulnerability, stability, and immunity from pain and sickness. The great and most subtle temptation for the good person lies in the implicitly self-aggrandizing notion that one can change the world (saviorism). Jeffers himself must have desperately fought this "demon," he writes about it so often. He saw love as an abnormality of an incestuous race, leading to many other insanities. One love is pure: the love of God who is indifferent to man. Piety lies in an undistracted regard for beauty, earthly and cosmic. Terrible beauty is the god who commands worship. The poet is one who creates as God creates (**"Apology for Bad Dreams"**), who reconciles existence for man, putting man's preoccupations with sin, guilt, corruption, pain, and all other confounding fears and desires into saving context. The "good person" is not the leader, rebel, or savior; he is the self-contained mystic, contemplating God and living out the necessary conspiracies of life with a certain aloofness (Tamar achieves this amidst her melodrama of family destruction).

Jeffers's art grew out of his life and vice versa; it was a consequence of his philosophy and of his sense of vocation. Once one grasps the dimensions of his beliefs, it becomes clear that Jeffers's poetry is incredibly centered and predictable. The theme of every poem, one way or another, is the divine beauty of the cosmos and the mutability of man. Jeffers has a deep sense of ritual, not only in nature's rites of death and renewal but in every rhythm of being. His ritual intent is strikingly evidenced in a letter to his editor in 1926, in which he explained that the movement

of his narratives was "more like the ceremonial dances of primitive people; the dancer becomes a raincloud, or a leopard, or a God . . . the episodes . . . are a sort of essential ritual, from which the real action develops on another plane" (*Selected Letters*). He embraces tragedy in its pre-Sophoclean sense of the inevitable, blameless fall which yields new beginnings. "All life is tragic" translates into "all life is cyclic." Though civilized man flees the metaphysical implications of cycle, primitive man seems to have accepted and celebrated them. Characteristically in Mediterranean fertility cults, each year the cycle god, Attis, Osiris, Tammuz, Dionysus, had to suffer the consequences of reentry into being; each was born in order to die (and be reborn ten thousand times). Decline and death were not blameworthy or cataclysmic but inevitable and natural. Death is perhaps Jeffers's most frequent theme; it is a truth to understand, accept, and move within.

Of course subordinate themes abound in Jeffers's poetry, but they all bear on the truth of the cycle—human mutability, reconciliation with evil, confrontation of pain, indifference born of cosmic perspective, acceptance of God on his own terms, desirability of death and annihilation, inevitability of processes, delusion of human effectiveness, presumptuousness of man's self-importance, the nature of the poet's art, the omnipresence and beauty of tragedy.

The poetics of Jeffers are fairly simple and direct. His is a poetry of the external landscape, not the landscape of the mind (**"Credo"**). After the lyrics and semi-narratives of his first two books, he consciously avoided meter and rhyme. He replaced the first with the larger, more supple rhythms of Hebrew and Old English verse and the second with symmetries of parallelism and alliteration. Ten-beat lines are common in the narratives although there are many variations; four-beat lines are more likely in the lyrics.

Much of Jeffers's poetic effect comes through word-choice or diction. He chose words for etymology and for their successive layers of meaning. He kept a huge unabridged dictionary by his side and pondered word possibilities, sometimes for days. His imagery makes a fascinating study. Most of it is taken from his immediate coastal experience: hawks, herons, wild swans, pelicans, mountain lion, deer, and cattle; redwood, cypress, grass, wildflowers, rock, ocean, headland, clouds, sky, stars, and planets. Hawks are godlike, totem birds, representing what is noble and fierce. Lion and deer are the predators and victims, metaphors for all victimhood, neither blameworthy. Flora and fauna almost always fill a twofold function in his narratives: they are part of the realistic backdrop for the action; they also foreshadow the tragedy imminent in all drama, recalling animal surrogates of the year-gods and the sacrificial flowers which sprang from the gods' blood. Rock is a consistent image of God, mysterious chthonic presence and stoic endurance; it is volcanic origins, the bones of motherearth. The sea is a mind-subduing expanse, life and death, matrix of all life, source of story, change of season. Mountain and headland are measure of the heavens and reminder of human life's precariousness. Storm represents elemental apocalyptic forces; earth, air, fire, water (quake, storm, holocaust, and deluge)—all are fearful agents in Jeffers's narratives. Clouds are a dream medium on which the poet projects human folly (**"The Great Sunset"**). Sky and stars are the universe beckoning. Stars are used both mythically, as in the constellation patterns of Orion and Scorpio in **"Tamar,"** but more often scientifically—gigantic atomic fusion furnaces whose lifespan predicts the fate of our sun and solar system (**"Nova"**). The far stars and galaxies are the ultimate actors of Jeffers's ultimate metaphor, the expanding and contracting universe which recycles every eighty-two billion years and is God's heartbeat (**"The Great Explosion," "At the Birth of an Age"**).

Jeffers wrote and spoke little of his poetics. His 1938 foreword to **Selected Poetry** declares his intent to reclaim the subject matter which poetry had surrendered to prose. He meant to write about permanent things or the eternally recurring (**"Point Joe"**). He promised to pretend nothing, neither optimism nor pessimism. He would avoid the popular and fashionable; he would write as he believed, whatever the consequences.

In **"Apology for Bad Dreams,"** an early *ars poetica* in lyric form, Jeffers indicates that he creates his narratives and dramas (bad dreams) principally for his own salvation. Using the vignette of a woman beating a horse amidst the magnificence of a coastal sundown, he attempts to reconcile man's perversity with the essential beauty of things. The landscape, he says, demands tragedy (pain, sacrifice, horror); the greater its beauty, the stronger the demand. It would seem that the poet wrote out these vicarious terrors in order to be spared the real terror of personal tragedy. Exactly what metaphysics is involved, Jeffers does not explain. He may write stories to educate himself to violence and the cycle, thus taking some of the terror out of the pain that he, as everyone, must endure. He may write as a form of therapy, letting out his inner violences, lest he act them out and beat horses himself. Or he may see in his writing a way of participating in being's ritual, acting out a discovery-process that parallels God's own creative process—a kind of "magic" (as he calls it).

Anyone who doubts the religious intent of Jeffers's poetry should read carefully the choric invocation in **"Tamar"** (section V), his first narrative poem of note. He calls on the god of natural beauty to enter into his "puppet" characters—a brother and sister who have just committed incest and the disintegrating family that surrounds them. God, Jeffers says, chooses the twisted and lame to be his signs and the agents of his revelation. For this same reason God has chosen him. The same kind of lyric interruption greets us in **"The Women at Point Sur,"** Jeffers's most tortured and convoluted narrative. Here again he has created human grotesques, he says, to praise God, "puppets" to speak of him; they "stammer the tragedy." There are other writers, Jeffers tells us in the "Prelude" to the poem, who will tell tales to entertain; his vocation is to slit open the eyeholes in mankind's mask. Human resistance to God and to integration into the organic whole of the universe can be broken only by dramatic means (**"Roan Stallion"**): disorienting vision, limit-vaulting desire, unnatural crime, inhuman science, and tragedy. "These break [the mould], these pierce

[the mask], these deify, praising their God shrilly with fierce voices: not in man's shape. He approves the praise" (**"Roan Stallion"**). Later Jeffers will clarify this view of storytelling and further its religious context in the lyric **"Crumbs or the Loaf"** where, in a parallel to Jesus's story of the sower and the seed (Matthew 13), he characterizes his narratives as parables, as contrasted with his lyrics which are confrontive apodictic pronouncements.

Jeffers's final statement on poetry comes toward the end of his writing career. In 1949, amidst the triumph of *Medea* and impending rejection of **The Double Axe,** he characterizes the truly great poet in an article for the *New York Times,* "Poetry, Gongorism and a Thousand Years." The poet, he says, stands alone. He renounces self-consciousness, over-learnedness, labored obscurity (by which Jeffers would probably have characterized most of contemporary poetry). He is direct and natural, saying what he must say clearly, out of the spirit of his time but as understandable for all times.

Elsewhere I have called Jeffers the "metaphysician of the West." Metaphysics is that most fundamental area of philosophy which studies being itself. Metaphysics has to deal with all that exists; it delves into the nature of all processes, of all that is—the workings and interactings of the universe and of the molecule and atom. **"Of the West"** suggests more than writing in and from the point of view of the West, or using its scenes as a setting. Jeffers does all these things, but his peculiar genius is his use of the West, the Far West, the continent's end and drop-off cliff of the world on which he perched his home, to explore the nature of being, the relevance of the human race, and the bridge between man and the furthermost expanses of the cosmos.

Jeffers represented his western landscape exactly; it stretched from Point Pinos in the north to Point Sur and Pfeiffer Beach in the south. This fifty miles of storm-scoured promontories, precipitous headlands, wave-wracked points, wind-twisted trees, and precarious beaches was known intimately to him. It was the subject for solitary walks and family pilgrimages. The place names in his poems are almost all right off the geological survey map: Point Pinos and Joe, Robinson Canyon, Carmel Beach, Point Lobos, Mal Paso Creek, Notley's Landing, Palo Colorado Canyon, Rocky Point, Soberanes Reef, Bixby's Landing, Mill Creek, Little Sur River, Point Sur. The terrain, the beaches, the weather, the flowers, the animals are all true-to-life re-creations. Jeffers Country is no mythical Yoknapatawpha County; only the characters' names are made up.

Yet, in their own way, Jeffers's characters are authentic, arising as they do from the violent legends of this forbidding and isolating terrain. Someone has suggested that the Big Sur country causes madness because of something in its dynamic which either produces or attracts the grotesque, the macabre. Robinson Jeffers himself suggests this in **"Apology for Bad Dreams."** Jeffers's characters are ranch families, self-exiled hermits in shacks, wandering Indian cowboys from a previous era.

The land has never been domesticated; it is inconceivable that it ever will be; this is not so much remote backpacking country as impenetrable space. As one can see from the Sierra Club photo book, *Not Man Apart,* the coast is an almost continuous headlong precipice. The Coast Highway, an engineering triumph of the 1930s, strung a precarious ribbon of asphalt just above the drop-off, dynamiting through shoulders of rock, leaping over creek gorges with delicate butterfly bridges. Almost every winter a storm carries a lane of the highway into the sea. Behind this coast road are a few grassy knolls and fields, backed by wilderness. As one passes over it in a flight from Los Angeles to San Francisco, one sees tightly corrugated peaks and gulleys choked with trees and brush—no roads, no lights, no water, no signs of life. This is wilderness in an almost mystic sense, a place to correspond to the empty places in the soul. One need not visit it; it was comforting to Jeffers just to know it was there and that it would never be humanized, subdivided, asphalted andfitted with sewer systems.

Very conscious of writing as a westerner, Jeffers perceived his land and his conscience as scarred with the vestiges of westward expansion. All around him were the ghosts of Indians who were too easy a victim to the white man's ambitions and diseases. San Carlos Mission, a few blocks from Tor House, presided over the death of local tribes. A spade on his knoll may turn over the remains of a tribal feast, abalone and clam shells and charcoal from their fires. Jeffers is conscious that his Carmel River mouth is the center of a line which marks the final coast of migrations which began millennia ago, first crossing Europe, then the Atlantic, and finally the American continent ("**Tamar,**" Section V, makes use of this, as do "**The Loving Shepherdess**" and "**Continent's End**"). Somehow this coast sums up all migrations and all that men have done for good or evil in their "progress." Jeffers's Doppelgänger, the self-stigmatizing hermit in "**A Redeemer,**" summed it up: "Not as a people takes a land to love it and be fed, / A little according to need and love and again a little; sparing the country tribes, mixing / Their blood with theirs, their minds with all the rocks and rivers, their flesh with the soil . . . Oh, as a rich man eats a forest for profit and a field for vanity, So you came west and raped / The continent and brushed its people to death. Without need the weak skirmishing hunters and without mercy."

Jeffers is not a regionalist in the usual sense of the word— one who writes knowingly of his geographic section, reflecting its genius and foibles, relating its topographic and climatic peculiarities, reciting its idiom and its philosophy. The California coast for him is not a region; it is a final statement, a philosophical, metaphysical study. There are neither enough people nor customs in his mountains for regionally, and the landscape is unearthly, not picturesque. The final frontier is an ontological statement, not a geographic or cultural one. It is final as the coast is final— to all of mankind's hopes and illusions and indirections. America's violence, its rape of the land, its betrayal of the Indians, its pillaging of resources—all of these must ultimately be faced here.

Before concluding a discussion of Jeffers's themes and aesthetics, it is important to confront some of the objections to his writing—not in order to excuse his faults but to clarify his intent and identify his genre so that judgments may be better focused. With regard to his narratives, one can merely repeat what has been said above: Jeffers is a tragedian; he cannot write comedy for he saw comedy as an unfinished story. His stories are grotesque and usually end in blood. Whether he succeeded or not, his intent is to write parables, to instruct and to move his readers beyond their limits. His genre is, at an important level, ritualistic: that is, the story represents a Dionysian process, illustrating the cycles of life and death. His central characters, he says (in "**My Loved Subject**"), are the landscape: "Mountain and ocean, rock, water and beasts and trees / Are the protagonists, the human people are only symbolic interpreters." His human characters therefore are not primarily psychological or humanistic studies. Actually Jeffers chooses a sort of stereotyping (he has consistently called his characters "puppets"): his men tend to be Appolonian, stoic, cerebral, presumptuous that their power and plans will carry the day; his women tend to be Dionysian, sudden, intuitive, destructive; they are divine agents. Stories tend to follow the pattern of Pentheus's destruction by Agave in *The Bacchae* (Jeffers's version: "Humanist's tragedy"). The reader must be cautious: Jeffers should never be identified with his characters; their attitudes and statements are rarely or never his. He has no heroes or heroines, only maimed, floundering "idols." At some points Tamar, Orestes, and Fayne Frazer might be exceptions.

With regard to the short poems several additional precautions should be noted. Jeffers has many voices, the most prominent of which is, by far, that of prophet, a voice which may have been familiar to him out of the Old Testament literature of his childhood. The prophet primarily proclaims the truth, no matter how bitter the consequences. The prophet is a man obsessed and desperate to communicate. He has a vision of holiness which he sees desecrated usually by a middle- or upper-class "establishment" who live by idolatry, injustice, and dishonesty. The prophet deals in exaggeration, overstatement, hyperbole. As Flannery O'Connor notes: For those who are almost blind, the prophet must write in huge caricatures; for those who are marginally deaf, he must shout. A prophet by definition must shock to communicate. But just as Isaiah did not rant and excoriate all of the time but also cajoled, admonished, comforted, and extolled, so Jeffers has other intonations and messages. At times he is pure mystic, praying to his God in the solitude of his tower as in "**Night.**" At other times he is a teacher, reasoning and unfolding, suggesting how to live, as in "**Signpost,**" "**The Answer,**" or "**Return.**" He can be a discerning philosopher as in "**Theory of Truth.**" He can even be autobiographic as in "**To His Father**" or "**The Bed by the Window.**" He could assume a sort of priesthood over the rituals of nature and celebrate their holiness and rhythms as in "**Salmon-Fishing**" and "**To the House.**" He could turn himself inward to purify his art and sharpen his focus, always questioning the validity of his message and examining his poetic talents from the perspective of eternity as in **"Self-Criticism in February"** or **"Soliloquy."** Often his tones take on the gravity of the ecologist, lamenting the imbalance and guilts perpetrated by his own nation, or the apocalyptist, judging cities the ultimate idolatry and forecasting global purgation.

By this it should be clear that Jeffers should be approached with some patience and informed understanding. He cannot be summed up in one poem nor is he heard well until he has been listened to in several voices. He has often been dismissed by critics and the general reader as a misanthropist, pessimist, or nihilist. Isaiah might fall under the same charges. As one rightly balances the vitriolic rhetoric of the Old Testament prophet's first chapters with his Book of Comfort (Isaiah, chapters 40ff.) or his suffering servant songs, so one needs to balance Jeffers's heavier poems (**"Summer Holiday,"** **"November Surf,"** **"What Are Cities For?",** **"Original Sin,"** for example) with the lighter, more positive statements: **"The Excesses of God"** or the final lines of **"The Beginning and the End."**

A final word on Jeffers's role as western writer. When one reviews the spectrum of themes from the literature of the West, one sees that Jeffers came to grips with all of them. he dealt with agrarian and pastoral types, the epic sweep of migrations, hero archetypes, violence, search for Eden, the disaster of the American Dream, Indian extermination, land and landscape, the mysticism of wilderness, immersion in nature, the folly of progress, the moral dilemmas of ownership, land-development, law, power, and greed. Grandson of an early pioneer of Ohio, he was inextricably involved in the nation's historical progress and in judgment upon it.

There is in his poetry a deep-seated ambivalence, arising from the clash between mystic and prophet. On the one hand he espouses an Eastern, Buddhist type of passivity and inner peace, assuming that nothing can be done. War, betrayal, moral and political corruption are variations of a natural process of decay that inevitably follows the cresting of nation's vitality and idealism. He can pronounce this process "not blameworthy" as in **"Shine, Perishing Republic."** On the other hand he can, and more often does, deal with it with a heavy prophetic hand. Though he rejected the savior syndrome, heacted in many ways the redeemer whom he pictured in the short narrative by that title, "here on the mountain making / Antitoxin for all the happy towns and farms, the lovely blameless children, the terrible / Arrogant cities." He tried to base his peace in the philosophy of inhumanism. At times he seemed to reject not only American life but the life of the race as well. Yet he is ever conscious of his roots, ever ready to pay his "birth-dues," to discover new meanings for his people. The westering experience was for him the exemplar of all journeys. Western motifs gave him vehicles for a larger philosophizing. The continent's end provided a yardstick to measure the divine cosmos. The western shore was full of life, yet inhospitable, ancient and yet young, violent yet serene, a platform above the Pacific set for tragedy.

Tim Hunt (essay date 1988)

SOURCE: An introduction, in *The Collected Poetry of Robinson Jeffers,* Vol. 1, Stanford University Press, 1988, pp. xvii-xxviii.

[*In the essay below, Hunt provides a biographical and critical overview of the Jeffers's life and work, focusing in particular on the poet's rejection of modernism.*]

By 1914 modernism was already transforming American poetry. Ezra Pound and Imagism were unavoidable presences; [T. S. Eliot's] "Prufrock," as yet unpublished, was four years old; and Wallace Stevens was about to write "Peter Quince" and "Sunday Morning." In 1914, though, Robinson Jeffers was still poetically adrift. Two years younger than Pound, a year older than Eliot, he was still imitating his Romantic and Victorian predecessors. His mature idiom was a full six years in the future, and **"Tamar,"** which would make his reputation, would not be completed until 1923. Even so, by 1914 Jeffers had (by his own report) already made his "final decision not to become a 'modern'" ["Introduction," **Roan Stallion, Tamar and Other Poems**]

Even if the modernist work Jeffers would have been reading in *Poetry* and other magazines was not yet *The Waste Land* or *The Cantos,* it already offered the one decisive alternative to nineteenth-century attitudes and techniques, and Jeffers' rejection of it is in some ways surprising. Why should he have chosen to write long narratives when the mode seemed hopelessly old fashioned? Why, in his shorter poems, to blend painstaking naturalistic detail with direct statement and forego the sophisticated formal experiments and indirection of his most talented contemporaries? Why, most simply, should he turn his back on the dynamic world of modern British and European art toconcentrate instead on the isolated landscape of California's Big Sur coast and the simple, though intense, people of the foothill ranches that surrounded his home in Carmel? Some have wanted to assume he was a California original, a primitive, looking west from the "continent's end" without realizing, or caring, what was behind him in New York or London or Paris. But Jeffers was not a primitive. Rather, the Calvinist faith of his minister father and his own immersion in the world of modern science helped direct his sophistication in a radically different direction from his modernist contemporaries.

Jeffers' early years were dominated by his father, a professor of Old Testament literature and biblical history at Western Theological Seminary, a Presbyterian school on the outskirts of Pittsburgh. Dr. William Hamilton Jeffers was a 46-year-old widower when he married Annie Robinson Tuttle, a church organist 22 years his junior. John Robinson Jeffers was born a year and a half later on January 10, 1887. Jeffers' only sibling, Hamilton, a prominent research astronomer, was born in 1894. Jeffers' father was a reserved man impatient of childish play. He introduced his first son to Latin, Greek, and the tenets of Presbyterianism early on, and Jeffers' first ten years were a succession of houses and schools as the elder Jeffers looked for the right combination of seclusion for himself and intellectual rigor for his son. In 1898 Jeffers entered the first of five Swiss boarding schools, and four years later, when he entered what is now the University of Pittsburgh, Jeffers already had a mastery of French, German, Greek, and Latin to go with his newest enthusiasm—Dante Gabriel Rossetti and poetry. After his first year of college, the family moved to Los Angeles for Dr. Jeffers' health. Jeffers enrolled at Occidental College, where he graduated two years later with coursework in astronomy and geology to supplement biblical literature and Greek. Then came a year and a half of graduate study, first at the University of Southern California and then the University of Zurich. Jeffers' courses included Old English, Dante, Goethe, Spanish Romantic poetry, and late nineteenth-century French literature.

When Jeffers returned from Zurich in September 1906, he was not yet twenty and already had what even Pound would have seen as a promising start for a modernist-to-be. Had Jeffers encountered a Santayana at this point, as did Stevens and Eliot at Harvard, or even an energetic and opinionated peer such as Pound, as did H.D. and Williams at Pennsylvania, his work might well have developed differently, but Jeffers spent the next six months translating German medical papers and then in 1907 enrolled in the USC medical school, where he excelled in physiology and earned an assistantship in his second and third years. He left in 1910 without completing his training and entered the University of Washington to study forestry. A year later he returned to Los Angeles, again, without completing his studies.

How seriously Jeffers considered either profession is not clear. Certainly he was already developing his interest in poetry. By 1911 he had already written a number of the imitative, dandyish poems of *Flagons and Apples,* which he issued privately in 1912 after receiving a small inheritance. Whatever his sense of vocation, though, medicine and forestry would have been a sharp contrast to his literary studies. Both emphasized direct and close observation of the actual world and involved alternative views of time and tradition. Moreover Jeffers' medical studies would have introduced him to modern biology in a more than casual manner, while his study of forestry would have strengthened his interest in a specifically Western landscape and offered a view of nature unmediated by poetic conventions.

Jeffers' early and mid-twenties were also years of personal turmoil. However much he may have resented the strict round of study imposed by his father, Jeffers was, through his boarding school years, a properly shy and studious minister's son who presumably acted from his sense of doctrine and belief, rather than mere obedience. But by the time Jeffers entered medical school at twenty his allegiance had begun to shift to the religion of art and the wine, women, and song appropriate to a turn of the century poet-to-be. This drift might have simply replaced his earlier views (it did for many of his generation) had he not become increasingly involved with a married woman, a situation which neither his father's values nor the priorities of his bohemianism seemed able to resolve. Jeffers met Una Call Kuster when both were literature students at USC.

She was three years older, and their relationship apparently started innocently and probably continued that way for a time. By 1910 the matter was a serious concern to both and likely a factor in Jeffers' decision to leave for Washington to study forestry. However, when he returned to Los Angeles at the end of that year, the affair began again and became known to Una's husband, a young Los Angeles attorney. Scandal and divorce followed.

On August 2, 1913, Robinson Jeffers and Una Call Kuster were married. Witty, vibrant, and ambitious, Una Jeffers became a prime force in her husband's life. She had faith in his talent as a writer and the will to discipline him to that faith. The crisis of courtship might have confirmed Jeffers' bohemianism. Instead it was the beginning of a renewed moral seriousness. This is not to suggest his affair left him guilty for his actions nor that he came to accept society's norms or his father's. Rather, the crisis seems to have combined with the deaths of his father and infant daughter and the discovery of the West as a subject for his writing to commit him to struggle with the question of whether actions have moral consequences in a world where the methods and discoveries of science had already undercut the pieties of the past.

It may seem odd to suggest Jeffers needed to discover the West when he had already spent a number of years in Los Angeles and Seattle. But Los Angeles took its cue from other centers of fashion. It was, that is, provincial. Los Angeles tyros read *The Smart Set* right along with their Chicago and New York counterparts, and their fantasies were of Europe. Jeffers, judging from his letters, even toyed with becoming a sort of Los Angeles F. Scott Fitzgerald. Certainly at the time of his marriage the West meant relatively little to him in terms of his writing. He and Una planned to settle in Europe and presumably would have done so had she not become pregnant. Their daughter, born in May 1914, survived only a day, and by the time the couple was ready to consider the move again, the war in Europe persuaded them to look closer to home.

In September of 1914, they traveled north to Carmel, probably because it was something of an artists' colony, a rustic and inexpensive spot of culture. The decisive factor that led them to settle there, though, and the decisive factor for Jeffers' work, was the landscape itself and the people of the isolated ranches and farms about it. These demanded to be viewed on their own terms, not through any European lens or lens of literary convention. As Jeffers wrote in the "Foreword" to *The Selected Poetry of Robinson Jeffers,* "for the first time in my life I could see people living— amid magnificent unspoiled scenery—essentially as they did in the Idyls or the Sagas, or in Homer's Ithaca. Here was life purged of its ephemeral accretions. . . . Here was contemporary life that was also permanent life; and not shut from the modern world but conscious of it and related to it." The intensity of this new landscape coming on top of his scientific training, courtship and marriage, the death of a child, and the first signs of Europe's political and cultural collapse led Jeffers, apparently within months, to his aesthetic declaration of independence. Whatever he would be as a poet, he would not be "a 'modern.'"

For Jeffers (reacting against the modernist work found in the little magazines of the time) the moderns were writing a poetry of form, not content, a poetry that indulged technique for its own sake. And if this work celebrated the imagination's power to remake the materials of the tradition, to him it did so, finally, be celebrating the aesthetic object's superiority over the ordinary and actual. His training in science, however, meant he could only be satisfied with an art that used the imagination to attend to the actual, not escape it. To Jeffers, that is, the work of the early Pound and others seemed a poetry of fashion, and the world he had discovered in Carmel was anything but fashionable. It was, though, in Jeffers' view, fundamental, authentic, and relevant to the larger world. It offered the freedom to be regional without being provincial, which Los Angeles did not, and just as importantly, Carmel suited the energetic severity of his temperament at a time when his training in the sciences had freed him to respond to it. Just as importantly, this new, yet archaic, world seemed to require a poetry of moral seriousness at a time when his own personal experience and the reality of world conflict seemed to make such seriousness imperative. . . .

The first phase of Jeffers' independence appeared in *Californians,* published by Macmillan in 1916. Like his later volumes, *Californians* featured several narratives of the rural West. Narrative gave Jeffers scope to portray this new landscape and even more importantly allowed him to explore the connection between the land itself and the people who inhabited it (or as he would later think of the matter, the people who expressed it). But these early narratives, though a decisive turn from his contemporaries and his own earlier work, are largely unsuccessful. Their traditional meters, rhyme, and diction fail to match the expansiveness of the material, and they read as if Jeffers, freed from the need to be technically fashionable, simply assumed he could borrow his form from tradition and allow the subject to make its own way. More importantly, the narratives of *Californians,* and those recently recovered from the few years following it, show Jeffers vacillating between a sentimental and a superficially nihilistic treatment of nature. In some of the poems nature offers a simplistic, if reassuring, moral norm to the human world. In others the world of nature moves with one logic while a seemingly disconnected human world moves with quite another; characters violate norms only to find that nature has no interest in their affairs and that society is unlikely to discover what they have done. In these poems Jeffers' sense of science freed him to look intensely and without preconception, but it also effectively divorced the human world from the natural. If his mood demanded a poetry of moral seriousness, the lesson of modern science seemed to deny that possibility. The perspective of science undercut any sense of a moral outcome to what he observed, even as it gave him access to his material and freed him from his contemporaries.

In the years immediately following *Californians,* Jeffers struggled with his work and the problem of the war. He temporarily abandoned narrative, trying his hand at an epic drama modeled on Hardy's *The Dynasts,* and then turning to sonnets. Both directions provided elegant, but stiff and mannered, comments on the moral and political crisis of Europe. Meanwhile Jeffers worried whether or not to enlist. Twin sons born in 1916, a wife, and a less than ample income argued no, but his application to serve was pending when the war ended. The war years, though, did confirm his desire to stay in Carmel. Shortly after the Armistice, he and Una purchased a headland on the south edge of Carmel and hired a local mason to build a low stone cottage from the granite about the site. Working with the masons, Jeffers discovered his other life's work—building with stone. After the house was completed, he began a six-year project, the construction of a two-and-a-half story stone tower, and he fell into the routine of his mature years—writing in the morning, stone work or planting and caring for his forest of trees in the afternoon.

Whether it was the war, the increased pattern and discipline of his life, or simply the trial and error of poem after poem, Jeffers' work began to coalesce shortly after the move into Tor House when he returned to writing narrative and working with local material. The first narratives after the war were written as ballads, the one after that in long-line couplets. None are fully successful, but they show Jeffers worrying again the problem of violence and nature, as he had in *Californians,* and pressing toward a resolution that came first in several short poems sometime in the early 1920's. The key was a minor, but telling, shift in emphasis in his sense of nature. In lyrics such as **"Natural Music"** he began to focus on nature itself and view it as a living organism, with man simply one of its elements, one of its expressions.

> Whatever future readers and historians may decide, it is clear that Jeffers made good his vow not to "be a 'modern,'" but it should also be clear that Jeffers, in his own quite different way, developed a distinctly modern poetry.
>
> —*Tim Hunt*

This shift in emphasis, from the life of individuals to the life of nature, enabled Jeffers to synthesize his sense of science with his Calvinist heritage, even as he discarded the latter's specific forms and justifications. Both Calvinism and science taught that man was not the measure of the world, and both, in different ways, taught that the world itself might be inherently beautiful and worthy of worship. Once Jeffers came to see the observation of nature and the observation of human actions, even perverse and violent ones, as inherently the same act of witness and to see the expression of them as a further witness to the inscrutable dynamism of nature, he began to overcome the dichotomy that had marred much of his earlier work. Poetry could not resolve, nor need it, the conflicts of nature or human experience. Poetry's task was to confront, reveal, and praise the grandeur of a universe in flux.

Jeffers apparently thought of this new mode at first primarily as one that allowed him to write lyrics that praised the beauty of nature in a new, more direct way. The lyrics that followed **"Natural Music"** show him quickly mastering the long, unrhymed accentual line that would be the basis of the rest of his writing. But sometime in 1922, perhaps quite early 1923, he seems to have realized his new sense of nature could be the basis of narrative as well. His reading of Freud and Jung likely played a role in this, along with his reading of the Cambridge anthropologists and their studies of ancient myth and ritual. Whatever the impetus, the return to narrative fulfilled the promise of his first sense of his Carmel material and resulted in the poem that would gain him recognition as a major poet.

Like his earlier narratives (and later ones) **"Tamar"** portrays a perverse, violent human world: Tamar's incest with her brother and her father, her father's earlier incest with his sister, the conflagration Tamar brings about to destroy herself, her brother, her father, and her lover. But in **"Tamar,"** unlike the earlier narratives, Jeffers came to view nature itself as fundamentally in conflict—a cycle of destruction and renewal—and this recognition allowed him, finally, to write poems that combined his sense of modern science and high moral seriousness, even though the lessons of **"Tamar"** were neither specifically scientific nor moral in the usual sense of those words. In Jeffers' scheme, human conflict is an analogue of the larger rhythms of conflict in the natural world. The human world, though, is often blind to its own status and thus dooms itself to play out the cycles in an unnecessarily perverse, violent, and empty manner. In the narratives, Jeffers' characters are largely unable to recognize or accept themselves as elements of nature, and this dooms them to suffer nature's power without experiencing the compensatory vision of its beauty (even if that beauty is itself of the painful motion of stars consuming in flame, of rock eroding, of hawk dropping to feed). The characters can become more or less aware of their cycle and can even, as Tamar does, hurry on destruction, but finally the real salvation in these poems is the one available to reader and poet and comes from recognizing our place in nature, which frees us to witness the transcendent beauty of destruction and renewal and to accept its liberating beauty, even if the cycle of renewal takes place on a scale that never renews (only destroys) the individual ego.

Initially, Jeffers seems not to have known what to do with **"Tamar."** He first considered grouping it with a series of poems written in response to the First World War, as if that violent episode would best explain the violence of this new work. He then, apparently, came to see this new direction in his narrative work as of a piece with his more recent lyrics, restructured the collection, and after some months of hesitation chose to issue the volume privately, even though the printer he'd hired was so impressed with the collection that he offered to act as publisher. When *Tamar and Other Poems* did finally appear in April 1924, it made no more impression initially than *Californians*. After nearly a year, though, chance brought it to the attention of several major reviewers, and Jeffers suddenly found himself compared to the Greek tragedians, Shakespeare,

Whitman, and a few others for good measure. Whatever the reviews left undone, *Tamar*'s scandalous plot finished, and when Boni & Liveright reissued it in November 1925 in an expanded edition as *Roan Stallion, Tamar and Other Poems,* Jeffers became a popular, as well as critical, success. Ten major trade collections followed between 1927 and 1954, first with Liveright and then with Random House.

In the years following *Tamar,* Jeffers was intensely productive. He explored the implications of his breakthrough in such pieces as **"The Tower Beyond Tragedy,"** a recasting of Aeschylus's *Oresteia,* and **"Roan Stallion,"** another narrative of the California coast. Jeffers' most ambitious project, though, was *The Women at Point Sur.* He apparently began working on early versions of it almost immediately after **"Tamar"** and struggled with what he hoped would be "the Faust of this generation" through early 1927. In *Point Sur* he explored a topic that would recur in a number of later poems, that of the savior who mistakenly turns from his vision of nature's power and beauty to seek control of disciples.

Jeffers' longest, and in many ways most complicated, poem, *The Women at Point Sur* was less favorably received than *Roan Stallion, Tamar and Other Poems*. But reviewers took his status as a major figure for granted, and his reputation remained strong through the rest of the 1920's and the early 1930's, as he produced *Cawdor and Other Poems* (1928), *Dear Judas and Other Poems* (1929), *Thurso's Landing and Other Poems* (1931), and *Give Your Heart to the Hawks and Other Poems* (1933). In these volumes Jeffers turned more to his characters' human dilemmas, the problems of guilt, of pain, of endurance. As a result, the narratives of this period tend to be more realistic, though less mythic, and to explore the characters' psychologies in more detail. These volumes, which refined and extended the directions implicit in his early work, have been among Jeffers' most popular.

After *Give Your Heart to the Hawks,* the narratives at least came more slowly. *Solstice and Other Poems* (1935), *Such Counsels You Gave to Me and Other Poems* (1937), and *Be Angry at the Sun* (1941), were generally less well received than the earlier volumes, though they contained some of Jeffers' finer short poems. Part of the problem may have been a kind of fatigue: Jeffers' work had consistently derived from his thematic perspective and formal principles of the early 1920's. Part of it may have been the Second World War. Jeffers' saw it coming earlier than most, and if the First World War had helped precipitate his mature work, this impending conflict threatened his creative equilibrium. Even though his vision of nature argued that war was a fact of nature, a part of the order of things, and so essentially beautiful and inevitable, the suffering it would bring and its futility challenged the answers of the early 1920's. As a result his work increasingly took the form of shorter meditations on contemporary politics or addressed explicitly the tenets of what he came to call in 1948 "Inhumanism," "a philosophical attitude" that called for "a shifting of emphasis and significance from man to not-man; the rejection of human solipsism and recognition of the transhuman magnificence." ["Prefact," *The Double Axe and Other Poems*].

A confirmed isolationist, Jefferson pleased few contemporary readers with his poems of this period, even though they have proved surprisingly prophetic. The war itself led to two of his most distinctive narratives, **"The Love and the Hate"** and **"The Inhumanist."** The first, written at the end of the war, is perhaps Jeffers' most controversial narrative, tracing the revenge of a soldier who physically returns from the dead to punish those whose blindness and hypocrisy have sent him to die. The second, perhaps Jeffers' most philosophical and allegorical narrative, examines the attempts of an isolated old man to maintain his integrity and balance despite the threats of society and its violence. Together **"The Love and the Hate"** and **"The Inhumanist"** made up the title sequence of *The Double Axe and Other Poems* (1948), a volume whose references to contemporary political figures, especially in its short poems, so upset his editors at Random House that they insisted on including an editorial disclaimer. Whether the editors properly understood the poems or the politics, the fact that the volume was published at all, even under such circumstances, suggests Jeffers was still regarded as a major figure in the late 1940's, though an increasingly isolated and troubling one. His other major project of the 1940's was his adaptation of Euripides' *Medea,* He had prepared the text in 1945 at the request of the tragic actress Dame Judith Anderson. The play was produced in late 1947 and was, like *Roan Stallion,* a major critical and commercial success.

Jeffers continued to write after *The Double Axe,* but intermittently. Traveling in Ireland in 1948, he nearly died from pleurisy. Shortly after that Una Jeffers began her own battle; she died of cancer in 1950. Jeffers' last narrative, the brief and poignant **"Hungerfield,"** shows how devastating this loss was. It was collected, along with several short poems and an adaptation of Euripides' *Hippolytus,* in *Hungerfield and Other Poems* (1954), the last volume Jeffers published. Although *Hungerfield* was received more positively than *The Double Axe,* it was less popular than most of his earlier volumes—perhaps because he had, by and large, ceased to be a topic of discussion. The New Criticism of the 1950's had little patience for either narrative or direct statement, and critics such as Yvor Winters and R. P. Blackmur condemned both Jeffers' ideas and what they took to be his slack line and inflated rhetoric. The work of Jeffers' final years was compiled by Melba Berry Bennet, his biographer, and appeared as *The Beginning and the End* in 1963, the year after his death on January 20, 1962. In the 25 years since, Jeffers has attracted a steadily growing readership and renewed critical and scholarly interest.

Whatever future readers and historians may decide, it is clear that Jeffers made good his vow not to "be a 'modern,'" but it should also be clear that Jeffers, in his own quite different way, developed a distinctly modern poetry. Chance and decision led him to an alternative model to Pound's, one that owed more to Milton, Wordsworth, Darwin, and modern astronomy than to Coleridge, Mallarmé,

Pater, and Hulme. Where the modernist aesthetic stressed the power of the imagination to transform perception, Jeffers' aesthetic stressed the paradoxical energy of consciousness and the way it allowed us to perceive our place in nature and yet, thereby, alienated us from it in self-consciousness. Where modernism emphasized the word as a thing to be valued for its own inherent properties, Jeffers treated it for its referential power. And where modernism viewed the poem as an aesthetic object, Jeffers viewed it as utterance, a kind of prophetic speech.

All of these matters reflect Jeffers' sense that poetry points to reality rather than transforming or replacing it and that poetry's task is to demonstrate the permanent and universal. At times these views give his work a didactic quality, but he saw no reason poems should not include direct statement. And if these attitudes placed him distinctly at odds with his modernist contemporaries and made his work, finally, technically more conservative than theirs, it may be that his sense of the interplay of culture and nature was in many ways more radical and forward looking. If Pound and others sought to make their poems permanent, Jeffers sought to make his reveal the permanences beyond the poem:

> Permanent things are what is needful in a poem,
>   things temporally
> Of great dimension, things continually renewed or
>   always present.
>
> Grass that is made each year equals the mountains
>   in her past and future;
> Fashionable and momentary things we need not see
>   nor speak of.
>
> Man gleaning food between the solemn presence of
>   land and ocean,
> On shores where better men have shipwrecked,
>   under fog and among flowers,
>
> Equals the mountains in his past and future; that
>   glow from the earth was only
> A trick of nature's, one must forgive nature a
>   thousand graceful subtleties.
>
>   **("Point Joe")**

Helen Vendler   (review date 1988)

SOURCE: "Huge Pits of Darkness, High Peaks of Light," in *New Yorker,* Vol. LXIV, No. 45, December 26, 1988, pp. 91-5.

[*In the following review of* Rock and Hawk, *Vendler provides an overview of Jeffers's career, concluding Jeffers "will remain a notable but minor poet."*]

The poet Robinson Jeffers (1887-1962) is periodically resurrected. Stanford University Press is bringing out his complete poems in four sumptuous volumes; and from the ashes of *The Selected Poetry* (1938), compiled by Jeffers himself, and of a second selection, compiled in 1965 by anonymous editors at Random House, there now arises a third, *Rock and Hawk* (Random House), selected by the Californian poet Robert Hass. Jeffers' own *Selected* ran to six hundred and twenty-two pages, the second to a hundred and eleven, and the new one—handsomely produced—is two hundred and ninety pages long and contains over a hundred short poems. Hass has dropped Jeffers' swollen narrative poems (ranging from fifty to ninety pages apiece), which have now sunk in critical estimation, though in the thirties they made Jeffers' name and brought him an adulation normally reserved for religious cult figures. Even reduced to his shorter works, Jeffers remains, it seems to me, a finally unsatisfying poet—coarse, limited, and defective in self-knowledge. Some modulation of intelligence or sensibility is missing from his writing. But because Jeffers was a man of very unusual linguistic equipment and literary training, because he felt so deeply compelled to poetry that he sequestered himself in Carmel and wrote obsessively, and because he had an extraordinary fame in both poetry and drama, his work asks for a scrutiny no one would bother to give to amateur writing. He has had warm defenders of his craggy philosophy—Czeslaw Milosz most recently—and impatient detractors, like Yvor Winters and Kenneth Rexroth (the California competition). It is not his opinions I would quarrel with. His descriptions of nature are made with an intent eye; his sensibility declares itself with apparent sincerity; his lexical range is enviable. And yet I resist grouping him not only with his greater contemporaries—Eliot and Frost—but even with such lesser contemporaries as Moore and Williams.

Robert Hass, in an earnest, intelligent, and winning essay prefacing this selection, gives an honest account of various unpleasant qualities he finds in Jeffers' work. Among the adjectives he resorts to are "pretentious," "repetitious," "bombastic," "humorless," "fuzzy," "obsessed," and "hysterical." Yet Hass's essay is fundamentally a defense of Jeffers, founded on his admiration for Jeffers' "truly obsessed and original imagination." Hass sets this internal power against what actually appeared from Jeffers' pen: "The most dangerous thing that can be said of him, I think, is that he was verbally careless." The risky division that Hass draws between imagination and writing may be dear to the heart of every poet; it is certainly, in some cases, dear to me. The extent to which any imaginative ardor outstrips its verbal after-image is commemorated in Shelley's vivid Biblical image: "The mind in creation is as a fading coal. . . . When composition begins, inspiration is already on the decline." Beloved poets are valued for their imagination even in their less accomplished moments. But the distinction between fire and fading is rarely invoked for the whole of a poet's work. Hass seems to want us to take Jeffers' entire œuvre as the work of a vivid imagination that never quite found its exact verbal body. Hass perhaps extrapolates backward to the glowing coal in Jeffers, while I see the fading embers, the extant works. It is not humorlessness or bombast I mind (after all, Coleridge accused Wordsworth of just these faults), nor is it hysteria and obsession (which are everywhere in, say, Eliot and Plath). Even pretentiousness and fuzziness might pass (they are not absent from Whitman).

In an attempt to explain objections to Jeffers, Hass suggests that modern critics, uncomfortable with poetic statement, were seeking, and not finding in Jeffers, the modernist hermetic symbol (Eliot's rose garden, Stevens' pigeons sinking downward to darkness). Yet that account is unsatisfactory: critics showed themselves willing to praise Frost's plain speaking and Eliot's long discursive passages in the "Quartets." What, then, is it that fails to compel acquiescence to Jeffers' verse? My short answer would be "His moral timidity." Since I mean that phrase to apply to the morality of art, and not only to the morality of practical life, it may need some explanation.

Jeffers, though he seems not to have realized it, had a painful childhood. His father was a clergyman whose first wife died; he married again, and he was forty-eight when "Robin" was born. Biographers agree that Jeffers believed he loved his parents, and equally agree that behind the violent and incestuous family dramas that appear in his plays and poems there may have been some troubled Oedipal feelings toward his mother, who was in her twenties when she bore him. They also surmise that Jeffers as a child confused his father (a professor of Old Testament at the Western Theological Seminary of Pittsburgh) with God, and that his subsequent fierce atheism and his philosophy of scientific "Inhumanism" were the other side of the Presbyterian beliefs of his childhood. After severe paternal instruction in Latin and Greek and after European travel with his parents, the young Jeffers was apparently too unusual to fit in with other Pittsburgh schoolchildren, and he had a lonely youth. Between the ages of twelve and fifteen, he attended European boarding schools while his parents roamed about Europe and the Near East. Eventually, the family moved to Pasadena, and at eighteen Jeffers graduated from Occidental College. He went on to U.S.C., and there met a young married woman, Una Call Kuster, whom he married eight years later, after she was divorced. Jeffers' graduate work was in science, and was perhaps undertaken in an attempt to find a comprehensive world view different from that of his father. In 1912, Jeffers published his first book of poems, at his own expense; in 1913, he married Una; in 1914, they went by stagecoach to Carmel, built a house, and settled in for life. Their first child, a daughter, died; they then had twin sons. During the ten years after the publication of his fourth book, *Roan Stallion* (1925), Jeffers became an internationally famous man: a consciously Byronic studio portrait by Edward Weston ornaments the 1938 *Selected Poetry,* and Hass tells us that in the thirties Jeffers appeared on the cover of *Time* and in the pages of *Vogue.* His reputation, though it was somewhat resuscitated by Judith Anderson's 1947 appearance in his *Medea,* has since declined; his achievements (praised by Edwin Arlington Robinson and Mark Van Doren in the early years but disputed even then by Yvor Winters and later by R. P. Blackmur) continue to perplex evaluation.

Once Jeffers had found his free-verse style and his topics—the sublimity of nature, sexual violence, and the pettiness or degeneracy of mankind—nothing further seems to have happened fundamentally to his mind or his writing. This is agreed on by all. Hass sees some superficial mellowing in the later work. "The mind has relaxed somewhat," he says of the poetry of the last years, but he adds that Jeffers "still hammers away at his religious convictions." Not much, in short, has changed at the center. This permanent arrest at the point of youthful self-discovery is the central fact to be confronted by any commentator on Jeffers.

It is not that Jeffers did not work on his art. He learned to purge out a good deal of his earlier grotesquerie, lines of the sort we find in, say, **"Tamar,"** where Tamar asks the dead:

> What shall I ask more? How it feels
>   when the last liquid morsel
> Slides from the bone? Or whether you see
>   the worm that burrows up through the
>   eye-socket, or thrill
> To the maggot's music in the tube of a
>   dead ear? You stinking dead.

More troubling than the surplus of the grotesque is Jeffers' never-purged sadism. Tamar's brother, sexually jealous, takes up a whip to flog her:

> Sickened to see the beautiful bare white
> Blemishless body writhe under [the whip]
>   before it fell . . .
>   the coppery pad of her hair
> Crushed on the shoulder-blades, while that
>   red snake-trail
> Swelled visibly from the waist and flank
>   down the left thigh. . . .
>   From her bitten lip
> A trickle of blood ran down to the pillow.

Passages like these suggest that a braver artist than Jeffers would have dared to bring his sadistic impulses under some reflective scrutiny. Jeffers, instead, simply continued to act them out in verse, and, worse, to find in them a justified contempt for the human. His sadism is accompanied by a fascination with the socially deviant. Even when he does attempt some analysis of this obsession (he speculates, for instance, that some psychological deformity prompts figures such as Jesus and the Buddha to form religions), the tone of hectic interest and covert excitement persists, unexamined. Jeffers' primary defense against his fantasies of sexual deviation, torture, dissolution, and sadism was an affectation of "coldness": while the narratives and plays run riot with incest, necrophilia, women sexually interested in stallions, and so on, the haughty poet watches aloofly. This Sadean reaction to sexual obsession and physical torture becomes a mechanical one in Jeffers—one by which he seems helplessly manipulated.

It is scarcely possible to prescribe a dose of intelligence to a poet so intelligent, or a dose of feeling to one so hopelessly trapped in a groove of feeling, or a deflection of obsession to one so obsessed. On the other hand, unanalyzed obsession is the opposite of moral intelligence, of aesthetic inquiry, and of that modulation of poetic rhythm and tone which makes for melody in verse as in music. Jeffers' anvil chorus is finally boring.

The argument against an *opera omnia* of dominant brasses and percussion is not—though it may appear so—solely a stylistic argument. A ceaselessly curious investigation of a chosen medium is the quality that above all distinguishes artists from the mass of other people (preachers, teachers, journalists) who spend time communicating thoughts, messages, and personal responses in prose and verse. It is true that Jeffers spent some years exploring language, and that he developed an early form of personal idiom. While in **Flagons and Apples** (1912) and **Californians** (1916) he stumbles along in apprenticeship to Swinburne and Yeats, and especially to Robinson (the chief begetter of Jeffers' long narratives), by the time of **Tamar and Other Poems** (1924) Jeffers' long-breathed style has become recognizably his own. Hass's selection begins with poems from this book, which appeared when Jeffers was thirty-seven:

> The clapping blackness of the wings of
>   pointed cormorants, the great indolent
>   planes
> Of autumn pelicans nine or a dozen strung
>   shorelong,
> But chiefly the gulls, the cloud-calligraphers of
>   windy spirals before a
>   storm,
> Cruise north and south over the sea-rocks
>   and over
> That bluish enormous opal.

This is Jeffers at his spacious and lofty best. In his seventies, he is writing lines that sound very much the same:

>   The cormorants
> Slip their long black bodies under the
>   water and hunt like wolves
> Through the green half-light. Screaming,
>   the gulls watch,
> Wild with envy and malice, cursing and
>   snatching.

In short, from thirty-five to seventy-five Jeffers did not change his writing in any artistically important way. By the time he was thirty-five, both his parents had died, and he had acquired his lifelong wife, his lifelong house, and his two children. Perhaps he was through with seeking, and was preoccupied with recording.

In what Hass calls an "explosion of work," Jeffers wrote between 1920 and 1938 "fifteen narrative poems ranging in length from ten to two hundred pages, four verse dramas, and almost two hundred lyric poems." A writer he certainly was: a modest private income and timely gifts from rich friends enabled him to live without a job, and he wrote every day. After shearing the "rhyme-tassels" (as he called them) from his verse, he devised his all-purpose unrhymed long line—a unit indebted, according to one of Jeffers' private notes, to Greek quantitative metres and to tidal rhythms. In this flexible line, which may also owe something to Whitman, Jeffers could say almost anything at any length, and did. The absence of a stanzaic exoskeleton sets problems for free-verse lyrics, since all poetic structure—tonal, logical, visual—must then come from an inner armature. Jeffers' turgid narratives (and Hass makes no brief for them) were carried by their violent plots, but plots of this sort could not govern his lyrics. In 1932, Jeffers sent some remarks on poetry versus prose to a student at Berkeley—remarks that seem to convey absolutely no idea of poetry as a form with a structure of its own, different from structures appropriate to narration or exposition. For Jeffers, poetry was simply more primitive, concrete, musical, emotional, imaginative, sensual, unspecialized, passionate, and celebratory than prose. It was, in fact, prose made rhythmic, intense, and exalted:

> Poetic content (the feeling, thought, and expression of poetry) may be found in prose also and is only distinguished from that of prose by having more of certain qualities and less of certain others. The thought is more primitive and less specialized. Language is more figurative, giving concrete images rather than abstract ideas and cares more for its own music. Poetry appeals rather to the emotions than to the intelligence and especially to the aesthetic emotion. It appeals more eagerly than prose does to the imagination and to the bodily senses. It deals with the more permanent aspects of man and nature.

When Jeffers pressed himself to go beyond such a feeble theory of poetic content, his remarks tended to be about what the poetic line should exhibit—rhythm and "singing emphasis," alliteration and assonance. It seems odd, given his long acquaintance with Greek and Latin poetry, that his comments never turned naturally to lyric genres, to larger compositional masses, to the structural supports of lyric, or to the modulation over time which is natural to a temporal art—not to speak of the qualities of concision, surprise, volatility, and intimacy so native to the lyric.

We can attribute Jeffers' indifference to such matters largely to the fact that he was not actually writing lyric. He was writing oratory—a rhythmical, emotional, sensual, and imaginative public prose he had absorbed from the Greek political tradition. And his oratorical stridency seems to me that of a timid man having to prove himself durable and masculine. Lyric for him is an oratorical sermon designed to persuade others—not a probe designed to investigate himself and his medium. A friend who was present at the reading Jeffers gave at Harvard in 1941 recalls that at the reception Jeffers turned to the wall, face averted from the crowd. The poet's attitude was at that time interpreted as hauteur; it could equally well be interpreted as the panicky ill-ease of a friendless, freakish boy (even though Jeffers was then over fifty).

Hass has omitted from his collection some poems once notorious—among them certain war poems of the forties, like "**The Bloody Sire**" and "**Cassandra**." In "**The Bloody Sire**" Jeffers asks the question that exposes nakedly his instinctive conjunction of beauty, sex, religion, and murder:

> Who would remember Helen's face
> Lacking the terrible halo of spears?
> Who formed Christ but Herod and Caesar,
> The cruel and bloody victories of Caesar?

> Violence, the bloody sire of all the world's
>   values.

And in "**Cassandra**" he places himself, as prophet, above both gods and men, who equally connive against "the truth" (a phrase, dear to ideologues, that comes easily to Jeffers' lips):

> Does it matter, Cassandra,
> Whether the people believe
> Your bitter fountain? Truly men hate the
>   truth; they'd liefer
> Meet a tiger on the road.
> Therefore the poets honey their truth with
>   lying. . . .
>   Poor bitch, be wise.
> No: you'll still mumble in a corner a crust
>   of truth, to men
> And gods disgusting.—You and I,
>   Cassandra.

Though the mellower Jeffers of the late sketches is an altogether more appealing fellow than this rigidly self-appointed denouncer of the degenerate mob, the essence of Jeffers' defensive and tormented personality lies more in the excessive poems (deleted, probably on grounds of taste, by Hass) than in the milder late woodnotes. Hass has also deleted the more maudlin of these, such as the posthumous speech of Jeffers' dead dog to him and his wife:

> I hope that when you are lying
>
> Under the ground like me your lives will
>   appear
> As good and joyful as mine.
> No, dears, that's too much hope: you are
>   not so well cared for
> As I have been.

By sparing us poems like this, Hass makes a better *Selected* than the 1965 one compiled by Random House. And in some late poems he shows us the Jeffers who had at the end of his life the grace to doubt the sufficiency of his aesthetic of brutality and its denigration of human life. In a glimpse of a sublimity not of nature (which he had always responded to) but of man the old Jeffers speculated:

> The hawks are more heroic but man has
>   a steeper mind,
> Huge pits of darkness, high peaks of light,
> You may calculate a comet's orbit or the
>   dive of a hawk, not a man's mind.

Perhaps he realized that all the California peaks and abysses he had spent his life describing were less "inhuman" and "objective" than he had suspected, since he transfers them here to interior steeps and pits, emblems of a perilous subjectivity like that admitted by Hopkins—"O the mind, mind has mountains; cliffs of fall / Frightful, sheer, no-man-fathomed." In his most honest piece of self-examination

Jeffers mused, late in life, on an anthology of Chinese poems—poems of a restrained aesthetic almost incomprehensible to him, since it got along without frenzied contempt, oratorical excess, lurid prophecy, or illogical lineation. His poem on the Chinese anthology is a genuine query, all defenses down. For the first time, Jeffers lifts his visor and gazes at Tu Fu and Li Po. In this most gentle of the late poems we see the Jeffers who might have been, relenting instead of relentless, curious rather than repudiatory, regretful instead of disdainful—damned, so to speak, to his own aesthetic of sublimity rather than boisterously electing it. Here is Jeffers' reluctant homage to discretion, gentleness, affection, friendship, and peace as aesthetic motives, and as a moral *summa* remote from his harsh Calvinism:

"On An Anthology of Chinese Poems"

Beautiful the hanging cliff and the wind-
    thrown cedars, but they have no weight.
Beautiful the fantastically
Small farmhouse and ribbon of rice-fields a
    mile below; and billows of mist
Blow through the gorge. These men were
    better
Artists than any of ours, and far better
    observers. They loved landscape
And put man in his place. But why
Do their rocks have no weight? They
    loved rice-wine and peace and friendship,
Above all they loved landscape and soli-
    tude,
—Like Wordsworth. But Wordsworth's
    mountains have weight and mass, dull
        though the song be.
Is it a moral difference perhaps?

Jeffers' plaintive question "But why / Do their rocks have no weight?" is the cry of the Christian against the Confucian. Pound, contemplating the same Chinese poems, decided to try a weightlessness of his own, in phrases floating unmoored from the British solidity of blank verse. Jeffers, timid and unballasted among people, felt secured and ballasted by stone, weight, long lines, mass. His bluster— what Blackmur called "the flannel-mouthed inflation in the metric of Robinson Jeffers with his rugged rock-garden violence"—needs to be read as the long-maintained armor protecting him against an investigation into his own private terrors. Jeffers condemned "introversion" as the decadent practice of decadent cultures:

> There is no health for the individual whose attention is taken up with his own mind and processes; equally there is no health for the society that is always introverted. . . . All past cultures have died of introversion.

He added, in a moment of monumental self-delusion, "I have often used incest as a symbol to express these introversions." Perhaps what this really means is that when he practiced introspection he found incest, and that the price of introspection was consequently too high. It might have been too high for any of us; but the price of finding intro-

spection too dangerous is in the layperson a self-stalled identity and in the poet a self-stalled art. Jeffers, it appears to me, will remain a notable minor poet, the first to give an adequate description in verse of the scenery of the California coast. His ambitions as a moralist and prophet were defeated by his lack of genuine moral curiosity and its counterpart, an original moral vision. If Jeffers' harsh contempt for human history had been tempered by personal insight, and framed in a flexible style, we might now read his poems as we read those of Milosz.

Robert Zaller   (essay date 1990)

SOURCE: "Spheral Eternity: Time, Form, and Meaning in Robinson Jeffers," in *Critical Essays on Robinson Jeffers,* G. K. Hall & Co., 1990, pp. 252-65.

[*In the following essay, Zaller discusses Jeffers's narratives in the context of Aristotelian tragedy.*]

Aristotle, that famous law-giver, laid it down that the action of a tragedy should occur within twenty-four hours. He was thus the first to inscribe an arrow in a circle—the accomplishment of a perfected sequence of events in the orbit of a day's passage. Robinson Jeffers has been faithful, in his fashion, to this dictum; and part of the fascination with ancient tragedy that appears both in his retelling of the Greek stories and in the California narratives that evoke them lies in the tension between human praxis and natural process that Aristotle found in tragedy and saw, with unerring insight, as its essence. To be sure, Jeffers's narratives do not keep to the single alternation of day and night prescribed by Aristotle, but his world is wider, and his notion of human fate and cosmic necessity is far less rigidly deterministic than that of the ancient poets. The essence of his art is still, however, like theirs, the inscription of human meaning within natural process.

If Jeffers owed his basic perception of the tensions between the human and the natural to the Greeks, he expressed it within a consciousness informed by Christian eschatology and the language of modern science. For the ancients, the relation of human time to that of cosmic process, however problematic, was linked by a shared nature. With the Christian appropriation of Neoplatonism, however, the temporal drama of human salvation was imposed on the natural world, subjecting it to a transcendent order that implicitly devalued and ultimately subsumed it. Jeffers regarded this as a vast and corrupting mistake, a myth that did not reflect or interpret reality but usurped it. The result was to obscure men from themselves no less than from the world. The Greeks had dealt frankly with incest and *familicide* as generically human violations of the natural order, and they sought to expiate them through tragic reenactment. Christianity repressed this painful but necessary consciousness as sin, subordinating all drama and ritual to the rite of redemption, as it had subordinated the temporality of natural process to that of divine history.

As Christianity had been (at least from this standpoint) a corruption of Neoplatonism, so secular humanism was a corrupted form of Christianity. Christianity had replaced the ancient relation between man and cosmos with a radical dichotomy between matter and spirit, self and world, time and eternity. The humanism which replaced a decadent Christianity in turn did not abandon the promise of salvation but recast it in political terms (from "Mother Church" to "Father State," as Jeffers sardonically put it) [*Selected Poetry of Robinson Jeffers*]. By making humanity the author of its own salvation, humanism fed what the ancients would have recognized as hubris, whose symptoms Jeffers described as introversion and the denial of temporal succession—in its extremest form, the denial of time itself—and which he depicted, as the Greeks had, by incest, sexual inversion, and familicide.

Humanism had captured not only politics (in the form of mass democracy, fascism, and communism) but philosophy as well. Kant had made reality a construct of the human intellect; by suppressing the transcendental pole of his thought, Marxists, utilitarians, pragmatists, and positivists made the real itself a product, in John Passmore's phrase, of the "community of finite selves." Set against this, however, was the enterprise of modern science. As humanism had contracted reality to the social organism, science expanded the cosmos forward in space and backward in time, dwarfing human presumption with a scale so vast as to humble the imagination. Jeffers saw science as ethically but not ontologically netural, for it proclaimed the cosmos as value, and by grounding itself in empirical observation and experiment it affirmed its material substratum as well. But science, too, was corruptible, and partook of its epoch; in **"Prescription of Painful Ends,"** Jeffers linked "the immense vulgarities of misapplied science and decaying Christianity," and, in a moment of disgust, he likened the human race to a "botched experiment." Harnessed to the destructive impulses of cultural introversion, science could only hasten the impending collapse. It afforded, perhaps, a refuge, but no escape.

Nonetheless, science provided Jeffers with a perspective that, like the cosmogonic speculations of Lucretius and Empedocles before him, was the basis of a redemptive vision. The perception of beauty and the contemplation of order, he contended, afforded satisfaction to the senses and the intellect, discipline to the will, and peace to the mind. Yet truth to tragedy—fidelity to lived experience—demanded that human time be related to sidereal time, demanded narrative. Between the individual and the cosmos, however, stood a third term, the measure of collective human activity called history. History gave perspective to the individual act as cosmic evolution did to the world's daily occasion. As humanity was comprehended in nature, so history was assimilated in the wider entelechy of the universe.

Broadly speaking, the three major modes in which Jeffers wrote—narrative, meditative, and lyric—corresponded to the three tropes of time—personal, historical, and cosmic—in which the drama of being had its play. The three modes were freely woven through the fabric of individual poems; the narratives were punctuated by lyric or meditative strophes, while the predominantly meditative poems frequently took lyric or dramatic observation as their point of departure, and the lyric ones seldom lacked a meditative or didactic point. Some of the poems—**"A Redeemer," "An Artist," "Steelhead,"** and **"Going to Horse Flats"** come to mind—are deliberately hybrid, consisting of lyric meditations set off by dramatic scenes. While particular poems may resist categorization, however, the modes remain distinct.

As the modes are mixed within the poems, so, consequently, are the temporal tropes that correspond to them. It would be difficult, if not bootless, to say which element was structurally primary, since temporal differentiation is always so present in Jeffers's consciousness. A mere glance at his titles will confirm not only his preoccupation with time but also its importance as an ordering principle in his verse and thought: **"The Year of Mourning," "Dream of the Future," "Ante Mortem," "Post Mortem," "Solstice," "The Cycle," "At the Birth of an Age," "At the Fall of an Age," "Birth and Death," "Birthday," "Return," "Now Returned Home," "Resurrection," "No Resurrection," "Time of Disturbance," "Believe History," "The Day Is a Poem," "Moments of Glory," "New Year's Dawn, 1947," "End of the World," "The Beginning and the End."**

As we have noted, Jeffers keeps to no set time scheme in his narratives, but their action tends to follow seasonal patterns and variations, often with a high degree of specificity. Thus, the opening of **"Tamar,"** depicting the drunken, near-fatal fall of Lee Cauldwell, is set not with calendral but sidereal time: "grave Orion / Moved northwest from the naked shore, the moon moved to meridian." It is only several stanzas later that this is converted into calendral time: "he that fell in December / Walked in the February fields." But Orion is invoked again as Lee's sister, Tamar, recalls that their aunt, Stella, had foreseen him lying injured under Orion's sky in a vision. (The association of the name *Stella* itself with the sky is too obvious to require comment.)

Lee dismisses Stella's prophecy as without significance, just as he interprets his accident as banally as possible, seeing it as a call to abjure his youthful sins and become "decent." It is Tamar who returns to the shore where her brother had fallen to undergo a symbolic purgation of her humanity, rising for an instant beyond good and evil to bear "a third part / With the ocean and keen stars in the consistence / And dignity of the world," The twist of perspective recalls Jeffers's comment in **"Thurso's Landing"** that humanity could shine "at stricken moments . . . terribly against the dark magnificence of things" and the observation on tragedy in a late poem, **"The World's Wonders"**: "Lear becomes as tall as the storm he crawls in." The willingness to suffer extremity, and even, as in Tamar's case, to willfully seek it, is tied to the sense of human destiny that tragedy reflects. Humanity is pathetic and admirable for the same reason, pathetic in its vulnerability to pain, but admirable, in singular individuals, in its ability to endure it. To quote the previously cited passage in full:

> I have learned that
> happiness is important, but pain *gives*
> importance.
> The use of tragedy: Lear becomes as tall as the
> storm he crawls in; and a
> tortured Jew became God.

But pain is never properly sought for itself; it is the by-product of action, and action is the product of desire. Only in the tragic poet are these instrumentalities welded together. For the tragic protagonist, in Jeffers's view, the satisfaction of desire is the end of action; for the poet, it is the means whereby the revelation of suffering is accomplished. Suffering in itself, of course, has no value, but suffering plus endurance—the tragic virtue—*is* value.

So central was the notion of accepted suffering to Jeffers that the conceived of God himself as ultimately Promethean, and being—the material emanation of Godhead—as a condition of pain. He expressed this vision most directly in the speech of the Hanged God in **"At the Birth of an Age"**:

> Without
> pressure, without conditions, without pain,
> Is peace. . . .
> I have chosen
> Being; therefore wounds, bonds, limits and pain; the
> crowded mind and
> the anguished nerves, experience and ecstasy.
> Whatever electron or atom or flesh or star or
> universe cries to me,
> Or endures in shut silence: it is my cry, my silence;
> I am the nerve, I am
> the agony,
> I am the endurance.

In God alone, however, was willed suffering a value for Jeffers, since God alone could not suffer *except* by willing. Suffering, he thought, was all we can know of God, since it was only in this attribute that he was intimately revealed to us, only this attribute that we could share, and only by participation in it that we could aspire towards him: "a tortured Jew became God."

We can thus begin to understand Jeffers's conception of humanity's place in the cosmos. Each person was, he said, one of God's sense-organs, immoderately alerted to feel"; but his distinguishing characteristic was consciousness:

> But man is conscious,
> He brings the world to focus in a feeling brain,
> In a net of nerves catches the splendor of things,
> Breaks the somnambulism of nature . . .
> ("**Margrave**")

Consciousness represented for Jeffers a principle of return from the created world towards its creator. In consciousness, the "splendor" of creation became apparent for the first time in the form of beauty, which Jeffers described as "the human mind's translation of the transhuman / intrinsic glory." But beauty posed, inevitably, the question of deri-

vation, and, with that, the quest for origin. Thus consciousness took God as its ultimate subject, while God, by the same token, objectified himself in humanity as well. Consciousness was in this sense a participation in the divine, and a vehicle of its self-transformation. The import of this process was not to be fathomed; as Jeffers remarked succinctly, "[God] being sufficient might be still." But the task it imposed on consciousness was not mere contemplative understanding but tragic action, the *imitatio Dei*. This was fulfilled—could only be fulfilled—in suffering.

We may now put Jeffers's vision of tragedy in perspective. The setting of his narratives is the California coast, but their space implies cosmic depth. Indeed, the coast itself assumed for Jeffers the aspect of a cosmic stage whose grandeur seemed to reflect the immanence of the divine agon:

> The platform is like a rough plank
> theatre-stage
> Built on the prow of the promontory: as if our
> blood had labored all
> around the earth from Asia
> To play its mystery before strict judges at last, the
> final ocean and sky . . .
> ("**Thurso's Landing**")

This coast crying out for tragedy like all beautiful
> places,
> (The quiet ones ask for quieter suffering: but here
> the granite cliff the
> gaunt cypresses crown
> Demands what victim? The dykes of red lava and
> black what Titan? The
> hills like pointed flames
> Beyond Soberanes, the terrible peaks of the bare
> hills under the sun,
> what immolation?)
> ("**Apology for Bad Dreams**")

Similarly, while strictly narrative time was the duration of accomplished action, significant time was the time necessary for the tragic protagonist to assume the burden of pain that bound him to the divine agon. The prototypically tragic figures for Jeffers were Oedipus and Lear, and, historically, Jesus:

> King Oedipus reeling blinded from the palace
> doorway, red tears pouring
> from the torn pits
> Under the forehead; and the young Jew writhing on
> the domed hill in the
> earthquake . . .
> I saw the same pierced feet, that walked in the same
> crime to its
> expiation; I heard the same cry.
> ("**Meditation on Saviors**")

Jeffers's tragic exemplars were Cawdor in the poem that bears his name, Reave Thurso in *Thurso's Landing,* and Lance Fraser in *Give Your Heart to the Hawks*. These protagonists—the first middle-aged, the other two young but prematurely grave—are all ranchers, bluff and stolid men who not only have no desire to transgress limits but seem almost obsessively determined to live within them. They seek not power but only control, and what betrays them is not hubris but jealousy and resentment.

Cawdor, a man of fifty, unwisely takes a young wife, Fera Martial. Fera falls in love with Cawdor's son Hood, who rejects her advances. Vengefully, she tells Cawdor that Hood has raped her, and he kills him in a fit of rage. Consumed by grief and despair, he becomes monumental in his anguish, and threatening to those around him. When Fera at last confesses the truth, he admits his own guilt, and forestalls the judgment of others by putting out his own eyes. Even this, however, seems to him "mere indulgence": "'I'd not the strength,'" he says, "'to do nothing.'"

A similar tale is told in *Give Your Heart to the Hawks*. Lance Fraser surprises his brother Michael making love to his wife Fayne after a druken picnic, and he hurls him over a cliff. Lance's instinct is to confess, but Fayne persuades him to keep silent: "'What we have done / Has to be borne. It's in ourselves and there's no escaping, / The state of California can't help you bear it.'" Fayne hopes that time will ease his sense of guilt, and Jeffers, in an ironic passage, seems to agree:

> Oh, ignorant penitents,
> For surely the cause is too small for so much
> anguish.
> To be drunk is a folly, to kill may call judgment
> down,
> But these are not enormous evils,
> And as for your brother, he has not been hurt.
> For all the delights he has lost, pain has been saved
> him;
> And the balance is strangely perfect,
> And why are you pale with misery?

Lance's guilt only intensifies, however. He seeks judgment from his father, but, finding none, gashes his hands to the bone on barbed wire in an attempt to divert himself from his moral agony, and finally leaps to his own death.

Reave Thurso, like Fraser and Cawdor, has an unfaithful wife, Helen. Reave's crime is not against law but against nature; wanting to control what he cannot possess, he forces Helen to return to a loveless marriage. His punishment is physical: attempting to cut the cable of his father's abandoned lime kiln that hangs like a symbol of his own failure above him, he is crushed and left paralyzed when it swings back on him. Lying helpless in a pain he can only assuage by the drugs he refuses to take, Reave discovers that "pain is the solidest thing in the world, it has hard edges, / I think it has a shape and might be handled." In Fraser and Cawdor, pain is mixed with guilt, and thus it distracts the will; for Reave, however, it becomes the will's very project, the most difficult and therefore the most necessary thing in the world to master. Paralysis has stripped away all else in his life, and pain is the only meaning left: if it ever ceased, he says, "I'd have to lie and burn my fingers with matches." Reave in fact dies unconquered; he is slain by Helen, who takes her own life in turn.

Cawdor, Thurso, and Fraser are all men on whom pain descends as a burden to be ceaselessly and immutably borne. Their endurance is not passive, however. It requires all the fortitude of which these supremely willful men are capable; it is, for all of them finally, the ultimate project of the will. In virtually all the narratives of Jeffers's classic phase, the action of the story may well be called a pretext for the occasion of pain; the crippling blow, be it physical or psychological, is the crux of the drama, and the remainder of the poem—in the extreme case of *Give Your Heart to the Hawks,* sixty-nine of eighty pages—is in each case devoted to the protagonist's struggle with pain and its effects on others. It is, needless to say, the moral character of this struggle that concerns Jeffers, and gives his depiction of agony the redeeming power of art.

With this in mind, we can more fully understand the choral apostrophe from *Give Your Heart to the Hawks* quoted above. Jeffers, addressing his own characters as "ignorant penitents," tells them that Lance Fraser has not "hurt" his brother in slaying him, for he has spared him the pain that would inevitably have been his lot in this life. These remarks seem to undermine the moral coherence of the poem, for they suggest that pain has no redemptive value and that grief should be temperate. But tragedy is precisely what exceeds the norm of life, and, by means of transfiguring pain, gives access to the divine. Were not certain natures predisposed to suffer this excess, the tragic epiphany, the *imitatio Dei,* would not be possible. Thus, while Jeffers's counsel to temper grief and avoid pain is entirely appropriate from an ordinary human perspective—indeed, is the only appropriate counsel from such a perspective—it has no applicability in the tragic realm; and the very function of the apostrophe is precisely to set off the merely human action of the poem from its tragic consequences.

In terms of our earlier distinction, Jeffers's tragic protagonists step from the arena of ordinary, personal experience—the place where, in the words of the prophet, there is to every thing a season—into the unbounded cosmos of the divine agon, where pain, as a manifestation of the divine essence, is inexhaustible and indivisible. Their suffering, that is, remains rooted in material cause—the act or event which, slight in itself from a cosmic perspective, casts them beyond atonement, and separates them from humanity. To those around them, their steadfast self-punishment seems monstrous and perverse. They seem fixated on a single deed that excludes all other meaning; in other words, they refuse to let time flow, and thereby heal. In the tragic realm, however, their acts *are* immitigable, because in this realm, the realm of epiphany, time does not flow, succession does not exist, and the divine wound is never stanched.

Tragic consciousness in this full and final sense, as the revelation of divinity, is beyond such men as Cawdor, Thurso, and Fraser, blunt skeptics who are, if anything, confirmed in their unbelief by the experience of suffering. They participate in the divine agon without realizing it, and their rejection of all consolation is the quality that perfects their suffering. They are "ignorant penitents," or, as Jeffers suggests elsewhere, the apes of God; and, like apes, their function is to mimic without understanding.

In so defining his heroes, Jeffers remained faithful to the spirit of Greek tragedy, in which the cosmic order can only be fully revealed by the acts which defy it. On the plane of history as well, he contended that the great religious founders were driven by inner shame or conflict, the epistemic equivalent of the tragic flaw. His paradigm was the figure of Jesus, which he explored in a number of poems, most notably the verse drama *Dear Judas,* a work contemporary with the California narratives we have considered here.

Dear Judas is set in the suspended time of Noh drama, whose protagonists enact their passions in the form of ritual. They are "nearly unfleshed of time," "fading" into eternity, Jeffers says; yet the Jesus-figure notes with exactitude that nineteen hundred years have passed since his passion first transpired, which places the poem in the historic present as well. This apposition seems to indicate the waning of Christian belief, whose final eclipse will release Jesus and his fellow performers from their purgatorial ritual. Jesus exists in both dimensions; he suffers his passion as if for the first time, and yet is conscious of it as repetition, repetition with a term.

This perception encapsulates Jeffers's view of historic time, which he saw, with Nietzsche, as a form of cyclical recurrence. Jeffers's concern was not whether exact persons or events would recur, but rather to assimilate historic time to cosmic process by showing homologous *patterns* of events. On the level of personal experience, this took the form of the archetypal passions incarnated by individuals; on the historic one, of the ebb and flow of great civilizations. Jeffers in fact pursued parallel projects in the 1920s and 1930s designed to illustrate this symmetry, alternating the narratives of the California coast, which depicted the fate of individuals, with the verse dramas (*Dear Judas, At the Fall of an Age, At the Birth of an Age, The Bowl of Blood*), which portrayed the crises of Western civilization.

At the same time, Jeffers commented on the relation between the great religious founders and their civilizations in such poems as **"Meditation on Saviors"** and **"Theory of Truth,"** and, in a series of meditative and didactic poems from **"The Broken Balance"** (1929) to **"Prescription of Painful Ends"** (1941), on the cyclical nature of historical experience and impending decline of the West. He was thus able to link personal to historical time, and the historical cycle to cosmic process, in an overarching pattern of recurrence. The latter relationship is evoked with particular effectiveness in **"Prescription of Painful Ends"**:

>   The future is a misted
>   landscape,
>   no man sees clearly, but at cyclic turns
>   There is a change felt in the rhythm of events, as
>   when an exhausted horse
>   Falters and recovers, then the rhythm of the running
>   hoofbeats is
>   changed: he will run miles yet,
>   But he must fall: we have felt it again in our own

>   life time, slip, shift and
>   speed-up
>   In the gallop of the world; and now perceive that,
>   come peace or war, the
>   progress of Europe and America
>   Becomes a long process of deterioration—starred
>   with famous
>   Byzantiums and Alexandrias,
>   Surely—but downward.

The image of the horse, with its portent of fatigue and collapse, is checked by that of the stars, whose duration is indefinite, though their extinction is certain. Jeffers thus combines gathering force and momentum with protracted duration, thereby suggesting the great scale of the event, and assimilating it to the cycles of cosmic change. At the same time, he suggests that the nature of historical process is necessarily concealed; the acceleration toward doom is portrayed as a mechanized advance ("slip, shift and speed-up"), and, by a deliberately archaized usage, "progress," the promise of improvement, is stood on its head as the process of decay.

The suggestion that historical decay inevitably masked itself as progress and enlightenment was the most radical aspect of Jeffers's cultural pessimism. In the modern world, this decadent progress manifested itself most clearly in the post-Nietzschean injunction to overthrow conventional restraints and personal inhibitions. The result was an exaltation of the will, portrayed by Jeffers in the personae of Tamar Cauldwell, the Clytemnestra of **"The Tower Beyond Tragedy,"** his verse adaptation of the *Oresteia,* and Arthur Barclay in *The Women at Point Sur*. If Cawdor, Thurso, and Fraser represent the negative exercise of the will as endurance, these earlier protagonists embody it as an assertion against the limits of existence as such. Tamar seeks nothing less than a reversal of the temporal ordinance itself. "All times are now," she declares, "to-day plays on last year and the inch of our future / Made the first morning of the world." Tamar not only assumes the temporal perspective of divinity, seeing the world as simultaneity and recurrence, but asserts a divine potency: "I am the fountain." When her megalomania (inevitably) collapses, she consumes the small world of her family and farmstead in a holocaust.

These key images of fire and fountain are repeated by Clytemnestra in her address to her lover, Aegisthus: "I'd burn the standing world / Up to this hour and begin anew. You think I am too much used for a new brood? Ah, lover / I have fountains in me." Aegisthus, a merely conventional sinner, counsels moderation: "We may pass nature a little, an arrow flight, / But two shots over the wall you come in a cloud upon the feasting Gods, lightning and madness." The "arrow" of individual action, even of vengeance and murder, must remain inscribed within the sphere of prescription. To come upon the gods is a catastrophe; to aspire towards them, unthinkable. But this is precisely what Clytemnestra does, and when she acknowledges that "It's not a little / You easily living lords of the sky require of who'd be like you," it is only to steel herself further for whatever may be necessary.

Unlike Tamar and Clytemnestra, who ultimately seek power on a merely personal level, Arthur Barclay is a savior, a man who would become a god *for* others. Such men—as Jeffers asserted in **"Meditation on Saviors"**—were the founders of great civilizations, which flourished as long as the metaphor of divinity they provided remained vivid. But the decadence of founding myths was as essential as their ripening; renewal could not come until the full course had been run. *The Women at Point Sur* was written in the aftermath of World War I, when Jeffers's sense of the West's decadence was particularly acute: "You kept the beast under till the fountain's poisoned, / He drips with mange and stinks through the oubliette window" (*CP*, 241). But Jeffers imagined Arthur Barclay as a product of his time's sickness, not as its cure. The West, as Jeffers had concluded by the time of **"Prescription of Painful Ends,"** had its Byzantiums and Alexandrias yet ahead of it, and many false prophets to follow before a new messiah might, perhaps, appear.

Jeffers was skeptical whether civilization could transcend its need for myth, the apprehension of the true by means of the false. Communal truth, he felt, would always be partial, distorted, and transitory; and history followed from that fact. But if every man were obliged to endure history, it did not follow that he was necessarily bound by it. Again and again, Jeffers counseled what he called finally a "reasonable detachment" from the historical moment. This detachment was not to be gained by denial of or indifference to the world. One had to live the life of one's time no less than the times of one's life, and quietism was no more acceptable a response on the historical plane than suicide was on the personal one. Rather, detachment was the fruit of a deep, contemplative engagement with the natural, nonhuman world, and the perception of divinity that was its basis:

> Things are so beautiful, your love will follow your
>   eyes;
> Things are the God, you will love God, and not in
>   vain,
> For what we love, we grow to it, we share its
>   nature.
>
>   ("Signpost")

Jeffers's own verse was the best testimony of his conviction that "Things are the God." For more than four decades, he celebrated the beauty of his chosen coast and the divinity he found manifested in it with the direct lyric earnestness of a religious witness. But if the natural world was the most immediate revelation of value, humanity too—as Jeffers never ceased to insist—was part of it, and to ignore the human pathos within the transhuman splendor was as much an error as the cultural self-absorption that had cut man off from his root in nature, and blocked the sight of God. The coast, as Jeffers noted, "cried out" for tragedy; man was implicated in landscape, and in a special (though not salvific) way, in divinity as well. Only by living all the times of man—the personal one of passional experience, the collective one of history, and the cosmic one of natural process and divine immanence—could the human condition be seen in proper perspective, and its terms accepted.

Jeffers did create one character who attains fully to such a perspective through purgative suffering and religious exaltation. In **"The Tower Beyond Tragedy,"** Clytemnestra represents the misdirected passion for power, and the prophetess Cassandra, who is punished by seeing divine motion through human eyes, the terror of an unmediated perception of cosmic process. The hero Orestes experiences both trials, and emerges with a vision of final cosmic order:

> I entered the life of the brown forest
> And the great life of the ancient peaks, the patience
>   of stone, I felt the
>   changes in the veins
> In the throat of the mountain, a grain in many
>   centuries, we have our own
>   time, not yours; and I was the stream
> Draining the mountain wood; and I the stag
>   drinking; and I was the stars
> Boiling with light, wandering alone, each one the
>   lord of his own summit;
>   and I was the darkness
> Outside the stars, I included them, they were a part
>   of me. I was mankind
>   also, a moving lichen
> On the cheek of the round stone . . . they have not
>   made words for it, to
>   go behind things, beyond hours and ages,
> And be all things in all time, in their returns and
>   passages, in the
>   motionless and timeless center,
> In the white of the fire . . . how can I express the
>   excellence I have found,
>   that has no color but clearness,
> No honey but ecstasy; nothing wrought nor
>   remembered; no undertone
>   nor silver second murmur
> That rings in love's voice, I and my loved are one;
>   no desire but fulfilled;
>   no passion but peace,
> The pure flame and the white, fierier than any
>   passion; no time but
>   spheral eternity . . .

Orestes' experience is not of a static order, but of one whose "eternity" is manifested in the flux and reflux of phenomena and bound by the sphere of recurrence. It is the vision of Jeffers's temporal beatitude, of a world that, perfected in God, is never finished. Such a world can only be expressed in terms of contradiction because it *is* a contradiction, a world which is both endless and bounded, active in repose, and "passionately at peace" (**"Night"**). The contradiction remains, too, between the individual and the historical community. "Let each man make his health in his own mind," Jeffers counsels in **"Meditation on Saviors,"** and Orestes, alone among all his creations, perhaps does this; but he writes as well in **"The Beaks of Eagles"** that "It is good for man / To try all changes, progress and corruption . . . not to go down the dinosaur's way / Until all his capacities have been explored"; to remain, to the last, the ape of God.

Nicholas Everett (review date 1994)

SOURCE: "The Inhumanist," in *Times Literary Supplement,* No. 4782, November 25, 1994, pp. 10-11.

[*In this review of The* Collected Poetry of Robinson Jeffers, *Everett finds Jeffers's doctrine of "inhumanism" incompatible with the demands of tragic narrative and suggests that the poet's lyric achievements will prove more enduring than his narratives.*]

Despite their commitment to transcendence, religious writers usually want to persuade us not only that there is an persuade us not only that there is an accessible higher plane of existence but that our lives within society will be all the richer for our efforts to reach it. Robinson Jeffers's religious vision was by contrast defiantly antisocial. Taking to its extreme the familiar mystical preference for the objects of awe over the objects of emotion, he saw nature as absolute reality and humanity as just one of its many ephemeral and negligible accretions. "It is easy to see that a tree, a rock, a star are beautiful", he explained in a letter to a puzzled student, but "hard to see that people are beautiful unless you consider them as part of the universe—the divine whole." His obsessive message was that we should "uncenter our minds from ourselves" and regard ourselves chiefly as parts of nature rather than as members of society. For Wordsworth, love of nature led to love of mankind; for Jefferson, love of nature was an end in itself, attended more often than not by scorn for mankind.

As several critics have suggested, this extreme, dualistic stance must have owed something to the Calvinism of his father (a Presbyterian minister and professor of theology) though Jeffers always maintained it was derived from, and consistent with, modern (i.e., late nineteenth-century) science, in whose expanding scheme human history occupied a newly insignificant place. Whatever its provenance, it played a large part in both making and breaking his poetic reputation. The first published work in which he developed these ideas—*Tamar and Other Poems,* privately printed in 1924 when he was thirty-seven, and the expanded commercial edition which appeared the following year—earned him sudden and enormous, if comparatively late, critical acclaim. In particular, the long narrative poems set in the mid-Californian coastal mountains (where Jeffers settled with his family in 1914 and remained until his death in 1962), **"Tamar"** and **"Roan Stallion"** (1925), and the dramatic narrative, **"The Tower Beyond Tragedy"** (1924), a version of the *Oresteia,* were celebrated for their powerful, elemental vision of human destructiveness. The eponymous heroine of **"Tamar"** (a considerably altered version of the story in the Book of Samuel), herself the product of incest, seduces her brother and father, then bars their exit from a burning house, perishing with them but with a strong suggestion that she will rise phoenix-like from the ashes to claim the lives of future generations. The daring choice of subject-matter seemed to have been more than justified by the sobriety and dignity of its treatment. Here, many felt, was an American poet who could compete with the ancient Greeks.

In fact, Jeffers had intended sexuality (the "furious longing to join the sewers of two bodies"), and especially incest, as symbols of human "introversion"—our obsessive interest with ourselves and each other at the expense of the broader world around us. Encouraged by his success, he was also bemused by the failure of even the most adulatory reviewers to understand what he was going on about. So, in fifteen years of extraordinary productivity, he published ten more tragic narratives, four more dramatic poems and dozens of shorter ones, making his message increasingly clear and finally giving it the provocative but unappealing title of "inhumanism". Not everyone could live with this twin battery of familial violence and austere philosophy; and for many who could, the poems occasioned by the Second World War proved too much, if not because of their neutral and isolationist stance then because of their callously detached perspective on specific sufferings. "A star gives light, / So does a burning city full of dead bodies" reflects the protagonist of **"Mara"**, "Warsaw's burning's no worse than Arcturus burning." Few could agree when Jeffers said of the possible nuclear conflict that "Pity and terror / Are not appropriate for events on this scale watched from this level; admiration is all." From what level, one wonders, and how did Jeffers get there?

If this is the "reasonable detachment" Jeffers advocated as "a rule of conduct", it is nevertheless not the inhuman truth he claimed it was but a human fantasy, and no more objective or scientific than the idea of a benevolent deity. Environmentalists have had to be very selective in adopting Jeffers as a champion of their cause, since, though he explicitly deplored urban encroachments on his beloved wilderness, his would-be universal perspective can be used just as logically to accept, and even justify, as to condemn the destruction of the planet's surface. It is also all but impossible to sustain, especially with regard to our own lives and the lives of those around us, a problem to which the longer narratives draw surprisingly strong attention.

Indeed, in this respect the long poems are the small print on the Jeffers manifesto: tedious, wordy, overlong but full of unignorable qualifications to the promises of his message. Mark van Doren can't have been the only reader who has taken one of them (in his case *The Women at Point Sur,* 1927) as a refutation of what it was intended to substantiate. Despite their sparsely populated mountainous settings, their atmosphere is predominantly claustrophobic, the scenes often inside a house or a character's head, the characters hemmed in by family and self; when they do escape into the vast landscape, they are liable to confront ghostly doubles who pull them back into the social and psychological conflicts they were running from.

Only three characters, in all, actually achieve the exalted inhumanist position while alive (Orestes in **"The Tower Beyond Tragedy"**, California in **"Roan Stallion",** and the Old Man in the first part of *The Double Axe,* 1948), and for each there is a considerable price to pay. California, for instance, must shoot the horse which has given her a mystical experience of transcendence because it has trampled her husband to death; she's glad to be rid of the husband, who was a brute himself, but can't stop herself reverting to type and taking the human side. Mostly, the characters can't rise above the human sphere except by dying, as the conclusion of *Give Your Heart to the Hawks* (1933) illustrates in a moment of unintended bathos. Fayne Fraser is exhorting her husband Lance to dismiss his guilt about murdering his brother by viewing the deed as one of the many inevitable and insignificant acts of violence in the earth's history; he patiently hears her out, admits she is right and leaps from a cliff to his death. Finally, in the later narratives, even death isn't enough to guarantee escape. The protagonist of "The Love and the Hate" (the first part of *The Double Axe*) has been killed in a Second World War battle, but can find no rest until he has dragged his rotting corpse, his stomach a gaping wound, back to California to murder his father for encouraging him to enlist.

Despite Jeffers's triumphant detachment, his vision belongs properly to the realm not of modern science but of ancient superstition, as he effectively admitted in **"Apology for Bad Dreams"**, his defence of the persistent violence in his stories:

> "Better invent than suffer: imagine victims
> Lest your own flesh be chosen the agonist, or you
> Martyr some creature to the beauty of the place."
>   And I said
> "Burn sacrifices once a year to magic
> Horror away from the house, this little house
>   here
> You have built over the ocean with your own
>   hands
> Besides the standing boulders: for what are we,
> The beast that walks upright, with speaking lips
> And little hair, to think we should always be fed,
> Sheltered, intact, and self-controlled? . . ."

The tragic narratives were ritual sacrifices designed to appease, and thus protect his family from, the random forces of destruction. Lending the term "omniscient narrator" a new and scary nuance, their author behaves like a jealous and increasingly predictable God, killing off family after family, as if he must repeatedly acknowledge his own powerlessness before the unpredictable violence of the universe. The impression that grows and solidifies as the stories unfold is that, for Jeffers, whether consciously or unconsciously, to imagine even the possibility of happiness would have been as good as inviting the wolves to the feast. It is hard to think of a more extended case in literature of imaging the worst to stop it from happening.

Admirably and humanly humble though these motives are, the lofty and careless vision of humanity is a skewed expression of them and remains unpersuasive and objectionable. It is one thing to adopt and recommend a theocentric view, but quite another to regard humanity as you imagine God does. "No one with impunity / gives himself the eyes of a God", says Czeslaw Milosz in his poem "To Robinson Jeffers". When Jeffers stops looking knowingly back on humanity from a wholly fantasized divine or "objective" standpoint and starts looking ignorantly towards God or nature, his poetry immediately becomes much more sympathetic, thereby confirming his essential point.

He rarely keeps this up for long in the shorter poems, though, before his prophetic aspirations get the better of him. Almost all his admirers praise his discursive and didactic manner, not least for going against the twentieth-century grain, and blame the rise of modernist and New Critical values—with their prejudice against a poetry of directly stated ideas—for diminishing his reputation. It is not the didactic method in itself, however, but its inappropriate conjunction with his message which accounts for the main weakness of his work. As he frequently insisted in his many poetic studies of saviours and artists, but failed to realize in his own practice, the inhumanist position is peculiarly inimical to clear rational exposition and explanation. Only so much can be said—that we should look outwards to nature, not inwards to ourselves. A central aim for many post-Romantic poets has been to discover effective metaphorical procedures to overcome the pathetic fallacy and present themselves as a function of existence rather than vice versa. Jeffers would have served his purpose much better had he not so often let impotent, abstract assertions compromise—and sometimes altogether replace—his attempts to do the same.

As far as the course of twentieth-century poetry is concerned, then, Jeffers's work is an exception that proves the rule. His poetry only really takes off when he can resist the temptations of facile pontification and stay with the rigours of descriptive lyric, "surrendering himself to unpolemical nature" (as the critic John Elder puts it) instead of telling others to do so. To this end, he developed an effective form derived in part from Anglo-Saxon verse and from Hopkins. Alternate long and short accentual lines (usually ten and five stresses respectively) combined with more or less heavy alliteration and assonance enable the poetry's occasional flights from its relaxed conversational base into more purely lyrical intensities; where metaphor matches form—as, for instance, in **"Birds"**, where the "cries of a couple of sparrowhawks" pierce like "arrows shot through a curtain the noise of the ocean / Trampling its granite"—the natural scene is suddenly and vividly arrested. Unfortunately, anthologists prefer the sensational poet ("I'd sooner, except the penalties, kill a man than a hawk") to the poet of sensation and so tend to neglect the lyrics, such as **"Return"**, in which thought and instruction yield to experience and desire:

> A little too abstract, a little too wise,
> It is time for us to kiss the earth again,
> It is time to let the leaves rain from the skies,
> Let the rich life run to the roots again.
> I will go down to the lovely Sur Rivers
> And dip my arms in them up to my shoulders.
> I will find my accounting where the alder leaf
>   quivers
> In the ocean wind over the river boulders.
> I will touch things and things and no more
>   thoughts,
> That breed like mouthless May-flies darkening
>   the sky,
> The insect clouds that blind our passionate
>   hawks
> So that they cannot strike, hardly can fly.

Things are the hawk's food and noble is the
                     mountain, Oh noble
Pico Blanco, steep sea-wave of marble.

Jeffers's minor lyric achievements will prove of more enduring value, I suspect, than the ambitious prophetic and narrative works for which he is still most famous. Like Edna St Vincent Millay and Edwin Arlington Robinson, contemporaries with whom he corresponded and shared poems, he didn't substantially extend but worked within Romantic tradition, adapting its forms and ideas all the same in his few really successful poems to apprehend the earthly wilderness in his own distinctive manner.

FURTHER READING

Bibliographies

Vardamis, Alex A. *The Critical Reputation of Robinson Jeffers: A Bibliographic Study*. Hamden, CT: The Shoe String Press, Inc., 1972, 301 p.
> Primary and secondary bibliography. Vardamis also analyzes critical reception to Jeffers's work in the introduction.

Biographies

Bennett, Melba Berry. *The Stone Mason of Tor House*. Los Angeles: Ward Ritchie Press, 1966, 264 p.
> Biography that includes a chronology of the poet's publications as well as a bibliography.

Karman, James. *Robinson Jeffers: Poet of California*. San Francisco: Chronicle Books, 1987, 149 p.
> Biography in which Karman emphasizes the influence the Big Sur coastline of California had on Jeffers's works.

Criticism

Ackerman, Diane. "Robinson Jeffers: The Beauty of Transhuman Things." *American Poetry Review* 12, No. 2 (March-April 1983): 16-18.
> Examines the transhumanance in Jeffers's poetry. Ackerman concludes: "[Jeffers's] fits an apocryphally definitive idea of the American mind: close to nature, to the universe, closer to them than to fellow-humans."

Bennett, Joseph. "The Moving Finger Writes." *The Hudson Review* XVI, No. 4 (Winter 1963-64): 624-33.
> Laudatory review of *The Beginning and the End and Other Poems* in which Bennett states: "This volume . . . contains some of the best work Jeffers has produced."

Brophy, Robert. "Robinson Jeffers." *Western American Literature* XX, No. 2 (August 1985): 133-50.
> Surveys Jeffers's life and career, concentrating on the influence of western American landscapes on his works.

———, ed. *Robinson Jeffers: Dimensions of a Poet*. New York: Fordham University Press, 1995, 248 p.
> Collection of critical essays.

Carpenter, Frederic I. *Robinson Jeffers*. New York: Twayne, 1962, 159 p.
> Detailed discussion of Jeffers's narrative and lyric poetry.

Coffin, Arthur B. *Robinson Jeffers: Poet of Inhumanism*. Madison: University of Wisconsin Press, 1971, 300 p.
> Studies major themes in Jeffers's works.

Conrad, Sherman. Review of *The Selected Poetry of Robinson Jeffers*. *The Nation* 148, No. 12 (3 June 1939): 651-52.
> Mixed review of *The Selected Poetry of Robinson Jeffers* in which Conrad discusses Jeffers's treatment of such themes as truth and art.

Davis, H. L. "Jeffers Denies Us Twice." *Poetry* 31, No. V (1928): 274-79.
> Mixed review of *The Women at Point Sur*. Davis praises the language and style but states that Jeffers seems to have wanted "to divorce his mind from . . . all things human."

Gioia, Dana. "Strong Counsel." *The Nation* 246, No. 2 (16 January 1988): 59-64.
> Review of *Rock and Hawk* in which Gioia discusses the lack of critical acceptance of Jeffers's works.

Hicks, Granville. "A Transient Sickness." *The Nation* 134, No. 3484 (13 April 1932): 433-34.
> Mixed review of *Thurso's Landing*.

Hunt, Tim. "A Voice in Nature: Jeffers' *Tamar and Other Poems*." *American Literature* 61, No. 2 (May 1989): 230-44.
> Examines how Jeffers's treatment of nature changed and evolved in the years after he abandoned rhymed verse.

Murphy, Patrick D. "Robinson Jeffers' Macabre and Darkly Marvelous Double Axe." *Western American Literature* XX, No. 3 (November 1985): 195-209.
> Analysis of *The Double Axe* in which Murphy states that while the work "is focused on the single thematic purpose of a poetic protest against the direction of the United States during and after World War II, it consists of two contrasting halves."

Nolte, William H. "Robinson Jeffers as Didactic Poet." *PMLA* 42, No. 2 (Spring 1966): 257-71.
> Examines the didacticism inherent in Jeffers's poetry, concluding "of all major modern poets, Robinson Jeffers came closest to expressing himself in a uniquely singular style."

Scott, Robert Ian. "From Berkeley to Barclay's Delusion: Robinson Jeffers vs. Modern Narcissism." *Mosaic* XV, No. 3 (September 1982): 55-61.
> Contrasts Jeffers's unsentimental view of humanity with the delusional narcissism of such modern poets as Sylvia Plath.

Schweizer, Harold. "Robinson Jeffers' Excellent Action." *American Poetry* 5, No. 1 (Fall1987): 35-58.
  Compares Jeffers's tragic vision to that of English writer and critic Matthew Arnold.

Squires, Radcliffe. *The Loyalties of Robinson Jeffers.* Ann Arbor: The University of Michigan Press, 1956, 198 p.
  Examines various influences on Jeffers's works, including philosophy, science, and other writers.

Thesing, William B., ed. *Robinson Jeffers and a Galaxy of Writers. Contemporary Literature.* Columbia: University of South Carolina Press, 1995, 218 p.
  Collection of essays in which the contributors compare Jeffers to other modern writers.

Zaller, Robert. *The Cliffs of Solitude: A Reading of Robinson Jeffers.* Cambridge: Cambridge University Press, 1983, 263 p.
  Extensive critical study in which Zaller attempts to "locate Jeffers's narrative impulse in a series of efforts to mediate Oedipal trauma and recurrent crises of personal autonomy."

Zaller, Robert, ed. *Centennial Essays for Robinson Jeffers.* Newark: University of Delaware Press, 1991, 282 p.
  Anthology of critical essays published in the past four decades.

Ben Jonson
1572?-1637

English dramatist, poet, masque writer, and critic.

INTRODUCTION

A prolific Elizabethan playwright and man of letters, Jonson is among the greatest writers and theorists of English literature. Highly learned in the classics, he profoundly influenced the coming Augustan age through his emphasis on the precepts of Horace, Aristotle, and other early thinkers. In his day, Jonson's professional reputation was often obscured by that of the man himself: bold, independent, aggressive, fashioning himself an image as the sole arbiter of taste, standing for erudition and the supremacy of classical models against what he perceived as the general populace's ignorant preference for the sensational. While he is now remembered primarily for his satirical comedies, he also distinguished himself as a seminal figure in English literary criticism, as a preeminent writer of courtly masques, and as a poet. Among his most enduring contributions to the latter form are the classically influenced lyrics of his *Epigrams* (1616) and the pastoral poem "To Penshurst" contained in his collection *The Forest* (1616).

Biographical Information

Jonson was born in London shortly after the death of his father, a minister who claimed descent from Scottish gentry. Despite a poor upbringing, he was educated at Westminster School under the renowned antiquary William Camden. He apparently left his schooling unwillingly to work with his stepfather as a bricklayer, and later served as a volunteer in the Low Countries during the Dutch war with Spain. Returning to England by 1592, Jonson married Anne Lewis about three years later. Although it appears that the union was unhappy, it produced several children, all of whom Jonson outlived. In the years following his marriage he became an actor, and wrote respected emendations and additions to Thomas Kyd's *The Spanish Tragedy* (1592). By 1597 he was writing for Philip Henslowe's theatrical company. That year, Henslowe employed Jonson to finish Thomas Nashe's satire *The Isle of Dogs* (now lost), but the play was suppressed for alleged seditious content and Jonson was jailed for a short time. In 1598 the earliest of his extant works, *Every Man in His Humour,* was produced by the Lord Chamberlain's Men. That same year he was again jailed for killing actor Gabriel Spencer in a duel. In 1602 he separated from his wife and was imprisoned a third time in 1605 for his work with John Marston (a former rival playwright) and George Chapman on *Eastward Hoe.* He wrote all of his major comedies between 1606 and 1616, the later date marking the publication of

his *Workes,* which, in addition to the plays, included the poetic collections *Epigrams* and *The Forest,* as well as his early masques produced with the collaboration of designer/architect Inigo Jones. That same year he was also named Poet Laureate, and for the next decade focused his energies on the production of masques at the court of King James I. Fire destroyed his library in 1623, and when James I died in 1625, Jonson lost much of his influence at court. In 1628 he suffered the first of several strokes that would later incapacitate him. Jonson died in 1637 and was interred at Westminster Abbey. His third collection of poems, *Underwood,* appeared posthumously in the 1640 edition of his *Workes.*

Major Works

Jonson's major poetic works combine the classical forms of lyric, epistle, ode, elegy, and epithalamion with the native English sense of affect or feeling. Many of them are poems of praise and written within the obligatory confines of the patronage system. From *Epigrams,* the short poems influenced by the verse of the Roman poet Martial,

"On My First Daughter" and "On My First Son" are personal lyric consolations. This collection also contains the tender "Epitaph on S. P., a Child of Q. Elizabeth's Chapel." *The Forest* includes the pastoral "To Penshurst," Jonson's country house poem celebrating the poetic and political largesse of the Sidney family; the work is regarded as a model of the topographical form. In *The Forest* are two versions of "Song: To Celia," one dramatizing the *carpe diem* sentiment expressed by Volpone in Jonson's play of the same name, the other known by its first line, "Drink to me only with thine eyes." *Underwood* contains "A Celebration of Charis in Ten Lyric Pieces," an experiment in voice and the transformative power of language, and the Pindaric Ode dedicated "To the Immortal Memory and Friendship of that Noble Pair, Sir Lucius Cary and Sir H. Morison." The plays *Sejanus His Fall* (1603) and *Catiline His Conspiracy* (1611) established Jonson's reputation as a political tragedian; he is perhaps best known, however, for his satiric comedies *Volpone* (1606), *Epicoene* (1609), *The Alchemist* (1610), and *Bartholomew Fayre* (1614), which are portraits of the greed and hypocrisy Jonson saw in contemporary London. His *Timber; or, Discoveries* (1641), is considered the first formulation of applied literary principles in English, and predates the critical works of John Dryden.

Critical Reception

Jonson's immediate poetic reputation is traceable to the highly imitative works of his literary followers, known as the "Sons" or "Tribe of Ben," which included Robert Herrick, Thomas Carew, and the later Cavalier poets. His works were highly regarded during his lifetime, although his later plays, "dotages" as Dryden called them, were not well received. His controlled lines were models for the eighteenth century verse of writers such as Alexander Pope, who once observed that Jonson "brought critical learning into vogue." The nineteenth century Romantics decried his lack of passion and thought his comedies better than his tragedies. In the twentieth century the New Critical movement overlooked Jonson's poems in favor of the work of the Metaphysicals. His work, including his long neglected poetry, has, however, enjoyed a renaissance of critical attention in the late twentieth century from new historical theorists interested in the material issues of patronage and censorship that inform his poetics.

PRINCIPAL WORKS

Poetry

*Epigrams 1616
*The Forest 1616
†Underwood 1640
The Complete Poems of Ben Jonson 1975

Other Major Works

The Case Is Alterd (drama) 1598
Every Man in His Humour (drama) 1598
The Comicall Satyre of Every Man out of His Humour (drama) 1599
Cynthia's Revels; or, The Fountain of Self-Love (drama) 1601
Sejanus His Fall (drama) 1603
Eastward Hoe [with George Chapman and John Marston] (drama) 1605
Masque of Blacknesse (masque) 1605
Hymenai (masque) 1606
Volpone; or, The Foxe (drama) 1606
Masque of Beauty (masque) 1608
Epicœne; or, The Silent Woman (drama) 1609
Masque of Queenes (masque) 1609
The Alchemist (drama) 1610
Catiline His Conspiracy (drama) 1611
Oberon, the Fairy Prince (masque) 1611
Bartholomew Fayre (drama) 1614
The Divell is an Asse; or The Cheater Cheated (drama) 1616
The Golden Age Restored (masque) 1616
The Workes of Benjamin Jonson (dramas and poetry) 1616
Pleasure Reconcild to Vertue (masque) 1618
Informations by Ben Jonson to W. D. When He Came to Scotland upon Foot [also published as *BenJonson's Conversations with William Drummond of Hawthornden*, revised edition, 1976] (conversations) 1619
The Gypsies Metamorphosed (masque) 1621
The Fortunate Isles and Their Union (masque) 1625
The Staple of News (drama) 1626
The New Inne; or, The Light Heart (drama) 1629
The Magnetick Lady; or, Humors Reconciled (drama) 1632
A Tale of a Tub (drama) 1633
The Workes of Benjamin Jonson, 2 vols. (dramas, poetry, and prose) 1640-41
Timber; or, Discoveries, Made upon Men and Matter as They Have Flowed out of His Daily Reading, or Had Their Reflux to His Peculiar Notion of the Times (prose) 1641
Ben Jonson 11 vols. (dramas, poetry, and prose) 1925-52
The Complete Masques of Ben Jonson. (masques) 1969
The Complete Plays of Ben Jonson. 4 vols. (dramas) 1981-82

*Printed in the 1616 folio of Jonson's *Workes*.

†Printed in the posthumous two-volume 1640 edition of Jonson's *Workes*.

CRITICISM

Hugh MacLean (essay date 1964)

SOURCE: "Ben Jonson's Poems: Notes on the Ordered Society," in *Essays in English Literature from the Renaissance to the Victorian Age*, edited by Millar MacLure and F. W. Watt, University of Toronto Press, 1964, pp. 43-68.

[In the following essay, MacLean discusses Jonson's poems as observations on civilized society, stressing friendship between good men, the ideal relationship between prince and poet, and the social actions befitting the ruling class.]

"The reputation of Jonson," Mr. Eliot once remarked, "has been of the most deadly kind that can becompelled upon the memory of a great poet. To be universally accepted; to be damned by the praise that quenches all desire to read the book; to be afflicted by the imputation of virtues which excite the least pleasure; and to be read only by historians and antiquaries—this is the most perfect conspiracy of approval" ["Ben Jonson," *Selected Essays, 1913-1932,* 1932]. Perhaps the prospect is not quite so gloomy now: "Jonson criticism has at last commenced to grow green," Jonas Barish observes, and the articles he has recently collected indicate, over a variety of critical approaches, some avenues that may be profitably explored [*Ben Jonson: A Collection of Critical Essays*, 1963]. But it is striking that no essay in his collection bears directly on the lyric and occasional verse. If the lawn of Jonson criticism is newly green, brown patches are still perceptible. That is not very surprising, of course, for *Timber* invites attention to the comedies:

> The *Poet* is the neerest Borderer upon the Orator, and expresseth all his vertues, though he be tyed more to numbers; is his equall in ornament, and above him in his strengths. And, (of the kind) the *Comicke* comes neerest: Because, in moving the minds of men, and stirring of affections (in which Oratory shewes, and especially approves her eminence) hee chiefly excells.

> [*Ben Jonson,* ed. Herford and Simpson,
> Vol. VIII, 1925-52]

Given this remark, and the elaborations that follow, to say nothing of the triumphant Jonsonian comedies themselves, later critics could hardly be expected to spare the poems more than an appreciative glance before passing to the main course of comedy. It has often been the fate of the poems to be praised chiefly (sometimes exclusively) for their formal virtues, while the best criticism of the comedies, more than ever since L. C. Knights's *Drama and Society in the Age of Jonson,* has kept steadily in view Jonson's comment that "the Study of [Poesy] (if wee will trust *Aristotle*) offers to mankinde a certaine rule, and Patterne of living well, and happily; disposing us to all Civill offices of Society."

That is rather curious, too. The comedies, by their nature, present this "certaine rule, and Patterne" indirectly, appealing (as Knights says) to the "sardonic contemplation" of an audience characterized by "a lively sense of human limitations." The epigrams, as a rule, repeat that method; but a significant number of the poems, particularly in ***The Forrest,*** deal explicitly and directly with "high and noble matter," with "the mysteries of manners, armes, and arts." Geoffrey Walton, following Leavis, remarks on Jonson's regular attention, in the poems, to "serious moral matters

in a social context" ["The Tone of Ben Jonson's Poetry," in *Seventeenth Century English Poetry,* ed. W. R. Keast, 1962]. I suggest that, while the plays deal principally in the satiric recognition and description of the factors that contribute to social disorder, we find in the poems (with the *Discoveries* behind, as theory to practice), not an explicit and detailed outline of the social order Jonson admired, but rather "notes" on particular elements that ought to mark a society properly ordered, as well as suggestions for conduct in the midst of a disordered one. The negative strictures of the comedies, accordingly, are supplemented and completed by positive advices in the poetry and the *Discoveries*.

One must be careful not to claim too much: no integrated grand design for society emerges from the "lesser theatre" of these poems, so often committed to compliment. But the recurrence of three related themes is striking. In brief, the poems lay stress on the virtue of friendship between good men, who are receptive by nature to the free exchange of opinion and counsel, and on the strongresource such friendships constitute for the ordered society and the secure state. They reflect also Jonson's views on the relationship that ought ideally to obtain between prince and poet, in the interest of the people at large. Finally, they indicate the social attitudes and actions befitting a "ruling class" which thoroughly understands the nature of its responsibilities and desires to make them effective. It is relevant to observe here also that, when Jonson speaks to this third question, he is apt to select the verse-epistle as a vehicle peculiarly suited to the poet who outlines, for the benefit of those in high place, "holy lawes / Of nature, and societie." In this, as in much else, "there must be a Harmonie, and concent of parts."

A dominant and recurring theme in the *Discoveries* is the humanistic insistence on man's power, in spite of his own nature and the vicissitudes of time, to maintain ethical standards, not in a spirit of reactionary opposition to change, but in large measure by adapting classical precepts to contemporary circumstance. "Rules," Jonson noted, "are ever of lesse force, and valew, then experiments"; men find truth by following "the *Ancients* . . . but as Guides, not Commanders." Still, Jonson never pretended that this would be easy. He knew all about the shortcomings of human nature; when the character of mankind is in question, a note of disenchantment is often heard. "*Envy* is no new thing, nor was it borne onely in our times. The Ages past have brought it forth, and the comming Ages will. So long as there are men fit for it . . . it will never be wanting." "*Natures* that are hardned to *evill,* you shall sooner breake, then make straight; they are like poles that are crooked, and dry: there is no attempting them." Human nature "oft-times dies of a *Melancholy,* that it cannot be vitious enough." It is clear too that Jonson recognized the threat of vice not merely to individuals but to the community much more.

> When too much desire, and greedinesse of vice, hath made the body unfit, or unprofitable; it is yet gladded with the sight, and spectacle of it in others: and for want of ability to be an Actor; is content to be a

Witnesse. It enjoyes the pleasure of sinning, in beholding others sinne; as in Dicing, Drinking, Drabbing, &c.

Indeed, "A native, if hee be vitious, deserves to bee a stranger, and cast out of the Common-wealth, as an Alien." It goes without saying that Jonson would never abandon the effort to improve matters by any available means. He gathers up, for instance, Quintilian's gentle suggestions about the best ways in education and in criticism. But in the final analysis, he depends on a continuing supply of naturally "*Good men* . . . the Stars, the Planets of the Ages wherein they live, [who] illustrate the times." The well-known observation, "Men are decay'd, and *studies:* Shee [Nature] is not," needs to be compared with less familiar passages in the poet's commonplace book: "They are ever good men, that must make good the times: if the men be naught, the times will be such." "A good life," for Jonson, "is a maine Argument."

It is in the light of these attitudes that we should read those poems in which Jonson turns his attention to friend-ship. Geoffrey Walton touches on this matter but does not come closely to grips with it, beyond an approving glance at a few of the poems addressed to friends in various walks of life; and while it is true that in these pieces "one can observe . . . [Jonson's] feeling for civ-ilized personal relationships," there is more to be said. For Jonson, friendship is the bond enabling those good men who illustrate their times to group together and, by means of their collected virtue, cast out or resist vice. So they serve each other; but they help to safeguard the state as well.

These views are, of course, not original with Jonson, who might have been influenced by any of a number of author-ities. But while it is not very feasible to suggest particular sources for his poetical comments on friendship (given their relatively orthodox detail, together with the wide range of his reading), it should at least be observed that Jonson, unlike Spenser, is not much interested in the conception of friendship "as a harmonizing and unifying principle of cosmic love operating in the realm of man to promote concord" [C. G. Smith, *Spenser's Theory of Friendship,* 1935]. As usual with him, metaphysical theory takes sec-ond place to, or is eclipsed by, moral and social consid-erations, Friendship matters to Jonson because it is a moral virtue and because it contributes to social stability. His position recalls, in particular, that of Aristotle's disserta-tion on friendship (*Ethics,* VIII-IX), which contains some passages that must certainly have called out Jonson's ap-proval, whether or not they directly influenced his poetry. Having classified the three categories of friendship in terms of its object ("what is good, pleasurable, or useful"), Aristotle, shows that friendships based on utility and plea-sure must soon dissolve; he concludes that the only "per-fect Friendship" subsists

between those who are good and whose similarity consists in their goodness: for these men wish one another's good in similar ways; in so far as they are good (and good they are in themselves); and those are specially friends who wish good to their friends for

their sakes, because they feel thus towards them on their own account and not as a mere matter of result; so the Friendship between these men continues to subsist so long as they are good; and goodness, we know, has in it a principle of permanence.

[J. A. Smith, ed., *The Ethics of Aristotle,* 1911]

"Some go so far as to hold that 'good man' and 'friend' are terms synonomous," he remarks in the same place, pointing out that "requital of Friendship is attended with moral choice which proceeds from a moral state." Rele-vant also is Aristotle's distinction between friendships moral and legal, and between elements within a "legal" friendship: "The Legal is upon specified conditions . . . the obligation is clear and admits of no dispute, the friendly element is the delay in requiring its discharge."

All this is reflected in Jonson's poems, which often repu-diate, as in **"An Epistle answering to one that asked to be Sealed of the Tribe of Ben"** (9-15, 25-7), friendships based on utility or pleasure.

> Let those that meerely talke, and never thinke,
> That live in the wild Anarchie of Drinke,
> Subject to quarrell only; or else such
> As make it their proficiencie, how much
> They'ave glutted in, and letcher'd out that weeke,
> That never yet did friend, or friendship seeke
> But for a Sealing . . .
>
>   . . . . .
>
> Let these men have their wayes, and take their times
> To vent their Libels, and to issue rimes,
> I have no portion in them. . . .

Flattery, the extreme of that "friendship whose motive is utility," Jonson condemns in a thoughtful phrase: "To flatter my good Lord" is "To lose the formes, and dig-nities of men" (*Under-Wood* XV, 146-7). The view that "those are specially friends who wish good to their friends for their sakes, because they feel thus towards them on their own account and not as a mere matter of result," informs poems as various as "Inviting a friend to sup-per" or the ode to a "high-spirited friend" (*Und.* XXVI); notable too is the **"Epistle to a friend"** (*Und.* XXXVII), where the quality of "friendship which no chance but love did chuse" is heightened by contrast (7-9) with that of

> Your Countrie-neighbours, that commit
> Their vice of loving for a Christmasse fit;
> Which is indeed but friendship of the spit. . . .

These and other poems repeatedly emphasize certain qual-ities of friendship: moderation, candour, generosity, mutu-al esteem. The opening lines of the **"Epigram: To a Friend, and Sonne"** (*Und.* LXIX), perhaps to Lucius Cary, summarize those qualities with terse dignity:

> Sonne, and my Friend, I had not call'd you so
> To mee; or beene the same to you; if show,
> Profit, or Chance had made us: But I know

What, by that name, wee each to other owe,
Freedome, and Truth; with love from those begot:
Wise-crafts, on which the flatterer ventures not.

The friendship is "attended with moral choice" is asserted by Jonson less emphatically than one might expect. Still, membership in the Tribe evidently involved selective distinction between suitable candidates and those who sought friendship "but for a Sealing"; and the poet seems to assume that his "high-spirited friend" cannot after all "mis-apply" the "wholsome Physick for the mind" prescribed by Jonson, but will in fact choose to accept the honest counsel of a friend. Another kind of moral choice emerges in *Under-Wood* XXXVII (25-30):

It is an Act of tyrannie, not love,
In practiz'd friendship wholly to reprove,
As flatt'ry with friends humours still to move.

From each of which I labour to be free,
Yet if with eithers vice I teynted be,
Forgive it, as my frailtie, and not me.

Friendship, in short, confers (or should confer) a capacity to recognize and accept some frailties in human nature, and so to overlook minor vices that may otherwise obscure or even destroy a relationship essentially virtuous: to resist vice, therefore, by a moral decision. One is struck by Jonson's recurring use of the term "free": true friends may fearlessly exchange ideas, give an opinion, advise, censure even. Men come to know liberty through friendship; or again, to be a friend is to free both oneself and one's friend. The term itself does not appear in yet another **"Epistle to a Friend"** (*Und.* XVII), on the distinction between legal and moral friendships, but the poem deals with the right use of that freedom which only friends can know (1-6, 11-16):

They are not, Sir, worst Owers, that doe pay
Debts when they can: good men may breake their
    day,
And yet the noble Nature never grude;
'Tis then a crime, when the Usurer is Judge.
And he is not in friendship. Nothing there
Is done for gaine: If't be, 'tis not sincere. . . .

. . . he that takes
Simply my Band, his trust in me forsakes,
And lookes unto the forfeit. If you be
Now so much friend, as you would trust in me,
Venter a longer time, and willingly:
All is not barren land, doth fallow lie.

The associations of friendship with moral virtue, however, are no less important for Jonson than the role of friendship in its social context. Aristotle had said that "Friendship seems to be the bond of Social Communities," and also that, if some forms of "Communion"

are thought to be formed for pleasure's sake, those, for instance, of bacchanals or club-fellows, which are with a view to Sacrifice or merely company . . . [yet] all

these seem to be ranged under the great Social one, inasmuch as the aim of this is, not merely the expediency of the moment but, for life and at all times. . . . So then it appears that all the instances of Communion are parts of the great Social one: and corresponding Friendships will follow upon such Communions.

In **"An Epistle answering to one that asked to be Sealed of the Tribe of Ben"** (*Und.* XLVII), Jonson draws his view of friendship between individuals together with a statement on the obligations of friends to the body politic. The poem suggests that Jonson regarded the Tribe, his own band of brothers, not at all as an association "formed for pleasure's sake . . . or merely company," but as a dependable nucleus of virtuous companions, secure in self-knowledge and the wit to eschew triviality, upon whom the state might rely in all honourable causes. No doubt, too, while he would endorse all friendly connections established between virtuous men, he was bound to pay particular respect to any such group including a majority of poets, whose art is that "*Philosophy*, which leades on, and guides us by the hand to Action. . . ." The title, with its scriptural allusion, and the lines glancing at heaven's purposes decorously reinforce the note of high seriousness recurrently dominant in this poem. While the **"Epistle"** is not precisely balanced in its structure, it seems to be true that Jonson deals at first (1-30) with the distinguishing features of men unfit for friendship, and in conclusion (51-78) with the characteristics of true friends. The intervening passage, for the greater part a contemptuous catalogue of trivia dear to gossiping courtiers, contains also (37-42, at the poem's centre, as it happens) a concise and plainspoken affirmation of the good citizen's obligation to act as a member of the larger community.

I wish all well, and pray high heaven conspire
My Princes safetie, and my Kings desire,
But if, for honour, we must draw the Sword,
And force back that, which will not be restor'd,
I have a body, yet, that spirit drawes
To live, or fall a Carkasse in the cause.

Fops chatter, men act. But the passage throws into high relief a more significant contrast. The wastrels described in the opening section of the poem may be "received for the Covey of Witts," but in fact no "ignorance is more then theirs." Their crass concerns mark them as slaves to passion. Knowing nothing of friendship, each cares for himself alone. Jonson's statement of personal principle that opens the concluding section (56-62) seems at first to assert merely another kind of self-centred aloofness. But the poet at once draws into his circle all men with whom "square, wel-tagde, and permanent" friendship is possible, men (that is) of Jonson's own stamp:

. . . all so cleare, and led by reasons flame,
As but to stumble in her sight were shame;
These I will honour, love, embrace, and serve:
And free it from all question to preserve.

So short you read my Character, and theirs
I would call mine. . . .

                                                                    (69-74)

Such men, devoted to principle not appetite, serve each other and the community; and on such men the state can rely when it is time to "draw the Sword." Through friendship, then, good men who understand the rights and duties of the freedom they enjoy, and who are prepared to act in defence of virtuous principles, form a reliable substratum upon which the state and society at large may depend for health and survival.

To match what may be called this broad "horizontal" principle of friendship among men of active virtue, one means of preserving a desirable social order, Jonson was impressed also (as the *Discoveries* chiefly show) by the need for a "vertical" king-post of order: the healthy relationship of king and people. Details of mutual rights and duties, however, interested him less than the establishment of conditions that would be likely to ensure good government. Critics have often noticed that *dispositio,* arrangement, in plays or poems, receives Jonson's particular attention; the *Discoveries* everywhere reflect this concern. In the state also, it is vital that administration be properly arranged, especially that the good prince shall be attended by good advisers; "for though the *Prince* himselfe be of most prompt inclination to all vertue: Yet the best *Pilots* have need of *Mariners,* beside Sayles, Anchor, and other Tackle," and "the good Counsellors to Princes are the best instruments of a good Age." "The best Counsellors," Jonson noted from Lipsius, "are books"; but the proposition implicit throughout the *Discoveries* is that, in fact, the best counsellor of all is the poet.

Most of the Renaissance commonplaces about the relations of king and people are present in the *Discoveries.* "*The vulgar . . .* commonly ill-natur'd; and always grudging against their *Governours,*" are like a many-headed beast; the good prince "is the Pastor of the people . . . the *soule* of the Commonwealth; and ought to cherish it, as his owne body"; "*After God,* nothing is to be lov'd of man like the Prince." Jonson is orthodox on rebellion too: "Let no man therefore murmure at the Actions of the Prince, who is plac'd so farre above him. If hee offend, he hath his Discoverer. *God* hath a height beyond him." For these views and others like them, there was plenty of authority in Seneca, Erasmus, Lipsius, and "the great *Doctor of State, Macchiavell,*" on whom he draws directly for a mordant passage about advisers to the prince. Yet if he recognizes Machiavellian wisdom in some things, Jonson does not give way to cynicism. "The *Princes* Prudence" (as he notes from Farnese) may well be "his chiefe Art, and safety"; but it is "the mercifull *Prince . . .* safe in love, not in feare," whom Jonson admires. "A *good King* is a publike Servant," by no means "(as it is in the Fable) a crowned Lyon." He can agree that "*the strength* of Empire is in Religion. . . . Nothing more commends the *Soveraigne* to the Subject, then it," but then his own voice breaks in, "For hee that is religious, must be mercifull and just necessarily. . . . Justice is the vertue, that *Innocence* rejoyceth in." The prudence that adjusts flexibly to change and circumstance, and yet serves virtue still, he thought an essential element of administration, that princely art. "*Wise,* is rather the attribute of a Prince, then *learned,* or *good*"; but the governor who is truly wise must in the nature of things be a good man too.

Well enough; yet, "*Princes* are easie to be deceiv'd . . . what wisdome can escape it; where so many Court-*Arts* are studied?" One answer recalls that of Lipsius: "A *Prince* without Letters, is a Pilot without eyes." But a more effective response is to choose the right sort of counsellor: "Soveraignty needs counsell." Jonson knew from Vives what to look for:

> In being able to counsell others, a Man must be furnish'd with an universall store in himselfe, to the knowledge of all *Nature:* That is the matter, and seedplot; There are the seats of all Argument, and Invention. But especially, you must be cunning in the nature of Man: There is the variety of things, which are as the *Elements,* and *Letters,* which his art and wisdome must ranke, and order to the present occasion. For wee see not all letters in single words; nor all places in particular discourses. . . . The two chiefe things that give a man reputation in counsell, are the opinion of his *Honesty;* and the opinion of his *Wisdome. . . . Wisedome* without *Honesty* is meere craft, and coosinage. And therefore the reputation of *Honesty* must first be gotten; which cannot be, but by living well.

And of all such persons, the poet is most clearly qualified:

> I could never thinke the study of *Wisdome* confin'd only to the Philosopher: or of *Piety* to the *Divine:* or of *State* to the *Politicke.* But that he which can faine a *Common-wealth* (which is the *Poet*) can governe it with *Counsels,* strengthen it with *Lawes,* correct it with *Judgements,* informe it with *Religion,* and *Morals;* is all these. Wee doe not require in him meere *Elocution;* or an excellent faculty in verse; but the exact knowledge of all vertues, and their Contraries; with ability to render the one lov'd, the other hated, by his proper embattaling them.

The prince is the apex, so to speak, of society's pyramid, but he needs the special insight of the poet, who combines "goodnes of natural wit" with the capacity ("as by a divine Instinct") to utter "somewhat above a mortall mouth." When the prince attends to the counsel of his best adviser, the learned poet (who ought also to be his truest friend), he serves his people as ideal example, almost in the fashion Jonson noted from Euripides: "Where the *Prince* is good . . . *God is a Guest in a humane body.*" Philosopher-kings and poet-princes are rare: for the rest, "no man is so wise, but may easily erre, if hee will take no others counsell, but his owne."

Jonson was ready and willing to advise the monarch: he said to Drummond, "so he might have favour to make one Sermon to the King, he careth not what yrafter should befall him, for he would not flatter though he saw Death." This was, perhaps, bravado, although the notes for a disquisition on kingship lay at hand in the *Discoveries,* and this poet, at least, enjoyed high favour, amounting almost to friendship, with James I. But Jonson was quite aware that the "free" exchange of advice and counsel natural to friends could scarcely be duplicated in these circumstances. He had read Vives on the problems of counselling kings, "especially in affaires of *State*." And of course his own encounters with officialdom, notably in connection with *Sejanus* in 1603, when Northampton accused him "both of popperie & treason," must sufficiently have impressed even the poet who "never esteemed of a man for the name of a Lord." In any event, although one could compose verse-epistles or odes to advise one's high-spirited friends, even, by judicious indirection, counsel a whole class of society, it was difficult to extend these methods to the monarch. A few pieces, however, are relevant to Jonson's prose observations on the conduct appropriate for the good prince; and these bear also on the poems to and about his patrons.

Most of the poems addressed by Jonson to royalty are "occasional" in a narrow sense; one or two others repeat the commonplace that a poet ensures fame or notoriety for his subjects. "The lesse-*Poetique* boyes" may expect "a Snake"; but "in the *Genius* of a *Poets* Verse, The Kings fame lives" (*Und.* LXXVI, LXVIII). **"The humble Petition of poore Ben: To . . . King Charles"** (*Und.* LXXVI), however, primarily a request for more money, takes care to stress the rationale of the poet's position (3-7):

> . . . your royall *Father,*
> James *the blessed,* pleas'd the rather,
> Of his speciall grace to *Letters,*
> To make all the Muses debters,
> To his bountie. . . .

That Jonson claims his due "for goodnesse sake" is apt enough, since the best princes know that poetry is "neerest of kin to Vertue." Another **"Epigram: To K. Charles . . . 1629"** (*Und.* LXII) varies the same theme:

> Great Charles, among the holy gifts of grace
> Annexed to thy Person, and thy place,
> 'Tis not enough (thy pietie is such)
> To cure the call'd *Kings Evill* with thy touch;
> But thou wilt yet a Kinglier mastrie trie,
> To cure the *Poets Evill,* Povertie. . . .

This poem, too, concludes on a note of nearly explicit advice:

> What can the *Poet* wish his *King* may doe,
> But, that he cure the Peoples Evill too?

Jonson, however, does not as a rule presume to counsel the prince in these poems even thus indirectly. He prefers to draw attention to the fact (illustrated, fortunately, in both James and Charles) that the character and actions of a prince should be exemplary and therefore instructive, and to indicate some suggestive parallels between king and poet. An **"Epigram: To . . . K. Charles"** of 1629 (*Und.* LXIV) makes the first point, in somewhat fulsome tones:

> Indeed, when had great *Britaine* greater cause
> Then now, to love the Soveraigne, and the Lawes?
> When you that raigne, are her Example growne,

And what are bounds to her, you make your owne?
When your assiduous practise doth secure
That Faith, which she professeth to be pure?
When all your life's a president of dayes,
And murmure cannot quarrell at your wayes?

More striking are two of the **Epigrams**. **"To King James"** (**IV**) all but proclaims the monarch that ideal "poet-prince" who needs no other counsel.

> How, best of Kings, do'st thou a scepter beare!
> How, best of *Poets,* do'st thou laurell weare!
> But two things, rare, the Fates had in their store,
> And gave thee both, to shew they could no more.
> For such a *Poet,* while thy dayes were greene,
> Thou wert, as chiefe of them are said t'have beene.
> And such a Prince thou art, wee daily see,
> As chiefe of those still promise they will bee.
> Whom should my *Muse* then flie to, but the best
> Of Kings for grace; of *Poets* for my test?

A second poem (**XXXV**) with the same title enlarges on the principle of rule.

> Who would not be thy subject, James, t'obay
> A Prince, that rules by example, more than sway?
> Whose manners draw, more than thy powers
>   constraine.
> And in this short time of thy happiest raigne,
> Hast purg'd thy realmes, as we have now no cause
> Left us of feare, but first our crimes, then lawes.
> Like aydes 'gainst treasons who hath found before?
> And than in them, how could we know god more?

The prince, then (who is the better ruler for a youthful poetic bent), governs, as the poet teaches, by persuasion and example; and at length, through the laws that reflect his wisdom, thesubjects discover for themselves that here indeed, "God is a guest in a human body."

That these poems are few in number was to be expected: even if wisdom had not checked the impulse to counsel a king, Jonson was not the man to lavish his talents on this particular variety of panegyric. But an attractive alternative remained. One could, if one were reasonably decorous, address a ruling class instead. Those members of aristocratic families who extended their patronage and support to Jonson, especially those with whom the poet could consider himself to be on terms at least relatively informal, must in any event be honoured in the poet's verse. While he could not ordinarily expect to be as candid (or blunt) as with his own colleagues, he could claim with some justice to have attained something like friendship with a number of highly placed individuals. Relatively free, therefore, from the limitations imposed where princes were in question, yet still addressing or chiefly complimenting persons regularly concerned, in various spheres, with the maintenance of order in social and political life, Jonson could counsel while appearing chiefly to praise. For young Sir William Sidney, the poet might assume an oracular tone; with others, the note of approbation or reminder would often be more fitting. Particularly in *The Forrest,* but elsewhere too, he incorporates in gracefully complimentary verse those principles of social responsibility which the actions of a ruling class ought in his view to reflect. The poet, in short, transfers his advisory function (properly directed to a prince) to that class from which, as a rule, the monarch will draw his counsellors; and he can address some of them, at least, in a manner formal and "easy" at once.

Jonson's attitude to his patrons is conditioned primarily by three factors. He needed their support, of course, but that is in some ways the least important of the three: poems that openly request or acknowledge financial support appear only in the last years, when the poet's fortunes were palled. As a rule, Jonson chose to ignore the subject, or to make it the occasion for a lacture on the art of giving and receiving, as in the **"Epistle to . . . Sacvile"** (*Und.* XIII), which strikes a characteristic note.

> You . . . whose will not only, but desire
> To succour my necessities, tooke fire,
> Not at my prayers, but your sense; which laid
> The way to meet, what others would upbraid;
> And in the Act did so my blush prevent,
> As I did feele it done, as soone as meant:
> You cannot doubt, but I, who freely know
> This Good from you, as freely will it owe;
> And though my fortune humble me, to take
> The smallest courtesies with thankes, I make
> Yet choyce from whom I take them. . . .   (7-17)

The lines reflect a cast of mind also apparent in Aubrey's allusion to "Mr. Benjamin Johnson (who ever scorned an unworthy patrone)" [John Aubrey, *Brief Lives,* ed. A. Powell, 1949]. No doubt unworthiness might consist in the refusal to honour a promise of support, as **Epigram LXV ("To my Muse")** may indicate. But the poem hints at deeper causes of scorn; and **Epigram X ("To my lord Ignorant")** is perhaps relevant:

> Thou call'st me *Poet,* as a terme of shame:
> But I have my revenge made, in thy name.

While the episode at Salisbury's table is familiar, there were others of the sort:

> Ben one day being at table with my Lady Rutland [Drummond writes], her husband comming in, accused her that she keept table to poets, of which she wrott a letter to him which he answered My Lord intercepted the letter, but never chalenged him.

A patron may be "unworthy" on several counts, but his failure to acknowledge the poet's right to a privileged place in society is particularly reprehensible. Finally, Jonson expected the patron and his class to exemplify virtuous conduct, and so to persuade a society and secure a state. The *Epigrams* are dedicated to Pembroke, "Great Example of Honor and Vertue"; and whatever Jonson thought of the man described by Clarendon as "immoderately given up to women," **Epigram CII** illustrates the poet's ideal.

> . . . thou, whose noblesse keeps one stature still,
> And one true posture, though besieg'd with ill
> Of what ambition, faction, pride can raise;
> Whose life, ev'n they, that envie it, must praise;
> That art so reverenc'd, as thy comming in,
> But in the view, doth interrupt their sinne;
> Thou must draw more: and they, that hope to see
> The common-wealth still safe, must studie thee.

More specifically (as the poems reveal), Jonson expected a patron to pay more than lip-service to the ideal of fraternity; to illustrate in thought and action the continuing virtue of ancient traditions; to renew in each age, by the wise application of inherited talent, the life and force of those traditions. When hard circumstance closed every other avenue, there remained an obligation to exemplify (if need be, "farre from the maze of custome, error, strife") the ideal of virtuous life appropriate to one's station.

Jonson, accordingly, looked for a good deal more than financial support from the highly placed persons who could sponsor him. And he "counselled" his patrons, directly and indirectly, in a good many genres, from the epigram to the ode. The verse-epistle in particular he found well suited to his personality and his purposes. As Trimpi shows, the genre by Jonson's time combined regard for a continuing stylistic tradition with an attitude toward the range of matter proper to the verse-epistle considerably more liberal than that of classical practice. Cicero's observations on the characteristics of the plain style in oratory, and the view of Demetrius that, in genres suited to the plain style (i.e., comedy, satire, epigram, epistle), "the diction throughout [will be] current and familiar," particularly that the epistle should "obey the laws of friendship, which demand that we should 'call a spade a spade,' as the proverb has it," contributed to a tradition of epistolary style endorsed by Lipsius, Vives, and John Hoskyns. On the other hand, Demetrius' opinion that "there are epistolary topics, as well as an epistolary style," and that "in the case of the plain style, we can no doubt point to subject matter which is homely and appropriate to the style itself," had gradually given way to the view that the range of topics proper to the epistle may extend to "all public, private, and domestic concerns."

A verse form at once traditional and evolving in this way suited Jonson very well. The manner of any one epistle will certainly vary with the occasion; one does not address a noble lord as one might ask a friend to dinner. Nor are we to expect advice directly given so much as the counsel implicit in the poet's approbation of the action and character he describes; for "it . . . behooves the giver of counsell to be circumspect." Still, the humanist who allowed Aristotle his due while insisting on the right to "make further Discoveries of truth and fitnesse," and who thought rules less forceful than experiments, recognized the suitability of the verse-epistle for precepts turning on the principle, "Newnesse of Sense, Antiquitie of voyce!" Again, it was an appropriate medium for the poet concerned to remind society and its leaders of the dangerous temptation to "rest / On what's deceast": rather (*Und.* **XIII,** 131-4),

'Tis by degrees that men arrive at glad
Profit in ought; each day some little adde,
In time 'twill be a heape; This is not true
Alone in money, but in manners too.

And, of course, for one whose sense of injur'd merit lay always ready to hand, the relatively plain-spoken style of the verse-epistle might usefully reinforce expressions hinting at an equality of merit, or even at actual friendship, between poet and the highly placed person addressed.

Evidently Jonson employs forms other than the verse-epistle proper to endorse or counsel the social actions of his patrons. It may be observed, however, that while **XII** and **XIII** in *The Forrest* are explicitly termed "epistles," III ("To Sir Robert Wroth") is surely one also. The **"Ode: To Sir William Sydney"** gives advice as directly as does the **"Epistle to a Friend, to perswade him to the Warres"** (*Und.* **XV**), or even the **"Epistle to . . . Sacvile."** And the *Epigrams* (among which appears **"Inviting a friend to supper"**) include several pieces not obviously representative of Jonson's taut standards for the epigram. Jonson was fond of mingling literary kinds, and in any event he had good classical precedents for the practice. That various formal labels attached to these poems should not obscure the fact that they all reflect his conviction that the poet has a clear right, a duty even, to speak out to his patron in a manly fashion. Perhaps one may risk the suggestion that Jonson found the verse-epistle especially congenial and that something of its character and tone often echoes in poems not formally so described. If he employs the verse-epistle to remind a ruling group of the constant standard it must uphold and of the continual adjustment to circumstance this will require, and to insist besides on the essential fraternity of a healthy society, poems called "odes" or "epigrams" reflect those elements too.

"To Penshurst," formally both ode and "country-house poem," has been rather thoroughly examined by G. R. Hibbard (and others), but since Jonson here explicitly considers the role of an aristocratic dynasty (in terms of one with which he felt particular sympathy), one or two points need emphasis. Penshurst, apt symbol of the Sidney line, instructively illustrates Jonson's social ideal in one aspect at least: the contrast with those more magnificent ancestral piles that betray pride and ambition points up Penshurst's vitality and their lack of it. But we are not regularly made aware of "the world outside" Penshurst in this poem, although opening and conclusion remind us of that world's existence: Jonson's emphasis falls deliberately on the positive ideal exemplified at Penshurst. That nature is everywhere compliant, even eager to serve man, effectively supplements the fraternal atmosphere prevailing in this household, where all classes are as welcome as the poet (45-50; 61-4):

> . . . though thy walls be of the countrey stone,
> They'are rear'd with no mans ruine, no mans grone,
> There's none, that dwell about them, wish them
>   downe;
> But all come in, the farmer, and the clowne:
> And no one empty-handed, to salute
> Thy lord, and lady, though they have no sute. . . .

[There] comes no guest, but is allow'd to eate,
Without his feare, and of thy lords owne meate:
Where the same beere, and bread, and self-same
  wine,
That is his Lordships, shall be also mine.

And while the family that acknowledges its social responsibilities spreads genial influence on all sides, so too it prepares for its successors, those aristocratic patrons of the next age, by properly educating and directing offspring who (96-8) may

> every day,
> Reade, in their vertuous parents noble parts,
> The mysteries of manners, armes, and arts.

If this is how a great family ought to act, Jonson remarks also on the conduct appropriate to individual members of that family. Of the various poems addressed to members of the clan, the **"Ode: To Sir William Sydney, on his Birth-day"** is of special interest; since the person addressed is at the point of transition from youth to manhood, his responsibilities to a noble line and to society at large are emphasized in conjunction. Jonson thought that "no perfect Discovery can bee made upon a flat or a levell"; also that "to many things a man should owe but a temporary beliefe, and a suspension of his owne Judgement, not an absolute resignation of himselfe, or a perpetuall captivity." These principles underlie his advice to the young Sidney (27-50):

> . . . he doth lacke
>   Of going backe
>   Little, whose will
>   Doth urge him to runne wrong, or to stand still.
> Nor can a little of the common store,
>   Of nobles vertue, shew in you;
>   Your blood
>   So good
>   And great, must seeke for new,
> And studie more:
>   Not weary, rest
>   On what's deceast.
>   For they, that swell
>   With dust of ancestors, in graves but dwell.
> 'T will be exacted of your name, whose sonne,
>   Whose nephew, whose grand-child you are;
>   And men
>   Will, then,
>   Say you have follow'd farre,
> When well begunne:
>   Which must be now,
>   They teach you, how.
>   And he that stayes
>   To live until to morrow' hath lost two dayes.

These poems clearly reflect important elements in Jonson's "theory of social order": they are guide-lines for a ruling class that collectively and individually cares about its responsibilities. But they lack a dimension. The bright perfection of a Sidney-world obscures the sombre social backdrop that requires to be regulated by Sidneys and those like them. Leaders cannot forever prevent the incursions of vice, after all, by exemplifying virtue at a cool remove; they must often descend into the arena and actively wrestle with the enemy. Perhaps Jonson felt some reluctance, for reasons of decorum, to present Sidneys in postures other than serene: one recalls the **"Epode"** (*Forrest,* XI):

> Not to know vice at all, and keepe true state,
>   Is vertue, and not *Fate*:
> Next, to that vertue, is to know vice well,
>   And her blacke spight expell.
>
>   (1-4)

In any case, other poems not addressed to members of the Sidney clan complement and amplify the views approved in **"Penshurst"** and counselled in the **"Ode."** And each presumes a context appropriate to the second couplet of the **"Epode."**

Epigram LXXVI ("On Lucy Countesse of Bedford") has often attracted the admiration of critics: "How to be" may be suggested as the theme of this poem, which wittily translates ideal into fact. Less often noticed, but more significant here, is **Epigram XCIV ("To Lucy, Countesse of Bedford, with Mr. Donnes Satyres")**, an equally polished piece, with the theme, "How to act."

> Lucy, you brightnesse of our spheare, who are
> Life of the *Muses* day, their morning-starre!
> If workes (not th'authors) their owne grace should
>   looke,
> Whose poemes would not wish to be your booke?
> But these, desir'd by you, the makers ends
> Crowne with their owne. Rare poemes aske rare
>   friends.
> Yet, *Satyres,* since the most of mankind bee
> Their un-avoided subject, fewest see:
> For none ere tooke that pleasure in sinnes sense,
> But, when they heard it tax'd, tooke more offence.
> They, then, that living where the matter is bred,
> Dare for these poemes, yet, both aske, and read,
> And like them too; must needfully, though few,
> Be of the best: and 'mongst these, best are you.
> Lucy, you brightnesse of our spheare, who are
> The *Muses* evening, as their morning-starre.

Here is a poem decorously circular in design, turning on the role appropriate to patrons and exemplified by Lucy, who is not simply "Life of the *Muses* day," but who has the wit to discern and distinguish: to be, in fact, one of those "rare friends" that "rare poems" demand, patrons who, by extending favour to the poet, acknowledge the quality of the poetry—one might say, pay court to it. Far from assuming an attitude of aloofness and hauteur, his patroness, who deliberately seeks out satirical poems for their "matter," is concerned with the moral character of all levels of society, not merely her own. As true aristocrat, the Countess of Bedford justifies her place in the social order by gaining knowledge, through the mirror held up to nature by the poet, of social conditions upon which she may then (Jonson seems to imply) bring her beneficent influence to bear. But even if she does not act in that way, her refusal to turn away from unpleasant or

disturbing aspects of society, her insistence on a full view, indicate the completeness of her own nature, one fit to be described as evening and morning star both: a "full constant light," in fact, perfectly exemplifying the recognition that ancient privilege never exempts from present responsibility.

"To Sir Robert Wroth" (*The Forrest,* III) parallels **"To Penshurst"** in its emphasis on the acquiescence of external nature in the pursuits of man ("A serpent river leades / To some coole, courteous shade"), and on the mingling in this household, when occasion arises, of all classes (53-8):

> The rout of rurall folke come thronging in,
>   (Their rudenesse then is thought no sinne)
> Thy noblest spouse affords them welcome grace;
>   And the great *Heroes,* of her race,
> Sit mixt with losse of state, or reverence.
> Freedome doth with degree dispense.

However, unlike the other, this poem continually reminds the reader of threatening and vicious forces at court and in the world environing Wroth's home; the "thousands" who (85-8)

> . . . goe flatter vice, and winne,
>   By being organes to great sinne,
> Get place, and honor, and be glad to keepe
>   The secrets, that shall breake their sleepe. . . .

The natural surroundings of Durrants provide, not a permanent haven, but merely a "securer rest," to which Wroth may intermittently retreat for spiritual refreshment and moral strength, before returning to the task Jonson considers appropriate to every leader: "To doe thy countrey service, thyselfe right." Further, while divine power and natural influences may direct Wroth and his highly placed fellows to peace of mind, and enable them to meet the temptations of city and court with equanimity, still (93-4)

> . . . when man's state is well,
>   'Tis better, if he there can dwell

These tentative expressions point to the fact that the life even of the good man is one of continual and rigorous struggle, to shore up or regulate social order, and also, through self-examination, to guard against the "subtle traines" (as the **"Epode"** has it) by which "severall passions invade the minde, / And strike our reason blinde."

The **"Epistle to . . . Sacvile"** (*Und.* XIII), in which social vice and disorder are once again extensively detailed, with special attention to "hunters of false fame," adds a final note of counsel to the active leader. It is not enough merely to hold at bay the forces making for disorder in society and in oneself. The point of struggle is to secure virtue or to alter a vicious situation: to make something happen. At the very least, one may demonstrate in one's own person what others may also achieve (135-44). ("They are ever good men, that must make good the times.")

> . . . we must more then move still, or goe on,
> We must accomplish; 'Tis the last Key-stone
> That makes the Arch. The rest that there were put
> Are nothing till that comes to bind and shut.
> Then stands it a triumphall marke! then Men
> Observe the strength, the height, the why, and when,
> It was erected; and still walking under
> Meet some new matter to looke up and wonder!
> Such Notes are vertuous men! they live as fast
>   As they are high; are rooted and will last.

All these poems counsel or approve social actions befitting persons responsible for the maintenance and direction of social order. But what if society, hardened in bad moulds, too toughly resists the efforts of dedicated leaders to redirect its course? For Jonson had read his Seneca: "Wee will rather excuse [a vice], then be rid of it. That wee cannot, is pretended; but that wee will not, is the true reason. . . . It was impossible to reforme these natures; they were dry'd, and hardned in their ill." The **"Epistle: To Katherine, Lady Aubigny"** (*The Forrest,* **XIII**) gives counsel for just such a situation. Not surprisingly, Jonson advises his patroness to profit by the poet's example: fortitude in adversity and confidence to endure in the midst of trial will both be required. The poem opens with a warning:

> 'Tis growne almost a danger to speake true
> Of any good minde, now: There are so few.
> The bad, by number, are so fortified,
> As what th'have lost t'expect, they dare deride.
> So both the prais'd, and praisers suffer. . . .

But the poet, "at fewd / With sinne and vice, though with a throne endew'd," does not recoil. "Though forsooke / Of *Fortune,*" Jonson proudly claims (15-20)

> [I] have not alter'd yet my looke,
> Or so my selfe abandon'd, as because
> Men are not just, or keepe no holy lawes
> Of nature, and societie, I should faint. . . .

The character of Lady Aubigny, "perfect, proper, pure and naturall" (for so her "beauties of the mind" are shown in the poet's mirror), enables her to take a stand analogous to that of the beleaguered poet. Even friendship may fail (53-8); but the individual's responsibility to virtue remains constant (51-2):

> 'Tis only that can time, and chance defeat:
> For he, that once is good, is ever great.

In an unregenerate world that "cannot see / Right, the right way," the virtuous individual may continue to influence others merely by being true to herself, as Jonson reminds Lady Aubigny (110-12),

> . . . since you are truly that rare wife,
> Other great wives may blush at: when they see
> What your try'd manners are, what theirs should bee.

But this, he knew, was rather to be wished than expected; and since even a poet might sing, in fierce adversity, "high,

and aloofe," the key passage of the poem (59-63; 121-4) advocates the pursuit of virtue in a larger context. When the times defy moral redemption, and friends fall off,

> This makes, that wisely you decline your life,
> Farre from the maze of custome, error, strife,
> And keepe an even, and unalter'd gaite;
> Not looking by, or backe (like those, that waite
> Times, and occasions, to start forth, and seeme) . . .

> Live that one, still; and as long yeeres doe passe,
> *Madame,* be bold to use this truest glasse:
> Wherein, your forme, you still the same shall finde;
> Because nor it can change, nor such a minde.

Exemplary action, therefore, may now and again be matched by an exemplary endurance that conquers time and circumstance.

The **"Epistle to Elizabeth Countesse of Rutland"** (*The Forrest,* **XII**), to conclude, draws together a number of views already noted, now with special reference to the poet's central role. The epistle touches on the "credentials" of the poet-counsellor and on the conditions most favourable for the exercise of his gifts. As Hercules, Helen, gods and men owed their lives beyond life "onely [to] *Poets,* rapt with rage divine," so Jonson's poetry (89-91) will undertake

> . . . high, and noble matter, such as flies
> From braines entranc'd, and fill'd with extasies;
> Moodes, which the god-like Sydney oft did prove. . . .

In an age when

>   . . . almightie gold . . .
> Solders crackt friendship; makes love last a day;
> Or perhaps lesse,

Sidney's daughter can be trusted to

> . . . let this drosse carry what price it will
> With noble ignorants, and let them still,
> Turne, upon scorned verse, their quarter-face:
> With you, I know, my offring will find grace.
> For what a sinne 'gainst your great fathers spirit,
> Were it to thinke, that you should not inherit
> His love unto the *Muses,* when his skill
> Almost you have, or may have, when you will?

But the poem intends more than this: by spelling out the nature of that fame awaiting patrons fortunate enough to hold a place in Jonson's verse, it establishes the claim of the poet to a seat among the highest ranks of the social community. Jonson can promise "strange *poems,* which, as yet, / Had not their forme touch'd by an English wit"; poems, however, that also recall and confirm the powers of Orphic song. Ancient truth will live again in modes newly suited to contemporary conditions and taste. This poet can, of course, assure the worthy patron of earthly fame, "like a rich, and golden *pyramede,* / Borne up by statues." But Jonson's commitment is more explicit (86-7): to

. . . show, how, to the life, my soule presents
Your forme imprest there. . . .

The exemplary form of virtue embodied in the Countess
of Rutland while she lived will not merely be remembered
through Jonson's verse, but truly re-created in it; as "godlike Sidney" had given the mark of the right poet to be his
capacity so to create another nature. "To flatter my good
Lord," we recall, is "To lose the formes, and dignities of
men." False friendship destroys life; but the poet, like a
true friend, preserves the "formes" of the men and women
he addresses in his poems. The true poet gives life, in
fact, as kings can "create new men" (*Ungathered Verse*,
XVI). And only such poets, whose art "hath a Stomacke
to concoct, divide, and turne all into nourishment," are
thoroughly qualified to counsel the princes and patrons
whose art is the ordering of society and the state. The
structure of society severely limits the extension of friendship proper, on the pattern of theTribe; that is a pity; but
community of interest among good men may serve instead. And Jonson's poems record his constant care for
that harmonious ideal.

G. A. E. Parfitt (essay date 1968)

SOURCE: "The Poetry of Ben Jonson" in *Essays in Criticism*, Vol. 18, No. 1, January, 1968, pp. 18-31.

[*In the following essay, Parfitt interprets Jonson's poems
in light of the chief functions of his best verse, "energy,
assuredness, and rhythmical alertness," contrasting their
tendency to simplify and exaggerate.*]

Although there is enough of it to occupy the bulk of a
volume of the Oxford edition of his works, Ben Jonson's
poetry does not receive much primarily critical attention.
Part of this neglect comes from the fact that the plays are
Jonson's main achievement (and even these live in the
deep shadow of Shakespeare) but one must also take account of the doubts critics have expressed concerning the
intrinsic merits of the poetry. These doubts usually take
the form of equating Jonson's 'classicism'—that most
protean of qualities—with dulness and alienation from any
English tradition of language and thought, or of the belief
that he lacked inspiration and was, in Coleridge's sense,
a poet of fancy. The first of these reservations has had
some recent attention and I cannot now take the discussion further, except to remark in passing that there is little
in Jonson's thought or use of language which lacks English antecedents and that where he is distinctively classical (mainly in the lack of supernatural emphasis in his
ethical thought and in the non-resonance and unusual directness of his use of language) it is in a way which does not
make him an isolated figure. The second point is, however,
the one I wish to take up here.

The suggestion that Jonson lacked inspiration is clear in
Gregory Smith's remark that his poetry is without 'that
spiritual suggestion which in master-verse lies behind the
magic of phrase and rhythm' and again in Swinburne's

comment that we can expect 'no casual inspiration, no
fortuitous impulse' [*Ben Jonson*, 1919]. The Romantic
background is clear enough—Arnold gone to seed—but,
although outdated, these remarks have not really been
displaced, as anyone who has read J. B. Bamborough's
British Council booklet will appreciate. Dr. Leavis speaks
well of Jonson's poetry and Yvor Winters sees his verse
as the culmination of 16th century plain-style poetry. In
addition one or two recent anthologies have included a
larger and more intelligent selection of his work, but there
is still little evidence that Jonson is being read more widely
or more wisely than he was 40 years ago; mainly, I think,
because he does not fit very well into the framework of
metaphysical poetry, lacking the more striking qualities of
that mode. Jonson, in fact, loses two ways: if we are critics
or critically-influenced readers of poetry we are likely to
look for, and most appreciate, density of texture displayed
in such forms as irony, paradox and ambiguity; if we are
more occasional readers of poetry or reactionaries we are
liable to be close to the Romantic critical tradition. In
neither case will Jonson be an obvious poet for us to
read—and, yet, if we will read him, as we should, with as
much attention and as few preconceptions as possible, we
can see that he offers a great deal. An attempt to demonstrate this will need to take further account of the possible
objections to Jonson, but it will be best to begin by asking
what qualities Jonson's poetry has and whether they amount
to anything very much.

It is important, first of all, to be aware of what acts as the
basic impulse in Jonson's poetry. Part of Shakespeare's
fascination is that the particular area of experience he is
examining seems to suggest and define the moral values
relevant to it. There is a remarkable lack of preconception
in Shakespeare which makes him perhaps the most non-
didactic poet in English, but it is a quality which appears
in most great poetry and is, I think, almost part of any
adequate definition of the term. Jonson, on the other hand,
works largely from values to experience, for his *a priori*
belief in certain ethical tenets governs his selection, analysis
and expression of material. This is strength, in the consistency, weight and conviction it lends to his poetry, but
also potential weakness in that it can lead to inflexibility
and one-sidedness. But this feature of Jonson's poems does
not make him that near-contradiction in terms, a purely
cerebral poet. His intellect is usually less obtrusive than
Donne's, acting mainly to keep the development of his
poems clear and to focus them on the topic in hand, and
the wrongheadedness of seeing him as a mainly intellectual
writer can be demonstrated in most of his major poems
(which, apart from '**To Penshurst**', are not those most
widely known). '**An Epistle to a Friend, to persuade
him to the Warres**' [*The Under-wood* XV] contains a
mass of satirical detail which has obviously been selected
to give a peculiar emotional slant to the poem: very little
attempt is made to convince us by discursive reasoning of
the alleged decadence of the society being examined, and
instead Jonson overwhelms us with the sheer emotional
weight of detail. In '**To Sir Robert Wroth**' [*The Forrest
III*] there is a clear antithesis between town and country
life and our intellectual reaction must be that the matter is
more complex than Jonson pretends. If we give assent to the

poem's vision it may partly be because our minds suggest an element of truth in Jonson's simplification, but it is mainly because his belief in this vision is made emotionally convincing by the pressure of the chosen details and by the impact of the confident rhythms. Although frigidity is a reasonable charge against some of the lyrics, a general reputation for intellectual pedantry is not justified in Jonson's poems and is an unnecessary blockage to appreciation.

But if Jonson's basic impulse is didactic in the way just suggested, what are the chief features of his best verse? The qualities I should stress are energy, assurance and rhythmical alertness, all of which can be found in the **'Epistle to a Friend'** already mentioned:

> Wake, friend, from forth thy Lethargie; the Drum
> Beates brave, and loude in Europe, and bids come
> All that dare rowse: or are not loth to quit
> Their vitious ease, and be o'erwhelm'd with it.
> It is a call to keepe the spirits alive
> That gaspe for action, and would yet revive
> Mans buried honour, in his sleepie life:
> Quickening dead Nature, to her noblest strife.

Energy here is present in the clarity and immediate impact of the basic conception, and also in the concentrated power of such words as 'dare', 'vitious', 'o'erwhelm'd', 'gaspe' and 'sleepie', while assurance is the conviction that this (to our eyes) unusual attitude is reasonable in this context and the weight with which this conviction is pressed home. The rhythmical alertness is the way in which the stresses and sense-units are varied so that a strong emotional appeal and an impression of reasoned argument can co-exist with a kind of idiomatic directness appropriate to the topic.

It would be misleading, however, to expect from Jonson energy in an obviously striking form: he is not normally a coiner of instantly memorable phrases, but he has a remarkable fundamental strength which makes itself felt in almost any extended passage, and, as we become familiar with his poems, we sense also the unobtrusive local energy. The opening lines of **'To Heaven'** [*The Forrest* XV] make their first impact because of their poise rather than of anything striking in the language:

> Good, and great God, can I not thinke of thee,
> But it must straight, my melancholy bee?
> Is it interpreted in me disease,
> That, laden with my sinnes, I seeke for ease?
> O, be thou witnesse, that the reynes dost know,
> And hearts of all, if I be sad for show,
> And judge me after. . . .

The words are self-effacing, passing one through to the overall meaning without asking to be examined minutely. But—and here another Jonsonian quality, precision of word-choice, needs emphasis—they can stand up to such examination, for while it will reveal few deep-seated associations and fewer ambiguities, it increases respect for the essential rightness of 'reynes' and 'interpreted' and

understanding of how the conventional adjectives 'good' and 'great', and the standard image in 'laden', gain weight and point from the confident rhythms, from careful placing, and ultimately from the wider context of Jonson's thought.

The same process, whereby we slowly come to feel the strength of detail in Jonson's poetry, is evident in **'An Epistle Mendicant'** [*The Under-wood* LXXI] where, rarely, there is a single formative image. The poem begins:

> Poore wretched states, prest by extremities,
> Are faine to seeke for succours, and supplies
> Of Princes aides, or good mens Charities.
> Disease, the Enemie, and his Ingineeres,
> Wants, with the rest of his conceal'd compeeres,
> Have cast a trench about mee, now five yeares.

The immediate appeal is emotional (sympathy for the bedridden old poet and admiration for the dignity of his request for help) but what is particularly impressive is how Jonson controls and defines his situation, almost objectively and without self-pity. This is achieved by the use of a single image with no immediately obvious conceptual or emotional contact with his plight, and by the careful description of this 'external' image rather than of the plight. It is applied to himself in 'cast a trench about me' and 'block'd up, and straightned, narrow'd in, Fix'd to the bed, and boords. . . . ', and the application is an imaginative one, but Jonson makes no attempt to strike logical sparks from it and there is nothing startling in the choice of descriptive language. Yet its exactness is clear, perhaps most in the simple adjectives of the very first phrase: poverty and misery are the two aspects of a besieged town which most demand humane attention, and they apply with equal force to Jonson himself. Again, the poem's assurance is marked by the easy movement between abstract and concrete: 'Disease' and 'Wants' 'cast a trench', and the image continues the description of siege while applying metaphorically to the poet's isolation and incapacitation. **'An Epistle Mendicant'** is a small-scale achievement but it is still impressive and the reasons why this is so provide a more general summary of Jonson's qualities as a poet. The technical achievement is one of economy, energy and exactness, together with control and rhythmical alertness. Behind this lie an ability to see the relevant experience in a wider context, and an ability to place it and to give it just the amount of emphasis and development it will bear, and no more. The achievement is a real one partly because it is small: Jonson will not inflate himself.

This discussion of Jonson's characteristics as a poet may have suggested how well his style is fitted to the demands made on it by the nature of his interest in the communication of an ethical attitude. A suitable style for this purpose must convince us of the validity of his ethical analysis, both by allowing direct and forceful comment upon the society being analysed and equally impressive description of that society. It must also seem serious without becoming so elevated that, in relation to the very ordinary people and activities under examination, it seems absurd. The style of Jonson's best poetry fits such a prescription well. It has the range for satirical detail:

Some alderman has power
Or cos'ning farmer of the customes so,
T'advance his doubtfull issue, and ore-flow
A Princes fortune. . . .

> [*The Forrest* XIII ll. 38-41]

and for impressive statement of what is praiseworthy:

Where comes no guest, but is allowed to eate,
Without his feare, and of the lordes owne meate:
Where the same beere, and bread, and selfe-same
   wine,
That is his Lordships, shall be also mine.

> [*The Forrest* II ll. 61-4]

It can condemn directly with conviction:

'Tis growne almost a danger to speake true
Of any good minde now: There are so few,
The bad, by number, are so fortified,
As what th'have lost t'expect, they dare deride.

> [*The Forrest* XIII ll. 1-4]

and can give advice with equal assurance:

Thy morning's and thy evening's vow
Be thankes to him, and earnest prayer, to finde
A body sound, with sounder minde;
To doe thy countrey service, thy selfe right;

> [*The Forrest* III ll 100-03]

The style and what it communicates should not too easily be set aside as trivial because, on the one hand, it shows little sign of inspired insights, or, on the other, because it yields little of the density of texture which we tend to admire so much. Not only is the style a fit vehicle for the content (I am aware of the oversimplification) but it often makes the sort of imaginative demand that we seek in poetry. Here is a passage of natural description from **'To Sir Robert Wroth'**:

The mowed meddowes, with the fleeced sheepe,
   And feasts, that either shearers keepe;
The ripened eares, yet humble in their height,
   And furrowes laden with their weight,
The apple-harvest, that doth longer last;
   The hogs return'd home fat from mast;
The trees cut out in log; and those boughs made
   A fire now, that lent a shade!

> [ll. 39-46]

The corn, although ripe and high, is humble because its weight makes it bow and because it functions to feed Man, while the trees provide him with first shade and later heat. Jonson is trying to convey a sense of a satisfying Man-Nature relationship and he does this through smooth and balanced rhythms. The sensuousness of the passage from which this extract is taken is as apt here as it would be inapt in most of Jonson's work and is far more important than any intellectual perception we may have about the relationship in question. We are made to feel, as well as to perceive, that the relationship exists and matters. Later

in the same poem there is another kind of imaginative demand:

Goe enter breaches, meet the cannons rage,
   That they may sleepe with scarres in age.
And shew their feathers shot, and cullors torne,
   And brag, that they were therefore borne.
Let this man sweat, and wrangle at the barre,
   For every price, in every jarre,
And change possessions, oftner with his breath,
   Then either money, warre, or death. . . .

> [ll. 69-76]

More by the rhythms than by direct statement Jonson re-invokes the folly and confusion of the life described at the beginning of the poem, and the even movement of the nature-passage just mentioned is replaced by a more disjointed motion, which brings out strongly the erratic nature of this kind of life and the contrast between energy expended and result obtained. Here again, the verse is embodying the imagined experience.

What does all this amount to? As already hinted it amounts to an attempt at the convincing communication of an ethical viewpoint, one which is not original but nevertheless coherent and consistently held and which has validity. The validity springs from its humanity and emphasis upon man as a social creature with social responsibilities: the fact that the strands which make up Jonson's ethical viewpoint are largely derivative, commonplaces of English, Roman or Greek thought, increases the validity because they represent centuries of thought and experience. We have seen that the ethical viewpoint is communicated less by discursive reasoning than by exactness of description and accumulation of detail, to which we must add restriction of the associative potential of words. The result is a kind of verse which is active and concrete, with a life which comes from simplification and restricted resonance. It is verse which makes no attempt to embody the full variety and uncertainty of experience, and hence has little use for such devices as irony, paradox and ambiguity. Eliot rightly argued that Jonson's is a genuine created world, but L. C. Knights's remark that 'Exclusion was the condition of Jonson's achievement' [*A Guide to English Literature,* ed. B. Ford, II, 1956] makes the vital point—to create an imagined world Jonson had to simplify. I am inclined to see the reason for this less in some deficiency in Jonson than as an inevitable consequence of having an ethical system regulating his selection and treatment of material. Simplification is a condition of his achievement, and in case too much should be made of this it may be as well to remember that Jonson's simplification is only an extreme form of any artistic attempt.

In the satirical poems this simplification is obvious enough, for selection and exaggeration is basic in satire, where all things must be black or white, with the black stressed, for if satire admitted the moral complexity of life it would cease to shock. But Jonson is not only a satirist, for he pays considerable attention to what he considers morally good, using similar simplification to describe this:

And such a force the faire example had,
  As they that saw
The good, and durst not practise it, were glad
  That such a Law
Was left yet to Mankind:
                              [*The Under-wood* LXX, ll. 117-21]

What Jonson speaks of in his poetry constitutes a created world because of the consistency and coherence already mentioned. Considering the bulk of his verse this is a remarkable fact, but it is more important to realise that the creation and sustaining of this world depends largely upon the restriction of the emotive and associational power of words. Such power leads naturally to complexity and this would introduce doubts and questions to a world which only exists by their exclusion. This in turn means that, almost by definition, Jonson is involved in a kind of poetry which must severely restrict the use of some of the poetic attributes most emphasized by modern critics. What is lost is the complexity and ambiguity of Shakespeare's world, and even of Donne's, where more of the full range of human experience is present (both in total and at any given moment) than in Jonson's world. But it is tempting to draw an obvious conclusion too readily, because the Jonsonian world illuminates certain areas of the real one more intensely because of the narrow focus and more emphatically because of the distortions. The best illustration is from the plays. Of course Volpone is inhuman, but his inhumanity depends upon the exaggeration of some human traits and the omission of others. A comparison of Volpone and Shylock which concludes that the latter is the greater creation because more human would be both correct and beside the point, because if Shylock is more human it is also true that Volpone shows us more of Man's capacity to exploit Man and is the more striking example of what happens when the humane virtues are ignored. If Volpone ever made the appeal to our sympathy which Shylock does in the trial scene of *The Merchant of Venice* the impact of Jonson's play would be diminished at once. It is only because the greed of Voltore, Corvino and Corbacchio is so absolute, and Volpone and Mosca are so faithless, selfish and ruthless, that the play is such a terrifying parable.

But the poems also illustrate that the simplification in Jonson serves a purpose. At its simplest this is evident in the brutality of the epigram **'On Spies'**:

> Spies, you are lights in State, but of base stuffe,
> Who, when you have burnt yourselves down to
>   snuffe,
> Stinke, and are throwne away. End faire enough.
>   [*Epigrammes* LIX]

We have heard enough about the modern spy to imagine that his Elizabethan counterpart was probably the same sad mixture of twisted idealism and greed, but Jonson allows us to see only the sordidness and expendability. The candle-image is made brutally one-sided but it illustrates certain aspects of the Spy's business with a degree of force which springs directly from the suppression of other aspects. We might also consider whether the impact of 'Stinke' (depending so much on placing), the contempt

of 'End faire enough' (depending so much on the rhyme), the compressed irony of 'lights in state', and the manner in which the potential associations of the candle-image are restricted (for candles give a pleasing light and rich shadows) do not constitute a real poetic achievement.

In a more complex way the selection and compression of detail in the satirical epistles evokes with great power, the frenzied futility of a life lived only on the surface:

> As if a Brize were gotten i' their tayle,
> And firke, and jerke, and for the Coach-man raile,
> And jealous each of other, yet thinke long
> To be abroad chanting some baudie song,
> And laugh, and measure thighes, then squeake,
>   spring, itch,
> Do all the tricks of a saut Lady Bitch. . . .
>   [*The Under-wood* XV, ll. 71-6]

Although this is a far from fair picture of humanity, or of any individual, the unfairness—mainly through accumulation of active belittling verbs—makes it a very effective expression of how crudely mechanical and inhuman our life can be. The poem, as a whole, extends our experience of ourselves in the manner of Juvenal or Breughel, or as Gillray does with the brutality of his cartoons.

I have suggested that there is a similar kind of valid simplification in Jonson's description of what he sees as morally good. This description often occurs in his complimentary poems, a *genre* in which we do not expect measured criticism, but Jonson is unusual in that the qualities he celebrates are always those which belong to his own ethical position: he never praises one man for qualities condemned in another and never praises actions or attributes which, on other evidence, he would normally condemn. This consistency, together with the deep personal feeling for a set of ethical beliefs, gives Jonson's complimentary verse a sense of conviction which it would otherwise lack. Nevertheless, the convention of the *genre* whereby only the good is mentioned, and the fact that the good celebrated refers outside the individual concerned to an ethical code which is by definition generalised, means that human material is simplified and idealised, so that morally good qualities stand out, like caricature in reverse:

> Jephson, thou man of men, to whose lov'd name
> All gentrie, yet, owe part of their best flame!
> So did thy vertue enforme, thy wit sustaine
> That age, when thou stood'st up the master-braine:
> Thou wert the first, mad'st merit know her strength,
> And those that lack'd it, to suspect at length,
> 'Twas not entayl'd on title.
>   [*Epigrammes* CXVI]

This is very ordinary Jonson, and in praise of an almost-forgotten man: it would be easy to leave it at that, except that the exaggerations contribute to a statement of one of Jonson's firmest beliefs (that merit and title are not synonymous) and that the assurance of the rhythms and weight of the language (entail, inform, sustain) communicate a seriousness which goes beyond mere flattery.

In a more ambitious poem like **'To Penshurst'** simplification operates in a less obvious way. The poem is Jonson's most successful attempt to create in verse his belief in moral good attained and sustained in society, but he makes no effort to convey a total impression of life at Penshurst. Instead he idealizes it. There is, of course, a firm grasp of physical detail, but the result is a firmly realized ideal, for Jonson presents no reservations and the only hints of anything non-ideal are there for contrast. There is exaggeration (especially in the description of the fish), while the attitude of the country people to the great house and the account of the Sidneys' hospitality are both clearly simplified. In the same way, the descriptions of the family-life at Penshurst and of the children's education are miniatures of Elizabethan ideals. It could be demonstrated that each of the aspects of Penshurst which Jonson emphasizes relates to a contemporary belief or problem: the poem's greatness is largely in the way in which Jonson has presented the ideal in active and precise detail. We see the ideal in operation and are almost convinced of its practicability, but the achievement is, of necessity perhaps, one of exclusion.

If my discussion of the qualities of Jonson's poetry, and of how these are used, is accepted, it follows that to demand a different kind of poetry, and to censure Jonson for not providing it, involves rejection of what his poetry, with its characteristic features of simplification and exaggeration, achieves. We cannot—as I hope I have made clear—distinguish between Jonson's style and his concerns, for the former is a condition of the latter. To say that Jonson's verse is poor poetry because it lacks 'inspiration', or because it is without that particular density of texture which we indicate by such words as 'ambiguity' and 'association' is to say that what is achieved as a result of these limitations is not sufficient to compensate for them.

At this point I begin to think of babies and bathwater, but let us put the 'inspiration' and 'ambiguity *et al.*' views as strongly as possible, before setting Jonson's achievement against them. For present purposes we may, I think, link them. Both point to a type of language which can and does communicate insights which impress us as true, but which are incapable of scientific proof, by a subtle, supremely delicate, use of words and rhythm. This use of language is able to give some degree of expression to the ineffable by exploiting facets of language (ambiguity, irony, paradox, association, rhythmical linking) which are usually seen as weaknesses in discursive usage. The theory of inspiration stresses the actual apprehension of non-scientific truth, while the modern critic of poetic texture emphasizes the embodying of such apprehension in word and rhythm. In neither case is Jonson an obvious poet to illustrate the relevant activity: he makes few apparent attempts to raid the unconscious or to achieve the startling but convincing insight, and the texture of his verse does not respond very much to searches for paradox, association, etc. The latter fact, in particular, suggests that Jonson is not after the sudden breakthrough or the moment of vision. Instead he makes a constant effort to embody in verse a coherent view of life based on ethical distinctions, and the result is a created world, simplified from the actual, but seldom untrue to aspects of

it and therefore always relevant to it. The relevance is of a valuable kind because the simplification and exaggeration of Jonson's poetic world highlights and probes aspects of the actual, leading to insights which spring directly from the application of a firmly-held ethical view to the society in which Jonson lived. Again, these insights are only possible because of the simplification: they do not occur in spite of it. Much of Shakespeare's appeal may lie in his extraordinary ability to set ethical values against individuals and situations, but this does not alter Man's need to accept some standards as conditionally true, and to guide his life by the analysis of it in accordance with these standards, Jonson's achievement is to show this process in action, by embodying the standards in concrete terms and by evoking a sense of their absence.

The achievement is an important one, but it may not be clearly poetic, and our view of this point will depend on how we define that word. I should prefer to put the matter negatively. If the type of textual density of which I have spoken is an essential criterion of the poetic Jonson is only a poet occasionally, and the same is true if the poetic must include the faculty of the startling insight. But the inspiration theory is notoriously difficult to be exact about and textual density is too exclusive a standard. I am happier with the remarks of T. E. Hulme:

> There are two things to distinguish, first the particular faculty of mind to see things as they really are, and apart from the conventional ways in which you have been trained to see them.... Second, the concentrated state of mind, the grip over oneself which is necessary in the actual expression of what one sees. To prevent one falling into the conventional curves of ingrained technique, to hold on through infinite detail and trouble to the exact curve you want. Wherever you get this sincerity, you get the fundamental quality of good art [*Speculations,* 1949].

Jonson certainly has this 'fundamental quality': his integrity to the experience he is trying to communicate, the honesty of the matter-and-manner relationship in his verse, and his notable sense of linguistic appropriateness make him an important poet, more so than is commonly realised and more so than some more fashionable writers.

Fred Inglis   (essay date 1969)

SOURCE: "Jonson the Master: Stones Well Squared," in *The Elizabethan Poets: The Making of English Poetry from Wyatt to Ben Jonson,* Evans Brothers Ltd., 1969, pp. 127-56.

[*In the following essay, Inglis investigates Jonson's love, religious, and social poetry in relation to the facts of the poet's life.*]

Given the eminence I ascribe to Jonson, it seems right that this [essay] should open with a brief biography. But the decision is not only a critical one; Jonson occupies a position of unusual historical importance, and since we lack so much of the biographical evidence for Shakespeare whose career would be important in similar ways, Jonson's life is one of the few of which we can describe enough to know what life was like for a full-time professional in the world of letters. For Jonson, like Shakespeare, lacked Sidney's advantages of birth and ignored the particular aspirations of Ralegh or Donne. After his early years he was a full-time writer, and he was fiercely proud of it and censorious of amateurs; he was neither a churchman nor a politician (which is not to say he neglects political and theological action). He is an early representative of spectacular success in a new social group—the independent writers, though his independence, which was vigorously temperamental as well as social, was qualified by patronage, censorship, and the powers of the aristocracy.

The success he won depended in his youth on access to social opportunity. One or two literary historians have made much of Jonson's origins as a bricklayer, and this may be misleading. His father, who died a month before Jonson's birth in 1572, was a clergyman; his stepfather was a master-bricklayer, and as a craft-master a man of some social standing. None the less it would seem that his concerns were strictly non-intellectual, for after Jonson had been sent (sponsored apparently by a family friend) to the great London grammar school at Westminster, his stepfather removed him shortly before he would have entered the sixth form to proceed to Oxford or Cambridge. The record of his life between leaving school and turning up in the London theatre in 1597 is rather blurred. He was briefly a soldier in the Flemish wars which lingered on through the last two decades of the century and which killed Sidney. No doubt he enlisted when he was hard up, but from his acquaintance Drummond's report and his own **Epigrams "107"** and **"108"** he was a forthright, competent soldier. During the missing years he also married a wife whom he later left, crisply describing her to Drummond as 'a shrew, yet honest', and fathered the two children whose deaths, at six months and seven years, prompted the two finest short epitaphs in the language.

In 1598, after joining the famous manager Henslowe's company in London, Jonson arrived dramatically in the news: his play *Every Man in His Humour* won a striking success, and he was prosecuted for murder. The play was the first of a line of vivid, original and penetrating comedies, each (apart from the last two or three) remarkable for boisterous knockabout and also for moral stringency solidly there in the clear, penetrating light which the judgment of the plays sheds upon human affairs. We cannot consider the plays here, but it is important to say that, in all their exuberance and inventiveness of characterisation one never loses sight of their maker and his steady scrutiny of moral behaviour. The tone of the plays and of the poems is extraordinarily consistent, and it is one which, while taking high delight in the peculiarities of the subject, is always poised to move easily into judgment. It is magisterial but never frosty. Jonson's moral judgments, which may be highly-coloured and angry, or may be coolly judicious, arise from his boundless vitality, his keen sense of actual living. It is not surprising that Dickens admired Jonson's plays so much, and the plays and poems are an entity; the work is the man.

The man was often an uncomfortable person to have around. Innumerable figures in his plays lampoon lesser rivals of the time, and he attacks them not only for stupidity and incompetence, but also for brute ignorance of the classical texts Jonson learned at Westminster and in which he so fully saturated his intelligence throughout his working life. The great teacher, classicist and historian William Camden taught Jonson at Westminster and, as that moving brief tribute **"To Camden" ("Epigram 14")** makes clear, Camden remained teacher and friend to Jonson for many years. Jonson remade the tradition of the ancient classics in his own terms and with tremendous intensity; he made the breadth and variety of that tradition his own possession, and it grew with him according to the lineaments of his personality. So in his work a whole tradition—the great tradition of Christian humanism—utters through a distinctive and inimitable voice.

Just how broad and varied is the work we can only see if we read through the canon—plays, masques and poems, summarised and commented on during his last bedridden years between about 1630 and 1637 in his prose commonplace book, *Timber, or Discoveries*. The greatest comedies, *Volpone* (1606), *The Alchemist* (1612), *The Silent Woman* (1609) and *Bartholomew Fair* (1614), receive their acknowledgement as a part of literature; the extremely powerful political drama *Sejanus* (1605) is underrated and deserves more reading: the stately Court masques which Jonson provided for his admiring patron King James, all of which contain bold, rich and sometimes lovely poems, are scarcely read at all. Yet they are a large part of Jonson's work, and no adequate appraisal of his craftsmanship, as well as that part of him which enjoyed sumptuousness and splendour, is possible without at least a reading of the *Masque of Beauty* (1608) and *The Golden Age Restored* (1615-16). In spite of the extent of his work and widespread ignorance of so much of it, I would argue that one comes most definitely to the heart of his greatness in a close scrutiny of the poems, and that this opinion, as the conversations with Drummond and *Timber* imply, would have been Jonson's as well. The rest of the work is part of his plenitude and vitality, but if the case for the short poem is secure and if it does provide best for the poet's gifts, then Jonson's poems supply the essential evidence for the critic, the historian, and the human being.

Jonson's manifold humanity becomes explicit in the poems. In part this explicitness is merely anecdotal and, though of absorbing autobiographical interest, not really a part of our study. Thus, after his satire on the trendsetters and the swinging young charlatans-about-London *The Poetaster* was performed in 1601, the uproar which followed obliged him to publish a palliating prologue. But the prologue was as bluntly outspoken and independent as the play, and Jonson (as he well knew) appeased nobody. The same bluntness transpires after the flop of *The New Inn* in 1629 when he published the **"Ode to Himself,"** fulminating bitterly upon the grossness of his critics and the persecution of his gifts. Time and again Jonson had to call upon his patrons for rescue from the embarrassment incurred by his own proper failure to mitigate censure of the stupid, arrogant or wicked. He spoke out without compromise, and made the payment demanded. There was probably an element of deliberate self-sacrifice in all this, as there must be in anyone who sets up as a candid, incorruptible moral critic, as there must be perhaps in any kind of lonely hero. And there is no doubt that Jonson was such a hero. The age which lacks its Ben Jonson, its Dr. Johnson, its Charles Dickens, its F. R. Leavis, has no conscience, and its moral sense atrophies.

But what matters to us is not the actual historical occasions, though these are fascinating, but the poems in which the history is grasped in terms of moral realities. These poems delineate the moral pattern latent within the accidents of his life, and construct from them a generalised coherence. In saying that, I do not mean that he falsified his life in the interests of an ideal order of experience, but that the details and the proper names in the poems don't finally matter. What matters is that the poems are rooted in a real life; the experience and the personality from which they grow are solid and deep, and in recognising this, we recognise the rare integrity which can so put the truth of the poems beyond question. Jonson's poems provide a case in which we know from the art what the man was like, and the qualities realised in the art are those of a remarkably strong man, generous and abundant in his life, not gifted in speculative dialectic nor a glittering wit, but direct, independent, loyal and plainspoken. Thus it is affirmative evidence which the context of the poems gives us. Jonson became the leader of a literary club, having long been the magnetic centre of literary London as it met in the intellectual public houses. The club called itself 'The Tribe of Ben' and the quality of the poems it provoked makes it clear how gaping a distance lies between it and (say) the intellectual gossip-mongers of colour-supplement London. 'The Tribe of Ben' counted fine poets like Carew, Godolphin and Herrick among its number, and among the rest some of the most penetrating intelligences of the time—Lord Falkland, William Cavendish, Sir Kenelm Digby. It met for food, drink, and talk at the feet of the master, and the terms of its relationships were such as to provide rich and large material for poetry. The human contact signalled in **"An Epistle, Inviting a Friend to Supper"** deserves cherishing. There seems no reason why such experience should not persist.

[Jonson's] poems are rooted in real life; the experience and the personality from which they grow are solid and deep, and in recognizing this, we recognize the rare integrity which can so put the truth of the poems beyond question.

—Fred Inglis

Jonson was the last of the great Elizabethans. He *was* the tradition to which the new poets turned, and his statements carried an oracular weight. The prose commonplaces in *Timber* and the notes Drummond made during Jonson's visit to his Scottish home near Edinburgh in 1618 (Jonson

walked there and back, from London, and stopped, fairly enough, each way in Darlington to buy new boots) serve as commentary both to the historical context in which the poems were written, and to their literary intention. There is not space to quote extensively from *Timber* or the *Conversations.* . . . A handful of remarks must serve to represent their characteristic inflexion and the tips they offer as to how to read both Jonson's and any other poetry, and to indicate how Jonson himself went to work, and what were his points of reference. Drummond thinly notes that in the first place Jonson was 'jealous of every word and action of those about him (especially after drink which is one of the elements in which he liveth)' (*Conversations 19*). The closest work and arguing went with canary wine as much as did the parties in the Devil Inn and the theatres. One recollection is challenging:

> his opinion of verses
>   that he wrote all his first in prose, for so his
> master Camden had learned him.
>   That verses stood by sense without either
>   colours or accent,
>   which yet other times he denied.
>
>   (15)

It sorts well with what we can see in his poems that they should start out from prose beginnings—as Ezra Pound wrote, 'poetry should be at least as well written as prose'. The poems intend a statement, and the original force of that statement inhere first in its 'sense', and if in Jonson's case the distinctive 'accent' of his 'sense' is inseparable from the sense itself, yet his deliberate strength is first a matter of moral force so that 'colours', figures of speech and elegance of numbers are subordinate. It is consistent that Jonson felt 'couplets to be the bravest sort of verses especially when they are broken and that cross rhymes and stanzas . . . were all forced' (I), and from this judgment is follows that 'Donne for not keeping of accent deserved hanging' (3) and that although 'he esteemeth John Donne the first poet in the world in some things' (7) 'Donne himself for not being understood would perish' (12). Jonson always intends clarity and the cutting away of ambiguity and obscurity from around the lines of the verse. The couplet makes for such hardness and precision, hence his preference (though Jonson, like most of his contemporaries, was a virtuoso in stanza forms).

There is only agreeable gossip value in pursuing Jonson's impenitent self-esteem—'That next himself only Fletcher and Chapman could make a masque' (3) and (accurately) 'he was better versed and knew more Greek and Latin than all the poets in England'. The last anecdotes ring with utter authenticity of his pigheaded bluntness and his robust independence, for 'he never esteemed of a man for the name of a Lord' (14):

> Jones [Inigo, with whom Jonson collaborated in Court masques] having accused him for naming him behind his back a fool, he denied it; 'But', says he, 'I said he was one arrant knave and I avouch it'.
>
>   (17)

Being at the end of my Lord Salisbury's table with Inigo Jones and demanded by my lord why he was not glad, 'My Lord', said he, 'you promised I should dine with you, but I do not . . . '

(13)

These last extracts do no more than endorse the tones of the more relevant literaryobservations we have seen. In turning to *Timber,* we find the same tones meditating far more serious issues. It is notable that in dozens of places *Timber* is a rewriting, idea for idea, of some of the great classical critics and theorists of literature, particularly as they were rephrased for the Renaissance by the critic Vives whose primers ran into dozens of editions and were certainly among the textbooks at Westminster School. But *Timber* is more than an annotation of Vives's theories: it is the redefinition of Vives in Jonson's cadences and with the weight of his experience behind the sentences. We do not need Drummond's reminder to know how close lay the rhythms of Jonson's verse and prose.

The quality of *Timber* cannot, I suppose, be fully judged without a reading of Vives's *De Disciplinis* (1531), a grand formulation of all that was best in classical humanism. But the matter opens again the question of Jonson's relation to his history, and the way the history and the man moved together. I quote Wallace Stevens's noble poem "The House Was Quiet and the World Was Calm" in the last chapter during an attempt to define our understanding of a particular poetic tradition, and the decisive choices we make in charting our tradition. The analysis I propose may apply to Jonson, in *Timber* and in many poems. The scrapbook of quotations is tightened and compacted beneath the conviction of the writer. Each reminiscence from Vives moves into the bone of Jonson's being; the teacher becomes the pupil, and the pupil surpasses the teacher in passion and intelligence. Thus continuity holds through. It is as though we read a gifted modern poet whose mind has sharply altered according to his response to a great modern critic. The whole business of 'influence' is much subtler than our crude use of the term allows. It is not a matter of 'agreement' with so-and-so; it is a matter of possession, after which 'agreement'—or disagreement—is redundant. Your sensibility has changed, while it is still your own. You borrow the vocabulary, the inflexions and gestures of another man, even, but they become yours, and filled with your identity. So in these splendid passages it is Jonson's voice we hear, and simultaneously that of the moral history of the language.

Early on he writes, 'A good life is a main argument'; it is in keeping that the metaphor for life comes from logic. A little later he proceeds:

A man should so deliver himself to the nature of the subject whereof he speaks, that his hearer may take knowledge of his discipline with some delight: and so apparel fair and good matter that the studious of elegancy be not defrauded; redeem arts from their rough

and braky seats . . . to a pure, open and flowery light, where they may take the eye and be taken by the hand.

There follows the famous passage applauded by Eliot (and, improbably, Swinburne) in which Jonson rehearses Vives's instruction to scrutinise but not worship the classics. "Truth lies open to all; it is no man's several. A gift of the verse here bequeathed to the prose is the habit of concise and incisive generalisation. And then, a fine and embattled stance struck for independence:

I am neither author, or fautor [patron] of any sect . . . if I have anything right, I defend it as truth's, not mine . . . it profits not me to have any man fence, or fight for me, to flourish, or take a side. Stand for truth, and 'tis enough.

It is the plainness, the forceful cadences which rescue this from platitude, and make it the writer's own. So, writing of acts of courtesy, he gives an aphorism roots in the tricks of his own London:

he that doth them merely for his own sake is like one that feeds his cattle to sell them: he hath his horse well-dressed for Smithfield.

Horsemeat was just as nasty then as now.

The passages that count most describe the right style for speech, in verse or prose; but these passages mingle easily with those on moral behaviour, and at times (as they should be) the remarks which describe how to live well cannot be separated from how to write well. And even where there is a distinction, good writing never fails to be commensurate with values.

Others, . . . in composition are nothing, but what is rough and broken . . . They would not have it run without rubs, as if that style were strong and manly that struck the ear with a kind of unevenness. These men err not by chance, but knowingly, and willingly. . . .

Thus he admires one who 'never forced his language, nor went out of the highway of speaking,' one (and he might be describing himself) whose 'language was . . . nobly censorious. No man ever spake more neatly, more pressly, more weightily, or suffered less emptiness, less idleness, in what he uttered. No member of his speech but consisted of the (*sic*) own graces. If we take this last, telling judgement and assimilate it to the following magnificent extract, we have a set of criteria against which to test Jonson and the finest English authors. Only masters pass.

The chief virtue of a style is perspicuity . . . A strict and succinct style is that where you can take away nothing without loss, and that loss to be manifest. The brief style is that which expresseth much in little . . . The congruent and harmonious fitting of parts in a sentence hath almost the fastening and force of knitting, and connection: as in stones well squared, which will rise strong a great way without mortar.

THE POEMS

As with Shakespeare's sonnets, it is hard to forbear quoting from *Timber,* I have held over one memorable pair of aphorisms to open discussion of the poems. He writes:

> Language most shows a man: speak that I may see thee . . . No glass renders a man's form or likeness so true as his speech.

I have spent some time describing the context of Jonson's work in order to recreate the remarkable force of the man and to suggest the points at which he felt his emotional and intellectual convictions as being at ease with the possibilities of the age. For his finest poems seem to me tothose which cherish and celebrate the most admirable parts of life, which make a statement about its richest sources, those which ensure continuity. Yet, as we have seen, Jonson was and is known for the harshness of his strictures upon contemporary life, for the blunt candour with which he spoke out against viciousness, malice and triviality, and in a few poems, for the traditional stoicism with which he put aside the claims of this world. In each case the language, as he asked, was true to the man, and the man was always amazingly true to his own sense of identity. The contradictions, as in all of us, were overcome as best he could; Jonson's finest poems meant that he reconciled the strong claims in him made by his classical traditions and by his immediate, vivid life in London. He brought to a full realisation a sense of history and a sense of the moment, and these issued in a statement to the future, in an offering made to posterity. And the statement is more than just a manifesto; it is the sum of a man's experience, deep, strong and engaged, which issues in the central parts of the work. Such an account would fit, I suppose, any great poet to whom we refer instinctively as a sure guide in charting our lives, but the example of Jonson is unusually pressing. He is himself so conscious of the poet's function, so determined that morality shall find its definitive utterance in poetry, and that the discovery, after strenuous exertion, shall come as a discovery of the right speech. It is this search and the consequent discoveries which concentrate his work. The job in hand is to find a kind of speech, a style in which to talk about ethical behaviour; it is the only honourable vocation for a man. Such a view of literature is as noble as it may be, and it belies as irrelevant the struggles of many subsequent poets to find subjects or forms. I do not wish to reduce the difficulties of being a poet, for they are many, but they may sometimes lie nearer home than some desperate endeavours suggest. Jonson saw the business as being explicitly moral and as so developing the powers of poetry that moral argument was sustained in the most deliberate and straightforward manner possible—a manner in which richness, subtlety and power proceed from the intelligence of the poet and not from the accidents of language or subject.

Now there are poems of Jonson's which treat a specific and local subject, and I shall admire one of these in particular, **"To Penshurst."** It may be objected that there he had a subject to hand—fine and rooted living—which later

poets are denied. But as the poem reveals, Jonson uses Penshurst as the actual approximation to an ideal of civilisation, and moves surely from personal to impersonal tribute, from description to celebration. In so far as we are heirs to the great humanist ideas of the Renaissance—as I believe we are, though the ideas have passed through the transfiguration of romantic socialism—then what **"To Penshurst"** offers us is not regret for lost ways of life, but an example of how to value life. The poet should speak out against what he hates, as Jonson does, but above that his duty is to lives and ways of life which he may define and celebrate. Jonson lives for us because he relishes the

> Jonson's finest poems meant that he reconciled the strong claims in him made by his classical traditions and by his immediate, vivid life in London.
>
> *—Fred Inglis*

duty. In speaking of this material Jonson is primarily making his own life, and making his life was to do with planning his work. We therefore return to the central issue which is to discover the unalterable way to say what must be said. Thiscalls for a knowledge of the history of literature and ideas, for experience of the actualities of one's time, for a solid grasp on the relationships between ideas and action, and between action and a style of writing; it calls for a command of technical detail, since slight technical details record the distinctions in moral perception. It therefore calls for genius. Hidden in **"A Celebration of Charis (I)"** are ten lines of Jonson's which render the task he saw for himself, and which in their beauty overcome it:

> Though I now write fifty years,
> I have had, and have my peers:
> Poets, though divine, are men;
> Some have loved as old again.
> And it is not always face,
> Clothes or fortune gives the grace,
> Or the feature, or the youth;
> But the language and the truth,
> With the ardour and the passion,
> Gives the lover weight and fashion.

I shall treat Jonson's poems in three groups: first, the slighter poems he wrote according to more conventional tastes than his own but for which he is well known and a few of which are as beautiful as any of his contemporaries'; second, poems, sometimes 'occasional', sometimes without formal prompting, which treat ethical or religious themes; third, poems arising from particular social contacts, with friends, patrons, fellow poets, or enemies. Obviously, all kinds of other groupings are feasible; one could work through the various volumes of the complete poems: *Epigrams, The Forest, The Underwood,* and the ungathered poems (a part of the complete poems was published with Jonson's preparation in 1616; the remainder three years after his death, in 1640). One could take the various forms one by one: epigrams, odes, songs, epistles and so on. Or one could just consider the best. In the groupings I propose there are a very few poems I would like to discard, and a few which are flawed; Jonson's greatest poems emerge about equally from his moral reflections and from his social life, and as they are great, they transcend a particular occasion, shake off the 'appropriate' manner, and speak of major matters in Jonson's major style. The poems are brief and various; the range of their experience is wide and their wisdom is profound and assured; Jonson omits the further reaches of experience and the vertiginous glimpses of the unknown we find in Shakespeare; if he neglects numinous mystery, none the less he holds on to values and reality with the peculiar patience of genius. His metaphysics (and they are there) are not those of Donne, the dazzling casuist, the lavish, incredibly rapid dialectician. Jonson's mind is 'mere English', working for clarity, for the empiricism of the English spirit, for a sceptical accuracy. The poems in which he achieves what he wants are also warm and human—no one could dilute Jonson's humanity. They are among the greatest poems in our literature.

Love Poems

The smaller love lyrics do as well as all that has gone before. One might suggest that Jonson took the native style as his point of departure for love poems in which to rival the Petrarchans, except that he has gone a long way beyond the bluntness of Gascoigne. He has learned the graces and the flexibilities of Sidney, he can match Campion for mischief and sensuous delicacy. The famous 18th-century setting of **"Drink to Me only with Thine Eyes"** with its fat, lush melody, outrages all the poem's tact, its declared lightness of tone. Reading the poem, and forgetting (if we can) the tune, is to encounter an act of affectionate and ironically indulgent courtesy. Comparable virtues bring to life the famous love song **"To Celia"** from *Volpone*, inviting, in the manner of a score of other, of Marvell's "To His Coy Mistress" and Herrick's "To The Virgins," the lady to oblige him while youth is on her side. . . . [These] poems all derive from Catullus's *Vivamus, mea Lesbia, atque amemus,* and we may grasp (even without knowing Latin) how Jonson even more than his contemporaries was soaked in the ancient classics. This saturation, as *Timber* makes clear, means that the Latin issues not as stilted translation or as pedantry, but as a presence which informs the writing even when that writing is at its easiest and most idiomatic. Thus here the movement of the poem is unmistakably real and independent of sponsors; it is brisk and alert as it gives out the coolness of Jonson's persuasion:

> Come my Celia, let us prove
> While we may, the sports of love;
> Time will not be ours for ever,
> He, at length, our good will sever.
> Spend not then his gifts in vain.
> Suns that set may rise again,
> But if once we lose this light,
> 'Tis with us, perpetual night.

Comparable but gentle and less licentious is another song **"To Celia"** in octosyllabic couplets. The previous one is ostensibly Volpone's; snatches of the next appear in *Volpone,* but as a whole it is independent. Again, the light playfulness is fully authentic. This is not a poem 'about' flirtation; it is the act of flirtation magically realised and, in the tone, placed and valued.

> Kiss me sweet: the wary lover
> Can your favours keep, and cover,
> When the common courting jay
> All your bounties will betray.
> Kiss again: no creature comes.
> Kiss, and score up wealthy sums
> On my lips . . .

Campion could not have bettered the amusement in Jonson's 'There you are!' when he wrote, 'Kiss again: . . .' He enforces the pause by the colon—then, 'no creature comes'. So, in abandonment and relief after the next 'kiss', the line soars right over the line-ending to 'lips' in the next. The refinement of this chaste style never falters, and any collection of Jonson's pieces in this vein would be ample enough to rival most poets whose reputation rests on their Courtly Love poetry alone. We do not find the passionate momentum of Shakespeare's sonnets in Jonson's love poetry, and this is partly because those subjects which pressed most heavily upon his creative powers did not emerge as love poetry. The stormy pleading of the sonnets strikes no answering note in Jonson's poetry.

The love poems do not confine themselves to mischief. The whole sequence **"A Celebration of Charis"** contains within its subtle couplets the quick, deft changes from disconsolation to delight and back. And in the fourth poem of the sequence, there occurs a stanza which is a touchstone for freshness and sharpness of imagery, speaking alike to Renaissance and Romantic criteria.

> Have you seen but a bright lily grow,
>   Before rude hands have touched it?
> Have you marked but the fall o' the snow
>   Before the soil hath smutched it?
> Have you felt the wool of the beaver?
>   Or swansdown ever?
> Or have smelt the bud o' the briar?
>   Or the nard in the fire?
> Or have tasted the bag of the bee?
> O so white! O so soft! O so sweet is she!

The radiant images are allowed to do their work without emphasis, enhanced only by the light touch of 'bright', the contrast of 'smutched'; the sensuous delight gathers to an ecstasy in the breathless rhythms of the second half of the stanza. Yet this is not really characteristic Jonson. We do not, as we may even with such a minute stylist as George herbert, think in Jonson's connection of original or daring imagery. Of course, there is a command of the musical resources of the language.

> Slow, slow, fresh fount, keep time with my salt tears;
>   Yet slower, yet; O faintly, gentle springs;

List to the heavy part the music bears,
　Woe weeps out her division when she sings.

The first line is utterly expert. The alliteration and the stresses are regularly struck yet so delayed and muted that they contribute only to the languour and loitering step of the line, and not at all to anything ponderous. The second line perfectly imitates the affected anguish of some fastidious conductor—'Yet slower, yet; O faintly, . . . '—as it also creates a tiny diversion in the plaintive melody. The song is a verbal equivalent of Dowland's wonderful *Lachrimae*. The varieties of speech-contour exactly suit the curve of feeling; Jonson's stanza-forms are as versatile as all the madrigalists'.

All the same, I think it is fair to say that in thinking of Jonson as an Elizabethan lyricist, we turn first to poems, sometimes from the masques, sometimes from elsewhere, of which **"The Hymn to Diana"** is representative:

Queen and huntress, chaste and fair,
Now the sun is laid to sleep,
Seated in thy silver chair
State in wonted manner keep:
　Hesperus entreats thy light,
　Goddess excellently bright.

Lay thy bow of pearl apart,
And thy crystal shining quiver;
Give unto thy flying hart
Space to breathe, how short soever,
　Thou that mak'st a day of night,
　Goddess excellently bright

This ritual liturgy belongs to the intricate stylisation of the masques, and it derives from the conventions of pastoral Petrarchanism and from Arcadia. The restraint and stateliness of this is Petrarchanism made public; Jonson catches exactly the hymnal simplicity needed for the procession which accompanies the queen. The profusion of Spenser is chastened; this language is at once silvered and ethereal and austerely controlled. Within the masque conventions, Jonson takes such writing with complete seriousness. His craftsmanship is impeccable. Yet it is not just Puritan to insist that in the end the convention is not serious, however professional the writer is about the writing. The chastity of the style is not won from writing this kind of thing, and however lovely it is, it is not as lovely as those poems of Campion's with more evident roots in the stuff of experience. These poems are part of Jonson's accomplishment, but he does not utter them from his depths.

One or two love poems come from the centre of the man. There is the famous **"On My Picture Left in Scotland"** which muses poignantly on his vanished physical charms and the failure of his verse to supplant the bright young Apollos. He glumly sees (though the total effect is more poised and deprecating than glum) that

　　　she cannot embrace,
My Mountain belly and my rocky face . . .

Religious Poems

But in turning from the love poems to the second group I marked out, the group which deals with ethical or religious themes, we move in the best examples from delicately minor poetry to work of outright greatness. I shall begin with one of the best, the poem **"To Heaven"**:

Good and great God, can I not think of Thee,
　But it must, straight, my melancholy be?
Is it interpreted in me disease,
　That, laden with my sins, I seek for ease?
O, be thou witness, that the reins dost know
　And hearts of all, if I be sad for show;
　And judge me after, if I dare pretend
　To aught but grace, or aim at other end.
　As thou art all, so be thou all to me,
First, midst, and last, converted One and Three;
　My faith, my hope, my love; and in this state,
　My judge, my witness, and my advocate.
　Where have I been this while exiled from thee?
　And whither rapt, now thou but stoop'st to me?
Dwell, dwell here still! O being everywhere,
　How can I doubt to find Thee ever here?
　I know my state, both full of shame and scorn,
　Conceived in sin, and unto labour born,
　Standing with fear, and must with horror fall,
And destined unto judgement, after all.
　I feel my griefs too, and there scarce is ground
　Upon my flesh to inflict another wound.
　Yet dare I not complain or wish for death
　With holy Paul, lest it be thought the breath
Of discontent; or that these prayers be
　For weariness of life, not love of thee.

(line 2. 'it must, straight, . . . ' i.e. onlookers think this. l. 3. The onlookers 'interpret in (him) disease . . . ' l. 5. reins: seat of emotion in Elizabethan physiology)

The style of this is plain and direct, as it is also sinewy and felicitous. The informing principle of the poem is expository, and the one objection that may be brought against it is that the poem starts out from a sense of personal affront. Jonson declares himself wearied by those who always interpret his moments of contemplation as moments of private melancholy. It is an appeal to God for vindication and it thus involves a touch of pique which taints the nobility of feeling. This fault apart, the styles and the matter are firm. The couplet has never been better handled; where Pope is most impressive there is likewise a breathtaking facility which puts gravity like this out of reach. Jonson's couplets are like 'stones well squared': they present a polished and impressive surface—there is no break in the texture. Yet the rhythmic control is never slack or in repose; he adjusts the subdued variations to the precise expression of the feeling. Thus in the first line the slight alliteration throws heavy, impressive weight on three of the first four syllables. Elsewhere the placing of the caesura consolidates the meaning, as in the last line where the essential opposition and paradox of the poem is held in balance, or as in lines 17-20 where the regular placing of the caesuras allows quiet but powerful feeling to accumulate in the repetition and to release itself in the long curve of line 20, halted in the finality, 'after all'. The triple units of lines 10-12 render the intellectual concept of the Trinity with exactitude and passion; the mystery of Three-in-One becomes immediate in the triple movements of single lines. A small device borrowed from the Petrarchans, such as 'everywhere'/'ever here' in 15-16, rises above a device, and becomes the only way to express the omnipresence of God. The poem states Jonson's own position with his habitual firmness: in line 17, 'I know', in line 21, 'I feel'; the movement of the couplets is assured, the argument confident, the tone crisp, and braced. But for all the steadiness of Jonson's stance, one cannot doubt its attendant grace and humility. The quickening of stresses in line 15, 'Dwell, dwell here still!' though logical ('where have I been . . . ?') has the suddenness of rapturous terror. The moment is overcome, andthe poet returns to the meditative statement of the behaviour open to him. Jonson faces the temptation of 'weariness of life' ('dare I not complain'), understands it, and puts it by; he overcomes gracelessness, and he wins, by command of the available arguments and checking them against experience, a stoic composure. Stoicism is not the only courage; it isn't even Jonson's only kind, but it is an honourable attitude, and here he gives it unforgettable expression. He transcends the exclusive truculence of Ralegh, the violence of feeling in some poems of Donne. **"To Heaven"** takes its place alongside the poems about death like Donne's "Hymn to God the Father" and George Herbert's "Church-Monuments" as living documents one can turn to endlessly; they uphold the high calling of the human mind.

These poems, and Jonson's with them, speak with the voice of the poet, and their power derives from his intelligence and his moral perception in an experience best understood by meeting it as straightforwardly as possible. Consequently, there is in such poems scarcely any imagery; the poem *is* its own image, and metaphor could do relatively little to help it. Control of diction and rhythm absorbs the poet. Another of Jonson's on a similar topic as **"To Heaven"** may, at the risk of repetition, illustrate the matter further. In **"To the World: A Farewell for a Gentlewoman, Virtuous and Noble"** Jonson gives his speech to a mature and disenchanted intelligence, commenting on the traps of her experience. Once more, the development is ordered by exposition; the metaphors are conventional, and the unifying principle is, apart from the argument, the attitude and tone of the speaker. The stanza form is one of the simplest in English: octosyllabic quatrains rhyming *abab,* yet the poem is in spite of the clarity not simple. The ease of manner, the mature acceptance of disillusion and death, rest upon a reality of felt experience which informs the poem. The cost exacted by life for maturity of attitude has been paid in full. The methods of Lord Vaux, Gascoigne, and Ralegh are now entire, replete with wisdom, subtle, sensitive, and definite. The last eight lines must suffice to demonstrate what the poem does. The language is typically lucid, the movement firm, the placing of the rhymes sure and relevant. The speaker knows where her identity lies and where her omissions, and she likewise turns, as we all do, back to the place where she belongs in order to meet the demands of time. There is no compromise, no stridency, no desperation.

> No, I do know that I was born
> To age, misfortune, sickness, grief;
> But I will bear these with that scorn
> As shall not need thy false relief.
> Nor for my peace will I go far,
> As wanderers do, that still do roam,
> But make my strengths, such as they are,
> Here in my bosom, and at home.

Other poems in this manner which deserve extremely close reading include **"The Mind of the Frontispiece to a Book"** (first printed in Ralegh's *The History of the World*), the **"Hymn to God the Father"**, the **"Epode"** 'Not to know vice at all . . .', and the faultless series of epitaphs. I shall close this brief examination of Jonson's religious poems by quoting the epitaph **"On My First Son"**, though the other, intolerably poignant epitaph **"On My First Daughter"** is no less piercing, closing as it does with this couplet:

> This grave partakes the fleshly birth—
> Which cover lightly, gentle earth.

Perhaps this next epitaph is more moving simply because his son was seven years old when he died, and his daughter only six months.

> Farewell, thou child of my right hand, and joy;
> My sin was too much hope of thee, loved boy.
> Seven years thou wert lent to me, and I thee pay,
> Exacted by thy fate, on the just day.
> O, could I lose all father, now! For why
> Will man lament the state he should envy?
> To have so soon 'scaped world's and flesh's rage,
> And, if no other misery, yet age!
> Rest in soft peace; and, asked, say: Here doth lie
> Ben Jonson his best piece of poetry—
> For whose sake, henceforth, all his vows be such,
> As what he loves may never like too much.

Again, Jonson plays off the closed, trim form of the couplets against the rhythms of speech. This poem seeks more immediately than is usual with Jonson to reconcile a conflict—between the personal pain at the loss of his son, and the consolations of Christian doctrine: 'For why/ Will man lament the state he should envy?' But man does, especially when he is a parent, and this poem records all the appropriate tenderness as well as the anguish. The poem is written in what *Timber* calls 'the concise style, which expresseth not enough, but leaves somewhat to be understood'; the phrase 'yet age!' is left for the reader to fill in; the question 'why will man lament?' is left unanswered: the poem finds it answerable. At the end, he can only turn upon the pain and vow to avoid such pain again by so disciplining himself as not to admit such love. It is a grim resolve. The composure won by this poem is won by repression and severity, and it is worth proposing that the resignation of poems like **"To the World"** and **"To Heaven"** is complemented in Jonson by a titanic generosity of spirit. He gave himself largely to the world, and was bruised so giving. The melancholy and the moroseness which he noted in himself (and parodied) came in those periods when he withdrew from the world in order to comprehend its cruelties. In the finest poems, the exuberance and the austerity come together and issue in the wise disillusion we have seen, or, more finely yet, in the unsentimental warmth and humane gratitude of active celebration. It is to poems of this kind that I now turn.

Social Poems

These poems arise from a variety of occasions. There are tributes paid to patrons, epistles to friends prompted by all kinds of causes some of which we have to guess at, and there are the writings specifically presented to 'The Tribe of Ben' which in one sense foreshadow the civil and sociable environment of the 18th-century coffee house, but which surpass the milieu of Dryden by a livelier as more profound justification for what they did. Jonson's poems for The Tribe, like (say) Carew's excellent reproach to the master beginning "Tis true (dear Ben) . . . ', carry within them not only social graces and ceremonies which are more than courtly, but also a grasp on the serious values, the sanctions without which the graces are frivolous games. Such attitudes made full and—if the word is not irretrievably disgraced—democratic contact possible. A man met another man openly, gladly.

The opening document for this sort of contact is the epistle **"Inviting a Friend to Supper."** It does not involve the intimacy of other poems to The Tribe—that will come—but it sets the easy, courteous frame of reference within which intimacy is possible. The gregariousness of the friends was not possessive; it permitted the distance which, though not aloof, is necessary to individual delicacy of organisation. Jonson would have felt the force of Henry James's declaration that:

> I believe only in absolutely independent, individual and lonely virtue, and in the serenely unsociable (or if need be at a pinch sulky and sullen) practice of the same; the observation of a lifetime having convinced me that no fruit ripens but under that temporarily graceless rigour . . .
>
> To John Bailey, 11 November 1912

The paradox is that Jonson, who is so often like his Augustan namesake Dr. Johnson, drew so much nourishment both from his solitude and his companionships. A tense balance of the two electrified his element. In the invitation, however, we see only the ease of company. Only by implication can we divine that such ease is the product of knowing how to speak to people without chumminess or reserve. The speech is hard to hit. Like all difficult art, you perfect it only by a combination of genius and civilisation. You begin here:

> Yet you shall have, to rectify your palate,
> An olive, capers, or some bitter salad
> Ushering the mutton; with a short-legged hen,
> If we can get her, full of eggs; and then
> Lemons, and wine for sauce . . .

The food is not everything; there is the talk:

> Howsoe'er, my man
> Shall read a piece of Virgil, Tacitus,
> Livy, or of some better book to us,
> Of which we'll speak our minds, amidst our meat;
> And I'll profess no verses to repeat . . .

And there is the drink—'which most doth take my muse and me . . . a pure cup of rich Canary wine'. But the evening will close, as it began, in comely moderation:

> Nor shall our cups make any guilty men,
> But at our parting, we will be as when
> We innocently met.

It is not merely Horation or hedonistic good-living Jonson is offering as a present; it issomething tougher than a wine and food society. The something else is invoked in this next poem where in honouring a marriage and recovery from a dangerous wound (apparently after the bridegroom has won his wife from a rival by duelling), Jonson tenders moral advice to a headstrong friend. He uses an ode-form but as we now expect transposes the high style of an ode into a key more friendly and, here, direct:

> High-spirited friend,
> I send nor balms nor cor'sives to your wound,
>   Your fate hath found
> A gentler and more agile hand to tend
> The cure of that which is but corporal,
> And doubtful days (which were named critical)
>   Have made their fairest flight,
>   And now are out of sight.
> Yet doth some wholesome physic for the mind
>   Wrapped in this paper lie,
> Which in the taking if you misapply,
>   You are unkind.
>   Your covetous hand,
> Happy in that fair honour it hath gained,
>   Must now be reined.
> True valour doth her own renown command
> In one full action; nor have you now more
> To do, than be a husband of that store.
>   Think but how dear you bought
>   This same which you have caught,
> Such thoughts will make you more in love with truth.
>   'Tis wisdom, and that high,
>   For men to use their fortune reverently,
>   Even in youth.

It is beautifully judged. The high rhetorical form is used to give the syntax hesitation and delicacy. This is spoken straightly, but with all the gentleness, affection and understanding in the world. The reproachful close of each stanza prefigures Herbert both in its judicious firmness and its mild cadence. The strong imperatives—'Must', 'Think'—check with the shifts of the form; the respectful candour with which the large terms—'truth', 'wisdom', 'valour'—are offered precludes priggishness. The lady is never directly spoken of, but in giving the advice Jonson manages at the same time to exclude her from any blame, and pay her the timely compliments concealed in 'gentler and more agile hand' and the oblique (but not bashful) references in the second stanza. It is a marvellous poem, and if today we cannot write one like it, then I suggest it is not because the movement of history (or whatever) has broken the concept of friendship, but simply because we do not try. And without civilising poems of this sort, we have no final standard by which to test our behaviour.

The many ideals latent in this poem abound in the epistles to his friends. Yet it misrepresents and abuses Jonson to speak as though one were hunting through his work for latent ideals. Each successful poem makes the ideals, the values and sanctions of an adult personality and a rich civilisation actual and vivid in a particular situation. It is one of Jonson's gifts to do this with a rare explicitness; the poems emerge from the life he led. He adopts no 'masks', no special *personae* worn for the poem, and then discarded. These procedures have their uses, but they shadow the poet in the poem. Jonson tries always to come at his utmost consistency and integrity of spirit in each one of his 'social' poems. He speaks from his full sense of himself to whoever it may be who listens. This means, given his imperfections, that he may be over-assertive or self-righteous in unseemly ways—the **"Ode to Himself"** is an example of this tendency. It means, as in several of the epigrams on Court figures, that he may be wantonly obscene or brutal, though sometimes the brutality may be called for, as in the savage epigram **"On Sir Voluptuous Beast,"** or that **"On Gut"**:

> *Gut* eats all day, and lechers all the night,
> So all his meat he tasteth over twice;
> And, striving so to double his delight,
> He makes himself a thoroughfare of vice.
> Thus in his belly can he change a sin,
> Lust it comes out, that gluttony went in.

A useful exercise in reading Elizabethan poetry would be to ponder the evidence of a training in logic, grammar, and rhetoric in this epigram. The finest 'social' poems, or poems of friendship, speak out with the same trenchancy in admiration of indispensable virtues. These poems not only recommend the virtues, they animate them; so that in reading the poem we experience the qualities. It is an active affair. So in the **"Epigram to Camden (14),"** a little awkwardly perhaps, he pays tribute to Camden's exemplary union of classical and modern scholarship:

> Camden, most reverend head, to whom I owe
> All that I am in arts, all that I know . . .
> Pardon free truth, and let thy modesty
> Which conquers all, be once o'ercome by thee.
> Many of thine this better could, than I,
> But for their powers, accept my piety.

Jonson bore witness, as a matter of honour, to his masters; he paid his dues to his pieties—it is a lesson worth learning now when the factions of contemporary intellectuals plagiarise under cover of toadying. Each time, Jonson's epistles sound out bravely and directly. Thus to John Selden, acknowledging his book received,

> I know to whom I write. Here, I am sure,
> Though I am short, I cannot be obscure.

The long tribute to the patronage of Sir Edward Sackville strikes a slightly more deferential note, yet Jonson is still (as we would expect) brisk and manly. The lines carry themselves with an erect assurance, as of a man who knows his worth:

> You cannot doubt but I, who freely know
> This good from you, as freely will it owe;
> And though my fortune humble me, to take
> The smallest courtesies with thanks, I make
> Yet choice from whom I take them; and would shame
> To have such do me good, I durst not name;
> They are the noblest benefits, and sink
> Deepest in man, of which when he doth think,
> The memory delights him more from whom
> Than what he hath received. Gifts stink from some
> They are so long a-coming, and so hard;
> Where any deed is forced, the grace is marred.

The personal note and the impersonal chime together; once again, what in other hands would be platitudes, here quicken to the strength and unshakable integrity of the man who speaks them. And so it is that we know from the art—in its organised and self-conscious fullness—what we would have admired in Jonson the man, had we known him. One could multiply the evidence. There is the striking **"Epitaph to Master Vincent Corbet"** in which lightness and gravity of touch justly combine in order to give us the subject, Corbet, and Jonson's valuation of him at the same time. There is the well-known, little-read and generous memorial to Shakespeare ('To draw no envy (Shakespeare) on thy name'). There is the handsome brevity of another poem to a patron, the epigram (76) on **"Lucy, Countess of Bedford,"** which demands quotation, though the poem is densely woven and selection must mutilate it. He describes his ideal patroness, and in a polished turn at the last couplet finds that the Countess fits his model:

> I meant she should be courteous, facile, sweet,
> Hating that solemn vice of greatness, pride;
> I meant each softest virtue there should meet,
> Fit in that softer bosom to reside.
>
> Only a learned and a manly soul
> I purposed her; that should, with even powers,
> The rock, the spindle, and the shears control
> Of destiny, and spin her own free hours.

It would be pedantic to say these things again were it not that Jonson's greatness has been sold so short. Once more, in the absence of developed metaphors, it is the mastery of tone and rhythmic control which resolves the poem. The style is entire, powerful and sensitive. The repetitions of 'I meant' make it clear that Jonson wishes to set his own mark on the poem, but he judges his own place in it. And while the terms of approbation are completely his own, especially in these trenchant lines—

I meant to make her fair and free and wise,
Of greatest blood, and yet more good than great—

his eye remains steadily upon the subject and does not turn aside either into little ceremonies or into decoration. The relevance, the intellectual closeness of the poem form his compliment. To be fully intelligent is to make his bow.

The last two poems I wish to discuss in this (roughly speaking) social group are the famous address **"To Penshurst,"** family seat of Sidney's brother and a centre of civilised discussion and thought, and the **"Elegy"** beginning 'Though beauty be the mark of praise'. **"To Penshurst"** is 102 lines in length, it is closely modelled upon a Latin poem by Martial, and Jonson as in most of the celebratory epistles writes in couplets. The poem represents one of the peaks of Renaissance civilisation: the author, a product of the finest kinds of classical and Elizabethan training, himself a sturdily original temperament as well as a mighty intelligence, pays homage to a kind of living which embodies the richest potentialities of human contact and co-operation. Necessarily, the art of living in **"To Penshurst"** is not 'democratic' as we would know it. But the poem cannot be treated in class terms at all. We are ourselves too quick to call conscientiously anxious clichés to mind when the word 'class' crops up; this poem realises for us the mutual ceremonies and sanctions of a coherent way of life, and if no local pattern of living could be the same today, yet the values implicit in what Jonson's steadfast affection and straightness of judgment make alive to us are still alive and recognisable in their different forms. I certainly have no wish to resurrect the kind of aristocratic hauteur and reckless riding to hounds of which W. B. Yeats so much regretted the loss. But Jonson's poem gives us—as a matter of felt life—a more robust, less socially specific code of behaviour, though the poem handles the stuff of a housewife's life with engaging familiarity. We move (in feeling and in action) with the firm cadences of Jonson's voice and attitudes as he speaks to the life he enjoys. We participate in a sort of ritual, a festivity; we pay our homage, with wit, gentleness, and dignity to forms of human decency and kindness. Why should we not write like this today?

And if the high-swol'n Medway fail thy dish,
Thou hast thy ponds, that pay thee tribute fish,
Fat, aged carps, that run into thy net.
And pikes, now weary their own kind to eat,
As loth the second draught or cast to stay,
Officiously, at first themselves betray.
Bright eels that emulate them, and leap on land,
Before the fisher, or into his hand.
Then hath thy orchard fruit, thy garden flowers,
Fresh as the air and new as are the hours.
The early cherry, with the later plum,
Fig, grape and quince, each in his time does come:
The blushing apricot and woolly peach
Hang on thy walls that every child may reach.

It is a grand vision, gently hyperbolic (about the fish) but rich with a sense of cultivated and deliberate plenty. The landscape is not only fertile, it is serene and ordered by human reason, human providence and affection. There is no brutality—

And though thy walls be of the country stone,
They're reared with no man's ruin, no man's groan,
There's none that dwells about them, wish them down;
But all come in, the farmer and the clown . . .

One attractive and reliable measure of Jonson's gift as a poet is the way in which here, as in **"Inviting a Friend to Supper,"** as, indeed, in *Volpone or The Alchemist,* he can use tasty, juicy food to express moral realities. Here the food is all goodness and giving. The poem fills with a sense of place, of wholesome and rooted living in a way of life which takes in farming, sport, marriage, and family love. Such a sense, as we find it here, in places in Pope, in Wordsworth, George Eliot, and Lawrence, is a keen and abiding mark of the Englishness of English literature. It is worth noting that Wordsworth knew **"To Penshurst"** by heart; I think it among the greatest of Nature poems, for its terms of reference take in so much more than the individual. The last two couplets, in their beautiful seriousness and irresistible precision of judgments—the old, censorious Jonson flashes out—come to rest upon a verb. The present indicative 'dwells' summarises the argument, and extends the poem onwards into time. It is fair to call such a faith in continuity, religious.

Now, Penshurst, they that will proportion thee
With other edifices, when they see
Those proud, ambitious heaps, and nothing else,
May say, their lords have built, but thy lord dwells.

The last poem, though smaller in scope, is flawless. The odd line in **"To Penshurst"** lumbers a little; the **"Elegy"** is brief, succinct and springy. It takes what it needs from the song tradition, and what it needs from Jonson's own grave cast of mind, and his training in classical economy and the native style. A study of this poem should illuminate all I have proposed about the making of English poetry.

Though beauty be the mark of praise,
And yours of whom I sing be such
As not the world can praise too much,
Yet is't your virtue now I raise.

A virtue like alloy, so gone
Throughout your form, as though that move,
And draw, and conquer all men's love,
This subjects you to love of one,

Wherein you triumph yet; because
'Tis of your self, and that you use
The noblest freedom, not to choose
Against or faith, or honour's laws.

But who should less expect from you,
In whom alone love lives again?
By whom he is restored to men,
And kept, and bred, and brought up true.

His falling temples you have reared,
The withered garlands ta'en away;
His altars kept from the decay
That envy wished and nature feared.

And on them burn so chaste a flame
With so much loyalty's expense,
As Love, to acquit such excellence,
Is gone himself into your name.

And you are he: the deity
To whom all lovers are designed,
That would their better objects find:
Among which faithful troop am I.

Who as an offering at your shrine,
Have sung this hymn, and here entreat
One spark of your diviner heat
To light upon a love of mine.

Which if it kindle not, but scant
Appear, and that to shortest view,
Yet give me leave to adore in you
What I, in her, am grieved to want.

The poem praises a friend, but explicitly sets aside the courtly convention; it is a poem about friendship, not about love, and it therefore avoids the temptations of mannerism and cliché. Yet he praises the friend's capacity to love and therefore can appropriately borrow the Petrarchan metaphors, especially the metaphorical deification, without sounding absurd. He honours the friend for her integrity in love at a time when love is become disreputable, and this integrity he catches and holds in the fragile, haunting rhythms of the fifth stanza. He perfectly justifies the stylised wardrobe by the fragile step of the movement, at delicate contrast with the stronger gallantry of the third stanza. But there is more than gallantry here: there is the power and fullness of a poet in absolute command of his theme. There is the richness and extraordinary subtlety of organisation available only to a poet of refinement as well as genius. There is the unimpeded voice of a great intelligence speaking on a serious subject with all the skill at his disposal. The language is naked, the argument true, the development impeccable, and the poem should move all of us, in so far as we are human beings and not sentimentalists, and move us in heart and mind alike. Such poetry nurtures and cherishes the human spirit, and gives it significance to live by; it fulfils a moral and literary tradition. It abides the intervening centuries, and it holds up now. The style and the man are one.

J. B. Bamborough (essay date 1970)

SOURCE: "Jonson's Poetry, Prose and Criticism," in *Ben Jonson,* Hutchinson & Co., Ltd., 1970, pp. 151-76.

[*In the following excerpt, Bamborough examines the stylistic, thematic, and idiosyncratic qualities of Jonson's poetry.*]

I

Considering that he wrote the best-known lyric in the English language, Jonson has had comparatively little attention as a poet. The reason for this is not hard to see. As with his plays, he had a very clear idea of what he wanted to do in poetry and what his principles were, and he remained largely independent of fashions and schools. In consequence his poetry does not quite fit into the usual categories of English literary history, and while its obvious qualities have always gained it respect, it has never been fully in accord with the taste of any period. Jonson yielded to no one in in the high value he placed on poetry, but he saw it as essentially an Art, rather than as the expression of personality or a way of conveying a unique perception of Truth. Skill was the quality most inescapably demanded of the poet. Certainly he had to be born a poet, and equally certainly he needed Inspiration, in some sense of that difficult word, but no man can rely on these alone and think

> hee can leape forth suddainely a *Poet,* by dreaming hee hath been in *Parnassus,* or, having washed his lipps (as they say) in *Helicon.* There goes more to his making, then so. For to Nature, Exercise, Imitation, and Studie, *Art* must be added, to make all these perfect. And, though these challenge to themselves much, in the making up of our Maker, it is Art only can lead him to perfection, and leave him there, as planted by her hand.

[*Discoveries,* 2488-95]

The position maintained is straightforwardly neo-classical. In order to write well, the first necessity was, as Horace had said, to master the subject; then, to know how other writers had treated it so as to be able to make use of their work. Originality and Inspiration, as the Romantics understood them, do not, or need not, enter into this. There is one poem of Jonson's—'**That women are but men's shadows**' (*Forrest,* **vii**)—which we know was written to order, having been given to him as a 'penance' by the Countess of Pembroke. It is not a very distinguished poem, but it has interest because it shows Jonson carrying out his precepts in practice; having been set his task, he looked for a suitable model to imitate, found it in a lyric by the early sixteenth-century Latinist Barhélemi Aneau, and adapted this to his purpose. This is in miniature the technique he used when he had to fulfill a commission for a masque, such as *The Masque of Blackness,* and indeed it seems to have been his natural method whenever he set himself to compose anything, large or small.

Mastery of the matter to be conveyed and familiarity with the best models for imitation were as important even in a brief lyric such as '**That women are but men's shadows**' as in Tragedy and Comedy. Next after them came the logical disposition of the matter and proper attention to detail. In the preface to *The Alchemist* Jonson draws a distinction between energetic but careless writing, and proper composition:

> . . . there is a great difference between those, that (to gaine opinion of *Copie* [that is, copiousness or fertility

of imagination]) utter all they can, however unfitly: and those that use election and a meane. For it is only the disease of the unskilfull, to think rude things greater than polish'd: or scatter'd more numerous than compos'd.

The true craftsman-poet must be ready to polish and revise, to 'bring all to the forge and file again', and if necessary to expunge, and this is what lies behind his comment when the players mentioned it as an honour to Shakespeare, 'that in his writing . . . he never blotted out line'. In rejoining: 'Would he had blotted a thousand' Jonson certainly did not mean that he wished there was less of Shake-speare's writing, but that he felt that Shakespeare managed his genius badly and would have been an even better writer if he had revised more. [*Discoveries*, 647-68]. In his own way Jonson would have accepted the dictum that poetry must possess all the virtues of good prose, and indeed he told Drummond that

> he wrott all his \<verses\> first in prose, for so his master Cambden had learned him.
>
> [*Conversations*, 377-78]

This sounds like an exaggeration—it is difficult to believe, for example, that all his lyrics can have begun in this way—but it may well be largely true, and there are certainly places where Jonson can in fact be seen to be versifying his own or others' prose.

The next demand that poetry had to meet was for perspicuity and naturalness of diction. Simplicity and directness, however, were not to decline into emptiness and insipidity. Jonson distinguished between what he called 'men's poets' and 'women's poets', the latter being typified for him by Daniel:

> Others there are, that have no composition at all; but a kind of tuneing, and riming fall, in what they write. It runs and slides, and onely makes sound. Womens-*Poets* they are call'd: as you have womens-*Taylors*.
>
> *They write a verse, as smooth, as soft, as creame;*
> *In which there is no torrent, nor scarce streame.*
>
> You may sound these wits, and find the depth of them, with your middle finger. They are *Creame-bowle*, or but puddle deepe.
>
> [*Discoveries*, 710-18]

For this kind of writing Jonson had no patience, but he objected as much to the other extreme of deliberately 'strong' or harsh poetry:

> Others, that in composition are nothing, but what is rough and broken: *Quae per salebras altaque saxa cadunt*. And if it would come gently, they trouble it of purpose. They would not have it run without rubs, as if that stile were more strong and manly, that stroke the eare with a kind of unevennesse.
>
> [*Discoveries*, 695-700]

This was a 'humour' like affecting a 'singularity' in the cut of one's beard; Jonsoncomplained of it in Donne, a poet whom he otherwise greatly admired (he told Drummond 'that Done for not keeping of accent deserves hanging' and that 'Done himself for not being understood would perish' [*Conversations*, 648-49; 196]).

In versification, then, Jonson desired what was 'numerous' or harmonious, but not boringly regular. He tried his hand at a number of different meters, even experimenting with the Pindaric Ode, a form little practised by the Elizabethans, and indeed not very well understood by them; Jonson's scholarship gave him an advantage here, though he was not temperamentally suited for such a rhapsodic form, and could only sometimes bring it off. In general he had no taste for wild and irregular beauties: he said of style that it should be

> smooth, gentle, and sweet; like a Table, upon which you may runne your finger without rubs, and your nayle cannot find a joynt; not horrid, rough, wrinckled, gaping, or chapt.
>
> [*Discoveries*, 2068-71]

Perhaps most revealing of all is a remark that Drummond records:

> That Southwell was hanged yett so he had written that piece of his ye burning babe he would have been content to destroy many of his.
>
> [*Conversations*, 180-2]

Southwell was a Catholic martyr, and for a long period of his life Jonson was a member of the Roman Church, but it was probably not so much the religious content of *The Burning Babe* that he admired as its combination of gravity of subject, fervour of feeling and firm stylistic control. In his own work the same combination of qualities can be found, as in his **'Epigram'** on the death of his first son:

> Farewell, thou child of my right hand, and joy;
>   My sinne was too much hope of thee, lov'd boy.
> Seven yeares tho'wert lent to me, and I thee pay,
>   Exacted by thy fate, on the just day. . . .

The union of smoothness and strength is especially valuable in this poem because it so successfully contains what might easily have become mawkish and sentimental; this is truly 'masculine' poetry.

Jonson defined his ideal diction clearly in *Discoveries* (in what is actually a paraphrase from Quintilian):

> Pure and neate language I love, yet plaine and customary.

He took his stand, that is, with Cheke, Ascham, Sidney and those other humanists who believed in 'dignifying the vernacular' by 'purifying' it, freeing it from obscurity, rusticity, clumsiness and affectation, whether this last took the form of self-conscious archaism or of pedantic importation from ancient or modern languages. English was to be transformed into an expressive and worthy literary language by revealing its true genius, not by divorcing it from the actual speech ofmen, 'upon the which', Jonson says in his unfinished *Grammar,* 'all precepts are grounded, and to the which they ought to be referred'. 'Custom' or usage was the ultimate sanction, but this did not mean accepting the standards of the vulgar:

> Yet when I name Custome, I understand not the vulgar Custome: For that were a precept no lesse dangerous to Language, then life, if wee should speake or live after the manners of the vulgar: But that I call Custome of speech, which is the consent of the Learned; as Custome of life, which is the consent of the good.

> [*Discoveries,* 1938-44]

As always the link between purity in diction and purity in life was a vital one to Jonson, and in neither sphere must the good man be corrupted by evil practices. On the other hand it was wrong to be too precious in diction, or to attempt to astonish by inflated grandness of style:

> The true Artificer will not run away from nature, as hee were afraid of her; or depart from life, and the likeness of Truth; but speake to the capacity of his hearers. And though his language differ from the vulgar somewhat; it shall not fly from all humanity, with the *Tamerlaines* and *Tamer-Chams* of the late Age, which had nothing in them but the *scenicall* strutting, and furious vociferation, to warrant them to the ignorant gapers. Hee knowes it is his onely Art, so to carry it, as none but Artificers perceive it.

> [*Discoveries,* 772-8]

Jonson's own vocabulary has been extensively studied, and the statistical evidence supports those who have emphasised the Englishness of his language against the older view expressed by Dryden—'he did a little too much romanise our tongue' [*Essays,* Vol. I]. The modern reader may well be struck by apparent Latinisms in Jonson, but it must be remembered that many words of Latin origin were common in the Renaissance but have since passed out of currency. Jonson himself is credited with the introduction of only about 100 words from Latin, many of which are now quite domesticated—'candidate', for example, 'connection', 'frugal', 'gesticulate', 'petulant', 'preside', 'reciprocate', and 'terse'. This incidence of borrowing is low for an Elizabethan writer, and, oddly, it is lowest in Jonson's Roman tragedies. As might be expected he borrowed less still from Greek, though here again some of his important loans are now naturalised—'analytic' is one, and so are 'exotic', 'heroine' and 'plastic' (as an adjective). More obvious than his importations is his usages of words derived from Latin or Greek in their original rather than their English meaning, such as his use of 'front' to mean 'forehead' or 'frequent' to mean 'crowded' or 'well-attended' ('a frequent Senate'). Many of these senses were common in his day, and, of course, to the educated among his audience, to whom Latin was as familiar as English, they would not have seemed strange.

In his actual vocabulary, then, Jonson may be classified as only moderately Latinate, and certainly well removed from the affected Latinism which he satirised in the characters of Juniper in *The Case is Altered* and Crispinus in *Poetaster.* His language is more often given an exotic appearance by his readiness to interrupt normal English word-order. The 'hanging' or misplaced clause is an example of this:

> If you had bloud, or vertue in you, gentlemen, you would not suffer such eare-wigs about a husband, or scorpions, to creep between man and wife. . . .

> (*Epicœne,* V.iv.6-8)

> If there be never a *Servant-monster* i'the *Fayre,* who can helpe it? he sayes; nor a nest of *Antiques?* . . .

> (*Bartholomew Fair,* Ind.127-8)

A similar strangeness may come from a more minor displacement of the expected run of a sentence, as when he notes in *Discoveries* that 'Men are decay'd, and *studies*', or refers in the dedication to *Volpone* to the 'invading interpreters' (or unauthorised commentators on others' work) 'who cunningly, and often, utter their owne virulent malice, under other mens simplest meanings', where we would expect 'often cunningly'. His ellipses also sometimes produce odd effects, as in these lines from the first Prologue to *Epicœne* (which also contain one of Jonson's characteristic negatives):

> Our wishes, like to those (make publique feasts)
> Are not to please the cookes tastes, but the guests.
> Yet, if those cunning palates hether come,
>   They shall find guests, entreaty, and good roome;
>   And though all relish not, sure, there will be some,
> That, when they leave their seates, shall make 'hem say,
>   Who wrote that piece, could so have wrote a play:
>   But that, he knew, this was the better way.

> (8-15)

Together with Jonson's frequently heavy punctuation, these idiosyncrasies often produce both in prose and verse a broken-up, jerky impression which may at first reading be difficult to follow (though the difficulty often disappears if the passages are heard or read aloud). Sometimes in the plays this can be justified as reproducing the movement of a character's thought or the forms of colloquial speech, but it is not always possible to maintain this. No doubt Jonson was affected by the movement of taste at the end of the sixteenth century away from the polished 'Ciceronian' style towards a rougher, more abrupt and colloquial-seeming manner. The older balanced and ornate mode appears in him only in parody, as in Puntarvolo's address to his wife's gentlewoman:

> To the perfection of complement (which is the Diall of the thought, and guided by the Sunne of your beauties) are requir'd these three specials: the *gnomon,* the *puntilio*'s, and the *superficies*: the *superficies,* is that we call, place; the *puntilio*'s, circumstance; and the *gnomon,* ceremony: in either of which, for a stranger to erre, 'tis easy and facile, and such am I.

> (*Every Man out,* II.ii.19-23)

Jonson wrote in both the stock forms of 'baroque prose', the 'curt,' most familiar to us from Bacon's *Essays,* and the 'loose' or 'dispersed', of which the extreme example is perhaps Burton's *Anatomy of Melancholy;* both are well illustrated in *Epicœne,* mainly by Truewit, who is something of a virtuoso of 'modern' eloquence. But Truewit to some extent parodies himself, and Jonson was aware, as Bacon was, that in the end those who set out to avoid the ornateness of the Ciceronian style might fall as easily as their predecessors into that error 'when men study words and not matter'. In all probability Jonson's experimenting with word-order was not so much a conscious attempt to be fashionable as a wish to give English the more flexible word-order of Latin, and in this sense perhaps he was a 'romaniser'. His ultimate principles were never in doubt: 'I would rather have a plaine down-right wisdome, than a foolish and affected eloquence' [*Discoveries,* 343-5].

Jonson's borrowings from foreign languages are few, and can usually be accounted for by the need to provide local colour. *Volpone,* for example, has a number of loans from Italian, and *The Devil is an Ass* many from Spanish, since in that play there is some incidental satire of the contemporary vogue for Spanish fashions and manners (of which Jonson, born and brought up in Elizabethan England, disapproved). Some of the words he introduced have become established: 'caress' (as a noun) and 'disgust' (as a verb), both from Italian; 'casuist' and 'responsible' from French; 'drill' and 'furlough' from Dutch—remembered perhaps from his days as a soldier. He has none of the excessive dependence on French and Italian which characterised some of his contemporaries, and indeed satirises it in his fops. He is similarly sparing in his use of dialect and archaism; his comment on Spenser is famous: 'in affecting the Ancients [he] writ no language'. [*Discoveries,* 1806-7] Altogether in the 'enrichment' of English he was conservatives—extremely conservative in comparison with Spenser or Shakespeare—and he was equally conservative in drawing on native resources. All writers of his period show an extraordinary facility in substituting one part of speech for another and in giving new meanings to established words. Jonson is the first recorded authority for over 1,000 such usages, but this is little in comparison with Shakespeare. Nor was he very inventive in coining compound nouns and adjectives, in which Elizabethan English was particularly rich. 'Book-worm' is one of his creations, and so are 'half-witted', 'pig-headed', and 'close-mouthed'. Some of his inventions have failed to survive, and this is perhaps a pity: 'egg-chinned', 'shrewd-bearded' and 'squirrel-limbed' might be useful additions to our vocabulary. Significantly he was most creative in constructing new terms of disparagement or abuse; the speeches of Tucca and Buffone are rich in this respect, and so are those of Face. But in general Jonson's strength lay not so much in the richness or fecundity of his language, as in its perspicuity, preciseness and straightforward vigour. . . .

The stylistic qualities which Jonson desired were those which we would tend to think of as the qualities of good, plain prose, but he looked to see them in poetry as well. The prescriptions he laid down were those for the 'plain' rather than the 'high' or ornate style, and this choice rad-

ically limited his range as a poet [W. Trimpi, *Ben Jonson's Poems,* 1962]. It prescribed the type of poem he wrote, for by the laws of Decorum the plain style was only appropriate to certain 'kinds', in general those that were at once 'familiar' and moral. Jonson's **Epigrams,** which he called 'the ripest of my studies', fall under this heading. They are not the bitter, sharp, 'snarling' epigrams fashionable at the time he wrote his first Humour plays, although some of them are satirical (Jonson never in fact uses 'satire' to describe any of his poems), nor are they always, or even usually, witty and pointed. The lack of wit was commented on by contemporary critics, and Jonson acknowledged the complaint. His second epigram, however, should have made it plain that he was not offering specimens of the *genre* so popular at the end of the previous century:

> *To My Booke*
> It will be look'd for, booke, when some but see
>   Thy title, *Epigrammes,* and nam'd of mee,
> Thou should'st be bold, licentious, full of gall,
>   Wormewood, and sulphure, sharpe, and tooth'd withall;
> Become a petulant thing, hurle inke, and wit,
>   As mad-men stones: not caring whom they hit.
> Deceive their malice, who could wish it so.
>   And by thy wiser temper, let men know
> Thou are not covetous of least selfe-fame,
>   Made from the hazard of anothers shame:
> Much lesse with lewd, prophane, and beastly phrase,
>   To catch the worlds loose laughter, or vaine gaze.
> He that departs with his owne honesty
>   For vulgar praise, doth it too dearely buy.

To the 'meere English Censurer' who complains that his poems are not true epigrams of the old-fashioned sort, Jonson retorts (**Epigram XVIII**) that they are not a new kind but in 'the old way and the true', and he seems to be thinking of the epigrams of Martial, who said that the epigram should constitute a kind of letter. Many of Jonson's epigrams are addressed to his friends, and except in length there is little difference between them and his longer 'Epistles'; even the shorter, more satirical epigrams are often addressed to imaginary recipients. 'Epigram' could also cover epitaph, and in fact the famous **'Epitaph on Salamon Pavy'** was printed among them; even this is in a way a letter, since it is addressed to the audience: 'Weepe with me all you that read/This little storie . . . ' . In tone and mood, however, Jonson is nearer Horace than Martial, and he may have been aiming at providing an English equivalent of Horace's *sermones*—'conversational poems' or, literally, 'talks'.

In Jonson's hand the epigram was a versatile 'instrument', and he added to it the ode, the elegy, the lyric, as well as some other poems not so easily classifiable. He was cut off, however, not only from Heroic poetry—so that the closest he comes to the Epic style is in his tragedies—but, by his own decision, from love poetry as well. In *Poetaster* he had relegated erotic poetry to a subordinate place in the canon, and we should not therefore expect to find him devoting his talents to it; in fact he seems to have tried to make himself the kind of poet he represents Horace as being in that play. Perhaps there were personal reasons as well, but if so we cannot now discover them: the little humorous poem **'Why I write not of love'**, which was printed as the first poem in **The Forrest** tells us nothing. In fact he did write some 'elegies' of love, but they form a very striking contrast to those of Donne, for example. They have little of Donne's wit, of which Jonson did not wholly approve, although he could at times approximate to it; more significantly they are hardly passionate, though sometimes fervent, and reveal little sensuous feeling. On the whole they use the language and manner of erotic verse with some skill, but with a kind of constraint. The group of poems **'To Charis'** in **The Underwood** may perhaps express some real incident in Jonson's own life, but they are marked by a note of self-conscious irony, and the last two are frankly humorous. Moral considerations probably came into play here; it was not the part of the truly good man to celebrate passion or sensuality, and one safeguard was to introduce the pose of one who 'ever cometh last in the dance of love' and does not take it all too seriously. The **Elegy No. XLII** of **The Underwood** sets Jonson's usual tone:

> Let me be what I am, as *Virgil* cold;
>   As *Horace* fat; or as *Anacreon* old;
> No Poets verses yet did ever move,
>   Whose Readers did not thinke he was in love.
> Who shall forbid me then in Rithme to bee
>   As light, and active as the youngest hee
> That from the Muses fountaines doth indorse
>   His lynes, and hourely sits the Poets horse?
> Put on my Ivy Garland, let me see
>   Who frownes, who jealous is, who taxeth me.
> Fathers, and Husbands, I doe claime a right
>   In all that is call'd lovely: take my sight
> Sooner then my affection from the faire.
>   No face, no hand, proportion, line, or Ayre
> Of beautie; but the Muse hath interest in:
>   There is not worne that lace, purle, knot or pin,
> But is the Poets matter: And he must,
>   When he is furious, love, although not lust . . .

Thereafter it turns into a satire on women. Jonson would not have the same reasons for restraint, however, in his religious poetry, where he sounds sincere enough, but equally frigid, and it becomes obvious that the real limitation was stylistic.

The criteria which Jonson imposed on his own style were directed towards clarity and harmony, but they virtually precluded a complex and plastic use of words. This results in what T. S. Eliot called the 'superficiality' of his poetry, noting that his words lack

> a network of tentacular roots reaching down to the deepest terrors and desires.
>
>   [T. S. Eliot, *Selected Essays*]

Eliot was writing especially of the poetry in the tragedies, but it is generally true that Jonson's poems provide little for the exegete using the methods of 'close reading'; he lacks the interlocking of connotation and evocation and the buried image-chains for which critics are now trained to look. The first stanza of **'Drink to me only with thine eyes'**, for example, has a reasonably complex structure of meaning—indeed Professor Empson brought it, perhaps a little forcedly, within the compass of *Seven Types of Ambiguity*. Eyes can be liquid; they can literally 'brim over' with tears; their gaze can be intoxicating. Kisses, too, are not inappropriate in a cup; we are accustomed to the idea of tasting someone's lips, drinking in beauty, and so on, and 'kisses like wine' has become a cliché. After this, however, the poem dwindles into little more than graceful compliment, although possibly a determined commentator might see in the conceit of the unwithered branch a suggestion not only of the immortality of love but of the mistress as a fertility goddess.

From this point of view Jonson is rather an unrewarding poet, just as he is unrewarding as a poetic playwright, and one disappointed critic has committed himself to the surely damning judgment:

> Jonson's imagery . . . resembles that of a philologist who could also write poetry.
>
>   [E. B. Partridge, *The Broken Compass,* 1958]

Jonson may well, like Joyce and Milton, have had a primarily verbal rather than pictorial imagination, although in any case his insistence on the logical disposition of the matter of a poem (to say nothing of the practice of first writing his poems out in prose) would militate against an unconscious logic of metaphor. The major point, however, is that Jonson's views of the proper use of words drove him towards what we should call a denotatory use of language, in which the 'dictionary meaning' is the most important aspect of the word. In this, as in some other aspects of his thought, Jonson anticipated the doctrines of the later seventeenth century; perhaps it would be truer to say that the movement to 'ennoble' the English language by purifying it, to which he belonged, was that which eventually triumphed over its rivals and emerged as the dominant force in the latter part of the century. In general terms the strength and weakness of Jonson's poetry are very much the strengths and weaknesses of the poetry of Dryden and Pope, although it could not be confused with theirs, and could only in a limited sense be called 'Augustan'. (To Dryden and Pope, Jonson's verse was insufficiently pure and refined, not correctly versified, and altogether lacking in 'politeness'; Jonson for his part would have disapproved, among other things, of Dryden's persistent use of the High Style for inappropriate subjects, and of Pope's devotion to epigram and paradox.)

One significant characteristic of Jonson's verse is that it often draws its strength from objects rather than giving strength to them. A good example is this stanza, from the fourth of the series of poems **'To Charis'**—"**Her Triumph**":

> Have you seene but a bright Lillie grow,
>   Before rude hands have touch'd it?

Have you mark'd but the fall o'the Snow
  Before the soyle hath smutch'd it?
Have you felt the wooll o' the Bever?
      Or Swans Downe ever?
Or have smelt o'the bud o'the Brier?
      Or the Nard i' the fire?
Or have tasted the bag o'the Bee?
O so white! O so soft! O so sweet is she!

                              (21-30)

There is no question of the effectiveness of this, but it depends on reminding us of the actual physical qualities of the objects mentioned, and then transferring the sense-traces thus evoked to the idea of the mistress; Jonson does not, through his language, *convey* the sensual impressions to us, or modify them in any way. The same is true of much of his pastoral poetry, in a lyric such as this (from *Pan's Anniversarie*):

Strew, strew, the glad and smiling ground
With every flower, yet not confound
The Prime-rose drop, the Springs own spouse,
Bright Dayes-eyes, and the lipes of Cowes,
    The Garden-star, the Queene of May,
    The Rose, to crowne the Holy-day.

Drop, drop, you Violets, change your hues,
Now red, now pale, as Lovers use;
And in your death go out as well
As when you liv'd, unto the smell;
    That from your odour all may say,
    This is the Shepherds Holy-day.

                              (11-24)

Apart from the rather subdued conceit of the violets' breathing their last in odour nothing *happens* to the flowers in the poem; they are not even described, or given any qualities, and the effect of the piece depends on the reader's recalling them to his memory and producing in himself the stock attitude towards them.

This is not to say that Jonson's use of language is never creative. Characteristically, however, he is most forcible when he is dealing with things which in themselves generate emotion, and correspondingly at his most effective when expressing the emotions which are most readily aroused by the actual physical presence of objects. Desire and Aversion are the feelings he can most readily convey, and he habitually does so through reference to physical objects. Volpone thus attempts to convey his feelings for Celia through a catalogue of the riches he will shower on her:

See, here, a rope of pearle; and each, more orient
Then that the brave *Egyptian* queene carrous'd:
Dissolve, and drinke'hem. See, a carbuncle,
May put out both the eyes of our *St. Marke;*
A diamant, would have bought *Lollia Paulina,*
When she came in, like star-light, hid with jewels,
That were the spoiles of provinces; take these,
And weare, and lose'hem . . .

                         (III.vii.191-8)

This seems natural in Volpone: we may be more surprised to find the Host in *The New Inn* celebrating a more 'spiritual' matter—the death of the happy lover—in similar terms:

          A death
For Emperours to enjoy! and the Kings
Of the rich East, to pawne their regions for;
To show their treasure, open all their mines,
Spend all their spices to embalme their corpse,
And wrap the inches up in sheets of gold,
That fell by such a noble destiny!

                       (II.vi.236-42)

Not only do sexual desire and Avarice seem closely connected in Jonson's mind; he seems to need the tangible symbols of wealth to convey passionate longing and the desire for possession.

Jonson is still more original in his expression of scorn, hatred or contempt, and is most likely in this mood to create images which stick fast in our minds. Critics usually illustrate his vitality in this respect from some of the famous pieces of description in his comedies—such as Face's description of Subtle's complexion:

Stuck full of black, and melancholique wormes,
Like poulder-corns, shot, at the *artillery-yeard* . . .
                         (*Alch.* I.i.30-1)

As well as their sonorous and dignified passages in the high style, however, the two tragedies have some sharp imagery of this kind. In *Sejanus* Jonson twice brilliantly evokes the shiftiness and cunning of the time-serving Roman politicians, once when Sabinus commented to Silius on their lack of pliancy and ambition:

Wee have no shifts of faces, no cleft tongues,
No soft, and glutinous bodies, that can sticke,
Like snailes, on painted walls;

                            (I.7-9)

and again when Arruntius describes a group of Senators anxiously whispering together:

I, now their heads doe travaile, now they worke;
Their faces runne like shittles, they are weaving
Some curious cobweb to catch flies.

                          (III.22-4)

In his non-dramatic verse, too, there is no doubt that a new note of vigour and urgency appears when Jonson is on the attack, as for example in the '**Expostulation with Inigo Jones'**, or the '**Execration upon Vulcan'**.

There is a critical fallacy to be avoided here. The modern reader is conditioned to find the violent and the sordid more exciting and therefore more 'real' than the harmonious and beautiful, and to think that what excites him most in a poet must be the produce of what is 'deepest' in that poet's personality. It is tempting to base interpretation of Jonson's own character on the fact that he seems most vital when he expresses desire or repugnance in terms of physical objects; it may be safer to accept the fact that his concept of poetry and his view of language were bound to limit the emotional range of what he wrote. He may have felt himself free to express emotion only when he was confident that this could be justified morally: the dramatic expression of inordinate desire by characters who are clearly held up for disapproval, and the satirical description of real or imaginary opponents of virtue were privileged occasions. We cannot ignore the presence of much fine verse of a generally philosophical or ethical kind among his poems and in his masques; that this moves us less may be partly because the ideas he expresses no longer mean much to us, and because theexpression of them is restricted by his demand for perspicuity and logic.

Jonson's best poems, naturally enough, are in those 'kinds' to which his critical theories were best adapted—the epistle and the lyric. An epistle such as that to Edward Sackville, Earl of Dorset, manages to combine the familiar and the grave in a balance that can properly be called 'masculine', as Jonson understood the term:

> If, *Sackvile,* all that have the power to doe
> Great and good turns, as wel could time them too,
> And knew their how, and where: we should have,
>   then,
> Lesse list of proud, hard, or ingratefull Men.
> For benefits are ow'd with the same mind
> As they are done, and such returnes they find:
> You then, whose will not only, but desire
> To succour my necessities, tooke fire,
> Not at my prayers, but your sense; which laid
> The way to meet, what others would upbraid;
> And in the Act did so my blush prevent,
> As I did feele it done, as soone as meant:
> You cannot doubt, but I, who freely know
> This Good from you, as freely will it owe;
> And though my fortune humble me, to take
> The smallest courtesies with thankes, I make
> Yet choyce from whom I take them; and would shame
> To have such doe me good, I durst not name:
> They are the Noblest benefits, and sinke
> Deepest in Man, of which when he doth thinke,
> The memorie delights him more, from whom
> Then what he hath receiv'd.
>
> (1-22)

The more famous **'To Penshurst'** has the same use of objects for the evocative power that resides in them as Jonson's poetry of Desire and Loathing, but here adapted to the creation of a picture of harmonious and civilised rusticity:

> Each banks doth yeeld thee coneyes; and the topps
>   Fertile of wood, *Ashore,* and *Sydney's* copp's,
> To crowne thy open table, doth provide
>   The purpled pheasant, with the speckled side:
> The painted partrich lyes in euery field,
>   And, for thy messe, is willing to be kill'd.
> And if the high-swolne *Medway* fails thy dish,
>   Thou has thy ponds, that pay thee tribute fish,
> Fat, aged carps, that runne into thy net.

> And pikes, now weary their owne kinde to eat,
> As loth, the second draught, or cast to stay,
>   Officiously, at first, themselves betray.
> Bright eeles, that emulate them, and leape on land,
>   Before the fisher, or into his hand.
> Then hath thy orchard fruit, thy garden flowers,
>   Fresh as the ayre, and new as are the houres.
> The earely cherry, with the later plum,
>   Fig, grape, and quince, each in his time doth come:
> The blushing apricot, and woolly peach
>   Hang on thy walls, that every child may reach.
>
> (25-44)

The list of fruits in the last few lines is more than a catalogue, for it is modified by the very last phrase, 'that every child may reach'; the fruit is harmless, it is freely bestowed, it is plucked in innocence. The tone established is intensified in the lines immediately following:

> And though thy walls be of the countrey stone,
>   They'are rear'd with no mans ruine, no mans grone,
> There's none, that dwell about them, wish them
>   downe;
>   But all come in, the farmer, and the clowne . . .
>
> (45-8)

This invocation of simple, innocent but ordered and cultivated rural living is far removed from the bustling city life of the comedies, but it echoes the atmosphere of *The Sad Shepherd* and of some of the masques. **'To Penshurst'** and the epigram **'Inviting a friend to supper'** (**No. CI**) are Jonson at his most urbane and 'Roman', and at his closest to the Augustans:

> To night, grave sir, both my poore house, and I
>   Doe equally desire your companie:
> Not that we think us worthy such a ghest,
>   But that your worth will dignifie our feast . . .

No one would deny that these poems represent a largely conventional pose, or that we may be closer to the 'real' Jonson in the nervous indignant energy of the **'Expostulation with Inigo Jones'**. They do represent, however, Jonson as he would have liked to see himself, and (more importantly) successfully writing the kind of poetry he set himself to write.

Even in the trifles [Jonson] retained the characteristics of a 'man's poet'— craftsmanship, plain language and sober meaningfulness.

—J. B. Bamborough

Jonson's reputation as a lyric poet has suffered much from Swinburne's judgment that he was 'a singer who could not sing'. This may seem an odd description of the poet who wrote the **'Hymn to Diana'** from *Cynthia's Revels* (*'Queene,* and *Huntresse,* chaste and faire'), and the less-known Echo's song from the same play:

> Slow, slow, fresh fount, keepe time with my salt
>   teares;
> Yet slower, yet, o faintly gentle springs:
> List to the heavy part the musique beares,
>   Woe weepes out her division, when shee sings.
>   Droupe hearbs, and flowres;
>   Fall griefe in showres;
>   Our beauties are not ours:
>   O, I could still
> (Like melting snow upon some craggie hill,)
>   drop, drop, drop, drop,
> Since natures pride is, now, a wither'd daffodil.
>
> (I.ii.65-75)

There are many other lyrics in the masques which could be quoted to refute Swinburne. His judgment requires the elucidation provided by another passage:

> The case of Ben Jonson is the great standing examle of a truth which should never be forgotten or overlooked: that no amount of learning, of labour, or of culture will supply the place of natural taste and native judgment. . . .
>
> [Swinburne, *A Study of Ben Jonson*]

There is no pretending that Jonson's lyrics read like 'the spontaneous overflow of powerful feelings'; they are undoubtedly 'artificial'—a term which Jonson would have taken as one of approval, as indicating the proper exercise of the craft of the artificer-poet—and they certainly evince learning and care. But they are not therefore bad, unless one is prepared to dismiss all poetry of this kind as inferior; they are certainly good examples of their 'kind'. The song from *Epicœne* is a fair representative:

> Still to be neat, still to be drest,
> As, you were going to a feast;
> Still to be pou'dred, still perfum'd:
> Lady, it is to be presum'd,
> Though arts hid causes are not found,
> All is not sweet, all is not sound.
>
> Give me a looke, give me a face,
> That make simplicitie a grace;
> Robes loosely flowing, haire as free:
> Such sweet neglect more taketh me,
> Then all th'adulteries of art,
> They strike mine eyes, but not my heart.
>
> (I.i.91-102)

This may be in praise of simplicity and artlessness, but it is certainly itself neither simple nor artless; nor does it pretend to be. Instead it offers a civilised and sophisticated attitude that is both cynical and moral—indeed it is a minor attack on the targets of Appearance and Opinion; in expression it is precise, pointed, graceful and musical, but at the same time direct and plain-spoken ('All is not sweet, all is not sound'). These are qualities shared in some degree by all Jonson's lyrics; even in trifles he retained the char-

acteristics of a 'man's poet'—craftsmanship, plain language and sober meaningfulness.

II

When he spoke of the lack of a 'third dimension' to Jonson's poetry Eliot (adapting a judgment of G. G. Smith's) pointed at a quality which is common to all Jonson's work. His poems are very 'self-contained', in the sense that whatever emotion they generate is strictly kept within the bounds of the poem; there is no diffusion or spilling-over of generalised emotional force irrelevant to the meaning of the poem (as there certainly is with Swinburne). This is a quality of which Eliot could approve, but it carries with it the limitation that Jonson's poems rarely, if ever, lead the mind beyond themselves, to explore remoter areas of emotion or thought. If Jonson is never flabbily evocative in his poetry, he is not often imaginatively stimulating. *Mutatis mutandis,* this is generally true of his writing. Throughout his work Jonson's firm intellectual grasp of the principles of his art and his rigorous discipline in following them were a source of weakness as well as strength. He very often achieved what he wished to accomplish, but he very seldom achieved more. The 'grace beyond the reach of art' is something which Jonson lacked; he is not often free from a sense of effort, and there is very little in his writing which we can believe is the result of some 'happy accident'. It is here that Swinburne's reference to his lack of 'natural taste' has point.

We cannot blame Jonson for being the man he was. We may suspect that if he had dropped his guard a little and relaxed his unvarying control he might have freed himself to write not only differently, but better. But we cannot prove this, and it is plainly unfair to criticise him for not writing as it would have been repugnant to his critical canons to write, or for failing to achieve what he did not want to achieve. On the other hand it is not a final defence of a writer to say that he succeeded in writing as he intended: the reader is perfectly justified in accepting this, but preferring something different. It has been Jonson's fate throughout the years to find his greatest contemporary preferred to him. For a time in the seventeenth century he held his own—indeed, was in the ascendent—but from the time of Dryden's comparison in the *Essay of Dramatic Poesie* with its final summing-up—'I admire him, but I love Shakespeare'—the verdict has never been in doubt. And, as Coleridge noted, because of our admiration for Shakespeare we undervalue Jonson in comparison with others of his contemporaries as well. Jonson's uniqueness in his period cannot be overstressed: he is the exception to almost any generalisation that can be made about the English drama of his time. Where other Jacobean playwrights are weak he is strong, especially in verisimilitude and constructive skill; but he is also weak where they are strong, most obviously in the vivid imaginative expression of dramatic emotion. Because we admire Shakespeare so highly, we tend to elevate above Jonson those writers, like Webster, who are stronger in these 'Shakespearean' ways; if Shakespeare had never lived, not only would Jonson be unchallenged as the greatest dramatist of his period, but the critical ranking of his contemporaries would be different.

We obtain an even fairer view of Jonson if we judge him outside the context altogether of Jacobean English drama and in the perspective of European comedy; he should be compared not with Shakespeare, but with Molière, Goldoni and Holberg, and in this company he will not be disgraced.

In the end, however, Jonson defies any attempt to place him in a 'tradition'. He was an original, *sui generis*. It was an originality arrived at by conscious thought, not the originality which, like that of a romantic poet, is the product of a unique imaginative vision of the world. It was conditioned, therefore, to produce works of art in a given period and answering certain critical demands, and outside that period, when these demands are no longer made, it seems alien, even monstrous. This quality of monstrosity was noted by Coleridge:

> It was not possible, that so bold and robust an intellect as that of Ben Jonson could be devoted to any form of intellectual Power vainly or even with mediocrity of Product. He could not but be a Species of himself: tho' like the Mammoth and Megatherion fitted and destined to live only during a given Period, and then to exist a Skeleton, hard, dry, uncouth perhaps, yet massive and not to be contemplated without that mix-ture of Wonder and Admiration, or more accurately, that middle between both for which we want a term. . . .

[*Coleridge on the Seventeenth Century*]

Jonson's first drive was to glorify his art, and to justify himself as an artist. In order to do this, he needed to write correctly, and this involved him in deciding what the proper rules were for Comedy, or Tragedy, or Masque, are whatever 'kind' with which he was concerned. He would never take these rules on trust: he was ready to study the works of others, *tamquam explorator,* to find out how they solved the problems, but the final judgment was always his own. There is in him an element of singularity, and therefore for the reader a need to understand what he was attempting before a judgment can be made. The need for understanding, however, produces its own dangers, as Eliot noted:

> . . . not many people are capable of discovering for themselves the beauty which is only found after labour; and Jonson's industrious readers have been those whose interest was historical and curious, and those who have thought that in discovering the historical and curious interest they had discovered the artistic value as well.

[*Selected Essays*]

It is inevitable that Jonson should attract the attention of scholars—indeed he set out to do so. It seems that he saw himself as a Crites or Horace writing for an audience of Wellbreds and Truewits, if not of Camdens and Donnes, and that it was in default of these auditors that he had to supply his own choric commentators. Not everything that he put into his work was meant to be understood at first glance, and modern scholars labouring at their tasks may console themselves that Jonson was one author at least who would approve of their efforts. He offers less satisfaction, however, to the interpretive critic. His intentions may not always be obvious, but they are definite, and all

his works are perfectly finished specimens of their kind. There is little scope for fresh interpretations, or imaginative reconstruction of what should be in his plays but is not, and in seeing his work through the press with such care he even removed the opportunity for bold textual emendation. From this point of view Jonson is a poor vaulting-horse for a critic's ambition. For the scholar the danger which Eliot saw remains—that the satisfaction of curiosity and the pleasure of acquiring understanding may be mistaken for genuine enjoyment.

Both scholarly investigation and imaginative effort are necessary, however, to enter Jonson's world. It was above all a moral world. There is no need to query the genuiness of Jonson's ethical views. No doubt he desired in theory a moral perfection which in his own life he was incapable of achieving; most people do. He certainly did not find it possible to maintain the calm, moderate Horatian pose which he desired, and he appears often ill-tempered, insensitive and uncharitable. Yet this need not invalidate his attraction towards the ideal, or make him a hypocrite. Again it is true that his attacks on the evils of Society, although they were violently, even brutally, expressed, were not as bold as they purported to be. Had he been a saint—or a revolutionary—he might have said more, and the remedies he proposed are certainly more conventional palliatives than radical specifics. In this he was hampered by the insecurity of his social position, but perhaps still more by the limitations of his own mind. His was a clear, logical and decided morality, but it was neither original nor profound. He saw no reason to challenge, at least publicly, the accepted ethical thought of his day, and he interpreted it rigidly rather than flexibly. No one would go to Jonson for the delicate probing of moral uncertainty or the subtle discrimination of confused motives; his is the world of appetite and energy, not of velleity and doubt. The firmness and clarity of his vision give his work its consistency and strength, but they shut out irony and ambiguity. Despite its apparent elaboration, his was a simple view of life, and he was simply not capable of the complex response to life evinced by greater writers, the kind of complexity we find in Chaucer and Shakespeare.

There is another dimension lacking in his world. We know that he suffered at least to some degree from the religious uncertainties of his age, passing from the English to the Roman church, and back again, and we would presume that he must have spent much thought on matters of faith and doubt. If so, nothing of it appears in his writings. The only religious comment in his comedies is contained in his attacks on the Puritans—and this could as well be motivated by professional interest as by any religious feeling; as a playwright the Puritans were his natural enemies. The religious poems give an impression of sincerity, but they are few and conventional. Perhaps he was restrained by prudential considerations, but it seems that, as a creative writer, at least, anything that might be termed religious was outside his range; he thought in terms of Right and Wrong, rather than Good and Evil (and this is one of the limitations of his tragedies). But if he fails to meet the highest demands we make of a writer, neither illuminating for us the shadowy recesses of the human personality nor enlarging the boundaries of our conception of reality, he was driven by a real desire to teach, to convey an interpretation of human existence, and his convictions seem to have been genuinely held. No one can read his comedies and tragedies without feeling the force of his horror at the manifestations of man's irrational pride and lust for power, or read the masques and poems without a sense of his reverence for the beauty and nobility of Reason and Virtue.

It is not this, however, that makes Jonson a great writer, nor was it all that drove him to write. He was committed, as a serious Renaissance writer, to instruct his public, but he was committed also, both as a popular playwright and a court poet, to entertain. As an entertainer he was sustained by two drives, an urge to record the idiosyncrasies of human character, and a desire to exploit the resources of the English language. As always with Jonson, there are limitations which we have to accept: there are aspects of character beyond his comprehension, and powers in words which he either could not, or would not, unleash. But his greatest work succeeds in spite of these limitations, or even because of them. *The Alchemist, Volpone,* and *Bartholomew Fair* could only have been created by a writer of Jonson's great if limited strength; the acceptance of any wider range of human activity or emotionwould have weakened their outline, the play of any greater psychological subtlety would have lessened their impact. Again, the vigour and the fullness of Jonsonian comedy may be the products of a limited sensibility, but they are also the expression of a creative urge as powerful as that of any writer. Jonson's kind of interest in human character was very English. Stripped of its theoretical trappings, the Comedy of Humours is simply based on that response to humanity evinced when any Englishman says of another that 'he is a character'; it is the expression of an instinctive relish for oddity and absurdity. The English have always preferred, unlike other European peoples, to describe character rather than analyse it, and to emphasise individuality rather than to generalise; of this tradition Jonson is a part, and indeed to some degree an originator. He was certainly an intellectual, by almost any definition of the term which can be offered, but abstract concepts were for him secondary to actual experience. Of his love of the English language little further need be said: in his use of it he had a range insufficiently appreciated by the ordinary reader, whose knowledge is confined to his best-known plays, and this points up a flaw in many judgments of Jonson. His work is much more varied than is often realised, although at the same time it has an essential unity. In part this unity comes from Jonson's consistently maintained moral and critical views, in part from a less easily detached and analysable quality of personality. A knowledge of all his works—what Eliot called an 'intelligent saturation' in them—is necessary for a full understanding of any one, and a partial familiarity may be confusing. *The Sad Shepherd,* for example, is inexplicable without a previous knowledge of *The Entertainment of Althorpe* and *Pan's Anniversarie,* and a realisation that Jonson was as interested in rustic life as he was in that of the city; his aims in his non-dramatic poetry can only be understood by reference both to the ideals expounded in *Poetaster* and to the notes he made in *Discoveries.* Jonson is not a writer easily summed up on brief acquaintance.

It is the strength of his personality and his personal vision which makes him a living force in our literature. Like Chaucer, though less subtly, he capitalised on his own idiosyncrasies and made himself a character in his own work, and this, together with the unmistakeable stamp he put on all he wrote, has made him a figure more real to most readers than, say, Wordsworth or Tennyson (and it matters little in his context how close to the real man this *persona* came). It is in some ways an odd and not always attractive personality. Jonson has good claims to be called the first English 'Man of Letters', the first professional writer, that is, wholly dedicated to his craft and relying on his exercise of it to establish his place in Society. This links him with Dryden, Pope and the eighteenth century, yet he retains not only the flavour of his own age but that of even earlier times. Because of his social position, and also by reason of his twin aim to Instruct and Delight, he retains something of the air of the medieval Court poet who, like Skelton or Dunbar, combined the qualities of the learned clerk and the jester or buffoon. Despite the dignity he desired for the poet, Jonson offers himself up at times for the amusement of his patrons, and he, too, has his 'flytings' and his beggings for money.

> It is the strength of his personality and his personal vision which makes him a living force in our literature. Like Chaucer, though less subtly, he capitalised on his own idiosyncrasies and made himself a character in his own work.
>
> —*J. B. Bamborough*

Again, as Dryden noticed, Jonson was the first Englishman to practise criticism as we understand it. He never published a complete account of his critical views, and what we have is scattered over his plays, prefaces and notebooks, but it is possible without difficulty to distinguish the outlines of a considered theory of literature, and a not ignoble one. In his actual critical observations about others, it is true, he seems to have been sometimes actuated by personal malice. This may be the unjust result of a haphazard preservation of his views—Coleridge thought Drummond to blame for having preserved Jonson's impromptu remarks about his contemporaries, made in confidence and without forethought. Jonson wrote hard things about his rivals, however, as well as saying them. Yet he was not always unjustified. Inspired as he was to justify and ennoble his art, he was right to attack cheap and careless writing, and although he was often ungenerous in not recognising merit in writers he disliked, he was not always wrong in pointing out their faults. Marston was indeed both scurrilous and bombastic; Dekker did lack an artistic conscience; Daniel is often empty and dull, and did not deserve his inflated reputation in his own day, which placed him above Spenser.

With some, to him more considerable writers, such as Chapman and Drayton, Jonson's relations were not always cordial, but were tinged with more respect; Chapman in particular he seems to have paid the courtesy of accepting as a rival for the favour of the learned. What is of most significance is that Jonson reserved his highest praise—and it is very generous, though never totally unqualified—for the three greatest writers of his age, Shakespeare, Donne and Bacon. Whatever Jonson's limitations in critical theory or personal feeling, they did not prevent him from recognising what was truly good. Envy expressed in malicious and ill-founded attack on writers was to him the progeny of Ignorance, and the greatest enemy of the Art which he tried to serve. He himself was not envious of the truly great artists that he knew: the same could not be said of all poets.

Drummond noted that Jonson was 'a great lover and praiser of himselfe, a contemner and Scorner of others', but he also jotted down that 'of all stiles he loved most to be named honest' [*Conversations*]. Honesty is a quality which Jonson frequently holds up for praise. To be 'honest', to him, was not simply to be trustworthy and frank, but to be exactly what one claimed to be—the exact sense in which Iago is *not* 'honest' (and in which Jonson recorded that Shakespeare was). It implied, therefore, a bluff readiness to speak one's mind, and this can easily appear brusqueness and conceit; but it implied also a readiness to state one's principles and abide by them. There is no doubt that this, as a writer, Jonson did. He was always explicit about his aims and methods, and he tried conscientiously to provide the satisfactions that he promised. In that sense he is one of the most 'honest' writers in our literature. This openness was in some ways a restraint upon him, and there were other, graver limitations in the scope of his creative mind. Yet Dryden's remark is true: 'he managed his strength to more advantage than any who preceded him'.

He set out to write at what appeared to be a great disadvantage, with the need to satisfy a volatile and largely uneducated public in a form which was generally despised. By establishing his own standards and relentlessly observing them, he managed to satisfy both public taste and critical precept—and also, and most importantly, his own artistic conscience. His efforts to please both the 'vulgar' and the 'judicious' were not uniformly successful, but at his best he produced plays which were—and still are—eminently rewarding both on the stage and in the study. It is impossible for us to regret, however much he himself may have done so, that circumstances forced him into the public theatre. If he had found a patron to support him he might have devoted himself exclusively to poetry and criticism, and would perhaps have written only closet drama, constructed according to the most stringent neoclassical rules. The result would no doubt have been interesting to the literary historian, but to no one else. But we cannot be sure that he would have been satisfied with this. Jonson was driven on by something more than a literary theorist's desire for 'correctness' and the moralist's urge to instruct; as F. R. Leavis has said, he

was as robustly interested in men and manners and his own talk as in literatures and the poetic art.

[F. R. Leavis, *Revaluation,* 1953]

He recognised himself that when his enemies wanted to attack him they did not do so on the grounds that his art was too abstract and intellectual, but because it was too close to real life:

> Alas, sir, *Horace!* hee is a meere spunge; nothing but humours, and observation; he goes up and downe sucking from every societie, and when hee comes home, squeazes himself drie again.
>
> [*Poetaster,* 4.3.104-107]

Jonson's dedication to Art was not a matter of intellectual conviction only, but was the product of an artist's desire to express his personality through his own vision of the world. Different artists achieve this in different ways; Jonson's chosen way was through stage illusion. It is this impulse that has given us his plays. That they are still alive, and that through them we can experience a world long since dead, is the true measure of his greatness.

Arthur F. Marotti (essay date 1972)

SOURCE: "All About Jonson's Poetry," in *ELH,* Vol. 39, No. 2, June, 1972, pp. 208-37.

[*In the following essay, Marotti reads Jonson's dramatic verse and masques along with his non-dramatic poetry in order to demonstrate the poet's stylistic virtuosity and his range between the extremes of copiousness and restraint.*]

> When we say that Jonson requires study, we do not mean study of his classical scholarship or of seventeenth-century manners. We mean intelligent saturation in his work as a whole; we mean that, in order to enjoy him at all, we must get to the centre of his work and his temperament, and that we must see him unbiased by time, as a contemporary.
>
> [T. S. Eliot, *Selected Essays,* 3rd ed., 1958]

It is only recently that Ben Jonson's poetry has begun to receive the kind of attention it truly deserves. Yet critics have usually segregated the non-dramatic poetry from the rest of the verse to consider it as a separate body of work—as though Jonson the poet and Jonson the dramatist were different men. Whatever the virtues or conveniences of such a strategy, it is responsible, I think, for a critical strait-jacketing of Jonson's art—to the end, perhaps, of demonstrating his adherence to the plain style, a neoclassical aesthetic, or an ethical vision. Unfortunately (but thankfully), Jonson's poetry and imagination are broader and more various than most contemporary discussions indicate. Considering the non-dramatic work alone, his poetry is an impossible hodge-podge—in subject matter, forms, styles, and quality: representing over four decades of artistic experimentation (his motto was "Tamquam explorator"), it is a radically uneven collection of "workes of divers nature,"some of which he called "my strange *poems,* which, as yet / Had not their forme touch'd by an English wit" [*For.* 12, ll. 81-82]. To flatten this poetry for the sake of ready definition or consistency of argument is to ignore the richness and inventiveness, as well as the heterogeneity, of his art.

In order to make some simple and basic observations about Jonson's imagination and the characteristics of his verse, I would like to give his poetry the broadest possible definition—to include the dramatic and masque verse along with the non-dramatic pieces. Jonson, after all, thought of himself as a poet in all his creative writing, specifically calling his plays dramatic "poems." Looking at this larger body of verse, we can, I think, better perceive Jonson's stylistic virtuosity, the way his poetry ranges between extremes of copiousness and restraint. Although I intend the remarks in the following pages to be critically descriptive rather than prescriptive (I am not so much interested in proving a thesis as re-exploring Jonson's work with open eyes), my focal points are two kinds of verse Jonson composed—the first a poetry of explosive imagery and perverse imagining, the second a poetry of more visible control, imagistically spare, prosodically tight, and intellectually lucid. Jonson is an artistic schizophrenic, with both a Dionysian and an Apollonian side.

I

Unlike Shakespeare, who left us no objective pronouncements on the arts of poetry and playwrighting, Jonson has bequeathed us a substantial body of criticism—by way of his posthumously-printed commonplace book, the *Discoveries,* the prefaces and prologues to his plays and masques, and the dramatic and extradramatic commentary in his plays, as well as through his conversations with William Drummond of Hawthornden, who recorded the most striking (sometimes obviously drunken) remarks the poet made during a visit in 1619. In some respects, this has proved more a burden than a help; for, too often, the temptation has been for some critics to demonstrate, with cart-before-the-horse logic, that Jonson's practice accords with his theory, and consequently, by a careful selection and somewhat easy use of evidence, to create an illusion of harmony between his criticism and art. It would, of course, be foolish to deny the many affiliations between the two: one must acknowledge Jonson's theoretical and practical classicism, his devotion to the rhetorical virtues of the plain style (brevity, perspicuity, life, and quickness), as well as his advocacy of the social and ethical values these artistic canons reflect. He certainly believed many of the things he said about poetry in his prose criticism or at least subscribed to them as statements of ideals. And yet the author of "the farce of the grand Devil arse" (*The Gypsies Metamorphosed*) was doing one thing in transmitting tribal wisdom—culled from the writings of Aristotle, Seneca, Cicero, Quintilian, and others—and quite another in composing much of his poetry.

We should be alerted to this fact by the obvious conflict between the real-life Jonson and some of his dignified artistic posturings. The self-image he projects in some of his more staid Roman performances is not that of the boisterously energetic and irascible man who enthusiastically drained the communion-cup on his reconversion to Anglicanism, who killed a fellow actor in a duel, and who boasted of giving John Marston a sound beating. The same poet who announced self-righteously in the dedicatory epistle to *Volpone* that it was impossible for anyone to be a good poet without first being a good man fondly reminisced with Drummond about some of his erotic escapades and was troubled, apparently, on his death-bed because he had profaned the Scriptures in his plays. There are striking inconsistencies between the literary dictator who is the spokesman for chaste art, traditional learning, and social values, and the real man.

I stress this conflict because it parallels the very real one between his theory and his practice. We would do well, I think, to come to terms with what Eliot called Jonson's "temperament"—to use his life as well as his criticism as a guide to his art; for it reveals some crucial aspects of his artistic make-up we might never discover in his theoretical writings. Take, for example, William Drummond's character sketch of Jonson at the end of the "Conversations," which presents an aspect of Jonson's creative temperament notably absent from the *Discoveries:*

> He is a great lover and praiser of himself, a contemner and Scorner of others, given rather to losse a friend, than a Jest, jealous of every word and action of those about him (especiallie after drink) which is one of the Elements in which he liveth) a dissembler of ill parts which raigne in him, a bragger of some good that he wanteth, thinketh nothing well bot what either he himself, or some of his friends, and Countrymen hath said or done. he is passionately kynde and angry, carelesse either to gaine or keep, Vindicative, but if he be well answered, at himself. . . . [he is] oppressed with fantasie, which hath ever mastered his reason, a general disease in many poets.

This last remark is particularly puzzling because one does not always think of Jonson—at least the Jonson of the non-dramatic poetry—as a man whose imagination "mastered his reason"; yet one thinks of the interesting anecdote in which Jonson says he "consumed a whole night in lying looking to his great toe, about which he hath seen tartars & turks Romans and Carthaginions feight in his imagination." This kind of nighttime daydreaming probably lay behind much of his work. His Horatian pose of sanity and moderation seems to have had little to do with the *genesis* of his art. One has only to recall how grotesque or unusual are some of the conceits he invents for his comedies: the obsessive fear of noise in *Epicoene,* the alchemical con-game in *The Alchemist,* the Boschian world of *Bartholomew Fair,* the staple of news, the magnetic lady. These are the products of a bizarre imagination flirting with a vision closer to madness than rational calm.

Jonson worried about this, I think, and exorcised his fears by dramatizing them in the infected imaginations of many of the characters in his plays: Morose of *Epicoene* with his daylight nightmares, Kitely of *Everyman In His Humour* who refers to his troublesome "imaginations" (III.iii.50), even a character like Littlewit of *Bartholomew Fair,* who exclaims with numbskull enthusiasm, "I do feel conceits coming upon me more than I am able to / turn tongue to" (I.i.31-3). As one of the below-stairs characters in *The New Inn* remarks: "We are all mortal, / And have our visions" (III.i.129-30). The compulsive Asper of *Everyman Out of His Humour* closely resembles the satirist-playwright in his moral vigilantism, reflecting Jonson's imagination in its most neurotic aspect.

If, in order to transform private vision into art, the creative writer must (as Freud suggests) soften the egotistical character of his daydream, Jonson accomplishes this by putting his poetry of the agitated imagination (the songs of the self-intoxicated ego) into the mouths of some of his dramatic characters. Immersed in their own dreams and imaginings, they often assume the poet's role and produce the very kind of verse Jonson supposedly would not allow himself, thus offering him the chance to express the fertile chaos of his brain in an artistically (and morally) legitimate way. Artistic vices Jonson specifically identifies in his criticism—rhetorical amplification and hyperbole, "faint, obscure, sordid, humble, improper, or effeminate *Phrase,*" farfetched metaphors, flagrant violations of decorum—these become, in the speeches of some of his characters, delightful viciousness. Take, for example, the veritable explosion of fancy in Volpone's seduction speech to Celia:

> The heads of parrats, tongues of nightingales,
> The braines of peacoks, and of estriches
> Shall be our food: and, could we get the phoenix,
> (Though nature lost her kind) shee were our dish.
> . . . . .
> Thy bathes shall be the iuyce of iuly-flowres,
> Spirit of roses, and of violets,
> The milke of vnicornes, and panthers breath
> Gather'd in bagges, and mixt with *cretan* wines.
> Our drinke shall be prepared gold, and amber;
> Which we will take, vntill my roofs whirle round
> With the *vertigo.* . . . .
>
> (III.vii.202-05, 213-19)

He elaborates his fantasy as he dreams of a succession of disguises he and Celia can wear for love-making, concluding his speech with the following:

> . . . we may so, trans-fuse our wandring soules,
> Out at our lippes, and score vp summes of pleasures,
> *That the curious shall not know,*
> *How to tell them, as they flow;*
> *And the enuious, when they find*
> *What their number is, be pind.*
>
> (III.vii.234-39)

Grotesquerie is metamorphosed into soft lyricism. Despite the protestations about the morality of art in Jonson's prefatory epistle to this play, we are obviously meant to enjoy this performance: Volpone's artful perversity is far more interesting than Celia's colorless virtue. His is the poetry of the drunken imagination of the auto-intoxicate;

but we relish its energy and inventiveness apart from any moral framework.

Probably the most fascinating poetry of this kind Jonson put into the mouth of Sir Epicure Mammon in *The Alchemist,* a man of "voluptuous mind" (IV. v.74), who is more spontaneously and hyperbolically fantastic than Volpone. His profligate imagination is excited, for example, when he dreams of the kind of life the philosopher's stone can create for him. Yearning for a luxury beyond luxury (for beds softer than down), he fantasizes the perfect setting for the banquet of sense: an "oual roome" (II.ii.42) filled with pornographic art, mirrors "Cut in . . . subtill angles, to disperse / And multiply the figures, as I walke / Naked betweene my *succubae*" (II.ii.46-8), perfumed mists, and baths "like pits to fall into" from which he and his harem can emerge to dry themselves "in gossamour and roses" (II.ii.52), cooled by eunuchs with the soft breezes of ostrich-tail fans. He is rapturous by the time he gets to the pleasures of taste:

> My meat, shall all come in, in *Indian* shells,
> Dishes of agate, set in gold, and studded,
> With emeralds, saphyres, hiacynths, and rubies.
> The tongues of carpes, dormise, and camels heeles,
> Boil'd i'the spirit of SOL, and dissolu'd pearle,
> (APICVS diet, 'gainst the *epilepsie*)
> And I will eate these broaths, with spoones of amber,
> Headed with diamant, and carbuncle.
> My foot-boy shall eate phesants, caluerd salmons,
> Knots, godwits, lamprey's: I my selfe will haue
> The beards of barbels, seru'd, in stead of sallades;
> Oild mushromes; and the swelling vnctuous paps
> Of a fat pregnant sow, newly cut off,
> Drest with an exquisite, and poynant sauce;
> For which, Ile say vnto my cooke, there's gold,
> Goe forth, and be a knight.
>
> (II.iii.72-87)

He wants shirts of "taffeta-sarsnet, soft and light / As cobwebs" (II.ii. 89-90), "gloues of fishes, and birds-skins, perfum'd / With gems of *paradise* and eastern aire" (II.ii. 93-4). Sir Epicure's fantasies are inexhaustible, an ever-bubbling comic Helicon. "Whom the disease of talking still once possesses," Jonson wrote elsewhere, "he can never hold his peace!" (*Disc.*, p. 574). And yet it is ultimately the poet himself who is vaporing here, as he tries to "make," in the words of Volpone, "so rare a musique out of discordes" (V.ii.18). When, towards the end of *The Alchemist,* the indulgent Lovewit relishes his butler Jeremy's "teeming wit" (V.i.16), Jonson is actually engaging in an indirect form of self-compliment; for it is the poet's copious imagination behind the play's prodigious variety of detail, expressed most clearly and energetically when the poetry, like Sir Epicure Mammon's, reflects the comic world in small.

These two speeches—which I have quoted at some length to give a sense of their imaginative leisureliness—reveal Jonson's peculiar interest in the poetry of catalogue, a characteristic manifestation of the prodigal fancy. Grotesque food fantasies stimulate the imaginations of Volpone and Sir Epicure most powerfully—the latter, in courting

Doll Common, rhapsodizes about pheasants' eggs, cockles in silver shells, and shrimp swimming in a butter made of dolphin's milk (IV.i.157-60). But the catalogue takes many other forms in Jonson's poetry: from the traditional flower-list in the masque *Pans Anniversarie* (Hereford and Simpson, VII, 530), to the vomiting of bad diction in *The Poetaster,* to the list of poets and their mistresses in *Underwood* 29, the collection of the jargon of alchemy recited by Surly in *The Alchemist* (II.iii.184 ff.), the inventory of the poet's burned study in **"An Execration upon Vulcan"** (*Und.* 45), and the account of the transmigration of Pythagoras' soul in *Volpone* (I.ii.1-62). Jonson's evident fascination with food and excrement images—for which Edmund Wilson has offered the obvious psychological explanation ["Morose Ben Jonson," in *Ben Jonson: A Collection of Critical Essays,* ed. Jonas Barish, 1963]—expresses itself readily in this medium. In fact, the catalogue itself, a sure sign of the collecting impulse, is as clear an indication of his "anality" as his pervasive gastro-intestinal imagery. And this is most striking, perhaps, in lines like the following from hiscatological mock-epic **"On the Famous Voyage"** (*Ep.* 133):

> The sinkes ran grease, and hair of meazled hogs
> The heads, houghs, entrailes, and the hides of dogs...
>
> . . . . .
>
> Cats there lay divers had been flead and rosted,
> And, after mouldie growne, again were tosted. . . .
>
> (145-46, 149-50)

Whether we find it in Rabelais, Skelton, Jonson, Pope, or Dickens, the excremental catalogue is a staple of comic and satiric literature. This passage, for example, has a later incarnation in the conclusion of Swift's "A Description of a City Shower":

> Sweepings from Butchers Stall, Dung, Guts, and
>   Blood,
> Drown'd Puppies, stinking Sprats, all drench'd in
>   Mud
> Dead cats and Turnip-Tops come tumbling down the
>   Flood.
>
> (61-63)
> [*Collected Poems of Jonathan Swift,* ed.
> Joseph Horrell, 1958]

The crammed catalogue tends, of course, to reduce everything to debris, clutter, the excremental (like the contents of Mrs. Jellyby's closet in *Bleak House*); and this accounts for some of the peculiar aesthetic repulsiveness of Volpone's and Sir Epicure Mammon's fantasies. Under a more strict control, however, this kind of poetry appears in Jonson's non-satiric verse. **Epigram 101, "Inviting a Friend to Supper,"** is, like Volpone's speech to Celia, a seduction poem; but the speaker offers his would-be guest a combination of festive freedom and sane moderation. Yet it is characteristic of Jonson, that the liveliest part of the piece is the poetic menu:

> An olive, capers, or some better sallade
> Ushering the mutton; with a short-leg'd hen,
> If we can get her, ful of egs, and then,

> Limons, and wine for sauce: to these, a coney
>   Is not to be despair'd of, for our money;
> And, though fowle, now, be scarce, yet there are
>   clarkes,
>   The skie not falling, think we may have larkes.
> Ile tell you more, and lye, so you will come:
>   Of partrich, phesant, wood-cock, of which some
> May yet be there; and godwit, if we can:
>   Knat, raile, and ruffe too.
>
> (10-20)

Here is the same imaginative fertility that underlies the more absured catalogues, even though, as one critic has put it, Jonson more obviously has "poetry on the leash" [Robert Sharp, *From Donne to Dryden,* 1940].

It is perhaps a bit perverse, in the context of this discussion, to mention Jonson's superb **"To Penshurst"** probably his best poem and a model of his neoclassical aesthetic. But it is as much thepoet of the "teeming wit," whose imagination contains a super-abundance of concrete details and expresses itself in the energetic particularity of the catalogue—it is as much this Ben Jonson behind Penshurst, as the Ben Jonson who was the sober admirer of Horace and Quintilian. Drawing its inspiration from the imaginatively rich fifty-eighth epigram of Martial's third book, this poem celebrates order and hierarchy, tradition and simple virtue—it is an historically exemplary piece of neoclassical verse—but Jonson does not bring his poetic materials under such a rigid control that all eruptive or disruptive energy is lost. As I see it, what would in itself be a pleasantly varied, if mostly generalized, account of the topography, flora and fauna, and way of life of the Penshurst estate, takes on a decidedly different character upon close examination. We are given a signal, I think, in the section on the Sidneys' hospitality, where the speaker particularly praises the kind of entertainment he receives because he can freely satisfy his great appetite:

> Here no man tells my cups; nor, standing by,
>   A waiter, doth my gluttony envy:
> But gives me what I call, and lets me eate,
>   He knowes, below, he shall finde plentie of meate,
> Thy tables hoord not up for the next day. . . .
>
> (67-71)

This humorous self-reference highlights the (unmistakably comic) elements of the preceding natural description: the fact that the speaker is a "glutton" forces us to recognize that the nature he has portrayed is essentially *an edible one* (an emphasis that is Jonson's and not that of the Martial epigram he imitates). He comes to nature by way of the dinner table:

> Thy copp's too, nam'd of *Gamage,* thou hast there,
>   That never failes to serve thee season'd deere,
> When thou wouldst feast, or exercise thy friends.
>
> . . . . .
>
> Each banke doth yeeld thee coneyes; and the topps
>   Fertile of wood, *Ashore,* and *Sydney's* copp's
> To crowne thy open table, doth provide
>   The purpled pheasant, with the speckled side:
> The painted partrich lyes in every field,

And, for thy messe, is willing to be killed.
And if the high swolne *Medway* faile thy dish,
  Thou hast thy ponds, that pay thee tribute fish,
Fat, aged carps, that runne into thy net.
  And pikes, now weary their owne kinde to eat,
As loth, the second draught, or cast to stay,
  Officiously at first, themselves betray.
Bright eeles, that emulate them, and leape on land,
  Before the fisher, or into his hand.
Then hath thy orchard fruit, thy garden flowers,
  Fresh as the ayre, and new as are the houres.
The early cherry, with the later plum,
  Fig, grape, and quince, each in his time doth come:
The blushing apricot, and wooly peach
  Hang on thy walls that every child may reach.

                      (19-21, 25-44)

Those over-obliging fish have struck readers before; but they are not merely a slight wrinkle in the poem's smooth surface. They are part of a larger method of handling details with what Jonson called elsewhere a "diligent kind of negligence and . . . sportive freedom" (*Disc.*). From one point of view, this whole passage is yet another comic food fantasy. And, when the poem moves from the world of nature to that of man, Jonson is reluctant to put an end to his list of edibles. Imitating nature's act of freely yielding its abundance, the peasants present their offerings to the Sidneys:

Some bring a capon, some a rurall cake,
  Some nuts, some apples; some that thinke they make
The better cheeses, bring 'hem; or else send
  By their ripe daughters, whom they would commend
This way to husbands; and whose baskets beare
  An embleme of themselves, in plum, or peare.

                      (51-56)

Capons, cakes, nuts, apples, cheeses, and ripe daughters. The use of plum and pear as sexual emblems helps to submerge the country girls in the extended food catalogue: here, as in the seduction scene of *Volpone,* Jonson's oral sensuality encompasses all. The speaker is at table long before he mentions the Sidneys' beer, bread, wine, and meat.

It would be misleading, of course, to place **"To Penshurst"** in the same category as Sir Epicure Mammon's surrcalistic gluttony; what I am suggesting is that it takes on a different complexion when one looks at it through the poetry of the agitated fancy rather than through Jonson's devotion to the plain style or our narrow notions of a neoclassical aesthetic. He creates a *concordia discors* in the poem—which is something other than the placid harmony of purling streams and painted meads. It is order with vitality, thematically and poetically.

In **"To Penshurst,"** Jonson exercises, in the words of one seventeenth-century commentator, his "judgment to order and govern fancy" [Clarendon's *History of the Rebellion,* in *Characters from the Histories and Memoirs of the Seventeenth Century,* ed. David Nichol Smith, 1918]. "The remedy of fruitfulnesse is easie," he writes in the *Discoveries,* "but no labour will helpe the contrary". The poet

must be able to "powre out the Treasure of his minde", but, afterwards, a stricter discipline must follow. Jonson had a passion for artistic economy, which he expressed in his famous remarks on Shakespeare:

> I remember the Players have often mentioned it as an honour to *Shakespeare,* that in his writing(whatsoever he penn'd) hee never blotted out line. My answer hath beene, Would he had blotted a thousand. . . . (I lov'd the man and doe honour his memory (on this side Idolatry) as much as any). Hee was (indeed) honest, and of an open, and free nature: had an excellent *Phantsie;* brave notions, and gentle expressions: wherein he flow'd with that facility, that sometime it was necessary he should be stopp'd. . . . His wit was in his owne power; would the rule of it had beene so too. . . .

Professional jealously aside, Jonson is really stating one of his own articles of faith here, his belief in meticulously careful composition.

II

Jonson was a notoriously slow writer, taking great pains to produce artistically economical works. He evidently felt the need for some powerful counterforce to his exploding imagination. But there was only so much he could do to discipline his poetry of "fantasie" without robbing it of its distinguishing characteristics: **"To Penshurst"** represents, perhaps, the most careful controlling and structuring of this kind of verse (its very arrangement reflects Jonson's conception of proper hierarchy). To achieve a stronger artistic control, he had to turn to a radically different poetry—one that escapes the artistic "vices" (as well as some of the particular virtues) of his more copious verse as it substitutes plain statement for metaphor, abstractions for things, and real objects for fantastic ones. These two (aesthetically incompatible) kinds of poetry bear some resemblance to Sidney's "*Eikastike*" and "*Phantastike*" verse—the first "figuring foorth good things" and the second "infect[ing] the fancie with vnworthy objects" ["An Apology for Poetry," in *Elizabethan Critical Essays*]. In some of Jonson's masques, we *experience* the change from one to the other in the movement from antimasque to masque (and vice versa) as a poetry of misrule yields to a poetry of order.

The same impulse that led Jonson to avoid (serious) romance and fantasy in his plays—to scorn "*Tales, Tempests,* and such like *Drolleries*" (*Bartholomew Fair,* "Induction," l. 30), dramas that appeal, like Shakespeare's tragicomedies, to our abilities to dream more wondrous things than nature can bring forth—lay behind his deep distrust of poetic ornamentation. In a sense, Jonson regards poetic images and conceits as self-indulgence and self-advertisement. The same poet who skillfully portrays the eloquent perversities of self-enclosed characters, rejects the poetry of private introspection and insists upon clear and simple communication—social, rather than private, verse. He objects to the poems of the mature Donne because they force the reader to follow closely the idiosyncratic mental processes of their author, whose working intellect is at the center of his verse. For Jonson, who remarked that Donne "for not being understood would perish" (*Conv.*), this was a sin of intellectual solipsism. Though he is surely one of the great literary egotists, Jonson is, at least in one respect, a self-effacing poet: his poetry usually appeals to a traditional wisdom in which we all share rather than, like Donne's, attempting to display the mental ingenuity of its creator (he disliked "selfe-boasting Rimes" [*Und.* 45, l. 26]).

In most of his non-dramatic verse, Jonson reveals an hostility to sensuous imagery as well as metaphoric inventiveness, which are to him impediments to communication, a disguising of subject matter he would like to represent in a more direct way. He might have found attractive Hegel's later definition of metaphor as "an interruption of the perceptive process and a continual distraction, because it generates and accumulates images not strictly relevant to the object" [Arnold Hauser, *Mannerism,* trans. Eric Mosbacher, 1965]. In **"An Epistle to Master John Selden"** (*Und.* 16), he writes:

> . . . I cannot be obscure:
> Lesse shall I for the Art or dressing care,
> Truth and the Graces best, when naked are.
>
> (2-4)

He announces, with unconcealed truculence, in the prefatory epistle to *Volpone:* " . . . *if my* Muses *be true to me, I shall raise the despis'd head of* poetrie *againe, and stripping her out of those rotten and base rags wherwith the Times have adulterated her form, restore her to her primitiue habit, feature, and maiesty, and render her worthy to be imbraced and kist, of all the great and master-*spirits *of our world.*" Abundant imagery, like inflated language, or cosmetics and garish fashions, is artistically (and morally) vicious.

Jonson stresses those characteristics poetry does not share with the visual arts; for he is conscious of the inferiority of poetry to painting as an imitation of physical reality—an awareness that is behind his quarrel with Inigo Jones over the relative merits of verse and scenery or costume in the masque. In a piece addressed to his painter-friend, Sir William Burlase, he says:

> you are he can paint; I can but write:
> A Poet hath no more but black and white,
> Ne knowes he flatt'ring Colours, or false light.
>
> (*Und.* 54, ll. 19-21)

In the *Discoveries,* he alludes to the intellectual commonplace, *ut pictura poesis,* but stresses the dissimilarity rather than the similarity of painting and poetry: "*Poetry,* and *Picture,* are Arts of a like nature; and both are busie about imitation. It was excellently said of *Plutarch, Poetry* was a speaking Picture, and *Picture* a mute Poesie. For they both invent, faine, and devise many things, and accommodate all they invent to the use, and service of nature. Yet of the two, the pen is more noble, then the Pencill. For that can speake to the Understanding; the other, but to the Sense" (*Disc.* This resembles the distinction he draws between the body and the soul of the masque in his preface to *Hymenaei.*)

In the third and fourth poems of the incomplete sequence dedicated to Lady Venetia Digby (*Und.* 86), Jonson deals at length with the question of sensuous imagery—in both painting and poetry. Here his anti-imagistic bias conflicts with his very real need for imagery, and the result is a kind of refined or "Platonic" imagery, an attempt to transcend, while at the same time compensating for the loss of, sensuous particularity. The first of the poems, **"Her Body,"** is addressed to van Dyke, who did Lady Digby's portrait, and it instructs the artist in the proper method of capturing her on canvas. He dismisses, at the outset, the kind of depiction of physical detail that would distract from rather than reveal the woman's beauty and the spiritual loveliness it reflects:

> Sitting, and ready to be drawne,
> What makes these Velvets, Silkes, and Lawne,
> Embroideries, Feathers, Fringes, Lace,
> Where every lim takes like a face?
>
> (1-4)

One recalls the graceful lyric from *Epicœne,* "Still to be neat, still to be drest," with its contempt for "th'adulteries of art". To paint Lady Digby's clothing is to paint a disguise: like poetry itself (and the connection is established when Jonson calls her his "*Muse*" [no. 4, l. 21]), she does not need the "suspected helps" (5) of particularized sensuous imagery. But, since the decorum of portraiture prevents the artist from rendering her in the nude, something must be "fitly interpos'd" (10) between her body and the viewer. So Jonson suggests an alternate kind of imagery in surely some of the strangest advice ever given a painter:

> Draw first a Cloud: all save her neck,
> And, out of that, make Day to breake;
> Till, like her face, it doe appeare,
> And men may thinke, all light rose there.
>
> Then let the beames of that, disperse
> The Cloud and show the Universe;
> But at such distance, as the eye
> May rather yet adore, then spy.
>
> Then Heaven design'd, draw next a Spring,
> With all that Youth, or it can bring:
> Foure Rivers branching forth like Seas,
> And Paradise confining these.
>
> Last, draw the circles of this Globe,
> And let there be a starry Robe
> Of Constellations 'bout her horld;
> And thou hast painted beauties world.
>
> (13-28)

This symbolic microcosm of beauty would not surprise us in Cesare Ripa's *Iconologia* or Jonson's own masques (in fact, this description has been compared to the figures Splendor and Perfection in *The Masque of Beauty*); but it would make for an unusual van Dyke.

Ultimately, Jonson makes the problem of depiction his own, not the painter's and, in the next poem, considers the place of imagery in the kind of poetic picture of Lady Digby's mind he feels better qualified to paint. He explains to van Dyke:

Not that your Art I doe refuse:
But here I may no colours use.
   Beside, your hand will never hit
   To draw a thing that cannot sit.
                       (1-8)

The pun on colors (pigments and rhetorical figures) harks back to Jonson's words to Burlase; but this poem works out the implications of an anti-imagistic bias more carefully. In refusing a painter's images or symbols, he rejects poetic metaphor:

You could make shift to paint an Eye,
   An Eagle towring in the skye,
   The Sunne, a Sea, or soundlesse Pit;
   But these are like a Mind, not it.
                     (9-12)

Practically these very same images satisfy Keats in the Elgin Marbles sonnet; yet they will not do for Jonson. As he begins to describe Lady Digby's mind, he demands some kind of equivalence, or the thing itself:

I call you *Muse;* now make it true:
   Henceforth may every line be you;
   That all may say, that see the frame,
   This is no Picture, but the same.
                  (21-24)

In some poems, Jonson pretends that a proper name can express a person's soul. He spends the whole epigram on Lucy, Countess of Bedford (*Ep.* 76) preparing to write something worthy of her; but the best he can do is (borrowing a trick from Sidney) to bring the full weight of the poem to bear on her name: "Such when I meant to faine, and wish'd to see, / My *Muse* bad, *Bedford* write, and that was shee" (17-18). In the Lady Digby poem, however, he ultimately finds imagery impossible to avoid. He moves from an adjectival mode—"A Mind so pure, so perfect fine, / As 'tis not radiant, but divine" (25-26)—to the quiet reintroduction of more visibly figurative language: her speech is "Musique to the eare," her "Voyce so sweet, the words so faire, / As some soft chime had stroak'd the ayre" (35, 37-38). Finally, the last stanzas, which portray Lady Digby's body as her mind's dwelling-place, return to an unashamed use of simile and metaphor:

Thrice happy house, that hast receipt
   For this so loftie forme, so streight,
   So polish, perfect, round, and even,
   As it slid moulded off from Heaven.

Not swelling like the Ocean proud,
   But stooping gently, as a Cloud,
   As smooth as Oyle pour'd forth, and calme
   As showers; and sweet as drops of Balme.
       . . . . .
In action, winged as the wind,
   In rest, like spirits left behind
   Upon a banke, or field or flowers,
   Begotten by the wind, and showers.
            (53-60, 65-68)

Jonson's rejection of sensuous particularity leads not—as it does elsewhere—to a near-total absence of imagery, but to the creation of a more generalized or rarefied variety, to Shelleyan rather than Keatsian imagery. These low-visibility images are closer to the world of thoughts than to the world of physical multiplicity and can, supposedly, better reflect spiritual realities. In his **"Epistle to Katherine, Lady Aubigny"** he boasts: "My mirror is more subtile, cleere, refin'd, / And takes, and gives the beauties of the mind" (*For.* 13, ll. 43-44). And yet this neoplatonic aesthetic (which he puts on from time to time like a clean shirt) accounts for some of the worst poetry Jonson wrote—much of his masque verse, for example.

Jonson (consciously or unconsciously) sought for and found suitable substitutes for vivid metaphors and lively images, other sources of variety, energy, and richness. Sometimes he enlivens his poetry of statement by creating what Phillip Wheelwright has called "semantic tension" [*The Burning Fountain: A Study in the Language of Symbolism,* rev. ed., 1968], either between a classical manner and a contemporary setting or between the values of a community of wise and virtuous men and the actual world of social turmoil in which they live. He also tries to make abstractions carry the burden images ordinarily bear. In the masques and in poems like the one prefaced to Raleigh's *Historie of the World* (**"The mind of the Frontispice to a Booke,"** *Und.* 26), the abstract ideas relate to concrete images outside the poetry itself: the costumes, music, and scenery of the masque and the elaborate frontispiece of Raleigh's book.

Jonson is able to tap a rich source of energy by employing what might be called the technique of anti-metaphor in some of his poems. Instead of defining something by saying what it is like, he says what it is not like. He uses this strategy in the poetry of praise, following a *via negativa* of complement. To define the virtue of Sir Robert Wroth, for example, he dissociates him from other men in his society:

Let others watch in guiltie armes, and stand
   The furie of a rash command. . . .
       . . . . .
Let this man sweat, and wrangle at the barre,
       . . . . .
Let thousands more goe flatter vice, and winne,
   By being organes to great sinne,
Get place, and honor, and be glad to keepe
   The secrets, that shall breake their sleepe:
       . . . . .
But thou, my *Wroth,* if I can truth apply,
   Shall neither that, nor this envy:
   Thy peace is made. . . .
      (*For.* 3, ll. 67-68, 73, 85-88, 91-93)

Jonson's masques, which define the values they celebrate by presenting their opposites in the antimasques, employ a similar strategy.

It is in the relationship of poetic form to content that Jonson finds a particularly rich source of tension and vitality.

Usually, however, he objected to poetic forms with high visibility, preferring couplets to all other kinds of verse. He wrote **"A Fit of Rime Against Rime"** (*Und.* 31) to demonstrate how form could get in the way of content. He "scorned Anagrams" (*Conv.* and acrostics, and disliked the sonnet because he thought it (paradoxically) encouraged needless amplification or too extreme compression. The comedy of much of his parodic verse (he was particularly addicted to Skeltonics) springs from the mismatch of form and content. Even in his serious attempt to compose an English Pindaric Ode, the poem to Cary and Morison (*Und.* 72), he betrays an uneasiness with high-definition form by including deliberate structural jokes: he ends one strophe with "Ben," and begins the next with "Jonson"; he stretches the word "twilight" over two lines. Highly patterned poetry, he felt, could muffle its own meaning by calling too much attention to its own artifice.

Still, he does exploit the relationship of form and content to good effect in at least one kind of poem, the epitaph. Conscious of the tight control it imposes, Jonson writes, at the start of his **Epitaph on Lady Elizabeth**:

> Wouldst thou heare, what men can say
>   In a little? Reader, stay.
> Under-neath this stone doth lye
>   As much beautie, as could dye. . . .
>   (*Ep.* **124**, ll. 1-4)

One critic has remarked: "The restraint of the style becomes a manifestation of inner restraint before the fact of death" [O. B. Hardison, Jr., *The Enduring Monument: A Study of the Idea of Praise in Renaissance Literary Theory and Practice*, 1962]. But it is the form itself that forces stylistic compression. One can detect this most clearly in those epitaphs which are apparently expressions of genuine feeling—such as the one occasioned by the death of his first son. Behind the composition of this poem is an interesting bit of biography we find in the *Conversations with Drummond*:

> When the king came in England, at that tyme the Pest was in London, he [Jonson] being in the Country at Sr Robert Cottons house with old Cambden, he saw in a vision his eldest sone (yn a child and at London) appear unto him wt ye Marke of a bloodie crosse on his forehead as if it had been cutted wt a sword, at which amazed he prayed unto God, and in ye morning he came to Mr. Cambdens chamber to tell him, who persuaded him it was but ane apprehension of his fantasie at which he sould not be disjected. In ye mean tyme comes yr letters from his wife of ye death of yt boy in ye plague. He appeared to him he said of a Manlie shape & of yt Grouth that he thinks he shall be at the resurrection.

Although Camden's diagnosis might be clinically correct, we can still sense, beneath the flat surface of Drummond's prose, how powerful an experience this must have been for Jonson. Yet when we read the epitaph he composed for the boy, we are struck as much by what he does not say as by what he does:

> Farewell, thou child of my right hand, and joy;
>   My sinne was too much hope of thee, lov'd boy.
> Seven yeeres tho'wert lent to me, and I thee pay,
>   Exacted by thy fate, on the just day.
> O, could I lose all father, now. For why
>   Will man lament the state he should envie?
> To have so soone scap'd worlds, and fleshes rage,
>   And, if no other miserie, yet age?
> Rest in soft peace, and, ask'd, say here doth lye
>   *Ben Jonson* his best piece of *poetrie*.
> For whose sake, hence-forth, all his vowes be such,
>   As what he loves may never like too much.
>   (*Ep.* 45)

Elaborate artistry, he implies, would be an unkindness to his son's memory; and so the poem both refuses to give ornate expression to a father's natural sorrow and it controls the poet's desire for artistic display: imagistic and emotional particularity are refined out of the poem. Still, the epigraph's miniature form (small in comparison to the formal elegy) interacts with the large emotion it adumbrates; in the words of one critic, "the neatness of its design is a part of the discipline of the speaker's feelings" [L. A. Beaurline, "The Selective Principle in Jonson's Shorter Poems," *Criticism* 8 (1966)]. This kind of tension seems to have been, for Jonson, one of the most attractive features of the classical epigram.

Jonson discovers a way of combining the energy of his fantasytormented characters with the artistic clarity and neatness of his simpler verse in those poems that exploit the figure of the poetic persona or the dramatic speaker. This is his most effective way of compensating for the loss of imagistic variety in much of his verse; for it springs from what is most basic and interesting in Jonson's art.

At the very center of Jonson's poetic world is the idea of imposture. It is basic to his world-view as a comic dramatist, and, curiously, to his concept of literary imitation as well. In his prose he reiterates the world-stage topos adding his own personal twist: "*I have considered, our whole life is like a Play: wherein every man, forgetfull of himselfe, is in travaile with expression of another. Nay, wee so insist in imitating others, as wee cannot (when it is necessary) returne to our selves: like Children, that imitate the vices of Stammerers so long, till at last they become such; and make the habit to another nature, as it is never forgotten*" (*Disc.*). This mysterious transformation of identity also occurs, Jonson implies, in the imitation of another author; in fact, it is *necessary* for the poet "to convert the substance, or Riches of another *Poet,* to his owne use. To make choise of one excellent man above the rest, and so to follow him, till he grow a very *Hee:* or, so like him, as the Copie may be mistaken for the Principall. Not, as a Creature, that swallowes, what it takes in, crude, raw, or indigested; but, that feedes with an Appetite, and hath a Stomacke to concoct, divide, and turne all into nourishment" (*Disc.*). Jonson digested Martial before he wrote his epigrams; he mimicked Horace in his verse epistles, and Catullus in his love poems; he played on "th'Alcaike Lute" and "Anacreons Lyre" (*U.P.* 53, 11, 42, 43); he translated the *Ars Poetica,* and passages from Petronius, Seneca, Cicero, and others. In the

Discoveries he practices a form of imposture by presenting as his own adaptations and translations from both classical authors and modern critics. The speaking voices we hear are *assumed;* Jonson's ventriloquism carries well beyond his plays. I stress this because critics have been too casual about calling these other voices Jonson's.

Critical discussions of imposture and role-playing in Jonson's dramas have concentrated upon three kinds of characters, partly because they serve, in different ways, as artist-figures: the moralists and virtuous men (like Crites of *Cynthia's Revels,* Horace of *The Poetaster,* Cordus of *Sejanus,* and Cicero of *Catiline*), the satirists (like Asper of *Everyman Out of his Humour,* Arruntius of *Sejanus,* Morose of *Epicoene,* Surly of *The Alchemist,* Sir Humphrey Wasp of *Bartholomew Fair*), and the dissembler-villains (like Volpone and Mosca or Subtle and Face of *The Alchemist*). The first type is too morally alienated from a vicious world to participate in it fully; the second is overwhelmed by and, in a way, becomes as corrupt as the world he tries to scourge; and the third is of the world, but tries to control its events by manipulating others much the way a good dramatist maneuvers his characters. The first two reappear in the epigrams and verse epistles. There is another type, however, at least as close to the author as the others, but relatively neglected because of the prevailing notion of Jonson as a serious-minded scholar-artist. This is the group of buffoons and practical jokers.

We know of at least one incident in Jonson's life that suggests a boyish delight in practical jokes and imposture. We read in the *Conversations with Drummond:* "with the consent of a friend [he] cousened a lady, with whom he had made an apointment to meet an old Astrologer in the suburbs, which she keeped & it was himself disguised in a longe Gowne & a whyte beard at the light of (a) dimm burning Candle up in a little Cabinet reached unto by a ladder" (*Conv.*). This is not very surprising from the author of *The Alchemist.* It is in his later works, however, that he most deliberately chooses the buffoon or jokester figure as his favorite artistic persona. The Induction to *The Staple of News* describes "the Poet" as follows:

> *Yonder he is within (I was i' the Tiring-house a while to see the* Actors *drest) rowling himselfe up and downe like a tun, i' the midst of 'hem, and spurges, never did vessel of wort, or wine work so! His sweating put me in minde of a good Shrouing dish (and I beleeue would be taken up for a service of state somewhere, an't were knowne) a stew'd* Poet!

(ll. 61-66)

Jonson's avatar in *The New Inn* is a mad host buffoon [see Northrop Frye, *Anatomy of Criticism,* 1957] who is described as "some round-growne thing! a Jug, / Fac'd with a beard, that fills out to the ghests, / And takes in, fro' the fragments o' their jestes" (I.iv.13-15).

In his non-dramatic poetry, Jonson puts one or another version of this comic persona to interesting uses. There are, of course, many poems (regarded as autobiographical) in which he seems merely to be indulging in playful self-reference. He calls attention in "**My Picture Left in Scotland**" (*Und.* 11) to his "mountaine belly" and his "rockie face" (l. 17); we learn in *Under-wood* 56 and 58 that he weighs approximately 280 pounds; he apologizes in one of his love elegies (*Und.* 40) for getting drunk and committing some unspecified social *faux pas* (this sounds like the Ben Jonson of legend). But, in converting life into art—and gaucherie into civility—Jonson stylizes this buffoon figure and creates a vivid contrast between his ungainly appearance and his beautiful language. Consider the fact that he placed the lovely song "Come my Celia" in the mouth of a malicious middle-aged lecher in *Volpone;* I find it difficult to read Jonson's other Catullan performances without imagining a similar speaker. In his love poetry, Jonson cannot resist calling attention to the contrast between the speaker and his language:

> Let me be what I am, as *Virgil* cold;
>   As *Horace* fat; or as *Anacreon* old;
> No Poets verses yet did ever move,
>   Whose Readers did not thinke he was in love.
> Who shall forbid me then in Rithme to bee
>   As light, and active as the youngest hee
> That from the Muses fountaines doth indorse
>   His lynes, and hourely sits the Poets horse?
> Put on my Ivy Garland, let me see
>   Who frownes, who jealous is, who taxeth me.

(*Und.* 44, ll. 1-10)

No matter how gross and clumsy the lover, he reminds us in another poem:

> . . . the Muse is one, can tread the Aire,
>   And stroke the water, nimble, chaste, and faire,
> Sleepe in a Virgins bosome without feare. . . .

(*Und.* 58, ll. 13-15)

Jonson masterfully exploits this contrast between an unhandsome speaker and sweet words in the famous "Charis" poems (*Und.* 4), a sequence I would like to examine in some detail. If we recall the first poem in *The Forrest,* "Why I write not of love" (a promise Jonson breaks, but only technically), it seems odd that he attempted these ten poems to a court lady. He usually comes across as a gruff antifeminist: virtually every time one of his female characters opens her mouth she makes a fool of herself. "**A Celebration of Charis in Ten Lyrick Peeces**" is a misleading title; Jonson does not suddenly abandon his typical attitude toward women to pay court to a noble mistress. He does, however, disguise his feelings for the better part of the sequence by hiding behind the mask of a comic speaker.

We can glimpse some of his innate hostility to the role he is playing as the court lover in the initial poem, "His excuse for loving." The figure he cuts is ridiculous—that of the infatuated fifty-year-old—a mask of folly concealing what proves to be a most alert aggressiveness; "Let it not your wonder move / Lesse your laughter; that I love" (1-2) he begins. Once again, Jonson combines an unhandsome speaker with sweet rhetoric:

And it is not always face,
Clothes, or Fortune gives the grace;
Or the feature, or the youth:
But the Language, and the Truth,
With the Ardor, and the Passion
Gives the Lover weight and fashion.

(7-12)

Although these lines invite us to forget the speaker's appearance and attend to his words, the rest of the sequence intrudes his presence upon our consciousness. Through a kind of studied clumsiness he reminds us of the contrast between the burly middle-aged lover and the delicacy of his Anacreontic lyricism and courtly dream world: "Farre I was from being stupid / For I ran and call'd on Cupid" (**No. 2**, ll. 5-6) he writes left-handedly. In this same poem, the second of the group, he becomes a figure of comic impotence, a rude misfit in the world of courtly gentility. Jonson immobilizes him in a comic tableau:

Cupids Statue with a Beard
Or else one that plaid his Ape,
In a *Hercules*-his shape. . . .

(30-32)

Exposed to public ridicule by Charis' rejection, he now converts the sequence from celebration to (subtle) revenge:

Looser-like now, all my wreake
Is, that I have leave to speake,
And in either Prose, or Song,
To revenge me with my Tongue,
Which how Dexterously I doe
Heare and make Example too.

(**No. 3**, ll. 21-26)

Now a kind of villain fool, he advertises the cleverness of his design, whose success depends largely on the disparity between his intentions and the role he has assumed. Yet in the next poem, surprisingly, he offers self-consciously stylized complement, done in the manner of much of the masque poetry. There is a clue to what he is doing in the last stanza, where he virtually assaults Charis (and the reader) with sensuous imagery:

Have you seen but a bright Lillie grow,
  Before rude hands have touch'd it?
Ha' you mark'd but the fall of the Snow
  Before the soyle hath smutch'd it?
Ha' you felt the wooll o' the Bever:
  Or Swans Downe ever?
Or have smelt o' the bud o' the Brier?
  Or the Nard in the fire?
Or have tasted the bag of the Bee?
O so white! O so soft! O so sweet is she!

(21-30)

Words like "rude hands" and "smutch'd" (the unconscious wish surfaces in the idea of defilement) and imagery from rustic and homely, rather than courtly, contexts ("wooll of the Bever," "bud o' the Brier," "bag of the Bee") clash with the mythological machinery of the rest of the poem, high-

lighting its artificiality or unreality. This poem's hyperbolic manner is exactly what Jonson satirizes in Ovid's praise of Julia in *The Poetaster* (I.iii.38-58); and the folksy imagery of this stanza resembles the more obvious parody found in Penyboy Jr.'s tongue-in-cheek blazon of Lady Pecunia in *The Staple of News:* "her smiles they are *Love*'s fetter! / Her brests his apples, her teats strawberries!" (I.ii.53-54). Like Lady Pecunia, Charis becomes "a theame that's overcome with her owne matter" (IV.ii.76-77).

The little drama between the speaker and Cupid in the fifth poem, with its extension of the hyperbolic praise begun in the previous lyric, is suspect because it looks, from the vantage point of the next poem, like an elaborate strategy to win a kiss, which it succeeds in doing:

Charis guesse, and doe not misse,
Since I drew a Morning kisse
From your lips, and suck'd an ayre
Thence, as sweet, as you are faire,
  What my Muse and I have done:
Whether we have lost or wonne. . . .

(1-6)

Love poems are lies, he intimates, and he concludes his flattery with:

  Guesse of these, which is the true;
And, if such a verse as this,
May not claime another kiss.

(34-36)

Judging from Jonson's inclusion of a "kiss poem" in *Cynthia's Revels* (IV.iii.242-53) as an outstanding example of effete court poetry, there is something strange about his presentation of this kind of lyric as the seventh piece in the Charis sequence. If we recall that the speaker is a kind of Silenus in a drawing-room, the comedy of the poem comes to life: "I'le taste as lightly as the Bee, / That doth but touch his flower and flies away" (5-6). Like Volpone, who poses as love's gentle gourmet but then tries to rape Celia, the speaker of this poem finally unmasks to confess the less delicate kind of kissing he'd prefer:

Joyne lip to lip, and try:
  Each suck others breath.
And whilst our tongues perplexed lie,
Let who will thinke us dead, or wish our death.

(15-18)

In these last three poems, he effectively aims the ridicule away from himself and at Charis. She is put on the defensive as he displays his own wit in the execution of artful poetic revenge. The eighth poem explicitly shifts attention from the lover to his mistress, who emerges now as that familiar Jonsonian satiric butt, the vain lady of fashion, who sits before her "Idoll Glass" (22) performing her cosmetic rites. And, to make matters worse, we learn here that she is a woman past her prime: "All your sweet of life is past" (28) he teases.

It is this shallow-brained, and aging, coquette who describes her man in the ninth poem—a man who is not a man, for, like Marvell's nymph, she is afraid of a real one. She prefers a boy with French fashions, "crisped haire / Cast in a thousand snares, and rings" (10-11), looking "wanton-wise, / Eye-brows bent like *Cupids* bow, / Front an ample field of snow" (16-18). Some of the very same images applied to Charis earlier now reappear. He should have "nose and cheeke . . . Smooth as is the Billiard Ball; / Chin as wooly as the Peach" (19-21). He should be sensual, but non-aggressive:

> And his lip should kissing teach,
> Till he cherish'd too much beard,
> And make *Love* or me afeard.
>
> (22-24)

Clearly, by the time she describes his inner qualities (which do not particularly excite her imagination), it is apparent she wants neither a man, nor love: only a boy and sensuality in small sips. This exposure of Charis, presented as her self-exposure, is the master-stroke of revenge. The short, final lyric in the sequence, spoken by another court lady, satirizes women from a different angle. Like Charis, this woman is taken with wealth, fashion, and youth; but, like the comic lover, she is interested in meatier sexual satisfaction. As she says to Charis: "What you please, you parts may call, / 'Tis one good part I'ld lie withall" (7-8). **"A Celebration of Charis in Ten Lyrick Peeces"** ends with a bawdy *double entendre*. Women are, finally, either vain and opportunistic flirts or callous libertines. Jonson transforms courtly love poetry into sophisticated satire; and he is able to do this largely through his adroit manipulation of his dramatic speaker.

III

Although I began writing about Jonson's poetry with no large thesis to prove—only with the conviction that it is not all of a piece, that the non-dramatic verse ought not to remain separate from the other poetry, and that Jonson's biography offers as many insights into his art as his criticism does—at this point one conclusion forces itself upon me: that the two basic kinds of poetry Jonson wrote are linked through the figure of the dramatic speaker and the idea of role-playing. If we think of a character like Sir Epicure Mammon, who speaks the most typical kind of poetry of the agitated fancy and compare him with Jonson's persona in (the first eight poems of) the Charis sequence, some interesting similarities appear: both are, for the poet, self-conscious roles, yet they both reveal Jonson's artistic mischievousness. He indulges his play instinct in two different ways: the main difference is that, in the former case, he does not block or seriously restrain the explosive force of his imagination, and, in the latter case, he does—but in such a way that he gives some sense of an underlying sensuality and perversity Sir Epicure Mammon offers him the opportunity to express. In poems like those of the Charis sequence, then, Jonson's Dionysian and Apollonian poetry approach one another. They actually meet in the figure of Volpone, who can shift from dreaming about eating nightingales' tongues and peacock brains to reciting the masterfully controlled lyric **"To Celia"** ("Come my *Celia,* let us prove"). Volpone's personality, which is, I think, a curious reflection of Jonson's, embraces the two poetic styles.

It is Jonson himself who finally becomes the central point of reference in any discussion of his art. He stands behind all the roles in his dramatic and non-dramatic poetry, variously playing a poverty-stricken scholar, a friend to the great, a latter-day Horace or Martial, a temperate moralist, an enraged satirist, a voracious epicure, a bungling lover, a delicate sensualist, even a (not very convincing) devout Christian. If we carefully examine either the author figures of the plays and masques or the speakers of the non-dramatic poems, we reach an essential paradox: Jonson is, like Robert Browning, none of his characters and all of them. From one point of view, to put it in Keats's terms, his poetical character "has no self—it is everything and nothing—It has no character. . . . The Poet . . . has no Identity." Yet negative capability is a strange characteristic to assign to such a self-advertising and egocentric artist; we would have to say also that, for us, Ben Jonson has one of the most clearly defined characters of any poet in the language. We feel we *know* him, in a way we do not know Shakespeare.

Jonson is a poet of fascinating contradictions and complexities: his imagination explodes in images, yet he despises imagery; he writes poetry "ramm'd with life" (*The Poetaster,* III.i.136), but he sometimes turns his back on the world of flesh and blood; his criticism is an inadequate and misleading guide to his art, but one must inevitably consult it; despite the distance between the real man and his artistic personae, he is felt in every one of them; like Wordsworth after him, he tried to clear poetry of cant, but few poets could make better poetry out of it. In the face of all this, one must be extremely hesitant about offering schematic frameworks for or pat generalizations about Jonson's poetry; the two basic kinds of verse I have defined are not intended as hard and fast categories, but as points of reference in our confrontation with an enormously varied and puzzling body of verse. I would like, however, to make one final suggestion. If Jonson is to cease being our greatest unread classic (as T. S. Eliot called him) we ought to feel free to walk about his literary landscape—not searching for evidence to prove an argument, but with eyes open to the unusual, the surprising, and the delightful. Then, perhaps, later on, much later on, everything will in some mad fashion come into focus.

Harris Friedberg (essay date 1974)

SOURCE: "Ben Jonson's Poetry: Pastoral, Georgic, Epigram," in *English Literary Renaissance,* Vol. 4, No. 1, Winter, 1974, pp. 111-36.

[*In the following essay, Friedberg analyzes Jonson's poems in terms of the classical literary tradition.*]

Like Donne, Jonson began his poetic career with the epigram. For a man like Jonson who believed that "it is onely the disease of the vnskilfull, to thinke rude things greater then polish'd: or scatter'd more numerous then compos'd," the epigram remains the perfect form, one that convinces by its point rather than its logic, and Jonson's *Epigrams* contain some of his most "polish'd" and effective writing. Many of the *Epigrams* provided subjects for his plays: there are epigrams "To Alchymists," "On Lieutenant Shift," "On Court-worme," "On Don Surly," "To Fine Lady Would-bee," poems which combine Jonson's considerable talent for lighting on the abuses of the town with a skeptical, almost metaphysical, wit. Yet mixed with these satires in miniature are commendatory poems, poems of public praise addressed to Jonson's friends at court and poems of private sorrow like those "On My First Daughter" and "On My First Sonne." The obverse to his satiric epigrams, these poems celebrate an ideal and redress the balance upset by the jaundiced eye of the satirist. Although they differ in tone, they conform to the same poetic and expound the same morality, the same attitude toward life and toward the profession of the poet. By adopting the epigram as his primary form and by reducing the epigram to the central act of naming the good man, Jonson commits himself to making his poem a perfect record of the world. Significance no longer resides in feigning; "making," the essential meaning of the poetic act which Jonson traces etymologically to the Greek *potein,* he understands as constructing rather than creating, an architectural rather than visionary activity. The poet's glory, to Jonson, comes from his ability to reflect the world, its brass as well as its gold, not his ability to transcend it. Sidney's great vision of the poet spurning the earth, renouncing its brazen nature for his own golden one, no longer seems possible to Jonson. Part of the reason for Jonson's retrenchment, his rejection of a visionary poetry for a poetry of reference, is temperamental, but part of that rejection is due to the new way in which the century sees language and especially the language of praise.

> By adopting the epigram as his primary form and by reducing the epigram to the central act of naming the good man, Jonson commits himself to making his poem a perfect record of the world.
>
> —*Harris Friedberg*

Jonson's poems of praise raise the same problems of sincerity and conviction which troubled Sidney in *Astrophil and Stella* and Shakespeare in those sonnets addressed to the friend. Two centuries of Petrarchanizing had reduced the poetry of praise to a mere formula which any poetaster could imitate. The court poet, as Touchstone knew, had won a reputation for "feigning" by showering his compliments on unworthy subjects. "Since men haue left to doe praise-worthy things," Jonson complained to the Earl of Suffolk, "Most thinke all praises flatteries. But truth brings / That sound, and that authoritie with her name, / As, to be rais'd by her, is onely fame" (*Epigrams* LXVII, 2-4). In language which recalls Shakespeare's greatest sonnets, Jonson shows how the flattering poet becomes infatuated with the false image of virtue he has created.

> Away, and leaue me, thou thing most abhord,
> That hast betray'd me to a worthlesse lord;
> Made me commit most fierce idolatrie
> To a great image through thy luxurie.
> (LXV, "To My Mvse," ll. 1-4)

Typically, Jonson's poems of praise begin with a discussion of the moral worth not of the subject but of the genre and finally raise more questions about the genre, and about the relationship between poetry and the acknowledgement of virtue, than about the person praised. Often their wit turns on poetry's failure to express what it should. Jonson's highest praise, like that he affords to Donne, is to insist that his subject transcends his poetry's ability to praise: "All which I meant to praise, and, yet, I would; / But leaue, because I cannot as I should!" (**XXIII**, 9-10).

Jonson's praise of Donne as beyond praise is, of course, the most gross and palpable flattery of all; it succeeds because it is so outrageous. Yet it marks an important theme in Jonson's poetry, the recognition that poetry is inadequate either to create or express real virtue, that its only function must be to recognize and proclaim the virtue it finds in the real world. Naming the virtuous man becomes a moral act, a poem in itself. To William Herbert, Earl of Pembroke and pretender to the title of Shakespeare's Mr. W. H. Jonson wrote: "I doe but name thee PEMBROKE, and I find / It is an *Epigramme,* on all mankind" (**CII**, 1-2). To Mary, Lady Wroth, Sir Philip Sidney's niece, Jonson addressed a poem which inverts the Petrarchan mode and tells the lady how little she needs a poet's praise to achieve the immortality of fame.

> How well, faire crowne of your faire sexe, might hee,
> That but the twi-light of your sprite did see,
> And noted for what flesh such soules were fram'd,
> Know you to be a SYDNEY, though vn-nam'd?
> And, being nam'd, how little doth that name
> Need any *Muses* praise to giue it fame?
> Which is, it selfe, the *imprese* of the great,
> And glorie of them all, but to repeate!
> (CIII, 1-8)

The poem begins like a Petrarchan sonnet; the word "crowne" invokes the Petrarchan metaphor of sovereignty, and the rhetorical questions which open the poem free Jonson from the flatterer's needs for assertion; he can praise his lady without seeming to flatter her, also a Petrarchan strategy. Yet in the third and fourth couplets Jonson turns on his Petrarchan model, his claim to be able to confer immortality on his subject. The Sidney name does not need the Muses to praise it; rather the poem derives its "glorie" from simply being able to repeat the name. The rhetorical question of ll. 5-6 emphasizes the tentative quality of the poem; its negative statement, continued throughout, questions the value of the poem, the purpose of praise, and not the lady herself. Compared to the accomplishments of the Sidney family, Jonson's poem is an admitted irrelevance; it is an *imprese,* a seal ring or emblem which is nothing by itself, a mere counter. Thus, Jonson's poem on its simplest level is but a repetition of the name of virtue, an acknowledgement of an ideal, not its creation. Unlike the

Petrarchans, those "lowdest praisers, who perhaps would find / For euery part a character assign'd" (**CIII,** 11-12), and spin a model of virtue out of their own witty conceits, Jonson admits he cannot manufacture virtue: "My praise is plaine, and where so ere profest, / Becomes none more then you, who need it least" (13-14). If poetry has a moral function, and if that moral function is to acknowledge goodness, he argues, then poetry is a form of naming, of designating virtue by giving it a name and by naming those men and women who embody it.

Jonson's insistence on the reference of poetry is perhaps clearest in his superb commendatory poem **"On Lucy Countesse of Bedford."** The poem has implicit connections with Elizabethan love poetry and the Petrarchan convention, and it opens with a formal invocation of the Muse. Yet the poem parodies the *afflatus* theory of poetry suggested by the invocation:

> This morning, timely rapt with holy fire,
>   I thought to forme vnto my zealous *Muse,*
> What kinde of creature I coulde most desire,
>   To honor, serue, and loue; as *Poets* use.
> I meant to make her faire, and free, and wise,
>   Of greatest bloud, and yet more good then great;
> I meant the day-starre should not brighter rise,
>   Nor lend like influence from his lucent seat.
> I meant shee should be curteous, facile, sweet,
> Hating that solemne vice of greatnesse, pride;
>   I meant each softest vertue, there should meet,
>   Fit in that softer bosome to reside.
> Onely a learned, and a manly soule
>   I purpos'd her; that should, with euen powers,
> The rock, the spindle, and the sheeres controule
>   Of destinie, and spin her owne free houres.
> Such when I meant to faine, and wish'd to see,
>   My *Muse* bad, *Bedford* write, and that was shee.
>
>   **(LXXVI)**

The poem confronts that timeless poetic rapture with the poet's situation in time. The overworked poet's schedule fortunately permits an early conference with his Muse: he is *"timely* rapt." The colloquial "This morning" which opens the poem gives it a scene and a time linking the act of writing poetry with the poet's humbler, quotidian experiences as a man, as much a part of his daily routine as eating or sleeping. Jonson's poet belongs to a social world of patronage and visits, the drawing-room milieu of *Epicœne*. Here a visit from Apollo or the Muses seems out of place. And Jonson connects this suggestion, that poetry is simply another human activity, with his rejection of the idea of the poet as a man apart, touched by the "holy fire" of divine inspiration. That poet's Muse is overworked, "zealous"; the figures he forms, those interchangeable Petrarchan ladies, are constructed according to formula, "as *Poets* use." Again, in this weak, deprecating afterthought, syntactically unrelated to the sentence, Jonson opposes convention to reality.

The same theme is present in the poem's progression of verbs, a series which describes the poetic act in terms of creation: "I thought to *forme,"* "I meant to *make,"* and "I

meant to *faine."* Each of these verbs, especially "faine," a loaded word which suggests fakery as well as poetic invention, develops the hint of the first lines, the falseness of the conception of the poet as a maker of another nature, a golden world. These infinitives suggest the factitious nature of poetic creation and cement the suggestion of unreality, the contrary-to-fact, conditional quality of "thought" and "meant." At the same time, as infinitives they represent frustrated action, incomplete predication. The turn of the poem, while completing the grammar, completes this sense. Words like "meant" and "purpos'd" express the poet's frustration, his inability to create what he imagines. His powers are limited; poetry cannot extend life or impose poetic justice, as the speaker would like (14-16). No matter how hard Jonson's poet tries to create his ideal lady, he is inadequate to the task. The final couplet reinforces the implication with which the poem begins, that the fact, Lucy herself, possesses greater power than poetic fancy. Poetry is frail, a realm of intention only; it cannot create fact. And in the poem of praise, reality will always triumph over the insufficiency of making things up.

"On Lucy Countesse of Bedford," like the epigram to Donne, contrasts two poets, the speaker or putative poet unequal to his task and the actual poet responsible for both *persona* and poem, who succeeds by acknowledging poetic weakness. Clearly the poem's literal statements about its intentions are strategic. While the speaker explains how he intends to praise his ideal lady, Jonson is actually praising Lucy; the poem is made out of materials which seem, temporally and logically, to precede its writing. The poem recounts the genesis of another poem, the poem the speaker intends to write but which he discovers is superfluous, unnecessary: "My *Muse* bad, *Bedford* write, and that was shee." As in Jonson's Induction to *Bartholomew Fair,* the curtain appears to have been raised too soon, before all the machinery has been put in place and the actors dressed. Jonson insists upon parading his half-dressed dramatic materials before his audience with their make-up off to include his audience in his creation of illusion. Much the same thing happens in **"Lucy Countesse of Bedford,"** where the premature curtain parts to reveal a *dramatis personae* of naked grammatical categories. Stripped to its essentials, the poem has three elements, which correspond to the grammatical categories of verb, adjective, and proper noun. Lines 4 and 5 contain two triplets, one verbal ("To honor, serue, and loue") and one adjectival ("faire, and free, and wise"). By placing these triplets in parallel, Jonson stresses the grammatical category of the words rather than their sense. And by stressing grammatical categories so early in the poem, he insists that the act of writing poetry is primarily a linguistic act of predication. The poem begins with the verb, with the desire to act; the verbs Jonson proposes, once purged of their Petrarchan associations, are highly moral. The parallel triplets suggest some relationship between the uncompleted moral action of the verbs and the hovering, unfocused adjectives, which take up the rest of the poem to the concluding couplet. Action, especially the kind of moral action Jonson demands from poetry, depends on the linguistic act of judgment contained in the predication of the adjective, the ascriptive function of linking adjective with noun, quality with substance. Comparing the moral qualities suggested by the ascriptive adjectives ("yet more good *then* great," "not *brighter* rise," "I meant each *softest* virtue, there should meet, / Fit in that *softer* bosome to reside") implies an act of judgment which can only be completed by locating these qualities in some substance, in Bedford or Penshurst or Sir Robert Wroth. And the poem enacts this search for substance, for the thing which corresponds to the word. The middle twelve lines of "Bedford" present unrealized qualities, adjectives not attached to any person. Jonson's *persona*, his speaker-poet, thinks this person must be created, but for Jonson himself and for the reader these lines amount to a search. In the final couplet this search is concluded, not in a world of Petrarchan Delias and Dianas feigned by the poet, but in a world of fact, of historical persons with last names and local addresses.

As the poems to the Earl of Pembroke, Lucy, Countess of Bedford, and Lady Mary Wroth demonstrate, many of Jonson's poems of praise proceed from his recognition of the limit of the poet's powers. The poet succeeds only when he acknowledges the realities of the quotidian world; when he attempts to create a realm of pure ideality, he fails. Thus Jonson employs the slightest of epideictic forms, the epigram. The etymology of the word "epigram" reflects its origin as inscription, literally attached to the subject upon which it commented, an origin, and a dependence, which the epigram never outgrew. Even after it abandoned its particular setting, its physical link to its subject, the epigram remained dependent on it. This dependence is reflected by the importance of the epigram's title or lemma; the title invokes the particular circumstances of the epigram, its absent subject, linking it irrevocably to some site or *locus*. And Jonson, if anything, strengthens the epigram's intrinsic dependence on the world outside of the poem. Not only does he insist upon the pallor of the fictive when it is held up to the real, but he reduces the epigram itself to a form of naming, until the poem merely traces the process of discovering the subject already announced in the lemma: "My *Muse* bad, *Bedford* write, and that was shee." The epigram, the poetic act, becomes superfluous, a mere repetition of its title. And Jonson recognizes this when he writes "To Robert Earle of Salisburie":

> What need hast thou of me? or of my *Muse*?
>   Whose actions so themselues doe celebrate;
> Which should thy countries loue to speake refuse,
>   Her foes enough would fame thee, in their hate.
> 'Tofore, great men were glad of *Poets*: Now,
>   I, not the worst, am couetous of thee.
>
>   **(XLIII, 1-6)**

His repeated concern with naming in the epigrams reflects his awareness of the irreducible distance between subject and poem, words and things, as well as his desire to equate them, to make the poem a perfect mirror of the real world, a true equivalent of its subject. In the act of naming, language circumvents its own inherent duplicity by establishing a uniquely perfect correspondence between word and object. Basically, names are circular. "In the code of English," writes Roman Jakobson, "'Jerry' means a person named Jerry . . . the name means anyone to whom this

name is assigned. . . . The general meaning of such words as *pup, mongrel,* or *hound* could be indicated by abstractions like puppihood, mongrelness, or houndness, but the general meaning of *Fido* cannot be qualified in this way. To paraphrase Bertrand Russell, there are many dogs called *Fido,* but they do not share any property of 'Fidoness'" ["Shifters, Verbal Categories, and the Russian Verb," *Selected Writings, II: Word and Language,* 1971]. In proper names language assumes a unique neutrality, a reduction to the level of pure counterness. Names reveal the arbitrary nature of the verbal sign, its purely conventional relation to the concept it designates. Small children often have trouble with names because they do not set off a class of attributes. Introduced to a second person named John, they search for some shared quality of John-ness ("You don't look like John") or reject the impostor altogether ("You aren't John"). Having learned that common nouns imply qualities (mongrelness from mongrel), they expect the same of proper nouns. But names lack the common noun's ability to generate concepts. What they gain in the designating function they lose in the conceptual function; they are more specific than common nouns, more precise in their pointing, but less general. (When names are turned into common nouns, they take the indefinite article: *a* Quisling rather than *the* Quisling.) In naming, then, language refers to itself. Names are language at its most purely diacritical; like the phonemes they are made of, they signify simple difference. To Jonson names are valuable because they designate so precisely. They provide the poet with a paradigm of unambiguous reference, a model of contact with the world outside of his poem.

What Jonson's poetry is, then, is a poetry which tests poetry, a search for a point of contact between the realms of poetic language and ordinary reality. To Jonson, poetry's visionary capability is called into question by its inability to find its visions confirmed by nature. He consciously restricts praise to its humblest vehicle, the epigram, while redefining the epigram as a superfluous act of naming, all in order to establish the poem's correspondence to a nonverbal reality. His rediscovery of Martial's form of the epigram is the result of a generic search for a poetry of reference linked to its origins in the realm of common experience. Reducing that form to mere naming results from a similar search conducted within language. The epigram is a genre of designation; naming locates the same designating function within language. Jonson resorts to both to test poetry, to demonstrate that it does refer. Already *poesis* has been redefined. It no longer means "making" in the sense of creating, the act of envisioning an imaginative kingdom of words, a heterocosm within language. Jonson admires the poet like Spenser who describes a realm of Platonic ideas beyond our imperfect sublunary existence. But he is uncomfortable with this kind of poet, with Sidney's conception of the poet, advanced in the *Apologie for Poetrie,* as a Maker not "captived to the truth of a foolish world" but free to people realms of his own making. Sidney attempts to answer Plato's objection that the poet, like the artist, merely imitates what the eye sees, that he is slavishly tied to the senses and unable to transcend the brazen stuff of nature. Sidney's poet is a true legislator of the imagination, a true metaphysician, not tied to the contingencies of nature and history and hence related by lineal descent to prophet and seer, to Orpheus and Holy David. Jonson retreats from this position under pressure. Poetry for him is a moral language related to the orator's, taking its authority not *ab numine,* from divine inspiration, but from its correspondence to the moral realities of the world. His poet is an arbiter in the court of public morals, not a seer. His gold must be sifted from nature's brass, not created anew through the poet's alchemy.

Jonson's implicit defense of the poet is unlike Sidney's because the poet comes under a different kind of attack from a different quarter. Plato attacks the poet for mastering illusions rather than forms. The poet is inferior to the philosopher because he deals in deceptions; even the lowly artisan knows more about the table he builds than the poet or painter who represents it. Later in the seventeenth century it will be these artisans and mechanics, that strange alliance of Puritans and Baconians, who lead the assault on mere verbiage in natural philosophy, the pulpit, and poetry. But Jonson, who knew Bacon at James's court and defended him as "the *marke* and *acme* of our language" whose works "may be compar'd, or preferr'd, either to insolent *Greece* or haughty Rome" in *Timber: or Discoveries,* in some sense anticipates the scientific revolution that sweeps England during the century. His reduction of the epigram to the act of naming reflects his awareness of the separation of fact and value. Facts require language, and poets, to express their values; the *locus* requires the inscription to make it speak. Pure designation fails to solve this epistemological problem, to locate qualities in substances, values in facts. Qualities are abstractions; they belong to the realm of mind and therefore to language. In their linguistic form, as adjectives, their designation is weaker than the designation of a name. An epigram like **"Lucy Countesse of Bedford"** turns the poetic act into a syntactical act of linkage, grammatical predication; it couples adjective with proper noun. The poem begins with copulatory intent; the poet's frustrated desire to ʾact, to predicate, shows itself in his verbal phrases: "I thought to forme," "I meant to make," and the verbal triplet "to honor, serue, and loue." Grammatically, these infinitives suspend predication; they describe a frustrated intention. The middle of the poem, beginning with the corresponding adjectival triplet "faire, and free, and wise" (5), catalogues the qualities the poet wants to predicate. The final couplet completes the predication suspended in the infinitives while providing a grammatical paradigm for the epigrams: "Such when I meant to faine, and wish'd to see" (17) returns to the infinitives which open the poem, contrasting visionary experience ("faine") with ordinary perception ("see"). The Muse then supplies the missing proper noun, the grammatical designation necessary to complete predication ("My *Muse* bad, *Bedford* write"), and the poem concludes with a poem-in-little, a grammatical model of predication ("that was shee") in which one pronoun designates qualities, the other substance.

Significantly, **"Lucy Countesse of Bedford"** sets up much the same hierarchy of grammatical categories that Bacon advances in the *Novum Organum* in 1620. There Bacon argues that words contain "certain degrees of distortion and error" and can be arranged accordingly: "One of the least faulty kinds is that of names of substances, especially of lowest species and well-deduced (for the notion of *chalk* and of *mud* is good, of *earth* bad); a more faulty kind is that of actions, as *to generate, to corrupt, to alter;* the most faulty is of qualities (except such as are the immediate objects of the sense) as *heavy, light, rare, dense,* and the like" (*Novum Organum* I.lx). Bacon's well-known antipathy to language is based on the fluidity of its designation. Words fail to represent the truths of nature accurately and precisely. They fail to correspond to things not just on the level of the sentence or discourse but, more damagingly, on the level of the individual word. Words stand for concepts, "notions" in Bacon's terminology, rather than things. Thus, language is open to two kinds of errors; it includes words which are "either names of things which do not exist (. . . to which nothing in reality corresponds), or they are names of things which exist, but yet [are] confused and ill-defined and hastily and irregularly derived from realities" (I.lx).

This duplicity of names led Bacon's followers in the Royal Society to formulate their famous motto, *nullius in verba,* and attempt to create an artificial, universal language in which the name of the thing would also express its nature. Seth Ward, professor of astronomy at Oxford, proposed such a project in 1654: "Such a Language as this (where every word were a definition and contain'd the nature of the thing) might not unjustly be termed a naturall Language, and would afford that which the *Cabalists* and *Rosycrucians* have vainely sought for in the Hebrew, And in the names of things assigned by Adam" [*Vindiciae Academiarum,* quoted in R. F. Jones, "Science and Language in England of the Mid-Seventeenth Century," *The Seventeenth Century,* 1951]. The Royal Society's dismemberment of spoken languages in favor of artificial ones culminates in John Wilkins' *Essay Towards a Real Character and a Philosophical Language,* sponsored by the Royal Society and published in 1668. Wilkins tried to create a system of symbols, compounded of straight lines, curves, loops, dots, and whirls, which would reveal the genus and species of each thing it designated. Imaginary creatures like fairies were given no symbols, insuring that language would represent material reality only. As Richard Foster Jones points out, Wilkins' undertaking carries Bacon's mistrust of language to its *absurdum;* it "representsthe lowest state to which language was degraded. Barred from representing the creations of the imagination and strippcd of all connotations from past usage, language was to become nothing more than the dead symbols of mathematical equations."

Poets, of course, suffered most from the attack on language. As Jones insists, "More than to any other linguistic defect, scientists objected to a word's possessing many meanings or the same meaning as another word, and especially to the use of metaphor. The desire to make the word match the thing, to be in a strict sense a description of a thing or action, explains their exaggerated antipathy to metaphors and such figures of speech." What Bacon rediscovers, and what Jonson tries to overcome, is that language is not co-extensive with reality. Seventeenth-century poets and philosophers alike reëxperience the curse of Babel, the withdrawal of the Logos. "In its original form," writes Michel Foucault, "when it was given to men by God himself, language was an absolutely certain and transparent sign for things, because it resembled them. The names of things were lodged in the things they designated . . . just as the influence of the planets is marked upon the brows of men: by the form of similitude. This transparency was destroyed at Babel as a punishment for men. Languages became separated and incompatible with one another only insofar as they had previously lost this original resemblance to the things that had been the prime reason for the existence of language" [Michel Foucault, *Les Mots et les Choses,* 1966, trans. as *The Order of Things: An Archaeology of the Human Sciences,* 1970]. In Eden words are things; the names that Adam gives to the animals in Genesis correspond to their natures. But since the fall of Babel values no longer reside in the names of things. In the fourth chapter of *Leviathan,* Hobbes gives the scriptural account a skeptical going over. He acknowledges that language has a divine origin: "The first author of Speech was *God* himself, that instructed *Adam* how to name such creatures as he presented to his sight." But he insists, in a diction that itself suggests a second loss of paradise, that since the fall of Babel our language is fallen, its Edenic perfection lost: "But all this language gotten, and augmented by *Adam* and his posterity, was again lost at the tower of Babel, when by the hand of *God,* every man was stricken for his rebellion, with an oblivion of his former language. And being hereby forced to disperse themselves into severall parts of the world, it must needs be, that the diversity of Tongues that now is proceeded by degrees from them" (London, 1651). Language is no longer a system of transparent signs but of arbitrary counters. Divorced from the first Word, fallen languages lose all traces of their divine origin and lapse into the babblings of human error. For Hobbes, as for Bacon, these words are mere counters, nothing in themselves: "The first use of names, is to serve for *Markes,* or *Notes* of remembrance" (p. 13); "words are wise mens counters, they do but reckon by them: but they are the mony of fooles, that value them by the authority of an *Aristotle,* a *Cicero,* or a *Thomas*" (p. 15). The kinds of meaning available through the manipulation of these counters came to seem more and more illusory. Their misuse, Hobbes states, has four results, two belonging to the word, two to the proposition: "First, when men register their thoughts wrong, by the inconstancy of the signification of their words: by which they register for their conceptions, that which they never conceived, and so deceive themselves. Secondly, when they use words metaphorically; that is, in another sense than that they are ordained for; and thereby deceive others. Thirdly, when by the word they declare that to be their will, which is not. Fourthly, when they use them to grieve one another." Hobbes is hardly alone in singling out metaphor for special abuse. The metaphoric properties of language, its ability to relate ideas and find resemblances among things through a *tertium quid,* a common term which applies to both parts of the metaphor in different senses, are no longer accepted as a valid means of penetrating the surfaces of things. For Bacon this use of a common name for different objects or actions becomes the primary occasion for error, the source of much of the deficiency of learning. "The *Idols of the Market-place* are the most troublesome of all," he writes in the *Novum*

Organum, "idols which have crept into the understanding through the alliance of words and names" (I.lix). A word is "nothing else than a mark loosely and confusedly applied to denote a variety of actions which will not bear to be reduced to any constant meaning" (I.lx), one name applied indifferently to things which are not of the same nature [Foucault, *The Order of Things*]. Thus words suggest phantom relationships between things which have no other likeness except the likeness of their names.

Jonson had dealt comically with this kind of purely linguistic control over nature in *The Alchemist,* where magic masquerades as science and things vibrate with the hermetic affinities and quintessences, secrets that can be unlocked with cabbalistic incantations. Face and Subtle are Jonson's linguistic entrepreneurs, purveyors of discredited metaphors to Sir Epicure Mammon, the man of imagination manqué. Jonson's epigrams, committed to matching qualities to substances, facts to values, test the metaphoric potentialities of a fallen language, the adequacy of names, the extent to which they reveal value. The deficiencies make the location of value difficult; things do not announce their natures through their names; resemblance is more often a source of error than a form of truth. Jonson's naming epigrams, therefore, present the poet's tentative search for true metaphors, names which reveal values.

The *Epigrams* initiate Jonson's testing of metaphor. Occasionally Jonson finds an abundance of allegorical names, names which are words as well as counters. These word-names identify both quality and substance, the individual and his nature, simultaneously; they repair the division between concrete fact and abstract value present in language since the fall of Babel. **Epigram XCI, "To Sir Horace Vere,"** opens:

> Which of thy names I take, not onely beares
>   A *romane* sound, but *romane* vertue weares,
> Illustrious VERE, or HORACE; fit to be
>   Sung by a HORACE, or a *Muse* as free.

In Latin, *Vere* means "truly"; with its English pronunciation, the name also puns on Latin *vir.* But it is not the "*romane* sound, but *romane* vertue" present in the name that excites Jonson. Here language is transparent, a system of signatures. As in allegory, name is also word, and Vere's name corresponds to his nature, announcing the existence both of an individual and a virtue, the unique (Vere) and the abstract (*vir, veritas, virtu*). Name identifies both the concrete and the universal and ties the Roman quality of *veritas* to the man. Language functions metaphorically, and the resemblances of sound and spelling reveal a deeper identity between Vere and Rome.

But names like Vere's, names which contain abstractions and which therefore potentially identify quality as well as substance, seem mere accidents. Words or names seldom announce essences; reality is only intermittently allegorical, and attempts to read it as such usually end, like Mammon's, in delusion. Even when presented with allegorical names Jonson remains cautious. The derivation of Lucy from the Latin *lux* or *lucifer* provides Jonson with his opening invention in **Epigram XCIV, "To Lucy, Countesse of Bedford, with Mr. Donnes Satyres"**: "LUCY, you brightnesse of our spheare, who are / Life of the *Muses* day, their morning-starre!" But the epigram turns on the Countess' patronage of Satire, an act which Jonson sees as proof of a moral nature. Here a metaphorical name, a linguistic revelation, is incidental to the poem's discovery of the subject's value. And in **Epigram CIII, "To Mary Lady Wroth,"** Jonson passes up a metaphorical given name to concentrate on the Sidney family name. Mary means "exalted," according to William Camden, Jonson's friend and master at Westminster School [*Remaines Concerning Britain,* 1637]. But Jonson instead structures the poem around the relationship between appearance and reality, inner and outer beauty, to question whether appearances can function as signs announcing meanings:

> How well, faire crowne of your faire sexe, might hee,
>   That but the twi-light of your sprite did see,
> And noted for what flesh such soules were fram'd,
>   Know you to be a SYDNEY, though vn-nam'd?
>
> (1-4)

The poem raises the problem of identifying values in a world of fact: how well can one correlate spirit and flesh, physical appearance and moral worth? Jonson couches the problem in terms borrowed from the Neoplatonists' dogma that physical beauty reflects moral beauty, that the light of the soul shines through the eyes. But he sees the spirit as locked in the flesh, unable to shine through. Even in the clearest cases, like Lady Wroth's, only a part of that spiritual radiance, a "twi-light of [the] sprite," is available to the senses. That is enough to identify Lady Wroth, Sir Philip Sidney's niece, as a Sidney, but the recognition of her moral worth depends on family resemblance, on the poet's recognition of her nurture, not her nature. Her name, not her beauty, reveals her goodness; name, not appearance, functions as emblem, "the *imprese* of the great." Like language, the visible world seldom embodies its moral worth, its essential meaning, in its appearance. To stress this, Jonson excuses himself from the symbolic Petrarchan *blazon:*

> Forgiue me then, if mine but say you are
>   A SYDNEY: but in that extend as farre
> As lowdest praisers, who perhaps would find
>   For every part a character assign'd.
>
> (9-12)

To Jonson the physical world does not reveal its essence symbolically, through its appearance. The Petrarchan invention of finding "characters," emblematic representations of moral qualities, in the lady's appearance becomes "lowdest praisers" but not scrious poets. It is a form of false wit, of wasted ingenuity. Like language the visible world is seldom a system of signs or hieroglyphs to Jonson.

Jonson's distrust of resemblance as a form of knowledge, a device for extracting value from the world of facts, severely limits his metaphorical resources. Even when presented with a name that seems to declare a moral genealogy, Jonson draws back from full-scale metaphoric identification. In **"To Susan Countesse of Montgomery,"** Jonson writes:

> Were they that nam'd you, prophets? Did they see,
>   Euen in the dew of grace, what you would bee?
> Or did our times require it, to behold
>   A new SVSANNA, equall to that old?
> Or, because some scarce thinke that storie true,
>   To make those faithfull, did the *Fates* send you?
>
> (CIV, 1-6)

This coincidence of names, biblical Susanna and contemporary Susan, seems to offer some clue to the Countess' qualities, even to allude to some divine allegory working through history, but Jonson is unable to read it. Jonson plays with the possibilities offered by the resemblance, but his praise resides only in the half-serious way in which he entertains the possible similitudes his imagination suggests. The hint that divine purposes are being revealed remains only a hint, a fantasy, and Jonson's exegesis stops short of identifying the Countess' role in history: "Iudge they, that can: Here I haue rais'd to show / A picture, which the world for yours must know" (13-14). Metaphor is discovered, developed, and then declined.

Jonson's rejection of his central metaphors in **"To Mary Lady Wroth"** and **"To Susan Countesse of Montgomery"** points up his sense of the dangers of resemblance, the difficulty of distinguishing true metaphor from false. In fact, in both poems he equates this rejection with the value of his praise. To Lady Wroth he apologizes for his reluctance to catalogue her virtues through her "parts," as "lowdest praisers" perhaps would do. But in his concluding couplet he insists: "My praise is plaine, and where so ere profest, / Becomes none more then you, who need it least." The plainness of his praise, his refusal to spin the fantastic metaphors of a more ornate style, is his highest praise; its value as praise derives from the poet's metaphoric restraint, and this restraint is the touchstone of Jonson's style. In his epigram to the Countess of Montgomery, Jonson declines the invention, the strategy of praise, that her name offers, leaving the question of its significance to rasher poets; the value of his poem resides rather in the accuracy of its portrait, "which the world for yours must know." Here, as in the epigrams to Lady Wroth and the Countess of Bedford, Jonson argues that its equivalence to its subject verifies his praise. And in the majority of his epigrams, what Jonson dramatizes is the poet's selection of equivalents to reveal his subject's inncr naturc. Thc act of praising, even the act of writing poetry, becomes an act of selection, of discriminating between false and true metaphors. In this act Jonson's style, its representation of the poet through his voice in the poem, functions as his primary instrument of discrimination. The poet's voice, firmly rooted in the world of fact, tests the metaphors that imagination and tradition provide. The *Epigrams* offer one instance of this testing; **"To Penshurst,"** which concerns itself with literary tradition more fully, offers another.

The country house poem that initiates the kind in English, **"To Penshurst"** (**II** of *The Forest*) is also a poem of praise. As in Jonson's shorter poems of praise, the real praise resides in the poem's tone of careful discrimination. Behind **"Penshurst"** lie Martial's epigrams, especially his praise of Faustinus' Baian villa (III.lviii). And through

Martial Jonson is able to celebrate a community which combines nature and nurture, Edenic innocence and classical learning. His details function simultaneously as description and allusion, acknowledging Penshurst's place in the real world while linking it, through his use of Martial, to Rome and its culture. Jonson expects his audience to catch both meanings, to note his Latin sources, and yet to acknowledge the essential seriousness in the poet's use of these hyperbolic *topoi* from the tradition of retirement poetry. Behind the "Bright eeles" that "leape on land, / Before the fishes, or into his hand" (37-38), for example, Jonson expects his audience to recognize both the lamprey from Martial's praise of the sea resort at Formiae, where "natat ad magistrum delicata muraena," and the presence of an Edenic reciprocity between man and nature, a natural fecundity so overwhelming that it justifies the sense of the hyperbole. These two meanings reinforce each other, and the presence, however slight, of Rome and the earthly paradise in the poem tempers its wit and redeems its hyperboles.

The structure of the poem can best be described as a search, conducted through different generic styles, for an adequate language of praise, a poetic style which will allow Jonson to express the values he finds in Penshurst without compromising its *locus* in the world of fact. Jonson's title, and his turning to Martial for so many of the poem's details, stress the poem's origin in inscription. But the poem's concern with the natural world, and especially with man's relations with nature, forces it into a complex relationship with the more fictive poetic genres of pastoral and georgic. In **"Penshurst"** Jonson describes a landscape in which real and ideal meet. The poem reveals him drawing on different generic resources to link that ideality to the real world. In the course of **"Penshurst"** genres are juxtaposed and revalued as Jonson searches for a decorum which will accommodate the several kinds of experience—literary, social, religious—that Penshurst embodies. At the same time, the poem shows Jonson trying to clarify his own attitude toward the literary traditions of the Renaissance, its return to fictive landscapes of pure symbol like pastoral, realms of pure value sanctified by the poets who dwelled in them but with only the most tenuous link to the world of fact.

"To Penshurst" opens with an eight-line part announcing two themes, the search for a language of praise and the conception of poet as arbiter. Here Jonson's syntactical habit of discrimination by negatives places Penshurst in a satiric context, anticipating how Pope will adapt the country house poem. Penshurst lacks the ostentation of other country houses; its value is hardly apparent, not embodied in an "enuious show" of wealth:

> Thou art not, PENSHURST, built to enuious show,
>   Of touch, or marble; nor canst boast a row
> Of polish'd pillars, or a roofe of gold:
>   Thou hast no lantherne, whereof tales are told;
> Or stayre, or courts; but stand'st an ancient pile,
>   And these grudg'd at, art reuerenc'd the while.
> Thou ioy'st in better markes, of soyle, of ayre,
>   Of wood, of water: therein thou art faire.
>   (1-8)

These lines present the problem of discriminating values hardly accessible to the sense which Jonson faced in the epigrams. As a building Penshurst is unimpressive; it does not proclaim its value in marble or gold. Subtly, in his diction, Jonson hints here that the values immanent in Penshurst are spiritual, invisible. Penshurst is "reuerenc'd" not for itself, but for its seat in the natural world, its marks of soil, air, wood, and water. Its value lies in its relationship to nature, not in its pillars orgold. And Jonson's negative definition points to the poetic and ethical difficulty of defining that value: It is easier to say what Penshurst is *not* than what it is. His negative definition acts as a metaphor for the poem's real subject, the act of discriminating value that the poet finally shares with the Sidney family, while suggesting the difficulty of finding a language or style which will permit Jonson to capture the invisible values of Penshurst.

Jonson first attempts to draw on literary resources. Invoking the mythological figures of pastoral, Jonson presents the landscape as a locus of unseen presences, a landscape of spirit as well as fact. These nature deities, though, inhabit a recognizable landscape, one located firmly in the empirical world, and not the generalized pleasance or *locus amœnus* of pastoral. Natives of Arcadia, these deities have been set down in Kent. Nymphs and satyrs frequent the oak where Lady Leicester began her labor pains: "And thence, the ruddy *Satyres* oft prouoke / The lighter *Faunes,* to reach thy Ladies Oke" (17-18). The Muses meet at a tree dedicated to Sir Philip Sidney; Pan and Bacchus feast on the Sidneys' "Mount." At Penshurst the realms of poetry and history miraculously intersect. The mythopoeic style allows Jonson to name the landscape's values; the pagan gods appear as the manifestation of their gifts [Maynard Mack, "Secretum Iter," in *The Garden and the City: Retirement and Politics in the Later Poetry of Pope, 1731-1743,* 1969], as the embodiments of a nature nearly strong enough to take on physical form:

> Thy *Mount,* to which the *Dryads* doe resort,
> Where PAN and BACCHUS their high feasts haue made,
> Beneath the broad beech, and the chest-nut shade.
>   (10-12)

The pagan gods identify the numen lurking in the shade of Penshurst's forests.

By superimposing one landscape on another, the purely fictive landscape of gods, nymphs, and satyrs on the actual landscape of Penshurst, Jonson defines its ideality while testing the reality of the literary tradition. Defining that tradition is difficult. Jonson adapted this section of **"Penshurst"** from one of Martial's epigrams (IX.LXI) celebrating Julius Caesar through an idealized description of a grove of trees planted by Caesar at his estate at Tartessus [William Dinsmore Briggs, "Source-Material for Jonson's *Epigrams and Forest,*" *CP,* 11 (1916)]. To Martial, writing over one hundred years after Caesar's death and deification, the presence of nymphs and dryads marked the site as sacred, a point of contact between gods and men sanctified by the man-god Caesar. His deities mark off the grove as numinous, a spot discontinuous with the rest of the landscape because of its associations with Caesar. Martial sets off the grove by filling it with figures from pastoral:

> Saepe sub hac madidi luserunt arbore Fauni
>   terruit et tacitam fistula sera domum:
> dumque fugit solos nocturnum Pana per agros,
>   saepe sub hac latuit rustica fronde Dryas.
>
> (11-14)

These pastoral figures emphasize the discontinuity; they stress Caesar's divinity, his difference from other men. Through the pastoral Martial moves from a *locus* in the real world, Tartessus, into the imaginative landscape of Arcadia. The movement in **"Penshurst,"** however, is more complex. From Martial Jonson learned the technique of invoking other, more numinous genres to identify values in the course of an epigram. But Jonson uses pastoral in **"Penshurst"** to suggest the essential identity of literary and real landscapes. Rather than separating the zone of the human and historical, the realm of fact, from the zone of the literary and symbolic as Martial does, Jonson superimposes them. The Sidneys share their walks with the Dryads, participating in the same natural rhythms of birth and feasting as these wood spirits. And through these pastoral allusions Jonson is able to show the harmony with the natural world that the middle section of the poem continues.

But Jonson's graceful compliment to his hosts does not stop there. The mythological figures in this section of the poem function not only as divinized forms of nature but also as allusions to a literary heritage with its origins in Rome and Roman culture. Penshurst thus stands in perfect harmony with both human history and nature. It is both a refuge from the world of affairs and a monument to classical culture. Here the Latin deities serve as metaphor both for a relationship with the landscape and with a cultural tradition; they are no mere ornaments, but part of the primary experience of the poem, mediating between natural and literary landscapes and stressing their essential oneness at Penshurst. Through Martial and his use of the pastoral kind, Jonson insists upon a rough equivalence, an important symmetry, between literary experience and all other kinds of experience. Through Martial Jonson verifies not only his sense of Penshurst as a mysterious merging of nature and culture, but also the value of his literary heritage.

In this first section, borrowing a domesticated version of pastoral from Martial, Jonson superimposes natural and literary landscapes to confirm Penshurst's claims to ideality. But this mythopoeic mode is essentially a foreign one to Jonson. Penshurst is the "resort" of Dryads, not their home, and Penshurst itself is capable of announcing its own value without relying on the poet's importation of a fictive landscape. Thus pastoral gives way to a more georgic mode. Now the countryside provides a norm for human behavior:

> Each banke doth yield thee coneyes; and the topps
>   Fertile of wood, ASHORE, and SYDNEY'S copp's,
> To crowne thy open table, doth prouide
>   The purpled pheasant, with the speckled side:
> The painted partrich lyes in euery field,
>   And, for thy messe, is willing to be kill'd.

And if the high-swolne *Medway* faile thy dish,
  Thou hast thy ponds, that pay thee tribute fish.

(25-32)

Here Jonson's controlling pattern of imagery seems to arise from the landscape before him. In this description the realm of fact unfolds its meaning. The images of "serue," "tribute," "crowne," and "yeeld" establish man as the monarch of creation and provide a model for the tenant-lord relationship in human society that Jonson treats later in the poem. Nature itself seems ordered; Jonson's description reveals "an underlying harmonic pattern in the scene" [Paul M. Cubeta, "A Jonsonian Ideal: 'To Penshurst'," *Philogical Quarterly* 42 (1963)] that seems to come as much from nature as from the poet:

> The lower land, that to the riuer bends,
> Thy sheepe, thy bullocks, kine, and calues doe feed:
> The middle grounds thy mares, and horses breed.
>
> (22-24)

Nature reassumes its Edenic transparency; physical details can be read as natural metaphors reuniting fact and value. And the entire landscape reveals a profound orientation toward man.

> The earely cherry, with the later plum,
>   Fig, grape, and quince, each in his time doth
>   come:
> The blushing apricot, and woolly peach
>   Hang on thy walls, that euery child may reach.
>
> (41-44)

The last detail, significantly, is reminiscent of a detail from Virgil's panegyric of the philosopher-poet and husbandman in the second Georgic. There the happy man "quos rami fructus, quos ipsa volentia rura / sponte tulere sua, carpsit" (II.500-01). And as in georgic proper, the metaphors that arise from Jonson's description of the landscape provide models for man's relationship with man. At Penshurst nature willingly sacrifices itself to serve its lord; the forests "proude" game, the Medway provides "tribute fish." And this willing service is mirrored in the tenant's relationship with his master. Here too there is no enforced tribute:

> And though thy walls be of the countrey stone,
>   They'are rear'd with no mans ruine, no mans
>   grone,
> There's none, that dwell about them, wish them
>   downe.
>   But all come in, the farmer, and the clowne:
> And no one empty-handed.
>
> (45-49)

The essence of georgic sections of **"Penshurst"** lies in the way it presents its emblematic relationship between human society and its model in the natural world. Jonson structures his poem to present his scenes of human society as the extensions of lessons learned from nature. The motives and values in the natural world identified through Jonson's descriptive metaphors provide **"Penshurst"** with an inner inevitability of design. The mythopoeic mode of the opening section, which points to the existence of a "spirit" in the natural world, a presence of intention and design in the natural world which in turn requires the presence of Jonson's classical deities to give that presence form, gives way to a georgic mode, in which similar values seem inherent in the very physical countenance that nature presents to man. The values that Jonson finds in nature— fecundity and willing service—point in turn to certain human values: hospitality, generosity, mutual respect. These themes, set in patterns of imagery which link sections of description, provide models for the interpretation of what the landscape teaches. But Jonson never insists on the validity of these models; his evaluation of Penshurst does not ultimately rest on the motifs arising out of the poem's descriptive sections, either on the poem's fictions or its metaphors, but on the explicit evaluation inthe poet's own voice with which the poem ends. **"Penshurst,"** despite its attempts to domesticate pastoral and georgic as instruments of discrimination, reverts in the end to genres, Horatian epistle and epigram, which stress the poet's speaking voice.

Again, for Jonson, the poem reduces itself to the ascriptive act, the act of uniting word with thing. In **"Penshurst"** Jonson meets the epistemological threat created by the disjunction between word and thing by evolving a poetic strategy which justifies the use of a fictive, ascriptive language. **"Penshurst"** uses the same structure as the epigrams, but with different terms. In the epigrams words without specific reference, an adjectival rhetoric of praise, are linked to the world through the poet's presence in the poem, through the act of recognizing value in the world outside of the poem, to which the poem refers and from which it derives its authority. The poem of praise thus presents an intersection of subjective quality, the adjective, and objective substance, the person or place. In **"Penshurst"** generic terms replace the grammatical categories of **"Lucy Countesse of Bedford."** The pastoral genre takes over the ascriptive function of the adjective; the pagan gods, names of things to which nothing in reality corresponds, stand for the numinous qualities of the landscape. The georgic middle section of the poem, like the verbs in **"Lucy Countesse of Bedford,"** serves a mediating, copulatory function; it provides a generic model for the linking of real and ideal, fact and value. But like the epigram, **"Penshurst"** is completed only by a return to naming, a generic return to the epigram form. Here, what Jonson does is to insist on the poet's role in tying quality to substance, on his individual role as arbiter.

The poet's presence in **"Penshurst"** is pervasive. Jonson lays a place for himself at Sidney's table (the poet is uninvited in Martial's description of Faustinus' Baian villa, from which Jonson takes this section of **"Penshurst,"** and hardly present in the poem). And Jonson's deviation from Martial is highly significant. His physical presence is not literary allusion; he is not there as the voice of Latin culture, but again as a man. The figure he presents of himself and of his table manners emphasize that he is no abstract type of the Poet. Once more, as in the negative references at the beginning and end of the poem, references beyond the Kentish landscape which emphasize the poet's moral choice, Jonson acknowledges an external world of

things to which his words must correspond. His knowledge does not have to be limited to the poem to sustain its world; the poem, while stressing those Edenic qualities of the *locus amœnnus,* while using the simple as a model of the complex, is not pastoral. And, too, the poet's presence shapes his metrics. Jonson told Drummond that "He had written a discourse of Poesie both against Campion & Daniel especially this Last, wher he proues couplets to be the brauest sort of Verses, especially when they are broken, like hexameters and that crosse Rimes and Stanzaes (becaus the purpose would lead him beyond 8 lines to conclude) were all forced." Jonson's couplets are syntactically open, so that the couplet form does not commit him to more lines than his subject requires [Wesley Trimpi, *Ben Jonson's Poems,* 1962], and his use of caesura is also quite free, as the last lines of **"Penshurst"** demonstrate. Thus Jonson's prosody is his own, forged by the requirements of his subject and not the property of his verse form. His rhythms, enjambements, and caesura placement are all dictated by the speaking voice, which is heard through the couplet.

> These, PENSHURST, are they praise, and yet not all.
>   Thy lady's noble, fruitfull, chaste withall.
> His children thy great lord may call his owne:
>   A fortune, in this age, but rarely knowne.
> They are, and haue beene taught religion: Thence
>   Their gentler spirits haue suck'd innocence.
> Each morne, and euen, they are taught to pray,
>   With the whole household, and may, euery day,
> Reade, in their vertuous parents noble parts,
>   The mysteries of manners, armes, and arts.
>   (89-98)

In this passage lies the essence of Jonson's verse. Jonson's rhythms slow to a formal cadence, and his couplets close. His moral peroration is delivered in the simplest diction, without much verbal patterning. There is a careful choice, almost a hesitation (produced by lingering on the monosyllables and the double caesurae in lines like 90 and 95) in Jonson's use of language; the rhythm creates the sense of a man pausing over almost every word: "Thy lady's noble, fruitfull, chaste withall." And through this style Jonson can point outward from the poem toward satire. He is speaking in his own voice, and through him the world beyond the Kentish countryside is present: "His children thy great lord may call his owne: / A fortune, in this age, but rarely knowne" (91-2). This brief hint of a corruption outside the garden gate provides the perspective in which the values of Penshurst become meaningful [J. C. A. Rathmell, "Jonson, Lord Lisle, and Penshurst," *ELR* 1 (1971)]. Another form of negative definition, like the opening lines of the poem which also contrast Penshurst to the great world outside, these lines refer to a world beyond the poem, outside of it, which verifies Penshurst. Jonson permits himself no retreat into the isolation of a classical heritage or a pastoral refuge. And the value of a Penshurst education, Jonson suggests, stems from its easy inclusion of the accomplishments of the court and public worlds, "The mysteries of manners, armes, and arts." Jonson finds his own values at Penshurst, and it is these that he praises.

"To Penshurst" presents Jonson's search for a language of praise that will discriminate the invisible values present at Penshurst and yet tie those values to a world of fact. To do this Jonson creates a poem which recapitulates literary history, moving through the mythopoeic mode of the poem's first section, where the pagan gods are superimposed on the Penshurst landscape to suggest its ability to sustain the values of the pastoral, to the georgic middle section, in which the landscape itself is read as a system of signs, a repository not only of intrinsic meanings but also of intrinsic values, ones which profoundly influence the human sphere at Penshurst. And finally, the poem ends in the familiar epigrammatic mode, in that realm of naming and plain speaking in which the *Epigrams* proper are set. Here the discrimination of values takes the form not of myth or metaphor, but of the poet speaking in his own voice. The poem's central metaphor, its praise of the Sidney family through their estate and the values that arise from the poet's presentation of their estate, gives way to the explicit discrimination of epigram. The Sidneys replace their landscape as emblems of their virtue, and finally they become the poem itself, its primary metaphor: "Reade, in their vertuous parents noble parts, / The mysteries of manners, armes, and arts" (97-8). Praising is reduced again to naming; the Sidneys become the text of their own panegyric, flesh made poem.

["To Penshurst"] traces a slow unfolding, a turning of the terms of art from its ownworld of myth to the poet's world of history.

—Harris Friedberg

"To Penshurst" enacts to a great degree the fate of the fictive classical genres in seventeenth-century poetry. Acknowledged as realms of value, they are nonetheless discarded as irrelevant in a world of fact. "Penshurst" initiates the movement, common in the seventeenth century, of turning from the creation of a second world of literary symbols, the heterocosms of myth and pastoral, as a statement of the values inherent in experience to the creation of a dramatic style, a speaking voice, which dramatizes the poet's selection, and rejection, of false resemblances. New classical genres are imported—Horatian epistle and satire, non-narrative epigram like Martial's rather than the looser Greek Anthology form, and georgic poetry which verifies the emblems it extracts from the landscape with passages of "historical retrospection or incidental meditation" in the poet's own voice—genres which are formally defined in terms of style and meter rather than in terms of their phenomenological content, their creation of self-sufficient worlds. The movement of Jonson's poem is outward from these self-sufficient literary worlds into the world of fact. The poem traces a slow unfolding, a turning of the terms of art from its own world of myth to the poet's world of history. Pastoral opens to georgic; the superimposition of landscapes of fact (the Penshurst landscape)

and value (the pastoral landscape of pagan deity and sacred grove) gives way to a genre in which value seems immanent in the world of fact. And as georgic gives way to epigram, Jonson presents the Sidneys themselves as emblems. He reunites the realms of fact and value by creating a plain style which stresses the poet's central role of discrimination in the poem; this is Jonson's great contribution to his contemporaries. Finally, he domesticates the literary tradition, by finding, as in "Penshurst," continuities between the poet's golden world and nature's brazen one.

Geoffrey Walton (essay date 1955)

SOURCE: "The Tone of Ben Jonson's Poetry," in *Ben Jonson and the Cavalier Poets: Authoritative Texts, Criticism,* edited by Hugh MacLean, W. W. Norton & Company, 1974, pp. 479-96.

[*In the following essay, Walton characterizes Jonson's poetry as a model of civility, exhibiting both its intellectual and moral values.*]

It is well known that Pope imitated the opening couplet of Jonson's **"Elegie on the Lady Jane Pawlet, Marchion: of Winton"**:

> What gentle ghost, besprent with *April* deaw,
> Hayles me, so solemnly, to yonder Yewgh?

in his own opening couplet of the **"Elegy to the Memory of an Unfortunate Lady"**:

> What beck'ning ghost, along the moonlight shade
> Invites my steps, and points to yonder glade?

The similarity and the difference between the grand style of Pope and the slightly Spenserian language of Jonson on this occasion are obvious. I have chosen to begin with a reference to this piece of plagiarism, however, because these two poems may be taken to mark, in so far as there are any beginnings and ends in literature, the limits of my study, and because the debt draws pointed attention to the dignified and courteous tone of Jonson's poetry, especially in his occasional verses. Several lines of elegy, which often intersect and blend, run between Jonson's epitaphs and formal eulogies and Pope's poem, which seems to gather up into itself all the various threads, the earlier Metaphysical and philosophic meditation of Donne, the formality of Cowley on Crashaw, the tenderness of Cowley on Hervey, the satire of Dryden in the ode on Anne Killigrew and the elegiac of Milton on the same Lady Jane. Pope inherited a large measure of Metaphysical wit coming from Donne, but the predominant aspect of his genius, the Augustan decorum, can be traced back to Donne's contemporary, Jonson.

Although Jonson's greatness as a poet is generally recognized, very little has been written on his lyric and other nondramatic poems. There is room for a detailed consideration of certain aspects of this work and for some redirection of attention towards poems hitherto neglected. Making a limited approach, I want to try to locate and define as clearly as possible his characteristic tone and civilized quality.

One often finds oneself trying, with a certain sense of frustration, to reconcile Professor C. H. Herford's morose rough diamond "with no native well-spring of verse music" and the kind of seventeenth-century Mallarmé implied by Mr. Ralph Walker. The coarse side of Jonson must not be forgotten. He was rooted in the English life of tavern and workshop in his life and in his art, besides being the friend of Selden and Lord Aubigny. We have to take into account **"The Voyage"** as well as the **"Hymn to Diana,"** and remember the last line of **"A Celebration of Charis."** Dr. Leavis places the odes to himself at the central point, as showing us both the independent, forthright working dramatist and the learned Horatian who brought out his plays annotated in folio.

I disagree with Dr. Leavis about the odes. "The racy personal force" and the "weighty and assertive personal assurance" are indeed present. The poems are eminently successful in the sense that they communicate their content without hesitation or vagueness. One can accept and applaud the fiercely contemptuous satire on dullness and ill will, but the final effect, I think, embarrasses still, as it seems to have embarrassed the "Tribe" and as the author in person had earlier embarrassed Drummond of Hawthornden. These odes are too personal and self-regarding. It is not the self-pity of a Shelley that is forced upon us, but self-assertion and unseemly pride:

> 'Twere simple fury still thyselfe to waste
>   On such as have no taste. . . .
> 'Tis crowne enough to vertue still, her owne
>   applause.

This is not redeemed by the finer aspiration of.

> Strike that disdaine-full heate
> Throughout, to their defeate,
> As curious fooles, and envious of thy straine,
> May, blushing, sweare no palsey's in thy braine.

Though Cartwright, Randolph and Cleveland approved, one can sympathize with that excellent literary critic, Thomas Carew, when he expostulates:

> 'Tis true (dear Ben) thy just chastizing hand
> Hath fixed upon the sotted Age a brand
> To their swolne pride, and empty scribbling due . . .
>   . . . but if thou bind,
> By Citie, or by *Gavell-kind,*
> In equall shares thy love on all thy race,
> We may distinguish of their sexe and place;
> Though one hand form them and though one brain
>   strike
> Souls into all, they are not all alike.
> Why should the follies then of this dull age
> Draw from thy Pen such an immodest rage,
> As seems to blast thy (else immortall) Bayes,
> When thine owne hand proclaims thy ytch of praise?

> The wiser world doth greater Thee confesse
> Than all men else, than Thyself only lesse.

Along with his mastery of the irregular Donnean couplet, Carew shows here a fineness of feeling and a regard for his poetic father, a polish of tone and an integrity of character, which represent all that was best in the class and way of life from which he came. Carew feels that the great intellectual leader has been ungentlemanly in a very deep sense; that ideal demanded a measure of humility; it was something rooted in the traditional code and which became obliterated in the more superficial, if more formally polite, Augustan age. In an ode on the same theme, not published until the present century, Jonson expresses a proud but far more admirable attitude towards the public:

> Yet since the bright and wise
>   *Minerva* deignes
> Uppon this humbled earth to cast hir eyes,
>   Wee'l rip our ritchest veynes
> And once more strike the Eare of tyme with those
>   fresh straynes:
>   As shall besides delight
>   And Cuninge of their grounde
> Give cause to some of wonder, some despight;
> But unto more despaire to imitate their sounde. . . .
>
>   Cast reverence if not feare
>   Throughout their generall brests
> And by their taking let it once appeare
> Who worthie come, who not, to be witts Pallace
>   guests.

However, the point to be emphasized is that Jonson at his best has a superlatively civilized tone, and it was, in fact, in him that Carew found models for the expression of such a tone in poetry. In Jonson it springs, of course, mainly from his classical culture, that culture which Carew and his class shared in a way corresponding to Jonson's participation in the social activities which produced the manners and the tone of their world. The tone which issues in Jonson's poetry from this double source is best exemplified in the following ode:

> High-spirited friend,
> I send nor Balmes, nor Cor'sives to your wound,
>   Your fate hath found
> A gentler, and more agile hand, to tend
> The Cure of that, which is but corporall,
> And doubtful Dayes, (which were nam'd *Criticall,*)
>   Have made their fairest flight,
>   And now are out of sight.
> Yet doth some wholesome Physick for the mind,
>   Wrapt in this paper lie,
> Which in the taking if you misapply
>   You are unkind.
>
>   Your covetous hand,
> Happy in that faire honour it hath gain'd
>   Must now be rayn'd.
> True valour doth her owne renowne command
> In one full Action; nor have you now more

To doe, then to be husband of that store.
   Thinke but how deare you bought
This same which you have caught,
Such thoughts wil make you more in love with truth.
    'Tis wisdom, and that high
For men to use their fortune reverently,
                  Even in youth.

This is no mere pindaric experiment. To whoever is addressed Jonson is giving extremely intimate personal advice, analysing a situation and a character instead of writing a conventional epithalamium, but his delicate movement and hesitating phrases, using the opportunities of the formal pattern, keep it free of all suggestion of patronage or importunity. There is great strength in the total effect of mature wisdom. Jonson is appealing to an ideal of human dignity and reasonable behaviour held in common with his reader which inspires frankness and at the same time sincere mutual respect. The ultimate basis is again at the old idea of courtesy. This was a quality of the spirit which made it possible to consider serious moral matters in a social context without losing sight of their seriousness or doing anything in what would later be called "bad form." This ode by itself seems to me a refutation of Professor Herford's opinion that Jonson "for all his generous warmth lacked the finer graces of familiarity." It has both.

The wit of Jonson, like that of Donne, manifests itself in many ways. As an intellectual force it has a disciplinary and clarifying rather than a free-ranging and elaborating effect, but the relationship between the two poets is shown in Jonson's admiration for Donne and in the common features of that group of elegies whose authorship has long been in dispute between them. In discussing the more social aspect of Jonson's wit, the tone that he handed on to his "sons," usually in the form of an economy and polish of technique, I think that one can claim that these "finer graces" form one of Jonson's great qualities as a poet. "High-spirited friends . . .": and "Fair friend . . ." that elegant, but closely reasoned and firmly phrased lyric, equally expressive of his distinctive classical urbanity, together give us the quintessence of Jonson's attitude towards his friends and fellow poets, his patrons and patronesses. It is not the formal decorum of a large polite world—such, in any case, did not yet exist—but one feels it to be, I think, the tone of small circles in which aristocratic and cultivated people knew each other intimately. One can back up these deductions by a short survey of Jonson's occasional and certain other verses and of imitations by his "sons." They have the kind of tone I have just noted, and they describe the life that contributed to produce that tone. Beside these poems much of the social verse, even of Pope, sounds brassy. One knows that life at Whitehall, particularly in the reign of James I, was often disorderly, not to say squalid, and that sports and pastimes on the bestordered country estate were rough and cruel, but the refinement was also there, sometimes in the same people. In the poetry it is preserved for ever.

The epigram, **"Inviting a Friend to Supper,"** is admirable social verse, besides being a document of the Jonson world, an offering of scholarly conversation with simple but good food and wine—Virgil and Tacitus with canary. A long series of epigrams and complimentary verses sketch in the type of men with whom Jonson liked to associate and the qualities that for him made up a civilized life. **"An Epistle, answering one that asked to be Sealed of the Tribe of BEN"** is unfortunately little more than satire on smart London life and the masques of Inigo Jones. **"An Epistle to a Friend, to persuade him to the Warres"** with its finely realized opening:

Wake, friend, from forth thy Lethargie: the Drum
Beates brave and loude in Europe and bids come
All that dare rowse . . .

is again mainly negative, a vigorous and racy denunciation of loose sexual morality and excessive drinking, but the ending sets up a heroic ideal of moral and physical valour, temperate, stoical and devout, the very reverse of the Renaissance braggart:

Goe, quit 'hem all. And take along with thee
Thy true friends wishes, *Colby,* which shall be
That thine be just, and honest; that thy Deeds
Not wound thy conscience, when thy body bleeds;
That thou dost all things more for truth, then glory
And never but for doing wrong be sory
That by commanding first thyselfe, thou mak'st
Thy person fit for any charge thou tak'st;
That fortune never make thee to complaine,
But what shee gives, thou dar'st give her againe;
That whatsoever face thy fate puts on,
Thou shrinke or start not, but be always one;
That thou thinke nothing great, but what is good,
And from that thought strive to be understood.
So, 'live so dead, thou wilt preserve a fame
Still pretious, with the odour of thy name.
And last, blaspheme not, we did never heare
Man thought the valianter, 'cause he durst sweare. . . .

The two poems to the brilliant young Earl of Newcastle, exalting his horsemanship and his fencing, show a kindred enthusiasm. As Professor Herford remarks, admiration for virility "gives eloquence to his verse." Vincent Corbet stands for graver and gentler virtues:

His Mind was pure, and neatly kept,
   As were his Nourceries; and swept
So of uncleannesse, or offence,
That never came ill odour thence:
   And add his Actions unto these,
   They were as specious as his Trees.
'Tis true, he could not reprehend,
His very Manners taught to 'mend,
   They were so even, grave, and holy;
   No stubbornnesse so stiffe, nor folly
To licence ever was so light
As twice to trespasse in his sight,
   His looks would so correct it, when
   It chid the vice, yet not the Men.
Much from him I confesse I wonne,
And more, and more, I should have done,

But that I understood him scant.
Now I conceive him by my want. . . .

The poet's self-criticism emphasizes the respectfulness of his attitude and deserves particular notice in this essay. In addressing Selden his verse is less distinguished, but it must be quoted for the attitude to himself shown in:

Though I confesse (as every Muse hath err'd,
and mine not least) . . .

and for the conception of scholarship and the literary life described:

Stand forth my Object, then, you that have beene
Ever at home: yet, have all Countries seene;
And like a Compasse keeping one foot still
Upon your Center, doe your circle fill
Of generall knowledge; watch'd men, manners too,
Heard what times past have said, scene what ours doe:
Which Grace shall I make love to first? your skill,
Or faith in things? or is't your wealth and will
T'instruct and teach? or your unweary'd paine
Of Gathering? Bountie'in pouring out againe?
What fables have you vext! what truth redeem'd!
Antiquities search'd! Opinions dis-esteem'd!
Impostures branded! and Authorities urg'd! . . .

In writing to Drayton, Jonson notes that they have not followed the custom of exchanging verses and continues:

And, though I now begin, 'tis not to rub
Hanch against Hanch, or raise a rhyming *Club*
About the towne.

"Butter reviewers," said Mr. Nixon to the young Hugh Selwyn Mauberley.

This quotation rounds off my references to Jonson's verses on himself as a writer and his relation to the literary world. One does not take everything in seventeenth-century commendatory verses at its face value. Drayton was no Homer, but it is worth studying what Jonson says—and, more important, does not say—about the lesser figures whom he honours. The most interesting lines in the eulogy of Shakespeare are those calling upon the shades of the Greek tragedians. Jonson's critical acumen here breaks through all his own and the age's prejudices. Sir Henry Savile was somewhat above the Jonson circle and receives a formal epigram, but the ideals admired as embodied in him correspond to those of the epistle to Selden, literary skill joined to integrity of character—a very solemn conception of the philosopher and the gentleman, to recall deliberately Addison's famous phrase:

We need a man that knows the severall graces
Of historie, and how to apt their places;
Where brevitie, where splendour, and where height,
Where sweetnesse is requir'd and where weight;
We need a man, can speake of the intents,
The councells, actions, orders and events
Of state, and censure them: we need his pen

Can write the things, the causes, and the men.
But most we need his faith (and all have you)
That dares nor write things false, nor hide
things true.

One sees in these poems the positive moral and intellectual values which are more usually merely implicit in the plays: young Wittipol in the *Devil is an Ass* emerges as a personality of somesolidity and life, but the majestic Cicero is never an adequate dramatic foil to the political gangsters in *Catiline*. In the poems one can observe, described and felt in the texture of the poetry itself, the cultural ideals that gave Jonson his assurance and intellectual dignity and at the same time his feeling for civilized personal relationships. His tone only fails him when personal bitterness or excessive indignation causes him to lose his bearings and his sense of fellowship in the republic of letters.

Jonson was, however, conscious of a larger community than that meeting at the Devil Tavern with connections at the universities. Some of his finest verse celebrates this social scene and the characters who inhabited it and, in fact, led the nation. Courthope remarks that in this mode "Jonson is unequalled by any English poet, except perhaps Pope at his best." We know from the plays what he thought of the projectors and of other pioneers of nascent capitalism. He held older ideals of social justice and responsibility. He saw the values he believed in embodied in certain noblemen and squires, and in statesmen and lawgivers such as Burleigh and Sir Edward Coke. The greatest document, and also the finest poem, in this connection is, of course, **"To Penshurst"**:

Thou are not, PENSHURST, built for envious show,
Of touch, or marble, nor canst boast a row
Of polish'd pillars, or a roofe of gold:
Thou hast no lanthorne, whereof tales are told;
Or stayre, or courts; but stand'st an ancient pile,
And these grudg'd at, are reverenc'd the while.

It is a medieval house—it happens to have been built about the year of Chaucer's birth. For Jonson a new genius presides over it from:

That taller tree, which of a nut was set,
At his great birth, where all the *Muses* met.

It was now the seat of Sir Philip Sidney's brother, and Sidney appears several times in similar poems as the representative of civilization. He brings the culture of *Il Cortegiano* to bear on the more active traditional idea of the gentleman expressed in, say, Langland's:

Kings and knightes • sholde kepe it by resoun,
Riden and rappe down • the reumes aboute,
And taken transgressores • and tyen hem faste,
Till treuthe had ytermyned • her trespas to ende,
That is the profession appertly • that appendeth for
knightes,
And nought to fasten on Fryday • in fyvescore wynter,
But holden with him and with her • that wolden al
treuthe,

And never leue hem for loue • ne for lacchying of
syluer.

[*Piers Plowman*. B., Passus I, 94-101]

Penshurst is surrounded by all the beauty and wealth of
nature, but it is much more than a house:

And though thy walls be of the countrey stone,
 They'are rear'd with no mans ruine, no mans
 grone,
There's none, that dwell about them, wish them
 downe. . . .
Where comes no guest, but is allow'd to eate,
 Without his feare, and of thy lords own meate:
Where the same beere, and bread, and self-same wine,
 That is his Lordships, shall be also mine.
And I not faine to sit (as some, this day,
 At great mens tables) and yet dine away.

Jonson sees it is an active centre of a patriarchal community
in which duties and responsibilities are as important as
rights, and of a way of life in which all classes, including
the poet—Jonson intimates that for him and for others
such hospitality is becoming a thing of the past—yet live
in close personal contact. **"To Sir Robert Wroth"** describes
a very similar scene at Durance with rather more emphasis
on the sporting life of the great estate—an aspect less
likely to be forgotten [quotes II. 21-58]. The Golden Age
is thus naturalized in the hall of an English mansion in a
real agricultural setting, and we end with an almost Homeric
scene of feasting, in which bounty and humanity have
temporarily overthrown the whole social hierarchy. Other
contemporary moralists and commentators lamented that
this old-fashioned "house-keeping" was dying out. In Selden's *Table Talk* the account of the Hall is significantly in
the past tense:

The Hall was the Place where the great Lord used to
eat, (wherefore else were Halls made so big?), where
he saw all his Servants and Tenants about him. He eat
not in private, except in time of sickness: when he
became a thing cooped up, all his greatness was spilled.
Nay, the King himself used to eat in the Hall, and his
Lords sat with him, and then he understood Men.

Inigo's Jones's Double Cube Room at Wilton, say, would
not have lent itself to such a life. It may sound cheap to
say that Jonson made the most of two worlds; he certainly
wrote at a time when a highly cultivated society still kept
in close contact with the community which supported it
and still preserved traditions which encouraged it to maintain
this kind of give and take, social, economic and cultural.

Nevertheless, despite changing architecture and changing
habits of life, the ideal persisted. Jonson initiated an extremely interesting line of what, borrowing a modern analogy, one may call documentary poetry. It deserves a brief
exploration. The most obvious imitations of his poems are
Carew's "To Saxham" and "To my Friend G. N., from
Wrest." No one is going to claim that Carew shared his
master's powers of social observation. The first poem is a
light and fanciful thing; the other, less well known, which

gives a detailed picture of the scene and of the social
organization represented there, illustrates a number of
points already made [quotes II. 19-24, 31-44, 61-69]. The
picture of the wine-press carries us away from the thoroughly
English scene; it shows the Cavalier taking his eye off the
object in order to classicize. But the mere fact that a man
like Carew, derivative as he clearly is, recognized the
existence—and the value—of such a scheme of things of
the point of writing about it shows that the rather artificial
culture of Charles I's court with its extravagant masques
and its Italian pictures and Flemish painters had also not
lost touch with its roots. Vandyck perhaps overdoes the
elegance and refinement in his portrait of Carew and Killigrew, but when William Dobson paints Endymion Porter
he shows us a florid country squire with beautiful laces
andalso dog and gun, leaning on a relief of muses and
with a classical bust of a poet in the background; it is a
superb and highly revealing work. Similarly Herrick in
The Hock-Cart starts on the shores of the Mediterranean
and then hurries home [quotes II 1-6, 26-29, 32-39]. As a
whole it is, with its colloquial language, a vivid picture of
a Devon harvest festival, and Herrick has suggested, in
the reference to the plough, the deeper meaning. Lovelace
shows us that he was something of a naturalist as well as
a chivalrous Kentish squire in those fanciful and moralized
descriptions of insects and in "The Falcon" for whom he
laments:

Ah Victory, uphap'ly wonne!
Weeping and Red is set the Sun,
Whilst the whole Fields floats in one tear,
And all the Air doth mourning wear:
Close-hooded all thy kindred come
To pay their Vows upon thy Tombe;
The *Hobby* and the *Musket* too,
Do march to take their last adieu.

The *Lanner* and the *Lanneret*,
The Colours bear as Banneret;
The *Goshawk* and her *Tercel*, rous'd
With Tears attend thee as new bows'd,
All these are in their dark array
Led by the various *Herald-Jay*.

But thy eternal name shall live
Whilst Quills from Ashes fame reprieve,
Whilst open stands Renown's wide dore,
And Wings are left on which to soar:
Doctor *Robbin*, the Prelate *Pye*
And the poetick *Swan* shall dye,
Only to sing thy Elegie.

Whatever personal significance this may have had for
Lovelace—it would seem to express a haunting regret for
lost causes—its interest for us in the present context lies
in his charming blend of the gentleman's knowledge of
field sports and heraldry with poetic traditions—one thinks
inevitably of the "Parlement of Foules." The idiom of these
poems is, as Sir Herbert Grierson has put it, "that of an
English gentleman of the best type, natural, simple, occasionally careless, but never diverging into vulgar colloqui-
alism . . . or into conventional, tawdry splendour." Several

contributors to *Jonsonus Virbius* make plain the influence of Jonson in favour of "right and natural language." This is a stream of English poetry, the gentleman writing as a gentleman about his position and responsibilities, his interests and pleasures, which, if we omit Byron who is in any case often both vulgar and tawdry, now for better or worse dries up.

Early Stuart governments made several attempts to arrest the decay of the patriarchal household and the drift to London. Sir Richard Fanshawe wrote "An Ode, upon His Majesties Proclamation in the Year 1630. Commanding the Gentry to reside upon their Estates in the Countrey." He sees what Jonson sees, and expresses the anxiety of those who realized how times were changing:

> Nor let the Gentry grudge to go
> Into those places whence they grew,
> But think them blest they may do so
>   Who would pursue.
>
> The smoky glory of the Town,
> That may go till his native Earth,
> And by the shining Fire sit down
>   Of his own hearth. . . .
>
> The Countrey too ev'n chops for rain:
> You that exhale it by your power,
> Let the fat drops fall down again
>   In a full shower. . . .

One thus sees embodied in verse of considerable distinction a picture of a social order, its natural setting and its occupations, and a sense of some of the dangers threatening it. The fact that it was written by men of very varying distinction of character and intelligence shows how widely the ideals expressed were held. That they were not always lived up to one may take for granted, though the enthusiasm of the verse seems to be more than merely literary. And as regards cultural standards there must have been, for a small number of houses like Penshurst, Wrest, Wilton, Great Tew or Bolsover, a very large number like that of Mrs. Henry Hastings or of far less individuality and long forgotten. The scheme of knightly prowess, literary and musical interests and public spirit set forth by Peacham in *The Compleat Gentleman* was not universally followed; he bitterly reproaches those who waste their substance in London, "appearing but as Cuckoes in the Spring, one time in the yeare to the Countrey and their tenants, leaving the care of keeping good houses at Christmas, to the honest Yeomen of the Countrey." However, one finds in this verse evidence of a climate of social opinion and, more important, feelings and habits which, with all their imperfections, were civilized in the narrower artistic sense, and also in the wider sense of having a foundation of social justice. This world provided Jonson with his larger *milieu*, or rather *milieux*, for its being made up of small groups is an important feature; he had lived in the house of Lord Aubigny and was a visitor at several others. One does not find this scene in English poetry after the Restoration. Though English noblemen never became, as Fanshawe feared they might, mere court sycophants or men about town, manners

in the widest sense changed in the era of the coffee-house. Life became more formally decorous. Pope, in the "Epistle to Boyle," presents an ideal vision comparable to Jonson's:

> His Father's Acres who enjoys in peace,
> Or makes his Neighbours glad if he increase:
> Whose chearful Tenants bless their yearly toil,
> Yet to their Lord owe more than to the soil;
> Whose ample Lawns are not asham'd to feed
> The milky heifer and deserving steed;
> Whose rising Forests, not for pride or show,
> But future Buildings, future Navies grow:
> Let his plantations stretch from down to down,
> First shade a Country, and then raise a Town.

But fine as it is, and central to Pope's work, it does not imply so intimate and personal a relationship between the classes as the earlier poetry. The whole domestic layout had altered as ideas changed, and the lord was benevolent from the portico or the church steps rather than from the dais in the hall. Nevertheless one finds the spirit still alive in the age of "Squire Allworthy," of Coke of Norfolk and of Dr. Johnson's Club, and it was the tradition of culture that died first.

It need hardly be said that Jonson used an independent tone towards his patrons—except when he was in extreme financial straits. He had opinions about his rightful place at table in an age when all knew their own degrees and had their rightful places by birth or merit; "my Lord," he says that he said to the Earl of Salisbury, evidently a more remote patron than Sir William Sidney, "you promised I should dine with you, but I do not." **"An Epistle to Sir Edward Sacvile, now Earl of Dorset"** treats, after Seneca, of the question of patronage and gratitude:

> You cannot doubt, but I, who freely know
> This Good from you, as freely will it owe;
> And though my fortune humble me, to take
> The smallest courtesies with thanks, I make
> Yet choyce from whom I take them; and would shame
> To have such doe me good, I durst not name:
> They are the Noblest benefits, and sinke
> Deepest in Man, of which when he doth thinke,
> The memorie delights him more, from whom
> Then what he hath receiv'd. Gifts stinke from some,
> They are so long a coming, and so hard;
> Where any Deed is forc't, the Grace is mard.

He goes on to analyse the characters of niggardly and ungracious patrons and those who sponge upon them. Jonson thought he knew who deserved his respect and why. In *Timber* he defines his conception of manners by implication, in the act of defining Courtesy in its euphemistic sense:

> *Nothing* is a courtesie, unless it be meant us; and that friendly, and lovingly. Wee owe no thankes to *Rivers*, that they carry our boats . . . It is true, some man may receive a Courtesie, and not know it; but never any man received it from him, that knew it not. . . . No:

The doing of *Courtesies* aright, is the mixing of the respects for his owne sake, and for mine. He that doth them meerly for his owne sake, is like one that feeds his Cattell to sell them: he hath his Horse well durst for *Smithfield*.

Good manners for Jonson were something that, while adorning the upper tiers of the social hierarchy, should yet permeate through it. He expected the same kind of consideration from a patronas he showed towards his "high-spirited friend," and he admired similar qualities in his friends in every sense.

The grace of Jonson's manner comes out in his addresses to noble ladies, especially the Countesses of Rutland, Montgomery, and Bedford, and Lady Mary Wroth. A consideration of them will form a conclusion to this study, for, though he flatters splendidly, he does not cringe. There were certain fixed viewpoints in Jonson's outlook.

He praises his patronesses partly for their beauty and their taste, partly for deeper qualities: He writes to Lady Mary Wroth with full Renaissance exuberance:

> Madame, had all antiquities beene lost,
>   All historie seal'd up, and fables crost;
> That we had left us, nor by time, nor place,
>   Least mention of a *Nymph,* a *Muse,* a *Grace,*
> But even their names were to be made a-new,
>   Who could not but create them all, from you?
> He, that but saw you weare the wheaten hat,
>   Would call you more than CERES, if not that:
> And, durst in shepherds tyre, who would not say:
>   You were the bright OENONE, FLORA, or *May?*
> If dancing, all would cry th'*Idalian* Queene,
>   Were leading forth the *Graces* on the greene:
> And, armed for the chase, so bare her brow
>   DIANA alone, so hit, and hunted so.

Lady Montgomery is a new Susanna, and in Lady Bedford he bows before qualities of character which belong peculiarly to his own vision [quotes **Epigram LXXVI**]. This beautifully polished epigram is a suitable vehicle for the presentation of a vision of aristocratic elegance, charm, virtue and intelligence—one notices the emphatic and subtle rhythm of the third quatrain—and the poet's admiration for them. One is reminded of the undirected, and possibly therefore more perfect, **"Elegie"**:

> Though Beautie be the Marke of Praise,
>   And yours of whom I sing be such
>   As not the Word can praise too much,
> Yet is't your vertue now I raise,

where the sense of the rarity and fragility of such qualities is delicately realized in the cadence of:

> His falling Temples you have rear'd,
>   The withered Garlands tane away;
>   His Altars kept from the Decay,
> That envie wish'd, and Nature fear'd.

The dangers and difficulties besetting his ideals of the lady are magnificently argued out in "Not to know vice at all . . . " and **"To the World. A farewell for a Gentlewoman, vertuous and noble"**:

> No, I doe know that I was borne
>   To age, misfortune, sicknesse, griefe:
> But I will beare these, with that scorne,
>   As shall not need thy false reliefe.

This is the simple but dignified Stoicism which conditions of the age made both necessary and desirable. Jonson admired it in others and possessed it himself. This moral strength and perception, along with his erudition and conscious art, discoursed on in *Timber,* and an ever-present sense of the whole gamut of living, combine with the tone of the Jacobean noble household, "curteous, facile, sweet," where in season "freedome doth with degree dispense," to support the brilliance of the famous lyrics. Like his gentlewoman he could say,

> Nor for my peace will I goe farre,
>   As wandrers doe, that still doe rome,
> But make my strengths, such as they are,
>   Here in my bosome, and at home.

The end of it all is realized with unerring taste in such things as:

> Would'st thou heare, what man can say
>   In a little? Reader, stay.
> Under-neath this stone doth lye.
>   As much beautie, as could dye:
> Which in life did harbour give
>   To more vertue, then doth live.
> If, at all, shee had a fault
>   Leave it buryed in this vault.
> One name was ELIZABETH,
>   Th' other let it sleepe with death:
> Fitter, where it dyed, to tell,
>   Then that it liv'd at all. Farewell.

I am brought back to my starting point, the **"Elegie on the Lady Jane Pawlet,"** through which the urbanity of Jonson links up directly with that of Pope, Jonson thought "couplets be the bravest sort of verses, especially when they are broken like hexameters," and he has an important place in their development, but, as regards regularity, he broke them with a caesura in varied places, and the following lines from one of his livelier occasional poems are worth remembering:

> To hit in angles, and to clash with time:
>   As all defence, or offence, were a chime!
> I hate such measur'd, give me metall'd fire. . . .

He liked a varied movement in poetry as well as fencing. The **"Elegie,"** like the other poems in couplets, bears this out:

> I doe obey you, Beautie! for in death
>   You seeme a faire one! O that you had breath,
> To give your shade a name! Stay, stay, I feele

A horrour in mee! all my blood is steele!
Stiffe! starke! My joynts 'gainst one another knock!
    Whose Daughter? ha? Great *Savage* of the
Rock? . . .
Her Sweetnesse, Softnesse, her faire Courtesie,
    Her wary guardes, her wise simplicitie,
Were like a ring of Vertues, 'bout her set,
    And pietie the Center, where all met.
A reverend State she had, an awful Eye,
    A dazling, yet inviting, Majestie:
What Nature, Fortune, Institution, Fact
    Could summe to a perfection, was her Act!
How did she leave the world? with what contempt?
    Just as she in it liv'd! and so exempt
From all affection! when they urg'd the Cure
    Of her disease, how did her soule assure
Her suffrings, as the body had beene away!
    And to the Torturers (her Doctors) say,
Stick on your Cupping-glasses, feare not, put
    Your hottest Causticks to, burne, lance, or cut:
'Tis but a body which you can torment,
    And I, into the world, all Soule, was sent!
Then comforted her Lord! and blest her Sonne!
    Chear'd her faire Sisters in her race to runne!
With gladness temper'd her sad Parents teares!
    Made her friends joyes to get above their
feares!
And, in her last act, taught the Standers-by,
    With admiration, and applause to die!
Let angels sing her glories, who can call
    Her spirit home, to her originall! . . .

It combines a slightly naïve declamatory manner at the start with Jonson's characteristic blend of urbanity, shrewd observation and simplicity in the description of the Marchioness's personality and an anticipation of the more formal high decorum of the Augustans towards the end; but no Augustan would have written her words to the doctors, overflowing as they are with "enthusiasm." Here in a lady at the top of the social hierarchy one notes the hierarchy of virtues. They correspond fairly to the qualities of men we have already seen portrayed. Together Jonson's lords and ladies form a brilliant, dignified, benevolent and gracious society, "dazling, yet inviting." We can see from the poems, and other evidence corroborates, that there was no impassable gap between the world of the poet's vision and Jacobean and Caroline England. "Eupheme" on the Lady Venetia Digby is usually held up as an example of hyperbole; a passage in a quiet key on the character of the Lady, whether true to life in this particular case or not, shows, with a characteristic note of irony, a picture of deportment which would be appropriate to any of the scenes or characters discussed:

              All Nobilitie,
    (But pride, that schisme of incivilitie)
She had, and it became her! she was fit
    T'have knowne no envy, but by suffring it!
She had a mind as calme, as she was faire;
    Not tost or troubled with light Lady-aire;
But, kept an even gate, as some streight tree
    Mov'd by the wind, so comely moved she.

And by the awfull manage of her Eye
    She swaid all bus'nesse in the Familie!

Jonson himself, as we have seen at the start, was sometimes guilty of "that schisme of incivilitie." He probably needed the stimulus of good company to bring out the full refinement of his literary culture. But it is brought out over and over again, and was, and is, a model of its kind. It is impossible finally to separate the qualities presented in the poems from the poet's attitude towards them; social manner and manners are infectious and the one seems to have evoked the other. We should need more biographical information than we possess to take the matter further but I do not think it is base to attribute to Jonson what might be called poetic "party manners."

> [Jonson's] poetry, even more than his plays, links seventeenth-century culture and the polite civilization of the Augustans to the better features of the medieval social order and to the half-religious ideal of Courtesy.
>
> —*Geoffrey Walton*

One cannot sum up an achievement such as Jonson's in a word. I have only touched in passing on his trenchancy and seriousness as a satirist and his strength and delicacy as a lyric poet. I wanted to deal at some length with his tone and accent because, in considering the meaning of wit, I believe that, though it changed from an intellectual to a social spirit as the century wore on, nevertheless a social spirit of a clear and peculiarly noble kind was present in poetry from the start and that this spirit is exemplified particularly in Ben Jonson. His poetry, even more than his plays, links seventeenth-century culture and the polite civilization of the Augustans to the better features of the medieval social order and to the half-religious ideal of Courtesy.

Claude J. Summers and Ted-Larry Pebworth (essay date 1982)

SOURCE: Introduction to *Classic and Cavalier: Celebrating Jonson and the Sons of Ben,* University of Pittsburgh Press, 1982, pp. xi-xvii.

[*In the following excerpt, Summers and Pebworth describe Jonson as a varied poet, viewing his idealism as the link between his neo-classical tendencies and his emotionalism.*]

The recent quickening of critical interest in Ben Jonson's nondramatic poetry has led to a new appreciation of his "subtile sport" and to a new willingness to read him on his own terms. His status as poet has risen steadily over the past two decades. After years of languishing in Donne's shadow, he is now recognized among the most important poets in the language. He is justly celebrated as a self-nominated arbiter of civilized values, as a public poet who articulates the "mysteries of manners, armes, and arts" in weighty judgment and broad generality, as, in fact, a thoroughgoing neo-classicist. But such a view, accurate though it is in basic outline, is at best only partial, even when buttressed with timeworn and misleading contrasts of a laborious, frigid Jonson with a gentle Shakespeare and a fiery Donne. The unqualified view of Jonson as neoclassicist neglects his frequent indulgences in emotional excess and self-dramatization, and—more positively—his ability to create poetry of individual sensation. What needs emphasis is that Jonson's carefully fashioned poetic commonwealth includes space for the personal and the private as well as for the general and the public. If Jonson is, as Arthur Marotti has characterized him, "an artistic schizophrenic, with both a Dionysian and an Apollonian side [Arthur Marotti, "All About Jonson's Poetry," *ELH* 39 (1972)], these divergent aspects of his personality are united by the idealism that animates the contradictory impulses of his poetry: wit and didacticism, self-assertion and social vision, rage and commendation, satire and celebration.

The variety of Jonson's poetry undoubtedly reflects the contradictions of his life. Stepson to a bricklayer, he became the defender of conservative, aristocratic tradition, yet also insisted that merit and high birth are not synonymous. A felon convicted of manslaughter, he promulgated a code of ethical behavior for an age he diagnosed as corrupt and in imminent danger of social and political collapse. A gregarious man who inspired the devotion of younger poets and wits, he also made numerous enemies and prosecuted many quarrels. He asserted "the impossibility of any mans being the good Poet, without first being a good man" (*Volpone*, Dedication), yet he was described by Inigo Jones as "the best of Poetts, but the worst of men" ("To his false friend mr: Ben Johnson"), and by William Drummond of Hawthornden as "a great lover and praiser of himself, a contemner and Scorner of others, given rather to losse a friend, than a Jest" (*Conversations*, 680-81). Proud of his learning and conscious of his dignity, he could nevertheless mock his physical appearance and freely reveal such idiosyncrasies as that "he heth consumed a whole night in lying looking to his great toe, about which he hath seen tartars & turks Romans and Carthaginions feight in his imagination" (*Conversations*, 322-24).

The many facets of Jonson's complex personality cohere in his carefully shaped yet various canon, wherein he adopts such dramatic voices as tactful adviser, genial host, urbane commentator, scornful satirist, grieving father, and vulnerable lover. For all his multiplicity of roles, however, Jonson nearly always reveals himself as insistently and self-consciously the poet. His confession to Drummondthat, "In his merry humor, he was wont to name himself the Poet" (*Conversations*, 636), both reveals his self-image and accords with his practice in the poems. But Jonson's creation of a poet-persona is not merely a self-promoting pose or simply a poetic strategy exploited deftly in such works as the verse epistles, the epitaphs on his children,

"A Celebration of Charis," "My Picture left in Scotland," the Cary-Morison ode, "To Penshurst," and "On Lucy Countesse of Bedford," among many others. It is also a reflection of the idealism that unites the disparate works of his canon and constitutes one of his greatest legacies to the "Tribe of Ben."

Jonson's idealism is rooted in his unswerving conviction of the true utility of poetry, that "dulcet, and gentle *Philosophy,* which leades on, and guides us by the hand to Action, with a ravishing delight, and incredible Sweetnes" (*Discoveries,* 2398-2400). Paraphrasing Cicero, he described poetry as an art which "nourisheth, and instructeth our Youth; delights our Age; adornes our prosperity; comforts our Adversity; entertaines us at home; keepes us company abroad, travailes with us; watches; divides the times of our earnest, and sports; shares in our Country recesses and recreations; insomuch as the wisest and best learned have thought her the absolute Mistresse of manners, and neerest of kin to Vertue" (*Discoveries,* 2389-96). Of the poet, he said, "Wee doe not require in him meere *Elocution;* or an excellent faculty in verse; but the exact knowledge of all vertues, and their Contraries; with ability to render the one lov'd, the other hated, by his proper embattaling them" (*Discoveries,* 1038-41). Implicit throughout Jonson's work is an abiding vision of human possibilities, a vision that poetry not only incorporates but also helps to realize. Poetry "offers to mankinde a certaine rule, and Patterne of living well, and happily" (*Discoveries,* 2386-7). And unlike wealth, beauty, and nobility, it offers the reward of immortality, as Jonson explains in his **"Epistle. To Elizabeth Countesse of Rutland"**:

> It is the *Muse,* alone, can raise to heaven,
>   And, at her strong armes end, hold up, and even,
> The soules, shee loves. Those other glorious notes,
>   Inscrib'd in touch or marble, or the cotes
> Painted, or carv'd upon our great-mens tombs,
>   Or in their windowes; doe but prove the wombs,
> That bred them, graves: when they were borne, they di'd,
>   That had no *Muse* to make their fame abide.
>
>   (41-48)

Jonson's trust in good verses sustained him throughout the vicissitudes of his life. "*Poetry,* in this latter Age, hath prov'd but a meane *Mistresse,* to such as have wholly addicted themselves to her" (*Discoveries,* 622-4), he complained. Yet he never lost his faith in the continuity of ethical principles, in the living relevance of timeless questions about the nature of the good life, or in the ability of poetry to re-create the past and to preserve the present for the future. Thus his real audience was never limited to his own time. He offered his work to posterity, confident of its verdict. "An other Age, or juster men," he wrote, "will acknowledge the vertues of [the poet's] studies: his wisdome, in dividing: his subtility, in arguing: with what strength hee doth inspire his readers; with what sweetnesse hee strokes them: in inveighing, what sharpnesse; in Jest, what urbanity he uses" (*Discoveries,* 786-91). Jonson's own poetry exemplifies those qualities of learning, subtlety, strength, and urbanity that he expected posterity to value.

But "Saint Ben's" legacy to his poetic sonsmay reside almost as much in the trust in good verses as in the verses themselves. Jonson's idealistic conception of the poet-priest is certainly not original; yet he more than anyone else in the early seventeenth century exemplified in life and in poetic practice the continuity of Orpheus's direct line. As Thomas Randolph wrote, in "A gratulatory to Mʳ. Ben. Johnson for his adopting of him to be his Son,"

> I am a kinne to *Hero's,* being thine,
> And part of my alliance is divine.

Robert C. Evans (essay date 1987)

SOURCE: "Literature as Equipment for Living: Ben Jonson and the Poetics of Patronage," in *CLA Journal,* Vol. 30, No. 3, March, 1987, pp. 379-94.

[*In the following essay, Evans contends that the poetry Jonson wrote within the patronage system was as psychologically necessary as it was financially enabling.*]

The impact of patronage on English Renaissance literature seems all the greater when one recognizes that literary patronage was only one aspect of a much larger, far more comprehensive system of patronage relationships. Patronage, broadly defined, was the central social system of the era. It dominated political life and permeated the structure of the church and universities. Its influence on the economy was enormous, and the assumptions behind it were reflected in religious thought, in cosmological speculation, and in the organization and daily detail of family life. Painting, architecture, music—in fact, all the arts and not just literature—were affected by a patronage culture so pervasive that no individual or sphere of life could entirely escape its effects. The connection between poetry and patronage, then, involved more than how writers were paid or how they made their livings. It involved, more fundamentally, how they lived their lives. The patronage system was more than simply a means of organizing the economy or of structuring politics, of arranging social life or of thinking about one's relationship with God. Because it was all these things, it was also a psychological system, in the sense that the assumptions behind a patronage culture inevitably affected how people thought about themselves, others, and their mutual interactions. Patronage, or one's place in the various interlocking patronage networks, went far towards defining not only one's social status, but also one's self-esteem. Making a secure and respected niche for oneself in the patronage system meant more than ensuring a healthy income. It meant winning an opportunity to participate most fully, most *really,* in the life of one's time.

In its broadest sense, the patronage system was simply the translation into practical social terms of the grand hierarchical "Elizabethan World Picture"—that set of assumptions, grounded in notions of subordination and degree, by which society was ostensibly ordered and its place in the universe conventionally explained. With God the Father at the head of an enormous chain of subordinate relationships, with the monarch as God's vice-regent on earth and as a father to his people, and with individual fathers as little sovereigns, minor masters of their own families and households, Renaissance culture formed a webwork of patriarchal relationships. Authority was vested inpowerful, mostly older male figures who exercised it over properly deferential inferiors. Gaining power meant propitiating those who held it, and at every level one's most important relations were less with one's equals or peers than with one's superiors and subordinates. "Horizontal" relations—friendships, for instance—were not insignificant; for one thing, they could provide some relief from, as well as some alternative to, the pressures or anxieties of participating in the patronage system. But the relief could never be total, the alternative never complete: no friendship, however satisfying, could in itself assure one a secure place in the social hierarchy. And one's friends, of course, were also themselves participants in the same system. Connections with them might in fact be useful in winning or maintaining patronage, but it was the relation with the patron that was of prime importance. Indeed, the very fact that friendships could provide a sense of refuge from the pressures of competition suggests how the patronage system could color the character of relationships seemingly separate from it. Even the link between man and wife was conceived less as a partnership of equals than as a subordination of the woman to the husband. In theology, politics, and domestic relations, patriarchy was the rule and patronage its reflection in practical life. It is precisely because literary patronage was not an isolated or peculiar arrangement, precisely because it reflected and replicated in one sphere the patterns of thinking and behavior dominant in society at large, that its effects on literature seem so potentially complex, important, and far-reaching. Paradoxically, it is only when one pulls back from a focus on literary patronage *per se* to a concern with the larger patronage system that the full implications of patronage for literature begin to become apparent.

Ideally patronage relationships were grounded in mutual reciprocity, but the translation from theory to practice was inevitably imperfect. While in theory the patronage system reflected the underlying hierarchical order of the universe, in practice it created numerous opportunities for tensions, contradictions, suspicions, and resentment. By its very nature the patronage system involved the accommodation of egos with different, sometimes contradictory interests. The actual operation of the "system," in fact, was neither simple nor rigidly systematic; relations among its participants were likely to be complex and dialectical rather than straightforwardly causal. The opportunities for irony, ambiguity, paradox, and equivocation existed not only in the literary works to which patronage relations gave birth, but in the relations themselves.

Over the course of a career that spanned four decades and the reigns of three very different monarchs, Ben Jonson became perhaps the most spectacularly successful patronage poet of his era. House-guest of well-connected nobles, perennial author of holiday masques, and recipient of royal grants of money and sack, Jonson by middle age had become a fixture at the Jacobean court. He had achieved the kind of fame and social influence that had always eluded Spenser; and although his fortunes diminished in his final years, at his death a parade of nobles escorted him to the grave. Many of his best poems were addressed to patrons, and many more deal explicitly with patronage as a theme. During the course of his long career he met many of the typical challenges and fulfilled most of the common functions of the patronage poet. His work represents, to an unsuspected extent, a repertoire of responses to patronage pressures and influences. Yet discussion of the impact of patronage on Jonson's poetry has rarely been as complicated or extensive as the impact itself.

For this, Jonson's success is partly responsible. If any Jacobean poet benefited from patronage, he did. Compared to others—Donne, for instance—his rise was meteoric and his status secure. Yearafter year he won lucrative commissions to write masques for James's court, so that in time his prosperity became almost its own best guarantee. Aspiring courtiers who noted Jonson's favor with the King employed him to help win or maintain similar status for themselves. And if Jonson's poetry could enhance the prestige of one aristocrat, he was likely to win the attention and encouragement of others. The more he became known and regarded at court, the more likely he was to continue flourishing there. Jonson's experience with patronage can thus seem at first glance unproblematic—hence uninteresting and comparatively unimportant.

But this account of Jonson's career is defectively simple. It substitutes the long view of literary history for Jonson's day-to-day *lived* experience. Looking back on his life from a distance of several centuries, it is much easier for us than it ever was for him to take his literary and social success for granted. Historical hindsight imposes a shape and thus a seeming inevitability on his career—an inevitability of which he was inevitably ignorant. His early years seem to have impressed upon him how uncertain and unpredictable life could be—the extent to which good fortune and status could depend upon chancy contingencies or luck. And his later experience as a competitor for patronage only reinforced that lesson. He sought patronage for the same reasons others did—to enhance his financial and social security— but he had the extra motive of winning back some of the status and concomitant self-esteem that his father's untimely death and mother's remarriage to a bricklayer had denied him.

Jonson's struggle for social acceptance was thus more than pragmatically important: it was psychologically imperative. It was waged, moreover, in the face of recurrent, sometimes rancorous competition. Even a short list of Jonson's competitors—men he seems to have threatened or felt threatened by—reads like a Who's Who of Jacobean letters: Alexander, Brome, Chapman, Daniel, Day, Dekker, Jones, Marston, Overbury, and (most controversial of all) Shakespeare. Not all these men directly competed with Jonson for patronage, but his relations with none of them can entirely be separated from patronage concerns. Nor were all his challengers themselves historically important: some rate footnotes only for having quarrelled with Jonson, while the names of others—some of those he attacks in his

Epigrammes, for instance—cannot be recovered. Yet the impact of such competition was immense, and no assessment of Jonson as a patronage poet can afford to ignore it. His patronage poems include not only those addressed to patrons, but those directed at the rivals who competed with him for their attention.

Even if Jonson had had no competitors to worry about, his position as a patronage poet would still not have been entirely secure. Patronage dependency, though more profitable and respectable than writing for the stage, was dependency nontheless and carried its own hazards. Indeed, in certain respects the transition from the stage to the court could leave a poet more exposed to uncertainties and anxieties than before. A play might fail in the theatre because it did not please, but a poet might fail at court if his personality were unpleasant. Because the patronage system during this period was tied so intimately to the predilections and characteristics of individual patrons, it lacked many of the checks and balances, the institutional safeguards typical of the more impersonal patronage practiced, for instance, by private foundations and government endowments in twentieth-century democracies. At any time, for any reason, a patron could take offense, lose interest, lose influence, or die. A poet could win the favor of a noble lady along with the jealousy of her husband. He could anger a patron by angering the patron's friend, while words innocently meant could easily be misinterpreted andheld against him. He could be used by an aristocrat while the aristocrat lived, then abused by the man's enemies when the patron passed away. These are not fanciful suppositions—all happened to Jonson at one time or another, and in most cases more than once. Poetry was never as important a concern to patrons as it was to the poets themselves, nor was the poet's actual social position ever as exalted as the poets wished. Unlike suitors with political or economic benefits to confer, the poet had relatively less to offer a patron and was thus relatively less secure. Even success, if it came, could breed anxieties of its own. The more acceptance Jonson found from patrons, for instance, the more his dependence on them grew and thus the more their possible rejection of him would have meant, financially and psychologically. By the closing years of James' reign, no one was more aware than Jonson himself how unusual his social position was: reason enough both to doubt its security and to fight to maintain it.

These twin sources of anxiety—the inherently unstable nature of the relationship between poet and patron, and the inevitable fact of continuous competition for patronage support—arguably had a profound, even determining influence on Jonson's life and art. Coupled with the uncertainties he experienced in his early years, such anxieties must have affected in minute fashion the ways in which he thought about, executed, and presented each of his poems. Of course, almost all writers will, with different degrees of self-consciousness, need to anticipate the possible reactions of their audiences. And such anticipation will affect not only what they write, but how. For the patronage poet, however—and for Jonson in particular—such considerations must have been more important than we can probably today appreciate. For him, each poem was quite literally a calculated risk; he could never confidently predict how his patrons or competitors might react to it, and yet he knew that their reactions would determine his future in fundamental ways. As such, the poem was invested with an immense amount of psychic energy and life; a patronage perspective on Jonson's works would be valuable if it did nothing other than return to use some sense of that kind of energy.

Yet the idea of Jonson as a fundamentally anxious poet is not one that has received much emphasis in Jonson criticism. Even when it *has* been mentioned, it has usually been dealt with in such a way as to underplay its significance. To stress that the audience Jonson was necessarily most responsive to was comprised primarily of patrons and potential patrons, of competitors and potential competitors; to argue that when Jonson wrote, distributed, or printed a poem he had to take the possible reactions of these readers into account—such an emphasis might seem to compromise the image Jonson presents of himself as a poet fundamentally independent of the social pressures of his day. And to compromise that image might seem to undermine Jonson's importance as a poet. Some of Jonson's readers, perhaps influenced by Romantic assumptions of poetry as self-expression, react with mild contempt or disdain to any poem that suggests too clearly its concern with patronage; for these readers Jonson's "begging" poems, or the official verse he churned out under Charles, make an embarrassing coda to the apparent independence of his earlier career. At the same time, they tend to be embarrassed by Jonson's personal feuds with other known literary figures of his age. Both reactions implicitly acknowledge a fact which Jonson himself could hardly afford to ignore: that his acceptance as a poet depended (and still depends) very much upon the right kind of *self*-presentation.

Our standard concepts of poetry, however—whether we like to think of it as didactic instruction, personal expression, the congealed spirit of its culture or age, or the free play of signifiers—leave little room, and provide almost no vocabulary, for thinking of it in terms of the poet's self promotion and individual advantage. The very idea seems a bit distasteful, for however "sophisticated" or "critical" or "distanced" our attitudes towards other conventional verities, the urge to enshrine the poet as a creative culture-hero, somehow set apart from and above ambition, remains strong. Nurtured over the centuries by poets themselves, it exercises an understandable appeal for critics as well. It helps account for the fact that recent discussion of poetic anxiety tends to focus less upon the poet's relations with contemporary competitors than on mental wrestlings with intellectual forebears. It partly explains why studies of poets and politics so frequently concentrated on their subjects' ideological commitments, or on major shifts of historical thought, rather than on the day-to-day power relations that consume so much of the energy and attention of so many ordinary people. In Jonson's case, it makes sense of the tendency to present his quarrel with Jones as primarily an aesthetic disagreement, and in almost every case it leads to an emphasis upon ideas in and of themselves, while neglecting their tactical serviceability—the

ways people use them against or direct them towards each other, and why. None of these approaches is illegitimate; each is valuable and contributes to our understanding of the authors involved. Yet none is adequate in and of itself, and all are inadequate to the extent that they ignore the power dimension of individual activity. This is not to say that an emphasis on that dimension can itself provide anything like a total, adequate explanation: to reduce human actions merely to power relations would be to falsify them. But neither can this dimension be ignored. It must take its place as part of any total explanation.

To emphasize the psychological importance of patronage to the poet, however, is not to suggest that the poet was completely dominated by the patron, or in any way incapacitated by his dependency. For although the poet depended upon the patron to a great degree for his sense of self-validation and self-esteem (especially in the face of competition from other poets), the patron to a lesser extent depended upon the poet to enhance his reputation in the face of competition among the patrons themselves. A skillful poet could take advantage of this fact and use the patron's interest in maintaining a healthy public reputation to advance his own interests. Jonson's inclusion of the Countess of Bedford in his important epistle to the Countess of Rutland (*The Forrest*, **XII**), for instance, allows him to set up a kind of quiet, understated competition between the two women to see which will prove the more deserving patron. He uses a variation of this same tactic in a less well-known poem to the Countess of Bedford herself. The work is brief enough to permit full discussion of it, not only in order to show the impact that the patronage situation could have on the aesthetic design of individual poems, but also in order to suggest how a patronage perspective can broaden and deepen our appreciation of the skill and accomplishment of even relatively minor examples of Jonson's writing:

> Madame, I told you late how I repented,
>   I ask'd a lord a buck and he denyed me;
> And, ere I could aske you, I was preuented:
>   For your most noble offer had supply'd me.
> Straight went I home; and there most like a *Poet*,
>   I fancied to my selfe, what wine, what wit
> I would haue spent: how euery *Muse* should know it,
>   And Phoebvs-selfe should be at eating it.
> O *Madame*, if your grant did thus transferre mee,
>   Make it your gift. See whither that will beare mee.

This is, of course, a much slighter poem than the "**Epistle**" to the Countess of Rutland, and the objective it seeks to obtain is much more immediate and practical, and much less important, than that sought in the longer poem. Yet Jonson himself seems to have fancied the work: Drummond of Hawthornden mentions it as one that the poet particularly liked to quote. Simply as a work of "art," it is hard to imagine why Jonson would have been so proud of it; but as an example of how one could skillfully manipulate a patron—itself an artful undertaking—it becomes easier to understand how a poet who gave evidence of valuing poems in such terms could think so highly of it. Seen in this way, it is a sophisticated work indeed.

Jonson uses the first quatrain to establish a clear opposition—in the mind of the Countess, and in the mind of anyone else to whom she or Jonson might show the poem, or quote it—between the niggardliness of the unnamed lord and the Countess' spontaneous generosity. In interpreting this poem, as in interpreting many others by Jonson, it is important to remember that the works of Renaissance poets were often "published" long before they were ever actually printed and sold. Manuscript circulation or readings of the poems in small groups could be far more significant in establishing a poet's reputation than merely selling copies of a printed book—especially if the manuscripts were circulated among or read to those who shaped the tastes and values of the poet's society. Manuscript publication and readings also meant that a poet could control—or try to control—the distribution of his work more effectively than if it were widely published in print. Proper interpretation of the poem might then depend upon the context the poet established during his reading of it. This point becomes especially significant when one is considering Jonson's satiric attacks on unnamed malefactors, as in the present work. Although the lord is left unnamed in the printed version, there is every reason to suspect that when Jonson read the poem or showed it around, his audience was made aware of the identity of the man he attacked.

Jonson claims that while the unnamed lord had denied his specific request, the Countess granted his desire before he could even make an appeal to her for it. He puns with the initial rhyme-words, "repented" and "preuented," seeming to suggest in the first line that *he* has something to feel sorry about, until it emerges in the next line that it is the unnamed lord who is at fault. Similarly, in claiming that he was "preuented" from asking the Countess for the buck, he seems for an instant to imply that someone squelched his intention, until it becomes obvious that he means that the Countess anticipated his need before he could voice it. Both puns emphasize the characteristic he ascribes to each of the aristocrats—the blameworthiness of the unnamed lord, the generosity of the Countess. In reminding Lucy of this event, however, he not only compliments her, but reminds her of his power to affect her own reputation. Just as he made known to her in conversation the illiberality of the lord whose name he disdains to mention in the poem, so her failure to fulfill the grant she offered him could lead to the same result. Indeed, the very poem in which he now compliments her generosity would then stand as a potentially public rebuke; the clear distinction established in the first quatrain between the Countess and the unnamed lord would collapse, and the Countess would even stand to seem *more* culpable, since she, after all, had explicitly promised Jonson the buck he sought. She would not simply be denying a request; she would be reneging on a promise.

In a sense, then, the Countess herself holds the key to how the poem will be interpreted: depending upon how she acts, it will either speak well or ill of her. Jonson gives the Countess an opportunity in this poem to prove herself a more worthy patron than the lord who at first refused him; yet the poem pressures her into seizing the opportunity lest she be thought even less worthy. To explain the effect of the poem in such terms, however, is to risk under-

emphasizing the subtle means by which the effect is achieved. It risks failing to notice how skillfully Jonson employs humorous self-deprecation—presenting himself as a somewhat silly, wine-guzzling poet with an overactive imagination—to minimize any overt sense of threat to the patron while making himself as lovably attractive a potential recipient as possible. He explicitly holds out to her the promise of public gratitude if she fulfills her grant "euery *Muse* should know it," and his willingness to print the present poem suggests that the poem itself discharges that promise, and therefore that the grant was indeed fulfilled. Yet the poem also serves to remind both the Countess and the unnamed lord of the poet's power to affect their reputations, while it demonstrates to a modern reader Jonson's ability to play the competing interests of individual members of the aristocracy off against each other to enhance his own.

In the Renaissance, all the arts could be used to celebrate a patron, but literature by its very nature could do more. A poem could be used not simply to extol the interaction between the writer and his patron; it could also be used to comment upon their relationship, to manipulate its nature and direction. In other arts the relationship between the artist and his benefactor occurred mostly outside the work (however indirectly and insistently the relationship might impinge upon it). Study of the relationship thus becomes mainly a problem for biography. But in many of Jonson's poems the relationship continues—is negotiated—*within* the work. The epigram to Lady Bedford is a slight but striking example. It suggests in a rather blatant way what might seem more subtly true of numerous other patronage poems—a view of the poem as a bargain, a compromise, an accommodation of egos. But precisely because this accomodation is carried out *within* or *through* the work, it becomes more than simply a matter for biographical study. It becomes a problem for aesthetics and criticism, a matter with definite implications for the success (and for the successful understanding) of the poem *as* poem.

As a vehicle for prosecuting the writer's interaction with his patron, a poem offered definite advantages. To a much greater degree than "spontaneous" conversation or the contacts of "everyday life," the tactics or structures of a poem could be calculated or premeditated. Indeed, it is precisely this studied, artful nature of the poem that makes a genuinely literary-critical approach to patronage verse possible. Because the poem *was* more stable, however, more permanent and more literally tangible than the fluid give-and-take of normal daily discourse, it was also in some ways more dangerous. The very ability to give lasting shape and expression to a thought—which was one of the poet's chief claims to importance and social recognition—meant that a tactical mistake or miscalculation in a poem would be less easy to correct or forget. A slip or faux pas in conversation might be erased in the very next moment by a smile, a glance, an explanatory phrase. But a blunder committed to paper was thereby both easier to recollect and harder to revoke. In their own works, Jonson's enemies often mocked lines he had written just months previously or many years before.

Paradoxically, the very effectiveness of the poem as an instrument for self-promotion meant that the writer who most obviously used it for that purpose was less likely to succeed. Not only did he make himself an easier target for antagonists; he was also more likely to arouse the suspicions or provoke he disdain of the person he addressed. Studying patronage poetry therefore often means studying strategies of indirection and implication. This is less true— there is less reason for it to be true—of the poems Jonson aimed at his rivals and enemies. There he can afford to speak more bluntly and abruptly. Even in those poems, however, he was writing for a larger audience than any particular antagonist. Just as when addressing a patron he always had to be aware of possible rivals and rivalries, so in attacking an enemy he could not forget that he was presenting an image of himself to a wider world.

Jonson could not write as more recent poets have been able to: primarily to express themselves, to shape their individual feelings, attitudes, and perceptions. Both his circumstances and his own instincts demanded that he play a more social role, but it was a role that was defined entirely neither by society nor by the poet himself. Constantly renegotiated, the role (like the poems that grew out of it) was complex and entangled, equivocal in the literal sense. The voice that speaks in Jonson's poems is a self-conscious voice, but more importantly it is a voice aware of other voices, to which it silently responds and adjusts itself. Studying Jonson as a patronage poet can help us better grasp not only the complications of his life, but the corresponding intricacies of his art. And it can help us begin to grasp the complex impact that the patronage system had not only on his work and career, but on the lives and writings of other Renaissance poets.

FURTHER READING

Bibliography

Judkins, David C., ed. *The Nondramatic Works of Ben Jonson: A Reference Guide*. Boston: G. K. Hall & Co., 1982, 260 p.

Contains a chronological listing of Jonson criticism from 1615 to 1978, including biographies, theses, dissertations, and manuscripts, with an introduction summarizing critical debates.

Criticism

Burt, Richard. *Licensed by Authority: Ben Jonson and the Discourses of Censorship*. Ithaca, N. Y.: Cornell University Press, 1993, 227 p.

A materialist study of Jonson's writings in relation to the working of seventeenth century censorship practices.

Dryden, John. "Essay of Dramatic Poesy." In *John Dryden: Selected Criticism*, edited by James Kinsley and George Parfitt, pp. 16-76. Oxford: Clarendon Press, 1970.

Discusses Jonson in relation to Shakespeare, and examines *Epicœne; or, the Silent Woman* with regard to the French classical tradition.

Eliot, T. S. "Ben Jonson." In *Ben Jonson: A Collection of Critical Essays,* edited by JonasA. Barish, pp. 14-23. Englewood Cliffs, N. J.: Prentice Hall, Inc., 1963.

Characterizes Jonson's poetry as superficial, yet with form and appealing to the mind.

Evans, Robert C. "'Games of Fortune, Plaid at Court': Politics and Poetic Freedom in Jonson's *Epigrams*." In *"The Muses Common-Weale": Poetry and Politics in the Seventeenth Century,* edited by Claude J. Summers and Ted-Larry Pebworth, pp. 48-61. Columbia: University of Missouri Press, 1988.

Analyzes three epigrams in light of Jonson's independence and the instability of the patronage system.

———. *Ben Jonson and the Poetics of Patronage*. Lewisburg, Pa.: Bucknell University Press, 1989, 334 p.

An extended study of the patronage system, covering such issues as freedom, flattery, the psychology of patronage, rivalry, and friendship.

Johnston, George Burke. *Ben Jonson: Poet*. New York: Columbia University Press, 1945, 175 p.

Evaluates Jonson's use of the mythological and religious in his poetry, along with his treatment of themes on women, chivalry, and courtly love. Includes a discussion of his relationship with Inigo Jones.

Jonson, Ben. *Ben Jonson: Poems,* edited by Ian Donaldson. London: Oxford University Press, 1975, 410 p.

Includes "Ungathered Verse" and poems from the plays and masques. Stresses Jonson's "confidence in moral continuities," which allowed him to draw upon the poetry of classical writers.

Knights, L.C. "Ben Jonson: Public Attitudes and Social Poetry." *A Celebration of Ben Jonson. Papers Presented at the University of Toronto in October 1972,* edited by William Blissett, Julian Patrick, and R. W. Van Fossen, pp. 167-87. Toronto: University of Toronto Press, 1973.

Examines Jonson's individual voice as it informs his social poetry.

McCanles, Michael. *Jonsonian Discriminations: The Humanist Poet and the Praise of True Nobility*. Toronto: University of Toronto Press, 1992, 306 p.

Focuses on Jonson's poetry in terms of *vera nobilitas,* true nobility, and in relation to aristocratic status, signs of nobility, praise, patronage, and courtship.

Miles, Rosalind. *Ben Jonson: His Life and Work*. London: Routledge & Kegan Paul, 1986, 306 p.

Chronological study of Jonson's major works.

———. *Ben Jonson: His Craft and Art*. London: Routledge & Kegan Paul, 1990, 303 p.

A Companion volume to Miles's 1986 book, it examines the entire Jonson corpus, including translations, works of criticism, and philology.

Nichols, J. G. *The Poetry of Ben Jonson*. London: Routledge & Kegan Paul, 1969, 177 p.

Discusses Jonson's poetry as idealistic and satirical, but not intentionally artful.

Parfitt, G. A. E. *Ben Jonson: Public Poet and Private Man.* London: J. M. Dent & Sons, Ltd., 1976, 181 p.

Contends that Jonson projects into his work both a classicist and a realist persona.

————. "The 'Strangeness' of Ben Jonson's *The Forest.*" *Leeds Studies in English* 18 (1987): 45-54.

Emphasizes the poems of *The Forest* as examples of paradox, simultaneously conservative and "strange."

Patterson, Annabel. "Lyric and Society in Jonson's *Underwood.*" *Lyric Poetry: Beyond New Criticism,* edited by Chaviva Hošek and Patricia Parker, pp. 148-63. Ithaca, N. Y.: Cornell University Press, 1985.

Remarks on the relation of the self to the state in Jonson's later lyrics.

Summers, Claude J. and Ted-Larry Pebworth, eds. *Classic and Cavalier: Essays on Jonson and the Sons of Ben.* Pittsburgh, Pa.: University of Pittsburgh Press, 1982, 290 p.

Compilation which includes essays on Jonson's poetry, on his contribution to the history of English literature, on his poetics, and on the poetic structures he shares with his "tribe."

Swinburne, Algernon Charles. *A Study of Ben Jonson.* London: Chatto & Windus, 1889, 181 p.

Categorizes Jonson's poetry as "incurably" stiff and irregular in terms of expressive texture and style.

Trimpi, Wesley. *Ben Jonson's Poems: A Study of the Plain Style.* Stanford, Calif.: Standford University Press, 1962, 292 p.

Comments on Jonson's adaptation of the anti-Ciceronian classical "plain style" which emphasizes content rather then expression, and denotation rather than connotation.

Additional coverage of Ben Jonson's life and career is contained in the following sources published by Gale Research, Inc.: *Concise Dictionary of British Literary Biography Before 1660; Dictionary of Literary Biography,* Vols. 62, 121; *DISCovering Authors; DISCovering Authors: British; Drama Criticism,* Vol. 4; *Literature Criticism from 1400 to 1800,* Vol. 6; and *World Literature Criticism, 1500 to the Present.*

Simon J. Ortiz
1941-

Native American poet, short story writer, essayist, and children's author.

INTRODUCTION

Ortiz is a highly respected Acoma Pueblo writer, recognized for his poetry infused with an awareness of Native American history, mythology, philosophy, and social concerns. The simple and direct language of Ortiz's poems reflects the oral storytelling tradition of his people, and typically offers the point of view of an observer, contrasting Indian and contemporary American lifestyles. Deeply grounded in his Native American heritage and identity, Ortiz often writes with an ironic or sorrowful tone as he comments on the racial, ideological, and material concerns of the late twentieth century. He tempers this mood in many of his poems, however, with his sustained humor, clarity, and optimism.

Biographical Information

Born near Albuquerque, New Mexico on the Acoma Pueblo homeland, Ortiz grew up in an artistic family, attending the Bureau of Indian Affairs day school and St. Catherine's Indian School in Santa Fe. After high school he worked in the uranium fields near Grants, New Mexico—an experience he drew upon for his book *Fight Back: For the Sake of the People, For the Sake of the Land* (1980). After serving in the U. S. Army, Ortiz earned his B. A. from the University of New Mexico and a Master of Fine Arts degree in writing in 1969 from the nationally acclaimed Writers' Workshop at the University of Iowa. His first full length collection of poems, *Going for the Rain,* appeared in 1976. He married Marlene Foster in 1981, and his three children, to whom he dedicates many of his poems, were born in the 1980s—a period during which Ortiz taught creative writing and American Indian literature at a number of American colleges and universities. Since 1982 he has served as consulting editor of the Pueblo of Acoma Press.

Major Works

Ortiz's first published collection, *Going for the Rain,* is significant for its emphasis on ritual in everyday life, its cyclical structure, and the appearance of the traditional cultural hero of several Native American tribes, Coyote. A humorous, powerful, and versatile figure, Coyote functions for Ortiz as both narrator and subject in many of his poems, and as an embodiment and lover of the natural world or as a symbol of survival. In *A Good Journey*

(1977), Ortiz writes extensively on the history of the Acoma Pueblo while addressing contemporary social and environmental issues. In several of the collection's poems, Ortiz relates the effects of the modern American lifestyle upon Indian consciousness. The poems of *From Sand Creek: Rising in This Heart Which Is Our America* (1981) recount Ortiz's personal experience as a patient in 1974-1975 in a Colorado Veterans Administration hospital and detail the 1864 massacre of Arapaho and Cheyenne people near Sand Creek by the U. S. Army. Although the book chronicles a history of violated trust, Ortiz manages to remain optimistic about the possibilities of his people reconnecting with the land and their heritage in the work. A similar theme informs *Fight Back: For the Sake of the People, For the Sake of the Land.* In this collection Ortiz records the personal and social transformations that occurred when railroads were built and uranium mines opened near the homeland of the Acoma Pueblo. Again Ortiz concludes the volume optimistically by predicting that a balance between human and environmental necessities will be successfully achieved. *After and Before the Lightning* (1994) is a journal-like collection of poems and poetic prose in which Ortiz records his stay on the Rosebud Sioux Indian Reservation in South Dakota. In these pieces, the poet focuses on the land and the Lakota people, paying tribute to both for their endurance.

Critical Reception

Critical reaction to Ortiz's poetry since the publication of *Going for the Rain* in the mid-1970s has been overwhelmingly positive. Some have applauded his groundedness, accessibility, and emphasis on the intersection between contemporary life, tradition, and history. Though the basis of his work is his personal and family life, most observers have noted that he typically relates these elements to larger social and political concerns, a quality that strengthens his writing by affording it a universal significance. Instead of being wholly consumed by his own individual struggles, some critics have noted that he grafts his concerns onto the larger body of historical issues, environmental concerns, and modern efforts toward political justice.

PRINCIPAL WORKS

Poetry

Going for the Rain 1976
A Good Journey 1977
Fight Back: For the Sake of the People, For the Sake of the Land (poetry and essays) 1980
From Sand Creek: Rising in This Heart Which is Our America 1981
A Poem Is a Journey 1981
Woven Stone: A 3-in-1 Volume of Poetry and Prose 1991
After and Before the Lightning 1994

Other Major Works

Howbah Indians (short stories) 1978
The People Shall Continue (juvenile literature) 1978
Song, Poetry, Language: Expression and Perception (essays) 1978
Blue and Red (juvenile literature) 1982
The Importance of Childhood (essay) 1982
Fightin': New and Collected Stories (short stories) 1983

CRITICISM

Harold Jaffe (review date 1982)

SOURCE: "Speaking Memory," in *The Nation*, April 3, 1982, pp. 406-08.

[*In the following review, Jaffe praises the politics and poetics of Ortiz's two collections,* Fight Back: For the Sake of the People, For the Sake of the Land *and* From Sand Creek.]

Although he has been publishing fine poetry since the mid-1960s, Simon Ortiz, an Acoma Pueblo born in 1941, was until recently read mainly by other American Indian writers and by a handful of small-press addicts. Ortiz's audience widened somewhat after Harper and Row published *Going for the Rain* in 1976. Here is a representative exchange from that volume:

> Q. "What would you say that the main theme of your poetry is?"
>
> A. ". . . to recognize the relationships I share with everything. "

American Indians have always known a good deal about relationships, communion; more than others, their relationships have been forcibly severed. Ortiz's fundamental theme concerns these sacred relationships—and their violations. Although his poems are usually about American Indians, the audience addressed in his work includes the poor, the dispossessed *and* the untranquilized middle class of various hues.

Both new volumes of poetry are testimonials: *Fight Back* to the revolt of the Pueblos (along with mestizos, mulatoes, Navahos and Apaches) against the Spanish colonialists in 1680; *From Sand Creek* marks the 1864 massacre of 133 Arapahoes and Cheyennes, nearly all women and children, in southeastern Colorado.

From Sand Creek is the more cohesive volume of the two. It contains forty-two poems on consecutive recto pages, with the same number of brief prose passages on the facing versos. The prose often introduces a theme or an image that is taken up in the corresponding poem or elsewhere in the volume. Most of the poems contain details about a Veterans Administration hospital in Fort Lyons, Colorado, where their narrator is a patient in 1974 and 1975.

What does the V.A. hospital have to do with Sand Creek? A good deal, really. According to Ortiz's accompanying note, the Cheyennes and Arapahoes who were camped on a bend of Sand Creek thought they were at peace with the whites. President Lincoln himself had presented Black Kettle, one of the guiding elders, with an American flag, which, the Indians were told, would protect them from attack. The flag was flying above Black Kettle's lodge on that cold November dawn when Colonel Chivington and more than 700 volunteers and troops from nearby Fort Lyons swooped down on the 600 Indians and wiped them out.

One-hundred-odd years later, the patients in the V.A. hospital in Fort Lyons include many young American Indians who, like their forebears, wished in some measure to trust the flag, and who fought for it in Vietnam. Those who returned, returned emptied of their trust in the U.S. government and, too often, of their ability to endure as aliens on their own soil.

The words and images with which Ortiz repeatedly characterizes the hospitalized Indians are *blood, dream, breath, shadow, compassion, memory, love, ghost.* Combined, these words have the impact of a mountain or tree rooted in the natural cycle, which, when unimpeded, is perpetual. Only there is impediment everywhere in Ortiz's poems, and his people are reduced to shadows striving, usually fruitlessly, to reconnect with their bodies, their earth, their birthright:

> Looking for Billy . . .
> He was the shadow.
> Memory was his lost trail.

Almost seamlessly, Ortiz imbues his sad, spare hospital scenes not only with the dreadful echo of the Sand Creek massacre but with a selective history of Native American faith, oppression and resistance. Yet the cumulative impression is, admirably, not of gloom and despair but of a renewed faith in the prospect of relationship with the land and solidarity among the dispossessed.

The single non-Indian literary precedent for these poems who comes to mind is Whitman during the Civil War, especially in his "Wound Dresser" letters from the veterans hospitals in Washington, D.C. Ortiz is himself a wound dresser, but unlike Whitman, whose rhapsodic brotherhood was often celebrated without identifiable basis, Ortiz's final affirmative, mined as it is from the grieving poems, glows with the luster of someone who has come through.

Ortiz owes much to the great body of invocation, song and prayer that is central to the Native American oral tradition. Aside from a modest number of books, such as Paul Radin's *The Autobiography of a Winnebago Indian* (1920) and Ruth Underhill's *Singing for Power* (1938), this "literature" has been largely unrecorded until recently. But contemporary American Indians have begun to draw on this tradition and to create an impressive canon of imaginative prose and poetry. Because the strongest of these writers (Ortiz, N. Scott Momaday, Vine Deloria, Leslie Marmon Silko, James Welch, Luther Standing Bear and others) have succeeded in fusing fractured present to coherent past, their writings are frequently more problematic than those of their forebears. In Ortiz, for example, the apparently simple, yet elusive, syntax sometimes seems fractionally off, as if the English were adapted from another language.

> They should have eaten
> whole buffalo.
> They should have,
> like the people wanted for them.

Fight Back seems a simpler volume than it is. Except for the 27-page **"No More Sacrifices,"** the poems are usually brief narratives about the Pueblos and Navahos and whites who live in the "Uranium Belt" west of Albuquerque, New Mexico. Ortiz shows us these people working in the uranium mines or the mills, riding in car pools, planting in a clayey soil, bathing in the sacred hot springs. We observe their distress, their joys and the persistent faith in the natural order that sustains them.

"No More Sacrifices" is the linchpin of the volume and one of the strongest poems in recent memory. Strictly speaking it is more prose then verse, part meditation, part sociopolitical analysis. The poet has climbed a volcanic mountain called Srhakaiya, west of the village that the white people named McCartys in which he was raised. Descending the mountain and walking home,

> I was sick
> feeling a sense of "otherness."
> How can I describe it?
> An electric current
> coursing in waves through me?
>   "Otherness."

It becomes clear that his disconnection was produced by his vision on the mountain. Not so much what he physically saw (though pollution and industrialization were visible) as what he saw through to: the history of the Acoma people from the days before the Spanish conquest to the Pueblo revolt. He saw the invasion of the "Mericanos" with their railroads and cavalry and uranium mines. And he saw the people's painful transition from productive land-laborers to wage slaves.

His vision sickens the poet, but then, while resting under a juniper on his walk home, the "otherness" recedes, and he sees something else:

> . . . horses.
> One was a pinto
> and the other was red.
> The sun had long set.
> The horses were alert
> to me as I passed by.
> Suddenly, they bolted,
> and galloped
> into the canyon . . .

The sight of the horses enforces his relationship with the land, even as it underscores his realization of what must be done for the future he envisions:

> The future will not be mad with loss
>   and waste though
> the memory will be there; eyes will
>   become kind
> and deep, and the bones of this nation
>   will mend. . . .

Kenneth Lincoln   (essay date 1983)

SOURCE: "The Now Day Indi'ns," in *Native American Renaissance,* University of California Press, 1983, pp. 183-221.

[In the following excerpt, Lincoln describes how Ortiz's poetry is built upon the traditions of his people and how it looks to the future of these traditions.]

In a southwest land of ancient syllables and stone monuments—Lukachukai Mountains, Ocotillo Wells, Chuksa Mountains, Many Farms—Simon Ortiz writes poems to teach his children, Rainy Dawn and Raho Nez, the old, time-trusted regards and ways of home. He says in **A Good Journey,** "Like myself, the source of these narratives is my home." What his father taught him of names, values, attentiveness, kinship, gentleness, respect, and building walls, this father as a poet now teaches his own children. "Be patient, child, be kind and not bitter." And again, another time: "Sing a bit, be patient. Wait."

This word-sender, hitchhiking to Colorado, offers up traveling song-prayers in natural acts of attention:

> Look, the plants with bells.
> Look, the stones with voices.

So, too, attend here: "Be patient, child, / quiet," as a Navajo woman "in the calm of her work at the loom." Simon Ortiz sings an inclusive poetry of walls and looms, carpentry and pottery, interwoven with teachings and observances, remembrances and prayers. His language appeals to the traditional moralities of "home" for any people—land, family, the elders, the clan, kin, animals, plants, stones, and the gods. These walls adjoin, rather than separate.

Ortiz perceives and articulates, in his own contemporary language, what it means to be Acoma Pueblo, among the "Acumeh" at "Acu," a people with a two-thousand-year-old sense of themselves.

—Kenneth Lincoln

Ortiz cares for all things in a natural religious regard, unscaffolded with theology or a monotheistic deity. This poet's religion calls upon a sense of the world as greater than man, multitudinous, spiritually alive, if Indian people ritually prepare and conduct themselves in a sacred manner. But "sacred" here infuses the "common" world, so that *this* world, the ordinary things now, come forward speaking of significances related to, yet apart from, man. The Indian world is reciprocal with people.

Walls testify to such kinship. Ortiz appeals continuously to the "good" life, as in the Navajo concept of *hózhó,* discussed by Gary Witherspoon: "*Hózhó* expresses the intellectual concept of order, the emotional state of happiness, the moral notion of good, the biological condition of health and well-being, and the aesthetic dimensions of balance, harmony, and beauty." The poet says it this way in **"Apache Love":**

> It is how you feel
> about the land.

> It is how you feel
> about the children.

> It is how you feel
> about the women.

> It is how you feel
> about all things.

> Hozhoni,
> in beauty.

> Hozhoni,
> all things.

> Hozhoni,
> for all time.

> Hozhoni,
> through all journeys.

For Simon Ortiz, poetry lyricizes experience. It is not so much a function of the words in themselves, poetry or prose, as a choice of subjects, and ways to see, and attitudes to think about things. He voices a complete act of seeing-in-saying-in-being. Ortiz recalls his father's songs as he carved wood: "I listen carefully, but I listen for more than just the sound, listen for more than just the words and phrases, for more than the various parts of the song. I try to perceive the context, meaning, purpose—all of these items not in their separate parts but as a whole—and I think it comes completely like that." For Simon Ortiz, then, language completes itself in the process of listening-and-speaking, not just in each word as product. He speaks toward and from a mind integrated within its culture: "that is, when a word is spoken, it is spoken as a complete word . . . not spoken in any *separate* parts."

Ortiz perceives and articulates, in his own contemporary language, what it means to be Acoma Pueblo, among the "Acumeh" at "Acu," a people with a two-thousand-year-old sense of themselves. "Acoma" means, according to the elders, a "place that always was." Tribal legend records occupation of the "Sky City" on Acoma Mesa before Christ. Archaeologists conservatively agree that Old Acoma has been peopled from at least A.D. 1200 to the present.

All this is a past continuous in the present, as in the poet's own family. "My father is a small man,"Ortiz begins his essay, "Song/Poetry and Language—Expression and Perception." "My father carves, dancers usually. What he does is find the motion of Deer, Buffalo, Eagle dancing in the form and substance of wood . . . his sinewed hands touch the wood very surely and carefully, searching and knowing." Before his death in 1978, Ortiz's father worked as a wood sculptor, a stonemason, a carpenter, a welder, and "one of the elders of the Antelope people who are in charge of all the spiritual practice and philosophy of our people, the Acumeh. He and his uncles are responsible that things continue in the manner that they have since time began for us, and in this sense he is indeed a 1,000 year old man."

Among his last acts at Acoma, Ortiz's father manually rebuilt the Antelope Society House, his son remembers.

As the father shaped wood and layered stone, so the son fits words. These are the traditional arts of natural and useful objects. A concrete language of necessary elements joins and particularizes the world. It makes experience both communal and special. Ortiz, in turn, fashions poems as a part of things and apart from things. Language co-joins the world, and is a medium in itself.

In **"A Story of How a Wall Stands"** the poet speaks of a four-hundred-year-old wall on an incline holding an ancient graveyard of "dirt and bones," the past interred and shored up through the craft of stones. The Pueblos listen back to "the old rocks, millions of years old," all the way back to Mesa Verde and Four Corners. The *Anasazi,* or "ancient" stones with voices, still carry inflections in ochre and sienna sandstone. The sun's light weathers these earth bones like a palette of sunset tempering the desert below. The poet's mason father tells him that

> "Underneath
> what looks like loose stone,
> there is stone woven together."

The hand that shapes the wall is so shaped itself, as the layered stones are knitted in the manner of bones inside the stonebuilder's hands.

> He tells me those things,
> the story of them worked
> with his fingers, in the palm
> of his hands, working the stone
> and the mud until they become
> the wall that stands a long, long time.

Here stands a wall "built that carefully" to last.

The poet's own young son, as well, will be "tasting forever" the dust of stones in his mouth at Canyon de Chelly, the oldest continuously inhabited "home" in the contiguous United States (**"Canyon de Chelly"** in *A Good Journey*). And in Rainy Dawn's birth, "You come forth / the color of a stone cliff / at dawn," so in her continuing life,

> relish
> the good wheat bread your mother makes,
> taking care that you should think
> how her hands move, kneading the dough,
> shaping it with her concern,
> and how you were formed and grew in her.
> **["To Insure Survival"** and **"Forming Child"]**

The key is to discover the fit. A person's body, tools, and spirit in making the world so, *are so made.*

> Essentially, it is how you fit
> into that space which is yourself,
> how well and appropriately.
> **["Four Dheetsiyama Poems"]**

Breathing native prayers, working among the people, dancing ceremonial songs: poetry then is organic. Verse is consistent with carving the designs *in* ("into" and "from") the grains of wood; rebuilding and rebinding ancient village walls; coiling, molding, firing, and decorating pottery. It is so with the stones interleaved and mortared in Anasazi walls; there is a continuity of flowing parts.

A wall transcends its own parts in the harmony and wholeness, hózhó, of separate stones that interlock. And, too, words complete their "sentence" when spoken, ritualized sequentially in song. They gather not as separate phonemes, but complete as whole syntactic movements. "For example, when my father has said a word—in speech or in a song—and I ask him, 'What does that word break down to? I mean breaking it down to the syllables of sound or phrases of sound, what do each of these parts mean?' And he has looked at me with exasperated—slightly pained—expression on his face, wondering what I mean. And he tells me, 'It doesn't break down into anything.'" It is so, as well, with the people, the stones, and the mortar made of earth—these elements that comprise a culture *are* earth. The flesh itself, made of dust, comes from the body of mother earth, and *is* her body.

In *A Good Journey* the earth-body extends even farther, to interconnect interior and exterior conditions of the tactile world. **"This Occurs To Me"** speaks of "how useful" Ortiz finds "dirt and stone," by way of his father's instruction, "what you can do with them." *Working* with the mystery of making things, *watching* light and shadow and animal movement and the strata of sediment, *touching*

> with foot and hand
> the tamp of sand
> against cliff wall,
> noting the undershadow
> of stone ledge.

The verb in the title, **"This *Occurs* To Me,"** implies the natural, participatory context of these observations. These things are. They register as "ordinary" perceptions, intrinsic, unassuming, almost conversational in import, but essential as poetry. Maria Chona, the Papago, told Ruth Underhill half a century ago. "My father went on talking to me in a low voice. That is how our people always talk to their children, so low and quiet, the child thinks he is dreaming. But he never forgets."

The Pueblos have always known walls, from Anasazi origins in cliff-dwellings within nature's own embracing walls, to adobe multiple dwellings with adjoining man-made walls, to earthpit kiva chambers down in the ground-wall itself. Tabletop exposure left the Anasazi cliff-dwellers vulnerable, and the mesa walls dropping into deep valleys offered protection sheltering the old ones from the elements and their enemies. These majestic walls cradled whole villages at Batatakin or Cliff Palace or White House. Families shared adjoining walls like clusters of nesting children. These walls did not divide, so much as fit form to function, like protective layers of durable cloth that contour to the body; indeed, weaver and mason both mold their materials to human needs. Ortiz then learns from his father the traditions of "weaving stone"—not piece work individually, no more than words exist separately, but a tapestry of stones, a pattern that connects. It is a mortaring, too, of son to father, inner to outer being, stone to spirit, concrete particle to organic design. Such a craftsman releases the intrinsic pattern in his materials.

"The words are the vision," *A Good Journey* opens in dedication to the poet's children, "by which we see out and in and around." The poems grow out of the natural language of daily prayer, memory, and thought.

> In the morning, take cornfood inside,
> say words within and without.
> Being careful, breathe in and out,
> praying for sustenance, for strength,
> and to continue safely and humbly,
> you pray.
> **["A San Diego Poem: January-February 1973"]**

Gary Witherspoon writes of Navajo language, art, and religion that "speech is the outer form of thought, and thought is the inner form of speech." Knowledge (inner) is to language as thought (inner) is to speech. The whole rests on a religious philosophy of the "in-standing wind soul" breathing life through all people and things. In short, words breathe the inner wind-soul into the world: "It was the wind that gave them life. It is the wind that comes out of our mouths now that gives us life. When this ceases to flow we die. In the skin at the tips of our fingers we see the trail of the wind; it shows us where the wind blew when our ancestors were created" (Navajo origin myth).

Simon Ortiz is not Navajo, but scholars note how the Diné culture grafted on beliefs from older Pueblo traditions; the Navajo expanded and made conscious what their ancient brothers left unsaid and implicit. So the father of Ortiz's sketch, "Something's Going On" in *Howbah Indians* (1978), "breathed in and out upon the cornmeal, motioning to the children that they were to follow along, giving it life so life would continue." Or as Ortiz himself speaks consciously of artistic processes, "The song is basic to all vocal expression. The song as expression is an opening from inside of yourself to outside and from outside of yourself to inside but not in the sense that there are separate states of yourself. Instead, it is a joining and an opening together."

Just as touching flesh-to-flesh, skin being the body's wall, acknowledges mutual need and separation, so the pueblo wall and the tribal word serve to bond the people, at the same time granting them privacy. A walled pueblo allows for communal distinctions where people share common, yet distinct places—compartments, clans, kivas—within the whole. Walls permit cohabitation. Inside to one family is outside to a neighbor, and vice versa. Once recognized as such in a *commun*-ity, neighbors acknowledge their mutual concerns for freedom within adjoining walls, reciprocal lives "inside/outside" across a continuum of time and space. These social dynamics are fusional in positive tensions, kiva circles fronting apartment rectangles, the old riddle of squaring the circle, the one and the many, the whole fitting *into* the natural wall of the earth.

Rooted in sandstone and clay, the old ones hugged the mesa walls and scaled, stone by stone, toward their fields and common sky overhead, never forgetting their spiritual origins down in the kiva *Shipapuni* or "place of emergence." So the old stories say. Pueblo ceremonial life took place underground in the kivas, and the people descended down a "water ladder" into the "water-filled" ritual chamber. The drama of this spiritual descent must be inferred, not at all obvious, through the small hole in the earth's surface wall.

What is said for his father's stonemasonry and ancestral dwellings could as well be carried over to Ortiz's mother and sisters making pottery. Foods and liquids contained *in* traditional vases are determined by the walls of their containers. Both walled container and contained space form the jar, with a functional inner surface adjoining an artistic outer design. And his father's wood carving, to turn the concept once again, exactly inverses this dynamic of pottery making, without losing the principle of common surfaces. In bringing forth the immanent design *in* the grain, the sculpted wood reveals the intrinsic spirit embedded in the grain. Surface both reflects and is substance here. Decoration and function lie contiguous in one "wall" of wood, as it were. "Indeed," Ortiz remarks of an Indian language of common walls, "the song was the road from outside of himself to inside—which is perception—and from inside of himself to outside—which is expression."

HORIZONS HOME

> The brown people losing trails
> and finding trails and losing them
> and finding again—
>
> the horizons
> and rains
> in the far distance.
> —Simon Ortiz

Outside the walls of family and past today, a horizon planes into the future. Will the walls hold? Across America, Ortiz's poetry journeys painfully through the ruins of the present, the despair and challenge of contemporary acculturations. Coyote, reality's credible fool, makes up an origin story to begin things in *Going for the Rain* (1976):

> "First of all, it's all true."
> Coyote, he says this, this way,
> humble yourself, motioning and meaning
> what he says

and then the old Trickster lopes off to another page. A gently attentive humor binds Ortiz's poems humanly together, acknowledging and partly "civilizing" the animal-who-wanders-in-man. This Indian poet declares **"The Significance of Veteran's Day"**:

that I am a veteran of at least 30,000 years
when I travelled with the monumental yearning
of glaciers, relieving myself by them,
growing, my children seeking shelter
by the roots of pines and mountains.

The trickster-poet's moon-singing laughter temporizes our
"b.s.-ing" human affairs, forgiving and reminding the people of their base natures, directing them on toward

> the continuance of the universe,
> the travelling, not the progress,
> but the humility of our being there.

"Are you really a poet?" someone asks this hitchhiker.
"Shore," Ortiz replies, like a cricket *is* simply a cricket.
Along that road where coyotes prowl and crickets scrape,
no more nor less than poets, the wandering pilgrim stops
over at **"Washyuma Motor Hotel"** where "The ancient
spirits tell stories / and jokes and laugh and laugh." These
things keep things going. They make up the cycles, the
"ups and downs," the jokes and pains, the continuities, as
time warps back into the circle of all things. This poet
centers on "continuance": laughter's survival, the old ways
persisting, a journey toward being, a joke, a tale, a song-
poem always unfolding before the people. "Why do you
write?" an anonymous voice asks in the preface to *A Good
Journey*. "The only way to continue is to tell a story and
that's what Coyote says," the poet returns, then considers
further, "your children will not survive unless you tell
something about them."

"Once, in a story, I wrote that Indians are everywhere.
/ Goddamn right." But a park ranger at the Florida state
line tells Ortiz, "This place is noted for the Indians /
that don't live here anymore" (**"Travels in the South"**).
The poet must scavenge for Indian survivals, "fugitive"
in San Diego, Chicago, Hollywood, and New York. He
hangs on desperately with bourbon and beer, gutting
out hitchhiking hungers, loneliness for home, a *sub*way
blues.

The contemporary Ortiz in *A Good Journey* writes throw-
away lines, fragments of notes, shards from **"The Poems
I Have Lost"**: "a long rambling / letter, called it a poem,
from Nashville."

> Memories, I guess they are,
> crowd me because of all the signals
> I've missed, the poems that keep
> coming back in pieces.

Prose voices and local Indian views come back to him, as
Eagle skips flint stones off Highway 66, sparking a summer night long ago in *Howbah Indians*. It is an eidetic
image for the Indian poet: ancient stones flaring off a
white man's *high*way penciling the Southwest. A billboard
fills the horizon over an Indian gas station, "WELCOME
HOWBAH INDIANS."

Ortiz travels Interstate 40 from Albuquerque to Gallup in
"Horizons and Rains"—

witness to the brown people
stumbling Sunday afternoon
northwards—

seeking a life-source on the desert. "Where's the rain that
feels so good?" The question means "rain," yes, but more
than rain: where is the good "way" gone? In this drought
of modern times, where are the native gods who wed earth
and sky, promising the futurity of spring?

"Where it has always been," Ackley says; the poet asserts
of a distance he journeys *into,* "The horizons are still
mine" ("**And The Land Is Just As Dry**'" in *A Good
Journey*). It is a time, then, to journey home.

The "good journey" to the horizon, "going for the rain,"
voices a traveling-prayer. The way of words becomes a
lifelong pilgrimage, a road one travels away from, and
back toward Acoma. "There are things he must go through
before he can bring back what he seeks, before he can
return to himself." Whatever word assigned—home, family, clan, tribe, history, time itself—the Pueblos seek a
place of origin, still alive in the "place where the spirits
enter the world." The underground *Shipapuni* is traceable
from the Rio Grande basin to the mesa tops and down into
the beginnings of the world, the primal Shipapu back with
the Anasazi. In **"Passing Through Little Rock,"**

> The old Indian ghosts—
>   "Quapaw"
> "Waccamaw"—
>   are just billboard words
> in this crummy town.
> "You know, I'm worrying a lot lately,"
> he says in the old hotel bar.
>
> "You're getting older and scared ain't you?"
>
> I just want to cross the next hill,
> through that clump of trees
> and come out the other side
>
> and see a clean river,
> the whole earth new
> and hear the noise it makes
> at birth.

A Good Journey records the coming back home of a poet
after *Going for the Rain*. "One step at a time to return,"
even if viewing dioramas of Pueblo "history" among Anasazi ruins, "I have to buy a permit to get back home" ("**A
Designated National Park**"). Coyote Old Man, "Pehrru"
the hungry one, goes tramping and shouting his head off,
"bragging" around Western-style as "the existential Man":

> Coyote, old man, wanderer,
> where you going, man?

The poet comes home to his children, packing conversations, anecdotes, advice, recipes, and traditions. His plain
speakings risk a prosaic voice; his homilies merge in common concerns.

This father-artist advises his daughter, first "learn how to make good bread." Here rest the old values—domestic virtures, homely moralities, humilities of prayer, laughter and weeping among blooded kin—still appropriate for a settled life and stable culture, no matter how apparently archaic by contemporary standards. The quest, for Ortiz, is always "a full life," a good journey, a bellyful of good food. He even jots down a prose poem, **"How to make a good chili stew."**

In the ongoing struggle with moneyed "foundations," who offer tractors and gas for mining rights to a culture, Indians thirst for trust,

> We are hungry for the good earth,
> the deserts and mountains growing corn.

While **"Apache Red"** and **"Mericano"** wrestle on one TV channel, and astronauts walk the moon on another channel, a *Howbah Indians* family talks across generations:

> "That's some story, Nana, but it's a dream.
> It's a dream but it's the truth, Faustin said.
> I believe you, Nana, his grandson said."

Somewhere in a bar in Cuba, New Mexico, the people come together to speak German, French, Navajo, Spanish, Acoma, and English all at one time: "We were a confluence of separate languages / and the common language of ourselves" (**"Place We Have Been"**). The word and the prayer, the struggle and the deed, register in the "continuances" of Simon Ortiz's children expressed in **"A Birthday Kid Poem"**:

> It shall end well.
> It shall continue well.
> It shall be.
> It shall.
> It shall.
> It shall.
> It shall.

Andrew Wiget (essay date 1986)

SOURCE: *Simon Ortiz,* Boise State University Press, 1986, 54 p.

[*In the following excerpt, Wiget provides a detailed analysis of the structure and content of* Going for the Rain, A Good Journey, Fight Back: For the Sake of the People, For the Sake of the Land *and* From Sand Creek.]

I.

. . . For Ortiz language is an energy, which has its own economy and circulation in the life of the community, an idea very common in oral cultures from ancient Israel to the Arctic. In this larger sense of language, all that lives and has breath also has language. As Ortiz speaks of it, language is not an exclusive attribute of human beings but a "spiritual force" which "uses" humans to circulate it: "When you regard the sacred nature of language, then you realize that you are a part of it and it is a part of you . . . and that if you do control some of it, it is not in your exclusive control" ("Song/Poetry").

The luxury to think about language abstractly is not frequently afforded those immersed in an oral culture. Language is never separated from a context of use. Ortiz recalls asking his father on one occasion to analyze the components of a word into the different constituents of meaning, a move the father resisted, saying that the word "doesn't break down into anything" (Ortiz "Song/Poetry"). For his father, the word was whole, the expression was whole, and its force derived from its fit with the situation in which it was uttered.

The impact of such an understanding of how language works is to attend in a special way to orality. In writing **"That's the Place Indians Talk About,"** Ortiz recollected the gestures of the old Paiute man and "the particular breathing that accompanied the words." Ortiz observes that "I 'sound' out the words and stanzas as I write them down, so that I become aware of the weight of the sounds and syllables and rhythms of speech. Line lengths are decided accordingly" ("Creative Process").

As Ortiz speaks it, language is not an exclusive attribute of human beings but a "spiritual force" which "uses" humans to circulate it.

—Andrew Wiget

This sense of language use which Ortiz brought to his own writing contrasts strongly with one of the more widely held notions of art in Anglo-American criticism which treats the poem as an artifact composed of parts which make a whole. (The nearest Western aesthetic analogue is perhaps Charles Olson's notion of "projective verse.") Even the most artful language forms in an oral tradition, however, can never be entirely comprehended apart from their contexts. This is clear in those traditional forms which undergird Ortiz' work—song, story, and conversation.

In a discussion of the creative process, Ortiz observed, "conversations have always been important beginning points for me. . . . How the voice is used, what gestures are made, the setting, the tonic, etc., all of these are important to the event of the 'conversation,' and when I listen and learn I see myself as a participant in the event." In reflecting on his free verse technique, he concluded, "the words and line order seemed to be a way of re-experiencing what was going on in the original sense. I realize that in another, very close way that it was not merely a reenactment of speech, emotion, setting and so forth, but actually a way of original experiencing in terms of words, language" (Ortiz, "The Creative Process"; hereafter "Process").

That literature could recover the force of its original moment, indeed that its force was precisely in that recovering, was brought home to Ortiz in an experience which figures in several places in his works. He recalled his father once remarking on finishing a song, "This song, I really like it for that old man." Ortiz understood this to mean:

> In my father's mind during the process of making the song and when he sang it subsequent times afterwards, he was reaffirming the affection he had for the old guy, the way "he danced like this." My father was expressing to me the experience of that affection, the perceptions of the feelings he had. Indeed, the song was the road from outside of himself to inside—which is perception—and from inside of himself to outside— which is expression. That's the process and product of the song, the experience and the vision that a song gives you. ("Song/Poetry")

The real nature of song, then, is not to be apprehended as a merely verbal form, but as an experience. "A song is made substantial by its context," Ortiz writes, "that is its reality, both that which is there and what is brought about by the song." It is a spiritual experience and "you are present in and part of it." But there are some constraints. "The context has to do not only with your being physically present, but it has to do also with the context of the mind, how receptive it is and that usually means familiarity with the culture in which the song is sung" ("Song/ Poetry"). In this concept of song as experience/expression, "singing is basically a way to understand and appreciate your relationship to all things. The song as language is a way of touching" ("Song/Poetry").

The use of language to "touch," to establish and affirm relationships by creating their context, is also why Ortiz favors writing poetry with a narratable content. "The narrative technique, which to me is simply the storytelling style of talking, is very effective because it provides its own setting, the particular mood intended, and requires a certain immediacy of language which is provided by the storyteller or narrator" ("Creative Process"). By assuming a visible presence in the poem through adopting a narrative voice, Ortiz feels he can better control the communication.

Of the stories he learned in school, he remarks, "I learned there were no Indians; they were visages of the historical past who rode painted ponies and attacked wagon trains . . . we were expected to identify with white American images of Dick and Jane and Spot and Puff and homes with white picket fences." The natural consequence for Ortiz was that he became "confused," but what is interesting in this description of the struggle for cultural integrity is that he chooses to cast it as a struggle of stories. "So I turned to language, the stories that always were; they were basic; they were knowledge which would help me . . . I regarded stories as a way I could deal with the world"

("Stories"). This same sense of the power of stories to structure a world is at the heart of his sense of himself as a poet. A story is a path for the future, and he commends his work to his audience in the Preface of *A Good Journey* in just those terms: "The only way to continue is to tell a story and there is no other way." Stories chart the way: "Your children will not survive unless you tell something about them—how they were born, how they came to this certain place, how they continued."

II. "A Place That is Common to Us . . ."

Perhaps the most important of many relationships which stories chart is the relationship of people to a certain place. Indeed it is only in the telling of a story, which associates a space with an event, that a space becomes distinguished from among the surroundings as a Place. This understanding of the power of stories, or more broadly, of "telling," to map the world in which we live is especially forceful in communities whose traditions trace their origins and history to particular landscapes. This is in fact the central theme of the Emergence myth and its migration sequel through which Puebloan peoples like Ortiz' Acoma assert their bond to the Earth, the Mother, the Beginning. Tribal traditions clearly spell out the particular place in the local landscape which is the Place of Emergence, the cervical opening of Mother Earth's birth canal. The bond is not metaphorical, but genetic. The Acoma are made of the stuff of the earth and born from her and through her intention, and it is not merely an unspecified earth, but the Earth of this Place.

Consequently, there is a fundamental difference between attitudes of Native American writers toward place and those of Western writers. The Euro-American cultural heritage either alienates the latter utterly from the land as a source of meaning (the Western positivistic or "scientific" perspective) or provides through the Adamic myth of Genesis an extremely generalized model by means of which one can claim a relationship to any piece of land. Unfortunately for other peoples, the generalizing power of the Genesis myth enables Europeans to disguise their imperial acts by legitimating their appropriation of others' lands with spiritual claims. It is a contest of ideologies, one place-specific and the other place-general, that is played out in several Western fictions, for example, in McMurtry's *Horseman, Pass By.*

Ortiz' encounters with the National Park mentality bring this difference home forcefully. Wanting to camp at Montezuma Castle he finds "This morning, / I have to buy a permit to get back home," and in the Kaibab Forest on the North Rim of the Grand Canyon, he must pay to gather firewood; he concludes: "This is ridiculous. / You gotta be kidding. / Dammit, my grandfathers / ran this place / with bears and wolves / . . . And I got some firewood / anyway from the forest, / mumbling, Sue me" (*A Good Journey*). In **"Under the L.A. Airport,"** Ortiz feels his identity dissolve as his sense of place evaporates. In the maze of tunnels under the terminal, he feels "lost." Because his dislocation is spiritual as well as physical, his "knowledge of where I am"—which is "under the

L.A. Airport, / on the West Coast, someplace called America,"—is "useless:"

> America has obliterated my sense of comprehension.
> Without this comprehension, I am emptied
> of any substance. America has finally caught me.
> I meld into the walls of that tunnel
> and become a silent burial. There are no echoes.
>
> (*A Good Journey*)

As a result of en/ac-culturation, both Anglo and Indian have been exposed to the power of Euro-American culture to alienate, dislocate, and remap. Against such debilitating forces, Ortiz feels keenly the need to reaffirm the historical bond between people and the land. In discussing one of his poems, he has written, "It is important for me to strive to have my poems reestablish and reaffirm relationships among ourselves as a community of people and that community to know itself in relationship to all other forms of life, especially the land. My audience in that sense is that community of land and people" ("Creative Process").

Ortiz approved when one of his audience, who happened to be a Sioux from South Dakota, came up to him after a reading of **"That's the Place Indians Talk About"** and asserted that he "knew" that place even though he had never visited it. For Ortiz what was important about that statement was that the man "knew that place that is common to us, that exists in all of us, that we all share with our concerns. It is something we can identify with, that place. And as I said, it does not mean only Indian people" ("Creative Process").

III. "Poems . . . are Political"

Because acculturation—the vast remapping and renaming operation which attends conquest—is a political activity, any attempt to reappropriate one's land and history is also political. Ortiz himself understands his work as "revolutionary" in that revisionary sense. When he began to write in college, he felt, "It was a revolutionary thought, at least to me, to write about my culture, history, and heritage, especially since there was nothing, not even a tiny bit of it, from a Native American perspective in previous works of literature. And it was indeed revolutionary to write about contemporary Native American people, not stereotyped visages from the past, but people who thrived in social-cultural struggle for equality, justice, democracy, and human rights" ("Stories"). In this sense Ortiz' poetry is clearly and consciously political.

As a member of a colonized society, he has been historically sensitized to what has only recently become for some in academe a critical commonplace:

> Often we hear that poetry is made "less poetic" if it expresses and insists upon a political point of view and purpose, but I suspect that designation is made by those who do not want to hear the truth spoken by those who defend the earth. . . . Poetry is a way of engendering life, and that is a political stand when it

is against what will take away life. . . . Naturally, this inspiration has been labelled dangerous in many cases—and unliterary and unpoetic as well—because it challenges the established oppressive ruling powers that be. Native American poets who speak from a tradition of resistance against oppression are speaking for land and life; their poems, personal and social, are political. ("Creative Process").

Ortiz is clear here. An "objective" aesthetic focussing on "inherent aspects of form" is an impossibility and clearly a ploy which institutionalizes the values of those in power, often through an unconscious conspiracy of silence which begs all questions of value. Against such canons, his poetry must seem not only politically but aesthetically unattractive. (Critics who assert that such an aesthetic presumption is self-serving ignore the fact that their assertion is itself self-serving. Interest and aesthetics are intertwined.) If it is true that oral cultures cannot afford the luxury of speaking of art and language in the abstract, it is equally true that literate, colonial powers cannot afford to speak of them as specified by history because it exposes uncomfortable connections between interest, power, and value. Consequently, it is in their interest to speak of the "inherent beauty of the work" because it absolutizes and authorizes their own culturally and historically relative values.

Ortiz sees this practice as essential to the formation of an American self-consciousness:

> The axiom
> would be the glory of America
> at last,
>   no wastelands,
> no forgiveness.
> The child would be sublime.
>
> (*From Sand Creek*)

In an economic and aesthetic instance of the end justifying the means, America need not ask forgiveness since it has exhausted both people and land in creating something it has chosen to call sublime.

In contrast to the received, institutionalized history of America, Ortiz offers in one of his children's books, *The People Shall Continue,* a different vision of history in which the struggles of all Indian peoples over time are understood as elements of a single struggle against the rich and the powerful. In this struggle, traditions, especially stories and songs, are nourishment and weapons for battle. Such a history takes little account of the cultural distinctions, even outright hostility, between Native peoples, but it does enable Ortiz to highlight economic motives in a way the received, institutionalized history frequently obscures. It also enables him to make appeals for solidarity among all economically oppressed people whatever their race and so enlarge the notion of The People from that first denoted by the title.

In the context of his appeal to the solidarity of oppressed peoples and his understanding of the act of writing/performing poetry as an implicitly political one, Ortiz has expectations for how his poetry will be received, how it ought to "work." A poem is a communication of energy circulating from writer/performer to reader/listener. As such it is expected to effect a union between the two. What he has written in a discussion of a particular poem (**"That's the Place Indians Talk About"**), I believe expresses his understanding of how the creative act generally takes place for him. "Decisions have to do with the selection of words, phrases, images, but it is more than that too. I wanted the poem to be meditative but also 'active,' in the sense that the reader can be inspired to make a decision, feel something of the message conveyed, and agree with the source of the 'moving power' [a phrase in the poem referring to the Earth as source of spiritual power]. That's why I decided to end [the poem] with the words 'listen' and 'hearing' set prominently featured and intended to be reinforced by the process that is involved in hearing and listening" ("Creative Process").

These—language, place, and poetry as political—are concepts fundamental to understanding Ortiz' work and his sense of himself as a writer. . . .

V. "Song . . . A Way of Touching"

Ortiz' poetry first appeared in a highly regarded regional journal when it was published in 1969 in the special Indian issue of *South Dakota Review* titled "The American Indian Speaks." Inclusion of his poems in several anthologies of Indian and ethnic writers soon followed, and in 1976 Ortiz' first book of poetry, *Going for the Rain,* was published by Harper and Row. The collection demonstrated the same concern for personal integration, cultural integrity, and attachment to the land which highlighted his fiction. The book opens with a Prologue, which locates the significance of the volume's title in Acoma terms. The *shiwanna* or rain priest is sought on a road made of prayer and song. These the *shiwanna* will heed and return to Acoma with rain and the power of giving life. Ortiz transforms this particular cultural sense into a quest metaphor, such that all living is a journeying to find meaning and a sense of self. When both senses are read together, the journey takes on special urgency, since it is only through individual quests for meaning that any life-giving is possible. So our stake in this economy of value and meaning is clear: if any man cannot find that which gives life, it is because it has been withheld by others, and we are the others who are both implicated and impoverished in that withholding.

The poems in the opening section, "Preparation," are governed by the principal metaphor of speech. The book's first poem, **"The Creation, According to Coyote,"** is a good example. It suggests that one's origins occur in a geographical place, but on reflection that place is more specifically cultural. It is located by a story, "the creation, according to Coyote," which is in fact embedded in another story (that of the book's journey which it inaugurates), which is itself implicitly part of another story (that of the reader, when s/he appropriates it). The inference, dawning here but enhanced subsequently, is that persons have meaning by virtue of their relationships, and that networks of relationships are founded upon belief in a governing story which establishes a Center. Clearly, if one loses faith in that Center, the networks of relationships disintegrate and one's sense of self collapses. This motion of establishment, strain, collapse and reintegration, imaged as a journey from the Center to the horizon and back to the Center, organizes the volume.

The movement is recapitulated individually in the second poem, **"Forming Child,"** which celebrates the imminent birth of Ortiz' second child. The poem articulates the many ways in which this child will take her "place," each place a story which she will know. Frequent in the poems in this first section are verbs like "sing," "respect," and "pray," which indicate actions that affirm, principally through speech, the context of meaning, the "world." In **"Language"** Ortiz celebrates hearing as sanctification, and what is "sanctified" is "the sphere / of who he or she is who is hearing / the poetry" (*Rain*). One senses in these lines that it is in the act of hearing/speaking that we are constituted as persons because hearing/speaking establishes relationships: "All language comes forth / outward from the center. Hits / the curve of your being. Fits" (*Rain*). The section concludes with the poet affirming his ability to see and hear all the faces and voices of the Earth.

The second section of *Going for the Rain* is entitled "Leaving." Most of the poems "map" the psyche with journeying motifs in which landscape features correlate with emotional states. The opening poem of the section announces this theme through a much more localized journey when the poet and his family "were trying to find / a place to start all over / but couldn't" (*Rain*). Each person sets out on many roads, mapped as relationships established between persons/points, he seems to say in **"Many Farms Notes,"** and the danger is losing track of the Center.

"Old Hills" is the first of many poems that address the reality of dis-placement, of a dissociation between geographical "place" and cultural "place." By virtue of this transformed sense of "place," it is possible, as Ortiz writes in **"Travels in the South,"** to say that "Indians are everywhere." Indeed, *he* does find them everywhere. But the same transformation provides for dis-placement, since being Indian gets you put into a particular "place" by Anglos which is other-than/different-from/absent-to the mental place where "Anglo" is located. As a result, Ortiz spends a good deal of time telling a hotel clerk "who I really wasn't," while a Florida Ranger affirms that a State Park "is noted for the Indians / that don't live here anymore" (*Rain*).

The key poem of this section, and to my mind one of Ortiz' most important, is **"Relocation,"** a title with at least three significations. The first makes the shift from the speaker's rural reservation environment to the city. This shift is occasioned in part by the second signification, which refers to a Federal program of the 1950s that promised to relocate Indians from impoverished areas to urban areas of higher employment and provide them with job skills, education, and other support systems. Rarely, at its best, the program had mixed results; more commonly, at its worst, it was a disaster. But this program originated in the context of the third and principal signification of the title, which is that ongoing enterprise of acculturation aimed at culturally relocating Indians within the Anglo-American value system. That "other" world is epitomized in one poem as by an "apartment / with five locks on Thirteenth Street, / Somewhere Else City, USA" (*Rain*). Bus stations, airports, and border towns, all the locations where the two "worlds" intersect are featured prominently in this section.

In **"For Those Sisters & Brothers in Gallup,"** Ortiz comes face to face on his journey with the living dead spewed out by that other world. Gallup is a northwestern New Mexico strip town with innumerable bars and a bad reputation for promoting alcoholism among, economic exploitation of, and police brutality toward Indians. The highway leading north from town has one of the highest single-car and hit-and-run fatality rates in the United States. When Ortiz runs over a lump on the road one night, he fears the worst. Discovering the lump to be a dog long since dead, he falls beside the road and prays. His encounter with a drunken woman confirms his identity: "O my god, I know what is my name: she stumbled like a stuffed dummy / against me . . ." (*Rain*). There is no escape from such encounters with these possible other selves, but he presses on despite the pain: "It's a duty with me, / I know, to find the horizons" (*Rain*).

"Returning" is the third section of *Going for the Rain*. In many of its poems, the speaker, having exposed the categories which imprison him, repudiates their value as legitimate alternatives. One of the most forceful of these poems is **"The Significance of Veteran's Day"** (*Rain*). Here Ortiz' experience of invisibility before others, like that of Ralph Ellison's invisible man, marks a turning point for him: "I never knew that feeling before, / calling for significance, / and no one answered." Though an Army veteran himself, the real issue is not military wars, but cultural ones, wars against "foreign disease, missionaries, / canned food, Dick & Jane textbooks, IBM cards, / Western philosophies, General Electric" and a host of other weapons of progress. As a "veteran of at least 30,000 years," he wants to celebrate "not the completion of our age. / . . . / but the humility of our being there"—even more, "how we have been able / to survive insignificance."

Having found his horizon of value, the speaker can begin his long journey home. The first step is to reappropriate the Earth as a cultural reality, which he accomplishes by juxtaposing it to "America." A principal image here is the Wisconsin Horse who finds himself looking from behind a chainlink fence across the street to a construction site at "America building something" (*Rain*). In other poems the speaker will juxtapose "the hills" to "America." That all is clear in poems like **"Wind and Glacier Voices"** wherein only Indians can hear the language of the earth. Since language is the principal sign of relationship, only Indians are in relation to the Earth. In the penultimate poem of this section, this relation to nature is localized further still in the person of his wife, Joy Harjo, by describing her as a landscape. The section concludes with a poem which writes him back into the life of this earth in a harmonious manner, indicating the fact of his return by "tracks / at river's edge, raccoon, / coyote, deer, crow, / and now my own" (*Rain*).

Going for the Rain's final section, "The Rain Falls," is marked by a sense of ease and acceptance at moving once again in a familiar environment. The first three poems recoup the speaker's sense of identity with the Earth and continually remind him of Relation: "I must remember / that I am only one part / among many parts" (*Rain*), an idea which becomes the theme of the prayer he teaches his children (*Rain*). This sense of being integrated among others is commensurate with his sense of being integrated within himself. In a discussion with Joy, he characterizes the idea of "presence" as "how you fit / into that space which is yourself, / how well and appropriately." The notion of "fit" is a useful one, since it calls to mind the feelings of inadequacy or constraint that come from not "fitting."

To accept the idea of an appropriate "place" for oneself is to create possibilities for Beauty (to find and exult in the ways in which one "fits") and a Future (how one can better "fit"). The peaceful tone of this last section derives from the easiness of the poet's relation to his "world." The harsh land can be "a pretty woman" when, like the bony dog his father brought home in a gunny sack, it is "loved . . . without question" (*Rain*). This doesn't mean that there are no questions to be asked, but that there must be some "givens," some accepted and unquestioned place to start, which for Ortiz, I think, is rooted in a sense of the natural relations that obtain between all beings. He agrees with his wife Joy, who explains a neighbor's limp by his habit of pouring charcoal fluid on anthills and burning them. Ortiz' values are those of the elders he meets, men of great age like 114-year-old Yuusthiwa and 101-year-old Curly Mustache: "live enjoying and appreciating / your life, taking care . . ." (*Rain*). The volume's concluding poem asserts, "It doesn't end," and of course, the journeying cannot. Having reestablished the Center in himself again, Ortiz will set off again to find the horizon of value.

The journeying motif is explicitly affirmed by the title of his second volume of poetry, *A Good Journey* (1977). In its Dedication Ortiz reiterates his belief that the Center from which the poet speaks is the Earth, and his voice the channel for the Earth's: "The stories and poems come forth / and I am only the voice telling them." So the poet's task is to give voice to the truth the Earth knows.

The first section of the book, entitled "Telling," locates the poet's own voice in the tradition of tellings from which he has received the stories that dramatize the values and meanings to which he subscribes. Many of the stories are about Coyote, the Trickster figure and shape-changer. The teller of these stories dramatizes the vanity behind Coyote's decision to amend the Earth's story by denying the fixity of the natural order, but he also empathizes with Coyote's need to do so. More precisely, recognizing that his own motives are much the same as Coyote's, the teller chooses the path of humility and compassion rather than judgment. This attitude of humility and compassion, this emphasis on attitude, on right relation, is central to this first section. In **"San Diego Poem"** it is imaged by the now familiar metaphor of displacement. Ortiz is not only physically but spiritually alienated from the Earth by the droning metal hulk which lofts him away, and on his arrival at the L.A. airport he feels entombed in the maze of tunnels and technology. At the opposite pole of engagement/alienation is **"How to make a good chili stew,"** a poem which calls our attention to a larger sense of what constitutes "the ingredients," so that we can appreciate the advantages of making chili in a certain place, at a certain time of day, and so on, to be engaged with the process, not just the outcomes.

In "Notes for My Child," the second section of *A Good Journey,* Ortiz invokes "the whole earth spirit," reminding himself that his relationship is one of "Breathing the earth!", participating by his hearing/speaking in that circulation of the spirit. This experiencing of Place is the necessary condition of faith and the ground for meaning to which the stories appeal:

> Here it is possible
> to believe legend,
> heroes praying on mountains,
> making winter chants,
> the child being born Coyote,
> his name to be the Christ.
> Here it is possible
> to believe eternity.

The poems in this section are acts of "passing on," of "sharing" and "making one" through communicating story and vision. While explicitly addressed to his children, they offer images which attempt to connect the experience of the child with some other story familiar to the reader. All of these poems assert the primacy of the Earth, our identification with the Earth (he compares his child to a young bird learning to fly), and our ability to violate the Earth (as in **"Burning River"**). The section concludes by telling another kind of story, one of "leaving," of alienation and exploitation, which sets up the next section.

In the third part of *A Good Journey,* "How Much He Remembered," the protagonist has been alienated to some degree from the Earth, and the distance is measurable by counting the losses. The section opens with a poem testifying to the physically absent but remembered beloved, and moves to other poems in which places or events evoke memories. Soon it becomes clear that if memory testifies in some measure to loss, the persistence of memory also constitutes a way in which that which is lost can be present. Several of these poems imagine that "being present" as a kind of clairvoyance in which the moment/person suddenly becomes transparent to reveal the mythical/cultural form by which it has meaning for the poet.

If it is true, as the previous section suggests, that events can have multiple meanings and evaluations, then the suppression of some meanings/values is an exercise of power, which understandably angers those victimized by it. This anger motivates Ortiz in *A Good Journey*'s next section, "Will Come Forth in Tongues and Fury," the principal aim of which is to re-assert the aboriginal naming, to speak the unspeakable and make visible the invisible. In poems like **"From Grants to Gallup, New Mexico"** and **"The State's Claim . . . ,"** Ortiz contrasts the effects of "civilization" as he sees them with the implicit claims made for the benefits of "progress," exposing the rhetoric's ability to disguise reality. In other poems he names the effects of "progress": water theft, war on animals, and alcoholism. Against implicit claims perhaps that he ought to do more, Ortiz addresses the spirits of birds killed by automobiles in the war on animals: "This, for now, is as much as I can do, / knowing your names, telling about you. / Squirrel. Flicker. Gold Finch. Blue Jay. / Our brothers."

"Telling," then, is a political act, so that when Ortiz names the final section of *A Good Journey,* "I Tell It To You Now," his passing on of the story, his informing of us, implicates the reader in what and how Ortiz knows. The section serves as a fitting conclusion, recapitulating the movement of the book as a whole. The first poems in the section, which recall experiences of naming and identification, speak of "fit," the sense of being located in a particular geographical and cultural space and being attentive to it. The second group of poems in this section are about his stay in the VA hospital and address the issue of alienation from one's past, one's sense of self: "There's always something that you almost / did that you should have done." The section takes its title from the final poem of the book, a title which suggests that telling has a healing/bonding function. Encountering an Isleta woman he is reminded of what he had always wanted to say but didn't, even in that moment of encounter. Now, in the moment of writing, he will tell her and effect a relationship: "These few things then, / I am telling you / because I do want you to know / and in that way / have you come to know me now." As always, for Ortiz, "telling" is healing.

Fight Back: For the Sake of the People, For the Sake of the Land (1980) might be called Simon Ortiz' third volume of poetry, though in fact it featured a mixture of prose and poetry formats, the entire distinction being compromised by Ortiz' commitment to orality. The book is specifically meant to commemorate the tricentennial of the Pueblo Revolt of 1680, when concerted efforts by Native Americans under the full moon in August 1680 forcibly expelled the Spaniards from New Mexico. The Spaniards were not able to reassert domination until Vargas' reconquest in 1696. The volume implicitly asks the reader to compare the present colonized state of Native Americans, particularly in New Mexico, with that earlier oppression and exploitation. It invites the reader to acknowledge him/herself "to be in a relationship that is responsible / and proper, that is loving and compassionate, / for the sake of the land and all people."

The earlier poems in the book mark out the ways in which Native peoples are currently being exploited in the Grants (New Mexico) Mineral Belt, an area of energy resource development with its roots in railroad and coal development but currently located by the Ambrosia Lake (underground) and Jackpile (open pit) uranium ore mines. Many of the poems recount personal experiences as type-stories, transforming reports of real events into the kind of local legend which serves to characterize the place. These events include being denied credit, meeting the first "hard core" bigot, having a friend crushed by heavy equipment, and the terrible anxiety which follows hard upon the company's casual disregard for health hazards associated with handling ore. The role of Indians in this economy is highlighted in **"It Was That Indian,"** which points out that the booming city of Grants was slow to give credit to a Navajo named Martinez who first came out of the hills with a sample of what would prove to be uranium, but when complaints of chemical poisonings, cave-ins, and deteriorating quality of life began to pile up, the same community rushed to blame "that Indian who started the boom." Indians constituted "the bottom," and an inexhaustible supply of cheap labor which grew as the economy made them increasingly wage-dependent. Under such circumstances, Indians were even let out of jail to serve as "scabs" to break strikes by Indian unionists.

But if conditions were, and are, very difficult, there remains, as the title suggests, hope for effective and necessary resistance. This resistance, Ortiz implies, will begin with identifying one's place in the system of exploitation which profits a few and injures many. **"To Change in a Good Way"** . . . suggests that what we have in common—the families we care about, the land we live on, the people we live among—is the place to start building relationships of compassion and responsibility that will bind the exploited together against the exploiters. Anger, too, can be mobilized for resistance. Ortiz recalls the great pain of families, having become wage-dependent, watching their husbands, fathers, brothers leaving for distant places, for long periods of time, to work on the railroad and waiting, hoping that this train will be the one to bring their loved ones home: "Love / and hope. O Daddy. Please train. / . . . / Never again those years. / . . . / Our own solution will be strength: hearts, blood, bones, skin, hope and love. The woman anger and courage risen as the People's voice again." And the knowledge of the earth and its power to be, endure, give life, this too is a source of hope, as expressed in **"That's the Place Indians Talk About."**

What Ortiz hopes for and believes in is an ideology of work which would see labor not as an opportunity for exploitation but as the occasion for renewing creative integration of relationships. He offers the examples of his parents and of Agee, an Indian union organizer who spoke up probably at the cost of his life to repudiate the categories of oppression that enslaved him and deprived him of his potency.

The last half of the book is an essay, in mixed prose/poetry format, entitled **"No More Sacrifices,"** which picks up Ortiz' recurrent theme that "telling" is a political action. It opens with a short poem in which Ortiz confesses a feeling of nausea that comes upon him in an existential moment while walking on the Acoma sacred mountain. He attributes the nausea to a wave of Otherness, and the distance that it implies and that he has internalized is the distance between what the Acumeh (Acoma people) are and what they have been made to be. In order to eliminate that distance, he must "take back" his history.

The essay unfolds by juxtaposing the Aaqcu names and categories with the Anglo ones through which they have been suppressed, and showing how the re-naming marks the history of oppression. The village in which he was born, Deetzeyamah (**"Northern Door"** because it can be seen from the top of Aaqcu by looking north between two mesas toward the sacred mountain), appears on maps as McCartys, named after "an Irishman who operated the water pumps which sucked water from the nearby chuna, Rio San Jose" to supply the railroad. Elsewhere he contrasts the stories of how the Aacumeh came down from the cities near Mesa Verde with the Park Service's story, complete with its exhibit of a recovered Anasazi corpse named "Esther." Maps, payrolls, and museums are examples of the instruments of objectification, which obscure the personal, human, and immediate realities of lives and families where history is "lived" instead of talked about. Such instruments are thus both the condition and the consequence of conquest.

Opposed to them, as always for Ortiz, stand "the stories," the Aacqumeh history of themselves: "The people insist on talking about the years when there was rain and when the grass was lush and tall. It is not with mere nostalgia that they speak because it is not memory that they refer to. Rather, it is a view of the struggle they have known." Consequently, it is appropriate that after a call to resistance, to taking back one's history and the sense of self which that history describes, that the book should end with a poem entitled **"A New Story."** In this poem, Ortiz refuses the invitation of a California Anglo pageant director to be the Indian who will welcome ashore Sir Francis Drake.

In *From Sand Creek* (1981), Ortiz articulated his vision of history in a powerful work of art, which won a 1982 Pushcart Prize for poetry published by a small press. Based on his experiences at home at the Ft. Lyons, Colorado, Veterans' Administration hospital after the Vietnam War had ended, it calls us back to the multiple meanings of being a veteran. Though America apparently survived its experience in Vietnam, those who remember the nightly body counts, who marched in the streets or shouldered M-16s in the steaming jungles, who saw whole quarters of major cities left to burn and prophetic voices stilled by assassins' bullets, they will understand Ortiz' urgency.

As his title suggests, the poetry is suffused with tremendous historical depth, juxtaposing images and headlines with his own personal history. Today few young people even know that My Lai has anything to do with Vietnam. And more to the point, almost no young Americans have heard of Sand Creek, Colorado, where in 1864 Americans brutally murdered 105 Cheyenne women and children and twenty-eight men while they camped under a flag of peace presented by President Lincoln himself. The Cheyenne corpses were mutilated for soldiers' war trophies. Such knowledge is not the center of Ortiz' poetry, however valuable and necessary the act of remembering, but the foundation of a compassionate vision that would transform grief and guilt into hope.

However much these poems are rooted in history, it is in their language that they come to life. Throughout the cycle of forty-five poems, each with an expository epigraph on the facing page, Ortiz carefully orchestrates recurring images of blood, stone, grass, steel, darkness, and other dream-like Wagnerian leitmotifs. Sometimes these are elaborated surrealistically, as when the soldiers are mesmerized by the flowing blood of battle:

> Spurting,
>   sparkling,
> splashing, bubbling, steady
> hot arcing streams.
>   Red.
> and bright and vivid
> unto the grassed plains.
> Steaming.
> So brightly and amazing.
> They were awed.
> It seemed almost magical
> that they had so much blood.

Other times he transforms the image. Bones, for instance, are split to provide marrow for nourishment. Then he displaces and negates this image so that "Dreams / thinned / and split / can only produce / these bones." In another poem blood steams from the ground, the steam becomes cloud, the cloud provides rain and renewal. By using images as motifs, Ortiz can link historical figures as diverse as Cotton Mather, aerospace engineers, Mennonite immigrants, and Kit Carson, toward the development of a common theme.

The theme of the cycle—the souring of the American Dream—is a familiar one, handled unfamiliarly:

> The axiom
> would be the glory of America
> at last,
>   no wastelands,
> no forgiveness.
>
> The child would be sublime.

Under Cotton Mather's tutelage, everything has been appropriated to our national, corporate, and personal interests ("no wastelands"), because we have been moved by the Biblical imperative to subdue and conquer the earth, an imperative that seemingly gives divine sanction ("no forgiveness" needed). The beauty of our handiwork, the bounty which is the visible mark of our blessing, would excuse our sins. Yet the arrogance and self-righteousness were unnecessary, Ortiz argues: "Like a soul, the land / was open to them, like a child's heart . . . If they had only acknowledged / even the smallest conceit." But to dreamers moved by fear, conquest seemed more reasonable than cooperation.

Turned against others, Americans began to turn against themselves. They separated themselves from the land: "Their cells / would no longer bother / to remember." They separated themselves from themselves, subjecting

everything to their overriding, self-justifying purpose: "Anger meant nothing to them, / not even an intellectual exercise."

In one poem this separation is brought home with particular force. In the quiet of the hospital, long after lights out, the night is shattered by a scream: "Far / below, far below, / the basement speaks / for Africa, Saigon, Sand Creek." Others who would calculate the odds of winning *this* war only see part of the picture: "They'll never know. / Indians stalk beyond the dike, / carefully measure the distance, / count the bullets."

Occasionally Ortiz is too doctrinaire, especially in the epigraphs: "Men and war and fortune and destiny—the real winner and culprit is the imperial one: the agents and men are only agents and men." Such oversimplification betrays the complexity of the situations which have entangled so many in pain. It also undermines itself when juxtaposed with the immediacy of the experiences conveyed in the poetry, as when "W., the Sioux, / blunted his fingers / on the wall. / [of the] Kit Carson Chapel at Ft. Lyons. / You know, we stood shivering / to some kind of error / that afternoon." And occasionally the abstract diction of political and sociological rhetoric insinuates itself into this poetry of experience.

More often, however, Ortiz speaks from a wounded heart. We cannot help being American, he says, including himself, but "love should be answerable for." *From Sand Creek* is his response to his own love for all that America could have been and could still be. It is this note of compassion, rising from a clear knowledge and a certain sense of shared pain, which finally dominates the epic breadth of his historical vision, suffusing it with intimacy and hope.

Much of [Ortiz's] sense of his location can be traced to his attitude toward tribal tradition, which he sees as offering a set of values and beliefs alternative to and legitimately competing with those of the Anglo-American.

—*Andrew Wiget*

As Simon Ortiz continues to write, certain clearly emerging themes and attitudes have given him a distinctive position in relationship to other Native American writers. He is, for one thing, unabashedly political, but his criticism of America is not that it has failed, but as Chesterton remarked of Christianity, it has yet to be really tried. What is wanting is the commitment and the humility that will give birth to hope. For another, he strikes a careful balance between the explicitly mythopoeic work of Leslie Silko and the almost equally explicit demythologization of Indians offered by James Welch. Much of this sense of his location can be traced to his attitude toward tribal tradition, which he sees as offering a set of values and beliefs alternative to and legitimately competing with those of the Anglo-American. The viability of those traditions is something Ortiz reinforces in almost every poem or story, by adopting a distinctly "oral" voice, directly addressing the reader, catching the local pronunciation, casting his work into narrative.

Like some of the current crop of Anglo writers of the American West who have rejected the romantic regionalist stereotypes as untruthful, Ortiz repudiates the several senses "Indian" has come to acquire in Anglo culture, for the Anglo concept has failed to provide for the truth which only he can speak. Where writers such as McMurtry might vehemently assert the death of that Old West, Ortiz might argue that his West, with its own sense of place and its own history, not only has never died, it was never "born" in the Anglo-American consciousness in the first place.

To provide a space in which an authentic voice may be heard, and in that hearing to evoke respect, compassion, and the promise of hope, this seems to me what the work of Simon Ortiz is all about. It is not about a race that is vanishing, a way of life that is passing, or a language that is dying, but about a nation of those who have preserved their humor, their love for the land that is their mother, and their sense of themselves as a distinctive people. It is about journeying, about survival, about the many significances of being a veteran.

Simon Ortiz with Joseph Bruchac (interview date 1987)

SOURCE: "The Story Never Ends: An Interview with Simon Ortiz," in *Survival This Way: Interviews with American Indian Poets,* University of Arizona Press, 1987, pp. 211-229.

[*In the following excerpt, Ortiz speaks of the influence his past has had on his poetry.*]

[Joseph Bruchac]: *What was your childhood like?*

[Simon Ortiz]: I grew up at Acoma Pueblo homeland in the small village of McCartys. And I grew up pretty normally as an Indian child. There were conditions, social and economic conditions, that resulted in our community being pretty poor. People, years and years ago, generations back, made their living by farming, but by the turn of the century agricultural occupations were no longer extensive or possible to make a living by. So people began to go for wage work. My father was a railroad worker. He was away from home quite a lot, working at jobs he could get like other men of the tribe.

My childhood was normal, but sometimes it was stressful. In Indian communities or other communities where people are poor, the conditions are sometimes not good. I mean people are poor, so they suffer. But, through it all, the sense of community, the sense of who I was as an Acoma person and what was meant for me to do as a person in that community, in my family, it was always there. Sometimes spelled out very deliberately. Other times, maybe most times, it was just the way you did things and the way you were. That was my childhood.

I lived there most of the time except a couple of times our family went to where my father worked, to Arizona and California. Then, when I was in the seventh grade, I went to boarding school—St. Catherine's Boarding School and Albuquerque Indian Boarding School—because the school at McCartys only went up to the sixth grade. After I was about nineteen, I basically left home to go to college, Army, work, et cetera. But you never really leave. You're always a part of there. Acoma is sixty-five miles west of here, Albuquerque, and all of this is really Acoma.

There's a sense in your work of being firmly grounded in who you are and in the tradition from which you come. I find this is a contrast to many non-Indian writers who are always searching for who they really are.

I think for Indian writers to be able to use their talent and their beings to write they have to know some *place*. And to know some place you have to *let yourself*. It's a choice, then, that you really have to make. Non-Indian writers, perhaps, don't have a choice partly because of their cultural upbringing. The kind of history this nation has and the philosophies developed in the Western tradition don't allow that. But for Indian people, who have grown up within an Indian community, something is there that insists you allow yourself that choice. That you make that choice. That you are affirmed for making that choice. Belonging somewhere is a real affirmation. Perhaps non-Indian writers are just not affirmed when they find a place or desire a place. I hope, though, this is coming for them. I can't really see any value in not knowing a place. You have to have it. Otherwise you are drifting. You remain at loose ends and you're always searching without ever knowing where you are or what you're coming to. I guess the background, the heritage of Native American people at least offers this opportunity to have a *place*. We have something that we can choose.

Can you compare the education you received in a traditional sense with the education you received in Western-style schools?

I was thinking of this as I was going across town to meet you. I thought about the experience one has within his family, his home, his community—which is the whole tribal group and its way of life. It's *experiential*. You live it, breathe it, talk it. You touch it. You are involved with the motion of it. When you're born you are of your family, you're of your clan, you're recognized, and you are given a very particular mission or duty to acknowledge this. You're then a living part of it, and you're always going to have to be aware of this. Otherwise your life has no value, no meaning, no real part of anything.

Then you go to school. I first went to school when I was about seven years old to learn to read and write English. You learn *about* it. You learn about life. You read about it, you study it, you solve problems. But it's not an experienced learning; rather, you acquire it. You learn it mentally. You learn mentally certain processes, procedures, and results, and it's something that's outside of you, almost. What this, of course, means is that you learn because you are alone. You learn not within a communal experience. You learn because you, as an individual, have solved this problem or looked in the dictionary and sought out the meaning of this particular word. That's one of the differences and it's an important difference. Now, of course, this other way of education is a part of us. I think some of it is good and some is totally useless. In fact, some of it is contradictory to what that other *experienced* life is—the gathering of knowledge into us and how we are a part of that knowledge.

How does writing—which is basically a Western form—fit into the work of an American Indian poet?

I look at it as just language itself. That's why listening is so important, because that's the way you learn language—listening as an experience. Listening not really to find any secrets or sudden enlightenment, but to be involved with that whole process and experience, that whole process and experience of language. That's the way we understand how we are, who we are, what we know, what we'll come to know. So, when I look at language in terms of writing, it's the language itself I'm concerned with, not that those symbols on a printed page have any meaning. What I try to be aware of is its core nature, the basic elements of language itself. So that writing is a furtherance or continuation of what is spoken, of what is emotion in terms of sound, meaning, magic, perception, reality . . . Native American people write of many, many things in various ways, in various forms.

There's something else you probably might want to ask with that question. What about the topics that have been chosen by Indian writers? I think we should write about anything and everything and that we should write a lot. In fact, we must! Indian people love knowledge and have always sought knowledge. I know that U.S. history, especially from the 1890s onward, has characterized Indians as not wanting to learn. But I know that knowledge and the seeking of knowledge is a main requirement for living a life that is fulfilling. Writing, using language—whether it's in speaking or singing or dancing or writing—is a way of using that knowledge. So we should write about everything. I don't think there's any real limit we should impose upon ourselves—as long as it's good. When I told my mother I was going to be a writer—I was about nineteen or twenty years old, around 1961—one of the first things she said to me was, "All right. As long as it's good!" I think she meant it on a very practical level—like don't write pornography or useless things. That was very good advice. My collection of short stories, *Fightin'*, is dedicated "For my mother—who told me years ago to write only for good things." I hope I have. But I think it's important to write in all areas of knowledge. We're talking mainly about poetry and fiction, but we need writers in history, economics, sociology, philosophy, any other areas of human experience.

When did you begin to write?

My first published poem was when I was in fifth grade. It was a Mother's Day poem. But I don't think I thought of it in terms of being a writer. But I loved to read. Once I learned how to read it was like a world just opened up in front of me, all around me. Again, I think this interest came about purely because of language. I would listen to stories when I was small. My life was always stories. I call them stories even though they may have just been talking about somebody—gossip, anecdotes, jokes. My father or my mother telling what they did that day. My aunt coming over and crying over some problem. Or an old man talking about how it was a long, long time ago and how it wasn't anymore. I call these stories, whatever they may have been, because that's the way they were experienced. But when I learned to read, that was the thing that was happening, I guess. I began to read almost anything, whatever we had. We didn't get much reading material. My father would bring the newspapers home sometimes and I would get books from the school at McCartys. Comic books, whatever. I read whatever was available. It was, I think, at about twelve or thirteen that I was inspired to write something. The thing I wrote was song lyrics, song lyrics in the folk music tradition. My father was a railroad worker and would sing songs, working kinds of songs he had learned in his travels. He was a good singer in Acoma, in English, in Spanish, and in other languages like Zuni and some Navajo. He had a beautiful voice. He was an inspiration to me. So writing song lyrics was really my beginning, but don't think I knew anything about what a writer was. I think it was in high school when I first began to be encouraged. As a skill, I knew it was something that I was good at, to express myself. I started out writing stories when I remember first consciously thinking of myself as a writer. That was partly because of the romanticization that came about when I read stories by F. Scott Fitzgerald, Ernest Hemingway, Thomas Wolfe. My background in writing had a lot to do with that. I also kept a diary when I went to St. Catherine's Indian School, a journal—a secret one. Being away from home, family, clan, community, life is very tenuous, especially being a preteen. You're scared and you're lonely and you're homesick, and so writing is a way to reassure yourself. That was part of it, how I came to be a writer.

By the time I was nineteen I was very aware that there was such a thing as a writer, that he was a certain kind of person. Probably I had that ideal of the American writer in the Western tradition, that he was a special person, an artist, a creator, an individual fighting the world, sitting in a garret composing his great novel. I got rid of that idea later. That period in the '50s was also the beatnik era. I read Jack Kerouac and Ginsberg and others—mostly the San Francisco poets. Snyder, Phillip Whalen, Rexroth. Those poets were very important to me. I'm not sure why. By the time I was twenty-one, I think I was committed. I would tell people that I was a writer, though I was still slated for a real job as a mechanic or something that seemed more real than a writer. By the time I was twenty-two, probably about 1963, I knew that's what I wanted to do as a profession and a career, though I didn't publish anything until '65 or so.

Why is there all this traveling in your work? Is a poem like a journey?

Yes, think it is. I use an image which is very prominent in my consciousness: *Heeyanih,* which is road. A road of life. A road of experience. A road of learning. A road on which one travels from the time he is born until he goes back into the earth. And there is a certain process. Another book of mine, **Going For the Rain,** has a preface which describes some of that process—the preparation, setting out on the journey, and returning. So, it's a motif that I am aware of throughout my work, particularly in the poems. I look at journeys as a way in which I can further experience knowledge. In my poems I note places that I've been, note people that I've met, conversations that I've had, experiences that I've had—some good, some bad, some absurd, some that shouldn't have been. But all this is part of that journey of setting out and returning.

You're always on a journey. Especially in this age. Indian people are much more mobile. I think Indian people were always mobile. Not that they weren't settled, not that they didn't live in one place and call it home, but that they didn't always just stay there all the time. The Pueblo people, Acoma people and others, have a mixture of various cultural traditions. Some are from Mexico, some from the seacoast. This means that people either came from the seacoast or we went to the seacoast. We went south to get the parrot feathers. There was a great movement of people who were on journeys, and it's still happening today. Some peoples, in the past, followed migrations of animals—buffalo hunters—and those were journeys. That didn't mean they were a homeless people. They belonged somewhere. But the journey was important. Those are some of the reasons I use the motif or symbol or theme of the journey in my work. I've been pretty much all over this United States and I've learned and I'm still learning a lot.

In 1970, I went looking for Indians. This relates to your question about education. You know there are Indians because you grew up with Indians, you were born with Indian parents, but formal, institutionalized, United States education tells you in very clear, though sometimes subtle, ways that there are no Indians. When I was a kid we weren't Indians. The picture books showed you Indians were in teepees and rode ponies and there were buffalo. At Acoma there are no buffalo and there are no teepees. There are ponies, but they are usually ridden by Indian cowboys, ranchers, people who had cattle. Some, something tells you that you're not a real Indian. Then, further, the books tell you there are no Indians in California. They all just disappeared. They tell you the same thing about the southeastern United States. They went to Indian Territory or they just disappeared. Where did they go? There was this feeling that there were no Indians, that the Indians you were growing up with were not really Indians. So, by 1970, I really wanted to find Indians again. I wanted to debunk the myth of the "Vanished American" finally, for all time, for myself. It was important for me. I wanted

to see for myself. I had Indian friends in the South I had met a couple of years before, Adolf Dial from South Carolina, a guy from the Seminole people in Florida, some people in Mississippi. I knew these people individually, but I wanted to see for myself. So I went through the South, starting out from Arizona, through Texas and Oklahoma, throughout the South: Louisiana, Georgia, Florida, South Carolina, North Carolina, Tennessee. Indians all over the place—all over the place! People who were mixed with black people, with white people, and some who were in communities who call themselves Indian. So, once and for all, the myth was cast aside. There are Indians everywhere! In one of my poems, I say, "You're damn right, there are Indians everywhere!"

Do you think of traditional ways as being threatened or disappearing as anthropologists often say?

I think the anthropologists are wrong. I think what they think is disappearing is their own version of Indians. Their own images of Indians, their own stereotype of Indians. One time up in Alaska, about six years ago, with the Before Columbus Foundation, we were conducting a workshop with a lot of emphasis on the oral tradition. There was a man from England who has written about Alaskan native literature who happened to be in Anchorage at the same time. On the panel he said something that was absolutely horrible and clear evidence of how anthropologists look at native people. He said, "There are no more storytellers. The last one spoke to me and he died." I just blew up! There were several young Alaskan native writers, Eskimo, Aleut, and Tlingit, sitting across the table from him and he says that there are no more native Alaskan storytellers! What he was referring to, of course, is that version in their own minds, the stereotyped Indians on the ponies, setting upon a wagon train. That's what they bemoan the loss of. Their version is unreal, it always was. It's best lost. Indian culture is dynamic culture; it's not a static culture. If Indian cultures were static, they would be gone. But cultures evolve and they evolve creatively. The fact that there are Native American writers, singers, dramatists, screenwriters is clear evidence that this tradition continues.

During the 1950s, especially after the period of termination and relocation, there seemed to be a period of real depression. I think we were forced to relocate mentally as well as emotionally, breaking away from the spiritual nature of our lives. People left to go to school because we were told there were no longer ways in which you could make the right standard of living at your home, your foods were no good for you, you had to go to San Francisco and eat commodity foods or starve because you were becoming an American. You were really learning how to be a "full and equal" citizen in this United States. It was a period of real depression in the '50s. But I've seen the '60s and the '70s and now the '80s. It has been a real growth period, a real affirmation back to what our values were, back to what those values meant to us. More people, young people especially, began to participate in dances. More people wanted to learn, to protest, to stand up for their Indian rights, their Indian identity, their Indian lands, and human rights in general. It's been a healthy period.

How do you define poetry?

Yesterday when I was up at the Four Seasons Elderly Care Center in Santa Fe I defined it pretty well. I forget now exactly how I said it. It had to do with that idea I talked about before—experience itself. I was talking about song as poetry, song as motion and emotion. Song as the way in which I can feel those rhythms and melodies and how those things give me energy or make me aware of an energy that is really the life force, a part of all things that we are part of. Then I said that song is poetry and poetry is the way in which those images become possible for me to obtain, that become realized in me. I think I also said that poetry is the way in which we make the connections between words, the connection between all things. Poetry is a way of reaching out to what is reaching for you. Poetry is that space in between what one may express and where it is received. Where there is another energy coming toward you—it's that space in between. Poetry is stories, certainly, for me. When I began to write poems I wrote them mainly because they were stories. Prose fiction was really my first love. I think, basically, it still is.

How can history be used in poems?

You have to use history. History is the experience we live. I suppose "history" in the Western definition means something that is really a kind of contrived information to support the present case, the present United States existence and aims. That it is a super power because in the past the groundwork was laid and we were destined to be great. Well when I use history I mean for this to happen: that history be studied, that history be acknowledged. We are a part of that, even though scholars, academicians, policy makers, corporations may not acknowledge it. Indian people built this country. Indian land, Indian labor, Indian resources built this land, and we have to say it, we have to study it, we have to look at what the motives were and are. We have to acknowledge that certain terrible things happened. If *they* don't want to say it, then we have to say it for them. If their writers, their historians, their sociologists, their artists, their minds don't want to accept it and say it, we have to say it for them.

To some extent, I think Indian people have not acknowledged this history, recorded history. For example, I know that it's usually difficult for Indian people, Pueblo people particularly, to acknowledge how we have been colonized, what those events in colonization were. It's really *hard* to talk about. Some people even go so far as to say those things didn't really happen. We were never slaves. Acoma was never burnt and razed. Yet history records it. When Onate's men in 1598 burned and destroyed Acoma, they killed people. They cut off their arms and legs and they took people to Mexico as slaves. This is the experience of all the Pueblos—and other Indian people. And then they don't really acknowledge certain things later on. We talked about education. That education was a device, a strategy, a policy by which we would become separated from each other, that we would be broken. And then we don't acknowledge that there was religious persecution. The reason why most of the religion is underground, why foreign-

ers are forbidden, is just because of that, because you had to hide and people are still hiding. For all public purposes, at Acoma and most of the other pueblos there are no native religions because it's still dangerous. People don't see and they don't admit to this danger readily. And why don't they do it readily? Because suppression and colonialism are still in effect here. There are still those pressures upon Indian people to hide and not to allow ourselves to see. I think that the only way in which we will become not scared anymore, not hide anymore, is to know the truth. And to know the truth of history and to acknowledge it, use it to foster knowledge, not only foster our own knowledge, but of non-Indians and those policymakers who have used ignorance against us and themselves. I know that when you tell the truth it's a political act. When you acknowledge history and point out such things as Sand Creek— maybe nobody wants to hear about Sand Creek—it is a political statement and the truth. It is necessary to talk about it because it's a part of how we are going to live, how we are going to fulfill ourselves on that journey. It has to happen for the national consciousness. If we don't, there will always be a black blot, a dark spot in our minds. There will be a continued sickness if you don't talk about it.

You think of your audience as not just Indian people, but American society?

Someone in Farmington, New Mexico, asked me that question once. I told them my audience was really everybody. Of course, I direct it, based on certain information to certain issues. Those two books, ***Fight Back*** and ***From Sand Creek***, certainly have to do with United States history. They point out conditions and circumstances and areas where people may be sensitive, and I address them to those people who *are* sensitive about those things. In *Sand Creek*, I address Indian people and non-Indian people. It's necessary to address Indian people. I don't say that I do it first of all for them or that it's my priority, but I think Indian people are the ones my words are intended for. That is partly because I am an Indian person and it's like I'm speaking to myself. I'm speaking *with* myself. Language is an important act which has to do with a re-affirmation of self, and so the poetry has that, is intended for that—to reaffirm one's self.

It's been said, though, that poetry doesn't reach many people in the United States.

Poetry is suspect all the time, I think. Poetry is suspect because this goes back to how art is seen, in general. Art is something extracurricular. Art is something you hang up on the wall. You can enjoy it only if you can afford it. That's a separation from reality. The idea becomes: I don't have time to appreciate art, I don't have time to appreciate poetry, much less write it. So, poetry doesn't reach an audience. It's suspect because it has nothing, supposedly, to do with your real life. Knowledge and intellect and aesthetic tastes are over here, removed, somewhere else, far removed. Poetry is not a part of our complete lives as compared to cultures where art is something that you do all the time, where language is important to you and you do it, you live it, you experience it, you communicate with it. I think the fact that Indian people are very artistic people—whether it's in certain crafts like pottery making or weaving or in music and drama—is evidence of art being a part of life and not separated. The act of living is art. But poetry isn't seen like that in United States society. Poetry is suspect and is only for weird and strange people like bohemians, Hippies, lost souls, and Indians.

So what do you do? Do you stop writing poetry and try to write things people will read?

I think you should become more determined. One of the things I've done lately is sing more and explain that this is poetry. For some reason, with singing you can make a real connection in spite of people's hesitancy about poetry, in spite of people's curtains and walls. Those are not really their own walls, but learned behavior. The song breaks down or goes through those walls. You can even sing about those walls and people will understand.

I think, also, to reach a wider audience poetry has to be somehow more conscious of the tradition of its oral source. That's one of the ways. Luci Tapahonso's poetry works in that manner. I tried to pattern my book *A Good Journey* almost wholly on the oral tradition, intentionally. I wanted the word *as act,* you know, poem *as act.* As close to it in its written form as possible. If poetry is to reach more people, this is one of the things that has to happen. It has to be aware consciously and insistently of its source in the oral tradition. And singing probably achieves this in a very definite way.

Your name is immediately recognized by Indian people wherever I go in the United States. Perhaps that is because within American traditions there's still that sense of art, that relationship to art?

And also to art as political statement. I think a lot of people know me because of that. I'm involved with events that are purely political in nature, which are statements about Indian people, lands, and what we must struggle for with all human people. The spirit of humanity is thriving and fighting back. I think a lot of people recognize that. The human spirit doesn't really stay in one place. In order to ensure a good future we must resist and have certain goals in mind. I think I suggest in *From Sand Creek* that we have to be revolutionary poets. Decolonization requires it, decolonization as African peoples, as the people in Central and Latin America, are determining for themselves. For the past ten years I've looked to African writers— Chinua Achebe, James Ngugi—and Ernesto Cardenal and Pablo Neruda of Latin America. What I think poetry means in a social, economic, political, cultural context in other countries is applicable here. I think people recognize me as a poet, but also as a person who is speaking for himself and maybe, in a sense, for them.

Yet even in your poems which depict those situations in which Indian people are brutalized, jailed, exposed to radiation, disenfranchised, I find a lack of obvious anger and bitterness. Why is this so?

It probably has to do with seeing the value that language has itself. You have to say certain things and what you say should be worth what you're saying. Perhaps how we can best say it is to affirm ourselves. We're not lost. We're not just fighting for survival. We're going beyond survival. There is meaning beyond mere breathing and walking.

It may be just a different style of saying it. I have a poem called **"Time to Kill in Gallup."** First of all that means just time to spend there. Other times, I have been angry enough to kill Gallup! There are certain things that point out, that say implicitly, that there is such an anger. But again, as you say, it doesn't come out and say "I'm going to go down the street and I'm going to get Whitey and put his children to death or hit them over the head with a piece of cement." I think the bitterness and anger *is* said, but I think it's said in a different style. Also, with what I said about language being a means of affirmation, that's quality we can't waste, we can't misuse. It's something we have to hold onto in whatever way we can. But there are angry poems I've written. The *From Sand Creek* poems are very understated. One of the poems says that they don't know that Indians are counting their bullets. Of course, that book ends with "that dream shall have a name after all."

You and Peter Blue Cloud are known for using Coyote in your poems. Who is Coyote and why does he visit your writing so frequently?

I think Peter writes more about Coyote than I do. I don't write much about Coyote anymore. Partly, I have a reputation for using Coyote because of *A Good Journey,* in which I used it a lot. Some of my early work used it. I have uion and its transformation into the present in writing—and the continuation of the oral tradition itself. Coyote *is* there all the time. I don't mean to say that I don't use Coyote anymore, absolutely. In fact, some of my recent poems have coyotes. Just the circumstances change. The events are different, but the figure is there. He may have a different name or she may have a different name, but the Coyote figure is there because they're stories. Coyote has, for me, been the creative act. The act of creation and beyond. It is something that never dies. It is a symbol, for me, of continuation. No matter what the circumstances are—like in the traditional stories when, through some mishap, maybe his fault, maybe another person's trickery, Coyote sort of dies. But something happens and he or she comes back. Maybe a skeleton fixer comes along and says, "Hey, I wonder whose bones those are. I think I'll put him back together." So he or she is brought back to life and the story goes on. The story never ends.

You *must* tell a story. That's the way I think it's possible for life to have meaning and for it to continue. That's how we have to maintain ourselves. And Coyote, for me, is a symbol of that continuation. Indian people have various totems—at least I've read so in anthropological journals. But there are figures—animals—who are relatives, who are our brothers and sisters in life through whom human qualities or lack of qualities speak. It's human aspiration and human desperation, but the human experience is spoken through some relative being; he may be Coyote or Raven or Bear or others that speak for us and with us. Peter Blue Cloud sent me some stories. I really like them because they are transformations of Coyote in present-day circumstances. This is evidence again that the story may be old, but you have to make it new in order for it to be useful now, in order for it to be healthy and useful in today's terms.

Talking of Peter reminds me that your name turns up in the poems of some other Indian poets. Mentioning each other's names seems about as common among Indian writers as it has been among the Beats or the New York School.

It's a big family, it's a big family. Naming each other and sharing each other in stories and poems has to do with a tradition. And, it being a mobile society, we're really all over the place. That Indian I met in Flagler Beach knew somebody, an Archembault from South Dakota whom I'd been with in the Army. You talk to somebody in California and you talk about New York and you mention names. You go to Alaska, you go to Phoenix, and you see somebody who knows somebody else. "Yeah, he's my kinfolk," or "He's my brother-in-law." It's amazing. It's more than just the fact that you're in a group like the beatnik generation. It has to do with that relationship between Indian peoples, a sense of community. Every place I go I know somebody who knows somebody and usually in a very close way. It really helps us to maintain that community— not necessarily as writers, but as people who share a common origin and will have a destiny that is communal and important because it is interconnected. That's why my name pops up every now and then—not just because of some crazy episodes, which sometimes have been the case. It's healthy to recognize each other. You're not alone, you're not separated from what's happening.

Simon Ortiz (essay date 1987)

SOURCE: "The Language We Know," in *I Tell You Now: Autobiographical Essays by Native American Writers,* edited by Brian Swann and Arnold Krupat, University of Nebraska Press, 1987, 185-94.

[*In the following excerpt, Ortiz discusses the importance of language in his work, and how straddling two cultures—Native and Anglo-American—affects his poetry.*]

I don't remember a world without language. From the time of my earliest childhood, there was language. Always language, and imagination, speculation, utters of sound. Words, beginnings of words. What would I be without language? My existence has been determined by language, not only the spoken but the unspoken, the language of speech and the language of motion. I can't remember a world without memory. Memory, immediate and far away in the past, something in the sinew, blood, ageless cell. Although I don't recall the exact moment I spoke or tried

to speak, I know the feeling of something tugging at the core of the mind, something unutterable uttered into existence. It is language that brings us into being in order to know life.

My childhood was the oral tradition of the Acoma Pueblo people—Aaquumeh hano—which included my immediate family of three older sisters, two younger sisters, two younger brothers, and my mother and father. My world was our world of the Aaquumeh in McCartys, one of the two villages descended from the ageless mother pueblo of Acoma. My world was our Eagle clan-people among other clans. I grew up in Deetziyamah, which is the Aaquumeh name for McCartys, which is posted at the exit off the present interstate highway in western New Mexico. I grew up within a people who farmed small garden plots and fields, who were mostly poor and not well schooled in the American system's education. The language I spoke was that of a struggling people who held ferociously to a heritage, culture, language, and land despite the odds posed them by the forces surrounding them since 1540 A.D., the advent of Euro-American colonization. When I began school in 1948 at the BIA (Bureau of Indian Affairs) day school in our village, I was armed with the basic ABC's and the phrases "Good morning, Miss Oleman" and "May I please be excused to go to the bathroom," but it was an older language that was my fundamental strength.

In my childhood, the language we all spoke was Acoma, and it was a struggle to maintain it against the outright threats of corporal punishment, ostracism, and the invocation that it would impede our progress towards Americanization. Children in school were punished and looked upon with disdain if they did not speak and learn English quickly and smoothly, and so I learned it. It has occurred to me that I learned English simply because I was forced to, as so many other Indian children were. But I know, also, there was another reason, and this was that I loved language, the sound, meaning, and magic of language. Language opened up vistas of the world around me, and it allowed me to discover knowledge that would not be possible for me to know without the use of language. Later, when I began to experiment with and explore language in poetry and fiction, I allowed that a portion of that impetus was because I had come to know English through forceful acculturation. Nevertheless, the underlying force was the beauty and poetic power of language in its many forms that instilled in me the desire to become a user of language as a writer, singer, and storyteller. Significantly, it was the Acoma language, which I don't use enough of today, that inspired me to become a writer. The concepts, values, and philosophy contained in my original language and the struggle it has faced have determined my life and vision as a writer.

In Deetziyamah, I discovered the world of the Acoma land and people firsthand through my parents, sisters and brothers, and my own perceptions, voiced through all that encompasses the oral tradition, which is ageless for any culture. It is a small village, even smaller years ago, and like other Indian communities it is wealthy with its knowledge of daily event, history, and social system, all that make up a people who have a many-dimensioned heritage. Our family lived in a two-room home (built by my grandfather some years after he and my grandmother moved with their daughters from Old Acoma), which my father added rooms to later. I remember my father's work at enlarging our home for our growing family. He was a skilled stoneworker, like many other men of an older Pueblo generation who worked with sandstone and mud mortar to build their homes and pueblos. It takes time, persistence, patience, and the belief that the walls that come to stand will do so for a long, long time, perhaps even forever. I like to think that by helping to mix mud and carry stone for my father and other elders I managed to bring that influence into my consciousness as a writer.

In my childhood, the language we spoke was Acoma, and it was a struggle to maintain it against the outright threats of corporal punishment, ostracism, and the invocation that it would impede our progress towards Americanization.

—Simon J. Ortiz

Both my mother and my father were good storytellers and singers (as my mother is to this day—my father died in 1978), and for their generation, which was born soon after the turn of the century, they were relatively educated in the American system. Catholic missionaries had taken both of them as children to a parochial boarding school far from Acoma, and they imparted their discipline for study and quest for education to us children when we started school. But it was their indigenous sense of gaining knowledge that was most meaningful to me. Acquiring knowledge about life was above all the most important item; it was a value that one had to have in order to be fulfilled personally and on behalf of his community. And this they insisted upon imparting through the oral tradition as they told their children about our native history and our community and culture and our "stories." These stories were common knowledge of act, event, and behavior in a close-knit pueblo. It was knowledge about how one was to make a living through work that benefited his family and everyone else.

Because we were a subsistence farming people, or at least tried to be, I learned to plant, hoe weeds, irrigate and cultivate corn, chili, pumpkins, beans. Through counsel and advice I came to know that the rain which provided water was a blessing, gift, and symbol and that it was the land which provided for our lives. It was the stories and songs which provided the knowledge that I was woven into the intricate web that was my Acoma life. In our garden and our cornfields I learned about the seasons, growth cycles of cultivated plants, what one had to think and feel about the land; and at home I became aware of how we must care for each other: all of this was encompassed in an intricate relationship which had to be maintained in order

that life continue. After supper on many occasions my father would bring out his drum and sing as we, the children, danced to themes about the rain, hunting, land, and people. It was all that is contained within the language of oral tradition that made me explicitly aware of a yet unarticulated urge to write, to tell what I had learned and was learning and what it all meant to me.

My grandfather was old already when I came to know him. I was only one of his many grandchildren, but I would go with him to get wood for our households, to the garden to chop weeds, and to his sheep camp to help care for his sheep. I don't remember his exact words, but I know they were about how we must sacredly concern ourselves with the people and the holy earth. I know his words were about how we must regard ourselves and others with compassion and love; I know that his knowledge was vast, as a medicine man and an elder of his kiva, and I listened as a boy should. My grandfather represented for me a link to the past that is important for me to hold in my memory because it is not only memory but knowledge that substantiates my present existence. He and the grandmothers before him thought about us as they lived, confirmed in their belief of a continuing life, and they brought our present beings into existence by the beliefs they held. The consciousness of that belief is what informs my present concerns with language, poetry, and fiction.

My first poem was for Mother's Day when I was in the fifth grade, and it was the first poem that was ever published, too, in the Skull Valley School newsletter. Of course I don't remember how the juvenile poem went, but it must have been certain in its expression of love and reverence for the woman who was the most important person in my young life. The poem didn't signal any prophecy of my future as a poet, but it must have come from the forming idea that there were things one could do with language and writing. My mother, years later, remembers how I was a child who always told stories—that is, tall tales—who always had explanations for things probably better left unspoken, and she says that I also liked to perform in school plays. In remembering, I do know that I was coming to that age when the emotions and thoughts in me began to moil to the surface. There was much to experience and express in that age when youth has a precociousness that is broken easily or made to flourish. We were a poor family, always on the verge of financial disaster, though our parents always managed to feed us and keep us in clothing. We had the problems, unfortunately ordinary, of many Indian families who face poverty on a daily basis, never enough of anything, the feeling of a denigrating self-consciousness, alcoholism in the family and community, the feeling that something was falling apart though we tried desperately to hold it all together.

My father worked for the railroad for many years as a laborer and later as a welder. We moved to Skull Valley, Arizona, for one year in the early 1950s, and it was then that I first came in touch with a non-Indian, non-Acoma world. Skull Valley was a farming and ranching community, and my younger brothers and sisters and I went to a one-room school. I had never really had much contact with white people except from a careful and suspicious distance, but now here I was, totally surrounded by them, and there was nothing to do but bear the experience and learn from it. Although I perceived there was not much difference between *them* and *us* in certain respects, there was a distinct feeling that we were not the same either. This thought had been inculcated in me, especially by an Acoma expression—*Gaimuu Mericano*—that spoke of the "fortune" of being an American. In later years as a social activist and committed writer, I would try to offer a strong positive view of our collective Indianness through my writing. Nevertheless, my father was an inadequately paid laborer, and we were far from our home land for economic-social reasons, and my feelings and thoughts about that experience during that time would become a part of how I became a writer.

Soon after, I went away from my home and family to go to boarding school, first in Santa Fe and then in Albuquerque. This was in the 1950s, and this had been the case for the past half-century for Indians: we had to leave home in order to become truly American by joining the mainstream, which was deemed to be the proper course of our lives. On top of this was termination, a U.S.government policy which dictated that Indians sever their relationship to the federal government and remove themselves from their lands and go to American cities for jobs and education. It was an era which bespoke the intent of U.S. public policy that Indians were no longer to be Indians. Naturally, I did not perceive this in any analytical or purposeful sense; rather, I felt an unspoken anxiety and resentment against unseen forces that determined our destiny to be un-Indian, embarrassed and uncomfortable with our grandparents' customs and strictly held values. We were to set our goals as American working men and women, singlemindedly industrious, patriotic, and unquestioning, building for a future which ensured that the U.S. was the greatest nation in the world. I felt fearfully uneasy with this, for by then I felt the loneliness, alienation, and isolation imposed upon me by the separation from my family, home, and community.

Something was happening; I could see that in my years at Catholic school and the U.S. Indian school. I remembered my grandparents' and parents' words: educate yourself in order to help your people. In that era and the generation who had the same experience I had, there was an unspoken vow: we were caught in a system inexorably, and we had to learn that system well in order to fight back. Without the motive of a fight-back we would not be able to survive as the people our heritage had lovingly bequeathed us. My diaries and notebooks began then, and though none have survived to the present, I know they contained the varied moods of a youth filled with loneliness, anger, and discomfort that seemed to have unknown causes. Yet at the same time, I realize now, I was coming to know myself clearly in a way that I would later articulate in writing. My love of language, which allowed me to deal with the world, to delve into it, to experiment and discover, held for me a vision of awe and wonder, and by then grammar teachers had noticed I was a good speller, used verbs and tenses correctly, and wrote complete sentences. Although I imagine that they might have surmised this as

unusual for an Indian student whose original language was not English, I am grateful for their perception and attention.

During the latter part of that era in the 1950s of Indian termination and the Cold War, a portion of which still exists today, there were the beginnings of a bolder and more vocalized resistance against the current U.S. public policies of repression, racism, and cultural ethnocide. It seemed to be inspired by the civil rights movement led by black people in the U.S. and by decolonization and liberation struggles worldwide. Indian people were being relocated from their rural homelands at an astonishingly devastating rate, yet at the same time they resisted the U.S. effort by maintaining determined ties with their heritage, returning often to their native communities and establishing Indian centers in the cities they were removed to. Indian rural communities, such as Acoma Pueblo, insisted on their land claims and began to initiate legal battles in the areas of natural and social, political and economic human rights. By the retention and the inspiration of our native heritage, values, philosophies, and language, we would know ourselves as a strong and enduring people. Having a modest and latent consciousness of this as a teenager, I began to write about the experience of being Indian in America. Although I had only a romanticized image of what a writer was, which came from the pulp rendered by American popular literature, and I really didn't know anything about writing, I sincerely felt a need to say things, to speak, to release the energy of the impulse to help my people.

My writing in my late teens and early adulthood was fashioned after the American short stories and poetry taught in the high schools of the 1940s and 1950s, but by the 1960s, after I had gone to college and dropped out and served in the military, I began to develop topics and themes from my Indian background. The experience in my village of Deetziyamah and Acoma Pueblo was readily accessible. I had grown up within the oral tradition of speech, social and religious ritual, elders' counsel and advice, countless and endless stories, everyday event, and the visual art that was symbolically representative of life all around. My mother was a potter of the well-known Acoma clayware, a traditional art form that had been passed to her from her mother and the generations of mothers before. My father carved figures from wood and did beadwork. This was not unusual, as Indian people know, there was always some kind of artistic endeavor that people set themselves to, although they did not necessarily articulate it as "Art" in the sense of Western civilization. One lived and expressed an artful life, whether it was in ceremonial singing and dancing, architecture, painting, speaking, or in the way one's social-cultural life was structured. When I turned my attention to my own heritage, I did so because this was my identity, the substance of who I was, and I wanted to write about what that meant. My desire was to write about the integrity and dignity of an Indian identity, and at the same time I wanted to look at what this was within the context of an America that had too often denied its Indian heritage.

To a great extent my writing has a natural political-cultural bent simply because I was nurtured intellectually and emotionally within an atmosphere of Indian resistance.

Aacquu did not die in 1598 when it was burned and razed by European conquerors, nor did the people become hopeless when their children were taken away to U.S. schools far from home and new ways were imposed upon them. The *Aaquumeh hano,* despite losing much of their land and surrounded by a foreign civilization, have not lost sight of their native heritage. This is the factual case with most other Indian peoples, and the clear explanation for this has been the fight-back we have found it necessary to wage. At times, in the past, it was outright armed struggle, like that of present-day Indians in Central and South America with whom we must identify; currently, it is often in the legal arena, and it is in the field of literature. In 1981, when I was invited to the White House for an event celebrating American poets and poetry, I did not immediately accept the invitation. I questioned myself about the possibility that I was merely being exploited as an Indian, and I hedged against accepting. But then I recalled the elders going among our people in the poor days of the 1950s, asking for donations—a dollar here and there, a sheep, perhaps a piece of pottery—in order to finance a trip to the nation's capital. They were to make another countless appeal on behalf of our people, to demand justice, to reclaim lost land even though there was only spare hope they would be successful. I went to the White House realizing that I was to do no less than they and those who had fought in the Pueblo Revolt of 1680, and I read my poems and sang songs that were later described as "guttural" by a Washington, D.C., newspaper. I suppose it is more or less understandable why such a view of Indian literature is held by many, and it is also clear why there should be a political stand taken in my writing and those of my sister and brother Indian writers.

The 1960s and afterward have been an invigorating and liberating period for Indian people. It has been only a little more than twenty years since Indian writers began to write and publish extensively, but we are writing and publishing more and more; we can only go forward. We come from an ageless, continuing oral tradition that informs us of our values, concepts, and notions as native people, and it is amazing how much of this tradition is ingrained so deeply inour contemporary writing, considering the brutal efforts of cultural repression that was not long ago outright U.S. policy. We were not to speak our languages, practice our spiritual beliefs, or accept the values of our past generations; and we were discouraged from pressing for our natural rights as Indian human beings. In spite of the fact that there is to some extent the same repression today, we persist and insist in living, believing, hoping, loving, speaking, and writing as Indians. This is embodied in the language we know and share in our writing. We have always had this language, and it is the language, spoken and unspoken, that determines our existence, that brought our grandmothers and grandfathers and ourselves into being in order that there be a continuing life.

[In the following review, Baxter approvingly assesses the poetry and prose of Woven Stone—*a volume containing Ortiz's first three collections.]*

It is a testament to Simon Ortiz's influential career that **Woven Stone** has been published: three of his books, long out of print, have now been collected into one volume. For those of you who have searched in vain for **Going For The Rain** (1976), **A Good Journey** (1977), and **Fight Back: For the Sake of the People, For the Sake of the Land** (1980), look no further. Reprinted in their entirety, these acclaimed works are now available along with an insightful, in-depth thirty-page preface which chronicles the author's life.

For those not familiar with Simon Ortiz's prolific career, **Going For The Rain** and **A Good Journey** are two works of poetry that use oral histories, narratives and stories. His memories of a traditional upbringing at Acoma Pueblo, New Mexico, intertwine with his encounters of rural and working-class Americans. These cyclical poems are told to us by Ortiz with Coyote's help and vice versa. An ironic sense of humor flows throughout tales of the contemporary world. Always committed to native survival and endurance, Ortiz's gift lies in making us aware of our own personal responsibility; these are not just words on a page, they are a call to political action.

Fight Back is a powerful and beautiful example that art and politics do mix. This book of poetry and prose focuses on the uranium mining in the Acoma-Grants-Laguna area in the early 1950s. Ortiz writes from historical perspectives (the most accurate history being the stories of the workers and their families) as well as from his own memories of working in the mines. The book speaks directly to the social, cultural and economic devastation of the surrounding region.

The introduction is a fascinating autobiographical essay. Ortiz honestly confronts his struggle with alcoholism and his encounters with the white world as a young boy and man from Acoma Pueblo. He also speaks about compassion and convictions—that within every poem lies a story, and that story must be told in order to ensure survival. He contends that we must expand our concerns globally to include indigenous peoples throughout the world. Our responsibility to one another does not end with political borders. Colonialism, poverty and spiritual loss remain critical concerns and, as artists, we can use our talents to not only love and respect each other but also to "fight back."

Simon Ortiz has given us indelible proof that the written word is indeed an effective weapon. And we are left with a sense of renewal and hope: "to behold with passion and awe the wonders and bounty and beauty of creation and the world around us."

Andrea-Bess Baxter (review date 1993)

SOURCE: A Review of *Woven Stone,* in *Western American Literature,* Vol. 28, No. 2, Summer, 1993, pp. 162-63.

Gary Soto (review date 1994-95)

SOURCE: A Review of *After and Before the Lightning* in *Hungry Mind Review,* Winter, 1994-95, pp. 56-7.

[In the following review, Soto comments favorably on the poetry of After and Before the Lightning, *but remarks that the volume's prose is occasionally flawed.]*

We are earthbound in this journal-like compilation of poems and poetic prose, [*After and Before the Lightning*] which begins on November 18 and ends on March 21 of an unnamed winter.

In his preface Ortiz states, "I felt like I was putting together a map of where I was in the cosmos," an ambitious calling indeed. Whenever a word like "cosmos" arises, a reader becomes suspicious, especially within a sentence such as the one uttered above, which is plainly without grace. But we can suspend such suspicion because those familiar with Ortiz's poetry have come to expect such usage. We have come to expect such words as "spirit," "dreams," "offerings," "vision," "vital brilliance." This is part of his cultural speech, which from a less-skilled poet could come off as the razzle-dazzle of a snake oil salesman. We also know to anticipate the effortless mingling of spirit and place, as when he writes in **"Morning, the Horizon"**:

> Later, east of Carter
> we travel on the horizon.
> We are finally the blue horizon
> of this high prairie.
> We've become the distance.

Ortiz succeeds in becoming the "distance" that he speaks of—"distance," "blue horizon," "high prairie," a metaphysical blending of self with the landscape—with little movement or frantic worry. He's keenly aware of place, so much so that the reader realizes that Ortiz is measuring his life to his surroundings, elegantly, as in "The low sun's light is a flat blade / on the black highway."

The Rosebud Sioux Reservation becomes not an exile but a march into the snowy interior of the Dakotas. In some ways, this collection resembles Cesare Pavese's *Hard Labor* in that the poet employs physical and spiritual courage during a bleak period in his life. Some of the poems are chants, such as **"Our Names"** and **"The Dreamer's Song,"** but most are lyrics and prose like narratives. Story is paramount.

But the book occasionally suffers from the prose entries that either preface or augment the poems. His descriptive power loses its voltage. While we have come to expect that poetry should be as well written as prose, a notion of Ezra Pound's, we should, conversely, expect prose to equal poetry in its grace and delivery. While not all of the entries are flawed, we feel the start of a yawn when we come across this passage:

> . . . an intense concentration, a focus on your eyes so you can't and don't want to hold his gaze for very long. His words are comical too at the same time, that is, he finds something humorous in you, that you all can laugh about. Because it's something you and he and everyone else can identify with. And still an honest and subject seriousness. Beyond this even, he is totally honest, totally subjective, and totally serious.

And the entry persists with a litany of other ambiguities. Still, we can forgive such passages amidst poems of a man redeemed by six months of living in snow.

Ortiz's use of nature and weather images:

Written in journal format complete with dates, Ortiz's [*After and before the Lightning*] takes the reader through a South Dakota winter, starting in mid-November when the snow is just beginning to fall and finishing in late March after a long season spent shivering. Ortiz is marvelously adept at capturing the moody stages of cabin fever, wonder for the endurance of the land, and the quiet humility of a semiforeign culture. Written while he lived on the Rosebud Sioux Indian Reservation, the book chronicles both nature and the resilience of the Lakota people. Although you might think the constant weather references would become tedious, they instead establish a soothing rhythm during a season when the weather is not merely unforgettable but potentially deadly. Ortiz provides a fascinating glimpse into a world of frozen laundry, prairie gumbo, and blue dawns, and although he admits the time recorded may have contained the darkest moments of his life, this collection frequently shines.

Elizabeth Gunderson, in Booklist, *Vol. 91, No. 1 September 1, 1994.*

Robert L. Berner (review date 1995)

SOURCE: A Review of *After and Before the Lightning* in *World Literature Today*, Spring, 1995, p. 409.

[In the following review, Berner calls After and Before the Lightning *Ortiz's "most powerful achievement to date."]*

The Acoma poet Simon Ortiz spent the winter of 1985-86—the date can be determined by his reference to the *Challenger* disaster of January 1986—as a visiting professor at Sinte Gleska College on the Rosebud Reservation in South Dakota. That year and the profound culture shock which he experienced, caused less by his dealings with the Lakota Sioux of the reservation than by the awesome Dakota prairie and its frightening weather, required a search for "a way to deal with the reality of my life and the reality in which I lived." The result is less a collection of poems, though it is that, than a poetic journal containing poems and prose notes dated from late autumn to the first day of the following spring—the Dakota winter between autumn's last lightning and the first lightning of spring.

The prairie Ortiz experienced is a hard place where brutal work is normal for those who hope to endure, where dreams are smashed, where even murder can occur, but above all where winter and the lonely landscape are a test of character; and to the child of the Great Plains who writes this review, the language Ortiz uses to render the reality of that world seems exactly right. It is a place of "blistering cold," the wind's "deeply throated frozen moan," and an "icy sunlight glistening off snow-fields," and the sun viewed through a few trees is "so low I have to bend down to see it." "Nothing," he says in one poem, "can measure distance here," and in "this South Dakota wind and snow, a destiny we cannot deny," Ortiz came to terms with himself, with his place and time, and with humanity's place in a cosmos which seems more immediate on the plains than anywhere else and where driving the long strip of US 18 is like "travelling on the farthest reaches of the galactic universe."

Some readers may think many of the poems too sketchy to stand by themselves; but they work in the context of the steady progression of the season they chronicle, and most of them in fact can stand by themselves and indeed are very strong. They deal with universal concerns: with the recognition of mortality while chopping wood (**"Comprehending"**) or driving blind for two seconds after a huge truck passes by in a storm (**"Blind Curse"**), with the mingled guilt and gratitude felt while cooking venison (**"What We Come to Know"**), with an abandoned farm and the poet's imagined farmer whose courageous story must be told (**"A Story of Courage"**). These poems, and for that matter Ortiz's book itself, must be considered his most powerful achievement to date, a major event in the current movement of American Indian poetry, and in fact a significant contribution to our literature in general.

FURTHER READING

CRITICISM

Gingerich, Willard. "The Old Voices of Acoma: Simon Ortiz's Mythic Indigenism." *Southwest Review* (Winter 1979): 18-30.

    Discussion of writing derived from native sources, and how Ortiz's work benefits from the weight of tradition and history.

Gleason, Judith. "Reclaiming the Valley of the Shadows." *Parnassus: Poetry in Review* 12, No. 1 (Fall/Winter 1984): 21-71.

    Includes lengthy reviews of Ortiz's *A Good Journey* and *From Sand Creek,* which Gleason discusses in terms of myth, history, and contemporary Native American Life.

Smith, Patricia Clark. "Coyote Ortiz: *Canis latrans latrans* in the Poetry of Simon Ortiz." In *Studies in American Indian Literature: Critical Essays and Course Designs,* edited by Paula Gunn Allen, pp. 192-210. New York: The Modern Language Association of America, 1983.

    Concentrates on manifestations of the Native-American Coyote myth used by Ortiz, especially in his collection *Going for the Rain.*

Wiegner, Kathleen. "Books: Poetry as Ritual." *American Poetry Review* 6, No. 1 (January-February 1977): 46.

    Praises Ortiz's first collection of poetry, *Going for the Rain,* for its recognition of the importance of ritual in life.

Additional coverage of Simon Ortiz's life and career is contained in the following sources published by Gale Research: *Contemporary Authors,* Vol. 134; *Contemporary Literary Criticism,* Vol. 45; *Dictionary of Literary Biography,* Vol. 120; *DISCovering Authors: Multicultural; DISCovering Authors: Poets;* and *Native North American Literature.*

Pier Paolo Pasolini
1922-1975

Italian poet, novelist, essayist, screenwriter, filmmaker, critic, editor, and short story writer.

INTRODUCTION

Pasolini has been called one of the most notable poets to have emerged from post-World War II Italy. Although recognized outside his country primarily as a filmmaker, Pasolini is well known in Italy for the outspoken views on Marxism and religion he presents in his poetry. Central to Pasolini's life and works is his despair over Italy's impoverished conditions and his anger over the indifference of the materialistic bourgeoisie. During the course of his controversial career, his observations on Catholicism, communism, and the existing social order have alternately pleased and angered conservatives and leftists alike and have earned Pasolini the title of "civil poet." Frank Capozzi noted, "In Pasolini one finds the lyricism of Pascoli, the aspiration of Rousseau, the revolt and the anguish of Rimbaud, the self-destruction of Genet. His . . . poems . . . will always be important for an understanding of post-war society."

Biographical Information

Pasolini was born in Bologna, the son of an army officer. His father's long absence as a prisoner of war in Kenya and his brother's execution as a partisan by the Fascists forced political awareness upon Pasolini at an early age. Having begun to write poetry when he was seven, Pasolini attended high school and university in Bologna, though he had lived in various parts of northern Italy during his youth. His childhood and early adult experiences in the poverty-stricken village of Casarsa, located in the province of Friuli, inspired his first book of Friulian dialect poetry, *Poesie a Casarsa* (1942) as well as his lifelong identification with the poor. Following a brief period with the Italian army, just before the Italian surrender to the Allied forces in 1943, Pasolini returned to Casarsa, where he was strongly influenced by the ideas of Karl Marx and Antonio Gramsci, the leading theoretician of Italian communism. In the late 1940s, Pasolini earned his doctorate degree and became a state high school teacher. He had kept his homosexuality a secret until a scandal in 1949, stemming from accusations that he had approached a male student, led to the loss of his teaching job and his membership in the Italian communist party. Pasolini escaped with his mother to Rome, where he became immersed in the slum life of that city. Subsequently the lives and views of its underclass youths would become central to his poetry and films. In 1955 Pasolini co-founded the review *Officina* in Bologna with friends Francesco Leonetti and Roberto Roversi, and

later joined Enzo Siciliano in the *Nuovi Argomenti*. In 1957 *Le ceneri di Gramsci* (*The Ashes of Gramsci*) was published, earning Pasolini a Viareggio Prize. In 1962 Pasolini was arrested on charges that he had insulted the church in his poetry and films. Later, two of his films, *I racconti di Canterbury* (1972) and *Salò o le centoventi giornate di Sodoma* (1975), were declared obscene. In 1975, at age 54, Pasolini was murdered in Ostia, outside Rome, by a 17-year-old male prostitute.

Major Works

Pasolini wrote his earliest poetry, collected in his first book, *Poesie a Casarsa,* in his native Friulian peasant language, in the hope of creating a literature accessible to the poor. Pasolini rejected the official language because he believed that it had been created by and for the bourgeoisie. These early poems appear in an expanded and revised version, *La meglio gioventù* (1954) and center on his renunciation of Catholicism and his endorsement of Marxist beliefs. Other early poems, along with some experiments in the tradition of religious poetry, are collected in the volume, *L'usignolo della Chiesa Cattolica* (1958).

The poetry of *Le ceneri di Gramsci* and *La religione del mio tempo* (1961) reflects, among other beliefs, Gramsci's idea of a "popular national literature." Pasolini broke away from the preceding generation of Italian poets by composing *Le ceneri di Gramsci* in *terza rima*—a subversive return to the traditional verse of Dante, Pascol, and the civic poets of the Risorgimento. Although he eventually abandoned *terza rima,* he later returned to it in "A Desperate Vitality," in *Poesia in forma di rosa* (1964). He revised many poems in *Friuliano* and published them in *La nuova gioventò* (1975). Pasolini's later poems are more autobiographical and confessional, yet the political concerns central to the majority of his works are still evident. In his last works Pasolini declared a kind of poetic bankruptcy as he attempted to renounce literature and his origins. Shortly before his death Pasolini repudiated a large part of his own work: "It's already an illusion to write poetry, and yet I keep doing so, even if for me poetry is no longer the marvelous classic myth that exalted my adolescence. I no longer believe in dialectic and contradiction, but only in opposition."

Critical Reception

Most critics agree that Pasolini's great contribution was the creation of a "civic" poetry, "the rational argument of a civilized mind." The adjective has also been used to describe Pasolini's verse as "public" poetry, even if there was not necessarily a consensus of acceptance by the public. Critics and intellectuals have considered Pasolini an "organic intellectual," a term used by Gramsci to designate a new kind of militant intellectual, linked to the working class, who worked through the apparatus of the party. The openness in Pasolini's poetry has been seen as a strength by some critics; others have commented on Pasolini's inability to resolve his inner conflicts in his work, and his tendency toward narcissism, egocentrism, and martyrdom. While some critics, noting Pasolini's strong narrative tendency and use of traditional metrics, have read his poetry as a conservative exercise which missed the 1960s avant-garde trend in Italy, Pasolini's poetry has been seen by some as immune to a historically-determined categorization. Stefano Agosti considered Pasolini's poetic language "a diction which is at once total and suspended, entirely involved and critically deferred."

PRINCIPAL WORKS

Poetry

Poesie a Casarsa 1942
I diarii 1945
Tal cour di un frut: Nel cuore di un fanciullo 1953
Dal diario, 1945-47 1954
La meglio gioventù 1954
Le ceneri di Gramsci [*The Ashes of Gramsci*] 1957
L'usignolo della Chiesa Cattolica 1958

Passione e ideologia, 1948-1958 (poetry and essays) 1960
Roma 1950: Diario 1960
La religione del mio tempo 1961
L'odore dell'India [*The Scent of India*] (poetry and prose) 1962
Poesia in forma di rosa 1964
Poesie dimenticate 1965
Trasumanar e organizzar 1971
La nuova giovento: Poesie friulane, 1941-1974 1975
La divina mimesis [*The Divine Mimesis*] 1975
Le poesie [*Poems*] 1975
Roman Poems: Bilingual Edition 1986
Poetry 1993

Other Major Works

Ragazzi di vita [*The Ragazzi*] (novel) 1955
Una vita violenta [*A Violent Life*] (novel) 1959
Accatone (screenplay) 1961
Il sogno di una cosa [*A Dream of Something*] (novel) 1962
Mamma Roma (screenplay) 1962
Il vangelo secondo Matteo (screenplay) 1964
Alì dagli occhi azzurri [*Roman Nights and Other Stories*] (short stories) 1965
Ucellacci e uccellini (screenplay) 1965
Edipo Re [*Oedipus Rex: A Film,* adapted from the tragedy by Sophocles] (screenplay) 1967
Teorema [*Theorem*] (novel and screenplay) 1968
Porcile [*Pigsty*] (screenplay) 1969
Medea [adapted from the tragedy by Euripides] (screenplay) 1970
Empirismo eretico [*Heretical Empiricism*] (essays) 1972
Calderón (drama) 1973
Il padre selvaggio (prose) 1975
Salò o le centoventi giornate di Sodoma (screenplay) 1975
Scritti corsari (essays) 1975
Trilogia della vita (Il Decamerone, I racconti di Canterbury, Il fiore delle Mille e una notte) (screenplays) 1975
Affabulazione (drama) 1977
Pilade (drama) 1977
The Letters of Pier Paolo Pasolini, 1940-1955 (letters) 1993

CRITICISM

Jean-Michel Gardair (essay date 1971)

SOURCE: An Interview with Pier Pasolini, in *Stanford Italian Review,* Vol. II, No. 2, Fall, 1982, pp. 46-8.

[*In the following interview, originally published in 1971, Pasolini discusses the poetic renewal that inspired* Trasumanar e organizzar.]

Pasolini the filmmaker had overshadowed for some time Pasolini the writer. Then, however, not only six tragedies and a collection of essays were published one after the other, but with *Trasumanar e organizzar* a poetic silence that had lasted since *Poesia in forma di rosa* (1964) was broken.

[Gardair]: *Was this silence due to circumstances or to some "poet's block"?*

[Pasolini]: Let's say that after *Poesia in forma di rosa* I had the feeling of having exhausted a certain linguistic world, the pleasure of certain choices, certain words. I didn't give up immediately, or rather I first tried to renew myself at any cost, but for this will power is not enough. There is no renewal without an interior renewal. Time is needed. So, meanwhile, I preferred to express myself through others: my actors, the characters of my tragedies. And when, about two years ago, I started to write poems again, I realized that the poetic renewal I had hoped for and pursued in vain had happened spontaneously. Most of the words and figures that were the base of my former poetry had completely disappeared from this last collection.

Isn't it due also to a widening of your cultural horizons?

You know, my cultural horizons in fact have shrunk. I am no longer the avid reader I was ten years ago. The cinema made me less civilized, less cultured, like all filmmakers. No, I am just older. And I discovered that getting older means having less future ahead, which in turn means being freer. It is the obsession with the future that keeps man from being free. He creates for himself thousands of duties to evade his intolerable freedom. In the same way, it is always the notion of future that perverts ideologies, Catholicism as well as Marxism or McLuhan-style liberalism, with its mythical perspective of undefined well-being. So for me it has been less an enrichment through new experiences and readings than freeing myself from the inevitably hypocritical, deceptive and unscrupulous young man who spoke in my first poems.

How does this evolution manifest itself in your poetry?

First through a certain humor. In my former films and novels, there could be comical touches, but never humor. It is due to a fact I could barely explain to myself: having lost most of my illusions, I am nevertheless living, acting and writing as if I still had them. For example, even if I no longer believe in the revolution, I want to stay on the side of the young who fight for it. Writing poems is another illusion, yet I keep writing even if poetry stopped long ago being the marvelous classical myth that exalted me as an adolescent. For a young poet of the forties or fifties, it was unthinkable to write for his contemporaries: he wrote inevitably for posterity with all the rhetoric that it involves.

In what ways are your poems formally different?

They are mostly written in the style of a diary, poems as notes, some sincere, direct, and others in bad faith, I mean composed with the esthetic feeling of writing notes.

What are they about?

I tried to classify them myself, although they are really a single poem, continuously resumed and interrupted. But it is possible to discern three relatively homogeneous groups. First the "civic" poems, dedicated for instance to Pope Pius XII as the promoter of a religion close to the Hitlerian ideology or to the Jewish law, one based on faith and hope but not at all on charity; to Panagoulis, to Rudi Dutschke's attack, to the deaths of Ho Chi Minh and Kennedy. A second group, more decidedly political, is about the ambiguity I just mentioned of my ties with the revolutionary youth of today, the leftist movement, etc. And a third group is a diary of my most intimate life that I have the impudence to show off in public. But, in a curious way, there are also a great number of poems inspired by my friendship with Maria Callas.

But to go back to your poems and to end with the question we should have started with, could you explain the title of your last collection?

"Trasumanar" is the term by which Dante designates the ineffability of the mystic askesis in *Paradiso*. "Organizzar" is of course its caricatural opposite. In fact I don't believe anymore in dialectics and contradictions, but in pure oppositions. I don't pretend at all to transcribe in verse the ineffability which only life permits us to live and apprehend. And since I myself am neither a mystic nor a saint, I don't have any experience of what a seventh-heaven rapture might be. But I am more and more fascinated with the exemplary union accomplished by the major saints, St. Paul for instance, between active and contemplative life. And it is that double face of the human, that double aspiration of the imaginary to both embody and reflect itself, that I try to capture through these notes torn from my daily life.

T. O'Neill (essay date 1975)

SOURCE: "Pier Paolo Pasolini's Dialect Poetry," in *Forum Italicum*, Vol. IX, No. 4, December 1975, pp. 343-67.

[*In the following essay, O'Neill comments on Pasolini's use of Friulian dialect in his poetry, and on his Spanish and Italian poetic influences.*]

Perhaps the best synthesis of the world of Pasolini's dialect poetry is that given, unconsciously, by the author himself in the important 1952 essay on *La poesia dialettale del Novecento,* talking of the Triestine poet, Giotti:

> Una povera storia, infinitamente più nuda e deserta
> che nei crepuscolari, poiché nella sua angoscia non c'è
> compiacimento o ripensamento da favola decadente,
> ma come un interno terrore, una nozione della morte
> e del disfacimento del mondo, delle cose care e degli
> affetti, che ha quasiun remoto accento leopardiano.

The "mondo" of which Pasolini speaks is that of Friuli, specifically Casarsa, the birthplace of his mother, to where his family had been evacuated in 1943, and where he remained until 1949, when, he moved, definitively, to Rome. But the Casarsa of Pasolini is not a precise, well-defined geographical location; it is not, in a word, realistically described and recognisable as such, like, say, the Tuscany or Umbria of Luzi: rather it has become, to adopt an expression of Silone's, the poet's *paese dell'anima.* Casarsa is not part of the geographical world, but rather the symbol of a world complete in itself, an absolute (and therefore perfect) idyllic world of youth and innocence: in the words of the poet himself, it is the world of "coloro che egli amava con dolcezza e violenza, torbidamente e candidamente," a "vita rustica, resa epica da una carica accorante di nostalgia"—"il calore puro e accecante dell'adolescenza" (*Passione e ideologia*). In this respect the *dedica* speaks clearly:

Fontana di aga dal me país.
A no è aga pí fres-cia che tal me país.
Fontana di rustic amòur.

(Fontana d'acqua del mio paese. Non c'è acqua più fresca che nel mio paese. Fontana di rustico amore.)

His poetry will be a celebration of the "país" in the absolute sense . . . , and the "fontana di rustic amòur," with its "aga fres-cia"—a recurring motif in the early poetry, perhaps of Machadian derivation—the concrete symbol of a world of innocence and purity, untrammeled by complications.

So too, just as Casarsa is his *paese dell'anima,* its young inhabitants—given in the infinite and evocative variations of the dialects: *nini* (fanciullo), *fì* (ragazzo), *zòvin* (giovane), *soranèl* (ragazzetto), *fantassùt* (giovinetto), *donzel* (giovinetto), *frut* (fanciullo)—are also simply, to use Eliot's term, objective correlatives of the poet himself, loaded with the emotion that is his, deriving from the consciousness he has of the fleeting nature of the world and its inhabitants which he contemplates. In this sense, the diminutive "fantassùt," used vocatively at the beginning of **"Ploja tai cunfins"** can legitimately be compared to the "corpo fanciulletto" of Foscolo's *A Zacinto,* and, perhaps more so, to the "fanciullo mio" of Leopardi's *Il sabato del villaggio,* both of which perform the same poetic function as Pasolini's "fantassùt"—that is to say, they are persons representing a state of innocence, of unawareness, and are attractive precisely because of these qualities, but at the same time they are poetically intensified by the awareness, as we shall see shortly, of a different reality on the part of the poet.

This nostalgic, memorial evocation of an idyllic, perfect world of youth and innocence, such as permeates Pasolini's early dialect poetry, is, of course, more than understandable in the climate of the early forties in Italy. Pasolini, to an extent, explains it himself in the concluding pages of *La poesia dialettale del Novecento,* where, talking of the regress from language to dialect in his own poetry, he says it was:

causato da ragioni più complesse, sia all'interno che all'esterno: compiersi da una lingua(l'italiano) a un'altra lingua (il friulano) divenuta oggetto di accorata nostalgia, sensuale in origine (in tutta l'estensione e la profondità dell'attributo) ma coincidente poi con la nostalgia di chi viva—e lo sappia—in una civiltà giunta a una sua crisi linguistica, al desolato, e violento, *"je ne sais plus parler"* rimbaudiano.

(*Passione e ideologia*).

The civilisation in linguistic crisis which, given the strong link in Pasolini between language and society, indicates a civilisation in crisis *tout court,* was, of course, that of fascism which, thanks to Mussolini's tactics, starting with the anti-semitic legislation of the summer of 1938, and continuing with the Rome-Berlin pact of the following year, was gradually drawing closer in form and outlook to Hitler's Germany. Pasolini's withdrawal into the Casarsa of his youth is, in its way, a withdrawal from the unacceptable reality of fascist Italy, a rejection of history. It too is part of that "evasività," which he attributes to Solmi, "che coincide, in parte, con quella ermetica dell'anteguerra" (*Passione e ideologia*).

Nor, besides this evident political cause, is his choice of subject matter strange in the light of the vogue in Italy at that period of two masterpieces in the literature of adolescence, Alain-Fournier's *Le grand Meaulnes* (1913) and Raymond Radiguet's *Le diable au corps* (1923). Nor . . . is there to be excluded the possible influence of the Spanish poet, Antonio Machado, whose memorial evocation of the Castille of his youth—*Mi juventud, veinte años en tierra de Castilla*—is not dissimilar in intention, and, on occasions, in style and vocabulary, to the Casarsa of Pasolini.

In the last analysis, however, neither political cause nor literary affinity completely explain Pasolini's choice of subject matter. His evocation of an adolescent world would seem to have deeper, perhaps more psychological roots, for, on examination, it can be seen to be a constant in his works. The *ragazzi di vita* of the "Roman" novels, in fact, although influenced by the Neapolitan Russo, and particularly by the Roman Belli, are still basically the *frutin* who populate his early poetry. It would seem to us that Pasolini himself wished to stress the constant importance the world of adolescence had for him, when, in reprinting his dialect poems in 1954, he chose as their title **La meglio gioventù,** stressing thereby his belief in it—youth—as the best period of one's life, conscious as he was then that, alas, it was—in the words of the *canto popolare* he was citing—"soto tera."

If the early dialect poetry of Pasolini, however, were simply a highly lyrical, descriptive evocation of youth, it is doubtful whether it would be able to hold our attention as it does. In fact, the world of youth and innocence evoked by the poet is, in many respects, only the framework of the collection, its "povera storia," to use his own expression. . . . [The] various youths who pass through his poetry are the objective correlatives of the poet himself. The objective world of Casarsa is simply one side of the coin. On the other side there stands the poet himself, remembering and endowing that world with a richness, complexity and ambiguity that is his. The "carica accorante di nostalgia" is counterbalanced by the consciousness or awareness of reality that he has. The awareness of what he is (reality), compared with what they are (nostalgia), brings in the consciousness of change, and, ultimately, of death. What we have, in effect, is a repetition of a well-known Leopardian situation, typical of the *grandi idilli*: namely, the nostalgic evocation of a situation, which nostalgic evocationcontains within itself the consciousness of its being no more. From this nostalgia, which is not anescape from reality but rather a sublimation of it, there derives that "nozione della morte e del disfacimento del mondo, delle cose care e degli affetti" that Pasolini sees in Giotti, and which we believe mirrors accurately his own poetry.

An examination of the opening poems from his first collection will illustrate this situation of nostalgia-consciousness. It is well illustrated in the volume's first poem following the *dedica*, **"Il nini muart"** (Il fanciullo morto):

> Sera imbarlumida, tal fossál
> a cres l'aga, na fèmina plena
> a ciamina pel ciamp.
>
> Jo ti recuardi, narcìs, ti vèvis il colòur
> de la sera, quand li ciampanis
> a sùnin di muart.
>
> (Sera luminosa, nel fosso cresce l'acqua, una donna
> incinta cammina per il campo. Io ti ricordo, Narciso,
> avevi il colore della sera, quando le campane suonano
> a morto. *La meglio gioventù.*)

The poem is divided into two tercets. The first one presents us with a simple scene, evoked with a few impressionistic strokes, reminiscent of Pascoli's *Myricae*, against which there stands out the "fèmina plena," symbol, like the water running in the ditch, of life. What at first sight may seem a simple, descriptive piece, takes on its full significance in the light of the second tercet, for there the poet's memory, through the unifying element of the "colòur / de la sera," leads to his awareness that that life, mirrored in the first tercet, cannot be separated from its necessary counterpart, death, and it is the awareness of death, inherent in that incipient life, that takes the first tercet (and the complete poem) beyond the bounds of a merely descriptive piece, and makes it, instead, a poetic vehicle for the intense emotion of the poet.

A similar situation is to be found in the poem immediately following, **"Ploja tai cunfins"** (Pioggia sui confini):

> Fantassùt, al plòuf il Sèil
> tai spolèrs dal to pais,
> tal to vis de rosa e mèil
> pluvisìn al nas il mèis.
>
> Il soreli scur di fun
> sot li branchis dai moràrs
> al ti brusa e sui cunfìns
> tu i ti ciantis, sòul, i muàrs.

Fantassùt, al rit il Sèil
tai barcòns dal to pais,
tal to vis di sanc e fièl
serenàt al mòur il mèis.

(Giovinetto, piove il Cielo sui focolari del tuo paese, sul tuo viso di rosa e miele, nuvoloso nasce il mese. Il sole scuro di fumo, sotto i rami del gelseto, ti brucia e sui confini, tu solo, canti i morti. Giovinetto, ride il Cielo sui balconi del tuo paese, sul tuo viso di sangue e fiele, rasserenato muore il mese. *La meglio gioventù.*)

In this poem, with its three quatrains of *ottonari* rhyming ABAB, CDCD, ABAB, the reader is once again confronted with the presence of life in the form of the "vis di rosa e mèil," standing out in contrast with the natural scene, the dismal, raining first day of the month, and here also, as in **"Il nini muart"** with its "sera imbarlumida" as a mirror of death, the nascent month already contains within itself, in the adjective "pluvisìn," underscored in the "soreli scur di fun" of the second quatrain, a premonition of what is to come. And so, with the inevitable passing of time, the life of the *fantassùt* wastes away, the initial "vis di rosa e mèil" becomes, with a neat assonance between "mèil" and "fièl," its opposite, "vis di sanc e fièl," contrasting with the "serenàt" of the month in the same way it had in the opening quatrain.

These opening poems [of *La meglio gioventù*], with their nostalgia-cum-consciousness situation centred on a life-death cycle, are exemplary in that they clearly delineate, right from the outset, what will be one of the constants in Pasolini's work.

—*T. O'Neill*

As a final example, let us examine the next poem, **"Dili"**:

> Ti jos, Dili, ta li cassis
> a plòuf. I cians si scunìssin
> pal plan verdùt.
>
> Ti jos, nini, tai nustris cuàrps,
> la fres-cia rosada
> dal timp pierdùt.
>
> (Vedi, Dilio, sulle acacie piove. I cani si sfiatano per
> il piano verdino. Vedi, fanciullo, sui nostri corpi la
> fresca rugiada del tempo perduto. *La meglio gioventù*).

Here too we have the same procedure as in **"Il nini muart"**: the evocation of the scene in the first tercet through a few impressionistic strokes, and the completion of that initial scene by the awareness of the poet in the second tercet, with its beautiful image of the "fres-cia rosada," of the fleeting nature of that scene and everything in it, including himself and Dilio, underlined by the rhyme between "verdùt" of the first tercet—the greenness and freshness of youth—and the truncated "pierdut" of the last line of the poem.

These opening poems, with their nostalgia-cum-consciousness situation centred on a life-death cycle, are exemplary in that they clearly delineate, right from the outset, what will be one of the constants in Pasolini's work. Usually reflected against a backcloth of seasonal change, the inevitable passing of time occurs again and again in *Poesie a Casarsa.* If one were to sum up the predominant sentiment present in these poems, one could do no better than cite—perhaps ironically—Pasolini himself, who, talking of Luzi's *Onore del vero,* said that the Florentine poet—and the judgement describes perfectly his own early poetry:

> si trova in possesso di una grande ricchezza, di un capitale inesauribile: la coscienza della morte. Profondamente originale e profondamente ovvio, il suo messaggio poetico non è che un "memento mori." (*Passione e ideologia*).

This consciousness of life being a "memento mori" has two results. On the one hand, the perfect, innocent world of youth, the "calore puro e accecante dell'adolescenza" evoked with the "carica accorante di nostalgia," subject as it is to the laws of time, will gradually be subjected to maturity, that is to say, to the imperfect, the impure, the corrupt which infiltrate it. This was already to be seen in **"Ploja tai cunfins,"** in the change from the "vis di rosa e mèil" to the "vis di sanc e fiel." More than a direct mutation from one state to another, however, more often than not there is a state of coexistence, indicative perhaps of the unwillingness of the author, although only too aware of the reality of the situation, to abandon the intensely loved world of his youth. Thus in **"O me donzel"** (O me giovinetto), the poet can define himself as a "lontàn frut peciadòur" (lontano fanciullo peccatore), where the first adjective and the noun are the attributes of innocent youth (or of nostalgia), whereas the second adjective is that of corrupt maturity (or reality). To this same category belong the "ridi scunfuartàt" (riso sconsolato) of the same poem—taken up in the "ridi pens" (grave riso) of **"David"**—and the autodefinition of the poet in **"Vilota"** as an "antìc soranel" (antico ragazzetto). This coexistence of youth-maturity, innocence-corruption, adumbrated in the poetry in dialect, will be developed fully in the Italian poems of *L'Usignolo della Chiesa Cattolica.*

On the other hand, even if there is present a consciousness of progression towards maturity and corruption, and even if this progression is only reluctantly accepted by the poet, who would prefer that his chosen world remain unchanged in its youthful innocence, there is also an increasing awareness on the poet's part that so to wish is to deny the march of history, of progress. The deliverance from maturity is at the same time a condemnation to a stunted existence. This dilemma, which will never really be resolved and which will appear constantly in all Pasolini's works, is present already in his *Poesie a Casarsa.*

Symptomatic of this is the poem **"Tornant al pais"** (Tornando al paese), constructed on a dialogue between the poet and a *fantassuta* in the town to which he now returns:

> Fantassuta, se i fatu
> sblanciada dongia il fòuc,
> coma una plantuta
> svampida tal tramònt?
> 'Jo i impiji vecius stecs
> e il fun al svuala scur
> disìnt che tal me mond
> il vivi al è sigur.'
> Ma a chel fòuc ch'al nulìs
> a mi mancia il rispìr,
> e i vorès essi il vint
> ch'al mòur tal pais. (I)
>
> . . . . .
>
> A fiesta a bat a glons
> il me país misdí.
> Ma pai pras se silensi
> ch'a puarta la ciampana!
> Sempre chè tu ti sos,
> ciampana, e cun passiòn
> jo i torni a la to vòus.
> 'Il timp a no'l si mòuf:
> jot il ridi dai paris,
> coma tai rams la ploja,
> tai vuj dai so frutíns.' (III)

(Giovinetta, cosa fai sbiancata presso il fuoco, come una pianticina che sfuma al tramonto? 'Io accendo vecchi sterpi, e il fumo vola oscuro, a dire che nel mio mondo il vivere è sicuro.' Ma a quel fuoco che profuma mi manca il respiro, e vorrei essere il vento che muore nel paese . . . Festoso nel mio paese rintocca il mezzogiorno. Ma sui prati che silenzio porta la campana! Sempre la stessa tu sei, campana, e con sgomento ritorno alla tua voce. 'Il tempo non si muove; guarda il riso dei padri, come nei rami la pioggia, negli occhi dei fanciulli.')

Here, in the opening stanza, we have the first sign of the awareness on the poet's part of the stunted existence of his beloved Casarsa in the contrast between the affectionately evoked "fantassuta" lighting the "vecius stecs" to indicate that "il vivi al è sigùr," and the poet who, although attracted by the fire, by its perfume, is also choked by its smoke. This awareness is heightened in the third stanza where the realisation that the bell ringing out across the town and the fields is that same bell of many years ago, brings home to the poet the fact that time has stood still for the folk of Casarsa. This realisation, however, is no longer a source of joy but rather a source of "passiòn" (sgomento), because the poet realises, in the words of the young girl, that "nualtris si vif, / a si vif quiès e muàrs" (noi si vive, si vive quieti e morti), where the adjective to be stressed is not so much "quiès" as "muàrs."

This awareness of condemnation inherent in the perfect, unchanging world of the Friuli, already hinted at in the poems of the first collection, will become progressively deeper in the volumes following. In **"La not di maj,"** (La notte di maggio), for example, of *Suite furlana,* the sense of time precipitating has become much more intense, and as a result of this the elegiac world of the first poems, "clar e fer" (chiaro e fermo), lightly covered with "la fres-cia rosada / dal timp pierdùt," is now reflected in the "rèit / di rujs insanganadis" (rete / di rughe sanguinose) of the young boy grownold as "àins scurìs / e nos dismintiadis / e passiòns soteradis" (anni oscuri / e notti dimenticate / e passioni sepolte), in a word, "Vita senza distìn, puartada via cu'l cuarp" (Vita senza destino, portato via col corpo).

The dilemma is perhaps presented in its clearest terms in the poem **"Mostru o pavea"** (Mostro o farfalla), with its two series of contrasting terms. On the one hand, there is the butterfly, "pavea di serèn" (farfalla di sereno), symbol of youthful innocence—"Pavea selesta sensa ombrenis" (Farfalla celeste senza ombre) which "A pausa viola ta li me violis / tal grin da li vualvis oris" (Si posa viola tra le mie viole, nel grembo delle ore uguali). On the other hand, the same butterfly is seen as a "mostru di seren" (mostro di sereno) which "mi cres / coma una nula" (mi cresce come una nube) and which "va cuntra di dut, fòut di dut, / al sporcia i flòurs di me frut" (va contro di tutto, fuori di tutto, sporca i fiori di me fanciullo). But perhaps the most telling lines of the poem are the final ones:

No, al è un mostru di speransa
tal vagu disperàt di Ciasarsa:
al mi fai no essi un omp cu'l nut
suspièt di no vej mai vivùt.

(No, è un mostro di speranza nel vuoto disperato di Casarsa: mi fa non essere un uomo col nudo sospetto di non aver mai vissuto.)

Here there is quite evidently the awareness of the harsh reality of the situation (vagu disperàt di Ciasarsa), and, along with this realisation, the consciousness of the stunted nature of a childhood not allowed to develop to maturity (nut / suspièt di no vej mai vivùt), but also, in spite of this, the inability of the poet to accept that reality, resulting in that *sineciosi*—"mostru di speransa"—that we have already seen to be a constant in his poetry.

The awareness of the existence of a different world from that of his youthful Friuli, a world of movement reflecting not only the cycle of life but also that of progress, and which therefore puts his Friuli in a completely different light, however contrasted it may be, . . . does nevertheless exist. And if proof were needed, it could be gleaned from the faint but noticeable insertion into his early poetry—of its nature essentially and highly lyrical: a poetry of mood, for the most part fragmentary and impressionistic—of a certain narrative tendency—in, for example, **"Pastorela di Narcis"** (Pastorella di Narciso)—and, along with this, a certain linguistic realism such as we find, for example, in the third stanza of **"Il diaul cu la mari"** (Il diavolo con la madre):

Bessòul al pompa l'aga, al glutàr
di aga ch'a cola cun un amàr
sunsàr tal giàtul; e al pissa
sot li stelis de la not lissa.

(Solo, pompa l'acqua, una sorsata d'acqua che cade con un amaro strepito nel rigagnolo; e piscia sotto le stelle della notte liscia.)

The tendency towards a narrative discourse, influenced no doubt by the poetry of Pavese and by the polemical, strongly realistic programmes of the numerous and, for the most part, ephemeral *riviste di poesia* of the post-war period, particularly **"La strada"**, was continued in the poems of **Romancero**. The poetry from being, as we have seen, prevalently fragmentary and impressionistic, tends now to the longer, narrative structure, rendered frequently, rhythmically, by a popular movement based to a great extent on repetition, exclamation, invocation, such as in **"Spiritual."** This tendency towards a narrative structure is accompanied by a much clearer tendency towards objectivity in which the protagonists of the poems exist in their own right and not simply as projections of the poet himself. Along with this, the dichotomy innocence-maturity, which we have seen on occasions of awareness configured as exclusion-inclusion in society in progress, is now, frequently, seen in a polemical note of poor-rich, whether it be in the anguished questions posed in **"Fiesta"**:

Aleluja aleluja aleluja!
Cui sìntia la vòus dai Anzuj?
Cui sàia la passiòn di un puòr?
Cui sìntia il ciant dai Anzuj?
E cui sàia il me nòn: Chin Cianòr?
        Cui ghi cròdia ai Anzuj?

(Aleluja aleluja aleluja! Chi sente la voce degli angeli? E chi sa il tormento di un povero? Chi sente il canto degli Angeli? E chi sa il mio nome: Chino Canòr? Chi crede negli Angeli?)

or, perhaps more clearly, in the contrast between Chino Canòr and the others, the "siòrs" (signori), emphasized polemically through repetition, in the concluding lines of the same poem:

Aleluja aleluja aleluja!
Li ciampanis a sunin pai siòrs,
jo i sint altris ciampanis:
ciampanis vissinis pai siòrs,
par me ciampanis lontanis
        coma i siòrs.

(Aleluja aleluja aleluja! Le campane suonano per i ricchi, io sento altre campane: campane vicine per i ricchi, per me campane lontane come i ricchi.)

And, as a result of this, the "dis perdut" become "dis robat" (giorni rubati) where, in the poem of that title, beauty, innocence and youth are now seen not as eternal but rather as an all too fleeting prelude to the harsh reality of maturity:

Nos ch'i sin puòrs i vin puòc timp
de zoventùt e de belessa:
mond, te pòus stà sensa de nos.
Sclafs da la nàssita i sin nos!

Pavèjs ch'a no àn mai vut belessa
muartis ta la galeta dal timp.

(Noi che siamo poveri abbiamo poco tempo di gioventù,
e di bellezza: mondo, tu puoi stare senza di noi. Schiavi
della nascita siamo noi! Farfalle che non hanno mai
avuto bellezza, morte nel bozzolo del tempo.)

This tragic note, accompanied by a polemical anti-bour-
geois tone, is best expressed in the naked realism, contrasting
with the unfulfilled dreams, of **"Vegnerà el vero Cristo"**:

No gò corajo de ver sogni:
il blú e l'onto de la tuta,
no altro tal me cuòr de operajo.

Mort par quatro franchi, operajo,
il cuòr, ti te gà odià la tuta
e pers i to piú veri sogni.

El jera un fiol ch'el veva sogni,
un fiol blú come la tuta.
Vegnerà el vero Cristo, operajo.

a insegnarte a ver veri sogni.

(Non ho coraggio di avere sogni: il blue e l'unto della
tuta, non altro nel mio cuore di operaio. Morto per due
soldi, operaio, il cuore, hai odiato la tuta e perso i tuoi
più veri sogni. Era un ragazzo che aveva sogni, un
ragazzo blu con la tuta. Verrà il vero Cristo, operaio,
a insegnarti ad avere veri sogni.)

This tendency to an ever-increasing awareness of a reality
outside of himself, alternating between acceptance and
rejection, accompanied, stylistically, by a movement from
the lyricism of the early Friulan *villotta* to the larger, epic-
narrative dimension in the later poems, culminating in the
novel *Il sogno di una cosa* of 1949-50, is undoubtedly a
reflection (or result) of the increasing ideological concern
in Pasolini—the discovery of Marx and Gramsci in 1949—
as well as a reflection of the study in those same years of
dialect and popular literature, leading to the publication of
La poesia dialettale del Novecento in 1952, and *La poesia popolare italiana* in 1955.

This thematic, stylistic development . . . in the dialect
poems from the early **Poesia a Casarsa** to those written in
Rome in the early fifties—coeval, . . . with his fundamental
critical studies of those years, and also, in part, it may be
added, with the first "Roman" novel, *Ragazzi di vita*—is
accompanied by a similar development in Pasolini's use
of dialect and his attitude towards it. . . .

Pasolini himself has briefly but succinctly described the
evolution of his use of dialect in two documents which,
taken together, provide the reader with all the necessary
details. These documents are the already cited autobiographical pages at the conclusion of *La poesia dialettale
del Novecento,* and the *nota* added to the various volumes
of dialect poetry gathered together and reprinted in
1954with the collective title of **La meglio gioventù**. . .

[Pasolini's adoption of] dialect in his novels . . . was an
attempt, a conscious attempt to resolve the linguistic impasse in which the ·literary language found itself in the
immediate post-war period. In this respect, his claim that
his regress to dialect was "coincidente . . . con la nostalgia
di chi viva—e lo sappia—in una civiltà giunta a una sua
crisi linguistica" is wholly acceptable. In addition to his
novels, the 1953 poems of **Romancero** should also be
included in this category, for there too the dialect is undoubtedly used, to adopt the poet's own expression, "nella
intera sua istituzionalità." In many respects, however, these
poems are the least interesting, the fruit of his research
into dialect and popular literature rather than of his lyrical
inspiration. What interests us more particularly here is his
use of dialect not in these later poems where, under the
ideological impetus of Gramsci and his concept of a "letteratura nazionale-popolare," Pasolini is already in the
process of developing those ideas on language which will
permeate his critical work in the fifties and have their
practical fruits in the two "Roman" novels, but rather his
use of it in the early **Poesie a Casarsa**. When Pasolini
states in the cited *nota* that "là—in the first edition, that
is to say—la 'violenza' linguistica (cui accennavo in una
noticina) tendeva a fare del parlato casarsese insieme una
koinè friulana e una specie di linguaggio assoluto, inesistente in natura, mentre qui il casarscse è riadottato nella
intera sua istituzionalità," what he says of his use of dialect in the first edition may be true, but what he says of
it in the second, namely that it is "riadottato nella intera
sua istituzionalità" is, I feel, resultant on hindsight rather
than on a radical change in the function of the casarsese
dialect used. What, then, if not "nella intera sua istituzionalità," is the way Pasolini uses dialect in these first
poems, and why is it so?

Why he uses it, of course, is easily explained. To the
absolute and perfect idyllic world of youth and innocence
there corresponds the absolute and perfect expression of
dialect. The private, unchanging world of the poet requires
a private, immutable language in order to adequately reflect the poet's chosen world of youth and innocence. In
this respect the regress "da un parlante—the poet—a un
parlante presumibilmente *più puro, più felice*" (italics mine)
is quite understandable.

More important than why he uses it, however, is *how* he
uses it, and, here again, the poet, perhaps, as I have suggested, with hindsight, lucidly accounts for his use of it.
This, he recognises, was "sensuale in origine (in tutta
l'estensione e la profondità dell'attributo)" and as such
had implicit in it both "un eccesso di ingenuità" and—
undoubtedly more important—"un eccesso di squisitezza"
with, later on, "qualche prevedibile involuzione verso più
pericolose zone letterarie (per es. Mallarmé e gli Spag-
nuoli)." It was undoubtedly this sensual, exquisite use of
dialect by him that made it, as he says in the *nota*, "una
specie di linguaggio assoluto, inesistente in natura," if one
likes, Pasolini's equivalent of what Pascoli in *Addio* calls
a "lingua di gitane, / una lingua che più non si sa." This
absolute, inexistent, if one likes, ideal rather than real
nature of the dialect is evidenced by the second paragraph
of the original *noticina*, where the poet calls upon the

non-Friulan reader to pay particular attention to certain words, which, he says, "nel testo italiano, ho variamente tradotti, ma che, in realtà, restano intraducibili."

If further confirmation of the sensual, exquisite nature of the dialect were required, it would be sufficient to note how Pasolini does not really, as he says, move from dialect in its sensual, exquisite aspects to dialect "nella intera sua istituzionalità," that is to say, from its hermetic, allusive qualitiesto its more realistic aspects in the period 1947-49, but rather how he deepens or extends the sensual, exquisite element by multiplying the choice of dialects. Thus, to the original *friulano di Casarsa,* which was itself, as he admitted in the original *noticina,* not "quello genuino, ma quello dolcemente intriso di veneto che si parla nella sponda destra del Tagliamento," there are added the Friulan of Valvasone, of Cordenons, of Cordovado, of Gleris and Bannia, as well as the Venetian dialects of Pordenone and Caorle, all used in the poems of 1947-49, and published in the 1949 edition, *Dov'è la mia patria* by the Academiuta at Casarsa. I also feel that his adoption of popular poetic forms, such as the Friulan *villotta* in the earlier poems, and, later on, the Piedmontese epico-lyrical *canzoni,* comes into the same category, that is to say, it is dictated by purely aesthetic considerations rather than a desire to adhere more closely to reality.

The sensual, exquisite, evocative musical qualities of the dialect and the poet's treatment of it (". . . non poche sono le violenze che gli ho usato per costringerlo ad un metro e a una dizione poetica") reveal close affinities both with the Symbolists and the Parnassians, a concern with heightened language and form, in a word, an adherence to *littérature.* As such Pasolini would clearly enter into that category of Italian literature, which, taking up a note of Gramsci, he defines as "una letteratura d'*élites* intellettuali, la cui storia stilistica è una storia d'individui protetti, nell'*inventio,* da una *koinè* già 'per letteratura,' da una parte, e dall'altra da una condizione sociale preservante l'io nella sua passione estetica a coltivare o le abnormità di tipo religioso o intimistico o l'*otium* classicheggiante o squisito." In other words, Pasolini too, at least at the outset of his literary career, belongs to "la torre d'avorio ermetica, implicante un'orgogliosa e in fondo condiscente religione delle lettere."

That this is so can be confirmed by the numerous influences which can be traced in his early poetry—corresponding, it may be said, to the main stages of the development of contemporary Italian poetry outlined by Luciano Anceschi in his *Le poetiche del Novecento in Italia*—and which range from Pascoli, through the *crepuscolari,* to Ungaretti and Montale, through Quasimodo and the Hermetics, to external literary influences, in the case of his early poetry, especially, I would suggest, that of Antonio Machado.

The all-pervading influence is, of course, that of Pascoli. Pasolini's interest in the poet of San Mauro and the influence of his poetry on him started early and can be quite clearly documented. From his *tesi di laurea* to the article in *Convivium* in 1947, and again in the opening number of *Officina* in 1955, Pascoli forms a constant *obbligato* in the critical writings of Pasolini and remains just as strongly an influence in **Le ceneri di Gramsci** as in the early poetry.

In his early poetry, of course, in addition to certain metrical borrowings, it is easy to see the link between Pasolini's world of youth and innocence and Pascoli's *poetica del fanciullino.* It is undoubtedly from this theory—and its practical results in poetry—that Pasolini's early verse derives its rich, detailed, impressionistic mixture of sound and colour that is so common in Pascoli's *Myricae.*

However, Pasolini's poetry is much more than a simple mimesis, much more, that is, than a simple external repetition of Pascolian stylistic features. Rather it is a conscious adoption of one of those features, what he calls "il particolare," which merits examination in some detail since it confirms, while stressing its Pascolian origin, what I individuated in the opening pages of this paper as Pasolini's use of the objective correlative. The source of Pasolini's theorization of this aspect of Pascoli's *poiesis* is his 1947 *Convivium* article "Pascoli e Montale." This essay, which is one of his earliest, is, perhaps because of its dating, almost as penetrating and acute as his slightly later one on Ungaretti, since both are singularly free from the strait jacket of ideology which was to characterize to a great extent his later essays of the fifties. Starting, as his mentor, Contini, would have done, from the individual word—in this case, the distinctly Pascolian vocabulary, *frullo, volo, grembo,* adopted in Montale's poem, *In limine:* "Il frullo che tu senti non è un volo / ma il commuoversi dell'eterno grembo"—Pasolini moves out to examine Pascoli's limited, because unconscious, use of "il particolare," especially its visual qualities, in the *Myricae* and the better poems of the *Canti di Castelvecchio;* and then goes on to examine how Montale, in the wake of the lesson of Symbolism, develops consciously what Pascoli had used unconsciously. He then illustrates how the "stupendo" in Pascoli, which was to all intents and purposes simply one of the aspects of the *poetica del fanciullino,* is, for the most part, innovative merely in language and not in substance, and how it is only in the better of his poems, that is in those "legati a un particolare visivo o, insomma, fisico, in cui si innesta una 'metafisica' tutta di parole" (Convivium), that he manages to do what Montale will later consciously and constantly do. In the second half of this essay, centred on a telling comparison between Pascoli's *Vischio* and Montale's *Casa dei doganieri,* he defines the "metafisica" of the "particolare" as:

> . . . lo scaturire improvviso nella coscienza di un pensiero, che era stato elaborato nel subcosciente, al contatto di un "riflesso condizionato," scelto e riconosciuto tra i simboli del mondo esteso; è il substrato emotivo che viene tratto alla luce secondo un canone puramente estetico.

I feel it is quite evident from this definition, from what he later individuates in both Pascoli and Montale as "la distensione del loro attimo lirico nella memoria, uno storicizzarsi della loro emozione," the similarity with the objectified, emotive, memorial movement . . . in some of Pasolini's own early poems.

Pascoli, in addition to providing the source of the Montalian element in Pasolini's poetry, is also the ultimate source of his crepuscular element, to wit, his sense of death. Starting from *Il giorno dei morti* of the *Myricae,* to the "estate fredda dei morti" of *Novembre,* and "il vanire e lo sfiorire, / e i crisantemi, il fiore della morte" of *I gattici,* Pascoli's poetry is continually permeated with a sense of death, of time inexorably passing, perhaps best summed up in the final lines of *Il ritardo:*

> Oh! tardi! Il nido ch'è due nidi al cuore,
> la fame in mezzo a tante cose morte;
> e l'anno è morto, ed anche il giorno muore,
> e il tuono muglia, e il vento urla più forte,
> e l'acqua fruscia, ed è già notte oscura,
> e quello ch'era non sarà mai più.

It is precisely this "interno terrore," this "nozione della morte e del disfacimento del mondo"—to use the poet's own terms from his essay on Giotti—, deriving from Pascoli, that Pasolini has in common not only with the poet of San Mauro but also with the *crepuscolari,* especially, I would say, with Corazzini; and which, as I have indicated earlier, is an indispensable complement to the world of adolescence evoked in the early poems.

The influence of Pascoli, and, through him, of the *crepuscolari* and Montale, can, as I would hope to have demonstrated, be fairly well substantiated from the text themselves, and is, as in the essays, the predominant influence. The influence of Ungaretti, and of Quasimodo and the strictly Hermetic line, is, although present, much more evanescent, and, consequently, more difficult to pin down with precision.

In general terms I would say that if the highly lyrical, fragmentary and impressionistic poetry of the early years, completely lacking in any narrative structure, is, in the final analysis, also derivative from Pascoli, where with the *Myricae* there was initiated that process of disintegration of the poetic form which was to characterize Italian poetry in the late nineteenth and early twentieth century, it is also, in no small part, a reflection of the hermetic, allusive nature of poetry in the thirties and forties, and as such, along with his choice of subject-matter (adolescence) and language (dialect), is a reaction against the incursions of the fascist régime on the autonomy of art.

More specifically the Hermetic influence is to be seen in specific images, consciously or unconsciously derivative from the Hermetic poets, and also, on occasions, in a daring use of language, again typical of the early Hermetics.

In the first category, that of the derivative image, one could include, for example, the first two stanzas of **"Ale-luja"** where, in the first, the dying goldfinch echoes Ungaretti's "Ma non morire di lamento / come un cardellino accecato" of *Agonia,* while, in the second, the image of the "fanciullo di luce" (frut di lus) would seem to be a direct borrowing from the opening lines of the 57 poem of Onofri's *Vincere il drago!:* "Con un'arancia in mano, abita il prato / un fanciullo di luce e d'aria tenue." **"La Domenica Uliva,"** the final poem of the first volume, although prefaced in its first edition with the opening lines of Ungaretti's

La madre, would in its dialogue between mother and son seem to be modelled rather on Quasimodo's *Laude 29 aprile 1945.* Similarly, in the next volume, **Suite furlana,** the introduction of a realistic note in, for example, **"Ciants di un muart"** (Canti di un morto,) with its precise date, "vuei XIII Zenar MCMXLIV" (oggi XIII gennaio MCMXLIV), would seem modelled on a similar technique used by Quasimodo in that same period in *Giorno dopo giorno:* in, for example, the titles of such poems as *19 gennaio 1944, Milano, agosto 1943, Anno Domini MCMXLVII.*

In the second category, that of a daring use of language, individual combinations of adjective and noun as, for example, in "colòur smarit" (colore smarrito) of **"Ciant da li ciampanis"** (Canto delle campane) belong to that typically Hermetic combination one frequently finds in Luzi's *Avvento notturno,* such as, for example, the "vie pensierose" of *Passi,* and the "albero increscioso" of *Periodo;* as do poems such as the **"Lengas dai frus di sera"** (Linguaggi dei fanciulli di sera) and, especially I would say, the complete section of **"Lieder."**

What, finally, of the influence of the contemporary Spanish poets, especially, I would suggest, Machado? That he was familiar with the Spanish poets in general is clear from that autobiographical-critical page I have already quoted, where he talks about "qualche prevedibile involuzione verso più pericolose zone letterarie (per es. Mallarmé e gli Spagnoli)"; that he was familiar, perhaps more especially, with Machado we can gather from the direct quotation from the Spanish poet's *Retrato* which prefaced **Suite furlana.** To be more specific, however, is somewhat hazardous. To be sure, in Pasolini's early poems the time of day that recurs most frequently is the evening, and this is very similar to the *tarde* of Machado. The very description of the evening given by Pasolini in **"Il nini muart":** "Sera imbarlumida" (Sera luminosa) may even be a direct calque of Machado's "¡Oh tarde luminosa!," the opening line of Poem LXXVI. Similarly the frequent recurrence of the fountain as a leit-motif in his early poetry—the "fontana di aga dal me pais" of the *Dedica*—may betray a Machadian influence as may the equally frequent recurrence of bells, although, in this latter case, their frequent presence in both Corazzini and, needless to say, Pascoli, makes any precise location of sources very difficult. The great wealth of visual detail that one finds in Machado's poetry and which is also evident in Pasolini's turns up frequently in Pascoli, so that it may not be inappropriate to say that Pasolini is attracted to and influenced by Machado precisely because of the Pascolian qualities of the Spanish poet's verse. In addition to this—and in more general terms—it may simply be that he is attracted to a poet who, regardless of differences that undoubtedly exist in detail, is, in his general development, very close to him: both poets' early work is, in many respects, based on a contrast between a past happiness and a present bitterness, centred around a memorial evocation of youthful innocence, mìrrored or identified with a precise geographical location: in Pasolini, Friuli with its "vita rustica, resa epica da una carica accorante di nostalgia;" in Machado, the province of Soria:

En la desesperanza y en la melancolía
de tu recuerdo, Soria, mi corazón se abreva,
Tierra de alma, toda, hacia la tierra mía,
por los floridos valles, mi corazón te lleva.

And just as Pasolini was to move, if ever so slightly, from
an evocative, memorial poetry to verse in a more realistic
vein as a result of the effect upon him of the Resistance,
so too Machado, as a result of the Spanish Civil War,
moved towards a more *engagé* poetry.

Perhaps, in conclusion, the best summation of **Poesie a
Casarsa,** thematically and stylistically, is provided by the
concluding lines of Maria Luisa Spaziani's *Sera di vento:*

Vorrei cogliervi tutte, o mie nel tempo
ebbre, sfogliate voci lungo l'arida
corona dell'inverno,
e ricomporvi in musica, parole
sopra uno stelo eterno.

—that is to say, the voices of youthful innocence, recollected in the winter of maturity, and translated and rescued from the laws of time in the style and form of poetry.

Norman MacAfee (essay date 1980-81)

SOURCE: "'I Am a Free Man': Pasolini's Poetry in
America," in *Italian Quarterly,* Vols. XXI-XXII, Nos. 82-
83, Fall-Winter, 1980-81, pp. 99-105.

[*In the following excerpt, MacAfee focuses on the appropriateness of Pasolini's civil poems to a post-fascist
society.*]

Pasolini's Italian poems were made as civil poems, in bright
contrast to the then still dominant mode of poetic discourse, hermeticism—whose style was, I think, a function
of its poets living under the growth and success of fascism.
Pasolini's Italian poems, from 1954 to his death, are discourse appropriate to a post-fascist society, and fully use
a climate of freer speech. Pasolini's long civil poems link
him to Whitman and Pound and Ginsberg, but he is a real
original—and just as the films of this film-poet have had
roughest going in America, of all the non-Communist
world, the poems will also upset some ideas about what a
poem can't be—but I think the soil is already prepared by
the three aforementioned American poets, and that Pasolini's poetry and career will have a deep effect on American poetry, and thus on American life.

American poetry 1980 is at a point of particular opportunity.
For at least ten years a network of poetry queries and magazines has been in the process of organizing itself. The out-
lets are there for publishing good and great work, as well as
the usual vast amount of mediocre writings. But hermeti-
cisms of all kinds abound, and an unworkable hermetic esthetic has hold of most of the organs that publish poetry. The
poet is still at the outskirts of the society, however. And
Pasolini's example of gaining and maintaining a central place

as poet in the society will I hope be noted by all poets.
I think his poetry will in fact have an effect on ours similar
to its impact on Italian poetry, because American poetry takes
its cues largely from master poets who are hermetics (Whitman, Pound, and Ginsberg excepted) rather than civil poets.
Though Pound supported fascism and Pasolini his own
form of "never-orthodox" Marxism, it was special versions of each, and both poets share many qualities—most
importantly, they included politics in their poetry, and they
were tireless in promoting the wellbeing of culture. . . .

More than anything else, what sets . . . most of Pasolini's
work apart from ways of thinking that collide with Power—
the power of the superpowers, for example—is the element of homosexuality. . . . Pasolini made an effort to be
honest about his homosexuality, if for no other reason
than to avoid the blackmail inevitable to those who have
something to hide. The boys and young men he was attracted to had mythic status for him; as he writes in a late
poem, "A boy in his first loves is none other than the
fecundity of the world." Two subproletarian boys spark
the long poem **"The Religion of My Time"** from 1959
which is one of the great visions of Italy and the world at
that time. His relations with peasant and subproletarian
males were completely in line with his politics. His behavior as lover of them and memorializer of them in film
and poem causes a whole group hitherto almost unseen in
art to be brought forward. . . . [The] long poem, **"A
Desperate Vitality,"** written in 1963, . . . illustrates the
method well: the poet has been interviewed by a newspaper
reporter. The poem is filled with cinematic touches, with
references to Godard's film *Contempt* (based on a story by
Alberto Moravia then being filmed in Rome; one of the first
lines is: "As in a film by Godard"); the reporter asks
"What's the function of the Marxist?" The poet answers and
the politics and homosexuality are brought together

There are two loves, . . . of the boy ("a boy in his first
loves is none other than the fecundity of the world"—that
is, the future) and "another love: life through the centuries"—
which is the same as the "fecundity of the world."

In another 1963 poem, **"Plan of Future Works,"** Pasolini
expressed the need for an alliance of minorities, and, as a
homosexual and outsider, his solidarity with other outcast
groups—such as blacks and Jews. Since Pasolini was an
outsider, and grew more and more self-reliant, his relationship with homosexuality in Italy was different from
what it might be here today. The drawing of homosexuals
into a political and social group is part self-protection.
Pasolini didn't have this kind of group situation in his
Italy till late in his life, and by then he was such an op-
poser it is doubtful he would have joined for long. In
America this tension between individual and group is usually tilted toward the individual, which makes organizing
homosexuals difficult. But the less regulated homosexual
life in Italy is fraught with the dangers of having a sexual
life outside the homosexual circle. He seems to have been
most attracted to young heterosexuals. This linked him to
the general life in Italy—the point at which young men
have left their parents and have not yet become parents,
but will, as their mark of virility. His killer's reason for

the murder is that he didn't want to be sodomized. Pelosi's refusal and subsequent crime and lenient punishment dovetail nicely. Sexually conventional or at least hypocritical society nods its head understandingly and gives the killer nine years.

I have seemed to stray far away from the original starting point, which was Pasolini's departure from hermeticism, and his celebration of free speech. But a true coming out from hermeticism entailed this other, homosexual, coming out.

I can only guess how Pasolini's poems will affect American poetry and culture, since only a few of the poems have appeared in magazines. . . .

Pasolini tends to concentrate not on things, as many moderns have—from Rilke to William Carlos Williams to Charles Simic—but rather on a general portrayal of the world—or at least an Italy not misrepresentative of the world in its conflicts and ideologies. And on a world full of people, whether the handsome teenagers maturing into mediocrity in **"Reality"** or the vulgar interviewer in **"A Desperate Vitality."**

Cinema as a mass art has affected all the other arts—the novel, the still photograph—and poetry has not been immune. Hart, Crane, Pound, Williams are early examples. Pasolini is the child not just of poetry but also of film. He wrote his first poem at seven and came into contact with both arts earlier than that. The films have outbursts of poetry—often verbal, as in *Porcile,* when Julian reveals his manias, in verse; and visual, in a directness that isn't documentary, in a subjectivity (the handheld camera). In the poems we have not only the obvious references of a film director in **"A Desperate Vitality"** but also the cinematic techniques in that poem's jump cuts, in the quick breathtaking shots of landscapes in **"The Ashes of Gramsci"** and the whole section of landscape writing in **"The Tears of the Excavator"** of 1956—a section that would be perhaps better filmed than written.

Pasolini, as word poet and film poet, dragged poetry further out of the cloister than any other great poet this century. In the poem **"Reality,"** he defines the title word as the "practical end of my poetry" and later in a 1968 interview talks of his coming to film as an "explosion of my love for reality." In a sense his film poetry was the "practical end" of his verse poetry. His poetry will bring some shibboleths into American poetry: "reality," for one; another: "class struggle." The 3-decade-long debate he had with Marxism humanized the poetry. This type of debate has been almost impossible in American poetry because of the bias against ideas—especially Marxist ideas—in poetry and in society at large, which most poetry merely reflects.

A further link between Pasolini and Americans is their common effort at creating roots. His earliest published poems were in the dialect of Friuli; he founded an Institute of Friulian Language to further the regional culture in 1946, he later edited anthologies of regional folk songs.

The structure of the long poems is astounding. A poem like the 30-page **"Religion of My Time"** holds together amazingly well. Perhaps only in his last two films—*Arabian Nights* and *Salò*—are the structural feats as astonishing.

[From] **"Reality,"** another major poem from 1963, [comes] the line "I am a free man." . . . [Three] pages after the line "I am a free man," there is this line, which should be taken much more as a simple description of the toll taken on one who is free than as a prophecy: "Free with a freedom that's massacred me."

Allen Mandelbaum (essay date 1980-81)

SOURCE: "'*Ah Mistica / Filologia!*' Rereading Pasolini," in *Italian Quarterly,* Vols. XXI-XXII, Nos. 82-83, Fall-Winter, 1980-81, pp. 95-8.

[*In the following essay, Mandelbaum comments on what he deems the "over-sympathetic relation between Pasolini and his audience."*]

Few poets have declared their own bankruptcy as resolutely as did Pasolini: *"Io? Io sono inaridito e superato,"* uttered in parentheses, parentheses less complex than Marvell's "my fruits are only flowers" but certainly *echt* Pasolini. Like Eliot's rueful assessment of "twenty years largely wasted" at the end of "east Coker"; or Swinburne's "least song" at the end of "By the North Sea"; or Montale's musings in "Mediterranee"; or the anti-pride of Pound in the *Pisan Cantos*—this is not a humility *topos,* but the product of what I should call an adherent I, an epistolary I (the I of Ungaretti's final strophe in "Monologhetto": *"Poeti, poeti, ci siamo messi—Tutte le maschere;—Ma uno non è che la propria persona."*)

But oxymoronically, no poet has so resolutely hedged himself against those who would even cite, let alone anatomize, these declarations of bankruptcy. The first of his *Umiliato e offeso* epigrams is addressed to Catholic critics, but one need not be Catholic to feel the force of the elbow—or the stiletto—in **"Ai critici cattolici"**

> Molte volte un poeta si accusa e calunnia,
>   esagera, per amore, il proprio disamore,
> esagera, per punirsi, la propria ingenuità,
>   è puritano e tenero, duro e alessandrino.
> E anche troppo acuto nell'analisi dei segni
>   delle eredità, delle sopravvivenze:
> ha anche troppo pudore nel concedere
>   qualcosa alla ragione e alla speranza.
> Ebbene, guai a lui! Non c'è un istante
>   di esitazione: basta solo citarlo!

So much defensiveness-aggressiveness and auto-aggressiveness consumed, preempted much vital space, space that was already apportioned among the novel, cinema, and critical prose in addition to poetry. Apportioned, but, of course, also augmented. And shadowed by Pasolini's deep awareness of the paralimnions of failure, of the marginal status of poetry itself, and of the solitude it necessarily involved.

But however—thematically—Pasolini's verse embraced that solitude, he was reluctant to center his life therein. But whatever the later reader can say is already comprehended in Pasolini's own depiction of that situation. See **"Versi del testamento"**:

> . . . il tuo desiderio di solitudine non potrebbe esser
> più soddisfatto,
> e allora cosa ti aspetta, se ciò che non è considerato
> solitudine
> è la solitudine vera, quella che non puoi accettare?
> Non c'è cena o pranzo o soddisfazione del mondo,
> che valga una camminata senza fine per le strade
> povere,
> dove bisogna essere disgraziati e forti, fratelli dei
> cani.

One may see-say-lament that out of that solitude there grew an *over*-sympathetic relation between Pasolini and his audience, a connubium not unlike that which overtook the later American Auden or the Eliot of the verse dramas—an overintimacy that promotes a forensic rhetorical dimension. (Witness Pasolini's **"In morte del realismo"** [281-283]—for me a poem of relapse and disturbing poetic inertia—where rhetorical, already overpercussive Shakespeare is brought back to Rome—and, there arrived, grows even more ponderous, overweight). Such overintimacy has the additional drawback of severely curbing both the metaphorical range and the impetus of lexical asymmetries, wrenchings, projections, volatile fountains (not quite **"Fontana di aga del me pais"**).

Unlike poets who do not break the bread of Catholicism with their audience, poets in secular climes where there is tremendous pressure on the word "all," generating the trombonelike ubiquitousness and—often—gratuitousness of "all," Pasolini, with a double *chiesa* at hand, has all the standard lexical mediations he needs, and he neglects few of them. In the 1950's, it is the clandestine capitalization of *"il puro"* even when *"puro"* masquerades as an adjective. Of *"il puro"* and of *"innocenza."* And then there is the panoply of explicit capitalizations: *Italia* (which is Dante's *umile Italia* and Petrarch's *Italia mia*); and then *Nazione Classe, Sogno, Popolo, Autorità, Anarchia, Commissione Interne, CGIL* (this last acronym consciously invoked as *Divinità Alata*), *Stato, Lingua, Ragione, Speranza.* How many personifications populate this world! A population richest in the clash of *amore* and *ragione*.

The counters acquired flesh when moved—by one of the astutest men of our time—not only across the poetic grid but across the meditative board where he who plays may indeed lose all. On rereading, these counters often lack the force of driven apparitions—the inevitable evocations that overtake the lectern, divan, or even the *prato* of the poet. Pasolini's answer to the query of the rereader would of course be: they were *always* oppressive, unsummoned specters; they never had any substance beyond the intertial weight of the real. Bureaucracy and organization had long since bloated and devalued them:

only the native or the *venduti* could ever have granted them visionary status. They formed, retroactively, part of a *"ridicolo decennio"* and *"ridicoli decenni."*

What did have visionary status, then? I suppose one would have to say toponomastics. What an enormous gazetteer of Italy—and not a gazetteer for gluteists, for those content to sit on their sedentary *chairs*. But a peripatetic gazetteer that ranges up and down the peninsula with a flow like that of Dante's Benaco or, for us, the orography of the Apennines seen from the air. And all those proper nouns carry an implicit vocative.

And yet, and yet. One's expectations seem often thwarted. When *compositio* is not problematic on a line by line basis, when the problem of form is not so obsessive (as has often been the case in this century), when a poet—as did Pasolini—has a relatively constant metrical module that need not be called into question at each point, then—one might think—the decreased pressures of *compositio* would give larger space to *inventio* in its modern sense. But that is not the case with Pasolini. One thing that blocks his *inventio*, is, I believe, the generic nature of some of the lexical counters I have referred to above. Another, a kind of brutal, even raw honesty in Pasolini that finds the sublime nauseating. And yet this same man is not reluctant to fall back on sententious, often Polonius-like but as often unforgettable conclusions to his poems—conclusions that summon *"tenerezza eroica d'un immortale stagione,"* *"il profumo del sole,"* *"piedi di Angeli,"* *"disperazione senza un po' di speranza."*

But there is, I think, a somewhat deeper layer, an implicit political fable, the one *inventio* that rises out of the varied ground that Pasolini seeded. That fable declares: There was a chance for political *inventio*, but it was not realized—*"la Rivoluzione non è più che un sentimento,"* The poet *can* become an aretologist—a praiser of the gods—but to do so would be to produce magical papyri, and as Arnold Ehrhardt has it: "Such a magic papyrus presents an unwholesome mixture of human, all too human, desires; meaningless so-called magic words; fanciful, sometimes disgusting magic actions and recipes; and finally invocations and prayers, which stand out by their higher stylistic level. All magic invocations, and ours are not exceptions to the rule, follow a line of combined blackmail and flattery." And I think that Pasolini is a man of the enlightenment, a rejector of magic papyri.

If poetic *inventio* is premature, it is not because history has ended but because it has not yet begun. Thus, in the *"ultima forma—storica di Roma"*—a phrase preceded by the *qui* of Pasolini (a *qui* that is not the pseudo-deictic *here* of Eliot's *Gerontion*)—that historic form is, for Pasolini, a *pre*-historic form. The image of Rome that haunted the foreigner and some Italians (witness the diligence of Morel-Fatio, who shows us a text of Janus Vitalis feeding into Castiglione, Du Bellay, and Quevedo, to which a bleary scrutinist might add Spenser, Pound, Lowell, and J. V. Cunningham) was an image of its ruins. Nor—some say—was Gibbon averse to meditating on ruins. But those were most often strangers seeking Rome in Rome and finding "naught of Rome in Rome at all." Pasolini almost finds all (or at least half of all: Franco Fido will have attended to the Friulian half earlier today). But Belli was not a stranger, and Pasolini knows only too well *"la papale itterizia del Belli"* as well as the Rome of Ungaretti, which we conventionally call Baroque. He knew the linguistic travail of Belli, and certainly Pasolini's dialect concerns in his 1952 Guanda volume were a little less elegiac in their mode and a little less putative than Mengaldo's recent dialect inclusions. But he would ask: When will the periphery become center? And can the poet ever abdicate his role as protagonist of the periphery without falling into banality? His, then, are the gods of house and place—or better, of the unhoused in an ineluctable place. And implicit in insisting on those gods of house and place is his remarkable renunciation of Italy's centrality of Europeanness or of any Italian equivalent to Gaullist *gloire*. In a world of English and Russian, Rome becomes linguistic romance. It does not preside over its subproletariat, Friulian, Provençal, the swarm of emarginated tongues— it joins them. But it joins them as a yet—and necessarily— imperfect instrument.

Marco Vallora tries to read a specific, unfuzzy mannerism and metaliterature into Pasolini. One can do that by day, but in a long night, it washes with difficulty. (But also see where *"non mi resta che fare ogetto della mia poesia la poesia"* is terminal pathos.) Politics infects language, but language is not capable of self-redemption or self-purgation or the solace of a *sistema di segni*—a system of signs. And for Pasolini, there were no hypersigns, no seductive as well as gratuitous systemic titanism. Though language can pour back into politics, possibly purifying it, Pasolini's invective against the users of language, himself included, is too resolute to apotheosize any *ars grammatica*. For him the *cucina* is not a *fucina*. *"Ah mistica/filologia"* is the vocative that may delude us now, but its full announcement awaits another *polis*—and other poets. If the early Lukàcs was aware not only of his predecessors, but of his successors, what I should call a John-the-Baptist syndrome, Pasolini shares that syndrome—consciously.

Anthony Oldcorn (essay date 1980-81)

SOURCE: "Pasolini and the City: *Rome 1950: A Diary*," in *Italian Quarterly*, Vols. XXI-XXII, Nos. 82-83, Fall-Winter, 1980-81, pp. 107-19.

[*In the following excerpt, Oldcorn examines the poet's formative years in Rome and how they are reflected in his work, particularly in the early verse journal,* Rome 1950: A Diary.]

The verse journal **Roma 1950, diario** (**Rome 1950: A Diary**) remained unknown until 1960, when it was published in a limited edition of 600 copies by Vanni Scheiwiller of Milan. This "book of hours," which chronicles the poet's state of mind in his moments of rest from servile work—his first awakenings, his evenings, holidays, the noontide siesta—is a slim volume of fifteen short poems

in more or less regular unrhymed hendecasyllables (the Italian equivalent of blank verse). With the same timid indecision that characterizes the psychological attitudes it represents, the volume hovers between tradition and innovation, between literary freedom and convention, between open and closed form. The number of lines varies from 11 to 28 (twice 14), though most of the compositions are closer to eleven lines than to twenty-eight, while the final poem is actually fourteen lines long. The average length makes us suspect that the ghost at least of the confessional sonnet form (". . . with this key—Shakespeare unlocked his heart; the melody—Of this small lute gave ease to Petrarch's wound . . .") lurks somewhere in the background. In an earlier age, another poet might well have unburdened himself of the emotions here expressed in a traditional sonnet sequence. The verse is not free. The classic Italian eleven-syllable line is respected (or almost always), although it is handled with the rhetoric of anti-rhetoric. The poems are in Standard Italian, not in the Friulian dialect Pasolini had previously favored. They do retain something of the introspective lyric atmosphere of the dialect poems, but, given the urban setting, they lack, apart from an occasional evocative Proustian aside, their pastoral imagery. The studied concern to avoid all undue emphasis and sublimity of diction, the bleached voice, the deliberate pushing of understatement to the limits of banality, show how important the stylization imposed by the dialect filter had been in creating the peculiarly rapt tone of the earlier poems. In saying this, I do not imply that the present poems are unprecious and unstylized. The preciosity is there, it is of a different order.

The poems document a moral crisis, precipitated by his recent experience of social ostracism, a crisis that remains essentially unresolved, despite the apparent movement toward some kind of resolution. It remains unresolved, I think, because the particular literary tradition in which Pasolini chose to address it did not offer the tools necessary to its solution. By the mid-twentieth century, the tradition, venerable though it was and elegant, was a bankrupt tradition a tradition of mystification. From the standpoint of true moral understanding, the tradition was, in Eldridge Cleaver's phrase, not part of the solution but part of the problem. The sense of physical confinement, of entrapment that pervades the poems corresponds to the poet's moral entrapment in a system and a discourse not of his own making, to his inability to free his thinking of the spurious Latin Catholic bourgeois standards by which he had been condemned. Instead of the "transvaluation of values" proposed by a writer like Sade, for instance, or by Rimbaud, or by Nietzsche, instead of transcending or jettisoning the traditional categories of moral judgment, Pasolini finds himself attempting merely to extend those categories to accommodate moral phenomena they were never meant to embrace, phenomena incompatible with them, which they were in fact devised to exclude. He fails to recognize that, by bourgeois standards, his homosexuality was a qualitative, and not simply a quantitative transgression. When he pleads that his was "a love repressed, astonished to be guilty," he seems to remain blind to the fact that the Romantic appeal for understanding ("pietà non che perdono") could only be advanced in the case of relations between the sexes. The homoerotic impulse is not excess but *other,* inadmissible on any grounds, anathema. Far from being the radical stance the occasion called for, Pasolini's is still, for want of a better word, a Petrarchan reaction, a palliative rather than a solution, in which the perfectly elegant and stylized statement of the dilemma is offered as a substitute for resolution. "Because the pain is eased in singing," "perché cantando il duol si disacerba." Pasolini attempts to come to terms with his guilt (I speak, of course, not of an objective state, but of a subjective feeling) rhetorically, not by defiantly asserting his "difference" (as he seems to do upon occasion, though by no means consistently, in his later career), but by arguing that his desire, far from being "unnatural," is in fact continuous with the desires sanctioned, even sanctified, by society. In condemning him, we are to conclude, society is revealing itself to be inconsistent. Yet another source of confusion are the poet's self-martyrizing tendencies, which lead him to cast himself in the role (a role he will frequently return to, at times with a more radical grasp of its potential for subversion) of the victimized and persecuted Christ—a Christ closer, it must be admitted, in the present instance, to Corazzini than to Jacopone or Matthew. If we have here a Romantic appeal to the morality of passion, all too readily the passion tends to become confused with the Passion. But, given the prevailing tone of calculated understatement, one is left ultimately with the impression, not of a supreme offering of self, so much as of a wounded, rebuffed and mortified sensuality.

[Rome] stands for life, ordinary everyday life in all its reassuring monotony, life from which Pasolini feels himself to be excluded.

—Anthony Oldcorn

A word now about Pasolini's immediate literary antecedents. One observes in these compositions a wilful rejection of the hieratic reigning models of modernism and the specifically Italian style of "hermeticism" (a preciously allusive variety of imagism), and a return, partial at least, to earlier, less aristocratic models. This trait Pasolini shares with the so-called neorealistic school of poets (with whom Pasolini had otherwise few sympathies), in particular with Cesare Pavese, who committed suicide in late August 1950, just as the poems of *Rome 1950* were being written (poem 11 mentions that it is October). Reading the first poem (**"Adulto? Mai,"** "An adult? Never?"), one cannot help remembering the Shakespearean epigraph to Pavese's last novel, *La luna e i falò*: "Ripeness is all!" The dominant tone of the poems, which Pasolini himself might have described as "epistolare" (familiar without being excessively colloquial) or "depresso" (in a minor key), is reminiscent, not so much of a vague and generic "crepuscolarismo" as of certain more distinctive poetic voices. One of these may be the voice of **"l'uomo di pena,"** Giuseppe Ungaretti, known to have been Pasolini's chief predilec-

tion at the time. But, more than of Ungaretti, one is reminded of those poets whom Pasolini calls the "masters in the shadows" ("maestri in ombra") of twentieth-century Italian poetry, the poets whose names are associated with the Florentine periodical *La Voce*—the breathless spiritual anxiety of Clemente Rebora, the resigned and astonished stoicism of Camillo Sbarbaro. Like the work of these pre-hermetic poets, these poems of Pasolini's have a primarily moral, abstract and spiritual, rather than a concrete pictorial dimension.

Although the volume is entitled *Rome 1950: A Diary,* the setting, such as it is, is an indoor one, a womb without much of a view, the objective correlative, we earlier suggested, of the poet's moral predicament. The city is outside, a backdrop, heard rather than seen, present to the speaker's meditation in its attenuated crepuscular emblems. The city stands for life, ordinary everyday life in all its reassuring monotony, life from which Pasolini feels himself to be excluded. The story the volume tells, if it can be said to tell a story (the story is in any case, as we have said, more intentional than actual), is one of *recueillement* and rebirth. In the final poems, we emerge, down "an old familiar corridor" (poem 13), into an alien, rather nightmarish Rome (poem 14), recognizable, albeit in the muted code of the present text, as the hallucinatory Rome of Pasolini's early expressionistic prose pieces. The prose poems were the direction of the future, the direction that would permit his true originality the scope it needed to come to the fore. In the rarefied lyric atmosphere of *Rome 1950,* the false path of self-pity and self-absorbed narcissism is exorcised. Was it because they were too personal that the poems were not published for a decade? By the time they did come out, Pasolini had emerged as a force to be reckoned with on the Italian literary scene. In publishing them, one imagines the poet looking back with his customary delicate urgency of compassion upon the vulnerability and fragility of this former self, a self he had buried deep within him, but not put behind him. To his readers he seems to be saying: Look how far I have come!

Wallace P. Sillanpoa (essay date 1981)

SOURCE: "Pasolini's Gramsci," in *Modern Language Notes,* Vol. 96, No. 1, January, 1981, pp. 120-37.

[*In the following excerpt, Sillanpoa investigates the influence of Antonio Gramsci on Pasolini's work.*]

When discussing those who perhaps most influenced the thought of the late Pier Paolo Pasolini, poet, novelist, critic and filmmaker, one critic recently spoke of "il *suo* Gramsci." Implied in this possessive is the highly personal interpretation that Pasolini attached to the example and writings of Antonio Gramsci, revolutionary political theorist whose famous notebooks survived their author's death in 1937 after eleven years of Fascist imprisonment. What follows attempts to qualify this implication through a survey of Pasolini's writings directly linked to a reading of Gramsci. Demonstration should emerge to bolster those claims of a subjective interpretation whose ultimate complexity can best be described generally as a curious admixture of confraternity and contradiction.

The closing section of **L'usignolo della Chiesa Cattolica** (1958), containing verse composed between 1943 and 1949, carries the subtitle, *La scoperta di Marx*. War and the Italian Partisan response had transformed Pasolini, leading him to the conviction that life demands "qualcos'altro che amore/per il proprio destino." For the young Pasolini, that "something other" prompted a probe into an alternative world view, grounded in reason, synthesized in Marx, and calling for a commitment to popular political struggle. Within a short period of time, this newly explored world view began to intrude upon the sentimental universe of the poet's earlier verse, linguistically and thematically circumscribed by his maternal Friuli.

Pasolini's idiolect thus evolved into the idiom of a wider historical and class perspective, but without ever causing the poet to dismiss his previous experience. Pasolini's topocentric perspective widened, that is, and allowed the peasant world of Friuli, a world of primitive innocence and religious fatality, to assume even greater mythic proportions in the course of this investigation of a Marxist rationalism. During these years, first as a witness to Partisan struggles, and then as a sympathizer to the uprisings of Friulan day laborers, Pasolini participated in the local politics of the Italian Communist Party. But also in these years, he helped found, together with other young Friulans, the *Academiuta de lengua furlana,* a small circle dedicated to the philological study and social diffusion of Friulan language and culture. Thus Pasolini's early formation joined a sentimental attachment to the linguistic and cultural environment of his adolescence to an examination of Marxist rationalism and political ideology. . . .

In 1948 Pasolini was forced to abandon his region and his people under personal and political circumstances that left deep scars. Amid the disinherited of Rome's shantytowns (*borgate*), he felt painfully torn from the world of his youth. That emotional and ethical energy previously nourished through his contact with Friuli was thus diverted to these emarginated urban poor who, lured by the promises of postwar industrial reconstruction, were leaving behind their Southern agrarian communities to find themselves amid the wretched conditions of those inhabiting the periphery of many large Italian cities. The poet's myth of an atemporal and a-rational Friuli was hence transferred to the neoprimitive and socially incohesive topography of Rome's dispossessed. Pasolini's presence among these poor of the Roman *borgate,* his passion for their dialect and street-wise slang, his fascination with their desperate vitalism and what he considered their prepolitical rebelliousness, supplanted his poeticized concept of Friuli. *Ragazzi di vita*, Pasolini's celebrated novel begun in 1950 and published in 1955, emerged from this newly uncovered social and linguistic reality.

At the same time, some of the verse Pasolini composed while in Rome marked the survival of his passionate attachment to the *locus amoenus* of his youth, through

memories populated by farm hands and shepherd boys at ease in the fields, mountains and wind-washed village squares of his mythic Friuli. Once removed from his native setting and confronted with the back-street humanity of Rome's periphery, however, Pasolini found it difficult to reconcile the poetic concepts of his earlier work to the expressive demands of his present writings. While Friuli quite often appeared in his verse as a natural utopia, by contrast, the Roman borgate of his novels *Ragazzi di vita* and *Una vita violenta* (1959) seem an inferno of degradation and disassociation. In his esthetic treatment of the socially downtrodden, Pasolini nonetheless tempered this hellish world with residues of primitive purity and adolescent innocence present beneath the coarse language and brutal(ized) faces of its inhabitants. In the end, death triumphs over the instinctual guile and bruised grace of these *ragazzi di vita,* as the novelist underscores the social and political pathos of this cast-off race and class. But, as just stated, Pasolini never dismissed the primordial virtues of a simpler world, and so it is in Rome during the early 1950's that he came to believe his primitive innocents the victims of a Neocapitalism that he claimed would eventually destroy the very humanity of these people as it swept away time-honored linguistic and social patterns.

In truth, that aforementioned rupture in Pasolini's poetry had already manifested itself to some extent at the time of his "discovery of Marx." One such example can be found in **"Testament Coran,"** a part of the verse in dialect written between 1947 and 1952. Here Pasolini depicts a young peasant in Friuli who joins the Partisans and is then captured and hung by the Nazis. While dying, the boy-soldier commits his image to the conscience of the rich, as he sadly salutes the courage, pain, and innocence of the poor.

Similarly, the underlying evangelism of **Poesie a Casarsa** (1941-1943) gradually replaced a traditional peasant demand for an avenging afterlife with a here-and-now vindication. In one poem, now part of **La meglio gioventù** containing all of Pasolini's verse in dialect, the peasants' figure of Christ crucified, index of a future retribution, takes on the workclothes and identity of a laborer who promises more than an atonement to come. . .

[The] passage of Pasolini's rhapsodized race from a natural-religious state to an historical-political one was greatly influenced by the catalytic intrusion of external events. The esthetic and sensual aura of a poeticized Friuli gave way to the cruel incandescence of the War and Resistance and stirred the poet's ethical consciousness. The Resistance, above all, deeply affected Pasolini (as it did an entire generation), modifying his poetic sensibility. In 1957, when censuring what he considered the political quietism of many writers during Fascism, Pasolini remarked:

> Lassi in reditàt la me imàdin
> te la cosientha dai sòrs.
> (. . .)
> Coi todescs no ài vut timoùr
> de lassà la me doventha.
> Viva el coragiu, el doloùr

e la nothentha dei puarèth!
                                             ["**La meglio gioventù**"]

El jera un fiol ch'el veva sogni,
un fiol blù come la tuta.
Vegnerà el vero Cristo, operajo,
a insegnarte a ver veri sogni.
       [**"Fine dell'engagement,"** *Passione e ideologia*]

La Resistenza ha soprattutto insegnato a credere
nuovamente nella storia, dopo le introversioni evasive
ed estetizzanti di un ventennio di poesia.

One must then see this 'historical lesson' in conjunction
with the poet's turn to Gramsci, for throughout the 1950's,
the example of the Sardinian revolutionary played an
important role in defining Pasolini's pronounced conflict
between the pull of a visceral and esthetic passion and a
call to rational, ideological exactitude. It was precisely
this conflict that became the ferment of much of Pasolini's
later works.

Le Ceneri di Gramsci

Although the volume's title poem was actually composed in
1954, *Le ceneri di Gramsci* was published in 1957. These
poems, written in Italian (and not in dialect) occupy a special
place in postwar Italian literature, for they signal a significant departure from pre- (and post-) war Hermeticism.

Contesting the Hermetics' mystique of the word, Pasolini
models his verse on a rejuvenation of certain traditional
stylistic modes (*e g*, adjectivization; the *terzina*, reminiscent of post-Dantean didactic and satirical verse; the *po-
emetto*, evoking the Romantic-patriotic poetry of the
Risorgimento), motivated by the desire for a return to a
'civil' poetry that might effectively challenge the Hermetic
postulates of absolute self-expression and pure lyricism.
At the same time, Pasolini's 'civil' poetry shares little
with various strains of postwar prose *à thèse*, nor does it
confuse reportage with poetic expression. Instead, his verse
proceeds from a conflict experienced between publiccom-
mitment and poetic predilection—instinct and reason
Within a context based on seemingly irreconcilable antitheses, Gramsci represents a world of reason and ideological precision both guiding and goading the poet. This world
clashes with Pasolini's visceral-irrational feelings that ultimately precede his ideology. Thus, *Le ceneri di Gramsci* records a struggle between reason (Gramsci) and passion (Pasolini).

"Le Ceneri di Gramsci"

A note to the text establishes Rome as the location of the
collection's title poem: specifically, the Testaccio (working-class) quarter; the English cemetery; Gramsci's grave.
It is an "autunnale/maggio" in the mid-1950's, a decade
once anticipated with hope by the Resistance: "la fine del
decennio in cui ci appare/tra la macerie finito il profondo/
e ingenuo sforzo di rifare la vita." The poet, "capitato/per
caso" into Rome's cemetery for non-Catholics, finds there
a "mortale/pace" that shuts out the industrious clatter of

the nearby proletarian neighborhood, providing a proper
situation for his colloquy with Gramsci. This setting lends
an immediate air of elegy that reduces all color and contour to an achromatic grey in a meeting of the living dead:
"e noi morti ugualmente, con te, nell'umido/giardino."

From the beginning, then, the poem's metaphoric progression rests on a series of contrasts. The juxtaposition of the
cemetery's quiet to the frenzy of the surrounding neighborhood is the first in succeeding analogical contrasts that
culminate in the poet's self-reflexion and refraction in his
hero—who is simultaneously his antagonist. Attraction and
repulsion result from Pasolini's thirst for vitalistic passion
and Gramsci's somber reminder of the need for rational
articulation:

    con la tua magra mano
    delineavi l'ideale che illumina
    (. . .)
          questo silenzio.
    (. . .)
    Lo scandalo del contraddirmi, dell'essere
    con te e contro te; con te nel cuore,
    in luce, contro te nelle buie viscere;
    del mio paterno stato traditore
    —nel pensiero, in un'ombra di azione—
    mi so ad esso attaccato nel calore
    degli istinti, dell'estetica passione

For Pasolini, Gramsci's "rigore" denoting the antithesis of
his own "violento/e ingenuo amore sensuale," has "scisso/
(. . .) il mondo" into opposing poles. Nonetheless, it
soon becomes clear that despite the poet's insistence on
living "nel non volere/del tramontato dopoguerra," of surviving through a refusal to choose between passion and
reason ("sussisto/perché non scelgo"), a decision has really
already been made:

    Mi chiederai tu, morto disadorno
    d'abbandonare questa disperata
    passione di essere nel mondo?

Elegy renders Pasolini's evocation of Gramsci the commemoration of a lost ideal, for Gramsci, as person and
precept, undergoes a figurative transformation. The force
of **"Le ceneri di Gramsci"** is discharged through an extension of personal conflict ("con te nel cuore,/in luce,
contro te nelle buie viscere") to a general, and generational,
crisis ("e noi/morti ugualmente, con te"). In bemoaning
the loss of the hopes and ideals of the Resistance, Pasolini
indirectly censures the *pisaller* of the 1950's, while implying that the 'committed' poet and critic of his times must
paradoxically operate within and without conventional political structures. Gramsci, meanwhile, must necessarily
remain a luminary ("in luce"), iconically remote and ideally
distant from the poet's inner torment: "Lì tu stai, bandito e
con dura eleganza/non cattolica, elencato tra estranei/morti:
Le ceneri di Gramsci." Thus Pasolini's Gramsci lives only
insofar as he is 'ashes'; insofar as his presence is experienced emblematically and at a defining distance. Without
this figure, Pasolini's visceral passion would have no bal-
last. Gramsci is thus made to assume the role of an ideolog-

ical counterpoise, keeping in check the grip of the poet's "calore/degli istinti" and "estetica passione."

As for the torment that lies outside, Pasolini identifies with the humble poor:

> Come i poveri povero, mi attacco
> come loro a umilianti speranze
> come loro per vivere mi batto
> ogni giorno.

But the poet's poor are the poor of a pre-proletarian state championed for their inbred and sacred vitalism: "come/ d'un popolo di animali, nel cui arcano/orgasmo non ci sia altra passione/che per l'operare quotidiano." Hence, again addressing Gramsci, Pasolini declares himself:

> attratto da una vita proletaria
> a te anteriore, è per me religione
> la sua allegria, non la millenaria
> sua lotta: la sua natura, non la sua
> coscienza

Moreover, Pasolini's apostrophe here is to a "giovane," . . . "non padre, ma umile/fratello." One should note that in an article of 1957, the year of the publication of *Le ceneri di Gramsci,* Pasolini called the Sardinian a "maestro." But here the emphasis on Gramsci's 'youth', his evocation as 'brother', and the strange erotic attraction that takes hold of the poet at graveside ("ebbra simbiosi/ d'adolescente di sesso con la morte") suggest a commutation of Pasolini's emblem. In effect, it appears that the poet is impressing on Gramsci the figure and force of his own dead brother, tragic youthful martyr to the Resistance. This commutation gives rise to a fundamental ambiguity surrounding the image of Gramsci as master and luminary and as shadow of the poet's dead young brother. Meanwhile, it should be observed that the one clear bio-bibliographical allusion to Gramsci focusses on the latter's presumed stoic character:

> sento quale torto
> —qui nella quiete delle tombe—e insieme
> quale ragione—nell'inquieta sorte
> nostra—t avessi stilando le supreme
> pagine nei giorni del tuo assassinio.

From the above it appears that pathos insures Gramsci's longevity. In fact, in yet another essay ["La libertà stilistica," *Passione e ideologia*] published the same year as the poem, Pasolini asserted that:

> (. . .) su qualsiasi altro, domina nella nostra vita politica lo spirito di Gramsci: del Gramsci 'carcerato', tanto più libero quanto più segregato dal mondo, fuori dal mondo, in una situazione suo malgrado leopardiana, ridotto a puro ed eroico pensiero.

Here, as in the poem, Pasolini elevates Gramsci to a symbolic, and hence metahistorical, plane. What he terms a reduction to "puro ed eroico pensiero" is really a dilation of the human and historical Gramsci (political revolution-

ary, jailed party leader, and philosopher of praxis) to an ideal interlocutor and rational censor. Pasolini's search to construct a 'civil' poetry requires this sort of Gramsci responding to the poet's existential and cognitive needs for such an ideal and exacting interlocutor, by necessity remote and at odds with his own inner feelings. . . .

Paul Colilli (essay date 1981-82)

SOURCE: "The Concept of Death in Pier Paolo Pasolini: A Philosophical Approach," in *Canadian Journal of Italian Studies,* Vol. 5, Nos. 1-2, Fall-Winter, 1981-82, pp. 91-7.

[*In the following essay, Colilli uses philological criticism to study the concept of death in Pasolini's poems.*]

The purpose of this paper is to investigate briefly the application of philological criticism to the study and interpretation of poetry, and in particular to a selected poem of Pier Paolo Pasolini in order to examine the claim by philological critics that a specific word is not used repetitively and randomly by the poet. In fact, as is generally believed by philological critics, a diachronic study of a specific word in its context of occurrence usually demonstrates that it contains a semantic configuration which forms a psycholinguistic frame, or "charge", that determines both lexical and overall poetic structure. In the present case we shall concentrate on lexical items based on the morpheme "mor-", hence the various forms of "morte", "morire", etc.

As is well known, Benedetto Croce believed artistic creation to be the result of pure inspiration and intuition: "L'arte è intuizione pura o pura espressione, non intuizione intellettuale alla Hegel. . . ." However, in line with proposals advanced by philological critics we intend to demonstrate that, in the case of Pasolini at least, a poet is indeed in possession of a systematic perception of poetic structure which manifests itself in all of his poetry. This sort of probe into the "zona della invenzione" is deemed by Fredi Chiappelli (a leading critic in this field) as a method to "verificare. . . la progressiva conquista del fantasma ispiratore e la valutazione della sua complessità attraverso la identificazione delle sue componenti". As Guiseppe De Robertis points out, this approach to poetry also allows one to ". . . entrare nel segreto dell'arte d'uno scrittore, a respirare nella sua aria, assai meglio che i voli pazzi della critica grandemente ispirata".

Philological criticism involves three basic steps, the first being the compilation of a concordance wherein the word to be studied is listed systematically every time it occurs along with the passage it is taken from. Our concordance, which was based on the following collections of Pasolini's poems: *Poesie a Casarsa, La meglio gioventù, Le ceneri di Gramsci, L'usignolo della Chiesa Cattolica, La religione del mio tempo,* and the poems **"Il Biondomoro"**, **"Marcia funebre"** and **"Fuga"** from *Ali' dagli occhi azzurri*, indicates that the various forms of the words based on "mor-" occur collectively 275 times.

The second step consists of an examination of the semantic constants of the word, which would be formulated from the concordance, for the purpose of ascertaining the meanings and concepts the poet attributes to it. In this regard the concordance suggests that the various forms of the words based on "mor-" are found in the same sentence or passage as words associated with songs and singing ("A bat Rosari, pai pras al si scunis: / jo i soj muàrt al ciant da li ciampanis.", **"Ciant da li ciampanis"**, *La meglio gioventù*); time, which is measured in terms of day, night, month, morning, season, century, etc. ("dissepolta da un fango di altri evi /—a farsi godere da chi può strappare / un giorno ancora alla morte . . .", **"Serata romana"**, *La religione del mio tempo*); life ("Ti vens cà di nualtris / ma nualtris si vif / a si vif quies e muars . . .", **"Tornant al pais"**, *La meglio gioventù*); silence ("Qui il silenzio della morte è fede / di un civile silenzio . . .", **"Le ceneri di Gramsci"**, *Le ceneri di Gramsci*); and the concept of light/clarity ("nell'acre luce di una Roma ignota, / la Roma appena affiorata dalla morte, . . .", **"Lacrime"**, *La religione del mio tempo*).

The various forms of "mor-" take on one or more of the above meanings or associations 73% of the time in the poems from which the concordance was compiled. A further breakdown of this data shows that in *Poesie a Casarsa* and *La meglio gioventù* "mor-" is associated with songs and light 60% of the time, but primarily with country life and notions of youth. In *Le ceneri di gramsci* "mor-" is connected, 67% of the time, with silence, life and time. In *L'usignolo della Chiesa Cattolica, la religione del mio tempo* and the poems from *Ali' dagli occhi azzuri* "mor-" takes on one or more of the five meanings 80% of the time.

What do these semantic constants indicate? Before we attempt to answer this question it should be explained that one of the dominant themes of Pasolini's poetic works is the motif of death and along with it also the life/death dichotomy. In fact, the theme of death in Pasolini's poetry is accounted for in the following way by Antonio Russi. ". . . Quanto al sentimento della morte, poi, Pasolini, forse per riflesso di certa poesia popolare friulana, ne' è come ossessionato. Ed anche si aggiunge sullo stesso piano dimesso e angoscioso, un rimpianto dell'infanzia. . . .". Mariella Betarini quotes the following passage from *Empirismo eretico* which delineates Pasolini's philosophical and, possibly, also his poetic stance on the life/death dichotomy: "Finchè io non sarò morto, nessuno potrà garantire di conoscermi veramente, cioè di poter dare un senso alla mia azione, che dunque, in quanto momento linguistico, è mai decifrabile . . . Solo grazie alla morte, la nostra vita ci serve ad esprimerci". In her own words Bettarini adds to this dichotomy that: "Una vita, attraversata da unamorte . . . diventa una storia".

In Pasolini's poetry the presence of death with life is only natural, as in the case of the Giovinetto who grows innocently, between the silence of life and death: "Il soreli scur di fun / sot li branchis dai moràrs / al ti brusa e sui

cunfins / tu i ti ciantis, soul, i muars" (**"Ploja tai cunfins"**, *La meglio gioventù*). Thus, in a condition of existence where life and death are omnipresent norms, the poem "Li letanis del bel fì" (*La meglio gioventù*), can be justified: "Jo i soj un bel fì / i rit dut il dì / ti prei, Jesus me / ah fami murì".

In effect, the life/death dichotomy is manifested as two concepts within the range of the above mentioned five semantic contexts: the first, expressing the notion of life, would include the lexical domains connected with songs and singing, since music is always jubilant even though the joy may be an illusion; and those associated with light/clarity and life, both for obvious reasons; the second, manifesting the death concept of the dichotomy, comprises the words associated with silence which in Pasolini's poetry signifies stasis and mortality. However, the notion of time belongs to both concepts for the following reason: our concordance indicates that time is measured frequently by both month and day, and that "Aprile" is the month which Pasolini mentions the most. As a result, "Aprile" may belong to the life concept, since that month gives rise to a new season, even though spring technically begins in late March; but it also belongs to the death concept since traditionally, and also in the context of Pasolini's poetry, as **"La Crocifissione"** (*L'usignolo della Chiesa Cattolica*), will attest, Christ died during that month. Also, the day was broken down into "mattino" and "sera", with the former being associated with the life concept and the latter belonging to the death concept of the dichotomy. From all of this information we can deduce that by associating the above five semantic constants or fields to the various forms of "mor-", Pasolini has made them a collective microcosm for his entire life/death polemic. Hence, we may concur with Walter Siti when he observes that in Pasolini's poetry: "Le opposizioni-base a livello tematico (vita-morte, buio-luce, antico nuovo) si ritrovano evidentemente con frequenza particolare anche a questo livello stilistico. . . ." Now we might also add that these "opposizioni" are used as lexical devices.

The final step in a philological approach to poetic criticism consists of an examination of the "varianti" and/or editions if such exist) of the author's poetical works on which the concordance was based. This allows the analyst to check for any variants that might affect the word under study. The objectives and value of the study of variants are affirmed by De Robertis in this manner: "lo studio delle varianti . . . oltre a offrire la prova d'un'acuta, inquieta e . . . vittoriosa ricerca della espressione . . . ci fa assistere al nascere della parola poetica. . . .".

The relevant variants involve only *Poesie a Casarsa* and *La meglio Gioventù* and they are as follows: in **"Ploja tai cunfins"**, (*La meglio gioventù*), we have: ". . . tu ti ciantis, suol, i muars. . . .", while in the *Poesie a Casarsa* version, it is: ". . . dut bessôl tu ciantis I". In the same poem we have: "sernàt al mour il mèis" in the *La meglio gioventù* edition, while in *Poesie a Casarsa* we have: ". . . dut sblanciat 'a mur il mèis'". In **"Tornant al pais"**, *La meglio gioventù*, we have: ". . . vores essi il vint / ch'al mour tal pais", whereas in *Poesie a Casarsa*, with the poem then entitled **"Per un ritorno al paese"**, it is ". . . voréss jèssi il vint c'al cole e al no si mòuf". Again, in the same poem, the *La meglio gioventù* edition reads: "Ti vens cà di nualtris / ma nualtris si vif / a si vif quiès e muàrs", while the *Poesie a Casarsa* edition has: "Cà, tu vens da noàltris / ma noàltris a si vîf / comel'àghe 'a consùme / chèl che tu no ti sâs".

The small number of variants are indicative of the fact that these poems had reached a somewhat definitive form in the original version. The variants that do exist, however, point to the fact that Pasolini was aiming for a concise language where the vague was substituted by the specific, that is, by a form of "mor-".

A more specific instance of the insights provided by philological criticism in the interpretation of poetry may be seen in **"Usignolo VI"** from *L'usignolo della Chiesa Cattolica,* where: ". . . domina il senso della morte che getta un'ombra cupa e desolata sul trepido ed esile descrittivismo paesistico di cui la parola pare illuminarsi e trasalire". This poem contains a synthesis of the five major semantic fields and associations that Pasolini attributes to the morphological manifestations of "mor-". In fact, here we have a vivid example of how the presence of "mor-" clearly influences the choice of words such as "sole", "vita", "Aprile", "silenzio", "luce", cantava", etc. As Siti observes, in Pasolini's poetry "la prosa forza la poesia, la discussione logica, il ritmo del discorso razionale ne invadono le strutture". Consequently, we may add that a word *per se* might influence the total structure of the poem. Specifically, the presence of "mor-" has influenced the structure of this poem in that the dialogue form genuinely mirrors and is an instrument of expression for the life/death dichotomy which is both at the heart of this poem and, as we've seen, intrinsic to the semantic structure of "mor-".

In this poem—dialogue the poet is trying to ascertain the nature of his own reality. It is not the choice between good and evil which is at hand, instead, we have VIVO which is the living present that would physically recapture the poet's youth but is totally unable to do so: "VIVO. Ti guardo quasi piangendo, o sole di Aprile: dieci Aprili e la vita. . ." (lines 1-2). MORTO is the dead past which would undermine any endeavor on the part of the present to recapture the poet's childhood: "MORTO. Taci, silenzio . . . Chi parla di morte? Senti come rido beato a dieci anni in un Aprile lontano." (lines 3-4). After vain attempts to penetrate the physical reality of the past ["VIVO. No! son io quel bambino che ride in un ciclo di Aprile, e ascolta, fermo, il canto di sua madre lontana. . ." (lines 8-9); "VIVO. Il mio paese! dove sono vivo e ridevo da bambino. Va via morto, va via" (lines 12-13)], VIVO realizes: "Che tempi lontani!" (line 15). However, as far as MORTO is concerned, he is the poet alive in the past: "MORTO. Vicini, oh tu più morto di me!, vicini. Il quieto Aprile fa nascere i fiori sulla tomba fresca" (lines 17-18). In the end though, VIVO's final effort is completely in vain: "VIVO. Sì, ma intanto, giovane infiammato, me ne sto qui nel paese a cantare" (lines 21-22). By giving MORTO the last words the poet demonstrates that he is aware of the

irretrievable nature of his long-lost world of innocence which is infinitely frozen in the past, and it is "Aprile" (which, as we've seen, encompasses both life and death) that is a constant reminder of this irreversible reality. Thus, the poet's past, in the guise of MORTO, is alive only in his memory, but dead—as implied by VIVO—to his corporeal present.

Primarily, this study has attempted to show that a word may indeed determine poetic structure. . . .

An important aspect of philological criticism is that one may not only successfully interpret a poem with the observations gained from this approach, but also ascertain the significance of the semantic constants within the context of the poetry. In fact, as the analysis of one specific poem, **"Usignolo VII",** demonstrates, an explanation of the poetic structure in terms of recurring semantic fields associated with a specific morpheme is indeed a plausible hermeneutic technique.

Stefano Agosti (essay date 1982)

SOURCE: "The Word Beside Itself," in *Stanford Italian Review,* Vol. II, No. 2, Fall, 1982, pp. 54-71.

[*In the following essay, Agosti presents a phenomenological analysis of Pasolini's poetry, seeing his verse as both conservative and innovative.*]

It is probable (it is, at least in part, already an established fact) that an attempt at historical collocation of Pier Paolo Pasolini's poetry—considered in terms of its most significant and most striking achievements: *Le ceneri di Gramsci,* 1957; *La religione del mio tempo,* 1961; some sections of *L'usignolo della Chiesa cattolica,* published in 1958 but containing work of the period 1943-1949—would lead to its finding itself firmly placed on the side of experiences that might be termed conservative as opposed to innovative or "eversive" experiences in twentieth-century literature; nor need this imply any doubt of its intrinsic worth if one admits that a considerable part of significant twentieth-century Italian literature (the perfect example, the prose of Cardarelli) falls into just this perspective, whereas the revolutionary landscape all too often houses products of uncertain alloy when they are not outright vulgar (a no less paradigmatic example of this, Marinetti and, in general, the Italian brand of Futurism). That Pasolini should be so placed two macroscopic immanent aspects of his poetic production might seem to justify: (1) its openly (indeed ostentatiously) *discursive and egocentric* dimension, which means that the experiment must be referred back to pre-twentieth-century, we might even say with suitable caution, to "romantic" positions; (2) its use of an outmoded metrical framework, e.g., the *terzina,* the distich *a rima baciata,* and even the stanza of the medieval *canzone* as used in particular by Dante. Critics have insisted, and from the outset, on just these aspects, going on to define them and investigate their relationships. Thus, where the discursive and egocentric dimension is concerned, it has proved possible to define more sharply its specific nature, expressible—macroscopically—in terms of an unceasing contradiction or antinomy—present explicitly and constantly at a thematic level throughout the text—between reason and passion (or rationality and visceral participation), history and nature, human and sub-human, and which comes to embrace more specifically ideological oppositions like Marxism and Catholicism, or psychological oppositions like perversion and innocence. (These latter are found essentially in work earlier than *Le ceneri di Gramsci,* i.e., in the collection of verses in Friuli dialect, *Poesie a Casarsa,* 1942, which from 1954 forms part of *La meglio gioventù,* and, particularly, in *L'usignolo della Chiesa cattolica.*) As for the outmoded metrical forms, some degree of critical awareness has shown that it is no merely passive appropriation when such forms are subjected to an incessant process of erosion of their integrity (or of calling in question of their normativity): rhyme almost constantly precipitates in an assonance which is often merely visual, or at the very least in striking irregularities; the rhythmical measure opens out or contracts with respect to the rule; while stanza composition frequently breaks free of the schemata fixed by the model. Inthe light of this, it has proved possible to postulate a relationship between two planes, so that "transgressions" met with on the formal, or more precisely metrical, plane, to the extent to which they represent a tension between norm and freedom, order and disorder, etc., would merely reproduce the state of antinomy existing on the content plane. Both planes of the manifestation are thus found to be mutually homologous within a typology of substantially expressive kind, where the nature of content conditions configuration on the formal plane.

Now, if the phenomenology of Pasolini's poetic experience is, in general terms, more or less that sketched out above, it may also lend itself to a totally different interpretation: one that would admit of its collocation historiographically in a perspective that is directly opposed to that in which the findings so far adduced would place it; it would then find itself on the side of innovative experiment, or, at least, of an experimentation characterized by exceptional cultural receptivity.

Let us look again at the data earlier referred to, for there are further qualifications which must at once be added.

The collocation of the experiment in a distinctively, ostentatiously discursive dimension, entirely centered on the Subject's consciousness as seen from close up, certainly removes it from the mainstream of twentieth- and late nineteenth-century experience, which was not experience of "discourse" but experience of "language." From Mallarmé and Rimbaud, and not from them alone but even from Pascoli (from Pascoli Pasolini derives the not unimportant notion of stylistically plural linguistic experimentation, though he remains unaware of the astonishing material elaboration of his text thanks to which Pascoli stands beside the most advanced of twentieth-century innovators, others who might flank him being found outside poetry in experiences like those of Dubuffet, of Fautrier) down to other key figures of

the twentieth century, creators of concentrated, or even highly concentrated, works (Ungaretti), but also of linguistically diffuse works (Eliot), poetry has come progressively to recognize as central a linguistic or, better, "verbal" dimension. So that, even in cases where it inclines, let us say, towards narration and the tale, it is elaboration of language that will be found determinate and dominant with respect to elaboration of meaning and concept (of discourse). If an example is called for we might think of the similar cases of Gozzano and Francis Jammes—usually designated as repositories of a "realistic" tradition in opposition to the practitioners of so-called "pure" poetry—where contents of humble-rural kind (Jammes) or intimistic-bourgeois-provincial kind (Gozzano), articulated as elementary patterns of *récit,* build up constructions of precise and weighty formal architecture identifiable, in the case of Jammes, with phenomena of iteration, and, in the case of Gozzano, with closed metrical form, to which are added significant techniques of quotation, which effect inside the composition striking phenomena of textual stratification, i.e., of language elaborating language.

The metrical-formal aspect in Pasolini, too, seen as a recuperation of archaic forms, and rightly interpreted by the critics as separable from the discourse, harks back to techniques no longer in vogue, though the resulting metrical aspect cannot be isolated from the experiment as a whole. In this case too, any contention that Pasolini's poetic experience is outdated would find support in the distinction proposed above regarding the central dimension of the "linguistic" (of the "verbal") aspect in twentieth-century poetry. To put it in other words, a privileged role is accorded the signifier (in its phonic, timbric, rhythmic, syntactic, lexematic aspects) seen as the "stage" whereon the poetic, the expressive, experience unfolds. So that what might be called the purely metrical aspect would fall into this order of things, and participate (conspicuously) in the complex typology of the signifier.

In substance, it might be affirmed that whereas the great narrative prose of the twentieth century, in its most revolutionary and innovative aspects, those typified by a Gadda or a Joyce, lends itself to ready collocation under the aegis of the experience of a Dante, of the Dante of the *Commedia* in particular, the great poetry concomitant with it finds more than one motive for taking its place appropriately, if not absolutely, within the ideal perimeter which the Petrarchan experience defines. It is not our intention here to reduce to partitions so drastic the multiplicity (in the last resort, indeed, irreducibility) of the phenomena. But there do come to mind—at least on a qualitative plane—poetical experiences deriving from an Ungaretti or a Valery, a Montale or a Salinas, a Guillén, or those that may be made collectively to derive from more recent avant-garde (neo-avant-garde) experiences, French in particular, not to mention certain individual, and highly significant, experiences of the middle generation—those of a Bonnefoy, of a Du Bouchet, a Zanzotto, a Celan—all of which may serve to give an idea of the extent to which the notion of a verbal absolute, in sovereign fashion scaling down the totality of experience—an absolute of just the kind on which the Petrarchan practice in the *Canzoniere* is founded—can lend itself to form a common basis for phenomena otherwise so dissimilar.

By developing a celebrated model proposed by Contini we might say, then, that in opposition to the extrovert, centrifugal, excessive plurilinguism of the (inimitable) pattern of Dante if assumed as protector and patron of twentieth-century experiences in prose, there stands, magnetically drawing the poetry to itself, the introvert, centripetal, absolutizing monolinguism of the (inimitable) pattern Petrarch provides. It was this pattern, moreover, that had already presided, magnificently though implicitly, over the greatest revolution ever effected in the history of poetry: that of Mallarmé.

At this point in our demonstration we might be strongly tempted to try to get beyond the notion of "outdatedness" which dogs Pasolini's poetry by proposing the hypothesis of an interpenetration of genres, which are, in our case, no less than the primary categories of expression: poetry, prose. In reality, other avenues are offering to lead us beyond this "outdatedness," and they are much more complex. It is a fact that the example of Dante persists in the background not only of Pasolini's poetic practice (with its experimentality within the genre, to say nothing of the explicit reference of the metrical schemes adopted, the *terzina* and the *canzone* stanza) but of his entire activity as well (experimentality of genres) and also, perhaps, of his "existential" itinerary of which traces are to be found in the preparatory sketches and the fragments of the recently published *La Divina Mimesis;* this does not, though, resolve the problem posed by the "discourse," by the use made of the "discourse." Pasolini's Dantism, in terms of this problem, which is no less than the central problem, appears, on the best hypothesis, as a fact of style (and, as such, always subordinate, even if "style" is to be understood to extend beyond its normal literary sense to include the living, or the existing).

If what we have termed language exercises are to be defined in terms of their meaning-constructing activity, or, better, of their deconstruction of meaning and construction (production) of sense, discourse will, for its part, be defined as the place wherein are manifested (or performed) meanings given from the outset, pre-existent and even, in extreme cases, hypostatic. By means of discursive performance, a world of natural or cultural, historical or individual meanings is taken over by the Subject, who thereby becomes their custodian, custodian of just so many meaning-truths. The meaning-truth, on the one hand, the Subject on the other, are the two constituent poles of discourse structure. This shows, in its poetic manifestation as well, the same series of characteristics that mark its manifestation in prose, most markedly (*a*) the univocal character of the meanings manifested (meaning-truths do not tolerate, by definition, ambiguity or semantic multivalency: insofar as they are "true" they must be recognized as self-identical); (*b*) the progressive unfolding of the sequences, which presupposes the existence of a principle or of a beginning of sense (*arch*) and, symmetrically, of a finality (*telos*); (*c*) the "property" of meaningful production, where the term is to be taken in its twofold value of "per-

tinence" and of "belongingness": "pertinence" in relation to the object, i.e., to the manifestation of the discourse, which cannot but be semantically *senseful* in virtue of the role of custodian exercised by the Meaning-Truth (by the Meaning-Origin) over hierarchically inferior orders; "belongingness" in relation to the Subject, who sees himself at one and the same time as proprietor of the discourse (*énonciation* exigencies) and as effect of the discourse (*énoncé* exigencies). The "meaningful" nature of the discourse, in fact, allows the Subject to circumscribe, through the act of uttering, the entire discursive production. This, on the other hand, since it is guaranteed in its "truth" by the Meaning of its meanings, will include among its sense effects the Subject as well. From this point of view, the Discourse plays, where the Subject is concerned, the same role of doubling and recognition played by the mirror for the child during the famous mirror phase (*"le stade du miroir"*) studied by Lacan.

Thus the "metaphysical" character of discourse in general (and *in se*) is stressed, not only in those cases where convention so predisposes it, e.g., in manifestations of philosophical, religious, juridical, political discourse and so forth, manifestations that, on the whole, do no more than exploit, in specific "senses," this fundamental character; but also in other cases where usage seems radically alien, as, for example, in all manifestations of instrumental or communicative discourse.

On the other hand, there is no way of doing without discourse. There exists no "direct" access to reality. Reality—one knows—is nothing less than the sum of infinite universes of discourse (of ideologies), each of which represents the actuation of a determined system of meanings. Giving verbal expression to reality means speaking inside, (from inside) one of these systems actuated in discourse: it means, in short, uttering a determined discourse-universe, i.e., a determined ideology, whose meanings are confirmed as just so many *truth objects or values*.

It is more or less on the basis of such considerations that, most particularly over the last twenty years and in France especially, a systematic "critical" investigation of institutionalized knowledge has been undertaken, knowledge that has coalesced to form the various universes of discourse. Such investigation finds its most striking and radical exemplification in the brilliant process of deconstruction of Western metaphysical discourse initiated by Jacques Derrida. Derrida's investigations go back, on the one hand, to the analyses of Freud—insofar as they are the construction of "other" texts by deconstruction of the texts manifested—and, on the other, to Nietzsche—insofar as they are knowingly "symptomatic" thought, the meeting place of "other" mental itineraries.

Now, the main current of late nineteenth-century and of twentieth-century poetry, the current that derives from Mallarmé and Rimbaud, and for which we have adopted the term "language exercises,"operates in the same direction; indeed, it exemplifies—according to what we might call the best possible techniques—that process of ideological (and metaphysical) deconstruction of the meaning to which the actual work of constructing the text corresponds: for the construction is without foundations, mobile, and fluctuating, and construction of the text is the process of producing its sense.

But just as for the pre-eminently discursive poetry contemporary with these experiences it is possible to speak of language effects of the same kind as those described above (our observations regarding the narrative-realistic current represented primarily by the work of Jammes and Gozzano), in identical fashion, or, at least, with the use of similar argumentation, it might be maintained that *all* poetry, and not merely poetry subscribing to a primarily formalistic tradition, operates (it may be unintentionally) in virtue of the fact that it is in opposition to discourse. It is sufficient to cite in this sense the non-rationalizable senses that are superimposed on the rational (discursive) semanticity of the utterances, senses that are represented by the elaboration of rhythms, timbres, and, more mysteriously, by the writing itself (formal and informal messages), an aspect earlier work of ours has dealt with.

Now Pasolini cannot be assimilated to any of the positions here formulated. Though far removed from what we have called "language exercises," the use he makes of the discourse does not involve either the corrective of modern experiments with language (which the Italian neo-avant-garde might exemplify) nor the "traditional" corrective of a non-rational and non-rationalizable supplement of sense, which is obtained through formal elaboration (metrical patterns, as we have pointed out, offering themselves in isolation from the discourse—they are not incorporated into it); hence its distance from the "actual" and present-day "language exercises" and linguistic experimentation within the discourse, which is, at one and the same time, distance from the "non-actual" as well, when these are represented by various currents of realistic, and what we might very approximately term "post-romantic," poetry.

If we now go on to foreground the phenomenon and bring it into focus, we might say that the use Pasolini makes of the discourse is a use "carried to extremes" in the sense that discourse seems here to be employed in its absolute state; secondly, that this poetically abnormal use of discourse, which is in the last analysis "unpoetical" corresponds to a desire *a parte subjecti* for *a total diction of reality.* Where by "diction" is meant both what is said (*niveau de l'énoncé*) and the act of its saying (*niveau de l'énonciation*), and where "total" means likewise both a phenomenology of the utmost range of contents (*niveau de l'énoncé*) and also the full involvement of the Subject in its own discourse (*niveau de l'énonciation*). In our case, where the utterance is concerned we will have a "reality" that moves from the world of the proletariat and the *Lumpenproletariat* of technological civilization to the archaic and prehistoric world of peasant and of primitive societies (the Veneto, Southern Italy, Africa, India); from biographical experience (caught, at one extreme, in its elegiac variant: Friuli and tender; at the other, in its "comic" variant: Rome and violent) to intellectual experience represented by an ideological and cultural discourse (this too embraced in its fullest range: popular ideology and cul-

ture— "decadent" ideology and culture) down to perfectly inward experience, recording both confessions of the most intimate nature and the most intimate lacerations of the personality, and also tranquil states of mind inclined to recollection and contemplation, with other more abrupt conscious states of lyrical-evocative kind or exclamation and interjection. Whereas, where the utterance act is concerned, first-person involvement in his own discourse on the part of the subject compels him to have recourse, in concomitance with the contents chosen, to a whole range of discursive typologies which bring into play, at one extreme—let us say at the "upper" extreme—the subordinate structures of logical-demonstrative discourse; and, at the "lower" extreme, the "grammatical" violence of lyrical concentration; while, in what we might call the middle zone, phenomena of evocative and contemplative parataxis are found and, generally, all the features of coordinative syntax relative to narrative expansions, to descriptions, to enumerations, and so forth.

Obviously the need to embrace all is not only to be found at an all-encompassing level, i.e., with regard to the sum total of the work or of its single components, where the different discursive typologies dealt with in the first person arrange themselves in terms of positionings foreseen and circumscribed by the contents treated; for it persists also, though not continuously, in the very texture of the text itself, where it is already active within the range of the single syntactical or rhythmical units. This is the phenomenon known as "stylistic expressivity" manifested in form of an interpenetration, or overlapping or coexistence side by side, of typologies of different kind or even reciprocally incompatible. A rapid survey, purely exemplificatory in scope, of several *incipit* should suffice—they are taken, almost in the order in which they appear, from the volume *Le ceneri di Gramsci,* and their range—macroscopic within the microscopic character of the samples— is expressed as an oscillation (or compresence) of "poetic" diction and "unpoetic" ("prosastic") diction: *Senza cappotto* ["impoetic" expression, of "humble" genre] *nell'aria di gelsomino* ["poetic" syntagm, given the ellipsis of the adjective], *Non è di maggio* [syntagm, or locution, of humble-ordinary genre] *questa impura aria* ["poetic" syntagm, given the anticipation of the epithet]; *Solo l'amare, solo il conoscere* [proverb-like statement, but of "ordinary communicative" genre] / *conta, non l'aver amato; / non l'aver conosciuto* [. . .] [highly elaborated sentence structure, thus "poetic," with double iteration of its elements and with variants of the negation and elements distributed into individual rhythmical units].

The desire for a total diction of the real actuated in the first-person discourse seems to find expression in more sophisticated forms as well. Not only, that is, through the plurality of the contents expressed and of the discursive typologies employed, both experimented to their most far-flung extremes, but also by means of processes of homologation (of mimesis) between discourse structures and the structures of reality. One of the most frequent processes of this type involves the setting up of a correspondence (of an equivalence) between the temporal aspect of the discourse and the temporal aspect of the real. See, for example, the opening of **"La ricchezza"** in *La religione del mio tempo,* where discourse time, segmented on the basis of alternations of narrative durations and meditative durations, seems to take the impress of the duration and bivalence of the physical time in terms of which the real story unfolds. A sort of *total rendering* of the event is thus effected (with results that are almost cinematographic, for it is the film sequence that can coincide point by point with a real sequence).

If this technique develops a type of correspondence between discourse and reality founded on what we might call a normal temporality, and aims at cinematographic effects of referential duration, there also exist other types of discursive homologation that involve what we might term "viewing time," and in particular "long-distance viewing" (here too there is fairly evident reference, or it may be a prelude, to the cinema). Here the discourse follows (reproduces) the movement of a hypothetical eye which dominates the real and whose temporality seems to take the form of the product of two different temporalities: cosmic time and memory time, i.e., an external, distant, neutral time, and a more intimate, closer, more secret time. Examples of this type of homologation are found in a score of Pasolini's most effective compositions, like **"L'Appennino"** (in *Le ceneri di Gramsci*), or **"L'Italia"** (from *L'usignolo della Chiesa cattolica*).

On the whole, though, mimesis of temporal duration and of spatial continuity (viewing time), insofar as these are structures underpinning perceived reality, is entrusted to the setting up of a syntactic *continuum,* achieved through a variety of expedients. In the specimen quoted, for example, it is obtained by referring to a simple object, at first given in a subordinate clause (the *bianchi litorali*), a series of attributes (in the order: *scuri, fragranti, sconvolti*), whose task it is to govern the respective noun clauses. Here, then, is the splendid passage from *Le ceneri di Gramsci* which we give in full from the point of view of the phenomenon described.

> [. . .] Come capisco il vortice
> dei sentimenti, il capriccio (greco
> nel cuore del patrizio, nordico
>
> villeggiante) che lo inghiotti nel cieco
> celeste del Tirreno; la carnale
> gioid dell'avventura, estetica
>
> e puerile: mentre prostrata l'Italia
> come dentro il ventre di un'enorme
> cicala, spalanca bianchi litorali,
>
> sparsi nel Lazio di velate torme
> di pini, barocchi, di giallognole
> radure di ruchetta, dove dorme
>
> col membro gonfio tra gli stracci un sogno
> goethiano, il giovincello ciociaro . . .
> Nella Maremma, scuri, di stupende fogne
> d'erbasaetta in cui si stampa chiaro

il nocciòlo, pei viottoli che il buttero
della sua gioventù ricolma ignaro.

Ciecamente fragranti nelle asciutte
curve della Versilia, che sul mare
aggrovigliato, cieco, i tersi stucchi,

le tarsie lievi della sua pasquale
campagna interamente umana,
espone, incupita sul Cinquale,

dipanata sotto le torride Apuane,
i blu vitrei sul rosa . . . Di scogli,
frane, sconvolti, come per un panico

di fragranza, nella Riviera, molle,
erta, dove il sole lotta con la brezza
a dar suprema soavità agli olii

del mare [. . .]

. . . How well I understand the vortex
of feelings, the whim (Greek
in the heart of the patrician, Nordic
holidaying) which swallowed him up in the blind
sky-blue of the Tyrrenian; the carnal
joy of adventure, ecstatic

and puerile; while prostrate Italy
as within the stomach of an enormous
cicala, opens out white beaches

scattered in Latium with its veiled herds
of pines, baroque, of yellowish
clearings of *ruchetta,* wherein sleeps

his member swollen in the rags a neoclassical
dream, the young lad of Ciociaria . . .
In the Maremma, dark, with its amazing trenches

of *erbasaetta* where stands out clear
the nut-tree, through tracks that the herdsman
fills unwittingly with his youth.

Blindly fragrant in the dry
curves of Versilia, which on the sea
tangled and blind, the clear stuccos,

the light inlay of its eastertide
countryside completely human,
spreads out, darkling on Cinquale

unwound under the torrid Apuane,
glassy blue on rose . . . With reefs,
landslides, disarrayed, as in a panic

of fragrance, in the Riviera, soft,
steep, where the sun struggles with the breeze
to give supreme lightness to the oil

of the sea [. . .]

The spatial *continuum* of the vision (imagined—recollected) thus influences—in this and in the other compositions quoted—the syntactic *continuum*. So that the discourse seems to offer itself outright as an *analogon* of the real whose basic structures are reproduced: i.e., the *continuous* structures of space and time. It is this that represents the point of maximum extension of "total diction" as Pasolini experiments it: the real is expressed not only to the point of the "unpoetical," but right down to its most general and non-meaningful structures.

Now it is at just this point, i.e., where the total diction might seem to coincide, reinforcing it to the limits of its potential, with the metaphysical character of the discourse, transforming the desire for (the will to) expressive totality into a total metaphysics of expression, it is at just this point that it becomes possible to bring to the surface of Pasolini's operation, as we have so far exemplified and described it, an impressive *active criticism of discourse.*

The example given above, in fact, as well as a syntactic *continuum* as mimesis of the *continuum* of viewing (of spatial-temporal reality) further offers a phenomenon of exactly opposite value: i.e., the suspension, the disorientation of the meaning brought about by the difficulty of seizing at once upon any agreement between the attributes of the object (*scuri, fragranti,* etc.)—whose function is to govern the single noun clauses—and the object itself (the *bianchi litorali*) whose outline recedes progressively to the point of disappearing behind the accumulation of the propositions, which thereby give the appearance of being acephalous. This indecisiveness, immediate enough, of the meaning calls into question the primary characteristic of the discourse, in virtue of which it presents itself as custodian of the "truth": of the univocal character of the meaning, its self-identity, non-ambiguity, etc.

Keeping back examples of this till later, we can at once insert under this heading the substantial thematic antinomy of Pasolini's poetry. Without insisting excessively on the aspect most treated of exegetically, it will be enough for us to observe that entire constellations of meanings, or vast and complex systems of meaning, seem to be contested by constellations of meaning (systems of meaning) of opposite value, so that the discourse can no longer act as depository of *one single* truth. Certain compositions (the short poem **"Le ceneri di Gramsci"** comes to mind, for example) are entirely based on, and articulated around, a macroscopic antinomy, which branches out capillary fashion to touch on all points of the text, not permitting it to settle on any one definition, on any one definite meaning.

But the second characteristic of the discourse, too, that relative to the progress of the sequences with their immanent exigencies of origin and finality, will be found to be called into question by the manner in which Pasolini's discourse is actuated. Here too, the relevant examples can easily enough be deduced from the occurrences of syntactic continuity themselves, for it is they that witness to the most advanced point reached by Pasolini in his will to total diction—examples whose significance here is twofold, in that the syntactic *continuum* seems to be nothing less than the progression itself. If, then, we go back to the

first of the examples mentioned in this regard, and precisely to the first part of the poem **"La ricchezza,"** it is readily enough established that on the temporal (narrative) *continuum* of which the text is effectively made up there is superimposed a different process which is perfectly antithetical: the iteration, or the recurrence, of determined elements that function as points of demarcation within the composition (as "semantic rhymes" as it were) so that, in addition to the forward movement (the movement *prorsus* of the "prose," of the "discourse") there is a further, and contrary movement, the movement, the ebb, *à rebours,* typical of the "poetic" (of the "verses," or *versus*). We refer to the metonymic pair *sguardo-luce,* further lexicalized on the basis of a narrow range of synonyms (*occhio-i, guardare,* etc., for *sguardo;* the archaic, and Dantesque, *lume* for *luce*), and then filtered down, once more metonymically, *Schiuma è questo sguardo*), in the word-image of *schiuma* and its derivatives *Schiuma gli sciami / di borghesi; Schiuma [. . .] gli stanchi rumori; Schiuma [. . .] questo fermento; Schiumeggia innocente l'ardore; [. . .] questo schiumeggiare della vita*). Here, as a demonstration, is a survey of the lexicalizations: [. . .] *lancia sospetti sguardi / di animale;* [. . .] *quegli occhi / scrutano intimoriti;* [. . .] *ai fiotti / del lume divino; un altro lume; quella pura / luce; l'umiliato sguardo; l'occhio cala; quei / poveri occhi; É una luce [. . .] che si spande; [E una luce] Che si spande; Schiuma è questo sguardo* [to these the occurrences of "schiuma" quoted above must be related]; *se ti guardi intorno.* We might further point out that the two verses that sum up this first part of the poem contain the word *cieco,* which is, admittedly, a word of very high frequency in Pasolini's poetry, though it is significant that in this case it is associated, however negatively, both with *sguardo* and also with *luce. E più cieco il sensuale rimpianto / di non essere senso altrui, sua ebrezza antica.*

If this demonstration is to be carried forward to the sections that follow in this same poem, where the progressive structures are in all respects analogous to those of the first part, the confirmation of a concomitant and oppositive process of iteration of elements will be seen to be striking.

Such iterations break up the progression of the discourse so that its movement, turning back upon itself, scanned by identical elements, is deprived of goal (of finality) and cut off from any hypothetical origin; while the complexity of the syntactic articulation, equally involved in the constitution of that mimetic *continuum* of which we have spoken, ends up rendering the meaning fluctuating, hindering a movement that would fix it on foreseen or foreseeable elements of the phrase. The "total diction" Pasolini seeks through his use of discourse is thereby revealed as, contemporaneously, a criticism of discourse; for the moment we might call it a criticism of discourse relative to the first two characteristics we have pointed out in it: criticism, that is, of meaning, and criticism of structures (linear, progressive, teleological structures).

Now, criticism of meaning and criticism of structures are no more than the consequence, observable respectively at the level of the utterance and at the level of the overall organization of the discourse, of *a generalized process of expropriation-falsification of the linguistic modulation.* If Pasolini's poetic discourse is modulated, *grammatically,* inside the voice of the Subject (shown in violent close-up), setting out from Meaning-Truths ("meanings" of history and biography; "truths" of ideology and culture, etc.), in fact, i.e., *semantically,* it will be found to be phase-displaced, built over a fracture: non-correspondence of the voice of the Subject and of the meanings it utters. The voice of the subject is rendered extraneous to the meaning by the interposing of a formal pattern (the outdated metrical and rhythmical patterns referred to already), and it is this pattern that breaks up the fundamental articulation on which the structure of the Discourse itelf is built: the Voice of the Subject-Meaning.

It is a schema, in fact, that does not offer itself either as a catalyzing element that would serve as a starting-point for unified definition of the discourse meanings and for the voice that expresses them insofar as they are "language" (see the discursive kind of poetic experiences earlier quoted: Gozzano, Jammes); nor is it the carrier of a supplement of sense thanks to which musical, material "authentication" can be attributed to the meanings borne by, "incarnated in," the sequences (as is the case, for example, in Romantic poetry. Compare, in this regard, the "murmuring" of Lamartine's poetry). In Pasolini's case, the formal pattern *acts from outside with respect to the discourse,* which it constrains to a movement, a torsion, not at one with its *cursus,* while, in its turn, it operates on the pattern to the point of disfiguring it under the pressure of its own exigencies (exigencies of syntax, of meaning positions, etc.).

Thus arise two reciprocally correlated complexities, which both remain unresolved: a syntactic complexity (the complexity of the "torsion" to which the discourse is subjected) which achieves no solution into "meaning"; and a formal complexity (the complexity of the metrical patterns, deformed and altered by the pressure of the discourse) which is never resolved into that higher effect of the sense which is "song." To define more narrowly still: on the one hand, we find a syntactic complexity which the constriction of formal patterns provokes acting on the meaning to the point of de-constructing it, of undoing it, through the multiplication of the connections and the complication of the structures, or through the increase (redundancy) of elements lexematically pressed into service to fill out the patterns; on the other, the formal lay-out, compromised and disfigured by discursive pressure, finds itself in no position to produce that semantic overdetermination of the discourse into which the sense of the text can be made to flow.

Dissipated "meanings" and unrealized "songs" thus represent the point from which the Voice of the Subject sets out to express its own particular linguistic modulation, a modulation that, as we have said, assumes a dual, overlapping and reciprocal phase-difference (non-fulfillment) of meaning and of song insofar as this is a state of defamiliarization and falsification (of expropriation), in virtue of which the discourse (the totality of the diction effected

through the discourse) becomes susceptible of moving from the Same to the Other as to the sole condition of its authenticity and identity.

This is the situation that characterizes Pasolini's poetry in its most striking achievements, in the central collections (*Le ceneri di Gramsci* and *La religione del mio tempo*) as well as some of the compositions of *L'usignolo della Chiesa cattolica* (like, for example, the already mentioned **"L'Italia,"** and the whole section **"Lingua"**). So that the examples that might be called on as proof of our contentions would coincide with all the texts and collections named. As the criterion so far adopted is one of economy (of space, of course) we shall continue in a rapid confirmatory glance by looking again at the lengthy quotation of *Le ceneri di Gramsci* given above.

Over and above what has already been arrived at in our investigation (instability and indecisive character of the meaning) the passage in question shows very clearly, in more general terms, that phase-difference and appropriation of the sense already referred to, in this case ascribable to the rigid segmentation into subordinated structures of single sentential blocks, wherein different grammatical subjects, the almost desinential collocation of lexematic elements (substantives, epithets), dislocation or elimination of verbs, all of which bring to a standstill any normal semantic itinerary. The itinerary is diffracted into a myriad of sense nuclei which cannot be immediately connected up, given that any kind of connection other than semantic connection is to be excluded—e.g., one effected by the melodic line—since there also exists an analogous, parallel disorientation of the formal framework. As a more precise verification, see the final verse quoted above and here, for the reader's convenience, reproduced:

1 . . . *Di scogli,*
2 *frane, sconvolti, come per un panico*
3 *di fragranza nella Riviera, molle,*
4 *erta, dove il sole lotta con la brezza*
5 *a dar suprema soavità agli olii*
6 *del mare . . .*

1 . . . with reefs
2 landslides, disarrayed, as in a panic
3 of fragrance, in the Riviera, soft,
4 steep, where the sun struggles with the breeze
5 to give supreme lightness to the oil
6 of the sea . . .

where units that are regular in formal terms (there are only two cases of hypermetric verses but they fall correctly into the hendecasyllabic computation, for the first—our verse 2—has a double unstressed syllabic termination, in consonance, in fact, with *Apuane;* while the second—our verse 4—elides its first syllable by synaloepha with the preceding *molle* at the end of verse 3) are in reality segmented into microsequences that undermine the overall rhythmical structures. The structures do not even find support in the demarcation points of timbric relations, when they present as here the paradigm *scogli: molle: olii,* aberrant from a grammatical and visual point of view and not merely phonetically (see, though, the further pattern *Apuane: panico*). Now, it if is allowed that such disorder, such formal disarray, is the product of the oppositive violence of the discourse which the metrical and rhythmical schemata should have, let us say, "interiorized" (or "rendered melodic"), there also exists—and it is a fact we have already pointed out—a quite opposite effect: i.e., a dismemberment of the discourse on the part of just these schemata, which appear as impregnably external to the discourse. Hence, the sentence no longer seems linear, but is broken up minutely to form a close network of propositional segments, whose constituent elements are custodians of different, contrasting or mutually opposed values. Thus we have only a nominal governance exercised by the adjective *sconvolti* over the now far-removed *litorali,* deferred with respect to its complements (the *scogli-frane* pair, whose elements are articulated around a masculine-feminine opposition, aided by violent enjambement; two circumstantials in adjoining succession though their value is different: a circumstantial of manner (*come per un panico,* etc.) and a circumstantial of place (*nella Riviera*), to whose substantive *Riviera* the desinental divarication of the pair of epithets is singularly well adapted, for they too are separated by enjambement; a successive proposition introduced by *dove,* where the presence of the verb gives the impression of opening a phrase which,though, it closes: thus it is that the whole sentence constitutes as it were an *exemplum* of *éclatement* of linearity and, thus, of the meaning of the discourse, whose formal framework, as we have seen, offers no solution of a hypersemantic order.

This double movement, this double and reciprocal complexity of Pasolini's text, *which determines its structure in point of semantic displacement, in point of expropriation of meaning with respect to the voice that administers the discourse,* so that the Subject's word ends up being, in a certain sense, beside itself, in a diction that is at once total and suspended, entirely involved and critically deferred, this double movement, this double complexity, is present even where one might think the formal dimension absent, in eclipse. For it persists, *deguisèe* though it be, even in the most free compositions like, for example, the poem **"La ricchezza,"** which is arranged, it would seem, as an uninterrupted flux of "free verse," though each of its sequences involves timbric links which tie together all its rhythmic units.

At times, the secret formal tie that constrains the continual flux of the discourse is characterized by an inflexible normativity. This is the case in the third part of **"La ricchezza,"** where the sumptuous, overwhelming, baroque "apparition" of Rome in the morning is linked in each of its rhythmic units to other units, while it is, at one and the same time, regulated in these relationships, and throughout the whole extension of the *laisse* (41 verses), by the submerged pattern of the *terzina* itself.

The same phenomenon is to be found for the **"Poesie incivili,"** the last section of *La religione del mio tempo,* where frank revelation of the Subject and more direct syllabation (with consequently accentuated manifestation of the discourse) are found side by side with the rigorous

schemata—subtly disguised, however—of the fourteenth-century *canzone.* Were it not for the fact that, in this case, we have already gone beyond the bounds of the phenomenon so far defined and described. In fact, the adoption of the formal pattern no longer acts on the discourse to suspend its meaning, impeding and interrupting its structural continuity; nor, on the other hand, does the complex elaboration of the schema seem to derive from the pressure brought to bear by the discourse. The reciprocal interaction of the two dimensions (the discursive and the formal dimensions) does not take place here where the discourse exists in its bare linearity, and where complexity of metrical-timbric elaboration must be ascribed simply to autonomous requirements of variation. The reactivation of the meaning is thus accompanied by adoption of what is in effect formalism; metrical forms that are refined in the sense that they are but scarcely functional. In Pasolini's next collection, **Poesia in forma di rosa,** the further step will be taken of inserting the discourse into the framework of an unrelated iconicity, sanctioning in the most striking fashion the reciprocal independence of the two structure. (Weakening of formal structure, in some parts of the book, will open the way for a *brute* inflow of meaning, for its "metaphysical" character—an aspect we have defined above—while preparing the way for the successive, and substantially unsuccessful, **Trasumanar e organizzar**.)

And so it is at this point that our demonstration may end, at its natural point of rest: internally, its tasks are done; externally, the *demonstranda* coincide with the bounds of the object. Bounds which, while they bring one experience to a close, do so in order to open another: the experience of an intense civil "presence" (or civil "pedagogics") carried on through the most widely varied means of communication: cinema and interviews, articles in the official press (*Corriere della Sera*) and "civil" poetry, as their author terms it, though it might just as well be called "uncivil."

The only thing that remains to be done is to furnish, or attempt to furnish, a cumulative interpretation of the phenomenon that works itself out with the **"Poesie incivili"**: this is its concluding section; nevertheless, it joins up, circlewise, with what had constituted the beginning: the poems in Friuli dialect, where use of dialect, looked at as the equivalent of a "dead language," strives towards exactly the same ends of formal excess reached by taking over, and refinedly elaborating, the patterns of *canzone* stanzas.

Well then, if twentieth-century poetry seems intent on transforming "discourse" into "language," aiming at the attainment of a pre-discursive position, which might be defined as no less than the *verbal character in itself,* in Pasolini's case, on the contrary, we are faced with an operation that tends in exactly the opposite direction. In a striving after totality he takes over the entire configuration of the discourse with its inherent specific characteristics (of meaning, of linearity, of "property") while articulating it in the complex and defamiliarizing terms of a structural antinomy—whence the semantic displacement that runs through the text, and that the voice of the Subject is called upon to "make his own"—so that he thereby sets in act an experiment that carries the entire expressive situation *beyond the discourse,* placing it *after the discourse.* In the first case, the poet, occupied with the de-construction of the discourse, moves towards the "atemporal" or towards the "origin," it may well be with the aim of experiencing its absence or its continual "deferment"; in Pasolini's case, the operator, while he keeps the discourse intact, while overdetermining it critically, seems to hint at the possibility of some "posthumous" dimension, where the effects of truth (of history, of temporality, of melodic centralization of lived experience) collapse into the defamiliarized sense, into the unformulated song of a word that has come to the point of circumscribing its own otherness: sheer mortality.

Keala Jane Jewell (essay date 1982)

SOURCE: "Reading Pasolini's Roses," in *Symposium,* Vol. XXXVI, No. 3, Fall, 1982, pp. 207-19.

[*In the following excerpt, Jewell examines the poems "A na fruta," "Poesia in forma di rosa," and "Nuova poesia in forma di rosa" in order to find a definition of Pasolini's poetic language.*]

Pier Paolo Pasolini initiated his literary education writing lyric poetry. Commentators have found elusive, inherent poeticity throughout his work. In fact it is possible to view the poetic as a key to the complexity and diversity of a production which included novels, plays, journalistic essays, drawings and films. I wish to examine moments of Pasolini's poetic practice and theory in order to find a definition of poetic language pertinent to Pasolini's artistic corpus. My point of reference is the long **"Poesia in forma di rosa,"** the title poem for a volume of collected verse from the years 1961-64. Two factors influenced my choice: the volume *Poesia in forma di rosa* is contemporary with the poet's first films and forms a point both of rupture and of transition and this volume in particular presents an interesting paradox. In it one follows the course of a "death" of poetry for Pasolini, as he becomes "poeta sul marciapiede" 'streetwalker poet,' and yet, simultaneously, the birth of an incipient "Cinema di poesia" (title of his theoretical article), as the "poetic" moves out of poetry and into cinema. To determine what constitutes poetic language and its powers for Pasolini, I shall study not only **"Poesia in forma di rosa"** in its two versions, but shall begin by shifting backwards to his earlier dialect "formazione" and then forward briefly to his cinematic theories. The itinerary for my readings follows three thematically compatible poems, each containing image of the rose of Pasolini's titles. The first poem is **"A na fruta,"** from *Poesie a Casarsa* (1942), the second is **"Poesia in forma di rosa,"** and the third **"Nuova poesia in forma di rosa"** (the last two are both dated 1961-64).

It is best to include the entire poem and its Italian translation, as close analysis of **"A na fruta"** yields essential characteristics of Pasolini's poetics:

Lontàn, cu la to pièl

sblanciada da li rosis
i ti sos una rosa
ch'vif e a no fevela.

Ma quant che drenti al sen
ti nassarà na vòus
ti puartaràs sidina
encia tu la me cròus.
Sidina tal sulisu
dal solàr, ta li s-cialis,
ta la ciera dal ort,
tal pulvin da li stalis . . .

Sidina ta la ciasa
cu li peràulis strentis
tal cour romai pierdút
par un troi di silensi.

A una bambina. Lontana, con la tua pelle sbiancata dalle rose, tu sei una rosa che vive e non parla.

Ma quando nel petto ti nascerà una voce, porterai muta anche tu la mia croce.

Muta sul pavimento del solaio, sulle scale, sulla terra dell'orto, nella polvere delle stalle . . .

Muta nella casa, con le parole strette nel cuore, ormai perduto per un sentiero di silenzio.

The volume's page presents two separated texts, one in the dialect of Friuli (the language of Pasolini's mother), and the other below it in Italian. It is important to note, by way of introduction, several facts concerning Pasolini's choice of the Friulan dialect. First, from the perspective of the history of culture, dialect was "consciously antagonistic toward the *logos* of standardized Italian, no one's mother tongue." Pasolini embraced the language and life of rural Friuli and its peasants as a counter-Italy in opposition to the fascistic myth of a unified empire and as an escape from the linguistic dictatorship of the day. Second, from the perspective of literary history, Pasolini's poems depart from the use made of dialect in both the bourgeois theatre, where dialect was the language of the audience, and in veristic narrative, where dialect has democratic and "realistic" connotations. Pasolini's poetic dialect is neither a communicative aperture nor the language of "reality," but what Mengaldo has called "una dialettalità introversa." Although a case can be made for anchoring Pasolini's use of dialect to a distinct literary tradition, a study of the specific textual characteristics of his dialect poems within both the thematic and symbolic structures is equally useful for an understanding of the foundation of his poetic practice.

The choice of **"A na fruta"** for close analysis is in some senses simply pragmatic. The poem contains a significant rose image and thus material for thematic comparison, with the pivotal **"Poesia in forma di rosa."** It also is a poem that provides insight into Pasolini's poetic theories. As regards the thematics, Pasolini made the roses of the early volumes *La meglio gioventù* and *L'usignolo della Chiesa Cattolica* into a poetic myth which might be linked to a long European lyric tradition beginning with the *Roman de la Rose,* and he made the rose into a figure which carried a number of more private associations. The rose throughout Pasolini's early poetry is in fact often associated with the figure of his mother. In one exquisite poem she discovers a delicate white rose left on the white sheets of her son's unmade bed. The rose becomes a special *trait-d'union* and Pasolini does not fail to exploit the connotation given in Christian iconography to the rose as Mary, the link between Heaven and Earth.

The poem **"A na fruta"** introduces a deceptively simple portrait of a young inhabitant (his mother as a young girl perhaps) of the idyllic realm of Casarsa, where Pasolini spent part of his youth. The speaker of the poem converses with the girl. A number of dynamic and provocative oppositions concerning this figure are established in the first quatrain and developed over the poem's fourteen lines. The girl's pale skin visually contrasts the red of the roses in "la tua pelle sbiancata dalle rose" (i.e., the skin appears whiter in comparison with the red roses). The poem then proceeds to attribute more abstract contrasting qualities to her: "tu sei una rosa che vive e non parla." The two traits of vitality and lack of speech initially seem puzzling, but the symbolic meanings become clearer when the poet explains the way in which the girl will paradoxically become mute when she gains a voice: "Ma quando nel petto ti nascerà una voce, porterai muta anche tu la mia croce."

The female figure's acquisition of a voice follows an itinerary not unlike that of the Passion it seems. However, Pasolini coupled the itinerary of redemption with the suggestion of the plucking of the rose. After the girl bears the cross borne also by the poet, she touches silence and loss suggestive of mere death and not the fullness of eternal life. As she begins to perform her Leopardian "opre femminili" in the third quatrain, her heart shall be "ormai perduto per un sentiero di silenzio." At the time of her sexual maturation, the girl becomes silent, despite her voice or her potential for speech. In this oppositional coupling of the two itineraries of Passion, the two separate paths lead to two views of life. One is the Christian view of the passage through life, implied in the symbol of the cross, in which true, eternal life comes from the individual bearing his own cross. The second is the itinerary followed by the girl and symbolized in the rose. Now the pattern of events of a movement to eternal life is reversed, and is linked also to the idea of the voice and speech.

The phrase "ti nascerà una voce" may provide a way of understanding Pasolini's unusual reversal of Christian symbolism. The notions of birth and voice would benefit from deeper and separate analysis, but can only be treated briefly here, as both pertain more to Pasolini's philosophy than to his poetics. Anna Panicale has pointed out that Pasolini views birth into the world as loss and expropriation, as an end to an infinity of possibilities and expectations present in a pre-existence which birth captures and wrestles into finite, coercive shapes. Because the path to death begins inexorably from the moment of birth, birth itself and existence come to signify to Pasolini the very impossibility of dreams and a future. Such is the fate of our "fruta." The negative implication in the phrase "ti nascerà una voce" become clearer when tied to the concept of birth outlined above. The birth of a voice is another, perhaps final step on the path away from the unbounded state or pre-life.

The topic of voice deserves further attention, since it sheds light on Pasolini's notion of a poetic voice, which is tied, as we shall see, to the rose image. The rose of the poem is in fact juxtaposed to speech. Pasolini writes "rosa che vive e non parla." The rose is on the positive side of juxtaposition of present vitality and the paradoxically silent and future voice. The rose symbolically evokes the qualities associated with a state which precedes (the opening word is "lontana") and is thus exempt from the *parlare,* from voice and, more globally, from language. From a psychoanalytic view, the rose suggests a vital unity which is lost when the child learns verbal language. Because the rose in Pasolini's early poetry is also associated with the mother and the rose of **"A na fruta"** contrasts with the onset of the voice, one could assert further that Pasolini links the separation from the mother indirectly with the onset of the voice in a manner reminiscent of Jacques Lacan's linking of the development of the psyche with the developments of language acquisition. If one regards the girl's silence not just as a possible early death but as repression both at a psychoanalytic and a societal level, one sees that to Pasolini the onset of language means beginning to learn the Rules, beginning to submit to the power of exterior authority (in Lacanian terms, the movement from the realm of the Imaginary to the Symbolic).

Because the path to death begins inexorably from the moment of birth, birth itself and existence come to signify to Pasolini the very impossibility of dreams and a future.

—Keala Jane Jewell

The choice of dialect as the vehicle for the poetry provides another link between the symbolic rose and the poetic as "pre-linguistic." First of all, the dialect poem is distant; like the girl/rose it is "afar" from Language, especially from the language of the hallowed (perhaps "dead") Italian lyric tradition. Contini justifiably writes of Pasolini's use of dialect as a "scandal," and Pasolini has variously been considered in some aspects Hermetic since Friulan is almost unintelligible to the majority of Italian readers, and Symbolist for his choice of a pure, private language as the language of poetry. The dialect poem is also literally distant from the Italian in a spatial sense: the printed page produces a peculiar effect, since the dialect demonstrates the traditional stanzaic shape and poetic traits, while the Italian text is relegated to the bottom of the page in smaller print and across several inches of white space which suggests the resistance between the two texts. In Pasolini's contradictory scheme of things, the dead language (Friulan and dialects are heading toward extinction) is the virgin, living one. Dialect is the language which deploys the poetic messages or form in music, meter, assonance, etc.; thus, poetry and dialect are inseparable and both counteract Language. Yet our understanding of the complexity of Pasolini's use of dialect grows if we take a further step and view the dialect and Italian texts as entering a dialectical relation.

Pasolini wrote the following in a note to an edition of his poems: "Le versioni in italiano a piè di pagina . . . fanno parte integrante del testo poetico: le ho perciò stese con cura e quasi, idealmente, contemporaneamente al frilano." While the bilingualism of the poetry indubitably is evidence of psychological struggle (between the "maternal" and "paternal" tongues) with social and cultural consequences, from the point of view of the reader, the poetic process is significantly imitated in the process of reading the double poems. The Italian text does not simply refer to some signifieds without first referring to some other verbal forms, the dialect ones. Each text refers to some words already formed in a text, rather than simply to some referent or to a stable, social, standard signified. That the Italian text sends the reader back to another anterior and more mysterious text is crucial. In this movement is the intersection of the thematics of regression and the poetics of regression. In an essay on Friulan poets Pasolini wrote of himself: "il suo regresso da una lingua all'altra—anteriore e infinitamente più pura—era un regresso lungo i gradi dell'essere. . . . Non potendo impadronirsi per le vie psicologicamente normali del razionale, non poteva che reimmergersi in esso: tornare indietro: rifare quel cammino in un punto del quale la sua fase di felicità coincideva con l'incantevole paesaggio casarsese."

The typographical juxtaposition on the page makes more explicit Pasolini's view of the problematic nature of translation. Just as in the movement of the formless into form something is always lost, so intranslation is something inevitably lost, or not grasped. One critic has even advanced the idea that the Italian text destroys the dialect. Pasolini warned his readers in a note to an early edition of words that "nel testo italiano, ho variamente tradotti, ma che in realtà restano intraducibili." Pasolini informs his readers that reality cannot be fully represented in all its originality, but he also presents a claim that dialect and poetry come closer to the real enigmatic text. Significantly, one word stands out in **"A na fruta"** because it passes untranslated from dialect into Italian and back: "rosa."

The particular linguistic status of the dialect helps us to understand why Pasolini holds it to be, as he has said, "più vicino al mondo." Tzvetan Todorov's [*Dictionnaire Encyclopedique des sciences du language*] classification of the principal and secondary meanings of language into typologies is useful in this regard. Todorov

notes that a secondary meaning can result from what he calls a contiguity of signifiers, and what Charles Bally named evocation by milieu (e. g., *pastiche*). In **"A na fruta,"** no matter what "sidina" denotes in dialect, the word would take on a special secondary meaning simply by virtue of its marked dialect status. This pinpoints why Pasolini attributes to dialect such an immediacy or closeness to reality: dialect is linked by its use in that milieu to the timeless world of the peasants of Friuli in a nearly Utopian way.

The second poem to be read here followed nearly ten years after **"A na fruta,"** and is the one which gives its name to the volume *Poesia in forma di rosa*. The volume was written after Pasolini's well-known narrative poem, **"Le Ceneri di Gramsci,"** after what has been called the "Roman period," which includes two novels written in the fifties and his earliest work in cinematic circles. During the years 1961-64, Pasolini's poetic and cinematic practices entered into complex exchanges, as the poet emerged, along with Christian Metz and Umberto Eco, as an important contributor to the debates at the Pesaro Film Festivals on the semiology of cinema. It is essential to understand that the volume *Poesia in forma di rosa* marks the disintegration of the poet's faith in the peasant world, or the sub-proletarians of the Roman novels, to withstand the onslaught of what Pasolini views as the homologizing forces of neo-capitalist consumerism, which came on the tails of the so-called "economic miracle" of the sixties in Italy. The latter is seen to blur class distinction, and hence to impede class struggle, turning even the peasantry into petit-bourgeois greedy for washing machines. The volume holds altogether new landscapes, often connected with travels in Pasolini's film directing to Guinea, Israel, and Africa which, to a certain extent, replaces Friuli and the Roman slums as the stronghold against the new forces of capitalism.

The volume is Pasolini's most autobiographical work, and draws the portrait of an alluring, powerful personality quite different from that of the influential public figure whose byline appeared on the front page of *Corriere della sera*. The poet mercilessly derides himself, ironically referring to himself as a "bestia ferita," a "Don Chisciotte di tre anni, un Orlando noioso." There are accounts of his night wanderings, of the judiciary proceedings he underwent. Fear of solitude and isolation pervades, with weeping confessions, which serve, as Enzo Siciliano has pointed out, to cure a division of self. The sense of marginality in the poet is so great that the narrative coherence of earlier poems of the fifties like **"Le Ceneri di Gramsci"** is eroded. At the same time, the probing of open wounds results in a strength when Pasolini holds up his own homosexual love, seen to separate him from the world, as "amore infecondo e purissimo." Single-handed, the self pitches a battle against the monster consumerism, with its mental and physical pollution. Pasolini alone must preserve everything that his young "fruta" had been, and ironically but half seriously he calls himself a "feto adulto."

"Poesia in forma di rosa" is nearly two hundred lines long and rather unwieldy. It was written in a modified *terza rima*, and is essentially a monologue with a tenuous narrative thread: a taxi ride from Fiumicino airport. Movement to disillusion constitutes a second narrative organization, reflected in a substructuring system, the form of the rose, as each of five roses or petals is plucked (each carries a certain thematic), until none are left. This "plucking of the rose" also suggests dismemberment of the poet, since the petals are said to be strewn on the taxi floor. The poet has become the place of oppositions and contradictions which form the subject matter of the poem. I shall have to limit my discussion of the thematic aspects, and focus on Pasolini's poetic language as it emerges here. It is useful to quote several stanzas:

> Ho sbagliato tutto, Fiumicino
> riapparso di tra nuvole di fango,
> è ancora più vecchio di me.

> I resti del vecchio Pasolini
> sui profili dell' agro . . . tuguri
> e ammassi di grattacieli . . .

> È una rosa carnale di dolore,
> con cinque rose incarnate,
> cancri di rosa nella rosa

> prima: in principio era il Dolore.
> Ed eccolo, Uno e Cinquino.
> La prima rosa seriore significa

> ah, una puntura di morfina! aiuto!

This rose is hardly the earlier fragrant white rose on white sheets, for the poet immediately evokes carnality and disease. A strange *contaminatio* generates this new, hybrid rose. Pasolini adopts the liturgical language of the holy mystery of the trinity, and a primal grief/rose supplants the biblical *verbum* of gospel beginnings. The rose is "uno e cinquino," with familiar primal unity. It is of the beginnings, an age before the word became flesh (reminiscent of the birth of **"A na fruta"**); it is pre-articulation. Despite the different, growing number of branches of the Unity (five rather than three), this rose is still the rose of poetry, "che vive e non parla," although she has been thrown into the mud. Pasolini's words again verge on heresy, but provide a clue to the nature of his religiosity, defined by Scalia as "l'ossessione della crisi di ogni re-ligio."

Another characteristic of the functioning of the language of **"Poesia in forma di rosa"** parallels that found in **"A na fruta."** The concept of evocation by milieu has been mentioned in connection with Pasolini's use of dialect, along with the notion that signification comes about by referring to an anterior text. Clearly, in **"Poesia in forma di rosa,"** the text evoked is St. John's Gospel. In the later poem, two texts in a problematic relationship (Pasolini's and the Bible) are not separated on the page as in the dialect poems, and stylization has slipped into parody. Nevertheless, the poetics and thematics of juxtaposition are present. The "sous-systèmes" of the poem call each other in turn into question, and their interaction says more than either could convey alone.
A brief excursion into stylistic analysis of the poem reveals

something of what the various sub-systems are. There appear to be two different textual movements: one in the direction of disorder, and one in the direction of order. Within the first category fall the fractured narrative discourse, the chaotic rhythms of Pasolini's hendecasyllables, and the ironic modes which engage ambiguity. In the second category falls the patterning of the *terza rima,* a return, though subversive, to tradition. The *terza rima* provides an appropriate vehicle for the narrative precisely because of its nature as a continuum. The second movement to order is found in the rose as the main element of structure. An internal form, it generates poetry and content because each of its petals carries a thematic, and each is sequentially dismissed. Furthermore, each petal spans roughtly five tercets, except the central one which contains ten tercets. The two movements in different directions, to order and its opposite, cannot easily be made homologous or concentric, although in a "contest," the movement to order in the straightforward structure of the rose tugs hardest, and the rose provides a substantial, if artificial, alternate organization of meaning.

Pasolini's concept of the poetic word is further elucidated in the contents of the third petal of the poem, a lengthy narration in which barbarians dressed in the American shirts of charity overrun Europe in a future pre-history dubbed "la Nuova Preistoria." The mysterious account reads like a prophecy, though at one level it stages a future decline of Neo-capitalism. Pasolini spoke of the prophetic aspect of this work as his "cursus del Vecchio Testamento." His coupling of the poetic and the prophetic (a series of poems in the volume has the title **"Profezie"**) reveals a new Pasolini-Jeremiah.

Maurice Blanchot writes that the prophetic word in the form of dreams, possession, the burning bush, "s'impose du dehors, elle est le dehors même, le poids et la souffrance du Dehors." The prophet's word also refers to a word already formed. In prophecy meaning is imperative, for "il n'y a pas de refuge contre ce sens qui partout nous poursuit, nous précède . . .The prophet and poet touch that totality of meaning and combat its reduction into the misleading Language. The imperative of meaning, and its difficult translation, is crucial to a comprehension of Pasolini's theory of the cinema as the written language of reality, what Pasolini calls the "magma," an overwhelming, beloved, impelling, and infinite exterior. In prophecy the word equals reality, though there may be a gap between the time of utterance and fulfillment. For Pasolini, the cinema and reality became synonomous. Anna Panicale is right when she states that Pasolini "chiede che la poesia si faccia uguale alla vita. . . ."

Pasolini called his second rendering of **"Poesia in forma di rosa"** the "imbarazzanti calligrammes / del mio vile piagnisteo." The stanzas of this "Nuova poesia in forma di rosa" resemble rose petals, but the iconic nature of this representation should not be exaggerated, since some of Pasolini's earlier poems in **L'usignolo della Chiesa Cattolica** appeared in a similar form. A single word opens each stanza and is centered. Underneath, two or three words are centered, and so on, until the pyramid structure reverses its order and diminishes and the last line is composed of a single word. The number of words per line grows until, at the center, they flow into prose stretching to both margins, and are ordered back into a reverse hierarchy. This visual organization subverts the syntactic reading, in what Giovanni Pozzi calls "una crisi di rapporti fra immagine e segno." Again, Pasolini challenges language as the power to dictate meaning, and an alternative production of meaning emerges as the iconic signs acquire a new role, symptomatic, perhaps of Pasolini's increasing use of the cinematic medium.

The **"Nuova poesia in forma di rosa"** leaves little room for any poetic mystery in its contents. Significantly, the plucking of petals doubles as a reading of the petals. Openly declaring the rose to be a text, Pasolini grieves in the last stanza: "sfogliai una vana rosa." Bitter irony prevails, as he calls up Dante's text this time, the opening lines of the heady Paradiso XXXI: "In forma dunque di candida rosa / mi si mostrava la milizia santa." Dante had contemplated tiers of illustrious souls in the Celestial Rose, angels swooping like bees to drink from the flower. Pasolini contemplates the motley troops of Italian literary life, his friends of the nineteen fifties and sixties: Leonetti "Da redattore rifatto formica": Roversi "come un monaco di clausura / diventato pazzo." Moravia who "ci lascia soli a dibatterci in questi spregevoli problemi letterari / vecchi come il cucco."

The dominance of the ironical mode signals a new direction in Pasolini's poetry. Later poems acknowledge the death of poetry. The poet lies down in solitude: "in ogni campo mona kateudo, eora tocca a altri" we read in *Le poesie*. Pasolini finds it fruitless to oppose poetry, with its connotations of freedom, to the pervasiveness of a system of repression by permissiveness and false sense of well-being. The *koiné* has consolidated its territory, and Pasolini seeks a new way to free poetry from its stylish service to the bourgeois class, which he feels has espoused and co-opted its problematic nature. In cinema, Pasolini will find a better instrument or technique to grasp the already formed and mysterious text of reality, to grasp and save it.

The subject of Pasolini's theory and practice of cinema is complex, and critics (especially his biographer Enzo Siciliano) have examined the significance of the poet's change of artistic medium at length. Pasolini's own views of his practice also evolved over a period of years. Factors worthy of note are: Pasolini's desire to protest against the Italian nation by choosing an artistic form he believed to be transnational; his belief that cinema is less institutional in its codes ("La sua operazione non può essere linguistica ma stilistica"); and his conviction that cinema, with its use of the image, provides a technique for "una specie di ritorno alle origini: fino a ritrovare nei mezzi tecnici del cinema l'originaria qualità onirica, barbarica, originale, irregolare, aggressiva, visionaria."

Perhaps the most controversial of his theoretical tenets was the claim that cinema constituted the written language of reality. An extract from his article "Res sunt nomina" illustrates Pasolini's idea, testifying to the lyrical nature of even his theoretical writings: "Prendiamo questo Joaquim: egli si presenta ai miei occhi, in un ambiente (la spiaggia di Barra, sotto il Corcovado), e si esprime, prima con la pura e semplice presenza fisica, il suo corpo; poi con la mimica (il modo di camminare non solo espressivo in sé, ma reso appositamente tale per comunicare certe cose in un certo modo all'osservatore), infine con la lingua orale. Ma questi tre mezzi non sono che tre momenti di un solo linguaggio: il linguaggio di Joaquim vivente. . ."

According to Pasolini, the cinema reproduces and best captures in images what has already been made a cipher, a pre-existing system. For him, Reality, now capitalized, forms an infinitely polysemous semiotic system, whose signs are objects subject to aesthetic organization, just as the signs of verbal language can be poetic. One has access to the text of Reality in several ways: Pasolini writes that the written-spoken language *evokes* Reality, referring to it "con tutto ciò di regressivo che ciò implica." This special form of translation stands in opposition to the cinema as "traduzioni per riproduzione." Antonio Costa finds that Pasolini tried to establish between visual and verbal signification the same kind of relationship which the poet previously posited between dialect and standard Italian. All systems attempting to capture the original text of Reality fall short, however, and "In realtà non c'é significato: perché anche il significato è un segno."

This endless chain of representing falls short of possessing what Andrea Zanzotto called Pasolini's "aldilà della lingua . . . quella totalità che il cinema vorrebbe essere e metaforizza." In his cinema Pasolini has changed the instruments of his incantation, but his activity is still that of a poet.

N. S. Thompson (review date 1982)

SOURCE: "Poet into man," in *The Times Literary Supplement*, No. 4,149, October 8, 1982, p. 1105.

[*In the following excerpt, Thompson notes the development of Pasolini from "civil poet" to "kinetic poet" in* Pier Paolo Pasolini: Poems.]

As a poet, Pier Paolo Pasolini was an arch-traditionalist; as a man, a "politikon z on", he was a radical romantic whom disillusion drove to despair. The man frustrated the poet and forced him, first, to relinquish his traditional means in favour of a freer approach to poetry, and later, to abandon his poetry—ostensibly, at least—for the cinema.

The present volume of *Poems*, . . . represents about a sixth of Pasolini's published work in Italian and none of his early lyrics in the Friulan dialect. It is based on a selection Pasolini himself made for an edition in 1970, and includes his introduction to this volume as an appendix. Certainly, making a first, rigorous choice from among the works of such a wide-ranging poet is an exceedingly difficult task, and, while this selection is inclusive, showing the move from rational public poet to tortured private man, the picture it presents is inevitably incomplete. . . .

What kind of a poet emerges? As may be expected of a writer who also painted, and later turned to film, a very visual one; the two long poems in *terza rima* are intense metaphysical meditations, but firmly located in time and place. A visit to the grave of Antonio Gramsci in the Protestant Cemetery in Rome is the setting for a scrupulously honest self-examination in the course of which the rational Communist finds that he does not want his beloved working class to change, to lose its traditional vital qualities; **"Two days of fever"** give rise to a scrutiny of his concepts of religion and love, where he remembers his earlier Catholicism, contrasting it with his present Marxism. In both poems, descriptions of his environment amplify and extend his state of mind. But, unlike the *ermetici*, Pasolini is not locked inside himself; the problems he examines, albeit from a personal, even private point of view, are universal: society, religion, social change. As most critics agree, Pasolini's great contribution was the creation of "una poesia civile", the rational argument of a civilized mind. But the adjective also carries the meaning of "civil": his is a public poetry, even if there is no consensus of acceptance by the public. After the strenuous effort to arrive at these well-reasoned, balanced poems of the 1950s, he changed direction, turning inwards to become a "kinetic poet": his subjective reactions are given first place, making for an engaging warmth, until they become the agony of his later years. However, in both modes, Pasolini was a skilled prosodist—especially in his resurrection of Dante's *terza rima*—who twisted and broke the rules to great effect. . . .

Reviewing Pasolini's first small book of dialect poetry in the *Corriere di Lugarno* in 1943, Gianfranco Contini, then a young professor, hit a prophetic note in remarking on the "scandal" which it introduced into the "annals of dialect literature". The scandal was in trying to use dialect for the expression of honest, personal sentiment rather than as a medium for folk tales.

Pia Friedrich (essay date 1982)

SOURCE: *"La meglio gioventù:* The Best Youth," in *Pier Paolo Pasolini,* Twayne Publishers, 1982, pp. 48-59.

[*In the following essay, Friedrich analyzes the imagery of Narcissus in Pasolini's Fruilian poems of* La meglio gioventù.]

La meglio gioventù [The best youth] is the volume, published in 1954, that brings together the entire first cycle of Friulian poems: most of the *Poesie a Casarsa* (1941-48); the *Suite furlana* (1944-49); a group of poems directly linked to the events of the Resistance entitled *Il Testament Coran* (1947-52); *Appendice* (1950-53); and *Romancero* (1953). The latter group includes, under the subtitle *I Colús*—the surname of the poet's mother's family—the "humble" story of the Friulian land.
The presentation in a single volume of a number of poetic

works, written during different periods even if thematically and linguistically tied, seems to indicate the author's desire to clarify *a posteriori* the psychological and cultural structure of his first literary attempts. The fundamental choice is that of the Friuli as "the early characterization of an essential rapport, of a bond with a geographical, social, and even biological matrix" conditioning the poet's whole discourse, up to the necessary ideal conclusion. Underlying the choice of the Friuli is the dialectal option shared by all the compositions of *La meglio gioventù* and constituting their most evident stylistic note. Speaking of himself in the third person, Pasolini has outlined the motives of the choice that made him assume the Friulian dialect as "his only mode of consciousness." In the essay "La poesia dialettale del Novecento" [Dialect poetry of the twentieth century, 1952], in the section on "Il Friuli" we read that

> at the sources of his sensuality there was an impediment to a form of direct knowledge from the inside out, from the bottom up . . . ; a screen had fallen between him and the world for which he felt such a violent, childlike curiosity. Being unable to possess it by the psychologically normal means of the rational, he could only re-immerse himself in it . . . return along that road, at that one point when his moment of happiness coincided with the enchanting landscape of Casarsa, with a rustic life made epic by a heartrending charge of nostalgia. Knowing was the same as expressing. And here is the linguistic break, the return to a language closer to the world.

The rejection of the official Italian language of the twentieth century thus imposes the retreat to a dialect which, for lack of other instruments of expression, becomes the chosen language. Regarding this option, it would be restrictive to neglect its political significance, albeit differently "political" with respect to the poet's whole later message, preceding as it does "the discovery of Marx". . . [Through] his adoption of dialect in the early poems, Pasolini exalted, with true anti-conformism, that which the Fascist regime intended not so much to oppress as to exclude, namely the regional idiosyncrasies, the vital originality of local cultures, and the innocent naturalness of the peasant world. Opting for a world left outside the institutions, the poet carried on his literary operation against the nationalistic centralism of Rome and against the pseudo-intellectualism descending from it.

Beyond the courage and purpose of a political statement, and in a certain sense in contradiction to them, the recourse to dialect implies a rather complex process of poetic stylization. In the first poems, namely those collected in the short volume published in Bologna in 1942 under the title *Poesia a Casarsa,* the linguistic medium is "a literary koiné" utilizing words and expressions from the dialect of Casarsa and its neighboring villages (those on the right side of the Tagliamento River). The young poet had sensed the creative autonomy and the integral vigor of that vernacular, still relegated to the status of a spoken language, which made it unique even within the sphere of the limited but tested Friulian linguistic and literary tradition. With the philological acumen that would always mark him, and through survey operations showing a technique based on the codified rules of university linguistics, Pasolini gathered the living language, emitted "from the mouths of native speakers." The attestation is once again his own:

> On a summer morning in 1941 I was on the wooden balcony outside my mother's house. . . on that balcony, I was either drawing . . . or I was writing verses. When there resounded the word *rosada* [dew]. It was Livio, a neighbor boy from across the street, one of the Socolaris, who spoke. A tall, large-boned boy. . . . Anyway Livio surely spoke of simple, innocent things. The word *rosada,* spoken on that sunny morning, was only an expressive bit of his oral vivacity. Certainly that word . . . *had never been written*. It had always only been a *sound*. Whatever I had been doing that morning . . . I stopped suddenly: this is part of the dazzling memory. And I immediately wrote some verses in that Friulian speech . . . which up to that point had been *only a bunch of sounds:* I began at first to make the work *rosada* graphic. That first experimental poem disappeared; the second, which I wrote the next day, remains: Sera imbarlumida, tal fossàl/ a cres l'aga . . ." [Luminous evening, in the ditch/ the water grows.]

However reliable the "dazzling memory" might be, what undoubtedly struck the poet, activating his imagination, was the expressiveness of the intimate spoken language and its phonic substance; and he benefited, as Giorgio Caproni has written, from "the fact of having assumed a language . . . not properly his own, which not only did not force him, precisely because it was not his own, to choose and love its particular physical and human territory with a redoubled 'spirit of love'; but, being almost virgin as far as literature is concerned, also permitted him a greater freedom of speech thanks to the newness of the words, which were not yet codified and therefore still malleable." ["Appunti," *Paragone Letteratura*].

As we learn in a "note" by the author in the 1954 edition, the compositions in Friulian that follow **Poesie a Casarsa** show some changes with respect to the first group ". . . while there the linguistic 'violence' tended to make of the Casarsan speech both a Friulian koiné and a sort of absolute language, nonexistent in nature . . . here Casarsan is readapted in its entire institutional quality." Several of the poems of the second group, furthermore, are based on other variants of the Friulian dialect: that of Valvasone, Cordenons, Gleris, etc.: all villages situated in the heart of the Friuli, on the right bank of the Tagliamento. The poet's philological attention to local variations is painstaking, and it is carried out through tonal differences pervading the various compositions and also in the use of similar— but not identical—words identifying or qualifying a single object, and in the multiformity of syntactical devices.

In my opinion, however, it is in **Poesie a Casarsa** that "the greater freedom of speech" permitted by words "not yet codified" is manifested more clearly, in the extraordinary richness of expressive variation afforded by the "speakers'" vocabulary and that of the poet.

To aid the average Italian reader and—given the special composite nature of the dialect in the earlyworks—the Fri-

ulian reader as well, Pasolini has provided, at the bottom of the page, an Italian version of the various compositions, stating in the note to the 1954 edition "the versions in Italian . . . are a part, and sometimes an integral part, of the poetic texts: I have therefore drafted them with care and almost, ideally, at the same time as the Friulian versions." With Pasolini, and contrary to the opinion of those critics who pointed out only the inevitable lack of "musical resonance" in the translations and the fact that they are only approximative interpretations (which, no doubt, is quite evident at times), I retain that they fulfill a notable structural function both within the individual compositions and in the collection as a whole. Within the full range of his Friulian works, the dialect text conveys the poet's yearning— originally lyrical—for a recovery of moral health to be acquired only through an immersion in the innocent naturalness of the peasant's world, the remoteness of which the poet feels with unconquerable melancholy. Detached from reality, taken on as a distant, absolute tongue, the dialect lives in its ability to evoke, evoking essence rather than existence. To the translation is given the task of "naming" in a recognizable fashion. In the pages of the book, the physical space between the dialect text and the translation the reader must consult in order to understand (a space which at times takes up most of the page) creates a further distancing from the poet's world.

This opposition—or juxtaposition—of dialect and translation can also be expressed as a contrast between the poetic functions of sound and meaning. Consider what Pasolini said about his first perception of the aural essence of Friulian: The dialect provides the poetic sound and substance, but we must resort to the translation to demystify the expression and to find access to its meaning.

Identification with nature and with people, the boy and the mother, the enchantment of the countryside, the arcane fascinations of religiosity and solitary sex constitute the general topics of the first part of the collection. They are placed between the polar presences of innocence and death. In the second part, which deals with adulthood (and the division is purely psychological), the same themes reappear, revealing, however, new interests, not so much social as moral, favoring the motifs of poverty as daily struggle, of a first, still-latent, and unconscious rebellion by the peasants against the rich, of a thirst for liberty understood as freedom from oppression of the natural right to be young and to be happy. The theme of the Resistance is also placed within this by-now-limiting framework, between youth and death.

In the economy of both parts, if to differing extent and with differing functional usage of stylistic elements within the whole of the text, the image of infancy and youth in all their attributes is preeminent, and the expressive richness of dialect assists the poet.

The lexical variants connoting children, boys, and youths are quite numerous, and the tonal shadings they express are, more often than not, impossible to render in translation; but they may be felt in the poetic context of dialect. The range of these expressions is again enlarged through adjectival qualifications.

Nini is the word connoting childhood. There follow those that designate early adolescence and youth: *frut, donzel* (of almost classic poetic stature), *fi, fantàt, zòvin,* and the variations *frutín, fantassín, fantassút, frutút, zuvinín.* The range of these locutions is further widened by qualifying expressions: *frut di lus* ("child of light"), *zòvin lizèir* ("light youth"), *bel fi* ("handsome lad"), *puòr zòvin* ("poor youngster"), *frut ch'al rit* ("laughing child"), *spirt di frut* ("boyish spirit"). (The more imaginative and affectionate of these variations are more numerous in the first part of the collection.)

The poem immediately following the **"Dedica"** [Dedication] to Casarsa introduces many if not all the allusive symbols of the collection, beginning with the title **"Il nini muàrt"** [The dead child] and the evocation of Narcissus. In the first tercet the landscape is luminously vital, marked by fertility expressed in nature and woman:

> Sera imbarlumida, tal fossàl
> a cres l'aga, na fèmina plena
> a ciamina pal ciamp . . .

> [Luminous evening, in the ditch the water grows, a woman with child walks through the field.]

Nevertheless, in the second part the picture dissolves and the luminous quality of the evening vanishes: "I remember you, Narcissus, you were the color of the evening, when the bells toll for the dead." The evocation of memory, and especially the past "you were," interrupt the peaceful contemplation. There is an implicit relationship between the "I" and Narcissus: the "I" establishes the scene and the memory, then evokes and calls Narcissus. Narcissus is the device permitting the introduction of both the poetic voice and the symbolic premonition of death. In an atmosphere of subdued resonances, in which the "luminous" evening of the first tercet becomes the mere color of itself, the end is linked to the title. The symbolic poles of the work are revealed through the structure of the poem and the overlapping of images.

NARCISSUS

The first boy to emerge from the poet's memory in **"Poesie a Casarsa"** is called **"Narcís,"** Narcissus. In other poems other boys and youths appear, and if their name is not Narcissus, they take Narcissus's lyric function. In *Poesie a Casarsa* and *Suite Furlana* (1944-49) especially, the name and presence of Narcissus return until they finally assume an unequivocal dimension:

> O me donzel! Jo i nas
> ta l'odòur che la ploja
> a suspira tai pras
> di erba viva . . . I nas
> tal spieli de la roja . . .

> [O my youngling! I am born in the smell that the rain breathes from the meadows of living grass . . . I am born in the mirror of the fosse . . .]

And under the title **"David"**:

> "Leaning against the wall, poor lad, you turn towards me your kind head, with a weary laughter in your eyes . . ."

up to the poem **"Suite furlana"** and the three variations of **"Dansa di Narcís"**:

> "A boy gazes at himself in the mirror, his eye laughs black . . ."

> . . . I arose among the violets
> while the dawn was breaking
> singing a forgotten song . . .
> I said to myself: "Narcissus"
> and a spirit with my face
> obscured the grass
> with the gleaming of his curls.

The motifs connected to the myth of Narcissus are not, in my opinion, peripheral to Pasolini's poetic work, but they encompass all the other themes. By this I do not intend to claim that the myth constitutes the poetic archetype, but rather that the fundamental elements of the myth of Narcissus and those accessory to it are present in most of the poems of the first two groups. In the later ones, when the first glimmers of the social problematics surface, the myth is present on another level and takes on other colors, but it does not lose its function as a basic structure. Consider the last poem of *Romancero* (1953), cited above, the poem with the same title— **"La miej zoventút"**—that ends the book *La meglio gioventù:*

> . . . Vegnèit, trenos puartaìt lontan la zoventút.

> [Come trains, take far away the youth.]

The poet's identification with the "merry youths" sent away from their land and condemned to laugh no more is obvious. Less evident is the link between the last poem in the collection and the first. If the Narcís of the first poem is a *nini muàrt, la miej zoventút* ("the best youth") of the last poem *va soto tera* ("goes under the earth"): This in fact is the following verse in an old Friulian folksong, from which the title is taken:

> Sul ponte di Bassano
> bandiera nera
> la meglio gioventù
> va soto tera

> [On the bridge of Bassano, banner of black, the best youth goes under the earth.]

The search for the elements of the myth of Narcissus in the compositions of *La meglio gioventù* reveals a singular balance between the energy and content of the poems and their formal characteristics. We find concrete presences: Narcissus and the other boys, the waters, the fountains, the tears, the mirrors, and—significantly in one of the last poems—*il flòur dal narcís* ("the narcissus flower"). One component above the level of verbal imagery that governs the form of the work, connecting it with the substance of the myth, is the atmosphere of total stillness that in many compositions permits the reflection of the image:

> I nas
> tal spieli de la roja.
> In chel spiele Ciasarsa
> —coma i pras di rosada—
> di timp antic a trima . . .
>
> [I am born in the mirror of the fosse. In that mirror Casarsa—like the meadows with dew—quivers with ancient time . . .]

The past within which the poet searches for himself is a reality retransmitted to us as a poetic image, and immobility is necessary so that the optical phenomenon of reflection may take place. Casarsa quivers "in the mirror of the fosse," but "like the meadows with dew" her stirring is placed within a poetic, figurative context that has the features of eternity. In the same way, "the woman with child" who yet "walks through the field" is immobilized as a characterizing pictorial element in the changeless scene in which Narcissus searches for and, in the dead child, recognizes himself.

Another stylistic structure that leads us back to the myth is the function of the echo. The Italian translation "echoes" the dialect text, and most of the poetry of the second drafting—*La nuova gioventù*—echoes that of the first version. Words and feelings become somewhat distorted, as words and sounds are when they are repeated by an echo. Thus the verse of the dedication "A no è age pí frescia che tal mi país" (There is no water fresher than in my village) becomes "A no è aga pí frescia che ta chel país" (There is no water older than in that village). And the verses of the first form of "Aleluja": "Adès/ ti sos/ un frut di lus" (Now you are a child of light) reecho: "Adès/ ti sos/ un frut mai vivút" (Now you are a child who never lived).

The meanings and the conclusive evidence of Pasolini's tormented narcissistic itinerary will be found in the pages of *La nuova gioventù*, all of them marked with the anguish of continual contradiction with reality.

—*Pia Friedrich*

If we continue reading *La meglio gioventù* examining the network of those metaphors that appear with high frequency, always in connection with the same ancient myth, we may glimpse the underlying affective forces and the decisive existential experiences that shaped them. We find the text invaluable in pointing out and exemplifying the author's persistence—up to the inevitable breaking point— in an attempt to realize (or simply to represent to himself) an

ideal self, absolutely lovable for its truth, beauty, and power:

> Io i soj un biel fí, . . .
>
> [I am a handsome lad, . . .]
>
> . . . io i soj un spirt di amòur,
> che al so país al torna di lontan.
>
> [. . . I am a spirit of love that to his place returns from afar.]
>
> Lus a è me vita, e a súnin
> di fiesta par me tal sèil nut, . . .
>
> [Light is my life, and they ring festively for me in the naked sky . . .]

The attempt to perpetuate a complete reproduction of himself and his own body is organized and concentrated around attributes or parts of his own physical concreteness. Of primary importance for the clarification of this aspect are the first two variations of **"Suite furlana,"** which I transcribe only in part:

> Un frut al si vuarda tal spieli
> il so vuli al ghi rit neri.
> No content tal redròus al olma
> par jodi s'a è un cuàrp chè Forma . . .
> [A boy gazes at himself in the mirror, his eye laughs black. Not content, he looks in the other side to see if that Form is a body . . .]

The refusal to accept the reduction to subjectivity, marked by limitation and difference, is seen in the last of the *Poesie a Casarsa,* first version:

> A plòuf un fòuc
> scur tal me sen:
> no'l è soreli
> e no l'è lus.
> Dis dols e clars
> a svùalin via,
> io i soj di ciar,
> ciar di frutút . . .
>
> [A dark fire trains in my breast: it is not sun and it is not light. Sweet clear days fly away, I am of flesh, flesh of a child . . .]

To conclude this analysis, . . . there remains to be pointed out that determining element which, in the economy of narcissistic expansion and fixation as it appears in *La meglio gioventù,* is represented by the figure of the Mother. She comes to assume the role of an oracle of wisdom and authority that merges with her natural and immediate role as the object of desire, an image that is an obvious sign of a substantially regressive ideal ego, to the point where such an image may be recalled in the intact, absolute form of "Child mother" and "Girl mother." In **"Pastorela di Narcís"** the representation of the mother as the sensual image of a young shepherdess is set beside that of a fourteen-year-old Narcissus:

> I olmi platàt . . .
> e al so post i soj jo:
> mi jot sintàt ta un soc
> sot i ram dal pòul.
> I vuj di mi mari
> neris coma il fons dal stali,
> il stomi lusínt
> sot da l'abit risínt
> e una man pojada sora il grin.

> [I spy hidden away . . . and in her place am I: I see
> myself seated on a stump, under the branches of the
> poplar. My mother's eyes, black as the bottom of the
> manger, shining body under the new dress, and one
> hand placed upon her lap.]

Exemplary of the mother's desire—desire by the mother—
and furthermore of extraordinary poetic effect is "Suspir
di me mari ta na rosa" [Sigh of my mother over a rose]:

> Rosuta di me fí,
> dulà ti àia ciolta,
> parsè ti àia ciolta,
> la man di me fi?

> [Little rose of my son, where did it pick you, why did
> it pick you, the hand of my son?]

Death, tenderly celebrated in *La meglio gioventù* (and in
different ways in all of Pasolini's works where a relationship and identification with innocence and youth are expressed), is necessarily left outside the myth. The death of
the archetypal Narcissus is not a real one, as the transition
from the body to the flower is a resurrection, and the
flower gives shape to the fundamental elements of transformation.

The meanings and the conclusive evidence of Pasolini's
tormented narcissistic itinerary will be found in the pages of *La nuova gioventù*, all of them marked with the
anguish of continual contradiction with reality. Mourning the elusive purity of virgin youth the poet will say
there:

> I no soj veciu jo
> al è veciu il mond
> che no murínt al lassa
> cui ch'a vif sensa fond . . .

> [I am not old; it is the world that is old, which, undying,
> leaves those who live without aground . . .]

And again:

> i no plaus parsè che chel mond a no'l torna pí
> ma i plaus parsè che il so tornè al è finít . . .

> [I do not weep because that world will not return, but
> I weep because its turning has ended.]

In the Friulian poems, essentially, Pasolini lives the para-

dox that the narrator—in Ovid's version of the myth—
points out to the young Narcissus: "What you seek is
nowhere; but turn yourself away, and the object of your
love will be no more. That which you behold is but the
shadow of a reflected form and has no substance of its
own. With you it comes, with you it stays, and it will go
with you—if you can go."

John Ahern   (essay date 1983)

SOURCE: "Pasolini: His Poems, His Body," in *Parnassus: Poetry in Review,* Vol. 11, No. 2, Fall/Winter, 1983-
Spring/Summer, 1984, pp. 103-26.

[*In the following excerpt, Ahern demonstrates how Pasolini's "whole poetic career can be seen as a doomed struggle with the violence of poetic language."*]

It is easy to forget that Pier Paolo Pasolini is a major poet.
Between 1950 and his death in 1975 he published four
volumes of vigorous criticism—social, political, cultural,
linguistic, and literary. Some of these pieces, just a few
years after newspaper publication, have already found their
way into anthologies. He wrote or directed over two dozen
compelling, highly personal movies. He translated Aeschylus
and Plautus, and wrote four plays of his own. He edited
two anthologies of poetry in Italian dialects. He produced
two linguistically remarkable novels. Given the bulk of
his work and the notoriety of his life and death, it is easy
to overlook his five volumes of Italian verse and his single
volume in the *Friulano* dialect. . . .

Pasolini was the adored son of an adored mother. His
tolerated, absent father was a career military man, a patriot
and enthusiastic Fascist. In his childhood the family moved
every two or three years, spending summers in Friuli, his
mother's region, a pastoral oasis in northeastern Italy
between Venice and Udine. Just before the Second World
War he studied at the University of Bologna with Roberto
Longhi, the art historian, and various eminent philologists.
A curious, enterprising student and a born organizer, had
he followed the course of least resistance—something this
courageous man rarely chose—he would have become a
great poet-philologist like Poliziano, Leopardi, Carducci,
or Pascoli. He spent the war in Friuli where he set up a
private school at home. His students wrote poems in *Friulano,* learned the Latin names of plants, memorized the
witty didactic verses he composed for them, and listened
to him read Verga, Chekhov, Black Spirituals, and *The
Spoon River Anthology*. He bicycled through the countryside, scientifically collecting its speech, which changed
every few kilometers, as if his mother's mother tongue
were the primal language and Friuli Eden. . . . He practised an aesthete's liturgical, uninstitutional Catholicism.
Friends noticed an innate puritanism. His younger brother,
after fighting with the partisans, was traitorously murdered
by rival Communist partisans. Like young intellectuals all
over the peninsula, Pasolini joined the Communist Party
soon after the war. He turned out brilliant propaganda
posters for it in Italian and *Friulano,* became its local
secretary, secured a regular job in a state high school,

organized a lively film club. Then a priest blackmailed him: either resign the party or his love affairs with boys would be revealed. He ignored the threat. The police were informed. Newsboys hawked the story on the piazza. The Party expelled him as "morally and politically untrustworthy." He lost his teaching job. He and his family faced despair and hysteria. One bleak winter dawn in 1949 the twenty-seven-year-old ex-school teacher escaped to Rome with his mother.

In these years he wrote many poems in various *Friulano* dialects—a choice Americans unfamiliar with Italy might find quixotic. When Italy attained national unity in 1870 eighty percent of its population spoke a dialect as the mother tongue, and sometimes, but not always, Italian as a second language. These dialects are as old as Italian and like it derive from Latin. They are not ignorant, fallen forms of Italian, but regional languages, sometimes with literatures of their own, which larger linguistic groups term "dialects." The Fascists repressed the dialects in favor of Italian more vigorously than even the first national governments. Poets and writers found themselves in a bind. Before the twentieth century, Italian was primarily a written language of Tuscan origin, static and insulated from daily life, a literary language in the worst sense. In the nineteenth century many writers, such as Manzoni and Verga, mastered Italian after childhood. The *milanesi,* for example, snickered at Verga's peculiar, heavily accented Italian, literally translated from Sicilian. Patriotism and the desire for large audiences led most writers to choose Italian, but they still found it difficult to create a living literature in a language few readers did their living in. For Pasolini, whose mother tongue was in fact Italian, the publication of poetry in *Friulano* between 1942 and 1954 was a polemical gesture. . . .

Pasolini chose dialect not to get a better grip on reality, but as an absolutely pure language, not found in nature, "which no one knows any more." His choice was neither provincial nor folkloric. He worried *Friulano* into a delicious music similar to that of the Parnassians and Symbolists. The spectre of Giovanni Pascoli's equally artificial but less decadent lyrics haunt these poems. Their ideal public could never have consisted of Friulano peasants. The enormous range of literary references, the rhyme schemes drawn from literatures far removed in time and space, the falsely ingenuous sensibility are simply too alien. To be savored fully these poems demand the most refined literary palate. Their ideal reader would register the pervasive influence of Antonio Machado's lyrical evocation of Castile, and hear behind *"O sera imbarlumida"* in **"Il nini muàrt"** (which Pasolini renders in Italian as *"O sera luminosa"*) Machado's *"O tarde luminosa!"* (Poem LXXVII). The bodies of doomed *kouroi* dominate all these precious anthems. At the heart of this timeless, fatherless world lies a Friulan Adonis—a *fantassút,* a *fanciullino.* Osiris, Narcissus, Jesus, and the adolescent poet himself—whose mother's rapt attention (the true ideal audience?) will modulate into mourning at the inevitable death of her sterile, parthogenetic son. His obscurely necessary sacrifice does not renew the world. . . .

Pasolini became a notorious public figure. He won prizes,

was tried for obscenity, pornography, and offending religion. It was the happiest, most fertile period of his life. He was, he thought, inventing a new poetic language, rooted in history and part of its slow rush towards revolution. Expelled from Eden into time, his happy fall brought him to Rome in a moment of national crisis, whose witness and protagonist he chose to become. . . .

Narcissus woke to find himself a revolutionary intellectual. In 1957 he printed his elegy for [Antonio] Gramsci, **"The Ashes of Gramsci,"** which he had composed two years before. It sold out immediately, and has since been rarely out of print. The preceding generation of poets, Montale, Ungaretti, and the Hermeticists, adopted a diffident, marginal stance before the world. They scrutinized the text of nature, not civilization: clouds, waves, the play of light and wind on water. Pasolini broke with all that. He took history and society as his texts. He composed his non-transcendental graveyard poem in the *terza rima* of Dante, Pascoli, and the civic poets of the Risorgimento, replacing full rhyme with assonance and eye-rhyme. He fashioned a tense, broken, adjective-laden narrative in violation of the abstemious Hermetic precepts, mixing the exquisite with the ordinary. He assumed the persona of a national poet measuring his private passions against a dead heroic thinker who represents perfect historical consciousness.

> [Pasolini] fashioned a tense, broken, adjective-laden narrative in violation of the abstemious Hermetic precepts, mixing the exquisite with the ordinary. He assumed the persona of a national poet measuring his private passions against a dead heroic thinker who represents perfect historical consciousness.
>
> —*John Ahern*

The scene: nightfall in the English Cemetery in Rome where Gramsci is buried with others whom Italian society excluded. Shelley, who is also buried there, is invoked as representing high, non-revolutionary nineteenth-century culture. Surrounding the cemetery is the teeming, subproletarian, historically unconscious neighborhood of Testaccio. The poem is a meditation on passion and ideology, pleasure and praxis: it neither embraces nor challenges Marxism. The poet establishes a permanent tension between the movements of history and individual desire. Marxism is one term in his oxymoron, he is the other. He enriches the vocabulary and syntax of contemporary spoken Italian with the lexica of bible, church, and historical materialism. At times divergent semantic charges converge powerfully in single words. *Coscienza* denotes historical and class consciousness, ethical and religious conscience, and consciousness broadly understood. **"Le ceneri di Gramsci"** is a prosaic, gnomic, memorable dialogue between light and dark, heart and guts (*viscere*).

> Ed ecco qui me stesso . . . povero, vestito

dei panni che i poveri adocchiano in vetrine

dal rozzo splendore, e che ha sbiadito
la sporcizia delle più sperdute strade,
delle panche dei tram, da cui stranito

è il mio giorno: mentre sempre più rade
ho di queste vacanze, nel tormento
del mantenermi in vita; e se mi accade
di amare il mondo non è che per violento
e ingenuo amore sensuale
così come, confuso adolescente, un tempo

l'odiai, se in esso mi feriva il male
borghese di me borghese: e ora, scisso
—con te—il mondo, oggetto non appare

di rancore e quasi di mistico
disprezzo, la parte che ne ha il potere?
Eppure senza il tuo rigore, sussisto

perché non scelgo. Vivo nel non volere
del tramontato dopoguerra: amando
il mondo che odio—nella sua miseria

sprezzante e perso—per un oscuro scandalo
della coscienza. . . .

("Le ceneri di Gramsci," III)

And here am I . . . poor, dressed in
clothes that the poor admire in store

windows for their crude splendors
and that filthy back streets and tram
benches (which daze my day)

have faded; while, less and less often, these
moments come to me to interrupt my torment
of staying alive; and if I happen

to love the world, it's a naïve
violent sensual love, just as I
hated it when I was a confused

adolescent and its bourgeois evils
wounded my bourgeois self; and now, divided—
with you—doesn't the world—or at least

that part which holds power—seem worthy only
of rancor and an almost mystical contempt?
Yet without your rigor I survive because

I do not choose. I live in the non-will
of the dead post-war years: loving
the world I hate, scorning it, lost
in its wretchedness—in an obscure scandal
of consciousness. . . .

The poet annexes the cultural and economic crises of the nation to the pulsating tension of his own moral and intellectual conflicts, and then expresses these contrary forces in breathless, seemingly artless discourse which is barely saved from rant by Latinate precision (*"senza il tuo rigore sussisto"*—'without your rigor I survive') in the midst of willfully banal fixed phrases (*"le più sperdute strade"*—'the most out of the way streets') and by the ghost of broken hypermetric hendecasyllables which haunts his prose into poetry. If his awesome self-dramatization succeeds, it is because we finally accept the outrageous language. Nor has he forgotten the lyricism of the *Friulano* verse. In the poem's famed apophatic opening he politicizes the chaste silence, subtle coloring, and luscious epithets of the Decadents and Hermeticists, while abandoning their terseness for manic wordiness.

Non è di maggio questa impura aria
che il buio giardino straniero
fa ancora piè buio, o l'abbaglia

con cieche schiarite . . . questo cielo
di bave sopra gli attici giallini
che in semicerchi immensi fanno velo

alle curve del Tevere, ai turchini
monti del Lazio. . . .   Spande una mortale
pace, disamorata come i nostri destini,

tra le vecchie muraglie l'autunnale
maggio. In esso c'è il grigiore del mondo
la fine del decennio in cui ci appare

tra le macerie finito il profondo
e ingenuo sforzo di rifare la vita;
il silenzio, fradicio e infecondo . . .

("Le ceneri di Gramsci," I)

It isn't May-like, this impure air
which darkens the foreigners' dark
garden still more, then dazzles it

with blinding sunlight . . . this foam-
streaked sky above the ocher roof
terraces which in vast semicircles veil

Tiber's curves and Latium's cobalt
mountains. . . .   Inside the ancient walls
the autumnal May diffuses a deathly

peace, disquieting like our destinies,
and holds the whole world's dismay,
the finish of the decade that saw

the profound naive struggle to make
life over collapse in ruins;
silence, humid, fruitless . . .

Pasolini moved from script-writing to directing. His first feature-length movie, *Accattone*, caused a scandal when it appeared in 1961. Moving pictures brought him far larger audiences and incomes than printed words. He continued to write poems. He collected the early poems in Italian in *The Nightingale of the Catholic Church* (1958). *The Religion of My Time* (1961) carried on the enterprise begun in *The Ashes of Gramsci*. Now that he was a filmmaker, he could not easily play the national poet with a rare, albeit Marxist, sensibility. In **Poems in the Shape of a Rose** (1964) he included a poem in the form of a film-script of an interview with a French journalist, the Cobra, a cautionary fictionalization of the reader as well brought up, middle-class ignoramus. The poem is *"in cursus"*—the rhetorical name for solemn rhythmical medieval Latin prose. . . .

(Senza dissolvenza, a stacco netto, mi rappresento
in un atto—privo di precedenti storici—di
"industria culturale.")
Io volontariamente martirizzato . . . e,
lei di fronte, sul divano:
campo e contracampo, a rapidi flash,
"Lei—so che pensa, guardandomi,
in più domestica-italica M.F.
sempre alla Godard—lei, specie di Tennessee!",
il cobra col golfino di lana
                  (col cobra subordinato
            che screma in silenzio magnesio).
Poi forte: "Mi dice che cosa sta scrivendo?"

"Versi, versi, scrivo! versi!
(maledetta cretina,
versi che lei non capisce priva com'è
di cognizioni metriche! Versi!)
VERSI NON PIÙ IN TERZINE!

           Capisce?
Questo è quello che importa: non più in terzine!
Sono tornato tout court al magma!
Il Neo-capitalismo ha vinto, sono
sul marciapiede
          come poeta, ah [singhiozzo]
          e come cittadino [altro singhiozzo]."
E il cobra con il biro:
"Il titolo della Sua opera?" "Non so . . .
[Egli parla ora sommesso come intimidito,
   rivestendo
la parte che il colloquio, accettato, gli impone di
fare: come sta poco
a stingere
la sua grinta
in un muso di mammarolo condannato a morte] . . .
               (from **"Una disperata vitalità,"** III)

(Without a dissolve, in a sharp cut, I portray
myself in an act—without historical precedents—
of "cultural industry.")

I, voluntarily martyred . . . and
she in front of me, on the couch:
shot and countershot in rapid flashes,
"You"—I know what she's thinking, looking at me,
a more domestic-Italian *Masculine-Feminine,*
always à la Godard— "you, sort of a Tennessee!"
the cobra in the light wool sweater
        (and the subordinate cobra
          gliding in magnesium silence).
Then aloud: "Tell me what you're writing?"
"Poems, poems, I'm writing! Poems!

(stupid idiot,
poems she wouldn't understand, lacking as she is
in metric knowledge! Poems!)
POEMS NO LONGER IN TERCETS!

      Do you understand?
This is what's important: no longer in tercets!
I have gone back, plain and simple, to the magma!
Neocapitalism won, I've
been kicked out on the street
        as a poet [boo-hoo]
        and citizen [another boo-hoo]."
And the cobra with the ballpoint:
"The title of your work?" "I don't know . . .
[He speaks softly now, as though intimidated,
   assuming
the role the interview, once accepted, imposes
on him: how little it takes
for his sinister mug
to fade into
the face of a mama's boy condemned to death] . . .
          (from **"A Desperate Vitality,"** III)

This poem, a self-deprecating apology for abandoning *terza rima,* written partially in *terza rima,* attempts to exorcise the poet's bad conscience at abandoning full-time dedication to writing and poetry to become a movie director and media personality. The usual systematic contamination of styles and media (*singhiozzo, singhiozzo,* sob, sob, is comic strip language) does not produce a convincing poem. The merciless self-portrait ("sinister mug," thinning hair) and self-revelation (masturbation until he bled) do not efface the disingenuousness in characterizing himself as success's "voluntary martyr on a couch.". . .

[In the 1960s] Pasolini feared that his domination over cultural life was waning. In Palermo in 1963 an "avant-garde" of university professors had attempted to unseat Italy's leading writers, including Pasolini and Calvino. They drew unflattering comparisons between the truly "experimental" poetry of Ezra Pound and that of Pasolini. In this period he worked on a Dantean pastiche, *The Divine Mimesis* (posthumously published in unfinished form in 1975), whose manuscript he claimed had been found on the corpse of a poet "beaten to death with a stick in Palermo in 1963." At the Venice premier of *Teorema* in 1968 he contrived to interview an ailing Ezra Pound in a bold attempt to win his public support. The two poets shared a love of Italy's landscape and literature, as well as eccentric political beliefs, a knack for cultural organization, and a tendency to rant. No interchange occurred. Chastened, humble, courteous, Pound left his *tempus tacendi* long enough to affirm the failure and incoherence of a life dedicated to poetry. This was exactly what Pasolini feared most, and would have none of it. Shortly before his own death seven years later he would repudiate a large part, if not all, of his work. . . .

[Pasolini's] literary life was also moving toward a crisis. His final, slack book of verse, **Trasumanar e organizzar** (1971), received few and poor notices. His own review of it conceded its "falsity, insincerity and awkwardness," but not its "unreality." He observed that "an Oedipal terror of coming to know and admit determines the strange unhappy fortune of this book and probably of all Pasolini's work." . . .

Hatred consumed him: hatred for himself, his boys, his utopian political visions. He revised many poems in *Friulano* and published them with the originals in **La nuova gioventù (The New Youth)** in Spring 1975. More than savage palinodes, they are an assault on the corpus of his verse. In the poem that follows — original first, then revision—his village's mulberry plantation (silkworms feed on mulberry leaves) has been covered with asphalt, people live in new apartment houses, no smoke rises from the hearths of the old houses. The poet, now just the 'spirit' of a boy rather than a real boy, hates his ancestors instead of singing them, and befouls his face: shit instead of roses, piss instead of blood. Sadism now touched the securest part of his literary corpus, as it did his actual body.

> Fantassút, al plòuf il Sèil
> tai spolers dal to país,
> tal to vis di rosa e mèil
> pluvisín al nas il mèis.
>
> Il soreli scur di fun
> sot li branchis dai moràrs
> al it brusa e sui confíns
> tu i it ciantis, sòul, i muars.
>
> Fantassút, al rit il Sèil
> tai barcòns dal to país,
> tal to vis di sanc e fièl
> serenàt al mòur il mèis.
>
>   **("Ploja tai cunfíns")**

> Lad, Heaven rains
> on the hearths of your town,
> on your face of rose and honey
> in drizzle the month is born.
>
> The sun, dark with smoke,
> beneath the mulberry branches
> burns you, and on all the borders
> you alone sing the dead.
>
> Lad, Heaven smiles
> on the balconies of your town,
> on your face of blood and gall,
> the month dies clear and bright.
>
>   **("Rain on the Borders")**

> Spirt di frut, al plòuf il Sèil
> tai spolers di un muàrt país,
> tal to vis di merda e mèil
> pluvisin a nas un mèis.
>
> Il soreli blanc e lustri
> sora asfàlt e ciasis novis
> al it introna, e fòur di dut
> non i it às pí amòur pai muàrs.
> Spirt di frut, al rit il Sèil

> ta un país sensa pí fun,
> tal to vis di pis e fèil,
> mai nassút, al mòur un mèis.
>
>   **("Ploja fòur di dut")**

> Spirit of a boy, Heaven rains
> on the hearths of a dead town,
> on your face of shit and honey
> in drizzle the month is born.
>
> The sun, white and glistening,
> over the asphalt and new houses,
> stuns you, and you, outside of everything,
> have no more love for the dead.
>
> Spirit of a boy, Heaven smiles
> on a town with no more smoke:
> in your face of piss and gall,
> the month, never born, dies.
>
>   **("Rain Outside of Everything")**

After 1968 when he said he would "throw his body into the struggle," the poet in him began to die. His greatest work, the Friulan poems, **The Ashes of Gramsci** and **The Nightingale of the Catholic Church,** was behind him. Filmmaking, journalism, and his lonely, prophetic politics took all his energy. Never had he seen his poems as making up a body of work exempt from the mortality of his actual body. Rather he looked upon them as extensions of that body and filled them with images of recently or soon-to-be-slaughtered bodies, all of which were eventually his. He had decided to be the "lamb slain from the foundation of the world." He appears really to have believed that the death of his body could make a difference in the world which no poem could ever hope to. Who dare criticize him for choosing physical courage over the humility of the poet's craft? . . .

Pasolini's death conferred on his poetry a retroactive coherence that almost nullified the retroactive meaninglessness of his "Repudiation of the *Trilogy of Life*" five months earlier. The closure which his death provided his texts resembles that given to the Hebrew Scriptures by Jesus' death—it cries out for and resists interpretation. [The Sicilian novelist Leonardo] Sciascia said that the Catholic elements in it annihilate the anarchic ones. Does he mean, one wonders, that Pasolini's death was a sacrifice like Jesus'? These lines from an early poem in **The Nightingale of the Catholic Church** will not be read today as they were first read over thirty years ago. In them Christ looks upon his crucifiers as would a sexually excited homosexual masochist:

> Cristo, il tuo corpo
> di giovinetta
> è crocefisso
> da due stranieri.
> Sono due vivi
> ragazzi e rosse
> hanno le spalle,
> l'occhio celeste.
> Battono i chiodi

e il drappo trema
sopra il Tuo ventre . . .

(from **"La passione"**)

Christ, your young
girl's body
is crucified
by two foreigners.
They are two living
boys and have
red shoulders,
blue eyes.
They hammer in the nails
and the cloth quivers
over Thy belly . . .

There are those who argue that the linguistic sign is by origin and forever sacrificial. The word "stands for" what it represents as a sacrificial victim "stands for" the people. Following this line of thought, poetry, as the highest form of language, is *ipso facto* its most violent manifestation. Thus Pasolini's death was more than just thematically implicit in his poetry. His whole poetic career can be seen as a doomed struggle with the violence of poetic language. Hence his attempt to transform Friulano into an ahistoric Adamic tongue. . . . Acoustic signifiers with no assignable signifieds imply a non-violent because non-signifying language. Unfallen tongues bespeak no bloodshed. Pasolini's tragedy was never to have found an untragic language. Yet whatever relations one posits between language and violence, Pasolini's violent death does not redeem his poetry, even though it seals forever its union with his life. His poems, films, essays, novels, articles, and interviews are microtexts which together constitute a single *persona,* or macrotext. As the central man of the central decades of this century in Italy, he compels us to read his poems. Could they be detached from his life (and it is exactly this that his death will not allow), to be read only for themselves, we would find them less compelling. Nothing, not even a poet's blood, quite replaces craft.

Robert Wells (review date 1984)

SOURCE: "Most Ancient of Youths," in *The Times Literary Supplement,* No. 4,253, October 5, 1984, p. 1130.

[*In the following excerpted review of* Selected Poems, *Wells notes that the strength of Pasolini's poetry derives from its openness and departure from hermetic lyric tradition.*]

"What strikes me is the realization of how ingenuous was the expansiveness with which I wrote them: it was as if I were writing for someone who could only love me a great deal. I understand now why I have been the object of so much suspicion and hatred".

The great strength of Pasolini's poetry is its openness, the desire "to have / the world before my eyes and not / just in my heart". Writing often in a loose *terza rima*

which derives from Dante, he broke with the hermetic lyric tradition to produce a civil poetry (innovatory in Italian because it is of the Left), exploring in his own "obscure scandal of consciousness" the difficulties of post-war Italy. At its best, in for example **"The Ashes of Gramsci",** he combines liveliness and gravity, the apprehension of a general predicament with beautifully observed and lived specifics. The world of his poetry is chiefly that of the Roman suburbs and a population of first or second-generation city-dwellers, still living by the values of the countryside from which they came. Pasolini celebrates an ideal of archaic ingenuousness belonging to an immemorial *civiltà contadina.* The ideal originated in his memories of his own youth, largely spent in the north Italian region of Friuli, in whose dialect his earliest poems were written. The cityscapes of his poems are often interrupted by his recollection of "footpaths the shepherd / unknowingly fills to the brim with his youth".

Pasolini managed the poise of **"The Ashes of Gramsci"** only rarely. His work is characterized by **"A Desperate Vitality"**—the title of one of his most technically interesting poems. The stress is as much on the desperation as the vitality. Pasolini has the restlessness and haste of the protagonists in many of his films or of the hordes of urchins who often run shrieking in their wake. In his poetry, he is not at rest within the language and often gives the impression that he has already moved beyond what he is saying; the words are thrown away as if casually and with impatience. His descriptions of tireless street-wandering are dominated by a feeling of sexual promise and distraction, and there are many glimpses of the boys, "always nearer the enchantment of the species / the norm that makes of sons tender fathers", whom he sought out as partners. The confusions recorded in the poetry resolve themselves elsewhere—and then symbolically or by pretext—in the temporary clarity of sex.

These encounters are partly a defiant assertion of his "difference", but they mean much more. What moves Pasolini and what he has to teach—his didactic intention requires the body as well as the mind to lie open to it—is a sense of historical and mythical continuity, experienced with carnal immediacy. His Mediterranean world is an ancient one, but its ancientness is continually made new in the young body, according to a knowledge involuntarily absorbed generation by generation. "Ah, antichissima gioventù" is the central exclamation of his poetry. The horror in his late political essays, which can be read back into the poetry, is that this inward continuity—barely touched by Fascism—was now being destroyed. . . .

[Pasolini's] writing is too rawly outgoing and of the moment to exist easily in English. . . . We need more of Pasolini's poetry in English, less for any self-sufficient literary pleasure which it offers than because it is important to understand what he is saying.

Achille Formis (essay date 1985)

SOURCE: A Review of *Selected Poems,* in *Modern Language Review,* Vol. 80, No. 4, October, 1985, pp. 959-61.

[In the following excerpted review of Selected Poems, *Formis finds that Pasolini's "fracture between moral vocation and inner feelings, between reason and instinct" is not resolved in his poetry.]*

Pasolini's death was tragic and at the same time dreary: a homosexual murdered by *ragazzi di vita.* The Italian media and over-zealous biographers exaggerated in giving details of the event. Here Pasolini's lifelong problem clearly comes to light: the fracture between moral vocation and inner feeling, between reason and instinct. I would not have brought this issue forward if the discrepancy were resolved in his poetry. But is it so? In my opinion Pasolini's style does not flow, rather it is like a diagram that oscillates up and down. The lyrical and autobiographical elements do not seem to blend consistently with that aspect of the poet as public figure making use of his accusatory and more narrative style. A considerable amount of narcissism is also very often apparent, generated by Pasolini's consciousness of being different both as intellectual and homosexual. Poetry slips then, with empty repetitive cries, to rhetoric, although Italian critics, always very clever with words and abstruse formulae, have glorified Pasolini's poetry, probably because they were scared of being hit by one of his cutting epigrams. It is not, for example, a very happy choice, right in the first poem of the book, **"Le Ceneri di Gramsci,"** to use the Dantesque terzina, which although very well exploited, forces the poet into some ostentatious repetitions ('maggio . . . quel maggio italiano') and sometimes not very convincing rhyming (*pederasti—casti, menta—spenta*), etc. It also stresses the difference between modern epithets and words and more literary ones (*straccetto rosso—terreno cereo,* for example)

Pasolini's drama is clearly stated at the beginning of Part IV of the poem, when he talks about 'Lo scandalo di contraddirmi', and this brings shadows to his style. His very choice of the stylistic device of oxymoron results sometimes in strained images ("Umana la luna da queste pietre/ raggelate trae un calore di alte passioni"). . . .

The reader who is a connoisseur of modern Italian history and literature will certainly find this parabola, as testified by one of its eminent protagonists, moving from the illusions of the early 1950s to the gloomy recent period, of absorbing interest. Pasolini called these modern times, dominated by capitalism-levelling society, 'anthropological genocide'. Leaving aside any formalistic debate one has to recognize Pasolini's merit in fighting for social causes, and with this intention in mind, in breaking, in Italy, the chains of pure lyric poetry.

He was certain, then, to find difficulties and to struggle towards better solutions, as this book of **Selected Poems** shows; see the beautiful **"Religion of My Time"** and the high points of **"Tears of an Excavator," "Prayer to My Mother," "Desperate Vitality,"** for instance. Searching more and more for action and 'a practical end' Pasolini will say, 'I'd simply like to live/ because life is expressed only with itself'. I'd like to express myself by examples./ To

throw my body into the struggle.' Or again: 'I will be a poet of things.' As Siciliano says [in his foreword,] 'This poet searched with pertinacity and anguish, day after day, year after year, experiment after experiment, risking the total destruction of his own lyric inspiration and the definitive laceration of his own instinctive sensibility for Italian verse in parallel with his never satisfied will to live'—so much so that Parolini ultimately ended up losing that harmony between contemplative life and active life which he admired so much in St. Paul, pursuing and trapped by his own paradox.

Naomi Greene (essay date 1990)

SOURCE: "Pasolini: 'Organic Intellectual'?" in *Italian Quarterly,* Vol. XXXI, Nos. 119-20, Winter-Spring, 1990, pp. 81-100.

[In the following excerpt, Greene surveys Pasolini's intellectual response to the thought of Antonio Gramsci, as reflected in his political verse.]

Pasolini's great debt to [Antonio] Gramsci (a debt he repeatedly acknowledged, defining himself at one point as "gramscian") was by no means an unususal phenomenon among members of his generation: as one historian has noted, the discovery of Gramsci's writings after the war "created a sub-renaissance within the wider re-awakening of Italian cultural life." But he may have been unique in that his response to Gramsci was always colored by a deep and complex ambivalence. It is this ambivalence, in fact, and the resulting tensions (which greatly intensified in the course of his career) that lie at the heart of one of his most famous poems, **"Le ceneri di Gramsci"** (**"The Ashes of Gramsci,"** the title poem in the collection which first won him national recognition as a poet when it appeared in 1954). These tensions have both existential and historical-political roots. On the personal level, Pasolini was torn by a life-long conflict between ideological awareness, commitment and history (represented by the heroic and martyred figure of Gramsci), and his own attraction (part of his bourgeois "exquisite" heritage) to the "innocence" and "primitive joy" of an ahistorical, vitalistic, almost mythic working-class and sub-proletarian world. In the poem he feels himself intellectually—ideologically, rationally—with Gramsci and the hopes for a new society; but he is instinctively, viscerally, passionately attached to a vitalistic and popular world which he cannot renounce for consciousness and "history" (understood as Marxism, ideology and the class struggle). Addressing himself to Gramsci, Pasolini describes this essential inner struggle which renders him incapable of action:

Lo scandalo del contraddirmi, dell'essere
con te e contro te; con te nel cuore,
in luce, contro te nelle buie viscere;

del mio paterno stato traditore

—nel pensiero, in un'ombra di azione—
mi so ad esso attaccato nel calore
degli istinti, dell'estetica passione;

attratto da una vita proletaria
a te anteriore, è per me religione

la sua allegria, non la millenaria
sua lotta: la sua natura, non la sua
coscienza; e la forza originaria

dell'uomo, che nell'atto s' è perduta,
a darle l'ebbrezza della nostalgia,
una luce poetica . . .

[The scandal of contradicting myself, of being
with you and against you; with you in my heart,
in the light, against you in my dark entrails.

traitor (in thought, on the rim
of action) to my paternal state,
knowing myself attached to it by the

heat of instincts and esthetic passion;
attracted by a proletarian life
anterior to you. Its joy,

not its age-old struggle, is
religion for me; its nature,
not its consciousness. It is man's

original vigor, lost in acting,
taking on nostalgia's intoxication,
a poetic light . . .]

But it is not only this essential existential tension which creates the poem's melancholy tone. Added to Pasolini's inner tensions is a bitter disillusion coming from the historical changes of the preceding decade, from the sense that the revolutionary hopes of the Resistance (hopes embodied in the poem by the figure of Gramsci and by that of the partisans) have been betrayed. With hope dispelled, the poet—caught—between the old bourgeois world and the future, still-to-be-realized society envisioned by Gramsci—is unable to make "choices," "commitments." Summing up this personal and historical dilemma in the final mediation of the poem, Pasolini declares:

    . . . Ma io, con il cuore cosciente

    di chi soltanto nella storia ha vita,
    potrò mai piú con pura passione operare
    se so che la nostra storia è finita?

    [. . . as for me, with a heart whose

    consciousness lives only in history,
    can I ever again act with pure passion,
    if I know that our history is finished?]

The sense of personal crisis and historical despair (a despair colored by nostalgia for an earlier time when hope was still alive) which marks this poem would grow deeper and more acute as the years went by. As the decades passed, Pasolini became increasingly convinced that the Gramscian hope that intellectuals might play a vital role in na-

tional life, that they might contribute to the creation of a new culture, were doomed to failure. But even as this sense of historical crisis grew ever more urgent and violent—a violence which exploded in his writings of the 1970s—Pasolini never ceased to write under the sign of Gramsci as he attempted to seize and articulate the crucial links between culture and politics. . . .

The mood of historical pessimism adumbrated in **"Le ceneri di Gramsci"** may have been particularly acute in Pasolini but it also reflected—as was almost always the case with him—important developments in Italian political and intellectual life. Postwar hopes for a new Italian society and culture had been crushed in 1948 by the defeat at the polls of the left-wing Popular Front; and, on the international scene, the swing towards repression came to a head in 1956 with the suppression of the Hungarian Revolution. By the early 1950s, neorealism (and the hopes it represented) had petered out, while the belief that intellectuals could help create a new society had grown increasingly suspect and in need of re-evaluation.

The sense of personal crisis and historical despair (a dispair colored by nostalgia for an earlier time when hope was still alive) which marks ["La ceneri di Gramsci"] would grow deeper and more acute as the years went by.

—*Naomi Greene*

It was in this climate that Pasolini and others began to re-examine the immediate artistic past, especially the cultural movement—neorealism—which, a decade earlier, had seemed to embody Gramsci's hope for a national-popular art. As they did so, they explored the possible roles still open to intellectuals, the cultural paths that could still be taken. Many of the most important discussions of these issues were published in the review *Officina,* which was founded in Bologna in 1955 by Pasolini and a few others. . . .

In his examination of past culture, Pasolini focuses on the two major Italian literary movements of the twentieth century: the hermetic, modernist and formalist literature (influenced by Mallarmé and the French symbolists) of the Fascist period, and the neorrealist reaction to it. Examining the language of both modernist and neorealist literature in terms of their respective social and ideological eras, Pasolini concludes that these two movements represent the two faces of bourgeois culture—and thus both are incapable of a new world vision. Modernist literature uses an irrational, mystical and precious language which, he feels, can deal only with the inner self, with feelings and words. Its incapacity to deal with the outer world, with history or the class struggle, and its "total adaptation to poetry," made it the perfect literature for the Fascist State; its seeming stylistic liberty was merely illusory because the antidemocratic Fascist involution was the result of the same decadence of liberal and romantic bourgeois ideology that has led to the literary involution of stylistic research done for its own sake, to a formalism filled only with its own esthetic consciousness . . . In a period of reactionary, centralist State politics, language had achieved a maximum of "fixation" perhaps never before seen in Italy [*Passione e ideologia*].

Pasolini nevertheless observes, demonstrating his refusal to schematize or simplify, that hermetic language also opposed Fascist values: as a language of the "elite," it resisted the Fascist desire for a language of great clarity accessible to all.

Contradictions and paradoxes also mark, in Pasolini's view, the language of neorealism. He grants, of course, that, in its reaction against the preciosity and rhetoric of modernist literature, neorealism did make important innovations designed to capture everyday reality and express historical events: hence it mixed styles, reproduced the "direct discourse" of the people, and emphasized the social and historical backdrop of events (this last element, Pasolini remarks, lent itself especially well to cinematic expression). Yet, despite these innovations and good intentions, neorealism did not, and perhaps could not, avoid certain pitfalls since, according to Pasolini, it was undermined by both the lack of a mass base and linguistic factors. In its attempt to find a "prose" language, neorealism fell back on the very language developed during the pre-Fascist period: "One can well ask how the literary embodiments of the notion of 'national-popular' could be realized in such a language, precisely the creation of the conservative bourgeoisie . . . that gave us Fascism" [*Passione e ideologia*]. Furthermore, because of its lack of concern with language and stylistics, neorealism was plagued by an involuntary tendency to incorporate some of the metaphorical, romantic and even religious and decadent elements of past literary language. Proceeding as if its literary, ethical and phenomenological vision were not in need of "research," neorealism found that its "will to innovate, stripped of an experimental covering, ended fatally . . . by readopting a superseded, often perishing, linguistic material" [*Passione e ideologia*]. In the end, neorealism fell prey to some of the same irrational remnants of past cultures which Pasolini perceived in Marxism itself: "The adoption of Marxist philosophy comes originally from a sentimental and moralistic impetus and is therefore continually permeable to the rising of the religious spirit" [*Passione e ideologia*].

But—and here we come to the tension and the personal issues at stake underlying Pasolini's analyses of past literature and culture—what implications does all this have for contemporary writers? Clearly, if they are committed and aware they must reject the language of both modernism and neorealism because of the ideologies implicit in them. But what, then, are writers to use in their place? Although Pasolini calls for "authentic experimentalism" and the adoption of a "plurilingual" language (one incorporating the different dialects of Italy, as opposed to a "monolingual" and abstract literary language) as well as a return to "premodernist" literary modes capable of expressing rationality and historicity, he is, nevertheless, distraught by his inability to finally answer this fundamental question in a satisfactory way, to define exactly what he means by "authentic experimentalism."

Moreover, this inability to envisage a new literature, a new culture, is part of a much greater dilemma. For, how can the writer envision a new literature and language when the society to which they correspond has still to be realized? And—what may be equally difficult—how can bourgeois intellectuals free themselves from the culture which formed them, a culture which, at least in Pasolini's case, was both hated and loved. (He always remained deeply attached to the symbolist, hermetic tradition of language and literature which had marked his youth). A Janus-like creature, he was torn between his nostalgia for the culture of the past he sought to renounce and his longing for a new society and culture not yet in existence. For Pasolini, the crisis of the bourgeois intellectual was lived *linguistically*—a crisis which an earlier generation, exemplified by Sartre, lived sentimentally. Voicing this crisis repeatedly in the poems and essays of the 1950s, Pasolini grappled with the conflict between his own bourgeois heritage and the awareness that Marxism had changed his perception of the world. The experience of the Resistance and the Liberation, and the discovery of Marx and Gramsci, had awakened in him (and in his generation) a heightened historical sense with the result that

> the world which was, at first, a pure source of sensations expressed by means of a ratiocinative and precious irrationalism, has now become an object of ideological, if not philosophical, awareness, and, as such, demands stylistic experiments of a radically new type [*Passione e ideologia*].

This crisis—the result of an awareness of Marxism and historical realities—had no easy resolution on any level whether ideological, existential or literary. For, unlike Gramsci, Pasolini was tormented by the knowledge that intellectuals like himself could not escape their own class; nor, could they believe any longer in the hopes raised by the Resistance (any fidelity to the "myth if the Resistance would be antihistorical"), or accept any of the "official" ideologies of the Left (i.e., the Communist Party). Writers, then, are trapped in an impasse: barred from both the "inner" poetry of the past and the "socialist realism" favored by "orthodox Marxists", they must also be wary of avant garde literature which inevitably emphasizes the divorce between the language of the people and that of the elites. Caught in an ideological limbo which renders literary experimentation somewhat gratuitous, the writer can only bear witness, through pain and struggle, to a period of unhappy transition. In an essay written in 1954, the same year as **"Le ceneri di Gramsci,"** the only glimmer of hope Pasolini raises (and even this glimmer was soon extinguished) is that from this very "pain" a new poetry will be born:

> Whether we cannot or do not want (it's the same thing) to be communists, the fact of finding ourselves placed in front of this new, important, social and moral measure, in front of this future perspective . . . acts within us—within us, we who have remained bourgeois with the violence and the inertia of a psychology determined by history . . . But this situation in which we live daily—of choices not completed, of dramas

unresolved due to hypocrisy or weakness, of false "relaxation," of discontent for every thing that has given a restless fullness to the generations preceding us— seems sufficiently dramatic to produce a new poetry [*Passione e ideologia*].

It has often been suggested that Pasolini's sense that literature had reached an historical impasse was one of the reasons he began making films. Although he himself refused to separate cinematic and literary experiments (for him, they were "analogous" rather than "antithetical" forms) he did observe that "the desire to express myself through cinema is part of my need to adopt a new, innovating, technique. It also signifies my desire to escape obsession." Later, in a more pessimistic vein, in a poem whose title **"Io, poeta delle Ceneri" ("I, Poet of the Ashes")** plays on that of **"Le Ceneri di Gramsci",** he noted that his embrace of cinema was an attempt to escape his "petit-bourgeois" origins:

> quante volte rabbiosamente e avventatemente
> avevo detto di voler riunciare alla mia cittadinanza
>   italiana!
> Ebbene, abbandonando la lingua italiana, e con essa,
> un po' alla volta, la letteratura,
> io riunciavo alla mia nazionalità.
> Dicevo no alle mie origini piccolo borghesi.

> [how many times in rage and without thinking
> I had said that I wanted to renounce my Italian
>   citizenship!
> Well, abbandoning the Italian language and with it,
> a little at a time, literature
> I renounced my nationality.
> I said no to my petit-bourgois origins.]

This attempt to renounce literature or his origins (although, in point of fact, he never stopped writing) did not mean that he could escape the two faces of past culture he had analyzed so lucidly in his *Officina* essays. . . .

In his eyes, "committed" art, or what was then often called "materialist" criticism . . . was no less bourgeois than "militant" film. By regarding books and films as "products," he said, such criticism furthers the values of neo-capitalism which values things (or products) more highly than people. Running counter to much left-wing theory and practice of those years, over and over he was to argue that "poetry" (symbolic, perhaps, of all authentic art) was not a "product."

> Poetry, in fact, is not produced "in a scrics": therefore it is not a product. And a reader of poetry can read a poem a thousand times: he will never consume it. Rather, strange to think perhaps, that the thousandth time, the poem might seem more strange, new, and scandalous than the first time [*Il Caos*].

This insistence on "poetry", on "authentic" art, was part of Pasolini's re-thinking of many of the formal issues first discussed at length in the *Officina* essays. But now his tone was increasingly desperate, signaling one of the violent swings of the pendulum that would mark his career. Convinced that national-popular literature was no

longer possible, that "committed" literature was bourgeois, and that most Marxist critics were simplistic and moralistic, he argued increasingly (and in this perhaps he was closer to Adorno than to Gramsci), that the "protest" embodied in a work of art lay in its "form" rather than its content. . . .

Despite his statements declaring the marginality of intellectuals and his professed disbelief in the possibility of political action, Pasolini by no means refrained from political action. From the late 1960s until his death, he published one "intervento" after another, usually in the mass press, concerning the vital political and social issues of those years. More than any other aspect of his work, it is probably these interventi—still debated hotly years after his death—that earned him the title of"organic intellectual." . . .

The first intervention to create a national controversy came in the wake of the 1968 student riots. The intervention, which he qualified and tempered in the course of the coming months and years, took the form of a poem entitled **"Il PCI ai giovani."** It was to become emblematic of the contradictory, infuriating and yet vital role Pasolini was to play in Italian cultural and political life until his death. In this pocm, Pasolini attacked the students because they, sons and daughters of the bourgeoisie, pitted themselves against the police, sons of peasants and the poor. The worldwide media, he claimed, favored the students because the media, too, was bourgeois. Furthermore, Pasolini now maintained, despite his long-standing criticisms of the Communist Party, that by rejecting the Party the students were turning away from the only instrument truly dangerous to their parents. The poem's well-known opening lines read:

> È triste. La polemica contro
> il PCI andava fatta nella prima metà
> del decennio passato. Siete in ritardo, figli.
> E non ha nessuna importanza se allora non eravate
>   ancora nati . . .
> Adesso i giornalisti di tutto il mondo (compresi
> quelli della televisione)
> vi leccano (come credo ancora si dica nel
>   linguaggio
> delle Università) il culo. Io no, amici.
> Avete facce di figli di papà.
> Buona razza non mente.
> Avete lo stesso occhio cattivo.
> Siete paurosi, incerti, disperati
> (benissimo!) ma sapete anche come essere
> prepotenti, ricattatori e sicuri:
> prerogative piccolo-borghesi, amici.
> Quando ieri a Valle Giulia avete fatto a botte
> coi poliziotti,
> io simpatizzavo coi poliziotti!

> [It's sad. The argument against
> the PCI should have been made in the first half
> of the past decade. You're late, children.
> And it's not important if you weren't born then . . .
> Now the journalists of the whole world (including

those of television)
kiss (as I think they still say in the language
of the University) your ass. Not I, friends.
You have the spoiled faces of your fathers.
A race doesn't lie.
You have the same evil eye.
You're afraid, uncertain desperate
(fine!) but you also know how to be
arrogant, black mailers and confident:
petit-bourgeois perogatives, friends.
Yesterday at the Valle Guilia when it came to blows
with the police,
I sympathized with the police!
Because the police are sons of the poor.]

Again and again throughout the 1970s, Pasolini repeated this role of "provocateur," of devil's advocate, towards the radical Left as he questioned ideologies and assumptions taken for granted. This was the same role that he had played earlier towards the Communist Party which by now, was part of the Establishment, soon to make its "historical compromise" with the Christian Democrats. Characteristically revealing the tensions which always pulled him in different directions, at the same time that Pasolini attacked the various positions taken by "New Left" groups, he also worked with them. . . . His obvious ambivalence toward these student radicals (and their militant filmmaking) revealed, in a sense, part of the difficulty he experienced in these tense years which were marked by inflation, worker demands and strikes, recession, aggravated political tensions and terrorism.

Chris Bongie (essay date 1991)

SOURCE. "A Postscript to Transgression," in *Exotic Memories: Literature, Colonialism, and the Fin de Siècle,* Stanford University Press, 1991, pp. 188-228.

[In the following excerpt, Bongie observes the importance of the "authentic experience" in Pasolini's poems.]

One cannot . . . speak of Pasolini during the early 1960's without taking into account the twenty-year path that led him to embrace the Third World as a radical solution to the problem of decadence. . . . If we consider his earlier (and without question most important) literary production, we find that the "outside" that will eventually become so necessary for Pasolini is anything but present there; it proves, in fact, irremediably absent. For the decadentist-tinged poetry of his first literary decade, the 1940's, this should come as no surprise. The young Pasolini was careful to situate himself firmly within Italian literary tradition: if this poetry—much of it indebted to the hermetic school that flourished during the fascist *ventennio*—succeeds, it is, quite clearly, only at the level of "a perfect stylistic success." There is no question of an "outside" in this work (or, rather, the motif is raised in the traditional and non-secular terms of religious transcendence).

One point about the early poetry does, however, need to be brought out before we examine some of the works written during the next decade—works that form the more immediate genealogy of Pasolini's *tiers-mondisme*. The novelty of this poetry resides in Pasolini's decision to write not only in Italian but also in the dialect of his mother's home region, the Friuli (to the northeast of Venice). In these poems—most of which were subsequently collected in 1954 as *La meglio gioventú—Pasolini* gives literary form to what might well be considered the sheer orality of dialect, a dialect that he himself had to learn as an anthropologist would that of a culture under study. Far from being a mimetic attempt at re-presenting this language, however, his written dialect, in its extreme literariness, places itself at a clear remove from the dialect spoken by the inhabitants of the Friuli. Pasolini's Friulan, in other words, turns out to be a metaphor of "real" Friulan; as Rinaldo Rinaldi, the author of far and away the most compelling account of Pasolini's work as a whole, puts it, "His dialect is a register of writing used as a metaphor for the negation of writing." By writing in dialect, Pasolini refers, metaphorically, to what is prior to that writing: to engage this spoken language is, inevitably, to put oneself at a distance from it, to evoke it in the form of what it is not—namely, writing.

Given its inevitably metaphorical form, the content of Pasolini's dialect poetry is also, of necessity, at a distance from what it purports to say; his "exotic" attachment to the Friuli—the identification of it as "my country," *me país,* as he calls it in the epigraph to *La meglio gioventú* must, for this reason, be read as a conceit, a rhetorical artifice. It is the artificiality of such identification with the Other that Pasolini's *tiers-mondisme* will fruitlessly contest—a contestation that is, indeed, anticipated during Pasolini's last years in the Friuli when he will attempt, in the wake of what he called his "discovery of Marx," to use dialect as the vehicle for his new political activism. This move toward a language of immanence is, however, abruptly curtailed when, in 1949, Pasolini is expelled from the local Communist party on moral grounds (having to do with his homosexuality). Forced to leave the Friuli, he relocates in Rome and, after several years of intense poverty, emerges as one of the most prominent, and scandalous, figures on the Italian cultural scene. . . .

The *poemetti* of *Le ceneri di Gramsci* (written from 1951 to 1956 and published in 1957) are of more immediate interest to us than the novels because of their obsession with a phantasmic past—not Gramsci himself but the ashes of Gramsci, the traces of an authentic experience. Poetry here turns away from a modernity to which it nonetheless remains attached: it assumes a memorial stature, setting itself the task of remembering a heroic world that has no place in our own. As such, it falls somewhere in between what Agamben, following Freud, has identified as the two related strategies of mourning and melancholy. . . .

The melancholic confers reality on an object that never was, mourning it, and thereby in a way giving life to its unreality. This is the essence of mourning itself since the real object, once it has ceased to exist, proves equally phantasmic, equally "unappropriable."

We can see this laceration of self and (real/unreal) object, one that history effects and writing records, at work in a poem like **"Canto popolare"** (1952), where an absolute distance is established between us ("noi")—the subjects of history—and the people ("popolo")—those who ingenuously repeat the past and who are not "blinded" ("abbagliato") by modernity because they are not exposed to its harsh light. These "people" are never drawn up ("tolto"), as it were, by the dialectic of enlightenment:

> . . . non abbiamo nozione
> vera di chi è partecipe alla storia
> solo per orale, magica esperienza;
> e vive puro, non oltre la memoria
> della generazione in cui presenza
> della vita è la sua vita perentoria.
>
> (. . . we have no true
> notion of who participates in history
> only through oral, magic experience;
> and lives pure, not beyond the memory
> of the generation in which presence
> of life is his peremptory life.)

The world of "oral, magic experience" is at a painful remove from the subject who desires its "presence." For all that he longs to come into contact with this other world, Pasolini un-realizes it, placing it at an insuperable distance from his own. He remembers it at the cost of a laceration: historical man "non ha più che la violenza / delle memorie, non la libera memoria" ("now has only the violence / of memories, not memory's freedom"). In *Le ceneri* what makes up for this absence is the belief that "our" world is not merely one of mourning but of hope: against the loss of this "libera memoria," this peremptory ground of experience, we can hope for a very different, redemptory sort of liberty.

The poet of *Le ceneri* is not, however, very interested in considering this future, which at once attracts and "repulses" him; the ethos of these poems is melancholic, directed toward a world anterior to "ours," one that has come before and yet remains with us, but only as trace—unreachable, if not in its absence. In **"Le ceneri di Gramsci"** (1954), Pasolini calls this trace "la forza originaria / dell' uomo, che nell'atto s'è perduta" ("the originary force / of man, which has been lost in the act")—a lost force that provokes both "l'ebbrezza della nostalgia" ("the rapture of nostalgia") and "una luce poetica" ("a poetic light"). Poetry and nostalgia unite, as they always have, to reveal/conceal what is hidden to "us." This insight is presented less compactly in an exemplary stanza from a poem written the same year, **"L'umile Italia":**

> Più è sacro dov'è più animale
> il mondo: ma senza tradire
> la poeticità, l'originaria
> forza, a noi tocca esaurire
> il suo mistero in bene e in male
> umano. Questa è l'Italia e
> non è questa l'Italia: insieme
> la preistoria e la storia che

> in essa sono convivano, se
> la luce è frutto di un buio seme.

> (The world is more sacred where it is
> more animal: but without betraying
> the poeticity, the originary
> force, we must exhaust
> its mystery in human good and
> evil. This is Italy and
> this is not Italy: together
> the prehistory and the history, which
> are in it, live—if
> light is the fruit of a dark seed.)

Here, "prehistory" differs considerably from what it will soon become for Pasolini in its Third World incarnation; the realm of the sacred, of animal nature, is lost to "us" as darkness is to light, as something that we can have no "true notion" about. Its "cohabitation" (*convivenza*) with history is nothing more than a phantasmic one, an imaginary relation between the real and the unreal.

We must not turn away from what has come before us, yet neither can we re-present its originary force. To deliver that force over to the present would be to betray its "poeticity." The light of poetry grounds itself in an unrepresentable absence of light that is anterior to it; the poet looks back upon this absence, interrogating it with what Pasolini would so often refer to as an *amor da lonh,* a love from afar. The poet through commemoration, seeks access to an origin that is always-already inaccessible: it might well be argued that this is the essential(izing) project of the European poetic tradition. Whatever one's definition of poetry, however, this is the central project in Pasolini's *Ceneri*. With an approximating language that simultaneously draws near and pushes back, Pasolini's overwhelming impulse in these poems is to articulate an unbridgeable gap: between the sacred, animal world of nature and a secular, human world; between a heroic people whose metonym is Gramsci and the ashen inferno of modernity.

A potential ambiguity inhabits Pasolini's idea of *convivenza,* however. For the poet of *Le ceneri,* the prehistoric is present only as phantasm, as an object to be mourned in the world of light and history; to bestow upon the prehistoric a real content would be to betray its originary force. It would, we can add, be to grasp (fetishistically) what is by essence ungraspable. But it is precisely this reality that Pasolini—increasingly unhappy with the prospect of mourning and equally uncomfortable with that extension of mourning we identified as modernism (a position that takes the absence of experience for granted)—will attempt to embrace, at the cost, as he had foreseen, of betraying "la poeticità." The *glas* of melancholy, as it were, has sounded too early for Pasolini's liking, and he will seize upon the apparent possibilities of mutual presence that a word like *convivenza* opens up despite the nostalgic intentions of (his) poetry. A period of relative optimism begins, in which his work attempts to conjure up first historical, and then prehistorical, alternatives to capitalism— openings of the sort that he had already theoretically envisioned in some of the essays of *Passione e ideologia*. During his brief *tiers-mondiste* period (roughly, 1958-63), Pasolini is buoyed up by the possibility of political and literary transgression, on both the domestic and the international front. He begins to explore the futural dimension that was almost entirely absent from the world of the *Ceneri*—a world where, as he puts it in **"Picasso"** (1953), remaining "inside the inferno with a marmoreal / will to understand it" appeared to offer the only chance of "salvation."

On the one hand, he adopts, or re-adopts, the traditional terms of the class struggle when speaking about the possibility of political change within Italy: modernity, he will claim, can be surpassed through a qualitative leap forward— as we see, for instance, in his account of the difference between "dissent" and "revolution." Dissent, he explains to the readers of *Vie nuove* (30 November 1961), is essentially religious, irrational, caught up within what it contests; however, all moments of dissent(and here he identifies three types: the heretical, the anarchical, and the humanitarian) prepare the way for the "qualitative leap," the "betrayal," of Marxism: "With this leap 'religiosity' loses every historical characteristic—irrationalism, individualism, metaphysical prospectivism—and acquires entirely new characteristics: rationalism, socialism, laical prospectivism." This epochal shift will establish "another culture," "another and entirely new point of view" ("un'altra cultura," "un altro punto di vista totalmente nuovo"), from which the ills of modern society will have disappeared. . . .

[Although] the first years of the 1960's are marked by one announcement after another of various novelistic projects, by the middle of the decade Pasolini is forced to admit that he has "renounced" the novel.

By this time, his poetic vein is also temporarily exhausted—arriving, although from a rather different direction, at the same neo-capitalist dead end. If his next collection of poetry is in many ways an extension of *Le ceneri* (just as *Una vita violenta* grows out of *Ragazzi di vita*), one fundamental difference resides in Pasolini's efforts to figure what had hitherto been the object of his melancholy as really present. Reworking the material of the previous collection, *La religione del mio tempo* (1961), establishes a direct contact between the poet and the "prehistoric" world that he had previously contemplated *da lonh*: Pasolini separates himself from the alienated historical subject of the *Ceneri* ("noi") in an attempt at opening up another point of view from a trans- or extra-historical perspective. The individual subject, it now transpires, can come into contact with Other worlds: in **"La ricchezza"** (1955-59), for instance, Pasolini the dandy ("il raffinato") assimilates himself to the urban "subproletariat," because they are

> entrambi fuori dalla storia,
> in un mondo che non ha altri varchi
> che verso il sesso e il cuore,
> altra profondità che nei sensi.
> In cui la gioia è gioia, il dolore dolore.

> (Both outside of history
> in a world whose only passageways lead
> toward sex and the heart,
> whose only depth comes from the senses.
> In which joy is joy, and sadness sadness.)

This alliance with the "frutti / d'una storia tanto diversa" ("fruit / of such a different story") is what Pasolini will seek to effect in the coming years, trying to operate outside the historical framework in and by which he nonetheless still feels himself engaged.

But in his earlier poetry he had already so effectually buried Italy's peasantry (*contadini*) and subproletariat under the ground of an unattainable "prehistory" that his literary efforts to recuperate a *convivenza* on the domestic front inevitably fall short of their goal, striking the reader as a painfully awkward projection of reality onto some phantasmic object—in other words, as essentially rhetorical. And it is precisely this sense of rhetoric that Pasolini most wants to avoid. Dissatisfiedwith these results and yet wishing to elaborate his vision of an alternative present, Pasolini extends his gaze beyond the boundaries of Italy to the emerging Third World and comes to the conclusion (in **"Alla Francia"** [1958]—an epigram inspired by Sékou Touré, then-president of Guinea):

> Forse a chi è nato nella selva, da pura madre,
> a essere solo, a nutrire solo gioia,
> tocca rendersi conto della vita reale.

> (Perhaps he who is born in the forest, of a pure
>　　mother,
> born to be alone, to nourish joy alone,
> will be the one to take real life into account.)

Pasolini turns away from Europe and the all-embracing world of neo-capitalism, in search of the once and future alternative—a poetic program that he announces at the end of one of the closing poems in *La religione del mio tempo,* the **"Frammento alla morte"** (1960):

> Sono stato razionale e sono stato
> irrazionale: fino in fondo.
> E ora . . . ah, il deserto assordato
> dal vento, lo stupendo e immondo
> sole dell' Africa che illumina il mondo.

> Africa! Unica mia
> alternativa. . . .

> (I have been rational and I have been
> irrational: right to the end.
> And now . . . ah, the desert deafened
> by the wind, the wonderful and filthy
> sun of Africa that illuminates the world.
> Africa! My only
> alternative. . . .)

That this fragmentary invocation to the new world is couched in a self-consciously Romantic style; that Pasolini must produce his alternative vision in a language that reeks of nineteenth-century exoticism; that he must ignore the clichéd nature of his project if he is to invest it with any degree of "authenticity": these are obvious ironies, signaling the a priori sterility of his neo-exoticist undertaking. It is this hopeless vacancy that Pasolini will discover in his literary and existential encounter with the Third World. This vacancy, we might add, is itself inscribed in the poem's final ellipsis: the future that would complete the present cannot be uttered; the words that would heal the poet's *male incurabile* are irretrievably absent from the discursive realm, covered over by a set of periods, each of which marks the same thing. That same thing is the end of the line.

FURTHER READING

Biography

Schwartz, Barth David. *Pasolini Requiem.* New York: Pantheon, 1992, 785 p.

  Detailed biography of Pasolini's life, career, and violent death.

Siciliano, Enzo. *Pasolini: A Biography,* translated by John Shepley. New York: Random House, 1982, 435 p.

  First translated biography of Pasolini.

Criticism

Allen, Beverly. "The Shadow of His Style." *Stanford Italian Review* II, No. 2 (Fall 1982): 1-6.

  Compares the "assertive uniqueness" of the Catholicism, Marxism, and sexuality present in Pasolini's films as well as in his poems and novels.

Capozzi, Frank. "Pier Paolo Pasolini: An Introduction to the Translations." *Canadian Journal of Italian Studies* 5, Nos. 1-2 (Fall-Winter 1981-1982): 109-13.

  A brief, one-page biographical sketch and introduction to four translated poems.

Gatt-Rutter, John. "Pier Paolo Pasolini." In *Writers and Society in Contemporary Italy: A Collection of Essays,* edited by Michael Caesar and Peter Hainsworth, pp. 143-65. New York: St. Martin's Press, 1984.

  Brief overview of Pasolini's career.

Jewell, Keala Jane. "Pasolini: Deconstructing the Roman Palimpsest." *Substance* 53, No. 2 (1987): 55-66.

  Comments on Pasolini's representation of Rome and its history in *Passione e ideologia* and the poems "Le ceneri di Gramsci" and "Il pianto della scavatrice."

McCarthy, Patrick. "A Friulian Freedom." *The Times Literary Supplement,* No. 4684 (January 8, 1993): 19.

  Reviews of *The Letters of Pier Paolo Pasolini,* the film version of *Theorem,* and *Poetry.* Calls Nico Naldini's biographical introduction to *Letters* "the best guide to Pasolini's early life" and commends Mazza's translations of Pasolini's difficult *Poetry.*

Peterson, Thomas E. "Parallel Derivations from Dante: Fortini, Duncan, Pasolini." *South Atlantic Review* 59, No. 4 (November 1994): 21-45.

  Compares the poetry of Pasolini to that of Franco Fortini and Robert Duncan in the context of their debt to Dante.

Pivato, Joseph. "Cultural Differences." *Canadian Literature,* Nos. 138-39 (Fall-Winter 1993): 146-47.

  Includes a review of *Poetry* that comments on the challenges of translating Pasolini, and notes that translator Antonio Mazza "has introduced a model for Italian-Canadian writers that is closer to the peasant origins of their immigrant parents."

Smith, Lawrence R. "Roman Poems: Pier Paolo Pasolini," *Sulfur* 6, No. 2 (November 1986): 126-29.

  Review of *Roman Poems* in which Smith notes the difficulty in capturing the essence of Pasolini's poems when translated into English and observes "Pasolini's strange mixture of aesthetic conservatism and radicalism."

Steele, Gary. "Pasolini: Complex Life, Bloody Death." *Los Angeles Times Book Review* (July 25, 1982): 7.

  Reviews Siciliano's *Pasolini: A Biography,* which Steele calls "a heroic labor in portraying this complex figure," and Pasolini's *Poems.*

White, Edmund. "Movies and Poems: Pier Paolo Pasolini." In *The Burning Library: Essays,* edited by David Bergman, pp. 141-44. New York: Alfred A. Knopf, 1994.

  Compares Pasolini's life, career, and works (particularly his poetry and films) to those of his "exact contemporary," the Japanese novelist Yukio Mishima, who also was a homosexual and suffered a violent death.

Interview

Stack, Oswald. *Pasolini on Pasolini: Interviews with Oswald Stack.* Bloomington: Indiana University Press, 1969, 176 p.

  The first chapter, "Background," deals with Pasolini's life and formation, the rest of the volume is a source of first-hand collected attestations on his cinemagraphic as well as his literary works. Includes a brief bibliography, mainly concerning his films.

Additional coverage of Pasolini's life and career is contained in the following sources published by Gale Research, Inc.: *Contemporary Authors,* Vols. 61-64, 93-96; *Contemporary Literary Criticism,* Vols. 20, 37; *Dictionary of Literary Biography,* Vol. 128; and *Major 20th-Century Writers.*

Charles Tomlinson
1927-

(Full name Alfred Charles Tomlinson) English poet, translator, editor, critic, and artist.

INTRODUCTION

A respected English poet whose verse focuses on the philosophic implications of sensory experience, Tomlinson uses acute observation and detailed description to explore the relationship between the external world and the self. Tomlinson suggests that through sensitive perception of natural phenomenon, human beings are able to gain an awareness "that teaches us not to try to reduce objects to our own image, but to respect their own otherness, and yet find our way into contact with that otherness." Tomlinson's admiration for the work of such American writers as Ezra Pound, William Carlos Williams, Wallace Stevens, and Marianne Moore is reflected in the clarity of his language, the musical cadences of his verse, his detached tone, and his objective point of view.

Biographical Information

Born in Stoke-on Trent in Staffordshire to a working-class family, Tomlinson attended Cambridge University from 1945-48, where he studied English literature. It was at Cambridge that he first developed an interest in American poetry, which became a significant influence on his work. In addition to his many well-regarded collections of verse, Tomlinson has translated works by such poets as Fyodor Tyutchev, Antonio Machado, and Cesar Vallejo; he has edited collections of poems and essays by Marianne Moore, William Carlos Williams, and Octavio Paz; and he has collaborated with Paz and other poets on two other books of verse, *Renga* and *Airborn/Hijos del aire*. An accomplished graphic artist, he has also published several volumes of his visual images, including *Eden: Graphics and Poetry*, which combines poetry and artwork.

Major Works

Tomlinson's first major collection, *Seeing is Believing*, was widely praised for its attention to landscape and visual detail and was noted for its emphasis on the need for disciplined and accurate observation. His succeeding volumes, *A Peopled Landscape* and *American Scenes and Other Poems*, reflect his exposure to American landscapes and his contacts with such American poets as George Oppen, Louis Zukofsky, Marianne Moore, and William Carlos Williams, whom he met during his travels across America from 1959 to 1960. Tomlinson's

concern with the natural world, with landscape, place and weather has, as critics observe, remained central to all of his work, but that concern was accompanied by an interest in the processes of time and history that came to figure more prominently in the volumes of the 1960s. In his next two major collections, *The Way of a World* and *Written on Water*, Tomlinson presents his themes through the recurring motifs of water and time. *The Way of a World* contains some of Tomlinson's best-known poems, including "Against Extremity" and the widely anthologized "Swimming Chenango Lake." In *The Way In and Other Poems*, he introduces personal elements into his verse while continuing to probe the nature of perception and reality. His poems in this volume reflect the shifting balance of constancy and change as he returns to the landscapes of England, creating imaginative portraits of familiar scenes in such poem as "At Stoke" and "The Marl Pits." The poems in his next book, *The Shaft*, contains the highly regarded "Lines Written in the Euganean Hills," in which the poet denounces human imposition on the natural world.

The Flood reflects his travels in England, North America, and Italy and displays a variety of literary styles, including elegiac and narrative verse and prose passages. In *Notes from New York and Other Poems*, he imaginatively recreates the urban landscapes of New York City. These poems attest to his concerns about the consequences of human interaction on the physical environment. Tomlinson's most recent collection, *Jubilation*, explores youth and aging, family life, and meditates on the dialectical relationship between rootedness and aging.

Critical Reception

Tomlinson is well-regarded for the precision, restraint, and originality of his verse, and is often praised for his deft explorations of the relationships between the external world and the self. His complex, philosophical poetry is also noted for its clarity of language, objective tone and view, and detailed imagery. Many commentators have examined the influence of American poets on his work, especially that of Ezra Pound, Wallace Stevens, Marianne Moore, and William Carlos Williams. Often faulted by some critics for being preoccupied with landscape and visual objects, he is also derided for a perceived lack of human warmth and passion in his work. Despite these charges, many scholars maintain the importance of his poetry; critic Calvin Bedient has described Tomlinson as "the most considerable English poet to have made his way since the Second World War."

PRINCIPAL WORKS

Poetry

Relations and Contraries 1951
The Necklace 1955
Seeing Is Believing 1958
A Peopled Landscape 1963
American Scenes and Other Poems 1966
The Way of a World 1969
Renga [with Octavio Paz, Jacques Roubaud and Edoardo Sanguineti] 1971
Written on Water 1972
The Way In and Other Poems 1974
Selected Poems, 1951-1974 1978
The Shaft 1978
Airborn/Hijos del aire [with Octavio Paz] 1981
The Flood 1981
Notes From New York and Other Poems 1984
Collected Poems 1985
The Return 1987
Selected Poems 1989

Other Major Works

Words and Images (graphics) 1972
In Black and White (graphics) 1976
Some Americans: A Personal Record (essays) 1981
Poetry and Metamorphosis (essays) 1983
Eden: Graphics and Poetry (graphics and poetry) 1985

CRITICISM

Hugh Kenner (essay date 1956)

SOURCE: "A Creator of Space," in *Poetry,* Vol. 88, No. 5, August, 1956, pp. 324-28.

[*In the following review of* The Necklace, *Kenner differentiates Tomlinson's poetry from that of other contemporary English poets.*]

What claims to be the "agreeable minor verse" of anonymous British culture—the sort of thing for instance that gets printed for filler in *The Listener*—traffics, as the patient inspector quickly discovers, in void gestures of rumination over themes that, until the ruminative process seized on them, barely existed as themes. A thousand unpretentious poems are amplified samples of the background noise that continually accompanies the chatter of our mental processes, insistent, like all background noise, when the talking machine pauses for a moment: bits of commonplace assimilation of one's environment, isolated and promoted as "poetic" because not crassly practical. This random example comes from *The Listener* for October 13, 1955 [elisions Kenner's]:

> Hesitate with letters, there by the pillar-box,
> Holding the gesture, Listen: . . .
>   . . ."It is the hour
> Of—" But of what? . . .
>   . . . You watch the wind
> Tumble the smoke, lift half the blossom of a tree,
> Twitching away April like a table-cloth.
> Sparrows occur. Wheels twinkle. Thin and high,
> High and continuing high like a violin,
> A vapour trail describes an enormous flower,
> Grown out, nudging the blue, into absolute silence . . .

This has a delectable post-Thermidor complacency. Tennyson need no longer be guillotined every Wednesday; poetry has outlived the phase of manifestoes and metrical Schrecklichkeit and can resume its normal business of distracting the middle classes. It is no longer quite the *same* poetry of course; even the incorruptible pentameter admits numerous hypermetric syllables, and it is licit for vapor-trails, flowers and violins to collapse into a simultaneous sensation. "Sparrows occur" is a very knowing bit of synthetic casualness, decidedly post-Auden. The revolution is consummated, Rupert Brooke is old hat, and we moderns (not of course glass-and-chrome moderns, but at any rate Eden's and Eisenhower's parishioners, not Bonar Law's) have our contemporary *poésie d'ameublement*. Civilization resumes its course. Time heals all things, even the schisms promoted by Vorticism. Mr. Wyndham Lewis gets a friendly nod now and then. And so on.

Under these circumstances the bored cisatlantic reader would have some excuse for supposing that Mr. Charles Tomlinson, with his apparatus of flutes, seashores and sunsets, was a member in good standing of the BBC party. Let the reader be undeceived; there could be no more convincing instance of the infallibility of the guardians of British public taste in distinguishing between the genuine and the specious than their unanimous condescension toward Mr. Tomlinson. A glance at the pages of *The Necklace* sufficed to persuade them that *all was not well*. Quite so: these mere fifteen poems constitute just such a flawlessly alert achievement in the joining of words, unassisted by rhetoric of form or empathy of theme, as the counter-Bohemian arbiters of the Queen's realm, though they go through the motions of prizing such criteria, must make it their business to proscribe.

> . . . But how shall one say so?—
> The fact being, that when the truth is not good
>   enough
> We exaggerate. Proportions
>
> Matter. It is difficult to get them right.
> There must be nothing
> Superfluous, nothing which is not elegant
> And nothing which is if it is merely that. . . .

This extract—both what it says and the quality of writing it typifies—will serve to illustrate Mr. Tomlinson's minimum virtue, not talking too much while not indulging in a mummery of laconism, epigrams, meaningful glances, knowing understatements. He functions, at his mildest, like a flute-player oblivious to listeners, in a tacit dialogue with his art, getting a short passage exactly right. When this intentness on the contours of a perception extends itself, we have such a poem as "**Observation of Facts**," which needs to be quoted intact:

> Facts have no eyes. One must
> Surprise them, as one surprises a tree
> By regarding its (shall I say?)
> Facets of copiousness.
>
> The tree stands.
>
> The house encloses.
>
> The room flowers.
>
> These are fact stripped of imagination:
> Their relation is mutual.
>
> A dryad is a sort of chintz curtain
> Between myself and a tree.
> The tree stands: or does not stand:
>
> As I draw, or remove the curtain.
>
> The house encloses: or fails to signify
> As being bodied over against one,
> As something one has to do with.
>
> The room flowers once one has introduced
> Mental fibre beneath its elegance,
> A rough pot or two, outweighing
> The persistence of frippery
> In lampshades or wallpaper.
>
> Style speaks what was seen,
> Or it conceals the observation

> Behind the observer: a voice
> Wearing a ruff.
>
> These facets of copiousness which I proposed
> Exist, do so when we have silenced ourselves.

This is elegant only in the sense in which a mathematician so praises a demonstration, or a physicist an experiment; its elegance denotes not a patent-leather glaze over a quotidian shoe, but the co-presence of the fewest possible components functioning with minimum waste. "**Observation of Facts**" isn't a surface but an action compact of surprises. The leap from "fact stripped of imagination" to "A dryad is a sort of chintz curtain" would have delighted Aristotle; and how finely weighed, in the vicinity of "dryad" and "curtain," is that "stripped"! And then we discover that we have paused too soon:

> A dryad is a sort of chintz curtain
> Between myself and a tree.

—only then and there, not always. Yet we need the pause, the half-joke of the first line in isolation. The line-ending *functions*; without it, without the shift of perspective it induces, the sentence would be merely fanciful. Dr. Williams once described Marianne Moore's "Marriage" as "an anthology of transit"; Mr. Tomlinson, though his affinities are rather with Miss Moore than with, say, Keats, doesn't display the copiousness of an anthology; he isn't culling a prickly heap of experiences. Nor is his world a stripped world; he doesn't arrive at it by subtraction, he builds from nothing; his world is a blank which he proceeds to furnish. He isn't a connoisseur of austerities, cultivating

> an Olympian *apathein*
> In the presence of selected perceptions;

or inviting us to share an effete predilection for items that dangle before the appreciative gaze, in Calderesque whimsicality. Rather the ideal reader assists at an athletic act of creation, where subtle and exact relationships, like the ones that occupy an oriental geomancer, are not being found but step by step established. Yet this creator of spaces is no Mondrian; he is blessedly free of the revolutionary itch.

This comes out clearly in Mr. Tomlinson's third category of poems, the ones where he isn't explicitly purifying thought processes but simply building: as in "**Nine Variations in a Chinese Winter Setting**." First we have the blank expectations aroused by the title; then we have, by fiat,

I

> Warm flute on the cold snow
> Lays amber in sound.

or a little later, with more aplomb than preciosity,

III

> The sage beneath the waterfall
> Numbers the blessing of a flute.

Water lets down
Exploding silk.

or later still, more intricate,

V

Pine-scent
In snow-clearness
Is not more exactly counterpoised
Than the creak of trodden snow
Against a flute.

One is constantly aware of what these poems are not;
they have in that respect an odd affinity with Augustan
satire, which works by just evading the regnant clichés.
Mr. Tomlinson's flutes, for instance, manage not to be
drawn into the convention of literary still-life; they are
neither bourgeois stage-props whimsically disposed, like
the guitars of the early cubist collages, nor are they a
refined equivalent. Picasso might have employed the flute
instead of the guitar if the matrix of his Romantic satire
had been that of, say, Proust instead of Pécuchet; the
flute would still have retained its connections with a
certain social world, though a high bohemia instead of a
sidewalk cafe. Mr. Tomlinson's flute on the cold snow
does nothing of the kind; it posits a quality of music and
so a quality of perception, and no more. The word "Chinese" in his title is merely part of the machinery for
detaching the flute and the snow from Anglo-Saxon clichés; the poem isn't transferred into the allied cliché-
world of chinoiserie.

Which explains in turn why this author's work differs so
radically from the staple minor British verse to which his
stock of images, his persistent synaesthesia, his preoccupation with moments of tranced half-attention would seem
at first glance to ally him.

It is neither between three and four
Nor is it the time for lamps:
It is afternoon—interminably.

—one wouldn't be *very* surprised to come across those
lines in a patch of versified filler. The difference is that
Mr. Tomlinson compels a wholly different kind of attention from the reader: so much so that it is grossly wrong
to speak of him as employing devices, or keeping images
in stock, or being preoccupied with anything the reader
is likely to remember from his own mental life. The lines
just quoted aren't a situation from which the poem starts,
a circumstance in which its meditations are carried on,
but a point of perception through which it passes after it
has been in movement for all of four lines. Which amounts
to saying that Mr. Tomlinson, building up his austere
little universes before our eyes, does something altogether different from the man who, pausing in the act of
mailing a letter, notes the commonplace novelties of the
sensual world ("Sparrows occur. Wheels twinkle.") and
so flatters a reader who has undergone such moments of
arrest himself. He also does something very different from
the Wallace Stevens who ravels out into cumbersome
frivolities, though his path has obviously intersected that
of the Stevens of "Thirteen Ways of Looking at a Blackbird." Even there, Stevens' unpeopled landscapes imply

an ache, an absence of the familiar *point d'appui,* whereas Mr. Tomlinson's "facets of copiousness" ignore the
inhabitant precisely because they "exist . . . when we
have silenced ourselves." This explains why he has none
of Stevens' itch for the grand style, nor the consequent
Stevens delight in jokes attendant on the grand style
gesturing in a void

(Yet that things go round and again go round
      Has rather a classical sound.)

His mind isn't on styles but on the blank paper and the
prospects of calligraphy.

It is hard to imagine where Mr. Tomlinson is going next;
the chief defect of his fifteen poems is their air of having
exhausted their method in a bare few hundred words. At
any rate *The Necklace* deserves circulation in this country.
It is neither applied art nor last season's dishwater. It
belongs in the small category of poetic acts which can
preserve us from being abused by the complacent rhetoric
of the genteel inconspicuous.

Hugh Kenner (essay date 1959)

SOURCE: "Next Year's Words," in *Poetry,* Vol. 93, No.
5, February, 1959, pp. 335-40.

[*In the following review of* Seeing is Believing, *Kenner
discusses the innovative nature and respect for tradition
in Tomlinson's poetry and acknowledges his debt to William
Wordsworth, Marianne Moore, and the Symbolist poets.*]

To be the best poet practicing in England is, these days,
to share a meaningless eminence with the wittiest statistician
in Terre Haute or the handsomest peacock ever hatched in
Idaho. It is therefore virtually useless to locate Mr. Tomlinson with reference to his contemporaries; not only because he is steadily on the move and they aren't, but because he manifests just that unmistakable combination of
radical originality and a sure impassioned civil intercourse
with the past that marks off the poet of genius from the
writers one merely places.

The sea
Whether it is "wrinkled" and "crawls"
Or pounds, plunders, rounding
On itself in thunderous showers, a
Broken, bellowing foam canopy
Rock-riven and driven wild
By its own formless griefs—the sea
Carries, midway, its burning stripe of light.

Such kinetic mastery earns the right of its allusion to
Tennyson's vignette. The dead poet is neither conscripted
not snubbed, he is enabled to cooperate in the task of
fixing perception. The onomatopoeia doesn't deflect a
hairsbreadth the forward dart of meaning; the sea does
pound, does plunder, does round on itself in thunderous
showers, and these are not fortunate occasions for poetic effect but the sea's salient qualities for the stanza's

purpose. Such unremitting intentness on the movement of the perceiving mind through sensate particulars, a movement plotted by establishing the identity of each particular as succinctly as may be—such self-effacing concern for the essential poetic *action,* which is an action of the mind, sustains and justifies the poet's extreme technical resourcefulness. Everything scintillates, nothing distracts.

Nine lines later, having traversed the "half-lies" of the guidebooks ("twenty minutes in a comfortable bus"), we arrive at the nub of this particular poem:

> The imagination cannot lie. It bites brick;
> Says: "This is steel—I will taste steel.
> Bred on a lie, I am merely
> Guidebooks, advertisements, politics."

It might add, poesy, "all this fiddle" which Miss Moore enjoins us to read with a perfect contempt. We are very seldom in the presence of verse which so persuades us that verse need not be "bred on a lie."

"Bred on a lie," as art, except for heroic particular acts, has been since before the Renaissance. The great falsifiers are household names; they maintained with passion that believing was indifferent to seeing, or exacted of themselves a frantic rivalry with the actual. It is this rivalry, obliterating with its impasto of opaque will the inexhaustible tensions and recesses of the visible, that **"Farewell to Van Gogh"** tactfully relegates to history:

> The quiet deepens. You will not persuade
>   One leaf of the accomplished, steady, darkening
> Chestnut-tower to displace itself
>   With more of violence than the air supplies
> When, gathering dusk, the pond brims evenly
>   And we must be content with stillness.
>
> Unhastening, daylight withdraws from us its shapes
>   Into their central calm. Stone by stone
> Your rhetoric is dispersed until the earth
>
>   Becomes once more the earth, the leaves
> A sharp partition against cooling blue.
>
> Farewell, and for your instructive frenzy
>   Gratitude. The world does not end tonight
> And the fruit that we shall pick tomorrow
>   Await us, weighing the unstripped bough.

The earth becomes once more the earth: things are what they are:

>   Stones act, like pictures, by remaining
> Always the same, unmoving, waiting on presence
> Unpredictable in absence, inhuman
> In a human dependence;

and as for the Universe,

> Sun is, because it is not you; you are
>   Since you are self, and self delimited

> Regarding sun. It downs? I claim? Cannot
>   Speech such as this gather conviction?
> Judge, as you will, not what I say
>   But what is, being said.

Mr. Tomlinson's insistent didacticism amounts to an injunction that we be conscious, and conscious with a mode of attention that entails the disciplined will to attend. It isn't preachy; it grows so naturally out of the articulated perceptions of his landscapes and still-lifes that it seems the voiced moral gravity of the things themselves. Seeing is more than acknowledging, it is believing. Things seen this poet knows as a painter must, in their surfaces, their relations to space, their interplay of irreducible presence. "Delicate, minute must be the inventory of truth," wrote Wyndham Lewis, another painter. This painter's vision, deliberately cultivated as a mode of poetic organization, is Mr. Tomlinson's parry to a long tradition of incanted verse, hollow oes and aes, the very word which is like a bell, old men in a dry month, darkling listeners. The eye, unlike the ear, cannot sponsor solipsism. Though there are seldom people in these poems, there is a concrete and embodies world whose objects unite with the capable eye in an inimitably kinetic dialogue. Thus the drop of a wave is dissociated into a sequence of Japanese prints—

> Launched into an opposing wind, hangs
>   Grappled beneath the onrush,
> And there, lifts, curling in spume,
>   Unlocks, drops from that hold,
> Over and shoreward. . . .

Thus, ultimately, a John Constable's inventory of visual facts—

> He admired accidents, because governed by laws,
>   Representing them (since the illusion was not his
>   end)
> As governed by feeling

—makes of landscape an art complete because human; human, despite the absence of people in the subject-matter, because

> . . . the looped pigments, the pin-heads of light
>   Securing space under their deft restrictions
> Convince, as the index of a possible passion.
>   As the adequate gauge, both of the passion
> And its object.

Whence the conclusion,

>   The artist lies
> For the improvement of truth. Believe him.

By comparison, Wordsworth's rendition of

>   these steep and lofty cliffs
> That on a wild secluded scene impress
> Thoughts of more deep seclusion, and connect
> The landscape with the quiet of the sky

is deficient in the equivalent of "looped pigments, pin-heads of light", lulled by received cadences, and prone to unite flaccid categories ("a wild secluded scene"; "thoughts of more deep seclusion") by ("impress"; "connect") perfunctory connective gestures, Mr. Tomlinson has returned Wordsworth's job with instruments perfected by Stevens, Pound, and Miss Moore, not to mention the Symbolists.

For the Symbolists have done for the twentieth century what they did for Yeats: they have rendered irrelevant the impasse, prepared by Locke and never solved by Wordsworth, between what is in front of me and what goes on in my mind as I confront it. Wordsworth, besieged by the problem, dissolved subject and object in an evasive syntax, refusing (as Mr. Empson has noted) to say what was more deeply interfused than what; and mingling notation and perception, the blue sky and the mind of man, produced a serviceable illusion of unity. Had he been equipped to do more than the very great deal that he did, the history of nineteenth century sensibility might have been totally different; but he had insufficient presence to inhibit the prestige of showier poets, and stands, to our backward gaze, like a basalt slab at the back of a Romanticism which disregarded his minatory grandeur while profiting from his interception of history. He apparently rendered eighteenth century poetics irrelevant; that came to be his polemic usefulness.

It was there that an important enterprise was choked off; and now that commune pre-romantic centuries have been reopened, Mr. Tomlinson has perceived the relevance of returning to Wordsworth's area of concern. He has also observed that art's status as the elucidator of perception was clarified, after Wordsworth, not by poets but by painters. That is why the range of painting that is germane to his purposes is bounded by Constable and Cézanne. It is also why the range of things observed in *Seeing Is Believing* is so sharply limited. The Atlantic, oxen ploughing, the Mediterranean, a mausoleum, the paring of an apple, reeds, a castle, a ruin: they are the subjects of yesterday's paintings.

To suppose that Mr. Tomlinson's talent is bound by these formulae would probably be as great a mistake as the supposition, in 1917, that Mr. Eliot was going to devote his career to writing quatrains. For one thing, *Seeing Is Believing* marks a change of method from that of his earlier volume, *The Necklace,* so radical as to suggest that his normal mode of operation is to wring a procedure dry and then leave it behind. For another thing, the present collection ends with a remarkable sequence called **"Antecedents"** which, in valediction to the Symbolists themselves, deserts the painterly approach for an unexpected virtuosity of wit and literary allusion.

> . . . We had our laureates, they
> Their full orchestra and its various music. To that
>
>   Enter
> On an ice-drift
> A white bear, the Grand Chancellor
> From Analyse, uncertain

> Of whom he should bow to, or whether
> No one is present. . . .

—quite like a Critic considering the Limits of Poetry.

Mr. Tomlinson's remarkable capacity for development is the most salient of his virtues. That he is intensely English, yet at present accessible chiefly to American readers; that he is invariably omitted from London Letters concerning English writing in the fifties, while the paper-doll warfare of the Angry Young Men and the University Wits passes for urgent literary history; that no British publisher's reader has been able to recognize his verse as even competent; that a blurb for the present volume concocted in a New York publisher's office summarizes his qualities more accurately than any British review of *The Necklace*; these are facts for a historian to ponder who would trace the sequel to that now distant age when a Robert Frost was compelled to go abroad and be discovered (by Ezra Pound, it is true) in London.

Donald Davie (essay date 1959)

SOURCE: "See, and Believe," in *Essays in Criticism,* Vol. IX, No. 2, April, 1959, pp. 188-95.

[*In the following review of* Seeing is Believing, *Davie commends the development of Tomlinson's verse, calling the collection a "landmark."*]

[*Seeing is Believing*] is Tomlinson's third collection of poems, but the first that is both substantial and representative. His first, published quite some years ago by the Hand & Flower Press, contains, as they say, 'prentice-work', promising, intelligent and various, but now interesting chiefly because it shows the poet casting about for the style he wanted. In *The Necklace,* fifteen poems published four years ago by the Fantasy Press, the style has been achieved completely, but appears a specialized instrument for very special purposes. Special, and limited. Of course. But not at all so limited as people thought. The proof is in this collection, where what is recognisably the same style has been adapted, refined and elaborated so as to serve a much wider range of experience—as wide a range, in fact, as anyone has the right to demand of any poets except the greatest.

The word which the reviewers found for *The Necklace* was 'imagist'. But it was the wrong word, as Geoffrey Strickland pointed out in this journal; for Tomlinson had entered into his landscapes with far more of himself than an Imagist poet could ever afford to deploy. What he aimed at and achieved was a sensuous apprehension more comprehensive and more comprehending than the Imagist programme, bound to the one sense of sight and the one stance of cool observer, could allow for. Tomlinson's attitude, as distinct from his techniques, was far nearer to Lawrence's (in a poem like 'Snake') than to Pound's or Hulme's. What prompted the word 'imagist' was the one thing no one could deny, however little he might value it:

the exquisitely accurate register of sense-impressions. What wasn't realised was that this scrupulous exactness wasn't there for its own sake, but as a discipline and a control; controlling an exceptionally passionate and whole-hearted response to the world, to a world that bore in, not just on the five senses, but also on a man's sentiments, a man's convictions. The American reviewers seem, some of them, to be making the same mistake with this collection.

But for heaven's sake let's not carp at the Americans. They have published, first in their magazines and now in this very elegant book, poems which (as I know) have for years been hawked in vain round the British magazines, the British anthologists and the London publishing houses. All honour to Miss Erica Marx and Mr. Oscar Mellor, and to those editors who have published Tomlinson in British magazines, even if they did choose to print mostly pieces which were marginal and untypical. The blunt fact remains: that *The Necklace* was unavoidably a slight and fugitive publication, and that otherwise this most original and accomplished of all our post-war poets, profoundly English as he is in his attitudes and nowadays his landscapes, had to wait for a transatlantic critic, Hugh Kenner, to discover him; for transatlantic magazines to publish him in bulk, pay him, and award him prizes; and for a transatlantic publisher to bring him out between hard covers. Your withers, of course, remain unwrung. Am I trying to pretend that this is a national disgrace? Nothing less. But anyhow, the case is no special one: the publication of this volume gives point to desultory arguments that have gone on for some time, about whether New Provincial isn't Old Parochial, whether the glibly cosmopolitan is any worse than the aggressively insular. For Tomlinson's models are largely French and American; that is, he refuses to join the silent conspiracy which now unites all the English poets from Robert Graves down to Philip Larkin, and all the critics, editors and publishers too, the conspiracy to pretend that Eliot and Pound never happened. Tomlinson refuses to put the clock back, to pretend that after Pound and Eliot, Marianne Moore and Wallace Stevens have written in English, the English poetic tradition remains unaffected. He refuses to honour even the first rule of the club, by sheltering snugly under the skirts of 'the genius of the language'; instead he appears to believe, as Pound and Eliot did before him, that a Valéry and a Mallarmé change the landscape of poetry in languages other than their own. No wonder he doesn't appeal to our Little Englanders.

This, the debt to the French, is the subject of the elaborate tail-piece to this volume, an eight-page poem in six parts entitled **'Antecedents'**. It is the only lineal descendent of Pound's 'Mauberley', and worthy of that great original, limited only as that is limited, by offending against Sidney's injunction that the poet should not confound himself with the historian. The hero is Jules Laforgue, introduced in the second section after a brilliant capsulated history of French symbolism as the logical consequence of the Romantic Movement, the whole orchestrated in terms of two arch-Romantic images, sunset and the call of a horn, conflated in a series of synaesthetic perceptions like those of the symbolists themselves ('Slow horn pouring through

dusk an orange twilight'). After Byron, Tennyson, Nietzsche, Wagner, Mallarmé, Baudelaire, enter Laforgue:

> We had our laureates, they
> Their full orchestra and its various music. To that
> > Enter
> On an ice-drift
> A white bear, the grand Chancellor
> From Analyse, uncertain
> Of whom he should bow to, or whether
> No one is present. It started with Byron, and
> Liszt, says Heine, bowed to the ladies. But Jules . . .
> Outside,
>
> > De la musique avant toute chose
> The thin horns gone glacial
> And behind blinds, partitioning Paris
> Into the rose-stained mist,
> He bows to the looking-glass. Sunsets.

Will Tomlinson be told to bear his learning more lightly? But where do we find a lighter touch than in the elegant fantasy (adapted from Laforgue himself) which makes of the blank white page and the blank space on the page a polar bear on an icefloe? Mallarmé said, 'L'armature intellectuelle du poème se dissimule et tient—a lieu—dans l'espace qui isole les strophes et parmi le blanc du papier: significatif silence qu'il n'est pas moins beau de composer que les vers.' If this is one of the most perceptive things said about the art of poetry in the last hundred years, how can we maintain that a professional poet should not know this, or that, if he does, he should conceal the fact? But he answers such objections himself:

> > Our innate
> Perspicacity for the moderate
> Is a national armory. 'I have not
> Read him. I have read about him':
> In usum delphini—for the use
> Of the common man. After Nietzsche
> (Downwards) Sartre, after whom
> Anouilh, dauphin's delight. And thus
> Rimbaud the incendiary,
> Gumin contemporary
> With Gosse, the gentleman
> Arrived late. He was dressed
> In the skin of a Welsh lion, or the lion
> Wore his—for the light
> Was dubious, the marsh softening
> And the company, willing to be led
> Back to the forsaken garden by a route
> Unfamiliar—yet as it wound
> Dimly among the fetishes, a bewilderment
> Of reminiscence. The force
> That through the green dark, drove them
> Muffled dissatisfactions. Last light, low among
> > tempests
> Of restless brass. Last music
> For the sable throne (She comes, she comes!)
> As the horns, one by one
> Extinguish under the wave
> Rising into the level darkness.

Except for the strident and typically Poundian pun ('del-phini' / 'dauphin's'), this is more Eliotic than Poundian, in the interlarded quotations of course, but more importantly in the Mallarméan syntax which acts out, for instance, the anachronism of Thomas playing in 1940 the Rimbaud game for which the right time was 1870:

> And thus
> Rimbaud the incendiary,
> Gamin contemporary
> With Gosse, the gentleman
> Arrived late.

This is wit that is something better than deprecating, because this is a poet with something better to write about than himself. Laforgue had nothing better—'He bows to the looking-glass'; and so **'Antecedents'** is, as the title says, at once 'A homage and a valediction'. Tomlinson is a post-symbolist poet, not a symbolist absurdly belated. And he is not going to make the mistake he diagnoses in Thomas, of playing Laforgue as Thomas played Rimbaud, a half-century too late.

What Tomlison aimed at and achieved was a sensuous apprehension more comprehensive and more comprehending than the Imagist programme, bound to the one sense of sight and the one stance of cool observer, could allow for.

—Donald Davie

How to utilise the Symbolist disciplines and procedures whileescaping from the Symbolists' solipsistic trap—this is spelled out in the last section of **'Antecedents',** as well as at other points. But Tomlinson's style (and I don't mean the specially contrived style of **'Antecendents'**) does better than spell out the answer; it exhibits it in living action. For the style which Tomlinson discovered in *The Necklace* and has here developed so flexibly is not just a way of writing, not at all a way of writing in any sense that is not also a way of perceiving, a way of responding. Central to this style of perceiving is a symbolist idea generally known to us only in the rather special version that Eliot gave of it when he spoke of the objective correlative. It is the idea that an arrangement of objects or events in the apparently external world may so correspond to a pattern of thought and feeling in the mind, that the latter may be expressed and defined in terms of the former. It is against the background of this conviction that Tomlinson can speak (as, to be sure, others have spoken) of 'a certain mental climate', of 'the moral landscape of my poetry in general'. These are something better than metaphors or, if they are metaphors, these metaphors underpin everything Tomlinson writes. Now it is obvious that the idea as just outlined permits of a two-way traffic between the poet's mind and the world: he may proceed from himself outward, starting with a state of feeling in himself and seeking an objective

correlative for it; or he may start with perceptions of the objective world, and move inward to find a subjective correlative for them in a state of feeling he induces or imagines. Symbolist poetry characteristically seems to have run the traffic all the first way, to the point indeed at which the reality of the supposedly objective world, as anything but a phantasmal reflection of the subjective, becomes highly questionable. Tomlinson too may run the traffic this way, as when he answers Amis's notorious 'Nobody wants any more poems about foreign cities', by conjuring up cities imagined so as to correspond to states of mind:

> Nor forgetting Ko-jen, that
> Musical city (it has
> Few buildings and annexes
> Space by combating silence),
> There is Fiordiligi, its sun-changes
> Against walls of transparent stone
> Unsettling all preconception—a city
> For architects (they are taught
> By casting their nets
> Into those moving shoals); . . .

But far more characteristically (and specifically so as to escape the Symbolist vertigo about whether the objective exists), Tomlinson runs the traffic the other way, insisting upon the irreducible Otherness of the non-human world, its Presence in the sense of its being present, its being bodied against the senses, as the irreplaceable first principle of all sanity and all morality. Of many statements of this (for it is after all what gives the book its title), I take **'Cézanne at Aix'**:

> And the mountain: each day
> Immobile like fruit. Unlike, also
> —Because irreducible, because
> Neither a component of the delicious
> And therefore questionable,
> Nor distracted (as the sitter)
> By his own pose and, therefore,
> Doubly to be questioned: it is not
> Posed. It is. Untaught
> Unalterable, a stone bridgehead
> To that which is tangible
> Because unfelt before. There
> In its weathered weight
> Its silence silences, a presence
> Which does not present itself.

Some objections may here be anticipated, and a concession made at no cost (which is that, yes, there are about five unsuccessful poems here, out of thirty-five). It will be objected that the poems are inhuman, that they never deal with people, human relations, human sentiments. In fact, the great advance on *The Necklace* is precisely here, in commenting (but by implication, always by implication from arrangements of sense-perceptions) on the life of man in history, especially on his communal life as registered by his buildings, by the nature and quality of his tools, by the landscapes he has modified. Secondly, it appears that the readers have difficulty with

Tomlinson's metres. Like most of Eliot (and how much else?), the metre is on the uncertain borderline between *vers libre* and loose (basically four-stress) accentual verse. For my part, I am sure that to count syllables as well as stresses is to have an instrument more delicate and various. But it is disingenuous to object to Tomlinson's metre while accepting Hopkins and Eliot—he is less emphatically muscle-bound than the one, more alert and vigorous than the other. The stops and starts of syntax play over against, and so tauten, the runs and pauses of rhythm; and there is a Hopkinsian (but again less emphatic and so more flexible) richness of orchestration in internal echoes and half-echoes of consonance and assonance, lacing clauses and lines together.

When I turn from these poems to work by highly and justly commended writers, such as R. S. Thomas, say, or even Edwin Muir, what dismays me about these is a pervasive slackness—not in perception nor in seriousness (for both are commonly as honest and truthful as Tomlinson is), but simply in artistic ambition. In their hands the medium is used scrupulously and well, to good and important ends; but it is *not wrought up to its highest pitch*. They do not say a thing once and for all, then move on fast to another thing. Their expressions could be, not more true, but more forcibly, more brilliantly and compactly true. What people don't realise is that in poetry there can be no question of choosing between the thing well done and the thing done consummately, conclusively. The art imposes its own laws: it demands to be pushed to the extreme, to be wrought up to the highest pitch it is capable of. There are degrees of meritorious performance, certainly, but there can be no question—not for the poet nor for the responsible reader—of preferring the less degree to the greater, as one may prefer weak tea to strong. Thus it is nonsense to say of Tomlinson, as some have said, that of course his diction and his music are choice and distinguished beyond the reach of his contemporaries, but nevertheless a coarser music may be better, a diction more vulgar may be more vigorous and so more valuable. The muse is not to be fooled, and vigour bought at that cost will be soon exhausted As an art, poetry cannot juggle with its own hierarchies. This is also the reason why it cannot stand still; why a poet who writes as if Pound and Mallarmé had never written may have merit, certainly, but other things being equal he can never have equal merit with a poet whose writing acknowledges the heights to which the art was wrought at those hands. This book, I am sure, is a landmark. What a pity it should mark a new peak in the obtuseness of the English to their own poets, as well as a new height gained in the long struggle back to English poetry considered by the poet as a way of spiritual knowledge.

Hayden Carruth   (essay date 1964)

SOURCE: "Abstruse Considerations," in *Poetry*, Vol. CIV, No. 4, July, 1964, pp. 243-44.

[*In the following positive review of* A Peopled Landscape, *Carruth explores the imitative structure of Tomlinson's verse.*]

At first, [*A Peopled Landscape*] offers the reader a curious, even excessive, medley of impressions. Its appearance is characteristic of the English taste in thin volumes of poetry; dun-white paper, type in an Old Style face, a binding of pale yellow linen stamped in gold leaf; the whole giving off an iodoformic smell which is always present, I don't know why, in new books of English manufacture. Appalling as it sounds, the composite is not unattractive. Then, however, one opens the book and turns the pages, finding that the poems, resting unread on the page, give a totally different impression, an American impression; and one remembers that Charles Tomlinson has been visiting in our country at some length recently. In particular, one notices the large number of poems in staggered tercets. Dr. Williams's form. His alone, one hastens to say; and these poems imitatively shaped, in Tomlinson's book, arouse an immediate hostility. At any rate they did in me, and I tried, without success, to think of a single self-respecting American poet who had *dared* to copy this form, at least for more than a poem or two.

As it turns out, though, the poems are English after all. I think Paul Goodman was the first to point out that Dr. Williams's tercets incline toward the pentameter. Tomlinson's incline toward the alexandrine. A world, or at least half a world, of difference lies between the two, perhaps even lengthened by the similarity of typography. Tomlinson's long rhythms, rather sonorous voicings, and elaborate grammar are unmistakable, and if they weren't, he clinches the matter by ending a good many poems in rhymed couplets. His subjects are what we expect, musings on life and death, art and passion, time and eternity, etc., usually set off by a "prospect" of the English countryside.

Once one accommodates oneself to the idea that Tomlinson is Tomlinson (and that the tercets are what they should be, gestures of respect), one can read these poems with pleasure and with admiration for his skill, which is evident and persuasive. A unified sensibility lies behind these poems. Having said this, however, I at once realize that a unified sensibility lies behind the work of every sane poet. What I miss in Tomlinson's poems are the points of conviction against which or upon which or around which the sensibility ought to consolidate. The conviction impelling these poems, as far as I can see, is none but the generalized esthetic conviction of an era vaporized in the attenuating myth of the artist as exclusive *homme d'esprit*. I am old-fashioned enough, or just possibly new-fashioned enough, to insist that the poem, if it is to be a work of art and not an article of consumption (to apply Hannah Arendt's distinction between work and labor), must sustain itself on convictions existing outside the poem, outside the art, and outside the artist considered in his artmaking capacity. Mind you, no incompatibility whatever intrudes between this view and the common iconographic definition of the poem as an autonomous structure.

Very likely these considerations appear as unhappily abstruse. But they lie at the heart of the current dissatisfactions and disagreements in the "world" of poetry, and all poets, certainly those as talented and intelligent as Charles Tomlinson, must think about them.

Denis Donoghue (essay date 1968)

SOURCE: "The Proper Plenitude of Fact," in *The Ordinary Universe: Soundings in Modern Literature,* The Macmillan Company, 1968, pp. 21-50.

[*In the following excerpt, Donoghue discusses the defining characteristics of Tomlinson's verse.*]

One might imagine a five-Act drama proceeding along these lines: (I) 'I see a mountain.' (2) 'The mountain exists, owing nothing to me.' (3) 'Now that it exists, however, it will register my feeling, receive its intimation.' (4) 'My feeling, when all is said, is more important than an inert mountain: the mountain will not mind diminishing itself to serve me.' (5) 'I shall now write my poem and it will take the place of the mountain; in this way, incidentally, I shall undo the work of Creation and be my own God. My faith in my own consciousness will move that mountain.' So Wallace Stevens wrote 'The Poem that Took the Place of a Mountain':

> There it was, word for word,
> The poem that took the place of a mountain.

The poem has replaced the mountain because the poet has needed 'a place to go to in his own direction', and he persists until the landscape is exactly 'right', answerable to his imperial mind. The rocks and pines are real now only, as an earlier voice said, 'if I make them so'. I am my world,' Wittgenstein says in the *Tractatus,* thus providing a formula that can be slanted in either direction; though later he says, 'The world is independent of my will.'

The imaginary five-Act play is designed to suggest, however, one of the dominant assumptions of modern literature, that nothing is real unless we have made it; the phenomena of earth are tokens of nothing but ourselves. The world is our oyster. Rejecting metaphysics, we make a metaphysics of our own, sometimes calling it an aesthetic theory, sometimes a Supreme Fiction. Meanwhile, as Lawrence said, 'To be, or not to be, is still the question.' Indeed, Lawrence's poems were written to resolve this problem, or at least to rebuke the imperial imagination. The novels confront the issue at last, in more problematic terms. In the poems Lawrence elucidates the relation of birds, beasts, and flowers, and shows a man acting graciously toward them. Hence the poems are parables, essays in civility, notes toward a proper mode of life. If Lawrence compares a pike, 'with smart fins/And grey-striped suit', to 'a lout on an obscure pavement', it is to show that the comparison is bogus. The fish is itself, different, 'fish-alive' in its own idiom; not you or I. We are to live in the world, Lawrence implies, remembering this. [In *God Without Thunder,* 1931] John Crowe Ransom has described the poetic attitude to the natural object as one in which 'we regard the endless mysterious fullness of this object, and respect the dignity of its objective existence after all—in

spite of the ambition to mastery that has become more and more habitual with us'. As James said in the Preface to *The Spoils of Poynton,* 'Always the splendid Things.'

One of the most lucid descriptions of such a world, proceeding under these auspices, is the poetry of Charles Tomlinson, especially the volume *Seeing is Believing*.

In the fourth part of '**Antecedents**,' in stern reply to, 'We lack nothing/But the milieu', Tomlinson says, 'We lack nothing/ But a significant sun.' Lacking this, he goes down to rock bottom, to the relation between the individual consciousness and the Other. This is something, a way out of the prison:

> Out of the shut cell of that solitude there is
> One egress, past point of interrogation.
> Sun is, because it is not you; you are
> Since you are self, and self delimited
> Regarding sun.

We must have it formulated with cool precision:

> You accept
> An evening, washed of its overtones
> By strict seclusion, yet are not secluded
> Witheld at your proper bounds.

The fine relation is an act of reverence, propriety, a sense of limits, identity, dialogue; it is pious, poetic, never predatory. In '**Cézanne at Aix**' the mountain is a mountain, irreducible, not an ambiguous reflection of the speaker or his consciousness; an object, independent of any use we may choose to make of it:

> And the mountain: each day
> Immobile like fruit. Unlike, also
> —Because irreducible, because
> Neither a component of the delicious
> And therefore questionable,
> Nor distracted (as the sitter)
> By his own pose and, therefore,
> Doubly to be questioned: it is not
> Posed. It is. Untaught
> Unalterable, a stone bridgehead
> To that which is tangible
> Because unfelt before. There
> In its weathered weight
> Its silence silences, a presence
> Which does not present itself.

The poem enacts, in the poise of its courtesy, a relationship equal in grace to that of the mountain and its 'scene'. The lines swing gently between precise notations, committed to the firm, modest duty of discrimination. The moral rhetoric, with its decorous emphases, has that unconscious fastidiousness in which, as Marianne Moore says, there is 'a great amount of poetry'. This is the tone of Tomlinson's best poems. The fine relation, the dialogue, acknowledged and pondered with a sense of its contractual harmonies, issues in genial assent. Tomlinson gives the supporting theory in a later poem:

> Distrust that poet
> Who must symbolize your stair
> Into an analogue of what was never there. Fact
> Has its proper plenitude that time and tact
> Will show, renew.

This is Tomlinson's reverence, acknowledging that we receive more than we give, and that we make up the difference—if we do—by tact, in wonder and local recognition:

> That which we were,
> Confronted by all that we are not,
> Grasps in subservience its replenishment.

So this poet, acknowledging his role in the scene of Being, is devoted to those relationships—seemingly chained to metaphors of aggression—which are open to more gracious formulation. The oxen and their master; the moss and the rock; the sea and the railway-tracks that seem to deny its glamour; the knifeblade and the apple; the bridge straddling vacancy as a girl's hand composes the air around it:

> At Luna
> There is a city of bridges, where
> Even the inhabitants are mindful
> Of a shared privilege: a bridge
> Does not exist for its own sake.
> It commands vacancy.

Stevens might have been thinking of such a poet as Tomlinson when he spoke of poetry [in *Opus Posthumous,* 1957] as 'an instrument of the will to perceive the innumerable accords, whether of the imagination or of reality, that make life a thing different from what it would be without such insights . . . a means by which to achieve balance and measure in our circumstances'.

We began with a persuasive relation, in Tomlinson's poems, between the individual consciousness and the Other. Outside the poems, this relationship more often than not is denied; or, if conceded, it seems restless, capricious: hence the temptation to be Master, to set up as God. In Tomlinson's poems the unifying motive is to translate these restless occasions into comelier terms of participation and harmony. The poems try to make marriages out of divorces. Tomlinson begins where Freud's *Civilization and its Discontents* leaves off, but he does not forget the sources of discontent. This is the determining figure of his poems; to find in experience justification for a pattern, guaranteed by the poise of its disclosure. The poems aspire to a condition of stillness, in which the self and the Other are acknowledged for what they are, separate but not alien. Like the bowl on a table:

> The laric world where the bowl glistens with
> presence
> Gracing the table on which it unfolds itself.

It is a 'wooing both ways', in Blackmur's phrase.

Or it is this when everything goes well, when a moral harmony is possible. Tomlinson is not content to enforce relationships, by fiat, setting the poem over against our experience of the daily world in which accords are often broken or frustrate. He brings the daily world as close as possible to the 'ideal' harmonies of the poem, by going back over the world's relationships and seeing whether at least some of the tangled ones are not, after all, open to more engaging interpretation. Stevens has argued for this, or something like it, as the essential poetic programme, to be 'in agreement with the radiant and productive world in which (the poet) lives'. Only when this proves impossible is Tomlinson defeated. Often, indeed, it is impossible, or too late. When the object is abused, there is no chance of liaison; we are baffled by guilt, watching defilement. Tomlinson thinks of such occasions as the wanton demolition of a house, or its defacement. In a ruines a focus for nothing:

> Within, wet from the failing roof,
> Walls greened. Each hearth refitted
> For a suburban whim, each room
> Denied what it was, diminished thus
> To a barbarous mean. . . .

A potentially vivid relation has been undermined. To speak of it in aesthetic terms is innocent if we bear in mind that for this poet aesthetic terms have weight only in a moral context of feeling.

But the fine relation can be subverted by the abuse or the exorbitance of its other member, the 'I'. The fact of 'otherness' is a beautiful necessity that invites recognition; if the 'I' turns back upon itself, it commits a breach of tact, falls from the condition of grace. This is the Symbolist impasse. Tomlinson has several poems that ponder the situation, and one that enacts its rebuke:

> She looks. And a flawed perfection
> Disburses her riches. She is watched
> And knows she is watched. The crimson reveals
> itself
> Recommending her posture and assured by it
> Both of her charm and her complicity: . . .

She has become a component of the delicious 'and therefore questionable'; distracted as the sitter—by her own pose and therefore 'doubly to be questioned'. Thus one poem glosses another in Tomlinson's single world.

To describe that world, we should consider its relations and its definitive terms. The terms of distaste include these: inert, mean, politician, romantic, prodigal, suburban, diminished, whim, ugly, waste, barbarous, negligence, empty, sullen, menial, excess. Some of the terms of praise are: replenishment, civil, order, ceremony, profuse, natural, consent, lucid, relation, stable, equable, comity, seasoned, human, stillness, recognition, temper, deft, haven, accomplished, supple, presence, dependence, grace. It is a Yeatsian vocabulary in the sense that Tomlinson, using such words as 'ceremony', 'civil', and 'accomplished', takes advantage of the resonance earned for them and their like in such poems as **'A Prayer for my Daughter'** and **'In Memory of Major Robert Gregory'**. This is a dependence, an acknowledged relation, rather than a debt; like the relation to Marianne Moore's 'Silence' in Tomlinson's **'The Castle'**. The world defined by Tomlinson's key-terms is a world of pieties and accords, a world of rooted men, gestures, pictures, cities, bridges, and apples. This is why he speaks, in one poem, of the release from 'knowing' to 'acknowledgement'.

I have mentioned situations apparently encased in aggression, ascribing to them a dominant force in modern literature. In many writers the only proof of reality, the only sign that can be taken seriously, is the mark of violence. But by now every trivial novelist knows how to forge the signs. Can anyone doubt that hundreds of contemporary novels are trading upon an induced violence, a mass-produced extremity? [*In Beyond Culture,* 1966] Lionel Trilling has recently entered a dispirited protest against the literature that features 'an accredited subversiveness, an established moral radicalism, a respectable violence'. Tomlinson distrusts this literature so deeply that his distrust has the defect of its quality: if his poems reveal a danger-sign, it is their tendency to retreat to a merely passive position in the moral world. Some time ago the poet endorsed Martin Buber's early redaction of certain Chinese emphases in philosophy as a timely critique of our own: in particular, the 'containment of the will' and the 'potentialities of quietude' sponsored in the *Tao*. It is obvious that the West has much to learn from the East in this respect, but the Taoist position itself is no real help. This is less China than chinoiserie: there must be a more Confucian way out. Tomlinson's own poems are not quietist: it is enough that they are quiet.

Perhaps at this point we might resort to the philosophers to rehearse the idiom of participation. Clearly, this idiom depends upon our acknowledgement of Being as the first commitment in an intelligible life. Before Stevens could posit a relation between his jar and Tennessee, he had to assent to the separate being of each, the ABC of being. As in his 'Study of Two Pears', 'The pears are not seen/As the observer wills.' This is provisional in Stevens, though he commits himself to it, as we shall see, in many of his last poems. [In *The Christian Philosophy of St. Thomas Aquinas,* 1956] Etienne Gilson has pointed out that, among the philosophers, Aquinas had a lively sense of the plenitude and continuity of being, but he remarks also that it is difficult to express this sense by the concept of Being. A philosopher who would being with that, and that alone, undertakes to deduce the concrete from the abstract. To avoid this difficulty he would try to enrich the concept by giving it the vigour of an existential intuition. Subject and object must be connected by an intuition of the 'act'. Otherwise, Gilson says, 'an essence is dead when it is deposited in the understanding as a quiddity, without preserving its contact with the act-of-being'. Let us say that the act of being must be acknowledged by a correspondingly 'active' sense. It is this sense, I would argue, that explains the eventfulness of Wordsworth's poems, the muscular exertion in Hopkins's poems, and the urge in some parts of Stevens and many parts of Tomlinson to render essence by deploying existents in lithe relationships. It is the relationship, the movement of energy between the objects, that certifies their participation in the act-of-being.

Rounding this out a little: we think of Aquinas and his modern pupil as supplying a theory in support of Hopkins's practice, with more cogency than the maverick Scotus normally invoked for this purpose. (But we revert to this later.) For Wordworth's moral ballads we have his own theory. Beside this we might place a passage from Ortega's *Meditations on Quixote,* where he discusses 'Things and their Meaning'. Things have their meaning, he says, in relation to themselves and to other things. 'The "meaning" of a thing is the highest form of its coexistence with other things—it is its depth dimension. No, it is not enough for me to have the material body of a thing; I need, besides, to know its "meaning", that is to say, the mystic shadow which the rest of the universe casts upon it.' Hence what we call Nature is only 'the maximum structure into which all material elements have entered'. For Stevens's poems we have his own theories, fabulous in their resource, with only this disability, that they are neater than the poems themselves in the matter of consistency. The poems flout the essays time and again, as perhaps they should. For Tomlinson's poems there is a certain amount of theory, often in his verse. But perhaps we might supplement it by recourse to two passages from older poets. There is a splendid letter in which Rilke, writing to his Polish translator, puts a case for Nature, he says, meaning all the objects of our context, is but a frail thing. But as long as we are here we should not abuse it. We should not "pollute and degrade the Actual', if for no other reason than this, that its transitoriness is held in common with our own. Many of the things which our grandfathers valued are disappearing; in their lives, almost every object with which they lived was 'a vessel in which they found something human or added their morsel of humanity'. These things have gone and cannot be replaced. 'We are perhaps the last to have known such things': we are already replacing them with things that resist our humanity. It is our responsibility not only to remember them but to endorse 'their human or "laric" value'. We may think that, in some of his later poems, Rilke freed himself a little from this admonition; but this is by the way. The second text to put beside Tomlinson's poem is a stanza from the *Song to David,* where Smart shows what laric value means by rendering the mutual relation of things:

> For ADORATION rip'ning canes,
> And cocoa's purest milk detains
>   The western pilgrim's staff;
> Where rain in clasping boughs inclos'd,
> And vines with oranges dispos'd,
>   Embow'r the social laugh.

I give this as an accompaniment to Tomlinson's poems, to emphasize a particular continuity of feeling at a time when dissociations are more often in the news. In the **'Ode to Arnold Schoenberg'** Tomlinson speaks of proceeding

> through discontinuities
>   to the whole in which
>   discontinuities are held
>   like the foam in chalcedony
>   the stone, enriched
>   by the tones' impurity.

This is the direction of his recent poems. He still retains the old liaisons, recognizable in such phrases as 'the mystery of fact', 'the trust of seeing', the marriage of eye and mind. In Machado's Castilian ilexes, Tomlinson finds, 'strength and humility agree'. It is entirely in keeping with these poems that, quoting *The Deserted Village,* he should invoke 'the seasons' sweet succession'.

On the first page of **American Scenes** Tomlinson speaks of 'terror and territory'; at the end of the book we read of 'pause and possibility'. Between these extremes we find him accepting every invitation of language, provided its terms are gracious and rational. It is a good omen, a sign of proper nonchalance. Some of Tomlinson's poems in the early years were a little too tight for their own ease. They refused to speak beyond their contract; as if, like Flaubert in Henry James's phrase, they felt of their vocation almost nothing but the difficulty. The recent poems are wrought with the old care, but they move more genially. There is no loss of their qualifying merit.

The collection is divided in four parts. The first, 'Negotiations', is continuous with the idiom of *A Peopled Landscape*. Sometimes the figures are rather monolithic, as if they were hired for the occasion to represent an aesthetic theory: they do not move with their own energy. A girl climbing a hill is a moral emblem, acting in that capacity before she is fully established as a girl climbing a hill. The second part, 'American Scenes', is Tomlinson's response to the landscapes of Arizona and New Mexico. Some of these poems are satirical, a new mode for this poet and still, it seems, difficult for him to gauge. In the weaker satires we hear an outraged English sensibility finding itself in Barstow, California, 'a placeless place' featuring an 'execrable conjunction/of gasoline and desert air'. A sensibility in pain may be allowed the privilege of roaring as loud as it wishes; and yet one thinks of Austin Clarke's satires, poems like 'Martha Blake' and 'The Loss of Strength', where the pain is given in the cadence. In 'American Scenes' the lovely poems are the memorials to people like Homer Vance, Thomas Eakins, Mr. Brodsky, Emily Dickinson. The third and fourth parts contain a group of Mexican poems and a longer Idyll from San Francisco. Some of these pieces are like short stories, incidents, things seen from a bus, a Chinese adolescent in San Francisco reading a book called *Success in Spelling.*

The nonchalance of this poetry is partly Tomlinson's readiness to accept the invitations of language, and partly an equal readiness to accept the casualties of event, whatever the day offers. He still pares his poetic apples with concern, but he is now responsive to the yield of chance. He takes things as they come. This was implicit in his terminology from the beginning, but held back by some scruple. Now it is free. Tomlinson trusts, of course, that things, as they come, will not come too violently: his poems are not yet ready for the big storms, the 'violence without', in Stevens's phrase. When things come, the poet receives them with the values already declared in the earlier books. So we hear of 'a loving lease/on sand, sun, rock', and the splendour of 'Castilian grace'. If we need a motto to hold these poems in mind, we have one: 'the tranquillity of

consciousness/forgotten in its object'. This may be Tomlinson's answer to those modern writers who insist upon remembering their consciousness, whatever the fate of the object. So Tomlinson proceeds, compiling an anthology of minor occaisions to endorse a pervading tact. His masters in this transaction are Ruskin, Lawrence, and Williams, so far as one can see: there is still a trace of Marianne Moore, but hardly a sign of Stevens, an early master. Ruskin is audible particularly in **'A Given Grace',** where two cups on a mahogany table are seen to 'unclench the mind, filling it with themselves', a figure elsewhere invoked for the tranquillity of consciousness. Lawrence seems to underwrite those poems in which the acknowledgement of separateness is a first step toward larger courtesies. Williams is invoked, mostly in the American scenes, to guide the younger poet in dealing with casualty and 'rankest trivia', the things that come into the poems because they are true, they were there at the time. In **'Chief Standing Water'** we read of the *Book of Mormon* for the same reason that in Marianne Moore's poem we are told of four quartz crystal clocks, because there were four, neither three nor five. The casual is not enough, as Stevens says, but the ability to receive the casual, giving it a flick of feeling, is rare in poets. Tomlinson's happiest development is in this direction. Seeing is still believing:

> To love
> is to see,
> to let be
> this disparateness
> and to live within
> the unrestricted boundary between.

We think of Isabel Archer, and of her interest, as James says, in 'the things that are not herself',

Calvin Bedient   (essay date 1970)

SOURCE: "Calvin Bedient on Charles Tomlinson," in *The Iowa Review,* Vol. 1, No. 2, Spring, 1970, pp. 83-100.

[*In the following essay, Bedient analyzes the innovative nature of Tomlinson's verse.*]

Charles Tomlinson is the most considerable English poet to have made his way since the second World War. There is more to see along that way, more to meditate, more solidity of achievement, more distinction of phrase, more success as, deftly turning, hand and mind execute the difficult knot that makes the poem complete, than in the work of any of Tomlinson's contemporaries. It is true that the way is strait; but Tomlinson would have it so. For his is a holding action: he is out to save the world for the curious and caring mind. And if he is narrow, he is only so narrow as a searching human eye and a mind that feeds and reflects on vision—an eye that to everything textured, spatial, neighboring, encompassing, humanly customary, and endlessly and beautifully modulated by light, dusk, weather, the slow chemistry of years, comes like a cleansing rain—as also like a preserving amber. The quality everywhere present in Tomlinson's poetry is a peculiarly astringent, almost dry, but deeply meditated love; this is true whether his subject is human beings, houses, lamplight, chestnuts, lakes, or glass. Tomlinson is a poet of exteriority and its human correlatives: the traditional, the universal, the unchangeable, the transparencies of reflection. And he is thus the opposite of a lyric or "confessional" poet. Yet what a mistake it would be to confuse this outwardness with superficiality. To read Tomlinson is continually to *sound*: to meet with what lies outside the self in a simultaneous grace of vision and love. Tomlinson's chief theme is, in his own phrase, "the fineness of relationships." And though his poetry is in great measure restricted to this theme, the theme itself is an opening and a wideness.

Tomlinson's theme, or his strict relation to it, is one with his originality; and this originality is most salient in his poems on the world's appearances. We have been asked to admire so many poets of "nature" that we can but sigh, or look blank, to hear it announced that still another one has come along; and we will greet with skepticism any claims to originality. But Tomlinson is unmistakably an original poet. There is in him, it is true, a measure of Wordsworth: the at-homeness in *being* as against *doing,* the wise passivity, the love of customariness, and what Pater spoke of as Wordsworth's "very fine apprehension of the limits within which alone philosophical imaginings have any place in true poetry." Both poets awaken, moreover, in Shelley's phrase, "a sort of thought in sense." But how different in each is the relation of sense to thought. In Wordsworth, sense fails into thought. Nature strikes Wordsworth like a bolt; it is the charred trunk that he reflects upon. His thought looks back to sense and its elation, hungering. In Tomlinson, by contrast, the mind hovers over what the eye observes; the two are coterminous. Together, they surprise a sufficiency in the present; and if passion informs them, it is a passion for objectivity. For the most part, Wordsworth discovers himself in nature—it is this, of course, that makes him a Romantic poet. Tomlinson, on the other hand, discovers the nature of nature: a classical artist, he is all taut, responsive detachment.

The sufficiency (or something very near it) of the spatial world to Tomlinson's eye, mind, and heart, the gratefulness of appearances to a sensibility so unusual as his, at once radically receptive and restrained, separates him from such poets as D. H. Lawrence and Wallace Stevens—though the latter, indeed, exerted a strong early influence. This marked spiritual contentment—which makes up the message and quiet power and healing effluence of Tomlinson's work—may be conveniently illustrated by one of his shorter poems, **"The Gossamers."**

Autumn. A haze is gold
By definition. This one lit
The thread of gossamers
That webbed across it
Out of shadow and again
Through rocking spaces which the sun
Claimed in the leafage. Now
I saw for what they were
These glitterings in grass, on air,

Of certainties that ride and plot
The currents in their tenuous stride
And, as they flow, must touch
Each blade and, touching, know
Its green resistance. Undefined
The haze of autumn in the mind
Is gold, is glaze.

This poem is in part a parable on the propriety of the self-forgetting mind. The mind—it seems to hint—is in itself a wealth, like a gold haze; the mind turned outward, however, is wealth piled upon wealth, a glaze upon particular things—a haze lighting up glittering gossamers. This reflection, which encloses the poem, forms part of its own wealth; and yet it is to the poem only what the enclosing haze is to the gossamers: an abstract richness outdone by and subservient to the vivid interest of the concrete. The poem is as good as its word: proclaiming the supremacy of the particular, it stands and delivers. To the tenuous intellect, it presents a living, green resistance. Tomlinson's poem discovers gossamers as a scientist might discover a new chemical; indeed, Tomlinson himself has quoted with covetous interest from Lévi-Strauss' *The Savage Mind* a phrase applicable to his own cast of thought: "the science of the concrete." Of course the phrase omits the grateful quality of Tomlinson's attention: a scientist observes, Tomlinson regards, has regard. The gossamers are his host, he their thankful guest. And as a consequence of this humble gratitude, of this self-abnegating attention, Tomlinson brings into the human record—as nothing else has ever done—the look and being of gossamers, an obscure yet precious portion of articulated space. Impossible, now, not to know how gossamers plot currents, ride air, tenuously stride, connect and resist. Modest as it is, the poem is as good as a front row, a microscope, the opening of a long-buried treasure.

With this example before us, we may perhaps approach to a sharper view of Tomlinson's originality as a poet of nature. Among such poets, he is the anchorite of appearances. To poetry about them he brings an unexpected, an unparalleled, selflessness and objectivity. An ascetic of the eye, Tomlinson pushes poetry closer to natural philosophy than it has ever been before—and at the same time prosyletizes for fine relationships with space, writes and persuades in earnestness, if not in zeal. Into an area crowded with hedonists, mystics, rapturous aesthetes, he comes equipped with a chaste eye and a mind intent upon exactitude. Nature may indeed be a Book; but not until now, say the chaste eye, the intent mind, has the book been more than scanned. The fine print, the difficult clauses, the subtle transitions, the unfamiliar words—Tomlinson will pore over them all. And his language will be as learned and meticulous, his dedication as passionate, his ego as subdued, as that of the true scholar—though mercifully he will also exercise, what few scholars possess, a deft and graceful feeling for form.

The clue to Tomlinson's originality lies in the apparent incongruity between his chosen subject and his temperament. In part, the subject is all the opulence of the visual world—jewelled glass, golden gossamers, fiery clouds. The temperament, by contrast, is strict and chaste, not far from sternness, flourishing only in an atmosphere of "fecund chill," of "temperate sharpness." It is akin to that grain of wheat which, unless it die, cannot bring forth fruit. Ordinarily, of course, men of such temperament turn to God, to the State, to the poor, to science, to learning. They would no sooner turn to the sensual earth than the pious would turn to the Devil. Or if they did, they would bring a scourge, not a strict curiosity indistinguishable from the most discrete and delicate love. A nature of which there is no "point" to seize, as the first of the **"Four Kantian Lyrics"** suggests, exists, after all, only to the senses; and the senses are notorious panders to the self, tributary streams of the torrential Ego. And yet what the chaste temperament desires is, precisely, to be selfless. Men of such mold would fall to the ground and emerge—something else, something richer. An anti-hedonist who cultivates his senses, an ascetic of

> the steady roar of evening,
> Withdrawing in slow ripples of orange,
> Like the retreat of water from sea-caves . . .

—these are patent contradictions in terms. Tomlinson, politely denying the contradiction, steps in among the hullabalooers and coolly and dedicatedly clears serious ground of his own in the region of the senses, in the forests and "further fields" of nontranscendent space. The result is a nature poetry as unique in its classical temperateness as in its consecration to the Being of Space, to the face and actions of our natural environment.

Tomlinson looks outward, and what he sees becomes, not himself exactly, but his content. Seeing discovers his limits—but they are the limits of a vase or a window, not of a prison. Indeed, to Tomlinson it is a happy circumstance that the world is "other"; were it identical with the self, there would be no refuge from solitude, nothing to touch as one reaches out.

> Out of the shut cell of that solitude there is
> One egress, past point of interrogation.
> Sun is, because it is not you; you are
> Since you are self, and self delimited
> Regarding sun.

Observer and observed stand apart, then, as the necessary poles of a substantiated being. The eye is the first of philosophers; seeing turns up the soil of ontology. Beholding thus applies to the spirit a metaphysical balm. The "central calm" of appearances, their very thereness, gives a floor to the world. So Tomlinson walks and looks, and he finds it enough. Philosophically, he begins in nakedness—in nakedness, not in disinheritance; for the scrutinizing eye detects no twilight of past dreams of transcendence, only a present wealth of finite particulars, an ever shifting but sharply focused spectacle. In Tomlinson, the spirit, as if ignorant of what once sustained it—Platonic forms, Jehovah, the Life Force, the whole pantheon of the metaphysical mind—finds bliss in trees and stones that are merely trees and stones. And doubtless this implies an especially fine, not a particularly crude, capacity for wonder. Tomlinson is one of the purest instances in literature of the contemplative, as distinct from the speculative, mind.

No poet has ever before regarded the intricate tapestry of Space with such patient and musing pleasure, with so little dread or anxiety to retreat through a human doorway or under the vaulted roof of a church. On the other hand, neither has any poet been less inclined to eat of the apples in his Eden. Tomlinson holds up to the tapestry a magnifying glass: he is all absorption, but, courteously, he keeps his place. And evidently his reward is a sense of answered or multiplied being. Let others—Dylan Thomas, D. H. Lawrence, E. E. Cummings—mount nature in ecstatic egoism. They will not really see her, except distortedly, through the heat waves of their own desire for union; they will not be companioned. Let still others—Thomas Hardy, Robert Frost, Philip Larkin—suspect the worst of her, dread her, hint at wrinkled flesh beneath the flowered dress. They, too, will be left with only themselves. Tomlinson, putting himself by, will gain the world.

What Tomlinson values in human beings is a similar facing-away from the self, a rock-like, disciplined submergence in *being*. For the most part, the people in his poems are either models of subservience to task or tradition, as in **"Return to Hinton," "The Farmer's Wife," "The Hand at Callow Hill Farm," "Oxen," "Geneva Restored," "Maillol"**—or examples of the discontent of desiring: the ambitious castellan of **"The Castle,"** the Symbolists of **"Antecedents,"** the **"Black Nude"** who is sullen until she learns the "truce" of the eye, the restless poet in **"Up at La Serra,"** and **"Mr. Brodsky,"** the American "whose professed and long / pondered on passion / was to become a Scot." Like the hills and seas of his poems, Tomlinson is conservative through and through. If he could, one feels, he would bring all the world to a halt; to the "luminous stasis" of contemplation. The dread he conveys is not of nature, nor even of human nature, but of the "rational" future and its present busy machines—of what is happening to the earth, our host, and to the distinctively human source of our contentment, the filaments of custom that hold us lovingly to place. Better a contented poverty, he believes, than a standardized prosperity:

> No hawk at wrist, but blessed by sudden sun
>   And with a single, flaring hen that tops the chair
> Blooming beside her where she knits. Before the
>   door
>   And in the rainsoaked air, she sits as leisurely
> As spaces are with hillshapes in them. Yet she is
>   small—
>   If she arrests the scene, it is her concentration
> That commands it, the three centuries and more
>   That live in her, the eyes that frown against the
>   sun
> Yet leave intact the features' kindliness, the
>   anonymous
>   Composure of the settled act. Sufficient to her day
> Is her day's good, and her sufficiency's the
>   refutation
>   Of that future where there'll be what there already
>   is—
> Prosperity and ennui, and none without the privilege
> To enjoy them both . . .
>   **("Portrait of Mrs. Spaxton")**

No doubt this leaves much to be said; but there is wisdom, passion, and sting in it, as well as beauty. In Tomlinson, the present as the latest and brimming moment of the past has both a first-rate poet and an able defender. "Farm-bred certainties," "ancestral certitude," or, as here, "three centuries and more"—these, to him, have the same sanctifying use as a beech tree or a mood of light: all are alike, for human beings, the conditions of an "anonymous / Composure." All conduce to, all are food for, a contemplative life.

The Tomlinson of these portrait poems beholds not so much his subjects' individuality as their fine or fumbled relation to time and place: he beholds, in other words, their beholding. He is thus himself once removed—though, in another sense, also himself twice over. In the remainder of his poems he beholds natural objects directly and minutely—standing back only so far as will allow him to reflect on the virtue of the eye. In either case, he is the poet of contemplation. It is this that gives him his strong and peculiar identity. The atmosphere of his work is that of a calm and cherishing attention. It is an atmosphere in which the objects of this world suddenly stand forth as part of the beautiful mystery of the founded. Whatever can be apprehended as the locus of a fine relation, dwelt on with intent devotion—whether gossamers slung in a haze, or a woman knitting in the rain-soaked air—becomes, to this poet, an "Eden image"; at once pristine and permanent, it radiates being. Tomlinson's sensibility homes to everything well established, and alights, and broods. And though it comes for grace, it comes also like a grace. It consecrates. This rare and valuable quality, never in excess but always temperate and chaste, is the essence of almost every Tomlinson poem.

It is this patient intention to consecrate that saves Tomlinson from the rapids of the senses. Indeed, it is doubtless a fear of the sensual and gluttonous Ego that gives thrust to the intention to consecrate. Accordingly—at least until lately—beholding in Tomlinson has seemed as much a discipline as a delight. In such recent poems as **"Clouds"** and **"In the Fullness of Time,"** Tomlinson comes through as impressively equal to what he contemplates—a large, gracious, and answering stability. In many of his early poems, by contrast, he seems a trifle *determined* to see chastely and feel calmly. Indeed, so little excitement, so little spontaneous joy do these poems convey that their seeing seems rather more a discipline than a delight. The description never blurs, but neither does it glow, with enthusiasm; no sentiment ever spills over the detail into a general, joyful reference. Not that Tomlinson's sensibility appears ever to have been in great need of restraint. Though exquisite, it is far from being abundant. But disciplined it nonetheless is. Adding its own kind of intensity to Tomlinson's poems is the reactive force of a self-rejection. Here contemplation is, in Tomlinson's own word, a shriving. Light, this poet says in **"Something: A Direction,"** is split by human need: accept the light, and you heal both the light and your need. At each dawn the sun is recovered

> in a shriven light
> And you, returning, may to a shriven self
> As from the scene, your self withdraws.

So it is that Tomlinson would make of beholding an *ascesis,* a chaste, chill atmosphere to cool the hot and clouding Ego.

In consequence, Tomlinson's poems have something of the severity of a religious cell. Whitewashed of the self, chill, close-packed as stone walls, they are rooms for intense and selfless meditation. Austerity marks both their language and their movement. The diction has the dryness of exposure to mental weather—though the dryness of living bark, not of stones. Learned and exact, it joins the concrete with academic abstraction: in **"Gossamers,"** for example, the sun is said to *claim* the spaces that *rock* in the leafage; and if the gossamers *ride* and *plot,* they are *certainties* that do so. Tomlinson's descriptions, accordingly, both feed and ration the eye. Seeing passes somewhat difficultly into thought and stops just short of an easy clarity. At the same time, the depictions give out only so much emotional warmth as they counter with the chill of a rational diction. Even when almost entirely concrete, this poet's delineations remain anatomy:

> A trailed and lagging grass, a pin-point island
> Drags the clear current's face it leans across
> In ripple-wrinkles. At a touch
> It has ravelled the imaged sky till it could be
> A perplexity of metal, spun
> Round a vortex, the sun flung off it
> Veining the eye like a migraine—it could
> Scarcely be sky . . .

Like a window that allows vision through only one side, this looks out lucidly toward surfaces, is blind and indifferent to the inner life. Concrete with respect to spatial things, it is abstract to feeling. Not that it fails to touch feeling; for there is delight here—the delight of detected resemblance and, deeper still, the pleasure that comes from perceiving that a thing has escaped being simply itself—"it could / Scarcely be sky. . . ." And this is to say that there is considerable imaginative life in the description—an aspect of the poetry that we must return to. All the same, Tomlinson analyzes and photographs the current as one who stands over against it, alien though not estranged. He neither attempts to become the water, as any number of poets might have done, nor leaves chinks in his description for sentiment. With Robbe-Grillet, his passage declares that "to describe things . . . is deliberately to place oneself outside them, facing them," and also that "there is in existence in the world something that is not man, that takes no notice of him." So the stream is itself, and the words merely serve its being. While Tomlinson stands over against the water, his language, as it were, stands over against him and on the side of what faces him. Indeed, until recently, it has even turned a deaf ear to itself, avoiding all but the most discrete self-echoing—as here, for instance, the tucked-away rhyme of "lagging" and "drag."

Meter is also, of course, a self-reference of sound, and Tomlinson's verse logically eschews it, is "free." It is not, however, free as the verse of D. H. Lawrence or William Carlos Williams is free: it is not free to empathize with its subjects. Empathic rhythm, like meter, awakens feeling: the difference, of course, is that where meter is emotionally introverted, empathic *vers libre* is extroverted. So the meter of Christina Rossetti's

> My heart is like a singing bird
>> Whose nest is in a water'd shoot;
> My heart is like an apple-tree
>> Whose boughs are bent with thick-set fruit . . .

turns feeling around and around, like a dancer in a music box, while the rhythm of Lawrence's "Fish,"

> Aqueous, subaqueous
> Submerged
> And wave-thrilled . . .

or Williams' "Rain,"

> the trees
> are become
> beasts fresh risen
> from
>> the sea—
> water
>
> trickles
> from the crevices of
> their hides . . .

sends feeling outward into objects. Tomlinson's rhythm, by contrast, is neither extroverted nor introverted, but emotionally suspended, stilled and poised in meditation. It springs free of the hypnotic spin of meter, but holds itself back from the emotional free-lancing of *vers libre*. It is free, not to dance new steps to the music of a vital happening, but free, precisely, from the tug and engulfing tide of feeling. Just as a rational element checks emotional participation in Tomlinson's descriptions, so an approximate accentual balance and a kind of sanity of isochronism reins in feeling in Tomlinson's rhythm—a rhythm that moves narrowly between the mind-lulling security of meter and the mind-dissolving fluidity of free verse:

> Two stand
> admiring morning,
> A third, unseen as yet
> approaches across upland
> that a hill and a hill's wood
> hide. The two
> halving a mutual good,
> both watch a sun
> entering sideways
> the slope of birches . . .

Here the first two lines have an approximate quantity or length; they also balance in beat. The next three add a beat and balance one another. The sixth, though it drops an accent, keeps the length with its two long vowels and caesura. And in the last two lines, the rhythm quickens back to its initial measure. Reading Tomlinson, one comes instinctively to look for this sort of rough yet reliable recurrence. Like the next bead in a rosary, the accentual repetition provides a necessary sense of stability. On the

other hand, shifting and uncertain as it is, it discourages complicities of the pulse. It leaves the mind strung, alert, and waiting.

This condition is heightened by the frequent breakage of the lines *against* phrasal expectations and unities. The lines end long or short, in mid air; and thus left jutting and jagged, they spur the mind to attention. So of the swan in **"Canal"** we read:

> . . . Sinuously
> both the live
> bird and the bird
> the water bends
> into a white and wandering
> reflection of itself,
> go by in grace
> a world of objects . . .

Obviously the lines here work against any sharing of the swans' sinuous motion. The swans may be all grace, but the lines, as such, are all stiff angles. Typically fragmenting sentences down to phrases, then further fragmenting some of the phrases, omitting expected and interjecting unexpected commas, Tomlinson's lines retard and brake the mind, suspend and distance its grasp, so that when full comprehension finally comes, it arrives, as it were, soundless and clear, unaccompanied by the resonant surge of an affective rhythm.

Altogether, then, there is in Tomlinson's slow, inorganic rhythm of stops and starts and precarious, uncertain balances no wave for imagination to surf on, no independence and autonomy of accent. And yet, for all that, it has character and charm; one acquires a taste for it. Toughly flexile, it introduces a new quality into verse, as if after centuries of beating the drum of the blood, a rhythm had at last been found for the mind. Anything more fluent and facile—so one feels while reading him—would be intolerably flaccid. Whether in short lines, as in **"Canal,"** or in medium lines like these,

> It happened like this: I heard
> from the farm beyond, a grounded
> churn go down. The sound
> chimed for the wedding of the mind
> with what one could not see,
> the further fields, the seamless
> spread of space . . .

or in the longer lines he has favored of late,

> Cloudshapes are destinies, and they
>> Charging the atmosphere of a common day,
> Make it the place of confrontation where
>> The dreamer wakes to the categorical call
> And clear cerulean trumpet of the air . . .

the movement serves as a kind of stiffening, not only standing the lines up to the mind but constituting in its own right an aesthetic value, a virility like starch in a formal shirt.

So it is that, in both his relation to his subject and his poetic manner, Tomlinson is an original—and what is more, with an originality that counts, that comes to seem, while we read him, and the more we read him, the very intelligence of the eye, the very rhythm of a chaste beholding. And the mainspring of this originality, it has been suggested, lies in the singleness of Tomlinson's contemplative purpose, the rigor of his attempt to make of the observation of nature through the medium of poetry a shriving of the self—a naked, though not unthoughtful, encounter with appearances.

To read Tomlinson is continually to *sound*: to meet with what lies outside the self in a simultaneous grace of vision and love.

—*Calvin Bédient*

What makes Tomlinson an important poet is partly his originality; but of course it is not his originality that makes him a poet. If his poetry contained observation alone, it would be of no more interest—though of no less interest, either—than a camera set rolling in a snowy field or by the sea. Tomlinson is a poet, in part, because of a consistent, masculine elegance of language, and also in part because of his feeling for rhythm. But mostly he is a poet because he uses, and excites, imagination, and because this imagination is not of a light or gratuitous kind, but steeped in feeling, organic, pregnant with a response to life. Deeply and richly conceived, Tomlinson's poems are neither the mere notations of a stenographic eye, nor cold slabs of reflection; they begin, they vault, and they conclude in feeling. "That art is selective," writes Dewey in *Art as Experience,* "is a fact universally recognized. It is so because of the role of emotion in the act of expression. Any predominant mood automatically excludes all that is uncongenial with it." And the unity of Tomlinson's poems is fundamentally the unity of a magisterial and imaginative mood.

To be sure, no magistrate was ever more humble or amenable while still retaining and exercising his proper powers. Tomlinson's imagination *attends* to observable reality with almost the patience that characterizes and gives distinction to his eye. Like a fine atmosphere, it can be gentle to the point of invisibility, so that objects and places, and not the poet himself, seem to be communicants of feeling. And when it does grow dense, it thickens as light thickens, making its objects as well as itself more vivid. Impossible to imagine a closer cooperation between the conceiving mind and the receiving eye, Tomlinson's imagination takes its cues, its colors, its composure, from the Persian carpet of the visual world itself.

From what has already been said, it will be seen at once that this delicate cooperation is a matter of strict principle. Indeed, it is largely the imagination—that genie and tempt-

ress of the self—that the straps of *seeing* are intended to confine. If Tomlinson's poems are imaginative, it is almost in their own despite. They are imaginative, so to speak, only because they must be in order to qualify as poetry. Granted their way, so it seems, they would be, instead, only a wondering silence. Nor does this principle of imaginative containment—so jealously adhered to—remain implicit. Several of the poems give a sharp rap to the skull of Romanticism, consistently conceived as an egoistic imagination bringing to birth frenzied and false worlds of its own. For example, **"Distinctions"** chides Pater for indicating that the blue of the sea gives way to "pinks, golds, or mauves," **"Farewell to Van Gogh"** patronizes that painter's "instructive frenzy," and **"Maillol"** glances at the "flickering frenzy of Rodin." Indeed, it is the fault of these, as well as of two or three other poems, that they seem to exist chiefly for the sake of their doctrine. Of course, all of Tomlinson is doctrinal—the bias toward passivity, receptivity, and self-effacement being as overwhelming as it is avowed, determined, and morally aggressive. But for the most part this doctrine proves unobjectionable, for the simple reason that poetry takes it over. In the anti-Romantic poems, however, the doctrine tends to tread the poetry down. And, left alone on the field, Tomlinson's vigilance against the self's excesses itself emerges as excessive. His strictures are too tight, they hold their breath in prim disapproval. "To emulate such confusion," he writes of a scuffle between wind and trees,

> One must impoverish the resources of folly,
>   But to taste it is medicinal.

And just as the first line, here, drops a demolition ball on the point, so the tasting in the second seems a trifle too fastidious. Similarly, **"The Jam Trap,"** which glances at harmful egoistic hedonism in its picture of flies immersed "Slackly in sweetness," comes through as so unfairly and extremely reductive that it makes Tomlinson, and not Romanticism, seem wrong-headed.

And yet, unobtrusive and stopped down as it is, Tomlinson's imagination is, as was suggested, precisely the gift and power that makes his poetry poetic. Though obviously far from being ample, headlong, or richly empowering, neither, on the other hand, is it faint or apologetic. It is as active as it is attentive, as forceful as it is discrete. As procreative mood, it is the tension and coherence that keeps the poems brimming, and the still depth that moves the detail toward us, magnified. As subjective transmutation, moreover, it is the gold, the glaze, that makes the detail glitter. Subtract it from the poems, and only sorry fragments would remain. Of course, the farther Tomlinson stands off from objects, the more conspicuous the mediation of his emotional and imaginative presence becomes, increasing like the green of deepening waters. Thus bare lines like these from **"The Hill,"**

> Do not call to her there,
> but let her go
> bearing our question
> in her climb: what does she
> confer on the hill, the hill on her?

are obviously tense with imaginative concentration: with the conceived drama of contemplation, and the conceived mystery of relationship. Yet, whether noticed or not, this controlling and conceiving element is nonetheless almost always present and always felt in Tomlinson's poems. Even the largely "factual" poems resonate under imagination's bow. Consider, for example, even so unambitious a poem as **"Letter from Costa Brava"**:

> Its crisp sheets, unfolded,
> Give on to a grove, where
> Citrons conduct the eye
> Past the gloom of foliage
> Towards the glow of stone. They write
> of a mesmeric clarity
> In the fissures of those walls
> And of the unseizable lizards, jewelled
> Upon them. But let them envy
> What they cannot see:
> This sodden, variable green
> Igniting against the gray.

In the knock and juxtaposition of these two glowing and gloomy landscapes, the one dryly sensual, the other soggily spiritual, what a fine effect is produced by the unexpected, proud, and lovin—so deftly made understandable for the puritanically passionate English scene. It was imagination that caught and conveyed both the similarity and the deep polarity of these scenes, their different registers in the life of the spirit. And of course it was imagination that produced here and there the fillip of metaphor, adding local intensities to the shaping tension of the whole: a stimulation felt most strongly in the adjectives and in the verbid *igniting,* so boldly yet so rightly qualifying the suggestion of *sodden.* And elsewhere in Tomlinson one finds equal felicities of the imaginative power of augmenting and interpreting appearances without denying them—for example, the rose in **"Frondes Agrestes,"** seen

> Gathered up into its own translucence
> Where there is no shade save colour . . .

or, in **"Prometheus,"** the trees that

> Continue raining though the rain has ceased
> In a cooled world of incessant codas . . .

However adverse Tomlinson may be to imagination, clearly there is no lack of it in his poetry.

By now it will have become apparent that Tomlinson is something less of the simple observer and something more of a poet than he himself seems inclined to believe. The view that he encourages of himself, through his poems, is neither accurate nor fully just. Listen to the poems and you will conclude that Tomlinson is but the servant or the guest of appearances. Experience the poems, on the other hand, and you will know that he is something more, and more difficult—namely, their abettor, their harvest, their fulfillment. And this is to say that there is a notable discrepancy, widening at times into a contradiction, between what the poems declare and what they are and do. They speak,

as it were, in ignorance of themselves. Thus, though they recommend passivity, it is through their own activity. Though they would teach us to conserve, they themselves are creative and therefore innovative. As they urge us to silence before the multiple voices of space, they impress us with a distinctively human voice. And as they praise nature as our replenishment, they replenish us. So it is that what the right hand gives, the left hand takes away. In **"Observation of Fact,"** to cite a specific instance, Tomlinson cautions:

> Style speaks what was seen,
> Or it conceals the observation
> Behind the observer: a voice
> Wearing a ruff . . .

and meanwhile delights us, in the concluding image, by speaking what has never been and never will be seen.

> I leave you
> To your one meaning, yourself alone . . .

he says of an upended tree in **"Poem"**; but what his vehemently anthropomorphic description actually leaves in the memory is not a tree but a creature crouching "on broken limbs / About to run forward." "Only we / Are inert," Tomlinson writes in **"In Defense of Metaphysics"**—and then, in observing that "Stones are like deaths. / They uncover limits," himself shows admirably more than inertia of mind. In **"Chateau de Muzot,"** he says of the stone mass,

> A shriven self
> Looks out at it. You cannot
> Add to this. Footholds for foison
> There are none. Across stoneface
> Only the moss, flattened, tightly-rosetted
> Which, ignorant of who gives
> Accepts from all weathers
> What it receives, possessed
> By the nature of stone . . .

Yet in so describing it, Tomlinson obviously and wonderfully adds to it, finding footholds not only for the imaginative "foison" of rosetted moss but for the whole parable-conceit of gift, acceptance, and possession. Examples could be multiplied.

Altogether, then, there is in Tomlinson a rebuke to the active, creative self that, coming from a poet, seems untutored. It is as if a Catholic priest were to celebrate, from the pulpit, with both passion and eloquence, the inward light: there is professional suicide in the sermon. What other poet is so insistently and recklessly forgetful of his own gift and its prerogatives? Virtually taking a giant erasure to his work, Tomlinson will write:

> Those facets of copiousness which I proposed
> Exist, do so when we have silenced ourselves.

Indeed, Tomlinson would thus erase more than his gift; he would erase human consciousness itself. For of course the only truly silenced human being is a dead one. Dewey is again to the point: as he observes, "nothing takes root in the mind when there is no balance between doing and receiving"; for "perception is an act of the going-out of energy in order to receive, not a withholding of energy," and though "the esthetic or undergoing phase of experience is receptive," an "adequate yielding of the self is possible only through a controlled activity that may well be intense." Though Tomlinson again and again salutes the "yielding," the "activity," as a rule, he leaves out of account. So in **"A Given Grace"** he commences:

> Two cups,
> a given grace,
> afloat and white
> on the mahogany pool
> of table. They unclench
> the mind, filling it
> with themselves . . .

And several lines later he concludes:

> you would not wish
> them other than they are—
> you, who are challenged
> and replenished by
> those empty vessels.

This is true, but only half true. For it is just as reasonable, and just as partial, to say that it is the empty vessels that have been filled, and filled by mind. Sophisticated poet though he is, Tomlinson yet falls into what Husserl calls "the natural unsophisticated standpoint" of consciousness, which assumes "an empty looking of an empty 'Ego.'" Consciousness can indeed be invested, but only in so far as it invests; as Husserl observes, it is the ego that invests "the being of the world . . . with existential validity." Apart from consciousness, after all, the world is but a sweep and waste of energy unseen, unfelt, unheard, and untasted. Of poets, moreover, it may be said that they invest appearances doubly—not only with their mind and senses but with their imagination as well. Thus in **"A Given Grace,"** while it is Tomlinson's eye that perceives and invests the two cups, it is his imagination that sees them floating in a mahogany pool, making them something other than they are. Facets of copiousness do indeed exist, but only in a dialectic between the self and the objective world.

It should be noted, however, that though Tomlinson has emphasized and done more than justice to the passive aspect of the self's liaison with space, he has managed to strike other notes of his theme as well. In fact, however unequally these may be pressed, the chord of his theme stands complete. Thus in a fairly recent poem, **"The Hill,"** Tomlinson celebrates at last—quite as if he had never doubted it (as perhaps he had not)—consciousness as itself a grace, a grace of giving. The female figure climbing the hill named in the title is a type of the being-investing consciousness:

> She
> alone, unnamed (as it were),
> in making her thought's theme
> that thrust and rise,
> is bestowing a name . . .

A still more recent poem, **"Adam,"** provides a partial gloss:

> We bring
> To a kind of birth all we can name . . .

So the hill stands forth, rounds out into being, through the generosity of the girl's attention. The grace of consciousness consists in its active intentionality: the girl *makes* her thought's theme that thrust and rise. It is, after all then, stones that are inert. Indeed, a recoiling spring, Tomlinson perhaps goes too far when, in **"The Hill,"** he adds:

> . . . do not call to her there:
> let her go on,
> whom the early sun
> is climbing up with to the hill's crown—
> she, who did not make it, yet can make
> the sun go down by coming down.

In this instance, of course, the "making" is only a manner of speaking. And yet here Tomlinson, for one rare and indulgent moment, encourages a solipsistic illusion. Putting by the domestic uniform it usually wears in his poems, the mind steps forward as almost a demi-urge, capable of making, by a simple withdrawal of attention, a heavenly body slide out of the sky.

Of course the true grace of any and every relationship is neither a giving nor a receiving, but an interchange and balance of the two. And toward this inclusive reciprocity Tomlinson may be said to have ripened. His early attempts to render it do not quite come off, and are, perhaps, not quite sincere, the self having been made too hollow a counter-weight to space. For example, in **"Reflections"** Tomlinson writes:

> When we perceive, as keen
> As the bridge itself, a bridge inlaying the darkness
> Of smooth water, our delight acknowledges our
> debt—
> To nature, from whom we choose . . .

But this would seem, rather, an instance of being chosen, and the declaration of self-determination does not convince. In some of the more recent poems, by contrast, the self seems genuinely erect before the world it experiences. Perhaps no statement and evocation—for the poem is both—of a pristine and yet not unsophisticated encounter with environment, the mind and space meeting as two equal and mysterious realities, could be at once more justly delicate and soberly beautiful than **"Swimming Chenango Lake."** Here, as in **"The Hill,"** the anonymous human figure is a type of consciousness—not, in this case, however, of consciousness as the only proud Climber of Creation, but as Creation's Swimmer, active in a dense, merciless element that "yet shows a kind of mercy sustaining him":

> . . . he has looked long enough, and now
> Body must recall the eye to its dependence
> As he scissors the waterscape apart

And sways it to tatters. Its coldness
  Holding him to itself, he grants the grasp,
For to swim is also to take hold
  On water's meaning, to move in its embrace
And to be, between grasp and grasping free.

Not only the mutuality of two alien orders of being, but the simultaneous doing and undergoing in human experience, finds in this poem a crystal paradigm. So it is that, here and there in Tomlinson, the self has come into its own. And still more is this true in a few of the poems addressed to art. Despite his animadversions against Romanticism, Tomlinson has shown himself quite ready to think of art—especially music—as a spiritual flowering beyond anything offered by reality. Thus in **"Flute Music"** he notes:

Seeing and speaking we are two men:
The eye encloses as a window—a flute
Governs the land, its winter and its silence.

An early poem, **"Flute Music"** may perhaps be written off as an accident of ventriloquism—the result of a saturation in Wallace Stevens. But in a later and more impressive poem, **"Ode to Arnold Schoenberg,"** the same theme sounds again. "Natural" meaning, according to the ode, does not suffice: art satisfies by pursuing "a more than common meaning." The "unfolded word" not only renews "the wintered tree" of previous art, but creates and cradles space, filling it with verdure. Is space ordinarily, then, a winter and a silence? Decisively, persuasively, the other poems answer "No." And yet the very fact that they were written bespeaks a painful and reluctant "Yes." The truth is that, beyond the discrepancy between what the poems say and what they are, yawns the still greater discrepancy between what they say and the fact that they are. Let them set nature before us as a sufficient spiritual end; still, their very existence as poetry, their very excess over nature, suggests that it is art, and not nature, that cures the ache of being. As both the beholder and the poet of nature, Tomlinson is the contemplative twice over; and just in that apparent superfluity, it seems, lies the fullness that the spirit requires. The poems confess that "those empty vessels" of space whet as much as they replenish; and what nature prompts, art concludes. Not so humble or subservient after all, the spirit relives its experiences, but recreates them from itself alone—positing, retrospectively, the space that once had nourished it. The hill it climbs becomes a subjective space, memory worked over by imagination. The essential confession of Tomlinson's art is, I believe, the essential confession of all art: that man is forced to be, and also needs to be, his own replenishment, perpetually renewed out of himself. So it is that, merely by existing, Tomlinson's poetry completes the real but limited truth—namely, the gratefulness of the world to the senses—whose thousand faces the poems seek out and draw.

Tomlinson, born in 1927, is still, it may be hoped, in mid-career. It is likely that he will deepen—indeed, he has already begun to do so; it is also likely that he will diversify his canon by throwing out more "sports," such as his recent, delightful poem on a personified **"Rumour";** but it is not at all likely that he will alter his course. Nor, I think, is it desirable that he should; for Tomlinson strikes one as a poet who has finally won through to himself, and were he now to become someone else, it would seem almost an act of violence.

It was in his third volume, *Seeing is Believing* (1960), that Tomlinson first became both the distinct and the distinguished poet that he is today. His first volume, *Relations and Contraries* (1951), is haunted by Yeats and Blake, and though brilliant in patches, is not of much consequence. Tomlinson next moved a good deal nearer to himself in *The Necklace* (1955), which ranks, at the least, as a prologue to his real achievement. It zeroes in on the great Tomlinson theme, but vitiates it by a kind of enameled elegance; it has Stevens's epicurean quality, but not his saving gusto and bravura. Precious in both senses of the word, *The Necklace* is a book to be valued, but—too beautiful, too exquisite—not to feel at home in: you must park your muddy shoes at the door. The very title of the third volume, *Seeing is Believing,* suggests a homely improvement over *The Necklace*. Here the earth takes on some of the earthiness that, after all, becomes it; and the manner is more gritty, rubs more familiarly with the world. In the subsequent two volumes, *A Peopled Landscape* (1962) and *American Scenes* (1966), the same manner—at once meticulous, prosaic, and refined (for Tomlinson's early elegance is roughened rather than lost)—is extended, as the titles indicate, to new subjects if not exactly to new themes. It is largely to the Tomlinson of these three volumes and of a fourth that is now, as I write, in the press, that I have addressed my remarks, and it is this Tomlinson who, as I began by declaring, has produced the most considerable body of poetry, to date, of any postwar English poet.

With the exception of Donald Davie—who, however, turns out more verse than poetry—no other English poet of Tomlinson's generation so strongly gives the impression of being an artist modestly but seriously at work—a poet equally intense about his message and his craft. Tomlinson's dedication is deep and unmistakable; and joined with his rare if quiet talent, it has created not only poetry of the highest quality, but success after success, in a period when the successes of more striking and seductive poets—Ted Hughes, R. S. Thomas, Philip Larkin—have seemed haphazard. Of all these gifted poets, it is Tomlinson who best survives the rub and wear of repeated readings; indeed, only Tomlinson's poetry improves under such treatment, like a fine wood under polish.

Part of the reason that Tomlinson tells slowly is that he has gone farther than any of his contemporaries—though Ted Hughes and Thomas Kinsella follow close—in outstaring and outmaneuvering facility. He waits in advance, as it were, of his readers, who, burdened with aging notions of what makes up poetic appeal, must labor to come abreast. In consequence, until Tomlinson is admired, he must be tolerated. His meticulous descriptions, so often hard to seize with the eye, his laconic meditations, his uncertain, demanding rhythms, his frustrations of expectations of various kinds—these one must struggle through as if through scrub, until one emerges, pleased and surprised, into the clearings that, in reality, the poems usually are. Because of both an increased dynamic clarity and a more definite music, Tomlinson's latest poems are probably his most readily accessible; they still, however, constitute a language to be learned, a flavor to be found, and to care about Tomlinson is to approve of this difficulty. Just as the later Yeats makes the early Yeats seem somewhat facile and obvious, so Tomlinson, asceticizing poetry as he has, gives one a new sense of what the art can be. His is the sort of modification of poetry that ultimately makes it incumbent on other poets to change, to make it new, to work passionately at their craft.

As for the sensibility that Tomlinson's poetry expresses, its value, I think, should be self-evident. The truth it has seized upon, indeed the truth that seems native to it, is the lesson implicit in art itself—that contemplation is the fulfillment of being. Of course we have always to know what needs to be changed; but we also do well to praise and reverence what is sufficient for the day and the vast design that, though it impinges on us, ultimately lies beyond our human agency. For without this reverence we can scarcely be committed to the value of being; it is the secret of what Pasternak called "the talent for life." Tomlinson is certainly out of season to recall us to the life of the moment conceived as an end in itself; and yet it is just this unseasonableness that puts him in harmony with what is lasting in our relations with the world.

Ronald Hayman (essay date 1970)

SOURCE: "Observation Plus," in *Encounter,* Vol. XXXV, No. 6, December, 1970, pp. 72-4.

[*In the following excerpt, Hayman provides a positive assessment of* The Way of a World.]

Though American critics have recognised the importance of Charles Tomlinson's achievement, it is still generally underrated in this country and almost without exception, reviews of his new book *The Way of a World* have been condescending, if not unfavourable. Just as an actor gets type-cast, a poet in our literary climate is all too liable to go on being discussed in the same terms that are applied to him in his first set of reviews. "Painterly," "visual," "microscopic"—the words were relevant to Tomlinson's 1955 collection *The Necklace,* but while he is no less precise an observer than he was, he has developed so much since then that to go on thudding out the same adjectives is to tell a small part of the truth.

The position he took in *The Necklace* is defined in its first two lines:

> Reality is to be sought, not in concrete,
> But in space made articulate

In the poems which follow and in his second book *Seeing is Believing,* the basic assumption is that clarity of vision

is the prerequisite for an adequate grasp on reality. *"When the truth is not good enough/We exaggerate."* The poems record and advocate the discovery and practice of a discipline by which distortion can be avoided. The poems observe not only the surfaces of things, but the play of light and shade in the spaces between them. In **"More Foreign Cities"** the lit space becomes as solid as the stone masses. But even these early poems are not narrowly "visual." They are constantly enlisting the other senses to refine and articulate the visual impressions.

> Warm flute on the cold snow
> Lays amber in sound.

Or:

> The girls (white as their prayer-books) are
>   released,
> Rustle in lavender and thyme
> From incense back to houses where
> Their white pianos cool each thirsty square.

This is poetry for all the senses, but its concern is to wake them up, not to put them to sleep with facile gratification. To become aware of a tree or a field or a house, to avoid the danger of seeing it as a reflection or extension of ourselves, we must empty our minds of everything else, imitating the patience and stillness of stone. If there seems to be a battle going on between the wind and the trees, we can only taste the confusion if we hold back from emulating it. It is characteristic of these two volumes that they hardly ever employ the first person, except inside quotation marks.

Instead of asserting himself subjectively, Tomlinson uses himself as a medium through which he realises natural life more vividly than any poet since Hopkins. No one writing today is more sensitive than Tomlinson to the turn of the seasons and though he most often opts for a winter setting, his attitude of reverent gratitude in face of the natural landscape which surrounds us and his keen awareness of the processes of self-renewal which are constantly and copiously at work in it put him emotionally at the antipodes of Beckett and the writers whose preoccupations are one-sidedly with decay, the gradual failing of the individual body's faculties.

The people in Tomlinson's next book, *A Peopled Landscape,* are integral parts of the landscape and one of the poems in *American Scenes* centres on the legend of an old Indian Chief transformed by death into a mountain. Featured in the lighter poems in this book are a New Mexican captured by the Apaches and trained by them to steal, a bagpipe-playing Jew and a converted Indian Chief—characters comically at odds with their environment. But it is only in *The Way of a World* that the assertion of the human will comes into the foreground of the serious poems. **"Assassin"** is by far the most dramatic poem Tomlinson has yet written: he projects himself into the consciousness of the Stalinist agent who killed Trotsky, recreating it almost as if it were a landscape, but subtly pinpointing the man's awareness of the passing moments before and after the murder, his reaction to the blood which he had steeled himself to expect and the details which catch him by surprise—Trotsky's animal cry and the papers snowing from his desk to the floor.

> Woven from the hair of that bent head,
>   The thread that I had grasped unlabyrinthed
> all—
> Tightrope of history and necessity—
>   But the weight of a world unsteadies
> my feet
> And I fall into the lime and contaminations
>   Of contingency; into hands, looks, time.

The opening poem **"Swimming Chenango Lake"** sets the tone and focus of the book. Knowing the approaching winter will soon have made the water too cold, the man hesitates on the brink and then

> Body must recall the eye to its dependence
>   As he scissors the waterscape apart
> And sways it to tatters. Its coldness
>   Holding him to itself, he grants the grasp,
> For to swim is also to take hold
>   On water's meaning, to move in its embrace
> And to be, between grasp and grasping, free.
>   He reaches in-and-through to that space
> The body is heir to, making a where
>   In water, a possession to be relinquished
> Willingly at each stroke. The image he has torn
>   Flows-to behind him, healing itself,
> Lifting and lengthening, splayed like the feathers
>   Down an immense wing whose darkening
>   spread
> Shadows his solitariness: alone he is unnamed
>   By this baptism, where only Chenango bears
>   a name

Surely this could hardly be bettered either as a description of a body moving in water or as an allegorical picture of an individual testing his environment, striking up an impermanent relationship with it. It tolerates his aggression, embraces him frigidly, circumscribes his liberty, partly gives him a sense of identity, partly takes it away.

This is only a beginning. In **"Prometheus"** Tomlinson not only sets up a more complex interrelationship between the visual, aural, and tactual references than before, but he develops a new rhythm, no less subtle but less reticent, more committed than in the earlier poems. Altogether this is a less private voice, a controlled rhetoric which claims and commands a wider space, ranges over a more impressive variety of tones than ever before.

> Cymballed firesweeps. Prometheus came down
>   In more than orchestral flame and Kérensky
>   fled
> Before it. The babel of continents gnaws now
>   And tears at the silk of those harmonies that
>   Seemed
> So dangerous once. You dreamed an end
>   Where the rose of the world would go out
>   like a close in music.

Inevitably there is some loss of precision and economy. "Tears" is too nearly a repetition of "gnaws" and the verbs and images in the last sentence could have been interrelated better. But in **"Night Transfigured"** the description of the nettles illuminated by torchlight is superb in its richness and exactness of descriptive detail. The title poem seizes with extraordinary clarity on a remembering mind groping for and grasping a particular movement of the wind, while **"Descartes and the Stove,"** equally admirable in its description, is most valuable for the complex outside the mind.

I have still said nothing of the prose poems, which are uneven but quite brilliant at their best, or of the short line poems like **"Before the Dance,"** which skilfully uses its impatient rhythm to generate the suspense of the moment before the beginning of the Indian dance at Zuni. Somehow the poem contrives a pre-echo of the sound which is not yet in the air.

Bill Ruddick   (essay date 1975)

SOURCE: A review of *The Way In,* in *Critical Quarterly,* Vol. 17, No. 2, Summer, 1975, p. 184.

[*In the following mixed review of* The Way In, *Ruddick praises Tomlinson's comedic sense.*]

Certain poems in Charles Tomlinson's **The Way In** show the dangers of the freewheeling approach. His Hebridean pieces are unmemorable and the title poem of the collection, though it shows sharp observation of externals in its description of the way a remembered place seems transformed out of all recognition as the poet drives past its high rise developments and the smoke of demolition men's fires, refuses to carry the reader in to the muted emotional climax which its author plainly intended:

> Perhaps those who have climbed into their towers
> Will eye it all differently, the city spread
> In unforeseen configurations, and living with this,
> Will find that civility I can only miss—and yet
> It will need more than talk and trees
> To coax a style from these disparities.

The idea is valid, but the verse is flat. Like the speedometer of the author's car at the beginning of the poem 'the needle point' of poetic intensity 'teeters at thirty'. But when Mr Tomlinson abandons his car for the pavements of his remembered Black Country childhood his inspiration stops teetering and surges ahead, as in **'Gladstone Street,'** a poem describing how a once proud Victorian street wore out and was finally wrecked by its residents in the 1950s:

> The housemaids lasted
> Until the war, then fed the factories.
> Flat-dwellers came and went, in the divided houses,
> Mothers unwedded who couldn't pay their rent.
> A race of gardeners died, and a generation
> Hacked down the walls to park their cars

Where the flowers once were. It was there it
  showed,
The feeble-minded style of the neighbourhood
Gone gaudily mad in painted corrugations,
Blotches of sad carpentry.

In addition, Mr Tomlinson brings to bear on his own re-membered self a fine sense of life's little ironies. The two **'Portrait of the Artist'** poems and **'Class'** are admirably sharp and pointed. Indeed the lethal satirical comedy **'Class,'** with its splendid jibe at 'the author of *The Craft of Fiction*', and the riotous **'Beethoven attends the C Minor Seminar'** at the end of the volume lead one to hope that Charles Tomlinson will go on exercising his obvious gift for satiric and social comedy.

Charles Tomlinson with Jed Rasula and Mike Erwin (interview date 1975)

SOURCE: An interview in *Contemporary Literature,* Vol. XVI, No. 4, Autumn, 1975, pp. 405-16.

[*In the following interview, Tomlinson discusses the role of politics in his poetry, the language he utilizes in his verse, and the function of poetry in society.*]

[Mike Erwin]: *In the Poem as Initiation you write, "there is no occasion too small for the poet's celebration—Williams' red wheelbarrow, or Wordsworth's 'naked table'—all ask, through the insistence of the poem's ritual celebration, to be recorded by us in their deeper significances." Is this an archetypal reality, something touching on the primary basis of existence (whatever your sense of that is); or in other words, does the particular contain the general or does the particular exist primarily in its own "isolate intensity"?*

[Charles Tomlinson]: In *The Poem as Initiation,* with twenty minutes or so in which to say my piece at the Phi Beta Kappa ceremony, I didn't really have time to differentiate the kinds of celebration that are possible for the poet. Rather than call the celebration that of an archetypal reality *tout court,* I should want to come down to the individual poet, the individual poem. For Williams, "so much depends" on the red wheelbarrow—but already I'm deforming by paraphrasing what he wrote:

so much depends
upon
a red wheel
barrow. . . .

Cut out the doubled preposition of "upon" and substitute "on" and you cut back the verbal force in the doubling, ignore the split between "wheel" and "barrow" straddling the line end and you are ignoring the fact that the dependence he's talking about is involved in slowing down the appearance of the separate words of the poem, letting them come into view only bit by bit. It's the form of language—the speed of meditation through written language *depends*

on the wheel/barrow. The celebration here is not only a celebration of objects but of the forms of language we choose to articulate the sense of objects bodied over against us.

Now, Wordsworth's "naked table"—"snow-white deal,/ Cherry or maple" as he goes on—is one of the domestic objects in Book One of *The Prelude* and it has its part in a life rich in essential things and unmindful of luxuries—"plain" and "seemly" are two other adjectives Wordsworth uses in this context. They play cards round this table in a cottage while winter is raging outside—rain and frost and splitting ice. So Wordsworth's contact with primal things and (I suppose) archetypal things. I suppose the very different sorts of celebration in Williams and Wordsworth do touch on "the primary basis of existence" as you call it; for both, the particular radiates outwards (and inwards), for both there is an ethical awareness approved and enacted by their verse, and the particular ballasts the ethics in common daily existence.

In my own case, I should add that the particular, rather than existing in its own isolate intensity, means first of all the demands of a relationship—you are forced to look, feel, find words for something not yourself—and it means, like all relationships, a certain forgetfulness of self, so that in contemplating something, you are drawn out of yourself towards that and towards other people—other people, because, though the words you use are *your* words, they are also *their* words: you are learning about the world by using the common inheritance of language. And once you are moving on into your poem, rather than "isolate intensity," you are aware of belonging among objects and among human beings and it is a great stay for the mind, this awareness. And a great chastener in that you realize that you in your *own* isolate intensity would be an egotist and a bore.

[Mike Erwin]: *There seems to be a noticeable lack of myth in your poetry. Why? What are your feelings about the use of myth in poetry in general, and in your own work (i.e., what can it convey, or does it tend instead to obstruct)?*

I think there's a lack of myth in my poetry because it usually arises directly from something seen. I want to register *that* in all its clarity or in all its implications. The nearest I come to myth is that word "Eden," which I can't seem to get rid of and that fits what I'm doing with its implication of primal things, fresh sensations, direct perceptions unmuddied. In a recent poem, **"The Way In"** (in the first number of *Poetry Nation*), I describe the demolition of parts of Bristol—humble and rather fine streets in their unpretentious way, neighborhoods never to be restored. I catch sight of an oldish couple dragging away scrap iron, old magazines, odds and ends in a battered perambulator and this I suppose is a use of myth, though I dislike the word "use." It's a use of myth in so far as I see them as Adam and Eve long-banished from Eden, but I wouldn't want to expand the thing to Wagnerian proportions.

Over twenty years ago I wrote in *The Necklace:*

A dryad is a sort of chintz curtain
Between myself and a tree.

The tree stands: or doesn't stand:
As I draw or remove the curtain.

This tends to be very much the case now—it is temperament, I imagine, plus the fact of also being a painter. In getting rid of the dryad I'm trying to realize something that has been left out of consciousness—we are great fixers of the contents of our consciousness and hence great fixers of our egos: we'll have it all on our own terms. . . . [elisions Rasula's and Erwin's] So I get rid of the dryad to see what is there. And this, I say, is in part temperamental; I could imagine a different sort of artist keeping *in* the dryad to realize something that has been left out of consciousness—which, I suppose, is why dryads first arose.

That dryad passage was a reference to the marvelous section in Buber's *I and Thou,* "I consider a tree," where he talks about various attitudes to trees seen as objects, then the moment when one becomes bound up in relation with the tree. I have that battered copy of *I and Thou* still on my shelves. Here's the passage:

> Everything belonging to the tree is in this: its form and structure, its colors and chemical composition, its intercourse with the elements and with the stars, are all present in a single whole.

And he goes on: "The tree is no impression, no play of my imagination, no value depending on my mood." That's what got me: "no value depending on my mood"; if you've ever tried to draw anything accurately, respecting its structure, you suddenly see how much mere mood would have left out. So, yes, I first worked out of a suspicion with myth, trusting sensation; and sensation, as people have been telling us for a long time, isn't just the naked impact of objects but already a grasping for significance.

In a recent article Donald Wesling isolates that astonishing passage from Coleridge's *Biographia Literaria,* where Coleridge seems to be agreeing with Hobbes and Hartley "that all real knowledge supposes a prior sensation" and suddenly moves out of associationism into phenomenology with "sensation itself is but vision nascent, not the cause of intelligence, but intelligence itself revealed as an earlier power in the process of self-construction." So in our trusting in the language of the senses we are constructing our selves. So much, once more, for "isolate intensity"—how could it ever exist? How much we bring to our moments of perception—how much our moments of perception bring to us—awarenesses already extensible, always offering new facets. Perhaps myth would have been mere superfluity for me, beginning where I did, and moving from the moment of perception into a world that was visual, geographical, historical.

[Jed Rasula]: *In* **"Swimming Chenango Lake"** *there is much attention paid to the sense of flux and permutation of form, usually thought of in terms of the passing of time. In two other poems in* **The Way of a World** *there are references to an arc; in* **"Tout Entouré de Mon Regard"** *the lines: "To see, is to feel at your back this domain of a circle whose power consists in evading and refusing to*

be completed by you." And in the poem **"In the Fullness of Time"** *you speak of*

> . . . That hesitant arc
> We must complete by our consent to time—
>   Segment to circle, chance into event:
> And how should we not consent? . . .

Is there an increased concern for this problem of permutation of form through time (with increased attention to water, also) in **The Way of a World** *and* **Written on Water**? *In other words, has the arc that resists completion become a central image in your work?*

I think there are two arcs in question here: first, the fact that, as I said, things are not given *absolutely,* so that there is much (necessarily) that escapes us, escapes the forms of language. And in this I rejoice. If you could close *that* circle, if language or consciousness could completely possess their objects, there would be no more room for literary endeavor and there would be no surprises, no discoveries. The second arc I speak of in that **"Fullness of Time"** poem is one we can convert into a circle by accepting things as given—in this poem by not attempting to escape from time or transcend it or search for the moment of intersection of the timeless with time, as Eliot does. The poem celebrates my friendship with Octavio Paz. Many chances led to our meeting; we had corresponded before but finally met *by chance* at Rome airport, then travelled together to Spoleto. Our friendship ripened through chance and time but we chose it also—and the arc became a circle and chance became "event," which in the poem rhymes with "consent." So my poetry is aware of time as a necessary medium for such things, and it's also aware of the flux of time though it pleads that there *are* human fidelities that survive mere flux and that they *need* the passage of time to become what they are.

The other arc that *resists* completion has been there implicitly since the early Stevens poems based on "Thirteen Ways of Looking at a Blackbird"—thirteen, the odd number, the series that could go on forever. My second arc the conversion of chance into event also links up with the fact of my painting—oddly enough the first booklength publication of some of my pictures in '75 will be introduced by Octavio Paz. Since 1968 I've done a lot of pictures, many of them based on chance beginnings—using decalcomania, the surrealist technique—then building out of that, choosing, either by use of brush and extension of the given idea or by use of scissors and extension via collage. I've also used photo-collage—destroying or transforming images and discovering other images among them quite different from what the original photograph was supposed to be. . . . [elisions Rasula's and Erwin's]

I do quite agree, though, that the question of time is very much there in **The Way of a World** and **Written on Water,** but it was there in early perceptive poems like **"Sea Change"** in **The Necklace** and it was there in the poems about ruined buildings in **Seeing is Believing** in a more specifically historic way. And history is certainly an arc that resists completion, though men are always trying to fix it through revolution or mystical transcendence. I see the assassination of Trotsky in *The Way of a World* ["Assassin"] as an attempt to transcend time, almost as a caricature of mysticism, an attempt to have the future *now* on one's own terms and the result of trying to complete *that* circle is inhumanity—as when Che Guevara for whatever "good" reasons decided "We must transform ourselves into cold and efficient killing machines."

[Mike Erwin]: *Are you much moved by world events? What responsibility do you feel the poet has for writing a political or publicly minded kind of poetry? Do you feel the private and the public impulse can be reconciled in poetry?*

I am much moved by the event of revolution. And I am anti-revolutionary. In *The Way of a World* there is a poem called **"Prometheus"** about the Russian revolution and the shadow it has cast over our history. I was much moved by the recent events in Chile, and now that Allende put back the cause of reform there by God knows how many years by pressing on dogmatically in the face of realities, I imagined people might see there are certain pragmatisms that ought not to be ignored. However, Allende has now become a martyr.

People tried political poetry in the '30s, didn't they? The only poem that comes anywhere near bringing it off to my mind is Hugh MacDiarmid's second of his three hymns to Lenin, but even MacDiarmid ends up in this poem by saying that poetry includes politics and should be "the greatest power among men." He thinks what Lenin is up to is pretty fine but concludes in praise of poetry: "Ah, Lenin, politics is bairns' play./ To what this maun be." I wouldn't exactly put it that way myself. I prefer Marvell's "Horatian Ode on Cromwell's Return from Ireland," which tries to sum up a whole phase of politics very close to the events. Then there's Dryden's *Absalom and Achitophel* written much more decidedly than Marvell's poem, from a given political point of view. I think these are indisputably fine poems but neither of them settles for easy partisanship.

What political poetry tends to more now is urging liberal sentiments (on Vietnam, for example, not so long ago) that everyone already agrees with anyway and, of course, as in Bly's political poems, heaping on top of that very ugly and inflated rhetoric that mistakes itself for poetry when all it is doing is enjoying a bath in its own righteous indignation. I see no reason why you shouldn't write a political kind of poetry but I don't see it in terms of merely urging opinions, or merely supporting the New Left, or trying with horrible self-conscious enthusiasm to ride along with youth as in that disastrous volume of Denise Levertov's *To Stay Alive*. Initially a lot of Vallejo's poetry is political, but it gets far beyond merely urging solutions— you have only to compare it with the naive point of view in his prose reportage of Russia in the 1930s where he seems to have swallowed every cliché.

I very much understand the feelings of my friend George

Oppen, who did live through the 1930s, was very much of the left, but reticent to write "political poetry." He saw that men needed feeding and as there was no easy way of doing that for them by writing poems he worked in poor relief. If that is the way one sees the priorities, that is what one does. Alternately, I am maybe the writer for whom it would be possible to see men were being fed *and* to go on writing poems. Ultimately, I think the private and the public impulse are reconciled in one's care for language—one's duty towards that is a duty to a thing at once public and private; one will so deal with language that insofar as it is in one's power, one will not issue a debased currency.

[Mike Erwin]: *In "Comedy" in Written on Water you write:*

> . . . If you sat still
> The horizontals plainly said
> You ought to be walking, and when you did
> All you were leaving behind you proved
> That you were missing the point. And the
> innumerable views
> Kept troubling him, until
> He granted them. Amen.

Are you implying that you believe in the overwhelming complexity and relativity of things (which the complexity of your own poetry would seem to belie) and that a unilateral political position is inadequate?

What I was saying in that poem in **Written on Water** was chiefly a philosophic comedy, not a question of politics. If expressing a unilateral political position means expressing a view on a given issue, I imagine a pamphlet, not a poem, would be the most effective weapon. After all, "expressing a position" means you more or less know in advance what you're going to say, whereas writing poetry is a less predictable undertaking. The views in that poem are views of landscape, not political views.

[Jed Rasula]: *In an interview with Peter Orr in 1961 you spoke of Ruskin, Wallace Stevens, and Marianne Moore as being of use in giving you an "openness to the creative universe in looking at the surfaces that it offers one." How exhaustively do you think the surfaces can be pursued? For instance, in one poem from **The Necklace** you write "Six points of vantage provide us with six sunsets," and in another poem: "To define the sea—/ We change our opinions/With the changing light." In The Poem as Initiation you have said "There is no occasion too small for the poet's celebration," and in **"A Process"** in **The Way of a World** you mention*

> that speech of islanders, in which, we are told, the sentence is never certainly brought to an end, its aim less to record with completeness the impression an event makes, than to mark its successive aspects as they catch the eye, the ear of the speaker.

Is your own work an attempt at such a language? How much can a certain area of material be covered before a change of consciousness is necessary, or a different sen-

sibility in ways of perceiving? Also, you seem to have been aware, perhaps, of the complications of these beliefs behind your poetry in the lines: ". . . And the innumerable views/ Kept troubling him, until/ He granted them" ("Comedy" in **Written on Water***). Has this been in fact a problem for you?*

We seem destined to keep returning to this little poem "**Comedy**." It merely expresses in comic vein what I said perhaps more urgently in "**Antecedents**" in *Seeing is Believing:* "Let be its being"—an attempt to calm the desire to be always anxiously seeking. After all, one doesn't always want to be wondering how many ways there are of looking at a blackbird. There ought to be times when one way is enough or the existence of *that* blackbird is enough. Consciousness that becomes merely a disease of prying, a bullying assertion of its own dear self, can be not merely obtrusive but comic—I think of some of Proust's more excessive moments.

That "speech of islanders" in "**A Process**" refers, I think to the characteristics of the language of (I may be misremembering this) the Trobriand Islanders. I had been thinking of the way the structures of Hopi and Navajo speech give one a so very different sense of space and time than our own language. Then a friend came up with this example from these islanders. The sentence "never certainly brought to an end" does remind one of the open-ended structure of much modern poetry which, in its turn, is very much aware of the way language stylizes our perception.

[Mike Erwin]: *How much does poetry, because of medium or practice or historical role, tend to shelter rather than stimulate? Or is the balance tending toward stimulation? Are these functions incompatible?*

When I look at all the pain that poetry has been able to admit and cope with in its long history, I don't see it as sheltering in any sense. Of course, some poems are more comfortable than others, as some moments are more comfortable than others. In painting there is Goya. But there is also Matisse. I think Matisse is stimulating as well as full of "luxe, calme et volupté" because his formal means are never just indulgent. You see something new in these oases of luxurious possibility he creates. Some poems of Eluard have a similar effect. There's room for patience and accepting the good that is given and art should not slight these.

[Mike Erwin]: *You suggest that aggressiveness or defensiveness toward the world is up to the reader in "Poem" from* **Seeing is Believing** *in the line "I leave you / To your own meaning, yourself alone." How does this relate to the problem of presentation/stimulation?*

"**Poem**" is about a fallen tree striking an impossibly romantic pose. I'm talking to the tree and the people who also fall into attitudes. The last line you quote has a misprint in the first edition and should read not "I leave you/ To your own meaning, yourself alone," but "I leave you to your *one* meaning. . . ." It is a reflection on the way posturing means bad faith, means loss of integrity in rela-

tionship and *that* applies to daily life or to writing a poem. For me, what you call the problem of presentation/stimulation can only be solved in poetry by the chastity of the formal means.

[Mike Erwin]: *In the poem "Beauty and the Beast" you write "Beauty is neither/Truth nor truth's reflection." Do you think art is more concerned with truth or with beauty?*

You may not have noticed, but I removed "**Beauty and the Beast**" from the second (British) edition of *Seeing is Believing* because I had come to feel that there was a lingering Nietzscheanism in that formulation, "Beauty is neither/Truth nor truth's reflection." I find it hard, also, to go on using that word "beauty" because it always seems to be heading you towards a stereotype—*Vogue,* the ghastly child on the back of the Pears Soup package, "preparing to be a *beautiful* lady": you know if she keeps that up she'll be finished by eighteen or whenever. I think art is concerned with truth and that truth begets beauties ("a terrible beauty," if you like, to use Yeats's formula) which were unforeseen. The very wrenched, compact poems of Ungaretti have a beauty that no one would have thought beautiful in, say, 1890. But we have killed that word: how can it adequately define the satisfaction one gets in Ungaretti's war poems from the exact fit of language and the event?

[Mike Erwin]: *How much inspiration do you draw from your painting when you write poetry?*

Poetry and painting are interdependent for me because I am the same person conducting both. They are different because painting is a silent world whereas poetry only uses silence to measure sound. At times—perhaps the teacher's occupational disease—the sheer vanity of so much talk, talk, talk, discussion, verbal evaluation, weighs one down. Take up a brush and then you are almost sure to do a good picture. But certainly my poems and pictures do come back to the same area of imagery: water, stones, light, space.

[Mike Erwin]: *Many of your poems seem to be in the form of an address. Do you have a reader in mind?*

To quote George Oppen once more. Some years ago he wrote me a letter on this topic of one's imaginary reader. I suggested that he could break up the prose into a verse lineation and this was the result:

> One imagines himself
> addressing his peers
> I suppose. Surely
> that might be the definition
> of "seriousness"? I would like,
> as you see,
> to convince
> myself
> that my pleasure in your response
> is not
> plain vanity
> but the pleasure of being heard,
> the pleasure

of companionship, which seems
more honorable.

Yes, I do always feel I'm speaking to someone. Though it
may, of course, take some time to reach him. There is
quite a lot of humor in my poems, though the reviewers
never seem to notice it, but I go on hoping it will be
heard.

[Mike Erwin]: *How much does what you choose to write
about determine length, form, and manner of poem—i.e.,
what limitations does the material itself pose? Do you
think there is material that is definitely limited or limitless?*

As to length, I can rarely predict it. As to form, I often use
a four stress line—basically four stress but capable of
variants up to six and down to three—because it gives me
something of the breadth of the iambic pentameter line,
yet leaves me free to use as many unstressed syllables as
I want. I like this medium. It has roominess and can carry
a lot of internal rhymes. I never really know what limitations the material itself imposes until I'm a good way on
with it. As to manner—"a man speaking to men," starting
as foursquare as possible, no special pleading, a clarity of
utterance and sometimes an urgency, no bludgeon, a respect
for the adulthood of the reader, no "howling," no theatri-
cality, but these aren't determined by what I *choose* to
write as you put it. These are the ethical base. I choose
surprisingly little. It usually hits me. Or you see something and decide to explore the situation—hawks mating,
a madwoman dancing on a London underground platform—
but is that in any exact sense a "choice"? There's an early
poem, **"Chateau de Muzot"** [*Seeing is Believing*] which
goes:

> Than a choice of subject
> Rather to be chosen by what has to be said
> And to say it. . . .

Yet I always want to unfold the subject, lift it up into
consciousness as far as I can, see its facets, set it into a
perspective of place and time.

[Jed Rasula]: *In the poem **"Reflections"** in **Seeing is
Believing** you say that nature and habit are blind and
that they lie—that we can get close to the truth of things
because what we reflect we choose. Do you think, then,
that the best and truest representation of experience in
poetry is achieved by an arrangement of perception, a
control exercised by the poet in trying to strike a balance
between the surfaces of what his eye sees and the depths
that the whole man perceives?*

Your quoting from **"Reflections"** seems to half refute what
is said in **"Chateau de Muzot."** Actually, **"Reflections"**
was an early poem and I kept feeling the need to argue
with its rather brusque formalism. We can, of course,
choose one point of vantage, choose to write or not to
write, but whether choice versus habit is the best way of
putting the matter I had come to doubt by the time I wrote
"Chateau de Muzot." Some balance, as you say, has to

be struck and an achieved poem in which the stresses, say,
have been counted and the rhymes rhymed is scarcely just
a direct slice of description. And yet many of my poems
have arisen by writing done very swiftly, before the object,
before the actual scene, what was perceived, just as a
painter might do a preliminary sketch from nature.

Often the thing seen embeds itself more and more in an
historical context or a context of thinking about what we
see or a context of memory. The thing seen (or heard) has
to beget its song, but that act of seeing and the act of
getting it over into words in the preliminary sketch are
also acts of thought—already in taking purchase on nature,
on attending to what Wordsworth and Coleridge call the
language of sense, the whole man is involved.

So I don't see it as a question of striking a balance between
the surfaces the eye sees and the depths that the whole
man perceives. Surfaces are already leading one into depths:
surfaces already are involved in space, light, texture, color,
resistance. The surface, say, of an Edward Weston photograph are *all* he has to say—and they are deep enough for
his purposes—evaluative purposes, purposes of thought
and feeling. I dislike making a dualism of that pair. "Sensation is but vision nascent," to get back to that Coleridge
already instanced. And, for me, the moment of sensation,
the taking hold on the physical moment, the melting of
person and presence, are what comes first in my poetry.

I'd always wanted to find some way of explaining how we
build our structures on the sensed and the given. Then one
day, in a friend's flat in New York, I turned up Merleau-
Ponty's *The Primacy of Perception* and the little essay in
that seemed to say all I'd wanted to say. It says it for
poetry and much more, and it makes one see how poetry
is of a piece with other human activities. I return, time and
again, to the central point of that essay where Merleau-
Ponty says,

> By these words, the "primacy of perception," we mean
> that the experience of perception is our presence at the
> moment when things, truths, values are constituted for
> us; that perception is a nascent logos; that it teaches
> us, outside all dogmatism, the true condition of
> objectivity itself; that it summons us to the tasks of
> knowledge and action. It is not a question of reducing
> human knowledge [and here I put in "poetry"] to
> sensation, but of assisting at the birth of this knowledge,
> to make it as sensible as the sensible, to recover the
> consciousness of rationality.

That, for me, with the whole essay behind it, is one of our
great defenses of poetry.

Michael Schmidt   (essay date 1978)

SOURCE: "In the Eden of Civility," in *The Times Literary Supplement,* December 1, 1978, p. 1406.

[*In the following favorable review of* Selected Poems *and*
The Shaft, *Schmidt explores Tomlinson's rejection of both*

Neo-romantic and Movement poetry and discusses the ways this conscious rejection informs his own work.]

In **"Small Action Poem"** (1966) Charles Tomlinson introduces Chopin "shaking music from the fingers". Chopin's art was second nature to him. Tomlinson is not that sort of artist. he is to an unusual degree fastidious. In *The Shaft,* his latest collection, there are poems which he characterizes as "bagatelles"—a genre he has frequently exploited, most memorably in *American Scenes* (1966) which gives the lie to those critics who dismiss him as "humourless". Tomlinson's humour is broad, short on fashionable local wit but rich in human observation. Yet the bagatelles are marginal in Tomlinson's work. At the centre is not anecdote but an acute perception of a common world with a history, a world of movement and process—two of his favourite words. The poetry is as much about perception as about the things perceived. Variety of experience is reflected in a variety of forms, tones and techniques which must strike anyone who picks up the new *Selected Poems 1951-1974* or *The Shaft*.

There is a unity of tone and theme throughout this diversity, but at the same time an impressive technical development from the flute tones of the first books to a more complex and rewarding orchestration. That development reaches its climax in poems of a directly civic character, especially the recent poems about the French Revolution which develop ideas first introduced in **"The Ruin"** and **"Up at La Serra"** (1963) and then, memorably, in **"Prometheus"** and **"Assassin"** (1969). Out of an aesthetic sharply opposed both to the excesses of neo-Romantic writing and to the defeatism of the ironizing school emerged a politics whose cardinal virtues are suggested in the words "civility", "style", "balance", "justice" "reconciliation" and "praise", terms for a private as well as a public code of action and perception.

It is not hard to think ourselves back to the poetic world of the early 1950s into which Tomlinson stepped as a writer. A rising generation was reacting to its immediate antecedents. Against an exhausted Bohemia and the popular rhetoric of Dylan Thomas, some young poets made head (as literary journalism has it) under the banner of the Movement. They set out to slay overstatement with irony, free-verse with tidy quatrains, banishing surrealism and the naked subconscious with bold declarations about common sense. Their irony was a stylistic device, not a thematic verity, and it proved a short-cut to a form of dishonesty more English, but quite as pernicious, as that of their rhetorical predecessors: the dishonesty of understatement, truncated response replacing the untempered surge of feeling. It was all in the language. The struggle of modernists such as Pound to renew the direct connection between words and the world of things and actions they named was of little consequence to them. Poetry was something one did with words, not something that one's words did with the primary world.

Tomlinson chose an alternative strategy. He did not suffer from the xenophobia of his young contemporaries. He could not swallow that famous maxim: "Nobody wants

any more poems about foreign cities". Amongst the discarded 1940s poets he found Keith Douglas, by whom he could take his bearings. And going further back, he found Edward Thomas. Looking abroad, in the work of Ungaretti, Tyuchev, Valéry, Marianne Moore and Wallace Stevens—as later of William Carlos Williams, Antonio Machado and Octavio Paz—he perceived alternatives to the narrow field his contemporaries were tilling. Their new decorum of subject-matter and tone pointed towards that now familiar genre, the Welfare State poem. Tomlinson shared with them, however, a distrust for the 1940s rhetoricians. He identified his distrust not in the quality of their statements or their sense of role but in the overbearing quality of their rhythms. Instead of irony, Tomlinson chose rhythmic modulation as his method of establishing due proportion and balance in his art. His was, and to a large extent still is, a phrased rather than a cadenced poetry. His rhythmic strategy meant that he retained the option of *vers libre,* the thematic resources of dream, and the technical resources of modernism. Tone and voice vary with the subject, and his entire effort is to "accord to objects their own existence", not to use objects or images in the service of a predetermined statement or form.

Yet the expression itself is precisely determined, each effect gauged to reveal some aspect of the object in its process of existing. Nowhere is this deliberateness more evident than in the rhythms themselves, always subtly managed. Take these five lines from **"Winter-Piece"**:

> Gates snap like gunshot
> as you handle them. Five-barred
>   fragility
> sets flying fifteen rooks who go
>   together
> Silently ravenous above this
>   winter-piece
> that will not feed them.

The third line is iambic, a pentameter with an extra unstressed syllable. It is the line of action, the flight of the birds. The rhythmically irregular phrased lines before and after build up to and then down from the action, set the scene and then resolve it. The manipulation of rhythms eases the image into action, and then into significance.

Such deliberate expression is no easy achievement, and the early poems are so carefully groomed that they occasionally achieve preciosity rather than a broader precision. Tomlinson had a point to make against his more publicly successful contemporaries. Various traits of the new ironists repelled him: their resignation, their middleclass *ennui,* their declared philistinism and their social condescension, the affectation of speaking for and as the common man. His early work was, I believe, distorted by an indignation which has never entirely left him. The distortion is towards a refinement which looks at times mannered, a scrupulous numbering of the streaks of the tulip.

He had not experienced in youth "the soft oppression of prosperity". Born in Stoke-on-Trent in 1927 into a working-class household, he made his way by scholarships to Cambridge. At each step music, works of art, films, the literature he encountered took him by surprise. He was drawn forward by the excitement of discovery. His "culture", like his aesthetic, is not an accidental advantage of birth but to a large extent acquired and assembled. Nothing is second nature to him. Even the natural world he has witnessed to is a chosen rather than a native environment. He returns to Stoke in elegiac, not nostalgic vein. It is not only travel that lends an exotic element to his poems of place, for even the English countryside is strange and new in the entirely unsentimental nature it reveals to him. His images he tries to disentangle as much as possible from the subjective perceiver. "Having mislaid it and then/ Found again in a changed mind/ The image": he sees, returns to look again, in a changed light, a changed mind, at the image, be it landscape or idea. In Tomlinson as in Geoffrey Hill ideas come to have the consistency of image.

From the outset Tomlinson was after "a civil language", a language resistant to subjective overstatement, with which to deal with a world of actualities. He tries in English to render thought sensuously. He envies French "its power of sensuous abstraction" and praises Valéry's "sensuous cerebration", exalting what he calls "passionate intellect". French poetry manages this with metrical resources he has largely denied himself.

The result in his work is a poetry of images which are paradoxically hard to visualize: they do not appear static but in process (those fluent clouds which traverse the sky of his imagination). Not only are they in movement: so, too, is the poet's perception of them. Synaesthesia is a common technique, even a theme, in his work. And the poems demand a quality of effort different from that which most modern work requires. They take some time to make themselves familiar to us. There is seldom conclusion, finality: they resolve on balance, on a taut clarity. They dts but establish relationships.

When I set out to fix in memory some particularly arresting passage in Tomlinson's work, the mnemonic device is therefore seldom rhythm. It may be the internal or end rhymes, but more often it is the process of imagery or thought—you might say the argument. Though the rhythms are distinctive, they are not emphatic, except in the "civic" poems. Were they regularly pronounced, they would tend to distort the object of the poem. This rhythmic tentativeness has its drawbacks. Tomlinson—always an attentive reader—is at times inclined to borrow rather than assimilate and transform a compelling literary experience. In **"John Maydew"**, an early poem in Williamsesque triplets, he seems to pour old wine into new bottles. The short, breathless free verse lines of Williams's unmediated observation become mannered in such passages as:

> He eyes the toad
>   beating
>   in the assuagement
> of his truth.

The deliberate diction is vitiated by an arbitrariness of lineation, with a rhythm all the more difficult to establish because of the elbowing enjambements. Objections to this mode are silenced by the success of such poems as **"Up at La Serra"** or the beguiling **"Picture of J. T. in a Prospect of Stone"**, where the skipping triplet answers the necessary delicacy of thought in dialogue form. The poem is a prayer for his daughter without the grandiloquence of Yeats, with much of the delicacy of Marvell (whom the title recalls) as well as the charm of Edward Thomas's poems for his children. Literary associations inevitably crowd the reader's mind in what is very much a genre poem. The triplets helped Tomlinson to un-tense his diction. Indeed, *American Scenes* (1966)—in which the triplet is often used—is the collection in which Tomlinson showed clearly the poet of broad concerns he was to become. His first major collection—*The Way of a World*—followed in 1969.

Rhythmic susceptibility has sometimes seriously betrayed him, and nowhere more so than in the **"Seasons"** section of *The Shaft*. There, and elsewhere in the collection, he follows not at a distance but almost mechanically the rhythmic patterns of Edward Thomas. This form of homage in Thomas's centenary year may have its point—but it worries me. Tomlinson's and Thomas's countrysides are very different worlds, and their poetries are fundamentally distinct. Thomas's images effortlessly carry a general and profound felt significance. Tomlinson's have the power of lucid particularity, but do not carry darkness or the conclusive charge which we experience in Thomas. Thomas wrote his poems because he must, but Tomlinson writes his Thomasesque poems because he wants to.

The tension in these ventriloquisms between Thomas's matter and rhythms and Tomlinson's processes leads to serious difficulties. Tomlinson is, in the best sense, a literary poet, while Thomas is anything but that. When Thomas borrows de la Mare's "clouds like sheep", it is to appropriate the image entirely in his poem. When Tomlinson borrows "Old Man", or a familiar Thomas rhythm, it carries too boldly the tag of its provenance. Such lapses in Tomlinson are not frequent, and *The Shaft* includes, especially in the **"Histories"** and **"In Arden"** sections, what must be among his best work to date.

The continuity of concern in Tomlinson's work is of a kind we associate with Ruskin or Adrian Stokes. **"The Ruin"** (1960) and **"Prometheus"** (1969) complement each other across a decade. **"At Holwell Farm"** (1960) and **"Movements (iv)"** (1972) worry at the same, fundamentally Tomlinsonian theme of creative perception, in different terms but with distinct rhythmic affinities. In these poems, the civic theme emerges from a complex of particular perspectives and images, suggesting the quality of imagination which is discriminating and in a valid sense conservative. At every stage of the poetry the merely subjective is frustrated: there is no wilful distortion of the perceived or the historical world, rather an attempt to realize it in all its complexity: poetry as sculpture, the poet approaching now from one angle and now from another. As well as **"Prometheus"** and **"Up at La Serra"**, **"Assassin,"** **"The Way In"**, and in Charlotte Corday and Jacques Louis David reveal an acute appreciation of human motive and consequence, the particular action and the general effect.

These poems seem to me to be part of Tomlinson's outstanding achievement, with a broad pertience. These poems, and Tomlinson's philosophical ruminations on perception and imagination, such as **"Movements"** from *Written on Water* (1972), continue to strike me as his best. They achieve that sensuous thought he strives for in our recalcitrant English. The "In Arden" section of *The Shaft* comes closer to defining Tomlinson's Eden of civility and balance than any of his earlier work. His Eden is a distillation, not a fabrication.

The new *Selected Poems* ends abruptly in 1974. Readers will still need to possess *The Way In* (1974) and—if they can get it—*Written on Water*. In selecting his work, Tomlinson has destroyed some of his best sequences, including **"Movements"**, which is a pity. One laments other absent friends: **"The Impalpabilities"**, **"Return to Hinton"**, **"The Fox"**, **"Processes,"** etc. Still, it is a generous selection--with about a hundred and fifty poems and a clutch of tentranslations, and if one wishes that the publisher had extended himself to a *Collected*, that is only to pay tribute to a poet whose work is never less than engaging and—in its varied subjects and techniques—often illuminating to an unusual degree, visionary with precision. The vision is of our common world seen as if for the first time.

Kathleen O'Gorman (essay date 1983)

SOURCE: "Space, Time, and Ritual in Charles Tomlinson's Poetry," in *Sagetrieb*, Vol. 2, No. 2, Summer-Fall, 1983, pp. 85-98.

[In the following essay, O'Gorman examines the function of ritual in Tomlinson's verse as well as his unique notion of space and time.]

> One might show, for example, that aesthetic perception too opens up a new spatiality, that the picture as a work of art is not the space which it inhabits as a physical thing and as a colored canvas . . . that the dance evolves in an aimless and unorientated space, that it is a suspension of our history. . . .
>
> Merleau-Ponty
> *Phenomenology of Perception*

In their most traditional aspects, space and time are important frames of reference for Charles Tomlinson. The farm at Hinton Blewett, a bridge in Venice, the historical allusions of **"Prometheus"** and of **"Assassin"** all bring the particular, a sense of rootedness, of solidity to the poems in which they appear. This particularity of reference—in space as in time—localizes and explores the relationship between perceiver and perceived, but does so always with respect to the "mutuality of the relation" realized [in Ruth Grogan's "Charles Tomlinson: The Way of His World," in *Contemporary Literature,* 1978]. Yet Tomlinson's poetry transcends the limits of the particular, so that notions of space and time become involved in a different way as the reader apprehends his own inherence in a world. Space and time become part of man's immediate awareness, his bodily presence in the world, not mere cognitive structures imposed on experience to define reality. Such immediacy in a work of art compels the reader's response to the rhythms of the interplay of verbal and visual textures with modulations of tone and meaning in a poem.

Tomlinson repeatedly affirms this concept of art. He begins *The Necklace* with the poem **"Aesthetic,"** the first two lines of which read, "Reality is to be sought, not in concrete, / But in space made articulate." He begins *A Peopled Landscape* with **"A Prelude"**:

> I want the cries of my geese
> To echo in space, and the land
> They fly above to be astir beneath
> The agreement of its forms.

In the next poem of the same volume, **"Return to Hinton,"** Tomlinson states, "Our language is our land." **"Aesthetic"** and **"Return to Hinton"** state more directly what **"A Prelude"** presents metaphorically: the idea that in poetry, language can create a reality different from that of everyday life. [In his *The Truth of Poetry: Tensions in Modern Poetry from Baudelaire to the 1960s,* 1972] Michael Hamburger says as much when he asserts that metaphor "lends itself to . . . transferences from one order of reality to another," and Harvey Gross, in his *Sound and Form in Modern Poetry* phrases it most succinctly: "The articulations of sound in temporal sequences, rhythms, and meters, present us with 'aesthetic surface'; it is this surface which our perception immediately engages." Poetic form itself then, the structure and texture of words in relation to each other and to the reader, creates verbal "space," as, simultaneously, sound and silence, movement, stress, and tension become "felt time, musical 'duration.'" Tomlinson shows a clear grasp of this in his own discussions of the poetic process as well as in his poetry itself:

> Rhythm, as it is felt in the act of writing, signifies the creation of a continuum, an imaginary space within which words and memories, the given and the possible can be felt as co-present, held over against each other, yet constantly crossing one another's paths. As the mind attends to the pulsation of the growing poem, it is as if it enters and shares this created space, which, filled by the invitations of movement and sound, seems at once landscape and music, perhaps more music than landscape [*Agenda,* 1972-73].

In creating "imaginary space" through a temporal continuum of sounds, the poet thus creates a new center of experience in relation to which man is defined and which is itself defined by that relationship. The lived experience of a poem—including the "felt time" and "imaginary space" it creates as well as the visual, aural and intellectual content it embodies—becomes for the reader a different order of reality, an experience of space and time analogous to, but not identical with, his everyday experience of extension and duration.

Tomlinson clarifies his own grasp of the significance of the aesthetic center of experience which space and time create in a poem when he defines a poem as a rite of initiation. [In his *The Poem as Initiation,* 1967] He states that a poem constitutes a "dwelling on the inner rhythms of events" which establishes a relationship between reader and poem, perceiver and perceived, which occurs outside of ordinary spatial extension and temporal duration. In Tomlinson's control of language especially, with his use of rhythmic structures as expressive forms, one is continually aware of the appeal of his poetry to a level of cognition different from the intellectual. Tomlinson's sense of the structures of sound in appealing immediately to the pre-reflective faculties, coupled with his awareness of the lived experience of the body as the primary locus of meaning, leads him to conceive of the function of poetry in terms of ritual, the experience of reading a poem, a "rite of passage." Tomlinson elaborates in his address to the Phi Beta Kappa Society of Colgate University:

> The poem, in itself, is a ceremony of initiation. . . . It is a rite of passage through a terrain which, when we look back over it, has been flashed up into consciousness in a way we should scarcely have foreseen.

From the start, then, for Tomlinson, the notion of rite or ritual necessarily involves the ideas of space and time: the rite of passage is "through a terrain," our awareness is a "looking back" through time and space, and even the notion of "a way we should scarcely have foreseen" binds together visual perceptions of space with an abstract concept of time. As Merleau-Ponty states, "Spatial outlines are also temporal: elsewhere is always something we have seen or might see" [*Phenomenology of Perception,* translated by Colin Smith, 1976]. Tomlinson describes the manner in which a poem compels the reader to "pause over the stages of the act" which it describes/embodies—again using terminology which refers to space and time to detail the workings of the poem as a rite—and concludes with an acknowledgement of the limits of ceremony, of ritual. To define poetry in such a way is to see that the poem has a power of its own, a capacity to engage the reader in its process.

To try to isolate the notions of space, time, and ritual, to try to dissect a work of art or a theory of aesthetics in terms of any one of these elements assumes an identity for each completely independent of the others. Such an assumption is false, as it relegates the terms "space," "time," and "ritual" to the realm of abstract formulation, and does not account for their embodied presence in man's lived experience of the world. As Merleau-Ponty asserts [in *Signs,* translated by Richard C. McCleary, 1964], and as Tomlinson agrees, our awareness of the world occurs at a pre-reflective level; in trying to conceptualize that awareness, "analytic thought . . . seeks in the mind the guarantee of a unity [of time and of space] which is already there when

we perceive." [In *Phenomenology of Perception*] The philosopher continually reminds us that space and time are a part of our "primordial encounter with being . . . [that] being is synonymous with being situated." Merleau-Ponty joins the ideas of space and time with that of ritual in his discussion of the rhythms of existence which are inherent in perception, pointing out that perception "ratifies and renews in us a 'prehistory,'" or a unity of the flux of spatial/temporal existence which is realized in the lived body, independent of any abstract notions of space and time. The correlation between this and Tomlinson's notions of space, time, and ritual is clear, particularly in Tomlinson's emphasis on the poem's "dwelling on the inner rhythms of events." Works such as **"Poem," "Eight Observations on the Nature of Eternity," "Distinctions," "Ode to Arnold Schoenberg," "Wind,"** and **"Swimming Chenango Lake"** suggest the complex relationship between time and space which the rite of the poem compels. They affirm, as do most of Tomlinson's poems, the concept of the body as the primary locus of meaning in the aesthetic experience. As philosopher and poet would have it, the actual impulses of meaning in a work of art, together with the visual and intellectual content, effect the transference from one order of reality to another. The "aesthetic surface which our perception immediately engages" initiates the reader into the way of a world in which

> We bring
> To a kind of birth all we can name
> And, named, it echoes in us our being.

Tomlinson makes real the ritualistic presence of the poem most clearly in those works whose subject matter itself concerns specific rites—those which mark the passage from a lower to a higher status, and those which mark recurrent events. Rites of initiation almost always designate an elevation in status, while those celebrating the "rhythmic forms of nature—the day, a season, the life of a blossom—" constitute cyclical rites. Tomlinson's poetry considers ritual in both of its forms and renders that which is considered in a rite of initiation of its own. Poems like **"Prelude," "Harvest Festival," "The Matachines,"** and **"Before the Dance,"** celebrate the cyclical events of nature, while **"A Death in the Desert,"** and **"Swimming Chenango Lake"** restore the proper relation between the passage of individuals from one state of being to another and mark the eternal recurrences of nature. A closer examination of several of these poems indicates the way in which Tomlinson views the ritual process and establishes the concept of space and time "indefinitely recoverable, indefinitely repeatable" which is the space and time of every ritual.

"Return to Hinton" incorporates both forms of ritual in a number of different ways. The speaker of the poem alludes throughout to rites of initiation marking passages from one important stage of life to another, and he surveys the farm and its inhabitants—their past and present—with reference to recurrent natural and religious cycles. The occasion of his return is the death of someone's father, and the visit calls to mind the idea of the mother as a bride (the speaker notices "The Bridal March" on the piano)—both instances of transitions which are marked by ceremonial rites of passage. He associates the traditional color, "white," with the Bridal March, and contrasts that with the "widow's silk" and the "blackened bellies" of the kettles in the kitchen. The speaker refers twice to doors, and in both cases sees them in their ceremonial role as points of passage or transition, again symbolically from one stage of life to another. The kitchen door is the first one considered, and this becomes the threshold between two different worlds:

> The television box
> is one,
>   the mullions and flagged floor
>   of the kitchen
> through an open door
>   witness a second
>   world in which
> beside the hob
>   the enormous kettles'
>   blackened bellies ride—
> as much the token of an order as
>   the burnished brass.
>   You live
> between the two. . . .

The ambiguous "between the two" can designate the point between the world of the television and that of the kitchen or between the worlds betokened by the blackened bellies and the burnished brass. It can indicate, also, the distinction between "a world (English and rural) that is stridently contrasted to the world of the U.S. whence the poet has returned." In any case, the open door allows for passage from one to the other. Appropriately, the second mention of a door refers to the widow's closing her door on despair, "as the gravestones tell [her] to." "Door" is used metaphorically in this instance to indicate the finality of the widow's acceptance of her husband's death, having "given / grief its due," and signifies also the woman's passage into a new order herself. It simultaneously reinforces the finality of the passage of her husband from life to death. The gravestones then serve as the literal reminder of that passage, the physical counterpart to the metaphysical reality.

Tomlinson's poetry transcends the limits of the particular, so that notions of space and time become involved in a different way as the reader apprehends his own inherence in a world.

—*Kathleen O'Gorman*

The passage of the individuals from one state of being to another—the woman from bride to widow, her husband, from life to death—takes place within a context of cyclical forms, religious and natural. The Bible, Genesis, prayer and "chapel gospel" are all specifically mentioned, and the phrase "'God / saw the light / that it was good'" works in several ways to underscore the ritualistic nature of the occasion. In quoting the passage, Tomlinson suggests the familiarity the family has with the Bible, "whose cadences became a part of one," but he also chooses a phrase which is repeated over and over in the Bible to suggest the ritualistic repetitions in the story of creation.

In addition to the religious references, the seasons, cycles of fertility of the land, the passing on of land from one generation to another and the return of the speaker to Hinton Blewett betoken an order beyond the immediate. The patterns of repetition in nature and in human lives move events beyond our everyday notions of space and time and allow for the lived experience of extension and duration, felt time and rhythmic cognition.

Just as the structure of a ritual compels the participants to "pause over the stages of the act," the occasion of the speaker's return compels him to meditate on the death of a man and its place in the rhythms of human experience, personal and impersonal. But the cadences of which that death is a measure are realized as well in the texture of the poem itself, so that the ritual process described becomes also the process rendered. The three-step line in which the poem is written forces the reader to pause over the stages of the act that is the poem, as does the repetition of words such as "death," "land," "door," and "certainty," coupled with the interplay of assonance and alliteration in lines like "express / won readiness / in a worn dress." The oppositions of life and death, suggested in the white and black of the woman's clothes, find counterparts in other oppositions referred to in the poem: poverty and prosperity, certain and uncertain enemies, past and future. Of the poem's subject matter, its visual suspense, the verbal and aural texture and the juxtapositions of opposites, it might easily be said that "It is through them and with them that we take this grip on significance," that the reader establishes relationship. In responding to the contours and measures of the poem, we grasp the way of a world; and the locus of meaning, as in all ritual, is in the lived experience of the body participating in the rite.

Equally complex in evoking the function of ritual is Tomlinson's poem "The Matachines". Again, ritual works in "The Matachines" on several different levels simultaneously: it defines the nature of the event which the poem treats, and it determines how the reader relates to the poem. The title refers to "a / dance of / multiform confusions" whose purpose even the Indians performing the ceremony no longer understand. In "The Matachines," Tomlinson embodies the tensions between a number of different elements. Catholic ceremonies and personages are set against those of the American Indians (references to Saint Anthony of Padua, the holy Virgin, a church with altar and crucifix, juxtaposed to the masked figures participating in the dance). The war between the Moors and the Spanish Christians is alluded to with references to the morris—"the Moorish dance"—"the way the Moors / were beaten in Spain," the daughter of the Moroccan emperor, again set in opposition to the Christian references. The Spanish and the Indians of Mexico are similarly related (Cortez, the Malinche, Moctezuma); male and female (the bull betrayed by the girl, the lines of men through which they dance); sexual indulgence and sexual abstinence (the Indian mistress and the holy Virgin); the past and the present (the confused events of a number of different histories made present in the dance). The tensions are realized in the poem in the evocation of the girl dancing, in the ritual which brings them all together. But the ritual of the poem, in addition to that described by it, constitutes an equally compelling encounter, a profoundly evocative center of experience.

Just as observer and dance create the encounter described, reader and poem mutually determine the aesthetic achievement of the experience of the reading. The suspended syntax, which only comes to rest in the final line of the poem, creates immediately a sense of anticipation which involves the reader with the poem in his attempt to resolve the verbal complexities. Tomlinson's frequent use of colons, semi-colons and dashes serves a similar function, visually as well as grammatically compelling a movement forward, as do the shorter lines which continually leave an idea or a phrase incomplete. The patterned repetition of key words and phrases—"the saint," "the Moors," "betrayal," "the dance," among others—echoes the recurrent ritual of the dance. This repetition becomes especially important at the beginning and end of the poem. The first line, "Where, but here," is repeated as the ninth line, and a variation of it, "where, / but in this / place" occurs nine lines after that. What begins as a question and establishes itself in the ear and mind of the reader echoes as a resolution in the phrase "we are here" (line 80), which signals the approaching conclusion of the poem and which later ends it. Beginning and end unite in a verbal cycle which renews itself and the aesthetic experience in every reading, just as the performance of the dance re-actualizes the events it commemorates. The repetition of the lines which follow "we are here" signifies an important change in the participants' perception of their performance and further complicates the patterns of meaning and sound which give the poem its ritualistic effect:

> we are here
> whatever we
> do or
> mean in this
> dance
> of the bull
> and the betrayal:
> whatever we
> do we mean
> as praise, praise
> to the saint
> and the occasion.

The change from "whatever we / do or / mean in this" to "whatever we / do we mean / as praise, praise" radically alters the participants' sense of the dance and the reader's response to the poem. The vagueness of the first proposition is reinforced with the emphasis on the conjunction "or" ending line 82 and on the demonstrative pronoun "this" ending line 83. That vagueness disappears completely when the lines are repeated in slightly altered form. Those who participate in the "dance of / multiform confusions" give it meaning themselves, and the decisiveness

of that act is underscored with the repetition of the word "praise" twice in one line. The lines "It is / done" also provide a tone of resolve towards the end of the poem, without sacrificing the tensions of the language and of the historical and religious events to which they refer. The declaration, "It is / done," follows the reference to the crucifix, calling to mind the last words of Christ; yet it establishes simultaneously that the ceremony of the dance is finished. Again the mutual oppositions assert themselves—Christian and Indian, especially—in an articulation of the relationship which defines them and which measures the ritualistic experience of the dance, the aesthetic experience of the poem. With the last line, "we are here," the poem comes full circle, and "here"—at a church, at an Indian ceremony, in the present—signifies as well all that has taken place outside of this particular church, in repetitions of this ceremony throughout the whole history of the Indians, in a time measured, not in hours or days, but rather in the rhythms of the seasons, in the pulses of a ritual dance.

Those pulses are transformed into impulses of meaning in **"Before the Dance"** and enrich the aesthetic surface to which the reader responds by making real the feeling of anticipation which it describes. **"Before the Dance"** details the sense of apprehension before a Navajo dance begins, acknowledging that

> the wait
> for the Indian
> is half the dance,
> and so they wait
> giving a quality
> to the moment
> by their refusal
> to measure it.

This suspense is made real in the visual suspense of the short lines and, again visually, in the repeated use of the colon throughout, signalling that more follows to complete the meaning of what has come before. The language of this poem too creates a continuum of sound with repetitions of several key words: "wait" recurs three times, "the dance," three times, and "the moment," three, while "begin," "the wind," and "the movement" are used twice each. The phrase "the moment / is expansible" occurs twice, and the effect of that repetition is particularly important. In its initial use, the phrase indicates the transformation of all sense of time which accompanies the ritual of waiting for the dance. The phrase recurs, however, separated into two phrases, each in parentheses: "(the moment)" and "(is expansible)." In its second occurrence, it is divided by a line of the poem: "on the earth floor." The passage reads

> they wait, sitting
> (the moment)
> on the earth floor
> (is expansible)
> saying very little.

The effect is three-fold. The parentheses and the double interruption of syntax give the reader the sense that he has

heard the phrase elsewhere, without putting undue emphasis on that fact. The appeal, clearly, is to the pre-reflective
level of cognition. Equally important, however, is the integration of the phrase into the passage in alternating lines.
"They wait, sitting / on the earth floor / saying very little"
describes the actual appearance of the people waiting for
the dance to begin. The separation of subject and subject
complement—"the moment" separated from "is expansible"—reinforces visually the notion of time which the statement describes. In addition, interrupting the parenthetical
phrases with the prepositional phrase, "on the earth floor,"
creates the effect of grammatical wholeness, with "on the
earth floor" modifying "moment." This links the concept
of time with the Indians' bodily presence on the earth and
emphasizes subtly the notion of lived time in which the
participants and the reader are both involved. As the poem
proceeds, the moment it describes becomes expansible for
the reader, and time and space take on qualities which
distinguish them from ordinary temporal duration and
spatial extension. The ritual time and space described
become, for the reader, those which he experiences in the
process of the reading. The poem itself, in its capacity to
make real that which it describes, joins Merleau-Ponty's
notion of the rhythms of existence inherent in all perception with generally accepted notions of the power of ritual
to re-actualize the time and presence which it celebrates.

This is not to suggest, however, that those poems concerned with the ritual process *per se* are the only ones in
which "restoration of the right relation" between man and
the world occurs. It is a measure of Tomlinson's achievement that his poetry consistently renews the process of
our encounter with the world, and does so regardless of
the subject matter. In those poems which are not specifically
about ritual, the actual rite of the poem is just as easily
understood. This rite consists of the transference from one
order of reality to another through the aesthetic experience; from the images and references of the poem, from
its visual and aural structures, as well as from the temporal
and spatial reality it creates with the reader, the meaning
emerges. One has only to examine briefly such poems as
"Venice," "Arizona Desert," and "Paring the Apple"
to sense how the commonplace becomes a part of that
transference, a part of the order of reality created in the
interaction between reader and poem.

We are made to dwell on the inner rhythms of the event
of a city's coming into being in "Venice," as the poem
creates the verbal time and space in which "the houses
assemble in tight cubes." Ordinary time and space are
displaced from the start as the abrupt, single-syllable "cut"
effects the perceptual upset it describes. Tomlinson's use
of three-stress and four-stress lines throughout the rest of
the poem continues to measure the event in "felt time,"
and the controlled unfolding of meaning and sound creates
an aesthetic surface which continually renews and reveals
the perceptual change which it effects, the transition from
one order of reality to another. Perceiver and perceived,
reader and poem, are both revealed in the process, as the
cadences which determine the space and time of the poem
become a part of the reader, re-defining him at a pre-
reflective level.

In "Arizona Desert," the reader is compelled to pause
over the stages of the act of seeing which the poem describes, in a time and place in which

> to be
> is to sound
> patience deviously
> and follow
> like the irregular corn
> the water underground.

The sound patterns of "Arizona Desert" are as complex
as those of "Nine Variations in a Chinese Winter Setting," and the irregular vowel and consonant patterns
become the verbal counterparts to the course of "water
underground" to which the poem refers. The images of
this poem are particularly arresting: "layers / of flaked
and broken bone / unclench into petals, / into eyelids of
limestone," "A dead snake / pulsates," and "Villages /
from mud and stone / parch back / to the dust they human-
ize." As the sound patterns move the reader forward, the
images and syntax slow his progress, so that together form
and content work to determine the pace at which the poem
takes on meaning for the reader. The reader, in perceiving
the poem as an intentional unity (that is, in the phenom-
enologists' sense of intentionality), "sound[s] patience
deviously" as he measures and weighs each poetic unit—
syllable, foot, line—at a pre-cognitive level and experiences each passage of the poem as a literal "passage" into
its own particular space and time, into an order of reality
grasped in his immediate experience of the poem.

There is the same immediacy in "Paring the Apple," and
in that poem, too, the "recognition" compelled is as much
the rite of the poem as it is the experience of the reader.
In this work especially, the suspense of syntax undermines
the reader's expectations of extension and duration, never
resolving the verbal tensions it creates.

> And then? Paring it slowly,
> From under cool-yellow
> Cold-white emerging. And . . . ?

It has been said of "Paring the Apple" that "the act [de-
scribed/embodied in the poem] becomes almost a ritualistic
gesture, a manual prayer, something sacerdotal. It takes
place in a space between human and inhuman" [in *London
Magazine,* 1981]. Yet here we must distinguish between
secular and religious notions of ritual. The secular is profoundly rooted in man's experience of the world, while
the religious is a manifestation of belief in and devotion
to a deity. The former has man as its central concern; the
latter, god(s). It is important to understand that in Tomlinson's poetry, the ritual realized is secular. Tomlinson is
careful always to focus on man's relationship with the
world, a relationship predicated on a profound respect for
the world as it is given to the senses, as it is known through
the body, and as man's relationship with it can be re-
actualized through language. To introduce the notion of a
deity would be to shift the focus entirely. Tomlinson himself cautions us against such a mistake in "A Process":
"One accords the process [of knowing the world] its reality,

one does not deify it." In his most recent interview, Tomlinson's response to an inquiry concerning his religious views again fixes his poetry firmly in the world of the secular:

> Place—this place—speaks to me more than the dogmas of any religion, and it speaks of very fundamental things: time, death, what we have in common with the animals, what things are like when you stop to look. . . .

As Tomlinson states in an early poem of *Seeing Is Believing,* "Place is the focus," and as he continually reminds us, it is the body which places us, which is the primary locus of meaning in all experience. Only through our bodily inherence in the world can we come to know the world truly, and only in that encounter can we come to know ourselves.

Tomlinson returns to the notion of the poem as a ritual in his address at Colgate University and speaks of the limits of ceremony:

> The Hopi [Indian] removal of masks confesses the limit of ceremony, but the very act of doing so is a ceremonial act which would have been impossible without the context of those masks and the rites of which they are a part. . . . We put down the book. We put aside the mask. But it is the book and it is the mask that bring to bear the mystery and the qualities of the process of living.

We should add that in Tomlinson's case, it is the poetry, the reader's interaction with the aesthetic surface with which Tomlinson presents him, which brings to bear that mystery, which renews the process of living. Though that is perhaps to confess the limits of ceremony, it is to do so with full appreciation for the work of art as an object in its own right and in full acceptance of our own existence as a perpetual process of becoming.

Michael Edwards   (essay date 1987)

SOURCE: "Charles Tomlinson's Seeing and Believing," in *Poetry and Possibility,* The Macmillan Press, 1987, pp. 154-68.

[*In the following excerpt, Edwards examines the religious aspects of Tomlinson's poetry.*]

Seeing, according to the title of Tomlinson's first full-length collection, is believing, but hasn't his point been missed? Not only is this more than a demand for evidence: the stress falls quite as much on the believing as on the seeing, for the adage has been sounded and then reversed. It declares, surely, in the light of the poems that follow, that what is achieved in seeing well is a kind of belief. Surprisingly, therefore, the poetry of this non-Christian will be partly concerned with the question of belief, in its relation to sight; and the concern appears to be increasing.

Seeing is clearly momentous for Tomlinson, no less than a matter, as far as one's being in the world is concerned,

of life or death. The whole of the self, mind, body and whatever else we are, is involved, and judged, in the act of seeing, and to see as one should (the obligations of seeing mingling indissolubly with its delights) is to enter a relationship with the other, to be measured and called out. Commentators are well aware of this seeing, but they don't consider it religious, whereas Tomlinson does. In the course of his lecture 'The Poet as Painter' (reprinted in *Eden*), he discusses the use in his early poetry of 'the artistic ethic of Cézanne', an ethic 'distrustful of the drama of personality' and capable of rescuing and celebrating 'the paradisal aspect of the visual', and adds: 'It seemed to me a sort of religion'. The term is loosely applied—the discipline and the outward-seeking energy do not lead, after all, to an encounter with any god—but it does seem legitimate. The burden of Tomlinson's poetry is the need to 'know thyself' in relation rather than in the privacy of selfconsciousness, and to deal with self by becoming a kind of personal-impersonal 'one'. There is a quite remarkable sentence at the opening of his essay 'To begin: Notes on Graphics' (from *In Black and White*), where he sets out an objective: 'To begin beyond the self. . . . To reconcile the I that is and the I that I am.' 'The I that is'. . . . If I have understood him, he is distinguishing the *I* experienced in the first person, in the 'I am' of self-awareness, and a third-person *I* known to be there, as an existence among others, inhabiting the world on a level with 'paint, water and paper'. This is not the Christian view of the person, of a man fallen from himself yet existing potentially as an utterly changed 'new man' (where the perfect statement is surely St. Paul's 'by the grace of God I am what I am', in 1 Corinthians 15:10); yet while that view is not difficult to repeat, Tomlinson is genuinely exploring the question, and his aim is equally demanding in terms of vigilance and abstention. His words continue to turn in the mind, jostling with Rimbaud's 'JE est un autre', and represent a wisdom to which the religious would do well to attend. They suggest, to a reader so inclined, that one might know oneself as other, as 'one' among many, as of concern not to oneself but to God. There is, I presume, a strong religious impulse in this recent stanza:

> this script that untangles itself
> out of wind, briars, stars unseen,
> keeps telling me what I mean
> is theirs, not mine.
>
> ('Poem', *The Flood*)

Intensity issues from wordplay, from the double syntax made possible by the omission, habitual with Tomlinson, of 'that' ('telling me *that* . . .') and from the double sense of 'what I mean'. It is already a severe lesson for a poet to acknowledge that the meanings he makes belong not to him but to the poem where they are made and, more importantly, to the world from which his writing 'untangles' itself. (Consider, nevertheless, how one is released by the consent.) It is a harsh lesson for a man to realise that his own meaning, 'what he means', is not in himself but out there, with the wind, briars, unseen stars.

For Tomlinson, in fact, 'who am I?' is less decisive than 'where am I?' On the most everyday level, and this *is* in part a poetry of daily living, his writing explores what it is like to dwell in a house, to drive a car; how one's perpetually changing surroundings impinge on the mind and its senses. So as to register those changes, and to convey the activity rather than passive stance of the person in the landscape—and also, no doubt, because that's what he noticed—many of the poems are about being in motion, about walking, driving, flying even. (*Notes from New York* opens and closes with the aerial views that have for the first time become commonplace for poets of Tomlinson's generation.) Yet the desire from the beginning has been to salute not merely a world outside but, after a diuturnity of the cult of inwardness, a 'reign of outwardness' (**'A Prelude'**, *A Peopled Landscape*). A Christian will presumably concur in this concern for the actualities and reciprocations of place, since the world is God's and a way to the intuition of paradise; and the word 'reign', which joins 'kingdom' in the subliminal ontological politics of Tomlinson's vocabulary, indicates that this poetry which is quite oblique to Christianity nevertheless enters that profounder dimension of place, of being somewhere.

For one thing, his poems often report, and as it were effect, a waking to a world suddenly there, with a conviction of discovering Eden. Reflected sunbeams from water on the floor of his flooded cottage lead past the Fall and its consequences: 'Primeval light undated the day / Back into origin, washed past stain / And staleness, to a beginning glimmer' (**'The Flood'**, in the volume of the same name). Or mountains seen one morning that on other mornings are invisible seem the re-enactment of Creation:

> Light touches the sense awake,
> First fiat crossing the aeons to an eye
>   That sees it is still good, its touch a healing
> Where yesterday revealed at this turn of the hill
>   Only a void and formlessness of sky.
>   (**'At a Glance'**, *Notes from New York*)

He writes often of this light, and it may be his painter's eye that sees it. Yet although he refers in 'The Poet as Painter' to the 'bringing of things to stand in the light of origin' as the basic project of his writing, such glimpses of Eden are occasional, and differ from the assumption about Edenic light in Pope. Moreover, while the intention of his poetry, like Wordsworth's, is restorative, its dynamic, again like Wordsworth's, faces the future, specifically in terms of sudden openings-out of time. To return to the early poems after reading the latest is to realise that those moments have always existed, and that they too have a religious bearing. The initial poem of *Seeing is Believing* itself, **'The Atlantic'**, having described, one might have thought, the tide coming in, concludes: 'That which we were, / Confronted by all that we are not, / Grasps in subservience its replenishment.' In the abrupt change, or conversion, from 'that which we were', provoked almost in the twinkling of an eye by an act of absorbed attention, of seeing and saying, comes not exactly a new self but a vision of possibility, where 'all that we are not' means, as well as ocean, sun, shore and wind over against one, the scope of what one might be. If Tomlinson's poetry reaffirms Blake's 'As a man is So he Sees', it also argues that as a man sees, so he becomes. In the second poem of the enlarged edition, **'Winter Encounters'**, it is the non-human world as well as the self that is launched into futurity: 'There is a riding-forth, a voyage impending/ In this ruffled air, where all moves . . . The world stirs forward, instinct with becoming, as if recreation, in Tomlinson's non-Christian understanding of it, were occurring here and now. And while the ruffled air, unlike Wordsworth's gentle breeze, carries no intimation of spirit, the closing lines do open to something more than physical: 'One feels behind / Into the intensity that bodies through them / Calmness within the wind, the warmth in cold.' What 'bodies through' in this verbally active incarnation: intensity, calmness, and warmth, remains undefined, yet, though it is certainly not supernatural, it doesn't seem entirely natural either.

There is a pointed challenge here, in the fact that Tomlinson emphasises our power over the world rather less than the power of the world to awaken us. In a book where I am considering poetry and change, it is right that one should encounter a poet who cries out for the recognition not only of the otherness but of the greater worth of what is not ourselves. Only when the light of the mind has been acknowledged to be poorer than the light out there (as it is in **'Of Beginning Light'** from *Written on Water*) can it offer to renew the world in its own space. Tomlinson prompts the thought that the Christian needs to agree more than anyone (and the Christian poet most of all) that the authority of God's world and its ability to rouse us is indeed of more significance than our ability to rouse and recreate the world. One needs to take the full force, moral and spiritual, of his comment about fishing which is so much more than a comment about fishing, where what is required is 'just learning to sit still and keep your shadow off the water' [in an article by Alan Ross, in *London Magazine*, 1981].

To see is to believe, to sight a world in its paradisal possibility and also to place the self. It is the possibility that most concerns me here, and since, in this poet who appears simple or at least straightforward because his poems usually say what they mean, its observing is in fact very complex, to explore it further we shall need to advance carefully. Chance is obviously of importance, and seems to replace, in the Christian scheme, both inspiration and providence. It is inspiration and providence. It is inspiration when it prompts and then binds the writer with the fortuities of linguistic suggestion, especially rhyme (**'The Chances of Rhyme'**, *The Way of a World*). It is providence when the world that he encounters works on the observer by sudden thwartings of expectation: it wakes him by the surprises of appearing vistas, shadows, reflections; it 'unblinds certitude' (**'The White Van'**, *Written on Water*). Its action, indeed, usually seems to be beneficent (it is usually a happy chance), as does that of circumstance. A poem of natural death and rebirth declares: 'The breath of circumstance / is warm' (**'One World'**, *American Scenes*), and although there is still no hint of the good will of the Spirit one nevertheless recalls the warmth in cold, and wonders again just what, in the now 'windless air', such a breath might be.

The latest version of chance occurs in **'The Mirror in the Roadway'** (*Notes from New York*), which begins: 'Nature here / is the multiplicity of luck.' Tomlinson is referring to street reflections in a mirror beside a furniture lorry, and writes 'Nature here' rather than 'Nature'; yet the slight, witty, urban incident bids to redefine, I think, the grandiose Nature of Pope or Wordsworth. The physical world is many things in Tomlinson, but 'the multiplicity of luck' (which also, one sees, is good luck) is an accurate way of describing that world as it discloses itself. Strangely enough, it would also seem an apt description of the state of affairs from a Christian point of view—of the impingements of Providence in a world and a life that are fallen.

One of the accompaniments of chance is similitude. Again we return to 'like'; who will write the history of comparison? Similitude has been an explicit concern for Tomlinson since the beginning, vital to the ontological venture of looking and writing, and also painting. According to his most probing thinking, the viewer is not alone in his observing of similitudes, for here too a kind of friendly providence is at work. Through the resemblances of objects one may be 'taken in', or deceived, on one's quest for, say, mushrooms—which, though not occurring in romance, do lead to a magic circle—mistaking for them stones or marks on the ground; yet one is also 'taken in', drawn in, that is, to the perception of affinities, to a more mysterious apprehension of what is there (**'Mushrooms'**, *The Shaft*). A resemblance too, says the poem, is 'real', and 'true' to 'the weft of seeing', as are the meanings that one reads even though they are 'not there'. In this delicate, understated poem, which ends, 'in the twilight coolness', with the mushrooms becoming 'stepping stones across a gross of water', reality and truth are found in what is not there and yet is there, observed by a seeing that believes, and whose scrupulous weft is perhaps tacitly distinguished from the warp of a vision merely distorted.

Another of chance's strange accompaniments, glanced at in passing, is the reflection. Reflections hold for Tomlinson much the same interest as for Bonnefoy, and he is quite as willing to go along with them. They too, numerous throughout his volumes, are present from the outset, and their first appearance, in **'Venice'**, the second poem of *The Necklace,* is the most radical. It ends:

> She is about to embark, but pauses.
> Her dress is a veil of sound
> Extended upon silence.
>
> Under the bridge,
> Contained by the reflected arc
> A tunnel of light
> Effaces walls, water, horizon.
>
> Floating upon its own image
> A cortège of boats idles through space.

The reflection is real enough (it may also be the first imprint of Cotman in Tomlinson's work), and the scene is observed in a named city; yet the mind, travelling the reflection and the image, sees and writes out a place that is both physical and mental, that reaches beyond itself, and that floats finally with that cortège. A townscape, at a moment of pause, of 'about to . . . ', has become soundless sound, silence, effacement, light, and visionary space; the boats 'in' the sky are material yet weightless. And is it extravagant to think that 'cortège', a French word that has been assimilated into English, acts in itself as the whole poem acts, as a strangeness that is also familiar, a foreignness not outside our experience?

When Tomlinson himself asks what are the appeal and the meaning of reflections, however, as he does in **'Below Tintern'** in *The Shaft* (his poetry often posing such large questions, and answering them), his conclusion is more complex. The poem begins:

> The river's mirrorings remake a world
> Green to the cliff-tops, hanging
> Wood by wood, towards its counterpart:
> Green gathers there as no green could
> That water did not densen.

Yes: the power of a reflection is not that it reproduces the world but that it 'remakes' it; its bearings, one might say, are Neoplatonic rather than Aristotelian, though it stays close enough to its model to be still a 'mimesis'. A reflection offers entry to the green world, where green attains a greenness beyond what is possible in the nature we see directly, and where 'densen' marvellously suggests a whole world become vivid and compact. A question, however: 'Yet why should mind / So eagerly swim down and through / Such towering dimness?' elicits a response from the poem which is far more ambivalent and, in its ambivalence, surely right. The answer: 'Because that world seems true?' is itself interrogative, and the mere seeming is apparently confirmed by wordplay when the reflections are said to 'lie' beneath the water, and when, with the sudden information that the scene is being looked at from a car which, to close the poem, 'bends by', the underwater sights become 'lost to reflection'. Another pun, of course, and one that Tomlinson probes elsewhere for its suggestion that the mind resembles reflections, and that, by reflecting on objects and also reflecting them, it reconstitutes them in a possible world. So the glimpses, says the poem, are 'true enough'; but just as we are registering a shrug of the shoulders, the other meaning of that phrase too, that the reflected world does have sufficient truth for us, breaks across in the eloquent celebration of 'Those liquid thresholds, that inverted sky / Gripped beneath rockseams by the valley verdure'. A reflection cannot be the world renewed and habitable, but neither is it dismissed as a fancy: the poem, while losing them, salutes the fact that such hints of renewal exist, in a world that is 'counter' to this one yet also a 'part' of it.

(The poem recalls these lines on the river Loddon in Pope's *Windsor-Forest*:

> Oft in her Glass the musing Shepherd spies
> The headlong Mountains and the downward Skies,
> The watry Landskip of the pendant Woods,
> And absent Trees that tremble in the Floods;

In the clear azure Gleam the Flocks are seen,
And floating Forests paint the Waves with Green.

The lines were added after the first writing of the poem, as Pope himself points out in a note. They occur in a context of metamorphosis, as if, to the story of a nymph transformed into the river of her own tears, Pope adds the river's transformation of the scene into a quite novel Arcadia. It is the shepherd who sees the reflection, and he does so perhaps because of a poetic inclination akin to Pope's that sets him 'musing'. I am not sure of the significance of the passage, but I do think that the most fascinating word, given Mallarmé, is 'absent'.)

The religious dimension of the sounding of possibility, of the pursuit of belief, is particularly clear when the encounter is with 'presence', which is also Bonnefoy's word, or indeed with 'mystery'. Presence in the earlier poetry may seem to proclaim the otherness of a physical world in strictly objective terms: doesn't the 'ethic of Cézanne' operate in the poem about him, **'Cézanne at Aix'** in *Seeing is Believing,* to indicate the Montagne Sainte-Victoire as neither delicious fruit nor posing sitter but a kind of there-ness of mountain? Indeed it does; yet the mountain, without being numinous—for that is precisely the sort of word that Tomlinson has no use for, and of which he has no need—is not simply there, or rather, its being simply there is itself more than factual. In the final lines:

> There
> In its weathered weight
> Its silence silences, a presence
> Which does not present itself

the very withholding stills one into a kind of awe.

And what of a bowl in the same volume that 'glistens with presence' (**'The Ruin'**)? It glistens with the presence of humans and their objects in a house, with that mutuality of presence which creates the 'laric world'. But isn't it also presence itself that glistens, or that would do if that world were reanimated, as the bowl opens to the sheer glory of being there? The bowl is also described as 'Gracing the table on which it unfolds itself'. Like Marianne Moore, Tomlinson moves from an aesthetic to a religious meaning of 'grace', but he is his own master in genuinely combining them, and finding in ordinary objects and their reciprocations an extraordinary grace and presence, a light, and a singular unfolding. The idea is essayed more fully in a later poem:

> Two cups,
> a given grace,
> afloat and white
> on the mahogany pool
> of table. They unclench
> the mind, filling it
> with themselves.
> Though common ware,
> these rare reflections,
> coolness of brown
> so strengthens and refines

> the burning of their white,
> you would not wish
> them other than they are—
> you, who are challenged
> and replenished by
> those empty vessels.
>> (**'A Given Grace'**, *American Scenes*)

Two cups on a table have been transfigured, by the combined powers of sight, mind and language, almost to a transcendence: they are afloat, and their whiteness burns. Yet they are still cups, for their renewal is not beyond but within them. That, indeed, is their power—that they change while remaining the same—and 'you would not wish/them other than they are', since in this real vision of them they have already achieved a state of grace. One discovers the same ontological ambition as in Pope: to gild without altering; one also realises that Christianity has been both used and set aside. The grace and the gift occur almost explicitly outside the faith, for these cups, these vessels, that replenish us with something more than a mere drink, recall the communion cup only to displace it.

Tomlinson sees the 'rare' in the 'common' (a recalling of Wordsworth) earning that almost mystical, almost oxymoronic apprehension, of a filling from what is empty, by the attentiveness, the openness, of his looking; and he sees the mysterious in the factual. He is drawn, indeed, to 'the mystery of fact' (**'Maillol'**, *A Peopled Landscape*), and one needs to remember such a phrase when reading the early poems especially, where the closeness of observation and description, with its often Pope-like delicacy, felicity, luxury ('A salver, stippled at its lip by light', 'as they unlink/The pendants of chandeliers into their winking suds'), trembles accurately on the edge of the mysterious. Even before the appearance of *Seeing is Believing,* moreover, he had reproved the *New Lines* poets for being unaware of 'the continuum outside themselves, of the mystery bodied over against them in the created universe'. Although the word 'created' may be used rather loosely, 'mystery' seems a very deliberate addition to the Buberian expression that he had also adopted earlier, in *The Necklace,* when referring to a house 'bodied over against one' (**'Observation of Facts'**). The physical universe for Tomlinson, the body of the world, is nothing less than the incarnation of a mystery.

Here is one of his approaches to it, a poem that seems to take its cue from Donald Davie's 'Turnstall Forest':

> We must anticipate the dawn one day,
> Crossing the long field silently to see
> The roe deer feed. Should there be snow this year
> Taking their tracks, searching their colours out,
> The dusk may help us to forestall their doubt
> And drink the quiet of their secrecy
> Before, the first light lengthening, they are gone.
> One day we must anticipate the dawn.
>> (**'The Roe Deer'**, *The Shaft*)

In a poem whose light and simple touch is of the kind one only reaches at a very great depth, and whose smallness mirrors the small things in the phenomenal world that are large with implication when they are well seen, a silence and secrecy of nocturnal creatures and the wondrousness not of their going but (a beautiful effect of grammar and syntax) of their being there, gone—in the presence of their absence—occur, one would say, at a limit of the world: not in another world but wherever it is one enters by arriving before the light. The near-repetition of the first line in the last, a musical return with variation, moves from the commonsense practical world in which, if you want to see deer feeding, you have to catch them early, to a kind of ontological wisdom about 'anticipating the dawn'.

The mystery does not lead, of course, to God, and Tomlinson's poetry has an intriguing way of indicating as much. Whereas numerous poets, . . . are concerned with the invisible, Tomlinson's concern is with the unseen. The invisible implies mysterious reaches behind or beyond the phenomenal world; the unseen surrounds a movement of penetration into the phenomenal ('To see', says 'The Poet as Painter', 'was also to see *within*') with an awareness of the no less mysterious distances that belong to the world itself, where unseen objects in their infinity continue in being and sustain one.

The physical world is a 'mystery bodied'; it is also a threshold, or it contains thresholds. They are the entry to the reflected world (in **'Below Tintern'**), and they also offer to usher one into the world's possibility, into its change. In **'Departure'**, also from *The Shaft,* the point where a brook disappears under a bridge-arch is described as a 'place of perpetual threshold'. As an 'image of perfection' it is poised between 'gloom and gold', and so between the dark and the light, between suffering and gladness, death and life. (For these opposites of experience the earlier poetry too devised alliterative antitheses, such as 'village graves / and village green', 'delight and death'). Again the poem may be read in two ways. According to the first, the instant is supreme because it precedes the exhilarating issuing-out of the stream into the daylight, so that in 'reflecting nothing but sun' the waters pass by the threshold and celebrate the everyday real; they overcome the gloom, while nevertheless acknowledging, since they are 'Tasseling and torn', the wound in the world's condition. The other reading, however, would say that 'it is here / That I like best' because the place and moment appeal to 'Thought', the glimpser of possibility, which finds in this 'perpetual' threshold and in the disappearance of the waters the hope, the idea, of one's emerging to a light somehow free of the contradiction. 'Nothing but sun' both salutes the all-conquering sun which supersedes this moment (this is the volume that contains the poem **'De Sole'**) and regrets that it is 'nothing but' the sun. A third reading would embrace the other two, and is presumably the poem's wisdom.

There is a theme of the threshold in Tomlinson, where one might not expect it, as there is in Bonnefoy, where one does. And, again as with Bonnefoy, doesn't the world in Tomlinson's poetry give ultimately on to death? In a radio interview of early 1984, having said: 'one does feel at the corners of what one is doing there are openings into a world beyond oneself, into a world of mystery', he went on to describe, as the ground that he shares with religion or the religious instinct, 'this area of the world which is waiting for admission, which is beyond the immediate circle, which is sometimes beyond the human, which is often subtly interwoven with one's sense of death'. Why death? Partly, no doubt, because death is the most mysterious of the mysteries. Is another reason, however, that death is where the world might change beyond itself—is the way to that change—so that one's awareness of the possible involves inevitably, though perhaps only gradually, a sense of death?

Death is a turning from the sun, and since the earth at night makes just that move, with it we enter, according to **'After a Death'**, 'the whole / Reverted side of things'. The poem is from *The Way In,* a title that deepens at this point, and is actually concerned with a moon just visible in the daytime. It closes a sequence, however, **'Under the Moon's Reign'**, whose first poem seems to explore that nocturnal reversion, in which each sign is 'transformed' and the heavens are no less than 'transfigured'. The moon reigns in a world of 'lightning' in darkness, of dream, of the closeness yet otherness of animal life, and finally of death: a world remade on the far side of this one. Even here, though, Tomlinson will not allow that the 'miracle', as he agrees to call it, is performed from elsewhere, in excess of human perception and the reality of place; with the result that the 'perfection of the scene' (of the seen) is only 'momentary'. The night-world is flooded with the imagination, but is no more than a glimpse of the death and transfiguration of the daylight world.

According to **'After a Death'**, moreover, to 'read' the world's reverse would require a special 'sense', which I take to mean that it is the body that must sense a world passed beyond death, but with a sense that we do not possess. Here is part of a later probing:

> Mindful of your death, I hear the leap
>   At life in the *resurrexit* of Bruckner's mass:
> For, there, your hope towers whole:
>   Within a body one cannot see, it climbs
> That spaceless space, the ear's
>   Chief mystery and mind's, that probes to know
> What sense might feel, could it outgo
>   Its own destruction.
>
> **('For Miriam'**, *The Flood*)

'A body one cannot see': the mysterious substance of music is surely being offered as a way of imagining a body that has been through death, its sounds seemingly on the edge of sensing what a resurrected body might sense. Music here is the analogy, in Christian terms, of a 'spiritual body', and is, at least in that comma-enclosed 'there', a genuine 'hope' of resurrection. In this startling passage, the Rilkean equation to which Tomlinson has turned many times, 'song is being', is reinterpreted to suggest that music reaches for being through and beyond the dissolution of the body, by being itself an indissoluble body. Not surprisingly, in that light, music becomes the 'chief' mystery of the mind as well as of the ear. The poem, to be sure, moves on, but it has paused on that thought.

If, as a way of reading Tomlinson, this sounds improbable, consider an even more recent poem, **'Crossing Brooklyn Ferry'** in *Notes from New York*. It begins:

> To cross a ferry that is no longer there,
> The eye must pilot you to the farther shore:
> It travels the distance instantaneously
> And time also: the stakes that you can see
> Raggedly jettying into nothingness . . .

Again like Bonnefoy, Tomlinson, one realises, has his ferryman. And the Charon to pilot one to that farther shore, to the *ulterior ripa* of death, is, of all things, the organ most prominent in his poetry, the eye itself. The mere looking across to the opposite bank of a river where there used to be a ferry has been transfigured into a journey of the mind, via another of the senses, into death. The crossing has been demythologised, and placed in the real New York of Whitman, but the seeing eye has also become visionary. (Part of what is involved here is a right use of the body. 'The Poet as Painter' declares: 'by trusting to sensation, we enter being'.) As a poem about the eye's mysterious traffic with death, **'Crossing Brooklyn Ferry'** sends back intimations of meaning to the earlier poems about seeing, and persuades one that 'mystical', though certainly unexpected, might not be too inaccurate a description of Tomlinson's writing, as indeed of his graphics.

There would be many things to say of Tomlinson's graphics: they seem to me among the most powerful visual images recently produced in England, though, like the radically innovative major influences on them, they are largely ignored. As seeings and believings, they are arguably the quintessence of his poetry. Their mysteriousness clearly borders the mystical (a comment he has made on a critical moment in his struggling with paint: 'I saw black become dazzling', takes one to the famous oxymoron in Vaughan's 'The Night': a 'deep, but dazzling darkness'); while a description, also in 'The Poet as Painter', of his decalcomania-collage 'The Sleep of Animals' leads vertiginously to death, and seemingly to a depth of all his graphic work: 'two skulls are filled by a dream of the landscapes the bird and animal presences have been moving through. The dream articulates the darkness. I try to suggest a whole in world in each head. There is the hint that this sleep is, perhaps, death in which both the head and nature are now one.' Death is where the mind and the mystery bodied over against one enter each other through a process of visionary change.

Tomlinson's art, his mysticism (as it were) of the real, is 'a sort of religion', though at a deliberate distance from Christianity. Another implication of 'seeing is believing' is, after all, that what constitutes belief is not faith in God but a certain quality of sight; and he has presented himself, with an unusual absence of reticence and in a context charged with human loss and theological drama (**'For Miriam'**), as 'I / A pagan'. Not Christian, his poetry is not secular either.

Only if one recognises this can one learn the lesson of his precision, his scrupulousness. He draws back from tran-scendence (perhaps through hesitation, suspicion, rather than rejection), and from a transformation of the world, for the sake of discovering the world as a kind of permanent possibility of becoming, a continuous creation—but not through fear of exceeding the verifiable: why should an opposite bank, after all, be 'the farther shore'? He probes, with intense alertness and honesty to experience, and where he does not know, he does not conclude. A Christian might argue that it is easier to write convincingly about, for instance, being sustained by the 'giant palm' of nature (**'The Hill'**, *American Scenes*) than by the 'everlasting arms' of God; he might want to reverse Tomlinson's dictum another way, and claim that believing is seeing, since to see fully one must first believe. Yet Tomlinson's exigence remains, as an invitation, not to stick to the facts but to reverence the real.

Coventry Patmore asserted, moreover: 'All realities will sing, nothing else will', and it is to the singing of the real, and indeed of fact, that Tomlinson returns one. When Ruskin writes in *Modern Painters,* quaintly it may now seem, of the 'truth of clouds', the 'truth of vegetation'; when Coleridge notes that the 'trout leaping in the sunshine spreads on the bottom of the river concentric circles of light'; when Tomlinson himself remarks, in the **'Ode to Arnold Schoenberg'** (*A Peopled Landscape*), that as the wind ruffles the water beneath a willow the 'swayed mirror/half-dissolves/and the reflection/yields to reflected light', one is persuaded how much there is to notice in the world, how capable of delighting even bare notations are, when they have their own fineness, and how just is a certain realism; and one is persuaded that a clear sighting of what is there, of what occurs, can be (can be) a form of worship. Tomlinson's poetry is a renewal both in its mystery and in its clarity; its vision is a clairvoyance—neither an inert looking nor a *voyance* but a sight that is a quite overwhelming insight.

Donald Wesling (essay date 1988)

SOURCE: "Process and Closure in Tomlinson's Prose Poems," in *Charles Tomlinson: Man and Artist,* edited by Kathleen O'Gorman, University of Missouri Press, 1988, pp. 125-34.

[*In the following essay, Wesling analyzes Tomlinson's experiments with the prose poem, maintaining that they "must serve in the end to reinforce one's belief that he is after all a traditional poet."*]

The prose poem has not been favored by English poets, perhaps because of the prestige and unquestioned greatness of their national tradition of line and rhyme. Those who with Charles Tomlinson have experimented with the prose poem, like Roy Fisher and Geoffrey Hill, have been a shade more internationalist in outlook, open to certain formal possibilities from France and America. Tomlinson himself has written only eight prose poems, all of them grouped in the section called **"Processes"** in *The Way of a World* (1969). The longish and very fine text titled

"Prose Poem," from *The Shaft* (1978), is in lines and rhymes and makes such a unique, separate case—teasingly defining prose as a subject matter and not as a kind of notational style—that I reserve it for last. My brief for the eight poems called **"Processes"** is that Tomlinson, admiring chance effects but not abandon, experiments with extreme caution, refusing to be drawn toward the form's anarchic possibilities. The difference between his themes and methods in the prose poems and in his other poems is minimal, though by no means trivial. That difference could not fail to be significant to someone who, both poet and graphic artist, has spent upward of thirty-five years practicing the sister arts of *line*.

A reading of Tomlinson's prose poems—texts in that hermaphroditic and avant-garde format—must serve in the end to reinforce one's belief that he is after all a traditional poet. He is traditional in the way of the painter Constable, whom he admires, accepting the evidences of perception, loving the world's physical presences, and trusting that the artist's materials (word, pigment) can graph what's seen and felt. The notation of the work of art would be, for him, accurate to the way of a world, and also public; no accuracy but one that is communicable. The hygiene of "deconstruction" is not unknown to him, with its privileging of ideas of absence, indeterminacy, the text as a "galaxy of signifiers" (Roland Barthes), but Tomlinson is after all British, midlands British—incorrigibly perception-based, an artist who watches climate and landscape with the kind of charged perception that, he once said (quoting Kafka), catches a glimpse of things as they may have been before they show themselves to the observer. Tomlinson's attraction to notions of absence and chance, to the deconstructing and dispersing maneuvers of the international avant-garde, is always chastened by his fact-noticing Englishness.

For this reason we often see him in dialogue with Stéphane Mallarmé, the strong deconstructive poet whose works precede by generations the philosophical deconstruction of Martin Heidegger, Jacques Derrida, and Paul de Man. There is an **"Homage and Valediction"** to Mallarmé, along with Laforgue and Eliot, in the six-part poem **"Antecedents"** in *Seeing Is Believing* (1960); and the title of one of Tomlinson's drawings of a seashell, dated 11 October 1968, is "Débat avec Mallarmé." More to the point here, the first and to my mind the most considerable of his prose poems in the Processes section is **"Oppositions: debate with Mallarmé"**:

The poet must rescue etymology from among the footnotes, thus moving up into the body of the text, "*cipher*: the Sanskrit word *sunya* derived from the root *svi*, to swell."

To cipher is to turn the thought word into flesh. And hence "the body of the text" derives its substance.

The master who disappeared, taking with him into the echo-chamber the ptyx which the Styx must replenish, has left the room so empty you would take it for fullness.

Solitude charges the house. If all is mist beyond it, the island of daily objects within becomes clarified.

Mistlines flow slowly in, filling the land's declivity that lay unseen until that indistinctness had acknowledged them.

If the skull is a memento mori, it is also a room, whose contained space is wordlessly resonant with the steps that might cross it, to command the vista out of its empty eyes.

Nakedness can appear as the vestment of space that separates four walls, the flesh as certain then and as transitory as the world it shares.

The mind is a hunter of forms, binding itself, in a world that must decay, to present substance.

Skull and shell, both are helmeted, both reconcile vacancy with its opposite. *Abolis bibelots d'inanité sonore.* Intimate presences of silent plenitude.

There are nine verset-like parts, six of them fully equivalent to a single sentence. The third and the ninth versets refer to Mallarmé, to whose sonnet, "Ses purs ongles très haut dédiant leur onyx," Tomlinson's poem is a reply. Mallarmé there conjures an empty room (second quatrain);

> nul ptyx,
> Aboli bibelot d'inanité sonore
> (Car le Maître est alle puiser des pleurs au Styx
> Avec ce seul objet dont le Néant s'honore.)
> [no ptyx,
> Abolished bibelot of sounding inanity
> (For the Master is gone to draw tears from the Styx
> With this sole object which Nothingness honours.)]

For Tomlinson, who was drawing skulls and shells in profusion at just this time of his debate-poem in 1968-1969, such hollow objects are, and are occasions for, reconciliations of outer and inner, presence and absence. Tomlinson's lightly joking use of converging words, *ptyx* and *Styx,* suggests another kind of reconciliation—rhyme forcing a strained semantic connection even in a prose poem, even when one of the terms is a neologism and the other an archaism.

The poem proceeds from a manifesto (verses 1-3) to instances of the union in the art-object of absence and presence (4-7), to a generalizing statement (8) and a direct rebuttal of Mallarmé's sentence fragment in French by Tomlinson's in English (9). Tomlinson arranges this argument-by-juxtaposition so as to have the last word himself, but Mallarmé's assertion of a sounding inanity, a Nothingness, is not treated by Tomlinson with irony, merely contradicted with severe insistence. The mingling of assertion and example is Tomlinson's way to defend (by speaking) the silent plenitude of such natural yet artful objects. His defense of presences in the final sentence is foreshadowed by a rhetoric of body and substance in all the earlier versets, but especially, I should say, in the pun on *present* both as a transitive verb meaning "give" and as an adjective meaning "immediate" (verset 8). This doubling effect, putting into doubt etymology and phonology, would not function in a metered poem, where relative stress on first or second syllable would tell the reader how to sound and therefore how definitively to interpret the word. The prose poem preserves the several meanings and thus, in this instance, actually comprises more meaning than a metered poem.

Charles Tomlinson shows himself convinced, for this poem anyway, that the world means, means well, and means through a linguistic sign so thoroughly motivated that its cipher can "turn the thought word into flesh" (verset 2). Ferdinand de Saussure and Jacques Derrida and I might take Mallarmé's side in the debate, in order to resist Tomlinson's defiant Cratylism, his hope, with its emblem the Sanskrit root, to charge the word with so much presence it actually protrudes toward the noticer. The poet seems positively to have encouraged such dissent by setting the poem up to make debating points—by pronouncing on the way of a world, his world. He does this often, too, in his line and rhyme poems, stating how the world is, but the prose poems seem to accept this argumentative, point-making approach somewhat more easily. (The exception, to my mind, is the last of the eight, **"A Process,"** which has a higher proportion of declaration to image than **"Oppositions."**) Sometimes, with Tomlinson, the reader wants to resist being told how the world is; what "we" see, feel, know can be finicky, coercive to a degree; manifestoes of seeing seem to take over to persuade the reader that perception is a profound and not altogether helpless form of moral cognition. But without these continuous, really rather unobtrusive injunctions to see! feel! know! our perceptions, Tomlinson would be a landscapist pure and meek. The injunctions are part of his whole effort as a writer, and hence his admiration for Ruskin; only when the injunctions begin to out-number the famous Tomlinsonian "instances" of charged perception on which they depend do they seem preacherly. The poem **"Oppositions"** is not, to my mind, coercive—rather argumentative and emphatic, in order to prepare the reader to receive the seven other poems in the section called **"Processes."**

These poems are processes because, like all prose poems, they foreground a structuring principle in post-romantic poetry that may tend to recede from view in verse-formats, namely, sequence itself, the reader's sense that the text is a narrative of consciousness and of grammar. The eighth and last of these is called **"A Process"** and states aesthetic principles of continuous change, walking boundaries to "lay claim to them, knowing all they exclude"— a process in the sense of a trial (French *procès*), a proceeding, a test of how something can be a "complication and . . . unravelling." The beginnings of such experimental works have, Tomlinson says here, "to be invented"; and the ends, he claims, are indeterminate, openings-out rather than terminations:

> A process; procession; trial.
>   . . . . .
> Its perfect accompaniment would be that speech of islanders, in which, we are told, the sentence is never

certainly brought to an end, its aim less to record with completeness the impression an event makes, than to mark its successive aspects as they catch the eye, the ear of the speaker.

That would be the verbal equivalent of the method of decalcomania Tomlinson had begun to experiment with in the late 1960s, black gouache spread unevenly on a glossy white sheet, covered with a sheet that is then removed slowly. That was his phase of the created chance, the unpredictable, the exploratory, but Tomlinson next covered his decalcomanias with masking sheets with windows scissored in them. He wrote in a letter to Octavio Paz, "Scissors! Here was the instrument of choice. I found I could draw with scissors, reacting *with* and *against* the decalcomania." As maker of prose poems and decalcomanias, Tomlinson's habit seems to have been to open his creative process to effects of chance, but always to round off the work by an explicit return to choice for the purpose of making a finished pattern.

Tomlinson's endings are not usually as forensic and emphatic as the one on **"Oppositions,"** but he does employ syntax and allusion to create maximal closure. The prose poem entitled **"Poem"** has six sentences, the first of which ends on an ellipse as if incomplete:

> The muscles which move the eyeballs, we are told, derive from a musculature which once occupied the body end to end.

And the last sentence, describing (as so often elsewhere in the prose poems and the lined poems) the interpenetration of outer and inner, perception and cognition, picks up, elaborates, and completes the first sentence:

> So that "over there" and "in here" compound a truce neither signed—a truce that, insensibly and categorically, grows to a decree, and what one hoped for and what one is, must measure themselves against those demands which the eye receives, delivering its writ on us through a musculature which occupies the body end to end.

In between the opening supposition and the closing declaration come the confirming Tomlinsonian instances of perception, sentences so stout and fine they help the reader accept what is to be declared. ("Sunblaze as day goes, and the light blots back the scene to iris the half-shut lashes.") The poem **"Autumn"** deals with a seasonal truce, a moment of poise before winter wins out over life and color; that poem ends as it has proceeded, with abrupt answer rephrasing abrupt question:

> There will be a truce, but not the truce of the rime with the oak leaf, the mist with the alders, the rust with the sorrel stalk or of the flute with cold.
> It will endure? It will endure as long as the frost.

"Tout Entouré De Mon Regard" deals with another truce, the one between what the glance can take in and the sustaining and balancing "darkness behind you," and the closure is emphatic by means of image, not statement:

> To see, is to feel at your back this domain of a circle
> whose power consists in evading and refusing to be
> completed by you.
> It is infinity sustains you on its immeasurable palm.

That, as in all Tomlinson, is a secular infinity, an infinity of possible perceptions like the one the poet approves in his epigraph from Jorge Guillén, which in my rough translation reads, "And the present gives so much / That the walking foot feels / The wholeness of the world." Presenced perception is the content, strong closure the method of these eight prose poems—different and dovetailing expressions of an optimism that human nature and outer nature have a vital relationship before language, and, fortunately for poetry, in language.

The prose poems are the second last section in *The Way of a World*. The last section contains two lined poems, as if to assert a larger closure that will place a final bracket around the less regular prose poems. **"The Chances of Rhyme"** and **"The End"** are not only in a section called coda but also in the very process of letting

> him know
> Who reads his time by the way books go,
> Each instant will bewry his symmetries.
>
> ("**The End**")

The two poems are also rich with closural allusions and ornate effects of terminal rhyme. While diminishing art's little subendings, in theory, such poems play them for all they are worth. So we may find a special caution in Tomlinson's writing and deployment of his prose poems. Though his sentences are ingenious and eventful, he refuses to explore the furthest limits of English sentence structure. Though his narratives of consciousness are exploratory, especially in their instance-packed middles, he is not a poet of the irrational leap, the dream-logic that flashes unrelated images in sequence. His attitude is teacherly or lawyerly, not bardic; his rhythms are typically choppy, with short paragraphs and abrupt turns.

A certain uneasiness with the rhapsodic possibility of the form is hinted like a countercurrent in one of the prose poems, **"Skullshapes,"** when Tomlinson writes,

> The skull of nature is recess and volume. The skull
> of art—of possibility—is recess, volume and also
> lines—lines of containment, lines of extension.

Perhaps containment is slightly preferred to extension? In lines of verse the containment is more certain, or at least more obvious.

Thus the assumptions of **"Prose Poem,"** Tomlinson's sendup or skirting of the whole issue, are not entirely playful. The poem, written a decade after the **"Processes"** section, is a philosophical narrative of opening a century-old apothecary's jar. This story the poet has set out in thirty-nine lines with admirably unpredictable rhymes:

> What had to be done
> If we were to undo it, was to pass
> A silk cord round the collar of glass
> And rub it warm—but this friction
> Must be swift enough not to conduct its heat
> Inside—the best protection against which
> (Only a third hand can ensure this feat)
> Is a cube of ice on top of the stopper.

The jar is presented from the poem's beginning as an example of an unresolved issue in aesthetics: in what sense are the useful arts art? In the poem, this is transposed into a question about prose and poetry: can prose be for contemplation, poetry for use, thus upsetting a traditional hierarchy? By showing the poem's first and last lines we can see how Tomlinson avoids resolving this issue by keeping the terms *use* and *contemplation* equal in value, privileging neither:

> If objects are of two kinds—those
> That we contemplate and, the remainder, use,
> I am unsure whether its poetry or prose
> First drew us to this jar . . .
>
> . . . . .
>
> There is one sole lack
> Now that jar and stopper are in right relation—
> An identifiable aroma: what we must do
> Is to fill it with coffee, for use, scent and
> contemplation.

The bottle on opening is put to ear and gives, the poet says, "a low, crystalline roar" that is neither seashell murmur nor emptiness, but "so full of electric imponderables, it could compare / Only with the molecular stealth when the jar / Had breathed."

Here the jar is personified ("breathed") but also, giving sound, made an analogue for poetry, made worthy of contemplation, though earlier it had been presented as sealed off, a product: "Its cylinder of glass, / Perfectly seamless, has the finality and satisfaction / Of the achieved act of an artisan." Plainly Tomlinson admires objects, including poems, that deconstruct the opposition between using and contemplating, artisan-work and poetic art. His title-term, **"Prose Poem,"** and the beginning and ending of the poem keep the uncertainty from being resolved on one side or the other.

However, there is provocation in giving this title to a poem in this format, as if the poet is faintly parodying those others, including his own earlier self, who might reserve the term for a specific formal procedure, a notation of justified margins (though with an aura, it may be, of a nonlogical sequence of images). If my earlier readings are correct, this poem's disjunction between title and format is the obverse procedure from the processes in *The Way of a World,* where prose poems follow the narrative of consciousness of emphatic closure one usually sees in the line-and-rhyme tradition in English lyric. We may conclude that line-and-rhyme, or verse as such, has no special privilege for Tomlinson, and no special subject-matter; his works share in the era's stylistic pluralism and its democracy of subject. What he privileges, instead, is "the finality and satisfaction / Of the achieved art of an artisan." Accordingly he has written few prose poems and those of maximal closure. His experiments are done with carefully polished and calibrated instruments.

Michael Kirkham   (essay date 1988)

SOURCE: "An Agnostic's Grace," in *Charles Tomlinson: Man and Artist,* edited by Kathleen O'Gorman, University of Missouri Press, 1988, pp. 153-81.

[*In the following essay, Kirkham explores the ways in which Tomlinson's more recent poetry modifies and extends the themes of his earlier poetry.*]

The evolution of Tomlinson's poetry has been gradual, organic, involving modifications and extensions but no disavowals of his past work. There have been changes over the years, but, as Tomlinson himself said to Michael Schmidt in 1977, "The underlying continuity remains the important thing."

In the late fifties, aspects of his work that caught the eye of contemporary readers were those contrasting most sharply on the one hand with the neo-romanticism of Dylan Thomas and on the other hand with the new "realism" of Philip Larkin (a marriage, rather, of "faithful and disappointing" realism with its complement, a disappointed romanticism). Tomlinson was evidently neither a romantic nor a defeated, reductive realist. His earliest poems conducted a polemic against the romanticism of the forties. Early influences in the formation of his personal style were the clean line and phrasing of the American modernists—Pound, Stevens, Moore, and later Williams—and the reasoned structures, civilities, and conceptual diction of the eighteenth-century English poets. Linguistic restraint, the ordering of confusion, and the moderation of expectations, submission of the eye to the objective world and of the mind to a consciousness of natural limits: a literary regimen of chastening, corrective severity was what these poems recommended and demonstrated. It was not, as we shall see, the complete picture. As for realism, if Larkin's theme was the disparity between reality and desire, Tomlinson's was plainly not self and its emotions at all but the reality that exceeds and includes man, the reality of nature and, it became clearer in the sixties, of history and of man's accommodations with history. He chose to measure the scope of being rather than to trace "the graph of pain"— a revealing phrase of the early seventies ("**Melody**"). It would no doubt be nearer the truth to say that this subject matter chose him, that it also signaled his conscious repudiation of the literary milieu for which Larkin became the unofficial laureate.

Tomlinson dared to be positive, and his voice carried what was in the fifties an unfamiliar note of authority. In "**A Meditation on John Constable**" he commends in the

painter "the labour of observation"; his own poetry has the same scrupulous respect for facts, but we are not allowed to forget that art is observation infused with "passion," that in effect "delight / Describes" ("**A Meditation on John Constable**"). In a later declaration this claim for art is strengthened and extended: "man / In an exterior, tutelary spirit / Of his own inheritance, speaks / To celebrate" ("**Movements V,**"). Yet this version articulates an instinct or conviction that has informed Tomlinson's work from the beginning. Neither romantic nor realist, he combines an Augustan vigor of mind with, say, Hopkins's passionate interest in sense experience rendered in a muscular, kinaesthetic language. For Tomlinson poetry was—and is— an exploration by the senses and the mind of the world before them. Though his poetic terrain has been primarily sense experience, his aim was not—the contrast I have in mind is the early poetry of Ted Hughes—immersion in sensation, the illusion of the "thing itself," but investigation of the world perceived and of the act of perception. The bias of his interest was and has remained evaluative: not mere seeing but seeing that is believing, right seeing, is his theme. The realms of aesthetics and ethics here border on each other: accuracy of eye and ear, which lies in the proper relations of foreground to background, part to whole, usually implies also in these poems the tempering of emotion to its object and the clarity and impartiality of the judicious mind. It is, in a word, normative poetry: it seeks to define norms of sensory perception, of feeling and thinking—ultimately of human dwelling, as when, in "**At Holwell Farm**" admiration of the handsome farmhouse includes appreciation of the humanity expressed in the building of it:

> this farm
> Also a house, this house a dwelling.
> Rooted in more than earth, to dwell
> Is to discern the Eden image, to grasp
> In a given place and guard it well
> Shielded in stone.

The phenomenal world, the reality of place, landscape, and weather, dominates *The Necklace* (1955) and *Seeing Is Believing* (1958, 1960). It kept its central position in Tomlinson's poetry of the next decade, and indeed it is the primary concern of all his work; but it is probably true to say that the processes of time and history, which received some attention in the fifties in such poems as "**On the Hall at Stowey**" figure more prominently in the three volumes he published during the sixties. "**John Maydew**" and "**Up at La Serra**" are notable examples in *A Peopled Landscape* (1963). In *American Scenes* (1966), "**The Snow Fences**" "**Arizona Desert**" and "**The Well**" are diverse treatments of man's "negotiations" with time. As well as "**Prometheus**" and "**Assassin**" poems about time, history, and revolutionary attitudes, *The Way of a World* (1969) contains "**In the Fullness of Time,**" Tomlinson's tribute to "the beauty of succession" and his "consent to time."

If my description of his early anti-romanticism suggests that in the fifties Tomlinson barricaded himself behind the ramparts of a defensive neo-Classicism, I have given a false impression. There was nothing defensive about it. "Moderation of expectations" was one phrase I used; but it is the poetic principle in question that might be less misleadingly defined as the measuring of expectations by the yardstick of both the actual *and* the possible. I also said, trying to avoid the limiting, doctrinaire impossible. I also said, trying to avoid the limiting, doctrinaire implications of a label like "objectivism," that "he chose to measure [what cannot be measured] the scope of being." In this and the amended definition, I am suggesting that "measure" (measurement *and* moderation) is practiced in the interest of liberation, not constraint. The measuring eye in **"Ponte Veneziano," "Stripping the vista to its depth,"** and in **"Tramontana at Lerici"** the mind that threatens the sentimental imprecision of "politicians and romantics" with a "clarity" and sharpness of "definition" "that could cut like steel," are also the perceiving intelligence that in the former poem "broods on the further light" and, having stripped the vista to its depth, tunnels into prospects beyond. In different versions, this image of the penetrant mind that uses keenness of sensory perception as a tool of the prospecting imagination recurs in poems of the sixties and seventies. "How it happened," the poem that closes the sequence of **"Four Kantian Lyrics,"** ends,

> no absolute of eye can tell
> the utmost, but the glance
> goes shafted from us like a well.

This in turn looks forward to **"The Well"** in *American Scenes* and **"The Shaft,"** the title poem of a recent volume. The note of praise and celebration, when it is sounded, is clearer and more confident in the last gathering of the sixties, *The Way of a World*; some titles are sufficiently revealing: **"Eden," "Adam,"** and **"Night Transfigured"**. The tendency signified by these titles finds an echo, ten years later, in a title that Tomlinson also adopts as his heading for a group of poems, "In Arden." *The Shaft* (1978), where the poem appears, groups its contents into five categories. They are, though not in this order, Seasons, Histories, Perfections, In Arden, and Bagatelles. The difference between images of perfection and Arden is touched on in that poem's opening line, "Arden is not Eden, but Eden's rhyme," and elaborated in the body of the poem.

In the collections of the seventies there is much that is familiar to the reader of Tomlinson; themes are not repeated, however, but renewed, refreshed. A subsidiary theme of **"Snow Signs,"** for example, is the complementary relationship of contraries. Snow that has retreated in thin lines and dots and, with "Touched-in contour and chalk-followed fold," "has left its own white geometry / To measure out for the eye the way / The land may lie," discovers what otherwise would be missed, "the fortuitous / Full variety a hillside spreads for us." The simplification of geometry sharpens the eye's sense of the scene's complexity, and the satisfaction of measurement, of taking mental possession by that means, enhances appreciation of what measurement leaves out, the illimitable, indefinable, unpredictable fullness and variety in what the eye sees. It is essentially the same surprising conjuction of the analytic

eye-and-mind and the questing imagination illustrated in the previous paragraph from **"Ponte Veneziano,"** or, to recall **"A Meditation on John Constable,"** of observation and delight. It seems a paradox that the measuring eye and the impartial mind should serve the motive of celebration.

In **"Snow Signs"** a large portion of his visual experience is, so to speak, reassembled; it is not a repetition but a reordering prompted by the stimulus of new particulars. The following passage refashions and lines up into a sequence thoughts about the interaction of subject and object that have been divided among many previous poems:

> Walking, we waken these at every turn,
> Waken ourselves, so that our walking seems
>   To rouse some massive sleeper out of winter
>   dreams
> Whose stretching startles the whole land into life,
>   As if it were us the cold, keen signs were
>   seeking
> To pleasure and remeasure, repossess
>   With a sense in the gathered coldness of heat
>   and
> height.

Looking discovers features unnoticed before; in turn the act of discovering, which is a kind of wakening or regeneration, wakens us, the onlookers, to new life. The increase of alertness and awareness is an intensification and expansion of self, as the poet's images and wordplay ("walking . . . waken") accentuate the reciprocal action. One could trace numerous connections between this and earlier poems. The "wakening" image, for instance, takes us back to the very early **"Poem,"** the only piece to be rescued from *Relations and Contraries,* a volume of youthful experiments, for inclusion in *Collected Poems* (1985). These lines also give a less emphatic, less epigrammatic rendering of "What he saw / Discovered what he was" ("**A Meditation on John Constable**"). Tomlinson's language has remained unashamedly intellectual, but where the style of the Constable poem, and of *Seeing Is Believing* generally, is formal, public, and favors the sculptured symmetries of ordered thinking, that of **"Snow Signs"**—and this makes it representative of his later verse—is, for all its careful elaboration and intricacy of syntax, nearer to a flowing speech. It is noticeable that a lighter wordplay replaces epigram, so that, for example, "Waken ourselves" does not so much stand in logical and paradoxical antithesis to the first "waken" as modify it, absorbing the potential contrast and transferring attention to the unity—it is almost interchangeability—of perceiver and perceived.

The next stage in the sequence is that, wakening and being awakened, we therefore seem to rouse a whole landscape from its winter sleep, and a few lines later the words "transfigured" and "resurrection" appear. But the poem leaves no doubt about the meaning of those words: they convey facts, the facts at once of an objective world and of subjective response. The vocabulary of religion is used to articulate the transformations of the imagination, and imagination is not for Tomlinson, as it was for Coleridge, an intermediary between the temporal and the eternal, the human and the divine, but the faculty that brings to what the senses perceive here and now an inner sense of its contrary. What is present is thereby complemented by what is absent, the visible by the invisible (meaning only what is not apparent): fact is completed by imagination to create a *whole* composed of what is and is not immediately apprehensible. The apprehension of wholeness, wholeness of vision, is Tomlinson's delight and purpose.

What is not-self, the reality of objects, is primary in Tomlinson's thought, but it is the relationship, the interchange, between self and not-self, subject and object—especially so in his later poetry—that receives the main emphasis. The insistence in the early poetry on the irreducible otherness of objects, the stubborn separateness of facts, a sense of things that has remained integral to Tomlinson's work, was nevertheless a tactical insistence in response to the provocation of a neo-romantic subjectivist poetic. In the later poetry there is perhaps a more acute sense that the double awareness constitutes a paradox: it creates an exhilarating tension between two ways of seeing the world—as simultaneously having an independent existence and depending on the observer for its meaning. The visible world as it is presented in "At the Edge" seethes with various interests for itself and for what it implies that is not visible:

> Edges are centres: once you have found
>   Their lines of force, the least of gossamers
> Leads and frees you, nets you a universe
>   Whose iridescent weave shines true
> Because you see it, but whose centre is not you. . . .

The contraries of self and not-self entail others: the apparent and the hidden, the part and the whole, contraries that are in fact complementarities in that they are mutually exclusive view-points and yet both true. Each polarity expresses the same paradox, that the world has its center simultaneously (not alternately) inside and outside the perceiver; edges are centers for the viewer, but they do not cease to be edges too, and the world's center is not you—the netted universe is private and common, particular and general.

The double focus in Tomlinson's poetry on the thing itself and on the whole of which it is a part or a sign is reflected in the "sensuous abstraction" of the language, a quality of the French language he has said in an interview with Michael Schmidt that he envies. It is also a notable quality of Augustan verse; "Condemned to Hope's delusive mine," the first line of Johnson's "On the Death of Dr. Robert Levet," is a memorable example. **"Foxes' Moon,"** which studies the transformation by moonlight of quotidian existence, "England's interrupted pastoral," and assimilates the disparity between the two Englands to the incongruity of the fox's night world with the adjacent human world ("These / Are the fox hours cleansed / Of all the meanings we can use . . ."), illustrates this quality of Tomlinson's language:

> The shapes of dusk
> Take on an edge, refined

> By a drying wind and foxes bring
>   Flint hearts and sharpened senses to
> This desolation of grisaille in which the dew
>   Grows clearer, colder.

The imagery, factual and figurative, is precisely, incisively sensuous, but even in the thought-connections that link "edge," "refined," "drying," "flint," "sharpened," and "grows clearer, colder," the control of the abstracting mind is evident; it becomes conspicuous in "this desolution of grisaille." The juxtaposition of the fact and its interpretation is more striking a few lines later:

>   they nose
> The garbage of the yards, move through
> The *white displacement* of a daily view
> Uninterrupted.
>
>   [Kinkham's Italics]

Representing the poetic search, in **"Movements II,"** as a "Grasping for more than the bare facts warranted," Tomlinson might easily be naming the motivating principle in a language of "sensuous abstraction." We might link it, also, to another image in **"At the Edge."** Watching the movements of a wren darting in and out of its hole, "It made me," he remarks of its visible energy, "measure all the force unspied / That stirred inside that bank." The extension of the concrete into the abstract is a similar leap of imagination, spurred by the need and the will to measure the immeasurable.

Tomlinson has always worked to incorporate in one vision the near and the far, the data of sense experience and the "something else" (**"Canal,"**) of imagination; repeatedly his poems trace a movement outward from the known to the edges of the known and just beyond   the "glance" of his poetry "goes shafted from [him] like a well." **"At the Edge"** gives us that movement in the rapid transition from a web's edge to a netted "universe"; but the delight in the "unspied," the attraction of hiddenness as such ("The offscape, the infolds, secreted / Waterholes in the boles of trees"), is, I think, a new mood, and as such it corresponds to a habit of camouflaging analogy that has become more common in his later poetry. This is difficult to illustrate without quoting extensively from a poem, so I have chosen as my example a short poem from *The Shaft,* **"The Roe Deer,"** which follows **"In Arden"** and precedes the title poem and is related in theme to both:

> We must anticipate the dawn one day,
> Crossing the long field silently to see
> The roe deer feed. Should there be snow this year
> Taking their tracks, searching their colours out,
> The dusk may help us to forestall their doubt
> And drink the quiet of their secrecy
> Before, the first light lengthening, they are gone.
> One day we must anticipate the dawn.

This has a *sotto voce* intimacy of tone that, though the voice is not the same, resembles in one respect the voice of Frost or of Edward Thomas: an undemonstrative quietness of manner that, as in their verse, is the medium chosen to convey intimations of "other meaning" than the surface one. It is as though the lowness of the voice makes audible the faint murmuring of an undervoice, which augments the overt text with a covert significance. The coexistence of the two levels can be shown best by a modified paraphrase of the poem. The roe deer partake of a secret life; to "drink the quiet of their secrecy," we must follow tracks leading in the twilight to a hidden, pre-dawn pristineness of which the deer are part and to which, in their exquisite sensitivity and alertness and delicacy of movement, they alone are privy; as, barred from Eden itself, Adam in nature's Arden "tastes [the] replenishings" of Eden's waters in springs brought underground. We must make our approach as silent as they and it are silent. We can resolve to enjoy this secret life only at a remove: the silence is easily broken, the deer easily scared away, and "they are gone" at "first light" with a quiet suddenness that suggests hallucination, as if they have no daylight existence. One could probe further and speculate whether "their doubt"— an oddly human word for animal wariness—is a transposition of a doubt felt by the poet and responsible for his hesitancy of approach to the Eden source; but I have gone far enough into the poem to bring out the reticent suggestiveness of this kind of latent analogy.

It is customary in discussions of Tomlinson's work to distinguish the poems of sense of sense experience—poems that direct attention to the natural world, to life in space— from the poems of human experience, which concentrate on the processes of time and history. The division exists, though it would be more accurate to say of the latter group that the poems are more *overtly* concerned with the human world than those of the former; for the poems that explore the perceptual world and the act of perception have human implications. "Inanimate or human, / The distinction fails," Tomlinson was able to demonstrate in **"Winter Encounters,"** a poem of the fifties; in the early seventies, **"The Witnesses,"** with its picture of "hillside woods" in summer as an "aerial city," produces the same fusion of the natural and the human. The poems I have examined so far belong, if one employs the conventional distinction, to the first category: they are primarily studies of nature and the world of perception, only indirectly or metaphorically of the human world. Yet, despite the obvious differences enshrined in the classification, there is no clear boundary between the two groups; indeed they resemble each other more than they differ, or what they have in common is of more significance than what separates them. Just as it is more important to stress continuity than change in Tomlinson's development, so it is potentially more illuminating to notice the homogeneity of his work than to distinguish its parts. His preoccupation with encounters—for example, encounters between self and not-self, the human and the non-human—is as characteristic of the one group as of the other.

Thus **"Mackinnon's Boat,"** which scrutinizes the work of two fishermen (not forgetting the dog) on a typical day's fishing, describing not only the sea itself and the light with the precise "sensuous abstraction" we should expect but also the journey out tothe site, the hauling in of the catch, the disentangling of unwanted "Crabs, urchins,

dogfish, and star," the rhythms of each task, is about "the daily dealings" of man with the nonhuman "underworld." The two environments are mutually repellent: the "flailing / Seashapes pincered to the baits" die in the air, "their breath all at once grown rare / In an atmosphere they had not known existed"; as for the dog, a solipsistic landlubber, the sea is virtually nonexistent—"he stays / Curled round on himself: his world / Ignores this waste of the in-between, / Air and rock . . . ." Only man negotiates the territory "in-between." The poem highlights on the one hand the encounter, the transaction, and on the other hand the absolute discreteness of the two realities and in particular the impenetrable otherness, inconceivable to the human mind, of the sea-world. This sea gives back not even a ragged, twisted *image* of the boat: "Black, today / The waters will have nothing to do with the shaping / Or unshaping of human things. . . . The visible sea / Remains a sullen frontier to / Its *unimaginable* fathoms" [Kirkham's italics].

Although the theme is familiar, among the "human poems" **"Mackinnon's Boat"** is in several respects a new venture. The length itself, ninety-eight lines, is unusual and makes possible an unusual expansiveness of treatment; comparison with **"On the Hall at Stowey"** would reveal in the more leisurely narrative of the later poem a greater readiness to let facts be their uninterpreted selves. The poem also extends the conception of not-self to include along with objects the impersonal world of labor. In their work the fishermen are anonymous, their anonymity corresponding to, and joining while it lasts, a reality that bears no human imprint; "making a time / Where no day has a name, the smells / Of diesel, salt, and tobacco mingle"—human purpose and pleasure, that is to say, mingle, in a temporary, evanescent blend of smells, with the salt that "at last must outsavour name and time / In the alternation of the forgetful waters." Serving a purpose beyond themselves, they are—like the separate stages in their rapid undoing, re-typing and new-baiting of the traps (and like a Tomlinson poem)— "The disparate links of [a] concerted action." Remembering the careful use of the word "articulate" in the early **"Aesthetic,"** we might adapt its statement to this context: "Reality is to be sought, not in concrete / But in [the wholeness of] space made articulate" in its parts. The self-annulment of physical labor is also a release from self into a common world. And when "Their anonymity, for a spell, / Is at an end," each one is "Free to be himself more / Sharing the rest that comes of labour," their cooperation in the impersonal task both reinvigorating their individual freedoms and renewing the human bond. The *wholeness* of this world is presented as an interdependence of realities that are unassimilably separate; the *wholesomeness* of occupying the territory between them comes of an "alternation," reproducing the ebb and flow of "the forgetful waters," of action and inaction, of journeying out from self and the human domain and returning to them.

Another new development is an adoption of the standards of wholesome living—life lived according to a proportionate, whole view of reality—to the judgment of further reaches of human action, notably in those poems Tomlinson has called **"Histories."** The most striking examples are portraits, at dramatic moments of their lives, of Charlotte Corday, assassin of Marat, and Danton, characters who played decisive parts in the French Revolution. (This kind of poem and its moral standards were anticipated in **"Assassin,"** the assassin there being Mercader, the murderer of Trotsky.) An enemy of tyranny, the selfless heroine who gave her life for others, who delivered "a faultless blow," and who at her trial and execution exhibited a "composure none could fault," Charlotte Corday had, and is represented by the poet as having, impressive "strength." Yet in terms of the poem's (Yeatsian and Lawrencian) morality, her faults ran deep: she had made a voluntary contraction of her full humanity and subjected it to an *idea*. When she came to murder "her tyrant," she saw not the man, who had "a mildness in him, even," but a Julius Caesar. She was "A girl whose reading made a heroine— / Her book was Plutarch, her republic Rome" (**"Charlotte Corday"**). She not only had lopped her feelings to fit her "whole / Intent" (a cramped wholeness!) but also, in her single-mindedness, had no clear whole view of the political situation, the outcome of which she had wished to determine—"How should she know / The Terror still to come?" Tomlinson points to the conflict in her between idealism (that is, possession by idea and ideal) and a full human responsiveness and awareness by means of one telling detail that recalls **"Assassin."** Unlike Mercader, she is that paradox, "a daggered Virtue," "innocence" directing a murderous "intent," one who, imitating the supreme sacrifice of Christ, also "believed her death would raise up France"; but, as Mercader's prepared impassivity was not proof against the sound of Trotsky's rustling papers and his animal death-cry, so the poet conjectures that her "composure" was almost breached by an unforeseen human incidental, the cry with which Catherine Marat at the trial "broke off her testimony."

"For Danton" passes the same judgment on its protagonist. Danton has invested the whole of himself in the partial satisfaction of enjoying "perfect power"—partial because in the pursuit of political power he has forfeited the "contrary perfection," receptiveness of the senses, the power of "seeings, savourings." This diagnosis of his moral sickness is inherent in the figure-ground composition of the picture: his egoism—he "thinks that he and not the river advances"—is set against the background of moral "consequence" acted out, metaphorically, in the inexorable progress of the river, an image for time and fate. The snatched pleasure of the river's "music," as he listens from the bridge's parapet, is set against "other sounds" of "past and future wrong." This proportionate way of seeing moments in a life is the human counterpart to an aesthetic of perception demonstrated everywhere in Tomlinson's poetry, but nowhere more explicitly than in **"Poem,"** the earliest piece in *Selected Poems*. Describing the sound of horses' hooves in the early morning air, it ends,

> Though space is soundless, yet creates
> From very soundlessness a ground
> To counterstress the lilting hoof fall as it breaks.

The implied standard in **"For Danton"** is a rounded life— the satisfaction of contrary impulses and their subordination to a sense of the whole of which they are part. The rounded life is also a full life, which needs for the realization of its possibilities a certain length of years. Early in his life, before leaving for the metropolis, Danton had made a choice between powers and is pictured at the end of his career paying a last visit to his birthplace. He had "Returned to this: to river, town and plain, / Walked in the fields and knew what power he'd lost," seeking, too late, to reverse that choice and to give to his unnurtured senses now "a life he has *no time* / To live" [Kirkham's italics]. Like Charlotte Corday, he has sacrificed fullness of humanity to the partiality of a conceived ambition; his will to power requiring the death of a king and her idealism requiring the assassination of Marat, their motives lie closer together than their respective histories and personalities would lead us to suspect. In both, the sacrifice of fullness requires that they voluntarily or involuntarily cut short their own lives. Of Charlotte Corday, as she approaches the scaffold, the poet asks, "What unlived life would struggle up against / Death died in the possession of such strength?" "Unlived life," in its double meaning, is Danton's tragedy too: on the one hand are tracts of personality uncultivated, of experience unexplored, on the other hand is deprival of time needed for cultivation and exploration. Time is important; life needs to be lived out: with quantity—a certain *number* of years—a certain quality of life is hardly to be achieved. "Ripeness is all" would outweigh for Tomlinson any persuasion to sacrifice.

I have been illustrating in Tomlinson's recent work the process of refocusing, modifying, and extending an already existing poetic world. Let me at this point gather together signs in the late sixties and the seventies of a slight shift in mood and approach, to which references have been scattered in the preceding paragraphs. Cumulatively they suggest that an attitude of *agnosticism* has become more prominent (agnosticism in its general sense, without specific reference to the question of religious belief, though, as we have seen in **"Snow Signs,"** it includes that). I have the impression that those words of reservation and circumspection characteristic of Tomlinson's approach to metaphor, "as if" and "seems," are a little more insistent; it is as though they are meant to draw attention to the aspect of illusion in the workings of imagination. The technique of implication rather than application of thought is one expression of this more pressing sense of the fictionality of poetry. In **"At the Edge"** I noted the delight shown in things hidden, in what cannot be *known* directly or with certainty. I would add that this corresponds to the poet's growing preoccupation with what cannot be *said* singly, firmly, unambiguously, and with how to say it. It is the theme of **"Nature Poem."** The creative confusions of perception, "this sound / Of water that is sound of leaves," "nature's stirrings and comminglings . . . recall / The way a poem flows":

> No single reading renders up complete
> Their shifting text—a poem, too, in this,
> They bring the mind half way to its defeat,
> Eluding and exceeding the place it guesses,
> Among these overlappings, half-lights, depths,
> The currents of this air, these hiddennesses.

The poet's consciousness of the obscurities and "half-lights" of experience (that elude the "guesses" of the interpreting mind and mock its rage for order and finality), which consequently tempers this aspiration to as much certainty as is reasonable with a readiness to advance hesitantly and tentatively, is, I think, related to a moderation, in such poems as **"Charlotte Corday"** and **"For Danton,"** of an earlier habitual severity of judgment. "We must have some comradeship with imperfection," says George Eliot in *Daniel Deronda,* a fastidious and judicious moralist; Tomlinson displays his comradeship in the same measure as the novelist's—only *some* comradeship, so much and no more; like her, he also has an interest in "perfections." A comparison of **"Charlotte Corday"** with the earlier **"Assassin"** would reveal an equal moral penetration, but a greater empathy enters into its delineation of human imperfection. We feel it in the question about her "unlived life." The question in the opening lines of **"For Danton"** has a similar quality: "Who is the man that stands against this bridge / And thinks that he and not the river advances?" A tone reflecting not pity but mild wonderment accompanies the firm passing of judgment. These two historical portraits only moderate their strictness: Tomlinson has not changed his colors. In the weighing of compassion and justice he is still as far from that strain of political thinking that originates in Rousseau's discussions of compassion as F. R. Leavis shows himself to be in *Nor Shall My Sword: Discourses on Pluralism, Compassion and Social Hope.*

The poems in **Seeing Is Believing** have the same manner of terse authority as their title: the tone is positive, the disciplined eye and mind take command. The poems are distinguished by their sensory and mental clarity, by their strictness of moral discrimination, and generally by the strenuous clearing of a ground of certainty in a world of lax behavior, disordered emotion, and confused understanding. A good deal of this remains in Tomlinson's later work, but it has been modified to make a place for uncertainties and confusions. In the Arden of "in-between" in which we live—the seasons of time and nature housing memories or hopes of a timeless Eden—"the contraries / Of this place are contrarily unclear: / A haze beats back the summer sheen / Into a chiaroscuro of the heat" (**"In Arden"**). For it is where the real and the possible interpenetrate and distinctions blur; "the depths of Arden's springs," supplied by underground streams from their source in Eden, "convey echoic waters—voices / Of the place that rises through this place." **"In Arden,"** on the one hand, finds a reason for celebration in this rich confusion of what is there with what is not there, the confusion of the real with the imagined. **"A Self-Portrait: David,"** on the other hand, concerned to express the same sense of double reality (to the extent of using the same form of words), is cautionary: "This is the face behind my face," expressing a truth that "puts by / The mind's imperious geometry";

> distrust
> Whatever I may do unless it show
> A startled truth as in these eyes' misgivings,
> These lips that, closed, confess "I do not know."

Celebratory or cautionary, the deepest place in these poems is where there is not finality but an open question. **"In the Balance"** sets the finality of a winter landscape after a snowfall—its photographic immobility and clarity of definition—against the questions it raises and the doubts it leaves in the observer's mind: "Will it thicken or thaw, this rawness menacing? / The sky stirs: the sky refused to say." The sky is poised between fixity and change:

> Brought to a sway, the whole day hesitates
> Through the sky of afternoon, and you beneath,
> As if questions of weather were of life and death.

"The whole day hesitates"—I think we may extract a little extra meaning out of "whole": wholeness is composed of *shifting* parts, nature is a "shifting text." If wholeness is always unpredictably rearranging itself or induces that expectation, then "you beneath," the speculative mind, must copy that hesitancy in sensitive attunement to the nature of things; and this holds true, too, for "questions . . . of life and death." Nature—likewise the nature poem—is, as we have seen, a "shifting text"; its shades and secrets "bring the mind half way to its defeat, / Eluding and exceeding the place it guesses"; and if "they ask to be / Written into a permanence," that is to say, "not stilled—" "a poem flows, its permanence is not fixity—" but given pulse and voice." A poem, in this view, has the changing permanence of life renewed with each new reading. The aim, then, is "not to seize the point of things"—an early statement of his position (**"Kantian Lyrics I"**)—but to catch the fugitive hint of Eden from the stream of time. He uses this image, without making it as overtly metaphorical as I have made it, in **"Departure"** when he reminds his recent guests of the "stream / Which bestows a flowing benediction and a name / On our house of stone" and adds:

> it is here
> That I like best, where the waters disappear
> Under the bridge-arch, shelving through coolness,
> Thought, halted at an image of perfection
> Between gloom and gold, in momentary
> Stay, place of perpetual threshold,
> Before all flashes out again and on
> Tasseling and torn, reflecting nothing but sun.

As it is a "place of perpetual threshold" for the stream, so for the contemplating mind it is a threshold between the known and the imagined.

The mind must practice a delicate hovering of attention to catch its images, but it is only a "*momentary* stay against confusion" (to complete the quotation from Frost), and the image is willingly relinquished, allowed to dissolve in the rush of waters. The poet balances appreciation of the mind's reflection, the stilled image, and enjoyment of the stream's flash of movement—"reflecting nothing but the sun." The stream bestows on the house two things, as separate and as inseparable as a baptism and a christening: "a *flowing* benediction" and an *unchanging* name, as fixed and permanent as the stone of which the house is built. The certainty of stone receives its benediction from the *living* flow of water. The clumsily sensitive movement of the stream is in immediate contrast with that of the jet which carries his guests to their destination, the trail of which "is scoring the zenith / Somewhere"; the language of water, "pushing / Over a fall, to sidle a rock or two / Before it was through the confine," feeling its way pliantly over and round obstacles toward its freedom, is more exemplary for the mind and will than the imperious rhetoric of the jet plane's insensibility to its surroundings. "Certainty of stone" is a phrase I have taken from another poem in *The Shaft,* "The Gap". What, asks the poet, is the meaning of your delight in noticing casually, as you are driving by, a gap in the stone wall "Where you'd expect to see / A field gate," through which

> All you see is space—that, and the wall
>   That climbs up to the spot two ways
> To embrace absence, frame skies:
>   Why does one welcome the gateless gap?
> As an image to be filled with the meaning
>   It doesn't yet have? As a confine gone?
> A saving grace in so much certainty of stone?

The answers are inherent in the questions: the wall thus lets in the whole expanse of space, releases imagination to its task of filling absences, opening vistas of possibility. To frame is not to contain skies—they are uncontainable; the gap creates a view the value of which is that, though at first meaningless to the viewer, it gives the eye freedom. It takes you beyond certainty, whether of stone or the oblivious certainty of a jet's flight, and leaves you in one of two conditions: either it is the agnostic's confession, "I do not know," or it sets you "at the edge" or on the threshold of "a saving grace," your redemption from the merely known. For Tomlinson, however, they are not distinct conditions but alternative names for the invitation to the imagination potential in any encounter of the familiar with the unexpected. Living at the frontier of the known and the unknown is its own justification: **"The Gap"** emphasizes not the "afterknowledge and its map" generated by the encounter but "the moment itself, abrupt / With the pure *surprise* of seeing" [Kirkham's italics]. The sudden invasion of the mind by an awareness of what is beyond its grasp is in itself a liberation and an enlargement. In the long view there is little significant difference between this abrupt surprise that admits a limitless world and the "startled truth," received with "misgivings," visible in the eyes of David's self-portrait. The agnostic is neither believer nor skeptic but a Janus facing both ways. "I do not know" may be said with misgiving or gratitude, but either way the saying opens a door for an eye trained on "the further light" (**"Ponte Veneziano"**) an ear attuned to distant echoes (**"In Arden"**).

The welcoming of uncertainties, ambiguities, even confusions, as potentially liberating or redemptive is the same kind of paradox as the fortunate Fall in Christian theology. The uncertainties in Tomlinson's work mainly arise from the shifting relations of the real and the imagined; the paradoxical reality—the fictional truth—of analogy, as opposed to the reality of fact, is consequently a central concern of his later poetry. It is, in a sense, the theme of **"Mushrooms,"** which presents the question of truth and illusion as a teasing conundrum. To mistake "A stone or stain, a dandelion puff" for the mushroom you are seeking is to be "played-with rather than deluded" by appearances; to be "taken in" is, rather, to be "taken beyond"

> This place of chiaroscuro that seemed clear,
> For realer than a myth of clarities
> Are the meanings that you read and are not there.

Memory plays a similar role in **"Dates: Penkhull New Road."** Recalling the street as it had been in his youth, a "gravely neat" memorial of mid-Victorian working-class civility, and regretting the subsequent violation of its character ("Something had bitten a gap / Out of the stretch we lived in,") in the piety of memory, he restores the interrupted continuity and gives it the permanence of a poem: "It took time to convince me that I cared / For more than beauty: I write to rescue / What is no longer there." What is no longer there once existed and still has a mental existence; what is not there, for example, the image of a mushroom in "a stone or stain," has also, if only, a mental existence, taking you beyond mere certainties. Therefore, the poet advises,

>   waste
> None of the sleights of seeing: taste the sight
> You gaze unsure of—a resemblance, too,
> Is real and all its likes and links stay true
> To the weft of seeing.
>
>   (**"Mushrooms"**)

Wordplay and sound-play, which is pervasive in Tomlinson's verse, function here to confuse the distinction between analogical and linear thinking—"likes and links" appears to assimilate them—and, in the transition from "links" to "weft" (chains to threads), the distinction between thinking and seeing.

Poems now not only draw attention to the element of illusion in the truth of poetry but also express relish of the disparities between fact and appearance exploited by poems—as, for instance, between bales of hay and the "scattered megaliths" they resemble (**"Hay"**). On the skyline at nightfall they seem to be—and this is what so delights the imagination—

> A henge of hay-bales to confuse the track
> Of time, and out of which the smoking dews
> Draw odours solids as the huge deception.

The metaphor, "henge of hay-bales," in *confusing* (the neutral word would be "identifying") the two things, wins a victory over time: the megalithic appearance in evening light is at once as "solid" as the thing itself—"a resemblance, too, / Is real"—and a "huge deception" that is appreciatively embodied in the "lavish" sensuousness of the whole poem. Imagination, says **"Hawks,"** enables us to do the impossible: namely, to share, though we cannot understand, the ecstasy of birds that "after their kind are lovers" and, in defiance of our earthbound limits, "ride where we cannot climb the steep / And altering air, breathing the sweetness / Of our own excess." The poet is doing what many poets have done with their skylarks and nightingales, eagles and windhovers, but never with quite this contented poise between doing it and knowing it can't be done. Specifically, the sense of immoderateness, of overstepping limits, in "excess" is qualified by the etymological meaning, appropriate here, of merely going beyond (compare "exceeding the place it guesses" in **"Nature Poem,"** quoted above). Going beyond ourselves "we are kinned / By space we never thought to enter": that kinship and that entry are at once real and illusory, the claim to them is at once sober truth, carefully measured in the language, and intemperateness. The poem is both a confession and a celebration of the imagination's inordinacy.

"Face and Image," in *American Scenes,* was the first poem to say openly, "Let be / this disparateness" between, for example, the face we see and our (loving) image of it:

> mouth, eyes and forehead,
> substantial things,
> advance their frontier
> clear against all imaginings.

The gap between "the buzzard's two-note cry" and our translation of its meaning, or for that matter between the interpretation of its presence implicit in the silence of the small birds and, swayed by our admiration of its beauty, the image *we* have of it, is the theme of **"Translating the Birds."** The difference between the two poems lies in the latter's emphasis on the fact of disparity rather than on the injunction to "let be"—widening rather than closing the gap, increasing the tension between the thing itself and poetry's humanization of it. The poem expresses ironical awareness of an opposition between the other reality of the buzzard, "Thrusting itself beyond the clasp of words," and man's desire, "eager always for the intelligible," to "instruct those throats what meanings they must tell"; the irony informs the contrast—in "Beauty does not stir them, realists to a man"—between man's aesthetic appreciation of the predator and the response of its potential victims. The poet's admiration of what the small birds "do not linger to admire," the imagination's gift to reality, is reflected in the poem's opulent language: "The flash of empery that solar fire / Lends to the predatory ease of flights." The sun, indeed, here performs the office of metaphor—leading to the bird an imperial stature and dignity that do not belong to it—and symbolizes the power and artifice of art, which in a *flash* of eloquence bestows on the buzzard's "predatory ease of flight" its own dominion over its created world. The "empery" of art recalls "the mind's imperious geometry" writing its "signature" on the unknowable in **"A Self-Portrait: David."** The mistrust conveyed by "imperious" is also admitted, with a certain *sang-froid* in **"Translating the Birds,"** when the poet predicts that men will credit "with arias, minstrelsy," the small birds "who've only sung in metaphor"; but the depreciatory realism of this phrase is modified—the *sang-froid* perfects the bland—by an equal delight in the triumphant exercise of imagination: metaphor, as man's link with the world he inhabits, is both arbitrary and indispensable; art is imperious but also imperial.

In many of the later poems skepticism and affirmation, as it were, exchange properties. The *fiction* of analogy is the subject of **"Fireflies,"** analogy that nevertheless serves to express the poet's enchantment with the seeming world created by the pinpoints of light in the darkness: "that close world lies/Pulsing within its halo, glows or goes . . . cosmos grows out of their circlings. . . . You could suppose the whole of darkness a forming rose". The scarcely avoidable pun on "lies," so placed, points to the fiction without discrediting it. The crisscross of outer and inner rhymes—the quoted lines and phrases only give a glimpse of the full effect—add a riddling confusion to the interplay between the real and the possible; the boundaries disappear between what is there and not there ("glows or goes"), between the solidity of "rose" and the conjectural existence of "suppose." It is appropriate that **"In Arden"** should provide a rationale for these echoes. "The depths of Arden's springs/Convey echoic waters," voicings of an unseen Eden

> Overflowing, as it brims its surfaces
>   In runes and hidden rhymes, in chords and keys
> Where Adam, Eden, Arden run together
>   And time itself must beat to the cadence of this river.

The "hidden rhymes" are runic connections created by the wizardry of poetry: magically, "Adam, Eden, Arden run together." The echoes increase the richness of interplay, enhance our pleasure in it at the same time as they enhance our consciousness of the artifice. It is clear now, almost explicit, that Eden is a creation of poetry, the concentration and aspiration of the mind; language itself is the master of time.

This perceptual, or epistemological, and linguistic agnosticism—the basic uncertainty about what can be known and what can be said that I have been illustrating—includes a specifically religious agnosticism, one that underlies all Tomlinson's poetry but has only become overt in recent collections. Yet here, too, agnosticism rings with the tones not of doubt but of affirmation. Sacramental language has long been a feature of Tomlinson's verse; what is new is that the Christian associations of certain key words in his poetic vocabulary, discreetly used, are not firmly separated from their supernatural significance. **"To See the Heron"** catches a moment of visual perfection in language that, as the poem proceeds, gradually increases its religious charge (the italics here and in the next quotation are mine): "To see the heron rise," "this *raised* torch," "this leisurely sideways / wandering *ascension*." No sooner is the heron's transfiguration into a resurrected body completed than it is immediately restored to earth. The heron untransfigured is nothing more than a bird searching for its prey:

> *risen*
> it is darkening now
> against the sullen sky blue,
> so let it go
> unaccompanied save by the thought
> that this is autumn and the stream

whose course its eye is travelling
the source of fish. . . .

The poem's intention, however, is to be not cynical but paradoxical: the heron is both itself and a vehicle of revelation. The paradox has the same elements as that represented by the gulls in **"The Faring"**, which were, in the poet's recollection of an extraordinary day, simultaneously birds in a storm "above seasonable fields," "intent/On nothing more than the ploughhand's nourishment," and seeming messengers from an "unending sea" of space, whose presence for the observing-participating poet "rhymed here with elsewhere."

Tomlinson's concern with the religious question is most noticeable—at least I have become more conscious of it—in a recent volume, *The Flood* (1981). Plainly in several poems poetry is being offered as a sufficient "recompense" for the failed promise of revealed truth. This, at least, is one way of "translating" the Wordsworthian episode recorded in **"The Recompense"**, resembling similar epiphanies in *The Prelude,* both in content and in narrative technique. The poet and his companion "climbed the darkness" to view the comet predicted for that night; they "waited" but "no comet came, and no flame thawed / The freezing reaches of [their] glance." "Unwillingly" they took themselves and their disappointment back down again, but, facing in the opposite direction, found in the "climbing brightness" of the "risen moon" "recompense for a comet lost": forfeiting the hoped-for prodigy, they turned instead to the opportunity of self-transcendence offered by the mere "rarenesses" (**"Images of Perfection,"** of sense experience. We

Could read ourselves into those lines
  Pulsating on the eye and to the veins,
Thrust and countercharge to our own racing down,
  Lunar flights of the rooted horizon.
                              (**"The Recompense"**)

In his fine elegiac sequence **"For Miriam"** Tomlinson recalls how he had played the advocate for traditional Christianity against the heresies of an eccentric woman preacher, not as a believer but as a "pagan" pleading for "poetry forgone"; in the light of his own sacramental imagery, it is interesting that he should muster all his "rhetoric" to defend specifically the doctrine of the incarnation.

Religious affirmation has been, so to speak, relocated. There are poems now, however, that proclaim their paganism not by appropriating and revaluing the language and images of Christianity but by contrasting the two ways of believing. **"Under the Moon's Reign,"** which gives its title to a group of poems in *The Way In,* is to the best of my knowledge the first poem to probe the implications of this antithesis: the contrast there is between the twilight that was "a going of the gods" and the transformation wrought by moonlight—let us call it, at the risk of banality, the moon of imagination. In the confusion of twilight we

Were looking still for what we could not see—
The inside of the outside, for some spirit flung
From the burning of that Götterdämmerung. . . .

But the moon's transfiguration of the landscape is effected by "no more miracle than the place / It occupied and the eye that saw it"; "Drawing all into more than daylight height" indicates, in a favorite construction (compare "more than earth" in **"At Holwell Farm,"** "more than bread" in **"A Farmer's Wife"**), that the seeming miracle of its "steady lightning" is not other than just an extension of natural and human existence. If this poem faintly recalls Elizabeth Bishop's "A Miracle for Breakfast," **"San Fruttuoso,"** in its form of offhand anecdotal narrative and its lightly sardonic wit, it distantly resembles another kind of Bishop poem. The poet takes the ferry in rough seas; divers don their suits and slip underwater: the two actions alternate in counterpoint. The poet's is a world of sun, bodies, "an ill-lit sky," and violent motion: the divers "assume / alternative bodies," pursuing purposes—"whatever it is draws them downwards"—that Tomlinson treats with an affectation of polite puzzlement and incredulity throughout. That "alternative" is a coolly disdainful substitution for "resurrected" becomes apparent in the whimsical description of the divers levitating around the sunken statue of *Cristo del mare,* "buoyed up by adoration" "like Correggio's sky— / swimming angels," performing "slow-motion pirouettes / forgetful of body, of gravity"—and we may be sure that gravity also means "proper seriousness." The poem begins with salt—"Sea salt has rusted the ironwork trellis"—and toward the end, thankfully after the uncertainties of his passage, the poet reaches the quay "with salted lips": the salt of corrosive time, then, the acrid taste of an unignorable reality, in the presence of which the charming antics of the divers seem the merest frivolity. It is in keeping that, in an implied comparison with the "baroque ecstatic devotion" of the circling divers in the postcard of *Cristo del mare,* Tomlinson should show a humorous preference for the mother who "has the placid / and faintly bovine look / of a Northern madonna." Juxtaposition of a late poem, **"Thunder in Tuscany"**, with a comparable early poem, **"Ponte Veneziano"** (from which I have already quoted), may serve to isolate this shift of focus in his recent work. Both depict stone figures in postures that in the eyes of the poet express and affirm exemplary attitudes. In **"Ponte Veneziano"** the fixed gaze of the two figures, "Tight-socketed in space . . . / Stripping the vista to its depth," projects strength of mind and will: undistractable concentration, unrelaxing singleness and tenacity of purpose, strictness of judgment, a disciplined commitment to what is necessary, and, as "It broods on the further light," the "utmost" of what is possible. Staring into the circle formed by a bridge-vault and its reflection,

They do not exclaim,
But, bound to that distance,
Transmit without gesture
Their stillness into its ringed centre.

In contrast with the steady light and stillness of **"Ponte Veneziano,"** the scene of **"Thunder in Tuscany"** is cinematically dramatic, and the figures, far from being "without gesture," are almost flamboyantly expressive: lightning illuminates a facade of "statues listening," giving fragmentary glimpses of features "Taut with the intent a body shapes through them / Standing on sheerness outlistening the storm." The "stillness" of the Venetian figures epitomizes the peculiar quality of their attention and stoicism: asort of stoicism also characterizes the mood of **"Thunder in Tuscany,"** but the image here projects tension and challenge. The illusion of an abyss conveyed by "sheerness"—recalling as it might the "slow abyss" eating away the fields, in **"The Compact: At Volterra,"** and the grit of those who farm the land up to the very edge, "Refusing to give ground before they must"—perhaps will justify the suggestion that the attitude in which these statues are caught "outlistening," looking to survive, with knowledge of something beyond the storm, is an image of post-Christian daring.

The obverse of Tomlinson's affirmative agnosticism is an *ironic* sense of the disparities—between fact and appearance, thing and image, reality and imagination—that his poetry has chosen to embrace and to celebrate. An incidental implication of my comments on **"Translating the Birds"** was that irony and celebration ride together; I would suggest that in the poems of the seventies they are never far apart. **"Translating the Birds"** balances the realistic, respectful silence of the small birds in the presence of the buzzard against the loud rhetoric of the aroused imagination and sets poetry's "eagerness" to translate what it sees and hears into the language of the mind against a precise perception of the mind's limits and a readiness to applaud what is "beyond the clasp of words"; only a slight shift in perspective transmutes the double consciousness at play here into the ironic poise of the so-called **"Histories"** grouped together in *The Shaft*. Irony is an insurance against the hubris of imagination. In poems that reflect and reflect on Tomlinson's experience, irony plays a muted accompaniment to the mind's eagerness to possess and to transform what it contemplates. Conversely, in his treatment of others' attempts to possess their lives—his portraits, for example, of the revolutionaries Charlotte Corday and Danton and his interpretation of the painter David's self-portrait—and in his humorous exposure of contemporary anecdote's failure to give coherence and meaning to the poet Denham's life, irony dominates. Contraries in **"Translating the Birds"** are welded into complementarities: the simultaneous acknowledgment and defiance of limitation hints an irony but leaves no crack for it to enter by. The disparity, however, between the foreground of Corday's and Danton's partial, subjective readings of reality and the impersonal background of time's "links of consequence," of history, which is the poet's knowledge of the *whole* story, is the gap that in those poems admits irony (for example, the gap between Corday's intention, "to have brought peace" by her "faultless blow," and "the Terror still to come," the future she could not foresee). The guillotine,

> the blade
> Inherited the future now and she
> Entered a darkness where no irony
> Seeps through to move the pity of her shade.
>
> (**"Charlotte Corday"**)

What she cannot feel the poem provides—irony leaves space for pity, restrained pity for the disproportion and incompleteness of her life. The combination of irony and pity in these portraits produces the equivalent of the balance of positive realism and (let us call it) positive romanticism in poems like **"Translating the Birds."**

The tragic irony of Danton's situation is that he has mistaken the part for the whole; he not only has exchanged his full humanity for the partial satisfactions afforded by political power but also, now that he realizes his mistake, pursues the opposite satisfaction of the senses with an equally unbalanced intensity:

> He fronts the parapet
> Drinking the present with unguarded sense:
>
> The stream comes on. Its music deafens him
> To other sounds, to past and future wrong.
>
> (**"For Danton"**)

I am reminded by the phrase "unguarded sense," implying values that can easily be misconceived, of certain emphases in Calvin Bedient's description of Tomlinson's imagination in *Eight Contemporary Poets*. It is not possible to summarize his lengthy examination of the subject, but a fair impression of the kind of balance he strikes in his assessment is conveyed by this sentence: "Though obviously far from being ample, headlong, or richly empowering, neither, on the other hand, is it faint or apologetic." I disagree: I find it ample and richly empowering. One wonders, however, what conception of imagination is implied by "headlong." If one knew, it might tell us why he thinks Tomlinson's is "unobtrusive and stopped-down." I want to conclude this essay with a brief consideration of the issues raised by this description. By implication, a *guarded* sense of the present is the standard by which, in the lines quoted above, Danton's attitude is being judged. It might be assumed that a guarded sense of things is what Mr. Bedient conceivably means by a "stopped-down" imagination. It is an understandable but wrong assumption. For "guarded" in this context would mean not defensive but circumspect— that is, attentive to all circumstances that may affect decision. And should circumspection seem a modest literary virtue, let me remind the reader of Eliot's definition of wit in his essay on Andrew Marvell: "a constant inspection and criticism of experience. It involves, probably, a recognition, implicit in the expression of every experience, of other kinds of experience which are possible." Circumspection is a part of wit. The "unguarded," *headlong*, oblivious immersion in the pleasures of the present shuts out consciousness of "past and future wrong" and hides from Danton the significance of the stream's inexorable progress ("the links of consequence / Chiming his life away"). The "unguarded" vision is one blind to the *whole* truth: conversely, a guarded vision would be one that opens the mind to *all* circumstances, to the present and its contraries. Imagination for Tomlinson is, as I have said, the faculty that brings to what the senses perceive an inner sense of what is not present—we may call them contraries or "other kinds of experience which are possible." The critical, vigilant, self-doubting—in a word, circumspect—approach to experience recommended in these lines, far from bottling up imagination (the genie in a bottle figure, I suspect, lurks somewhere in the shadows of Mr. Bedient's prose), is precisely what *empowers* and gives it *ample* range.

Michael Ponsford   (essay date 1989)

SOURCE: "'To Wish Back Eden': The Community Theme in Charles Tomlinson's Verse," in *The Midwest Quarterly,* Vol. XXX, No. 3, Spring, 1989, pp. 346-60.

[*In the following essay, Ponsford maintains that Tomlinson's interest in the idea of community is directly related to his growing concern with the idea and ideal of Eden.*]

Charles Tomlinson is one of Britain's most admired poets, and one of her most prolific. His [*Collected Poems*] represent four decades of intense poetic activity; yet his has never been a household name, and even among his admirers, he is still regarded with some suspicion. Readers, perhaps, are discomforted by the inclusiveness of his verse, which ranges over vast geographical and intellectual landscapes. He describes a familiar English pastoral, the rural West Country, in a decidedly modern setting; but he is also the poet of New Mexico and New York, Arizona and Maine. He delves into the past, be it his own childhood in a Midlands industrial town, the rituals of American Indians, or the echoes of history which resound through a particular dwelling. He is a fine—and underrated—comic poet; but he also has mystical tendencies, moving from the immediately visible to the mystery beyond. He speaks with a clear, contemporary voice, yet he has a traditional interest in the natural world that sometimes recalls Georgianism. Tomlinson's poetry, then, is difficult to place. Nevertheless, it is possible to discern a common concern running through the ten volumes that make up *Collected Poems*, and that is Tomlinson's perennial fascination with places.

The publication of the *Collected Poems* has given us a broader perspective of Tomlinson's achievement. [In *Eight Contemporary Poets,* 1974] Calvin Bedient once remarked that the poet was "too strange an amphibian, too Americanized, too peopleless to be trusted." It is difficult to know what Bedient means by "Americanized," but an overall view of Tomlinson's work shows that his poetry has by no means remained "peopleless." The idea of the community, in the familiar images of the village and the city, has become one of Tomlinson's central concerns; while it is true that these images are by no means a new aspect of his work, the sociological interest attached to them is. Tomlinson shares interests with the planner and the social worker: he is concerned with how and where people live, exploring the relationships between people and places, and between our natural and our created environments. To these he adds a poet's concern, the relationship between our perception of the community and its reality. These concerns, as I hope to show in this [essay], are directly related to the poet's increasing preoccupation with the idea, and the ideal, of "Eden."

It is interesting, but presumably coincidental, that Bedient's observation on the "peopleless" quality of Tomlinson's verse should appear in the same year—1974—as *The Way In,* a volume which did a great deal to answer that complaint. The title poem of the volume introduces a section called **"Manscapes"** (though this sub-heading is not retained in the *Collected Poems*), and describes the evidence of change as the poet drives through an old residential area of a city: the "Kerb-side signs / For demolitions and new detours, / A propped pub, a corner lopped." Such sights have been familiar enough in British cities during the last decade or so, as urban re-development has flattened old communities to make way for newer and more impersonal slums. While he focuses on a particular social concern, Tomlinson regrets that "Bulldozers / Gobble a street up" not because of the street's intrinsic worth, but for its familiarity: "I thought I knew this place, this face / a little worn, a little homely," he laments.

For the poet, the ideal community is marked by its urbanity: it is a place civilized and humanized by contact with people, whose perception is part of its development. But this city is now deprived of "the look that shadows softened / And the light could grace"; the congruency that existed between the inhabitants and their habitation has been destroyed, symbolized by the old couple who are moving out, hauling their belongings with them:

> Slowing, I see the faces of a pair
>   Behind their load: he shoves and she
> Trails after him, a sexagenarian Eve,
>   Their punishment to number every hair
> Of what remains.

These are the archetypal Adam and Eve, cast out of an urban paradise—or, rather, leaving a paradise that has disintegrated around them. Tomlinson looks ahead to what might replace that Eden, the penultimate stanza discussing whether the redevelopment will furnish a subject fit for poetry. He decides that it cannot: others, concedes the poet, might "find that civility I can only miss," but his conclusion is scathing: "It will need more than talk and trees / To coax a style from these disparities." Indeed, the phrase "talk and trees" suggests the disparity, echoing the proverbial incongruents, "chalk and cheese." Tomlinson realizes that the relationships that meshed and defined the community have been lost, and the poem expresses the pervasive contemporary anxieties, rootlessness, and alienation.

In an interview published in *Contemporary Literature* in 1975, Charles Tomlinson has discussed **"The Way In"** in the context of his new concern with myth. He notes that he "first worked out of a suspicion with myth, trusting sensation," but acknowledges that his recent poetry has involved a mythical dimension. "The nearest I come to myth," he says, "is that word 'Eden,' which I can't seem to get rid of and which fits what I'm doing with its implication of primal things, fresh sensations, direct perceptions unmuddied." More specifically, he remarks on the fugitive old couple in **"The Way In"** that here is "a use of myth in so far as I see them as Adam and Eve long-banished from Eden, but I wouldn't want to expand the thing to Wagnerian proportions." Wagnerian proportions or not, Tomlinson's comment indicates a tendency to view the community mythically, aware of its potential to become an Eden, but conscious, too, of the limitations to such idealism. It is a tendency that has surfaced often in his recent volumes.

Tomlinson draws a close parallel between the destruction of a place and the decline of relationships among people: both are aspects of the lapsed Edenic community. In another poem from *The Way In,* **"Dates: Penkhull New Road,"** there is an idealistic nostalgia for a place the poet knew in his childhood, a place of little privacy, but where the daily routines of work and leisure were closely integrated, where there were close bonds between and within families, and where there was a sense of a traditional stability. He contends that this social fabric had survived intact from the time of the street's construction, in 1860, until his own childhood. The Victorian terraced street, he recalls, was essentially "a civil place," in which it was acceptable

> to be standing shouting out there
> Across to the other side—the side
> I envied, because its back-yards ran sheer
> To the factory wall.

Tomlinson's vision of these Victorian streets is still rather unconventional, though the architecture and social fabric of the terraced house and street are currently of much interest among scholars, and it is profitable to read Tomlinson's poem (and others in the **"Manscapes"** section of *The Way In*) with reference to Stefan Muthesius's authoritative book, *The English Terraced House.* Tomlinson voices no familiar protest against the dehumanizing effect of the industrial revolution, nor against the ugliness of the urban landscape it spawned. Rather, he sees the Victorian age as introducing an era of community spirit, and of a sense of belonging; Muthesius, too, defines such streets as "places for communication, for promenading, or just for looking at what was happening." But for Tomlinson, the street parties that celebrated peace in 1945 were the last expression of this era, for the end of the war ushered in a new age; his poem continues with another date, and a change of tone:

> I returned
> In seventy-three. Like England,
> The place had half-moved with the times—the
>   'other side'
> Was gone. Something had bitten a gap
> Out of the stretch we lived in. Penkhull still
>   crowned
> The hill, rebuilt to a plan—may as well scrap
> The architectural calendar: that dream
> Was dreamed up by the insurance-man
> And we've a long time to live it yet.

The poem closes with a statement of Tomlinson's changed aesthetic—he can no longer uphold his earliest poetic attitude, that "seeing is believing":

> It took time to convince me that I cared
> For more than beauty. I write to rescue

> What is no longer there—absurd
> A place should be more fragile than a book.

But fragile these places are, subject to time, to the whims of planners, and to changing taste. Tomlinson finds it increasingly difficult to locate communities which are based on an Edenic balance of people, place, and time, for the merest tremble in history upsets this balance, anticipating the collapse of Eden. The contemporary sociologist of the community must talk, as Lyn Lofland does, "about the massive growth of population and urbanization, about increasing spatial mobility, about the growing numbers who put down their roots not in a place, but in a profession." It is now clear, Lofland continues, that "what was once an environment of personally known others is becoming . . . a world of unknown others." These broad historical trends are filtering through society to affect every community, and they have proved dynamic enough to take Tomlinson out of his accustomed poetic themes.

This is not to say, of course, that there is no foreshadowing of such a development in Tomlinson's earlier work. There, in the pastoral paradigm, the poet turned to the rural world to discover a balance of people, place and time—the idea that country people live lives closer to their environment is a persistent one. **"Winter Encounters,"** a poem from *Seeing is Believing* (1960), is replete with reconciliatory language, emphasized by the balanced decorum of the opening lines:

> House and hollow; village and valley-side.
>   The ceaseless pairings, the interchange
> In which the properties are constant.

Intricate relationships bind every aspect of the scene proposed in this first stanza. The house does not merely fit into its site; it also "reposes" as part of the farmland community, "meshed / Into neighbourhood by such shifting ties." Similarly, in **"At Holwell Farm"** from the same volume, there is a further thoughcomplementary insight into

> a pattern of utilities—this farm
> Also a house, this house a dwelling.
>   Rooted in more than earth, to dwell
> Is to discern the Eden image.

Here, Tomlinson's vision of Eden is part of the tradition of English poetry, finding the ideal existence in the interaction of people with a rural landscape.

But Tomlinson is a poet who has persistently tested his insights against new experiences, and his early travel poetry has taken up his preoccupation with Edenic places in Britain. In particular, he has turned his attention to the United States, publishing a volume called *American Scenes* in 1966. In a country that represents contemporary culture almost exclusively, Tomlinson has found its anxieties of rootlessness and alienation thrown into sharp relief. The clash of cultures which has inevitably resulted from America's diverse heritage forms the basis of several poems: there is the shifting between English, Spanish, and slang

American of the speakers in **"Las Trampas U.S.A."** for example. And there is the sadly comic **"Mr Brodsky,"** who, in his absurd desire to become a Scot, arranges a Burns Night gathering in New Mexico, complete with "the Balmoral Pipers of Albuquerque," who "play in the haggis / out of its New York tin."

"At Barstow," however, is the most complete analysis of a particular place in the *American Scenes* volume. The poem depicts a community which is not a fallen paradise, as Penkhull New Road in a sense was, but a town that has never attained the civility that should characterize a community. The problem with Barstow is that it has no sense of stability, because people belong there only briefly, if at all:

> Nervy with neons, the main drag
> was all there was. A placeless place.
> A faint flavour of Mexico in the tacos
> tasting of gasoline. Trucks refuelled
> before taking off through space. Someone lived
> in the houses with their houseyards wired
> like tiny Belsens.

References to the holocaust of Nazi Germany use hyperbole to underpin the idea of the failure of civilization. The poet notes that Roy Rogers once stayed at a motel in Barstow, and tries to imagine the scene:

> his dustless, undishonoured stetson rode
> beside the bed,
> glowed in the pulsating, never-final twilight
> there, at the execrable conjunction
> of gasoline and desert air.

No relationship can exist between this created place and its environment, or between the place and its inhabitants. The present is not conjoined with the past; no culture has grown out of the environment—indeed, there is strong parody in the juxtaposed tacos and gasoline. Finally, the brash lighting ensures that night is merely a "never-final twilight," so that even the natural stability of time is disturbed.

Tomlinson emerges as a poet with a quest: how to realize more fully those occasional glimpses of Eden which only reveal its inaccessibility.

—*Michael Ponsford*

America is portrayed more favorably in Charles Tomlinson's later poetry, however. *Notes From New York and Other Poems,* published in 1984, still shows an interest in the cultural complexity of America, in poems like **"Ice Cream at Blaunberg,"** with its opening anachronisms:

> The restaurant serving Char-Broiled Meats
> Flavored in Flame, Welsh Farms Ice Cream,

> Stands at a four-way stop between
> A Dutch cemetery and an antique shop.

But there is a different interest in this volume, too. Tomlinson's developing focus on people enables him to discover that overtones of Eden can exist in what might seem to be an inhospitable community. In the first poem of the sequence, **"The Landing,"** New York is viewed with an unusual perspective—from an aircraft—which contributes to the idealizing of the city:

> Manhattan
> Beyond us is holding on to the rays
> Of a tawny strip of sun of late afternoon,
> That catches on spire and pinnacle and then
> Shafts out the island entire.

The poet's view of the city has the quality of a mystical apprehension, in lines like "we / In our circling the only ones to see / The total and spreading scope of it," and the exuberant tone combined with the light imagery gives New York the aura of a heavenly city.

This attitude is difficult to sustain except by distance, although Tomlinson does succeed in celebrating the city in several of the New York poems, even as he is aware of its failings. In **"What Virginia Said,"** a poem that cleverly intertwines dialogue and narrative, we see the city from two perspectives: the poet notices "the drunks, the sleepy / addicts, the derelicts," while Virginia talks about how much safer she feels in the crowd than in the quietness of a college town. The poem, then, suggests that the way we feel about a place is more significant than the reality: it is a deception that sustains the relationship between people and place. The same idea, that our attitude to the city can rediscover a lost Edenic existence, is suggested by another poem in *Notes From New York,* **"On Madison."** It is true that the opening description stresses alienation by the mist, together with forgetfulness of the city's true condition—the unseen homelessness, the loss of community in its most extreme form. But the poem is nevertheless a celebration:

> We savour the wine of the solitude of spaces
> In the same instant as we choose the street
> That seems like a home returned to, grown
> Suddenly festive as we enter it
> With the odour of chestnuts on the corner braziers.

"On Madison" thus discovers a precarious, fragile Eden to counter the sense of alienation that prevails in the modern world. But Tomlinson's problem is one that he shares with mystics—how to reconcile the "instant" of insight, when the Eden image is glimpsed, with the flux of time that destroys that image.

The passage of time is seen by Tomlinson as a subtle destroyer of the relationships and cultures upon which a community depends. The poet does not wish to transcend time, however, but to come to terms with it: in a poem called **"In Arden"** from *The Shaft* (1978), he describes the Forest of Arden—"Arden" being a variation of "Eden," as the opening line, "Arden is not Eden, but Eden's rhyme" makes clear—as a place that reconciles time and eternity. The poet recognizes in Arden's springs

> 　　　　voices
> Of the place that rises through this place
> Overflowing, as it brims its surfaces.
> 　　In runes and hidden rhymes, in chords and keys
> Where Adam, Eden, Arden run together
> 　　And time itself must beat to the cadence of this
> 　　river.

In **"Hay,"** from his 1981 volume, *The Flood,* Tomlinson returns to the countryside and its rituals, to discover a close relationship between time and eternity. The poem has a Keatsian richness of language that is unusual in Tomlinson's work: "The air at evening thickens with a scent / That walls exude and dreams turn lavish on." The scent of the mown hay seems to dominate the scene symbolically. It suggests not only the sacramental significance of the harvest, but also the permanence of its value, for it "hangs perpetual over the changes." There is, too, a sense of order in the reaped field's "parallels of grass, sweet avenues." The yearly repetition of the harvest is itself a means of translating time into stillness, imaged in the final "huge deception," The reapers' activity, sanctified by time, brings forth a sense of their prehistoric ancestors, who celebrated such seasonal rituals in the building of stone circles; by nightfall, the reapers have created a "henge of hay-bales to confuse the track of time." And it is of no consequence that the scene, dependent on a trick of the light and a suggestive similarity of shape, is really a deception. For, as he says in **"Mushrooms,"** from *The Shaft* (1978), "realer than a myth of clarities / Are the meanings that you read and are not there." In this poem, Tomlinson's rejection of the "myth of clarities" is really an adaptation of his early belief that "seeing is believing." **"Mushrooms"** outlines his new conviction: "A resemblance, too, / Is real, and all its likes and links stay true / To the weft of seeing."

Tomlinson, then, will not attempt to impose meaning on what he sees, finding that perception itself is a guarantee that meaning will emerge. Thus, like a mystic, he puts his confidence in the moment of insight, and so can be confident that Eden is recoverable, even if only briefly and in an attenuated form. This idea was put forward as early as 1969, in **"Eden,"** from *The Way of a World*: "I have seen Eden. It is a light of place / As much as the place itself; not a face / Only, but the expression on that face." The opening movement of **"Eden"** stresses the sense of relationships, particularly in a correspondence between earth and sky, and suggests the civility of Eden, where the "avenues of light" are "copious enough / To draft a city from". The poem states that "Eden / Is given one," though warning that "Despair of Eden is given, too." Recovery of Eden, then, depends on an attitude:

> 　There is no
> Bridge but the thread of patience, no way
> But the will to wish back Eden, this leaning
> 　To stand against the persuasions of a wind

That rings with its meaninglessness where it sang its meaning.

It is apparent that Tomlinson's early countryside poems contain within their depths mystical overtones; **"Eden"** demonstrates how these have become more and more explicit as the poet has explored the Eden theme. With *The Way In* of 1974, his idealism is given more concrete expression: in **"The Greeting,"** for example, Tomlinson suggests that perception of a scene is not enough in itself to discover an Edenic significance, as some sort of relationship between perceiver and scene must exist. The poem describes someone glancing "idly" at a scene, and proposes that

> Space and its Eden
> of green and blue
> warranted more watching
> than such gazing through:
>
> but the far roofs gave
> a "Good day" back,
> defeating that negligence
> with an unlooked for greeting.

The perceiver, then, suddenly becomes aware of a relationship between the external scene and the inner self, and it is significant that the final vision of "space / one whole without seam" results from a glimpse of "far roofs," signs that people are integrated with the environment. For whether it is in a rural or an urban landscape, the basis of the Edenic community is a sense of civility.

But Tomlinson's recent work shows that his attitude toward the countryside communities, the subtle relationships of which he described in early poems such as **"At Holwell Farm,"** is now deeply ambivalent. The celebratory tone of **"Hay"** is challenged by **"Hedgerows"** (from *Notes From New York and Other Poems*), which laments the disappearance, in some areas, of the hedges that are so much a part of the rural English landscape. "Once they begin to disappear / You see what an urbanity hedgerows are," says the poem; "they contain, compel as civilly as stanzas". The words, of course, are carefully chosen; for Tomlinson, urbanity and civility—signs that a place has been humanized—are hints of Eden.

But the first two "other poems" in the same volume press home Tomlinson's ambivalence in even greater measure. If the poet has been most inclined to search for Eden, or to recognize a lost paradise, in a social setting—the image of the community, **"From the Motorway"** and **"To Ivor Gurney"** explore the value of an unpopulated or empty Eden. These two are companion poems: both take as their starting point a scene glimpsed from a motorway. Complaints about the motorway designers' contempt for aesthetics have always flourished, and Tomlinson's **"From the Motorway"** takes up these complaints, but with a fresh perception. He notes how the building of a junction isolates an empty triangle of land. Its separation from people is stressed; it is "never to be named: / No one will ever go there," and even the road-builders are an unidentified, depersonalized "they." Tomlinson initially laments a loss: "How / Shall we have it back, a belonging shape?" he asks, lamenting, too, that "it will breed no ghosts" suggesting a pattern of procreation and mortality now denied to this land. The sense of loss undescored by the final image of the lights' "sodium glow on winter evenings / As inaccessible as Eden" recalls Tomlinson's horror, in **"At Barstow,"** at the power of artificial light to desecrate the natural processes of day and night. What the poet glimpses from the motorway is a lost paradise, its inaccessibility a sign that it has been denied to humanity.

"To Ivor Gurney" in part balances this lament. Tomlinson is travelling north through countryside that would have been familiar to Gurney, the composer, though the poet is detached from the landscape. He describes the hills he views from the road as "Edens that lay / Either side of this interminable roadway" the use of the past tense suggesting a paradise that has failed since the lifetime of the composer (Gurney died in 1937). The poet identifies this failure implicitly with the building of the road and explicitly with the intrusion of artificial lights. "You would recognize [the hill shapes] still," he says, "but the lanes / Of lights that fill the lowlands, brim / To the Severn and glow into the heights." However, the beauty of the image belies the lament and strengthens the ambiguity: "night is never to be restored / To Eden and England spangled in bright chains." Here the diurnal pattern has been replaced by the more positive spiritual connotations of perpetual light, and the "lanes of lights" have become, in their ordered beauty, symbolic of a recreated Eden. There is, in these two poems, a tension between the movement of the poet travelling on the motorway and the stasis of the landscape through which he travels. This new perspective allows a fresh insight into the idea of Eden, developing what might be called the aesthetic of inaccessibility. Although a more optimistic poem than **"From the Motorway,"** **"To Ivor Gurney"** nevertheless finds a form of Eden in a landscape devoid of people.

Tomlinson's glimpses of Eden, then, are qualified by its elusiveness. The poet cultivates the aesthetic of inaccessibility because it is precisely in those inaccessible areas of his consciousness that he recognizes an urbane balance of people, place, and time—in a wasteland glimpsed from a motorway, in a street that exists only as a childhood memory, in a community laid waste by the blight of town-planning. He explores the same theme through various personae—displaced characters like Mr. Brodsky and Virginia, or those, like the speaker of **"Jemez,"** who lament a lost community. Tomlinson is harshly critical of what we have made of our world and as such has a strong moral to impart. But he also emerges as a poet with a quest: how to realize more fully those occasional glimpses of Eden which only reveal its inaccessibility. Tomlinson's poetry is both the record of a search and a response to the world the poet sees around him. The search is inevitably idealistic, and as we consider Tomlinson's aesthetic of inaccessibility, we are inevitably reminded of Calvin Bedient's complaint that Tomlinson is perhaps "too peopleless to be trusted". The poet's tendency to idealize the landscape by denuding it of the human is one that many readers, I suspect, will find disturbing.

Ruth Grogan   (essay date 1989)

SOURCE: "Tomlinson, Ruskin, and Moore: Facts and Fir Trees," in *Twentieth-Century Literature,* Vol. 35, No. 2, Summer, 1989, pp. 183-94.

[*In the following essay, Grogan discusses John Ruskin's influence on Tomlinson, especially the attention to detail and faithfulness to visual surfaces.*]

Charles Tomlinson is undoubtedly one of England's most distinguished living poets and critics. The accumulated work of four decades—his *Collected Poems* published by Oxford in 1985, his many translations (from Vallejo, Tyutchev, Machado, and Paz, to name only a few), his large body of criticism and memoirs, his exhibitions of graphic work and the three resulting volumes of reproductions—has been accompanied by honors, prizes, and invitations to read and lecture in many countries. As a poet and artist deeply rooted in his native England, and at the same time an internationalist and multilinguist, he lays claim to our closest attention.

Tomlinson has frequently cited John Ruskin, that most English of seers, as a key precursor. Although he was attracted to modern American poets—Williams, Stevens, and Moore among others   well before they were generally known in England, it was only under Ruskin's auspices, a few years later, that he began to integrate their voices into his own. At the back of his reading was always "the sheet anchor of having read Ruskin." Recalling his early response to Marianne Moore [in an interview in *The Poet Speaks,* edited by Peter Orr, 1966] he said, "she has this Ruskinian openness to the creative universe in looking at the surfaces it offers one." Wallace Stevens' poetry, on the other hand, had to be resisted despite its allure: "I was arguing for a kind of exactness in face of the object, which meant an exactness of feeling in the writer. It meant that you must enter into a relationship with things, that you must use your eyes. . . . I learned this lesson from Ruskin—chiefly from the evocations of leaves, clouds, water in *Modern Painters*" [*London Magazine,* 1981]. That Tomlinson continues to find Ruskin's prose of inexhaustible interest is witnessed by a recent poem of 1987 entitled "Ruskin Remembered."

A study of the affinities between Ruskin and Tomlinson would have to begin with the eye. Tomlinson has quoted Ruskin's memorable description of the eye as possessing an "intellectual lens and moral retina," and it is clear that for both writers their delicate, rigorously objective descriptions of cloud, stone, and water arise from the profound conviction that the visual imagination is intimately and inseparably allied to the intellectual and moral faculties. There are strong divergences between them as well. Whereas Ruskin almost always judged art in terms of verisimilitude, and nature in terms of its revelations of divine purpose, Tomlinson is an heir of the early modernist movement, with its concern with collage, discontinuity, and indeterminacy. Tomlinson looks back at Ruskin through the lens of Cézanne.

Though the assimilations and repudiations of Ruskin in Tomlinson's work are complex, in this essay I wish to turn from these larger questions in order to make a study of intertextual minutiae. My focus will be on a cluster of anecdotes and images arising from and centering on two passages of Ruskin's prose, both of them descriptions of fir trees. Over the years traces of these images reappear in Tomlinson's poetry, criticism, reading, and discussions with friends—often, oddly enough, in an American connection. In their intertextual and transatlantic combinations they offer significant insights into the workings of Tomlinson's imagination.

We pick up the trail by going back to November 1956, when Hugh Kenner paid a visit to the Tomlinsons in their (then) home in Somerset. Knowing of Kenner's delight in imaginative factuality, Tomlinson read him a passage from Ruskin:

> There is, perhaps, no tree which has baffled the landscape painter more than the common black spruce fir. It is rare that we see any representation of it other than caricature. It is conceived as if it grew in one plane, or as a section of a tree, with a set of boughs symmetrically dependent on opposite sides. It is thought formal, unmanageable, and ugly. It would be so, if it grew as it is drawn. But the Power of the tree is not in that chandelier-like section. It is in the dark, flat, solid tables of leafage, which it holds out on its strong arms, curved slightly over them like shields, and spreading towards the extremity like a hand. It is vain to endeavour to paint the sharp, grassy, intricate leafage, until this ruling form has been secured; and in the boughs that approach the spectator, the foreshortening of it is like that of a wide hill country, ridge just rising over ridge in successive distances; and the finger-like extremities, foreshortened to absolute bluntness, require a delicacy in the rendering of them.

At this same meeting Kenner gave Tomlinson a gift he had brought along from New York—a copy of Marianne Moore's most recent book of poems, *Like a Bulwark*. It was an appropriate gift, for Tomlinson had been interested in Moore since his undergraduate days, and it was all the more appealing for having been inscribed to Tomlinson in her own hand.

The account of this meeting is in Tomlinson's charming memoir of his transatlantic friendships, *Some Americans*. With a bit of unaccented humor, he adds that the spruce tree must have stuck in Kenner's mind, for it reappeared almost twenty years later in *A Homemade World* (1975), still associated with Marianne Moore. What Kenner claims in this later citation is not that Moore quoted or even knew the passage, but rather that it demonstrates a relation of eye and language that her poems share. The metaphors in Ruskin's description—the arms, shields, hands—are neither personification of the tree nor some sort of recipe for a painter. What we have is "a tree of language, not of nature or of painting: it exists only on Ruskin's printed page. It got there by an effort of attention, commanding the resources of the whole being, that devised and traversed a half-dozen analogies, analogies not for a stolid tree but for a tree's fancied kinetic act, and the eye's act responding." Tomlinson's Ruskin passage prompted Kenner

to reflect on the transmutations of visual perception and language and the morality of self-forgetfulness necessary for this accomplishment. It is not surprising, then, that Kenner's comments on Ruskin and Moore should be unintentionally but acutely relevant to Tomlinson as well.

Tomlinson and Kenner were not the first to have given this passage an effort of attention. Another was Graham Hough, whose introduction to Ruskin in *The Last Romantics* (1949) Tomlinson would certainly have read in the early days of his interest in Ruskin. Hough quotes this same "patient and minute study" of the spruce, his purpose being to show how Ruskin trains the eye to overcome perceptual conventions and discover the exquisite repetitiveness of natural form, in this case the way the curves of the foreshortened boughs are echoed in the distant hills. In the following passage from Tomlinson's poetry, the observing eye has assimilated the lessons of Ruskin's common black spruce, though it has carried them to a continent Ruskin never knew and applied them to a different kind of fir:

> Dakota's rock—
>   the Chinese
> predicted
>   and depicted this
>   where cream-white
> rises into a wall
>   which pinestems (red)
>   horizontally of branch
> and leaf-mass (rhythmically repeated)
>   "decorate" is the word.

The discipline of sight, as exercised in Ruskin's description, becomes according to Hough "a morally and metaphysically important occupation." What Ruskin is striving to bring about is nothing less than a "psychological revolution," one that will release the sense of sight "from the bondage to utility and convention and . . . set it free to operate in its own way; he is vindicating the rights of the senses." Behind all of Tomlinson's work, both graphic and verbal, lies the same conviction.

The spruce passage had struck someone else to different effect many years earlier. The unnamed "student of Ruskin" who wrote the introduction to the 1907 edition of *The Elements of Drawing* (a work that Tomlinson has read, and very likely in this popular Everyman edition) also quotes it. He considers it essential to understanding the clearing of the artist's "working vision" which was Ruskin's purpose in *The Elements of Drawing*. But he expands its significance by juxtaposing it with another, apparently contradictory passage. In this second passage Ruskin exhorts his disciple to draw exactly what he sees; but be sure this is what you are doing, Ruskin urges, "for otherwise you will find yourself continually drawing, not what you *see*, but what you *know*." Try drawing the appearance of something a few feet away, books on your bookcase perhaps, or a bit of patterned muslin, or a bank of grass with all its blades, "and you will soon begin to understand under what a universal law of obscurity we live, and perceive that all *distinct* drawing must be *bad* drawing, and that nothing can be right, till it is unintelligible."

Juxtaposing Ruskin's law of obscurity with the careful visual distinctions of the spruce-tree passage is not willful paradox, according to the "student": for clearing the vision means, precisely, recognizing "the illusions and the veracities and the innocences of the eye." Seeing the fir tree means clearing away what you know, or thought you knew, about the fir tree—that Christmas-card fir in one plane, with its "set of boughs symmetrically dependent on opposite sides." In the end, as the reader is bound to infer, the clearer the vision, the more it comes up against mystery, not mystical or symbolic or transcendental mystery, but a practical one—one that resides in the limitations of our optical equipment. It marks a point, as Ruskin elaborates elsewhere, at which the painter must abandon the deceptions of mere verisimilitude for the even more difficult tasks of suggesting the optical mysteries of space, mist, design, motion, and infinity.

Ruskin's sense of the artist's double obligation—to see clearly and therefore to see where clarity fails and becomes unintelligible—is undoubtedly one of Tomlinson's major themes. What Tomlinson calls the "double mystery" of sight arises in that "daily experience" of not being able to "make out what precisely it is that one is looking at." It is the subject, to take only one example, of his prose poem called **"Skullshapes"**:

> Shadow explores them. It sockets the eye-holes with black. It reaches like fingers into the places one cannot see. Skulls are a keen instance of this duality of the visible: it borders what the eye cannot make out, it transcends itself with the suggestion of all that is there beside what lies within the eyes' possession: it cannot be possessed.

There are indications throughout this meditation that Tomlinson is transforming his precursor's work to his own ends. Not least of the clues is its reference to "Ruskin's blind man struck suddenly by vision," a parable in *The Elements of Drawing* about the necessity of innocent vision, uncluttered by learned preconceptions. Tomlinson asserts his revisionary rights by quarreling with Ruskin's interpretation. The eye is never innocent, he says. It is always swayed by memory and conception, for "it is what the mind sees."

On the border of what the eye possesses is what the eye cannot possess. In a remarkable poem entitled **"The Impalpabilities,"** Tomlinson explores this border area:

> It is the sense
>   of things that we must include
>   because we do not understand them
> the impalpabilities

The two opposing meanings of "sense"—intuitional and physical—expose the difference between what the senses possess and what they fail to possess, between palpabilities and impalpabilities. As the poem demonstrates, however, the poet does not *banish* the visible or palpable in order to reach the invisible or impalpable; he traces it watchfully, meticulously, to its very edge, waiting till it dissolves in the twilight, metamorphoses into something more metaphorical:

> and so the wood
> advances before the evening takes it—
>   branches
>   tense in a light like water,
> as if (on extended fingers)
>   supporting the cool immensity
>   while we meditate the strength
> in the arms we no longer see.

The ghost of Ruskin's spruce lingers here. It is not just that there are branches like arms and fingers. A reader who searches for the spruce-tree passage in the original will find it in *The Seven Lamps of Architecture*, in the chapter entitled "The Lamp of Power"; and will find, moreover, that the Lamp of Power has to do with nobility, majesty, mystery—in a word, sublimity. The Ruskinian context brings us to the surprising realization that the gathering darkness of the wood in Tomlinson's poem, the "cool immensity," the numinous "strength / in the arms we no longer see" constitute a modern version of the sublime.

When Tomlinson first started reading Ruskin, in 1949 or 1950, it was a little volume called *Frondes agrestes*, a selection of passages from *Modern Painters* put together in 1875 by a Coniston friend of Ruskin's. In a rueful footnote added to his friend's selection, Ruskin said: "Almost the only pleasure I have, myself, in re-reading my old books, is my sense of having at least done justice to the pine." The example he pointed to was the following:

> Magnificent! nay, sometimes almost terrible. Other trees, tufting crag or hill, yield to the form and sway of the ground, clothe it with soft compliance, are partly its subjects, partly its flatterers, partly its comforters. But the pine rises in serene resistance, self-contained; nor can I ever without awe stay long under a great Alpine cliff, far from all house or work of men, looking up to its companies of pines, as they stand on the inaccessible juts and perilous ledges of the enormous wall, in quiet multitudes, each like the shadow of the one beside it—upright, fixed, spectral, as troops of ghosts standing on the walls of Hades, not knowing each other, dumb for ever. You cannot reach them, cannot cry to them: those trees never heard human voice; they are far above all sound but of the winds. No foot ever stirred fallen leaf of theirs: all comfortless they stand, between the two eternities of the Vacancy and the Rock; yet with such iron will, that the rock itself looks bent and shattered beside them,—fragile, weak, inconsistent, compared to their dark energy of delicate life, and monotony of enchanted pride— unnumbered, unconquerable.

> Then note farther their perfectness. The impression on most people's minds must have been received more from pictures than reality, so far as I can judge, so ragged they think the pine; whereas its chief character in health is green and full *roundness*. It stands compact, like one of its own cones, slightly curved on its sides,

finished and quaint as a carved tree in some Elizabethan garden; and instead of being wild in expression, forms the softest of all forest scenery, for other trees show their trunks and twisting boughs; but the pine, growing either in luxuriant mass, or in happy isolation, allows no branch to be seen. Summit behind summit rise its pyramidal ranges, or down to the very grass sweep the circlets of its boughs; so that there is nothing but green cone, and green carpet. Nor is it only softer, but in one sense more cheerful than other foliage, for it casts only a pyramidal shadow.

"When [Ruskin] describes the pine-tree," Tomlinson has commented [in the *Sewanee Review,* 1962], "we know that we have never yet looked at one. Poets have realized that this was where to follow Ruskin."

To see how some poets have indeed followed Ruskin we must return to 1949. That year, at about the same time he was reading *Frondes agrestes,* Tomlinson borrowed a copy of Marianne Moore's *Selected Poems* of 1935. It was not an insignificant acquisition, for the two or three Marianne Moore poems, or bits of poems, he had encountered during and since his Cambridge days had begun to act as what he called "talismans" in his imagination. With both books now on his bookshelf, he spotted a link. Two lines of Moore's poem "An Octopus," scrupulously enclosed in quotation marks and with a footnote simply saying "Ruskin," he would have recognized as a slightly revised snippet from the pine-tree passage in *Frondes agrestes.* Here are Moore's borrowed trees:

> austere specimens of our American royal families,
> "each like the shadow of the one beside it.
> The rock seems frail compared with their dark
>   energy of life"

The Moore-Ruskin conjunction remained in Tomlinson's memory until 1969 when he was writing the introduction to a collection of critical essays on Moore. There he cites the lines from "An Octopus" as an instance of her discrimination, her capacity for making out the way a thing looks. She is, he adds, a poet "for whom fact has its proper plenitude." This is an oblique allusion to his own poem **"The Farmer's Wife: at Fostons Ash,"** where, in a Ruskinian tribute to "fact," to the fecund geography of the farm's lofts, cellars, orchards, and all the blessings they hold and inherit, he says:

> Distrust
> that poet who must symbolize
>   your stair into
>   an analogue
> of what was never there.
>   Fact
>   has its proper plenitude
> that only time and tact
>   will show, renew.

There are two camps then: the Ruskinian poets, such as Moore, for whom "fact" and "tact" are an aural and conceptual rhyme, and the symbolists, their representative here obviously Yeats.

Fourteen years later, in 1983, the shadowy ghost of the pine tree appears to Tomlinson again, this time while writing a review of Elizabeth Bishop's *Complete Poems.* Her poem "At the Fishhouses," contains the Ruskin particle in a different setting:

>   Back, behind us,
> the dignified tall firs begin.
> Bluish, associating with their shadows,
> a million Christmas trees stand
> waiting for Christmas. The water seems suspended
> above the rounded gray and blue-gray stones.
> I have seen it over and over, the same sea, the
>   same,
> slightly, indifferently swinging above the stones.

Tomlinson suggests that what is passed on from Moore to her younger friend Bishop is something more subtle than "influence"; what is betokened by the image of the fir is fidelity to visual appearances, economy of means, personal reticence—just those aesthetic and moral values that Tomlinson's readers know to be his as well.

In the 1983 review, however, he elaborates more freely on the "plenitude" of Ruskin's pine-tree passage. It suggested to Moore, he speculates, that

> if only Ruskin's wit could be rescued from his eloquence, the twentieth-century poet could write of nature free of the egotistical sublime. Ruskin witty? Take his pine trees—"each like the shadow of the one beside it— upright, fixed, spectral, as troops of ghosts standing on the walls of Hades, not knowing each other. . . . The rock itself looks bent and shattered beside them,— fragile, weak, inconsistent, compared to their dark energy of delicate life, and monotony of enchanted pride—unnumbered, unconquerable." The shadow at the beginning of this passage, that fantasy of the ghosts, the pre-Lawrentian "dark energy of delicate life" all pull against the miscalculated organ notes of "unnumbered, unconquerable."

Moore "sheers away at all this" in "An Octopus," seizing only what to her seems essential—the shadows, the frail rocks, the dark energy of life. Tomlinson sees Bishop, too, as having her own revisionary purposes—making of the image something "darker, post-imagist," with a "suggestion of threat in it," giving "a hint of the darkness about to fall, a margin of the sad and the inexplicable that refuses to be exorcized by her brave wit."

Tomlinson's remarks are as unexpectedly revealing about his own sensibility as they are about Ruskin, Moore, and Bishop. The emphasis on wit is odd, especially as the original Ruskin comparison of the pine trees to troops of ghosts seems more gothic than witty. But by "wit" he means the placing of one sharp edge against another as in collage, with that effect of discontinuity, incalculableness, and often humor that he himself achieves in many poems, his Mexican and American pieces being preeminent examples. Equally interesting is his observation on the marginal shadow and darkness in Bishop's poem, for it arises from his own awareness of shadows, reflections, and doubleness, the obscurity at the margins of the visible, and "the darkness about to fall."

Marianne Moore features once more in the circuitry of fir-tree images. In April 1959, just two-and-a-half years after receiving *Like a Bulwark* and while in the United States on a writer's fellowship, Tomlinson was invited to meet Moore in her Brooklyn apartment. The conversation turned to Ruskin, and they talked about the Ruskinian elements in "An Octopus" and "The Steeple-Jack," about a portrait of Ruskin by Millais that Moore recalled having seen somewhere, and about a visit Moore had made as a girl to Ruskin's home in Coniston, where she remembered a peacock feather on display. The meeting recorded in *Some Americans* had been commemorated many years earlier in **"Over Brooklyn Bridge"**:

> Goodbye
> Miss Moore
>   I hope
>   the peacock's feather you once saw
> at the house of Ruskin
>   has kept its variegations.

They also discussed what Tomlinson in his *Some Americans* account calls his "Ruskin piece." In that very Ruskinian volume **Seeing Is Believing,** which owed its 1958 publication in the United States to Kenner and a copy of which either Kenner or Tomlinson would undoubtedly have sent to Moore, there are two poems actually about Ruskin: **"Geneva Restored"** and **"Frondes Agrestes: On re-reading Ruskin."** Almost certainly, the latter is meant. First published in late 1957, about a year after Tomlinson received the inscribed copy of *Like a Bulwark,* it is a collage—Moore-fashion—of quotations from Ruskin's *Frondes agrestes*:

> A leaf, catching the sun, transmits it:
> "First a Torch, then an emerald."
>
> "Compact, like one of its own cones":
> The round tree with the pyramid shadow.
>
> First the felicities, then
> The feelings to appraise them:
>
> Light, being in its untempered state,
> A rarity, we are (says the sage) meant
> To enjoy "most probably" the effects of mist.
>
> Nature's difficulties, her thought
> Over dints and bosses, her attempts
> To beautify with a leopard-skin of moss
> The rocks she has already sculpted,
> All disclose her purposes—the thrush's bill,
> The shark's teeth, are not his story.
>
> Sublimity is. One awaits its passing,
> Organ voice dissolving among cloud wrack.
> The climber returns. He brings
> Sword-shaped, its narrowing strip
> Fluted and green, the single grass-blade, or

> Gathered up into its own translucence
> Where there is no shade save colour, the
>   unsymbolic rose.

The various snippets of the collage serve different purposes. Some pay homage to Ruskin's observant eye; some mock, with a Moore-like tartness, his lapses into sublimity and his effusiveness about Nature's grand purposes. The concluding image of the unsymbolic and shadeless rose is a transcription of the image which Tomlinson happened upon the first time he opened *Frondes agrestes,* and which, in its accuracy and beauty, convinced him that he must read further in Ruskin. The two lines on the fir tree are a tribute to Ruskin's observation of recurrences in natural forms (the shape of the tree echoed differently in its cone and in its shadow). And, given the available plenitude of images in Ruskin's lengthy description of the pine, it is significant that Tomlinson's eye should fall yet again on shadow.

The two lines on shadow are of course particles from the description of pine trees that Moore had rifled for "An Octopus." A tribute to and critique of Ruskin undoubtedly, the poem is by inference also a tribute to Moore's discriminating eye and mind, which she must have recognized when they talked about it in her Brooklyn apartment.

We have seen the fir trees reflected in and refracted through a number of texts by other writers, and have seen these texts themselves observed and reflected on by Tomlinson over five decades, from the late Forties to 1983. Like molecules entering new chemical combinations, they have combined with and drawn attention to several aspects of Tomlinson's imagination: the perception of design and recurrent form in nature, the shaping of visual perception by language, the submergence of the ego necessary to these perceptions, the concept of wit and disjunction, the sense of mystery in visual phenomena (optical at first, then edging toward metaphysical). A number of critics have noted Ruskin's presence in Tomlinson's discernment of detail and his fidelity to visual surfaces. But the fir-tree fragments have unexpectedly led us further, to an enterprise equally Ruskinian, though not part of the stock conception of Ruskin—that is, to Tomlinson's sense of the shadows and obscurity at the edge of the visual, and to an intimation of his profound *critique* of visual appearances.

Michael Edwards (essay date 1989)

SOURCE: "Providence and the Abyss," in *The Times Literary Supplement,* December 22-28, 1989, p. 1417.

[*Below, Edwards provides a laudatory review of* Annuciations.]

Annunciations is the book in which Charles Tomlinson makes explicit what has always been the case, that his poetry looks to this world to provide the "religious" sense of life which Christianity for him can no longer sustain. The Christian vocabulary remains, but only to describe art as a return to Eden, and nature itself as a process of resurrection or a heaven. The "annunciation" of a larger-than-life presence in the world, of a reality which has preceded us and will outlast us, of a mystery ceaselessly entering local chance and circumstance, comes not from beyond but from within the world, often in the form of light from the sun and moon.

Everything is a message from a physical universe to the mind made alert. The poetry opens to a kind of adoration of the light, to a paganism which celebrates the teeming of the earth and sky, and which travels back in time through the vast material otherness to what Tomlinson memorably calls "the grail of origin". The shaping of his poetry finds its *raison d'être* in this vision. His poems often move forward as the sounds of words beget other words (a blade of light "cut / in two the land / it was lancing. Then / as I stood, / the shaft shifted . . ."), while rhymes tend to rove through the verse without necessarily falling at line-ends. The poem advances as the world advances, through recurrence but also through apparent haphazard. In the absence of God, providence is an onward meshing of experience and of the world, as in the poetry a car drives by, a plane flies over. *Annunciations* offers the pleasures, in fact, of a style now completely achieved and possessed, where an ostensibly effortless and inevitable phrasing also produces certain lines to which all of his poetry seems to have led: "The sense that we are here, that it is now", "In a world imagined that is really there".

This vision is also embodied in Tomlinson's own reading (*Annunciations* is the twelfth cassette of his *Complete Poems* which the enterprising Richard Swigg has been recording in the English Department of the University of Keele). Tomlinson concentrates on articulating with extreme precision the sounds and the developing argument of the poems, maybe over-emphatically in the long run but with an unwavering attention to the patterns of meaning and with a complete absence of afflatus. His Staffordshire accent also reminds one of the riches which still exist in all those regional Englishes which have not collapsed into Londonese.

Tomlinson's poetry is altogether of our century in its desire, in a world apparently deserted by the divine, to find another way to "the reconciling of our dreams / With what is there". An underlying sadness also surfaces, and an occasional bitterness, and one should not be prevented by the playful religious parody of the liminary poem from recognizing the volume's growing disquiet, its resentment at death, its invasion by images of winter and snow, of "the abyss beneath", of "an endlessly descending causeway", and its quite serious opposition to God. *Annunciations* emerges, indeed, from thoroughly human emotions—from compassion also and perhaps fear as well as delight—and from a warm experience of the earth and its animals and plants. It arises from daily living and from things that Tomlinson has met with on his travels. Everything in it is real, and it is astonishing that his poetry is not more popular.

Robert Potts (essay date 1992)

SOURCE: "Tomlinson Stands Up," in *The Times Literary Supplement,* December 18, 1992, p. 19.

[*In the following mixed review of* The Door in the Wall, *Potts explores Tomlinson's continued interest in landscape.*]

Charles Tomlinson's poetry has benefited, perhaps perversely, from his frustrated interest in a career in cinema and his often frustrating progress as an artist, and almost fulfils that vexatious Horatian dictum, *ut pictura poesis*. Firmly categorized now as a poet of landscape, Tomlinson has for over forty years produced his careful, Impressionist pieces, combining a painter's precision and sensitivity with the cinematic facility for recording the passage of time. Whether in the free verse which formerly suited him so well for Mexican and American vistas, or in the more formal metres which he handles with extraordinary fluency, Tomlinson continues, in **The Door in the Wall,** to concentrate on the minute details of change and flux in landscape, which are played out against the more reliable constancies of seasonal iteration and immutable landmarks.

There is a reverence in his work which has always been close to religiosity—one poem, **"Blaubeuren"**, breaks startlingly into something like prayer—but his are resolutely secular devotions, closer to Gaia than theism or even humanism. From his earliest mature work Tomlinson sought a sublimation of his own ego, "putting aside some of the more violent claims of personality". Having eliminated himself from his enquiries, Tomlinson invests his poems with a sensibility rather than a presence, refusing to privilege the relationship between man and environment over the myriad relationships within that environment: the poet as component rather than colonist.

The Door in the Wall, as the title implies, maintains a focus on the unstable thresholds of a world in motion, delighting in the tension between boundary and passage, often drawn in terms of forces such as light or snow, which disregard or even recast landscapes and thoroughfares. **"The Operation"**, a description of a forest clearance, elevates the labour to an artistic process of honing and alteration, elsewhere an elegantly rendered Neoplatonism tests the potential and limitations of Tomlinson's poetic metamorphoses, aspiring to a vision beyond the empirical: "we live in a place always just out of reach." His suitably leaky stanzas, bounded by gentle enjambments, carry the filtered light and sound which washes through buildings, streets and unfenced spaces; Tomlinson is quietly intoxicated by the luminous and material traffic which paradoxically confirms "the integrity of the planet." His Eden is an attitude of undamaging appreciation, not a place, and he cites Octavio Paz as saying "there are no gardens . . . except / for those we carry with us."

This husbandry, which carries a tacit political or philosophical correlative, earns respect through the weight of Tomlinson's own regard for the subjects he presents with such dignified and attentive detail. It is a stance which has led to accusations of coldness, because Tomlinson's passion is communicated in an anti-Romantic spirit, which equates extremity of faith or feeling with arrogant violence. *The Door in the Wall* retains traces of this concern— poems recalling Paris in 1969, Siena in 1968—but without the vigour with which Tomlinson used to employ assassination as a motif for senseless homicide in the name of Utopia. When he does refer to Trotsky, in support of his distinctly personal credo that colour might determine one's choice of homeland, the passage sounds faintly batty read outside the context of his previous work: "I think when Mercader killed Trotsky, / the colours of that garden in Coyoacan / counted for little . . ."

These lines are taken from a letter to Paz which discusses their reasons for remaining in their own countries. Tomlinson's decision not to emigrate to the United States is couched in pedagogic terms; "I thought that I could teach my countrymen to see / The changing English light, like water / That drips off a gunwale". The tense of the sentence perhaps implies the thwarting of that particular desire. There is an otherworldly quality about Tomlinson's Zen aestheticism which has sometimes made him seem almost uninterested in people and history; and his latest work does nothing to dispel this impression of unease. His **"Ode to San Francisco"** remarks "It is strange to live in a city where one third of the males may die of the same disease," in an infelicitously curious tone, not helped by the doubtlessly well-meant fogeyism of "I used to think it gay / (that damaged word)."

Perhaps it is apt that so self-effacing a writer is most obtrusive in his parentheses; the occasional pettifogging footnote or disruptive qualification can only partly be attributed to a nervous regard for precision. The volume contains more of these tics and clumsinesses than one is used to from Tomlinson. **"At Hanratty's"** heavy-handedly extends his interest in mutability to a New York of immigrants learning the roles of a new nationality after an unusually prolix and rambling disquisition, and **"Crossing Aguadilla"** is no less programmatic in its final juxtapositions of McDonald's and a "Jesus is coming" sign. These are relatively trifling points, and to quibble over Tomlinson's treatment of human beings is not unlike criticizing Turner for not painting portraits. The majority of these poems, as always, command the reciprocation of their own painstaking contemplation, the beauty of their visions more than matched by the skill of their execution.

John Redmond (essay date 1995)

SOURCE: "Stirring Your Tea is Only a Normal Activity if You Stop Doing it Relatively Quickly," in *The London Review of Books*, Vol. 17, No. 13, July 6, 1995, p. 19.

[*In the following excerpt, Redmond provides a favorable review of* Jubilation, *calling it an old-fashioned but well-crafted, precise, and intelligent book of poetry.*]

Charles Tomlinson's **Jubilation** is a very old-fashioned poetry book. His sense of the line, his diction and his

subject-matter at times are reminiscent of the Georgians and, indeed, there are a couple of references to Edward Thomas and Ivor Gurney. When he is not referring to a timeless landscape and noting the effects of the seasons, he is describing medieval buildings or people from another time. **'Durham in March,'** for instance, which sees the landscape from a moving train, records the relics of a time before there were trains: a castle, a viaduct, 'a trinity of towers.' But there is nothing to stop an old-fashioned book of poems being very good, and **Jubilation** is, for the most part, excellent. Tomlinson's rhythmical control is superior to that of any of the other poets reviewed here, and it allows him, by the simplest means, to achieve complicated emotional effects, as in the very first stanza of the book:

> Four of the generations are taking tea,
> Except that one of them is taking milk:
> It is an English, autumnal afternoon,
> The texture of the air half serge, half silk.

Tomlinson does have his weaknesses. He is rather too fond of the quadripartite line which Eliot made his own ('the infirm glory of the positive hour'), using it to end several poems on a High Note: 'In the great cycle of the sleepless year', 'The Sabine promise of your open door,' 'The distant boom of a departing plane.' And landscape poets are always in danger of dropping the most commonplace of metaphors with a great thump: sunset equalling death, a green shoot equalling rebirth. Occasionally, Tomlinson allows such ready-made images to overtake the accuracy of his observations:

> the ties of blood
> Rooting us in place, not unlike the unmoving
>   trees,
> And yet, as subject to earth, water, times
> As they, our stay and story linked in rhyme.

But lapses of this kind are an exception in this well-crafted book. **Jubilation** is Tomlinson's fourth collection since his *Collected Poems* in 1987 and the title, so the dustjacket informs me, is a pun on the Spanish word for 'retirement', *jubilación*. Given the many qualities which this book displays—intelligence, precision and formal mastery— one hopes that the retirement which Tomlinson contemplates will not be from poetry.

FURTHER READING

Criticism

Brown, Merle. "Intuition and Perception in the Poetry of Charles Tomlinson." *The Journal of Aesthetics and Art Criticism* 37, No. 3 (Spring 1979): 277-93.
    Discusses Tomlinson's poem "Under the Moon's Reign," calling it his most ambitious work to date.

Edwards, Michael. "Charles Tomlinson: Notes on Tradition and Impersonality." *The Critical Quarterly* 15, No. 2 (Summer 1973): pp. 133-44.

Examines the diverse ways Tomlinson's poetry utilizes the themes of chance, tradition, and impersonality.

Getz, Thomas H. "Charles Tomlinson's Manscapes." *Modern Poetry Studies* 11, No. 3 (1983): 207-18.
Traces the Tomlinson's exploration of natural environments from *American Scenes* to *The Way In*.

Grogan, Ruth. "Charles Tomlinson: Poet as Painter." *Critical Quarterly* 19, No. 4 (Winter 1977): 71-7.
Relates Tomlinson's art to his verse.

———. "Charles Tomlinson: The Way of His World." *Contemporary Literature* 19, No. 4 (Autumn 1978): pp. 472-96.
Provides an overview of Tomlinson's poetry.

———. "Tomlinson, Ruskin, and Language Scepticism." *Essays in Literature* 17, No. 1 (Spring 1990): 30-42.
Determines the effect of post-Saussurean literary theory on Tomlinson's poetry.

———. "The Fall into History: Charles Tomlinson and Octavio Paz." *Comparative Literature* 44, No. 2 (Spring 1992): 144-59.
Contends that Tomlinson's poetry is enriched when approached in terms of his long-standing philosophical dialogue with Octavio Paz.

Hirsch, Edward. "The Meditative Eye of Charles Tomlinson." *The Hollins Critic* XV, No. 2 (April 1978): pp. 1-12.
Overviews Tomlinson's poetry and maintains that his early anti-romantic impulses deepen into a meditative attitude that reflects an allegiance to both the unshaped world and the shaping imagination.

Lea, Sydney. "To Use and Transform: Recent Poetry of Charles Tomlinson." *The Hudson Review* 46, No. 4 (Winter 1994): 731-40.
Asserts that Tomlinson's later poetry is more wrought in both subject matter and form than his earlier poetry, but that it is still technically inventive.

O'Gorman, Kathleen, ed. *Charles Tomlinson: Man and Artist.* Columbia: University of Missouri Press, 1988, 253 p.
Collection of critical essays on Tomlinson and his work.

Rosenthal, M. L. "Contemporary British Poetry." In *The New Poets: American and British Poetry Since World War II*, pp. 244-51. New York: Oxford University Press, 1967.
Determines the American influence on Tomlinson's poetry.

Stanton, Robert J. "Charles Tomlinson an the Process of Defining Relationships." *North Dakota Quarterly* 43, No. 3 (Summer 1977): 47-60.
Examines the major themes of Tomlinson's poetry.

Wilkinson, D. R. M. "Charles Tomlinson and the Narrative Voice." *Dutch Quarterly Review of Anglo-American Letters* 14, No. 2 (1984): 110-24.
Explores the narrative element in Tomlinson's poetry.

Young, Alan. "Rooted Horizon: Charles Tomlinson and American Modernism." *Critical Quarterly* 24, No. 4 (Winter 1982): 67-73.
Positive review of *Some Americans: A Personal Record* and *The Flood*.

Interviews

Meyer, Bruce. "A Human Balance: An Interview with Charles Tomlinson." *The Hudson Review* 43, No. 3 (Autumn 1990): 437-48.
Discusses John Ruskin's influence on Tomlinson, the effects that translating the poetry of others has had on his poetry, his interest in film, and the themes of Eden in his work.

Ross, Alan. "Words and Water: Charles Tomlinson and His Poetry." *London Magazine* 20, No. 10 (January 1981): 22-39.
Describes Tomlinson's working-class background, his experiences at Cambridge, the strong American interest in his poetry, the influences on his work, and his graphic art.

Additional coverage of Tomlinson's life and career is contained in the following sources published by Gale Research: *Contemporary LIterary Criticism*, Vols. 2, 4, 6, 13, 45; *Contemporary Authors*, Vols. 5-8R; *Contemporary Authors New Revision Series*, Vol. 33; *DISCovering Authors: Poets Module*; and *Dictionary of Literary Biography*, Vol. 40.